VAT Acts

2006

Value Added Tax

Tottel
publishing

VAT Acts

2006

Value Added Tax

Editor **Brian Butler**

Head of VAT
A & L Goodbody, Solrs

Tottel
publishing

Tottel Publishing, Maxwelton House, 41–43 Boltro Road, Haywards Heath, West Sussex, RH16 1BJ

A CIP Catalogue record for this book is available from the British Library.

ISBN 1 845922859

ISBN 1-84592-285-9

9 781845 922856

Typeset in Dublin by Marie Armah-Kwantreng
Printed and bound in Great Britain by Antony Rowe, Chippenham, Wiltshire

CONTENTS

Contents

Orders

Repealed orders are shown in *italics*.

Statements of practice
Repealed statements of practice are shown in *italics*.

Contents

European Union Legislation

Directives
Repealed directives are shown in *italics*.

Decisions

Regulations

HOW TO USE THIS WORK

Tracing legislation

This book sets out consolidated versions of the Value Added Tax Act 1972 together with the non-amending sections of the Finance Acts from 1973 to 2006 inclusive, and related regulations, orders and European law. Each section is annotated in respect of amendments, cross-references, definitions, construction, statutory instruments, statements of practice and former enactments.

The legislation is set out in the following manner:

(*a*) the full text of an amending provision is normally omitted, but effect is given to the amendment in the amended provision;

(*b*) the full text of a repealing provision is normally omitted, but effect is given to the repeal in the repealed provision.

Section and schedule headings of repealed or amended legislation are retained for the purposes of clarity.

For ease of reference, section and schedule numbers are conspicuously marked at the top of the page. If the section or schedule is known, it can be found immediately because the legislation is printed in chronological order. Where only the subject matter is known, it may be traced through the index. The marginal notes in the Value Added Tax Act 1972 are direct cross-references to the Sixth Directive. The marginal notes in the Sixth Directive are direct cross-references to the Value Added Tax Act 1972.

For additional ease of reference, explanatory headings are added to some subsections of the Value Added Tax Act 1972. These headings are not part of the legislation and are distinguished by italics and parentheses.

Standard abbreviations

The following are the standard abbreviations used in Tottel tax publications:

General

s, ss	section (or sections) of an Act
subs, subss	subsection (or subsections) of a section
Sch	Schedule to an Act
para, paras	paragraph (or paragraphs) of a Schedule
subpara, subparas	subparagraph (or subparagraphs) of a Schedule
Pt	Part (of an Act)
Ch	Chapter (or a Part of an Act)
r, reg	regulation (of a statutory instrument)

Statutes

CA	Companies Act
CATCA 2003	Capital Acquisitions Tax Consolidation Act 2003
CGTA 1975	Capital Gains Tax Act 1975

CGTAA 1978	Capital Gains Tax (Amendment) Act 1978
CTA 1976	Corporation Tax Act 1976
FA	Finance Act
F(No 2)A	Finance (No 2) Act
F(MP)A	Finance (Miscellaneous Provisions) Act
IA 2005	Interpretation Act 2005
IRRA 1890	Inland Revenue Regulation Act 1890
ITA 1967	Income Tax Act 1967
PCTA 1927	Provisional Collection of Taxes Act 1927
TCA 1997	Taxes Consolidation Act 1997
TD(SC)A 1942	Taxes and Duties (Special Circumstances) Act 1942
VATA 1972	Value Added Tax Act 1972
VATAA 1978	Value Added Tax Amendment Act 1978

Statutory Instruments

ITER	Income Tax (Employments) Regulations
SI 28/1960	Statutory Instrument Number 28 of 1960
IT(CC)R	Income Tax (Construction Contracts) Regulations
VATR 1979	Value Added Tax Regulations 1979

Practice

SP	Statement of Practice

Case law

ITR	Irish Tax Reports
IR	Irish Reports
STC	Simon's Tax Cases
TC	Tax Cases
TL	Tax Leaflet
ITC	Irish Tax Cases
ECJ	European Court of Justice

CURRENT VAT RATES

How to use this chart: With effect from 1 January 2004, there are four VAT rates: 0% (the zero rate), 4.4% (the flat-rate), 13.5%, and 21%. Goods and services the supply of which is not exempt (VATA 1972, Sch 1) or liable at 0% (VATA 1972, Sch 2), 4.4% (VATA 1972, s 11), or 13.5% (VATA 1972, Sch 6) are, by default, liable at 21% (VATA 1972, s 11). This chart summarises goods and services that are exempt or liable at 0%, 4.4% or 13.5%. Therefore, if the supply is not shown on this chart it will most likely be liable at 21%.

Goods

Exempt (Sch 1)
Blood and organ banks (xviii)
Cultural bodies (viia)
Non-deductible goods sold (xxiv)
Philanthropic societies (xxii)
Political parties (xxii)
Religious societies (xxii)
Trade unions (xxii)
Welfare services (non-profit) (viii)
(Goods *closely related* to the body's activities)

0% (Sch 2)
Aircraft (international transport) (v)(*b*)
Aircraft (international transport) equipment (va)
Aircraft (international transport) fuel etc (vb)
Animal feed (not pet food)(vii)
Animal medicine (oral) (xiv)
Artificial body parts (xixa) (*b*)
Books (xva)
Candles (plain white) (xx)
Children's clothes (xvii)
Drink (coffee, tea, etc) (xii)
Exports (i)
Exporters (supplies to) (vi*a*)
Fertiliser (farm) (vii)
Food (not confectionery, sweets) (xii)
Gold bullion (supplied to Central Bank) (x)
Imports (non-EC, consigned to EC State) (iiib)
Medicine (oral) (xiii)
Plants and seeds (food producing) (xv)
Ships (commercial seagoing, over 15 tons)(v)(*a*)
Tampons (xviii)
Wheelchairs (xixa)(*a*)

13.5% (Sch 6)
Antiques (xvia)
Art works (xvia)
Biscuits (not chocolate) (xxxi)(*b*)
Buildings (new) (xxviii)
Cakes (xxxi)(*a*)
Coal (fuel) (i)(*a*)
Concrete ready to pour (xxxii)
Concrete blocks (xxxiii)
Electricity (i)(*b*)
Gas (heating) (i)(*c*)
Magazines (xii)
Newspapers (xii)
Nursery plants (xia)
Oil (home heat) (i)(*d*)
Peat (fuel) (i)(*a*)
Photographs etc (xxii)

4.4% (s 11(1))
Cattle
Deer
Goats
Greyhounds
Horses
Pigs
Sheep

Services

Exempt (Sch 1)
Banks (i)
Betting businesses (xv)
Blood and organ banks (xviii)
Circuses (no food or drink) (viii)
Creches (non profit making) (vi)
Cultural bodies (viii*a*)
Dental technicians (iii*a*)
Dentists (iii*b*)
Doctors (iii)
Financial service agents (ix)(*d*)
Funeral undertaking (xix)
Hospitals (v)
Hospital meals (xxv)
Insurance agents (ix)(*b*), (*c*)
Insurance businesses (xi)
Landlords (short leases) (iv)
Lottery businesses (xvi)
Musical shows (no food or drink) (viii)
Nursing home (v)
Nursing home meals (xxv)
Opticians (iii*b*)
Passenger transport(xiv)
Philanthropic societies (xxii)
Philosophical societies (xxii)
Political parties (xxii)
Postal services (An Post) (xi*a*)
Radio broadcasts (RTÉ) (xiii)
Religious societies (xxii)
Schools (ii)
School meals (xxv)
Sporting events (xvii)
Sports facilities (non-profit) (xxiii)
Stockbrokers (i)(*a*)
Television broadcasts (RTÉ) (xiii)
Trade unions (xxii)
Travel agents (ix)(*a*)
Theatres (no food or drink) (viii)
Universities (ii)
Welfare services (non-profit) (vii)

0% (Sch 2)
Aircraft (int'nl transport) equipment repairs (v*a*)
Aircraft repairs (v)(*b*)
Airport services (iv)
Export agent services (vi)
Haulage to/from EC (iii)
Import agent services (iv)
Lifeboat services (xi)
Lighthouse services (ix)
Port services (iv)
Ship repairs (v)(*a*)
Work on non-EC goods (xvi)

13.5% (Sch 6)
Agricultural services (xi)
Boat hire (under five weeks) (xv)(*b*)
Building work (xxix)
Campsite facilities (xiii)
Caravan hire (under five weeks) (xv)(*d*)
Car hire (under five weeks) (xv)(*a*)
Cinemas (v)
Cleaning buildings etc (xxx)
Drink (vending machines) (ii)(*a*)
Driving lessons (xxvii)
Exhibitions (cultural etc) (ix)
Fairground entertainers (vii)
Food (vending machines) (ii)(*a*)
Guesthouse accommodation (xiii)
Hairdressers (xix)
Health studios (xix)
Holiday home accommodation (xiii)
Hotel accommodation (xiii)
Jockeys (xx)
Meals (hot, takeaway etc) (iv)
Meals (restaurant etc) (ii)(*b*)–(*c*),(iii)
Musical shows (food, drink) (vi)
Photographers (xxiii)
Photographic services (xxv)
Repair services (xviii)
Sports facilities (commercial) (vii*a*)
Theatres (food, drink) (vi)
Tour guides (xiv)
Veterinary surgeons (x)
Waste removal services (viii)

REVENUE ADDRESSES

Opinions & Statutory Clearance Queries

Name	Address	Telephone	Fax	e-mail
VAT Interpretation Branch	Dublin Castle, Dublin 2.	01–674 8858	01–6795236 01-6793814	vatinfo@revenue.ie

Revenue District Contact Points

Region	Regional Office & Districts	Address	Telephone	Fax	E-mail
Dublin	Regional Office	Apollo House, Tara Street, Dublin 2	01-6330890	01-6330607	dublinregoff@revenue.ie
	City Centre (Dublin City postal areas 1&2)	14/15 Upper O'Connell Street, Dublin 1	01-8655000	01-8746079	dublincitycentre@revenue.ie
	South City (Dublin City south of the Liffey excluding postal area 2)	85/93 Lower Mount Street, Dublin 2	01-6474000	01-6616510	dublinsouthcity@revenue.ie
	North City (Dublin City north of the Liffey excluding postal area 1)	14/15 Upper O'Connell Street, Dublin 1	01-8655000	01-8746079	dublinnorthcity@revenue.ie
	South County (Local Authority Area)	Plaza Complex, Belgard Road, Tallaght, Dublin 24	01-6470700	01-6341882	dublinsouthcounty @revenue.ie
	Fingal (Local Authority Area)	Block D, Ashtown Gate, Navan Road, Dublin 15	1890 678456	01 8277080	dublinfingal@revenue.ie
	Dun Laoghaire/ Rathdown (Local Authority Area)	Lansdowne House, Lansdowne Road, Dublin 4	01-6316700	01-6329618	dunblindunlrathdowncusserv @revenue.ie
South West	Regional Office	Government Offices, Sullivan's Quay, Cork	021-4325000	021-4325488	swregoffice@revenue.ie
	Cork East (includes City Centre, North City and North County east of the Mallow Road)	Government Offices, Sullivan's Quay, Cork	021-4325000	021-4310600	swregoffice@revenue.ie

	Cork South West (includes South City and South County)	Government Offices, Sullivan's Quay, Cork	021-4325000	021-4310600	corksouthwest@revenue.ie
	Cork North West (includes rest of City and County)	Government Offices, Sullivan's Quay, Cork	021-4325000	021-4310600	corknorthwest@revenue.ie
	Clare	River House, Charlotte's Quay, Limerick	061-212700	061-417863	claredistrict@revenue.ie
	Limerick	River House, Charlotte's Quay, Limerick	061-212700	061-417863	limtax@revenue.ie
	Kerry	Government Offices, Spa Road, Tralee, Co. Kerry	066-7183100	066-7121895	kerrydistrict@revenue.ie
Border Midlands West	Regional Office	Custom House, Flood Street, Galway	091-536300	091-536385	galway@revenue.ie
	Galway County	Hibernian House, Eyre Square, Galway	091-536000	091-566352	galwaycounty@revenue.ie
	Galway/ Roscommon (includes Galway City and Co. Roscommon)	Hibernian House, Eyre Square, Galway	091-536000	091-566352	galwayroscommon @revenue.ie
	Mayo	Michael Davitt House, Castlebar, Co. Mayo	094-9037000	094-9024221	mayo@revenue.ie
	Sligo (includes counties Sligo, Leitrim and Longford)	Government Offices, Cranmore Road, Sligo	071-9148600	071-9143987	sligo@revenue.ie
	Donegal	Government Offices, High Road, Letterkenny, Co. Donegal	074-9169400	074-912775	donegal@revenue.ie
	Westmeath/Offaly	Government Offices, Pearse Street, Athlone, Co. Westmeath	0906-421800	0906-492699	westmeathoffaly@ revenue.ie

	Louth	Government Offices, Millennium Centre, Dundalk, Co. Louth	042-9353700	042-9353385	louth@revenue.ie
	Cavan/Monaghan	Government Offices, Millenium Centre, Dundalk, Co. Louth	042-8353700	042-9353780	cavanmonaghan@revenue.ie
East & South East	Regional Office	Government Offices, The Glen, Waterford	051-862700	051-877483	wfordtax@revenue.ie
	Tipperary	Government Offices, Stradavoher, Thurles, Co. Tipperary	0504-28700	0504-21475	thurles@revenue.ie
	Kilkenny (includes counties Kilkenny, Carlow and Laois)	Government Offices, Hebron Road, Kilkenny	056-7760700	056-7760888	kilkenny@revenue.ie
	Waterford	Government Offices, The Glen, Waterford	051-862700	051-877483	waterford@revenue.ie
	Wexford	Government Offices, Anne Street, Wexford	053-63300	053-22045	wexford@revenue.ie
	Kildare, Meath & Wicklow	Grattan House, Lower Mount Street, Customer Service, Dublin 2	01- 6474000		kmw@revenue.ie
	Wicklow Audit/Compliance	4 Claremont Road, Sandymount, Dublin 4	01- 6316500	01 6606768	wicklow@revenue.ie
	Kildare Audit/Compliance	Plaza Complex, Belgard Road, Tallaght, Dublin 24	01- 6470700	01-6341882 01-6341880	Kildare@revenue.ie

Meath Audit/Compliance	Block D, Ashtown Gate, Navan Road, Dublin 15	01- 8277000	01-8277480	meath@revenue.ie

Other Revenue Contact Points

Large Cases Division	Business Units	Address	Telephone	Fax	E-mail
	Food	Francis Street, Sarsfield House, Limerick	061-488400	061-401011	icdfoodindustry@revenue.ie
	All other units	Setanta Centre, Nassau Street, Dublin 2	01-6470710	01-6716668	largecasesdiv@revenue.ie
VAT Repayments (registered) **(re VAT repayments to persons who are registered for VAT)**		Government Offices, Kilrush Road, Ennis, Co. Clare	065-6849000	065-6841366	regvat@revenue.ie
VAT Repayments (unregistered) **(re VAT repayments to persons who are not registered for VAT)**		Government Offices, Kilrush Road, Ennis, Co. Clare	065-6849000	065-6849248	unregvat@revenue.ie

Collector General's Division

Section	Address	Telephone	e-mail
Collector General, Payment Processing, Debt Management, tax payment queries (Business & Self-Employed)	Collector General, Sarsfield House, Francis Street, Limerick	1890 20 30 70	cg@revenue.ie

Useful Websites

Dept of Finance	http://www.ir/gov.ie/finance/
Revenue Commissioners	http://www.revenue.ie/

TAXPAYER'S CHARTER OF RIGHTS

GET TO KNOW YOUR RIGHTS

In your dealings with the Revenue Commissioners, you are entitled to:

COURTESY AND CONSIDERATION

– to expect that Revenue staff will at all times carry out their duties courteously and considerately.

PRESUMPTION OF HONESTY

– to be presumed to have dealt with your tax affairs honestly unless there is reason to believe to the contrary and subject to the Revenue Commissioners' responsibility for ensuring compliance with the law.

INFORMATION

– to expect that every reasonable effort will be made to give you access to full, accurate and timely information about Revenue law and your entitlements and obligations under it. So that they can do this, Revenue staff are entitled to expect that you will give them all the facts and the full co-operation which they need to deal with your affairs.

IMPARTIALITY

– to have your affairs dealt with in an impartial manner by Revenue staff who seek to collect only the correct amount of tax or duty, no more or no less.

PRIVACY AND CONFIDENTIALITY

– to expect that personal and business information provided by you will be treated in strict confidence and used only for purposes allowed by law.

INDEPENDENT REVIEW

– to object to a charge to tax or duty if you think the law has been applied incorrectly and to ask that your case be reviewed. If the matter cannot be resolved to your satisfaction by Revenue officials you have rights in law to independent review.

COMPLIANCE COSTS

– to expect that the Revenue Commissioners and their staff recognise the need to keep to the minimum necessary the costs you incur in complying with Revenue law, subject to their responsibility to carry out their functions efficiently and economically.

CONSISTENT ADMINISTRATION

– to expect that the Revenue Commissioners will administer the law consistently and apply it firmly to those who try to evade paying their lawful share.

OUR OBJECTIVE

The objective of the Revenue Commissioners is to collect the taxes, duties and other charges placed under our care and management in an efficient way and at the least possible cost to the public. This objective is to be achieved in a manner which:

- fosters the highest degree of public confidence in our integrity, efficiency and fairness, and

- encourages voluntary compliance with Revenue law and deters evasion and avoidance.

LEGISLATION

PROVISIONAL COLLECTION OF TAXES ACT 1927

(1927 Number 7)

ARRANGEMENT OF SECTIONS

Section

AN ACT TO GIVE STATUTORY EFFECT FOR A LIMITED PERIOD TO RESOLUTIONS OF THE COMMITTEE ON FINANCE OF DÁIL ÉIREANN IMPOSING, RENEWING, VARYING, OR ABOLISHING TAXATION, AND TO MAKE PROVISION WITH RESPECT TO PAYMENTS, DEDUCTIONS, ASSESSMENTS, CHARGES, AND OTHER THINGS MADE OR DONE ON ACCOUNT OF ANY TEMPORARY TAX IN ANTICIPATION OF THE RENEWAL OF THE TAX BY THE OIREACHTAS. [19TH MARCH, 1927]

1 Definitions

In this Act—

the expression **"Committee on Finance"** means the Committee on Finance of Dáil Éireann when and so long as such Committee is a committee of the whole House;

[the expression **"new tax"** when used in relation to a resolution under this Act means a tax which was not in force immediately before the date on which the resolution is expressed to take effect or, where no such date is expressed, the passing of the resolution by Dáil Éireann;][1]

the expression **"permanent tax"** means a tax which was last imposed without any limit of time being fixed for its duration;

the expression **"temporary tax"** means a tax which was last imposed or renewed for a limited period only;

the expression **"normal expiration"** when used in relation to a temporary tax means the end of the limited period for which the tax was last imposed or renewed;

the word **"tax"** includes duties of customs, duties of excise, income tax, ...[2] ...[3] [and Value Added tax][4] [and capital gains tax][5] ...[6] [and corporation tax][7] [and gift tax and inheritance tax][8] [and residential property tax][9] [and stamp duties][10] [and gift tax and inheritance tax][11] but no other tax or duty.

Amendments

1. Definition of "new tax" substituted by FA 2002, s 139(*a*) with effect from 25 March 2002.
2. Words "and super-tax" repealed by FA 1974, s 86 and Sch 2 Pt I for 1974–75 and later tax years.
3. Words "and also turnover tax" repealed by VATA 1972, s 41.
4. Inserted by VATA 1972, s 38.
5. Inserted by CGTA 1975, s 50.
6. Words "and wealth tax" deleted by FA 1978, s 38.
7. Inserted by CTA 1976, s 6.
8. Inserted by CATA 1976, s 69.
9. Inserted by FA 1983, s 114(1).
10. Inserted by FA 1986, s 100.
11. Inserted by CATCA 2003, s 115(1).

2 Certain resolutions to have statutory effect

Whenever a resolution (in this Act referred to as a resolution under this Act) is passed by [Dáil Éireann][1] resolving—

(*a*) that a new tax specified in the resolution be imposed, or

(*b*) that a specified permanent tax in force [immediately before the date on which the resolution is expressed to take effect or, where no such date is expressed, the passing of the resolution by Dáil Éireann][2] be increased, reduced, or otherwise varied, or be abolished, or

(*c*) that a specified temporary tax in force [immediately before the date on which the resolution is expressed to take effect or, where no such date is expressed, the passing of the resolution by Dáil Éireann][2] be renewed (whether at the same or a different rate and whether with or without modification) as from the date of its normal expiration or from an earlier date or be discontinued on a date prior to the date of its normal expiration,

and the resolution contains a declaration that it is expedient in the public interest that the resolution should have statutory effect under the provisions of this Act, the resolution shall, subject to the provisions of this Act, have statutory effect as if contained in an Act of the Oireachtas.

Amendments

1. Substituted by FA 1974, s 85(1)(*a*) with effect from 23 October 1974 (SI 312/1974); previously "the Committee on Finance".
2. Substituted by FA 2002, s 139(*b*) with effect from 25 March 2002; previously "immediately before the end of the previous financial year".

3 Application of general taxing enactments

(1) Whenever a new tax is imposed by a resolution under this Act and such resolution describes the tax as a duty of customs or as a duty of excise or as an income tax ...[1], the enactments which [immediately before the date on which the resolution is expressed to take effect or, where no such date is expressed, the passing of the resolution by Dáil Éireann][2] were in force in relation to customs duties generally, or excise duties generally, or income tax generally, ...[3] (as the case may require) shall, subject to the provisions of this Act, apply to and have full force and effect in respect of such new tax so long as the resolution continues to have statutory effect.

(2) Whenever a permanent tax is increased, reduced, or otherwise varied by a resolution under this Act, all enactments which were in force with respect to that tax [immediately before the date on which the resolution is expressed to take effect or, where no such date is expressed, the passing of the resolution by Dáil Éireann]² shall, so long as the resolution continues to have statutory effect and subject to the provisions of this Act, have full force and effect with respect to the tax as so increased, reduced, or otherwise varied.

(3) Whenever a temporary tax is renewed (whether at the same or a different rate and whether with or without modification) by a resolution under this Act, all enactments which were in force with respect to that tax [immediately before the date on which the resolution is expressed to take effect or, where no such date is expressed, the passing of the resolution by Dáil Éireann]² shall, so long as the resolution continues to have statutory effect and subject to the provisions of this Act, have full force and effect with respect to the tax as renewed by the resolution.

Amendments

1 Words "or as a super-tax" repealed by FA 1974, s 86 and Sch 2 Pt 1 for 1974–75 and later tax years.

2 Substituted by FA 2002, s 139(*b*) with effect from 25 March 2002; previously "immediately before the end of the previous financial year".

3 Words "or super-tax generally" repealed by FA 1974, s 86 and Sch 2 Pt 1 for 1974–75 and later tax years.

4 Duration of statutory effect of resolution

[A resolution under this Act shall cease to have statutory effect upon the happening of whichever of the following events first occurs, that is to say:

[(*a*) subject to section 4A of this Act, if a Bill containing provisions to the same effect (with or without modifications) as the resolution is not read a second time by Dáil Éireann—

    (i) where Dáil Éireann is in recess on any day between the eighty-second and the eighty-fourth day after the resolution is passed by Dáil Éireann, within the next five sitting days of the resumption of Dáil Éireann after that recess,

    (ii) in any other case, within the next eighty-four days after the resolution is passed by Dáil Éireann,]¹

(*b*) if those provisions of the said bill are rejected by Dáil Éireann during the passage of the Bill through the Oireachtas;

(*c*) the coming into operation of an Act of the Oireachtas containing provisions to the same effect (with or without modification) as the resolution;

(*d*) [subject to section 4A of this Act]² the expiration of a period of four months from that date on which the resolution is expressed to take effect or, where no such date is expressed, from the passing of the resolution by Dáil Éireann.]³

Amendments

1 Para (*a*) substituted by Appropriation Act 1991, s 2(*a*)(i).

2 Inserted by Appropriation Act 1991, s 2(*a*)(ii).

3 Section 4 substituted by FA 1974, s 85(1)(*b*) with effect from 23 October 1974 (SI 312/1974).

4A Effect of dissolution of Dáil Éireann

[Where Dáil Éireann, having passed a resolution under this Act, has been dissolved on the date the resolution was so passed or within four months of that date, then the period of dissolution shall be disregarded for the purposes of calculating any period to which paragraph (*a*) or (*d*) of section 4 of this Act relates.][1]

Amendments

[1]   Section originally inserted by Appropriation Act 1991; substituted by FA 1992, s 250.

Definitions

"Dáil Éireann": IA 2005, Sch.

5 Repayment of certain payments and deductions

(1) Whenever a resolution under this Act ceases to have statutory effect by reason of the happening of any event other than the coming into operation of an Act of the Oireachtas containing provisions to the same effect (with or without modification) as the resolution, all moneys paid in pursuance of the resolution shall be repaid or made good and every deduction made in pursuance of the resolution shall be deemed to be an unauthorised deduction.

(2) ...[1].

(3) Whenever an Act of the Oireachtas comes into operation containing provisions to the same effect with modifications as a resolution under this Act and such resolution ceases by virtue of such coming into operation to have statutory effect, all moneys paid in pursuance of such resolution which would not be payable under such Act shall be repaid or made good and every deduction made in pursuance of such resolution which would not be authorised by such Act shall be deemed to be an unauthorised deduction.

Amendments

[1]   Subs (2) repealed by FA 1974, s 85(1)(*c*) with effect from 23 October 1974 (SI 312/1974).

6 Certain payments and deductions deemed to be legal

(1) Any payment or deduction on account of a temporary tax to which this section applies made within two months after the expiration of such tax in respect of a period or event occurring after such expiration shall, if such payment or deduction would have been a legal payment or deduction if the tax had not expired, be deemed to be a legal payment or deduction subject to the conditions that—

    (*a*)   if a resolution under this Act renewing the tax (with or without modification) is not passed by [Dáil Éireann][1] within two months after the expiration of the tax, the amount of such payment or deduction shall be repaid or made good on the expiration of such two months, and

    (*b*)   if (such resolution having been so passed) an Act of the Oireachtas renewing the tax (with or without modification) does not come into operation when or before such resolution ceases to have statutory effect, the amount of such payment or deduction shall be repaid or made good on such cesser, and

    (*c*)   if (such Act having been so passed) the tax is renewed by such Act with such modifications that the whole or some portion of such payment or deduction is not a legal payment or deduction under such Act, the whole or such portion (as the case may be) of such payment or deduction shall be repaid or made good on the coming into operation of such Act.

(2) This section applies only to a temporary tax which was last imposed or renewed for a limited period not exceeding eighteen months and was in force immediately before the end of the financial year next preceding the financial year in which the payment or deduction under this section is made.

Amendments

1   Substituted by FA 1974, s 85(1)(*d*) with effect from 23 October 1974 (SI 312/1974); previously "the Committee on Finance".

7 Repeal

The Provisional Collection of Taxes Act, 1913, is hereby repealed.

8 Short title

This Act may be cited as the Provisional Collection of Taxes Act, 1927.

FINANCE ACT 1928

(Number 11 of 1928)

34 Care and management of taxes and duties

...

(2) Any information acquired, whether before or after the passing of this Act, by the Revenue Commissioners in connection with any tax or duty under their care and management may be used by them for any purpose connected with any other tax or duty under their care and management.

Cross-references

European Communities (Mutual Assistance in the Field of Value Added Tax) Regulations 1980 (SI 407/1980).

FINANCE ACT 1968

(Number 33 of 1968)

ARRANGEMENT OF SECTIONS

PART I
INCOME TAX

AN ACT TO CHARGE AND IMPOSE CERTAIN DUTIES OF CUSTOMS AND INLAND REVENUE (INCLUDING EXCISE), TO AMEND THE LAW RELATING TO CUSTOMS AND INLAND REVENUE (INCLUDING EXCISE) AND TO MAKE FURTHER PROVISIONS IN CONNECTION WITH FINANCE. [29TH JULY, 1968]

PART I
INCOME TAX

6 Obligation to keep certain records

[(1) In this section—

"linking documents" means documents that are drawn up in the making up of accounts and which show details of the calculations linking the records to the accounts;

"records" includes accounts, books of account, documents and any other data maintained manually or by any electronic, photographic or other process, relating to—

(*a*) all sums of money received and expended in the course of the carrying on or exercising of a trade, profession or other activity and the matters in respect of which the receipt and expenditure take place,

(*b*) all sales and purchases of goods and services where the carrying on or exercising of a trade, profession or other activity involves the purchase or sale of goods or services,

(*c*) the assets and liabilities of the trade, profession or other activity referred to in paragraph (*a*) or (*b*), and

(*d*) all transactions which constitute an acquisition or disposal of an asset for capital gains tax purposes.

(2) (*a*) Every person who, on his own behalf or on behalf of any other person, carries on or exercises any trade, profession or other activity the profits or gains of which are chargeable under Schedule D, or who is chargeable to tax under

Schedule D or Schedule F in respect of any other source of income, or who is chargeable to capital gains tax in respect of chargeable gains, shall keep, or cause to be kept on his behalf, such records as will enable true returns to be made, for the purposes of income tax and capital gains tax, of such profits or gains or chargeable gains.

(*b*) The records shall be kept on a continuous and consistent basis, that is to say the entries therein shall be made in a timely manner and be consistent from one year to the next.

(*c*) Where accounts are made up to show the profits or gains from any such trade, profession or activity or in relation to a source of income, of any person, that person shall retain, or cause to be retained on his behalf, linking documents.

(*d*) Where any such trade, profession or other activity is carried on in partnership, the precedent partner, within the meaning of section 69 of the Income Tax Act, 1967, shall, for the purposes of this section, be deemed to be the person carrying on that trade, profession or other activity.

(3) Records required to be kept or retained by virtue of this section, shall be kept—

(*a*) in written form in an official language of the State, or

(*b*) subject to section 113(2) of the Finance Act, 1986, by means of any electronic, photographic or other process.

(4) Linking documents and records kept pursuant to the preceding provisions of this section shall be retained by the person required to keep the records for a period of 6 years after the completion of the transactions, acts or operations to which they relate or, in the case of a person who fails to comply with section 10 (1) of the Finance Act, 1988, requiring the preparation and delivery of a return on or before the specified return date for a year of assessment, until the expiry of a period of 6 years from the end of the year of assessment in which a return has been delivered showing the profits or gains or chargeable gains derived from the said transactions, acts or operations:

Provided that, this subsection shall not—

(*a*) require the retention of linking documents and records in respect of which the inspector notifies in writing the person who is required to retain them that retention is not required, or

(*b*) apply to the books and papers of a company which have been disposed of in accordance with section 305(1) of the Companies Act, 1963.

(5) Any person who fails to comply with the provisions of subsection (2), (3) or (4) in respect of any records or linking documents in relation to a return for any year of assessment shall be liable to a penalty of £1,200:

Provided that a penalty shall not be imposed under this subsection if it is proved that no person is chargeable to tax in respect of the profits or gains for that year of assessment.][1]

Amendments

[1]   Section substituted by FA 1992, s 231.

Cross-references

Value added tax, equivalent obligations: VATA 1972, s 16.

Case law

Linking documents are taxpayer's property: *Quigley v Burke* (IV) ITR (332).

Definition

"person": IA 2005, s 18(c); "profession": TCA 1997, s 2(1); "trade": TCA 1997, s 3(1); "year of assessment": TCA 1997, ss 2(1), 5(1).

PART VII
MISCELLANEOUS

47 Care and management of taxes and duties

All taxes and duties imposed by this Act are hereby placed under the care and management of the Revenue Commissioners.

48 Short title, construction and commencement

(1) This Act may be cited as the Finance Act, 1968.

(2) Part I and (so far as relating to income tax, ...[1]) sections 34 to 39 and section 41 of this Act shall be construed together with the Income Tax Acts.

...

(4) ...[2].

(5) Part I and sections 34 to 39 of this Act shall, save as is otherwise expressly provided therein, be deemed to have come into force and shall take effect as on and from the 6th day of April, 1968.

(6) Any reference in this Act to any other enactment shall, except so far as the context otherwise requires, be construed as a reference to that enactment as amended by or under any other enactment, including this Act.

Amendments

[1]   Words "including sur tax" deleted by FA 1974, s 86 and Sch 2 Pt I for 1974–75 and later tax years.

[2]   Subs (4) repealed by CTA 1976, s 164 and Sch 3 Pt II.

Definition

"commencement": IA 2005, Sch; "Income Tax Acts": TCA 1997, s 1(2).

VALUE ADDED TAX ACT 1972

(1972 Number 22)

ARRANGEMENT OF SECTIONS

FIRST SCHEDULE
EXEMPTED ACTIVITIES

SECOND SCHEDULE
GOODS AND SERVICES CHARGEABLE AT THE RATE OF ZERO PER CENT

THIRD SCHEDULE
GOODS AND SERVICES CHARGEABLE AT THE RATE SPECIFIED IN SECTION 11(1)(*c*)[10%]

FOURTH SCHEDULE
SERVICES THAT, WHERE TAXABLE ARE TAXED WHERE RECEIVED

FIFTH SCHEDULE
PART I: ANNEX A OF COUNCIL DIRECTIVE NO 77/388/EEC OF 17 MAY, 1977

LIST OF AGRICULTURAL PRODUCTION ACTIVITIES

PART II
Annex B of Council Directive No.77/388/EEC of 17 May, 1977:
List of agricultural services

SIXTH SCHEDULE
GOODS AND SERVICES CHARGEABLE AT THE RATE SPECIFIED IN SECTION 11(1)(*d*)[12.5%]

SEVENTH SCHEDULE

EIGHTH SCHEDULE
WORKS OF ART, COLLECTORS ITEMS AND ANTIQUES CHARGEABLE AT THE RATE SPECIFIED IN SECTION 11(1AA) [12.5%]

AN ACT TO CHARGE AND IMPOSE CERTAIN DUTIES OF INLAND
REVENUE (INCLUDING EXCISE), TO AMEND THE LAW RELATING
TO INLAND REVENUE (INCLUDING EXCISE) AND TO MAKE
FURTHER PROVISIONS IN CONNECTION WITH FINANCE.
[*26th JULY, 1972*]

1 Interpretation

(1) In this Act, save where the context otherwise requires—

...[1]

["**agricultural produce**" has the meaning assigned to it by section 8;][2]   Annex A

["**agricultural service**" has the meaning assigned to it by section 8;][3]   Annex B

["**ancillary supply**" means a supply, forming part of a composite supply, which is not physically and economically dissociable from a principal supply and is capable of being supplied only in the context of the better enjoyment of that principal supply;][4]

["**antiques**" has the meaning assigned to it by section 10A;][5]

"**Appeal Commissioners**" means persons appointed in accordance with section [section 850 of the Taxes Consolidation Act, 1997],[6] to be Appeal Commissioners for the purpose of the Income Tax Acts;

["**assignment**", in relation to an interest in immovable goods, means the assignment by a person of that interest in those goods or of any part of those goods to another person:

Provided that where that other person at the time of the assignment retains the reversion on that interest in those goods, that assignment shall be a surrender;][7]

"**body of persons**" means any body politic, corporate, or collegiate, and any company, partnership, fraternity, fellowship and society of persons, whether corporate or not corporate;

"**business**" includes farming, the promotion of dances and any trade, commerce, a 4(2) manufacture, or any venture or concern in the nature of trade, commerce or manufacture, and any profession or vocation, whether for profit or otherwise;

["**clothing**" does not include footwear;][8]

"**Collector-General**" means the Collector-General appointed under [section 851 of the Taxes Consolidation Act, 1997];[9]

["**collectors' items**" has the meaning assigned to it by section 10A;][10]

["**Community**", except where the context otherwise requires, has the same meaning as it has in Article 3 of Council Directive No 77/388/EEC of 17 May

1977 (as last amended by Council Directive No 92/111/EEC of 14 December 1992), and cognate references shall be construed accordingly,][11]

["**composite supply**" means a supply made by a taxable person to a customer comprising two or more supplies of goods or services or any combination of these, supplied in conjunction with each other, one of which is a principal supply;][12]

["**contractor**", in relation to contract work, means a person who makes or assembles movable goods;

"**contract work**" means the service of handing over by a contractor to another person of movable goods made or assembled by the contractor from goods entrusted to the contractor by that other person, whether or not the contractor has provided any part of the goods used;][13]

"**the customs-free airport**" means the land which under the Customs-Free Airport Act 1947, for the time being constitutes the Customs-free airport;

"**development**", in relation to any land, means—

(*a*) the construction, demolition, extension, alteration or reconstruction of any building on the land, or

(*b*) the carrying out of any engineering or other operation in, on, over, or under the land to adapt it for materially altered use,

and "**developed**" shall be construed correspondingly [, and in this definition, "**building**" includes, in relation to a transaction, any prefabricated or like structure in respect of which the following conditions are satisfied:

(*a*) the structure—

(i) has a rigid roof and one or more rigid walls, and except in the case of a structure used for the cultivation of plants, a floor,

(ii) is designed so as to provide for human access to, and free movement in, its interior,

(iii) is for a purpose that does not require that it be mobile or portable, and

(iv) does not have or contain any aids to mobility or portability,

and

(*b*) (i) neither the agreement in respect of the transaction nor any other agreement between the parties to that agreement contains a provision relating to the rendering of the structure mobile or portable or the movement or re-location of the structure after its erection, and

(ii) the person for whom the structure is constructed, extended, altered or reconstructed signs and delivers, at the time of the transaction, to the person who constructed, altered or reconstructed the structure a declaration of his intention to retain it in the site on which it is at that time located;][14]

["electronically supplied services" includes—

    (*a*) website supply, web-hosting, distance maintenance of programmes and equipment,

    (*b*) supply of software and updating of it,

    (*c*) supply of images, text and information, and making databases available,

    (*d*) supply of music, films and games, including games of chance and gambling games, and of political, cultural, artistic, sporting, scientific and entertainment broadcasts and events, and

    (*e*) supply of distance teaching,

and **"electronic service"** shall be construed accordingly, but where the supplier of a service and his or her customer communicates by means of electronic mail, this shall not of itself mean that the service performed is an electronic service;][15]

...[16];

["establishment"][17] means any fixed place of business, but does not include a place of business of an agent of a person unless the agent has and habitually exercises general authority to negotiate the terms of and makes agreements on behalf of the person or has a stock of goods with which he regularly fulfils on behalf of the person agreements for the supply of goods;

["excisable products" means the products referred to in section 104 of the Finance Act, 1992;][18]

"exempted activity" means —

    (*a*) a [supply][19] of immovable goods in respect of which pursuant to section 4(6) tax is not chargeable, and

    (*b*) a [supply of any goods or services][20] of a kind specified in the First Schedule or declared by the Minister by order for the time being in force under section 6 to be an exempted activity;

["exportation of goods" means the exportation of goods to a destination outside the Community and, where the context so admits, cognate words shall be construed accordingly;][21]

["farmer" has the meaning assigned to it by section 8;][22]   a 25

["flat-rate addition" has the meaning assigned to it by section 12A;][23]   a 25

["flat-rate farmer" has the meaning assigned to it by section 12A;][24]   a 25

["footwear" includes shoes, boots, slippers and the like but does not include stockings, under-stockings, socks, ankle-socks or similar articles or footwear without soles or footwear which is or incorporates skating or swimming equipment;][25]

["free port" means the land declared to be a free port for the purposes of the Free Port Act, 1986 (No 6 of 1986), by order made under section 2 of that Act;][26]

[**"fur skin"** means any skin with the fur, hair or wool attached except skin of woolled sheep or lamb;][27]

"goods" means all movable and immovable objects, but does not include things in action or money and references to goods include references to both new and [used][28] goods;

...[29]

"hire", in relation to movable goods, includes a letting on any terms including a leasing;

...[30];

"immovable goods" means land;

[**"importation of goods"** means the importation of goods from outside the Community into [the State][31] either—

  (*a*) directly, or

  (*b*) through one or more than one other Member State where value added tax referred to in Council Directive No 77/388/EEC of 17 May 1977 has not been chargeable on the goods in such other Member State or Member States in respect of the transaction concerned,

and, where the context so admits, cognate words shall be construed accordingly;][32]

[**"individual supply"** means a supply of goods or services which is a constituent part of a multiple supply and which is physically and economically dissociable from the other goods or services forming part of that multiple supply, and is capable of being supplied as a good or service in its own right;][33]

"inspector of taxes" means an inspector of taxes appointed under [section 852 of the Consolidation Act, 1997];[34]

a 29a(3)

[**"intra-Community acquisition of goods"** has the meaning assigned to it by section 3A;][35]

"livestock" means live cattle, [horses,][36] sheep, [goats, pigs and deer][37];

"local authority" has the meaning assigned to it by section 2(2) of the Local Government Act 1941, and includes a health board established under the Health Act, 1970;

[**"margin scheme"** has the meaning assigned to it by section 10A;][38]

...[39];

"the Minister" means the Minister for Finance;

[**"monthly control statement"** has the meaning assigned to it by section 17;][40]

"movable goods" means goods other than immovable goods;

[**"multiple supply"** means two or more individual supplies made by a taxable person to a customer where those supplies are made in conjunction with each other for a total consideration covering all those individual supplies, and where those individual supplies do not constitute a composite supply;][41]

["**new means of transport**" means motorised land vehicles with an engine a 28a(2) cylinder capacity exceeding 48 cubic centimetres or a power exceeding 7.2 kilowatts, vessels exceeding 7.5 metres in length and aircraft with a take-off weight exceeding 1,550 kilogrammes—

(*a*) which are intended for the transport of persons or goods, and

(*b*) [(i) which in the case of vessels and aircraft were supplied three months or less after the date of first entry into service and in the case of land vehicles were supplied six months or less after the date of first entry into service, or][42]

(ii) which have travelled [6,000 kilometres][43] or less in the case of land vehicles, sailed for 100 hours or less in the case of vessels or flown for 40 hours or less in the case of aircraft,

other than vessels and aircraft of the kind referred to in paragraph (v) of the Second Schedule;][44]

["**a person registered for value added tax**" means, in relation to another Member State, a person currently issued with an identification number in that State for the purposes of accounting for value added tax referred to in Council Directive No. 77/388/EEC of 17 May 1977 and, in relation to the State, means a registered person;][45]

["**principal supply**" means the supply of goods or services which constitutes the predominant element of a composite supply and to which any other supply forming part of that composite supply is ancillary;][46]

"**registered person**" means a person who is registered in the register maintained under section 9;

"**regulations**" means regulations under section 32;

... [47];

... [48];

["**second-hand goods**" has the meaning assigned to it by section 10A;][49]

"**secretary**" includes such persons as are mentioned in [section 1044(2) of the Taxes Consolidation Act, 1997],[50] and section 55(1) of the Finance Act 1920;

"**the specified day**" means the day appointed by the Minister by order to be the specified day for the purpose of this Act;

["**supply**", in relation to goods, has the meaning assigned to it by section 3 and, a 5, 6 in relation to services, has the meaning assigned to it by section 5, and cognate words shall be construed accordingly;][51]

["**surrender**", in relation to an interest in immovable goods, means the surrender by a person (hereafter referred to in this definition as "**the lessee**") of an interest in those goods or any part of those goods to the person (hereafter referred to in this definition as **"the lessor"**) who at the time of the surrender retains the reversion on the interest in those goods and also includes the abandonment of that interest by the lessee and the failure of the lessee to exercise any option of the type referred to in subsection (1)(*b*) of section 4 in relation to that interest and surrender of an interest also includes the recovery by the lessor of that interest in those goods by ejectment or forfeiture prior to the date that that interest would, but for its surrender, have expired;][52]

"tax" means value added tax chargeable by virtue of this Act;

[**"taxable dealer"**—

(*a*) in relation to supplies of gas through the natural gas distribution system, or of electricity, has the meaning assigned to it by section 3(6A),

(*b*) in relation to supplies of movable goods other than a means of transport, has the meaning assigned to it by section 10A, and

(*c*) in relation to supplies of means of transport, has the meaning assigned to it by section 12B;][53]

"taxable goods", in relation to any [supply, intra-Community acquisition or importation][54], means goods the [supply][19] of which is not an exempted activity;

"taxable period" means a period of two months beginning on the first day of January, March, May, July, September or November [provided that the taxable period immediately following that commencing on the 1st day of May, 1973, shall be the period commencing on the 1st day of July, 1973, and ending on the 2nd day of September, 1973, and the next succeeding taxable period shall be the period commencing on the 3rd day of September, 1973, and ending on the 31st day of October, 1973][55];

a 4   [**"taxable person"** has the meaning assigned to it by section 8;][56]

"taxable services" means services the [supply][19] of which is not an exempted [activity;][57]

[**"telecommunications services"** means services relating to the transmission, emission or reception of signals, writing, images and sounds or information of any nature by wire, radio, optical or other electromagnetic systems and includes—

(*a*) the related transfer or assignment of the right to use capacity of such transmission, emission or reception, and

(*b*) the provision of access to global information networks;][58]

[**"vessel"**, in relation to transport, means a waterborne craft of any type, whether self-propelled or not, and includes a hovercraft.][59]

[**"works of art"** has the meaning assigned to it by section 10A.][60]

(2) In this Act references to moneys received by a person include references to—

(*a*) money lodged or credited to the account of the person in any bank, savings bank, building society, hire purchase finance concern or similar financial concern, and (*b*)   money, other than money referred to in paragraph (*a*), which, under an agreement, other than an agreement providing for discount or a price adjustment made in the ordinary course of business or an arrangement with creditors, has ceased to be due to the person, and

[(*bb*)   money due to the person which, in accordance with the provisions of [section 1002 of the Taxes Consolidation Act, 1997],[61] is paid to the Revenue Commissioners by another person and has thereby ceased to be due to the person by that other person, and][62]

[(*c*)   money, which, in relation to money received by a person from another person has been deducted in accordance with the provisions of—

   (i)   [Chapter 1 of Part 18 of the Taxes Consolidation Act, 1997],[63] or

   (ii)   [Chapter 2 of Part 18 of the Taxes Consolidation Act, 1997],[64]

   and has thereby ceased to be due to the first-mentioned person by the other person,][65]

and money lodged or credited to the account of a person as aforesaid shall be a 3 deemed to have been received by the person on the date of the making of the lodgment or credit and money which has ceased to be due to a person as aforesaid shall be deemed to have been received by the person on the date of the cesser.

[(2A) In this Act, save where the context otherwise requires, a reference to the a 3 territory of a Member State has the same meaning as it has in Article 3 (inserted by Council Directive No. 91/680/EEC of 16 December 1991 of Council Directive No. 77/388/EEC of 17 May 1977, and references to Member States and cognate references shall be construed accordingly.][66]

(3) Any reference in this Act to any other enactment shall, except so far as the context otherwise requires, be construed as a reference to that enactment as amended or extended by any subsequent enactment.

(4) In this Act—

(*a*)   a reference to a section or Schedule is to a section or Schedule of this Act, unless it is indicated that reference to some other enactment is intended, and

(*b*)   a reference to a subsection, paragraph or subparagraph is to the subsection, paragraph or subparagraph of the provision (including a Schedule) in which the reference occurs, unless it is indicated that reference to some other provision is intended.

Amendments

[1]   Definition of "accountable person" deleted by VATAA 1978, s 2(*a*) with effect from 1 March 1979; prior to its deletion it read: "accountable person" means a person who is accountable in accordance with section 8.

[2]   Definition of "agricultural produce" inserted by VATAA 1978, s 2(*c*) with effect from 1 March 1979.

[3]   Definition of "agricultural service" inserted by VATAA 1978, s 2(*c*) with effect from 1 March 1979.

[4] Definition of "ancillary supply" inserted by FA 2006, s 93(1)(*a*) with effect from such day as the Minister for Finance may appoint.

[5] Definition of "antiques" inserted by FA 1995, s 119(*a*) with effect from 1 July 1995.

[6] Substituted by TCA 1997, s 1100 and Sch 31; previously "156 of the Income Tax Act, 1967".

[7] Definition of "assignment" inserted by FA 1997, s 96(*a*) as on and from 26 March 1997.

[8] Definition of "clothing" inserted by FA 1984, s 85(*a*) with effect from 1 May 1985.

[9] Substituted by TCA 1997, s 1100 and Sch 31; previously "section 162 of the Income Tax Act 1967".

[10] Definition of "collectors' items" inserted by FA 1995, s 119(*b*) with effect from 1 July 1995.

[11] Definition of "Community" substituted by EC(VAT)R 1992, r 4(*a*) with effect from 1 January 1993; previously: "Community" means European Economic Community (VATAA 1978, s 2(*c*)).

[12] Definition of "composite supply" inserted by FA 2006, s 93(1)(*b*) with effect from such day as the Minister for Finance may appoint.

[13] Definitions of "contractor" and "contract work" inserted by FA 1996, s 88(*a*) with effect from 1 January 1996.

[14] Definition of "development" extended by FA 1981, s 43 with effect from 1 November 1972.

[15] Definition of "electronically supplied services" inserted by FA 2003, s 113 with effect from 1 July 2003.

[16] Definition of "established" deleted by VATAA 1978, s 2(*a*) with effect from 1 March 1979; prior to its deletion it read: "Established" means having a permanent establishment.

[17] Substituted by VATAA 1978, s 2(*b*) with effect from 1 March 1979; previously "permanent establishment".

[18] Definition of "excisable products" inserted by EC(VAT)R 1992, r 4(*b*).

[19] Substituted by VATAA 1978, s 30(2) and Sch 2 with effect from 1 March 1979; previously "delivery".

[20] Substituted by VATAA 1978, s 30(2) and Sch 2 with effect from 1 March 1979; previously "delivery of any goods or a rendering of any services".

[21] Definition of "exportation of goods" inserted by FA 1992, s 165(*a*)(i) with effect from 1 January 1993.

[22] Definition of "farmer" inserted by VATAA 1978, s 2(*c*) with effect from 1 March 1979.

[23] Definition of "flat-rate addition" inserted by VATAA 1978, s 2(*c*) with effect from 1 March 1979.

[24] Definition of "flat-rate farmer" inserted by VATAA 1978, s 2(*c*) with effect from 1 March 1979.

[25] Definition of "footwear" inserted by FA 1984, s 85(*b*) with effect from 1 May 1984.

[26] Definition of "free port" inserted by FA 1986, s 80 with effect from 27 May 1986.

[27] Definition of "fur skin" inserted by FA 1976, s 61 and Sch 1 Pt II with effect from 1 March 1976.

[28] Substituted by FA 1996, s 88(*b*) with effect from 15 May 1996; previously "second-hand".

[29] Definition of "hotel" deleted by FA 1991, s 77 with effect from 1 January 1992; previously it read: "hotel" includes any guest house, holiday hostel, holiday camp, motor hotel, motel, coach hotel, motor inn, motor court, tourist court, caravan park or camping site.

[30] Definition of "harbour authority" deleted by FA 1992, s 165(*a*)(ii) with effect from 28 May 1992; previously it read "harbour authority" has the meaning assigned to it by section 2 of the Harbours Act 1946.

[31] Substituted by FA 1996, s 88(*c*) with effect from 15 May 1996; previously "a Member State".

[32] Definition of "importation of goods" inserted by FA 1992, s 165(*a*)(iii) with effect from 1 January 1993.

[33] Definition of "individual supply" inserted by FA 2006, s 93(1)(*c*) with effect from such day as the Minister for Finance may appoint.

[34] Substituted by TCA 1997, s 1100 and Sch 31; previously "section 161 of the Income Tax Act, 1967".

[35] Definition of "intra-Community acquisition of goods" inserted by FA 1992, s 165(*a*)(iv) with effect from 1 January 1993.

[36] Inserted by FA 1990, s 98 with effect from 30 May 1990.

[37] Substituted by FA 1987, s 39(*a*)(i) with effect from 9 July 1987; previously "and pigs" (FA 1973, s 90 and Sch 10 with effect from 3 September 1973); previously "pigs and horses".

[38] Definition of "margin scheme" inserted by FA 1995, s 119(*c*) with effect from 1 July 1995.

[39] Definition of "manufacturer" deleted by VATAA 1978, s 2(*a*) with effect from 1 March 1979.

[40] Definition of "monthly control statement" inserted by FA 1992, s 165(*a*)(v) with effect from 1 November 1992.

[41] Definition of "multiple supply" inserted by FA 2006, s 93(1)(*d*) with effect from such day as the Minister for Finance may appoint.

[42] Subs (*b*)(i) in the definition of "new means of transport" substituted by FA 1994, s 91(*a*) with effect from 1 January 1995.

[43] Substituted by FA 1994, s 91(*b*) with effect from 1 January 1995; previously "3,000 kilometres".

[44] Definition of "new means of transport" inserted by FA 1992, s 165(*a*)(vi) with effect from 1 January 1993.

[45] Definition of "a person registered for value added tax" inserted by FA 1992, s 165(*a*)(vii) with effect from 1 January 1993.

[46] Definition of "principal supply" inserted by FA 2006, s 93(1)(*e*) with effect from such day as the Minister for Finance may appoint.

[47] Definition of "rendering" deleted by VATAA 1978, s 2(*a*) with effect from 1 March 1979; previously: "rendering", in relation to a service has the meaning assigned to it by section 5.

[48] Definition of "residing" deleted by VATAA 1978, s 2(*a*) with effect from 1 March 1979; previously: "residing", in relation to an individual, means resident for the purposes of the Income Tax Acts.

[49] Definition of "second-hand goods" substituted by FA 1995, s 119(*d*) with effect from 1 July 1995.

[50] Substituted by TCA 1997, s 1100 and Sch 31; previously "section 207(2) of the Income Tax Act 1967".

[51] Definition of "supply" inserted by VATAA 1978, s 2(*c*) with effect from 1 March 1979.

[52] Definition of "surrender" inserted by FA 1997, s 96(*b*) as on and from 26 March 1997.

[53] Subs (1)(definition of "taxable dealer") substituted by FA 2004, s 55; para (*a*) with effect on and from 1 January 2005 (previously "'taxable dealer', in relation to supplies of movable goods other than means of transport, has the meaning assigned to it by section 10A and, in relation to supplies of means of transport, has the meaning assigned to it by section 12B;"); paras (*b*) and (*c*) with effect from 25 March 2004.

[54] Words "supply, intra-Community acquisition or importation" substituted by FA 1992, s 165(*a*)(viii) with effect from 1 January 1993.

[55] Inserted by FA 1973, s 90 and Sch 10 with effect from 3 September 1973.

[56] Definition of "taxable person" inserted by VATAA 1978, s 2(*c*) with effect from 1 March 1979

[57] Substituted by FA 1992, s 165(*a*)(ix) with effect from 1 January 1993.

[58] Definition of "telecommunications services" substituted by FA 2000, s 108 with effect from 23 March 2000.

[59] Definition of "vessel" inserted by FA 1992, s 165(*a*)(x) with effect from 1 January 1993.

[60] Definition of "works of art" inserted by FA 1995, s 119(*f*) with effect from 1 July 1995.

[61] Substituted by TCA 1997, s 1100 and Sch 31; previously "section 73 of the Finance Act, 1988".

[62] Subs (2)(*bb*) inserted by FA 1988, s 60 with effect from 1 October 1988.

[63] Substituted by TCA 1997, s 1100 and Sch 31; previously "Chapter III of Part I of the Finance Act, 1987".

[64] Substituted by TCA 1997, s 1100 and Sch 31; previously "section 17 of the Finance Act, 1970".

[65] Subs (2)(*c*) inserted by FA 1987, s 39(*a*) with effect from 6 June 1987.

[66] Subs (2A) inserted by FA 1992, s 165(*b*) with effect from 1 January 1993.

Orders

Specified day: 1 November 1972, Value Added Tax (Specified Day) Order 1972 (SI 180/1972).

Definition

"land": IA 2005, Sch; "person": IA 2005, s 18(*c*).

Notes

Subs (2A): OJ L367, 31 December 1991, page 1.

2 Charge of value added tax

(1) With effect on and from the specified day a tax, to be called value added tax, shall, subject to this Act and regulations, be charged, levied and paid—

(Supply of goods and services within the State)

a 2(1)   [(*a*) on the supply of goods and services effected within the State for consideration by a taxable person in the course or furtherance of any business carried on by him, and][1]

(Importation into the State)

a 2(2)   (*b*) on goods imported into the State.

(Intra-Community acquisitions)

[(1A) Without prejudice to subsection (1), with effect on and from the 1st day of January, 1993, value added tax shall, subject to this Act and regulations, be charged, levied and paid—

a 28a(1)(a)   (*a*) on the intra-Community acquisition of goods, other than new means of transport, effected within the State for consideration by a taxable person, and

a 28a(1)(b)   (*b*) on the intra-Community acquisition of new means of transport effected within the State for consideration.][2]

(2) ...[3.]

Amendments

[1]   Subs (1)(*a*) substituted by VATAA 1978, s 3 with effect from 1 March 1979.

[2]   Subs (1A) inserted by FA 1992, s 166 with effect from 1 January 1993.

[3]   Subs (2) deleted by VATAA 1978, s 30(1) with effect from 1 March 1979.

Cross-references

Exempted activity (para (*a*)), special provisions in relation to immovable goods: s 4(8).

Goods in transit, new Member States after 1 January 1994 (subs (1)(*b*)): s 15B(1)(*b*), (5).

Intra-Community acquisition of goods: s 3A.

Margin scheme goods (subs (1)(*a*)): s 10A(3).

Special scheme for auctioneers (subs (1)(*a*)): s 10B(3).

Supply of goods: s 3; supply of services: s 5; imports: s 15.

Case law

Subject	*Case*	*Case reference*
Supplies by insurance intermediaries, restriction of exemption	*Card Protection Plan v The Commissioners C & E*	25 February 1999, C–349/96, [1999] BTC 5121, [1999] BVC 155
Illegality of sales does not prevent VAT being due; sales of counterfeit perfume are liable to VAT	*Regina v Goodwin & Unstead*	C–3/97, 4 June 1998
Renting out of space in a coffee shop for the sale of narcotic drugs falls within the scope of the 6th Directive	*Staatssecretaris van Financien v Coffeeshop "Siberië" vof*	29 June 1999, C–158/98
Factoring company purchasing debts and assuming the risk of debtors	*MKG-Kraftfahrzeuge Factoring Gmbh v Finanzamp Gross-Gerau*	26 June 2003, C–305/01

Admission of a member to a partnership in consideration of payment of a contribution in kind	*KapHag Renditefonds v Finannzamt Charlottenburg*	26 June 2003, C–442/01
Abuse of rights	*Halifax Plc v Commissioners of Customs & Excise*	21 February 2006, C–255/02
Abuse of rights	*University of Huddersfield Higher Education Corporation v Commissioners of Customs & Excise*	21 February 2006, C–233/02
Abuse of rights	*BUPA Hospitals Ltd v Commissioners of Customs & Excise*	21 February 2006, C–419/02

Regulations

Subject	*Regulation*
Free Port	Value Added Tax (Free Ports) Regulation (SI 275/87).

Orders

Subject	*Regulation*
Specified day: 1 November 1972	Value Added Tax (Specified Day) Order 1972 (SI 180/72).
Commencement of 1978 Act: 1 March 1979	Value Added Tax (Amendment) Act 1978 (Commencement) Order 1979 (SI 8/79)

Revenue precedent

Issue: Is sponsorship of sporting activities taxable?
Decision: No. Sport is not viewed as being carried on in the course or furtherance of business.
Issue: Computer system supplied within the State for training and testing before being exported by the company out of the State.
Decision: Authorisation given to zero rate the supply of the computer system to the company.
Issue: A UK company with no presence in Ireland sends PBX system to a factory in this State. A Dublin company supplies component to the foreign company but it is delivered directly to the factory in the State. VAT at 21% would normally apply to such a supply. The component is soldered into a finished product and sent back to the UK.
Decision: Provided the supplier has evidence that the goods have been transferred to OMS then the zero rate can apply.
Issue: Sports — taxable or not taxable?
Decision: Sporting activities are not deemed to be carried on in the course of business.

Revenue publications

Guide to Value Added Tax (Revenue Commissioners): Chapter 1.
No VAT loss: Tax Briefing, Issue 27.

Definition

"business": s 1(1); "Community": s 1(1); "goods": s 1(1); "intra-Community acquisition of goods: ss 1(1), 3A; "new means of transport": s 1(1);"person": IA 2005, s 18(*c*); "regulations": s 1(1), 32; "the specified day": s 1(1); "supply": s 1(1); "tax": s 1(1); "taxable person": s 1(1), 8.

3 [Supply] of goods

(1) [In this Act **"supply"**, in relation to goods, means—][1]

    (*a*) the transfer of ownership of the goods by agreement [other than the transfer of ownership of the goods to a person supplying financial services of the kind specified in subparagraph (i)(*e*) of the First

a 5

a 5(1)

Schedule, where those services are supplied as part of an agreement of the kind referred to in paragraph (*b*) in respect of those goods]²,

(Supplies by auctioneers)

a 5(4)(c)   [(*aa*) the sale of movable goods pursuant to a contract under which commission is payable on purchase or sale by an agent or auctioneer who concludes agreements in such agent's or auctioneer's own name but on the instructions of, and for the account of, another person,]³

(Hire purchase and credit sales transactions)

a 5(4)(b)   (*b*) the handing over of the goods to a person pursuant to an agreement which provides for the renting of the goods for a certain period subject to a condition that ownership of the goods shall be transferred to the person on a date not later than the date of payment of the final sum under the agreement,

(Goods processed from materials supplied by customer)

   [(*c*) the handing over by a person (in this paragraph referred to as the developer) to another person of immovable goods which have been developed from goods entrusted to the developer by that other person for the purpose of such development, whether or not the developer has supplied any part of the goods used,]⁴

(Compulsory purchase)

   (*d*) the transfer of ownership of the goods pursuant to—

a 5(4)(a)   (i) their acquisition, otherwise than by agreement, by or on behalf of the State or a local authority, or

        (ii) their seizure by any person acting under statutory authority,

(Supply of goods for exempt/part exempt activity – "self supply")

a 5(7)   [(*e*) the application (otherwise than by way of disposal to another person) by a person for the purposes of any business carried on by him of the goods, being goods which were developed, constructed, assembled, manufactured, produced, extracted, purchased[, imported or otherwise acquired]⁵ by him or by another person on his behalf, except where tax chargeable in relation to the application would, if it were charged, be wholly deductible under section 12 ...,⁶

(Use of goods for non business purpose — "self supply")

a 5(6)   [(*f*) the appropriation of goods by a taxable person for any purpose other than the purpose of his business or the disposal of goods free of charge by a taxable person where—

        (i) tax chargeable in relation to those goods—

            (I) upon their purchase, intra-Community acquisition or importation by the taxable person, or

            (II) upon their development, construction, assembly, manufacture, production, extraction or application under paragraph (*e*),

        as the case may be, was wholly or partially deductible under section 12, or

(ii)   the ownership of those goods was transferred to the taxable person in the course of a transfer of a business or part thereof and that transfer of ownership was deemed not to be a supply of goods in accordance with subsection (5)(*b*), and]⁷]⁸

(Intra-Community transfer of goods — no change in ownership)

[(*g*)   the transfer by a person of goods from his business in the State to the territory of another Member State for the purposes of his business, [or a transfer of a new means of transport by a person in the State to the territory of another Member State,]⁹ other than for the purposes of any of the following: a 28a(5)(b)

(Exceptions:)

(i)   the transfer of the goods in question under the circumstances specified in paragraph (*b*)[, (*cc*)]¹⁰ or (*d*) of subsection (6),

[(ii)   the transfer of goods to another person under the circumstances specified in paragraph (i) of the Second Schedule and the transfer of the goods referred to in paragraphs (v), (*va*), (*vb*) and (x) of the Second Schedule,]¹¹

...¹²

[(iii*a*)   the transfer of goods for the purpose of having a service carried out on them:

Provided that the goods which were so transferred by the person are, after being worked upon, returned to that person in the State,]¹³

(iv)   the temporary use of the goods in question in the supply of a service by him in that other Member State,

(v)   the temporary use of the goods in question, for a period not exceeding 24 months, in that other Member State, where the importation into that other Member State of the same goods with a view to their temporary use would be eligible for full exemption from import duties.]¹⁴

(Self-supplies cont:)

[1A] Anything which is a supply of goods by virtue of paragraph [(*e*), (*f*) or (*g*)]¹⁵ of subsection (1) shall be deemed, for the purposes of this Act, to have been effected for consideration in the course or furtherance of the business concerned: a 5(7)

Provided however, that the following shall not be deemed to have been effected for consideration, that is to say:

(Gifts)

(*a*)   a gift of goods made in the course or furtherance of the business (otherwise than as one forming part of a series or succession of gifts made to the same person) the cost of which to the donor does not exceed a sum specified for that purpose in regulations,   a 5(6)

(Samples)

(*b*) the gift, in reasonable quantity, to the actual or potential customer, of industrial samples in a form not ordinarily avail able for sale to the public.]¹⁶

(Supplies of power)

a 5(2) [(1B) The provision of electricity, gas and any form of power, heat, refrigeration or ventilation shall be deemed, for the purposes of this Act, to be a supply of goods and not a supply of services.]¹⁷

(Chain of sellers)

(2) If three or more persons enter into agreements concerning the same goods and fulfil those agreements by a direct [supply]¹⁸ of the goods by the first person in the chain of sellers and buyers to the last buyer, then the [supply]¹⁸ to such last buyer shall be deemed, for the purposes of this Act, to constitute a simultaneous [supply]¹⁸ by each seller in the chain.

...¹⁹

(Agent/auctioneer — point of acquisition)

a 5(4)(c) [(4) Where an agent or auctioneer makes a sale of goods in accordance with paragraph (*aa*) of subsection (1) the transfer of those goods to that agent or auctioneer shall be deemed to be a supply of goods to the agent or auctioneer at the time that that agent or auctioneer makes that sale.]²⁰

(Exceptions:)

(Hire purchase and credit sales transactions)

(5) (*a*) The transfer of ownership of goods pursuant to a contract of the kind referred to in subsection (1)(*b*) shall be deemed, for the purposes of this Act, not to be a [supply]¹⁸ of the goods.

(Transfer of ownership: loans, debts, sale)

(*b*) The transfer of ownership of goods—

(i) as security for a loan or debt, or

(ii) where the goods are held as security for a loan or debt, upon repayment of the loan or debt, or

[(iii) being the transfer to a taxable person of a totality of assets, or part thereof, of a business even if that business or part thereof had ceased trading, where those transferred assets constitute an undertaking or part of an undertaking capable of being operated on an independent basis,]²¹

shall be deemed, for the purposes of this Act, not to be a [supply]¹⁸ of the goods ...²².

[(*c*) Where a person, in this subsection referred to as an **"owner"**

(i) supplies financial services of the kind specified in subparagraph (i)(*e*) of the First Schedule in respect of a supply of goods within the meaning of paragraph (*b*) of subsection (1), being goods which are of such a kind or were used in such circumstances that no part of the tax, if any, chargeable on that supply of those goods was deductible by the person to whom that supply was made, and

(ii) enforces such owner's right to recover possession of those goods,

then the disposal of those goods by such owner shall be deemed for the purposes of this Act not to be a supply of goods.][23]

(Place of supply of goods)

[(*d*) The disposal of goods by an insurer who has taken possession of them from the owner of those goods, in this subsection referred to as the "insured", in connection with the settlement of a claim under a policy of insurance, being goods—

(*a*) in relation to the acquisition of which the insured had borne tax, and

(*b*) which are of such a kind or were used in such circumstances that no part of the tax borne was deductible by the insured,

shall be deemed for the purposes of this Act not to be a supply of goods.][24]

[(6) The place where goods are supplied shall be deemed, for the purposes of this Act, to be—

(Point of despatch)

(*a*) in the case of goods dispatched or transported and to which paragraph a 8(1)(a) (*d*) does not apply, the place where the dispatch or transportation to the person to whom they are supplied begins,

(Imports from outside Community)

[Provided that where the goods are dispatched or transported from a a 8(2) place outside the Community, the place of supply by the person who imports the goods and the place of any subsequent supplies shall be deemed to be where the goods are imported,][25]

(Installation and assembly)

(*b*) in the case of goods which are installed or assembled, with or without a a 8(1)(a) trial run, by or on behalf of the supplier, the place where the goods are installed or assembled,

(Location of goods)

(*c*) in the case of goods not dispatched or transported, the place where the a 8(1)(b) goods are located at the time of supply,

(Aircraft/vessels/trains travelling within Community)

[(*cc*) in the case of goods supplied on board vessels, aircraft or trains during a 8(1)(c) transport, the places of departure and destination of which are within the Community, the place where the transport began,][26]

(Distance selling arrangements)

(*d*) notwithstanding paragraph (*a*) or (*b*), in the case of goods, other than new means of transport, dispatched or transported by or on behalf of the supplier—

(i) (I) from the territory of another Member State, or

(II)   from outside the Community through the territory of another Member State into which the said goods have been imported,

to a person who is not a taxable person in the State, or

(ii)   from ...[27] the State to a person in another Member State who is not registered for value added tax,

a 28bB(1)

the place where the goods are when the dispatch or transportation ends:

(Exceptions: Place of supply is point of despatch)

[Provided that this paragraph shall not apply to the supply of goods, other than goods subject to a duty of excise, where the total consideration for such supplies does not exceed or is not likely to exceed—

(A)   in the case of goods to which subparagraph (i) relates, [€35,000][28] in a calendar year, unless the supplier, in accordance with regulations elects that it shall apply, and

a 28bB(2)

(B)   in the case of goods to which subparagraph (ii) relates, the amount specified in the Member State in question in accordance with Article 28b.B(2) (inserted by Council Directive No 91/680/ EEC of 16 December 1991) of Council Directive No 77/388/ EEC of 17 May 1977 unless the supplier elects that it shall apply and registers and accounts for value added tax in that Member State in respect of [such supplies,][29][30]][31]

[(e)   in the case of the supply of gas through the natural gas distribution system, or of electricity, to a taxable dealer, whether in the State, or in another Member State of the Community, or outside the Community, the place where that taxable dealer has established the business concerned or has a fixed establishment for which the goods are supplied, or in the absence of such a place of business or fixed establishment the place where that taxable dealer has a permanent address or usually resides,

(f)   in the case of the supply of gas through the natural gas distribution system, or of electricity, to a customer other than a taxable dealer, the place where that customer has effective use and consumption of those goods; but if all or part of those goods are not consumed by that customer, then the goods not so consumed shall be deemed to have been supplied to that customer and used and consumed by that customer at the place where that customer has established the business concerned or has a fixed establishment for which the goods are supplied or in the absence of such a place of business or fixed establishment, the place where that customer has a permanent address or usually resides,][32]

[(6A) In subsection (6) **"taxable dealer"** means a taxable person whose principal business in respect of supplies of gas through the natural gas distribution system, or of electricity, received by that person, is the supply of those goods for consideration in the course or furtherance of business and whose own consumption of those goods is negligible.][33]

(Liquidators and receivers)

[(7) (i) Where, in the case of a business carried on, or that has ceased to be a 5(c) carried on, by a taxable person, goods forming part of the assets of the business are, under any power exercisable by another person, including a liquidator and a receiver, disposed of by the other person in or towards the satisfaction of a debt owed by the taxable person, or in the course of the winding up of a company, they shall be deemed to be supplied by the taxable person in the course or furtherance of his business.

(ii) A disposal of goods under this subsection shall include any disposal which is deemed to be a supply of immovable goods under section 4(2).][34]

(Intra-Community trade — simplification arrangement)

[(8) Where a taxable person who is not established in the State makes an intra- a 28bA(2) Community acquisition of goods in the State and makes a subsequent supply of those goods to a taxable person in the State, the person to whom the supply is made shall be deemed for the purposes of this Act to have made that supply and the intra-Community acquisition shall be disregarded:

Provided that this provision shall only apply where—

(a) the taxable person who is not established in the State has not exercised his option to register in accordance with section 9 by virtue of section 8(3D), and

(b) the person to whom the supply is made is registered in accordance with section 9.][35]

Amendment

[1] Substituted by VATAA 1978, s 4(*u*) with effect from 1 March 1979; previously "In this Act, "delivery", in relation to goods, shall, subject to subsection (1A) include—".

[2] Inserted by FA 1995, s 120(*a*) with effect from 2 June 1995.

[3] Subs (1)(*aa*) substituted by FA 1996, s 89(*a*)(i) with effect from 15 May 1996.

[4] Subs (1)(*c*) substituted by FA 1996, s 89(*a*)(ii) with effect from 1 January 1996.

[5] Substituted by FA 1992, s 167 previously "or imported".

[6] Deleted by FA 1992, s 167(*a*)(i)(II) with effect from 1 January 1993; previously "and".

[7] Subs (1)(*f*) substituted by FA 1998, s 105 with effect from 27 March 1998.

[8] Subs (1)(*e*)–(*f*) substituted by VATAA 1978, s 4(*a*) with effect from 1 March 1979; subs (1)(*e*) previously substituted by FA 1976, s 51.

[9] Inserted by FA 1993, s 82.

[10] Inserted by EC(VAT)R 1992, r 5(*a*)(i) with effect from 1 January 1993 (SI 413/1992).

[11] Subs (1)(*g*)(ii) substituted by FA 1999, s 120(*a*) with effect from 25 March 1999.

[12] Subs (1)(*g*)(iii) deleted by FA 1996, s 89(*a*)(iii)(I) with effect from 1 January 1996.

[13] Subs (1)(*g*)(iii*a*) substituted by FA 1996, s 89(*a*)(iii)(II) with effect from 1 January 1996.

[14] Subs (1)(*g*) inserted by FA 1992, s 167(*a*)(iii).

[15] Substituted by FA 1992, s 167(*b*) with effect from 1 January 1993; previously "(*e*) or (*f*)".

[16] Subs (1A) inserted by FA 1973, s 78 with effect from 3 September 1973.

[17] Subs (1B) inserted by VATAA 1978, s 4 with effect from March 1 1979.

[18] Substituted by VATAA 1978, s 30(2); previously "delivery".

[19] Subs (3) deleted by FA 1996, s 89(*b*) with effect from 15 May 1996.

[20] Subs (4) substituted by FA 1996, s 89(*c*) with effect from 15 May 1996.

[21] Subs (5)(*b*)(iii) substituted by FA 2005, s 99 with effect from 25 March 2005.

[22] Subs (5)(*c*) inserted by FA 1999, s 120(*b*) with effect from 25 March 1999.

[23] Words "unless the goods are goods of a kind specified in the Fourth Schedule and the supply of the goods is one in relation to which tax at either of the rates for the time being specified in section 11(1)(*c*) is chargeable" deleted by VATAA 1978, s 30(1) and Sch 1 with effect from 1 March 1979.

[24] Subs (5)(*d*) inserted by FA 2001, s 182(*b*) with effect from 6 April 2001.

[25] Subs (6)(*a*)(proviso) inserted by EC(VAT)R 1992, r 5(*b*)(i) with effect from 1 January 1993.

[26] Subs (6)(*cc*) inserted by EC(VAT)R 1992, r 5(*b*)(ii) with effect from 1 January 1993.

[27] Deleted by EC(VAT)R 1992, r 5(*b*)(iii)(I) with effect from 1 January 1993; previously "a taxable person".

[28] Substituted by FA 2001, s 240 and Sch 5 Part 4 with effect from 1 January 2002; previously "£27,565"; previously "27,000" (FA 1999, s 120(*c*): 25 March 1999).

[29] Substituted by FA 2004, s 56(*a*) with effect on and from 1 January 2005; previously "such supplies.".

[30] Subs (6)(*d*)(proviso) substituted by EC(VAT)R 1992, r 5(*b*)(iii)(II) with effect from 1 January 1993.

[31] Subs (6) substituted by FA 1992, s 167(c) with effect from 1 January 1993.

[32] Subs (6)(*e*) and (*f*) inserted by FA 2004, s 56(*a*) with effect on and from 1 January 2005.

[33] Subs (6A) inserted by FA 2004, s 56(*b*) with effect on and from 1 January 2005.

[34] Subs (7) inserted by FA 1983, s 78.

[35] Subs (8) inserted by EC(VAT)R 1992, r 5(*c*) with effect from 1 January 1993.

Cross-references

Auctioneers, special scheme (subs (6)(*d*)): s 10B(8).

Boats, caravans, vehicles etc, short term hire of (subs (1)(*b*)): Sch 6 para (xv).

Business gifts under £15 exempt: VATR 1979, r 31.

Hire purchase transactions (subs (1)(*b*)), obligation of supplier to issue invoice to finance provider: s 17(1)(proviso).

Exporters, zero rating of supplies to (subs (3)(1)(*e*), (*f*)): Sch 2 para (vi*a*).

Immovable goods (subs (1)(*f*), (5)), special provisions: s 4(2C).

Margin scheme goods (subs (6)(*d*)): s 10A(11).

Option not to apply (subs (6)(*d*)(proviso)), Revenue may prescribe circumstances: s 32(1)(ii).

Supplier of goods also supplying financial services (subs (1)(*b*); Sch 1 para (i)(*e*)), taxable amount: s 10(4C).

Taxable dealers supplying means of transport, special scheme (subs (6)(*d*)): s 12B(6).

Waiver of exemption (subs (5)(*b*)(iii)): s 7(3)(*b*).

Case law

Subject	Case	Case reference
VAT recovery entitlement where related services relate to a transfer of a business	*Abbey National plc v Commissioners of Customs & Excise*	22 February 2001, C–408/98
Fuel management agreement	*Auto Lease Holland BV v Bundesamt für Finanzen*	6 February 2003, C–185/01
Transfer of business	*S O'Cúlacháin, Inspector of Taxes v Stylo Barratt Shoes Ltd*	[2003] ITR (77)
Transfer of a totality of assets	*Zita Modes SARL v Administration de l'Enregistrement et des Domains*	27 November 2003, C–497/01
Services by intermediaries — place of supply	*Staatssectretaris van Financien v D Lipjes*	27 May 2004, C–68/03

Regulations

Subject	Regulation
Contract work	European Communities (Value Added Tax) Regulation 1995 (SI 363/95)
Single market introduction	European Communities (Value Added Tax) Regulations 1992 (SI 413/92)
Business gifts exemption	Value Added Tax Regulations 1979 (SI 63/79) Reg 31

Revenue precedent

Issue: Treatment of lease transactions between taxable persons.

Decision: In a case involving sale of lease rentals it was agreed to treat the payment as an advance payment of lease payments.

Issue: Disposal of a hotel to a partnership of 85 investors on whose behalf a holding company is set up as agent. A separate company will run hotel.

Decision: Section 3(5)(*b*)(iii) applied to disposal subject to receipt from company operating hotel that it would take responsibility for VAT on behalf of the various investors.

Issue: Transfer of goodwill or other intangible assets.

Decision: Transfer of goodwill or other intangible assets of an exempt activity to a person engaged in the same activity is regarded as a transaction which is not liable to VAT.

Issue: The supply and installation of plant in the State is a service requiring a foreign company to register in this State.

Decision: In a particular case which came to light after the event. On the understanding that the plant was supplied for a single consideration, and there was no separate charge for assembly, and that no installation work was carried out by the company concerned, then VAT registration in the State was not pursued.

Revenue publications

Business gifts: Statement of Practice VAT 3/94.

Distance selling: Statement of Practice VAT 14/92 (Replaced by Information Leaflet No 8/01).

Guide to Value Added Tax (Revenue Commissioners): Chapter 3.

Leasing assets — VAT treatment: Tax Briefing, Issue 24.

Transfer of a Business or Part Thereof — Information Leaflet 1/02.

Transfer of a Business or Part Thereof — VAT Implications: Tax Briefing, Issue 51.

Definition

"business": s 1(1); "Community"; s 1(1); "development": s 1(1); "developed": s 1(1); "goods": s 1(1); "livestock": s 1(1); "local authority": s 1(1); "intra-Community acquisition of goods": s 1(1), 3A; "new means of transport": s 1(1);"person": IA 2005, s 18(*c*); "regulations": s 1(1), 32; "supply": s 1(1); "tax": s 1(1);"taxable person": s 1(1), 8.

3A Intra-Community acquisition of goods

(Definition)

[(1) In this Act **"intra-Community acquisition of goods"** means the acquisition of—   a 28a(3)

    (*a*) movable goods, other than new means of transport, supplied by a person a 28a(3) registered for value added tax in a Member State [, [or by a person obliged to be registered for value added tax in a Member State,][1] or by a person who carries on an exempted activity in a Member State,][2] [or by a flat-rate farmer in a Member State,][3] to a person in another Member State (other than an individual who is not a taxable person or who is not entitled to elect to be a taxable person [, unless the said individual carries on an exempted activity][4]) and which have been dispatched or transported from the territory of a Member State to the territory of another Member State as a result of such supply, or

a 28a(2),
a 28c(A)

[(b) new means of transport supplied by a person in a Member State to a person in another Member State and which has been dispatched or transported from the territory of a Member State to the territory of another Member State as a result of being so supplied.][5]

(Exception:)

[(1A) An intra-Community acquisition of goods shall be deemed not to occur where the supply of those goods is subject to Value Added tax referred to in Council Directive No. 77/388/EEC of 17 May 1977 in the Member State of dispatch under the provisions implementing Article 26a or 28o (inserted by Council Directive No. 94/5/EC of 14 February 1994) of that Directive in that Member State.][5]

(Tax point/place of supply)

a 28b
(A)(1)

(2) (a) The place where an intra-Community acquisition of goods occurs shall be deemed to be the place where the goods are when the dispatch or transportation ends.

a 28b
(A)(2)

(b) Without prejudice to paragraph (a), when the person acquiring the goods quotes his value added tax registration number for the purpose of the acquisition, the place where an intra-Community acquisition of goods occurs shall be deemed to be within the territory of the Member State which issued that registration number [, unless the person acquiring the goods can establish that that acquisition has been subject to value added tax referred to in Council Directive No 77/388/EEC of 17 May 1977 in accordance with paragraph (a)][7].

(Deeming provisions)

(3) For the purposes of this section—

a 28a(7)

(a) a supply in the territory of another Member State shall be deemed to have arisen where, under similar circumstances, a supply would have arisen in the State under section 3, and

[(aa) an activity in another Member State shall be deemed to be an exempted activity where the same activity, if carried out in the State, would be an exempted activity, and

(ab) a person shall be deemed to be a flat-rate farmer in another Member State where, under similar circumstances, the person would be a flat-rate farmer in the State in accordance with section 12A, and][8]

(b) a person shall be deemed to be a taxable person or a person who is entitled to elect to be a taxable person in another Member State where, under similar circumstances, the person would be a taxable person or entitled to elect to be a taxable person in the State in accordance with section 8.

(Imports into other Member States by unregistered persons within another EU State)

(4) Where goods are dispatched or transported from outside the Community to a ᵃ²⁸ᵃ⁽³⁾ person in the State who is not registered for tax and who is not an individual, and value added tax referred to in Council Directive No. 77/388/EEC of 17 May 1977 is chargeable on the importation of the said goods into another Member State then, for the purposes of subsection (1), the person shall be deemed to be registered for value added tax in that other Member State and the goods shall be deemed to have been dispatched or transported from that other Member State.]⁹

[(5) Paragraph (*b*) of subsection (2) shall not apply where—

(Intra-Community trade)

    (i) a person quotes the registration number assigned to him in accordance with section 9 for the purpose of making an intra-Community acquisition and the goods are dispatched or transported from the territory of a Member State directly to the territory of another Member State, neither of which are the State,

(Triangulation)

    (ii) the person makes a subsequent supply of the goods to a person registered for value added tax in the Member State where the dispatch or transportation ends,

    (iii) the person issues an invoice in relation to that supply in such form and containing such particulars as would be required in accordance with section 17(1) if he made the supply of the goods in the State to a person registered for value added tax in another Member State, and containing an explicit reference to the EC simplified triangulation arrangements and indicating that the person in receipt of that supply is liable to account for the value added tax due in that Member State, and

(Vies statements)

    (iv) in accordance with regulations, the person includes a reference to the supply in the statement referred to in section 19A as if it were an intra-Community supply for the purposes of that section.]¹⁰

Amendments

¹   Inserted by FA 1997, s 97 as on and from 10 May 1997.
²   Inserted by FA 1993, s 83(*a*).
³   Inserted by EC(VAT)R 1992, r 6(*a*)(i) with effect from 1 January 1993.
⁴   Inserted by EC(VAT)R 1992, r 6(*a*)(ii) with effect from 1 January 1993.
⁵   Subs (1)(*b*) substituted by FA 1993, s 83(*b*).
⁶   Subs (1A) inserted by FA 1995, s 121 with effect from 1 July 1995.
⁷   Inserted by EC(VAT)R 1992, r 6(*b*) with effect from 1 January 1993.
⁸   Subs (3)(*aa*)–(*ab*) inserted by EC(VAT)R 1992, r 6(*c*) with effect from 1 January 1993.
⁹   Section 3A inserted by FA 1992, s 168 with effect from 1 January 1993.
¹⁰ Subs (5) inserted by EC(VAT)R 1992, r 6(*d*) with effect from 1 January 1993.

Regulations

Subject	*Regulation*
Intra-Community Acquisitions	European Communities (Value Added Tax) Regulations 1992 (SI 25/92)

Revenue publications

Guide to Value Added Tax (Revenue Commissioners): Chapter 11.

EU imports by Government departments, local authorities, etc: Statement of Practice VAT 11/92 (replaced by Information Leaflet No 11/01).

Intra-Community Acquisitions by Government Departments, Local Authorities etc: Information Leaflet No 11/01.

Postponed accounting and intra-Community Acquisitions: Statement of Practice VAT 15/92.

Single market intra-Community transactions in goods by traders: Leaflet September 92

Schemes for retailers concerning treatment of intra-Community acquisitions: Leaflet March 93.

Triangular Trade within the EU Single Market: Leaflet July 1992.

Definition

"Community": s 1(1); "exempted activity": s 1(1); "flat-rate farmer": s 1(1), 12A; "goods": s 1(1); "new means of transport": s 1(1); "person": IA 2005, s 18(c); "a person registered for value added tax": s 1(1); "taxable person": s 1(1), 8.

3B Alcohol products

[(1) Where alcohol products are supplied while being held under a duty-suspension arrangement then any such supply effected while the products are held under that arrangement, other than the last such supply in the State, shall be deemed not to be a supply for the purposes of this Act other than for the purposes of section 12 and any previous—

> (*a*) intra-Community acquisition, or

> (*b*) importation,

of such products shall be disregarded for the purposes of this Act.

(2) Where tax is chargeable on a supply referred to in subsection (1) then, notwithstanding section 19(1), the tax on that supply shall be due at the same time as the duty of excise on the products is due:

Provided that this subsection shall not apply to a supply of the kind referred to in subparagraph (*a*)(I), (*b*) or (*cc*) of paragraph (i) or in paragraph (i*a*) of the Second Schedule.

(3) Where, other than in the circumstances set out in section 8(2B)(*b*), a taxable person makes an intra-Community acquisition of alcohol products and by virtue of such acquisition, and in accordance with Chapter II of Part II of the Finance Act, 1992, and any other enactment which is to be construed together with that Chapter, the duty of excise on those products is payable in the State, then, notwithstanding section 19(1A), the tax on the said intra-Community acquisition shall be due at the same time as the duty of excise on the products is due.

(4) Where tax is chargeable on the importation of alcohol products, which are then placed under a duty-suspension arrangement then, notwithstanding section 15(6), the tax on that importation shall be due at the same time as the duty of excise on the products is due.

(5) Notwithstanding subsections (1) and (1A) of section 10 and section 15(3), where the provisions of subsection (2), (3) or (4) apply, the amount on which tax

is chargeable shall include the amount of the duty of excise chargeable on the products on their release for consumption in the State.

(6) Notwithstanding any other provision to the contrary contained in this Act, where the provisions of subsection (2), (3) or (4) apply then—

> (*a*) the tax shall be payable at the same time as the duty of excise is payable on the products,

> (*b*) the provisions of the statutes which relate to the duties of excise and the management thereof and of any instrument relating to duties of excise made under statute, shall, with any necessary modifications and exceptions as may be specified in regulations, apply to such tax as if it were a duty of excise, and

> (*c*) the person by whom the tax is payable shall complete such form as is provided for the purposes of this subsection by the Revenue Commissioners.

(7) In this section—

"alcohol products" means the excisable products referred to at subsections (*a*), (*b*), (*c*), (*d*) and (*e*) of section 104 of the Finance Act, 1992;

"duty-suspension arrangement" has the meaning assigned to it by section 103 of the Finance Act, 1992.]¹

Amendment

¹ Section 3B inserted by FA 1993, s 84 with effect from 1 August 1993.

Cross-references

Deductible tax: s 12(1)(*a*)(iic).

Revenue publications

Guide to Value Added Tax (Revenue Commissioners): Ch 6.3.
Payment of VAT on alcohol products at time of payment of excise duty: Statement of Practice VAT 3/93.

Definitions

"excisable products": s 1(1); "intra-Community acquisition of goods": s 1(1), 3A; "person": IA 2005, s 18(*c*); "regulations": s 1(1), 32; "supply": s 1(1); "tax": s 1(1); "taxable person": s 1(1).

---

4 Special provisions in relation to the [supply] of immovable goods

(What is vatable property?)

(1) (*a*)   This section applies to immovable goods—

> (i) which have been developed by or on behalf of the person [supplying]¹ them, or

> (ii) in respect of which the person [supplying]¹ them was, or would, but for the operation of section 3(5)(*b*)(iii), have been at any time entitled to claim a deduction under section 12 for any tax borne or paid in relation to a [supply]² or development of them.

(What is interest?)

[(*b*) In this section **"interest"**, in relation to immovable goods, means an estate or interest therein which, when it was created was for a period of at least ten years or, if it was for a period of less than ten years, its terms contained an option for the person in whose favour the interest was created to extend it to a period of at least ten years, but does not include a mortgage, and a reference to the disposal of an interest includes a reference to the creation of an interest, and an interval of the type referred to in subsection (2A) shall be deemed to be an interest for the purposes of this section.][3]

(Option to extend an interest)

[(*c*) Where an interest is created and, at the date of its creation, its terms contain one or more options for the person in whose favour the interest was so created to extend that interest, then that interest shall be deemed to be for the period from the date of creation of that interest to the date that that interest would expire if those options were so exercised.][4]

(Scope of supply of property)

(2) Subject to ...[5], paragraphs (*c*), (*d*), (*e*) and (*f*) of section 3(1), section 19(2) and subsections (3), (4) and (5), a [supply][2] of immovable goods shall be deemed, for the purposes of this Act, to take place if, but only if, a person having an interest in immovable goods to which this section applies disposes [(including by way of surrender or by way of assignment)],[6] as regards the whole or any part of those goods, of that interest or of an interest which derives therefrom.

(VAT treatment of surrendered lease followed by disposal)

[(2A) Where the surrender of an interest in immovable goods is chargeable to tax, and those goods have not been developed since the date of creation of that interest (hereafter referred to in this subsection as a **"surrendered interest"**), and the person to whom the surrendered interest was surrendered subsequently disposes, as regards the whole or any part of those goods, of an interest or of an interest which derives therefrom on a date before the date on which the surrendered interest would, but for its surrender, have expired, then that disposal shall be deemed to be a supply of immovable goods, for the purposes of this Act, and where the interest (hereafter referred to in this section as a **"subsequent interest"**) disposed of is for a period which extends beyond the date on which the surrendered interest would, but for its surrender, have expired, the disposal of that subsequent interest shall be treated, for the purposes of this Act, as if it were the disposal of an interest for the period equal to the interval between the date of the disposal of the subsequent interest and the date on which the surrendered interest would, but for its surrender, have expired (a period hereafter referred to in this section as an **"interval"**), and where such interval is for a period of less than ten years, that disposal shall be treated as a supply of immovable goods to which subsection (6) applies:

Provided that the person, who disposes of a subsequent interest in which the interval is for a period of less than ten years, may opt, subject to and in accordance with regulations, if any, to have that disposal treated as a supply of immovable goods to which subsection (6) does not apply.

(New lease following surrender-reversion)

(2B) Where a person disposes of a subsequent interest in such circumstances that such person retains the reversion on the interest disposed of, then—

(*a*) if the subsequent interest expires on or after the date on which the surrendered interest which enabled that person to dispose of a subsequent interest (hereafter referred to in this subsection as "**the surrendered interest**") would, but for its surrender, have expired, the provisions of subsection (4) shall not apply to that reversion;

(*b*) if the subsequent interest expires prior to the date on which the surrendered interest would, but for its surrender, have expired, the provisions of subsection (4) shall apply to that reversion and that reversion shall be deemed for the purposes of subsection (4) to be for the period between the date of expiry of the subsequent interest and the date on which the surrendered interest would, but for its surrender, have expired.

(Surrender of lease and subsequent non-taxable use of property:)

(2C) Where the surrender of an interest in immovable goods is chargeable to tax, and those goods have not been developed since that interest was created and the person to whom the interest that was surrendered surrenders possession of those goods or any part thereof, on a date before the date on which the interest that was surrendered would, but for its surrender, have expired, in such circumstances that that surrender of possession does not constitute a supply of goods, that surrender of possession shall be deemed for the purposes of section 3(1)(*f*), to be an appropriation of the goods or of the part thereof, as the case may be, for a purpose other than the purpose of that person's business except where such surrender of possession is made—

(*a*) in accordance with an agreement for the leasing or letting of those goods where the person surrendering possession is chargeable to tax in respect of the rent or other payment under the agreement, or

(*b*) in connection with a transfer which, in accordance with section 3(5), is deemed, for the purposes of this Act, not to be a supply.][7]

(Self-supplies of property)

(3) (*a*) [Subject to paragraphs (*aa*) and (*b*)][8], where a person having an interest in immovable goods to which this section applies surrenders possession of those goods or of any part thereof in such circumstances that the surrender does not constitute a [supply][2] of the goods for the purposes of subsection (2), the surrender shall be deemed, for the purposes of section 3(1)(*f*), to be an appropriation of the goods or of the part thereof, as the case may be, for a purpose other than the purpose of his business.

[(*aa*) Where a person having an interest in immovable goods to which this section applies surrenders possession of those goods or of any part thereof in such circumstances that the surrender does not constitute a supply of the goods for the purposes of subsection (2), the provisions of paragraph (*a*) shall not apply when this paragraph and paragraph (*ab*) take effect pursuant to section 95(2) of the Finance Act 2005.

(*ab*) Subject to paragraph (*b*), where a person having an interest in immovable goods to which this section applies surrenders possession of those goods or any part thereof in such circumstances that the surrender does not constitute a supply of the goods for the purposes of subsection (2), that person shall be liable for an amount, in this paragraph referred to as a deductibility adjustment, which shall be payable as if it were tax due by that person in accordance with section 19 for the taxable period in which the surrender occurred, and that deductibility adjustment shall be calculated in accordance with the following formula:

$$\frac{T \times (Y\text{-}N)}{Y}$$

where—

T   is the amount of tax which the person who surrenders possession of the goods was entitled to deduct in accordance with section 12 in respect of that person's acquisition of the interest in and development of the goods the possession of which is being surrendered,

Y   is 20 or, if the interest when it was acquired by the person who surrenders possession of the goods was for a period of less than 20 years, the number of full years in that interest, and

N   is the number of full years since that person acquired the interest in the immovable goods being surrendered or, if the goods were developed since that interest was acquired, the number of full years since the most recent development:

but if that N is greater than that Y, such deductibility adjustment shall be deemed to be nil.][9]

(Exceptions re: self-supply:)

(*b*) This subsection shall not apply to—

(i) any such surrender of possession made in accordance with an agreement for the leasing or letting of the goods if the person surrendering possession is chargeable to tax in respect of the rent or other payment under the agreement, or

(ii) a surrender in connection with a transfer which, in accordance with section 3(5), is declared, for the purposes of this Act, not to be a [supply][2].

[(3A)(*a*) Where a person having an interest in immovable goods to which this section applies surrenders possession of those goods or of any part of them by means of a disposal of that interest or of an interest which derives from that interest, and where the value of the interest being disposed of is less than its economic value then for the purposes of this Act such disposal—

(i) shall be deemed not to be a supply of immovable goods for the purposes of subsection (2), but

(ii) shall be deemed to be a letting of immovable goods to which paragraph (iv) of the First Schedule applies.

(*b*) This subsection does not apply to the disposal of a freehold interest.

(*c*) Where a person establishes to the satisfaction of the Revenue Commissioners that the value of an interest in immovable goods being disposed of by such person is less than the economic value of those immovable goods because of an unforeseen change in market conditions affecting the value of that interest since such person acquired and developed those goods, then the Revenue Commissioners may determine that that disposal be treated as a supply of immovable goods for the purposes of subsection (2).

(*d*) For the purposes of this subsection—

"economic value", in relation to an interest in immovable goods being disposed of, means [the total amount on which tax was chargeable][10] to the person disposing of that interest [in respect of or in relation to][11] that person's acquisition of that interest and [in respect of or in relation to][11] any development of those immovable goods by or on behalf of that person since that acquisition; but if—

(i) there was no development of those immovable goods by or on behalf of that person since that person's acquisition of that interest, and

(ii) that person disposes, including by way of surrender or assignment, of an interest (in this subsection referred to as a "lesser interest") which is derived from the interest which that person acquired (in this subsection referred to as a "greater interest"), and

(iii) the lesser interest is an interest of not more than 35 years,

then the economic value of the lesser interest shall be deemed to be the amount calculated in accordance with the following formula:

$$E \times \frac{N1}{N2}$$

where—

E   is the economic value of the greater interest,

N1   is the number of full years in the lesser interest, and

N2   is the number of full years in the greater interest, but if the number of full years in the greater interest exceeds 35 or if the greater interest is a freehold interest then N2 shall be deemed to be equal to 35, but where—

(I) the disposal of the lesser interest is not a disposal by way of surrender or assignment, and

(II) the amount so calculated is less than 75 per cent of the economic value of the greater interest,

then the economic value of the lesser interest shall be deemed to be 75 per cent of the economic value of the greater interest;

"the value of an interest being disposed of" means the amount on which tax would be chargeable in accordance with section 10 if that disposal were deemed to be a supply of immovable goods in accordance with subsection (2).][12]

(Reversions)

(4) Where a person having an interest in immovable goods to which this section applies disposes, as regards the whole or any part of those goods, of an interest which derives from that interest in such circumstances that he retains the reversion on the interest disposed of, he shall, in relation to the reversion so retained, be deemed, for the purposes of section 3(1)(*f*), to have made an appropriation of the goods or of the part thereof, as the case may be, for a purpose other than the purpose of his business.

(Development of sites)

[(5) Where a person disposes of an interest in immovable goods to another person and in connection with that disposal a taxable person enters into an agreement with that other person or person connected with that other person to carry out a development in relation to those immovable goods, then—

(*a*) the person who disposes of the interest in the said immovable goods shall, in relation to that disposal, be deemed to be a taxable person,

(*b*) the disposal of the interest in the said immovable goods shall be deemed to be a supply of those goods made in the course or furtherance of business, and

(*c*) the disposal of the interest in the said immovable goods shall, notwithstanding subsection (1), be deemed to be a disposal of an interest in immovable goods to which this section applies.][13]

(Non-VATable/exempt property)

[(6) (*a*) Tax shall not be charged on the supply of immovable goods—

(i) which were used in such circumstances so that the person making the supply had no right to deduction under section 12 in relation to tax borne or paid on the acquisition or development of those goods, or

(ii) which have been occupied before the specified day and had not been developed between that date and the date of the supply.

(*b*) Paragraph (*a*) does not apply to a supply of immovable goods, being goods —

(i) to which subsection 5 applies, or

    (ii) which were acquired by the person making the supply as a result of a transfer in accordance with section 3(5)(*b*)(iii) and if tax had been chargeable on such transfer the person making the supply would have had a right to deduction under section 12 in relation to such tax.]¹⁴

(Turnover limits)

(7) The provisions of section 8(3) shall not apply in relation to a person who makes a [supply]² of goods to which this section applies.

(Reverse charge)

[(8) (*a*) Where tax is chargeable in relation to a supply of immovable goods which is a surrender of an interest in immovable goods or an assignment of an interest in immovable goods to—

    (i) a taxable person,

    (ii) a Department of State or a local authority, or

    (iii) a person who supplies immovable goods of a kind referred to in paragraph (*a*) of the definition of "exempted activity" in section 1 or services of a kind referred to in paragraphs (i), (iv), (ix), (xi), (xi*a*), (xiii) and (xiv) of the First Schedule, in the course or furtherance of business,

then, the person to whom those goods are supplied shall be accountable for and liable to pay the tax chargeable on that supply and the said tax shall be payable as if it were tax due by that person in accordance with section 19 for the taxable period within which the supply to the person took place and for these purposes the person to whom the goods are supplied shall be a taxable person and the person who made the surrender or assignment shall not be accountable for or liable to pay the said tax.

  (*b*) Notwithstanding subsection (2A)(*a*) of section 8, if the supply referred to in paragraph (*a*) is to a Department of State or a local authority, that Department of State or local authority shall be accountable for and liable to pay the tax referred to in that paragraph.

  (*c*) (i) A surrender or assignment of immovable goods referred to in paragraph (*a*) shall be treated as a supply of goods made by the person to whom the goods are supplied.

    (ii) Upon the surrender or assignment of immovable goods referred to in subparagraph (i), the person who makes the surrender or assignment shall issue a document to the person to whom the surrender or assignment is made indicating the value of the interest being surrendered or assigned and the amount of tax chargeable on that surrender or assignment.

    (iii) For the purposes of section 12, that section shall apply as if this paragraph had not been enacted.

(9) (*a*) Where an interest in immovable goods is created in such circumstances that a reversion on that interest (hereafter referred to in this subsection

as a "reversionary interest") is created and retained, then any subsequent disposal to another person of that reversionary interest or of an interest derived entirely therefrom shall be deemed to be a supply of immovable goods to which subsection (6) applies, provided that, since the date the first-mentioned interest was created, those goods have not been developed by, on behalf of, or to the benefit of, the person making such subsequent disposal: but the provisions of this subsection shall not be construed as applying to a disposal of an interest which includes an interval.

(*b*) The Revenue Commissioners may make regulations specifying the circumstances or conditions under which development work on immovable goods is not treated, for the purposes of this subsection, as being on behalf of or to the benefit of a person.]¹⁵

(Post-letting expenses)

[(10)(*a*) Where a disposal of an interest in immovable goods is chargeable to tax and the person who acquires that interest is obliged to pay rent to another person (hereafter referred to in this subsection as **"the landlord"**) under the terms and conditions laid down in respect of that interest, the landlord—

  (i) shall, notwithstanding the provisions of section 8, be deemed not to be a taxable person in respect of transactions in relation to those immovable goods other than—

    (I) supplies of those immovable goods on which tax is chargeable in accordance with the provisions of this section, or

    (II) supplies of other goods or services effected for consideration by the landlord, or

    (III) post-letting expenses in respect of that interest,

  (ii) shall not be entitled to deduct tax in respect of transactions in relation to those immovable goods other than—

    (I) supplies of those immovable goods on which tax is chargeable in accordance with the provisions of this section other than subsection (4), or

    (II) supplies of other goods or services effected for consideration by the landlord, or

    (III) post-letting expenses in respect of that interest,

  (iii) shall be deemed, where that landlord is not the person who made the disposal of the interest, to be a taxable person in respect of post-letting expenses in relation to that interest and shall in relation to those post-letting expenses be entitled to deduct tax, in accordance with section 12, as if those post-letting expenses were for the purposes of the landlord's taxable supplies.

(Examples of post letting expenses)

(*b*) For the purposes of this subsection post-letting expenses in relation to an interest in immovable goods are expenses which the landlord incurs—

(i) in carrying out services which the landlord is obliged to carry out under the terms and conditions of the written contract entered into on the disposal of the interest which was chargeable to tax but does not include transactions the obligation to perform which is not reflected in the consideration on which tax was charged on the disposal of that interest, or

(ii) which directly relate to the collection of rent arising under the contract referred to in subparagraph (i), or

(iii) which directly relate to a review of rent where the terms and conditions of the contract referred to in subparagraph (i) provide for such a review, or

(iv) which directly relate to the exercise of an option to extend the interest or to exercise a break-clause in relation to that interest where the terms and conditions of the contract referred to in subparagraph (i) provide for such an option or such a break- clause,

but do not include any expenses relating to goods or services of the type specified in section 12(3).][16]

Amendments

[1] Substituted by VATAA 1978, s 30(2) with effect from 1 March 1979; previously "delivering".

[2] Substituted by VATAA 1978, s 30(2) with effect from 1 March 1979; previously "delivery".

[3] Subs (1)(*b*) substituted by FA 1997, s 98(*a*)(i) as on and from 26 March 1997.

[4] Subs (1)(*c*) inserted by FA 1997, s 98(*a*)(ii) as on and from 26 March 1997.

[5] Deleted by VATAA 1978, s 30(1) with effect from 1 March 1979; previously "section 2(2)".

[6] Inserted by FA 1997, s 98(*b*) as on and from 26 March 1997.

[7] Subss (2A)–(2C) inserted by FA 1997, s 98(*c*) as on and from 26 March 1997.

[8] Substituted by FA 2005, s 100(*a*) with effect from such day as the Minister for Finance may, by order, appoint; previously "Subject to paragraph (*b*)". By virtue of SI 225/2005, 1 May 2005 appointed as start date.

[9] Subs (3)(*aa*)–(*ab*) inserted by FA 2005, s 100(*b*) with effect from such day as the Minister for Finance may, by order, appoint. By virtue of SI 225/2005, 1 May 2005 appointed as start date.

[10] Substituted by FA 2003, s 114(*a*) with effect from 28 March 2003; previously "the amount on which tax was chargeable".

[11] Substituted by FA 2003, s 114(*b*) with effect from 28 March 2003; previously "in respect of".

[12] Subs (3A) inserted by FA 2002, s 99 with effect from on and from 25 March 2002.

[13] Subs (5) substituted by FA 1995, s 122(*a*) with effect from 1 July 1995.

[14] Subs (6)(*a*) substituted by FA 2005, s 100(*c*) with effect from 25 March 2005.

[15] Subss (8)–(9) substituted by FA 2005, s 100(*d*) with effect from 25 March 2005.

[14] Subs (10) inserted by FA 1998, s 106 with effect from 27 March 1998.

Cross-references

Tax (subss (1)(*a*)(ii) and (6)(*a*)) charged at 0% (s 11(1)(*b*)) by virtue of Sch 2 para (vi*a*) is deemed to be deductible under s 12: s 13A(7).

Valuation of interests in immovable goods, Revenue may make regulations: s 32(1)(*t*); regulations: VATR 1979, r 19.

Meaning of assignment: s 1(1).

Meaning of "surrender" (subs (1)(*b*)): s 1(1).

Waiver of exemptions (subs (2C)(*a*)): s 7(1).

Taxable amount (subs (1)): s 10(10).

Tax deductible (subs (8)): s 12(1)(*a*)(iii*c*)–(iii*d*).

Case law

Subject	Case	Case reference
Property unit trust, deductibility of pre and post lease expenditure	*Erin Executor and Trustee Company v Revenue Commissioners*	16 Dec 1997, Supreme Court 363 and 369/94, (II) ITR (3)
The mere acquisition of ownership in and the holding of bonds and the receipt of income therefrom cannot be regarded as economic activities within meaning of Art 4(2)	*Finanzamt Augsburg-Stadt v Markegemeinde Welden*	6 February 1997, C–247/95
Reverse premium in relation to lease	*Mirror Group plc v Commissioners of Customs & Excise*	9 October 2001, C–409/98
Inducement payment in relation to the assignment of a lease	*Cantor Fitzgerald International v Commissioners of Customs & Excise*	9 October 2001, C–108/99
Member State entitlement regarding treatment of "low value" leases of property as supplies of goods	*Stichting "Goed Wonen" v Staatssecretaris van Financien*	4 October 2001, C–326/99

Regulations

Subject	Regulation
Waiver of exemption	Value Added Tax Regulations 1979 (SI 63/79) Reg 4
Waiver of exemption	Value Added Tax (Waiver of Exemption) (Amendment) Regulations, 1998 (SI 228/98)
Valuation of interest	Value Added Tax Regulations 1979 (SI 63/79) Reg 19
Valuation of interest	Value Added Tax (Valuation of Interests in Immovable Goods) (Amendment) Regulations 1998 (SI 482/98)

Revenue precedent

Issue: Sale and leaseback transactions.

Decision: Not taxable, subject to conditions. This treatment was extended to unregistered entities. Section 4 does not apply.

Issue: Two registered entities sell properties to a State body as trustee who in turn sells to a third party who is VAT-registered. Can the invoices be raised by the first-named to the latter? (one contract involved).

Decision: It was agreed that the invoices could be raised by the first-named to the last-named, ignoring the State body.

Issue: In a sale and leaseback situation the entity who leased the property back were allowed deductibility on post-lease development expenditure as the latter related directly to the completion of the development of the property.

Decision: Deductibility allowed subject to usual criteria and to the fact that the enhanced value was reflected in the value of the interest disposed of.

Issue: Supplemental deed created in exchange for surrender of portion of original property subject of main deed. Rent remained unchanged.

Decision: The said exchange was disregarded for the purposes of VATA 1972, s 4. No VAT arises.

Issue: Company with two subsidiaries, one has the freehold reversion, the second has a long leasehold interest. The latter creates long leases to another party whilst the former carries out the redevelopment work and sells the freehold interest to a pension fund. Company with freehold reversion is treated as a taxable person as regards disposal.

Decision: Joint venture registration allowed between the holder of the leasehold interest and the developer who holds the reversion.

Issue: Bakery transferred its trade to a wholly owned subsidiary and allowed it to use premises and equipment without a lease. Parent company later sell freehold interest and equipment to subsidiary, who in turn sell to a third party who will carry on bakery trade.

Decision: Technically the initial surrender of possession gives rise to a self-supply, however, the provisions of s (3)(5)(*b*)(iii) apply.

Issue: Do short term lettings of a taxable property within a VAT group give rise to a self-supply?

Decision: As there is no supply within a VAT group a self-supply would not arise.

Revenue publications

Building and Associated Services: Leaflet No 2 of 1999.

"Economic Value Test": Tax Briefing Issue 55.

"Erin Executor" Case: Tax Briefing Issue 32.

Finance Act 2005 issues: Tax Briefing 60.

Goods and services supplied through landlords: Leaflet May 1985.

Multiplier: Leaflet 2004.

Repayment claims arising from "Erin Executor" Supreme Court judgment: Leaflet No 3 1998.

Revenue VAT Guide, Chs 3, 4 and 6.

Reverse Charge: Leaflet June 2004.

Post Letting Expenditure: VAT recovery position: Leaflet No 4 1998.

Surrenders and Assignments: Tax Briefing Issue 56.

VAT Multiplier: Tax Briefing Issues 47 and 55

VAT on Property Transactions: FA 1997 Changes: Revenue Guide.

VAT on Property Transactions: Leaflet July 1980.

VAT Multiplier: Tax Triefing Issue 33.

Waiver of Exemption: Tax Briefing Issue 33.

10% Rule: Leaflet June 2004.

"10% Rule": Tax Briefing Issue 56.

Definition

"assignment": s 1(1); "business": s 1(1); "development": s 1(1); "developed": s 1(1); "goods": s 1(1); "immovable goods": s 1(1); "person": IA 2005, s 18(*c*); "a person registered for value added tax": s 1(1); "regulations": s 1(1), 32; "the specified day": s 1(1); "supply": s 1(1); "surrender": s 1(1); "tax": s 1(1); "taxable person": s 1(1), 8.

4A Person liable to pay tax in relation to certain supplies of immovable goods

(Scope for use of reverse charge)

[(1) Subject to the provisions of subsection (3), where tax is chargeable in respect of the letting of immovable goods which is deemed to be a supply of goods in accordance with section 4 and the lessee would, but for the operation of this section, have been entitled to claim a deduction under section 12(1)(*a*)(i) for all the said tax borne in relation to that supply, the lessor shall not be liable to pay the said tax and, in that case, the lessee shall be liable to pay the said tax as if the lessee had supplied the goods in the course or furtherance of business.

(Application for facility to use reverse charge)

(2) Where, in relation to a supply, the lessor and the lessee wish the provisions of subsection (1) to apply they shall—

    (*a*)   complete such application form as may be provided by the Revenue Commissioners for that purpose,

    (*b*)   certify the particulars shown on such form to be correct, and

    (*c*)   submit to the Revenue Commissioners the completed and certified application form, together with such further information in support of the application as may be requested by the said Commissioners.

(Notification by Revenue)

(3) Where, in relation to a supply of goods referred to in subsection (1), the lessor and lessee have furnished the particulars referred to in subsection (2), the Revenue Commissioners shall, where they are satisfied that it is in order to apply the provisions in subsection (1) in relation to that supply, notify the lessor and the lessee by notice in writing that the provisions of subsection (1) are to be applied in relation to that supply.

(Invoicing requirements)

(4) Where the provisions of subsection (1) apply in relation to a supply, the invoice issued by the lessor in accordance with section 17 shall show the following endorsement in lieu of the amount of tax chargeable:

> "In accordance with section 4A of the Value Added Tax Act, 1972, the lessee is liable for the Value Added tax of £X.",

and, in that endorsement, the lessor shall substitute the amount of tax chargeable in respect of that supply of goods for ["€X"][1].

(Record keeping)

(5) Every notification received by a taxable person, which has been issued to that person by the Revenue Commissioners in accordance with subsection (3), shall be part of the records which that person is required to keep in accordance with section 16.

(Authorised officers)

(6) For the purposes of this section, and subject to the direction and control of the Revenue Commissioners, any power, function or duty conferred or imposed on them may be exercised or performed on their behalf by an officer of the Revenue Commissioners.

(Definitions)

(7) In this section–

"lessee" means the person who receives the goods referred to in subsection (1);

"lessor" means the person who supplies the goods referred to in subsection (1).][2]

Amendments

[1]   Substituted by FA 2001, s 240 and Sch 5 Part 4 with effect from 1 January 2002; previously "£X".

[2]   Section 4A inserted by FA 1994, s 93 with effect from 7 July 1995 (the date appointed by the Minister for Finance — Finance Act 1994 (Commencement of Sections 93 and 96(*a*)) Order 1995, SI 184/95).

Revenue publications

Section 4A applications: Tax Briefing Issue 40.
Surrender and leaseback: Tax Briefing Issue 45.

Definitions

"business": s 1(1); "immovable goods": s 1(1); "supply": s 1(1); "tax": s 1(1); "taxable person": s 1(1).

5 [Supply] of services

(Definition)

[(1) In this Act **"supply"**, in relation to a service, means the performance or a 6 omission of any act or the toleration of any situation other than the supply of goods and other than a transaction specified in section 3(5).

(Catering — food and drink)

(2) The provision of food and drink, of a kind specified in paragraph (xii) of the Second Schedule, in a form suitable for human consumption without further preparation—

(*a*) by means of a vending machine,

(*b*) in the course of operating a hotel, restaurant, cafe, refreshment house, canteen, establishment licensed for the sale for consumption on the premises of intoxicating liquor, catering business or similar business, or

(*c*) in the course of operating any other business in connection with the carrying on of which facilities are provided for the consumption of the food or drink supplied,

shall be deemed, for the purposes of this Act, to be a supply of services and not a supply of goods.

(3) Any of the following shall, if so provided by regulations, and in accordance therewith, be deemed, for the purposes of this Act, to be a supply of services by a person for consideration in the course or furtherance of his business—

(Self-supply of services)   a 6(2)

[(*a*) the use of goods forming part of the assets of a business—

(i) for the private use of a taxable person or of such person's staff, or

(ii) for any purposes other than those of the taxable person's business,

where the tax on such goods is wholly or partly deductible,

(*b*) the supply of services carried out free of charge by a taxable person for such person's own private use or that of the staff of such person or for any purposes other than those of such person's business,

(*c*) the supply by a taxable person of services for the purposes of such a 6(3) person's business where the tax on such services, were they supplied by another taxable person, would not be wholly deductible.]¹

(Receipt of services from abroad)

[(3A) Where a person is in receipt of a service, other than a service [specified in paragraphs (*f*) and (*g*) of subsection (6) or in the Fourth Schedule]², for the purposes of his business and the circumstances are such that value added tax referred to in Community Council Directive No.77/388/EEC is not payable on the supply or, if it is payable, is, in accordance with the laws of the country in which the supplier has his establishment, repayable to or deductible by the person, that person shall be deemed, for the purposes of this Act, to have himself supplied the service for consideration in the course or furtherance of his business and shall be liable for tax on the supply except where such tax, if it were chargeable, would be wholly deductible under section 12.]³

(Undisclosed agent)

a 6(4) (4) The supply of services through a person (in this subsection referred to as the agent) who, while purporting to act on his own behalf, concludes agreements in his own name but on the instructions of and for the account of another person, shall be deemed for the purposes of this Act, to constitute a supply of the services to and simultaneously by the agent.

(Special provision — (services of a barrister))

[(4A) Where services are supplied by a person and the person is not legally entitled to recover consideration in respect of or in relation to such supply but moneys are received in respect of or in relation to such supply, the services in question shall be deemed, for the purposes of this Act, to have been supplied for consideration and the moneys received shall be deemed to be consideration that the person who supplied the services in question became entitled to receive in respect of or in relation to the supply of those services.][4]

(Legal services supplied to persons indemnified under policies of insurance)

[(4B) Where a person is indemnified under a policy of insurance in respect of any amount payable in respect of services of a barrister or solicitor, those services shall be deemed, for the purposes of this Act, to be supplied to, and received by, the said person.][5]

(Place of supply of services — general rule)

a 9(1) (5) Subject to subsection (6) and (7), the place where a service is supplied shall be deemed, for the purposes of this Act, to be the place where the person supplying the service [has established his business or][6] has his establishment or (if more than one) the establishment of his which is most concerned with the supply or (if he has no establishment) his usual place of residence.

(Place of supply of services — special rules)
(Immovable goods)

a 9(2)(a) (6) (*a*) The place of supply of services connected with immovable goods, including the services of estate agents, architects and firms providing on-site supervision in relation to such goods, shall be deemed, for the purposes of this Act, to be the place where the goods are situated.

(Transport services)

a 9(2)(b) [(*b*) Transport services, with the exception of intra-Community transport of goods, shall be deemed, for the purposes of this Act, to be supplied where the transport takes place.][7]

a 9(2)(c) (*c*) The following services shall be deemed, for the purposes of this Act, to be supplied where they are physically performed:

a 28(b)(D) (i) cultural, artistic, sporting, scientific, educational, entertainment or similar services,

[(ii) ancillary transport activities such as loading, unloading and handling, with the exception of activities ancillary to the intra-Community transport of goods received by a person registered for value added tax in any Member State,][8]

(iii) valuation of movable goods, [except where the provisions of subparagraph (iv) of paragraph (*f*), apply][9],

(iv)   work on movable goods [including contract work, except where the provisions of subparagraph (iv) of paragraph (*f*) apply][10].

(Hiring out of movable goods by non-EU person)

[(*d*)   In confirmation of the provisions contained in the Value Added Tax a 9(3)(b) (Place of Supply of Certain Services) Regulations, 1985 (SI No 343 of 1985), which regulations are hereby revoked, the place of supply of services consisting of the hiring out of movable goods by a person established outside the Community shall be deemed to be the place where the movable goods are, or are to be, effectively used.]][11]

(Telecommunications services supplied by non-EU suppliers)

[(*dd*)   Notwithstanding the provisions of subparagraph (v) of paragraph (*e*), w a 9(3)(b) here a person supplies a telecommunications service [, or a telephone card as defined in subsection (6A),][12] [or a radio or television broadcasting service,][13] in the course or furtherance of business from outside the Community to a person in the State who is not a person to whom the provisions of subparagraph (ii), (iii) or (iv) of paragraph (*e*) apply, the place of supply of that service shall be deemed, for the purposes of this Act, to be the State.][14]

(Telecommunications services supplied to non- EU residents)

[(*ddd*)   The place of supply of a telecommunications service or of a telephone a 9(3)(b) card as defined in subsection (6A) shall be deemed, for the purposes of this Act, to be the State when that service is supplied by a taxable person from an establishment in the State and it is received, otherwise than for a business purpose, by a person whose usual place of residence is situated outside the Community, and it is effectively used and enjoyed in the State.][15]

[(*dddd*)   Notwithstanding the provisions of subsection (5), the place of supply of services consisting of the hiring out of means of transport by a person established in the State shall be deemed to be outside the Community where such means of transport are, or are to be, effectively used and enjoyed outside the Community.][16]

(Fourth Schedule Services)

(Place of supply)

[(*e*)   The place of supply of services of any of the descriptions specified in a 9(2)(e) the Fourth Schedule [with the exception of the supply of services referred to in paragraphs (*ddd*) and (*ee*) [paragraphs (*ddd*), (*ee*) and (*eee*)][17] in the circumstances specified in those paragraphs respectively and],[18] (with the exception of services of the description specified in paragraph (*ia*) of the said Schedule supplied by a person who has his establishment outside the Community,) shall be deemed, for the purposes of this Act to be—

(i)   in case they are received, otherwise than for a business purpose, by a person whose usual place of residence is situated outside the Community, the place where he usually resides,

(ii) in case they are received, for the purposes of any business carried on by him, by a person—

    (I) who has his establishment outside the Community and has not also an establishment in the Community, or

    (II) who has his establishment in the Community but does not have his establishment or, if he has more than one establishment, his principal establishment in the country in which, but for this subparagraph, the services would be deemed to be supplied, [or][19]

    [(III) who has an establishment in the State and his principal establishment in the country in which, but for this subparagraph, the services would be deemed to be supplied,][20]

the place where he has his establishment or, if he has more than one establishment, the establishment of his at which or for the purposes of which the services are most directly used or to be used, as the case may be,

(iii) in case they are received, for the purposes of any business carried on by him, by a person resident in the Community who has no establishment anywhere, the place where he usually resides,

[(iii*a*) in case they are received, otherwise than for a business purpose, by a person in the State (referred to in this subparagraph as the "recipient") and are supplied by a person who has his establishment in another Member State of the Community, in circumstances in which Value Added tax referred to in Council Directive No 77/388/ EEC of 17 May 1977 is not payable in that Member State because the recipient held himself out or allowed himself to be held out as a taxable person within the meaning of Article 4 of that Directive in respect of such supplies, the State,][21]

(iv) in case they are received by a department of State, by a local authority or by a body established by statute, and are supplied—

    (I) by a person who has his establishment outside the Community and has not also an establishment in the Community, or

    (II) by a person who has his establishment in another Member State of the Community, in circumstances in which value added tax referred to in Community Council Directive No.77/388/EEC is not payable in that Member State in respect of the supply,

the State,

(v) in any other case, the place specified in subsection (5) that is appropriate to the circumstances.][22]

[(*ee*) The place of supply of services of the description specified in paragraph (v) of the Fourth Schedule shall be deemed, for the purposes of this Act, to be the State, when those services are supplied by a person in the course or furtherance of business established in the State and they are received, otherwise than for a business purpose, by a person whose usual place of residence is situated outside the Community, and they are effectively used and enjoyed in the State.]²³

[(*eea*) Where money transfer services are provided to a person in the State and are effectively used and enjoyed in the State, the place of supply of intermediary services provided in respect of or in relation to such money transfer services to a principal established outside the Community, shall be deemed, for the purposes of this Act, to be the State.]²⁴

[(*eee*) The place of supply of services of the description specified in paragraph (iii*c*) of the Fourth Schedule shall be deemed, for the purposes of this Act, to be the State when those services are supplied from outside the Community in the course or furtherance of business by a person who has an establishment outside the Community ...²⁵ and are received, otherwise than for a business purpose, by a person whose usual place of residence is the State.]²⁶

(Place of supply of transport services)

[(*f*) The place of supply of the following services received by a person registered for value added tax in a Member State shall be deemed, for the purposes of this Act, to be within the territory of the Member State that so registered the person for value added tax, that is to say: a 28bC

(i) the intra-Community transport of goods,

(ii) activities ancillary to the intra-Community transport of goods such as loading, unloading and handling, a 28bD

(iii) services of an agent acting in the name and on behalf of another person in the arrangement of services other than those specified in paragraph (vii) of the Fourth Schedule. a 28bE(1)

[(iv) valuation of or work on movable goods, including contract work, in cases where the goods are dispatched or transported out of the Member State where the valuation or work was physically carried out.]²⁷ a 28bF

(*g*) The place of supply of the following services supplied to persons other than those specified in paragraph (*f*) shall be deemed for the purposes of this Act to be—

(i) the place of departure in the case of—

(I) the intra-Community transport of goods, a 28bC(2) a 28bE(1)

(II) services of an agent acting in the name and on behalf of another person in the arrangement of intra-Community transport of goods, and

(ii) the place where they are physically performed in the case of services of an agent acting in the name and on behalf of another person in the arrangement of services other than those specified in subparagraph (i)(II) of this paragraph and paragraph (vii) of the Fourth Schedule. a 28bE(2)

a 28dC(1)

(*h*) In this subsection—

> **"intra-Community transport of goods"** means transport where the place of departure and the place of arrival are situated within the territories of two different Member States;

> **"the place of departure"** means the place where the transport of goods actually starts, leaving aside distance actually travelled to the place where the goods are;

> **"the place of arrival"** means the place where the transport of goods actually ends.][28]

(The supply of telephone cards — special rules re: deduction procedure)

[(6A)(*a*) Subject to paragraph (*b*), where the supply of a telephone card is taxable within the State and that telephone card is subsequently used outside the Community for the purpose of accessing a telecommunications service, the place of supply of that telecommunications service shall be deemed to be outside the Community and the supplier of that telephone card shall be entitled, in the taxable period within which that supplier acquires proof that that telephone card was so used outside the Community, to a reduction of the tax payable by that supplier in respect of the supply of that telephone card, by an amount calculated in accordance with paragraph (*c*).

(*b*) Where the supply of a telephone card is taxable in the State and the person liable for the tax on that supply is a person referred to in section 8(2)(*a*) who—

    (i) is not entitled to a deduction, in accordance with section 12, of all of the tax chargeable in respect of that supply, or

    (ii) is entitled to a deduction, in accordance with section 12, of the tax chargeable in respect of that supply because that card was acquired for the purposes of resale,

and that telephone card is subsequently used outside the Community for the purpose of accessing a telecommunications service, the place of supply of that telecommunications service shall be deemed to be outside the Community and the person who is taxable in respect of that supply of that telephone card shall be entitled, in the taxable period within which that person acquires proof that that telephone card was so used outside the Community, to a reduction of the tax payable in respect of that supply of that telephone card to the extent that that telephone card was so used.

(*c*) For the purposes of this subsection the amount of the reduction referred to in paragraph (*a*) shall be calculated as follows:

$$A \times \frac{B}{B + 100}$$

where—

A equals the tax inclusive price charged by the supplier for that part of the right contained in the telephone card which was consumed in accessing the telecommunications service which was deemed to be supplied outside the Community,

B equals the tax inclusive price charged to the supplier for that part of the right contained in the telephone card which was consumed in accessing the telecommunications service which was deemed to be supplied outside the Community, and

C is the percentage rate of tax chargeable on the supply of the telephone card at the time of that supply by that supplier.

(*d*) Where a telephone card is used to access a telecommunications service, the value of the telephone card so used shall, for the purposes of section 10(2), be disregarded.

(Telephone card — a definition)

(*e*) In this subsection "telephone card" means a card or a means other than money which confers a right to access a telecommunications service and for which, when the card or other means is supplied to a person other than for the purposes of resale, the supplier is entitled to a consideration in respect of the supply and for which the user of that card or other means is not liable for any further charge in respect of the receipt of the telecommunications service accessed by means of that card or other means.]²⁹

(7) Provision may be made by regulations for varying, in relation to services generally or of a description specified therein, the rules for determining their place of supply, and for that purpose the Fourth Schedule may be added to or varied.

[(8) (*a*) The transfer of goodwill or other intangible assets of a business, in connection with the transfer of the business or part thereof, even if that business or that part thereof had ceased trading, [or in connection with a transfer of ownership of goods in accordance with section 3(5)(*b*)(iii)]³⁰ by—

(i) a taxable person to another taxable person or a flat-rate farmer, or

(ii) a person who is not a taxable person to another person,

shall be deemed, for the purposes of this Act, not to be a supply of services.

(*b*) For the purposes of this subsection, taxable person" shall not include a ₐ 6(5) person who is a taxable person solely by virtue of subsections (1A) and (2) of section 8.]³¹]³²

Amendments

¹ Subs (3)(*a*)-(*d*) substituted by FA 2006, s 94 with effect from 31 March 2006.
² Substituted by FA 1992, s 169(*a*) with effect from 1 January 1993; previously "specified in the Fourth Schedule".

3   Subs (3A) inserted by FA 1986, s 81 with effect from 27 May 1986.

4   Subs (4A) inserted FA 1982, s 76 with effect from 1 September 1982.

5   Subs (4B) inserted by FA 1989, s 54 with effect from 1 March 1989.

6   Inserted by FA 1995, s 123 with effect from 2 June 1995.

7   Subs (6)(*b*) substituted by FA 1992, s 169(*b*)(i) with effect from 1 January 1993.

8   Subs (6)(*c*)(ii) substituted by FA 1992, s 169(*b*)(ii) with effect from 1 January 1993.

9   Inserted by FA 1996, s 90(*a*)(i) with effect from 1 January 1996.

10   Inserted by FA 1996, s 90(*a*)(ii) with effect from 1 January 1996

11   Subs (6)(*d*) inserted by FA 1986, s 81 with effect from 27 May 1986.

12   Inserted by FA 1998, s 107(*a*)(i) with effect from 1 May 1998.

13   Inserted by FA 2003, s 115(*a*) with effect from 1 July 2003.

14   Subs (6)(*dd*) inserted by FA 1997, s 99 as on and from 1 July 1997.

15   Subs (6)(*ddd*) inserted by FA 1998, s 107(*a*)(ii) with effect from 1 May 1998.

16   Subs (6)(*dddd*) inserted by FA 1999, s 121 with effect from 25 March 1999.

17   Substituted by FA 2003, s 115(*b*) with effect from 1 July 2003; previously "paragraphs (*ddd*) and (*ee*)".

18   Inserted by FA 1998, s 107(*a*)(iii) with effect from 1 May 1998.

19   Inserted by FA 1990, s 100 with effect from 30 May 1990.

20   Subs (6)(*e*)(ii)(III) inserted by FA 1990, s 100 with effect from 30 May 1990.

21   Subs (6)(*e*)(iii*a*) inserted by FA 2001, s 183(*a*) with effect from 6 April 2001.

22   Subs (6)(*e*) substituted by FA 1986, s 81 with effect from 27 May 1986.

23   Subs (6)(*ee*) inserted by FA 1998, s 107(*a*)(iv) with effect from 1 May 1998.

24   Subs (6)(*eea*) inserted by FA 2005, s 101(*a*)(i) with effect from 25 March 2005.

25   Deleted by FA 2005, s 101(*a*)(ii); previously "and has not also an establishment in the Community" with effect from 25 March 2005.

26   Subs (6)(*eee*) inserted by FA 2003, s 115(*c*) with effect from 1 July 2003.

27   Subs (6)(*f*)(iv) inserted by FA 1996, s 90(*b*) with effect from 1 January 1996.

28   Subs (6)(*f*)–(*h*) inserted by FA 1992, s 169(*b*)(iii) with effect from 1 January 1993.

29   Subs (6A) inserted by FA 1998, s 107(*b*) with effect from 1 May 1998.

30   Inserted by FA 2005, s 101(*b*) with effect from 25 March 2005.

31   Subs (8) inserted by FA 2001, s 183(***b***) with effect from 6 April 2001.

32   Section 5 substituted by VATAA 1978, s 5 with effect from 1 March 1979.

Cross-references

Self-supplied services (subs (3)), Revenue may make regulations: s 32(1)(*b*); Regulations (staff meals): VATR 1979, r 24.

Regulations (subs (7)) require consent of Minister for Finance: s 32(2A).

Tax due and payable (subs (6)(*e*)): s 19(2A).

Case law

Subject	*Case*	*Case reference*
Insurance legal services held to be supplied to the insurer not the insured	*Bourke v Bradley and Sons*	(IV) ITR (117); subs (4B) inserted to reverse the effect of this decision
Administration of copyright in sound recordings, a service	*Phonographic Performance (Ireland) Ltd v Somers*	(IV) ITR (314)
Place of supply of hire of means of transport held to be at establishment of lessor	*Aro Lease BV v Inspector der Belastngdienst Grote Ouderingen, Amsterdam*	ECJ C190/95
Place of supply of services — no fixed establishment in another Member State merely by virtue of hiring out or leasing cars to clients in that Member State	*Lease Plan Luxembourg S\A v The State of Belgium*	7 May 1998, C–390/96

Place of supply of services deemed to be the place of the supplier's business or fixed establishment etc	*Maatschap MJM Lindhorst, KPPG Powels & Scheres v Inspecteur der Omzetbelastingdienst Ondermingen*	6 March 1997, C–167/95
Community definition of a lawyer. Supply of the services of an arbitrator would be where that arbitrator established his business	*Von Hoffmann v Finanzamt Trier*	September 1997, C–145/96
Transfer of business	*S O'Cúlacháin, Inspector of Taxes v Stylo Barratt Shoes Ltd*	(2003) ITR (77)
Services by intermediaries — place of supply	*Staatssectretaris van Financien v D Lipjes*	27 May 2004, C–68/03
Transfer of softwear and related services	*Levob Verzekeringen BV v Staatssecretaris van Financiën*	27 October 2005, C–41/04

Regulations

Subject	Regulation
Catering services for employees	Value Added Tax Regulations 1979 (SI 63/79)

Revenue precedent

Issue: In the context of a multi-national group of companies, a transfer of a business takes place between three companies at the same time the intermediary one of which is not registered.

Decision: The fact that the intermediary company was unregistered in this State, did not preclude the application of a VAT free transfer under s 3(5)(*b*)(iii).

Issue: Sale of confectionery with a cup of coffee/tea in a pub.

Decision: 21%, coffee/tea not considered a meal.

Issue: The provision of relief milking service and relief farm work on a dairy farm are taxable services as provided by Co-operatives.

Decision: Decisions made that: 1. Relief milking services are not taxable; and 2. that relief farm work on a dairy farm will be chargeable to VAT as follows. 70% not taxable as relating to the relief milking. 30% chargeable at 12.5%. The treatment was given to the Co-operatives because of the social services being provided by these organisations.

Issue: Sale of theatre tickets by a booking agency which are bought in bulk from the theatre at a discount and sold at face value. The difference between the discount amount and the face value of the ticket forms the agency's commission.

Decision: Commission exempt from VAT as it was regarded as part of the cost involved in supplying those exempt theatre tickets.

Issue: Co-op undertaking a milk recording service on behalf of the State.

Decision: Decision made that one-third of the fee for the milk recording scheme to be taxed. It was regarded that two-thirds of the fee was in respect of non-taxable activities on behalf of the State and the balance as being in respect of taxable supplies by the local Co-op.

Issue: Reverse Premium — an amount paid by a landlord to a tenant as an inducement to take up a lease.

Decision: No supply is deemed to have been made.

Issue: Sale or lease of a milk quota without land in excess of £20,000 by an unregistered/flat-rate farmer.

Decision: 21%, however the farmer will be allowed retain his flat-rate status in all other respects.

Issue: Contract work carried out in this State for customers in other Member States who provide their own labels and packaging materials that are incorporated in the final product.

Decision: It was agreed that the contract work would be extended to include packaging and labelling.

Revenue publications

Advertising services: Statement of Practice VAT 3/92.
Agricultural services: Statement of Practice VAT 5/92 (replaced by Information Leaflet No 23/01).
Certain services received from abroad: Statement of Practice VAT 1/90.

Certain services received from abroad: Statement of Practice VAT 5/94 (Replaced by Information Leaflet No 9/01).

Dances: Statement of Practice VAT 6/92 (Replaced by Information Leaflet No 20/01).

Food and drink supplied through catering business, hotel, restaurant, pub, take-away etc, rates of VAT: Statement of Practice VAT 10/92.

Intra-Community goods transport and ancillary services from 1 January 1993: Statement of Practice VAT 12/92 (Replaced by Information Leaflet No 16/02).

International leasing of means of transport: Leaflet No 3 of 1999.

Rates of VAT on services from 1 March 1991: Statement of Practice VAT 1/91.

Rates of VAT on services from 1 March 1992: Statement of Practice VAT 1/92.

Revenue VAT Guide: Ch 4.

Solicitors: Leaflet April 1998.

Sports facilities: Statement of Practice VAT 4/92.

Staff canteens: Tax Briefing: Issue 29.

Staff Canteens: Tax Briefing Issue 62.

Supply and installation of goods: Tax Briefing Issue 58.

Transfer of a Business or Part Thereof — VAT Implications: Tax Briefing, Issue 51.

Treatment of Cultural, Artistic and Entertainment Services Supplied by Non-Established Persons — Information Leaflet 3/02.

Definition

"business": s 1(1); "Community": s 1(1); "goods": s 1(1); "immovable goods": s 1(1); "local authority": s 1(1); "movable goods": s 1(1); "establishment": s 1(1); "person": IA 2005, s 18(*c*); "a person registered for value added tax": s 1(1); "regulations": s 1(1), 32; "supply": s 1(1); "tax": s 1(1); "taxable person": s 1(1), 8.

Notes

Subs (3A): OJ L145/1 (13.6.1977).

5A Special scheme for electronic services

[(1) In this section—

"electronic services scheme" means the special arrangements for the taxation of electronically supplied services provided for in Article 26c of Council Directive No 77/388/EEC of 17 May 1977;

"EU Value Added tax" means Value Added tax referred to in Council Directive No 77/388/EEC of 17 May 1977 and includes tax within the meaning of section 1;

"identified person" has the meaning assigned to it by subsection (5);

"Member State of consumption" means the Member State in which the supply of the electronic services takes place according to Article 9(2)(*f*) of Council Directive No 77/388/EEC of 17 May 1977;

"Member State of identification" means the Member State which the non-established person chooses to contact to state when his or her activity within the Community commences in accordance with the provisions of the electronic services scheme;

"national tax number" means a number (whether consisting of either or both numbers and letters) assigned to a non-established person by his or her own national taxation authorities;

"non-established person" means a person who has his or her establishment outside the Community and has not also an establishment in the Community and who is not otherwise required to be a person registered for Value Added tax within the meaning of section 1;

"scheme participant" means a non-established person who supplies electronic services into the Community and who opts to use the electronic services scheme in any Member State;

"VAT return" means the statement containing the information necessary to establish the amount of EU Value Added tax that has become chargeable in each Member State under the electronic services scheme.

(2) Subject to and in accordance with the provisions of this section, a non-established person may opt to apply the electronic services scheme to his or her supplies of electronic services to non-taxable persons within the Community.

(3) The Revenue Commissioners shall set up and maintain a register, referred to in this section as an "identification register", of non-established persons who are identified in the State for the purposes of the electronic services scheme.

(4) A non-established person who opts to be identified in the State for the purposes of the electronic services scheme shall inform the Revenue Commissioners by electronic means in a manner specified by them, when his or her taxable activity commences and shall, at the same time, furnish them electronically with the following information—

(a) the person's name and postal address,

(b) his or her electronic addresses, including website addresses,

(c) his or her national tax number, if any, and

(d) a statement that the person is not a person registered, or otherwise identified, for Value Added tax purposes within the Community.

(5) Where a person has furnished the particulars required under subsection (4), the Revenue Commissioners shall register that person in accordance with subsection (3), allocate to that person an identification number and notify such person electronically of it, and, for the purposes of this section, a person to whom such an identification number has been allocated shall be referred to as an "identified person".

(6) An identified person shall, within 20 days immediately following the end of each calendar quarter, furnish by electronic means to the Revenue Commissioners a VAT return, prepared in accordance with, and containing such particulars as are specified in, subsection (7), in respect of supplies made in the Community in that quarter and shall at the same time remit to the Revenue Commissioners, into a bank account designated by them and denominated in

euro, the amount of EU Value Added tax, if any, payable by such person in respect of such quarter in relation to—

(a) supplies made in the State in accordance with section 5(6)(*eee*), and

(b) supplies made in other Member States in accordance with the provisions implementing Article 9(2)(*f*) of Council Directive No 77/388/EEC of 17 May 1977 in such other Member States:

but if the identified person has not made any such electronic supplies to non-taxable persons into the Community within a calendar quarter that person shall furnish a nil VAT return in respect of that quarter.

(7) The VAT return referred to in subsection (6) shall be made in euro and shall contain the following details—

(a) the person's identification number,

(b) for each Member State of consumption where EU Value Added tax has become due—

(i) the total value, exclusive of EU Value Added tax, of supplies of electronic services for the quarter,

(ii) the amount of the said value liable to EU Value Added tax at the applicable rate, and

(iii) the amount of EU Value Added tax corresponding to the said value at the applicable rate,

and

(c) the total EU Value Added tax due, if any.

(8) Notwithstanding section 10(9A), where supplies have been made using a currency other than the euro, the exchange rate to be used for the purposes of expressing the corresponding amount in euro on the VAT return shall be that published by the European Central Bank for the last date of the calendar quarter for which the VAT return relates, or, if there is no publication on that date, on the next day of publication.

(9) Notwithstanding section 12, a scheme participant who supplies services which are deemed in accordance with section 5(6)(*eee*) to be supplied in the State shall not, in computing the amount of tax payable by him or her in respect of such supplies, be entitled to deduct any tax borne or paid in relation to those supplies but shall be entitled to claim a refund of such tax in accordance with, and using the rules applicable to, Council Directive 86/560/EEC of 17 November 1986, notwithstanding Articles 2(2), 2(3) and 4(2) of that Directive.

(10) A scheme participant who supplies services which are deemed in accordance with section 5(6)(*eee*) to be supplied in the State shall be deemed to have fulfilled his or her obligations under sections 9, 16 and 19 of this Act if such participant has accounted in full in respect of such supplies in any Member State under the provisions of the electronic services scheme.

(11) For the purposes of this Act, a VAT return required to be furnished in accordance with the electronic services scheme shall, in so far as it relates to

supplies made in accordance with section 5(6)(*eee*), be treated, with any necessary modifications, as if it were a return required to be furnished in accordance with section 19.

(12)(*a*) An identified person shall—

(i) keep full and true records of all transactions covered by the electronic services scheme which affect his or her liability to EU Value Added tax,

(ii) make such records available, by electronic means and on request, to the Revenue Commissioners,

(iii) make such records available, by electronic means and on request, to all Member States of consumption, and

(iv) notwithstanding section 16, retain such records for each transaction for a period of 10 years from the end of the year when that transaction occurred.

(*b*) A scheme participant who is deemed to supply services in the State in accordance with section 5(6)(*eee*) shall be bound by the requirements of subparagraphs (i), (ii) and (iv) in relation to such supplies.

(13) An identified person shall notify the Revenue Commissioners of any changes in the information submitted under subsection (4) and shall notify them if his or her taxable activity ceases or changes to the extent that such person no longer qualifies for the electronic services scheme. Such notification shall be made electronically.

(14) The Revenue Commissioners shall exclude an identified person from the identification register if—

(*a*) they have reasonable grounds to believe that that person's taxable activities have ended, or

(*b*) the identified person—

(i) notifies the Revenue Commissioners that he or she no longer supplies electronic services,

(ii) no longer fulfils the requirements necessary to be allowed to use the electronic services scheme, or

(iii) persistently fails to comply with the provisions of the electronic services scheme.

(15) The Revenue Commissioners may make regulations as necessary for the purpose of giving effect to the electronic services scheme.][1]

Amendments

[1]   Section 5A inserted by FA 2003, s 116 with effect from 1 July 2003.

Revenue Publications

Electronically supplied services: Tax Briefing Issues 52 and 53.

a 13   **6 Exemptions**

(1) Tax shall not be chargeable in respect of any exempted activity.

(What decrees an activity as exempt)

(2) (*a*)   The Minister may by order declare the [supply of goods or services][1] of any kind to be an exempted activity.

   (*b*)   The Minister may by order amend or revoke an order under this subsection, including an order under this paragraph.

   (*c*)   An order under this subsection shall be laid before Dáil Éireann as soon as may be after it is made and, if a resolution annulling the order is passed by Dáil Éireann within the next twenty-one days on which Dáil Éireann has sat after the order is laid before it, the order shall be annulled accordingly, but without prejudice to the validity of anything previously done thereunder.

Amendments

[1]   Substituted by VATAA 1978, s 30(2) with effect from 1 March 1979; previously "delivery of goods of any kind or the rendering of a service".

Cross-references

Exempted activities: Sch 1.
European Communities (Exemption from Value Added Tax on the Permanent Importation of Certain Goods) Regulations 1985 (SI 183/85).

Regulations

Subject	*Regulation*
Permanent importations	European Communities (Exemption from Value Added Tax on the Permanent Importation of Certain Goods) Regulations 1985 (SI 183/85)
Investment gold	Value Added Tax (Waiver of Exemption on Supplies of and Supplies relating to Investment Gold) Regulations 1999 (SI 440/99)

Definition

"Dáil Éireann": IA 2005, Sch; "exempted activity": s 1(1); "goods": s 1(1); "the Minister": s 1(1); "supply": s 1(1); "tax": s 1(1).

6A Special scheme for investment gold

[(1) (*a*)   In this section—

   "intermediary" means a person who intervenes for another person in a supply of investment gold while acting in the name and for the account of that other person;

   "investment gold" means—

   (i)   gold in the form of—

      (I)   a bar, or

      (II)   a wafer,

      of a weight accepted by a bullion market and of a purity equal to or greater than 995 parts per one thousand parts, and

(ii) gold coins which—

(I) are of a purity equal to or greater than 900 parts per one thousand parts,

(II) are minted after 1800,

(III) are or have been legal tender in their country of origin, and

(IV) are normally sold at a price which does not exceed the open market value of the gold contained in the coins by more than 80 per cent.

(b) For the purposes of the definition of investment gold in paragraph (a), gold coins which are listed in the "C" series of the Official Journal of the European Communities as fulfilling the criteria referred to in that definition in respect of gold coins shall be deemed to fulfil the said criteria for the whole year for which the list is published.

(2) The provisions of this section shall apply to—

(a) [investment gold, including investment gold which is represented by securities]¹ or represented by certificates for allocated or unallocated gold or traded on gold accounts and including, in particular, gold loans and swaps, involving a right of ownership or a claim in respect of investment gold, and

(b) transactions concerning investment gold involving futures and forward contracts leading to a transfer of a right of ownership or a claim in respect of investment gold.

(3) Notwithstanding subsection (1) of section 6, a person who produces investment gold or transforms any gold into investment gold, may, in accordance with conditions set out in regulations, waive such person's right to exemption from tax on a supply of investment gold to another person who is engaged in the supply of goods and services in the course or furtherance of business.

(4) Where a person waives, in accordance with subsection (3), such person's right to exemption from tax in respect of a supply of investment gold, an intermediary who supplies services in respect of that supply of investment gold may, in accordance with conditions set out in regulations, waive that intermediary's right to exemption from tax in respect of those services.

(5) (a) Where a person waives, in accordance with subsection (3), such person's right to exemption from tax in respect of a supply of investment gold, then, for the purposes of this Act, the person to whom the supply of investment gold is made shall, in relation thereto, be a taxable person and be liable to pay the tax chargeable on that supply as if such taxable person had made that supply of investment gold for consideration in the course or furtherance of business and the person who waived the right to exemption in respect of that supply shall not be liable to pay the said tax.

(*b*)   Where a person is liable for tax in accordance with paragraph (*a*) in respect of a supply of investment gold, such person shall, notwithstanding the provisions of section 12, be entitled, in computing the amount of tax payable by such person in respect of the taxable period in which that liability to tax arises, to deduct the tax for which such person is liable on that supply, if such person's subsequent supply of that investment gold is exempt from tax.

(6) (*a*)   A taxable person may, in computing the amount of tax payable by such person in respect of any taxable period and notwithstanding section 12, deduct—

     (i)   the tax charged to such person during that period by other taxable persons by means of invoices, prepared in the manner prescribed by regulations, in respect of supplies of gold to such person,

     (ii)   the tax chargeable during that period, being tax for which such person is liable in respect of intra-Community acquisitions of gold, and

     (iii)   the tax paid by such person, or deferred, as established from the relevant customs documents kept by such person in accordance with section 16(3) in respect of gold imported by such person in that period,

   where that gold is subsequently transformed into investment gold and such person's subsequent supply of that investment gold is exempt from tax.

(*b*)   A person may claim, in accordance with regulations, a refund of—

     (i)   the tax charged to such person on the purchase of gold, other than investment gold, by such person,

     (ii)   the tax chargeable to such person on the intra-Community acquisition of gold, other than investment gold, by such person, and

     (iii)   the tax paid or deferred on the importation by such person of gold other than investment gold,

   where that gold is subsequently transformed into investment gold and such person's subsequent supply of that investment gold is exempt from tax.

(7) (*a*)   A taxable person may, in computing the amount of tax payable by such person in respect of a taxable period and notwithstanding section 12, deduct the tax charged to such person during that period by other taxable persons by means of invoices, prepared in the manner prescribed by regulations, in respect of the supply to the first-mentioned person of services consisting of a change of form, weight or purity of gold where that person's subsequent supply of that gold is exempt from tax.

(*b*)   A person may claim, in accordance with regulations, a refund of the tax charged to such person in respect of the supply to such person of services consisting of a change of form, weight or purity of gold where such person's subsequent supply of that gold is exempt from tax.

(8) (*a*) A taxable person who produces investment gold or transforms any gold into investment gold may, in computing the amount of tax payable by such person in respect of a taxable period and notwithstanding section 12, deduct—

  (i) the tax charged to such person during that period by other taxable persons by means of invoices, prepared in the manner prescribed by regulations, in respect of supplies of goods or services to the first-mentioned person,

  (ii) the tax chargeable during that period, being tax for which such person is liable in respect of intra-Community acquisitions of goods, and

  (iii) the tax paid by such person, or deferred, as established from the relevant customs documents kept by such person in accordance with section 16(3) in respect of goods imported by such person in that period,

  where those goods or services are linked to the production or transformation of that gold, and such person's subsequent supply of that investment gold is exempt from tax.

(*b*) A person who produces investment gold or transforms any gold into investment gold may claim, in accordance with regulations, a refund of—

  (i) the tax charged to such person on the purchase by such person of goods or services,

  (ii) the tax chargeable to such person on the intra-Community acquisition of goods by such person, and

  (iii) the tax paid or deferred by such person on the importation of goods by such person,

  where those goods or services are linked to the production or transformation of that gold, and such person's subsequent supply of that gold is exempt from tax.

[(9) Every trader in investment gold shall establish the identity of any person to whom such trader supplies investment gold when the total consideration which such trader is entitled to receive in respect of such supply, or a services of such supplies which are or appear to be linked, amounts to at least 15,000 euros, and such trader shall retain a copy of all documents used to identify the person to whom the investment gold is supplied as if they were records to be kept in accordance with section 16(1A) of this Act.]²]³

Amendments

1   Substituted by FA 2000, s 109(*a*) with effect from 23 March 2000; previously "investment gold which is represented by securities".

2   Subs (9) inserted by FA 2000, s 109(*b*) with effect from 23 March 2000.

3   Section 6A inserted by FA 1999, s 122 with effect from 1 January 2000.

Regulations

Subject	Regulation
Investment Gold	Value Added Tax (Waiver of Exemption on Supplies of and Supplies relating to Investment Gold) Regulations 1999 (SI 440/99)

Revenue publications

Tax Briefing: Issue 39.

a 13C

7 Waiver of exemption

(Definition)

[(1)(*a*)][1] Where, but for the provisions of section 6, tax would be chargeable in respect of the [supply][2] of any of the services [to which paragraph (iv) of the First Schedule relates][3], a person [supplying][4] any such services may, in accordance with regulations, waive his right to exemption from tax in respect thereof. Any such waiver shall extend to all the [services to which the said paragraph (iv) relates][5] that the person [supplies][6].

    [(*b*) A waiver of exemption from tax under this subsection shall not apply or be extended to any disposal of an interest in immovable goods which is deemed to be a letting of immovable goods to which paragraph (iv) of the First Schedule applies by virtue of section 4(3A)(*a*)(ii).][7]

[Provided that where a person waives his right to exemption from tax in respect of the leasing or letting of goods which are subject to an agreement of the type referred to in section 4(2C)(*a*) then that waiver shall only apply to the supply of services under that agreement.][8]

(Date of waiver and cancellation)

(2) A waiver of exemption under subsection (1) shall have effect from the commencement of such taxable period as may be agreed between the person making the waiver and the Revenue Commissioners and shall cease to have effect at the end of the taxable period during which it is cancelled in accordance with subsection (3).

(Cancellation)

[(3) Provision may be made by regulations for the cancellation, at the request of a person, of a waiver made by him under subsection (1) and for the payment by him to the Revenue Commissioners as a condition of cancellation of such sum (if any) as when added to the total amount of tax (if any) due by him in accordance with section 19 in relation to the supply of services by him to which the waiver applied is equal to the total of—

    (*a*) the amount of tax deducted by him in accordance with section 12 in respect of tax borne or paid in relation to the supply of such services,

    [(*aa*) the amount of tax deducted by him in accordance with section 12, prior to the commencement of the letting of the immovable goods to which the waiver relates, in respect of or in relation to his acquisition of his interest in, or his development of, those immovable goods,][9]

    (*b*) the amount of tax that would be deductible by him in accordance with section 12 if tax had been chargeable on the transfer of ownership of goods to him in respect of which the provisions of section 3(5)(*b*)(iii) were applied, and those goods were used by him in the supply of such services, and

(*c*) the amount of tax that would be deductible by him in accordance with section 12 if tax had been chargeable on the supply to him of goods or services in respect of which the provisions of paragraph (vi*a*) of the Second Schedule were applied, and those goods or services were used in relation to the supply of services by him to which the waiver applied.][10]

(4) Where exemption has been waived under subsection (1) in respect of the [supply][2] of any such service, tax shall be charged in relation to the person making such waiver during the period for which such waiver has effect as if the service to which the waiver applies was not specified in the First Schedule.

Amendments

[1] Subs (1) renumbered as (1)(*a*) by FA 2002, s 100(*a*) with effect from 25 March 2002.

[2] Substituted by VATAA 1978, s 30(2) with effect from 1 March 1979; previously "rendering".

[3] Substituted by FA 1991, s 78 with effect from 1 January 1992; previously "specified in paragraphs (iv) and (x) of the First Schedule".

[4] Substituted by VATAA 1979, s 30(2) with effect from 1 March 1979; previously "rendering".

[5] Substituted by FA 1991, s 78 with effect from 1 January 1992; previously "services specified in the paragraph or paragraphs".

[6] Substituted by VATAA 1979, s 30(2) with effect from 1 March 1979; previously "renders".

[7] Subs (1)(*b*) inserted by FA 2002, s 100(*b*) with effect from 25 March 2002.

[8] Subs (1)(proviso) inserted by FA 1997, s 100(*a*) as on and from 26 March 1997.

[9] Subs (3)(*aa*) inserted by FA 2003, s 117 with effect from 28 March 2003.

[10] Subs (3) substituted by FA 1997, s 100(*b*) as on and from 26 March 1997.

Cross-references

Revenue may make regulations: s 32(1)(*a*).
Waiver of exemption procedure: VATR 1979, r 4.
Supply of services: s 5.

Regulations

Subject	Regulation
Waiver of Exemption	Value Added Tax Regulations 1979 (SI 63/79) Reg 4
Waiver of Exemption	Value Added Tax (Waiver of Exemption) (Amendment) Regulations 1998 (SI 228/98)

Revenue Publication

Treatment of Cultural, Artistic and Entertainment Services Supplied by Non-Established Persons: Information Leaflet 3/02.
Waiver of exemption: Tax Briefing Issue 58.

Revenue precedent

Issue: Recovery of inputs in relation to restoration work on a castle garden open to the public.
Decision: Waiver of exemption allowed but only from a current date. Full recovery of inputs in the exceptional circumstances.
Issue: Group registration and waiver of entitlement to exemption.
Decision: The group is regarded as a single taxable entity.

Definition

"person": IA 2005, s 18(*c*); "regulations": ss 1(1), 32; "supply": s 1(1); "tax": s 1(1); "taxable period": s 1(1).

8 Taxable persons

(Definition — who is a taxable person)

a 4   [(1) A person who, otherwise than as an employee of another person, engages in the supply, within the State, of taxable goods or services in the course [or furtherance]¹ of business shall, in addition to the persons referred to in section 4(5) and [subsections [1A),]² (2), (2A) and (8)]³˒ be a taxable person and shall be accountable for and liable to pay the tax charged in respect of such supply [, but a person not established in the State who supplies [goods in the State in the circumstances set out [in paragraph (*f*) or (*g*) of subsection (1A)]⁴ or supplies a service in the State in the circumstances set out in subsection (2)(*aa*),]⁵ shall not be a taxable person and shall not be accountable for or liable to pay the tax chargeable in respect of such supply]⁶.]⁷

(Persons making intra-Community acquisitions)

[(1A)(*a*) Where a person engages in the intra-Community acquisition of goods in the State in the course or furtherance of business he shall be a taxable person and shall be accountable for and liable to pay the tax chargeable.

(*b*)   Subject to subsection (2), and notwithstanding paragraph (*a*), a person for whose intra-Community acquisitions of goods (being goods other than new means of transport or goods subject to a duty of excise) the total consideration for which has not exceeded and is not likely to exceed [€41,000]⁸ in any continuous period of 12 months shall not, unless he otherwise elects and then only during the period for which such election has effect, be a taxable person:

Provided that where the provisions of subsection (1) apply to that person, this paragraph shall not apply unless the provisions of subsection (3) also apply to him

(Farmers)

(*c*)   A person who is a taxable person by virtue of this subsection and who is a person referred to in paragraph (*a*) or (*b*) of subsection (3) shall be deemed to be a taxable person only in respect of—

(i)   intra-Community acquisitions of goods which are made by him, and

(ii)   any services of the kind referred to in subsection (2) which are received by him:

Provided that a person may elect that this paragraph shall not apply to him.

(Racehorse trainers)

(*d*)   A person who is a taxable person by virtue of this subsection and who is a person referred to in subsection (3A) shall be deemed to be a taxable person only in respect of—

(i)   intra-Community acquisitions of goods which are made by him,

(ii) racehorse training services which are supplied by him, and

(iii) any services of the kind referred to in subsection (2) which are received by him:

Provided that a person may elect that this paragraph shall not apply to him.

(State)

(*e*) For the purposes of this subsection, where an intra-Community acquisition is effected in the State by—

(i) a Department of State or local authority,

(ii) a body established by statute, or

(iii) a person for the purpose of any activity [specified in the First Schedule]⁹,

the acquisition shall be deemed to have been effected in the course or furtherance of business.]¹⁰

[(*f*) Where a person not established in the State supplies goods in the State which are installed or assembled, with or without a trial run, by or on behalf of that person, and where the recipient of the supply of those goods is—

(i) a taxable person,

(ii) a Department of State or local authority,

(iii) a body established by statute, or

(iv) a person who receives that supply for the purpose of any activity specified in the First Schedule,

then that recipient shall in relation to that supply of those goods be a taxable person or be deemed to be a taxable person and shall be liable to pay the tax chargeable as if that recipient supplied those goods in the course or furtherance of business.]¹¹

[(*g*) Where a taxable person not established in the State supplies gas through the natural gas distribution system, or electricity, to a recipient in the State and where such recipient is—

(i) a taxable person,

(ii) a Department of State or local authority,

(iii) a body established by statute, or

(iv) a person who receives that supply for the purpose of any activity specified in the First Schedule,

then that recipient shall in relation to that supply be a taxable person or be deemed to be a taxable person and shall be liable to pay the tax chargeable as if that recipient supplied those goods in the course or furtherance of business.]¹²

[(2)(*a*) Where by virtue of [subparagraph (ii), (iii) [, (iiia)]¹³ or (iv) of a 21(1)(b) paragraph (*e*), or paragraph (*f*), of subsection (6) of section 5]¹⁴ a taxable service that, apart from that provision, would be treated as supplied abroad, is deemed to be supplied in the State, the person who receives the service shall, in relation thereto, be a taxable person and be liable to pay the tax charged as if he had himself supplied the service for consideration in the course or furtherance of his business.][15]

[(*aa*) Where a person not established in the State supplies a cultural, artistic, entertainment or similar service in the State, then any person, other than a person acting in a private capacity, who receives that service shall—

(i) in relation to it, be a taxable person or be deemed to be a taxable person, and

(ii) be liable to pay the tax chargeable as if that taxable person had in fact supplied the service for consideration in the course or furtherance of business;

but where that service is commissioned or procured by a promoter, agent or other person not being a person acting in a private capacity, then that promoter, agent or person shall be deemed to be the person who receives the service

(*ab*) Where the person who receives the services referred to in paragraph (*aa*) is a body that has received funding from the Arts Council in the 3 years prior to the passing of the Finance Act, 2002, the Revenue Commissioners may, at the request of such body, authorise the application of that paragraph in respect of such services received by that body to be deferred to a time not later than 1 March 2003.][16]

[(*b*) A person who is a taxable person by virtue of this subsection and who is a person referred to in paragraph (*a*) or (*b*) of subsection (3) shall be deemed to be a taxable person only in respect of—

(i) any intra-Community acquisitions of goods which are made by him, and

(ii) services of the kind referred to in this subsection which are received by him:

Provided that a person may elect that this paragraph shall not apply to him.

(*c*) A person who is a taxable person by virtue of this subsection and who is a person referred to in subsection (3A) shall be deemed to be a taxable person only in respect of—

(i) any intra-Community acquisitions of goods which are made by him,

(ii) racehorse training services which are supplied by him, and

(iii) services of the kind referred to in this subsection which are received by him:

Provided that a person may elect that this paragraph shall not apply to him.][17]

[(*d*) (i) Where a person who owns, occupies or controls land (in this subsection referred to as a "premises provider") allows, in the course or furtherance of business, a person not established in the State to supply goods for consideration in the course or furtherance of business (in this subsection referred to as a "mobile trader") on that land for a period of less than seven consecutive days, then the premises provider shall, not later than fourteen days before the day when the mobile trader is allowed to supply goods on that land, furnish to the Revenue Commissioners, at the office of the Revenue Commissioners which would normally deal with the examination of the records kept by the premises provider in accordance with section 16, the following particulars—

    (I)   the name and address of the mobile trader,

    (II)   the dates on which the mobile trader intends to supply goods on the premises provider's land,

    (III)   the address of the land referred to in clause (II), and

    (IV)   any other information as may be specified in regulations.

(ii) Where a premises provider allows, in the course or furtherance of business, a promoter not established in the State to supply on the premises provider's land a cultural, artistic, entertainment or similar service which in accordance with section (2)(*aa*) is deemed to be supplied by that promoter, then the premises provider shall, not later than fourteen days before such service is scheduled to begin, furnish to the Revenue Commissioners, at the office of the Revenue Commissioners which would normally deal with the examination of the records kept by the premises provider in accordance with section 16, the following particulars—

    (I)   the name and address of the promoter,

    (II)   details, including the dates, duration and venue, of the event or performance commissioned or procured by the promoter in the provision of that service, and

    (III)   any other information as may be specified in regulations.

(iii) Where a premises provider fails to provide to the Revenue Commissioners true and correct particulars as required in accordance with subparagraph (i) or (ii), then the Revenue Commissioners may, where it appears necessary to them to do so for the protection of the revenue, make such premises provider jointly and severally liable with a mobile trader or promoter, as the case may be, for the tax chargeable in respect of supplies made by that mobile trader or promoter on the premises provider's land, and in those circumstances the Revenue Commissioners shall notify the premises provider in writing accordingly.

(iv) A premises provider who has been notified in accordance with subparagraph (iii) shall be deemed to be a taxable person and shall be liable to pay the tax referred to in that subparagraph as if it were tax due in accordance with section 19 by the premises provider for the taxable period within which the supplies are made by the mobile trader or promoter, but the premises provider shall not be liable to pay tax referred to in subparagraph (iii) which the Revenue Commissioners are satisfied was accounted for by a mobile trader or promoter.]¹⁸

(State and local authorities)

4(5)   (2A)(*a*) The Minister may, following such consultations as he may deem appropriate, by order provide that the State and every local authority shall be taxable persons with respect to specified categories of supplies made by them of goods or services and accordingly, during the continuance in force of any such order, but not otherwise, the State and every local authority shall be accountable for and liable to pay tax in respect of any such supplies made by them as if the supplies had been made in the course of business.

[Provided that, where supplies of the kind referred to in, subject to subsection (3E), paragraph (xxiii) of the First Schedule or in paragraph (viic) of the Sixth Schedule are provided by the State or by a local authority, an order under this subsection shall be deemed to have been made in respect of such supplies by the State or by the local authority.]¹⁹

(*b*) The Minister may by order amend or revoke an order under this subsection, including an order under this paragraph.

(*c*) An order under this subsection shall be laid before Dáil Éireann as soon as may be after it is made and, if a resolution annulling the order is passed by Dáil Éireann within the next twenty-one days on which Dáil Éireann has sat after the order is laid before it, the order shall be annulled accordingly, but without prejudice to the validity of anything previously done thereunder.

(Private individuals)

a 28a(4) [(2B)(*a*) Where a person is a taxable person only because of an intra-Community acquisition of a new means of transport, then the person shall not, unless he so elects, be a taxable person for any purposes of this Act with the exception of subsection (4) of section 19.

(*b*) Where

(i) a person is a taxable person only because of an intra-Community acquisition of excisable products, and

(ii) by virtue of this acquisition, and in accordance with Chapter II of Part II of the Finance Act, 1992, and any other enactment which is to be construed together with that Chapter, the duty of excise on those products is payable in the State, the person shall not, unless he so elects, be a taxable person for any purposes of the Act with the exception of subsection (5) of section 19.][20]

(Exclusion/election as a taxable person)

[(3) [Subject to subsections (1A) and (2), and notwithstanding the provisions of a 24, 25 subsections (1)]][21], the following persons shall not, unless they otherwise elect and then only during the period for which such election has effect, be taxable persons—

(Farmers)

[(*a*) a farmer, for whose supply in any continuous period of twelve months of—

(i) agricultural services, other than insemination services, stock-minding or stock-rearing, the total consideration has not exceeded and is not likely to exceed [€27,500][22], or

[(i*a*) goods being [bovine][23] semen, the total consideration has not exceeded and is not likely to exceed [€55,000][24] and, in calculating that total consideration, supplies of [bovine][23] semen to—

(I) any other farmer licensed as an artificial insemination centre in accordance with the provisions of the Live Stock (Artificial Insemination) Act, 1947, or

(II) a taxable person over whom that farmer exercises control,

shall be disregarded, or][25]

(Agricultural services)

(ii) goods of the type specified in paragraph (xi*a*) of the Sixth Schedule to persons who are not engaged in supplying those goods in the course or furtherance of business, the total consideration has not exceeded and is not likely to exceed [€55,000][26], or

(iii) [services specified in subparagraph (i) and either or both of goods of the type specified in subparagraph (i*a*) and goods of the type specified in subparagraph (ii) supplied in the circumstances set out in that subparagraph],[27] the total consideration has not exceeded and is not likely to exceed [€27,500][28],][29] [or][30]

[(iv) goods of the type specified in subparagraph (i*a*) and goods of the type specified in subparagraph (ii) supplied in the circumstances set out in that subparagraph, the total consideration has not exceeded and is not likely to exceed [€55,000][31],][32]

(Fishermen)

(*b*) a person whose supplies of taxable goods or services consist exclusively of—

(i) supplies to taxable persons and persons to whom section 13(3) applies of fish (not being at a stage of processing further than that of being gutted, salted and frozen) which he has caught in the course of a seafishing business, or

(ii) supplies of the kind specified in subparagraph (i) and of either or both of the following, that is to say:

(I) supplies of machinery, plant or equipment which have been used by him in the course of a sea-fishing business, and

[(II) supplies of other goods and services the total consideration for which is such that such person would not, because of the provisions of paragraph (c) or (e), be a taxable person if such supplies were the only supplies made by such person,][33]

(c) (i) subject to subparagraph (ii), a person for whose supply of taxable goods (other than supplies of the kind specified in section 3(6)(d)(i)) and services the total consideration has not exceeded and is not likely to exceed [€55,000][34] in any continuous period of 12 months,

(ii) subparagraph (i) shall apply if, but only if, not less than **90 per cent**, of the total consideration referred to therein is derived from the supply of taxable goods (not being goods chargeable at any of the rates specified in [paragraphs (a), (c), and (d)][35] of subsection (1) of section 11 which were produced or manufactured by him wholly or mainly from materials chargeable at the rate specified in paragraph (b) of that subsection),

(d) ...[36]

(e) a person, other than a person to whom paragraph (a), (b) or (c) applies, for whose supply of taxable goods and services the total consideration has not exceeded and is not likely to exceed [€27,500][37] in any continuous period of twelve months:

(Connected persons — "anti-fragmentation" provision)

Provided that—

(i) where in the case of two or more persons one of whom exercises control over one or more of the other persons, supplies of goods of the same class or of services of the same nature are made by two or more of those persons, the total of the consideration relating to the said supplies shall, for the purposes of the application of paragraphs (c) and (e) in relation to each of the persons aforesaid who made the said supplies be treated as if all of the supplies in question had been made by each of the last-mentioned persons;

[(ia) where a farmer supplies services or goods of the kind specified in paragraph (a)(i) [, (a)(ia)][38] or (a)(ii), subparagraph (i) of this proviso shall be deemed to apply to those supplies, notwithstanding that the provisions of that subparagraph do not otherwise apply to supplies by a farmer;][39]

[(ii) the provisions of this subsection shall not apply to a supply of the kind referred to in subsection (2).][40][41]

(Racehorse training)

[(3A) Where a person who supplies services consisting of the training of horses for racing, the consideration for which has exceeded [€27,500][42] in any continuous period of 12 months, would, but for the supply of such services be a farmer, he shall be deemed to be a taxable person only in respect of the supply of those services [and any intra-Community acquisitions of goods made by him and any services of the kind referred to in subsection (2) received by him][43] and, in the absence of an election, shall, in relation to the supply of any of the goods and services specified in paragraph (*a*) and subparagraphs (i) and (iii) of paragraph (*b*) of the definition of **"farmer"** in subsection (9), be deemed not to be a taxable person][44]

(Control — a definition)

[(3B) In this section **"control"**, in relation to a body corporate, means the power of a person to secure, by means of the holding of shares or the possession of voting power in or in relation to that or any other body corporate, or by virtue of any powers conferred by the articles of association or other document regulating that or any other body corporate, that the affairs of the first-mentioned body corporate are conducted in accordance with the wishes of that person, and, in relation to a partnership, means the right to a share of more than one-half of the assets, or of more than one-half of the income, of the partnership.][45]

(Dances)

[(3C)(*a*) The licensee of any premises (being premises in respect of which a licence for the sale of intoxicating liquor either on or off those premises was granted) shall be deemed to be the promoter of any dance held, during the subsistence of that licence, on those premises and shall be deemed to have received the total money, excluding tax, paid by those admitted to the dance together with any other consideration received or receivable in connection with the dance.

(*b*) For the purposes of this subsection **"licensee"** means—

(i) where the licence is held by the nominee of a body corporate, the body corporate, and

(ii) in any other case, the holder of the licence.][46]

(Persons not established in the State)

[(3D)(*a*) The provisions of paragraphs (*b*), (*c*) and (*e*) of subsection (3) shall not apply to a person who is not established in the State.

(*b*) A person who is not established in the State shall, unless he opts to register in accordance with section 9, be deemed not to have made an intra-Community acquisition or a supply of those goods in the State where the only supplies by him in the State are in the circumstances set out in section 3(8).][47]

(Normally exempt sports which may be taxable)

[(3E)(*a*) Notwithstanding the provisions of section 6(1) and of subsection (1), and subject to the provisions of subsection (3), where—

(i) a person supplies services which are exempt in accordance with section 6 and paragraph (xxiii) of the First Schedule, or

(ii) the State or a local authority supplies services of the kind referred to in paragraph (xxiii) of the First Schedule,

then an authorised officer of the Revenue Commissioners shall—

(I) where such officer is satisfied that such supply of such services has created or is likely to create a distortion of competition such as to place at a disadvantage a commercial enterprise which is a taxable person supplying similar-type services, or

(II) where such officer is satisfied that such supply of such services is managed or administered by or on behalf of another person who has a direct or indirect beneficial interest, either directly or through an intermediary, in the supply of such services,

make a determination in relation to some or all of such supplies as specified in that determination deeming—

(A) such person, the State or such local authority to be supplying such supplies as specified in that determination in the course or furtherance of business,

(B) such person, the State or such local authority to be a taxable person in relation to the provision of such supplies as specified in that determination, and

(C) such supplies as specified in that determination to be taxable supplies to which the rate specified in section 11(1)(*d*) refers.

(Notification of ruling)

(*b*) Where a determination is made under paragraph (*a*), the Revenue Commissioners shall, as soon as may be after the making thereof, issue a notice in writing of that determination to the party concerned, and such determination shall have effect from such date as may be specified in the notice of that determination:

Provided that such determination shall have effect no sooner than the start of the next taxable period following that in which the notice issued.

(*c*) Where an authorised officer is satisfied that the conditions that gave rise to the making of a determination under paragraph (*a*) no longer apply, that officer shall cancel that determination by notice in writing to the party concerned and that cancellation shall have effect from the start of the next taxable period following that in which the notice issued.

(*d*) In this subsection **"authorised officer"** means an officer of the Revenue Commissioners authorised by them in writing for the purposes of this subsection.]⁴⁸

(Increases in revenue — requirements to register)

[(4) Where, by virtue of subsection (3) or (6), a person has not been a taxable person and a change of circumstances occurs from which it becomes clear that he is likely to become a taxable person, he shall be deemed, for the purposes of this Act, to be a taxable person from the beginning of the taxable period commencing next after such change]⁴⁹

(Cancellation of registration)

(5) Provision may be made by regulation for the cancellation, by the request of a person, of an election made by him under this section and for the payment by him to the Revenue Commissioners of such a sum as a condition of cancellation as when added to the net total amount of tax (if any) paid by him in accordance with section 19 in relation to the [supply of [goods or services, other than services of the kind referred to in paragraph (xiii) of the Sixth Schedule,]⁵⁰]⁵¹ [and the tax deductible under section 12 in respect of intra-Community acquisitions made by him during such period]⁵² by him in the period for which the election had effect is equal to [the sum of]⁵³ the amount of tax repaid to him during such period in respect of tax borne or paid in relation to the [supply of [goods or services, other than services of the kind referred to in paragraph (xiii) of the Sixth Schedule.]⁵⁴]⁵⁵

[(5A)(*a*) Notwithstanding subsection (5), provision may be made by regulation for the cancellation, by the request of a person who supplies services of the kind referred to in paragraph (xiii) of the Sixth Schedule, of an election made by such person under this section and for the payment by such person to the Revenue Commissioners, in addition to any amount payable in accordance with subsection (5), of such an amount (hereafter referred to in this subsection as the "cancellation amount"), as shall be determined in accordance with paragraph (*b*), as a condition of cancellation and the cancellation amount shall be payable as if it were tax due in accordance with section 19 for the taxable period in which the cancellation comes into effect.

(*b*) (i) Where the person referred to in paragraph (*a*)—

(I) was entitled to deduct tax in accordance with section 12 in respect of the acquisition, purchase or development of immovable goods used by that person in the course of a supply of services of a kind referred to in paragraph (xiii) of the Sixth Schedule, or

(II) would be entitled to deduct tax in accordance with section 12 in respect of the acquisition, as a result of a transfer to that person, of immovable goods used by that person in the course of a supply of services of a kind referred to in paragraph (xiii) of the Sixth Schedule, if that tax had been chargeable but for the application of the provisions of section 3(5)(*b*)(iii) on that transfer,

then, in respect of each such acquisition, purchase or development, an amount (hereafter referred to in this subsection as the "adjustment amount") shall be calculated in accordance with subparagraph (ii) and the cancellation amount shall be the sum of the adjustment amounts so calculated or, if there is only one such adjustment amount, that amount: but if there is no adjustment amount, the cancellation amount is nil.

(ii) The adjustment amount shall be determined by the formula—

$$\frac{A \times (10 - B)}{10}$$

where—

A is

  (I)   the amount of tax deductible in respect of the said acquisition, purchase or development of the said immovable goods, or

  (II)   the amount of tax that would be deductible in respect of the said acquisition of the said immovable goods if the provisions of section 3(5)(*b*)(iii) had not applied to the transfer of those immovable goods,

and

B is the number of full years for which the said goods were used by the person in the course of the supply of services of a kind referred to in paragraph (xiii) of the Sixth Schedule: but if the said number of full years is in excess of 10, such adjustment amount shall be deemed to be nil.

and

(*c*) For the purposes of paragraph (*b*) a full year shall be any continuous period of 12 months.][56]

(Decline in turnover — cancellation of registration)

[(6) A taxable person, other than a person to whom subsection (5) [or subsection (5A)][57] applies, may, in accordance with regulations, be treated, for the purposes of this Act, as a person who is not a taxable person if the Revenue Commissioners are satisfied that, in the absence of an election under subsection (3), he would not be a taxable person.][58]

(Clubs and similar organisations)

[(7) Where any goods or services are provided by a club or other similar organisation in respect of a payment of money by any of its members, then, for the purposes of this Act, the provision of the goods or services shall be deemed to be a supply by the club or other organisation of the goods or services (as the case may be) in the course or furtherance of a business carried on by it and the money shall be deemed to be consideration for the supply.][59]

(Group registration)

[(8) (*a*) Where the Revenue Commissioners are satisfied that two or more a 4(4) persons established in the State are closely bound by financial, economic and organisational links and [where it seems necessary or appropriate to them for the purpose of efficient and effective administration, including collection, of the tax]⁶⁰ to do so then, subject to such conditions as they may impose by regulations, the said Commissioners, for the purpose of this Act, may—

(i) by notice in writing to each of the persons concerned, deem the activities relating to those links to be carried on by any one of the persons, and all transactions by or between such persons shall be deemed, for that purpose, to be transactions by that one person and all rights and obligations under this Act shall be determined accordingly [and the persons so notified shall be regarded as being in a group for as long as this paragraph applies to them,]⁶¹ and

(ii) make each such person jointly and severally liable to comply with all the provisions of this Act and regulations (including the provisions requiring the payment of tax) that apply to each of those persons and subject to the penalties under this Act to which they would be subject if each such person was liable to pay to the Revenue Commissioners the whole of the tax chargeable, apart from regulations under this subsection, in respect of each such person:

Provided that this subsection shall not apply in the case of:

(I) the supply of immovable goods by any such person to any other such person, or

[(IA) the requirement to issue an invoice or other document, in accordance with section 17, in respect of supplies to persons other than supplies between persons who are jointly and severally liable to comply with the provisions of this Act in accordance with subparagraph (ii), or

(IB) the requirement to furnish a statement in accordance with section 19A, or]⁶²

(II) the transfer of ownership of goods specified in section 3(5)(*b*)(iii) from any such person to any other such person, except where, apart from the provisions of this subsection, each of the persons whose activities are deemed to be carried on by that one person is a taxable person.

(*b*) The Revenue Commissioners may by notice in writing to each of the persons whose activities are, by virtue of a notification issued in accordance with paragraph (*a*)(i), deemed to be carried on by one of those persons, and as on and from the date specified in the notice (which date shall not be earlier than the date of issue of the notice) cancel the notification under the said paragraph; and as on and from the date specified in the said notice the provisions of the Act and regulations shall apply to all the persons as aforesaid as if a notification under the said paragraph had not been issued, but without prejudice to the liability of any of the persons for tax or penalties in respect of anything done or not done during the period for which the said notification was in force.

(c) The Revenue Commissioners may, for the purpose of this subsection, deem a person engaged in the supply of non-taxable goods or services in the course or furtherance of business to be a taxable person.

[(d) Where a person in a group (in this subsection referred to as the "landlord") having acquired an interest in, or developed, immovable goods to which section 4 applies, whether such acquisition or development occurred before or after the landlord became a person in the group, subsequently surrenders possession of those immovable goods, or any part of them, to another person in the group (in this subsection referred to as the "occupant") where the surrender of possession if it were to a person not in the group would not constitute a supply of immovable goods in accordance with section 4, and either the landlord or the occupant subsequently ceases to be a person in the group (in this subsection referred to as a "cessation") then, if that landlord does not have a waiver of his or her right to exemption from tax in accordance with section 7 still in effect at the time of the cessation—

(i) the surrender of possession, or

(ii) if that landlord surrendered possession of those immovable goods more than once to another person in the group, the first such surrender of possession,

shall be deemed to occur when that first such cessation takes place, but if such a landlord's waiver of his or her right to exemption from tax in accordance with section 7 has been cancelled before a surrender of possession of immovable goods to another person in the group ends, that surrender of possession shall be deemed to take place on the date of the said first such cessation.]⁶³]⁶⁴

(Definitions)

[(9) In this Act—

a 25(2) **"agricultural produce"** means, in relation to a farmer, goods, other than ...⁶⁵ live greyhounds, produced by him in the course of an Annex A activity;

"agricultural service" means, in relation to a farmer, any Annex B service supplied by him using his own labour or that of his employees or effected by means of machinery, plant or other equipment normally used for the purposes of an Annex A activity carried on by him;

"Annex A activity" means any activity of a description specified in Annex A (which is set out in Part I of the Fifth Schedule) of Council Directive No 77/388/EEC of 17 May, 1977 (OJ No.L145/1 13.6.1977);

"Annex B service" means any service of a description specified in Annex B (which is set out in Part II of the Fifth Schedule) of the said Council Directive;

[**"farmer"** means a person who engages in at least one Annex A activity and—   a 25(2)

(*a*) whose supplies consist exclusively of either or both of the following, that is to say:

(i) supplies of agricultural produce, or

(ii) supplies of agricultural services, or

(*b*) whose supplies consist exclusively of either or both of the supplies specified in paragraph (*a*) and of one or more of the following, that is to say:

(i) supplies of machinery, plant or equipment which has been used by him for the purposes of an Annex A activity,

(ii) supplies of services consisting of the training of horses for racing the total consideration for which has not exceeded and is not likely to exceed [€27,500]⁶⁶ in any continuous period of 12 months, or

[(iii) supplies of goods and services other than those referred to in subparagraphs (i) and (ii) or paragraph (*a*), the total consideration for which is such that such person would not, because of the provisions of paragraph (*c*) or (*e*) of subsection (3), be a taxable person if such supplies were the only supplies made by such person.]⁶⁷]⁶⁸]⁶⁹

Amendments

1 Words inserted by FA 1984, s 86 with effect from 23 May 1984.

2 Inserted by FA 1992, s 170(2)(*a*) with effect from 1 January 1993.

3 Inserted by FA 1991, s 79 with effect from 29 May 1991.

4 Substituted by FA 2004, s 58(*a*) with effect on and from 1 January 2005; previously "in subsection (1A)(*f*)".

5 Substituted by FA 2003, s 118(*a*) with effect from 28 March 2003; previously "a service in the State in the circumstances set out in subsection (2)(*aa*)".

6 Inserted by FA 2002, s 101(*a*) with effect on and from 25 March 2002.

7 Subs (1) substituted by VATAA 1978, s 6 with effect from 1 March 1979.

8 Substituted by FA 2001, s 240 and Sch 5 Part 4 with effect from 1 January 2002; previously "£32,000".

9 Substituted by FA 1994, s 94(*a*) with effect from 23 May 1994.

10 Subs (1A) substituted by FA 1993, s 85(*a*).

11 Subs (1A)(*f*) inserted by FA 2003, s 118(*b*) with effect from 28 March 2003.

12 Subs (1A)(*g*) inserted by FA 2004, s 58(*b*) with effect on and from 1 January 2005.

13 Inserted by FA 2001, s 184 with effect from 6 April 2001.

14 Substituted by FA 1992, s 170(2)(*c*) with effect from 1 January 1993; previously "section 5(6)(*e*)(ii),(iii) or (iv)".

15 Subs (2)(*a*) transposed from subs (2) by FA 1993, s 85(*b*); previously substituted by VATAA 1978, s 6 with effect from 1 March 1979.

16 Subs (2)(*aa*) inserted by FA 2002, s 101(*b*)(i) with effect from 25 March 2002.

17 Subs (2)(*b*)–(*c*) inserted by FA 1993, s 85(*b*)(ii).

18 Subs (2)(*d*) inserted by FA 2002, s 101(*b*)(ii) with effect from 25 March 2002.

19 Subs (2A)(*a*)(proviso) inserted by FA 1995, s 124(*a*) with effect from 1 January 1996.

[20]   Subs (2B) substituted by EC(VAT)R 1992, r 7(*b*) with effect from 1 January 1993; originally inserted by FA 1992, s 170(2)(*d*).

[21]   Substituted by FA 1993, s 85(*c*)(i); previously "Notwithstanding the provisions of subsections (1) and (1A)".

[22]   Substituted by FA 2006, s 95(*a*) with effect from 1 May 2006; previously "€25,500".

[23]   Substituted by FA 1999, s 123 with effect from 25 March 1999; previously "livestock".

[24]   Substituted by FA 2006, s 95(*a*) with effect from 1 May 2006; previously "€51,000".

[25]   Subs (3)(*a*)(i*a*) inserted by FA 1998, s 108(*a*)(i) with effect from 1 July 1998.

[26]   Substituted by FA 2006, s 95(*a*) with effect from 1 May 2006; previously "€51,000".

[27]   Substituted by FA 1998, s 108(*a*)(ii) with effect from 1 July 1998.

[28]   Substituted by FA 2006, s 95(*a*) with effect from 1 May 2006; previously "€25,500".

[29]   Subs (3)(*a*) substituted by FA 1997, s 101(*a*) as on and from 1 September 1997 (Finance Act, 1997 (Commencement of Sections 101 and 113) Order, 1997).

[30]   Inserted by FA 1998, s 108(*a*)(iii) with effect from 1 July 1998.

[31]   Substituted by FA 2006, s 95(*a*) with effect from 1 May 2006; previously "€51,000".

[32]   Subs (3)(*a*)(iv) inserted by FA 1998, s 108(*a*)(iv) with effect from 1 July 1998.

[33]   Subs (3)(*b*)(ii)(II) substituted by FA 1994, s 94(*b*)(ii) with effect from 1 July; previously

>   "(II)   supplies of other goods and services the total consideration for which has not exceeded and is not likely to exceed £15,000 in any continuous period of 12 months,".

[34]   Substituted by FA 2006, s 95(*a*) with effect from 1 May 2006; previously "€51,000".

[35]   Substituted by FA 1993, s 85(*c*)(ii) with effect from 1 March 1993; previously "paragraphs (*a*), (*c*), (*d*) and (*e*)".

[36]   Subs (3)(*d*) deleted by FA 1993, s 85(*c*)(iii).

[37]   Substituted by FA 2006, s 95(*a*) with effect from 1 May 2006; previously "€25,500".

[38]   Inserted by FA 1998, s 108(*b*) with effect from 1 July 1998.

[39]   Subs (3)(proviso)(i*a*) inserted by FA 1997, s 101(*b*) as on and from such date as the Minister for Finance may by order appoint.

[40]   Subs (3)(proviso)(ii) substituted by FA 1993, s 85(*c*)(iv).

[41]   Subs (3) substituted by FA 1992, s 170(2)(*e*) with effect from 1 January 1993.

[42]   Substituted by FA 2006, s 95(*a*) with effect from 1 May 2006; previously "€25,500".

[43]   Inserted by FA 1993, s 85(*d*).

[44]   Subs (3A) inserted by FA 1982, s 77 with effect from 1 September 1982.

[45]   Subs (3B) inserted by FA 1984, s 86 with effect from 23 May 1984.

[46]   Subs (3C) inserted by FA 1992, s 170(1)(*b*) with effect from 28 May 1992.

[47]   Subs (3D) inserted by EC(VAT)R 1992, r 7(*c*) with effect from 1 January 1993.

[48]   Subs (3E) inserted by FA 1995, s 124(*b*) with effect from 1 January 1996.

[49]   Subs (4) substituted by F(No 2)A 1981, s 11 with effect from 20 November 1981.

[50]   Substituted by FA 2000, s 110(*a*)(i) with effect from 23 March 2000; previously "such goods or services".

[51]   Substituted by VATAA 1978, s 30(2) with effect from 1 March 1979; previously "delivery of such goods or the rendering of such services".

[52]   Inserted by FA 1993, s 85(*e*)(ii).

[53]   Inserted by FA 1993, s 85(*e*)(i).

[54]   Substituted by FA 2000, s 110(*a*)(ii) with effect from 23 March 2000; previously "goods or services.".

[55]   Substituted by VATAA 1978, s 30(2) with effect from 1 March 1979; previously "delivery of goods or the rendering of services".

[56]   Subs (5A) inserted by FA 2000, s 110(*b*) with effect from 23 March 2000.

[57]   Inserted by FA 2000, s 110(*c*) with effect from 23 March 2000.

[58]   Subs (6) substituted by FA 1992, s 170(2)(*f*) with effect from 28 May 1992.

[59]   Subs (7) substituted by VATAA 1978, s 6 with effect from 1 March 1979.

[60]   Substituted by FA 2006, s 95(*b*) with effect from 31 March 2006; previously "that it would be expedient in the interest of efficient administration of the tax".

[61]   Inserted inserted by FA 2002, s 101(*c*)(i) with effect from 25 March 2002.

[62] Subs (8)(*a*)(Proviso (IA)–(IB)) inserted by EC(VAT)R 1992, r 7(*d*) with effect from 1 January 1993.

[63] Subs (8)(*d*) inserted by FA 2002, s 101(*c*)(ii) with effect on and from 25 March 2002.

[64] Subs (8) substituted by FA 1991, s 79 with effect from 29 May 1991.

[65] Words "live horses and" deleted by FA 1990, s 101 with effect from 1 January 1991.

[66] Substituted by FA 2006, s 95(*a*) with effect from 1 May 2006; previously "€25,500".

[67] Subs (3)(*b*)(iii) substituted by FA 1994, s 94(*d*)(ii) with effect from 1 July 1994.

[68] Definition of "farmer" substituted by FA 1982, s 77 with effect from 1 September 1982.

[69] Subs (9) substituted by VATAA 1978, s 6 with effect from 1 March 1979.

Cross-references

Alcohol products (subs (2B)(*b*)), intra-EU acquisitions of: s 3B(3); payment of tax: s 19(5).

Deemed group registration, right of appeal: s 25(1)(*aa*).

Election to be taxable, Revenue may prescribe manner: s 32(1)(*d*); regulations: VATR 1979, r 3.

Failure to register, penalty: s 26(2).

Flat-rate farmers (subss (3A), (9)): s 12A(2)(*c*).

Group registration, procedure: VATR 1979, r 5.

Immovable goods, special provisions (subs (2A)(*a*)): s 4(8).

No right to deduct (subss (1A)(*c*) and (2)(*b*)): s 12(1)(*a*)(proviso); flat-rate farmers: s 12A(2)(*b*).

No right to deduct (subss (1A)(*d*) and (2)(*c*)): unless tax relates to racehorse training services supplied by him: s 12(1)(*a*)(proviso).

Unregistered person issuing invoice, penalty: s 26(2).

Case law

Subject	*Case*	*Case reference*
Mere acquisition of ownership in and the holding of bonds and the receipt of income therefrom cannot be regarded as economic activities within the meaning of a 4(2)	*Finanzamt Augsbur-Stradt v Marktgemeinde Welden*	6 February 1997, C–247/95
Concept of taxable person — place where services are supplied SICAV	*Banque Bruxelles Lambert SA v the Belgian State*	21 October 2004, C–8/03

Regulations

Subject	*Regulation*
Election to be taxable	Value Added Tax Regulations 1979 (SI 63/79), r 3
Group registration	Value Added Tax Regulations 1979 (SI 63/79), r 5

Revenue precedent

Issue: VAT grouping of fund management company with all the funds and unit trusts under its management.

Decision: In the circumstances of this case and in consideration of previous decisions made concerning the criteria establishment in relation to group registration it was agreed to allow group registration in this case.

Issue: Is sponsorship of sporting activities taxable.

Decision: No — Sport is not viewed as being carried on in the course or furtherance of business.

Issue: Company with two subsidiaries, one has the freehold reversion, the second has a long leasehold interest. The latter creates long leases to another party whilst the former carries out the redevelopment work and sells the freehold interest to a pension fund. Company with freehold reversion is treated as a taxable person as regards disposal.

Decision: Joint venture registration allowed between the holder of the leasehold interest and the developer who holds the reversion.

Issue: Group registration and waiver of entitlement to exemption.

Decision: The group is regarded as a single taxable entity.

Issue: Company disposes of over 40 units to investors (unreg) by way of 9000 year leases. The investors in turn will lease to tenants with 37 year leases. (Most tenants would be registered).

Decision: To relieve compliance costs — it was agreed that the investors would not be required to register but all VAT obligations would be looked after by the development company.

Issue: Does turf or peat extracted from own land constitute "agricultural produce".

Decision: It was considered that for the purposes of the flat-rate addition system turf and peat should be regarded as agricultural produce. This decision was extended to gravel and stone from 10 April 1987.

Issue: Jockeys and jockeys' valets were officially brought into tax net from 1 January 1991.

Decision: Period of grace granted, registration deferred until 1/9/91.

Issue: VAT liability of commercial golf clubs.

Decision: Two months period of grace granted to such golf clubs to allow them to effect registration for the first time.

Issue: French airline sell aircraft while it is on ground in Dublin. Are they required to register?

Decision: No, concessionally, not required to register for VAT.

Issue: The conditions for group registration require members to be bound by financial, economic and organisational links.

Decision: (*a*) VAT grouping allowed where the managed company is passive, and did not have any independent management capabilities.

Issue: VAT grouping of companies linked either financially or organisationally where their business is not economically linked.

Decision: In exceptional case a group arrangement allowed for VAT purposes on the basis of economic links even though the actual business of the companies involved were not in themselves economically linked.

Issue: Grouping for VAT purposes.

Decision: Revenue accepts that there is no taxable supply of services by an overseas head office to its Irish branch within the same legal entity. Extended to services supplied by affiliate companies in a VAT group via head office based overseas for onward supply to its Irish branch. The concession does not apply to services supplied by affiliate companies via an overseas branch to an Irish head office.

Issue: Joint and several liability.

Decision: The joint and several liability requirement was relaxed in group situations in IFSC provided group registration conditions were met.

Issue: Can individuals who invest in forestry be regarded as "farmers" for VAT purposes?

Decision: No — investment in forestry is not sufficient to deem a person to come within the meaning of the term "farmer".

Revenue publications

Agricultural services: Statement of Practice VAT 5/92. (Replaced by Information Leaflet No 23/01).

Certain services received from abroad: Statement of Practice VAT 1/90.

Certain services received from abroad: Statement of Practice VAT 1/94.

Dances: Statement of Practice VAT 6/92 (Replaced by Information Leaflet No 20/01).

Distance selling: Statement of Practice VAT 14/93

Foreign traders and Construction Contracts: Tax Briefing, Issue 29.

Guide to Value Added Tax (Revenue Commissioners): Chapter 2.

Horticultural retailers Statement of Practice VAT 1/97 (Replaced by Information Leaflet No 24/01).

Intra-community acquisitions by Government Departments, local authorities etc: Statement of Practice VAT 11/92 (Replaced by Information Leaflet No 11/01).

Live horses: Statement of Practice VAT 3/90.

Racehorse trainers: Leaflet 1985.

Revenue powers: Statement of Practice GEN/1/94, May 1994.

Sports facilities: Statement of Practice VAT 4/92.

State and local authorities, certain services received from abroad: Statement of Practice VAT 1/90.

Supply and istallation of goods: Tax Briefing Issue 58.

Definition

"agricultural produce": s 1(1); "agricultural service": s 1(1); "business": s 1(1); "Dáil Éireann": IA 2005, Sch; "excisable products": s 1(1); "goods": s 1(1); "immovable goods": s 1(1); "intra-

Community acquisition of goods: ss 1(1), 3A; "local authority": s 1(1); "the Minister": s 1(1); "new means of transport": s 1(1); "person": IA 2005, s 18(*c*); "regulations": ss 1(1), 32; "supply": s 1(1); "tax": s 1(1); "taxable goods": s 1(1); "taxable period": s 1(1); "taxable person": s 1(1); "writing": IA 2005, Sch.

9 Registration

(Definition of the register)

[(1) The Revenue Commissioners shall set up and maintain a register of persons a 22(1) who may become or who are taxable persons [or who are persons who dispose of goods which pursuant to section 3(7) are deemed to be supplied by a taxable person in the course or furtherance of his business][1]][2].

(Registration numbers)

[(1A) The Revenue Commissioners shall assign to each person registered in accordance with subsection (1) a registration number.][3]

(Who must register?)

(2) Every person who on the appointed day or on any day thereafter would be [a taxable person][4] if tax were chargeable with effect as on and from the appointed day shall, within the period of thirty days beginning on the appointed day or on the day thereafter on which the person first becomes [a taxable person][4] or would become such a person if tax were chargeable as aforesaid, furnish in writing to the Revenue Commissioners the particulars specified in regulations as being required for the purpose of registering such person for tax.

(Requirements for liquidators and receivers)

[(2A) Every person who disposes of goods which pursuant to section 3(7) are deemed to be supplied by a taxable person in the course or furtherance of his business shall, within fourteen days of such disposal, furnish in writing to the Revenue Commissioners the particulars specified in regulations as being required for the purpose of registering such person for tax][5].

(Exceptions to subsection (2))

(3) Any person who on the appointed day was registered for the purposes of turnover tax on the basis of particulars furnished in accordance with section 49(2) of the Finance Act, 1963, shall be deemed, unless he notifies the Revenue Commissioners in writing that he does not wish to be so deemed, to have furnished the particulars required by subsection (2).

(1 Sept 1972)

(4) In this section **"the appointed day"** means the day appointed by the Minister by order to be the appointed day for the purposes of this section.

Amendments

1 Inserted by FA 1983, s 80 with effect from 1 September 1983.
2 Subs (1) substituted by VATAA 1978, s 7 with effect from 1 March 1979.
3 Subs (1A) inserted by FA 1992, s 171 with effect from 28 May 1992.
4 Words substituted by VATAA 1978, s 30(2) with effect from 1 March 1979; previously "an accountable person".
5 Subs (2A) inserted by FA 1983, s 80 with effect from 1 September 1983.

Cross-references

Failure to register (subs (2)), penalty: s 26(1).

Fraud, negligence (subs (1A)): penalties: s 27(1).

Registration particulars, Revenue may prescribe: s 32(1)(c); registration details: Value Added Tax (Registration) Regulations 1993 (SI 30/93).

Regulations

Subject	Regulation
Registration details	Value Added Tax (Registration) Regulations 1993 (SI 30/93)

Orders

Subject	Order
"appointed day"	1 September 1972: Value Added Tax (Appointed Day) Order 1972 (SI 192/72).

Case law

Subject	Case	Case reference
A non-resident company engaging in a single trading transaction within the State was held entitled to be registered	*WLD Worldwide Leather Diffusion Ltd v Revenue Commissioners*	[1994] ITR 165

Revenue precedent

Issue: Is an Irish company acting as an agent for foreign companies obliged to register separately for transactions carried out as agent?

Decision: In the particular circumstances registration was not required and a company acting as an agent could use its own VAT number to import and claim credit on such goods on behalf of a foreign company.

Revenue publications

Foreign Firms Doing Business in Ireland: Leaflet No 1 of 1999.

Guide to Value Added Tax (Revenue Commissioners): Chapter 2.

Electronically Supplied Services: Tax Briefing Issues 52 and 53.

Registration and Repayment Addresses: Tax Briefing Issue 30.

Definition

"business": s 1(1); "farmer": s 1(1); "goods": s 1(1); "the Minister": s 1(1); "person": IA 2005, s 18(c); "regulations": ss 1(1), 32; "tax": s 1(1); "taxable person": ss 1(1), 8; "writing": IA 2005, Sch.

10 Amount on which tax is chargeable

(General rule)

a 11A(1)   [(1) The amount on which tax is chargeable by virtue of section 2(1)(a) shall, subject to this section, be the total consideration which the person supplying goods or services becomes entitled to receive in respect of or in relation to such supply of goods or services, including all taxes, commissions, costs and charges whatsoever, but not including value added tax chargeable in respect of the supply.

(Intra-Community acquisitions)

a 28e   [(1A) The amount on which tax is chargeable on the intra-Community acquisition of goods by virtue of section 2(1A) shall, subject to this section, be the total consideration, including all taxes, commissions, costs and charges whatsoever, but not including value added tax chargeable, in respect of that acquisition.][1]

(Consideration not in money)

(2) If the consideration referred to in [subsections (1) or (1A)]² does not consist of or does not consist wholly of an amount of money, the amount on which tax is chargeable shall be the total amount of money which might reasonably be expected to be charged if the consideration consisted entirely of an amount of money equal to the open market price:

...³

(Consideration less than market value)

(3) [(*a*)   If for any non-business reason the actual consideration in relation to—

   (i)   the supply of any goods or services, or

   (ii)   the intra-Community acquisition of goods,

   is less than the open market price or there is no consideration, the a 11 amount on which tax is chargeable shall be the open market price.]⁴

(Consideration greater than entitlement)

   (*b*)   If the consideration actually received in relation to the supply of any goods or services exceeds the amount which the person supplying the goods or services was entitled to receive, the amount on which tax is chargeable shall be the amount actually received, excluding tax chargeable in respect of the supply.

(Provision for bad debts)

   (*c*)   If, in a case not coming within paragraph (*a*), the consideration actually a 11C(1) received in relation to the supply of any goods or services is less than the amount on which tax is chargeable or no consideration is actually received, such relief may be given by repayment or otherwise in respect of the deficiency as may be provided by regulations.

   [Provided that in any event this paragraph shall not apply in the case of the letting of immovable goods which is a taxable supply of goods in accordance with section 4.]⁵

(Provision for discounts and allowances)

   [(*d*)   If, following the issue of an invoice by a taxable person in respect of a supply of goods or services, the person who issued the invoice allows a reduction or discount in the amount of the consideration due in respect of that supply, the relief referred to in paragraph (*c*) shall not be given until the person who issued the invoice issues the credit note required in accordance with the provisions of section 17(3)(*b*) in respect of that reduction or discount.]⁶

(Self supplies and seized goods)

(4) The amount on which tax is chargeable in relation to a supply of goods a 11A(1) referred to in paragraph (*d*)(ii), (*e*) or (*f*) of section 3(1) or a supply of services by virtue of regulations made for the [for the purposes of paragraph (*a*) or (*b*) of section 5(3)]⁷ shall be the cost, excluding tax, of the goods to [the person supplying or acquiring the goods]⁸ or the cost, excluding tax, of supplying the services, as the case may be[, and the amount on which tax is chargeable in

relation to a supply of services by virtue of regulations made for the purposes of section 5(3)(c) shall be the open market price of the services supplied][9].

[Provided that where the supply in question is a supply of immovable goods, (hereafter referred to in this proviso as **"appropriation"**), the cost to the person making that appropriation shall include an amount equal to the amount on which tax was chargeable on the supply of those goods to that person, being the last supply of those goods to that person which preceded the appropriation.][10]

(Excise duty)

[(4A) Where goods chargeable with a duty of excise [, other than alcohol products within the meaning of section 3B,][11] are supplied while warehoused, and before payment of the duty, to an unregistered person, the amount on which tax is chargeable in respect of the supply shall be increased by an amount equal to the amount of duty that would be payable in relation to the goods if the duty had become due at the time of the supply.][12]

(Transfer of business goods abroad)

[(4B) The amount on which tax is chargeable in relation to the supply of goods referred to in section 3(1) (g) shall be the [cost of the goods to the person making the supply or, in the absence of such a cost, the cost price of similar goods in the State, and where an intra-Community acquisition occurs in the State following a supply of goods in another Member State which, if such supply was carried out in similar circumstances in the State would be a supply of goods in accordance with section 3(1)(g), then the amount on which tax is chargeable in respect of that intra- Community acquisition shall be the cost to the person making the supply in that Member State or, in the absence of a cost to that person, the cost price of similar goods in that other Member State].[13]][14]

(Hire purchase and credit sales transactions)

[(4C) In the case of a supply of goods of the type referred to in section 3(1)(b), where, as part of an agreement of the kind referred to in that provision, the supplier of the goods is also supplying financial services of the kind specified in subparagraph (i)(e) of the First Schedule in respect of those goods, the amount on which tax is chargeable in respect of the supply of the goods in question shall be either—

(a) the open market price of the goods, or

(b) the amount of the total consideration as specified in subsection (1) which the person supplying the goods becomes entitled to receive in respect of or in relation to such supply,

whichever is the greater.][15]

(Fourth Schedule services)

(5) The amount on which tax is chargeable in relation to services for the tax chargeable on which the recipient is, by virtue of section 8(2), liable shall be the consideration for which the services were in fact supplied to him.

(Intra-Community acquisitions in more than one Member State)

[(5A) Where,

    (*a*)   an intra-Community acquisition is deemed to have taken place in the territory of another Member State in accordance with section 3A(2)(*a*),

    (*b*)   the intra-Community acquisition has been subject to value added tax, referred to in Council Directive No. 77/388/EEC of 17 May 1977, in that other Member State, and

    (*c*)   the intra-Community acquisition is also deemed to have taken place in the State, in accordance with section 3A(2)(*b*),

then the consideration for the intra-Community acquisition to which paragraph (*c*) relates shall be reduced to nil.][16]

(Gift vouchers and tokens)

(6) [Subject to subsection (6A), where][17] a right to receive goods or services [, other than telecommunications services,][18] for an amount stated on any token, stamp, coupon or voucher is granted for a consideration, the consideration shall be disregarded for the purposes of this Act except to the extent (if any) that it exceeds that amount.

[(6A) Notwithstanding the provisions of subsection (6), where—

    (*a*)   a supplier

        (i)   supplies a token, stamp, coupon or voucher, which has an amount stated on it, to a person who acquires it in the course or furtherance of business with a view to resale, and

        (ii)   promises to subsequently accept that token, stamp, coupon or voucher at its face value in full or part payment of the price of goods,

    and

    (*b*)   a person who acquires that token, stamp, coupon or voucher, whether from the supplier referred to in paragraph (*a*) or from any other person in the course or furtherance of business, supplies it for consideration in the course or furtherance of business,

then in the case of each such supply the consideration received shall not be disregarded for the purposes of this Act and when such token, stamp, coupon or voucher is used in payment or part payment of the price of goods, the face value of it shall, for the purposes of section 10(2), be disregarded.][19]

(Consideration to be fixed)

(7) Provision may be made by regulations for the purpose of determining the amount on which tax is chargeable in relation to one or more of the following:

    (*a*)   supplies of goods and services to which an order under section 8(2A) applies,

    (*b*)   supplies of stamps, coupons, tokens or vouchers when supplied as things in action (not being stamps, coupons, tokens or vouchers specified in subsection (6)),

(c) [subject to subsection [(6A) or][20] (7A),][21] supplies of goods or services wholly or partly in exchange for stamps, coupons, tokens or vouchers of a kind specified in subsection (6) or paragraph (b),

...[22]

and such regulations may, in the case of supplies referred to in paragraph (b), provide that the amount on which tax is chargeable shall be nil.

(Discounts/coupons/vouchers)

[(7A)(a) Where a supplier sells a voucher to a buyer at a discount and promises to subsequently accept that voucher at its face value in full or part payment of the price of goods purchased by a customer who was not the buyer of the voucher, and who does not normally know the actual price at which the voucher was sold by the supplier, the consideration represented by the voucher shall, subject to regulations, if any, be the sum actually received by the supplier upon the sale of the voucher.

(b) Paragraph (a) is for the purpose of giving further effect to Article 11A.1.(a) of Council Directive No. 77/388/EEC of 17 May 1977 (OJ No L145 of 13 June 1977, p 1), and shall be construed accordingly.][23]

(The two-thirds rule)

(8) (a) Where the value of movable goods (not being goods of a kind specified in paragraph (xii) of the Second Schedule) provided under an agreement for the supply of services exceeds two-thirds of the total consideration under the agreement for the provision of those goods and the supply of the services, other than transport services in relation to them, the consideration shall be deemed to be referable solely to the supply of the goods and tax shall be charged at the appropriate rate or rates specified in section 11 on the basis of any apportionment of the total consideration made in accordance with paragraph (b).

(Differing rate classifications?)

(b) Where goods of different kinds are provided under an agreement of the kind referred to in paragraph (a), the amount of the consideration referable to the supply of goods of each kind shall be ascertained for the purposes of that paragraph by apportioning the total consideration in proportion to the value of the goods of each kind provided.

(Re: immovable property)

(c) This subsection shall also apply to an agreement for the supply of immovable goods and, accordingly, the references in paragraphs (a) and (b) to an agreement for the supply of services shall be deemed to include a reference to such an agreement.

(Property, construction and development services)

a
11A(1)(a)

(9) (a) On the supply of immovable goods and on the supply of services consisting of the development of immovable goods, the value of any interest in the goods disposed of in connection with the supply shall be included in the consideration.

(*b*) The value of any interest in immovable goods shall be the open market price of such interest.

[Provided that where a surrender or an assignment of an interest in immovable goods is a supply of immovable goods which is chargeable to tax, the open market price of such interest shall be determined as if the person who surrendered or assigned that interest were disposing of an interest in those goods which that person had created for the period between the date of the surrender or assignment and the date on which that surrendered or assigned interest would, but for its surrender or assignment, have expired.][24]

[(*c*) Where the Revenue Commissioners wish to ascertain the open market price of an interest in immovable goods, they may authorise a person to inspect the immovable goods and to report to them the open market price of such interest in those goods for the purposes of this Act, and a person having custody or possession of those goods shall permit the person so authorised to inspect the goods at such reasonable times as the Revenue Commissioners consider necessary.

(*d*) Where the Revenue Commissioners require a valuation to be made by a person named by them, the costs of such valuation shall be defrayed by the Commissioners.][25]

(Exchange rates)

[(9A) In relation to the tax chargeable by virtue of section 2(1)(*a*) or 2(1A), a 11C(2) where an amount is expressed in a currency other than the currency of the State the exchange rate to be used shall be—

(*a*) unless paragraph (*b*) applies, the latest selling rate recorded by the Central Bank of Ireland for the currency in question at the time the tax becomes due,

(*b*) where there is an agreement with the Revenue Commissioners for a method to be used in determining the exchange rate, the exchange rate obtained using the said method:

Provided that where paragraph (*b*) applies the method agreed in accordance with that paragraph shall be applied for all transactions where an amount is expressed in a currency other than that of the State until the agreement to use such method is withdrawn by the Revenue Commissioners.][26]

(Definitions)

[(10) In this section—

"interest", in relation to immovable goods, and **"disposal"** in relation to any such interest, shall be construed in accordance with section 4(1), provided that for the purposes of determining the open market price of a surrendered or assigned interest in accordance with the proviso to paragraph (*b*) of subsection (9), an interest in immovable goods shall also mean an estate or interest which, when it was created, was for a period equal to the period referred to in that proviso, regardless of the duration of that period;

"the open market price"—

a 11A(1)   (*a*)   in relation to the value of an interest in immovable goods which is not a freehold interest, means the price, excluding tax, which the right to receive an unencumbered rent in respect of those goods for the period of the interest would fetch on the open market at the time that that interest is disposed of, and

(*b*)   in relation to the supply of any other goods or services or the intra-Community acquisition of goods, means the price, excluding tax, which the goods might reasonably be expected to fetch or which might reasonably be expected to be charged for the services if sold in the open market at the time of the event in question;

"unencumbered rent", for the purposes of valuing an interest in immovable goods, means the rent at which an interest would be let, if that interest was let on the open market free of restrictive conditions.][27]][28]

Amendments

1   Subs (1A) inserted by FA 1992, s 172(*a*) with effect from 1 January 1993.
2   Substituted by FA 1992, s 172 with effect from 1 January 1993; previously "subsection (1)".
3   Subs (2)(proviso) deleted by FA 1995, s 125(*a*) with effect from 1 July 1995.
4   Subs (3)(*a*) substituted by FA 1992, s 172(*d*) with effect from 1 January 1993.
5   Subs (3)(*c*)(proviso) inserted by FA 1994, s 95 with effect from 23 May 1994.
6   Subs (3)(*d*) inserted by FA 1997, s 102(*a*) as on and from 10 May 1997.
7   Substituted by FA 2006, s 96(*a*) with effect from 31 March 2006; previously "for the purposes of section 5(3)".
8   Substituted by FA 1992, s 172(*e*) with effect from 1 January 1992; previously "the person supplying the goods".
9   Words ", and the amount on which tax is chargeable in relation to a supply of services by virtue of regulations made for the purposes of section 5(3)(*c*) shall be the open market price of the services supplied" inserted by FA 2006, s 96(*b*) with effect from 31 March 2006.
10   Subs (4)(proviso) inserted by FA 1997, s 102(*b*) as on and from 26 March 1997.
11   Inserted by FA 1993, s 86.
12   Subs (4A) inserted by FA 1982, s 78 with effect from 1 September 1982.
13   Substituted by FA 1999, s 124 with effect from 25 March 1999; previously "open market price".
14   Subs (4B) inserted by FA 1992, s 172(*f*) with effect from 1 January 1993.
15   Subs (4C) inserted by FA 1995, s 125(*b*) with effect from 2 June 1995.
16   Subs (5A) inserted by FA 1992, s 172(*g*) with effect from 1 January 1993.
17   Substituted by FA 2002, s 102(*a*) with effect on and from 1 May 2002; previously "Where".
18   Inserted by FA 1998, s 109 with effect from 1 May 1998.
19   Subs (6A) inserted by FA 2002, s 102(*b*) with effect from 25 March 2002.
20   Inserted by FA 2002, s 102(*c*) with effect from 25 March 2002.
21   Inserted by FA 1997, s 102(*c*)(i) as on and from 10 May 1997.
22   Subs (7)(*d*) deleted by FA 1997, s 102(*c*)(ii) as on and from 10 May 1997.
23   Subs (7A) inserted by FA 1997, s 102(*d*) as on and from 10 May 1997.
24   Subs (9)(*b*)(proviso) inserted by FA 1997, s 102(*e*) as on and from 26 March 1997.
25   Subs (9)(*c*)–(*d*) inserted by FA 2005, s 102 with effect from 25 March 2005.
26   Subs (9A) inserted by EC(VAT)R 1992, r 8 with effect from 1 January 1993.
27   Subs (10) substituted by FA 1997, s 102(*f*) as on and from 26 March 1997.
28   Section 10 substituted by VATAA 1978, s 8 with effect from 1 March 1979.

Cross-references

Alcohol products (subss (1), (1A)): s 3B(5).
Bad debts, discounts etc: VATR 1979, r 8.

Immovable goods, valuation of interests in: VATR 1979, r 19.

Margin scheme goods: s 10A(3); special scheme for auctioneers: s 10B(3).

Staff canteens: VATR 1979, r 24.

Stamps, coupons etc supplies of: VATR 1979, r 32; supplies in exchange for: VATR 1979, r 33.

Case law

Subject	Case	Case reference
Retail scheme, excise duty could not be included at 0%	*D.H. Burke & Sons Ltd v Revenue Commissioners*	HC 4 February 1997
Where goods are exchanged for vouchers VAT is chargeable on the sum received regardless of vouchers face value	*Argos Distributors v C & E Commissioners*	ECJ C288/94
Refusal of C & E to refund tax where unpaid consideration is not expressed in money – UK government had exceeded its authority.	*Goldsmiths (Jewellers) Ltd v The Commissioners C & E*	3 July 1997, C–330/95
Taxable amount involving credit sale of goods with credit granted by third party at no cost to customer	*Primback v Commissioners of Customs & Excise*	15 May 2001, C–34/99
Service Charges	*EC Commission v France*	29 March 2001, C–404/99
Treatment of Grants	*Keeping Newcastle Warm Ltd v Commissioners of Customs & Excise*	13 June 2002, C–353/00
Taxable Amount — Reduction Coupons	*Yorkshire Co-operatives Ltd v Commissioners of Customs & Excise*	16 January 2003, C–398/99
Taxable Amount — Money-Off Coupons	*Commission v Federal Republic of Germany*	15 October 2002, C–427/98
Taxable Amount — Competition Entry Fees	*Town & County Factors Ltd v Commissioners of Customs & Excise*	17 September 2002, C–498/99

Regulations

Subject	Regulation
Adjustments for bad debts, discounts/rebates etc	Value Added Tax Regulations 1979 (SI 63/79), r 8
Catering services for employees	Value Added Tax Regulations 1979 (SI 63/79), r 24
Supplies in exchange for stamps	Value Added Tax Regulations 1979 (SI 63/79), r 33
Supplies in exchange for stamps, coupons, tokens, vouchers etc	Value Added Tax Regulations 1979 (SI 63/79), r 24
Valuation of interest in property	Value Added Tax Regulations 1979 (SI 63/79), r 19
Valuation of interest in property	Value Added Tax (Valuation of Interests in Immovable Goods) (Amendment) Regulations 1998 (SI 482/98), r 8

Revenue precedent

Issue: Position relating to the levying of tax on facilities provided free of charge to employees in the catering trade.

Decision: The value for VAT purposes of meals and accommodation supplied "free of charge to the trade" may be assessed at £1 per week per employee.

Issue: Two-thirds rule applicable to repair and maintenance on motor vehicles and agricultural machinery.

Decision: Two-thirds rule will not apply to qualifying repair and maintenance services of vehicles and agricultural machinery.

Issue: Taxable amount re amusement arcade machines.

Decision: Only the money remaining after disbursement of winnings (i.e. net takings) is taxable.

Revenue publications

ECJ judgments in relation to Business Promotional Schemes: Leaflet No 6 of 1998.
Guide to Value Added Tax (Revenue Commissioners): Chapter 5.
Staff canteens: Tax Briefing Issue 29.
VAT and VRT: Tax Briefing Issue 40.

Definition

"business": s 1(1); "Community": s 1(1); "development" s 1(1); "goods": s 1(1); "immovable goods": s 1(1); "intra- Community acquisition of goods": ss 1(1), 3A; "movable goods": s 1(1); "person": IA 2005, s 18(*c*); "regulations": ss 1(1), 32; "second-hand": s 1(1); "supply": s 1(1); "tax": s 1(1).

10A Margin scheme goods

(Definitions)

[(1) In this section—

"antiques" means any of the goods specified in paragraph (xvia) of the Sixth Schedule or in paragraph (iii) of the Eighth Schedule;

"collectors' items" means any of the goods specified in paragraph (ii) of the Eighth Schedule;

"margin scheme" means the special arrangements for the taxation of supplies of margin scheme goods;

[**"margin scheme goods"** means any works of art, collectors' items, antiques or second-hand goods supplied within the Community to a taxable dealer—

(*a*) by a person, other than a person referred to in paragraph (*c*), who was not entitled to deduct, under section 12, any tax in respect of that person's purchase, intra-Community acquisition or importation of those goods:

Provided that person is not a taxable person who acquired those goods from—

(i) a taxable dealer who applied the margin scheme to the supply of those goods to that taxable person, or

(ii) an auctioneer within the meaning of section 10B who applied the auction scheme within the meaning of section 10B to the supply of those goods to that taxable person,

or

(*b*) by a person in another Member State who was not entitled to deduct, under the provisions implementing Article 17 of Council Directive No. 77/ 388/EEC of 17 May 1977, in that Member State, any Value Added tax referred to in that Directive in respect of that person's purchase, intra-Community acquisition or importation of those goods, or

(*c*) by another taxable dealer who has applied the margin scheme to the supply of those goods or applied the provisions implementing Article

26a (inserted by Council Directive No. 94/5/EC of 14 February 1994) of Council Directive No. 771388/EEC of 17 May 1977, in another Member State to the supply of those goods,

and also includes goods acquired by a taxable dealer as a result of a disposal of goods by a person to such taxable dealer where that disposal was deemed not to be a supply of goods in accordance with [paragraphs (*c*) and (*d*) of subsection (5) of section 3]¹.]²

"precious metals" means silver (including silver plated with gold or platinum), gold (including gold plated with platinum), and platinum, and all items which contain any of these metals when the consideration for the supply does not exceed the open market price, as defined in section 10, of the metal concerned;

"precious stones" means diamonds, rubies, sapphires and emeralds, whether cut or uncut, when they are not mounted, set or strung;

"profit margin" means the profit margin in respect of a supply by a taxable dealer of margin scheme goods and shall be deemed to be inclusive of tax and shall be an amount which is equal to the difference between the taxable dealer's selling price for those goods and the taxable dealer's purchase price for those goods:

Provided that, in respect of that supply, where the purchase price is greater than the selling price, the profit margin shall be deemed to be nil;

"purchase price", in relation to an acquisition of margin scheme goods, means the total consideration including all taxes, commissions, costs and charges whatsoever, payable by a taxable dealer to the person from whom that taxable dealer acquired those goods;

"second-hand goods" means any tangible movable goods which are suitable for further use either as they are or after repair, other than means of transport [agricultural machinery (within the meaning of section 12C),]³ works of art, collectors' items, antiques, precious metals and precious stones;

"selling price" means the total consideration which a taxable dealer becomes entitled to receive in respect of or in relation to a supply of margin scheme goods including all taxes, commissions, costs and charges whatsoever and Value Added tax, if any, payable in respect of the supply;

"taxable dealer" means a taxable person who in the course or furtherance of business, whether acting on that person's own behalf, or on behalf of another person pursuant to a contract under which commission is payable on purchase or sale, purchases or acquires margin scheme goods or the goods referred to in paragraphs (*b*) and (*c*) of subsection (4), with a view to resale, or imports the goods referred to in paragraph (*a*) of subsection (4), with a view to resale, and a person in another Member State shall be deemed to be a taxable dealer where, in similar circumstances, that person would be a taxable dealer in the State under this section;

"works of art" means any of the goods specified in paragraph (xvi), or subparagraph (*a*) of paragraph (xxii), of the Sixth Schedule or in paragraph (i) of the Eighth Schedule.

(Application of margin scheme)

(2) Subject to and in accordance with the provisions of this section, a taxable dealer may apply the margin scheme to a supply of margin scheme goods.

(Taxable amount)

(3) Where the margin scheme is applied to a supply of goods, then notwithstanding section 10, the amount on which tax is chargeable by virtue of section 2(1)(*a*) on that supply shall be the profit margin less the amount of tax included in the profit margin.

(Deemed margin scheme goods)

(4) Subject to such conditions (if any) as may be specified in regulations, a taxable dealer may, notwithstanding subsection (2), opt to apply the margin scheme to all that dealer's supplies of any of the following as if they were margin scheme goods—

   (*a*) a work of art, collector's item or antique which the taxable dealer imported, or

   (*b*) a work of art which has been supplied to the taxable dealer by its creator or the creator's successors in title, or

   (*c*) a work of art which has been supplied to the taxable dealer by a taxable person other than a taxable dealer, where the supply to that dealer is of the type referred to in section 11(1AA)(*b*)(ii):

   Provided that where a taxable dealer so opts in accordance with this subsection, such option shall be for a period of not less than two years from the date when such option was exercised.

(Imported works of art — purchase price)

(5) Where a taxable dealer exercises the option in accordance with subsection (4), in respect of the goods specified at paragraph (*a*) thereto, then notwithstanding the definition of purchase price in subsection (1), the purchase price for the purposes of determining the profit margin in relation to a supply of those goods shall be an amount equal to the value of those goods for the purposes of importation determined in accordance with section 15 increased by the amount of any tax payable in respect of the importation of those goods.

(Restriction on input tax credits)

(6) Subject to subsection (7) and notwithstanding section 12, a taxable dealer who exercises the option in respect of the supply of the goods specified in subsection (4) shall not be entitled to deduct any tax in respect of the purchase or importation of those goods.

(Scope to apply normal VAT rules — ignore margin scheme)

(7) Where a taxable dealer exercises the option in accordance with subsection (4), that dealer may, notwithstanding the proviso to subsection (4), in respect of any individual supply of the goods specified in subsection (4), opt not to apply the margin scheme to that supply, and in such case the right to deduction of the

tax charged on the purchase, intra-Community acquisition or importation of those goods shall, notwithstanding section 12, arise only in the taxable period in which the dealer supplies those goods.

(Special rule — low value margin scheme goods)

(8) (*a*)   Notwithstanding subsection (3), and subject to and in accordance with regulations (if any)—

(i)   where a taxable dealer acquires low value margin scheme goods in job lots or otherwise, the amount of tax due and payable in respect of that dealer's supplies of low value margin scheme goods shall, in respect of a taxable period, be the amount of tax included in that dealer's aggregate margin, or margins, for that period and the amount of tax in each aggregate margin shall be determined by the formula:

$$A \times \frac{B}{B + 100}$$

where—

A is the aggregate margin for the taxable period in question, and

B is the percentage rate of tax chargeable in relation to the supply of those goods, and

(ii)   where the taxable dealer referred to in paragraph (i) in any taxable period makes supplies which are subject to different rates of tax, that taxable dealer shall calculate separate aggregate margins for that taxable period in respect of the supplies at each of the relevant rates.

(*b*)   Subject to, and in accordance with regulations (if any), where a taxable dealer supplies a low value margin scheme good for an amount in excess of [€635]⁴ then—

(i)   notwithstanding the definition of low value margin scheme goods in paragraph (*c*), the supply of that good shall be deemed not to be a supply of a low value margin scheme good,

(ii)   in determining the aggregate margin for the taxable period in which the supply occurs, the taxable dealer shall deduct the purchase price of that good from the sum of the taxable dealer's purchase prices of low value margin scheme goods for that period, and

(iii)   the purchase price of that good shall be used in determining the profit margin in relation to the supply of that good.

(Definitions)

(*c*)   In this subsection—

"aggregate margin", in respect of a taxable period, means an amount which is equal to the difference between the taxable dealer's total turnover in that period from supplies of low value margin scheme goods, to which the same rate of tax applies, less the sum of that taxable dealer's purchase prices of low value margin scheme goods to which that rate of tax applies to the supply thereof, in that taxable period:

Provided that where the sum of that dealer's said purchase prices is in excess of the said total turnover, the appropriate aggregate margin shall be deemed to be nil and subject to, and in accordance with, regulations (if any), the amount of the excess shall be carried forward and added to the sum of that dealer's purchase prices for low value margin scheme goods for the purposes of calculating that dealer's appropriate aggregate margin for the immediately following taxable period;

"low value margin scheme goods" means margin scheme goods where the purchase price payable by the dealer for each individual item is less than [€635][5].

(Invoicing with respect to margin scheme)

(9) Notwithstanding section 17, a taxable dealer shall not, in relation to any supply to which the margin scheme has been applied, indicate separately the amount of tax chargeable in respect of the supply on any invoice or other document in lieu thereof issued in accordance with that section.

(Selling goods abroad)

(10) Where the margin scheme is applied to a supply of goods dispatched or transported from the State to a person registered for Value Added tax in another Member State, then notwithstanding paragraph (i)(*b*) of the Second Schedule, the provisions of section 11(1)(*b*) shall not apply, unless such goods are of a kind specified elsewhere in the Second Schedule.

(Place of supply)

(11) Notwithstanding section 3(6)(*d*), where the margin scheme is applied to a supply of goods dispatched or transported, the place of supply of those goods shall be deemed to be the place where the dispatch or transportation begins.

(Time of supply)

(12) Where a taxable dealer applies the margin scheme to a supply of goods on behalf of another person pursuant to a contract under which commission is payable on purchase or sale, the goods shall be deemed to have been supplied by that other person to the taxable dealer when the said taxable dealer supplies those goods.

(Sales to taxable persons of margin scheme goods)

(13) Notwithstanding paragraph (xxiv) of the First Schedule, where a taxable person acquires goods to which the margin scheme has been applied and that person subsequently supplies those goods, the provisions of that paragraph shall not apply to that supply.][6]

Amendments

[1]   Substituted by FA 2001, s 185 with effect from 6 April 2001; previously "section 3(5)(*c*)".

[2]   Definition of "margin scheme goods" substituted by FA 1999, s 125(*a*) with effect from 1 September 1999.

[3]   Inserted by FA 1999, s 125(*b*) with effect from 1 September 1999.

⁴   Substituted by FA 2001, s 240 and Sch 5 Part 4 with effect from 1 January 2002; previously "£500".

⁵   Substituted by FA 2001, s 240 and Sch 5 Part 4 with effect from 1 January 2002; previously "£500".

⁶   Section 10A inserted by FA 1995, s 126 with effect from 1 July 1995.

Cross-references

Antiques supplied by taxable dealer, other than in accordance with subss (3), (8): Sch 6 para (xvi*a*).

Concrete blocks supplied by taxable dealer, other than in accordance with subss (3), (8): Sch 6 para (xxxiii).

Concrete ready to pour supplied by taxable dealer, other than in accordance with subss (3), (8): Sch 6 para (xxxii).

Works of art supplied by taxable dealer, other than in accordance with subss (3), (8): Sch 6 para (xvi).

Regulations, Revenue power to make in order to determine conditions for taxable dealer to opt to apply the margin scheme (subs (4)): s 32(1)(*da*); in order to determine aggregate margin (subs (8)): s 32(1)(*db*).

Restriction of deduction (subss (3), (8)): s 12(3A)(*a*).

Revenue publication

Margin scheme/second hand goods: Leaflet December 1994.

Margin scheme goods: Tax Briefing, Issue 30.

Definitions

"Community": s 1(1); "goods": s 1(1); "importation of goods": s 1(1); "intra-Community acquisition of goods": s 1(1); "second-hand goods": s 1(1); "supply": s 1(1); "taxable person": s 1(1).

10B Special scheme for auctioneers

(Definition and scope of scheme)

[(1) In this section—

"auctioneer" means a taxable person who, in the course or furtherance of business, acting on behalf of another person pursuant to a contract under which commission is payable on purchase or sale, offers tangible movable goods for sale by public auction with a view to handing them over to the highest bidder;

"auctioneer's margin" means an amount which is equal to the difference between the total amount, including any taxes, commissions, costs and charges whatsoever, payable by the purchaser to the auctioneer in respect of the auction of auction scheme goods and the amount payable by the auctioneer to the principal in respect of the supply of those goods and shall be deemed to be inclusive of tax;

"auction scheme" means the special arrangements for the taxation of supplies of auction scheme goods;

"auction scheme goods" means any works of art, collectors' items, antiques or second-hand goods sold by an auctioneer at a public auction while acting on behalf of a principal who is—

    (*a*)   a person, other than a person referred to in paragraph (*c*), who was not entitled to deduct, under section 12, any tax in respect of that person's purchase, intra-Community acquisition or importation of those goods:

           Provided that person is not a taxable person who acquired those goods from—

(i) an auctioneer who applied the auction scheme to the supply of those goods to that taxable person, or

(ii) a taxable dealer who applied the margin scheme to the supply of those goods to that taxable person,

[(*aa*) an owner within the meaning of section 3(5)(*c*) who enforced such owner's right to recover possession of those goods under the circumstances set out in section 3(5)(*c*), or]¹

[(*aaa*) an insurer within the meaning of section 3(5)(*d*) (inserted by this Act) who took possession of those goods in connection with the settlement of a claim under a policy of insurance and whose disposal of the goods is deemed not to be a supply of the goods in accordance with section 3(5)(*d*) (inserted by this Act).]²

or

(*b*) a person in another Member State who was not entitled to deduct, under the provisions implementing Article 17 of Council Directive No. 77/388/EEC of 17 May 1977, in that Member State, any Value Added tax referred to in that Directive in respect of that person's purchase, intra-Community acquisition or importation of those goods, or

(*c*) a taxable dealer who applied the margin scheme to the supply of those goods or applied the provisions implementing Article 26a (inserted by Council Directive No. 94/5/EC of 14 February 1994) of Council Directive No. 77/388/EEC of 17 May 1977, in another Member State to the supply of those goods;

"principal" means the person on whose behalf an auctioneer auctions goods;

"purchaser" means the person to whom an auctioneer supplies auction scheme goods.

(Application of margin scheme)

(2) Subject to and in accordance with the provisions of this section, an auctioneer shall apply the auction scheme to any supply of auction scheme goods.

(Taxable amount)

(3) Notwithstanding section 10, the amount on which tax is chargeable, by virtue of section 2(1)(*a*), on a supply by an auctioneer of auction scheme goods shall be the auctioneer's margin less the amount of tax included in that auctioneer's margin.

(Details/documentary requirements)

(4) Where auction scheme goods are auctioned, the auctioneer shall issue, subject to such conditions (if any) as may be specified in regulations, to both the principal and the purchaser, invoices or documents in lieu thereof setting out the relevant details in respect of the supply of the auction scheme goods.

(Invoicing requirements)

(5) Notwithstanding section 17, an auctioneer shall not, in relation to any supply to which the auction scheme has been applied, indicate separately the amount of tax chargeable in respect of the supply on any invoice or other document in lieu thereof issued in accordance with that section.

(Invoicing requirements — simplification)

(6) Where auction scheme goods are auctioned by an auctioneer on behalf of a principal who is a taxable person, the invoice or document in lieu thereof issued to the principal in accordance with subsection (4) shall be deemed to be an invoice for the purposes of section 17, and the said principal shall be deemed to have issued same.

(Rate of VAT application)

(7) Where the auction scheme is applied to a supply of goods dispatched or transported from the State to a person registered for Value Added tax in another Member State then, notwithstanding paragraph (i)(*b*) of the Second Schedule, the provisions of section 11(1)(*b*) shall not apply, unless such goods are of a kind specified elsewhere in the Second Schedule.

(Place of supply)

(8) Notwithstanding section 3(6)(*d*), where the auction scheme is applied to a supply of goods dispatched or transported, the place of supply of those goods shall be deemed to be the place where the dispatch or transportation begins.

(Time of supply)

(9) Where an auctioneer supplies [auction scheme goods][3] by public auction, the principal shall be deemed to have made a supply of the auction scheme goods in question to the auctioneer when the said auctioneer sells those goods at a public auction.

(Sales to taxable persons of auction scheme goods)

(10) Notwithstanding paragraph (xxiv) of the First Schedule, where a taxable person acquires goods to which the auction scheme has been applied and that person subsequently supplies those goods, the provisions of that paragraph shall not apply to that supply.][4]

Amendments

[1]   Subs (1)(*aa*) inserted by FA 1999, s 126 with effect from 25 March 1999.

[2]   Subs (1)(*aaa*) inserted by FA 2001, s 186 with effect from 6 April 2001.

[3]   Substituted by FA 1996, s 91 with effect from 15 May 1996.

[4]   Section 10B inserted by FA 1995, s 127 with effect from 1 July 1995.

Cross-references

Antiques supplied by taxable dealer, other than in accordance with subs (3): Sch 6 para (xvi*a*).

Concrete blocks supplied by taxable dealer, other than in accordance with subs (3): Sch 6 para (xxxiii).

Concrete ready to pour supplied by taxable dealer, other than in accordance with subs (3): Sch 6 para (xxxii).

Regulations, Revenue power to make in order to determine form of invoice (subs (4)): s 32(1)(*dc*).

Restriction of deduction (subs (3)): s 12(3A)(*a*).

Works of art supplied by taxable dealer, other than in accordance with subs (3): Sch 6 para (xvi).

Regulations

Subject	Regulation
Second hand goods	Value Added Tax (Furniture, Silver, Glass and Porcelain) Regulations 1989 (SI 304/89)

Revenue Publications

Auctioneers and Auction and Agency Sales: Leaflet No 5 of 1998.

Definitions

"antiques": s 1(1); "business": s 1(1); "collectors' items": s 1(1); "Community": s 1(1); "goods": s 1(1); "importation of goods": s 1(1); "intra-Community acquisition of goods": s 1(1); "second-hand goods": s 1(1); "supply": s 1(1); "taxable dealer": s 1(1); "taxable person": s 1(1); "works of art": s 1(1).

a 12

11 Rates of tax

[(1) Tax shall be charged, in relation to the supply of taxable goods or services [, the intra-Community acquisition of goods][1] and the importation of goods, at whichever of the following rates is appropriate in any particular case—

(Irish VAT rates and their application)

    (*a*) **[21 per cent]**[2] of the amount on which tax is chargeable other than in relation to goods or services on which tax is chargeable at any of the rates specified in paragraphs (*b*), (*c*), (*d*) ...[3] and (*f*),

    (*b*) **zero per cent** of the amount on which tax is chargeable in relation to goods in the circumstances specified in paragraph (i) [or (i*a*)][4] of the Second Schedule or of goods or services of a kind specified in paragraphs (iii) to (xx) of that Schedule,

    (*c*) **10 per cent** of the amount on which tax is chargeable in relation to goods or services of a kind specified in the Third Schedule,

    (*d*) **[13.5 per cent]**[5] of the amount on which tax is chargeable in relation to goods or services of a kind specified in the Sixth Schedule, [and][6]

    ...[7]

    (*f*) **[4.8 per cent]**[8] of the amount on which tax is chargeable in relation to the supply of livestock and live greyhounds and to the hire of horses.][9]

(Guideline for application of rate)

[(1A)(*a*) The rate at which tax shall be chargeable shall, in relation to tax chargeable under [subsection (1)(*a*) or (1A) of section 2],[10] be the rate for the time being in force at the time at which the tax becomes due in accordance with [subsection (1), (1A) or (2)],[11] as may be appropriate, of section 19.

(Clarification regarding exclusion from a Schedule)

    (*b*) Goods or services which are specifically excluded from any paragraph of a Schedule shall, unless the contrary intention is expressed, be regarded as excluded from every other paragraph of that Schedule, and shall not be regarded as specified in that Schedule.

(Eighth Schedule goods)

[(1AA) Notwithstanding subsection (1), tax shall be charged at the rate specified in section 11(1)(*d*) of the amount on which tax is chargeable in relation to—

    (*a*) the importation into the State of goods specified in the Eighth Schedule,

    (*b*) the supply of a work of art of the kind specified in paragraph (i) of the Eighth Schedule, effected—

        (i) by its creator or the creator's successors in title, or

    (ii) on an occasional basis by a taxable person other than a taxable dealer where—

        (I) that work of art has been imported by the taxable person, or

        (II) that work of art has been supplied to the taxable person by its creator or the creator's successors in title, or

        (III) the tax chargeable in relation to the purchase, intra-Community acquisition or importation of that work of art by the taxable person was wholly deductible under section 12,

  and

  (*c*) the intra-Community acquisition in the State by a taxable person of a work of art of the kind specified in paragraph (i) of the Eighth Schedule where the supply of that work of art to that taxable person which resulted in that intra-Community acquisition is a supply of the type that would be charged at the rate specified in section 11(1)(*d*) in accordance with paragraph (*b*), if that supply had occurred within the State.]¹²

(Contract work)

[(1AB) Notwithstanding subsection (1), the rate at which tax is chargeable on a supply of contract work shall be the rate that would be chargeable if that supply of services were a supply of the goods being handed over by the contractor to the person to whom that supply is made:

Provided that this subsection shall not apply to a supply of contract work in the circumstances specified in paragraph (xvi) of the Second Schedule.]¹³

(Rate determination and appeals procedures)

[(1B)(*a*) On receipt of an application in writing from [a taxable person]¹⁴ the Revenue Commissioners shall, in accordance with regulations and after such consultation (if any) as may seem to them to be necessary with such person or body of persons as in their opinion may be of assistance to them, make a determination concerning—

    (i) whether an activity of any particular kind carried on by the person is an exempted activity, or

    [(ii) the rate at which tax is chargeable in relation to the supply or intra-Community acquisition by the person of goods of any kind, the supply or intra-Community acquisition of goods in any particular circumstances or the supply by the person of services of any kind.]¹⁵

  (*b*) The Revenue Commissioners may, whenever they consider it expedient to do so, in accordance with regulations and after such consultation (if any) as may seem to them to be necessary with such person or body of persons as in their opinion may be of assistance to them, make a determination concerning—

    (i) whether an activity of any particular kind is an exempted activity, or

    [(ii) the rate at which tax is chargeable in relation to the supply or intra-Community acquisition of goods of any kind, the supply or intra-

Community acquisition of goods in any particular circumstances or the supply of services of any kind.][16]

(Date of application of rate)

[(*c*)   A determination under this subsection shall have effect for all the purposes of this Act—

(i)   in relation to a taxable person who makes an application for the determination, as on and from the date which shall be specified for the purpose in the determination communicated to the taxable person in accordance with paragraph (*e*)(i), and

(ii)   in relation to any other person, as on and from the date which shall be specified for the purpose in the determination as published in the Iris Oifigiúil.][17]

(*d*)   The Revenue Commissioners shall not make a determination under this section concerning any matter which has been determined on appeal under this Act or which is for the time being governed by an order under section 6(2) or 11(8), and shall not be required to make such a determination in relation to any of the matters referred to in an application under paragraph (*a*) if—

(i)   a previous determination has been published in regard to the matter, or

(ii)   in their opinion the subject matter of the application is sufficiently free from doubt as not to warrant the making and publication of a determination.

(Notification of determination)

(*e*)   (i)   A determination under paragraph (*a*) shall, as soon as may be after the making thereof, be communicated to the person who made the application therefor by the service on him by the Revenue Commissioners of a notice containing particulars of the determination.

(ii)   A determination under paragraph (*a*) may and a determination under paragraph (*b*) shall be published in the *Iris Oifigiúil* and, in that event, it shall also be published in at least one daily newspaper published in the State.

(Appeals)

(*f*)   A person, aggrieved by determination under paragraph (*a*) made pursuant to an application by him, may, on giving notice in writing to the Revenue Commissioners within the period of twenty-one days beginning on the date of service on him of notice of the determination in accordance with paragraph (*e*)(i), appeal to the Appeal Commissioners.

(*g*)   Any [taxable person][18] who, in the course of business, [supplies goods or makes an intra-Community acquisition of goods, or supplies services][19] of a kind or in circumstances specified in a determination under paragraph (*a*) or (*b*) may, on giving notice in writing to the Revenue Commissioners within the period of twenty-one days beginning on the date of the publication of the determination in the *Iris Oifigiúil*, appeal to the Appeal Commissioners.][20]

(2) ...[21].

(Package of goods/services liable to different rates)

[(3) (*a*) Subject to section 10(8)—

(i) in the case of a composite supply, the tax chargeable on the total consideration which the taxable person is entitled to receive for that composite supply shall be at the rate specified in subsection (1) which is appropriate to the principal supply, but if that principal supply is an exempted activity, tax shall not be chargeable in respect of that composite supply,

(ii) in the case of a multiple supply, the tax chargeable on each individual supply in that multiple supply shall be at the rate specified in subsection (1) appropriate to each such individual supply and, in order to ascertain the taxable amount referable to each individual supply for the purpose of applying the appropriate rate thereto, the total consideration which the taxable person is entitled to receive in respect of that multiple supply shall be apportioned between those individual supplies in a way that correctly reflects the ratio which the value of each such individual supply bears to the total consideration for that multiple supply.

(*b*) In the case where a person acquires a composite supply or a multiple supply by means of an intra-Community acquisition, the provisions of this subsection shall apply to that acquisition.

(*c*) The Revenue Commissioners may make regulations as necessary specifying—

(i) the circumstances or conditions under which a supply may or may not be treated as an ancillary supply, a composite supply, an individual supply, a multiple supply or a principal supply,

(ii) the methods of apportionment which may be applied for the purposes of paragraphs (*a*) and (*b*),

(iii) a minimum amount, or an element of a supply, which may be disregarded for the purposes of applying this subsection.][22]

(Goods produced from customer's materials)

[(4) Where goods for the manufacture of which materials have been supplied by or on behalf of any person are [supplied][23] by the manufacturer to that person and the rate of tax chargeable in relation to the [supply][24] of the goods exceeds that which would be chargeable in relation to a [supply][24] within the State of the materials, the person who [supplies][25] the goods shall, in respect of the [supply][24] of such goods, be liable, in addition to any other liability imposed on him by this Act, to pay tax on the value of the materials [provided][26] to him at a rate equivalent to the difference between the two aforementioned rates.][27]

(Supply of service using food and drink supplied by customer)

[(4A) Where—

(*a*) goods of a kind specified in paragraph (xii) of the Second Schedule are used by a person in the course of the supply by him of taxable services, and

(*b*) the goods are provided by or on behalf of the person to whom the services are supplied,

the person who supplies the taxable services shall be liable in respect thereof, in addition to any other liability imposed on him under this Act, to pay tax on the value of the goods so used at the rate specified in [section 11(1)(*d*)][28].][29]

...[30]

(Letting of plant and machinery)

(6) Where immovable goods consisting of machinery or business installations are let separately from other immovable goods of which they form part, tax shall be chargeable in respect of the transaction at the rate which would be chargeable if it were a hiring of movable goods of the same kind.

...[31].

(Power to vary Schedules)

(8) [(*a*) The Minister may by order vary the [Second, Third, or Sixth Schedule][32] by adding to or deleting therefrom descriptions of goods or services of any kind or by varying any description of goods or services for the time being specified therein, ...[33] but no order shall be made under this section for the purpose of increasing any of the rates of tax or extending the classes of activities or goods in respect of which tax is for the time being chargeable.][34]

(*b*) The Minister may by order amend or revoke an order under this subsection, including an order under this paragraph.

(*c*) An order under this subsection shall be laid before Dáil Éireann as soon as may be after it has been made and, if a resolution annulling the order is passed by Dáil Éireann within the next twenty-one days on which Dáil Éireann has sat after the order is laid before it, the order shall be annulled accordingly, but without prejudice to the validity of anything previously done thereunder.

(9) ...[35].

Amendments

[1]   Inserted by FA 1992, s 173(3)(*a*) with effect from 1 January 1993.

[2]   Substituted by FA 2002, s 103(*a*) with effect on and from 1 March 2002; previously "20 per cent".

[3]   Deleted by FA 1993, s 87(*a*)(i) with effect from 1 March 1993; previously ", (*e*)".

[4]   Inserted by EC(VAT)R 1992, r 9 with effect from 1 January 1993.

[5]   Substituted by FA 2003, s 119 with effect from 1 January 2003; previously "12.5 per cent".

[6]   Inserted by FA 1993, s 87(*a*)(ii)with effect from 1 March 1993.

[7]   Subs (1)(*e*) deleted by FA 1993, s 87 with effect from 1 March 1993.

8 Substituted by FA 2005, s 103 with effect from 25 March 2005: previously "4.4 per cent" (FA 2004, s 59); previously "4.3 per cent" (FA 2001, s 187(*b*)); previously "4.2 per cent" (FA 2000, s 111); previously "4 per cent" (FA 1999, s 127); previously "3.6 per cent" (FA 1998, s 110); previously "3.3 per cent" (FA 1997, s 103(*a*)); previously "2.8 per cent" (FA 1996, s 92(*a*)); previously "2.5 per cent" (FA 1993, s 87(*a*)(iv)); previously "2.7 per cent".

9 Subs (1) substituted by FA 1992, s 173(2) with effect from 28 May 1992.

10 Substituted by FA 1992, s 173(3)(*b*) with effect from 1 January 1993; previously: "section 2(1)(*a*)".

11 Substituted by FA 1992, s 173(3)(*b*) with effect from 1 January 1993; previously: "subsection (1) or (2)".

12 Subs (1AA) inserted by FA 1995, s 128(*a*) with effect from 1 July 1995.

13 Subs (1AB) inserted by FA 1996, s 92(*b*) with effect from 1 March 1996.

14 Substituted by VATAA 1978, s 30(2) with effect from 1 March 1979; previously "an accountable person".

15 Subs (1B)(*a*)(ii) substituted by FA 1992, s 173(3)(*c*)(i) with effect from 1 January 1993.

16 Subs (1B)(*b*)(ii) substituted by FA 1992, s 173(3)(*c*)(ii) with effect from 1 January 1993.

17 Subs (1B)(*c*) substituted by FA 2006, s 97(1)(*a*) with effect from 31 March 2006.

18 Substituted by VATAA 1978, s 30(2) with effect from 1 March 1979; previously "accountable person".

19 Substituted by FA 1992, s 173(3)(*c*)(iii) with effect from 1 January 1993; previously: "supplies goods or services".

20 Subss (1A)–(1B) inserted by FA 1973, s 80 with effect from 3 September 1973.

21 Subs (2) deleted by FA 1985, s 43 with effect from 1 March 1985.

22 Subs (3) substituted by FA 2006, s 97(1)(*b*) with effect from such day as the Minister for Finance may appoint by order; previously

"(Package of goods/services liable to different rates)

[(3) Subject to section 10(8) [in relation to supplies of goods and services]²¹ where—

   (*a*) supplies of different kinds are made for a consideration in money which is referable to all the supplies [or intra-Community acquisitions]²² and not separately to the different kinds of supplies [or intra-Community acquisitions]²² and

   (*b*) one or both of the following subparagraphs applies or apply, that is to say—

        (i) but for this subsection, tax would not be chargeable in respect of one or more (but not all) of the supplies,

        (ii) but for this subsection, tax would ...²³ fall to be charged at two or more of the rates specified in subsection (1) in respect of the supplies [or intra-Community acquisitions]²²

   then, unless regulations provide for apportionment of the consideration—

   (Rule re: taxable and exempt goods in package)

   (*c*) where subparagraph (i) (but not subparagraph (ii)) of paragraph (*b*) applies, tax shall be chargeable in respect of all the supplies [or intra-Community acquisitions]²² at the rate specified in subsection (1) appropriate to the supply of taxable goods or services [, or intra-Community acquisition of goods]²⁴ included in the supplies [or intra- Community acquisitions].²²

   (*d*) where subparagraph (ii) of paragraph (*b*) applies (whether alone or with subparagraph (i) of that paragraph), tax shall be chargeable in respect of all the supplies [or intra-Community acquisitions]²² at the higher or highest rate (as the case may be) specified in subsection (1) appropriate to the supply of any taxable goods or services [, or any intra-Community acquisition of goods]²⁵ included in the supplies [or intra-Community acquisitions]²²:

Provided that, where goods—

   (I) are chargeable with tax at different rates,

   (II) are packaged for sale as a unit, and

   (III) are offered for sale for a consideration in money which is referable to the package as a whole and not to the different kinds of goods included therein,

the inclusion in the package of goods chargeable at a particular rate shall not be taken into account for the purpose of the preceding provisions of this subsection where the total tax-exclusive value of such goods does not exceed **50 per cent** of the total tax-exclusive consideration for the package or [25 pence]²⁶[40 cent]²⁷, whichever is the lesser, and, in any such case, the rate of tax chargeable in relation to the package shall be determined by reference to the other goods included therein.]²⁸

Amendments

²¹ Inserted by FA 1992, s 173(3)(*d*)(i) with effect from 1 January 1993.

²² Inserted by FA 1992, s 173(3)(*d*)(ii) with effect from 1 January 1993.

²³ Words '(apart from subsection (2))' deleted by FA 1985, s 43 with effect from 1 March 1985.

²⁴ Inserted by FA 1992, s 173(3)(*d*)(iii) with effect from 1 January 1993.

²⁵ Inserted by FA 1992, s 173(3)(*d*)(iv) with effect from 1 January 1993.

²⁶ Substituted by FA 1997, s 103(*b*) as on and from 10 May 1997; previously '5 pence'.

²⁷ Substituted by FA 2002, s 138 and Sch 6 para 1(*a*) with effect on and from 25 March 2002; previously '40 cents'.

²⁸ Subs (3) substituted by VATAA 1978, s 9 with effect from 1 March 1979.".

²³ Substituted by VATAA 1978, s 30(2) with effect from 1 March 1979; previously "delivered".

²⁴ Substituted by VATAA 1978, s 30(2) with effect from 1 March 1979; previously "delivery".

²⁵ Substituted by VATAA 1978, s 30(2) with effect from 1 March 1979; previously "delivers goods or services".

²⁶ Substituted by VATAA 1978, s 30(2) with effect from 1 March 1979; previously "rendered".

²⁷ Subs (4) substituted by FA 1975, s 51 with effect from 16 January 1975.

²⁸ Substituted by FA 1993, s 87(*b*); previously "section 11(1)(*c*)".

²⁹ Subs (4A) substituted by VATAA 1978, s 9 with effect from 1 March 1979.

³⁰ Subs (5) deleted by FA 1995, s 128(*b*) with effect from 2 June 1995.

³¹ Subs (7) deleted by FA 1992, s 173(2)(*b*) with effect from 28 May 1992.

³² Substituted by FA 1993, s 87(*c*); previously "Second, Third, Sixth or Seventh Schedule".

³³ Words "and may, in like manner, vary the Fourth Schedule by deleting therefrom descriptions of goods of any kind or by varying any description of goods for the time being specified therein" deleted by VATAA 1978, s 30(1) with effect from 1 March 1979.

³⁴ Subs (8)(*a*) substituted by FA 1973, s 80 with effect from 3 September 1973.

³⁵ Subs (9) repealed by VATAA 1978, s 30(1) with effect from 1 March 1979.

Cross-references

Apportionment of taxable consideration (subs (3)), Revenue may prescribe manner: s 32(1)(*e*); apportionment: VATR 1979, r 34.

Distortion of competition, Revenue may determine a person to be a taxable person (subs (1)(*d*)): s 8(3E)(*a*).

Exported goods, remission of tax (subs (1)(*b*)): s 13(1A).

Income tax appeal procedures (subs (1B)) applied by s 25(2)(*k*); determination of rate, Revenue may prescribe manner: s 32(1)(xxx); Value Added Tax (Determination in Regard to Tax) Regulations 1992 (SI 278/92).

Margin scheme goods, subs (1)(*b*) does not apply unless goods are otherwise zero-rated: s 10A(10); option to apply margin scheme (subs (1AA)(*b*)(ii)): s 10A(4)(*c*).

Residual tax deductible by taxable dealer when acquiring means of transport: s 12B(4)(*a*), (7), (8).

Special scheme for auctioneers, subs (1)(*b*) does not apply unless goods are otherwise zero-rated: s 10B(7).

Regulations

Subject	Regulation
Apportionment of consideration	Value Added Tax Regulations 1979 (SI 63/79), r 34

Order

Subject	Order
Fishermen	Value Added Tax (Reduction of Rate) (No 2) Order 1972 (SI 326/72)
Sea rescue services	Value Added Tax (Reduction of Rate (No 3) Order 1973 (SI 69/73)

Revenue precedent

Issue: VAT rate applicable to supply of fuel to be used in aircraft engaged in training flights.

Decision: The zero rate of VAT may be applied to duty-free supplies of fuel to aircraft engaged in training flights at Shannon duty-free airport. This applies to fuel supplied on or after 1 July 1975.

Issue: Computer system supplied within the State for training and testing before being exported by the company out of the State.

Decision: Authorisation given to zero rate the supply of the computer system to the company.

Issue: A UK company with no presence in Ireland sends PBX system to a factory in this State. A Dublin company supplies component to the foreign company but is delivered directly to the factory in the State. VAT at 21% would normally apply to such a supply. The component is soldered into a finished product and sent back to the UK.

Decision: Provided the supplier has evidence that the goods have been transferred to OMS then the zero rate can apply.

Issue: Inhaled anaesthetic drugs.

Decision: Zero %, Medicines administered by inhalation similar to asthmatic inhalers.

Issue: Antibiotic.

Decision: Zero rate even though it can be administered both orally and by injection.

Issue: Throat and mouth spray.

Decision: Zero % a licensed medicine for oral consumption Second Schedule para (xiii).

Issue: A specific chewing gum to help a person stop smoking.

Decision: Zero %, as coming within meaning of Second Schedule para (xiii).

Issue: Inhaler (asthma) (aerosol and dry powder).

Decision: Zero % comes within meaning of Second Schedule para (xiii).

Issue: Psychotherapist.

Decision: 12.5% applies.

Issue: Powder product to be mixed with a liquid and drank.

Decision: Zero %, as it is marketed as a meal replacement and as a result is considered food.

Issue: Butter and Chocolate Croissants, Fat content exceeds 2%.

Decision: Zero %.

Issue: Pasties filled with meat/salad etc.

Decision: Zero per cent. Pastry deemed incidental to the meat etc, filling (basic food).

Issue: Intravenous products.

Decision: Zero rate applies to supply of such products provided they have no pharmacological action and are purely nutritional.

Issue: Organic breads containing honey of less than 2% instead of sugar.

Decision: Zero rated as honey is a natural substituted for sugar.

Issue: Bread rolls and Vienna rolls fat content exceeds 2% limit of the weight of the flour included in dough.

Decision: Zero rate. Allow zero rating as fat content was only 2.35% (generally where 5% to 6% by weigh of sugar and/or fats added, no account to be taken of such small quantities).

Issue: Flavoured syrups/food supplements for babies/infants, supplying Vitamin C and consumed in dosage form.

Decision: Zero rate as they could not be described as drinks or for use in the taking of drinks or refreshments.

Issue: Croissants fat content exceeds 2%.

Decision: Zero rate allowed.

Issue: Kiddies' rides — VAT liability on receipts from same.

Decision: 12.5% rate, because of a type supplied in a fairground or amusement park.

Issue: VAT rate on TV aerials.

Decision: High Court Judge ruled that aerials are fixtures.

Issue: Increase on VAT rate.

Decision: Agreed for a limited period deferment of application of increase in VAT rate to certain bills in exceptional circumstances.

Issue: Active balance therapist (alternative/complimentary medicine).

Decision: 12.5% not coming within the meaning of First Schedule para (iii).

Issue: Hypnotherapist, aromatherapist, reflexologist, homeotherapist, accupuncturist and holistic services.

Decision: 12.5% not coming within the meaning of First Schedule para (iii).

Issue: Clothing designed for disabled children — sized by height.

Decision: The zero rate of VAT applies on garments up to and including size 152 cm. Garments in excess of 152 cm liable to VAT at 21%.

Issue: Sculpture (work of art).

Decision: 12.5% also applies to limited editions of original works of art made from the original cast/bust. Does not include mass produced works of art.

Issue: The supply of equipment normally subject to the standard rate of VAT to the owner of an over 15 ton vessel.

Decision: Zero rating allowed where we are satisfied that the item will be installed in a particular over 15 ton fishing vessel which should be named on the invoice.

Issue: Chocolate drink.

Decision: Zero % as product contains 57% semi-skimmed milk.

Issue: Agricultural consultants — R.E.P.S. Scheme.

Decision: Liable to VAT at 12.5 % on the understanding that it contains advice on matters such as waste control, management of water courses, wells, hedgerows, etc.

Issue: Goods supplied in the State by Irish traders for bulk export for promotion purposes.

Decision: Such goods were zero-rated subject to the proof of export being retained by the supplier.

Issue: Combined supply and sowing of seeds for the production of food.

Decision: The supply of polythene when used in the combined supply and sowing of maize seeds liable to VAT at zero rate regarded as integral part of growing of maize crop.

Issue: Foreign lessor leases government jet to Irish airline for onward leasing. Whether to register foreign lessor for VAT and whether to allow Irish airline to import aircraft at zero rate.

Decision: Foreign lessor not required to register for VAT, Irish airline allowed to import aircraft at zero rate as if or its airline business.

Issue: Application of zero rate to lease of aircraft to an intermediary company for subsequent onward leasing to qualifying airline.

Decision: Agreed to "look through" the intermediary, provided it is clear at outset that ultimate lessee is qualifying airline and regard first lease as also qualifying for zero rate in accordance with Second Schedule para (v)(*b*).

Issue: Musical card and a £1 lottery ticket.

Decision: Apportionment allowed VAT at 21% on value of card.

Issue: In a marketing campaign a small bottle of wine is supplied with tubs of spread for an all inclusive price.

Decision: Provided the items in question are listed separately showing the different rates of VAT applying on the invoice the "package rule" is not invoked.

Issue: Food hampers which contain both zero, 12.5 and 21 per cent goods.

Decision: Apportionment allowed — provided supplier keeps an accurate record of the goods supplied at the various rates.

Issue: Freeze-dried human blood component supplied with saline, a transfer needle and an infusion set in kit form should be subject to the "package rule" as provided for in VATA 1972, s 11(3).

Decision: Confirmed that the supply of the kit in question is exempt from VAT.

Issue: The sale of films at a price inclusive of the cost of processing. In such a supply where there is a rate difference between the supply of goods (i.e. the films) and a service (i.e. the processing) the "cocktail rule" should apply thereby attracting the higher rate of VAT.

Decision: Decision made on a method of apportionment of the consideration for the film and processing between the standard and lower rate of VAT.

Issue: Service charge with regard to door to door milk deliveries.

Decision: Seen as consideration for the supply of milk. Zero rate applies. Section 11(3) disregarded.

Issue: Rental/laundering of linen such as uniforms, overalls, towels etc.

Decision: Where a particular quantity of specified linen is hired to a customer and there is a separate contract for the laundering of the same linen, 12.5% applies to the laundry charge.

Issue: Christmas party night dinner.

Decision: Entire charge treated as liable to VAT at 12.5%. (Dancing facilities can be regarded as incidental to the supply of the meal.)

Issue: Is supply of custodial services a composite or multiple service.

Decision: Services supplied by a custodian can be disaggregated and each part considered an independent supply for determining VAT liability.

Revenue publications

Application of zero rating to intra-Community supplies: Statement of Practice VAT 8/92.

Commissioned framed photography: Tax Briefing Issue 39.

Dances: Statement of Practice VAT 6/92 (Replaced by Information Leaflet No 20/01).

Farmers agricultural services: Statement of Practice VAT 5/92 (Replaced by Information Leaflet No 23/01).

Food and drink supplied through catering business, hotel, restaurant, pub etc: Statement of Practice VAT 10/92.

Golf and other sporting activities: Statement of Practice VAT 1/95.

Guide to Value Added Tax (Revenue Commissioners): Chapters 15, 16.

Live horses: Statement of Practice VAT 3/90.

Rates of VAT on services from 1 March 1991: Statement of Practice VAT 1/91.

Rates of VAT on services from 1 March 1992: Statement of Practice VAT 1/92.

Services rates of VAT: Statement of Practice VAT 1/92.

Sports facilities: Statement of Practice VAT 4/92.

VAT rates on Revenue website: Tax Briefing Issue 45.

Zero rating of sales of goods to other EC States after 1 January 1993: Statement of Practice VAT 8/92.

Definition

"Appeal Commissioners": s 1(1); "body of persons": s 1(1); "business": s 1(1); "Dáil Éireann": IA 2005, Sch; "exempted activity": s 1(1); "goods": s 1(1); "hire": s 1(1); "immovable goods": s 1(1); "intra-Community acquisition of goods": ss 1(1), 3A; "livestock": s 1(1); "the Minister": s 1(1); "movable goods": s 1(1); "person": IA 2005, s 18(c); "regulations": ss 1(1), 32; "supply": s 1(1); "tax": s 1(1); "taxable goods": s 1(1); "taxable person"; s 1(1), 8; "writing": IA 2005, Sch.

12 Deduction for tax borne or paid

a 17,18,19

(Definition of input credits)

[(1) (*a*) In computing the amount of tax payable by him in respect of a taxable period, a taxable person may, insofar as the goods and services are used by him for the purposes of his taxable supplies or of any of the qualifying activities, deduct [, subject to making any adjustment required in accordance with section 12D,][1]—

(What input VAT is deductible?)

    (i)   the tax charged to him during the period by other taxable persons by a 17(2)(a) means of invoices, prepared in the manner prescribed by regulations, in respect of supplies of goods or services to him,

    (ii)   in respect of goods imported by him in the period, the tax paid by a 17(2)(b) him or deferred as established from the relevant customs documents kept by him in accordance with section 16(3),

    [(i*a*)   the amount in respect of tax indicated separately on a document issued during the period in accordance with section 17(1AA) in respect of a supply of goods to him.][2]

    [(ii*a*)   subject to such conditions (if any) as may be specified in regulations, the tax chargeable during the period, being tax for which he is liable in respect of intra-Community acquisitions of goods,

(ii*b*) subject to and in accordance with regulations, in respect of goods supplied under section 3(1)(*g*) an amount equal to any residual tax included in the consideration for the supply,]³

[(ii*c*) subject to such conditions (if any) as may be specified in regulations, in respect of goods referred to in section 3B, the tax due in the period in accordance with that section,]⁴

(iii) the tax chargeable during the period in respect of goods [other than supplies of goods referred to in section 3(6)(*d*))]⁵ treated as supplied by him in accordance with section 3(1)(*e*),

[(iii*a*) the tax charged to him during the period by other taxable persons in respect of services directly related to the transfer of ownership of goods specified in section 3(5)(*b*)(iii),]⁶

[(iii*b*) the tax chargeable during the period, being tax for which he is liable by virtue of section 4A (1), in respect of goods received by him.]⁷

[(iii*c*) the tax chargeable during the period, being tax for which the taxable person is liable by virtue of section 4(8), in respect of a supply to that person of immovable goods,]⁸

...]⁹

[(iii*e*) the tax chargeable during the period, being tax for which he is liable by virtue of section 6A(5)(*a*) in respect of investment gold (within the meaning of section 6A) received by him,]¹⁰

(iv) the tax chargeable during the period in respect of services treated as supplied by him for consideration in the course or furtherance of his business in accordance with section 5(3)(*d*),

(v) the tax chargeable during the period, being tax for which he is liable by virtue of section 5(3A), in respect of services received by him,

[(v*a*) the tax chargeable during the period, being tax for which the taxable person is liable by virtue of section 8(1A)(*f*) in respect of goods which are installed or assembled; but this subparagraph shall apply only where the taxable person would be entitled to a deduction of that tax elsewhere under this subsection if that tax had been charged to such person by another taxable person,]¹¹

[(v*b*) the tax chargeable during the period, being tax for which the taxable person is liable by virtue of section 8(1A)(*g*) in respect of the supply to such person of gas through the natural gas distribution network, or of electricity; but this subparagraph shall apply only where the taxable person would be entitled to a deduction of that tax elsewhere under this subsection if that tax had been charged to such person by another taxable person,]¹²

[(vi) subject to and in accordance with regulations (if any), residual tax referred to in section 12B,]¹³ [(vi*a*) the residual tax referred to in section 12C, being residual tax contained in the price charged to him for the purchase of agricultural machinery (within the meaning of section 12C), by means of invoices issued to him during the period by flat-rate farmers,][14]

[(vi*b*) the residual tax referred to in section 12C, being residual tax contained in the price charged to the taxable person for the purchase of agricultural machinery (within the meaning of section l2C), by means of documents issued to that person during the period in accordance with section 12C(1B),][15]

(vii) the tax chargeable during the period, being tax for which he is liable by virtue of section 8(2), in respect of services received by him, and

(viii) [flat-rate addition, which shall be deemed to be tax,][16] charged to him during the period by means of invoices prepared in the manner prescribed by regulations and issued to him in accordance with section 12A.   a 25(6)(a)

[Provided that this paragraph shall not apply to—

(I) a taxable person referred to in subsection (1A)(*c*) or (2)(*b*) of section 8, or

(II) a taxable person referred to in subsection (1A)(*d*) or (2)(*c*) of section 8 unless the tax relates to racehorse training services supplied by him.]][17]

(Qualifying activities — a definition)

(*b*) In paragraph (*a*) **"qualifying activities"** means—

(i) transport outside the State of passengers and their accompanying baggage,

[(i*a*) supplies of goods which, by virtue of section 3(6)(*d*), are deemed to have taken place i n the territory of another Member State: a 17(3)(a)

Provided that the supplier is registered for value added tax in that other Member State,][18]

[(i*b*) the operation, in accordance with Commission Regulation (EC) No 2777/2000 of 18 December 2000, of the Cattle Testing or Purchase for Destruction Scheme, by a body who is a taxable person by virtue of the Value Added Tax (Agricultural Intervention Agency) Order, 2001 (SI No 11 of 2001).][19]

(ii) services specified in paragraph (i), (ix) ...[20] (*d*), or (xi), of the First Schedule, supplied—   a 17(3)(c)

(I) outside the Community, or

(II) directly in connection with the export of goods to a place outside the [the Community,][21]

[(ii*a*) services consisting of the issue of new stocks, new shares, new debentures or other new securities by the taxable person in so far as such issue is made to raise capital for the purposes of the taxable person's taxable supplies, and][22]

a 17(3)(a)   (iii) supplies of goods or services outside the State [, other than services consisting of the hiring out of motor vehicles (as defined in subsection (3)(*b*)) for utilisation in the State,][23] which would be taxable supplies if made in the State.][24]

(Election to taxable person — stock in trade relief)

[(1A)(*a*) A person who, by election or in accordance with the provisions of sections 8(4) is deemed to become [a taxable person],[25] shall, in accordance with regulations, be entitled, in computing the amount of tax payable by him in respect of the first taxable period for which he is so deemed to be [a taxable person][25] to treat as tax deductible under subsection (1) such part of the value of the stock-in-trade (within the meaning of section 34) held by him immediately before the commencement of that taxable period as could reasonably be regarded as the amount which he would be entitled to claim under the said subsection (1) if he had been [a taxable person][25] at the time of the delivery to him of such stock-in-trade.

(Denial of double input credit)

(*b*) No claim shall lie under this subsection for a deduction for the tax relating to any stock-in-trade (within the meaning of section 34) if, and to the extent that, a deduction under subsection (1) could be claimed apart from this subsection.

(*c*) This subsection shall have effect in relation to taxable periods commencing on or after the 3rd day of September, 1973.][26]

(Excess input credit in a taxable period)

a 18(4)   (2) If, in relation to any taxable period, the total amount deductible under this section exceeds the amount which, but for this section, would be payable in respect of such period, the excess shall be [refunded to the taxable person in accordance with section 20(1)][27] [, but subject to [sections 20(1A) and 20(5)].[28]][29]

(Non-deductible input tax)

a 17(6)   [(3) (*a*) Notwithstanding anything [in this section, a deduction of tax under this section][30] shall not be made if, and to the extent that, the tax relates to—

(i) the provision of food or drink, or accommodation or other personal services, for the taxable person, his agents or his employees, except to the extent, if any, that such provision constitutes a supply of services in respect of which he is accountable for tax,

[(i*a*) expenditure incurred by the taxable person on food or drink, or accommodation or other entertainment services, where such expenditure forms all or part of the cost of providing an advertising service in respect of which tax is due and payable by the taxable person,][31]

(ii) entertainment expenses incurred by the taxable person, his agents or his employees,

(iii) the [purchase, hiring, intra-Community acquisition or importation][32] of motor vehicles otherwise than as stock-in-trade or for the purposes of a business which consists in whole or part of the hiring of motor vehicles or for use, in a driving school business, for giving driving instruction, ...[33]

(iv) the purchase [intra-Community acquisition or importation][34] of petrol otherwise than as stock-in-trade, or

[(iv*a*) the procurement of a supply of contract work where such supply consists of the handing over of goods to which this paragraph applies.][33]

(v) ...[35].

(Motor vehicles — a definition)

(*b*) In paragraph (*a*) of this subsection **"motor vehicles"** means motor vehicles designed and constructed for the conveyance of persons by road and sports motor vehicles, estate cars, station wagons, motor cycles, motor scooters, mopeds and auto cycles, whether or not designed and constructed for the purpose aforesaid, excluding vehicles designed and constructed for the carriage of more than 16 persons (inclusive of the driver), invalid carriages and other vehicles of a type designed for use by invalids or infirm persons.][36]

[(*c*) In subparagraph (i) of paragraph (*a*), reference to the provision of accommodation includes expenditure by the taxable person on a building, including the fitting out of such building, to provide such accommodation.

(*d*) In subparagraph (ii) of paragraph (*a*), **"entertainment expenses"** includes expenditure on a building or facility, including the fitting out of such building or facility, to provide such entertainment.][37]

[(3A) Notwithstanding anything in this section, where—

(Non-deductible tax margin schemes)

(*a*) the provisions of subsection (3) or (8) of section 10A or subsection (3) of section 10B have been applied to a supply of goods to a taxable person, or

(*b*) a taxable dealer deducts residual tax, in accordance with subsection (1)(*a*)(vi), in respect of a supply of a means of transport to a taxable person,

that taxable person shall not deduct, in accordance with subsection (1), any tax in relation to the supply to that person.][38]

(Apportionment of input credit)

[(4) (*a*) In this subsection—

"deductible supplies or activities" means the supply of taxable goods or taxable services, or the carrying out of qualifying activities as defined in subsection (1)(*b*);

"**dual-use inputs**" means goods or services (other than goods or services on the purchase or acquisition of which, by virtue of subsection (3), a deduction of tax shall not be made) which are not used solely for the purposes of either deductible supplies or activities or non-deductible supplies or activities;

"**non-deductible supplies or activities**" means the supply of goods or services or the carrying out of activities other than deductible supplies or activities;

"**total supplies and activities**" means deductible supplies or activities and non-deductible supplies or activities.

(*b*)   Where a taxable person engages in both deductible supplies or activities and non-deductible supplies or activities then, in relation to that person's acquisition of dual-use inputs for the purpose of that person's business for a period, that person shall be entitled to deduct in accordance with subsection (1) only such proportion of tax, borne or payable on that acquisition, which is calculated in accordance with the provisions of this subsection and regulations, as being attributable to that person's deductible supplies or activities and such proportion of tax is, for the purposes of this subsection, referred to as the "proportion of tax deductible".

(*c*)   For the purposes of this subsection and regulations, the proportion of tax deductible by a taxable person for a period shall be calculated on any basis which results in a proportion of tax deductible which correctly reflects the extent to which the dual-use inputs are used for the purposes of that person's deductible supplies or activities and has due regard to the range of that person's total supplies and activities.

(*d*)   The proportion of tax deductible may be calculated on the basis of the ratio which the amount of a person's tax-exclusive turnover from deductible supplies or activities for a period bears to the amount of that person's tax- exclusive turnover from total supplies and activities for that period but only if that basis results in a proportion of tax deductible which is in accordance with paragraph (*c*).

(*e*)   Where it is necessary to do so to ensure that the proportion of tax deductible by a taxable person is in accordance with paragraph (*c*), a taxable person shall—

(i)   calculate a separate proportion of tax deductible for any part of that person's business, or

(ii)   exclude, from the calculation of the proportion of tax deductible, amounts of turnover from incidental transactions by that person of the type specified in paragraph (i) of the First Schedule or amounts of turnover from incidental transactions by that person in immovable goods.

(*f*)   The proportion of tax deductible as calculated by a taxable person for a taxable period [shall][39] be adjusted in accordance with regulations, if, for the accounting period in which the taxable period ends, that proportion does not correctly reflect the extent to which the dual-use inputs are used for the purposes of that person's deductible supplies or activities or does not have due regard to the range of that person's total supplies and activities.][40]

[(5) At the time when a person disposes of an interest in immovable goods the possession of which that person had previously surrendered in circumstances where the person had paid a deductibility adjustment in accordance with section 4(3)(*ab*), that person is entitled to increase the amount of tax deductible for the taxable period within which the disposal is made, by an amount calculated in accordance with the following formula:

$$\frac{T \times (Y\text{-}N)}{Y}$$

where—

T   is the amount of tax which the person who previously surrendered possession of the goods was entitled to deduct in accordance with this section, prior to that surrender of possession, in respect of that person's acquisition of the interest in and the development of those goods,

Y   is 20 or, if the interest when it was acquired by the person who surrendered possession of the goods was for a period of less than 20 years, the number of full years in that interest when it was so acquired, and

N   is the number of full years since that person acquired the interest in the immovable goods being disposed of or, if the goods were developed since that interest was acquired, but before the deductibility adjustment in accordance with section 4(3)(*ab*) was payable, the number of full years since that development:

but if that N is greater than that Y, such amount shall be deemed to be nil.][41]

Amendments

[1]   Inserted by FA 2001, s 188(*a*) with effect from 6 April 2001.

[2]   Subs (1)(i*a*) inserted by FA 1996, s 93(*a*) with effect from 1 July 1996.

[3]   Subs (1)(*a*)(ii*a*)–(ii*b*) inserted by FA 1992, s 174(*a*) with effect from 1 January 1993.

[4]   Subs (1)(*a*)(ii*c*) inserted by FA 1993, s 88(*a*) with effect from 1 August 1993.

[5]   Inserted b y EC(VAT)R 1992, r 10(*b*) with effect from 1 January 1993.

[6]   Subs (1)(*a*)(iii*a*) inserted by FA 1991, s 81 with effect from 29 May 1991.

[7]   Subs (1)(*a*)(iii*b*) inserted by FA 1994, s 96(*a*) with effect from such date as the Minister for Finance may appoint.

[8]   Subs (1)(*a*)(iii*c*) substituted by FA 2005, s 104(*a*)(i) with effect from 25 March 2005.

[9]   Subs (1)(*a*)(iii*d*) deleted by FA 2005, s 104(*a*)(ii) with effect from 25 March 2005.

[10] Subs (1)(*a*)(iii*e*) inserted by FA 1999, s 128(*a*) with effect from 1 January 2000.

[11] Subs (1)(*a*)(v*a*) inserted by FA 2004, s 60 with effect from 25 March 2004.

[12] Subs (1)(*a*)(v*b*) inserted by FA 2004, s 60 with effect on and from 1 January 2005.

[13] Subs (1)(*a*)(vi) substituted by FA 1995, s 129(*a*) with effect from 1 July 1995.

[14] Subs (1)(*a*)(vi*a*) inserted by FA 1999, s 128(*b*) with effect from 1 January 2000.

[15] Subs (1)(*a*)(vi*b*) inserted by FA 2000, s 112(*a*) with effect from 23 March 2000.

[16] Substituted by FA 1993, s 88(*b*) with effect from 17 June 1993; previously "tax".

[17] Subs (1)(*a*)(proviso) inserted by FA 1993, s 88(*c*) with effect from 17 June 1993.

[18] Subs (1)(*b*)(i*a*) inserted by EC(VAT)R 1992, r 10(*a*) with effect from 1 January 1993.

[19] Subs (1)(*b*)(i*b*) by FA 2001, s 188(*b*) with effect from 8 January 2001.

[20] Deleted by FA 2002, s 138 and Sch 6 para 1(*b*) with effect from 25 March 2002; previously "(*b*), (*c*) or".

[21] Substituted by FA 2006, s 98(*a*) with effect from 31 March 2006; previously "the Community, and".

[22] Subs (1)(*b*)(ii*a*) inserted by FA 2006, s 98(*b*) with effect from 31 March 2006.

[23] Inserted by FA 1998, s 111(*a*) with effect from 27 March 1998.

[24] Subs (1) substituted by FA 1987, s 41 with effect from 1 November 1987.

[25] Substituted by VATAA 1978, s 30(2) with effect from 1 March 1979; previously "an accountable person".

[26] Subs (1A) inserted by FA 1973, s 81 with effect from 3 September 1973.

[27] Substituted by FA 1981, s 44 with effect from 28 May 1981; previously "repaid to the taxable person".

[28] Substituted by FA 1998, s 111(*b*) with effect from 27 March 1998; previously "section 20(1A)".

[29] Inserted by FA 1986, s 84 with effect from 27 May 1986.

[30] Substituted by FA 1987, s 41 with effect from 1 November 1987; previously "in subsection (1), a deduction of tax under that subsection".

[31] Subs (3)(*a*)(i*a*) inserted by FA 1994, s 96(*b*)(i) with effect from 23 May 1994.

[32] Substituted by FA 1992, s 174(*b*)(i) with effect from 1 January 1993; previously "acquisition (including hiring)".

[33] Word "or" deleted and subs (3)(*a*)(iv*a*) inserted by FA 1996, s 93(*b*) with effect from 15 May 1996.

[34] Inserted by FA 1992, s 174(*b*)(ii) with effect from 1 January 1993.

[35] Subs (3)(*a*)(v) deleted by FA 1987, s 41 with effect from 1 November 1987.

[36] Subs (3) substituted by VATAA 1978, s 10 with effect from 1 March 1979.

[37] Subs (3)(*c*)–(*d*) inserted by FA 1994, s 96(*b*)(ii) with effect from 23 May 1994.

[38] Subs (3A) inserted by FA 1995, s 129(*b*) with effect from 1 July 1995.

[39] Substituted by FA 2001, s 188(*c*) with effect from 6 April 2001; previously "may".

[40] Subs (4) substituted by FA 2000, s 112(*b*) with effect from 23 March 2000.

[41] Subs (5) inserted by FA 2005, s 104(*b*) with effect from such a day as the Minister for Finance may, by order, appoint. By virtue of SI 225/2005, 1 May 2005 appointed as start date.

Cross-references

Apportionment between deductible and non-deductible tax (subs (4)), Revenue may determine method: s 32(1)(x); method: VATR 1979, r 16.

Art works, rate of tax: s 11(1AA)(*b*).

Auction scheme goods, defined: s 10B(1).

Exported goods, remission of tax (subs (1)(*a*)): s 13(1C).

Exporter (subs (3)(*b*)), charge of tax at 0% to, "qualifying goods" means all taxable goods excluding motor vehicles within the meaning of this subsection (and petrol): s 13A(1).

Intra-EU acquisitions (subs (1)(*a*)(ii*a*)), Revenue may prescribe manner of deduction of tax: s 32(1)(*aa*).

Motor vehicles (subs (3)(*b*)), taxable dealers supplying means of transport, special scheme: s 12B(10).

Person not entitled to deduction under this section, intra-Community acquisitions of new vehicle, boat or plane: s 19(4)(*a*).

Regulations (subs (1)(*a*)(vi)) require Minister for Finance's consent: s 32(2A).

Residual tax (subs (1)(*a*)(ii*b*)), Revenue may prescribe manner of calculation: s 32(1).

Second-hand motor vehicles bought from non taxable persons: Value Added Tax (Second-hand Motor Vehicles) Regulations 1988 (SI 121/88).

Stock relief on registering (subs (1A)), Revenue may prescribe amount to be given: s 32(1)(xx); relief: VATR 1979, r 22.

Taxable dealers supplying means of transport (subs (1)(*a*))(vi)), special scheme: s 12B(1), (2), (4); Revenue may prescribe manner of deduction of tax: s 32(1)(*dd*).

Tax (subs (1)(*b*)), charged at 0% (for the purposes of s 4(1)(*a*) or 4(6)(*a*)) by virtue of Sch 2 para (vi*a*) is deemed to be deductible: s 13A(7).

Waiver of exemption: s 7(3).

Case law

Subject	Case	Case reference
Conditions for exercise of right to deduct input tax — requirement to hold invoice	*Finanzamt Gummersbach v Gerhard Bockemuhl*	1 April 2004, C–90/02
Right to deduct VAT incurred on expenditure relating to transfer of business	*Finanzamt Offenbach am Main-Land v Faworld Vorgrundungsgesselschaft Peter Hunninghausen und Wolfgang Klein GbR*	29 April 2004, C–137/02
Right to deduct input tax — conditions of exercise	*Terra Baubedarf-Handel GmbH v Finanzamt Osterholz-Scharmbeck*	29 April 2004, C–152/02
Share issues	*Kretzetchnik AG v Finanzamt Linz*	26 May 2005, C–465/03

Regulations

Subject	Regulation
Apportionment of VAT incurred	Value Added Tax Regulations 1979 (SI 63/79), r 16
Second hand motor vehicles	Value Added Tax (Second-hand Motor Vehicles) Regulations 1988 (SI 121/66)
Stock relief start-up	Value Added Tax Regulations 1979 (SI 63/79), r 22

Revenue publications

Guide to apportionment of input credit: Tax Briefing Issue 46.

Guide to Value Added Tax (Revenue Commissioners): Chapter 6.

Motor cars and petrol — no deduction: Tax Briefing, Issue 33.

Revenue information leaflet: Share Acquisitions, *Tax Briefing 54*, December 2003.

Shares, VAT not deductible: Statement of Practice VAT 2/90.

Case law

Subject	Case	Case reference
Property unit trust, deductibility of pre and post lease expenditure	*Erin Executor and Trustee Company Ltd v Revenue Commissioners*	[1994] ITR 179
Television aerial regarded as a fixture when installed	*Maye v Revenue Commissioners*	(III) ITR (332)
Taxable person has valid right to recover input tax even if subsequently unable to make the planned taxable supplies due to circumstances beyond his control	*Belgium v Ghent Coal Termminal NV*	15 January 1998, C–37/95
Possession of an invoice. A Member State must accept a copy invoice where there is no risk of fraud and no risk of further application for the same refund	*Société Generales des Grandes Sources d'Eaux Minerals v Bundesmt fur Finanzen*	June 1998, C–367/98
Kingdom of the Netherlands should not allow employer VAT recovery in respect of employee allowance	*Commission v Netherlands*	8 November 2001, C–338/98
Expenditure incurred in connection with acquisition of shareholdings in subsidiaries is attributable to general business overheads	*Cibo Participations SA*	27 September 2001, C–16/00

Revenue precedent

Issue: Right to input credit.

Decision: Two decisions: (1) Where an employer is responsible under contract for meeting costs of services, and the relevant invoices are issued in his name, he is entitled to input credit. (2) However, services supplied to the trustees for the purpose of their business would not be allowable.

Issue: VAT paid by shipping agents at importation on goods subsequently exported.

Decision: Input credit can be taken by shipping agent in their next VAT return subject to certain conditions.

Issue: Accommodation non-deductible for VAT-registered persons.

Decision: Airline companies allowed deductibility for accommodating passengers in hotels etc because of flight conditions.

Definition

"business": s 1(1); "Community" s 1(1); "goods": s 1(1); "intra-Community acquisition of goods": s 1(1), 3A; "person": IA 2005, s 18(c); "regulations": ss 1(1), 32; "second-hand": s 1(1); "supply": s 1(1); "tax": s 1(1); "taxable period": s 1(1); "taxable person": s 1(1), 8.

a 25(5)   **12A Special provisions for tax invoiced by flat-rate farmers**

(Invoicing requirements)

[(1) Where a flat-rate farmer supplies agricultural produce or an agricultural service to a person, the farmer shall, subject to section 17(2), issue to the person an invoice indicating the consideration (exclusive of the flat-rate addition) in respect of the supply and an amount (in this Act referred to as **"a flat-rate addition"**) equal to **[4.8 per cent]**[1] of the said consideration (exclusive of the said addition) ...[2]

[(2) In this Act **"flat-rate farmer"** means—

(Definitions)

    (*a*)   a farmer who is not a taxable person,

    (*b*)   a farmer who is a taxable person referred to in subsection (1A)(*c*) or (2)(*b*) of section 8, or

    (*c*)   a person who, in accordance with section 8(3A), is deemed not to be a taxable person in relation to the supplies specified in the definition of "farmer" in section 8(9).][3]

Amendments

[1]   Substituted by FA 2005, s 105 with effect from 1 January 2005: previously "4.4 per cent" (FA 2004, s 61); previously "4.3 per cent" (FA 2001, s 189); previously "4.2 per cent" (FA 2000, s 113); previously "4 per cent" (FA 1999, s 129); previously "3.6 per cent" (FA 1998, s 112); previously "3.3 per cent" (FA 1997, s 105 with effect from 1 March 1997); previously "2.8 per cent" (FA 1996, s 94 with effect from 1 March 1996); previously "2.5 per cent" (FA 1993, s 89(*a*) with effect from 1 March 1993); previously "2.7 per cent" (FA 1992, s 175(1) with effect from 1 March 1992); previously "2.3 per cent" (FA 1990, s 103, with effect from 1 January 1991); previously "2 per cent".

[2]   Words "and the person shall, if he is a taxable person, be entitled to treat the flat-rate addition as tax deductible under section 12 subject, however, to any restrictions imposed by or under subsection (3) or (4) of that section" deleted by FA 1992, s 175(2) with effect from 1 January 1993.

[3]   Subs (2) substituted by FA 1993, s 89(*b*).

Cross-references

Non compliance, penalties: s 26(1), (2A).

Revenue publications

Flat-rate farmers and the Single Market: Statement of Practice VAT 2/93 (Replaced by Information Leaflet No 12/01).
Repayments to unregistered persons: Statement of Practice VAT 2/94 (Replaced by Information Leaflet No 18/01).
Revenue VAT Guide: Chapter 7.

Revenue precedent

Issue: Can Government departments be regarded as farmer.
Decision: Governments departments are entitled to the flat-rate addition to their sales of agricultural produce.

Definition

"agricultural produce": s 1(1); "agricultural service": s 1(1); "farmer": ss 1(1), 8; "person": IA 2005, s 18(c); "supply": s 1(1); "tax": s 1(1); "taxable person": ss 1(1), 8.

12B Special scheme for means of transport supplied by taxable dealers

(Residual tax)

[(1) Where a taxable dealer supplies a means of transport, the residual tax which is deductible in accordance with section 12(1)(a)(vi) shall be deemed to be tax and shall be the amount referred to in subsection (4).

(2) The entitlement to deduct residual tax referred to in subsection (1) shall arise only where a taxable dealer purchases or acquires [(other than in the circumstances where an owner as referred to in paragraph (c) of subsection (5) of section 3, enforces such owner's right to recover possession of a means of transport)]¹⁻

(a) a means of transport from a person, other than a person referred to in subsection (10), who was not entitled to deduct, under section 12, any tax in respect of that person's purchase, intra-Community acquisition or importation of that means of transport, or

[(aa) a means of transport from a person where the disposal of that means of transport by such person to such taxable dealer was deemed not to be a supply of goods in accordance with [paragraphs (c) and (d) of subsection (5) of section 3]², or]³

(b) a means of transport other than a new means of transport from a person in another Member State who was not entitled to deduct, under the provisions implementing Article 17 of Council Directive No. 77/388/EEC of 17 May 1977 in that Member State, any Value Added tax referred to in that Directive in respect of that person's purchase, intra-Community acquisition or importation of that means of transport, or

(c) a means of transport from a taxable person who has exercised the entitlement under section 12(1)(a)(vi) to deduct the residual tax in respect of that person's supply of that means of transport to the said dealer, or

(d) a means of transport other than a new means of transport from a taxable dealer in another Member State who has applied the provisions implementing Article 26a or 28o (inserted by Council Directive No. 94/

5/EC of 14 February 1994) of Council Directive No. 77/388/EEC of 17 May 1977 to the supply of that means of transport, in that other Member State.

(Definitions)

(3) In this section—

"taxable dealer" means a taxable person who in the course or furtherance of business, whether acting on that person's own behalf, or on behalf of another person pursuant to a contract under which commission is payable on purchase or sale, purchases or acquires means of transport as stock-in-trade with a view to resale, and a person in another Member State shall be deemed to be a taxable dealer where, in similar circumstances, that person would be a taxable dealer in the State under this section;

"means of transport" means motorised land vehicles with an engine cylinder capacity exceeding 48 cubic centimetres or a power exceeding 7.2 kilowatts, vessels exceeding 7.5 metres in length and aircraft with a take-off weight exceeding 1,550 kilogrammes, which are intended for the transport of persons or goods, other than [agricultural machinery (within the meaning of section 12C), and][4] vessels and aircraft of the kind referred to in paragraph (v) of the Second Schedule.

(Calculation of residual tax)

(4) The residual tax which may be deducted by a taxable dealer in accordance with section 12(1)(a)(vi) shall be the residual tax deemed to be included in the purchase price payable by such dealer when acquiring a means of transport and shall be determined by the formula—

$$A \times \frac{B}{B + 100}$$

where—

A is the purchase price of the means of transport, and

B is the percentage rate of tax specified—

> (*a*) in section 11(1)(*a*) where the means of transport is deemed to be supplied within the State to the taxable dealer, or

> (*b*) in provisions implementing Article 12(1) of Council Directive No. 77/388/EEC of 17 May 1977 in another Member State where the means of transport is deemed to be supplied within that Member State to the taxable dealer:

> Provided that, subject to subsection (8), where the amount so calculated is in excess of the tax chargeable on the supply by the taxable dealer of the means of transport, the residual tax shall be an amount equal to the amount of tax chargeable on that supply.

(Invoicing requirements)

(5) Notwithstanding section 17, where a taxable dealer deducts residual tax referred to in subsection (1) in respect of a supply of a means of transport, that

dealer shall not indicate separately the amount of tax chargeable in respect of that supply on any invoice or other document issued in lieu thereof in accordance with that section.

(Place of supply for tax purposes)

(6) Notwithstanding section 3(6)(*d*), in the case of a supply of a means of transport which is dispatched or transported and where—

(*a*) a taxable dealer deducts residual tax referred to in subsection (1) in respect of the supply of that means of transport, or

(*b*) a taxable dealer in another Member State has applied the provisions implementing Article 26a or 28o of Council Directive No. 77/388/ EEC of 17 May 1977 in that other Member State, to the supply of that means of transport,

the place of supply shall be deemed to be the place where the dispatch or transportation begins.

(Zero rate application)

(7) Where a taxable dealer deducts residual tax referred to in subsection (1) in respect of a supply of a means of transport, then, subject to subsection (8), the provisions of section 11(1)(*b*) shall not apply in respect of that supply.

(New means of transport — intra-Community supply)

(8) Notwithstanding subsection (7), where a taxable dealer deducts residual tax referred to in subsection (1) in respect of the supply of a new means of transport dispatched or transported by the supplier to a person in another Member State, the provisions of section 11(1)(*b*) shall apply, and in determining the amount of the residual tax in accordance with subsection (4) the proviso to that subsection shall not apply.

(Time of supply — agent involvement)

(9) Where a taxable dealer supplies a means of transport on behalf of another person pursuant to a contract under which commission is payable on purchase or sale, the means of transport shall be deemed to have been supplied by that other person to the taxable dealer when the said taxable dealer supplies that means of transport.

(Onward sale of goods acquired under the special scheme)

(10) Notwithstanding paragraph (xxiv) of the First Schedule, the provisions of that paragraph shall not apply to—

(*a*) a supply by a taxable person of a means of transport, other than a motor vehicle as defined in section 12(3)(*b*), which that person acquired from a taxable dealer who deducted residual tax in respect of the supply of that means of transport to that person, ...[5]

(*b*) a supply by a taxable person other than a taxable dealer of a motor vehicle, as defined in section 12(3)(*b*), which that person acquired as stock-in-trade or for the purposes of a business which consists in whole or part of the hiring of motor vehicles or for use, in a driving school business, for giving driving instruction, from a taxable dealer who deducted residual tax in respect of the supply [of that motor vehicle to that person, and][6]

[(c) a supply by a taxable dealer of a means of transport being a motor vehicle as defined in section 12(3)(b) which has been declared for registration in accordance with section 131 of the Finance Act 1992 on that dealer's own behalf, unless it can be shown to the satisfaction of the Revenue Commissioners that, on the basis of the use to which that means of transport has been put by that taxable dealer, the provisions of subsection (11)(b) should not apply to that supply.][7]

[(11)(a) Where a means of transport which is a motor vehicle as defined in section 12(3)(b) is declared for registration to the Revenue Commissioners in accordance with section 131 of the Finance Act 1992 by a taxable dealer on that dealer's own behalf and on which deductibility in accordance with section 12 has been claimed by that dealer, then that means of transport shall be treated for the purposes of this Act as if it were removed from stock-in-trade and such removal is deemed to be a supply of that means of transport by that taxable dealer for the purposes of section 3(1)(e).

(b) At the time when a taxable dealer supplies to another person a means of transport which is deemed to have been supplied in accordance with paragraph (a), then that means of transport is deemed to be re-acquired by that dealer as stock-in-trade and, notwithstanding subsection (2), the taxable dealer is entitled to deduct residual tax referred to in subsection (1) and in that case for the purposes of the formula in subsection (4) the residual tax is calculated as if "A" were equal to the total of—

   (i) the amount on which tax was chargeable on the supply of that means of transport to the dealer,

   (ii) the tax which was chargeable on the supply referred to at subparagraph (i), and

   (iii) the vehicle registration tax accounted for by that dealer in respect of the registration of that means of transport, and, apart from the cases provided for in paragraph (c), the amount referred to in subparagraph (i) is the amount on which tax was chargeable on the supply of that means of transport in accordance with section 3(1)(e).

(c) Where a taxable dealer declares a means of transport for registration in the circumstances described in paragraph (a) but does not claim deductibility in accordance with section 12 in respect of that means of transport, then paragraph (b) applies when that dealer supplies that means of transport to another person.][8][9]

Amendments

[1]   Inserted by FA 1999, s 130(a)(i) with effect from 25 March 1999.
[2]   Substituted by FA 2001, s 190 with effect from 6 April 2001; previously "section 3(5)(c)".
[3]   Subs (2)(aa) inserted by FA 1999, s 130(a)(ii) with effect from 25 March 1999.
[4]   Inserted by FA 1999, s 130(b) with effect from 1 September 1999.

5   Deleted by FA 2003, s 120(*a*) with effect from 1 May 2003; previously "and".
6   Substituted by FA 2003, s 120(*a*) with effect from 1 May 2003; previously "of that motor vehicle to that person.".
7   Subs (10)(*c*) inserted by FA 2003, s 120(*a*) with effect from 1 May 2003.
9   Section 12B inserted by FA 1995, s 130 with effect from 1 July 1995.

Cross-references

Deductible tax: s 12(1)(*a*)(vi).

Regulations

Subject	*Regulation*
Cars, intra-Community acquisitions	Value Added Tax (Payment of Tax on Intra-Community Acquisitions of Means of Transport) Regulations 1992 (SI 412/92)
Cars, intra-Community acquisitions	Value Added Tax (Payment of Tax on Intra-Community Acquisitions of Means of Transport) Regulations 1993 (SI 248/93)
Cars	Value Added Tax (Special Scheme for Means of Transport; Documentation) Regulations 1996 (SI 201/96).

Revenue precedent

Issue: Motor dealer buying second-hand agricultural machinery and equipment from unregistered farmer claiming residual input credit under Seventh Directive mechanism required to issue specially endorsed invoice "Special Scheme".
Decision: Dealer allowed to reclaim the residual VAT and to issue VAT invoices on onward sale of such machinery and equipment. This arrangement applies only in respect of machinery and equipment on which a farmer if he were registered for VAT could claim VAT deductibility.

Revenue publications

Revenue information leaflet: VAT Treatment of second-hand vehicles, *Tax Briefing 22*, June 1996.
Revenue information leaflet: VAT Treatment of vehicles registered by dealers, *Tax Briefing 53*, August 2003.

Definitions

"business": s 1(1); "Community": s 1(1), "person": IA 2005, s 18(*c*); "supply": s 1(1); "tax": s 1(1); "taxable person": s 1(1).

12C Special Scheme for agricultural machinery

[(1) A taxable dealer who purchases agricultural machinery from a flat-rate farmer shall, subject to the provisions of this section and in accordance with subparagraph (via) of paragraph (*a*) of subsection (1) of section 12, be entitled to deduct the residual tax contained in the price payable by such taxable dealer in respect of that purchase.

[(1A) A taxable dealer who purchases agricultural machinery from a person where the disposal of that agricultural machinery by such person to such taxable dealer was deemed in accordance with [3(5)(*c*) or (*d*)]¹ not to be a supply of goods shall, subject to the provisions of this section and in accordance with subparagraph (vib) of paragraph (*a*) of subsection (1) of section 12, be entitled to deduct the residual tax, determined by the formula in subsection (3), contained in the price payable by such taxable dealer in respect of that purchase.

(1B) A person who disposes of agricultural machinery to a taxable dealer where the disposal of that agricultural machinery by such person to such taxable dealer was deemed in accordance with [3(5)(*c*) or (*d*)][1] not to be a supply of goods shall issue a document to the taxable dealer to whom the disposal is made and shall indicate on the document—

(*a*)   that person's name and address,

(*b*)   the name and address of the taxable dealer,

(*c*)   the date of issue of the document,

(*d*)   a description of the agricultural machinery, including details of the make, model and, where appropriate, the year of manufacture, the engine number and registration number of that machinery,

(*e*)   the consideration for the disposal of the agricultural machinery,

(*f*)   confirmation that the disposal is deemed in accordance with [3(5)(*c*) or (*d*)][1] not to be a supply of goods, and

(*g*)   such other particulars as may be specified by regulations, if any.][2]

(2) A flat-rate farmer who supplies agricultural machinery to a taxable dealer shall, subject to section 17(2A), issue an invoice in respect of that supply.

(3) The residual tax referred to in subsection (1) shall be determined by the formula

$$A \times \frac{B}{B + 100}$$

where—

A   is the purchase price of the agricultural machinery payable by the taxable dealer, and

B   is the percentage rate of tax specified in section 11(1)(*a*).

(4) Where a taxable dealer supplies agricultural machinery in respect of which such dealer was entitled to deduct residual tax and where the tax chargeable in respect of that supply is less than the residual tax deducted by that dealer in respect of the purchase of that machinery, then the excess of the residual tax over the tax payable on that supply shall be deemed to be tax chargeable in respect of that supply.

(5) In this section—

"agricultural machinery" means machinery or equipment, other than a motor vehicle as defined in subsection (3) of section 12, which has been used by a flat-rate farmer for the purpose of such farmer's Annex A activity in circumstances where any tax charged on the supply of that machinery or equipment to that farmer would have been deductible by such farmer if such farmer had elected to be a taxable person at the time of that supply of the machinery or equipment to such farmer;

"taxable dealer" means a taxable person who in the course or furtherance of business, whether acting on that person's own behalf, or on behalf of another person pursuant to a contract under which commission is payable on purchase or sale, purchases agricultural machinery as stock-in-trade with a view to resale.][3]

Amendments

1   Substituted by FA 2002, s 138 and Sch 6 para 1(*c*) with effect from 25 March 2002; previously
     "3(5)(*c*)".

2   Subss (1A)–(1B) inserted by FA 2000, s 114 with effect from 23 March 2000.

3   Subs 12C inserted by FA 1999, s 131 with effect from 1 September 1999.

Regulations

Subject	*Regulation*
Agricultural machinery documentation	Value Added Tax (Agricultural Machinery) (Documentation) Regulations 1999 (SI 443/99)

Revenue Publications

Tax Briefing: Issue 39.

12D Adjustment of tax deductible in certain circumstances

[(1) For the purposes of this section—

"full year" shall be any continuous period of twelve months;

"interest" in relation to immovable goods has the meaning assigned to it by section 4.

(2) Where—

(*a*)   a person makes a transfer of an interest in immovable goods in accordance with section 3(5)(*b*)(iii), and

(*b*)   but for the application of that section, tax would have been chargeable on the transfer, and the person (referred to in this section as a "transferor") was entitled to deduct part of the tax charged on the most recent purchase or acquisition of an interest in, or the development of, the immovable goods subject to that transfer,

that transferor shall, for the purposes of section 12, be entitled to increase the amount of tax deductible for the taxable period within which the transfer is made by an amount calculated in accordance with the following formula:

$$\frac{(T-TD)\ (Y-N)}{Y}$$

where—

T   is the tax chargeable on that most recent purchase or acquisition of an interest in, or that development of, the immovable goods,

TD   is the tax that the transferor was entitled to deduct on that most recent purchase or acquisition of an interest in, or that development of, the immovable goods,

Y   is 20 or, if the interest when it was created in the immovable goods being transferred was for a period of less than 20 years, the number of full years in that interest, and

N is the number of full years since the interest was created or, if the goods were developed since that interest was created, the number of full years since the most recent development:

but if that N is greater than that Y, such an amount calculated shall be deemed to be nil.

(3) Where a transferor acquired an interest in immovable goods as a result of a transfer in accordance with section 3(5)(*b*)(iii) and the transferor did not develop those immovable goods since the acquisition then, for the purposes of subsection (2), the amount by which that transferor shall be entitled to increase the amount of tax deductible, in accordance with section 12, for the taxable period in which the transferor transfers those goods, shall be calculated in accordance with the following formula:

$$\frac{A \times (Y-N)}{Y}$$

where—

A is the amount which the transferor was required to calculate and reduce his or her deductible amount by, in accordance with subsection (4), when the transferor acquired the interest in those goods,

Y is 20 or, if the interest when it was created in the immovable goods being transferred was for a period of less than 20 years, the number of full years in that interest, and

N is the number of full years since the interest was created or, if the goods were developed since that interest was created, the number of full years since the most recent development:

but if that N is greater than that Y, such an amount calculated shall be deemed to be nil.

(4) Where a person receives an interest in immovable goods as a result of a transfer and the person would not have been entitled to deduct all the tax that would have been chargeable on the transfer but for the application of section 3(5)(*b*)(iii), that person shall [calculate an amount which shall be payable as if it were tax due by that person in accordance with section 19 for the taxable period within which the transfer was made, and that amount shall be calculated][1] in accordance with the following formula:

$$\frac{(T1-TD1) \times (Y-N)}{Y}$$

where—

T1 is the amount of tax that would have been chargeable on the transfer if section 3(5)(*b*)(iii) did not apply,

TD1 is the amount of tax that would have been deductible by the transferee if section 3(5)(*b*)(iii) had not applied to the transfer,

Y is 20 or, if the interest when it was created in the immovable goods being transferred was for a period of less than 20 years, the number of full years in that interest, and

N   is the number of full years since the interest was created or, if the goods were developed since that interest was created, the number of full years since the most recent development:

but if that N is greater than that Y, such an amount calculated shall be deemed to be nil.]²

Amendments

1   Inserted by FA 2002, s 104 with effect from 1 September 2002.

2   Section 12D inserted by FA 2001, s 191 with effect from 6 April 2001.

---

13 Remission of tax on goods exported, etc

a 15, 16, 17

(Definitions)

[(1) Regulations may make provision for remitting or repaying, subject to such conditions (if any) as may be specified in the regulations or as the Revenue Commissioners may impose, the tax chargeable in respect of the supply of goods, or of such goods as may be specified in the regulations, in cases where the Revenue Commissioners are satisfied—

(*a*)   that the goods have been or are to be exported,

(*b*)   that the goods have been shipped on board an aircraft or ship proceeding to a place outside the State,

(*c*)   that the goods are, or are to be used in, a fishing vessel used or to be used for the purposes of commercial sea fishing.

(Retail export scheme)

[(1A) The Revenue Commissioners shall, subject to and in accordance with regulations (if any), allow the application of paragraph (*b*) of subsection (1) of section 11 (hereafter referred to in this section as **"zero-rating"**) to—

(*a*)   the supply of a traveller's qualifying goods, and

(*b*)   the supply of services by a VAT refunding agent consisting of the service of repaying the tax claimed by a traveller in relation to the supply of a traveller's qualifying goods or the procurement of the zero-rating of the supply of a traveller's qualifying goods,

where they are satisfied that the supplier of the goods or services as the case may be—

(i)   has proof that the goods were exported by or on behalf of the traveller by the last day of the third month following the month in which the supply takes place,

(ii)   repays, within such time limit as may be specified in regulations, any amount of tax paid by the traveller and claimed by that person in respect of goods covered by the provisions of paragraph (i),

(iii)   notifies the traveller in writing of any amount (including the mark-up) charged by the supplier for procuring the repayment of the amount claimed or arranging for the zero-rating of the supply [and where an amount so notified is expressed in terms of a percentage or a fraction, such percentage or fraction shall relate to the tax remitted or repayable under this subsection,]¹

(iv) uses, as the exchange rate in respect of monies being repaid to a traveller in a currency other than the currency of the State, the latest selling rate recorded by the Central Bank of Ireland for the currency in question at the time of the repayment, or where there is an agreement with the Revenue Commissioners for a method to be used in determining the exchange rate, the exchange rate obtained using the said method, and

(v) has made known to the traveller such details concerning the transaction as may be specified in regulations.

(VAT refund agents)

(1B) Regulations may make provision for the authorisation, subject to certain conditions, of tax-able persons or a class of taxable persons for the purposes of zero-rating of the supply of a traveller's qualifying goods or to operate as a VAT refunding agent in the handling of a repayment of tax on the supply of a traveller's qualifying goods and such regulations may provide for the cancellation of such authorisation and matters consequential to such cancellation.

(VAT refund agents — refundable VAT)

(1C) A VAT refunding agent acting as such may, in accordance with regulations, treat the tax charged to the traveller on the supply of that traveller's qualifying goods as tax that is deductible by the agent in accordance with paragraph (*a*) of subsection (1) of section 12, provided that that agent fulfils the conditions set out in subsection (1A) in respect of that supply.]²

(Export associated services — deductions)

(2) Regulations may make provision for remitting or repaying, subject to such conditions (if any) as may be specified in the regulations or as the Revenue Commissioners may impose, the tax chargeable in respect of the supply of all or any one or more (as may be specified in the regulations) of the following services:

(*a*) services directly linked to the export of goods or the transit of goods from a place outside the State to another place outside the State,

(*b*) the repair, maintenance and hiring of plant or equipment used in a vessel or an aircraft specified in paragraph (v) of the Second Schedule,

(*c*) the repair, maintenance and hiring of a vessel used, or of plant or equipment used in a vessel used, for the purposes of commercial sea fishing.

(Refunds to foreign businesses)

(3) (*a*) The Revenue Commissioners shall, in accordance with regulations, repay to a person to whom this subsection applies, deductible tax chargeable in respect of supplies of goods or services to him or in respect of goods imported by him.

a 17(4)   (*b*) This subsection applies to a person who shows to the satisfaction of the Revenue Commissioners that he carries on a business outside the State and that he supplies no goods or services in the State [other than services for which in accordance with section 8(2) the person who receives them is solely liable for the tax chargeable]³.

(*c*) In this subsection **"deductible tax"**, in relation to a person to whom this subsection applies, means tax chargeable [(including any flat-rate addition)][4] in respect of goods or services used by him for the purposes of any business carried on by him to the extent that such tax would be deductible by him under section 12 if the business were carried on by him within the State but does not include tax chargeable in respect of goods for supply within the State [[or in respect of motor vehicles (as defined in section 12(3)(*b*))][5] for hiring out for utilisation within the State][6] ...[7].

(Export of new means of transport)

[(3A)(*a*) The Revenue Commissioners shall, in accordance with regulations, repay to a person to whom this subsection applies the residual tax included in the consideration for supply of a new means of transport, where such new means of transport is subsequently dispatched or transported to another Member State.

(*b*) This subsection applies to a person not entitled to a deduction under section 12 of the tax borne or paid by him on the purchase, intra-Community acquisition or importation of the goods in question.][8]

(Definition)

[(3B) In this section—

"traveller" means a person whose domicile or habitual residence is not situated within the Community and includes a person who is normally resident in the Community but who, at the time of the supply of the goods intends to take up residence outside the Community in the near future and for a period of at least 12 consecutive months;

"traveller's qualifying goods" means goods, other than goods transported by the traveller for the equipping, fuelling and provisioning of pleasure boats, private aircraft or other means of transport for private use, which are supplied within the State to a traveller and which are exported by or on behalf of that traveller by the last day of the third month following the month in which the supply takes place;

"VAT refunding agent" means a person who supplies services which consist of the procurement of a zero-rating or repayment of tax in relation to supplies of a traveller's qualifying goods.

(Powers of the Revenue Commissioners)

(3C) For the purposes of this section, and subject to the direction and control of the Revenue Commissioners, any power, function or duty conferred or imposed on them may be exercised or performed on their behalf by an officer of the Revenue Commissioners.][9]

(4) ...[10]

(5) ...[10].][11]

Amendments

[1]   Inserted by FA 1999, s 132 with effect from 1 May 1999.

[2]   Subss (1A)–(1C) inserted by FA 1997, s 106(*a*) as on and from 1 July 1997.

[3]   Inserted by FA 2002, s 105 with effect from 25 March 2002.

[4]   Inserted by FA 1992, s 176(*a*) with effect from 1 January 1993.

[5]   Substituted by FA 1998, s 113 with effect from 27 March 1998; previously "or in respect of means of transport".

[6]   Inserted by FA 1987, s 43 with effect from 9 July 1987.

[7]   Words "or for hiring out for utilisation within the State" deleted by FA 1985, s 45 with effect from 30 May 1985.

[8]   Subs (3A) inserted by FA 1992, s 176(*b*) with effect from 1 January 1993.

[9]   Subss (3B)–(3C) inserted by FA 1997, s 106(*b*) as on and from 1 July 1997.

[10]   Subss (4)–(5) deleted by FA 1982, s 82 with effect from 1 September 1982.

[11]   Section 13 inserted by VATAA 1978, s 12; previously repealed by FA 1976, s 81.

Cross-references

Appeal (subs (3B)): s 25(1)(*ad*).

Fishing boats, etc, tax refund procedures: VATR 1979, r 29.

Foreign traders (unregistered), refund procedures: VATR 1979, r 30.

Goods allegedly exported liable to forfeiture: ss 27(9), (9A).

Residual tax (subs (3A)), Revenue may prescribe manner of calculation and repayment: s 32(1)(*ac*).

Regulations (subss (1)–(2)) require consent of Minister for Finance: s 32(2A).

Retail exporters (goods sold to tourists etc): Value Added Tax (Retail Export Scheme) Regulations 1998 (SI 34/98).

Traveller (subs (3B)), meaning applied: Sch 2 para (i)(*a*)(I).

Traveller's qualifying goods (subs (3B)), meaning applied: Sch 2 para (i)(*f*), (vi*b*).

Regulations

Subject	Regulation
Tourist VAT refunds	Value Added Tax (Retail Export Scheme) Regulations 1998 (SI 34/98)
Refunds to Foreign Traders	Value Added Tax Regulations 1979 (SI 63/79), r 30
Refunds regarding fishing vessels and equipment	Value Added Tax Regulations 1979 (SI 63/79), r 29

Revenue publications

Automated entry processing for imports/exports: Statement of Practice VAT 2/91.

Guide to Value Added Tax (Revenue Commissioners): Chapter 14.

Retail schemes: Tax Briefing, Issues 23, 27.

Tax free purchases for non-EU tourists: Leaflet April 1998.

Definition

"business": s 1(1); "flat-rate addition": ss 1(1), 12A; "goods": s 1(1); "intra-Community acquisition of goods": ss 1(1), 3A; "new means of transport": s 1(1); "person": IA 2005, s 18(*c*); "regulations": ss 1(1), 32; "supply": s 1(1); "tax": s 1(1); "vessel": s 1(1).

a 16   **13A Supplies to, and intra-Community acquisitions and imports by, certain taxable persons**

(Definitions)

[(1) For the purposes of this section and paragraph (vi*a*) of the Second Schedule—

"authorised person" means a qualifying person who has been authorised in accordance with subsection (3);

(How to qualify?)

"qualifying person" means a taxable person whose turnover from his supplies of goods made in accordance with [subparagraphs (*a*)(I), (*aa*), or (*b*)]¹ of paragraph (i) of the Second Schedule [, supplies of contract work where the place of supply is deemed to be a Member State other than the State and supplies of contract work made in accordance with paragraph (xvi) of the Second Schedule]² amounts to, or is likely to amount to, **75 per cent** of his total annual turnover from his supplies of goods and services:

Provided that the turnover from a supply of goods to a taxable person which are subsequently leased back from that person is excluded from the total annual turnover for the purposes of establishing whether the person is a qualifying person;

"qualifying goods" means all taxable goods excluding motor vehicles within the meaning of section 12(3)(*b*) and petrol;

"qualifying services" means all taxable services excluding the provision of food or drink, accommodation, other personal services, entertainment services or the hire of motor vehicles within the meaning of section 12(3)(*b*).

(Method of application to become an authorised person)

(2) A person who wishes to become an authorised person shall—

(*a*)   complete such application form as may be provided by the Revenue Commissioners for that purpose,

(*b*)   certify the particulars shown on such form to be correct, and

(*c*)   submit to the Revenue Commissioners the completed and certified application form, together with such further information in support of the application as may be requested by them.

(Authorisation certificate from Revenue Commissioners)

(3) (*a*)   Where a person has furnished the particulars required under subsection (2), the Revenue Commissioners shall, where they are satisfied that he is a qualifying person, issue to that person in writing an authorisation certifying him to be an authorised person.

(Period of validity)

(*b*)   An authorisation issued in accordance with paragraph (*a*) shall be valid for such period as may be determined by the Revenue Commissioners.

(Cancellation of authorisation)

(*c*)   Where a person who has been authorised in accordance with paragraph (*a*) ceases to be a qualifying person, he shall, by notice in writing, advise the Revenue Commissioners accordingly not later than the end of the taxable period during which he ceased to be a qualifying person.

(*d*)   The Revenue Commissioners shall, by notice in writing, cancel an authorisation issued to a person in accordance with paragraph (*a*) where they are satisfied that he is no longer a qualifying person and such cancellation shall have effect from the date specified in the notice.

(Issuing certificates to suppliers)

(4) An authorised person shall furnish a copy of the authorisation referred to in subsection (3) to each taxable person in the State who supplies taxable goods or taxable services to him.

(Invoicing requirements)

(5) A taxable person who supplies goods or services in circumstances where the provisions of paragraph (v*i*a) of the Second Schedule apply, shall, in addition to the details to be included on each invoice, credit note or other document required to be issued in accordance with section 17, include on such invoice, credit note or other document a reference to the number of the authorisation issued to the authorised person in accordance with subsection (3).

(Imports — compliance issues)

(6) In relation to each consignment of goods to be imported by an authorised person at the rate specified in section 11(1)(*b*) by virtue of paragraph (v*i*a) of the Second Schedule the following conditions shall be complied with—

(*a*) a copy of the authorisation referred to at subsection (3) shall be produced with the relevant customs entry; and

(*b*) the relevant customs entry shall incorporate—

(i) a declaration by the authorised person, or by his representative duly authorised in writing for that purpose, that he is an authorised person in accordance with this section for the purposes of paragraph (v*i*a) of the Second Schedule, and

(ii) a claim for importation at the rate specified in section 11(1)(*b*).

(Immovable goods)

(7) For the purposes of subsections (1)(*a*)(ii) and (6)(*a*) of section 4, the tax charged at the rate specified in section 11(1)(*b*) by virtue of paragraph (v*i*a) of the Second Schedule shall be deemed to be tax which is deductible under section 12.

(Non-deductible items)

(8) Where an authorised person is in receipt of a service in respect of which, had the provisions of paragraph (v*i*a) of the Second Schedule not applied, tax would have been chargeable at a rate other than the rate specified in section 11(1)(*b*) and all or part of such tax would not have been deductible by him under section 12, then the authorised person shall, in relation to such service, be liable to pay tax as if he himself had supplied the service for consideration in the course or furtherance of his business to a person who is not an authorised person.

(Implementation by Revenue Commissioners)

(9) For the purposes of this section, and subject to the direction and control of the Revenue Commissioners, any power, function or duty conferred or imposed on them may be exercised or performed on their behalf by an officer of the Revenue Commissioners.][3]

Amendments

1   Substituted by FA 2001, s 192 with effect from 6 April 2001; previously "subparagraph (*a*)(I) or (*b*)".

2   Inserted by FA 1996, s 95 with effect from 1 January 1996.

3   Section 13A inserted by FA 1993, s 90 with effect from 1 August 1993.

Cross-references

Charge of tax at 0% to authorised persons: Sch 2 para (vi*a*).

Revenue precedent

Issue: Can a VAT-registered lessee, who holds 13A authorisation of shop and office property, obtain a deduction for VAT charged on services/goods through landlords.
Decision: Yes, in these circumstances the landlord may register for VAT and recover the VAT suffered on the service charges on an annual basis.
Issue: Do receipts from the supply of Fourth Schedule services constitute turnover for the purposes of 13A scheme.
Decision: It was not the intention to discriminate against companies that were essentially exporting companies. It was decided that receipts derived from Fourth Schedule supplies outside the State would be ignored when calculating turnover for qualification under new scheme.

Revenue publications

Form 13B — Exports: Tax Briefing, Issue 29.
Guide to Value Added Tax (Revenue Commissioners): Chapter 13.
Zero-rating of goods in accordance with section 13A of the VAT Act: Statement of Practice VAT 1/93.

Definitions

"excisable products": s 1(1); "intra-Community acquisition of goods": s 1(1), 3A; "person": IA 2005, s 18(*c*); "regulations": s 1(1), 32; "supply": s 1(1); "tax": s 1(1); "taxable person": s 1(1).

14 Payment based on cash receipts

[(1) A person who satisfies the Revenue Commissioners that—

(*a*)   taking one period with another, not less than 90 per cent. Of such person's turnover is derived from taxable supplies to persons who are not registered persons, or

(*b*)   the total consideration which such person is entitled to receive in respect of such person's taxable supplies has not exceeded and is not likely to exceed [€635,000][1] in any continuous period of twelve months,

may, in accordance with regulations, be authorised to determine the amount of tax which becomes due by such person during any taxable period (or part thereof) during which the authorisation has effect by reference to the amount of the moneys which such person receives during such taxable period (or part thereof) in respect of taxable supplies.][2]

(Tax amount due)

[(1A) Where an authorisation to which subsection (1) relates has not been cancelled under subsection (2), then—

(*a*)   the rate of tax due by the person concerned in respect of a supply shall be the rate of tax chargeable at the time the goods or services are supplied,

(b) if tax on a supply has already been due and payable under any other provisions of this Act prior to the issue of such authorisation, tax shall not be due again in respect of any such supply as a result of the application of subsection (1), and

(c) if no tax is due or payable on a supply made prior to the issue of such authorisation, tax shall not be due in respect of any such supply as a result of the application of subsection (1).][3]

(Ministerial Order)

[(1B)(a) The Minister may, by order—

(i) increase the amount specified in subsection (1)(b), or

(ii) where an amount stands specified by virtue of an order under this paragraph, including an order relating to this subparagraph, further increase the amount so specified.

(b) An order under paragraph (a) shall be laid before Dáil Éireann as soon as may be after it is made and, if a resolution annulling the order is passed by Dáil Éireann within the next twenty-one sitting days on which Dáil Éireann has sat after the order is laid before it, the order shall be annulled accordingly, but without prejudice to the validity of anything previously done thereunder.][4]

(Cancellation of authorisation)

(2) The Revenue Commissioners may, in accordance with regulations, cancel an authorisation under ...[5] subsection (1), and may, by regulations exclude from the application of [that subsection][6]...[7] any tax due in respect of specified descriptions of supplies of goods or services and any moneys received in respect of such supplies.

[(3) This section shall not apply to tax provided for by subsection (1)(b) [or (1A)][8] of section 2.][9]][10]

Amendments

[1]   Substituted by FA 2001, s 240 and Sch 5 Part 4 with effect from 1 January 2002; previously "£500,000"; previously "£250,000" (Value Added Tax (Eligibility to Determine Tax Due by Reference to Moneys Received) Order 1997 (SI 316/1997): 17 July 1997).

[2]   Subs (1) substituted by FA 1994, s 97(a) with effect from 23 May 1994.

[3]   Subs (1A) inserted by FA 1992, s 177(1)(b) with effect from 28 May 1992.

[4]   Subs (1B) inserted by FA 1995, s 131 with effect from 2 June 1995.

[5]   Deleted by FA 1994, s 97(b)(i) with effect from 23 May 1994; previously "paragraph (a) of".

[6]   Substituted by FA 1994, s 97(b)(ii) with effect from 23 May 1994; previously "the said paragraphs (a)".

[7]   Words "and (b)" deleted by FA 1992, s 177(1)(c) with effect from 1 January 1993.

[8]   Words "or (1A)" inserted by FA 1992, s 177(2) with effect from 1 January 1993.

[9]   Subs (3) inserted by FA 1992, s 177(1)(d) with effect from 28 May 1992.

[10]   Section 14 substituted by VATAA 1978, s 13 with effect from 1 March 1979.

Cross-references

Cash basis, Revenue may prescribe how determined, and adjustments required: s 32(1)(*g*); regulations: Value Added Tax (Determination of Tax Due by Reference to Moneys Received) Regulations 1992 (SI 306/92).

Regulations

Subject	Regulation
Cash receipts basis	Value Added Tax (Determination of Tax Due by Reference to Money Received) Regulations 1986 (SI 298/86)
Cash receipts basis	Value Added Tax (Determination of Tax Due by Reference to Money Received) Regulations 1992 (SI 93/92)
Cash receipts basis	Value Added Tax (Determination in Regards to Tax) Regulations 1992 (SI 278/92)
Cash receipts basis	Value Added Tax (Determination of Tax Due by Reference to Money Received) Regulations 1992 (SI 306/92)
Cash receipts basis	Value Added Tax (Determination of Tax Due by Reference to Money Received) (Amendment) Regulations 1994 (SI 1259/94)

Orders

Subject	Order
Cash receipts basis	Value Added Tax (Eligibility to Determine Tax Due by Reference to Money Received) Regulations 1986 (SI 1298/86)

Revenue publications

Cash receipts basis: Tax Briefing, Issue 30.
Cash receipts basis; eligibility, change in operation with effect from 1 January 1993: Statement of Practice VAT 16/92.
Guide to Value Added Tax (Revenue Commissioners): Chapter 8.
Moneys received basis of accounting: Statement of Practice VAT 2/92.
Money received basis of accounting: Statement of Practice VAT 16/92.

Definition

"Dáil Éireann": IA 2005, Sch; "goods": s 1(1); "the Minister": s 1(1); "moneys received": s 1(2); "person": IA 2005, s 18(*c*); "regulations": ss 1(1), 32; "the specified day": s 1(1); "supply": s 1(1); "tax": s 1(1); "taxable goods": s 1(1); "taxable period": s 1(1).

15 Charge of tax on imported goods

(Rate of tax applicable to imports)

[(1) Tax shall be charged on the importation of goods at whichever of the rates a 14 specified in section 11(1) is the appropriate rate in respect of such goods.][1]

(2) ...[2]

(Valuation of imported goods)

(3) The value of imported goods for the purposes of this section shall be their a 11B value determined in accordance with the acts for the time being in force adopted by the institutions of the Community relating to the valuation of goods for customs purposes, modified by the substitution of references to the territory of the State for references to the customs territory of the Community, together with any taxes, duties [, expenses resulting from the transport of the goods to another place of destination within the Community, if that destination is known at the time of the importation,][3] and other charges levied either outside or, by reason of

importation, within the State (except value added tax) on the goods and not included in the determination.

(4) ...[4]

(Relief from import VAT)

(5) The Revenue Commissioners may, in accordance with regulations, remit or repay, if they think fit, the whole or part of the tax chargeable—

> (*a*)　on the importation of any goods which are shown to their satisfaction to have been previously exported,
>
> (*b*)　on the importation of any goods if they are satisfied that the goods have been or are to be re-exported,
>
> (*c*)　on the importation of any goods from the customs-free airport by an unregistered person who shows to the satisfaction of the Revenue Commissioners that he has already borne tax on the goods,

(Refund of import VAT on imports consigned to other Member States)

a 28a(3)　[(5A) The Revenue Commissioners shall, in accordance with regulations, repay the tax chargeable on the importation of goods where the goods have been dispatched or transported—

> (*a*)　to another Member State from outside the Community, and
>
> (*b*)　to a person, other than an individual, who is not registered for value added tax in that other Member State:

Provided that this subsection shall only apply where it is shown to the satisfaction of the Revenue Commissioners that the goods in question have been subject to value added tax referred to in Council Directive No. 77/388/EEC of 17 May 1977 in that other Member State.][5]

(Customs law applies)

(6) Subject to the foregoing provisions of this section, the provisions of the Customs Consolidation Act, 1876, and of other law in force in the State relating to customs shall apply with such exceptions and modifications (if any) as may be specified in regulations, to tax referred to in this section as if it were a duty of customs.

(Changes on imports by registered persons)

[(6A) Regulation 26 of the Value Added Tax Regulations, 1979 (SI No 63 of 1979), is hereby revoked and tax charged under section 2(1)(*b*) shall, in accordance with the provisions of the Customs Consolidation Act, 1876, and of other law in force in the State relating to customs, as applied to tax by subsection (6) and regulations thereunder, be paid in the manner and at the time that it would have been payable if that regulation had not been made][6].

(Postponement of VAT on imports)

(7) Regulations may—

> (*a*)　make provision for enabling goods imported by registered persons or by such classes of registered persons as may be specified in the regulations for the purposes of a business carried on by them to be delivered or

removed, subject to such conditions or restrictions as may be specified in the regulations or as the Revenue Commissioners may impose, without payment of the tax chargeable on the importation, and

(*b*) provide that the tax be accounted for by the persons or classes of persons aforesaid in the return, made by them under section 19(3), in respect of the taxable period during which the goods are so delivered or removed.][7]

Amendments

[1] Subs (1) substituted by FA 1992, s 178(*a*) with effect from 28 May 1992.

[2] Subs (2) deleted by FA 1992, s 178(*b*) with effect from 28 May 1992.

[3] Inserted by FA 1996, s 96 with effect from 1 January 1996.

[4] Subs (4) deleted by FA 1985, s 46 with effect from 1 March 1985.

[5] Subs (5A) inserted by FA 1992, s 178(*c*) with effect from 1 January 1993.

[6] Subs (6A) inserted by FA 1982, s 84 with effect from 1 September 1982.

[7] Section 15 substituted by VATAA 1978, s 14 with effect from 1 March 1979.

Cross-references

Alcohol products (subss (3) and (6)): s 3B(5) and (4).

Imports (subs (7)): Value Added Tax (Imported Goods) Regulations 1992 (SI 439/92).

Repayment of tax charged at import (subs (5A)), Revenue may make regulations: s 32(1)(*ad*).

Regulations (subss (6)–(7)) require consent of Minister for Finance: s 32(2A).

Transport services relating to importation of goods, where value of service is included in taxable amount (subs (3)): Sch 2 para (xvi*a*).

Regulations

Subject	Regulation
Imports	Value Added Tax (Imported Goods) Regulations 1982 (SI 279/82)
Imports	Value Added Tax (Imported Goods) Regulations 1983 (SI 129/83)
Imports	European Communities (Exemption from Import Charges of Certain Vehicles etc Temporarily Imported) Regulations 1983 (SI 422/83)
Imports personal	European Communities (Exemption from Import Charges of Certain Personal Property) Regulations 1983 (SI 423/83)
Imports	Taxable Amount Value Added Tax (Remission and Repayment of Tax on Certain Importation) Regulations 1985 (SI 344/85)
Imports temporary	European Communities (Value Added Tax) (Exemption on Temporary Importations of Certain Goods) Regulations 1986 (SI 264/86)
Imports	Value Added Tax (Imported Goods) Regulations 1992 (SI 439/92)
Imports	Value Added Tax (Imported Goods) (No 2) Regulations 1992 (SI 440/92)
Imports	Value Added Tax (Imported Goods) (Amendment) Regulations 2001 (SI 628/01)

Sixth Directive

Imports: a 7; chargeable event: a 10; within the territory of the country: a 11; exemptions on importation: a 14; persons liable to pay tax to the authorities: a 21; obligations under the internal system: a 22; obligations in respect of imports: a 23.

Case law

Subject	Case	Case reference
Taxable status of credit card commission	*SA Chasseures Bally v The Belgium State*	25 May 1993, C–18/92

| Importation into the Netherlands from the Netherlands Antilles deemed to be an importation into the EC | *Van der Kooy v Staatsecretaris van Financien* | 29 January 1999, C–181/97 |
| Imports — Removal of Goods from Customs Arrangements | *Liberexim BV v Staatssecretaris van Financiën* | 11 July 2002, C–371/99 |

Revenue publications

Guide to Value Added Tax (Revenue Commissioners): Chapter 13.

Definition

"business": s 1(1); "Community": s 1(1); "the customs-free airport": s 1(1); "goods": s 1(1); "importation of goods": s 1(1); "livestock": s 1(1); "person": IA 2005, s 18(*c*); "regulations": ss 1(1), 32; "tax": s 1(1); "taxable period": s 1(1).

a 28n

15A Goods in transit

(Goods in transit at 1 January 1993)

(1) Where—

    (*a*) goods from another member State were imported into the State on or before the 31st day of December, 1992, and

    (*b*) the tax referred to in section 2(1)(*b*) was not chargeable because the goods were, at the time of such importation, placed under one of the arrangements referred to in subparagraph (*b*) or (*c*) of paragraph 1 of Article 14, or subparagraph A of paragraph 1 of Article 16, of Council Directive No 77/388/EEC of 17 May 1977, and

    (*c*) the goods are still subject to such an arrangement on the 1st day of January, 1993,

then, the provisions in force at the time the goods were placed under the arrangement shall continue to apply in relation to those goods until such time as, in accordance with those provisions, the goods cease to be covered by those arrangements.

(Deemed importation)

(2) (*a*) Notwithstanding the definition of "importation of goods" in section 1, an importation within the meaning of that definition shall be deemed to occur in the following cases:

      (i) where goods have been placed under an internal Community transit operation in another Member State before the 1st day of January, 1993, and the operation terminates in the State on or after that date;

      (ii) where goods referred to in subsection (1) cease to be covered by the arrangements referred to in that subsection;

      (iii) where goods are returned to the State after the 1st day of January, 1993, being goods which were exported from the State before that date and imported into another member State in accordance with any of the arrangements referred to in subsection (1)(*b*).

  (*b*) In this subsection **"internal Community transit operation"** means the dispatch or transport of goods under cover of the internal Community transit arrangement referred to in paragraph 3 of Article 1 of Council

Regulation (EEC) No 222/77 of 13 December 1976, or under the cover of a T2L or equivalent document provided for in that Regulation and includes the sending of goods by post.

(Non-VATable imports)

(3) The tax referred to in section 2(1)(*b*) shall not be chargeable in the cases referred to in subsection (2) where—

(*a*) the goods are dispatched or transported outside the Community,

(*b*) the goods are other than a means of transport and are being returned to the State and to the person who exported them from the State, or

(*c*) the goods are a means of transport which was acquired or imported before the 1st day of January, 1993, and in respect of which value added tax referred to in Council Directive No 77/388/EEC of 17 May 1977 has been paid in a Member State and that value added tax has not subsequently been refunded because of exportation from that Member State of the means of transport:

Provided that this paragraph shall be deemed to be complied with where it is shown to the satisfaction of the Revenue Commissioners that the first use of the means of transport was prior to the 1st day of January, 1985, or that the tax due does not exceed [€130][1].

(4) In this section, references to subparagraph (*b*) or (*c*) of paragraph 1 of Article 14, and to subparagraph A of paragraph 1 of Article 16, of Council Directive No 77/388/EEC of 17 May 1977 shall be deemed to be references to those provisions of the Directive immediately prior to their amendment by Council Directive 91/680/EEC of 16 December 1991.][2]

Amendments

[1] Substituted by FA 2001, s 240 and Sch 5 Part 4 with effect from 1 January 2002; previously "£100".

[2] Section 15A inserted by EC(VAT)R 1992, r 11 with effect from 1 January 1993.

Definition

"Community": s 1(1); "goods": s 1(1); "importation of goods": s 1(1).

Notes

Subs (2)(*b*): OJ No L38, 9 February 1977.

15B Goods in transit (additional provisions)

a 28n

(Goods in transit at 1 January 1995 — expansion of Community)

[(1) Where—

(*a*) goods from a new Member State were imported into the State [before the date of accession][1], and

(*b*) the tax referred to in section 2(1)(*b*) was not chargeable because the goods were, at the time of such importation, placed—

(i) under an arrangement for temporary importation with total exemption from customs duty, or

      (ii) under one of the arrangements referred to in clauses (*a*), (*b*), (*c*) and (*d*) of subparagraph B of paragraph 1 of Article 16, of Council Directive No 77/388/EEC of 17 May 1977, and

  (*c*) the goods are still subject to such an arrangement on the [date of accession]²,

then, the provisions in force at the time the goods were placed under that arrangement shall continue to apply until the goods leave that arrangement on or after the [date of accession]².

(2) (*a*) Where—

      (i) goods were placed under the common transit procedure or under another customs transit procedure in a new Member State [before the date of accession]¹, and

      (ii) those goods have not left the procedure concerned before the [date of accession]²,

      then the provisions in force at the time the goods were placed under that procedure shall continue to apply until the goods leave that procedure on or after the [date of accession]².

  (*b*) In this subsection **"common transit procedure"** means the procedure approved by the Council of the European Communities by Council Decision No 87/415/EEC of 15 June 1987, approving the Convention done at Interlaken on the 20th day of May, 1987, between the European Community, the Republic of Austria, the Republic of Finland, the Republic of Iceland, the Kingdom of Norway, the Kingdom of Sweden, and the Swiss Confederation on a common transit procedure, the text of which is attached to that Council Decision.

(3) Where goods were in free circulation in a new Member State prior to entry into the State, an importation into the State shall be deemed to occur in the following cases:

  (*a*) the removal, including irregular removal, within the State of the goods referred to in subsection (1) from the arrangement referred to in subparagraph (i) of paragraph (*b*) of that subsection;

  (*b*) the removal, including irregular removal, within the State of the goods referred to in subsection (1) from the arrangement referred to in subparagraph (ii) of paragraph (*b*) of that subsection;

  (*c*) the termination within the State of any of the procedures referred to in subsection (2).

(4) An importation into the State shall be deemed to occur when goods, which were supplied within a new Member State [before the date of accession]¹, and which were not chargeable to a value added tax in that new Member State, because of their exportation from that new Member State, are used in the State on or after the [date of accession]², and have not been imported before that date.

(5) The tax referred to in section 2(1)(*b*) shall not be chargeable where—

(*a*) the imported goods referred to in subsections (3) and (4) are dispatched or transported outside the enlarged Community,

(*b*) the imported goods referred to in paragraph (*a*) of subsection (3) are other than means of transport and are being returned to the new Member State from which they were exported and to the person who exported them, or

(*c*) the imported goods referred to in paragraph (*a*) of subsection (3) are means of transport which were acquired in or imported into a new Member State before the [date of accession]² in accordance with the general conditions of taxation in force on the domestic market of that new Member State and which have not been subject by reason of their exportation to any exemption from or refund of a value added tax in that new Member State:

...³.

[(5A) Subsection (5)(*c*) shall be deemed to be complied with where it is shown to the satisfaction of the Revenue Commissioners that—

(i) the date of the first use of the means of transport was before 1 January 1987 in the case of means of transport entering the State from the Republic of Austria, the Republic of Finland (excluding the Aland Islands) or the Kingdom of Sweden,

(ii) the date of the first use of the means of transport was before 1 May 1996 in the case of means of transport entering the State from the Czech Republic, the Republic of Estonia, the Republic of Cyprus, the Republic of Latvia, the Republic of Lithuania, the Republic of Hungary, the Republic of Malta, the Republic of Poland, the Republic of Slovenia or the Slovak Republic, or

(iii) the tax due by reason of the importation does not exceed €130.]⁴

(6) The provisions of section 15A shall not apply to goods imported or deemed to be imported from a new Member State.

(7) (*a*) In this section—

["**date of accession**" means 1 January 1995 in respect of the Republic of Austria, the Republic of Finland (excluding the Aland Islands) and the Kingdom of Sweden or 1 May 2004 in respect of the Czech Republic, the Republic of Estonia, the Republic of Cyprus, the Republic of Latvia, the Republic of Lithuania, the Republic of Hungary, the Republic of Malta, the Republic of Poland, the Republic of Slovenia and the Slovak Republic;]⁵

"**the enlarged Community**" means the Community after the accession of the new Member States;

["**new Member State**" means any state referred to in the definition of "**date of accession**" with effect from the relevant date.]⁶

(*b*) A word or expression that is used in this section and is also used in Council Directive No 94/76/EC of 22 December 1994, has, unless the contrary intention appears, the meaning in this section that it has in that Council Directive.][7]

Amendments

1   Substituted by FA 2004, s 62(*a*) with effect on and from 1 May 2004; previously "on or before the 31st day of December, 1994".

2   Substituted by FA 2004, s 62(*b*) with effect on and from 1 May 2004; previously "1st day of January, 1995".

3   Subs (5)(*c*)(proviso) deleted by FA 2004, s 62(*c*) with effect on and from 1 May 2004.

4   Subs (5A) inserted by FA 2004, s 62(*d*) with effect on and from 1 May 2004.

5   Subs (7)(*a*)(definition of "date of accession") inserted by FA 2004, s 62(*e*)(i) with effect on and from 1 May 2004.

6   Subs (7)(*a*)(definition of "new Member State") substituted by FA 2004, s 62(*e*)(ii) with effect on and from 1 May 2004.

7   Section 15B inserted by EC(VAT)R 1994, r 4 with effect from 1 January 1995.

Definition

"Community": s 1(1); "goods": s 1(1); "importation of goods": s 1(1); "new means of transport": s 1(1).

Notes

Subs (2)(*b*): OJ No L26, 13 August 1977.

_{a 22(2)} **16 Duty to keep records**

(Scope of requirements)

(1) Every [taxable person][1] shall, in accordance with regulations, keep full and true records of all transactions which affect or may affect his liability to tax.

[(1A) Every person who trades in investment gold (within the meaning of section 6A) shall, in accordance with regulations, keep full and true records of that person's transactions in investment gold.][2]

(Retention of invoices by unregistered persons)

(2) Every person, other than [a taxable person][3,] who [supplies goods or services in the course or furtherance of any business][4] shall keep all invoices issued to him in connection with the [supply of goods or services][5] to him for the purpose of such business ...[6]

(Records required and period of retention)

(3) Records ...[7] kept by a person pursuant to this section and any books [invoices, [monthly control statements,][8] copies ...[9] of customs entries][10,] credit notes, debit notes, receipts, accounts, vouchers, bank statements or other documents whatsoever which relate to the [supply of goods or services,][11] [the intra-Community acquisition of goods][12] [, or the importation of goods][13] by the person and are in the power, possession or procurement of the person and, in the case of any such book, invoice, [monthly control statement,][14] credit note, debit note, receipt, account, voucher, or other document which has been issued by the person to another person, any copy thereof which is in the power, possession or procurement of the person shall [, subject to subsection (4),][15] be retained in his power, possession or procurement for a period of six years from the date of the

latest transaction to which the [records, invoices, monthly control statements]¹⁶ or any of the other documents relate:

Provided that this section shall not require the retention of records or invoices or any of the other documents in respect of which the Revenue Commissioners notify the person concerned that retention is not required, nor shall it apply to the books and papers of a company which have been disposed of in accordance with section 305(1) of the Companies Act, 1963.

[(4) Notwithstanding the retention period specified in subsection (3) the following retention periods shall apply:

(*a*) where a person acquires or develops immovable goods to which section 4 applies, the period for which that person shall retain records pursuant to this section in relation to that person's acquisition or development of those immovable goods shall be the duration that such person holds a taxable interest in such goods plus a further period of six years,

(*b*) where a person exercises a waiver of exemption from tax in accordance with section 7, the period for which that person shall retain records pursuant to this section shall be the duration of the waiver plus a further period of six years.]¹⁷

Amendments

1 Substituted by VATAA 1978, s 30(2) with effect from 1 March 1979; previously "accountable person".

2 Subs (1A) inserted by FA 1999, s 133 with effect from 1 January 2000.

3 Substituted by VATAA 1978, s 30(2) with effect from 1 March 1979; previously "an accountable person".

4 Substituted by VATAA 1978, s 30(2) with effect from 1 March 1979; previously "delivers goods in the course of business or renders services in the course of business".

5 Substituted by VATAA 1978, s 30(2) with effect from 1 March 1979; previously "delivery of goods or the rendering of services".

6 Words "and, in respect of goods imported by him, copies, stamped on behalf of the Revenue Commissioners, of the relevant customs entries" deleted by FA 1992, s 179(*a*) with effect from 1 January 1993.

7 Words "and invoices" deleted by FA 1982, s 85 with effect from 1 September 1982.

8 Inserted by FA 1992, s 179(*b*)(iii) with effect from 1 November 1992.

9 Words ", stamped on behalf of the Revenue Commissioners," deleted by FA 1992, s 179(*b*)(i) with effect from 28 May 1992.

10 Inserted by FA 1982, s 85 with effect from 1 September 1982.

11 Substituted by VATAA 1978, s 30(2) with effect from 1 March 1979; previously "delivery of goods by the person or the rendering of services".

12 Inserted by FA 1992, s 179(*b*)(ii) with effect from 1 January 1993.

13 Words inserted by FA 1982, s 85 with effect from 1 September 1982.

14 Inserted by FA 1992, s 179(*b*)(v) with effect from 1 November 1992.

15 Inserted by FA 2003, s 121(*a*) with effect from 28 March 2003.

16 Substituted by FA 1992, s 179(*b*)(iv) with effect from 1 November 1992: previously "records or invoices".

17 Subs (4) inserted by FA 2003, s 121(*b*) with effect from 28 March 2003.

Cross-references

Fraud, negligence: penalties: s 27(1).

Hire purchase transactions, supplier (who is obliged to issue invoice to financial service provider) is a taxable person for the purposes of this section: s 17(1AB)

Non compliance, penalty: s 26(1); obligation to keep records: FA 1968, s 6.

Records to be kept, Revenue may prescribe details and retention period: s 32(1)(*h*); regulations: VATR 1979, r 9.

Regulations

Subject	Regulation
Accounts/records	Value Added Tax Regulations 1979 (SI 63/79), r 9
Records	Value Added Tax (Record of transactions in Investment Gold) Regulations 1999 (SI 349/99)
Agricultural machinery	Value Added Tax (Agricultural machinery) Regulation 1999 (SI 443/99)

Revenue publications

Guide to Value Added Tax (Revenue Commissioners): Chapter 10.

Revenue powers: Statement of Practice GEN 1/94, May 1994.

Revenue powers: Statement of Practice GEN 1/94.

Definition

"business": s 1(1); "goods": s 1(1); "intra-Community acquisition of goods: ss 1(1), 3A; "monthly control statement": ss 1(1), 17; "person": IA 2005, s 18(*c*); "regulations": ss 1(1), 32; "supply": s 1(1); "tax": s 1(1); "taxable person": ss 1(1), 8.

a 22(3)   # 17 Invoices

(Issuing of invoices)

(1) [A taxable person][1] who [supplies goods or services][2] to another [taxable person][3] [or to a Department of State or local authority or to a body established by statute or to a person who carries on an exempted activity][4] [or ...[5] to a person, other than an individual, in another Member State of the Community][6] in such circumstances that tax is chargeable [at any of the rates specified in section 11(1), [or who supplies goods or services to a person in another Member State who is liable to pay Value Added tax pursuant to Council Directive No 77/388/EEC of 17 May 1977 on such supply,][7] [or who supplies goods to a person in another Member State of the Community in the circumstances referred to in section 3(6)(*d*)(ii),][8] ...[9]][10] shall issue to that [person][11] in respect of each such [supply of goods or services][12] an invoice in such form and containing such particulars as may be specified by regulations.

[Provided that, where goods are supplied in accordance with the terms of paragraph (*b*) of subsection (1) of section 3, and the ownership of those goods is transferred to a person supplying, in respect of those goods, financial services of the kind specified in subparagraph (*e*) of paragraph (i) of the First Schedule, the taxable person making the supply of the goods in question shall issue the invoice to the person supplying the said financial services in lieu of the taxable person to whom the supply of the goods is made and that invoice shall include the name and address of the person supplying those financial services.][13]

(Use of electronic invoicing)

[(1A)(*a*) An invoice or other document required to be issued by a person under this section shall, subject to paragraph (*b*), be deemed to be so issued by that person if the particulars which are required by regulations to be contained in such invoice or other document are recorded, retained and transmitted electronically by a system or systems which ensures the integrity of those particulars and the authenticity of their origin, without the issue of any invoice or other document containing those particulars.

(*b*) An invoice or other document required to be issued under this section shall not be deemed by paragraph (*a*)to be so issued unless the person, who is required to issue such invoice or other document, complies with such conditions as are specified by regulations and the system or systems used by that person conforms with such specifications as are required by regulations.

(*c*) The person who receives a transmission referred to in paragraph (*a*) shall not be deemed to be issued with an invoice or other document required to be issued under this section unless the particulars which are required by regulations to be contained in such invoice or other document are received electronically in a system which ensures the integrity of those particulars and the authenticity of their origin and unless the system conforms with such specifications as are required by regulations and that person complies with such conditions as are specified by regulations.]¹⁴

(Arrangements for hire purchase/credit sales transactions)

[(1AA) Where the proviso to subsection (1) applies, the person supplying the financial services in question shall issue a document to the person to whom the supply of goods is made and shall indicate thereon—

(*a*) the amount which is set out in respect of tax on the invoice issued to the person supplying the financial services in accordance with the said proviso in respect of that supply of goods, and

(*b*) such other particulars as are specified by regulations in respect of an invoice issued in accordance with subsection (1).

(Record requirements for financing institutions)

[(1AAA) Where a person, referred to in this subsection as the **"owner"**, supplies financial services of the kind specified in subparagraph (i)(*e*) of the First Schedule in respect of goods which are supplied within the meaning of section (3)(1)(*b*), being goods which are handed over from a person in another Member State to a taxable person acting as such in the State, referred to in this subsection as the **"acquirer"**, then the owner shall issue a document to the acquirer and shall indicate thereon—

(*a*) that the acquirer is liable to account for the tax, if any, due in respect of the intra-Community acquisition of those goods, and

(*b*) such other particulars as are specified by regulations in respect of an invoice issued in accordance with subsection (1).]¹⁵

(1AB) Where any person issues a document for the purposes of [subsections (1AA), (1AAA)][16] [or section 12C (1B)][17] that person shall, in respect of the document, be treated as a taxable person for the purposes of sections 16 and 18.][18]

(Monthly control statements)

[(1B) A taxable person who supplies goods to another taxable person in such circumstances that tax is chargeable at any of the rates specified in section 11(1) shall issue to that other taxable person a single document in this Act referred to as a monthly control statement in respect of all such supplies to that other taxable person during each calendar month, and every such statement shall be in such form, contain such particulars, and be issued within such time as may be specified by regulations:

[Provided that this provision shall not apply—

(*a*) to taxable persons whose taxable turnover in respect of supplies of goods to other taxable persons has not exceeded £2,000,000 in the previous period of 12 months, and

(*b*) in any event, in respect of all such supplies made in the taxable periods commencing on or after the 1st day of May, 1995.][19]][20]

(Flat-rate farmers — invoice requirements)

a 22(3)   [(2) A flat-rate farmer who, in accordance with section 12A, is required to issue an invoice in respect of the supply of agricultural produce or an agricultural service shall, in respect of each such supply, issue an invoice in the form and containing such particulars (in addition to those specified in the said section 12A) as may be specified by regulations if the following conditions are fulfilled:

(*a*) the issue of an invoice is requested by a [purchaser],[21]

(*b*) the [purchaser][19] provides the form for the purpose of the invoice and enters the appropriate particulars thereon, and

(*c*) the [purchaser][19] gives to the flat-rate farmer a copy of the invoice,

but may issue the invoice if those conditions or any of them are not fulfilled.][22]

[(2A) A flat-rate farmer who, in accordance with section 12C, is required to issue an invoice in respect of a supply of agricultural machinery shall, in respect of each supply, issue an invoice in the form and containing such particulars as may be specified by regulations if the following conditions are fulfilled:

(*a*) the issue of the invoice is requested by the taxable dealer,

(*b*) the taxable dealer provides the form for the purpose of the invoice and enters the appropriate particulars thereon, and

(*c*) the taxable dealer gives to the flat-rate farmer a copy of the invoice,

but may issue the invoice if those conditions or any one of them are not fulfilled.][23]

(Supplementary invoices and credit notes)

(3) Where, subsequent to the issue of an invoice by a person [to another person][24] in accordance with subsection (1), the consideration as stated in the invoice is increased or reduced, or a discount is allowed, whichever of the following provisions is appropriate shall have effect:

- (*a*) if the consideration is increased, the person shall issue [to that other person][25] another invoice in such form and containing such particulars as may be specified by regulations in respect of such increase,

- (*b*) if the consideration is reduced or a discount is allowed, the person shall issue [to that other person][26] a document (in this Act referred to as a credit note) containing particulars of the reduction or discount in such form and containing such other particulars as may be specified by regulations, [and, if that other person is a taxable person, the amount][27] which the [taxable person][3] may deduct under section 12 shall, in accordance with regulations, be reduced by the amount of tax shown on the credit note.

(Incorrect rate of VAT charged on invoice)

[(3A) Notwithstanding subsections (5) and (9), where a person issues an invoice in accordance with subsection (1) which indicates a rate of tax and subsequent to the issue of that invoice it is established that a lower rate of tax applied, then—

- (*a*) the amount of consideration stated on that invoice shall be deemed to have been reduced to nil,

- (*b*) the provisions of subsection (3)(*b*) shall have effect, and

- (*c*) following the issue of a credit note in accordance with the provisions of subsection (3)(*b*), the person shall issue another invoice in accordance with this Act and regulations made thereunder.][28]

(Incorrect hire purchase/credit sales invoices)

[(3AB) Where any person supplying financial services receives a credit note issued under the terms of paragraph (*b*) of subsection (3) in respect of a supply of goods to which the proviso to subsection (1) applies, that person shall, within seven days of receipt of such credit note, issue to the person to whom the goods in question were supplied, a document corresponding to that credit note indicating such particulars as are specified by regulations in respect of the issue of such credit notes, and the amount which the taxable person to whom the goods were supplied may deduct under section 12 in respect of that supply shall be reduced by the amount in respect of tax shown in the document.][29]

(Flat-rate farmers invoices — amending procedures)

[(4) Where subsequent to the issue by a flat-rate farmer of an invoice in accordance with subsection (2), the consideration as stated on the invoice is increased or reduced, or a discount is allowed, whichever of the following provisions is appropriate shall have effect:

(Undercharge)

- (*a*) in case the consideration is increased, the flat-rate farmer shall issue another invoice (if the conditions referred to in subsection (2) are fulfilled in relation to it) containing particulars of the increase and of the flat-rate addition appropriate thereto and in such form and containing such other particulars as may be specified by regulations and such other invoice shall be deemed, for the purposes of section 12, to be issued in accordance with section 12A, but the said farmer may not issue the invoice if the said conditions or any of them are not fulfilled,

(Overcharge)

(*b*) in case the consideration is reduced or a discount is allowed, the flat-rate farmer shall, ...[30] issue a document (in this section referred to as "**a farmer credit note**") containing particulars of the reduction or discount and in such form and containing such other particulars as may be specified by regulations, [and the amount which the person may deduct under section 12 or is entitled to be repaid under section 13 shall,][31] in accordance with regulations, be reduced by an amount equal to the amount of the flat-rate addition appropriate to the amount of the reduction or discount][32].

(Incorrect VAT on VAT documents)

(5) If [a taxable person][1] issues an invoice stating a greater amount of tax than that properly attributable to the consideration stated therein, or issues a credit note stating a lesser amount of tax than that properly attributable to the reduction in consideration or the discount therein, he shall be liable to pay to the Revenue Commissioners the excess amount of tax stated in the invoice or the amount of the deficiency of tax stated in the credit note.

(Incorrect VAT on hire purchase documents)

[(5A) If any person issues a document for the purposes of subsection (1AA) in relation to a supply of goods indicating a greater amount in respect of tax than the amount of tax invoiced in accordance with the proviso to subsection (1) in relation to that supply, that person shall, in relation to that excess, be deemed for the purposes of this Act to be a taxable person and a person to whom subsection (5) applies, and that excess shall be deemed to be tax.][33]

(VAT documents issued by unregistered persons)

(6) A person who is not a registered person and who, ...,[34] issues an invoice stating an amount of tax shall, in relation to the amount of tax stated, be deemed, for the purposes of this Act, to be [a taxable person][1] and shall be liable to pay the amount to the Revenue Commissioners.

(Incorrect use of flat-rate addition)

[(6A)(*a*) If a person, other than a flat-rate farmer, issues an invoice stating an amount of flat-rate addition, he shall be liable to pay to the Revenue Commissioners as tax the amount of flat-rate addition stated and shall, in relation to such amount, be deemed, for the purpose of this Act, to be a taxable person.

(*b*) If a flat-rate farmer issues an invoice stating an amount of flat-rate addition otherwise than in respect of an actual supply of agricultural produce or an agricultural service or in respect of such a supply but stating a greater amount of flat-rate addition than is appropriate to the supply, he shall be liable to pay to the Revenue Commissioners as tax the amount or the excess amount, as the case may be, of the flat-rate addition stated and shall, in relation to such amount or such excess amount, be deemed, for the purposes of this Act, to be a taxable person.

(*c*) If a flat-rate farmer, in a case in which he is required to issue a farmer credit note under subsection (4)(*b*), fails to issue the credit note within the time allowed by regulations or issues a credit note stating a lesser amount of flat-rate addition than is appropriate to the reduction in consideration or the discount, he shall be liable to pay to the Revenue Commissioners as tax the amount of flat-rate addition which should have been stated on the credit note or the amount of the deficiency of flat-rate addition, as the case may be, and shall, in relation to such amount or such deficiency, be deemed, for the purposes of this Act, to be a taxable person.][35]

(Time limits for issuing VAT documents)

(7) An invoice or credit note shall be issued within such time after the date of [supplying goods or services][36] as may be specified by regulations and an amendment of an invoice pursuant to subsection (4)(*b*) shall be affected within such time as may be specified by regulations.

[(7A) A document required to be issued in accordance with subsection (1AA) shall be issued within twenty-two days next following the month of supply of the goods.][37]

(Early payments/prior to completion of supply)

(8) Notwithstanding anything in subsection (7), where payment for the [supply of goods or services][38] [, other than supplies of the kind specified in subparagraph (*b*) or (*c*) of paragraph (i) of the Second Schedule][39] is made to a person, either in full or by instalments, before the [supply][40] is completed, the person shall issue an invoice in accordance with subsection (1) [or subsection (2), as may be appropriate,][41] within such time after the date of actual receipt of the full payment or the instalment as may be specified by regulations.

(Discounts allowed/consideration reduced)

(9) (*a*) Notwithstanding anything in subsection (3), where, subsequent to the issue to a registered person of an invoice in accordance with subsection (1), the consideration stated in the invoice is reduced or a discount is allowed in such circumstances that, by agreement between the persons concerned, the amount of tax stated in the invoice is unaltered, paragraph (*b*) of the said subsection (3) shall not apply in relation to the person by whom the invoice was issued.

[(*aa*) Paragraph (*a*) shall not apply where the person who issued the invoice referred to therein was, at the time of its issue, a person authorised, in accordance with section 14(1), to determine his tax liability in respect of supplies of the kind in question by reference to the amount of moneys received.][42]

(*b*)   In a case to which paragraph (*a*) applies—

    (i)   the reduction or discount concerned shall not be taken into account in computing the liability to tax of the person making the reduction or allowing the discount,

    (ii)   subsection (5) shall not apply, and

    (iii)   the amount which the person in whose favour the reduction or discount is made or allowed may deduct in respect of the relevant transaction under section 12 shall not be reduced.

(Settlement vouchers)

(10) Where—

(*a*)   ...[43] agricultural produce or agricultural services are supplied to a registered person by a flat-rate farmer][44] ...[45] and

(*b*)   the person to whom the [[agricultural produce][46] or services are supplied][47] issues to the other person, before the date on which an invoice is issued by that other person, a document (in this Act referred to as a settlement voucher) in such form and containing such particulars as may be specified by regulations, then, for the purposes of this Act—

    (i)   the person who issues the settlement voucher shall, if the person to whom it is issued accepts it, be deemed to have received from the person by whom the voucher was accepted an invoice containing the particulars set out in the voucher, and

    (ii)   the person to whom the settlement voucher is issued shall, if he accepts it, be deemed to have issued to the person from whom the voucher was received an invoice containing the particulars set out in the voucher.

(Debit notes)

(11) Where a person who is entitled to receive a credit note under subsection (3)(*b*) from another person issues to that other person, before the date on which a credit note is issued by that other person, a document (in this subsection referred to as "debit note") in such form and containing such particulars as may be specified by regulations, then, for the purposes of this Act—

(*a*)   the person who issues the debit note shall, if the person to whom it is issued accepts it, be deemed to have received from the person by whom the note was accepted a credit note containing the particulars set out in such debit note, and

(*b*)   the person to whom such debit note is issued shall, if he accepts it, be deemed to have issued to the person from whom the debit note was received a credit note containing the particulars set out in such debit note.

(Farmer debit notes)

[(11A) Where a person who is entitled to receive a farmer credit note under subsection (4)(*b*) from another person issues to that other person, before the date on which a farmer credit note is issued by that other person, a document (in this section referred to as **"a farmer debit note"**) in such form and containing such particulars as may be specified by regulations, then, for the purposes of this Act—

(*a*) the person who issues the debit note shall, if the person to whom it is issued accepts it, be deemed to have received from the person by whom the debit note was accepted a farmer credit note containing the particulars set out in such debit note, and

(*b*) the person to whom such debit note is issued shall, if he accepts it, be deemed to have issued to the person from whom the debit note was received a farmer credit note containing the particulars set out in such debit note.][48]

(Written evidence of tax paid for refund purposes)

(12)(*a*) [A taxable person][1] shall—

(i) if requested in writing by another person and if the request states that the other person is entitled to repayment of tax under section 20(3), give to that other person in writing the particulars of the amount of tax chargeable [by the taxable person][49] in respect of the [supply][50] by him of the goods specified in the request or of the [supply][51] by him of the services so specified,

(ii) if requested in writing by another person and if the request states that the other person is entitled to repayment of tax under [section 13],[52] give to that other person in writing the particulars specified in regulations for the purposes of subsection (1) in respect of the [goods or][53] services [supplied][54] by the [taxable person][3] to that other person that are specified in the request, and

(iii) if requested in writing by another person and if the request states that that other person is entitled to repayment of tax under section 20(2), give to that other person in writing the particulars of the amount of tax chargeable [by the taxable person][55] in respect of the [supply][2] by him of the radio broadcasting reception apparatus and parts thereof that are specified in the request.

[(*ai*) A flat-rate farmer shall, if requested in writing by another person and if the request states that the other person is entitled to repayment of the flat-rate addition under section 13, give to that other person in writing the particulars specified in regulations for the purpose of subsection (2) in respect of the goods or services supplied by the flat-rate farmer to that other person that are specified in the request.][56]

(*b*) A request under paragraph (*a*) shall be complied with by the person to whom it is given within thirty days after the date on which the request is received by him.

(Guidelines for Farmer credit and debit notes)

[(13) The provisions of this Act (other than this section) relating to credit notes and debit notes issued under subsection (3) and (11), respectively, of this section shall apply in relation to farmer credit notes and farmer debit notes as they apply in relation to the credit notes and debit notes aforesaid.][57]

[(14)(*a*) An invoice required under this section to be issued in respect of a supply by a person, in this subsection referred to as the "supplier", is deemed to be so issued by that supplier if that invoice is drawn up and issued by the person to whom that supply is made, in this subsection referred to as the "customer", where—

(i)   there is prior agreement between the supplier and the customer that the customer may draw up and issue such invoice,

(ii)   the customer is a person registered for Value Added tax,

(iii)   any conditions which are imposed by this Act or by regulations on the supplier in relation to the form, content or issue of the invoice are met by the customer, and

(iv)   agreed procedures are in place for the acceptance by the supplier of the validity of the invoice.

(*b*)   An invoice, which is deemed to be issued by the supplier in accordance with paragraph (*a*), is deemed to have been so issued when such invoice is accepted by that supplier in accordance with the agreed procedures referred to in paragraph (*a*)(iv).

(*c*)   An invoice required to be issued by a supplier under this section shall be deemed to be so issued by that supplier if—

(i)   that invoice is issued by a person who acts in the name and on behalf of the supplier, and

(ii)   any conditions which are imposed by this Act or by regulations on the supplier in relation to the form, content or issue of the invoice are met.

(*d*)   Any credit note or debit note issued in accordance with this section which amends and refers specifically and unambiguously to an invoice is treated as if it were an invoice for the purposes of this subsection.

(*e*)   The Revenue Commissioners may make regulations in relation to the conditions applying to invoices covered by this subsection.

(15)(*a*) A person who issues, or is deemed to issue, an invoice under this section shall ensure that—

(i)   a copy of any invoice issued by such person,

(ii)   a copy of any invoice deemed to be issued by such person in the circumstances specified in subsection (14), and

(iii)   any invoice received by such person, is stored, and for the purposes of section 16(1) the reference to the keeping of full and true records therein shall be construed accordingly in so far as it relates to invoices covered by this section.

(*b*)   Any invoice not stored by electronic means in a manner which conforms with requirements laid down by the Revenue Commissioners shall be stored within the State, but subject to the agreement of the

Revenue Commissioners and any conditions set by them such invoice may be stored outside the State.]⁵⁸

Amendments

1   Substituted by VATAA 1978, s 30(2) with effect from 1 March 1979; previously "an accountable person".
2   Substituted by VATAA 1978, s 30(2) with effect from 1 March 1979; previously "delivers goods or services".
3   Substituted by VATAA 1978, s 30(2) with effect from 1 March 1979; previously "accountable person".
4   Inserted by FA 2003, s 122(*a*) with effect from 1 January 2004.
5   Word "goods" deleted with effect from 1 January 1993 by EC(VAT)R 1992, r 12.
6   Inserted by FA 1992, s 180(*a*)(i) with effect from 1 January 1993.
7   Inserted by FA 2004, s 63 with effect from 25 March 2004.
8   Inserted by FA 1993, s 91(*a*).
9   Words ", including the rate of zero per cent," deleted by FA 1992, s 180(*a*)(ii) with effect from 1 January 1993.
10 Inserted by FA 1973, s 90 with effect from 3 September 1973.
11 Substituted by FA 1992, s 180(*a*)(iii) with effect from 1 January 1993; previously "other taxable person".
12 Substituted by VATAA 1978, s 30(2) with effect from 1 March 1979; previously "delivery of goods or rendering of services".
13 Subs (1)(proviso) inserted by FA 1996, s 97(*a*) with effect from 1 July 1996.
14 Subs (1A) substituted by FA 2001, s 193(*a*) with effect from 6 April 2001.
15 Subs (1AAA) inserted by FA 2001, s 193(*b*) with effect from 1 July 2001.
16 Inserted by FA 2000, s 115 with effect from 23 March 2000.
17 Substituted by FA 2001, s 193(*c*) with effect from 1 July 2001; previously "subsection (1AA)".
18 Subss (1AA)–(1AB) inserted by FA 1996, s 97(*b*) with effect from 1 July 1996.
19 Subs (1B)(proviso) substituted by FA 1995, s 132 with effect from 2 June 1995.
20 Subs (1B) inserted by FA 1992, s 180(*c*) with effect from 1 November 1992.
21 Substituted by FA 1992, s 180(*d*) with effect from 1 January 1993; previously "taxable person".
22 Subs (2) inserted by VATAA 1978, s 15 with effect from 1 March 1979; previously repealed by FA 1976, s 81 with effect from 1 March 1976.
23 Subs (2A) inserted by FA 1999, s 134 with effect from 1 September 1999.
24 Substituted by FA 1992, s 180(*e*)(i) with effect from 1 January 1993; previously "to a taxable person".
25 Substituted by FA 1992, s 180(*e*)(ii) with effect from 1 January 1993; previously "to the taxable person".
26 Substituted by FA 1992, s 180(*e*)(iii)(I) with effect from 1 January 1993; previously "to the taxable person".
27 Substituted by FA 1992, s 180(*e*)(iii)(xx) with effect from 1 January 1993; previously "the amount".
28 Subs (3A) inserted by FA 1993, s 91(*b*).
29 Subs (3AB) inserted by FA 1996, s 97(*c*) with effect from 1 July 1996.
30 Words ", if the person to whom the supply was made is a taxable person," deleted by FA 1992, s 180(*f*)(i) with effect from 1 January 1993.
31 Substituted by FA 1992, s 180(*f*)(ii) with effect from 1 January 1993; previously "and the amount which the taxable person may deduct under section 12 shall,".
32 Subs (4) inserted by VATAA 1978, s 15 with effect from 1 March 1979; previously repealed by FA 1976, s 81 with effect from 1 March 1976.
33 Subs (5A) inserted by FA 1996, s 97(*d*) with effect from 1 July 1996.
34 Words "otherwise than as required by section 13," deleted by FA 1976, s 81 with effect from 1 March 1976.
35 Subs (6A) inserted by VATAA 1978, s 15 with effect from 1 March 1979.

36   Substituted by VATAA 1978, s 30(2) effect from 1 March 1979; previously "delivering goods or rendering services".
37   Subs (7A) inserted by FA 1996, s 97(e) with effect from 1 July 1996.
38   Substituted by VATAA 1978, s 30(2) with effect from 1 March 1979; previously "delivery of goods or the rendering of services".
39   Inserted by FA 1992, s 180(g) with effect from 1 January 1993.
40   Substituted by FA 1978, s 30(2) with effect from 1 March 1979; previously "delivery or rendering".
41   Inserted by VATAA 1978, s 15 with effect from 1 March 1979.
42   Subs (9)(aa) inserted by VATAA 1978, s 15 with effect from 1 March 1979.
43   Deleted by FA 2003, s 122(b) with effect from 1 January 2004; previously "goods or services are supplied]⁴² to a registered person by another registered person or
      42   Substituted by VATAA 1978, s 30(2) with effect from 1 March 1979; previously 'goods are delivered or services are rendered'.".
44   Inserted by VATAA 1978, s 15 with effect from 1 March 1979.
45   Words "but who is required under section 13(1) to issue an invoice to a registered person" deleted by FA 1976, s 81 with effect from 1 March 1976.
46   Substituted by FA 2003, s 122(c) with effect from 1 January 2004; previously "goods".
47   Substituted by VATAA 1978, s 30(2) with effect from 1 March 1979; previously "goods are delivered or the services are rendered".
48   Subs (11A) inserted by VATAA 1978, s 15 with effect from 1 March 1979.
49   Substituted by FA 2006, s 127(a) and Sch 2 para 8 with effect from 31 March 2006; previously "to the taxable person".
50   Substituted by VATAA 1978, s 30(2) with effect from 1 March 1979; previously "delivery".
51   Substituted by VATAA 1978, s 30(2) with effect from 1 March 1979; previously "rendering".
52   Substituted by VATAA 1978, s 30(2) with effect from 1 March 1979; previously "section 5(4)".
53   Inserted by VATAA 1978, s 15 with effect from 1 March 1979.
54   Substituted by VATAA 1978, s 30(2) with effect from 1 March 1979; previously "rendered".
55   Substituted by FA 2006, s 127(a) and Sch 2 para 8 with effect from 31 March 2006; previously "to the taxable person".
56   Subs (12)(ai) inserted by FA 1992, s 180(h) with effect from 1 January 1993.
57   Subs (13) inserted by VATAA 1978, s 15 with effect from 1 March 1979.
58   Subss (14) and (15) inserted by FA 2003, s 122(d) with effect from 1 January 2004.

Cross-references

Appeal (subss (5)–(6)): s 25(1)(a).

Auctioneer, special scheme, tax not to be shown separately: s 10B(5); invoice deemed to be issued (subs (4)) by principal where goods auctioned on his behalf: s 10B(6).

Authorised persons (exporters, charge of tax at 0% to), authorisation number to be shown on invoice: s 13A(5).

Bad debts, discounts, goods returned: Revenue may prescribe manner of adjustment: s 32(1)(s); adjustments: VATR 1979, r 8.

Computer and microfilm based records: FA 1986, s 113.

Hire purchase transactions, deductible tax where supplier invoices financial service provider (subs (1AA)): s 12(1)(a)(ia).

Fraud, negligence; penalties: s 27(1).

Invoices etc, Revenue may prescribe particulars to be shown: s 32(1)(i); details: Value Added Tax (Invoices and Other Documents) Regulations 1992 (SI 275/92); time limits: Value Added Tax (Time Limits for Issuing Certain Documents) Regulations (SI 276/92); electronic transmission: Value Added Tax (Electronic Data Exchange and Storage) Regulations 1992 (SI 269/92).

Monthly control statement, Revenue may prescribe particulars to be shown: VATA 1972, s 32(1)(i); details: Value Added Tax (Monthly Control Statement) Regulations 1992 (SI 230/92).

Non compliance, penalty: s 26(1); (subs (4)(a)), penalty: s 26(2A).

Taxable amount (subs (3)(b)): s 10(3)(d).

Taxable dealers supplying means of transport, tax not to be shown separately: s 12B(5).

Regulations

Subject	Regulation
Adjustments for bad debts, discounts/rebates etc	Value Added Tax Regulations 1979 (SI 63/79), r 8
Monthly control statements	Value Added Tax (Monthly Control Statements) Regulations 1992 (SI 230/92)
Electronic invoicing	Value Added Tax (Electronic Data Exchange and Storage Regulations 1992 (SI 269/92)
Invoices, credit notes etc format	Value Added Tax (Invoices and Other Documents) Regulations 1992 (SI 275/92)
Invoices, credit notes etc time limits	Value Added Tax (Time Limits for Issuing Certain Documents) Regulations 1992 (SI 275/98)
Invoices, credit notes etc	Value Added Tax (Invoices and Other Documents) (Amendments) Regulations 1998 (SI 489/98)
Agricultural machinery documentation	Value Added Tax (Agricultural Machinery) (Documentation) Regulations 1999 (SI 443/99)
Electronic Invoicing and Storage	Value Added Tax (Electronic Invoicing and Storage) Regulations 2002 (SI 504/02)

Case law

Subject	Case	Case reference
Member State to regard credit notes as a document serving as an invoice if all necessary information included 17 September 1997	*Finanzamt Osnabuck- Land v Langhorst*	C–141/96
Member State to regard credit notes as a document serving as an invoice if all necessary information included:	*Finanzamt Osnabruck — Land v Langhorst*	17 September 1997, C–141/96

Revenue precedent

Issue: Authorisation to use electronic invoicing between traders in the State who are participating in a purchasing card scheme.

Decision: It was agreed, for ease of administration, to allow the letter of agreement on the purchasing card scheme to be accepted as simultaneous authorisation provided to all suppliers and purchasers within the scheme to use electronic invoicing.

Revenue publications

Delayed invoices, Revenue policy: *Tax Briefing 24*, December 1996

Electronic invoicing: authorisation procedure, system capacity, keeping of records, etc: Statement of Practice VAT 9/92.

Guide to Value Added Tax (Revenue Commissioners): Chapter 9.

Invoices — Time limits: Tax Briefing Issue 24.

Issue of credit notes: Tax Briefing Issue 47.

Monthly control statement: details to be included, use of commercial statement, etc: Statement of Practice VAT 7/92.

New EU rules on invoicing: Tax Briefing Issue 46.

VAT invoicing and other documents: Leaflet October 1992.

VAT treatment of Invoicing: Information Leaflet No 1/06.

Definition

"agricultural produce": s 1(1); "agricultural service": s 1(1); "farmer": s 1(1); "flat-rate addition": ss 1(1), 12A; "flat- rate farmer": ss 1(1), 12A; "goods": s 1(1); "monthly control statement": ss 1(1), 17; "person": IA 2005, s 18(*c*); "registered person": s 1(1); "regulations": ss 1(1), 32; "supply": s 1(1); "tax": s 1(1); "taxable person": ss 1(1), 8; "writing": IA 2005, Sch.

18 Inspection and removal of records

(Scope of powers to enter premises, search and remove records)

a 22(8)   [(1)(a)   For the purposes of this Act and regulations, an authorised officer may at all reasonable times enter any premises or place where he has reason to believe that business is carried on or anything is done in connection with business and—

(i) may require that person carrying on the business, or any person on those premises or in that place who is employed by the person carrying on the business or who is associated with him in the carrying on of the business, to produce any books, records, accounts or other documents relating to the business or to any other business which he has reason to believe may be, or have been, connected with the said business or have, or have had, trading relations with the said business,

(ii) may, if he has reason to believe that any of the books, records, accounts or other documents, which he has required to be produced to him under the provisions of this subsection have not been so produced, search in those premises or that place for those books, records, accounts or other documents,

a 22(8)   [(iia) may, if he has reason to believe that a person is carrying or has in his possession any records which may be required as evidence in criminal proceedings in accordance with [section 1078 of the Taxes Consolidation Act, 1997],[1] in relation to the tax, request the person to produce any such records, and if that person should fail to do so, the authorised officer or a member of the Garda Síochána may search that person:

Provided that—

(A) the officer or the member of the Garda Síochána conducting the search shall ensure, as far as practicable, that the person understands the reason for the search,

(B) the search is conducted with due regard to the privacy of that person,

(C) the person being searched shall not be searched by an officer or member of the Garda Síochána of the opposite sex, and

(D) the person being searched shall not be requested to remove any clothing other than headgear or a coat, jacket, glove or a similar article of clothing.][2]

(iii) may, in the case of any such books, records, accounts or other documents produced to or found by him, take copies of or extracts from them and remove and retain them for such period as may be reasonable for their further examination or for the purposes of any proceedings ...[3] in relation to tax,

(iv) may, if he has reason to believe that goods connected with taxable supplies [, intra-Community acquisitions]⁴ or importations are held on those premises or in that place and that particulars of such goods have not been kept and retained, as required by this Act or by regulations, in the books, records, accounts or other documents of the business or of any other business similarly required to keep and retain particulars of those goods, search those premises or that place for the said goods and, on their discovery, examine and take particulars of them,

(v) may require the person carrying on the business, or any person on those premises or in that place, who is employed by the person carrying on the business or who is associated with him in the carrying on of the business, to give the authorised officer all reasonable assistance [, including providing information and explanations and furnishing documents in connection with the business, as required by the authorised officer]⁵.

(*b*) Nothing in this subsection shall be construed as requiring any person carrying on a profession, or any person employed by any person carrying on a profession, to produce to an authorised officer any documents relating to a client, other than such documents as are material to the tax affairs of the person carrying on the profession, and, in particular, he shall not be required to disclose any information or professional advice of a confidential nature given to a client]⁶.

(Customers and supplies)

[(1A) A taxable person shall, on request from an authorised officer, furnish to that officer, in respect of a specified period, the following information:

(Customers details)

(*a*) the name and address of each of his customers and the total consideration payable in respect of supplies of goods and services made by him to each customer and the tax thereon [and the value and description of any gifts or promotional items given by him to any person in connection with such supplies or any other payments made by him to any person in connection with such supplies]⁷, and

(Supplier details)

(*b*) the name, address and registration number of each of his suppliers and the total consideration payable in respect of goods and services supplied to him from each supplier and the tax thereon.

(Definition of records)

(1B) In this section "records" means any document, or any other written or printed material in any form, including any information stored, maintained or preserved by means of any mechanical or electronic device, whether or not stored, maintained or preserved in a legible form, which a person is required to keep, retain, issue or produce for inspection or which may be inspected under any provision relating to tax.]⁸

(2) ...⁹.

(Obstruction/delay of an officer)

(3) A person shall not wilfully obstruct or delay an authorised officer in the exercise of his powers under this section.

(Obligation to show authorisation on request)

(4) Where, in pursuance of this section, an authorised officer enters any premises, carries out any search or requests production of any documents, he shall, on request, show his authorisation for the purpose of this section to the person concerned.

(Definition of an authorised officer)

(5) In this section **"authorised officer"** means an officer of the Revenue Commissioners authorised by them in writing for the purposes of this section.

Amendment

¹   Substituted by TCA 1997, s 1100 and Sch 31; previously "section 94 (as amended by section 243 of the Finance Act, 1992) of the Finance Act, 1983".

²   Subs (1)(iia) inserted by FA 1992, s 181(a)(i) with effect from 1 January 1993.

³   Words "for the recovery of a penalty" deleted by FA 1992, s 181(a)(ii) with effect from 28 May 1992.

⁴   Inserted by FA 1992, s 181(a)(iii) with effect from 1 January 1993.

⁵   Inserted by FA 1992, s 181(a)(iv) with effect from 28 May 1992.

⁶   Subs (1) substituted by FA 1984, s 89 with effect from 23 May 1984.

⁷   Inserted by FA 1995, s 133 with effect from 2 June 1995.

⁸   Subss (1A)-(1B) inserted by FA 1992, s 181(b) with effect from 28 May 1992.

⁹   Subs (2) deleted by FA 1984, s 89 with effect from 23 May 1984.

Cross-references

Books etc to be kept: VATR 1979, r 9.

Fraud, negligence: penalties: s 27(1).

Hire purchase transactions (supplier who is obliged to issue invoice to financial service provider) is a taxable person for the purposes of this section: s 17(1AB).

Information, disclosure regarding supplies made, Revenue may make regulations: s 32(1)(n); regulations: VATR 1979, r 35.

Intra-Community acquisition of goods: s 3A.

Revenue may make regulations regarding nomination of officers to perform functions: s 32(1)(k).

non compliance (subs (3)), penalty: s 26(3A).

Regulations

Subject	Regulation
Accounts/records	Value Added Tax Regulations 1979 (SI 63/79), r 9
Disclosure of information to the Revenue	Value Added Tax Regulations 1979 (SI 63/79), r 35

Revenue publications

Commissioned framed photography: Tax Briefing Issue 39.

Guide to Value Added Tax (Revenue Commissioners): Chapter 10.10.

Revenue powers: Statement of Practice GEN/1/94, May 1994.

Revenue powers: Statement of Practice GEN/1/99.

VAT rates on Revenue website: Tax Briefing 45.

Definition

"business": s 1(1); "goods": s 1(1); "person": IA 2005, s 18(c); "regulations": ss 1(1), 32; "tax": s 1(1); "taxable person": ss 1(1), 8; "writing": IA 2005, Sch.

---

19 Tax due and payable

a 10

(Time when tax becomes due)

(1) Tax chargeable under section 2(1)(*a*) shall be due—

(*a*) in case an invoice is required under section 17 to be issued, at the time of issue of the in voice, or if the invoice is not issued in due time, upon ^a 10(2) the expiration of the period within which the invoice should have been issued;

(*b*) in case a person is liable under subsection (5) or (6) of section 17 to pay an amount of tax by reference to an invoice or credit note issued by him, at the time of issue of such invoice or credit note, ...[1]

[(*bb*) in the case of continuous supplies being supplies of telecommunications services, electricity, or gas which has the meaning assigned to it in paragraph (i)(*c*) of the Sixth Schedule, for which a statement of account issues periodically, supplied to a person other than a person to whom an invoice is required under section 17 to be issued, at the time of issue of the statement of account in respect of those supplies, and in this paragraph **"statement of account"** means a balancing statement, or a demand for payment which issues at least once every 3 months, and][2]

(*c*) in any other case, at the time the [goods or services are supplied][3]:

...[4].

(Intra-Community acquisitions)

[(1A) Tax chargeable under section 2(1A) shall be due—

(*a*) on the fifteenth day of the month following that during which the intra- a 28d Community acquisition occurs;

(*b*) in case an invoice is issued before the date specified in paragraph (*a*) by the supplier in another Member State to the person acquiring the goods, when that invoice is issued.][5]

(Receipt of advance payments)

(2) Notwithstanding anything in this Act, the tax chargeable under section 2(1)(*a*) [, other than tax chargeable in respect of supplies of the kind specified in subparagraph (*b*) or (*c*) of paragraph (i) of the Second Schedule,][6] or the relevant part thereof, shall fall due not later than the time when the amount in respect of which it is payable has been received either in full or in part and where the amount is received in full or in part before the [supply of the goods or services][7] to which it relates, a [supply][8] for a consideration equal to the amount received of such part of the goods or services as is equal in value to the amount received, shall be deemed, for the purposes of this Act, to have taken place at the time of such receipt. [However this subsection does not apply to the tax chargeable in respect of supplies of goods or services where tax is due in accordance with [paragraph (*a*), (*b*) or (*bb*)][9] of subsection (1) by a taxable person who is not authorised under section 14 to account for tax due by reference to the amount of the moneys received during a taxable period or part thereof.][10]

(Prepayments for telecommunication services — 1 July 1997)

[(2A) Where a payment is made prior to the 1st day of July, 1997, in respect of a telecommunications service which is to be supplied by a person in the course or furtherance of business from outside the State on or after that date and the place of supply of that service is deemed by virtue of paragraph (*e*) of subsection (6) of section 5 to be, at the time of its supply, the State, then that payment shall be deemed, for the purposes of subsection (2), to be made on that date.]¹¹

(Rules and obligations re: VAT returns)

(Bi-monthly return)

a 22(4)   [(3) (*a*)   Subject to paragraph (*b*), a taxable person shall, within 9 days immediately after the tenth day of the month immediately following a taxable period, furnish to the Collector-General a true and correct return prepared in accordance with regulations of the amount of tax which became due by him during the taxable period, not being tax already paid by him in relation to goods imported by him, and the amount, if any, which may be deducted in accordance with section 12 in computing the amount of tax payable by him in respect of such taxable period and such other particulars as may be specified in regulations, and shall at the same time remit to the Collector-General the amount of tax, if any, payable by him in respect of such taxable period.

         ...¹²

(Annual return)

[(*aa*)   (i)   In this paragraph:

["**accounting period**" means a period, as determined by the Collector-General from time to time in any particular case, consisting of a number of consecutive taxable periods not exceeding six or such other period not exceeding a continuous period of twelve months as may be specified by the Collector- General:

Provided that—

(I)   where an accounting period begins before the end of a taxable period, the period of time from the beginning of the accounting period to the end of the taxable period during which the accounting period begins shall, for the purposes of this paragraph, be treated as if such period of time were a taxable period, and

(II)   where an accounting period ends after the beginning of a taxable period, the period of time from the beginning of the taxable period during which the accounting period ends to the end of the accounting period shall, for the purposes of this paragraph, be treated as if such period of time were a taxable period,

and any references in this paragraph to a taxable period shall be construed accordingly;]¹³

"**authorised person**" means a taxable person who has been authorised in writing by the Collector-General for the purposes of this paragraph and "**authorise**" and "**authorisation**" shall be construed accordingly.

(Powers of Collector-General)

(ii) Notwithstanding the provisions of paragraph (*a*)—

(I) the Collector-General may, from time to time, authorise in writing a taxable person for the purposes of this paragraph, unless the taxable person objects in writing to the authorisation,

and

(II) an authorised person may, within nine days immediately after the tenth day of the month immediately following an accounting period furnish to the Collector-General a true and correct return prepared in accordance with regulations of the amount of tax which became due by him during the taxable periods which comprise the accounting period not being tax already paid by him in relation to goods imported by him, and, the amount, if any, which may be deducted in accordance with section 12 in computing the amount of tax payable by him in respect of such taxable periods and such other particulars as may be specified in regulations, and at the same time remit to the Collector- General any amount of tax payable by him in respect of such taxable periods, [and, in the case of an authorised person referred to in subparagraph (iv)(III) that amount shall be the balance of tax remaining to be paid, if any, after deducting from it, the amount of tax paid by him by direct debit in respect of his accounting period,][14] and, where the authorised person concerned so furnishes and remits, he shall be deemed to have complied with the provisions of paragraph (*a*) in relation to the said taxable periods.

(iii) For the purposes of issuing an authorisation to a taxable person, the Collector-General shall, where he considers it appropriate, have regard to the following matter—

(I) he has reasonable grounds to believe that—

(A) the authorisation will not result in a loss of tax, and

(B) the taxable person will meet all his obligations under the authorisation,

and

(II) the taxable person has—

(A) been a registered person during all of the period consisting of the six taxable periods immediately preceding the period in which an authorisation would, if it were issued, have effect, and

(B)   complied with the provisions of paragraph (*a*).

(iv)   An authorisation may—

(I)   be issued either without conditions or subject to such conditions as the Collector-General, having regard in particular to the considerations mentioned in subparagraph (iii), considers proper and specified in writing to the taxable person concerned when issuing the authorisation,

(II)   without prejudice to the generality of the foregoing, require an authorised person to remit to the Collector-General, within nine days immediately after the tenth day of the month immediately following each taxable period (other than the final taxable period) which is comprised in an accounting period, such an amount as may be specified by the Collector-General.

[(III)   without prejudice to the generality of the foregoing, require an authorised person to agree with the Collector-General a schedule of amounts of money which he undertakes to pay on dates specified by the Collector-General by monthly direct debit from his account with a financial institution and the total of the amounts specified in that schedule shall be that person's best estimate of his total tax liability for his accounting period and he shall review on an on-going basis whether the total of the amounts specified in that schedule is likely to be adequate to cover his actual liability for his accounting period and where this is not the case or is not likely to be the case, he shall agree a revised schedule of amounts with the Collector-General and adjust his monthly direct debit amounts accordingly.]¹⁵

(v)   The Collector-General may, by notice in writing, terminate an authorisation and, where a taxable person requests him to do so, he shall terminate the authorisation.

(vi)   For the purposes of terminating an authorisation the Collector-General shall, where he considers it appropriate, have regard to the following matters:

(I)   he has reasonable grounds to believe that the authorisation has resulted or could result in a loss of tax, or

(II)   the taxable person—

(A)   has furnished, or there is furnished on his behalf, any incorrect information for the purposes of the issue to him of an authorisation, or

(B)   has not complied with the provisions of paragraph (*a*) or of this paragraph, including the conditions, if any, specified by the Collector-General under subparagraph (iv) in relation to the issue to him of an authorisation.

(vii) In relation to any taxable period in respect of which he has not complied with the provisions of paragraph (*a*), a person whose authorisation is terminated shall be deemed to have complied with paragraph (*a*) if, within [fourteen][16] days of issue to him of a notice of termination, he furnishes to the Collector-General the return specified in paragraph (*a*) and at the same time remits to the said Collector-General the amount of tax payable by him in accordance with that paragraph.

(viii) (I) An authorisation shall be deemed to have been terminated by the Collector-General on the date that an authorised person—

    (A) ceases to trade (except for the purposes of disposing of the stocks and assets of his business), whether for reasons of insolvency or any other reason,

    (B) being a body corporate, goes into liquidation, whether voluntarily or not, or

    (C) ceases to be a taxable person or a registered person, dies or becomes bankrupt.

(II) A taxable person to whom this subparagraph relates shall, in relation to any taxable period (or part of a taxable period) comprised in the accounting period which was in operation in his case on the date to which clause (I) of this subparagraph relates, be deemed to have complied with paragraph (*a*) if he furnishes to the Collector-General the return specified in subparagraph (ii)(II) and at the same time remits to the said Collector-General the amount of tax payable by him for the purposes of that subparagraph as if he were an authorised person whose accounting period ended on the last day of the taxable period during which the termination occurred:

Provided that the personal representative of a person who was an authorised person shall be deemed to be the taxable person concerned.][17]

(Liquidators' and receivers' guidelines)

(*b*) A person who disposes of goods which pursuant to section 3(7) are deemed to be supplied by a taxable person in the course or furtherance of his business—

(i) shall within 9 days immediately after the tenth day of the month immediately following a taxable period furnish to the Collector-General a true and correct return, prepared in accordance with regulations, of the amount of tax which became due by such taxable person in relation to the disposal, and such other particulars as may be specified in regulations, and shall at the same time remit to the

Collector-General the amount of tax payable in respect of the taxable period in question,

(ii) shall send to the person whose goods were disposed of a statement containing such particulars as may be specified in regulations, and

(iii) shall treat the said amount of tax as a necessary disbursement out of the proceeds of the disposal.

(c) The owner of goods which pursuant to section 3(7) are deemed to be supplied by a taxable person in the course or furtherance of his business shall exclude from any return, which he is or, but for this subparagraph, would be, required to furnish under this Act, the tax payable in accordance with paragraph (b).

[(d) (i) A return required to be furnished by a taxable person under this subsection may be furnished by the taxable person or another person acting under the taxable person's authority for that purpose and a return purporting to be a return furnished by a person acting under a taxable person's authority shall be deemed to be a return furnished by the taxable person, unless the contrary is proved.

(ii) Where a return in accordance with paragraph (i) is furnished by a person acting under a taxable person's authority the provisions of any enactment relating to Value Added tax shall apply as if it had been furnished by the taxable person.][18]][19]

(Rules re: Tax due on new means of transport)

[(4) (a) Notwithstanding subsection (3), where—

(i) a person makes an intra-Community acquisition of a new means of transport, other than a vessel or aircraft, in respect of which he is not entitled to a deduction under section 12, then—

(I) the tax shall be payable at the time of payment of vehicle registration tax or, if no vehicle registration tax is payable, at the time of registration of the vehicle [or, if section 131 of the Finance Act, 1992, does not provide for registration of the vehicle, at a time not later than the time when the tax is due in accordance with subsection (1A)],[20]

(II) the person shall complete such form as may be provided by the Revenue Commissioners for the purpose of this subsection, and

(III) the provisions relating to recovery and collection of vehicle registration tax shall apply, with such exceptions and modifications (if any) as may be specified in regulations, to tax referred to in this subparagraph as if it were vehicle registration tax,

and

(ii) a person makes an intra-Community acquisition of a new means of transport which is a vessel or aircraft, in respect of which he is not entitled to a deduction under section 12, then—

    (I)   the tax shall be payable at a time and in a manner to be determined by regulations, and

    (II) the provisions relating to the recovery and collection of a duty of customs shall apply, with such exceptions and modifications (if any) as may be specified in regulations, to tax referred to in this subparagraph as if it were a duty of customs.

(Definitions)

(*b*) In this subsection—

"registration of the vehicle" means the registration of the vehicle in accordance with section 131 of the Finance Act, 1992;

"vehicle registration tax" means the tax referred to in section 132 of the Finance Act, 1992.][21]

(Treatment of excisable goods)

[(5) Notwithstanding the provisions of subsection (3), where the provisions of section 8(2B)(*b*) apply, the tax shall be payable at the time of payment of the duty of excise on the goods and the provisions relating to recovery and collection of that duty of excise shall apply, with such exceptions and modifications (if any) as may be specified in regulations, to tax referred to in this subsection as if it were that duty of excise.][22]

...[23]

[(6) Notwithstanding the provisions of subsection (3), in cases where the provisions of section 5A are applied, the tax shall be payable at the time the VAT return is required to be submitted in accordance with section 5A(6).][24]

Amendments

1   Deleted by FA 2005, s 106(*a*)(i) with effect from 25 March 2005 : previously "and".

2   Subs (1)(*bb*) inserted by FA 2005, s 106(*a*)(ii) with effect from 25 March 2005.

3   Substituted by VATAA 1978, s 30(2) with effect from 1 March 1979; previously "goods are delivered or the services are rendered".

4   Subs (1)(proviso) repealed by VATAA 1978, s 30(1) with effect from 1 March 1979.

5   Subs (1A) inserted by FA 1992, s 182(*a*) with effect from 1 January 1993.

6   Inserted by FA 1992, s 182(*b*) with effect from 1 January 1993.

7   Substituted by VATAA 1978, s 30(2) with effect from 1 March 1979; previously "delivery of the goods or the rendering of the service".

8   Substituted by VATAA 1978, s 30(2) with effect from 1 March 1979; previously "delivery or rendering".

9   Substituted by FA 2005, s 106(*b*) with effect from 25 March 2005: previously "paragraph (*a*) or (*b*)".

10   Inserted by FA 2002, s 106(*a*) with effect from 1 May 2001.

11   Subs (2A) inserted by FA 1997, s 107(*a*) as on and from 10 May 1997.

12   Subs (3)(*a*)(proviso) deleted by FA 107(*b*) as on and from 7 November 1996.

13   Substituted by FA 1995, s 134 as on and from 1 September 1996 (Finance Act 1995 (s 134(1)) (Commencement) Order 1996 (SI 231/96)).

14   Inserted by FA 2001, s 194(*a*) with effect from 6 April 2001.

15   Subs (3)(*aa*)(iv)(III) inserted by FA 2001, s 194(*b*) with effect from 6 April 2001.

[16] Substituted by FA 2002, s 138 and Sch 6 para 1(*d*) with effect from 25 March 2002; previously "twenty-one".

[17] Subs (3)(*aa*) inserted by FA 1989, s 58 with effect from 24 May 1989.

[18] Subs (3)(*d*) inserted by FA 2002, s 106(*b*) with effect from 25 March 2002.

[19] Subs (3) substituted by FA 1983, s 84 with effect from 1 September 1983.

[20] Inserted by FA 1999, s 135 with effect from 25 March 1999.

[21] Subs (4) substituted by FA 1993, s 92(*b*) with effect from 1 September 1993.

[22] Subs (5) substituted by FA 1993, s 92(*c*).

[23] Subs (6) deleted by FA 1997, s 107(*c*) as on and from 7 November 1996.

[24] Subs (6) inserted by FA 2003, s 123 with effect from 1 July 2003.

Cross-references

Alcohol products (subss (1)–(1A)): s 3B(2), (3).

Fraud, negligence; penalties: s 27(1).

Intra-Community acquisition of goods: s 3A.

Refund of tax (subs (6)(*a*)): s 20(1)(proviso).

Returns, particulars required, Revenue may prescribe: s 32(1)(*j*); details: VATR 1979, r 12.

Statement of intra-EU supplies: Value Added Tax (Statement of Intra-Community Supplies) Regulations 1993 (SI 54/93).

Time and manner in which tax payable (subs (4)), Revenue may prescribe: s 32(1)(*ae*).

Waiver of exemption: s 7(3).

Regulations

Subject	*Regulation*
Intrastat	European Communities (INTRASTAT) Regulations 1993 (SI 136/93)
Returns	Value Added Tax (Returns) Regulations 1993 (SI 247/93)
Returns	Value Added Tax (Returns) Regulations 1996 (SI 294/96)
Advance VAT	European Communities (Value Added Tax) Regulations 1993 (SI 345/93)
Electronic data exchange and storage	Value Added Tax (Electronic Data Exchange and Storage) (Amendment) Regulations 1998 (SI 489/98)
Returns	Value Added Tax (Returns) Regulations 2002 (SI 267/02).

Order

Value Added Tax (Threshold for Advance Payment) Order 1993 (SI 303/93)

Value Added Tax (Threshold for Advance Payment) Order 1994 (SI 342/94)

Revenue precedent

Issue: Request to account for VAT on start up lease of capital equipment.

Decision: On application VAT on new leases may be accounted for at commencement of lease and customer invoiced for tax in one lump sum. Concession subject to condition that tax will be accounted for on the "invoice" basis.

Issue: Breaches in time limit for issue of invoices.

Decision: Revenue prepared to accept minor breaches, i.e. invoices issued before the end of the calendar month following the month supplies were made, subject to certain conditions.

Issue: Lease documents held in escrow pending tenant fitting out unit to landlord's satisfaction/ specification.

Decision: The date of supply of taxable leases is the date the signed lease documents are released from escrow.

Revenue publications

A Letter of Expression of Doubt — Information Leaflet 2/02.

Flexible Annual Accounting: Tax Briefing, Issue 22.

Guide to Value Added Tax (Revenue Commissioners): Chapter 7.

Increase in VAT Rate — Credit Notes: Tax Briefing, Issue 51.

VAT Returns Made by Agents: Tax Briefing, Issue 47.

Definition

"business": s 1(1); "Collector-General": s 1(1); "goods": ss 1(1), 32; "new means of transport": s 1(1);"person": IA 2005, s 18(c); "registered person": s 1(1); "regulations": s 1(1); "supply": s 1(1); "tax": s 1(1); "taxable period": s 1(1); "taxable person": s 1(1), 8; "writing": IA 2005, Sch.

19A Statement of intra-Community supplies

(VIES Return)

[(1) Subject to subsections (2) and (3), a taxable person shall by the last day of a 22(6), the month immediately following the end of each calendar quarter, furnish to the (12) Revenue Commissioners a statement of his intra-Community supplies in that quarter prepared in accordance with, and containing such other particulars as may be specified in, regulations.

(Monthly statements (VIES))

(2) The Revenue Commissioners shall, on request, authorise a taxable person to furnish by the last day of each month a statement of his intra-Community supplies in the previous month prepared in accordance with, and containing such other particulars as may be specified in, regulations.

(Annual Statements (VIES))

(3) The Revenue Commissioners may, on request, authorise a taxable person, whose supplies do not exceed or are not likely to exceed, in a calendar year, an amount or amounts specified in regulations, to furnish by the last day of January following that calendar year a statement of such intra-Community supplies prepared in accordance with and containing such other particulars as may be specified in regulations.

(Nil Statement (VIES))

(4) Notwithstanding the provisions of subsections (1), (2) and (3), a taxable person who made no intra-Community supplies in the relevant period, but who was liable to furnish a statement in respect of a previous period, shall, unless authorised by the Revenue Commissioners, furnish to them within the relevant time limit a statement indicating that he made no such supplies in that period.

(Cancellation of authorisation)

(5) The Revenue Commissioners may, in accordance with regulations, cancel an authorisation under subsection (2) or (3).

(Definition)

[(6) In this section **"intra-Community supplies"** means supplies of goods to a person registered for value-added tax in another Member State.]¹]²

Amendments

¹   Subs (6) substituted by FA 2005, s 107 with effect from 25 March 2005.

²   Section 19A inserted by FA 1992, s 183 with effect from 1 January 1993.

Cross-references

Form of statement, Revenue may prescribe: s 32(1)(af).

Fraud, negligence; penalties: s 27(1).

Return, particulars required, Revenue may prescribe: s 32(1)(j); details: Value Added Tax (Statement of Intra- Community Supplies) Regulations 1993 (SI 54/93).

Regulations

Subject   *Regulation*

VIES returns   Value Added Tax (Statement of Intra-Community Supplies) Regulations 1993 (SI 54/93)

Revenue publications

Guide to Value Added Tax (Revenue Commissioners): Chapter 11.

Definition

"person": IA 2005, s 18(*c*); "a person registered for value added tax": s 1(1); "regulations": s 1(1), 32; "taxable person" ss 1(1), 8.

19B Letter of expression of doubt

[(1) *(a)*   Where a taxable person is in doubt as to the correct application of any enactment relating to Value Added tax (in this section referred to as "the law") to a transaction which could give rise to a liability to tax by that person or affect that person's liability to tax or entitlement to a deduction or refund of tax, then that taxable person may, at the same time as the taxable person furnishes to the Collector-General the return due in accordance with section 19 for the period in which the transaction occurred, lodge a letter of expression of doubt with the Revenue Commissioners at the office of the Revenue Commissioners which would normally deal with the examination of the records kept by that person in accordance with section 16, but this section shall only apply if that return is furnished within the time limits prescribed in section 19.

(*b*)   For the purposes of this section "letter of expression of doubt" means a communication received in legible form which—

(i)   sets out full details of the circumstances of the transaction and makes reference to the provisions of the law giving rise to the doubt,

(ii)   identifies the amount of tax in doubt in respect of the taxable period to which the expression of doubt relates,

(iii)   is accompanied by supporting documentation as relevant, and

(iv)   is clearly identified as a letter of expression of doubt for the purposes of this section,

and reference to an expression of doubt shall be construed accordingly.

(2) Subject to subsection (3), where a return and a letter of expression of doubt relating to a transaction are furnished by a taxable person to the Revenue Commissioners in accordance with this section, the provisions of section 21 shall not apply to any additional liability arising from a notification to that person by the Revenue Commissioners of the correct application of the law to the said transaction, on condition that such additional liability is accounted for and remitted to the Collector-General by the taxable person as if it were tax due for the taxable period in which the notification is issued.

(3) Subsection (2) does not apply where the Revenue Commissioners do not accept as genuine an expression of doubt in respect of the application of the law to a transaction, and an expression of doubt shall not be accepted as genuine in particular where the Revenue Commissioners—

(*a*) have issued general guidelines concerning the application of the law in similar circumstances,

(*b*) are of the opinion that the matter is otherwise sufficiently free from doubt as not to warrant an expression of doubt, or

(*c*) are of the opinion that the taxable person was acting with a view to the evasion or avoidance of tax.

(4) Where the Revenue Commissioners do not accept an expression of doubt as genuine they shall notify the taxable person accordingly, and the taxable person shall account for any tax, which was not correctly accounted for in the return referred to in subsection (1), as tax due for the taxable period in which the transaction occurred, and the provisions of section 21 shall apply accordingly.

(5) A taxable person who is aggrieved by a decision of the Revenue Commissioners that that person's expression of doubt is not genuine may, by giving notice in writing to the Revenue Commissioners within the period of twenty-one days after the notification of the said decision, require the matter to be referred to the Appeal Commissioners.

(6) A letter of expression of doubt shall be deemed not to have been made unless its receipt is acknowledged by the Revenue Commissioners and that acknowledgement forms part of the records kept by the taxable person for the purposes of section 16.

(7) (*a*) For the purposes of this section "taxable person" includes a person who is not a registered person and is in doubt as to whether he or she is a taxable person in respect of a transaction and in that case references to a return and records are to be construed as referring to a return that would be due under section 19 and records that would be kept for the purposes of section 16, if that person were in fact a taxable person.

(*b*) A person whose expression of doubt concerns whether he or she is a taxable person shall lodge that expression of doubt for the purposes of applying subsection

(2) not later than the nineteenth day of the month following the taxable period in which the transaction giving rise to the expression of doubt occurred.][1]

Amendments

[1]   Section 19B inserted by FA 2002, s 107 with effect from 25 March 2002.

---

20 Refund of tax

(Refund of excess input credit)

(1) [[Subject to subsections (1A) and (1B)][1], where][2] in relation to a return lodged under section 19 or a claim made in accordance with regulations, it is

shown to the satisfaction of the Revenue Commissioners that, as respects any taxable period, the amount of tax, if any, actually paid to the Collector-General in accordance with section 19 together with the amount of tax, if any, which qualified for deduction under section 12 exceeds the tax, if any, which would properly be payable if no deduction were made under the said section 12, they shall refund the amount of the excess less any sums previously refunded under this subsection or repaid under section 12 and may include in the amount refunded any interest which has been paid under section 21.][3]

...[4]

(Deferment of refunds)

[(1A) Where the Revenue Commissioners apply the provisions of section 8(8) to a number of persons they may defer repayment of all or part of any tax refundable under subsection (1) to any one or more of the said persons prior to the application of those provisions, where any one or more of the said persons have not furnished all returns and remitted all amounts of tax referred to in section 19(3) at the time of such application.][5]

(Requirement of security re: refunds)

[(1B) The Revenue Commissioners may, where it appears requisite to them to do so for the protection of the revenue, require as a condition for making a refund in accordance with subsection (1) the giving of security of such amount and in such manner and form as they may determine:

Provided that the amount of such security shall not, in any particular case, exceed the amount to be refunded.][6]

(Provision of radios for the blind)

(2) Notwithstanding anything in this Act, a refund of the tax paid in respect of radio broadcasting reception apparatus and parts thereof belonging to an institution or society may be made to the institution or society if, but only if—

    (*a*) in the opinion of the Revenue Commissioners, it has for its primary object the amelioration of the lot of blind persons, and

    (*b*) it shows, to the satisfaction of the Revenue Commissioners, that the goods in question are intended for the use of blind persons.

(Other refunds — Ministerial Order)

(3) [(*a*) The Minister may by order provide that a person who fulfils to the satisfaction of the Revenue Commissioners such conditions as may be specified in the order shall be entitled to be repaid so much, as is specified in the order, of any tax borne or paid by him as does not qualify for deduction under section 12.][7]

    (*b*) The Minister may by order amend or revoke an order under this subsection, including an order under this paragraph.

  [(*bb*) An order under this subsection may, if so expressed, have retrospective effect.][8]

    (*c*) An order under this subsection shall be laid before Dáil Éireann as soon as may be after it is made and, if a resolution annulling the order is passed by Dáil Éireann within the next twenty-one days on which Dáil

Éireann has sat after the order is laid before it, the order shall be annulled accordingly, but without prejudice to the validity of anything previously done thereunder.

(Time limits for application for refunds)

[(4) (*a*) In relation to any taxable period ending before the [1 May 2003][9], no refund shall, subject to paragraph (*b*), be made under this section or any other provision of this Act or regulations unless a claim for that refund is made within the period of [six years][10] from the end of the taxable period to which the claim relates.

  (*b*) In relation to any taxable period commencing on or after the 1[1 May 2003][11], and on or after the [1 January 2005][12], in relation to any other taxable period, no refund shall be made under this section or under any other provision of this Act or regulations unless a claim for that refund is made within the period of [four years][13] from the end of the taxable period to which that claim relates.][14]

(Unjust enrichment)

(Right to request refund)

[(5)[(*a*) Where, due to a mistaken assumption in the operation of the tax, whether that mistaken assumption was made by a taxable person, any other person or the Revenue Commissioners, a person

  (i) accounted, in a return furnished to the Revenue Commissioners, for an amount of tax for which that person was not properly accountable, or

  (ii) did not, because that person's supplies of goods and services were treated as exempted activities, furnish a return to the Revenue Commissioners and, therefore, did not receive a refund of an amount of tax in accordance with subsection (1), or

  (iii) did not deduct an amount of tax in respect of qualifying activities, as defined in section 12(1)(*b*), which that person was entitled to deduct,

  then, in respect of the total amount of tax referred to in subparagraphs (i), (ii) or (iii) (in this subsection referred to as the "overpaid amount") that person may claim a refund of the overpaid amount and the Revenue Commissioners shall, subject to the provisions of this subsection, refund to the claimant the overpaid amount unless that refund would result in the unjust enrichment of the claimant.][15]

(Unjust enrichment — a definition)

  (*b*) Unjust enrichment of the claimant for the purposes of this section means the refund to a claimant of an overpaid amount or any part of an overpaid amount in circumstances where the cost of such overpaid amount or part thereof was, for practical purposes, passed on by the claimant to other persons in the price charged by the claimant for goods or services supplied by the claimant.

(Claims for compensation)

    (*c*) Where, in relation to any claim under paragraph (*a*), the Revenue Commissioners have withheld an amount of the overpaid amount claimed under paragraph (*a*) as it would result in the unjust enrichment of the claimant the Revenue Commissioners shall, notwithstanding the provisions of paragraph (*a*), refund to the claimant out of the amount withheld, the amount quantified at paragraph (*d*)(iii) which would appropriately compensate the claimant for any loss of profits due to the mistaken assumption made in the operation of the tax, where the Revenue Commissioners are satisfied that the conditions in paragraph (*d*) have been met.

(Conditions required for compensation)

    (*d*) The conditions referred to in paragraph (*c*), are that the claimant must—

        (i) establish, based on an economic analysis which takes into account the price elasticity of demand of the goods or services supplied by the claimant, that the claimant's business has suffered [a loss of demand for those goods or services, for the period for which the claim is being made][16] due to the mistaken assumption made in the operation of the tax,

        (ii) quantify the extent of that loss,

        (iii) quantify the extent of the claimant's loss of profits due to that [loss of demand].[17]

(Refund of overpaid VAT)

    (*e*) Where, in relation to any claim under paragraph (*a*), the Revenue Commissioners have withheld an amount of the overpaid amount claimed under paragraph (*a*) as it would result in the unjust enrichment of the claimant the Revenue Commissioners shall, notwithstanding the provisions of paragraph (*a*), refund to the claimant that part of the withheld amount [together with any interest payable in accordance with section 21A][18] which the claimant has undertaken to repay to the persons to whom the cost of the overpaid amount was passed on where they are satisfied that the claimant has adequate arrangements in place to identify and repay those persons.

(Failure to reimburse customers)

    (*f*) Where a claimant receives a refund in accordance with paragraph (*e*) and fails to repay the persons concerned at the latest by the thirtieth day next following the payment by the Revenue Commissioners of that refund, then any amount not so repaid shall, for the purposes of this Act, be treated as if it were tax due by the claimant for the taxable period within which that day falls.][19]

(Methods of refund)

[(6) Where the Revenue Commissioners refund any amount due under subsection (1) or subsection (5), they may if they so determine refund any such amount directly into an account, specified by the person to whom the amount is due, in a financial institution.][20]

[(7) The Revenue Commissioners shall not refund any amount of tax except as provided for in this Act, or any order or regulation made under this Act.][21]

Amendments

[1]   Substituted by FA 1992, s 184(1)(*a*) with effect from 28 May 1992; previously "Subject to subsection (1A)".

[2]   Substituted by FA 1986, s 87 with effect from 27 May 1986; previously "Where".

[3]   Subs (1) substituted by FA 1981, s 45 with effect from 28 May 1981.

[4]   Subs (1)(proviso) deleted by FA 1997, s 108 as on and from 7 November 1996.

[5]   Subs (1A) substituted by FA 1991, s 83 with effect from 29 May 1991.

[6]   Subs (1B) inserted by FA 1992, s 184(1)(*b*) with effect from 28 May 1992.

[7]   Subs (3)(*a*) substituted by FA 1992, s 184(1)(*c*) with effect from 1 January 1993.

[8]   Subs (3)(*bb*) inserted by FA 2000, s 116(*a*) with effect from 23 March 2000.

[9]   Substituted by FA 2003, s 124(*a*)(i) with effect from 1 November 2003 (Finance Act 2003 (Commencement of Sections 124,125,129 and 130(*b*)) Order 2003); previously "the 1st day of May, 1998".

[10]   Substituted by FA 2003, s 124(*a*)(ii) with effect from 1 November 2003 (Finance Act 2003 (Commencement of Sections 124,125,129 and 130(*b*)) Order 2003), appoint; previously "ten years".

[11]   Substituted by FA 2003, s 124(*b*)(i) with effect from 1 November 2003 (Finance Act 2003 (Commencement of Sections 124,125,129 and 130(*b*)) Order 2003); previously "the 1st day of May, 1998".

[12]   Substituted by FA 2003, s 124(*b*)(ii) with effect from 1 November 2003 (Finance Act 2003 (Commencement of Sections 124,125,129 and 130(*b*)) Order 2003); previously "the 1st day of May, 1999,".

[13]   Substituted by FA 2003, s 124(*b*)(iii) with effect from 1 November 2003 (Finance Act 2003 (Commencement of Sections 124, 125, 129 and 130(*b*)) Order 2003), appoint; previously "six years".

[14]   Subs (4) substituted by FA 1998, s 114(*a*) with effect from 27 March 1998.

[15]   Subs (5)(*a*) substituted by FA 2000, s 116(*b*) with effect from 23 March 2000.

[16]   Substituted by FA 2000, s 116(*c*) with effect from 23 March 2000; previously "a loss of turnover".

[17]   Substituted by FA 2000, s 116(*d*) with effect from 23 March 2000; previously "loss of turnover".

[18]   Inserted by FA 2003, s 124(*c*) with effect from 1 November 2003 (Finance Act 2003 (Commencement of Sections 124,125,129 and 130(*b*)) Order 2003).

[19]   Subs (5) substituted by FA 1998, s 114(*b*) with effect from 27 March 1998.

[20]   Subs (6) inserted by FA 1995, s 135 with effect from 2 June 1995.

[21]   Subs (7) inserted by FA 2003, s 124(*d*) with effect from 1 November 2003 (Finance Act 2003 (Commencement of Sections 124,125,129 and 130(*b*)) Order 2003).

Cross-references

Existing orders under this section remain valid: FA 1992, s 184(2).

Fraud, negligence; penalties: s 27(1).

Revenue power to make regulations: s 32(1)(*m*).

Regulations

Subject	Regulation
Disabled driver vehicles	Disabled Drivers and Disabled Passengers (Tax Concessions) Regulations 1994 (SI 353/94)
Fishermen, boats	Value Added Tax Regulations 1979 (SI 63/79), r 29

Refund procedures   Value Added Tax Regulations 1979 (SI 63/79), r 17

Sea rescue groups (boats and boat   Value Added Tax (Refund of Tax)(No 18) Order 1985 (SI 192/85)
houses)

Touring coaches   Value Added Tax (Refund of Tax)(No 28) Order 1996
                                     (SI 98/96)

Offset of Repayments   Taxes (Offset of Repayments) Regulations 2002 (SI 471/02).

Orders

Subject   *Order*

Disabled persons' aids   Value Added Tax (Refund of Tax)(No 15) Order 1981 (SI 428/81)

EuroControl (purchases by)   Value Added Tax (Refund of Tax)(No 7) Order 1974 (SI 290/74)

European Space Agency   Value Added Tax (Refund of Tax) (No 11) Order 1980
(purchases by)   (SI 239/80)

Farm buildings and drainage   Value Added Tax (Refund of Tax)(No 25) Order 1993
(unregistered farmers)   (SI 266/ 1993)

Marine diesel   Value Added Tax (Refund of Tax)(No 16) Order 1983
                                     (SI 234/ 1983)

Hospital equipment (bought   Value Added Tax (Refund of Tax)(No 23) Order 1992
through voluntary donations)   (SI 58/92)

Medical research equipment   Value Added Tax (Refund of Tax)(No 27) Order 1995
                                     (SI 38/95)

Mobile home (to be used as   Value Added Tax (Refund of Tax)(No 12) Order 1980
residence)   (SI 262/80)

Philanthropic organisations   Value Added Tax (Refund of Tax)(No 21) Order 1987
(exported goods)   (SI 308/87)

Case law

Subject	*Case*	*Case reference*
A disabled plaintiff who obtained a VAT refund on a specially adapted car was refused an excise duty refund on the basis that he was not wholly without the use of his legs (as required by regulations). His claim (by judicial review) that he had a "legitimate expectation" to a refund was refused as he should have known he did not meet the requirements	*Wiley v Revenue Commissioners*	(IV) ITR (170)
Teacakes sold as standard rated biscuits rather than zero rate cakes. Claimed for £3.5m in tax wrongly paid. Tribunal agreed C & E that most of tax cost passed to customer so to refund more than 10% would be unjust enrichment:	*Marks & Spencers plc v The Commissioners C & E*	January 1997, Tribunal 14692
Boys socks sold at standard rate rather than zero rate. Claimed repayment of full amount of overpaid VAT. C & E claimed that payment of more than 10% of the amount would unjustly enrich M & S. Tribunal found for M & S as the overpaid VAT had not been passed on to the customers	*Marks & Spencers plc v The Commissioners C & E*	January 1997, Tribunal 14693

Repayment of dock dues unjust enrichment	*Société Comateb & Others v Director Generale des Douanes et Droits Indirects*	14 January 1997, C–192 to C–218/95
VAT Repayments — Time Limits	*Marks & Spencer plc v Commissioners of Customs & Excise*	11 July 2002, C–62/00

Revenue precedent

Issue: Refund of VAT on respiration monitors.
Decision: In strict terms, Order No 15 of 1981 provides for repayment of tax borne or paid on supply or importation of goods. Case in question referred to services.
Issue: Agent acting on behalf of Community Institution.
Decision: Agent allowed remission of VAT subject to limit that would be allowed if the Community Institution had conducted transaction.

Revenue publications

Repayments to unregistered persons: Statement of Practice VAT 2/94 (Replaced by Information Leaflet No 18/01).
Refund direct to bank accounts: Tax Briefing Issue 45.
Revenue VAT Guide: Chapter 7

Definition

"Collector-General": s 1(1); "Dáil Éireann": IA 2005, Sch; "goods": s 1(1); "the Minister": s 1(1); "person": IA 2005, s 18(c); "regulations": ss 1(1), 32; "supply": s 1(1); "tax": s 1(1); "taxable period": s 1(1).

21 Interest

(Interest on late payment of tax due)

[(1) *(a)* Where any amount of tax becomes payable under section 19(3) and is not paid, simple interest on the amount shall be paid by the taxable person, and such interest shall be calculated from the date on which the amount became payable and at a rate of 0.0322 per cent for each day or part of a day during which the amount remains unpaid.

(b) Where an amount of tax is refunded to a person and where—

(i) no amount of tax was properly refundable to that person under section 20(1), or

(ii) the amount of tax refunded is greater than the amount properly refundable to that person under section 20(1),

simple interest shall be paid by that person on any amount of tax refunded to that person which was not properly refundable to that person under section 20(1), from the date the refund was made, at the rate of 0.0322 per cent for each day or part of a day during which the person does not correctly account for any such amount refunded which was not properly refundable.][1]

[(1A) Where the amount of the balance of tax remaining to be paid in accordance with section 19(3)(*aa*)(ii)(II) by an authorised person referred to in section 19(3)(*aa*)(iv)(III) (in this subsection referred to as the **"balance"**) represents more than 20 per cent of the tax which the authorised person became accountable for in respect of his accounting period, then, for the purposes of this subsection, that balance shall be deemed to be payable on a day (in this subsection referred to as the **"accrual day"**) which is 6 months prior to the final day for the furnishing of a return in accordance with section 19(3)(*aa*)(ii)(II) and simple interest in accordance with this section shall apply from that accrual day, however, where an authorised person can demonstrate to the satisfaction of the Collector-General that the amount of interest payable on the balance, in accordance with this subsection, is greater than the sum of the amounts of interest which would have been payable in accordance with this section if—

(*a*) the authorised person was not so authorised,

(*b*) the person had submitted a return in accordance with section 19(3)(*a*) for each taxable period comprising the accounting period, and

(*c*) the amounts which were paid by direct debit during a taxable period are deemed to have been paid on the due date for submission of that return for that taxable period,

then that sum of the amounts of interest is payable.][2]

(Interest on estimated tax due)

(2) Subsection (1) shall apply—

(*a*) to tax recoverable by virtue of a notice under section 22 as if the tax were tax which the person was liable to pay for the respective taxable period or periods comprised in the notice, and

[(*b*) to tax recoverable by virtue of a notice under section 23 as if (whether a notice of appeal under that section is received or not) the tax were tax which the person was liable to pay for the taxable period or, as the case may be, the later or latest taxable period included in the period comprised in the notice][3].

Amendments

[1] Subs (1) substituted by FA 2002, s 108 with effect from 1 September 2002.

[2] Subs (1A) substituted by FA 2001, s 195 with effect from 6 April 2001.

[3] Subs (2)(*b*) substituted by FA 1976, s 56 with effect from 27 May 1976.

Cross-references

Revenue may make regulations allowing remission of small amounts of interest: s 32(1)(*o*); regulations: VATR 1979, r 18.

Regulations

Subject	Regulation
Remission of small amount of tax/interest	Value Added Tax Regulations 1979 (SI 63/79), r 18

Revenue publications

Guide to Value Added Tax (Revenue Commissioners): Chapter 7.

Definition

"person": IA 2005, s 18(*c*); "tax": s 1(1); "taxable period": s 1(1); "taxable person": ss 1(1), 8.

21A Interest on refunds of tax

[(1) For the purposes of this section—

"claimant" means a person who submits a valid claim for a refundable amount;

determination against the claim, the estimated tax specified in the notice shall be recoverable in the same manner and by the like proceedings as if the person had furnished, within the prescribed period, a true and correct return, in accordance with regulations, for the [period]² to which the estimate relates, showing as due by him such estimated tax,

(*c*) if at any time after the service of the notice the person furnishes a return, in accordance with regulations, in respect of the [period]² specified in the notice and pays tax in accordance with the return, together with any interest and costs which may have been incurred in connection with the default, the notice shall, subject to paragraph (*d*), stand discharged and any excess of tax which may have been paid shall be repaid,

(*d*) where action for the recovery of tax specified in a notice under subsection (1), being action by way of the institution of proceedings in any court or the issue of a certificate under section 485 of the Income Tax Act 1967,⁵ has been taken paragraph (*c*) shall not, unless the Revenue Commissioners otherwise direct, apply in relation to that notice until the said action has been completed.

(Estimates for more than one period)

(3) A notice given by the Revenue Commissioners under subsection (1) may extend to two or more taxable periods.

Amendments

1   Substituted by VATAA 1978, s 30(2) with effect from 1 March 1979; previously "an accountable person".

2   Substituted by FA 2000, s 117 with effect from 23 March 2000; previously "taxable period".

3   Subs (1)(proviso) substituted by FA 2003, s 126 with effect from 28 March 2003.

4   Substituted by FA 2001, s 196 with effect from 6 April 2001; previously "twenty-one".

5   "section 485 of the Income Tax Act 1997" should be read as "section 962 of the Taxes Consolidation Act 1997".

Cross-references

Appeal: s 25(2)(*k*).

Estimates, Revenue may accept: s 32(1)(*r*); acceptance: VATR 1979, r 13; Revenue may make: s 32(1)(*u*); regulations: Value Added Tax (Estimation and Assessment of Tax Due) Regulations 1992 (SI 277/92).

Service of notices, Revenue may make regulations: s 32(1)(*q*).

Time limits for estimates: s 30(4)–(5).

Regulations

Subject	Regulation
Estimates	Value Added Tax (Estimation and Assessment of Tax Due) Regulations 1992 (SI 277/92)
Estimation of Tax Payable	Value Added Tax (Estimation of Tax Payable and Assessment of Tax Payable or Refundable) Regulations 2000 (SI 295/2000).

Revenue publications

Guide to Value Added Tax (Revenue Commissioners): Chapter 7.

Definition

"Appeal Commissioners": s 1(1); "person": IA 2005, s 18(*c*); "regulations": ss 1(1), 32; "tax": s 1(1); "taxable period": ss 1(1), 8; "taxable person": s 1(1); "writing": IA 2005, Sch.

22A Generation of estimates and assessments by electronic, photographic or other process

[For the purposes of this Act and regulations, where an officer of the Revenue Commissioners nominated in accordance with regulations for the purposes of section 22 or an inspector of taxes or an officer of the Revenue Commissioners authorised for the purposes of section 23, or any other officer of the Revenue Commissioners acting with the knowledge of such nominated officer or such inspector or such authorised officer causes to issue, manually or by any electronic, photographic or other process, a notice of estimation or assessment of tax bearing the name of such nominated officer or such inspector or such authorised officer, that estimate or assessment to which the notice of estimation or assessment of tax relates shall be deemed—

(*a*) in the case of an estimate made under section 22, to have been made by such nominated officer, and

(*b*) in the case of an assessment made under section 23, to have been made by such inspector or such authorised officer, as the case may be, to the best of such inspector's or such authorised officer's opinion.][1]

Amendments

1   Section 22A inserted by FA 1999, s 136 with effect from 25 March 1999.

23 Assessment of tax due for any period

(Authorisation to assess tax due)

[(1) Where, in relation to any period ...,[1] [the inspector of taxes, or such other officer as the Revenue Commissioners may authorise to exercise the powers conferred by this section (hereafter referred to in this section as **"other officer"**), has reason to believe][2] that an amount of tax is due and payable to [the Revenue Commissioners][3] by a person in any of the following circumstances:

(*a*) the total amount of tax payable by the person was greater than the total amount of tax (if any) paid by him,

(*b*) the total amount of tax refunded to the person in accordance with section 20(1) was greater than the amount (if any) properly refundable to him, or

(*c*) an amount of tax is payable by the person and a refund under section 20(1) has been made to the person,

then, without prejudice to any other action which may be taken, [the inspector or other officer may][4], in accordance with regulations but subject to section 30, make an [assessment][5] in one sum of the total amount of tax which in [his][6] opinion should have been paid or the total amount of tax (including a nil amount) which in accordance with section 20(1) should have been refunded, as the case may be, in respect of ...[7] such period and may serve a notice on the person specifying—

(i)   the total amount of tax so [assessed][8],

(ii) the total amount of tax (if any) paid by the person or refunded to the person in relation to the said period, and

(iii) the total amount so due and payable as aforesaid (referred to subsequently in this section as **"the amount due"**).

(Right of appeal)

(2) Where notice is served on a person under subsection (1), the following provisions shall apply:

(*a*) the person may, if he claims that the amount due is excessive, on giving notice to the Revenue Commissioners within the period of twenty-one days from the date of the service of the notice, appeal to the Appeal Commissioners, and

(*b*) on the expiration of the said period, if no notice of appeal is received or, if notice of appeal is received, on determination of the appeal by agreement or otherwise, the amount due, or the amended amount due as determined in relation to the appeal, shall become due and payable as if the tax were tax which the person was liable to pay for the taxable period during which the period of fourteen days from the date of the service of the notice under subsection (1) expired or the appeal was determined by agreement or otherwise, whichever taxable period is the later.

(Payment due pending determination of appeal)

[(3) Where a person appeals an assessment under subsection (1), within the time limits provided for in subsection (2), he shall pay to the Revenue Commissioners the amount which he believes to be due, and if—

(*a*) the amount paid is greater than **80 per cent** of the amount of the tax found to be due on the determination of the appeal, and

(*b*) the balance of the amount found to be due on the determination of the appeal is paid within one month of the date of such determination, interest in accordance with section 21 shall not be chargeable from the date of raising of the assessment.][9][10]

Amendments

1   Deleted by FA 2000, s 118(*a*) with effect from 23 March 2000; previously "consisting of one taxable period or of two or more consecutive taxable periods".

2   Substituted by FA 1985, s 47 with effect from 30 May 1985; previously "Revenue Commissioners have reason to believe".

3   Substituted by FA 1985, s 47 with effect from 30 May 1985; previously "them".

4   Substituted by FA 1985, s 47 with effect from 30 May 1985; previously "they may".

5   Substituted by FA 1992, s 185(*a*)(i) with effect from 28 May 1992; previously "estimate".

6   Substituted by FA 1985, s 47 with effect from 30 May 1985; previously "their".

7   Deleted by FA 2000, s 118(*b*) with effect from 23 March 2000; previously "the taxable period or periods comprised in".

8   Substituted by FA 1992, s 185(*a*)(ii) with effect from 28 May 1992; previously "estimated".

9   Subs (3) inserted by FA 1992, s 185(*b*) with effect from 28 May 1992.

10   Section 23 substituted by VATAA 1978, s 17 with effect from 1 March 1979.

Cross-references

Advance payment of tax (year end): s 19(6)(*c*)(proviso).

Appeal: s 25(2)(*k*).

Estimates, Revenue may accept: s 32(1)(*r*); acceptance: VATR 1979, r 13; Revenue may make: s 32(1)(*u*); regulations: Value Added Tax (Estimation and Assessment of Tax Due) Regulations 1992 (SI 277/92).

Service of notices, Revenue may make regulations: s 32(1)(*g*).

Time limits for estimates: s 30(4)–(5).

Regulations

Subject	*Regulation*
Estimates	Value Added Tax (Estimation and Assessment of Tax Due) Regulations 1992 (SI 277/92)
Estimation of Tax Payable	Value Added Tax (Estimation of Tax Payable and Assessment of Tax Payable or Refundable) Regulations 2000 (SI 295/2000).

Revenue publications

Guide to Value Added Tax (Revenue Commissioners): Chapter 7.

Definition

"Appeal Commissioners": s 1(1); "inspector of taxes": s 1(1); "person": IA 2005, s 18(*c*); "regulations": ss 1(1), 32; "tax": s 1(1); "taxable period": s 1(1).

23A Security to be given by certain taxable persons

(Requirement of security)

[(1) The Revenue Commissioners may, where it appears requisite to them to do so for the protection of the revenue, require a taxable person, as a condition of his supplying goods or services under a taxable supply, to give security, or further security, of such amount and in such manner and form as they may determine, for the payment of any tax which is, or may become, due from him from the date of service on him of a notice in writing to that effect.

(Right of appeal)

(2) Where notice is served on a person in accordance with subsection (1) the person may, on giving notice to the Revenue Commissioners within the period of twenty-one days from the date of the service of the notice, appeal the requirement of giving any security under subsection (1) to the Appeal Commissioners.][1]

Amendments

[1]   Section 23A inserted by FA 1992, s 186 with effect from 28 May 1992.

Cross-references

Appeal: s 25(2)(*k*).

Non compliance, penalty. s 26(3B).

Service of notices, Revenue may make regulations: s 32(1)(*g*).

Definition

"Appeal Commissioners": s 1(1); "person": IA 2005, s 18(*c*); "supply": s 1(1); "tax": s 1(1); "taxable person": ss 1(1), 8: "writing": 1A 2005, Sch.

24 Recovery of tax

(Application of income tax law)

(1) [(*a*) Without prejudice to any other mode of recovery, the provisions of any enactment relating to the recovery of income tax and the provisions of any rule of court so relating shall, subject to any necessary modifications, apply to the recovery of any tax payable in accordance with this Act and the regulations thereunder as they apply in relation to the recovery of income tax.][1]

(*b*) In particular and without prejudice to the generality of paragraph (*a*), that paragraph applies the provisions of [sections 962, 963, 964(1), 966, 967 and 998 of the Taxes Consolidation Act, 1997].[2]

...[3]

(Certificates of tax due and payable)

(2) In proceedings instituted under this section or any regulations for the recovery of any amount of tax—

(*a*) a certificate signed by an officer of the Revenue Commissioners which certifies that a stated amount of tax is due and payable by the defendant shall be evidence, until the contrary is proved, that that amount is so due and payable, and

(*b*) a certificate certifying as aforesaid and purporting to be signed by an officer of the Revenue Commissioners may be tendered in evidence without proof and shall be deemed, until the contrary is proved, to have been signed by an officer of the Revenue Commissioners.

(Recovery of interest due)

(3) Any reference in the foregoing subsections to an amount of tax includes a reference to interest payable in the case in question under section 21.

(Rules of Court)

(4) Subject to this section, the rules of the court concerned for the time being applicable to civil proceedings shall apply to proceedings by virtue of this section or any regulation under this Act.

(Court Officers Act)

(5) Where an order which was made before the passing of this Act under section 12 of the Court Officers Act, 1945, contains a reference to levy under a certificate issued under [under section 962 of the Taxes Consolidation Act, 1997],[4] that reference shall be construed as including a reference to levy under a certificate issued under the said [section 962][5] as extended by this section.

Amendments

[1] Subs (1)(*a*) substituted by VATA 1972, s 108(1)(*a*) with effect from 25 March 2005.

[2] Substituted by TCA 1997, s 1100 and Sch 31; previously "sections 480, 485, 486, 487, 488 and 491 of the Income Tax Act, 1967".

[3] Subs (1)(*c*) deleted by VATA 1972, s 108(1)(*b*) with effect from 25 March 2005, regulations made under VATA 1972 and to which VATA 1972, s 24(1)(*c*) related shall continue in force and may be amended or revoked accordingly.

[4] Substituted by TCA 1997, s 1100 and Sch 31; previously "section 485 of the Income Tax Act, 1967".

[5] Substituted by TCA 1997, s 1100 and Sch 31; previously "section 485".

Regulations

Subject	Regulation
Mutual assistance	European Communities (Value Added Tax) (Mutual Assistance as Regards the Recovery of Claims) Regulations 1980 (SI 406/80)
Mutual assistance	European Communities (Mutual Assistance in the Field of Value Added Tax) Regulations 1980 (SI 407/80)
Application of income tax provision	Value Added Tax Regulations 1979 (SI 63/79), r 15

Definition

"person": IA 2005, s 18(*c*); "regulations": ss 1(1), 32; "rule of court": IA 2005, Sch; "tax": s 1(1).

25 Appeals

(VAT matters which can be appealed)

(1) Any person aggrieved by a determination of the Revenue Commissioners in relation to—

    (*a*) a liability to tax under subsection (5) or (6) of section 17,

  [(*aa*) the treatment of one or more persons as a single taxable person in accordance with section 8(8),][1]

    ...[2]

  [(*ac*) a determination under section 8(3E),][3]

  [(*ad*) the refusal of an application for authorisation to operate as a VAT refunding agent (within the meaning assigned by section 13(3B)) or the cancellation of any such authorisation,][4]

  [(*ae*) the treatment of a person who allows supplies to be made on land owned, occupied or controlled by that person, as jointly and severally liable with another person, in accordance with section 8(2)(*d*),

   (*af*) the application of section 4(3A)(*c*),][5]

   (*b*) a charge of tax in accordance with regulations, or

   (*c*) a claim for repayment of tax,

against which an appeal to the Appeal Commissioners is not otherwise provided for under this Act may, on giving notice in writing to the Revenue Commissioners within twenty-one days after the notification to the person aggrieved of the determination, appeal to the Appeal Commissioners.

(Decisions on taxable status)

[(1A) Where a person is aggrieved by a decision of the Revenue Commissioners that such person is not a taxable person then such person may, on giving notice in writing to the Revenue Commissioners within twenty-one days after the notification of that decision to such person, appeal to the Appeal Commissioners.][6]

(Application of income tax law)

(2) The provisions of the Income Tax Acts relating to—

(Guidelines)

    (*a*) the appointment of times and places for the hearing of appeals;

(*b*) the giving of notice to each person who has given notice of appeal of the time and place appointed for the hearing of his appeal;

(*c*) the determination of an appeal by agreement between the appellant and an inspector of taxes or other officer appointed by the Revenue Commissioners in that behalf;

(*d*) the determination of an appeal by the appellant giving notice of his intention not to proceed with the appeal;

[(*dd*) the refusal of an application for an appeal hearing;][7]

(*e*) the hearing and determination of an appeal by the Appeal Commissioners, including the hearing and determination of an appeal by one Appeal Commissioner;

[(*ee*) the publication of reports of determinations of the Appeal Commissioners;][8]

[(*f*) the determination of an appeal through the failure of a person who has given notice of appeal to attend before the Appeal Commissioners at the time and place appointed;

(*ff*) the refusal of an application for the adjournment of any proceedings in relation to an appeal, and the dismissing of an appeal, by the Appeal Commissioners;][9]

(*g*) the extension of the time for giving notice of appeal, and the readmission of appeals by the Appeal Commissioners;

(*h*) the rehearing of an appeal by a judge of the Circuit Court and the statement of a case for the opinion of the High Court on a point of law;

(*i*) the payment of tax in accordance with the determination of the Appeal Commissioners notwithstanding that an appeal is required to be reheard by a judge of the Circuit Court or that a case for the opinion of the High Court on a point of law has been required to be stated or is pending;

(*j*) the payment of tax which is agreed not to be in dispute in relation to an appeal; and

(*k*) the procedures for appeal;

[shall, subject to the modifications set out hereunder and to other necessary modifications, apply to a claim under section 22 or an appeal under [section 11(1B), 23 or 23A][10] or this section as if the claim or appeal were an appeal against an assessment to income tax:

(i) a reference to a year of assessment shall include a reference to the [periods][11] concerned,

(ii) a reference to a return of income shall include a reference to a return required to be made under section 19,

(iii) a reference to interest shall include a reference to interest payable under section 21][12].

Amendments

1   Subs (1)(*aa*) inserted by FA 1991, s 84 with effect from 29 May 1991.
2   Subs (1)(*ab*) deleted by FA 2002, s 109(*a*) with effect from 25 March 2002.
3   Subs (1)(*ac*) inserted by FA 1995, s 137(*a*) with 1 January 1996.
4   Subs (1)(*ad*) inserted by FA 1997, s 109 as on and from 1 July 1997.
5   Subs (1)(*ae*) substituted and subs (1)(*af*) inserted by FA 2002, s 109(*b*) with effect from 25 March 2002.
6   Subs (1A) inserted by FA 1995, s 137(*b*) with effect from 2 June 1995.
7   Subs (2)(*dd*) inserted by FA 1995, s 137(*c*) with effect from 2 June 1995.
8   Subs (2)(*ee*) inserted by FA 1998, s 134(2) with effect from 27 March 1998.
9   Subs (2)(*f*)–(*ff*) substituted by FA 1983, s 85 with effect from 8 June 1983.
10 Substituted by FA 1992, s 187(*b*) with effect from 28 May 1992; previously "section 11(1B) or 23".
11 Substituted by FA 2000, s 119 with effect from 23 March 2000; previously "taxable periods".
12 Substituted by FA 1983, s 85 with effect from 8 June 1983.

Revenue publications

Guide to Value Added Tax (Revenue Commissioners): Chapter 7.

Definition

"Appeal Commissioner": s 1(1); "Circuit Court": IA 2005, Sch; "High Court": IA 2005, Sch; "inspector of taxes": s 1(1); "person": IA 2005, s 18(*c*); "regulations": ss 1(1), 32; "tax": s 1(1); "taxable period": s 1(1); "writing": IA 2005, Sch; "year of assessment": TCA 1997, ss 2(1), 5(1).

26 Penalties generally

(Non-compliance with Act)

[(1) A person who does not comply with section 9(2), 11(7), 12A, 16, 17, ...[1] [, 19 or 19A][2] or any provision of regulations in regard to any matter to which the foregoing sections relate shall be liable to a penalty of [€1,520][3].][4]

(Unauthorised charging of tax)

(2) A person who is not a registered person and who, on or after the specified day, ...[5] issues an invoice in which an amount of tax is stated shall be liable to a penalty of [€950][6].

(Unauthorised charging of flat-rate tax)

[(2A) Any person who, otherwise than under and in accordance with section 12A or 17(4)(*a*), issues an invoice in which an amount of flat-rate addition is stated shall be liable to a penalty of [€950][7].][8]

(Body of persons)

(3) Where a person mentioned in subsection (1) or (2) [or (2A)][9] is a body of persons, the secretary shall be liable to a separate penalty of [€950][10].

(Obstruction of an officer)

[(3A) A person who does not comply with [subsection (3) of section 18 or with a requirement of an authorised officer under that section][11] shall be liable to a penalty of [€1,265][12].][13]

[(3AA) Where a person is authorised in accordance with section 10(9)(*c*) to inspect any immovable goods for the purpose of reporting to the Revenue Commissioners the open market price of an interest in those goods and the person having custody or possession of those goods prevents such inspection or obstructs the person so authorised in the performance of his or her functions in relation to the inspection, the person so having custody or possession shall be liable to a penalty of €1,265.]¹⁴

(Supplies without security (Revenue Commissioners))

[(3B) A person who supplies taxable goods or services in contravention of the requirement of security specified in section 23A shall be liable to a penalty of [€1,520]¹⁵ in respect of each such supply.]¹⁶

(Proceedings for recovery of penalties)

(4) All penalties under this section may, without prejudice to any other method of recovery, be proceeded for and recovered summarily in the same manner as in summary proceedings for recovery of any penalty under any Act relating to the excise, and, notwithstanding section 10(4) of the Petty Sessions (Ireland) Act, 1851, summary proceedings under this section may be instituted within three years from the date of the incurring of the penalty.

(5) ...¹⁷.

(Certificates issued by Revenue Commissioner)

(6) In proceedings for recovery of a penalty under this section—

(*a*) a certificate signed by an officer of the Revenue Commissioners which certifies that he has inspected the relevant records of the Revenue Commissioners and that it appears from them that, during a stated period, stated particulars or stated returns were not furnished by the defendant shall be evidence until the contrary is proved that the defendant did not, during that period, furnish the particulars or return,

(*b*) a certificate signed by an officer of the Revenue Commissioners which certifies that he has inspected the relevant records of the Revenue Commissioners and that it appears from them that a stated document was duly sent to the defendant on a stated day shall be evidence until the contrary is proved that that person received that document in the ordinary course,

(*c*) a certificate signed by an officer of the Revenue Commissioners which certifies that he has inspected the relevant records of the Revenue Commissioners and that it appears from them that a stated notice was not issued by them to the defendant shall be evidence until the contrary is proved that the defendant did not receive the notice in question,

[(*d*) a certificate signed by an officer of the Revenue Commissioners which certifies that he has inspected the relevant records of the Revenue Commissioners and that it appears from them that, during a stated period, the defendant was [a taxable person]¹⁸ or was a registered person or was not a registered person shall be evidence until the contrary is proved that, during that period, the defendant was [a taxable person]¹⁸ or was a registered person or was not a registered person, as the case may be,

(*e*) a certificate certifying as provided for in paragraph (*a*), (*b*), (*c*) or (*d*) and purporting to be signed by an officer of the Revenue

Commissioners may be tendered in evidence without proof and shall be deemed, until the contrary is proved, to have been signed by an officer of the Revenue Commissioners][19].

(Rules of Court)

(7) Subject to this section, the rules of the court concerned for the time being applicable to civil proceedings shall apply to proceedings pursuant to this section.

Amendments

[1] Words "18(2)" deleted by FA 1984, s 90 with effect from 23 May 1984.

[2] Substituted by FA 1992, s 188(*a*)(i) with effect from 1 January 1993; previously "or 19".

[3] Substituted by FA 2001, s 240 and Sch 5 Part 4 with effect from 1 January 2002; previously "£1,200"; previously "£800" (FA 1992, s 188(*a*)(ii): 28 May 19).

[4] Subs (1) substituted by FA 1982, s 86 with effect from 1 September 1982.

[5] Words "otherwise than under and in accordance with section 13," deleted by FA 1976, s 81 with effect from 1 March 1976.

[6] Substituted by FA 2001, s 240 and Sch 5 Part 4 with effect from 1 January 2002; previously "£750"; previously "£500" (FA 1992, s 188((*b*): 28 May 1992).

[7] Substituted by FA 2001, s 240 and Sch 5 Part 4 with effect from 1 January 2002; previously "£750"; previously "£500" (FA 1992, s 188(*c*): 28 May 1992).

[8] Subs (2A) inserted by VATAA 1978, s 18 with effect from 1 March 1979.

[9] Inserted by VATAA 1978, s 18 with effect from 1 March 1979.

[10] Substituted by FA 2001, s 240 and Sch 5 Part 4 with effect from 1 January 2002; previously "£750"; previously "£500" (FA 1992, s 188(*d*): 28 May 1992).

[11] Substituted by FA 1984, s 90 with effect from 23 May 1984; previously "section 18(3)".

[12] Substituted by FA 2001, s 240 and Sch 5 Part 4 with effect from 1 January 2002; previously "£1,265"; previously "£800" (FA 1992, s 188(*e*): 28 May 19).

[13] Subs (3A) inserted by FA 1973, s 83 with effect from 3 September 1973.

[14] Subs (3AA) inserted by FA 2005, s 109 with effect from 25 March 2005.

[15] Substituted by FA 2001, s 240 and Sch 5 Part 4 with effect from 1 January 2002; previously "£1,200".

[16] Subs (3B) inserted by FA 1992, s 188(*f*) with effect from 28 May 1992.

[17] Subs (5) deleted by FA 1982, s 86 with effect from 1 September 1982.

[18] Substituted by VATAA 1978, s 30(2) with effect from 1 March 1979; previously "an accountable person".

[19] Subs (6)(*d*)–(*e*) substituted by FA 1976, s 57 with effect from 27 May 1976.

Cross-references

Fraud, negligence; penalties: s 27(1).

Revenue offences: FA 1983, s 94; tax defaulters, publication of names: FA 1983, s 23.

Time limits: s 30(1).

Revenue publications

Revenue VAT Guide: Chapter 7.

Definition

"body of persons": s 1(1); "flat-rate addition": ss 1(1, 12A; "person": IA 2005, s 18(*c*); "registered person": s 1(1); "regulations": ss 1(1), 32; "rule of court": IA 2005, Sch; "secretary": s 1(1); "the specified day": s 1(1); "tax": s 1(1); "taxable person": ss 1(1), 8.

---

27 Fraudulent returns, etc

(Penalties for fraud and negligence)

(1) Where a person fraudulently or negligently, for the purposes of this Act or of regulations, produces, furnishes, gives, sends or otherwise makes use of, any incorrect return, invoice, [registration number, monthly control statement, claim,][1] credit note, debit note, receipt, account, voucher, bank statement, estimate, statement, information, book, document, record or declaration, he shall, subject to subsection (2), be liable to a penalty of—

　　(*a*)　[€125][2], and

　　[(*b*)　the amount ...[3] of the difference between—

　　　　(i)　the amount of tax properly payable by, or refundable to, such person if the said return, invoice, registration number, monthly control statement, claim, credit note, debit note, receipt, account, voucher, bank statement, estimate, statement, information, book, document, record or declaration had been correct, and

　　　　(ii)　the amount of tax (if any) paid, or claimed by way of refund.][4]

[(1A) Where a person fraudulently or negligently fails to comply with a requirement in accordance with this Act or regulations to furnish a return, that person shall be liable to a penalty of—

　　(*a*)　€125, and

　　(*b*)　the amount ...[5] of the difference between—

　　　　(i)　the amount of tax properly payable by such person if such return had been furnished by that person and that return had been correct, and

　　　　(ii)　the amount of tax (if any) paid in respect of the taxable period for which the said return was not furnished.][6]

(Body of persons)

(2) Where a person mentioned in the [subsection (1) or (1A)][7] is a body of persons—

　　(*a*)　[any reference in those subsections][8] to [€125][9] shall be construed as a reference to [€630][10], or, in the case of fraud, [€1,265][11], and

　　(*b*)　the secretary shall be liable to a separate penalty of [€125][12], or, in the case of fraud, [€250][13].

(Corrections of errors)

(3) Where any such return, invoice, [registration number, monthly control statement, claim,][14] credit note, debit note, receipt, account, voucher, bank statement, estimate, statement, information, book, document, record or declaration as is mentioned in subsection (1) was made or submitted by a person neither fraudulently nor negligently and it comes to his notice (or, if he has died, to the notice of his personal representative) that it was incorrect, then, unless the error is remedied without unreasonable delay, the return, invoice, [registration number, monthly control statement, claim,][14] credit note, debit note, receipt, account, voucher, bank statement, estimate, statement, information, book,

document, record or declaration shall be treated for the purposes of this section as having been negligently made or submitted by him.

(Improper imports)

[(4) If a person, in a case in which he represents that he is a registered person or that goods imported by him were so imported for the purposes of a business carried on by him, improperly procures the importation of goods without payment of tax in circumstances in which tax is chargeable, he shall be liable to a penalty of [€630][15], and, in addition, he shall be liable to pay to the Revenue Commissioners the amount of any tax that should have been paid on the importation.][16]

[(4A) If a person acquires goods without payment of Value Added tax (as referred to in Council Directive No 77/388/EEC of 17 May 1977) in another Member State as a result of the declaration of an incorrect registration number, that person shall be liable to a penalty of [€630][17] and, in addition, that person shall be liable to pay to the Revenue Commissioners an amount equal to the amount of tax which would have been chargeable on an intra-Community acquisition of those goods if that declaration had been the declaration of a correct registration number.][18]

(Fraudulent/negligent use of invoices/credit notes)

[(5) A person who fraudulently or negligently—

    (*a*)   issues an invoice in which an amount of tax is stated, in such circumstances that, apart from his liability under subsection (5) or (6) of section 17, the said amount does not represent the amount of tax (if any) which becomes due by him in respect of the transaction to which the invoice relates, or

    (*b*)   issues a credit note showing an amount of tax other than that properly applicable to the transaction to which the credit note relates,

shall be liable to a penalty of

    (i)   [€125][19], and

    (ii)   the amount ...[20] of his liability under the said subsection (5) or (6), as the case may be, in respect of the issue of any such invoice or credit note.][21]

(Time limits)

(6) Notwithstanding anything in section 30, proceedings for the recovery of any penalties under this section shall not be out of time by reason that they are commenced after the time allowed by the said section 30.

(Presumption of knowledge)

(7) For the purposes of this section, any return, invoice, [registration number, monthly control statement, claim,][22] credit note, debit note, receipt, account, voucher, bank statement, estimate, statement, information, book document, record or declaration submitted on behalf of a person shall be deemed to have been submitted by that person unless he proves that it was submitted without his consent or knowledge.

(Interest)

(8) ...[23]

(Goods "exported")

[(9) Where, in the pursuance of regulations made for the purposes of section 13(1)(*a*), tax on the supply of any goods has been remitted or repaid and—

(*a*) the goods are found in the State after the date on which they were alleged to have been or were to be exported, or

(*b*) any condition specified in the regulations or imposed by the Revenue Commissioners is not complied with,

and the presence of the goods in the State after that date or the non-compliance with the condition has not been authorised for the purposes of this subsection by the Revenue Commissioners, the goods shall be liable to forfeiture and the tax which was remitted or repaid shall be charged upon and become payable forthwith by the person to whom the goods were supplied or any person in whose possession the goods are found in the State and the provisions of section 24(1) shall apply accordingly, but the Revenue Commissioners may, if they think fit, waive payment of the whole or part of that tax.][24]

(Forfeiture of goods)

[(9A)(1) Where goods—

(Which goods are liable to forfeiture)

(*a*) were supplied at the rate of **zero per cent**. Subject to the condition that they were to be dispatched or transported outside the State in accordance with subparagraph (*a*), (*b*) or (*c*) of paragraph (i) of the Second Schedule and the goods were not so dispatched or transported,

(*b*) were acquired without payment of value added tax referred to in Council Directive No. 77/388/EEC of 17 May 1977 in another Member State as a result of the declaration of an incorrect registration number, or

(*c*) are being supplied by a taxable person who has not complied with the provisions of section 9(2),

the goods shall be liable to forfeiture.

(Powers of Revenue Commissioners)

(2) Whenever an officer authorised by the Revenue Commissioners reasonably suspects that goods are liable to forfeiture in accordance with subsection (1) the goods may be detained by the said officer until such examination, enquiries or investigations as may be deemed necessary by the said officer, or by another authorised officer of the Revenue Commissioners, have been made for the purpose of determining to the satisfaction of either officer whether or not the goods were so supplied or acquired.

(Time limits)

(3) When a determination referred to in subsection (2) has been made in respect of any goods, or upon the expiry of a period of two months from

the date on which the said goods were detained under the said subsection, whichever is the earlier, the said goods shall be seized as liable to forfeiture or released.][25]

[(4) [For the purposes of this section][26], "the declaration of an incorrect registration number" means–

(*a*) the declaration by a person of another person's registration number,

(*b*) the declaration by a person of a number which is not an actual registration number which he purports to be his registration number,

[(*bb*) the declaration by a person of a registration number which is cancelled,][27]

(*c*) the declaration by a person of a registration number which was obtained from the Revenue Commissioners by supplying incorrect information, or

(*d*) the declaration by a person of a registration number which was obtained from the Revenue Commissioners for the purposes of acquiring goods without payment of Value Added tax referred to in Council Directive No. 77/388/EEC of 17 May, 1977, and not for any bona fide business purpose.][28]

(Customs Act provisions)

(10) The provisions of the Customs Acts relating to forfeiture and condemnation of goods shall apply to goods liable to forfeiture under [subsection (9) or (9A)][29] as if they had become liable to forfeiture under those Acts and all powers which may be exercised by an officer of Customs and Excise under those Acts may be exercised by officers of the Revenue Commissioners authorised to exercise those powers for the purposes of [the said subsections and any provisions in relation to offences under those Acts shall apply, with any necessary modifications, in relation to the said subsections][30].][31]

(Rights to arrest)

[(11) Where an officer authorised by the Revenue Commissioners for the purposes of this subsection or a member of the Garda Síochána has reasonable grounds for suspecting that a criminal offence has been committed under the provisions of [section 1078 of the Taxes Consolidation Act, 1997],[32] in relation to tax, by a person who is not established in the State, or whom he believes is likely to leave the State, he may arrest that person.][33]

Amendments

[1]   Inserted by FA 1992, s 189(*a*)(i) with effect from 1 November 1992.

[2]   Substituted by FA 2001, s 240 and Sch 5 Part 4 with effect from 1 January 2002; previously "£100".

[3]   Deleted by FA 2005, s 110(*a*) with effect from 25 March 2005: previously ", or in the case of fraud, twice the amount".

[4]   Subs (1)(*b*) substituted by FA 1992, s 189(*a*)(ii) with effect from 1 November 1992.

[5]   Deleted by FA 2005, s 110(*b*) with effect from 25 March 2005: previously ", or in the case of fraud twice the amount,".

[6]   Subs (1A) inserted by FA 2003, s 127(*a*) with effect from 28 March 2003.

7 Substituted by FA 2003, s 127(*b*)(i) with effect from 28 March 2003; previously "the foregoing subsection".

8 Substituted by FA 2003, s 127(*b*)(ii) with effect from 28 March 2003; previously "the reference in paragraph (*a*) of that subsection".

9 Substituted by FA 2001, s 240 and Sch 5 Part 4 with effect from 1 January 2002; previously "£100".

10 Substituted by FA 2001, s 240 and Sch 5 Part 4 with effect from 1 January 2002; previously "£500".

11 Substituted by FA 2001, s 240 and Sch 5 Part 4 with effect from 1 January 2002; previously "£1,000".

12 Substituted by FA 2001, s 240 and Sch 5 Part 4 with effect from 1 January 2002; previously "£100".

13 Substituted by FA 2001, s 240 and Sch 5 Part 4 with effect from 1 January 2002; previously "£200".

14 Inserted by FA 1992, s 189(*b*) with effect from 1 November 1992.

15 Substituted by FA 2001, s 240 and Sch 5 Part 4 with effect from 1 January 2002; previously "£500".

16 Subs (4) substituted by VATAA 1978, s 19 with effect from 1 March 1979.

17 Substituted by FA 2001, s 240 and Sch 5 Part 4 with effect from 1 January 2002; previously "£500".

18 Subs (4A) inserted by FA 2001, s 197(*a*) with effect from 6 April 2001.

19 Substituted by FA 2001, s 240 and Sch 5 Part 4 with effect from 1 January 2002; previously "£100".

20 Deleted by FA 2005, s 110(*c*) with effect from 25 March 2005: previously ", or, in the case of fraud, twice the amount".

21 Subs (5) substituted by FA 1973, s 84 with effect from 3 September 1973.

22 Inserted by FA 1992, s 189(*b*) with effect from 1 November 1992.

23 Subs (8) deleted by FA 2000, s 120 with effect from 23 March 2000.

24 Subs (9) inserted by VATAA 1978, s 19 with effect from 1 March 1979.

25 Subs (9A) inserted by FA 1992, s 189 with effect from 1 January 1993.

26 Substituted by FA 2001, s 197(*b*)(i) with effect from 6 April 2001; previously "For the purposes of subparagraph (*b*) of paragraph (1)".

27 Subs (9A)(4)(*bb*) inserted by FA 2001, s 197(*b*)(ii) with effect from 6 April 2001.

28 Subs (9A)(4) inserted by FA 1994, s 98 with effect from 23 May 1994.

29 Substituted by FA 1992, s 189(*d*)(i) with effect from 1 January 1993; previously "subsection (9)".

30 Substituted by FA 1992, s 189(*d*)(ii) with effect from 1 January 1993 previously "the said subsection".

31 Subs (10) inserted by VATAA 1978, s 19 with effect from 1 March 1979.

32 Substituted by TCA 1997, s 1100 and Sch 31; previously "section 94 (as amended by section 243 of the Finance Act, 1992) of the Finance Act, 1983".

33 Subs (11) inserted by FA 1992, s 189(*e*) with effect from 1 January 1993.

Cross-references

Revenue offences: FA 1983, s 94; tax defaulters, publication of names: FA 1983, s 23.
Time limits: s 30(1).

Case law

Subject	*Case*	*Case reference*
Subs (9A): No grounds for seizure of oil tanker lorry (alleged breach of Hydrocarbon Oil (Rebated Oil) Regulations 1961, r 8)	*McCrystal Oil Company Ltd v Revenue Commissioners*	(IV) ITR (386)

Revenue Publications

Revenue VAT Guide: Chapter 7.

Definition

"body of persons": s 1(1); "business": s 1(1); "goods": s 1(1); "monthly control statement": ss 1(1), 17; "person": IA 2005, s 18(*c*); "registered person": ss 1(1), 9; "regulations": ss 1(1), 32; "secretary": s 1(1); "supply": s 1(1); "tax": s 1(1).

28 Assisting in making incorrect returns, etc

(Penalties/fines)

Any person who assists in or induces the making or delivery, for the purposes of tax, of any return, invoice, [monthly control statement, claim,]¹ credit note, debit note, receipt, account, voucher, bank statement, estimate, statement, information, book, document, record or declaration which he knows to be incorrect shall be liable to a penalty of [€950]².

Amendments

¹   Inserted by FA 1992, s 190(*a*) with effect from 1 November 1992.

²   Substituted by FA 2001, s 240 and Sch 5 Part 4 with effect from 1 January 2002; previously "£750"; previously "£500" (FA 1992, s 190(*b*): 28 May 1992).

Cross-references

Revenue offences: FA 1983, s 94; tax defaulters, publication of names: FA 1983, s 23.

Revenue Publications

Revenue VAT Guide: Chapter 7.

Definition

"monthly control statement": ss 1(1), 17: "person": IA 2005, s 18(*c*); "tax": s 1(1).

29 Proceedings in High Court in respect of penalties

(Authorised officer's ability to sue)

(1) Without prejudice to any other mode of recovery of a penalty under this Act, an officer of the Revenue Commissioners, authorised by them for the purposes of this subsection, may sue in his own name by civil proceedings [for the recovery of the penalty in any court of competent jurisdiction as a liquidated sum, and, where appropriate, section 94 of the Courts of Justice Act 1924 shall apply accordingly.]¹.

(Authorisation to substitute officer)

(2) If an officer who has commenced proceedings pursuant to this section, or who has continued the proceedings by virtue of this subsection, dies or otherwise ceases for any reason to be an officer authorised for the purposes of subsection (1) of this section—

   (*a*)   the right of such officer to continue the proceedings shall cease and the right to continue them shall vest in such other officer so authorised as may be nominated by the Revenue Commissioners,

   (*b*)   where such other officer is nominated under paragraph (*a*) of this subsection, he shall be entitled accordingly to be substituted as a party to the proceedings in the place of the first mentioned officer, and

   (*c*)   where an officer is so substituted, he shall give notice in writing of the substitution to the defendant.

(Certificate of authority)

(3) In proceedings pursuant to this section, a certificate signed by a Revenue Commissioner certifying the following facts, namely, that a person is an officer of the Revenue Commissioners and that he has been authorised by them for the purposes of subsection (1), shall be evidence until the contrary is proved of those facts.

(Substitution of officers)

(4) In proceedings pursuant to this section, a certificate signed by a Revenue Commissioner certifying the following facts, namely, that the plaintiff has ceased to be an officer of the Revenue Commissioners authorised by them for the purposes of subsection (1), that another person is an officer of the Revenue Commissioners, that such other person has been authorised by them for the purposes of subsection (1) and that he has been nominated by them in relation to the proceedings, for the purposes of subsection (2), shall be evidence until the contrary is proved of those facts.

(Presumption of validity of certificates)

(5) In proceedings pursuant to this section, a certificate certifying the facts referred to in subsection (3) or (4) and purporting to be signed by a Revenue Commissioner may be tendered in evidence without proof, and shall be deemed, until the contrary is proved, to have been so signed.

(High Court Rules apply)

(6) Subject to this section, [the rules of court]² for the time being applicable to civil proceedings shall apply to proceedings pursuant to this section.

Amendments

¹   Substituted by FA 2003, s 128(*a*) with effect for civil proceedings commenced on or after 28 March 2003; previously "for the recovery of the penalty in the High Court as a liquidated sum and the provisions of section 94 of the Courts of Justice Act, 1924, shall apply accordingly.".

²   Substituted by FA 2003, s 128(*b*) with effect for civil proceedings commenced on or after 28 March 2003; previously "the rules of the High Court".

Revenue Publications

Revenue VAT Guide: Chapter 7.

Definition

"the High Court": IA 2005, Sch; "person": IA 2005, s 18(*c*); "writing": IA 2005, Sch.

---

30 Time limits

(Imposed on Revenue Commissioners)

(General rule)

(1) Subject to subsection (3) and sections 26(4) and 27(6), proceedings for the recovery of any penalty under this Act may be commenced at any time within six years next after the date on which it was incurred.

(Liability of personal representatives in case of deceased)

(2) Where the person who has incurred any penalty has died, any proceedings under this Act which have been or could have been commenced against him may be continued or commenced against his personal representative and any penalty

awarded in proceedings so continued or commenced shall be a debt due from and payable out of his estate.

(Proceedings following death of a taxable person)

[(3) Proceedings may not be commenced by virtue of subsection (2) against the personal representative of a deceased person at a time when, by virtue of paragraph (*b*) of subsection (5), an estimation [or assessment][1] of tax may not be made on the said personal representative in respect of tax which became due by such person before his death.][2]

(General limits on estimates)

(4)[(*a*)   (i)   In relation to any taxable period ending before [1 May 2003][3], an estimation or assessment of tax under section 22 or 23 may, subject to subparagraph (ii), be made at any time not later than [six years][4] after the end of the taxable period to which the estimate or assessment relates or, where the period in respect of which the estimate or assessment is made consists of two or more taxable periods, after the end of the earlier or earliest taxable period comprised in such period.

        (ii)   In relation to any taxable period commencing on or after [1 May 2003][5], and on or after [1 January 2005][6], in relation to any other taxable period, an estimation or assessment of tax under section 22 or 23 may be made at any time not later than [four years][7] after the end of the taxable period to which the estimate or assessment relates or, where the period in respect of which the estimate or assessment is made consists of two or more taxable periods, after the end of the earlier or earliest taxable period comprised in such period.

   (*aa*)   Notwithstanding paragraphs (*a*)(i) and (*a*)(ii) in a case in which any form of fraud or neglect has been committed by or on behalf of any person in connection with or in relation to tax, an estimate or assessment as aforesaid may be made at any time for any period for which, by reason of the fraud or neglect, tax would otherwise be lost to the Exchequer.][8]

(Neglect — a definition)

   (*b*)   In this subsection **"neglect"** means negligence or a failure to give any notice, to furnish particulars, to make any return or to produce or furnish any invoice, [monthly control statement,][8] credit note, debit note, receipt, account, voucher, bank statement, estimate [or assessment][10], statement, information, book, document, record or declaration required to be given, furnished, made or produced by or under this Act or regulations:

      Provided that a person shall be deemed not to have failed to do anything required to be done within a limited time if he did it within such further time, if any, as the Revenue Commissioners may have allowed; and where a person had a reasonable excuse for not doing anything required to be done, he shall be deemed not to have failed to do it if he did it without unreasonable delay after the excuse had ceased.

(Limits on estimates against personal representatives)

(5) (*a*) Where a person dies, an estimation [or assessment]¹ of tax under section 22 or 23 (as the case may be) may be made on his personal representative for any period for which such an estimation [or assessment]¹ could have been made upon him immediately before his death, or could be made upon him if he were living, in respect of tax which became due by such person before his death, and the amount of tax recoverable under any such estimation [or assessment]¹ shall be a debt due from and payable out of the estate of such person.

(Time limits applying)

[(*b*) No estimation [or assessment]¹ of tax shall be made by virtue of this subsection later than three years after the expiration of the year in which the deceased person died, in a case in which the grant of probate or letters of administration was made in that year, and no such estimation [or assessment]¹ shall be made later than two years after the expiration of the year in which such grant was made in any other case, but the foregoing provisions of this subsection shall have effect subject to the proviso that where the personal representative—

(i) after the year in which the deceased person died, lodges a corrective affidavit for the purposes of assessment of estate duty or delivers an additional affidavit under [section 48 of the Capital Acquisitions Tax Consolidation Act 2003],¹¹ or

(ii) is liable to deliver an additional affidavit under the said [section 48],¹² has been so notified by the Revenue Commissioners and did not deliver the said additional affidavit in the year in which the deceased person died,

such estimation [or assessment]¹ may be made at any time before the expiration of two years after the end of the year in which the corrective affidavit was lodged or the additional affidavit was or is delivered]¹³.

Amendments

¹ Inserted by FA 1992, s 191(*a*) with effect from 28 May 1992.

² Subs (3) substituted by VATAA 1978, s 20 with effect from 1 March 1979.

³ Substituted by FA 2003, s 129(*a*)(i) with effect from 1 November 2003 (Finance Act 2003 (Commencement of Sections 124,125,129 and 130(*b*)) Order 2003); previously "the 1st day of May, 1998".

⁴ Substituted by FA 2003, s 129(*a*)(ii) with effect from 1 November 2003 (Finance Act 2003 (Commencement of Sections 124,125,129 and 130(*b*)) Order 2003); previously "ten years".

⁵ Substituted by FA 2003, s 129(*b*)(i) with effect from 1 November 2003 (Finance Act 2003 (Commencement of Sections 124,125,129 and 130(*b*)) Order 2003); previously "the 1st day of May, 1998".

⁶ Substituted by FA 2003, s 129(*b*)(ii) with effect from 1 November 2003 (Finance Act 2003 (Commencement of Sections 124,125,129 and 130(*b*)) Order 2003); previously "the 1st day of May, 1999,".

⁷ Substituted by FA 2003, s 129(*b*)(iii) with effect from 1 November 2003 (Finance Act 2003 (Commencement of Sections 124,125,129 and 130(*b*)) Order 2003), appoint; previously "six years".

⁸ Subs (4)(*a*) substituted by FA 1998, s 115 with effect from 27 March 1998.

⁹ Inserted by FA 1992, s 191(*c*) with effect from 1 November 1992.

[10]   Inserted by FA 1992, s 191(*b*) with effect from 28 May 1992.

[11]   Substituted by CATCA 2003, s 119 and Sch 3; previously "section 38 of the Capital Acquisitions Tax Act 1976".

[12]   Substituted by CATCA 2003, s 119 and Sch 3; previously "section 38".

[13]   Subs (5)(*b*) substituted by VATAA 1978, s 20 with effect from 1 March 1979.

Cross-references

Fraud, negligence; proceedings not "out of time" in such cases: s 27(6).

Revenue Publications

Revenue VAT Guide: Chapter 7.

Definition

"affidavit": IA 2005, Sch; "monthly control statement": ss 1(1),17; "person": IA 2005, s 18(*c*); "regulations": ss 1(1), 32; "tax": s 1(1); "taxable period": s 1(1); "year": IA 2005, Sch.

31 Application of section 512 of the Income Tax Act, 1967

The provisions of [section 1065 of the Taxes Consolidation Act, 1997],[1] shall apply to any penalty incurred under this Act.

Amendments

[1]   Substituted by TCA 1998, s 1100 and Sch 31; previously "section 512 of the Income Tax Act, 1967".

Note

This section allows the Revenue Commissioners to mitigate penalties awarded by a court or to order the release from jail of a convicted tax defaulter.

Revenue Publications

Revenue VAT Guide: Chapter 7.

32 Regulations

(Revenue powers to make regulations)

(1) The Revenue Commissioners shall make such regulations as seem to them to be necessary for the purpose of giving effect to this Act and of enabling them to discharge their functions thereunder and, without prejudice to the generality of the foregoing, the regulations may make provision in relation to all or any of the following matters—

(Rules for application)

   (*a*)   the manner in which exemption in respect of certain services may be waived under section 7 and any such waiver may be cancelled, and the adjustments, including a charge of tax, which may be made as a condition of any such cancellation;

[(*aa*)   the deduction of tax chargeable in respect of intra-Community acquisitions;

  (*ab*)   the manner in which residual tax referred to in section 12(1)(*a*)(ii*b*) may be calculated and deducted;

  (*ac*)   the manner in which residual tax referred to in section 13(3A) may be calculated and repaid;

  (*ad*)   the repayment, in accordance with section 15(5A), of tax chargeable on the importation of goods;

(*ae*) the time and manner in which tax shall be payable in respect of the goods referred to in section 19(4);

(*af*) the form particulars to be specified therein and the amount or amounts to be applied for the purposes of section 19A(3);

(*ag*) the supply of goods ...¹ in accordance with paragraph (i*a*) of the Second Schedule;

(*ah*) the importation of goods consigned to another Member State in accordance with paragraph (iii*b*) of the Second Schedule;

(*ai*) the circumstances in which a person may elect not to apply the proviso to subsection (6)(*d*) of section 3;]²

[(*b*) the treatment under section 5(3) of the use and services specified therein as services supplied by a person for consideration in the course of business;]³

[(*ba*) the manner in which the electronic services scheme referred to in section 5A shall operate;]⁴

(*c*) the particulars required for registration and the manner in which registration may be effected and cancelled;

(*d*) the manner in which a person may elect to be [a taxable person]⁵ and any such election may be cancelled, the treatment of [a taxable person]⁵ as a person who is [not a taxable person]⁶, and the adjustments, including a charge of tax, which may be made as a condition of any such cancellation or treatment;

[(*da*) the conditions for a taxable dealer to opt to apply the margin scheme to certain supplies in accordance with section 10A(4);

(*db*) the determination of the aggregate margin in accordance with section 10A(8);

(*dc*) the form of the invoice or other document that shall be issued in accordance with section 10B(4);

(*dd*) the manner in which residual tax referred to in section 12(1)(*a*)(vi) may be deducted;

(*de*) the particulars to be furnished in relation to antiques as specified in paragraph (xvia) of the Sixth Schedule or paragraph (iii) of the Eighth Schedule;]⁷

[(*e*) (i) the manner in which any amount may be apportioned, including the methods of apportionment which may be applied for the purposes of paragraphs (*a*) and (*b*) of section 11(3),

     (ii) the circumstances or conditions under which a supply may or may not be treated as an ancillary supply, a composite supply, an individual supply, a multiple supply or a principal supply,

    (iii) a relatively small amount, or an element of a supply, which may be disregarded for the purposes of applying section 11(3);]⁸

(*f*) ...⁹;

[(*g*) the determination, under section 14, of a person's tax liability for any period by reference to moneys received and the adjustments, including a charge of tax, which may be made when a person becomes entitled to determine his tax liability in the manner aforesaid or, having been so entitled, ceases to be so entitled or ceases to be a taxable person;][10]

(*h*) the keeping by [taxable persons][11] of records and the retention of such records and supporting documents [or other recorded data][12];

[(*ha*) the keeping by persons trading in investment gold (within the meaning of section 6A) of records and the retention of such records and supporting documents or other recorded data;

(*hb*) the conditions under which a person may waive his right to exemption from tax on the supply of investment gold (within the meaning of section 6A);

(*hc*) the conditions under which an intermediary (within the meaning of section 6A) may waive his right to exemption from tax on his supply of services;

(*hd*) the conditions under which a person may claim a refund of tax in accordance with subsections (6)(*b*), (7)(*b*) and (8)(*b*) of section 6A, and the manner in which such refund may be claimed;][13]

[(*i*) the form of invoice, [monthly control statement,][14] credit note, debit note and settlement voucher, including electronic form, required to be used for the purposes of this Act, the particulars required to be inserted in such documents or electronically recorded and the period within which such documents or electronic data are required to be issued or transmitted and such other conditions in relation to the issue or receipt, in any form, of an invoice, [monthly control statement,][14] credit note, debit note and settlement voucher as may be imposed by the Revenue Commissioners;][15]

(*j*) the furnishing of returns and the particulars to be shown thereon;

(*k*) the nomination by the Revenue Commissioners of officers to perform any acts and discharge any functions authorised by this Act to be performed or discharged by the Revenue Commissioners;

(*l*) the manner in which tax is to be recovered in cases of default of payment;

(*m*) the refund of tax in excess of the amount required by law to be borne, or paid to the Revenue Commissioners;

[(*ma*) the conditions governing a person's entitlement to interest in accordance with section 21A;][16]

(*n*) disclosure to the Revenue Commissioners of such information as they may require for the ascertainment of liability to tax;

(*o*) the remission at the discretion of the Revenue Commissioners of small amounts of tax and interest;

[(*p*) matters consequential on the death of a registered person or his becoming subject to any incapacity including the treatment of a person of such class or classes as may be specified in the regulations as a person carrying on the business of the deceased or incapacitated person;][17]

(*q*) service of notices;

(*r*) the acceptance of estimates (whether or not subject to subsequent review) of the amount of tax payable or of any amounts relating to such tax;

(*s*) the adjustment of the liability of [a taxable person][5] who [supplies goods or services][18] and of the liability of [a taxable person][5] to whom [goods or services are supplied][19] where goods are returned, the consideration is reduced, a bad debt is incurred or a discount is allowed;

(*t*) the valuation of interests in or over immovable goods;

[(*ta*) specifying the circumstances or conditions under which development work on immovable goods is not treated as being on behalf of, or to the benefit of, a person;][20]

(*u*) the estimation of tax due for a taxable or other period;

[(*uu*) the adjustments to be made by [a taxable person][5] of any apportionment referred to in paragraph (*x*) or deduction under section 12 previously made, being adjustments by reference to changes, occurring not later than five years from the end of the taxable period to which the original apportionment or deduction relates, in any of the matters by reference to which the apportionment or deduction was made or allowed, and the determination of the taxable period in and from which or in which any such adjustment is to take effect;][21]

(*v*) the relief for stock-in-trade held on the specified day;

[(*w*) the determination of average build for the purposes of paragraph (xvii) of the Second Schedule;][22]

[(*ww*) the determination of average foot size for the purposes of paragraph (xix) of the Second Schedule;][23]

[(*www*) the circumstances, terms and conditions under which a letting of immovable goods constitutes a letting in the short-term guest sector or holiday sector, or under which accommodation is or is not holiday accommodation (within the meaning of paragraph (xiii) of the Sixth Schedule);][24]

(*x*) the apportionment between the tax which may be deducted under section 12 and tax which may not be deducted under that section, the review, by reference to the circumstances obtaining in any period not exceeding one year, of any such apportionment previously made, the charge or repayment of tax consequent on any such review and the furnishing of particulars by [a taxable person][5] to the Revenue Commissioners for the purpose of any such review;

[(*xx*)   the relief (if any) to be given to [a taxable person][5] in respect of tax borne or paid by him on stock-in-trade held by him immediately before the commencement of the first taxable period for which he is deemed to become [a taxable person][5];

(*xxx*)   the manner in which a determination may be made for the purposes of section 11(1B);][25]

(*y*)   the particulars to be furnished and the manner in which notification is to be given to the Revenue Commissioners by a person who intends to promote a dance, and the manner in which the Revenue Commissioners shall notify the proprietor of any premises in regard to dances proposed to be promoted in such premises.

(Flexibility of Regulations)

(2) Regulations under this section may make different provisions in relation to different cases and may in particular provide for differentiation between different classes of persons affected by this Act and for the adoption of different procedures for any such different classes.

(Ministerial consent)

[(2A) Regulations under this section for the purposes of section 5(7), [subsection 1(*a*)(vi) of section 12][26] subsection (1) or (2) of section 13 [subsection (6) or (7) of section 15 or paragraph (*ia*) of the Sixth Schedule][27] [or in relation to the [matters specified in [paragraph (*w*), (*ww*) or (*www*) of subsection (1)][28]][29]][30] shall not be made without the consent of the Minister for Finance.][31]

[(2B) Regulations under this Act may contain such incidental, supplementary and consequential provisions as appear to the Revenue Commissioners to be necessary for the purposes of giving full effect to—

(*a*)   Council Directive No 77/388/EEC of 17 May 1977 (OJ No L145 of 13.6.1977, p 1),

(*b*)   Council Directive No 79/1072/EEC of 6 December 1979 (OJ No L331 of 6.12.1979, p11),

(*c*)   Council Directive No 86/560/EEC of 17 November 1986 (OJ No L326 of 21.11.1986, p 40).][32]

(Government approval)

(3) Every regulation made under this section shall be laid before Dáil Éireann as soon as may be after it is made and, if a resolution annulling the regulation is passed by Dáil Éireann within the next twenty-one days on which Dáil Éireann has sat after the regulation is laid before it, the regulation shall be annulled accordingly, but without prejudice to the validity of anything previously done thereunder.

Amendments

1   Deleted by FA 2000, s 121 with effect from 1 July 1999; previously "by tax-free shops".
2   Subs (1)(*aa*)–(*ai*) inserted by FA 1992, s 192(*a*) with effect from 1 January 1993.
3   Subs (1) substituted by VATAA 1978, s 21 with effect from 1 March 1979.
4   Subs (1)(*ba*) inserted by FA 2003, s 130(*a*) with effect from 1 July 2003.
5   Substituted by VATAA 1978, s 30(2) with effect from 1 March 1979; previously "an accountable person".

[6] Substituted by VATAA 1978, s 30(2) with effect from 1 March 1979; previously "not accountable".

[7] Subs (1)(*da*)–(*de*) inserted by FA 1995, s 138 with effect from 2 June 1995.

[8] Subs (1)(*e*) substituted by FA 2006, s 99(1)(*a*) with effect from such day as the Minister for Finance may appoint by order; previously

"[(*e*) the manner in which notwithstanding section 11(3), any amount may be apportioned;][8]

Amendments

[8] Subs (1)(*e*) substituted by VATAA 1978, s 21 with effect from 1 March 1979.".

[9] Subs (1)(*f*) repealed by FA 1976, s 81 with effect from 1 March 1976.

[10] Subs (1)(*g*) substituted by VATAA 1978, s 21 with effect from 1 March 1979.

[11] Words substituted by VATAA 1978, s 30(2) with effect from 1 March 1979; previously "accountable persons".

[12] Inserted by FA 1986, s 88 with effect from 27 May 1986.

[13] Subs (*ha*)–(*hd*) inserted by FA 1999, s 137 with effect from 25 March 1999.

[14] Inserted by FA 1992, s 192(*b*) with effect from 1 November 1992.

[15] Subs (1)(*i*) substituted by FA 1986, s 88 with effect from 27 May 1986.

[16] Subs (1)(*ma*) inserted by FA 2003, s 130(*b*) with effect from 1 November 2003 (Finance Act 2003 (Commencement of Sections 124,125,129 and 130(*b*)) Order 2003).

[17] Subs (1)(*p*) substituted by VATAA 1978, s 21 with effect from 1 March 1979.

[18] Substituted by VATAA 1978, s 30(2) with effect from 1 March 1979; previously "delivers goods or renders services".

[19] Substituted by VATAA 1978, s 30(2) with effect from 1 March 1979; previously "goods are delivered or services are rendered".

[20] Subs (1)(*ta*) inserted by FA 2005, s 111(*a*) with effect from 25 March 2005.

[21] Subs (1)(*uu*) inserted by FA 1976, s 58 with effect from 27 May 1976.

[22] Subs (1)(*w*) inserted by FA 1984, s 91 with effect from 1 May 1984.

[23] Subs (1)(*ww*) inserted by FA 1985, s 48 with effect from 1 March 1985.

[24] Subs (1)(*www*) inserted by FA 2005, s 111(*b*) with effect from 25 March 2005.

[25] Subs (1)(*xx*)–(*xxx*) inserted by FA 1973, s 85 with effect from 3 September 1973.

[26] Inserted by FA 1987, s 44 with effect from 9 July 1987.

[27] Substituted by FA 1989, s 60 with effect from 24 May 1989; previously "or subsection (6) or (7) of section 15".

[28] Substituted by FA 2005, s 111(*c*) with effect from 25 March 2005: previously "subsection (1)(*w*) or (1)(*ww*)".

[29] Substituted by FA 1985, s 48 with effect from 1 March 1985; previously "matter specified in subsection (1)(*w*)".

[30] Inserted by FA 1984, s 91 with effect from 1 May 1984.

[31] Subs (2A) inserted by VATAA 1978, s 21 with effect from 1 March 1976.

[32] Subs (2B) inserted by FA 2006, s 99(1)(*b*) with effect from 31 March 2006.

Cross-references

Subs (1)(*aa*): Intra-Community acquisitions, deduction of tax.

Subs (1)(*ab*): residual tax, calculations.

Subs (1)(*ac*): residual tax, calculation.

Subs (1)(*ad*): repayment of tax on imports.

Subs (1)(*af*): Form of statement of Intra-Community supplies.

Subs (1)(*ag*): supply of goods by tax free shops.

Subs (1)(*ah*): Imported goods consigned to another EC State.

Subs (1)(*ai*): Goods supplied where transport ends:

Regulations

Subject	Regulation
Subs (1)(*a*): Waiver of exemption	Value Added Tax Regulations 1979 (SI 63/79), r 4
Subs (1)(*b*): Self-supplied services	Value Added Tax Regulations 1979 (SI 63/79), r 24

Subs (1)(*c*): Registration particulars   Value Added Tax (Registration) Regulations 1993
(SI 30/93)

Subs (1)(*d*): Election to be taxable   Value Added Tax Regulations 1979 (SI 63/79), r 3

Subs (1)(*e*): Apportionment of amounts Value Added Tax Regulations 1979 (SI 63/79), r 34

Subs (1)(*g*): Cash basis   Value Added Tax (Determination of Tax Due by Reference
to Moneys Received) Regulations 1992 (SI 306/92)

Subs (1)(*h*): Books, records to be kept   Value Added Tax Regulations 1979 (SI 63/79), r 9

Subs (1)(*i*): Invoice etc, particulars   Value Added Tax (Invoices and Other Documents)
Regulations 1992 (SI 275/ 1992)
Value Added Tax (Monthly Control Statement) Regulations
1992 (SI 230/92)
Value Added Tax (Time Limits for Issuing Certain
Documents) Regulations 1992 (SI 276/92)
Value Added Tax (Electronic Data Exchange and Storage
Regulations, 1992 (SI 269/92)

Subs (1)(*j*): Return, particulars   Value Added Tax Regulations 1979 (SI 63/79), r 12
Value Added Tax (Statement of Intra-Community Supplies)
Regulations 1993 (SI 54/93)

Subs (1)(*k*): Nomination of officers   Value Added Tax Regulations 1979 (SI 63/79), r 38

Subs (1)(*l*): Recovery of tax arrears   Value Added Tax Regulations 1979 (SI 63/79), r 15

Subs (1)(*m*): Repayment of tax   Value Added Tax Regulations 1979 (SI 63/79), r 17

Subs (1)(*n*): Disclosure of information Value Added Tax Regulations 1979 (SI 63/79), r 35
to Revenue

Subs (1)(*o*): Remission of small   Value Added Tax Regulations 1979 (SI 63/79), r 18
amounts of tax

Subs (1)(*p*): Personal representatives   Value Added Tax Regulations 1979 (SI 63/79), r 36

Subs (1)(*q*): Service of notices   Value Added Tax Regulations 1979 (SI 63/79), r 37

Subs (1)(*r*): Acceptance of estimates   Value Added Tax Regulations 1979 (SI 63/79), r 13

Subs (1)(*s*): Adjustments for goods   Value Added Tax Regulations 1979 (SI 63/79), r 8
returned, bad debts, discounts

Subs (1)(*t*): Valuation of interest in land Value Added Tax Regulations 1979 (SI 63/79), r 19
and buildings

Subs (1)(*u*): Estimates of tax due   Value Added Tax (Estimation and Assessment of Tax Due)
Regulations 1992 (SI 277/92)

Subs (1)(*v*): Stock relief (1 November   Value Added Tax Regulations 1979 (SI 63/79), r 21
1972)

Subs (1)(*x*): Apportionment between   Value Added Tax Regulations 1979 (SI 63/79), r 16
taxable and exempt turnover

Subs (1)(*xx*): Stock relief   Value Added Tax Regulations 1979 (SI 63/79), r 20

Subs (1)(*xxx*): Determination of tax   Value Added Tax (Determination in Regards to Tax)
rate, manner of   Regulations 1992 (SI 278/92)

Subs (1)(*y*): Dance promotions,   Value Added Tax Regulations 1979 (SI 63/79), r 20
particulars

Revenue Publications

Revenue VAT Guide: Chapter 12.

Definition

"antiques": s 1(1); "business": s 1(1); "commencement": IA 2005, Sch; "Dáil Éireann": IA 2005, Sch; "goods": s 1(1); "immovable goods": s 1(1); "monthly control statement": ss 1(1),17; "the Minister": s 1(1); "person": IA 2005, s 18(c); "registered person": s 1(1); "regulations": ss 1(1), 32; "the specified day": s 1(1); "tax": s 1(1); "taxable dealer": s 1(1); "taxable period": s 1(1); "taxable person": ss 1(1), 8.

33 Officer responsible in case of body of persons

(Responsibility of officer)

(1) The secretary or other officer acting as secretary for the time being of any body of persons shall be answerable in addition to the body for doing all such acts as are required to be done by the body under any of the provisions relating to tax.

(Rights of officer)

(2) Every such officer as aforesaid may from time to time retain out of any money coming into his hands, on behalf of the body, so much thereof as is sufficient to pay the tax due by the body and shall be indemnified for all such payments made in pursuance of this section.

(Timescales for notice)

(3) Any notice required to be given to a body of persons under any of the provisions relating to tax may be given to the secretary or other officer acting as secretary for the time being of such body.

(Definitions)

(4) In this section **"the provisions relating to tax"** means—

    (a)   the provisions of this Act and regulations, and

    (b)   the provisions relating to tax of any subsequent Act.

Definition

"body of persons": s 1(1); "person": IA 2005, s 18(c); "secretary": s 1(1); "tax": s 1(1).

34 Relief for stock-in-trade held on the specified day

(Allowable deductions)

(1) In computing the amount of tax payable by [a taxable person][1], the following amounts may, subject to subsections (3) and (4), in addition to the deductions authorised by section 12, be deducted on account of stock-in-trade which has been [supplied][2] to, and has not been [supplied][2] by, him before the specified day and which is held by him at the commencement of that day, or incorporated in other stock-in-trade held by him at such commencement, that is to say:

    (a)   in case the [taxable person][3] was, immediately before the specified day, not registered for turnover tax under the provision of section 49 of the Finance Act, 1963, nor required under the provisions of that section to furnish the particulars specified for registration, and was not registered for wholesale tax under the provisions of section 4 of the Finance (No. 2) Act, 1966, nor required under the provisions of that section to furnish the particulars specified for registration, an amount equal to the sum of the amounts which he would be liable to pay on account of turnover tax and wholesale tax if,

(i) he had been accountable for each of those taxes,

(ii) he had on the day immediately preceding the specified day sold the whole of his stock-in-trade aforesaid in the course of business to a person who was carrying on the same activities as his own and who had not given him, in accordance with section 50 of the Finance Act, 1963, a statement in writing quoting the turnover tax registration number of the person nor given him, in accordance with section 5 of the Finance (No. 2) Act, 1966, a statement in writing quoting the wholesale tax registration number of the person, and

(iii) he had on the said day immediately preceding the specified day received from the person mentioned in subparagraph (ii) payment for the stock-in-trade so deemed to have been sold of an amount equal to the cost to the [taxable person][3] of such stock or the market value thereof, whichever is the lower, and

(b) in case, immediately before the specified day the [taxable person][3] was registered for turnover tax under the provisions of section 49 of the Finance Act, 1963, or required under the provisions of that section to furnish the particulars specified for registration, but was not registered for wholesale tax under the provisions of section 4 of the Finance (No.2) Act, 1966, nor required under the provisions of that section to furnish the particulars specified for registration, an amount equal to the amount of wholesale tax which he would be liable to pay if,

(i) he had been [a taxable person][1] for the purposes of wholesale tax

(ii) he had on the day immediately preceding the specified day sold the whole of his stock-in-trade aforesaid in the course of business to a person who was carrying on the same activities as his own and who had in accordance with section 50 of the Finance Act, 1963, given him a statement in writing quoting the registration number of the person but had not given him, in accordance with section 5 of the Finance (No. 2) Act, 1966, a statement in writing quoting the wholesale tax registration number of such person, and

(iii) he had on the said day immediately preceding the specified day received from the person mentioned in subparagraph (ii) payment for the stock-in-trade so deemed to have been sold of an amount equal to the cost to the [taxable person][3] of such stock or the market value thereof, whichever is the lower.

(2) Where [a taxable person][1]—

(a) is not such a person as is mentioned in paragraph (a) or (b) of subsection (1) but was such a person at any time during the year ended the day immediately preceding the specified day or (*b*) is such a person as is mentioned in paragraph (*a*) or (*b*) of subsection (1) and was such a person during a part of the year ended the day immediately preceding the specified day but was not such a person during another part of that year,

the Revenue Commissioners may allow such deduction or make such restriction in the deduction which would otherwise be allowable as in their opinion is just and reasonable having regard to the nature of the business carried on, the period during the year ended on the day immediately preceding the specified day during which the business was carried on and the period during the said year during which the person was such a person as is mentioned in the said paragraph (*a*) or (*b*) of subsection (1).

(Time limits and procedure)

(3) A claim for a deduction under this section shall be made in accordance with regulations and the amount authorised to be deducted may be deducted by equal instalments in computing the amount of tax payable in respect of each of the taxable periods beginning on the first day of the first and second taxable periods next following that in which the specified day occurs.

(Non-deductible expenses)

(4) No deduction shall be granted under this section for any amount which is referable to turnover tax or wholesale tax on immovable goods on the [supply]⁵ of which tax is, by virtue of section 4(6), not chargeable or to wholesale tax on newspapers or periodicals, [or second-hand goods]⁴.

(5) In this section—

(Definion of stock-in-trade)

"stock-in-trade" means, in relation to any person, goods which are either—

[(*a*) movable goods of a kind that are [supplied]⁸ by the person in the ordinary course of his business being goods which are actually held for [supply]⁵ (otherwise than by virtue of section 3(1)(*e*)) or which would be so held if they were mature or if their manufacture, preparation or construction were complete, or]⁶

(*b*) materials incorporated in immovable goods of a kind that are [supplied]⁸ by the person in the ordinary course of his business and that have not been [supplied]⁸ by him since the goods were developed, but are actually held for [supply]⁵ or would be so held if their development were complete, or

(*c*) consumable materials incorporated in immovable goods by the person in the course of a business consisting of the [supply]⁷ of a service of constructing, repairing, painting or decorating immovable goods where that service has not been completed, or

(*d*) materials which have not been incorporated in goods and are such as are used by the person in the manufacture or construction of goods of a kind that are delivered by the person in the ordinary course of his business or, where his ordinary business consists of repairing, painting or decorating immovable goods, are used by him as consumable materials in the course of that business;

materials referred to in paragraph (*b*) of the definition of **"stock-in-trade"** shall, for the purposes of subsection (1), be regarded as having been [supplied][8] to the same extent as the immovable goods into which they have been incorporated can be regarded as having been [supplied][8];

materials referred to in paragraph (*c*) of the definition of **"stock-in-trade"** shall be regarded as having been [supplied][8] to the extent that the service in relation to which they have been used has been [supplied][8];

(Definition — cost)

"cost" means, in relation to stock-in-trade, the total of the money payable by the person for the [supply][5] of the stock, including any addition made for turnover tax or wholesale tax, but excluding any discount or allowance deducted or deductible on payment for the stock.

Amendments

[1] Substituted by VATAA 1978, s 30(2) with effect from 1 March 1979; previously "an accountable person".

[2] Substituted by VATAA 1978, s 30(2) with effect from 1 March 1979; previously "delivered".

[3] Substituted by VATAA 1978, s 30(2) with effect from 1 March 1979; previously "accountable person".

[4] Substituted by VATAA 1978, s 30(2) with effect from 1 March 1979; previously "second-hand goods or any goods of a kind specified in the Fourth Schedule".

[5] Word substituted by VATAA 1978, s 30(2) with effect from 1 March 1979; previously "delivery".

[6] Substituted by FA 1976, s 59 with effect from 27 May 1976.

[7] Substituted by VATAA 1978, s 30(2) with effect from 1 March 1979; previously "rendering".

[8] Substituted by VATAA 1978, s 30(2) with effect from 1 March 1979; previously "rendered".

Cross-references

Revenue may make provision for stock relief: s 32(1)(v), (xx).

Regulations

Subject	Regulation
Form of claim for deduction	Value Added Tax Regulation 1979, r 21
Relief for stock in trade held at commencement of taxability	Value Added Tax Regulation 1979, r 22
Stock relief start-up	Value Added Tax Regulation 1979, r 63

Orders

Subject	Order
VAT commencement day	Value Added Tax (Specified Day) Order 1972 (SI 180/72)

Definition

"business": s 1(1); "development": s 1(1); "developed": s 1(1); "goods": s 1(1); "immovable goods": s 1(1); "movable goods": s 1(1); "person": IA 2005, s 18(*c*); "regulations": ss 1(1), 32; "second-hand": s 1(1); "the specified day": s 1(1); "supply": s 1(1); "tax": s 1(1); "taxable period": s 1(1); "taxable person": ss 1(1), 8; "writing": IA 2005, Sch.

35 Special provisions for adjustment and recovery of consideration

(Recovery of turnover and wholesale tax)

(1) (*a*) Notwithstanding the repeal by this Act of the provisions relating to turnover tax and wholesale tax, sums due on account of turnover tax or wholesale tax under a contract entered into before the specified day, together with any additional sums which might be recoverable by virtue of the provisions of section 9 of the Finance (No. 2) Act, 1966, section 7 of the Finance (No. 2) Act, 1968, section 58 of the Finance Act, 1969, section 51 of the Finance Act, 1970, or section 4 of the Finance (No.2) Act, 1970, shall, in the absence of agreement to the contrary, but subject to subsection (2), be recoverable as if the said provisions relating to turnover tax and wholesale tax had not been repealed.

(Pre-VAT contracts)

(*b*) (i) Subject to subparagraph (ii), where, under an agreement made before the specified day, [a taxable person][1] [supplies goods or services][2] on or after that day in such circumstances that tax is chargeable, the consideration provided for under the agreement shall, in the absence of any agreement to the contrary, be adjusted by excluding therefrom the amount, if any, included on account of turnover tax or wholesale tax or both of those taxes, as the case may be, and including therein an amount equal to the amount of the tax so chargeable, and the consideration as so adjusted shall be deemed to be the consideration provided for under the agreement.

(ii) The consideration provided for under an agreement for the delivery of immovable goods or the rendering of a service consisting of a development made before the specified day shall, in the absence of agreement to the contrary, be deemed, for the purposes of this paragraph, to include an amount of turnover tax and wholesale tax combined equal to the amount of tax chargeable in respect of the transaction.

(*c*) ...[3].

(Adjustment of price subsequent to change in tax rate)

[(1A)(*a*) Where, after the making of an agreement for the [supply of goods or services][4] and before the date on which under subsection (1) or (2), as may be appropriate, of section 19 any tax in respect of the transaction [falls due][5], there is a change in the amount of tax chargeable on the [supply][6] in question, then, in the absence of agreement to the contrary, there shall be added to or deducted from the total amount of the consideration and any tax stated separately under the agreement an amount equal to the amount of the change in the tax chargeable.

(*b*) References in this subsection to a change in the amount of tax chargeable on the [supply of goods or services][4] include references to a change to or from a situation in which no tax is being charged on the [supply][6].][7]

(VAT is part of price)

(2) Where, in relation to a [supply of goods or services][8] by [a taxable person][1], the person issues an invoice in which the tax chargeable in respect of the transaction is stated separately, the tax so stated shall, for the purpose of its recovery, be deemed to be part of the consideration for the transaction and shall be recoverable accordingly by the person:

Provided that, if the invoice is issued pursuant to section 17(1), this subsection shall not apply unless it is in the form and contains the particulars specified by regulations.

(Flat-rate provisions)

a 21(1)(a) [(3) (*a*)   Where, under an agreement made before the commencement of section 12A, a flat-rate farmer supplies agricultural produce or an agricultural service after such commencement to any person, the consideration provided for under the agreement shall, in the absence of agreement to the contrary, be increased by an amount equal to the flat- rate addition appropriate to the said consideration.

a 13A(1)   (*b*)   Where, in relation to a supply of agricultural produce or an agricultural
(b), (c), (d),   service by a flat-rate farmer, the flat-rate farmer issues an invoice in
(e),   which the flat-rate addition is stated separately, the flat-rate addition so
a 13A(1)(b)   stated shall, for the purpose of its recovery, be deemed to be part of the
                           consideration for the transaction and shall be recoverable accordingly
                           by the flat-rate farmer.][9]

Amendments

[1]   Substituted by VATAA 1976, s 30(2) with effect from 1 March 1979; previously "an accountable person".
[2]   Substituted by VATAA 1978, s 30(2) with effect from 1 March 1979; previously "delivers goods or renders services".
[3]   Subs (1)(*c*) repealed by FA 1976, s 81 with effect from 1 March 1976.
[4]   Substituted by VATAA 1978, s 30(2) with effect from 1 March 1979; previously "delivery of goods or the rendering of services".
[5]   Substituted by VATAA 1978, s 30(2) with effect from 1 March 1979; previously "would, if the proviso to the said subsection (1) were disregarded, fall due".
[6]   Substituted by VATAA 1978, s 30(2) with effect from 1 March 1979; previously "delivery or rendering".
[7]   Subs (1A) inserted by FA 1973, s 86 with effect from 3 September 1973.
[8]   Substituted by VATAA 1978, s 30(2) with effect from 1 March 1979; previously "delivery of goods or a rendering of services".
[9]   Subs (3) inserted by VATAA 1978, s 22 with effect from 1 March 1979.

Cross-references

Specified day: 1 November 1972, Value Added Tax (Specified Day) Order 1972 (SI 180/72).

Order

Subject	Order
VAT commencement day	Value Added Tax (Specified Day) Order 1972 (SI 180/72)

Definition

"agricultural produce": s 1(1); "agricultural service": 1(1); "commencement": IA 2005, Sch; "development": s 1(1); "farmer": s 1(1); "flat-rate addition": s 1(1); "flat-rate farmer": ss 1(1), 12A; "goods": s 1(1); "immovable goods": s 1(1); "person": IA 2005, s 18(*c*); "regulations": ss 1(1), 32; "the specified day": s 1(1); "supply": s 1(1); "tax": s 1(1); "taxable person": ss 1(1), 8.

36 Special provision for deliveries made prior to the specified day

Amendments

Section 36 repealed by VATAA 1978, s 30(1) with effect from 1 March 1979.

37 Substitution of agent, etc., for person not resident in State

[Where a taxable person not established in the State supplies goods or services, [a 21(1)(a)] the Revenue Commissioners may, where it appears requisite to them to do so for the protection of the revenue, deem a person who—

(*a*) acts or has acted on behalf of the taxable person in relation to such supplies, or

(*b*) allows or has allowed such supplies to be made on land owned, occupied or controlled by him,

to have made such supplies in the course or furtherance of business from the date of service on him of a notice in writing to that effect.][1,2]

Amendments

1   Section 37 substituted by FA 1992, s 193 with effect from 28 May 1992.
2   Section 37 will be repealed by FA 2001, s 198 with effect from 1 January 2002.

Cross-references

Right of appeal: s 25(1)(*ab*).

Sixth Directive

Persons liable to pay tax to the authorities: a 21.

Revenue precedent

Issue: Is an Irish company acting as an agent for foreign companies obliged to register separately for transactions carried out as agent?
Decision: In the particular circumstances registration was not required and a company acting as an agent could use its own VAT number to import and claim credit on such goods on behalf of a foreign company.

Revenue Publications

Revenue VAT Guide: Chapter 12.

Definitions

"business": s 1(1); "land": IA 2005, Sch; "person": IA 2005, s 18(*c*); "tax": s 1(1); "taxable person": s 1(1), 8; "writing": IA 2005, Sch.

38 Extensions of certain Acts

(1) Section 1 of the Provisional Collection of Taxes Act, 1927, is hereby amended by the insertion of "and value added tax" before "but no other tax or duty".

(2) Section 1 of the Imposition of Duties Act, 1957, is hereby amended by the insertion in paragraph (*gg*) (inserted by the Finance Act, 1963) after "turnover tax" of "or value added tax", but no order shall be made under that Act for the purposes of increasing any of the rates of tax or extending the classes of activities or goods in respect of which tax is for the time being chargeable.

(3) Section 39 of the Inland Revenue Regulations Act, 1890, is hereby amended by the insertion of "value added tax," before "stamp duties".

(4) The First Schedule to the Stamp Act, 1891, shall have effect as if the following exemption were inserted therein under the heading "Bill of Exchange or Promissory Note":

> "Bill drawn on any form supplied by the Revenue Commissioners for the purpose of remitting amounts of value added tax".

Definitions

"goods": s 1(1); "tax": s 1(1).

39 Consequential adjustments in regard to capital allowances

Amendments

Repealed by FA 1975, s 29(3) with effect from 6 April 1975.

40 Increase of excise duty on betting

Note

This section is not relevant for Value Added Tax.

41 Repeals

Note

This section refers to repeals in Sch 5. This is not the existing Sch 5 but an earlier one. The section has no significance in relation to the existing Sch 5.

42 Collection of tax

Tax shall be paid to and collected and levied by the Collector-General.

Definition

"Collector-General": s 1(1); "tax": s 1(1).

43 Care and management of tax

Tax is hereby placed under the care and management of the Revenue Commissioners.

Definitions

"tax": s 1(1).

44 Short title

This Act may be cited as the Value Added Tax Act, 1972.

FIRST SCHEDULE
Exempted Activities

[(i)   Financial services consisting of—

(*a*)   the issue, [other than the issue of new stocks, new shares, new debentures or new securities made to raise capital, the]¹ transfer or a 13B(d) receipt of, or any dealing in, stocks, shares, debentures and other securities, other than documents establishing title to goods,

(*b*)   the arranging for, or the underwriting of, an issue [of stocks, shares, debentures and other securities, other than documents establishing title to goods,]²

(*c*)   the operation of any current, deposit or savings account [and the negotiation of, or any dealings in, payments, transfers, debts, cheques and other negotiable instruments excluding debt collection and factoring]³,

(*d*)   the issue, transfer or receipt of, or any dealing in, currency, bank notes and metal coins, in use as legal tender in any country, excluding such bank notes and coins when supplied as investment goods or as collectors' pieces,

[(*e*)   the granting and the negotiation of credit and the management of credit by the person granting it,]⁴

(*f*)   the granting of, or any dealing in, credit guarantees or any other security for money and the management of credit guarantees by the person who granted the credit,

[(*g*)   [the management of an undertaking specified in one of the following clauses, and such management may comprise any of the three functions listed in Annex II to Directive 2001/107/EC of the European Parliament and Council (being the functions included in the activity of collective portfolio management) where those functions are supplied by the person with responsibility for the provision of the functions concerned in respect of the undertaking, and which is—]⁵

     [(I)   a collective investment undertaking as defined in section 172A of the Taxes Consolidation Act 1997 (as amended by section 59 of the Finance Act 2000), or]⁶

     [(I*a*)   a special investment scheme within the meaning of section 737 of the Taxes Consolidation Act, 1997, or]⁷

     (II)   administered by the holder of an authorisation granted pursuant to the European Communities (Life Assurance) Regulations, 1984 (SI No 57 of 1984), or by a person who is deemed, pursuant to Article 6 of those regulations, to be such a holder, the criteria in relation to which are the criteria specified in relation to an arrangement administered by the holder of a licence under the Insurance Act, 1936, in section 9(2) of the Unit Trusts Act, 1990, or

(III)   a unit trust scheme established solely for the purpose of superannuation fund schemes or charities, or

(IV)   determined by the Minister for Finance to be a collective investment undertaking to which the provisions of [this subparagraph apply, or][8][9]

[(V)   an undertaking which is a qualifying company for the purposes of section 110 of the Taxes Consolidation Act 1997;][10]

(*gg*)   ...[11];

(*h*)   services supplied to a person under arrangements which provide for the reimbursement of the person in respect of the supply by him of goods or services in accordance with a credit card, charge card or similar card scheme;][12]

a 13A
(1)(i), (j)
(ii)   [children's or young people's education,][13] school or university education, and vocational training or retraining (including the supply of goods and services incidental thereto [, other than the supply of research services][14]), provided by educational establishments recognised by the State, and education, training or retraining of a similar kind [, excluding instruction in the driving of mechanically propelled road vehicles other than vehicles designed or constructed for the conveyance of goods with a capacity of 1.5 tonnes or more,][15] provided by other persons;

a 13A(1)
(b),(c), (e)
[(iii)   professional services of a medical nature, other than services specified in paragraph (iii*b*), but excluding such services supplied in the course of carrying on a business which consists in whole or in part of selling goods;][16]

a 13A(1)
(e)
a 13A(1)
(e)
[(iii*a*)   supply by dental technicians of services of a dental nature and of dentures or other dental prostheses;][17]

[(iii*b*)   professional services of a dental or optical nature;][18]

a 13B(b)
(iv)   letting of immovable goods [(which does not include the service of allowing a person use a toll road or a toll bridge)][19] with the exception of—

(*a*)   letting of machinery or business installations when let separately from any other immovable goods of which such machinery or installations form part;

[(*b*)   letting of the kind to which [paragraph (ii) of the Third Schedule or paragraph (xiii) of the Sixth Schedule][20] refers;][21]

[(*bi*)   provision of facilities of the kind to which paragraph (vii*a*) of the Sixth Schedule refers;][22]

(*c*) provision of parking accommodation for vehicles by the operators of car parks; and

(*d*) hire of safes;

(v) hospital and medical care or treatment provided by a hospital, nursing home, clinic or similar establishment; <small>a 13A (1)(b), (c), (d), (e)</small>

(vi) services for the protection or care of children and young persons, and the provision of goods closely related thereto, provided otherwise than for profit [and the supply of services for the protection or care of children and young persons, and the provision of goods closely related thereto, provided by persons whose activities may be regulated by regulations made under [Part VII or Part VIII of the Child Care Act 1991]²³;]²⁴ <small>a 13A (1)(h)</small>

(vii) supply of goods and services closely related to welfare and social security by non-profit making organisations; <small>a 13(1)(g)</small>

[(viii) promotion of and admissions to live theatrical or musical performances, including circuses, but not including— <small>a 13A (1)(n)</small>

    (*a*) dances ...²⁵, or

    (*b*) performances in conjunction with which facilities are available for the consumption of food or drink during all or part of the performance by persons attending the performance;]²⁶

[(viii*a*) supply of cultural services and of goods closely linked thereto by any cultural body, whether established by or under statute or otherwise, which is recognised as such a body by the Revenue Commissioners for the purposes of this paragraph, not being services to which paragraph (viii) relates;]²⁷ <small>a 13A (1)(n)</small>

(ix) agency services in regard to—

    (*a*) the arrangement of passenger transport or accommodation for persons, [and]²⁸ ...²⁹ <small>Annex F 27, a 28(3)(b)</small>

    ...³⁰

    ...³¹

    [(*d*) services specified in paragraph (i),]³²

[excluding ...³³ management and safekeeping services in regard to the services specified in paragraph (i)(*a*), not being services specified in [subparagraph [(g)]³⁴ of paragraph (i)]³⁵;]³⁶

(x) ...³⁷

[(xi) insurance and reinsurance transactions, including related services performed by insurance brokers and insurance agents and, for the purposes of this paragraph, **"related services"** includes the collection of insurance premiums, the sale of insurance, and claims handling and claims settlement services where the supplier of the insurance services delegates the authority to an agent and is bound by the decision of that agent in relation to that claim;][38]

a 13A(1)   [(xi*a*)   public postal services (including the supply of goods and services
(a)   incidental thereto) supplied by An Post including postmasters, or by persons licensed in accordance with section 73 or subsection (1) of section 111 of the Postal and Telecommunications Services Act, 1983;][39]

         (xii)   ...[40]

a 13A(1)(q)   (xiii)   the national broadcasting and television services, excluding advertising;
Annex F 17,
a 28(3)(b)   (xiv)   transport of passengers and their accompanying baggage;

a 13B(f)   [(xv)   the acceptance of bets subject to excise duty imposed by section 67 of the Finance Act2002 and of bets exempted from excise duty by section 68 of the Finance Act 2002;][41]

         ...[42]

a 13B(f)   (xvi)   issue of tickets or coupons for the purpose of a lottery;

        [(xvii)   promotion of (other than in the course of the provision of facilities of the kind specified in paragraph (viia) of the Sixth Schedule), or the admission of spectators to, sporting events;][43]

a 13A(1)(d)   (xviii)   collection, storage [, supply, intra-Community acquisition or importation][44] of human organs, human blood and human milk;

     [(xviii*a*)   supply, intra-Community acquisition and importation of investment gold (within the meaning of section 6A) other than supplies of investment gold to the Central Bank of Ireland;

     (xviii*b*)   supply of services of an intermediary (as defined in section 6A) acting in that capacity;][45]

Annex F 6,   (xix)   funeral undertaking;
28(3)(b)
         (xx)   ...[46]

         (xxi)   ...[46]

a 13A(1)(b)   (xxii)   supply of services and of goods closely related thereto for the benefit of their members by non-profit making organisations whose aims are primarily of a political, trade union, religious, patriotic, philosophical, philanthropic or civic nature where such supply is made without payment other than the payment of any membership subscription;

a 13A(1)(f)[(xxii*a*)   supply of services by an independent group of persons (being a group which is an independent entity established for the purpose of administrative convenience by persons whose activities are exempt from or are not subject to tax) for the purpose of rendering its members the services directly necessary for the exercise of their activities and where the group only recovers from its members the exact reimbursement of each member's share of the joint expenses;][47]

(xxiii) provision of facilities for taking part in sporting and physical education activities, and services closely related thereto, provided ...[48] by non-profit making organisations [with the exception of facilities to which paragraph (viib) or (viic) of the Sixth Schedule refers][49]; a 13A(1)(m)

(xxiv) supply of goods [other than [a supply of immovable goods to which section 3(1)(c) or 4 relates, or][50] a supply of goods of a kind specified in section 3(1)(g),][51] by a person being goods— a 13B(c)

   (a) which were used by him for the purposes of a business carried on by him,

   (b) in relation to the acquisition or application of which he had borne tax, and

   (c) which are of such a kind or were used in such circumstances that no part of the said tax was deductible under section 12;

(xxv) catering services supplied— a 13A(1)(b)

   (a) to patients of a hospital or nursing home in the hospital or nursing home, and

   (b) to students of a school in [the school;][52][53]

[(xxvi) the importation of gas through the natural gas distribution system, or the importation of electricity.][54]

Amendments

[1] Words "other than the issue of new stocks, new shares, new debentures or new securities made to raise capital, the" inserted by FA 2006, s 100(a) with effect from 31 March 2006.

[2] Substituted by FA 2006, s 100(b) with effect from 31 March 2006; previously "specified in subparagraph (a),".

[3] Inserted by FA 1991, s 85 with effect from 29 May 1991.

[4] Para (i)(e) substituted by FA 1995, s 139(a) with effect from 2 June 1995.

[5] Substituted by FA 2004, s 64(a)(i) with effect from 25 March 2004; previously "the management of an undertaking which is—".

[6] Para (i)(g)(I) substituted by FA 2002, s 138 and Sch 6 para 1(e) with effect from 25 March 2002.

[7] Para (i)(g)(I)–(i)(g)(Ia) inserted by FA 1999, s 138(a) with effect from 25 March 1999.

[8] Substituted by FA 2004, s 64(a)(ii) with effect from 25 March 2004; previously "this subparagraph apply;".

[9] Para (i)(g) substituted by FA 1991, s 85 with effect from 29 May 1991.

[10] Para (i)(g)(V) inserted by FA 2004, s 64(a)(iii) with effect from 25 March 2004.

[11] Para (i)(gg) deleted by FA 1991, s 85 with effect from 29 May 1991.

[12] Para (i) substituted by FA 1987, s 45 with effect from 1 November 1987.

[13] Inserted by FA 1997, s 110(a) as on and from 1 May 1997.

[14] Inserted by FA 2001, s 199(a) with effect from the 1 September 2001.

[15] Inserted by FA 1990, s 106 with effect from 30 May 1990.

[16] Para (iii) substituted by FA 1989, s 61 with effect from 1 November 1989.

[17] Para (iiia) inserted by FA 1986, s 89 with effect from 1 July 1986.

[18] Para (iiib) inserted by FA 1989, s 61 with effect from 1 November 1989.

[19] Inserted by FA 2001, s 199(b) with effect from the 1 September 2001.

[20] Substituted by FA 1993, s 94 with effect from 1 March 1993; previously "paragraph (vi) of the Third Schedule".

[21] Para (iv)(b) inserted by FA 1991, s 85 with effect from 29 May 1991.

[22] Para (iv)(bi) inserted by FA 1992, s 194(1)(a) with effect from 1 July 1992.

[23]   Substituted by FA 2003, s 163 and Sch 6 para 2 with effect from 28 March 2003; previously "Part VII of the Child Care Act 1991".

[24]   Inserted by FA 1997, s 110(*b*) as on and from 1 May 1997.

[25]   Words "to which section 11(7) relates" deleted by FA 1992, s 194(1)(*b*) with effect from 28 May 1992.

[26]   Para (viii) inserted by FA 1985, s 49 with effect from 1 March 1985.

[27]   Para (viii*a*) inserted by FA 1990, s 106 with effect from 30 May 1990.

[28]   Inserted by FA 2001, s 199(*c*) with effect from the 1 May 2001.

[29]   Word "and" deleted by FA 1987, s 45 with effect from 1 November 1987.

[30]   Para (ix)(*b*) deleted by FA 2001, s 199(*d*)(i) with effect from the 1 May 2001.

[31]   Para (ix)(*c*) deleted by FA 2001, s 199(*d*)(ii) with effect from the 1 May 2001.

[32]   Para (ix)(*d*) substituted by FA 1987, s 45 with effect from 1 November 1987.

[33]   Deleted by FA 2001, s 199(*d*)(iii) with effect from the 1 May 2001; previously "the services of loss adjusters and excluding".

[34]   Substituted by FA 1991, s 85 with effect from 29 May 1991; previously "(*g*) or (*gg*)".

[35]   Substituted by FA 1989, s 61 with effect from 1 July 1989; previously "paragraph (i)(*g*)".

[36]   Words inserted by FA 1987, s 45 with effect from 1 November 1987.

[37]   Para (x) deleted by FA 1991, s 85 with effect from 1 January 1992.

[38]   Para (xi) substituted by FA 2001, s 199(*e*) with effect from 1 May 2001.

[39]   Para (xi*a*) inserted by FA 1991, s 85 with effect from 1 January 1992.

[40]   Para (xii) deleted by FA 1987, s 45 with effect from 1 November 1987.

[41]   Para (xv) substituted by FA 2005, s 112(*a*) with effect from 25 March 2005.

[42]   Para (xv*a*) deleted by FA 2005, s 112(*b*) with effect from 25 March 2005.

[43]   Para (xvii) substituted by FA 1992, s 194(1)(*c*) with effect from 1 July 1992.

[44]   Substituted by FA 1992, s 194(2)(*a*) with effect from 1 July 1992; previously "supply and importation".

[45]   Paras (xviii*a*)–(xviii*b*) inserted by FA 1999, s 138(*b*) with effect from 25 March 1999.

[46]   Paras (xx) and (xxi) deleted by FA 1990, s 106 with effect from 1 January 1991.

[47]   Para (xxii*a*) inserted by FA 1990, s 106 with effect from 30 May 1990.

[48]   Words "for its members" deleted by FA 1992, s 194(1)(*e*) with effect from 1 July 1992.

[49]   Inserted by FA 1995, s 139(*b*) with effect from 1 January 1996.

[50]   Inserted by FA 2005, s 112(*c*) with effect from 25 March 2005.

[51]   Inserted by FA 1992, s 194(2)(*b*) with effect from 1 January 1993.

[52]   Substituted by FA 2004, s 64(*b*) with effect from 25 March 2004; previously "the school".

[53]   Sch 1 substituted by VATAA 1978, s 24 with effect from 1 March 1979.

[54]   Para (xxvi) inserted by FA 2004, s 64(*c*) with effect from 25 March 2004.

Cross-references

Apportionment of tax, Revenue may specify method: s 32(1)(*x*); method: VATA 1979, r 16.

Paras (i), (iv), (ix), (xi), (xi*a*), (xiii), (xiv): special provisions in relation to immovable goods: s 4(8).

Para (i)(*e*) taxable amount: s 10(4C); invoice requirements: s 17(1)(proviso).

Para (i)(*gg*): special investment schemes: FA 1993, s 13(6)(*a*)(i) (see *Tax Acts*).

Para (xxiii): Minister may provide that State and local authority may be taxable persons: s 8(2A)(*a*)(proviso); Revenue may make determination regarding such services: s 8(3E)(*a*).

Para (xxiv): margin scheme goods: s 10A(13); auctioneers, special scheme: s 10B(10); taxable dealers supplying means of transport: s 12B(10).

Case law

Subject	Case	Case reference
Financial services provided by third parties to banks are exempt from VAT	*Sparekassernes Datacenter (SDC) v Skatteministeriet*	C–2/95
Para (i)(*h*): Charge card company denied judicial review of its exempt status	*The Diners Club Ltd. v Revenue Commissioners*	(III) ITR (680)

Whether provision of "call centre" services considered as exempt transactions in securities	*CSC Financial Services Ltd v Commissioners of Customs & Excise*	13 December 2001, C–235/00
Treatment of toll roads	*Commission of the European Communities v Ireland*	12 September 2000, C–358/97
Meaning of "non-profit making organisations"	*Kennemar Golf & Country Club v Staatssecretaris van Financien*	21 March 2002, C–174/00
Research activities of public-sector higher-education establishments	*Commission v Germany*	20 June 2002, C–287/00
Exemption of care provided by capital companies	*Ambulanter Pfegedienst Kügler GmbH v Finanzamt für Körperschaften I in Berlin*	10 September 2002, C–141/00
Cultural Services by a Soloist	*Matthias Hoffman v Bundesgerichtshof (Germany)*	3 April 2003, C–144/00
Letting of Immovable Property (Prefabricated Building)	*Rudolf Maierhofer v Finanzamt Augsburg-Land*	16 January 2003, C–315/00
Exemption for medical care provided in the exercise of the medical and paramedical professions — expert medical report	*Margarete Unterpertinger v Pensionsvarsicherungsanstalt der Arbeiter*	20 November 2003, C–212/01
Letting of immovable property — cigarette vending machine installed in commercial premises	*Sinclair Collins v Commissioners of Customs and Excise*	12 June 2003, C–275/01
Phychotherapeutic treatment given in an out-patient facility provided by a foundation governed by private law	*Christoph-Dornier-Stiftung fur Klinische Psychologie v finanzamt Giesen*	6 November 2003, C–45/01
Medical care provided in the exercise of the medical and paramedical professions	*Dr Peter L d'Ambremunil, Dispute Resolution Services Ltd v Customs and Excise*	20 November 2003, C–307/01
Letting of immovable property — Licence to occupy	*Belgian State v Temco Europe SA*	18 November 2004, C–284/03
Outsourcing insurance related services — agency services	*Staatssectretaris van Financien v Arthur Andersen & Co*	3 March 2005, C–472/03
Share issues	*Kretzetchnik AG v Finanzamt Linz*	26 May 2005, C–465/03

Revenue precedents

Issue: Receipts from card games in public house.

Decision: Exempt — letting.

Issue: Breakdown of a fund management service into separate elements, for one overall charge.

Decision: The service agreement may be regarded as a package of separately identifiable activities and the fee may be apportioned between the separate elements provided that these are identified in the service agreement and that the basis for apportionment is realistic.

Issue: The supply of administration (back-office) services to specified funds.

Decision: Where administration services are provided to a fund by an administrator under licence from the IFSC authorisation body, as part of the statutory structure of the fund, then the service may be regarded as part of the exempt management function. Consequently, administration in these circumstances becomes a financial service and Fourth Schedule.

Issue: Company providing medical services.

Decision: Exempt, as company is run by doctors (medical).

Issue: Osteopaths and Chiropractors.

Decision: Exempt. First Schedule para (iii).

Issue: Chiropodists.

Decision: Exempt, Appeal Commissioner decision.

Issue: Nursing consultant.

Decision: Exempt.

Issue: Commission payable to agents selling lottery cards.

Decision: Commission exempt. Treatment is made possible through the broader interpretation of the phrase "issue of tickets or coupons for the purpose of a lottery".

Issue: Group treatment of management companies and special purpose companies, captive finance companies and captive insurance companies.

Decision: Group treatment agreed provided the managed entities are passive and not operationally involved in any activities and that the managed entities do not have any independent management capabilities. Relaxation of the joint and several liability requirement extended the managed entities operating in IFSC, provided, they have been approved for group treatment.

Issue: Services bought in from overseas by the managers of specified funds.

Decision: Certain services received from outside the State may qualify for the exemption applying to fund management services, provided Revenue are satisfied that those services form part of the management function.

Issue: Management of a qualifying fund partially subcontracted to commodity trading advisors outside the State.

Decision: In a particular case Revenue accepted that services were supplied to the investment manager outside the State for onward supply to the qualifying funds. Fees payable were not related to services received in the State.

Issue: Admission fees to historic houses and gardens.

Decision: On foot of appeal case admissions exempt under First Schedule para (iv).

Issue: Treatment of agency services in relation to issue, transfer or receipt of, or any dealing in stocks and shares.

Decision: Transfer agency services insofar as they have to do with purchase and redemption of shares, provided as a fully integrated service, qualify as exempt under First Schedule paras (i)(*a*) and (ix)(*d*). Registration services as a separate supply are taxable.

Issue: Management of ATCs in IFSC.

Decision: To the extent that an ATC is engaged in exempt financial transactions the manager can also be regarded as engaged in exempt financial transactions.

Issue: Management of credit card transactions.

Decision: Provision of management as a total servicing system for credit card transactions is regarded as single composite supply within the meaning of First Schedule para (ix)(*d*).

Issue: Is claims handling an insurance service/agency service in relation to insurance.

Decision: Agent has no authority to conclude contracts either as principal or agent on behalf of insurer. Services are supplied to the insurer and not regarded as exempt activities under First Schedule para (xi) or (ix)(*c*).

Issue: Promotion of certain film festivals in the course of business.

Decision: Festival company regarded as cultural body for the purposes of (viii*a*) and exempt for VAT.

Issue: Global custodial services.

Decision: On the basis that the taxable element constitutes a negligible part of the total cost of supplying the global custody service, Revenue accept that the service is an exempt financial service. Supply of purely physical service of safekeeping is not exempt.

Issue: VAT on inputs in relation to the exempt activities of a company that is involved in both taxable and exempt activities is non-deductible.

Decision: Deductibility allowed on certain inputs deemed attributable to the taxable activities of the company.

Issue: Fees received by solicitors in relation to arranging for issue of shares.

Decision: Insofar as solicitors actively participate in the arranging for and the issue of specific shares and are involved from the start, their fees are exempt.

Issue: Should tour operators be treated the same as travel agents?

Decision: Yes. (This followed discussions and agreement with the trade).

Revenue publications

Factoring and invoice discounting: Tax Briefing Issue 59.

Guide to Value Added Tax (Revenue Commissioners): Chapter 15.

Insurance related services: Tax Briefing Issue 45.

Shares, VAT not deductible: Statement of Practice VAT 2/90.

Share issues: Tax Briefing 61.

Sports facilities: persons liable, "sport facilities" defined etc: Statement of Practice VAT 4/92.

VAT treatment of the promotion of and admission to live theatrical and musical events (including performances by non-established performers): Information Leaflet No 2/06.

Definition

"business": s 1(1); "goods": s 1(1); "hire": s 1(1); "immovable goods": s 1(1); "the Minister": s 1(1); "establishment": s 1(1); "person": IA 2005, s 18(*c*); "regulations": ss 1(1), 32; "supply": s 1(1); "tax": s 1(1).

SECOND SCHEDULE

a 15, 16, 18

GOODS AND SERVICES CHARGEABLE AT THE RATE OF ZERO PER CENT

[(i) The supply of goods—

(*a*) subject to a condition that they are to be transported directly by or on behalf of the person making the supply—

[(I) outside the Community: a 15(1)

Provided that this subparagraph shall not apply to a supply of goods to a traveller (within the meaning assigned by section 13(3B)) which such traveller exports on behalf of the supplier and such supply shall be deemed to be a supply of the type referred to in subparagraph (*f*), or]²

(II) to a registered person within the customs-free airport,

[(*aa*) subject to a condition that they are to be dispatched or transported directly outside the Community by or on behalf of the purchaser of the goods where that purchaser is established outside the State,]¹

(*b*) dispatched or transported from the State to a person registered for a 28cA(a) value added tax in another Member State,

(*c*) being new means of transport dispatched or transported directly by a 28cA(b) or on behalf of the supplier to a person in the territory of another Member State,

[(*cc*) being excisable products dispatched or transported from the State to a 28cA(c) a person in another Member State when the movement of the goods is subject to the provisions of Chapter II of Part II of the Finance Act, 1992, and any other enactment which is to be construed together with that Chapter, which implement the arrangements specified in paragraph 4 and 5 of Article 7, or Article 16, of Council Directive No. 92/12/EEC of 25 February 1992,]³

(*d*) by a registered person within a free port to another registered person within a free port,

(*e*) by a registered person within the customs-free airport to another registered person within the customs-free airport or a free port;

[(*f*) which are a traveller's qualifying goods (within the meaning assigned by subsection (3B) of section 13), provided that the provisions of subsection (1A) of that section and regulations (if any) made thereunder are complied with;]⁴

[(i*a*) subject to such conditions and in such amounts as may be specified in regulations,—

(*a*) the supply of goods, in a tax-free shop approved by the Revenue Commissioners, to travellers departing the State for a place outside the Community, or

(*b*) the supply, other than by means of a vending machine, of food, drink and tobacco products on board a vessel or aircraft to passengers departing the State for another Member State, for consumption on board that vessel or aircraft;]⁵]⁶

(ii) ...⁷;

(iii) the carriage of goods in the State by or on behalf of a person in execution of a contract to transfer the goods to ...⁸ a place [outside the Community]⁹;

a 28cC   [(iii*a*) intra-Community transport services involving the carriage of goods to and from the Azores or Madeira;

a 28cD   (iii*b*) subject to and in accordance with regulations, the importation of goods which, at the time of the said importation, are consigned to another Member State;]¹⁰

(iv) the provision of docking, landing, loading or unloading facilities, including customs clearance, directly in connection with the disembarkation or embarkation of passengers or the importation or exportation of goods;

[(v) the supply, modification, repair, maintenance and hiring of—

a 15(5)   (*a*) sea- going vessels of a gross tonnage of more than 15 tons being vessels used or to be used—

(I) for the carriage of passengers for reward,

(II) for the purposes of a sea fishing business,

(III) for other commercial or industrial purposes, or

(IV) for rescue or assistance at sea, or

a 15(6)   (*b*) aircraft used or to be used by a transport undertaking operating for reward chiefly on international routes;]¹¹

a 15(6)   [(v*a*) the supply repair, maintenance and hiring of equipment incorporated or used in aircraft to which subparagraph (*b*) of paragraph (v) relates;]¹²

[(v*aa*) subject to and in accordance with regulations, if any, the supply, hiring, repair and maintenance of equipment incorporated or for use in sea-going vessels to which subparagraph (*a*) of paragraph (v) relates;]¹³

a 15(4),   [(v*b*) the supply of goods for the fuelling and provisioning of sea-going
15(7)   vessels and aircraft of the kind specified in paragraph (v) [but not including goods for supply on board such vessels or aircraft to

passengers for the purpose of those goods being carried off such vessels or aircraft];[14]]15

[(vc) the supply of navigation services by the Irish Aviation Authority to meet a 15(9) the needs of aircraft used by a transport undertaking operating for reward chiefly on international routes;]16

[(vi) services, supplied by an agent acting in the name and on be half of a 15(14) another person, in procuring—

(a) the export of goods ...17;

(b) services specified in paragraphs (iii), [(iiia)]18 (iv), (v) or (x), or

(c) the supply of goods or services outside the [Community]19;]20

[(via) subject to and in accordance with section 13A, the supply of qualifying goods and qualifying services to, or the intra-Community acquisition or importation of qualifying goods by, an authorised person in accordance with that section, excluding supplies of goods within the meaning of paragraph (e) or (f) of subsection (1) of section 3;]21

[(vib) the supply of services in procuring a repayment of tax due on the supply of a traveller's qualifying goods (within the meaning assigned by subsection (3B) of section 13) or the application of the provisions of subparagraph (i)(f) of this Schedule to that supply of goods, provided that the provisions of subsection (1A) of that section and regulations (if any) made thereunder are complied with;]22

(vii) animal feeding stuff, excluding feeding stuff which is packaged, sold or otherwise designated for the use of dogs, cats, cage birds or domestic pets;

(viii) fertiliser (within the meaning of the Fertilisers, Feeding Stuffs and Mineral Mixtures Act, 1955) which is [supplied]23 in units of not less than 10 kilograms and the sale or manufacture for sale of which is not prohibited under section 4 or 6 of the said Act;

(ix) services provided by the Commissioners of Irish Lights in connection with the operation of lightships, lighthouses or other navigational aids;

[(x) gold supplied to the Central Bank of Ireland;]24   a 15(11)

(xi) life saving services provided by the Royal National Lifeboat Institution including the organisation and maintenance of the lifeboat service;

[(xii) food and drink of a kind used for human consumption, other than the supply thereof specified in [paragraph (iv) of the Sixth Schedule]25, excluding—

(a) beverages chargeable with any duty of excise specifically charged on spirits, beer, wine, cider, perry or Irish wine, and preparations thereof, [(*b*)   other beverages, including water and syrups, concentrates, essences, powders, crystals or other products for the preparation of beverages, but not including—

(I)   tea and preparations thereof,

(II)   cocoa, coffee and chicory and other roasted coffee substitutes, and preparations and extracts thereof,

(III)   milk and preparations and extracts thereof, or

(IV)   preparations and extracts of meat, yeast, or egg;][26]

[(*c*)   ice cream, ice lollipops, water ices, frozen desserts, frozen yoghurts and similar frozen products, and prepared mixes and powders for making any such product or such similar product;][27]

(*d*)   (I)   chocolates, sweets and similar confectionery (including ...[28], glacé or crystallized fruits), biscuits, crackers and wafers of all kinds, and all other confectionery and bakery products [, whether cooked or uncooked,][29] excluding bread,

(II)   in this subparagraph **"bread"** means food for human consumption manufactured by baking dough composed exclusively of a mixture of cereal flour and any one or more of the ingredients mentioned in the following subclauses in quantities not exceeding the limitation, if any, specified for each ingredient—

(1)   yeast or other leavening or aerating agent, salt, malt extract, milk, water, gluten,

(2)   fat, sugar and bread improver, subject to the limitation that the weight of any ingredient specified in this subclause shall not exceed **2 per cent** of the weight of flour included in the dough,

(3)   dried fruit, subject to the limitation that the weight thereof shall not exceed **10 per cent** of the weight of flour included in the dough,

other than food packaged for sale as a unit (not being a unit designated as containing only food specifically for babies) containing two or more slices, segments, sections or other similar pieces, having a crust over substantially the whole of their outside surfaces, being a crust formed in the course of baking [, or frying][30] or toasting, and

[(*e*)   any of the following when supplied for human consumption without further preparation, namely—

(I)   potato crisps, potato sticks, potato puffs and similar products made from potato, or from potato flour or from potato starch,

(II)   savoury products made from cereal or grain, or from flour or starch derived from cereal or grain, pork scratchings, and similar products,

(III) popcorn, and

(IV) salted or roasted nuts whether or not in shells;]³¹]³²

(xiii) medicine of a kind used for human oral consumption;

(xiv) medicine of a kind used for animal oral consumption, excluding medicine which is packaged, sold or otherwise designated for the use of dogs, cats, cage birds or domestic pets;

(xv) seeds, plants, trees, spores, bulbs, tubers, tuberous roots, corms, crowns and rhizomes, of a kind used for sowing in order to produce food;

[(xva) printed books and booklets including atlases but excluding—

(a) newspapers, periodicals, brochures, catalogues [, directories]³³ and programmes,

(b) books of stationery, cheque books and the like,

(c) diaries, organisers, yearbooks, planners and the like the total area of whose pages consist of **25 per cent** or more of blank spaces for the recording of information,

(d) albums and the like, and

(e) books of stamps, of tickets or of coupons.]³⁴

[(xvi) the supply of services consisting of work on movable goods acquired or imported for the purpose of undergoing such work within the Community and dispatched or transported out of the Community by or on behalf of the person providing the services]³⁵

[(xvia) the supply of transport services relating to the importation of goods where the value of such services is included in the taxable amount in accordance with section 15(3);]³⁶

[(xvii) articles of children's personal clothing of sizes which do not exceed the sizes of those articles appropriate to children of average build of 10 years of age (a child whose age is 10 years or 10 years and a fraction of a year being taken for the purposes of this paragraph to be a child of 10 years of age), but excluding—

(a) articles of clothing made wholly or partly of fur skin other than garments merely trimmed with fur skin, unless the trimming has an area greater than one-fifth of the area of the outside material, and

(b) articles of clothing which are not described, labelled, marked or marketed on the basis of age or size;]³⁷

[(xviii) sanitary towels and sanitary tampons;]³⁸

[(xix) articles of children's personal footwear of sizes which do not exceed the size appropriate to children of average foot size of 10 years of age (a child whose age is 10 years or 10 years and a fraction of a year being taken for the purposes of this paragraph to be child of 10 years of age), but excluding footwear which is not described, labelled, marked or marketed on the basis of age or size;][39]

[(xix*a*) medical equipment and appliances being—

(*a*) invalid carriages, and other vehicles (excluding mechanically propelled road vehicles), of a kind designed for use by invalids or infirm persons,

(*b*) orthopaedic appliances, surgical belts, trusses and the like, deaf aids, and artificial limbs and other artificial parts of the body excluding artificial teeth [, corrective spectacles and contact lenses][40],

(*c*) walking frames and crutches,

(*d*) parts or accessories suitable for use solely or principally with any of the goods specified in subparagraphs (*a*), (*b*) and (*c*) of this paragraph;][41]

[(xx) (*a*)...[42],

(*b*) wax candles and night-lights which are white and cylindrical, excluding candles and night-lights which are decorated, spiralled, tapered or perfumed.][43]][44]

Amendments

[1] Para (i)(*aa*) inserted by FA 1999, s 139 with effect from 1 July 1999.

[2] Para (i)(*a*)(I) substituted by FA 1997, s 111(*a*)(i) as on and from 1 July 1997.

[3] Para (i)(*cc*) inserted by EC(VAT)R 1992, r 14 with effect from 1 January 1993.

[4] Para (i)(*f*) inserted by FA 1997, s 111(*a*)(ii) as on and from 1 July 1997.

[5] Para (i*a*) substituted by FA 2000, s 123(*a*) with effect from 1 July 1999.

[6] Para (i) substituted by FA 1992, s 195(2)(*a*) with effect from 1 January 1993.

[7] Para (ii) repealed by VATAA 1978, s 30(1) with effect from 1 March 1979.

[8] Words "or from" deleted by FA 1996, s 98(*a*) with effect from 15 May 1996.

[9] Substituted by FA 1992, s 195(2)(*b*) with effect from 1 January 1993, previously "outside the State".

[10] Paras (iii*a*)–(iii*b*) inserted by FA 1992, s 195(2)(*c*) with effect from 1 January 1993.

[11] Para (v) substituted by VATAA 1978, s 25 with effect from 1 March 1979.

[12] Para (v*a*) inserted by FA 1992, s 195(1)(*a*) with effect from 28 May 1992.

[13] Para (v*aa*) inserted by FA 2001, s 200 with effect from 6 April 2001.

[14] Inserted by FA 2000, s 123(*b*) with effect from 1 July 1999.

[15] Para (v*b*) inserted by FA 1993, s 95(*a*).

[16] Para (v*c*) inserted by FA 1998, s 116(*a*) with effect from 1 March 1998.

[17] Words "from the State" deleted by FA 1992, s 195(2)(*d*)(i) with effect from 1 January 1993.

[18] Inserted by FA 1992, s 195(2)(*d*)(ii) with effect from 1 January 1993.

[19] Substituted by FA 1992, s 195(2)(*d*)(iii) with effect from 1 January 1993; previously "State".

[20] Para (vi) substituted by VATAA 1978, s 25 with effect from 1 March 1979.

[21] Para (vi*a*) inserted by FA 1993, s 95(*b*).

[22] Para (vi*b*) inserted by FA 1997, s 111(*b*) as on and from 1 July 1997.

[23] Substituted by VATAA 1978, s 30(2) with effect from 1 March 1979; previously "delivered".

[24] Para (x) substituted by VATAA 1978, s 25 with effect from 1 March 1979.

[25] Substituted by FA 1992, s 195(1)(*b*)(i) with effect from 28 May 1992; previously "paragraph (xi*c*) of the Sixth Schedule".

[26] Para (xii)(*b*) substituted by FA 1992, s 195(1)(*b*)(ii) with effect from 1 November 1992.

[27] Para (xii)(*c*) substituted by FA 1992, s 195(1)(*b*)(iii) with effect from 1 July 1992.

[28] Word "drained" deleted by FA 1987, s 46 with effect from 1 July 1987.

[29] Inserted by FA 1992, s 195(1)(*b*)(iv)(I) with effect from 1 July 1992.

[30] Inserted by FA 1992, s 195(1)(*b*)(iv)(II) with effect from 1 July 1992.

[31] Para (xii)(*e*) substituted by FA 1992, s 195(1)(*b*)(v) with effect from 1 July 1992.

[32] Para (xii) substituted by FA 1985, s 50 with effect from 1 March 1985.

[33] Inserted by FA 2000, s 123(*c*) with effect from 23 March 2000.

[34] Para (xv*a*) inserted by FA 1998, s 116(*b*) with effect from 1 May 1998.

[35] Para (xvi) substituted by FA 1996, s 98(*b*) with effect from 1 January 1996.

[36] Para (xvi*a*) inserted by FA 1996, s 98(*c*) with effect from 1 January 1996.

[37] Para (xvii) substituted by FA 1984, s 92 with effect from 1 May 1984.

[38] Para (xviii) substituted by FA 1984, s 92 with effect from 1 May 1984.

[39] Para (xix) substituted by FA 1985, s 50 with effect from 1 March 1985; previously "(xviii*a*) and (xix)".

[40] Words ", corrective spectacles and contact lenses" inserted by FA 1989, s 63 with effect from 1 November 1989.

[41] Para (xix*a*) inserted by Value Added Tax (Reduction of Rate) (No 5) Order 1981 (SI 53/81) with effect from 1 March 1981.

[42] Para (xx)(*a*) deleted by FA 1988, s 63 with effect from 1 March 1992.

[43] Para (xx) substituted by FA 1983, s 86 with effect from 1 May 1983.

[44] Sch 2 substituted by FA 1976, s 60(*b*) with effect from 1 March 1976.

Cross-references

Para (i)(*a*)(I): alcohol products: s 3B(2); zero rating of sales to authorised exporters: s 13A(1).
Para (i)(*b*): alcohol products: s 3B(2); zero rating of sales to authorised exporters: s 13A(1); margin scheme goods: s 10A(10); auctioneers, special scheme: s 10B(7).
Para (i)(*cc*): alcohol products: s 3B(2).
Para (i*a*): alcohol products: s 3B(2); tax free shops, Revenue may regulate: s 32(1)(*ag*).
Para (iii*b*): import of goods consigned to another EC State: s 32(1)(*ah*).
Para (v): repair etc of movable goods: Sch 6 para (xviii)(*b*).
Para (v*a*): repair etc of movable goods: Sch 6 para (xviii)(*b*).
Para (vi*a*): zero rating of sales to authorised exporters: s 13A(5)–(8); waiver of exemption: s 7(3)(*c*).
Para (xii) (other than (subparas (*c*) or (*e*)(II)): rate on food: Sch 6 para (xxxi).
Para (xv): nursery or garden stock other than under this para: Sch 6 para (xi*a*).
Para (xvi): repair etc of movable goods: s 11(1AB) and Sch 6 para (xviii)(*b*).
Para (xvii): clothing, average size, Revenue may determine: s 32(1)(*w*).
Para (xix): footwear, average size, Revenue may determine: s 32(1)(*ww*).

Case law

Subject	Case	Case reference
Meaning of "aircraft used by airlines operating chiefly on international routes"	*Cimber Air A/S v Skatteministeriet*	16 September 2004, C–382/02

Regulations

Subject	Regulation
Abolition of duty free shops	European Communities (Value Added Tax) Regulations 1999 (SI 196/99)
Abolition of duty free shops	European Communities (Value Added Tax) Regulations 1999 (SI 197/99)

Revenue publications

Agricultural services: Statement of Practice VAT 5/92 (Replaced by Information Leaflet No 23/01).
Books: Statement of Practice VAT Apr 1/98.
Food and drink: Statement of Practice VAT 10/92.
Footwear: Information leaflet March 1998.
Footwear: Tax Briefing, Issues 27 and 32.
Footwear and clothing: Leaflet September 1987.
Guide to Value Added Tax (Revenue Commissioners): Chapter 15.
Intra-community zero rating: Statement of Practice VAT 8/92.
Printing and printed matter: Leaflet No 2 of 1998.
Rates of VAT on services from 1 March 1991: Statement of Practice VAT 1/91.
Rates of VAT on services from 1 March 1992: Statement of Practice VAT 1/92.
Services: Statement of Practice VAT 1/92.
Zero rating intra-Community supplies: Statement of Practice VAT 8/92.

Definition

"business": s 1(1); "Community": s 1(1); "clothing": s 1(1); "the customs-free airport": s 1(1); "establishment": s 1(1); "excisable products": s 1(1); "exportation of goods": s 1(1); "footwear": s 1(1); "free port": s 1(1); "fur skin": s 1(1); "goods": s 1(1); "movable goods": s 1(1); "new means of transport": s 1(1);"person": IA 2005, s 18(*c*); "a person registered for value added tax": s(1); "registered person": s 1(1); "supply": s 1(1); "vessel": s 1(1).

THIRD SCHEDULE
GOODS AND SERVICES CHARGEABLE AT THE RATE
SPECIFIED IN SECTION 11(1)(*C*)

[(i) Immovable goods being a domestic dwelling for which a contract with a private individual has been entered into before the 25th day of February, 1993, for such supply;

(ii) services specified in paragraph (xiii) of the Sixth Schedule, under an agreement made before the 25th day of February, 1993, and at charges fixed at the time of the agreement for such supply;

(iii) services specified in subparagraph (*a*) of paragraph (xv) of the Sixth Schedule, under an agreement made before the 25th day of February, 1993, and at charges fixed at the time of the agreement for such supply.][1]

Amendments

[1] Sch 3 substituted by FA 1993, s 96 with effect from 1 March 1993.

Revenue publications

Agricultural services: Statement of Practice VAT 5/92 (Replaced by Information Leaflet No 23/01).
Rates of VAT on services from 1 March 1992: Statement of Practice VAT 1/92.

Definition

"development": s 1(1); "goods": s 1(1); "immovable goods": s 1(1); "movable goods": s 1(1); "establishment": s 1(1); "person": IA 2005, s 18(c); "tax": s 1(1); "vessel": s 1(1); "week": IA 2005, Sch.

FOURTH SCHEDULE
SERVICES THAT, WHERE TAXABLE ARE TAXED WHERE RECEIVED

a 9(2)(e)

[(i)   Transfers and assignments of copyright, patents, licences, trade marks and similar rights;

[(i*a*) hiring out of movable goods other than means of transport;][1]

(ii)   advertising services;

(iii) services of consultants, engineers, consultancy bureaux, lawyers, accountants and other similar services, data processing and provision of information (but excluding services connected with immovable goods);

[(iii*a*) telecommunications services;][2]

[(iii*b*) radio and television broadcasting services;

(iii*c*) electronically supplied services;][3]

[(iii*d*) the provision of access to, and of transport or transmission through, natural gas and electricity distribution systems and the provision of other directly linked services;][4]

(iv) acceptance of any obligation to refrain from pursuing or exercising in whole or in part, any business activity or any such rights as are referred to in paragraph (i);

(v)   banking, financial and insurance services (including re-insurance [and financial fund management functions][5], but not including the provision of safe deposit facilities);

(vi) the provision of staff;

(vii) the services of agents who act in the name and for the account of a principal when procuring for him any services specified in paragraphs (i) to (vi).][6]

Amendments

1   Para (i*a*) inserted by FA 1985, s 52 with effect from 30 May 1985.
2   Para (iii*a*) inserted by FA 1997, s 112 as on and from 1 July 1997.
3   Paras (iii*b*) and (iii*c*) inserted by FA 2003, s 131 with effect from 1 July 2003.
4   Para (iii*d*) inserted by FA 2004, s 65(*a*) with effect on and from 1 January 2005.
5   Inserted by FA 2004, s 65(*b*) with effect from 25 March 2004.
6   Sch 4 substituted by VATAA 1978, s 27 with effect from 1 March 1979.

Cross-references

Para (iii): professional services in connection with land etc are taxed where the land etc is located: s 5(6)(*a*).

Place of supply of Fourth Schedule services: s 5(6)(*e*).

Case law

Subject	Case	Case reference
Place of supply — advertising services	*Design Concept SA v Flanders Expo SA*	5 June 2003, C–438/01
Transfer of softwear and related services	*Levob Verzekeringen BV v Staatssecretaris van Financiën*	27 October 2005, C–41/04

Sixth Directive

Supply of services: Art 9(2)(*e*).

Revenue precedent

Issue: Custodial services.
Decision: These are not Fourth Schedule services.

Revenue publications

Advertising: Statement of Practice VAT 3/92.
Commissioned Framed Photography: Tax Briefing Issue 39.
Fourth Schedule Services Information Leaflet No 1 of 2005.
Guide to Value Added Tax (Revenue Commissioners): Chapter 4.
Telecommunication services: Tax Briefing, Issues, 27, 35.

Definition

"business": s 1(1); "goods": s 1(1); "immovable goods": s 1(1); "movable goods": s 1(1).

FIFTH SCHEDULE

PART I

ANNEX A OF COUNCIL DIRECTIVE NO 77/388/EEC OF 17 MAY, 1977
LIST OF AGRICULTURAL PRODUCTION ACTIVITIES

[I. CROP PRODUCTION

1. General agriculture, including viticulture
2. Growing of fruit (including olives) and of vegetables, flowers and ornamental plants, both in the open and under glass
3. Production of mushrooms, spices, seeds and propagating materials; nurseries

II. STOCK FARMING TOGETHER WITH CULTIVATION

1. General stock farming
2. Poultry farming
3. Rabbit farming
4. Beekeeping
5. Silkworm farming
6. Snail farming

III. FORESTRY

IV. FISHERIES

1. Fresh-water fishing
2. Fish farming
3. Breeding of mussels, oysters and other molluscs and crustaceans
4. Frog farming

V. Where a farmer, processes, using means normally employed in an agricultural, forestry or fisheries undertaking, products deriving essentially from his agricultural production, such processing shall also be regarded as agricultural production.

PART II
ANNEX B OF COUNCIL DIRECTIVE NO.77/388/EEC OF 17 MAY, 1977
LIST OF AGRICULTURAL SERVICES

Supplies of agricultural services which normally play a part in agricultural production shall be considered the supply of agricultural services, and include the following in particular:

— field work, reaping and mowing, threshing, baling, collecting, harvesting, sowing and planting
— packing and preparation for market, for example drying, cleaning, grinding, disinfecting and ensilage of agricultural products
— storage of agricultural products
— stock minding, rearing and fattening
— hiring out, for agricultural purposes, of equipment normally used in agricultural, forestry or fisheries undertakings
— technical assistance
— destruction of weeds and pests, dusting and spraying of crops and land
— operation of irrigation and drainage equipment
— lopping, tree felling and other forestry services.][1]

Amendments

[1]   Sch 5 inserted by VATAA 1978, s 28 with effect from 1 March 1979.

Cross-references

A "farmer" is defined as a person who carries on at least one Annex A activity: s 8(9).

Definition

"farmer": ss 1(1), 8(*a*); "land": IA 2005, Sch; "supply": s 1(1).

SIXTH SCHEDULE
GOODS AND SERVICES CHARGEABLE AT THE RATE SPECIFIED IN SECTION 11(1)(*d*)[13.5%]

[(i) (*a*) Coal, peat and other solid substances held out for sale solely as fuel,
  (*b*) electricity:

Provided that this subparagraph shall not apply to the distribution of any electricity where such distribution is wholly or mainly in connection with the distribution of communications signals,

  (*c*) gas of a kind used for domestic or industrial heating or lighting, whether in gaseous or liquid form, but not including [motor vehicle gas within the meaning of section 42(1) of the Finance Act, 1976][1], gas of a kind normally used for welding and cutting metals or gas sold as lighter fuel, (*d*) hydrocarbon oil of a kind used for domestic or industrial heating, excluding gas oil (within the meaning of the Hydrocarbon (Heavy) Oil Regulations, 1989 (SI No 121 of 1989)), other than gas oil which has been duly marked in accordance with Regulation 6(2) of the said Regulations;

(ii) the provision of food and drink of a kind specified in paragraph (xii) of the Second Schedule in a form suitable for human consumption without further preparation—

    (*a*) by means of a vending machine,

    (*b*) in the course of operating a hotel, restaurant, cafe, refreshment house, canteen, establishment licensed for the sale for consumption on the premises of intoxicating liquor, catering business or similar business, or

    (*c*) in the course of operating any other business in connection with the carrying on of which facilities are provided for the consumption of the food or drink supplied;

(iii) the supply, in the course of the provision of a meal, of goods of a kind specified in subparagraph (*c*), (*d*) or (*e*) of paragraph (xii) of the Second Schedule, and fruit juices other than fruit juices chargeable with a duty of excise—

    (*a*) in the course of operating a hotel, restaurant, cafe, refreshment house, canteen, establishment licensed for the sale for consumption on the premises of intoxicating liquor, catering business or similar business, or

    (*b*) in the course of operating any other business in connection with the carrying on of which facilities are provided for the consumption of the food or drink supplied;

(iv) the supply of food [(other than bread as defined in subparagraph (*d*), of paragraph (xii) of the Second Schedule][2] and drink (other than beverages specified in subparagraph (*a*) or (*b*) of paragraph (xii) of the Second Schedule) which is, or includes, food and drink which—

    (*a*) has been [heated, enabling][3] it to be consumed at a temperature above the ambient air temperature, or

    (*b*) has been retained [heated after cooking, enabling][4] it to be consumed at a temperature above the ambient air temperature, or

    (*c*) is supplied, while still warm after cooking, ...[5] enabling it to be consumed at a temperature above the ambient air temperature,

and is above the ambient air temperature [at the time it is provided to the customer][6];

(v) promotion of and admissions to cinematographic performances;

   (vi)   promotion of and admissions to live theatrical or musical performances, excluding—

      (*a*)   dances, and

      (*b*)   performances specified in paragraph (viii) of the First Schedule;

[(vii)   amusement services of the kind normally supplied in fairgrounds or amusement parks:

      Provided that this paragraph shall not apply to–

      (I)   services consisting of dances,

      (II)   services consisting of circuses,

      (III)   services consisting of gaming, as defined in section 2 of the Gaming and Lotteries Act, 1956 (including services provided by means of a gaming machine of the kind referred to in section 43 of the Finance Act, 1975), or

      (IV)   services provided by means of an amusement machine of the kind referred to in section 120 of the Finance Act. 1992;][7]

[(vii*a*)   the provision by a person other than a non-profit making organisation of facilities for taking part in sporting activities;][8]

[(vii*b*)   the provision by a member-owned golf club of facilities for taking part in golf to any person, other than an individual whose membership subscription to that club at the time the facilities are used by that individual entitles that individual to use such facilities without further charge on at least 200 days (including the day on which such facilities are used by that individual) in a continuous period of twelve months, where the total consideration received by that club for the provision of such facilities has exceeded or is likely to exceed [€27,500][9] in any continuous period of twelve months and, for the purposes of this paragraph, the provision of facilities for taking part in golf shall not include the provision of facilities for taking part in pitch and putt;

(vii*c*)   the provision by a non-profit making organisation, other than an organisation referred to in paragraph (vii*b*), of facilities for taking part in golf to any person where the total consideration received by that organisation for the provision of such facilities has exceeded or is likely to exceed [€27,500][10] in any continuous period of twelve months and, for the purposes of this paragraph, the provision of facilities for taking part in golf shall not include the provision of facilities for taking part in pitch and putt;][11]

 (viii)   services consisting of the acceptance for disposal of waste material;

   (ix)   admissions to exhibitions, of the kind normally held in museums and art galleries, of objects of historical, cultural, artistic or scientific interest, not being services of the kind specified in paragraph (viii*a*) of the First Schedule;

    (x) services [of a kind]^{12} supplied in the course of their profession by veterinary surgeons;

  (xi) agricultural services consisting of—

      (*a*) field work, reaping, mowing, threshing, baling, harvesting, sowing and planting,

    [(*ai*) stock-minding, stock-rearing, farm relief services and farm advisory services [(other than farm accountancy or farm management services)]^{13},]^{14}

      (*b*) disinfecting and ensilage of agricultural products,

      (*c*) destruction of weeds and pests and dusting and spraying of crops and land,

    [(*d*) lopping, tree felling and similar forestry services;]^{15}

 [(xi*a*) nursery or garden centre stock consisting of live plants, live trees, live shrubs, bulbs, roots and the like, not being of a type specified in paragraph (xv) of the Second Schedule, and cut flowers and ornamental foliage not being artificial or dried flowers or foliage;]^{16}

 [(xi*b*) animal insemination services;

  (xi*c*) livestock semen;]^{17}

  (xi*d*) live poultry and live ostriches;]^{18}

[[(xii) printed matter consisting of:

      (*a*) newspapers and periodicals;

      (*b*) brochures, leaflets and programmes;

      (*c*) catalogues, including directories, and similar printed matter;

      (*d*) maps, hydrographic and similar charts;

      (*e*) printed music other than in book or booklet form;

      but excluding:

      (i) other printed matter wholly or substantially devoted to advertising,

      (ii) the goods specified in subparagraphs (*b*) to (*e*) of paragraph (xv*a*) of the Second Schedule, and

      (iii) any other printed matter;]^{19}

 [(xiii) subject to and in accordance with regulations, if any—

      (*a*) the letting of immovable goods (other than in the course of the provision of facilities of the kind specified in paragraph (viia))—

        (I) in the hotel or guesthouse sector, or

        (II) being a letting of all or part of a house, apartment or other similar establishment when that letting is provided in the short-term guest sector or holiday sector, or

        (III) in a caravan park, camping site or other similar establishment,

      or

      (*b*) the provision of holiday accommodation;]^{20}

(xiv) tour guide services;

(xv) the hiring (in this paragraph referred to as **"the current hiring"**) to a person of—

    (*a*) a vehicle designed and constructed, or adapted, for the conveyance of persons by road,

    (*b*) a ship, boat or other vessel designed and constructed for the conveyance of passengers and not exceeding 15 tonnes gross,

    (*c*) a sports or pleasure boat of any description, or

    (*d*) a caravan, mobile home, tent or trailer tent,

under an agreement, other than an agreement of the kind referred to in section 3(1)(*b*), for any term or part of a term which, when added to the term of any such hiring (whether of the same goods or of other goods of the same kind) to the same person during the period of 12 months ending on the date of the commencement of the current hiring, does not exceed 5 weeks;

[(xvi) a work of art being—

    (*a*) a painting, drawing or pastel, or any combination thereof, executed entirely by hand, excluding hand-decorated manufactured articles and plans and drawings for architectural, engineering, industrial, commercial, topographical or similar purposes,

    (*b*) an original lithograph, engraving, or print, or any combination thereof, produced directly from lithographic stones, plates or other engraved surfaces, which are executed entirely by hand, or

    (*c*) an original sculpture or statuary, excluding mass-produced reproductions and works of craftsmanship of a commercial character,

but excluding the supply of such work of art by a taxable dealer in accordance with the provisions of subsection (3) or (8) of section 10A or by an auctioneer within the meaning of section 10B and in accordance with the provisions of subsection (3) of section 10B;][21]

[(xvi*a*) antiques being, subject to and in accordance with regulations, articles of furniture, silver, glass or porcelain, whether hand-decorated or not, specified in the said regulations, which are shown to the satisfaction of the Revenue Commissioners to be more than 100 years old, other than goods specified in paragraph (xvi), but excluding the supply of such antiques by a taxable dealer in accordance with the provisions of subsection (3) or (8) of section 10A or by an auctioneer within the meaning of section 10B and in accordance with the provisions of subsection (3) of section 10B;][22]

(xvii) literary manuscripts certified by the Director of the National Library as being of major national importance and of either cultural or artistic importance;

(xviii) services consisting of—

    (*a*) the repair or maintenance of movable goods, or

(*b*) the alteration of [used]²³ movable goods, other than [contract work or]²⁴ such services specified in paragraph (v), (v*a*) or (xvi) of the Second Schedule, but excluding the provision in the course of any such repair, maintenance or alteration service of—

    (I)   accessories, attachments or batteries, or

    (II)   tyres, tyre cases, interchangeable tyre treads, inner tubes and tyre flaps, for wheels of all kinds;

(xix)   services consisting of the care of the human body, excluding such services specified in the First Schedule, but including services supplied in the course of a health studio business or similar business;

(xx)   services supplied in the course of their profession by jockeys;

[(xx*a*)   greyhound feeding stuff, which is packaged, advertised or held out for sale solely as greyhound feeding stuff, and which is supplied in units of not less than 10 kilograms;]²⁵

(xxi)   the supply to a person of photographic prints (other than goods produced by means of a photocopying process), slides or negatives, which have been produced from goods provided by that person;

(xxii)   goods being—

    (*a*)   photographic prints (other than goods produced by means of a photocopying process), mounted or unmounted, but unframed,

    (*b*)   slides and negatives, and

    (*c*)   cinematographic and video film,

which record particular persons, objects or events, supplied under an agreement to photograph those persons, objects or events;

(xxiii)   the supply by a photographer of—

    (*a*)   negatives which have been produced from film exposed for the purpose of his business, and

    (*b*)   film which has been exposed for the purposes of his business;

(xxiv)   photographic prints produced by means of a vending machine which incorporates a camera and developing and printing equipment;

(xxv)   services consisting of—

    (*a*)   the editing of photographic, cinematographic and video film, and

    (*b*)   microfilming;

(xxvi)   agency services in regard to a supply specified in paragraph (xxi);

(xxvii)   instruction in the driving of mechanically propelled road vehicles, not being education, training or retraining of the kinds specified in paragraph (ii) of the First Schedule;

(xxviii)   immovable goods;

(xxix)   services consisting of the development of immovable goods and work on immovable goods including the installation of fixtures, where the value of movable goods (if any) provided in pursuance of an agreement in relation to such services does not exceed two-thirds of the total amount on which tax is chargeable in respect of the agreement;

(xxx) services consisting of the routine cleaning of immovable goods;

[(xxxi) food of a kind used for human consumption, other than that included in paragraph (xii) of the Second Schedule, being flour or egg based bakery products including cakes, crackers, wafers and biscuits, but excluding—

(a) wafers and biscuits wholly or partly covered or decorated with chocolate or some other product similar in taste and appearance,

(b) food of a kind specified in subparagraph (c) or (e)(II) of paragraph (xii) of the Second Schedule, and

(c) chocolates, sweets and similar confectionery;][26]

(xxxii) concrete ready to pour [but excluding the supply of such goods by a taxable dealer in accordance with the provisions of subsection (3) or (8) of section 10A or by an auctioneer within the meaning of section 10B and in accordance with the provisions of subsection (3) of section 10B][27];

(xxxiii) blocks, of concrete, of a kind which comply with the specification contained in the Standard Specification (Concrete Building Blocks, Part 1, Normal Density Blocks) Declaration, 1987 (Irish Standard 20: Part 1: 1987) [but excluding the supply of such goods by a taxable dealer in accordance with the provisions of subsection (3) or (8) of section 10A or by an auctioneer within the meaning of section 10B and in accordance with the provisions of subsection (3) of section 10B][28].][29][30]

Amendments

[1] Substituted by FA 1993, s 97(1)(a) with effect from 1 March 1993; previously "gas of a kind specified in paragraph (i) of the Seventh Schedule".

[2] Inserted by FA 2005, s 113(a)(i) with effect from 25 March 2005.

[3] Substituted by FA 2005, s 113(a)(ii); previously "heated for the purpose of enabling" with effect from 25 March 2005.

[4] Substituted by FA 2005, s 113(a)(iii); previously "heated after cooking for the purpose of enabling" with effect from 25 March 2005.

[5] Deleted by FA 2005, s 113(a)(iv); previously "for the purpose of" with effect from 25 March 2005.

[6] Substituted by FA 2005, s 113(a)(v); previously "at the time of supply" with effect from 25 March 2005.

[7] Para (vii) substituted by FA 1994, s 101(a) with effect from 1 July 1994.

[8] Para (viia) inserted by FA 1992, s 197(3)(a) with effect from 1 July 1992.

[9] Substituted by FA 2006, s 101 with effect from 31 March 2006; previously "€25,500".

[10] Substituted by FA 2006, s 101 with effect from 31 March 2006; previously "€25,500".

[11] Paras (viib)–(viic) inserted by FA 1995, s 140(a) with effect from 1 January 1996.

[12] Inserted by FA 1994, s 101(b) with effect from 1 July 1994.

[13] Substituted by FA 1994, s 101(c) with effect from 23 May 1994; previously "(not being services of the kind specified in paragraph (xxii) of the Seventh Schedule)".

[14] Para (xi)(ai) inserted by FA 1992, s 197(3)(b) with effect from 1 July 1992.

[15] Para (xi)(*d*) substituted by FA 1993, s 97(1)(*b*) with effect from 1 March 1993; previously "lopping, tree felling and similar forestry services.".

[16] Para (xi*a*) inserted by FA 1997, s 113 as on and from such date as the Minister for Finance may by Order appoint.

[17] Paras (xi*b*)–(xi*c*) inserted by FA 1998, s 117(*a*) with effect from 1 July 1998.

[18] Para (xi*d*) inserted by FA 1998, s 117(*a*) with effect from 1 May 1998.

[19] Para (xii) substituted by FA 1998, s 117(*b*) with effect from 1 May 1998.

[20] Para (xiii) substituted by FA 2005, s 113(*b*) with effect from 1 July 2005.

[21] Para (xvi) substituted by FA 1995, s 140(*b*) with effect from 1 July 1995.

[22] Para (xvi*a*) inserted by FA 1995, s 140(*c*) with effect from 1 July 1995.

[23] Substituted by FA 1995, s 140(*d*) with effect from 1 July 1995; previously "second-hand".

[24] Inserted by FA 1996, s 99 with effect from 1 January 1996.

[25] Para (xx*a*) inserted by FA 1995, s 140(*e*) with effect from 1 July 1995.

[26] Paras (xii)–(xxxi) inserted by FA 1993, s 97(1)(*c*).

[27] Inserted by FA 1995, s 140(*f*) with effect from 1 July 1995.

[28] Words "but excluding the supply of such goods by a taxable dealer in accordance with the provisions of subsection (3) or (8) of section 10A or by an auctioneer within the meaning of section 10B and in accordance with the provisions of subsection (3) of section 10B" inserted by FA 1995, s 140(*g*) with effect from 1 July 1995.

[29] Para (xxxi) substituted and paras (xxxii)–(xxxiii) inserted by FA 1993 97(2) with effect from 1 July 1993.

[30] Sch 6 substituted by FA 1992, s 197(2) with effect from 28 May 1992.

Cross-references

Para (vii*c*): Minister may provide that State and local authority may be taxable persons: s 8(2A)(proviso).

Para (xi*a*): taxable persons, farmer: s 8(3)(*a*).

Para (xiii): agreements prior to 25 February 1993: Sch 3 para (ii).

Para (xvi): margin scheme goods: s 10A(1).

Para (xvi*a*): margin scheme goods: s 10A(1), Sch 8 para (iii); Revenue may make regulations as regards particulars to be furnished in relation to antiques: s 32(1)(*de*).

Para (xv)(*a*): agreements prior to 25 February 1993: Sch 3 para (iii).

Para (xxii): margin scheme goods: s 10A(1), Sch 8 paras (i)(*f*), (iii).

Case law

Subject	Case	Case reference
Para (i)(*b*): Transmission of cable television and radio signals not supply of electricity	*Brosnan v Cork Communications Ltd*	(IV) ITR (349)
Cable installation a separate service	*Cablelink Limited, Cablelink Waterford Limited and Galway Cable Vision v Revenue Commissioners*	C–155/2003

Revenue publications

Agrimonetary Compensation: Tax Briefing Issue 29.

Commissioned framed photography: Tax Briefing Issue 39.

Gold and other sporting activities: Statement of Practice VAT 1/95.

Horticultural Retailers: Statement of Practice VAT 3/92.

Rates of VAT on services from 1 March 1992: Statement of Practice VAT 1/92.

Revenue VAT Guide: Chapter 15 and Appendix.

VAT treatment of the promotion of and admission to live theatrical and musical events (including performances by non-established performers): Information Leaflet No 2/06.

Veterinary services: Statement of Practice VAT 3/91.

Waste disposal services: Tax Briefing 60.

Definitions

"antiques": s 1(1); "business": s 1(1); "clothing": s 1(1); "footwear": s 1(1); "fur skin": s 1(1); "goods": s 1(1); "immovable goods": s 1(1); "land": IA 2005, Sch; "movable goods": s 1(1); "establishment": s 1(1); "person": IA 2005, s 18(*c*); "regulations": ss 1(1), 32; "second-hand": s 1(1); "supply": s 1(1); "taxable dealer": s 1(1); "works of art": s 1(1).

SEVENTH SCHEDULE

Amendments

¹   Sch 7 repealed by FA 1993, s 98 with effect from 1 March 1993.

EIGHTH SCHEDULE
WORKS OF ART, COLLECTORS' ITEMS AND ANTIQUES CHARGEABLE AT THE RATE SPECIFIED IN SECTION 11(1)(*d*) IN THE CIRCUMSTANCES SPECIFIED IN SECTION 11(1AA)

[(i)   Works of art:

Every work of art being—

(*a*)   a picture (other than a painting, drawing or pastel specified in paragraph (xvi) of the Sixth Schedule), collage or similar decorative plaque, executed entirely by hand by an artist, other than—

   (I)   plans and drawings for architectural, engineering, industrial, commercial, topographical or similar purposes,

   (II)   hand-decorated manufactured articles, and

   (III)   theatrical scenery, studio back cloths or the like of painted canvas,

(*b*)   a sculpture cast the production of which is limited to eight copies and supervised by the artist or by the artist's successors in title provided that, in the case of a statuary cast produced before the 1st day of January, 1989, the limit of eight copies may be exceeded where so determined by the Revenue Commissioners,

(*c*)   a tapestry or wall textile made by hand from original designs provided by an artist, provided that there are not more than eight copies of each,

(*d*)   individual pieces of ceramics executed entirely by an artist and signed by the artist,

(*e*)   enamels on copper, executed entirely by hand, limited to eight numbered copies bearing the signature of the artist or the studio, excluding articles of jewellery, goldsmiths' wares and silversmiths' wares, or

(*f*)   a photograph taken by an artist, printed by the artist or under the artist's supervision, signed and numbered and limited to 30 copies, all sizes and mounts included, other than photographs specified in paragraph (xxii)(*a*) of the Sixth Schedule;

(ii) Collectors' items:

Every collectors' item being one or more—

(*a*) postage or revenue stamps, postmarks, first-day covers, pre-stamped stationery and the like, franked, or if unfranked not being of legal tender and not being intended for use as legal tender, or

(*b*) collections and collectors' pieces of zoological, botanical, mineralogical, anatomical, historical, archaeological, palaeontological, ethnographic or numismatic interest;

(iii) Antiques:

Every antique being, subject to and in accordance with regulations, one or more goods which are shown to the satisfaction of the Revenue Commissioners to be more than 100 years old, other than goods specified in paragraph (xvi), (xvi*a*) or (xxii)(*a*) of the Sixth Schedule or in paragraph (i) or (ii) of this Schedule.]¹

Amendments

¹   Sch 8 inserted by FA 1995, s 141 with effect from 1 July 1995.

Cross-references

Para (i): margin scheme goods: s 10A(1); rate of tax: s 11(1AA)(*b*)–(*c*).

Para (iii): margin scheme goods: s 10A(1); Revenue may make regulations as regards particulars to be furnished in relation to antiques s 32(1)(*de*).

Definitions

"antiques": s 1(1); "collectors' items": s 1(1); "works of art": s 1(1).

Revenue Publications

The margin scheme/secondhand goods: Leaflet December 1994.

FINANCE ACT 1973

(Number 19 of 1973)

ARRANGEMENT OF SECTIONS

PART V
VALUE ADDED TAX

TENTH SCHEDULE
AMENDMENT OF ENACTMENTS

AN ACT TO CHARGE AND IMPOSE CERTAIN DUTIES OF CUSTOMS AND INLAND REVENUE (INCLUDING EXCISE), TO AMEND THE LAW RELATING TO CUSTOMS AND INLAND REVENUE (INCLUDING EXCISE) AND TO MAKE FURTHER PROVISIONS IN CONNECTION WITH FINANCE. [4TII AUGUST 1973]

PART V
VALUE ADDED TAX

76 Commencement (Part V)

This Part (other than section 90, in so far as it amends the definition of **"manufacturer"** in section 1(1) of the Principal Act) shall come into operation on the 3rd day of September, 1973.

77 "Principal Act"

In this Part **"the Principal Act"** means the Value Added Tax Act, 1972.

78 Amendment of section 3 (supply of goods) of Principal Act

Notes

This amendment provided that the supply of food and drink by means of a vending machine, or in the course of a catering service was to be treated as the supply of a service. It has since been superseded.

---

79 Amendment of section 5 (supply of services) of Principal Act

Notes

This amendment provided that certain services (staff meals) self supplied by a taxable person, in connection with his business activities, were to be taxable. The two-thirds rule was not to apply to catering services. The changes have since been superseded.

80 Amendment of section 11 (rates of tax) of Principal Act

Notes

Paras (*a*)–(*c*), by amending VATA 1972, s 11, increased the VAT rates from 5.26% to 6.75%, 16.37% to 19.5% and 30.26% to 36.75% and imposed VAT on dinner dances. These rate changes have since been superseded.
Para (*d*), by inserting VATA 1972, s 11(1A) provided rules for determining the VAT rate when a change in rate takes place. A new VATA 1972, s 11(1B) empowered the Revenue Commissioners to make determinations regarding the VAT rate applicable to a supply of goods or services (or whether a supply was exempt) and provided a right of appeal against such determinations. Para (*e*), by inserting VATA 1972, s 11(4A) introduced a tax charge on food provided by a customer but prepared by a caterer. Para (*f*) substituted VATA 1972, s 11(8)(*a*) empowered the Minister for Finance to reduce VAT rates.

81 Amendment of section 12 (deduction for tax borne or paid) of Principal Act

Notes

Para (*a*) by inserting VATA 1972, s 12(1A) introduced stock relief on commencement for newly-registered traders.

82 Amendment of section 19 (tax due and payable) of Principal Act

Notes

This amendment has been superseded.

83 Amendment of section 26 (penalties generally) of Principal Act

Notes

This amendment has been superseded.

84 Amendment of section 27 (fraudulent returns etc) of Principal Act

Notes

This section substituted VATA 1972, s 27(5).

85 Amendment of section 32 (regulations) of Principal Act

Notes

This section inserted VATA 1972, s 32(1)(*xx*) and (*xxx*).

86 Amendment of section 35 (special conditions for adjustment and recovery of consideration) of Principal Act

Notes

This section by inserting VATA 1972, s 35(1A) provided rules for dealing with adjustments in contract prices following a change in the VAT rate.

87 Amendment of First Schedule (exempted activities) to Principal Act

Notes

This section exempted catering services in hospitals and schools, the supply and importation of live horses and greyhounds, and the insemination of cattle, sheep and pigs. The changes have since been superseded.

88 Amendment of Second Schedule (goods and services chargeable at the rate of zero per cent) to Principal Act

Notes

The net effect of these changes was to extend the 0% rate to most food and drink for human consumption, oral medicines, animal feed, food producing seeds etc, and life-saving services provided by the Royal National Lifeboat Institution.

89 Amendment of Third Schedule to Principal Act

Notes

This amendment has been superseded.

90 Miscellaneous amendments of Principal Act

The Principal Act is hereby amended as specified in column (3) of the Tenth Schedule to this Act.

97 Care and management of taxes and duties

All taxes and duties (except the excise duties on mechanically propelled vehicles) imposed by this Act are hereby placed under the care and management of the Revenue Commissioners.

98 Short title, construction and commencement

(1) This Act may be cited as the Finance Act, 1973.

...

(5) Part V of this Act shall be construed together with the Value Added Tax Act, 1972.

...

(7) Any reference in this Act to any other enactment shall, except so far as the context otherwise requires, be construed as a reference to that enactment as amended by or under any other enactment including this Act.

TENTH SCHEDULE
AMENDMENT OF ENACTMENTS

Notes

Amended: definitions of "livestock" and "taxable period" in VATA 1972, s 1(1); inserted "for the time being specified in section 11(1)(*c*)" in VATA 1972, s 3(5)(*b*); inserted "at any of the rates specified in section 11(1)..." in VATA s 17(1). Other amendments in this Schedule are now superseded by subsequent legislation.

FINANCE ACT 1975

(Number 6 of 1975)

ARRANGEMENT OF SECTIONS

PART I
INCOME TAX, SUR-TAX AND CORPORATION PROFITS TAX

CHAPTER V
Miscellaneous

AN ACT TO CHARGE AND IMPOSE CERTAIN DUTIES OF CUSTOMS AND INLAND REVENUE (INCLUDING EXCISE) TO AMEND THE LAW RELATING TO CUSTOMS AND INLAND REVENUE (INCLUDING EXCISE) AND TO MAKE FURTHER PROVISIONS IN CONNECTION WITH FINANCE.
[14th MAY, 1975]

PART I
INCOME TAX, SUR-TAX AND CORPORATION PROFITS TAX

CHAPTER V
Miscellaneous

28 Interest on unpaid taxes

(1) This section applies to interest chargeable under —

   (*a*)   ...[1],

   (*b*)   section 129 of the Income Tax Act, 1967,

(*c*)   section 550 of the said Income Tax Act, 1967,

(*d*)   section 17(6A) of the Finance Tax Act, 1970,

(*e*)   section 20(2) ...² of the Finance Act, 1971, and

(*f*)   section 21 of the Value Added Tax Act, 1972.

(2) Where any interest to which this section applies is chargeable for any month commencing on or after the 6th day of April, 1975, or any part of such a month, in respect of tax due to be paid or remitted whether before, on or after such date, such interest shall be chargeable at the rate of **1.5 per cent** for each month or part of a month instead of at the rate specified in the said sections and those sections shall have effect as if the rate aforesaid were substituted for the rates specified in those sections.

(3) In this section **"tax"** means income tax, sur-tax, ...³ or value added tax, as may be appropriate.

Amendments

1   Words "section 14 of the Finance Act, 1962" repealed by CTA 1976, s 164 and Sch 3 Pt II.

2   Words "and 50(2)" repealed by CTA 1976, s 164 and Sch 3 Pt II.

3   Words "corporation profits tax" repealed by CTA 1976, s 164 and Sch 3 Pt II.

Definition

"month": IA 2005, Sch.

29   Adjustment of capital allowances by reference to value added tax

(1) In computing any deduction, allowance or relief, for any of the purposes of —

(*a*)   Parts XIII to XVIII, inclusive, of the Income Tax Act, 1967,

(*b*)   section 22 of the Finance Act, 1971,

(*c*)   the Finance (Taxation of Profits of Certain Mines) Act, 1974, or

(*d*)   section 22 of the Finance Act, 1974,

the cost to a person of any machinery or plant, or the amount of any expenditure incurred by him, shall not take account of any amount included in such cost or expenditure for value added tax in respect of which the person may claim —

(i)   a deduction under section 12 of the Value Added Tax Act, 1972, or

(ii)   a refund of value added tax under an order under section 20(3) of that Act.

(2) In calculating, for any of the purposes of Part XVI of the Income Tax Act, 1967, the amount of sale, insurance, salvage or compensation moneys to be taken into account in computing a balancing allowance or balancing charge to be made to or on a person, no account shall be taken of the amount of value added tax (if any) chargeable to the person in respect of those moneys.

Cross-references

Petroleum taxation, exploration expenditure: this section applied by FA 1992, s 84(15).

Definition

"person": IA 2005, s 18(*c*).

PART V
VALUE ADDED TAX

50 Amendment of section 10 (amount on which tax is chargeable) of Value Added Tax Act, 1972

Notes

This amendment was an anti avoidance provision dealing with sales by manufacturers to associated companies of televisions, record players etc (old Sch 4). It has since been superseded.

51 Amendment of section 11 (rates of tax) of Value Added Tax Act, 1972

Notes

Para (*a*), which imposed an additional tax on supplies by manufacturers of goods produced from materials supplied by customers, is now irrelevant as VATA 1972, s 11(2) was subsequently deleted by FA 1985, s 43. Para (*b*) substituted VATA 1972, s 4.

52 Amendment of section 13 (special provisions for tax invoiced by farmers and fishermen) of Value Added Tax Act, 1972

Notes

This amendment, which suspended the then 1% flat-rate credit for unregistered farmers, has been superseded.

53 Amendment of Third Schedule to Value Added Tax Act, 1972

Notes

This amendment is now irrelevant as VATA 1972, Sch 3 was replaced by FA 1991, s 86.

PART VI
MISCELLANEOUS

55 Amendment of Provisional Collection of Taxes Act, 1927

Notes

This section amended PCTA 1927, s 4(*a*).

56 Care and management of taxes and duties

All taxes and duties imposed by this Act are hereby placed under the care and management of the Revenue Commissioners.

57 Short title, construction and commencement

(1) This Act may be cited as the Finance Act, 1975.

...

(6) Any reference in this Act to any other enactment shall, except so far as the context otherwise requires, be construed as a reference to that enactment as amended by or under any other enactment including this Act.

Definition

"commencement" IA 2005, Sch.

FINANCE (NO 2) ACT 1975

(Number 19 of 1975)

ARRANGEMENT OF SECTIONS

AN ACT TO CHARGE AND IMPOSE CERTAIN DUTIES OF INLAND
REVENUE, TO AMEND THE LAW RELATING TO INLAND REVENUE AND
TO MAKE FURTHER PROVISIONS IN CONNECTION WITH FINANCE.
[30th JULY, 1975]

2 Amendment of Value Added Tax Act, 1972

Notes

This section extended the 0% rate to certain clothing, material for clothing, footwear and fuel. The changes have since been superseded.

FINANCE ACT 1976

(Number 16 of 1976)

ARRANGEMENT OF SECTIONS

PART IV
VALUE ADDED TAX

AN ACT TO CHARGE AND IMPOSE CERTAIN DUTIES OF CUSTOMS AND INLAND REVENUE (INCLUDING EXCISE), TO AMEND THE LAW RELATING TO CUSTOMS AND INLAND REVENUE (INCLUDING EXCISE) AND TO MAKE FURTHER PROVISIONS IN CONNECTION WITH FINANCE.
[27th MAY, 1976]

PART IV
VALUE ADDED TAX

49 Commencement

This Part, other than sections 51, 52, 54 to 62, shall be deemed to have come into operation as on and from the 1st day of March, 1976.

50 Definitions (Part IV)

In this Part—

"the Act of 1973" means the Finance Act, 1973;

"the Principal Act" means the Value Added Tax Act, 1972.

51 Amendment of section 3 (delivery of goods) of Principal Act

Notes
This section which substituted VATA 1972, s 3(1)(e) (self supply to exempt activity) has been superseded.

52 Amendment of section 10 (amount on which tax is chargeable) of Principal Act

Notes
This amendment, which provided that potential customs or excise duty was part of the chargeable consideration for VAT has since been superseded.

53 Amendment of section 11 (rates of tax) of Principal Act

Notes
This section by amending VATA 1972, s 11(1), changed the 6.75% VAT rate to 10%, the 19.5% VAT rate to 20% and the 36.75% VAT rate to 35% and 40%. New provisions for VAT on dances were also introduced. The changes have since been superseded.

54 Amendment of section 12 (deduction for tax borne or paid) of Principal Act

Notes
This section restricted the right to a purchases VAT deduction on televisions, radios, records, record players (old Sch 4). The changes have since been superseded.

55 Amendment of section 15 (charge of tax on imported goods) of Principal Act

Notes
This section provided a new method of calculating the tax value of imported goods. The change has since been superseded by FA 1985, s 46.

56 Amendment of section 21 (interest) of Principal Act

Notes
This section substituted VATA 1972, s 21(2)(b).

57 Amendment of section 26 (penalties generally) of Principal Act

Notes
This section, by substituting VATA 1972, s 26(6)(e)–(f), provided a revised wording for form of evidence in connection with recovery of penalties.

58 Amendment of section 32 (regulations) of Principal Act

Notes
This section, by inserting VATA 1972, s 32(1)(uu), allowed the Revenue Commissioners to make regulations relating to certain purchases tax credit apportionments.

59 Amendment of section 34 (relief for stock-in-trade held on the specified day) of Principal Act

Notes

This section substituted VATA 1972, s 34(5)(*a*).

60 Substitution of new Schedules for First, Second, Third and Fourth Schedules (exempted activities and rates of tax) to Principal Act

Notes

These amendments listed the goods liable at 0%, 10% and 20% with effect from 1 March 1976. The changes have since been superseded.

61 Consequential amendments

In consequence of the amendments specified in sections 53 and 60 and the repeals specified in Part II of the Fifth Schedule, the Principal Act is hereby further amended as specified in Part II of the First Schedule.

62 Priority in bankruptcy and winding-up

(1) There shall be included among the debts which, under section 4 of the Preferential Payments in Bankruptcy (Ireland) Act, 1889, are to be paid in priority to all other debts in the distribution of the property of a person, being a bankrupt, arranging debtor, or person dying insolvent, any tax for which the person is liable in relation to taxable periods which shall have ended within the period of 12 months next before the date on which the order of adjudication of the bankrupt was made, the petition of arrangement of the debtor was filed, or, as the case may be, the person died insolvent and any interest payable by the person under section 21 of the Principal Act.

(2) (*a*) There shall be included among the debts which, under section 285 of the Companies Act, 1963, are to be paid in priority to all other debts in the winding-up of a company any tax for which the company is liable in relation to taxable periods which shall have ended within the period of 12 months next before the relevant date and any interest payable by the company under section 21 of the Principal Act.

(*b*) Paragraph (*a*) shall, for the purposes of section 98 of the Companies Act, 1963, be deemed to be contained in section 285 of that Act.

(*c*) In paragraph (*a*) **"the relevant date"** has the same meaning as it has in section 285 of the Companies Act, 1963.

Definition

"taxable period": VATA 1972, s 1(1).

63 Transitional provisions in respect of motor vehicles

(1) In this section—

"qualified vehicles" means vehicles which, on or before the 29th day of February, 1976, were delivered to or imported by a person other than a manufacturer of goods of the kind so delivered or imported in such circumstances that tax at the rate of 36.75 per cent. was chargeable in relation to such delivery or importation;

"relevant delivery" means a delivery of any qualified vehicles in such circumstances that, but for this section, tax at the rate of 10 per cent. would be chargeable;

"vehicles" means goods (other than second-hand goods) of a kind specified in Part I of the Fourth Schedule (inserted by this Act) to the Principal Act.

(2) During the period which commenced on the 1st day of March, 1976, and ended on the 30th day of April, 1976, notwithstanding the provisions of section 11 of the Principal Act, tax shall, in relation to a relevant delivery, be chargeable and be deemed to have been chargeable at the rate of 6.75 per cent.

(3) Notwithstanding the provisions of section 12(1) of the Principal Act, the amount deductible by a person under that section in relation to—

    (*a*)   any qualified vehicles, and

    (*b*)   the delivery or importation of any vehicles (not being qualified vehicles) in relation to the consideration for a delivery of which by him tax was charged at the rate of 6.75 per cent.,

shall not exceed, in the case of a delivery of such goods to him, 6.75 per cent. of the consideration payable by him exclusive of any tax payable in respect of the delivery by the person making the delivery and, in the case of an importation, 6.75 per cent. of the value of the goods calculated in accordance with section 15(4) of the said Act.

PART VI
MISCELLANEOUS

81 Repeals

...

(2) The enactment mentioned in column (2) of Part II of the Fifth Schedule to this Act is hereby repealed to the extent specified in column (3) of that Schedule.

(3) ...

    (*b*)   Subsection (2) of this section shall be deemed to have come into operation on the 1st day of March, 1976.

82 Care and management of taxes and duties

All taxes and duties (except the excise duties on mechanically propelled vehicles) imposed by this Act are hereby placed under the care and management of the Revenue Commissioners.

83 Short title, construction and commencement

(1) This Act may be cited as the Finance Act, 1976.

...

(5) Part IV of this Act shall be construed together with the Value Added Tax Act, 1972, and the enactments amending or extending that Act

...

(7) Any reference in this Act to any other enactment shall, except so far as the context otherwise requires, be construed as a reference to that enactment as amended by or under any other enactment including this Act.

FIRST SCHEDULE
Amendment of enactments

PART II
Amendments consequential on certain amendments of Value Added Tax Act, 1972

Notes

Inserted definition of **"fur skin"** in VATA 1972, s 1(1); substituted "either of the rates" in VATA 1972, s 3(5)(*b*).

Other amendments in this schedule are now irrelevant having been superseded by subsequent legislation.

FIFTH SCHEDULE
Enactments repealed

PART II

Notes

Repealed: VATA 1972, ss 11(1)(*b*), 12(1)(*b*), 13, 17(2) and (4), 17(6) [words "otherwise than as required by section 13,"], 17(7) [words from "and an amendment of an invoice" to the end of the subsection]; 17(10)(*a*) [words from "or goods or services" to "to a registered person]; 26(1) [numerals 13], 26(2) [words "otherwise than under and in accordance with section 13"]; 32(1)(*f*); 35(1)(*c*).

VALUE ADDED TAX (AMENDMENT) ACT 1978

(Number 19 of 1978)

ARRANGEMENT OF SECTIONS

Section

FIRST SCHEDULE
ENACTMENTS REPEALED

SECOND SCHEDULE
CONSEQUENTIAL AMENDMENTS

AN ACT TO AMEND THE VALUE ADDED TAX ACT, 1972, AND THE ACTS AMENDING THAT ACT AND TO PROVIDE FOR RELATED MATTERS. [20TH DECEMBER, 1978]

1 Principal Act

In this Act **"the Principal Act"** means the Value Added Tax Act, 1972.

2 Amendment of section 1 (interpretation) of Principal Act

Notes

This Act implemented in the State the provisions of the Sixth Council Directive 77/388/EEC on the harmonisation of VAT regimes in EC Member States, with effect from 1 March 1979.

This section deleted the definitions of "accountable person", "established", "manufacturer", "rendering" and "residing" from VATA 1972, s 1. The section also substituted "establishment" for "permanent establishment" and inserted definitions of "agricultural produce", "agricultural service", "community", "farmer", "flat-rate addition", "flat-rate farmer", "supply" and "taxable person" in VATA 1972, s 1.

The main change is that an "accountable person" became a "taxable person" and the old terms "delivery of goods" and rendering of services" have been replaced by the new term "supply" which is used in relation to goods and services throughout the EC.

---

3 Amendment of section 2 (charge of value added tax) of Principal Act

Notes

This section substituted in VATA s 2(1)(a). The charge of tax is restricted to transactions within the State.

4 Amendment of section 3 (supply of goods) of Principal Act

Notes

Para (a) amended VATA 1972, s 3(1) and substituted VATA 1972, s 3(1)(e)–(f) (self supply of goods to exempt activity, self supply of goods to non business use); para (b) substituted VATA 1972, s 3(1A) (small business gifts relieved of tax); para (c) by inserting VATA 1972, s 3(1B) provided that electricity, gas, power etc are deemed to be supplies of goods, not services. Para (d) by substituting VATA 1972, s 3(3) provided that auctioneers fees on auctioned livestock, greyhounds, fruit, vegetables, poultry, fish and eggs are to be taxed at the same rate as the rate applicable to the goods. Similarly an agent dealing in livestock or greyhounds has his fee or commission taxed on at the rate applicable to the goods he is selling.

5 Supply of services

Notes

This section substituted VATA 1972, s 5, providing new rules for place of supply of services, and providing that certain services supplied through an undisclosed agent are deemed to have been supplied by that agent.

6 Amendment of section 8 (taxable persons) of Principal Act

Notes

This section substituted VATA 1972, s 8(1), (2), (7), (8) and (9) and inserted VATA 1972, s 8(2A), redefining the old "accountable person" as "taxable person". Also by amending VATA 1972, s 8(3), the section increased the registration limits: this change has since been superseded.

7 Amendment of section 9 (registration) of Principal Act

Notes

This section substituted VATA 1972, s 9(1).

8 Amount on which tax is chargeable

Notes

This section substituted VATA 1972, s 10.

9 Amendment of section 11 (rates of tax) of Principal Act

Notes

This section substituted VATA 1972, s 11(3) and (4A). The main effect was to abolish the 35% and 40% VAT rates, with effect from 1 March 1979.

10 Amendment of section 12 (deduction for tax borne or paid) of Principal Act

Notes

This section substituted VATA 1972, s 12(1) and (3). VATA 1972, s 12(1) was subsequently substituted by FA 1987, s 41.

11 Special provisions for tax invoiced by flat-rate farmers

Notes

This section by inserting VATA 1972, s 12A restored the 1% flat-rate credit for unregistered farmers with effect from 1 March 1979.

12 Remission of tax on goods exported, etc.

Notes

This section inserted VATA 1972, s 13.

13 Determination of tax due by reference to cash receipts

Notes

This section, by substituting VATA 1972, s 14, provided new rules for deciding entitlement to the cash basis.

14 Charge of tax on imported goods

Notes

This section, by substituting VATA 1972, s 15, introduced "postponed accounting" for VAT at import with effect from 1 March 1979.

15 Amendment of section 17 (invoices) of Principal Act

Notes

Para (*a*) inserted VATA 1972, s 17(2); para (*b*) inserted VATA 1972, s 17(4); para (*c*) inserted VATA 1972, s 17(6A) para (*d*) amended VATA 1972, s 17(8); para (*e*) inserted VATA 1972, s 17(9)(*aa*); para (*f*) amended VATA 1972, s 17(10)(*a*); para (*g*) inserted VATA 1972, s 17(11A), para (*h*) amended VATA 1972, s 17(12)(*a*)(ii); para (*i*) inserted VATA 1972, s 17(13).

The changes in invoicing procedures are to harmonise Irish invoicing procedures with the stricter provisions of the Sixth Directive.

16 Amendment of section 19 (tax due and payable) of Principal Act

Notes

This amendment which introduced penalties for import/export offences, has been superseded as VATA 1972, s 19(3) was subsequently substituted by FA 1983, s 84.

17 Determination of tax due

Notes

This section substituted VATA 1972, s 23.

18 Amendment of section 26 (penalties generally) of Principal Act

Notes

This section amended VATA 1972, s 26(1); inserted VATA 1972, s 26(2A) and amended VATA 1972, s 26(3). The new penalties relate to invoices etc (see s 15).

19 Amendment of section 27 (fraudulent returns, etc) of Principal Act

Notes

This section substituted VATA 1972, s 27(4) and inserted VATA 1972, s 27(9)–(10) (penalties for import/ export offences).

20 Amendment of section 30 (time limits) of Principal Act

Notes

This section substituted VATA 1972, s 30(3) and (5)(*b*).

21 Amendment of section 32 (regulations) of Principal Act

Notes

This section substituted VATA 1972, s 32(1)(*b*), (*e*), (*g*) and (*p*), deleted VATA 1972, s 32(1)(*w*) and inserted VATA 1972, s 32(2A). A new VATA 1972, s 32(1)(*w*) was subsequently inserted by FA 1984, s 91.

22 Amendment of section 35 (special provisions for adjustment and recovery of consideration) of Principal Act

Notes

This section inserted VATA 1972, s 35(3).

23 Amendment of section 29 (adjustment of capital allowances by reference to value added tax) of Finance Act 1975

Notes

This section substituted FA 1975, s 29(1) para (ii).

24 Exempted activities

Notes

This section substituted VATA 1972, Sch 1.

25 Amendment of Second Schedule to Principal Act

Notes

This section substituted VATA 1972, Sch 2 paras (v), (vi) and (x). Amendments to paras (i) and (xvi) have been superseded by FA 1992, s 195.

26 Amendment of Third Schedule to Principal Act

Notes

This amendment is now irrelevant as VATA 1972, Sch 3 was replaced by FA 1991, s 86.

27 Services that are taxed where received

Notes

This section substituted VATA 1972, Sch 4. The old Sch 4 listed "luxury" goods: televisions, radios, record players and records liable at 35%/40%.

28 "Annex A activities" and "Annex B services"

Notes

This section substituted VATA 1972, Sch 5.

28 Amendment of Imposition of Duties Act, 1957

30 Repeals and consequential amendments

(1) The enactment mentioned in column (2) of the First Schedule is hereby repealed to the extent specified in column (3) of that Schedule.

(2) In consequence of the amendments of the Principal Act and of the repeals specified in the First Schedule, the Principal Act is hereby further amended by the substitution of the word or expression mentioned in column (3) of the Second Schedule at any reference number for the word or expression mentioned in column (2) of that Schedule at that reference number wherever it occurs in the provision of the Principal Act mentioned in column (4) of that Schedule at that reference number.

31 Transitional provisions

(1) (*a*)   The register that immediately before the commencement of this Act, was the register of persons who may become or who are accountable persons shall, as on and from such commencement, become and be the register of persons who may become or are taxable persons under section 9 of the Principal Act as amended by this Act and the persons who, immediately before such commencement, were registered in the former register shall, upon such commencement, stand registered in the latter register.

(*b*)   A person who, immediately before the commencement of this Act, was authorised to treat-

(i)   the moneys which he received in respect of the delivery of taxable goods or rendering of taxable services as the consideration in respect of such delivery of goods or rendering of services, and

(ii)   the moneys he received in respect of the rendering of taxable services as the consideration for the rendering of such services, shall be deemed (if he could be so authorised) to have been so authorised to determine his tax liability in respect of supplies of goods and services or supplies of services, as the case may be, under section 14 of the Principal Act as amended by this Act.

(*c*)   A person who, immediately before the commencement of this Act, was an accountable person and who, upon such commencement, would not, unless he so elected under section 8(3) of the Principal Act, be a taxable person, shall, upon such commencement, be deemed to have so elected and shall be a taxable person until the time when the election is cancelled or he permanently ceases to supply taxable goods and services, whichever is the later.

(2) In relation to a person who, immediately before the commencement of this Act, was an accountable person—

(*a*) references in subsection (3) of section 7 of the Principal Act to a waiver shall be deemed to include references to a waiver made under subsection (1) of the said section 7 before such commencement,

(*b*) references in subsection (5) of section 8 of the Principal Act to an election shall be deemed to include references to an election made under subsection (3) of the said section 8,

(*c*) references in the said subsection (3) of the said section 7 to the supply of services shall be deemed to include references to the rendering of services before such commencement, and

(*d*) references in the said subsection (5) and subsection (6)(*b*) of the said section 8 to the supply of goods or services shall be deemed to include references to the delivery of goods, or the rendering of services, before such commencement.

32 Short title, commencement, collective citation and commencement

(1) This Act may be cited as the Value Added Tax (Amendment) Act, 1978.

(2) The Value Added Tax Act, 1972, and (in so far as they relate to value added tax) the Finance Act, 1973, the Finance Act, 1975, the Finance (No. 2) Act 1975, the Finance Act, 1976, the Finance Act, 1978 and this Act shall be construed together as one Act and may be cited together as the Value Added Tax Acts, 1972 to 1978.

(3) This Act, other than section 29 shall come into operation on such day as the Minister may by order appoint.

FIRST SCHEDULE
ENACTMENTS REPEALED

Notes

Repealed: VATA 1972, s 2(2); VATA 1972, s 4(2) [words "section 2(2)"]; VATA 1972, s 11(8)(*a*) [words "and may, in like manner, vary the Fourth Schedule by deleting therefrom descriptions of goods of any kind or by varying any description of goods for the time being specified therein,"]; VATA 1972, s 11(9), VATA 1972, s 19(1)(proviso), VATA 1972, s 36 and VATA 1972, Sch 2 para (ii). Other repeals have been superseded by subsequent legislation.

SECOND SCHEDULE
CONSEQUENTIAL AMENDMENTS

Notes

This schedule is principally concerned with setting out the changes in terminology introduced by this Act. "Supply", "supplied", "supplying" and "supplies" are substituted throughout VATA 1972 in place of "delivery", "delivered", "delivering" and "delivers" respectively in relation to goods and in place of "render", "rendered", "rendering" and "renders" respectively in relation to services. Similarly "taxable person" is substituted for "accountable person" throughout VATA 1972. Other amendments relate to cross-references in VATA 1972.

FINANCE ACT 1978

(Number 21 of 1978)

ARRANGEMENT OF SECTIONS

PART VII
MISCELLANEOUS

AN ACT TO CHARGE AND IMPOSE CERTAIN DUTIES OF CUSTOMS AND INLAND REVENUE (INCLUDING EXCISE), TO AMEND THE LAW RELATING TO CUSTOMS AND INLAND REVENUE (INCLUDING EXCISE) AND TO MAKE FURTHER PROVISIONS IN CONNECTION WITH FINANCE.
[5TH JULY 1978]

46 Interest on unpaid taxes

Amendments

[1]   Repealed by FA 1998, s 133(3) in so far as it relates to value added tax.

---

53 Care and management of taxes and duties

All taxes and duties imposed by this Act are hereby placed under the care and management of the Revenue Commissioners.

54 Short title, construction and commencement

(1) This Act may be cited as the Finance Act, 1978.

...

(9) Any reference in this Act to any other enactment shall, except so far as the context otherwise requires, be construed as a reference to that enactment as amended by or under any other enactment including this Act.

FINANCE ACT 1979

(Number 11 of 1979)

ARRANGEMENT OF SECTIONS

PART III
VALUE ADDED TAX

Section

PART V
MISCELLANEOUS

AN ACT TO CHARGE AND IMPOSE CERTAIN DUTIES OF CUSTOMS AND INLAND REVENUE (INCLUDING EXCISE), TO AMEND THE LAW RELATING TO CUSTOMS AND INLAND REVENUE (INCLUDING EXCISE) AND TO MAKE FURTHER PROVISIONS IN CONNECTION WITH FINANCE.
[1st JUNE 1979]

PART III
VALUE ADDED TAX

48 Amendment of section 18 (inspection and removal of records) of Value Added Tax Act 1972

Notes

This amendment is now irrelevant as VATA 1972, s 18(1) was subsequently substituted by FA 1984, s 89.

49 Amendment of Third Schedule to Value Added Tax Act 1972

Notes

This amendment is now irrelevant as VATA 1972, Sch 3 was replaced by FA 1991, s 86.

PART V
MISCELLANEOUS

58 Care and management of taxes and duties

All taxes and duties imposed by this Act are hereby placed under the care and management of the Revenue Commissioners.

59 Short title, construction and commencement

(1) This Act may be cited as the Finance Act, 1979.

...

(4) *Part III* of this Act shall be construed together with the Value Added Tax Acts, 1972 to 1978, and may be cited together therewith as the Value Added Tax Acts, 1972 to 1979.

...

(7) Any reference in this Act to any other enactment shall, except so far as the context otherwise requires, be construed as a reference to that enactment as amended by or under any other enactment including this Act.

FINANCE ACT 1980

(Number 14 of 1980)

ARRANGEMENT OF SECTIONS

PART III
VALUE ADDED TAX

AN ACT TO CHARGE AND IMPOSE CERTAIN DUTIES OF CUSTOMS AND INLAND REVENUE (INCLUDING EXCISE), TO AMEND THE LAW RELATING TO CUSTOMS AND INLAND REVENUE (INCLUDING EXCISE) AND TO MAKE FURTHER PROVISIONS IN CONNECTION WITH FINANCE.
[25th JUNE, 1980]

PART III
VALUE ADDED TAX

80 Increase of rate of tax on certain goods and services

Notes

This section, by amending VATA 1972, s 11(1)(*c*) increased the standard rate from 20% to 25% with effect from 1 May 1980. The change has since been superseded.

81 Amendment of section 8 (taxable persons) of Value Added Tax Act, 1972

Notes

This amendment, which provided increased registration limits, has since been superseded.

82 Amendment of First Schedule to Value Added Tax Act, 1972

Notes

This section, by substituting VATA 1972, Sch 1 para (xv), restricted the scope of the exemption for betting businesses.

PART VI
MISCELLANEOUS

95 Care and management of taxes and duties

All taxes and duties imposed by this Act are hereby placed under the care and management of the Revenue Commissioners.

96 Short title, construction and commencement

(1) This Act may be cited as the Finance Act, 1980.

...

(4) *Part III* of this Act shall be construed together with the Value Added Tax Acts, 1972 to 1979, and may be cited together therewith as the Value Added Tax Acts, 1972 to 1980.

...

(8) Any reference in this Act to any other enactment shall, except so far as the context otherwise requires, be construed as a reference to that enactment as amended by or under any other enactment including this Act.

FINANCE ACT 1981

(Number 16 of 1981)

ARRANGEMENT OF SECTIONS

PART III
VALUE ADDED TAX

Section

PART VI
MISCELLANEOUS

AN ACT TO CHARGE AND IMPOSE CERTAIN DUTIES OF CUSTOMS AND INLAND REVENUE (INCLUDING EXCISE), TO AMEND THE LAW RELATING TO CUSTOMS AND INLAND REVENUE (INCLUDING EXCISE) AND TO MAKE FURTHER PROVISIONS IN CONNECTION WITH FINANCE.
[28TH MAY 1981]

PART III
VALUE ADDED TAX

42 Principal Act

In this Part "the Principal Act" means the Value Added Tax Act, 1972.

43 Amendment of section 1 (interpretation) of Principal Act

Notes

This section extended the definition of "development" in VATA 1972, s 1(1) to include prefabricated buildings.

44 Amendment of section 12 (deduction for tax borne or paid) of Principal Act

Notes

This section made a technical amendment to VATA 1972, s 12(2) to provide that repayments formerly dealt with under VATA 1972, s 12(2) are now dealt with under VATA 1972, s 20(2).

45 Amendment of section 20 (refund of tax) of Principal Act

Notes

This section made a technical amendment to VATA 1972, s 20(2) to provide that repayments formerly dealt with under VATA 1972, s 12(2) are now dealt with under VATA 1972, s 20(2).

PART VI
MISCELLANEOUS

53 Care and management of taxes and duties

All taxes and duties imposed by this Act are hereby placed under the care and management of the Revenue Commissioners.

54 Short title, construction and commencement

(1) This Act may be cited as the Finance Act, 1981.

...

(4) *Part III* of this Act shall be construed together with the Value Added Tax Acts, 1972 to 1980, and may be cited together therewith as the Value Added Tax Acts, 1972 to 1981.

...

(8) Any reference in this Act to any other enactment shall, unless the context otherwise requires, be construed as a reference to that enactment as amended by or under any other enactment including this Act.

FINANCE (NO 2) ACT 1981

(Number 28 of 1981)

ARRANGEMENT OF SECTIONS

PART II
VALUE ADDED TAX

Section

PART IV
MISCELLANEOUS

AN ACT TO CHARGE AND IMPOSE CERTAIN DUTIES OF CUSTOMS AND INLAND REVENUE (INCLUDING EXCISE), TO AMEND THE LAW RELATING TO CUSTOMS AND INLAND REVENUE (INCLUDING EXCISE) AND TO MAKE FURTHER PROVISIONS IN CONNECTION WITH FINANCE. [20th NOVEMBER, 1981]

PART II
VALUE ADDED TAX

10 Definitions (Part II)

In this Part—

"the Act of 1978" means the Value Added Tax (Amendment) Act, 1978;

"the Principal Act" means the Value Added Tax Act, 1972.

11 Amendment of section 8 (taxable persons) of Principal Act

Notes

This section substituted VATA 1972, s 8(4) (turnover limits for compulsory registration). Other amendments have been superseded.

---

12 Amendment of section 11 (rates of tax) of Principal Act

Notes

This section increased the 10% VAT rate to 15% with effect from 1 September 1981. The change has since been superseded.

---

13 Amendment of section 12A (special provisions for tax invoiced by flat-rate farmers) of Principal Act

Notes

This section increased the 1% flat-rate credit for unregistered farmers to 1.5% with effect from 1 September 1981. The change has since been superseded.

14 Relief for hotels etc

(1) In this section "qualifying service" means a service consisting of the supply, for the benefit of persons not resident in the State, under an agreement made before the 1st day of January, 1981, of sleeping accommodation, with or without board or of motor cars upon hire, boats upon hire or entertainment, at charges fixed at the time of the making of the agreement, to persons carrying on the business of travel agent, tour operator or the hiring out of motor cars or boats.

(2) In respect of taxable periods commencing on the 1st day of November, 1981, notwithstanding the provisions of section of the Principal Act (as amended by this Act) tax shall, in relation to the supply of a qualifying service, be chargeable, and be deemed to have been chargeable, at the rate of 10 per cent.

15 Transitional provisions

A person who, immediately after the passing of this Act, was a taxable person and who, upon such passing, would not, unless he so elected under section 8(3) of the Principal Act, be such a person, shall, upon such passing, be deemed to have so elected and shall be a taxable person until the time when the election is cancelled or he permanently ceases to supply taxable goods and services, whichever is earlier.

PART IV
MISCELLANEOUS

19 Care and management of taxes and duties

All taxes and duties imposed by this Act are hereby placed under the care and management of the Revenue Commissioners.

20 Short title, construction and commencement

(1) This Act may be cited as the Finance (No 2) Act, 1981.

...

(3) *Part II* of this Act shall be construed together with the Value Added Tax Acts, 1972 to 1981, and shall be included in the collective citation "the Value Added Tax Acts, 1972 to 1981".

...

(5) Any reference in this Act to any other enactment shall, except so far as the context otherwise requires, be construed as a reference to that enactment as amended by or under any other enactment including this Act.

FINANCE ACT 1982

(Number 14 of 1982)

ARRANGEMENT OF SECTIONS

PART III
VALUE ADDED TAX

AN ACT TO CHARGE AND IMPOSE CERTAIN DUTIES OF CUSTOMS AND INLAND REVENUE (INCLUDING EXCISE), TO AMEND THE LAW RELATING TO CUSTOMS AND INLAND REVENUE (INCLUDING EXCISE) AND TO MAKE FURTHER PROVISIONS IN CONNECTION WITH FINANCE.
[17th JULY, 1982]

PART III
VALUE ADDED TAX

74 Interpretation (Part III)

In this Part—

"the Principal Act" means the Value Added Tax Act, 1972;

"the Act of 1976" means the Finance Act, 1976;

"the Act of 1978" means the Value Added Tax (Amendment) Act, 1978;

"the Act of 1981" means the Finance Act, 1981.

75 Amendment of section 3 (delivery of goods) of Principal Act

Notes

This section substituted VATA 1972, s 3(3) (land and buildings supplied through auctioneer or estate agent no longer taxed at 3%).

76 Amendment of section 5 (rendering of services) of Principal Act

Notes

This section inserted VATA 1972, s 5(4A). Barristers' services, the fees for which are not technically recoverable in law, (as the barrister cannot sue for unpaid fees) are taxable (with effect from 1 September 1982: see s 87).

77 Amendment of section 8 (accountable persons) of Principal Act

Notes

This section, by inserting VATA 1972, s 8(3A), provided that a racehorse trainer is a taxable person when his turnover from racehorse training exceeds (or is likely to exceed) £15,000 per annum. The section also substituted a revised definition of "farmer" in VATA 1972, s 8(9).

78 Amendment of section 10 (amount on which tax is chargeable) of Principal Act

Notes

This section inserted VATA 1972, s 10(4A) to clarify the chargeable amount on sales (of dutiable goods: beer, whiskey etc) "in warehouse", to unregistered persons.

79 Amendment of section 11 (rates of tax) of Principal Act

Notes

This section increased the 15% VAT rate to 18% and the 25% VAT rate to 30% with effect from 1 May 1982. The 3% effective rate was applied to professional services supplied to farmers.

80 Amendment of section 12 (deduction for tax borne or paid) of Principal Act

Notes

This amendment, which is connected with s 15, provided a deduction in the VAT return for VAT paid at import (after 1 September 1982) for registered traders.

81 Amendment of section 12A (special provisions for tax invoiced by flat-rate farmers) of Principal Act

Notes

This section, by substituting VATA 1972, s 12A(2) increased the flat-rate compensation for unregistered farmers from 1.5% to 1.8% with effect from 1 May 1982, and introduced a new definition of "flat-rate farmer".

82 Amendment of section 13 (remission of tax on goods exported etc) of Principal Act

Notes

This section deleted VATA 1972, s 13(4)–(5) (sales in bond).

83 Amendment of section 14 (determination of tax due by reference to cash receipts) of Principal Act

Notes

This change has since been superseded.

84 Amendment of section 15 (charge of tax on imported goods) of Principal Act

Notes

This section reintroduced VAT at import with effect from 1 September 1982.

85 Amendment of section 16 (duty to keep records) of Principal Act

Notes

Para (*a*) amended VATA 1972, s 16(2), to provide that importers must keep copies of customs documents to verify claims for deduction for VAT paid at import. Para (*b*) amended VATA 1972, s 16(3) to provide that the customs documents must be kept for six years.

86 Amendment of section 26 (penalties generally) of Principal Act

Notes

This section substituted VATA 1972, s 26(1) and deleted VATA 1972, s 26(5) (General increase in penalties).

87 Amendment of First Schedule to Principal Act

Notes

The net effect of the changes is that services provided by actuaries, accountants, barristers, solicitors etc and debt collectors are no longer exempt, with effect from 1 September 1982.

88 Amendment of Second Schedule to Principal Act

Notes

This section reduced the scope of the 0% rate for sales by VAT registered persons in the Shannon customs free airport and the section also reduced the rate of VAT on books to 0%.

89 Amendment of Third Schedule to Principal Act

Notes

This amendment reduced the VAT rate on furniture, carpets, lino and coffins from 25% to 18% with effect from 1 May 1982.

90 Relief for hotels etc

(1) In this section **"qualifying service"** means a service consisting of the supply, for the benefit of persons not resident in the State, under an agreement made before the 1st day of January, 1982, of sleeping accommodation, with or without board, or of motor cars upon hire, boats upon hire or entertainment, at charges fixed at the time of the making of the agreement, to persons carrying on the business of travel agent, tour operator or the hiring out of motor cars or boats.

(2) In respect of the taxable periods commencing on the 1st day of May, 1982, the 1st day of July, 1982, the 1st day of September, 1982 and the 1st day of November, 1982, notwithstanding the provisions of section 11 of the Principal Act (as amended by this Act), tax shall, in relation to the supply of a qualifying service, be, and be deemed to have been, chargeable, at the rate of **15 per cent**.

PART VI
MISCELLANEOUS

104 Care and management of taxes and duties

All taxes and duties imposed by this Act are hereby placed under the care and management of the Revenue Commissioners.

105 Short title, construction and commencement

(1) This Act may be cited as the Finance Act, 1982.

...

(4) *Part III* of this Act shall be construed together with the Value Added Tax Acts, 1972 to 1981, and may be cited together therewith as the Value -Added Tax Acts, 1972 to 1982.

...

(8) *Part III* of this Act shall, save as is otherwise expressly provided therein, come into force as on and from the 1st day of September, 1982.

(9) Any reference in this Act to any other enactment shall, except so far as the context otherwise requires, be construed as a reference to that enactment as amended by or under any other enactment including this Act.

FINANCE ACT 1983

(Number 15 of 1983)

ARRANGEMENT OF SECTIONS

PART I
INCOME TAX, INCOME LEVY, CORPORATION TAX AND CAPITAL GAINS TAX

CHAPTER IV
Anti-avoidance and anti-evasion

AN ACT TO CHARGE AND IMPOSE CERTAIN DUTIES OF CUSTOMS AND INLAND REVENUE (INCLUDING EXCISE), TO AMEND THE LAW RELATING TO CUSTOMS AND INLAND REVENUE (INCLUDING EXCISE) AND TO MAKE FURTHER PROVISIONS IN CONNECTION WITH FINANCE.
[8th JUNE, 1983]

PART I
INCOME TAX, INCOME LEVY, CORPORATION TAX AND CAPITAL GAINS TAX

CHAPTER IV
Anti-avoidance and anti-evasion

22 Obligation to show tax reference number on receipts, etc

(1) In this section —

"business" means —

    (*a*)   a profession, or

(*b*)   a trade consisting solely of the supply (which word has in this paragraph the same meaning as in the Value Added Tax Acts, 1972 to 1983) of a service and includes, in the case of a trade part of which consists of the supply of a service, that part, and also includes, in the case of a trade the whole or part of which consists of the supply of a service which incorporates the supply of goods in the course of the supply of that service, that trade or that part, as the case may be;

"specified person", in relation to a business, means —

(*a*)   in case the business is carried on by an individual, that individual, and

(*b*)   in case the business is carried on by a partnership, the precedent partner;

"tax reference number", in relation to a specified person, means each of the following:

(*a*)   the Revenue and Social Insurance (RSI) Number stated on any certificate of tax-free allowances issued to that person by an inspector, not being a certificate issued to an employer in respect of an employee of that employer,

(*b*)   the reference number stated on any return of income form or notice of assessment issued to that person by an inspector, and

(*c*)   the registration number of that person for the purposes of Value Added tax.

(2) The specified person in relation to a business shall ensure that his tax reference number or, if he has more than one tax reference number, one of his tax reference numbers or, if he has not got a tax reference number, his full names and his address is or are stated on any document (being an invoice, credit note, debit note, receipt, account, statement of account, voucher or estimate relating to an amount of £5 or more) issued on or after the 1st day of September, 1983, in the course of that business.

(3) ...

Definition

"inspector": TCA 1997, ss 2(1), 5(1), 852; "profession": TCA 1997, s 2(1); "trade": TCA 1997, s 3(1).

---

23 Publication of names of tax defaulters

(1) In this section **"the Acts"** means —

(*a*)   the Tax Acts,

(*b*)   the Capital Gains Tax Acts,

(*c*)   the Value Added Tax Act, 1972, and the enactments amending or extending that Act,

(*d*)   the Capital Acquisitions Tax Act, 1976, and the enactments amending or extending that Act,

(*e*)   the statutes relating to stamp duty and to the management of that duty, and

(*f*)   Part VI,

and any instruments made thereunder.

[(2) The Revenue Commissioners shall, as respects each relevant period (being the period beginning on the 1st day of January, 1997, and ending on the 30th day of June, 1997, and each subsequent period of three months beginning with the period ending on the 30th day of September, 1997), compile a list of names and addresses and the occupations or descriptions of every person—

(*a*) upon whom a fine or other penalty was imposed by a court under any of the Acts during that relevant period,

(*b*) upon whom a fine or other penalty was otherwise imposed by a court during that relevant period in respect of an act or omission by the person in relation to tax, or

(*c*) in whose case the Revenue Commissioners, pursuant to an agreement made with the person in that relevant period, refrained from initiating proceedings for recovery of any fine or penalty of the kind mentioned in paragraphs (*a*) and (*b*) and, in lieu of initiating such proceedings, accepted, or undertook to accept, a specified sum of money in settlement of any claim by the Revenue Commissioners in respect of any specified liability of the person under any of the Acts for—

(i) payment of any tax,

(ii) payment of interest thereon, and

(iii) a fine or other monetary penalty in respect thereof.]¹

[(3) Notwithstanding any obligation as to secrecy imposed on them by the Acts or the Official Secrets Act, 1963—

(*a*) the Revenue Commissioners shall, before the expiration of three months from the end of each relevant period, cause each such list referred to in subsection (2) in relation to that period to be published in Iris Oifigiúil, and

(*b*) the Revenue Commissioners may, at any time, cause any such list referred to in subsection (2) to be publicised in such manner as they shall consider appropriate.]²

(4) Paragraph (*c*) of subsection (2) does not apply in relation to a person in whose case—

(*a*) the Revenue Commissioners are satisfied that, before any investigation or inquiry had been commenced by them or by any of their officers into any matter occasioning a liability referred to in the said paragraph of the person, the person had voluntarily furnished to them complete information in relation to and full particulars of the said matter, or

[(*aa*) the provisions of section 72 of the Finance Act, 1988, or section 3 of the Waiver of Certain Tax, Interest and Penalties Act, 1993, apply, or]³

(*b*) the specified sum referred to in the said paragraph (*c*) does not exceed £10,000 or was paid on or before the 31st day of December, 1983.

(5) Any such list as is referred to in subsection (2) shall specify in respect of each person named in the list such particulars as the Revenue Commissioners think fit —

(*a*) of the matter occasioning the fine or penalty of the kind referred to in subsection (2) imposed on the person or, as the case may be, the liability of that kind to which the person was subject, and

(*b*) of any interest, fine or other monetary penalty, and of any other penalty or sanction, to which that person was liable, or which was imposed on him by a court, and which was occasioned by the said matter.

(6) In this section **"tax"** means income tax, capital gains tax, corporation tax, Value Added tax, gift tax, inheritance tax, residential property tax and stamp duty.

Amendments

1   Substituted by FA 1997, s 158(*a*) for 1997 and later years.
2   Substituted by FA 1997, s 158(*b*) for 1997 and later years.
3   Subs (4)(*aa*) substituted by WCTIPA 1993, s 3(7); originally inserted by FA 1988, s 72(7).

Definition

"Tax Acts":TCA 1997, s 1(2).

PART III
VALUE ADDED TAX

77 Interpretation (Part III)

In this Part—

"the Principal Act" means the Value Added Tax Act, 1972;

"the Act of 1976" means the Finance Act, 1976;

"the Act of 1978" means the Value Added Tax (Amendment) Act, 1978;

"the Act of 1981" means the Finance (No 2) Act, 1981;

"the act of 1982" means the Finance Act, 1982.

78 Amendment of section 3 (delivery of goods) of Principal Act

Notes

This section, by inserting VATA 1972, s 3(7), provided that the disposal of business assets by a liquidator or receiver in the course of winding up the business, is taxable.

79 Amendment of section 8 (accountable persons) of Principal Act

Notes

This amendment, which reduced the VAT registration limits, has been superseded.

80 Amendment of section 9 (registration) of Principal Act

Notes

Para (*a*), by amending VATA 1972, s 9(1), and para (*b*), by inserting VATA 1972, s 9(2A), provided that liquidators, receivers etc who dispose of taxable goods in the course of winding up a business, must register for VAT.

81 Amendment of section 11 (rates of tax) of Principal Act

Notes

This section increased the effective 3% rate to 5%, the 18% rate to 23%, and the 30% rate to 35%, with effect from 1 March 1983. Fuels for home heat etc, previously liable at 0% became taxed at 5%.

82 Amendment of section 12A (special provisions for tax invoiced by flat-rate farmers) of Principal Act

Notes

This section increased the farmers flat-rate VAT compensation from 1.8% to 2.3% with effect from 1 March 1983.

83 Amendment of section 15 (charge of tax on imported goods) of Principal Act

Notes

This amendment provided that heating fuels, liable at 5% with effect from 1 March 1983, would be liable at 5% at importation.

84 Amendment of section 19 (tax due and payable) of Principal Act

Notes

This section, by substituting VATA 1972, s 19(3), provides that when a liquidator disposes of taxable goods in the course of winding up a business, he must make the necessary VAT returns, and pay any tax arising on the disposal of the goods by the due date.

85 Amendment of section 25 (appeals) of Principal Act

Notes

This section substituted VATA 1972, s 25(2)(f), (ff) and (k). The changes correspond to the income tax changes made by FA 1983, s 9, which were intended to prevent the appeal procedure being used to delay payment of tax.

86 Amendment of Second Schedule to Principal Act

Notes

This section removed heating fuels that were made taxable at 5% with effect from 1 March 1983 (s 81) from the list of zero rated goods.

87 Amendment of Third Schedule to Principal Act

Notes

This amendment has been superseded.

88 Insertion of Sixth Schedule to Principal Act

Notes

This section inserted VATA 1972, Sch 6, listing goods liable at the new 5% rate. The change has since been superseded.

89 Relief for hotels etc

(1) (*a*) In this section **"qualifying service"** means a service consisting of the supply, for the benefit of persons not resident in the State, under an agreement made before the 1st day of January, 1983, of sleeping accommodation, with or without board, or of motor cars upon hire, boats upon hire or entertainment, at charges fixed at the time of the making of the agreement, to persons carrying on the business of travel agent, tour operator or the hiring out of motor cars or boats.

(*b*) In respect of the taxable periods commencing on the 1st day of March, 1983, the 1st day of May, 1983, the 1st day of July, 1983, the 1st day of September, 1983 and the 1st day of November, 1983, notwithstanding the provisions of section 11 of the Principal Act (as amended by this Act), tax shall, in relation to the supply of a qualifying service, be, and be deemed to have been, chargeable at the rate of 18 per cent.

(2) Notwithstanding the provisions of section 11 of the Principal Act (as amended by this Act), the rate of tax chargeable in relation to the letting of immovable goods specified in paragraph (iv)(*b*) of the First Schedule to the Principal Act shall be **18 per cent**.

PART V
REVENUE OFFENCES

94 Revenue offences

(1) In this Part —

"the Acts" means —

(*a*) the Customs Acts,

(*b*) the statutes relating to the duties of excise and to the management of those duties,

(*c*) the Tax Acts,

(*d*) the Capital Gains Tax Acts,

(*e*) the Value Added Tax Act, 1972, and the enactments amending or extending that Act,

(*f*) the Capital Acquisitions Tax Act, 1976, and the enactments amending or extending that Act,

(*g*) the statutes relating to stamp duty and to the management of that duty, and

(*h*) Part VI,

and any instruments made thereunder and any instruments made under any other enactment and relating to tax;

[**"an authorised officer"** means an officer of the Revenue Commissioners authorised by them in writing to exercise any of the powers conferred by the Acts;][1]

"tax" means any tax, duty, levy or charge under the care and management of the Revenue Commissioners.

(2) A person shall, without prejudice to any other penalty to which he may be liable, be guilty of an offence under this section if, after the date of the passing of this Act, he —

(*a*) knowingly or wilfully delivers any incorrect return, statement or accounts or knowingly or wilfully furnishes any incorrect information in connection with any tax,

(*b*) knowingly aids, abets, assists, incites or induces another person to make or deliver knowingly or wilfully any incorrect return, statement or accounts in connection with any tax,

(*c*) claims or obtains relief or exemption from, or repayment of, any tax, being a relief, exemption or repayment to which, to his knowledge, he is not entitled,

(*d*) knowingly or wilfully issues or produces any incorrect invoice, receipt, instrument or other document in connection with any tax,

[(*dd*) (i) fails to make any deduction required to be made by him under section 32(1) of the Finance Act, 1986,

(ii) fails, having made the deduction, to pay the sum deducted to the Collector-General within the time specified in that behalf in section 33(3) of that Act, or

(iii) fails to pay to the Collector-General an amount on account of appropriate tax (within the meaning of Chapter IV of Part I of that Act) within the time specified in that behalf in section 33(4) of that Act,]²

[(*ddd*) (i) fails to make any deduction required to be made by him under section 18(5) of the Finance Act, 1989, or

(ii) fails, having made the deduction, to pay the sum deducted to the Collector-General within the time specified in paragraph 1(3) of the First Schedule to that Act]²,

(*e*) knowingly or wilfully fails to comply with any provision of the Acts requiring —

(i) the furnishing of a return of income, profits or gains, or of sources of income, profits or gains, for the purposes of any tax,

(ii) the furnishing of any other return, certificate, notification, particulars, or any statement or evidence, for the purposes of any tax,

(iii) the keeping or retention of books, records, accounts or other documents for the purposes of any tax, or

(iv) the production of books, records, accounts or other documents, when so requested, for the purposes of any tax,

[(*ee*) knowingly or wilfully, and within the time limits specified for their retention, destroys, defaces, or conceals from an authorised officer—

(i) any documents, or

(ii) any other written or printed material in any form, including any information stored, maintained or preserved by means of any mechanical or electronic device, whether or not stored, maintained or preserved in a legible form, which a person is obliged by any provision of the Acts to keep, to issue or to produce for inspection,][4]

(f) fails to remit any income tax payable pursuant to Chapter IV of Part V of the Income Tax Act, 1967, and the regulations thereunder, or section 7 of the Finance Act, 1968, and the said regulations, or Value Added tax within the time specified in that behalf in relation to income tax or Value Added tax, as the case may be, by the Acts, or

(g) obstructs or interferes with any officer of the Revenue Commissioners, or any other person, in the exercise or performance of powers or duties under the Acts for the purposes of any tax.

(3) A person guilty of an offence under this section shall be liable —

[(a) on summary conviction to a fine of £1,000 which may be mitigated to not less than one fourth part thereof or, at the discretion of the court, to imprisonment for a term not exceeding 12 months or to both the fine and the imprisonment, or][5]

(b) on conviction on indictment, to a fine not exceeding £10,000 or, at the discretion of the court, to imprisonment for a term not exceeding 5 years or to both the fine and the imprisonment.

(4) Section 13 of the Criminal Procedure Act, 1967, shall apply in relation to an offence under this section as if, in lieu of the penalties specified in subsection (3) of the said section 13, there were specified therein the penalties provided for by subsection (3) (a) of this section, and the reference in subsection (2)(a) of the said section 13 to the penalties provided for in the said subsection (3) shall be construed and have effect accordingly.

(5) Where an offence under this section is committed by a body corporate and the offence is shown to have been committed with the consent or connivance of any person who, when the offence was committed, was a director, manager, secretary or other officer of the body corporate, or a member of the committee of management or other controlling authority of the body corporate, that person shall also be deemed to be guilty of the offence and may be proceeded against and punished accordingly.

(6) In any proceedings under this section, a return or statement delivered to an inspector or other officer of the Revenue Commissioners under any provision of the Acts and purporting to be signed by any person shall be deemed, until the contrary is proved, to have been so delivered, and to have been signed, by that person.

(7) Notwithstanding the provisions of any other enactment, proceedings in respect of an offence under this section may be instituted within 10 years from the date of the commission of the offence or incurring of the penalty (as the case may be).

(8) Section 1 of the Probation of Offenders Act, 1907, shall not apply in relation to offences under this section.

(9) The provisions of section 128(4), 500(4), 501(3), 502(3), 506 and 507 of the Income Tax Act, 1967, and sections 26(6) and 27(7) of the Value Added Tax Act, 1972, shall, with any necessary modifications, apply for the purposes of this section as they apply for the purposes of those provisions, including, in the case of such of those provisions as were applied by the Capital Gains Tax Act, 1975, the Corporation Tax Act, 1976, or Part VI, the purposes of those provisions as so applied.

Amendments

1   Definition inserted by FA 1992, s 243(*a*)(i).

2   Subs (2)(*dd*) inserted by FA 1986, s 40(2).

3   Subs (2)(*ddd*) inserted by FA 1989, s 18 and Sch 1 para 3(2).

4   Subs (2)(*ee*) inserted by FA 1996, s 132(1) and Sch 5 Pt I para 13(2); it had been erroneously inserted by FA 1992, s 243(*a*)(ii) in sub-s (1).

5   Subs (3)(*a*) substituted by FA 1992, s 243(*b*).

Case law

Meaning of "criminal matter": *Director of Public Prosecutions v Seamus Boyle*, (IV) ITR (395).

Subs (2)(*e*): District Justice not entitled to conclude, on basis of Revenue certificate, that taxpayer had "knowingly and wilfully" failed to submit return of income; taxpayer not present at District Court hearing and was entitled to defend himself: (IV) ITR (478).

Cross-references

Collective investment undertakings, failure to deduct tax from payment to unit holder: FA 1989, s 18(5).

Self-assessment, notice of attachment, incorrect debtor's return treated (in cases of fraud or negligence) as a Revenue offence: FA 1988, s 73(5); failure to make debtor's return not a Revenue offence: FA 1988, s 73(9).

Subss (4), (6), (7), (8): tax amnesty, penalties applied by: WCTIPA 1993, s 9(2); false statement to obtain allowance: WCTIPA 1993, s 11(3).

Definition

"inspector": TCA 1997, ss 2(1), 5(1), 852; "month": IA 2005, Sch; "profits": TCA 1997, s 4(1); "Tax Acts": TCA 1997, s 1(2).

PART VII
Miscellaneous

121 Care and management of taxes and duties

All taxes and duties imposed by this Act (apart from income levy collected by health boards) are hereby placed under the care and management of the Revenue Commissioners.

122 Short title, construction and commencement

(1) This Act may be cited as the Finance Act, 1983.

...

(4) Part III and (so far as relating to value added tax) *Parts I* and *V* shall be construed together with the Value Added Tax Acts, 1972 to 1982, and maybe cited therewith as the Value Added Tax Acts, 1972 to 1983.

...

(7) Part III (other than sections 77 to 80, 81(1), 82, 84 and 85) shall be deemed to have come into force and shall take effect as on and from the 1st day of May, 1983, and the said sections 77, 81(1) and 82 shall be deemed to have come into force and shall take

effect as on and from the 1st day of March, 1983, and the said sections 78, 80, and 84 shall come into force and shall take effect as on and from the 1st day of September, 1983.

(8) Any reference in this Act to any other enactment shall, unless the context otherwise requires, be construed as a reference to that enactment as amended by or under any other enactment including this Act.

(9) In this Act, a reference to a Part, section or schedule is to a Part or section of, or schedule to, this Act, unless it is indicated that reference to some other enactment is intended.

(10) In this Act, a reference to a subsection, paragraph or sub-paragraph is to the subsection, paragraph or subparagraph of the provision (including a schedule) in which the reference occurs, unless it is indicated that reference to some other provision is intended.

FINANCE ACT 1984

(Number 9 of 1984)

ARRANGEMENT OF SECTIONS

PART III
VALUE ADDED TAX

AN ACT TO CHARGE AND IMPOSE CERTAIN DUTIES OF CUSTOMS AND INLAND REVENUE (INCLUDING EXCISE), TO AMEND THE LAW RELATING TO CUSTOMS AND INLAND REVENUE (INCLUDING EXCISE) AND TO MAKE FURTHER PROVISIONS IN CONNECTION WITH FINANCE.
[23rd MAY 1984]

PART III
VALUE ADDED TAX

84 Interpretation (Part III)

In this Part—

"the Act of 1976" means the Finance Act, 1976;

"the Act of 1983" means the Finance Act, 1983;

"the Principal Act" means the Value Added Tax Act, 1972.

85 Amendment of section 1 (interpretation) of Principal Act

Notes

This section inserted definitions of "clothing" and "footwear" in VATA 1972, s 1(1).

86 Amendment of section 8 (Accountable persons) of Principal Act

Notes

Para (*a*) amended VATA 1972, s 8(1) and para (*c*) inserted VATA 1972, s 8(3B), an anti-avoidance provision to counteract "turnover splitting" between controlled businesses. Other changes have since been superseded.

87 Amendment of section 11 (rates of tax) of Principal Act

Notes

This section introduced VAT on adult clothes at 8% with effect from 1 May 1984.

88 Amendment of section 15 (charge of tax on imported goods) of Principal Act

Notes

This section introduced VAT on imported adult clothes at 8% with effect from 1 May 1984.

89 Amendment of section 18 (inspection and removal of records) of Principal Act

Notes

This section substituted VATA 1972, s 18(1) and deleted VATA 1972, s 18(2).

90 Amendment of section 26 (penalties generally) of Principal Act

Notes

This section amended VATA 1972, s 26(1) and (3A), providing revised penalties in relation to the new powers for authorised officers.

91 Amendment of section 32 (regulations) of Principal Act

Notes

This section inserted VATA 1972, s 32(1)(w) (power to make regulations determining the average build of a child of 10 years of age: the cut-off age for children's clothes, which are still liable at 0%).

92 Amendment of Second Schedule to Principal Act

Notes

This section removed adult clothing (other than sanitary towels, tampons etc) from the list of goods liable at 0%, with effect from 1 May 1984.

93 Amendment of Third Schedule to Principal Act

Notes

This section removed concrete from the list of goods liable at 23% (to be liable at 5%). The hire of clothes remained liable at 23%.

94 Amendment of Sixth Schedule to Principal Act

Notes

This section included concrete, and live theatrical and musical performances in the list of goods/services liable at 5%.

95 Insertion of Seventh Schedule to Principal Act

Notes

This inserted VATA 1972, Sch 7 (since deleted) listing adult clothes as liable at 8%.

96 Rate of tax in relation to short-term hiring of certain goods

Notwithstanding the provisions of section 11 of the Principal Act, the rate of value added tax chargeable on the following services shall be **18 per cent** of the amount in respect of which tax is chargeable in relation to those services:

(*a*) the service specified in paragraph (ii) of Part II of the Third Schedule to the Principal Act, and

(*b*) the service consisting of the hiring to a person, under an agreement of the kind specified in the said paragraph (ii) of a tent or of a vehicle designed and constructed, or adapted, for the conveyance of persons by road.

PART VI
MISCELLANEOUS

115 Care and management of taxes and duties

All taxes and duties imposed by this Act are hereby placed under the care and management of the Revenue Commissioners.

116 Short title, construction and commencement

(1) This Act may be cited as the Finance Act, 1984.

...

(4) Part III shall be construed together with the Value Added Tax Acts, 1972 to 1983, and maybe cited therewith as the Value Added Tax Acts, 1972 to 1984.

...

(8) Part III other than sections 84, 86, 89, 90, 93(*a*)(i), 94 and 96 shall be deemed to have come into force and shall take effect as on and from the 1st day of May, 1984, and the said sections 84, 93(*a*)(i), 94 and 96 shall be deemed to have come into force and shall take effect as on and from the 1st day of March, 1984.

(9) Any reference in this Act to any other enactment shall, unless the context otherwise requires, be construed as a reference to that enactment as amended by or under any other enactment including this Act.

(10) In this Act, a reference to a Part, section or schedule is to a Part or section of, or schedule to, this Act, unless it is indicated that reference to some other enactment is intended.

(11) In this Act, a reference to a subsection, paragraph or sub-paragraph is to the subsection, paragraph or subparagraph of the provision (including a Schedule) in which the reference occurs, unless it is indicated that reference to some other provision is intended.

FINANCE ACT 1985

(Number 10 of 1985)

ARRANGEMENT OF SECTIONS

PART III
VALUE ADDED TAX

PART VI
MISCELLANEOUS

AN ACT TO CHARGE AND IMPOSE CERTAIN DUTIES OF CUSTOMS AND
INLAND REVENUE (INCLUDING EXCISE), TO AMEND THE LAW
RELATING TO CUSTOMS AND INLAND REVENUE (INCLUDING EXCISE)
AND TO MAKE FURTHER PROVISIONS IN CONNECTION WITH FINANCE.
[30th MAY 1985]

41 Interpretation (Part III)

In this Part—

"the Principal Act" means the Value Added Tax Act, 1972;

"the Act of 1976" means the Finance Act, 1976;

"the Act of 1978" means the Value Added Tax (Amendment) Act, 1978;

"the Act of 1983" means the Finance Act, 1983;

"the Act of 1984" means the Finance Act, 1984.

42 Amendment of section 5 (rendering of services) of Principal Act

---

Notes

This section implemented the Tenth Directive 84/386/EEC (place of hire of movable goods) in Irish VAT law.
The change as since been superseded.

---

43 Amendment of section 11 (rates of tax) of Principal Act

Notes

With effect from 1 March 1985, this section abolished the 5%, 8%, 18% and 35% VAT rates, replacing them
with 10% and 25%. Goods and services, the supply of which was liable at 5% (other than live theatre etc) or
8% became taxed at 10%, and goods and services the supply of which was liable at 23% or 35% became taxed

293

at 25%. Concrete blocks and newspapers (previously liable at 23%) became taxed at 10%. Adult footwear, previously liable at 0%, became taxed at 10%. Section 54 below provided a two month deferment of the 5% increase on houses under construction. A new 2.2% rate was introduced for livestock.

44 Amendment of section 12A (special provisions for tax invoiced by flat-rate farmers) of Principal Act

Notes

This section provided a 2.2% flat-rate compensation for unregistered farmers, with effect from 1 March 1985.

45 Amendment of section 13 (remission of tax on goods exported etc) of Principal Act

Notes

This section amended VATA 1972, s 13(3)(c), dealing with repayment of tax to traders not established in the State, implementing the Tenth Directive (place of hire of movable goods).

46 Amendment of section 15 (charge of tax on imported goods) of Principal Act

Notes

This amendment provided that VAT would be charged at import on goods at the new VAT rates of 2.2%, 10% and 25% introduced by s 43.

47 Amendment of section 23 (determination of tax due) of Principal Act

Notes

This section amended VATA 1972, s 23(1) and VATA 1972, s 23(2)(a) to transfer the power to make VAT estimates from the Revenue Commissioners to inspectors of taxes and other authorised Revenue officers.

48 Amendment of section 32 (regulations) of Principal Act

Notes

This section inserted VATA 1972, s 32(1)(ww) and amended VATA 1972, s 32(2A), enabling the Revenue Commissioners to make regulations determining the average foot size of a child of 10 years of age (the cut off age for children's shoes: liable at 0%).

49 Amendment of First Schedule to Principal Act

Notes

This section inserted VATA 1972, Sch 1 para (viii) to exempt live theatre and music performances, previously liable at 5%.

50 Amendment of Second Schedule to Principal Act

Notes

This section substituted VATA 1972, Sch 2 paras (xii) and (xix) to remove adult shoes from the list of goods liable to VAT at the 0% rate.

51 Miscellaneous amendments (Third, Sixth and Seventh Schedules) to the Principal Act

Notes

This section deleted VATA 1972, Sch 3 (23% rate goods and services) and Sch 7 (8% rate goods: adult clothes) and substituted VATA 1972, Sch 6 (new list of goods liable at 10%).

52 Amendment of Fourth Schedule to Principal Act

Notes

This section inserted VATA 1972, Sch 4 para (i*a*) (hire of movable goods), implementing the terms of the Tenth Directive 84/386/ EEC in the State.

53 Repeals

Section 89(2) of the Act of 1983 and section 92 of the Act of 1984 are hereby repealed.

54 Deferment of increase in rate of tax (private dwellings)

(1) For the purposes of this section-

"dwelling" means a house, or an apartment, flat, penthouse or similar unit of accommodation;

"qualifying supply" means the supply on or before the 30th day of April, 1985, to a person, being an individual acting on his own behalf, of a service consisting of the development of immovable goods, being the construction of a dwelling designed for the private use of, and occupation by, such person, and includes a supply of immovable goods to that person on or before the said date in connection with the supply of the said service.

(2) In this section reference to the construction of a dwelling does not include reference to the conversion, reconstruction, alteration or enlargement of any existing building or buildings.

(3) In respect of the taxable period commencing on the 1st day of March, 1985, notwithstanding the provisions of section 11 of the Principal Act (as amended by this Act), value added tax shall, in relation to a qualifying supply, be, and be deemed to have been, chargeable, at the rate of **5 per cent**.

PART VI
MISCELLANEOUS

70 Care and management of taxes and duties

All taxes and duties imposed by this Act are hereby placed under the care and management of the Revenue Commissioners.

71 Short title, construction and commencement

(1) This Act may be cited as the Finance Act, 1985.

...

(4) Part III shall be construed together with the Value Added Tax Acts, 1972 to 1984, and maybe cited therewith as the Value Added Tax Acts, 1972 to 1985.

...

(8) Part III (other than sections 42, 45, 47 and 52) shall be deemed to have come into force and shall take effect as on and from the 1st day of May, 1985.

(9) Any reference in this Act to any other enactment shall, unless the context otherwise requires, be construed as a reference to that enactment as amended by or under any other enactment including this Act.

(10) In this Act, a reference to a Part, section or schedule is to a Part or section of, or schedule to, this Act, unless it is indicated that reference to some other enactment is intended.

(11) In this Act, a reference to a subsection, paragraph or sub-paragraph is to the subsection, paragraph or subparagraph of the provision (including a Schedule) in which the reference occurs, unless it is indicated that reference to some other provision is intended.

FINANCE ACT 1986

(Number 13 of 1986)

ARRANGEMENT OF SECTIONS

PART III
VALUE ADDED TAX

AN ACT TO CHARGE AND IMPOSE CERTAIN DUTIES OF CUSTOMS AND INLAND REVENUE (INCLUDING EXCISE), TO AMEND THE LAW RELATING TO CUSTOMS AND INLAND REVENUE (INCLUDING EXCISE) AND TO MAKE FURTHER PROVISIONS IN CONNECTION WITH FINANCE.
[27th MAY, 1986]

PART III
VALUE ADDED TAX

79 Interpretation (Part III)

In this Part—

"the Principal Act" means the Value Added Tax Act, 1972;

"the Act of 1978" means the Value Added Tax (Amendment) Act, 1978;

"the Act of 1985" means the Finance Act, 1985.

80 Amendment of section 1 (interpretation) of Principal Act

Notes

This section inserted definition of "free port" in VATA 1972, s 1(1).

---

81 Amendment of section 5 (rendering of services) of Principal Act

---

Notes

Para (*a*) inserted VATA 1972, s 5(3A). Para (*b*) (i) inserted VATA 1972, s 5(6)(*d*) and para (*b*)(ii) substituted VATA 1972, s 5(6)(*e*). The changes dealt with the place of supply of services received from abroad.

---

82 Amendment of section 8 (accountable persons) of Principal Act

Notes

This amendment dealt with the accountability for tax of persons in receipt of services from abroad.

83 Amendment of section 11 (rates of tax) of Principal Act

Notes

Para (*a*) increased the livestock rate from 2.2% to 2.4% and the standard rate from 23% to 25% with effect from 1 March 1986.

84 Amendment of section 12 (deduction for tax borne or paid) of Principal Act

Notes

This section inserted VATA 1972 12(1)(*dd*) to allow a purchases VAT deduction for taxable persons in respect of certain services received from abroad.

85 Amendment of section 12A (special provisions for tax invoiced by flat-rate farmers) of Principal Act

Notes

This section increased the flat-rate deduction for unregistered farmers from 2.2% to 2.4% with effect from 1 March 1986.

86 Amendment of section 17 (invoices) of Principal Act

Notes

This section inserted VATA 1972, s 17(1A) to provide for electronic invoicing.

87 Amendment of section 20 (refund of tax) of Principal Act

Notes

This section by inserting VATA 1972, s 20(1A), provides the Revenue Commissioners with power to defer repayment in certain circumstances.

88 Amendment of section 32 (regulations) of Principal Act

Notes

Para (*a*) amended VATA 1972, s 32(1)(*h*) and para (*b*) substituted VATA 1972, s 32(1)(*i*). The changes allow the Revenue to make regulations regarding electronic invoicing.

89 Amendment of First Schedule to Principal Act

Notes

This section inserted VATA 1972, Sch 1 para (iiia), exempting the services (and related goods) supplied by dental technicians.

90 Amendment of Second Schedule to Principal Act

Notes

This section provided that sales within a free port would be liable at 0%, and removed take away food from list of goods liable at 0%.

91 Amendment of Sixth Schedule to Principal Act

Notes

This section included catering services, hot take away food, cinema admissions, repair of movable goods, and body care services in the list of goods and services liable at 10%, and provided a revised definition of "newspapers".

PART VI
Miscellaneous

113 Use of electronic data processing

(1) In this section —

"the Acts" means

   (*a*)   the Tax Acts,

   (*b*)   the Capital Gains Tax Acts,

   [(*c*)   the Value Added Tax Act, 1972,][1]

   (*d*)   the Capital Acquisitions Tax Act, 1976, and the enactments amending or extending that Act, and

   (*e*)   Part VI of the Finance Act, 1983,

and any instruments made thereunder;

"records" means documents which a person is obliged by any provision of the Acts to keep, to issue or to produce for inspection, and any other written or printed material;

"tax" means income tax, corporation tax, capital gains tax, value added tax or residential property tax, as the case may be.

(2) Subject to the agreement of the Revenue Commissioners, records may be stored, maintained, transmitted, reproduced or communicated, as the case may be, by any electronic, photographic or other process approved of by the Revenue Commissioners, and in circumstances where the use of such process has been agreed by them and subject to such conditions as they may impose.

(3) Where, in pursuance of subsection (2), records are preserved by electronic, photographic or other process, a statement contained in a document produced by any such process shall, subject to the rules of court, be admissible in evidence in any proceedings, whether civil or criminal, to the same extent as the records themselves.

(4) Notwithstanding anything in the Tax Acts, duplicates of assessments need not be made, transmitted or delivered.

(5) The entering by an inspector or other authorised officer of details of an assessment and the tax charged therein in an electronic, photographic or other record from which the Collector-General may extract such details by electronic, photographic or other process shall constitute transmission of such details by the inspector or other authorised officer to the Collector-General.

(6) In any proceedings in the Circuit Court, the District Court or the High Court for or in relation to the recovery of any tax, a certificate signed by the Collector-General or other authorised officer certifying that, before the institution of proceedings, a stated sum of tax as so transmitted became due and payable by the defendant —

> (*a*) (i) under an assessment which had become final and conclusive,
>
> (ii) under the provisions of section 429(4) (inserted by the Finance Act, 1971) of the Income Tax Act, 1967, or
>
> (iii) under the provisions relating to the specified amount of tax within the meaning of section 30 of the Finance Act, 1976,
>
> and
>
> (*b*) that demand for the payment of the tax has been duly made,

shall be *prima facie* evidence, until the contrary has been proved, of those facts and a certificate certifying as aforesaid and purporting to be signed by the Collector-General or other authorised officer may be tendered in evidence without proof and shall be deemed, until the contrary is proved, to have been signed by the Collector-General or other authorised officer.

Amendments

1   Subs (1)(*c*) substituted by FA 1993, s 99.

Definition

"Circuit Court": IA 2005, Sch; "District Court": IA 2005, Sch; "High Court": IA 2005, Sch; "inspector": TCA 1997, ss 2(1), 5(1), 852; "person": IA 2005, s 18(*c*); "rules of court": IA 2005, Sch; "Tax Acts": TCA 1997, s 1(2).

---

114 Amendment of provisions relating to payment of interest on tax overpaid

---

Notes

This section, by amending ITA 1967, s 429(4)(proviso)(*a*), reduced the general rate of interest chargeable on unpaid tax from 1.25 per cent per month (or part of a month) to 1 per cent; it also inserted ITA 1967, s 429(6) to provide that the Minister for Finance may change, by ministerial order, the rate of interest chargeable on outstanding tax.

---

115 Liability to tax etc, of holder of fixed charge on book debts of company

[(1) Subject to the other provisions of this section, where a person holds a fixed charge (being a fixed charge which is created on or after the passing of this Act) on the book debts of a company (within the meaning of the Companies Act, 1963), such person shall, if the company fails to pay any relevant amount for which it is liable, become liable to pay such relevant amount on due demand, and on neglect or refusal of payment may be proceeded against in like manner as any other defaulter:

Provided that—

(*a*) this section shall not apply—

(i) unless the holder of the fixed charge has been notified in writing by the Revenue Commissioners that a company has failed to pay a relevant amount for which it is liable and that, by reason of this section, the holder of the fixed charge—

(I) may become liable for payment of any relevant amount which the company subsequently fails to pay, and

(II) where subparagraph (iii) does not apply, has become liable for the payment of the relevant amount that the company has failed to pay,

(ii) to any amounts received by the holder of the fixed charge from the company before the date on which the holder is notified in writing by the Revenue Commissioners in accordance with subparagraph (i), and

(iii) where, within 21 days of the passing of the Finance Act, 1995, or of the creation of the fixed charge, whichever is the later, the holder of the fixed charge furnishes to the Revenue Commissioners a copy of the prescribed particulars of the charge delivered or to be delivered to the registrar of companies in accordance with the provisions of section 99 of the Companies Act, 1963, to any relevant amount which the company was liable to pay before the date on which the holder is notified in writing by the Revenue Commissioners in accordance with subparagraph (i),

and

(*b*) the amount or aggregate amount which the person shall be liable to pay in relation to a company in accordance with this section shall not exceed the amount or aggregate amount which that person has, while the fixed charge on book debts in relation to the said company is in existence, received, directly or indirectly, from that company in payment or in part payment of any debts due by the company to that person.

(1A) The Revenue Commissioners may, at any time and by notice in writing given to the holder of the fixed charge, withdraw, with effect from a date specified in the notice, a notification issued by them in accordance with the provisions of subsection (1):

Provided that such withdrawal shall not—

(i) affect in any way any liability of the holder of the fixed charge under this section which arose prior to such withdrawal, or

(ii) preclude the issue under subsection (1) of a subsequent notice to the holder of the fixed charge.

(1B) The Revenue Commissioners may nominate any of their officers to perform any acts and discharge any functions authorised by this section to be performed or discharged by the Revenue Commissioners.][1]

(2) In this section **"relevant amount"** means any amount which the company is liable to remit—

    (*a*)   under Chapter IV of Part V of the Income Tax Act, 1967, and

    (*b*)   under the Value Added Tax Act, 1972.

Notes

[1]   Subs (1)–(1B) inserted by FA 1995, s 174 with effect from 6 April 1995.

117 Care and management of taxes and duties

All taxes and duties imposed by this Act are hereby placed under the care and management of the Revenue Commissioners.

118 Short title, construction and commencement

(1) This Act may be cited as the Finance Act, 1986.

...

(4) Part III shall be construed together with the Value Added Tax Acts, 1972 to 1985, and may be cited therewith as the Value Added Tax Acts, 1972 to 1986.

...

(7) Part VI ...(so far as relating to value added tax) shall be construed together with the Value Added Tax Acts, 1972 to 1986.

...

(9) In Part III sections 79, 83(*a*) and 85 shall be deemed to have come into force and shall take effect as on and from the 1st day of March, 1986, and sections 83(*b*) and 89 to 91 (other than paragraph (*a*) of section 91) shall come into force on the 1st day of July, 1986.

(10) Any reference in this Act to any other enactment shall, unless the context otherwise requires, be construed as a reference to that enactment as amended by or under any other enactment including this Act.

(11) In this Act, a reference to a Part, section or schedule is to a Part or section of, or schedule to, this Act, unless it is indicated that reference to some other enactment is intended.

(12) In this Act, a reference to a subsection, paragraph or sub-paragraph is to the subsection, paragraph or subparagraph of the provision (including a Schedule) in which the reference occurs, unless it is indicated that reference to some other provision is intended.

FINANCE ACT 1987

(Number 10 of 1987)

ARRANGEMENT OF SECTIONS

PART III
VALUE ADDED TAX

PART VI
MISCELLANEOUS

AN ACT TO CHARGE AND IMPOSE CERTAIN DUTIES OF CUSTOMS AND INLAND REVENUE INCLUDING EXCISE), TO AMEND THE LAW RELATING TO CUSTOMS AND INLAND REVENUE (INCLUDING EXCISE) AND TO MAKE FURTHER PROVISIONS IN CONNECTION WITH FINANCE.
[9th JULY, 1987]

38 Interpretation (Part III)

In this Part—

"the Principal Act" means the Value Added Tax Act, 1972;

"the Act of 1978" means the Value Added Tax (Amendment) Act, 1978;

"the Act of 1985" means the Finance Act, 1985;

"the Act of 1986" means the Finance Act, 1986.

39 Amendment of section 1 (interpretation) of Principal Act

Notes

Para (*a*)(i) amended the definition of "livestock" in VATA 1972, s 1(1) to include goats and deer. Para (*a*)(ii) by inserting VATA 1972, s 1(2)(*c*) revised the definition of "moneys received" to include professional withholding tax. Para (*b*) revoked The Imposition of Duties (No 283)(Value Added Tax) Order 1986 (SI 412/1986) which had provided that live deer were liable at 2.4% with effect from 1 January 1987. The order is no longer necessary following the legislative amendment.

40 Amendment of section 11 (rates of tax) of Principal Act

Notes

This section reduced the rate on livestock from 2.4% to 1.7% with effect from 1 May 1987.

41 Amendment of section 12 (deduction for tax borne or paid) of Principal Act

Notes

Para (*a*) substituted VATA 1972, s 12(1); para (*b*) amended VATA 1972, s 12(3)(*a*) and para (*c*) by substituting VATA 1972, s 12(4) provided amended rules of apportionment between taxable and exempt activities.

42 Amendment of section 12A (special provisions for tax invoiced by flat-rate farmers) of Principal Act

Notes

This amendment reduced the farmer flat-rate compensation from 2.4% to 1.7% with effect from 1 May 1987.

43 Amendment of section 13 (remission of tax on goods exported etc) of Principal Act

Notes

This section amended VATA 1972, s 13(3)(*c*) providing amended rules for repayment of tax to foreign traders.

44 Amendment of section 32 (regulations) of Principal Act

Notes

This section amended VATA 1972, s 32(2A) to provide that certain regulations cannot be made without the Minister's consent.

45 Amendment of First Schedule to Principal Act

Notes

Para (*a*) substituted VATA 1972, Sch 1 para (i), extending the definition of exempt financial services. Para (*b*)(i) amended VATA 1972, Sch 1 para (ix)(*a*) redefining insurance agency services. Para (*c*) amended VATA 1972, Sch para (xi)(*d*) (insurance services) and para (*d*) removed VATA 1972, Sch 1 para (xia) which had been inserted by the Value Added Tax (Exempted Activities) (No 1) Order 1985 to exempt credit card company services. The exemption is now contained in the revised VATA 1972, Sch 1 para (i).

46 Amendment of Second Schedule to Principal Act

Notes

This section deleted the word "drained" from VATA 1972, Sch 2 para (xii)(*d*)(I); this means that drained fruit qualifies as zero rated food.

47 Amendment of Sixth Schedule to Principal Act

Notes

This section included driving lessons, exhibition admissions, photographic services, tour guide services and waste disposal services in the list of goods and services liable at 10%.

PART VI
MISCELLANEOUS

54 Care and management of taxes and duties

All taxes and duties imposed by this Act are hereby placed under the care and management of the Revenue Commissioners.

55 Short title, construction and commencement

(1) This Act may be cited as the Finance Act, 1987.

...

(4) Part III shall be construed together with the Value Added Tax Acts, 1972 to 1986, and maybe cited therewith as the Value Added Tax Acts, 1972 to 1987.

...

(8) In Part III sections 40 and 42 shall be deemed to have come into force and shall take effect as on and from the 1st day of May, 1987, section 39(*a*)(ii) shall be deemed to have come into force and shall take effect as on and from the 6th day of June, 1987, sections 46 and 47 shall be deemed to have come into force and shall take effect as on and from the 1st day of July, 1987, and sections 41 and 45 shall come into force on the 1st day of November, 1987.

(9) Any reference in this Act to any other enactment shall, unless the context otherwise requires, be construed as a reference to that enactment as amended by or under any other enactment including this Act.

(10) In this Act, a reference to a Part, section or schedule is to a Part or section of, or schedule to, this Act, unless it is indicated that reference to some other enactment is intended.

(11) In this Act, a reference to a subsection, paragraph or sub-paragraph is to the subsection, paragraph or subparagraph of the provision (including a Schedule) in which the reference occurs, unless it is indicated that reference to some other provision is intended.

FINANCE ACT 1988

(Number 12 of 1988)

ARRANGEMENT OF SECTIONS

PART III
VALUE ADDED TAX

AN ACT TO CHARGE AND IMPOSE CERTAIN DUTIES OF CUSTOMS AND INLAND REVENUE (INCLUDING EXCISE), TO AMEND THE LAW RELATING TO CUSTOMS AND INLAND REVENUE (INCLUDING EXCISE) AND TO MAKE FURTHER PROVISIONS IN CONNECTION WITH FINANCE.
[25th MAY, 1988]

PART III
VALUE ADDED TAX

59 Interpretation (Part III)

In this Part **"the Principal Act"** means the Value Added Tax Act, 1972.

60 Amendment of section 1 (interpretation) of Principal Act

Notes

This section, by inserting VATA 1972, s 1(2)(*bb*) in the definition of "moneys received" provided that money not actually received because it has been paid directly to the Revenue on foot of an attachment notice (in respect of a defaulting taxpayer) is deemed to have been received.

---

61 Amendment of section 11 (rates of tax) of Principal Act

Notes

This section introduced a 5% rate on electricity, and reduced the livestock rate from 1.7% to 1.4%, with effect from 1 March 1988.

---

62 Amendment of section 12A (special provisions for tax invoiced by flat-rate farmers) of Principal Act

---

Notes

This section reduced the farmer flat-rate compensation from 1.7% to 1.4% with effect from 1 March 1988.

---

63 Amendment of Second Schedule to Principal Act

Notes

This section, by deleting VATA 1972, Sch 2 para (xx)(*a*), excluded electricity from the list of goods and services liable at 0%.

PART VI
MISCELLANEOUS

76 Care and management of taxes and duties

All taxes and duties imposed by this Act are hereby placed under the care and management of the Revenue Commissioners.

77 Short title, construction and commencement

(1) This Act may be cited as the Finance Act, 1988.

...

(4) Part III shall be construed together with the Value Added Tax Acts, 1972 to 1987, and maybe cited therewith as the Value Added Tax Acts, 1972 to 1988.

...

(9) Part III, other than section 60 shall be deemed to have come into force and shall take effect as on and from the 1st day of March, 1988, and the said section 60 shall take effect as on and from the 1st day of October, 1988.

(10) Any reference in this Act to any other enactment shall, unless the context otherwise requires, be construed as a reference to that enactment as amended by or under any other enactment including this Act.

(11) In this Act, a reference to a Part, section or schedule is to a Part or section of, or schedule to, this Act, unless it is indicated that reference to some other enactment is intended.

(12) In this Act, a reference to a subsection, paragraph or sub-paragraph is to the subsection, paragraph or subparagraph of the provision (including a Schedule) in which the reference occurs, unless it is indicated that reference to some other provision is intended.

FINANCE ACT 1989

(Number 10 of 1989)

ARRANGEMENT OF SECTIONS

PART III
VALUE ADDED TAX

AN ACT TO CHARGE AND IMPOSE CERTAIN DUTIES OF CUSTOMS AND INLAND REVENUE (INCLUDING EXCISE), TO AMEND THE LAW RELATING TO CUSTOMS AND INLAND REVENUE (INCLUDING EXCISE) AND TO MAKE FURTHER PROVISIONS IN CONNECTION WITH FINANCE.
[24th MAY, 1989]

PART III
VALUE ADDED TAX

53 Interpretation (Part III)

In this Part—

"the Principal Act" means the Value Added Tax Act, 1972;

"the Act of 1978" means the Value Added Tax (Amendment) Act, 1978;

"the Act of 1985" means the Finance Act, 1985;

"the Act of 1988" means the Finance Act, 1988.

54 Amendment of section 5 (supply of services) of Principal Act

---

Notes

This section inserted VATA 1972, s 5(4B) to reverse the decision in *Bourke v Bradley and Sons*, unreported, HC, 28 July 1988, where it was held that barrister's services were provided to the insurance company and not the insured person. The new provision deems the services to have been supplied to, and received by, the insured person.

---

55 Amendment of section 8 (accountable persons) of Principal Act

---

Notes

Para (*a*) (i) substituted "£15,000" for "£12,000" in VATA 1972, s 8(3)(*b*).
Para (*a*) (ii) substituted "£32,000" for "£25,000" in VATA 1972, s 8(3)(*c*).

Para (*a*) (iii) substituted "£15,000" for "£12,000" in VATA 1972, s 8(3)(*e*).

Para (*b*) substituted "£15,000" for "£12,000" in VATA 1972, s 8(3A).

Para (*c*) substituted "£15,000" for "£12,000" in VATA 1972, s 8(9).

The net effect of the changes is to increase, with effect from 1 July 1989, the VAT registration limits from £25,000 to £30,000 (for persons whose turnover in the preceding 12 months derives as to 90% or more from the supply of goods) and from £12,000 to £15,000 (for persons whose turnover does not derive as to 90% or more from the supply of goods — service businesses).

56 Amendment of section 11 (rates of tax) of Principal Act

Notes

This section inserted VATA 1972, s 11(1)(*bb*) (new 5% rate on electricity, but not in connection with communication signals) and increased the rate on livestock from 1.4% to 2% with effect from 1 March 1989.

57 Amendment of section 12A (special provisions for tax invoiced by flat-rate farmers) of Principal Act

Notes

This section increased the farmer flat-rate compensation from 1.4% to 2% with effect from 1 March 1989.

58 Amendment of section 19 (tax due and payable) of Principal Act

Notes

This section, by inserting VATA 1972, s 19(3)(3)(*aa*), provided that certain traders, authorised by the Collector General would be permitted to submit annual VAT returns.

59 Amendment of section 20 (refund of tax) of Principal Act

Notes

This is a technical amendment to VATA 1972, s 20(3) which enables the Minister for Finance to make Orders that provide for the repayment of VAT (usually to unregistered persons). The current valid orders are included later in this book.

60 Amendment of section 32 (regulations) of Principal Act

Notes

This section amended VATA 1972, s 32(2A), to provide that regulations made by the Revenue Commissioners in relation to heating fuels etc must have the consent of the Minister for Finance.

61 Amendment of First Schedule to Principal Act

Notes

Para (*a*), by inserting VATA 1972, Sch para (i)(*gg*) added the management of a collective investment undertaking to the list of exempted activities, with effect from 1 July 1989. Paras (*b*) and (*c*), by substituting VATA 1972, Sch 1 para (iii) and inserting VATA 1972, Sch 3 para (iii*b*) with effect from 1 November 1989 provide that professional services of an optical nature continue to be exempt, but the supply of spectacles is not exempt. Such a supply becomes liable at 10% (see ss 62 and 63).

62 Amendment of Second Schedule to Principal Act

Notes

This section, by amending VATA 1972, Sch 2 para (xixa)(*b*), removed spectacles from the category of artificial body parts, thus excluding spectacles from being included at the 0% rate, now that the supply of spectacles as part of a professional optician service, is no longer exempt.

63 Amendment of Sixth Schedule to Principal Act

Notes

This amendment includes antiques, art works, and literary manuscripts in the list of goods and services liable at 10%, with effect from 1 July 1989. Corrective spectacles are included in the list of goods and services liable at 10% with effect from 1 November 1989 (no longer exempt: see s 61; not liable at 0%: see s 62).

PART VII
MISCELLANEOUS

92 Tax concessions for disabled drivers

(1) Notwithstanding anything to the contrary contained in any enactment, the Minister for Finance may, after consultation with the Minister for Health and the Minister for the Environment, make regulations providing for—

   (*a*)   the repayment of excise duty and value added tax and the remission of road tax in respect of a motor vehicle used by, and

   (*b*)   the repayment of excise duty relating to hydrocarbon oil used for combustion in the engines of vehicles, to be specified in the regulations, by, a severely and permanently disabled person-

      (i)   as a driver, where the disablement is of such a nature that the person concerned could not drive any vehicle unless it is specially adapted to take account of that disablement, or

      (ii)   as a passenger, where the vehicle has been specially constructed or adapted to take account of the passenger's disablement, and where the vehicle is adapted, the cost of such adaptation consists of not less than [20 per cent][1] of the value of the vehicle excluding tax and excise duty, or such lesser percentage in respect of certain cases as may be specified by regulations in respect of the repayment of any tax relating to adaptation costs only.

(2) Regulations under this section shall provide for—

   (*a*)   the criteria for eligibility for the remission of the taxes specified in subsection (1), including such further medical criteria in relation to disabilities as may be considered necessary,

   (*b*)   subject to subsection (3)(*b*), the procedures to be used in relation the primary medical certification of a disabled person and to appeals against such certification,

   (*c*)   the procedures for certification of vehicles to which the regulations relate,

   (*d*)   the amount of value added tax and excise duty repayable in respect of a vehicle to which the regulations relate,

(e) the maximum engine size or sizes to which the regulations relate,

(f) the limits on the frequency of renewal of a vehicle for the purposes of obtaining a refund of tax or excise duty, and

(g) in the case of the driver concerned, evidence that the vehicle is for his personal use and evidence of his driving capacity,

and the regulations may provide for such other matters as the Minister for Finance considers necessary or expedient for the purposes of giving effect to this section.

(3) (a) Upon the first coming into operation of regulations under this section, section 43(1) of the Finance Act, 1968, shall cease to have effect.

(b) Any person who, at the passing of this Act, was the registered owner of a motor vehicle, being a motor vehicle in respect of which such a person was entitled to and had received a refund of motor tax or excise duty by reference to section 43(1) of the Finance Act, 1968, shall be deemed to be a person who possesses a primary medical certificate which, subject to compliance with the non medical requirements set out in the regulations, entitles him to a similar repayment of tax or excise duty by reference to this section.

(4) Regulations made under this section shall be laid before Dáil Éireann as soon as may be after they are made, and if a resolution annulling the regulations is passed Dáil Éireann within the next subsequent 21 days on which Dáil Éireann has sat after the regulations have been so laid, the regulations shall be annulled accordingly, but without prejudice to the validity of anything previously done thereunder.

(5) In this section—

"medical practitioner" means a medical practitioner registered under the Medical Practitioners Act, 1978;

"primary medical certification" means medical certification by a medical practitioner who is the holder of a post in a health board, being the post commonly known as the post of Director of Community Care and Medical Officer of Health, in the area in which the person to whom the certification relates ordinarily resides and **"primary medical certificate"** shall be construed accordingly.

Amendments

[1] Substituted by FA 1991, s 124; previously "30 per cent".

Regulations

Disabled Drivers (Tax Concessions) Regulations 1989 (SI 340/1989).

---

99 Care and management of taxes and duties

All taxes and duties imposed by this Act are hereby placed under the care and management of the Revenue Commissioners.

100 Short title, construction and commencement

(1) This Act may be cited as the Finance Act, 1989.

...

(4) Part III shall be construed together with the Value Added Tax Acts, 1972 to 1988, and maybe cited therewith as the Value Added Tax Acts, 1972 to 1989.

...

(8) Part III other than sections 54, 55, 56(*a*) and 58 to 63 shall be deemed to have come into force and shall take effect as on and from the 1st day of March, 1989, paragraphs (*a*) and (*d*) of section 61 and section 63 shall take effect as on and from the 1st day of July, 1989, and paragraphs (*b*) and (*c*) of section 61 and sections 62 and 63(*b*) shall take effect as on and from the 1st day of November, 1989.

(9) Any reference in this Act to any other enactment shall, unless the context otherwise requires, be construed as a reference to that enactment as amended by or under any other enactment including this Act.

(10) In this Act, a reference to a Part, section or schedule is to a Part or section of, or schedule to, this Act, unless it is indicated that reference to some other enactment is intended.

(11) In this Act, a reference to a subsection, paragraph or sub-paragraph is to the subsection, paragraph or subparagraph of the provision (including a Schedule) in which the reference occurs, unless it is indicated that reference to some other provision is intended.

FINANCE ACT 1990

(Number 10 of 1990)

ARRANGEMENT OF SECTIONS

PART III
VALUE ADDED TAX

AN ACT TO CHARGE AND IMPOSE CERTAIN DUTIES OF CUSTOMS AND INLAND REVENUE (INCLUDING EXCISE), TO AMEND THE LAW RELATING TO CUSTOMS AND INLAND REVENUE (INCLUDING EXCISE) AND TO MAKE FURTHER PROVISIONS IN CONNECTION WITH FINANCE.
[30th MAY, 1990]

PART III
VALUE ADDED TAX

97 Interpretation (Part III)

In this Part—

"the Principal Act" means the Value Added Tax Act, 1972;

"the Act of 1978" means the Value Added Tax (Amendment) Act, 1978;

"the Act of 1985" means the Finance Act, 1985;

"the Act of 1986" means the Finance Act, 1986;

"the Act of 1989" means the Finance Act, 1989.

98 Amendment of section 1 (interpretation) of Principal Act

Notes

This section, by inserting the word "horses" in the definition of "livestock" in VATA 1972, s 1(1) provided that the supply of live horses became liable at 2.3% with effect from 1 January 1991. This was as a result of the deletion of the Sixth Directive Annex F para 4 (77/388/EEC) by the Eighteenth Directive Art 1(2)(*c*), with effect from 1 January 1991.

---

99 Amendment of section 3 (delivery of goods) of Principal Act

Notes

This section deleted the words "live horses" from VATA 1972, s 3(3)(*a*) and (*b*). The words are no longer needed as the supply of live horses became liable at 2.3% with effect from 1 January 1991 (see s 98).

100 Amendment of section 5 (supply of services) of Principal Act

Notes

Para (*a*) amended VATA 1972, s 5(6)(*e*)(ii)(II) and para (*b*) inserted VATA 1972, s 5(6)(*e*)(ii)(III), to provide that a recipient of services received from abroad who is established in the State and also in the State of the supplier, must "self account" on such services if they are used for the Irish establishment.

101 Amendment of section 8 (accountable persons) of Principal Act

Notes

This section deleted the words "live horses and" from the definition of "agricultural produce" in VATA 1972, s 8(9). This amendment is related to ss 98–99. The supply of live horses became liable at 2.3% (as livestock) with effect from 1 January 1991.

102 Amendment of section 11 (rates of tax) of Principal Act

Notes

This section reduced the 25% rate to 23%, increased the 2% rate to 2.3% and increased the (electricity) 5% rate to 10%, with effect from 1 March 1990. The wording for the 2.3% rate was amended to include live greyhounds and horses, with effect from 1 January 1991.

103 Amendment of section 12A (special provisions for tax invoiced by flat-rate farmers) of Principal Act

Notes

This section increased the flat-rate compensation for unregistered farmers from 2% to 2.3%, with effect from 1 March 1990.

104 Amendment of section 15 (charge of tax on imported goods) of Principal Act

Notes

This section provided that live greyhounds would be liable to 2.3% VAT at import with effect from 1 January 1991.

105 Non-application for a limited period of section 15 (invoices) of Principal Act

In respect of the period from the 1st day of October, 1990, to the 31st day of December, 1990, the provisions of section 17 of the Principal Act shall not apply in the case of the supply of services specified in paragraph (va) (inserted by this Act) of the Sixth Schedule (inserted by the Act of 1985) to the Principal Act.

Notes

This section gives Éircom time to adjust to its systems to the strict invoicing requirements of VATA 1972, s 17, following the introduction of VAT at 10% on telecommunications services, with effect from 1 October 1990.

106 Amendment of First Schedule to Principal Act

Notes

Para (*a*), by amending VATA 1972, Sch 1 para (ii) removes general driving lessons (driving lessons other than for goods vehicles with a capacity of 1.5 tonnes or more) from the list of exempted activities. Para (*b*), by inserting VATA 1972, Sch 1 para (viii*a*), provides that the supply of cultural services (and the supply of goods closely related to such services) is exempt from VAT with effect from 1 March 1990. Para (*c*), by deleting VATA 1972, Sch 1 paras (xx) and (xxi), provided that with effect from 1 January 1991 the supply of live horses or greyhounds is no longer included in the list of exempted activities (see ss 98–99). Para (*d*), by inserting VATA 1972, Sch 1 para (xxii*a*) with effect from 1 March 1990 includes services provided by independent administrative entities (set up by persons carrying on exempted activities) in the list of exempted activities.

107 Amendment of Sixth Schedule to Principal Act

Notes

Para (*a*) included electricity (see s 102) in the list of good and services liable at 10% with effect from 1 March 1990. Para (*b*) included telecommunications services (see s 105) in the list of goods and services liable at 10% with effect from 1 October 1990. Para (*c*), with effect from 1 March 1990, excluded services provided by independent administrative entities (set up by persons carrying on exempted activities) from the list of goods and services liable at 10%, as such services are exempt (see s 106).

PART VII
MISCELLANEOUS

139 Care and management of taxes and duties

All taxes and duties imposed by this Act are hereby placed under the care and management of the Revenue Commissioners.

140 Short title, construction and commencement

(1) This Act may be cited as the Finance Act, 1990.

...

(4) Part III shall be construed together with the Value Added Tax Acts, 1972 to 1989, and maybe cited therewith as the Value Added Tax Acts, 1972 to 1990.

...

(9) Part III (other than sections 98 to 101, paragraph (*c*)(ii) of section 102, sections 104 to 106 and paragraphs (*b*) to (*d*) of section 107) shall be deemed to have come into force and shall take effect as on and from the 1st day of March, 1990, paragraph (*c*) of section 107 shall take effect as on and from the 1st day of July, 1990, paragraph (*c*) of section 107 shall take effect as on and from the 1st day of October, 1990, and sections 98, 99 and 101, paragraph (*c*)(ii) of section 102, section 104 and paragraph (*c*) of section 106 shall take effect as on and from the 1st day of January, 1991.

(10) Any reference in this Act to any other enactment shall, except so far as the context otherwise requires, be construed as a reference to that enactment as amended by or under any other enactment including this Act.

(11) In this Act, a reference to a Part, section or schedule is to a Part or section of, or schedule to, this Act, unless it is indicated that reference to some other enactment is intended.

(12) In this Act, a reference to a subsection, paragraph or sub-paragraph is to the subsection, paragraph or subparagraph of the provision (including a Schedule) in which the reference occurs, unless it is indicated that reference to some other provision is intended.

FINANCE ACT 1991

(Number 13 of 1991)

ARRANGEMENT OF SECTIONS

PART III
VALUE ADDED TAX

AN ACT TO CHARGE AND IMPOSE CERTAIN DUTIES OF CUSTOMS AND INLAND REVENUE (INCLUDING EXCISE), TO AMEND THE LAW RELATING TO CUSTOMS AND INLAND REVENUE (INCLUDING EXCISE) AND TO MAKE FURTHER PROVISIONS IN CONNECTION WITH FINANCE [29th MAY, 1991]

PART III
VALUE ADDED TAX

76 Interpretation (Part III)

In this Part—

"the Principal Act" means the Value Added Tax Act, 1972;

"the Act of 1978" means the Value Added Tax (Amendment) Act, 1978;

"the Act of 1985" means the Finance Act, 1985;

"the Act of 1986" means the Finance Act, 1986;

"the Act of 1987" means the Finance Act, 1987.

77 Amendment of section 1 (interpretation) of Principal Act

Notes

This section deleted the definition of "hotel" in VATA 1972, s 1(1) with effect from 1 January 1992. A broader definition, which includes guesthouses, holiday home accommodation and campsite facilities, is included in the list of goods and service liable at 10% (new VATA 1972, Sch 3 para (vi)) with effect from 1 January 1992. The old definition did not include short-term letting of apartments, holiday cottages etc.

---

78 Amendment of section 7 (waiver of exemption) of Principal Act

Notes

This section amended VATA 1972, s 7(1) to provide that after 1 January 1992 veterinary surgeons will no longer have the right to waive their exemption from VAT. This is because services supplied by veterinary surgeons became taxable at the new 12.5% rate with effect from 1 January 1992 (see s 87).

79 Amendment of section 8 (accountable persons) of Principal Act

Notes

Para (*a*) amended VATA 1972, s 8(1) and para (*b*) substituted VATA 1972, s 8(8), to provide that where the Revenue take the view that certain persons are "connected" they may "deem" such persons to be members of a VAT group. This section, combined with s 83, allows the Revenue to "defer" VAT repayments to members of such groups.

80 Amendment of section 11 (rates of tax) of Principal Act

Notes

This section reduced the 23% rate to 21%, and increased the 10% rate (on certain goods and services) to 12.5%, with effect from 1 March 1991. The 10% rate remains for goods and services listed in the new VATA 1972, Sch 3.

81 Amendment of section 12 (deduction for tax borne or paid) of Principal Act

Notes

This section inserted VATA 1972, s 12(1)(*a*)(iiia) to provide that VAT charged "in respect of services directly related to" the transfer of a business (or part thereof) to another taxable person (VATA 1972, s 3(5)(*b*)(iii)) is deductible in the purchases part of the VAT return. This means that the VAT on liquidator's fees etc is deductible in purchases part of the liquidator's return (see VATA 1972, s 3(7) and 19(3)((*b*)–(*c*)).

82 Amendment of section 15 (charge of tax on imported goods) of Principal Act

Notes

With effect from 1 March 1991, this section provided that the goods liable at 10% (listed in the new VATA 1972, Sch 3) would be liable at the same rate on importation.

83 Amendment of section 20 (refund of tax) of Principal Act

Notes

This section, by substituting VATA 1972, s 20(1A), provides that where the Revenue take the view that certain persons are "connected" they may "deem" such persons to be members of a VAT group. This section, combined with s 79, allows the Revenue to "defer" VAT repayments to members of such groups.

84 Amendment of section 25 (appeals) of Principal Act

Notes

This section, by inserting VATA 1972, s 25(1)(*aa*), provides a right of appeal against a deemed group registration (see ss 79, 83).

85 Amendment of First Schedule to Principal Act

Notes

Para (*a*) (i), by amending VATA 1972, Sch 1 para (i)(*c*), includes dealing in negotiable instruments in the list of exempted activities (financial services) with effect from 1 March 1991.

Para (*a*), by substituting VATA 1972, Sch 1 para (i)(*g*), deleting VATA 1972, Sch 1 para (i)(*gg*), and amending VATA 1972, Sch 1 para (ix), redefine the management of a unit trust, which is already an exempted activity (financial services), to reflect the repeal of the Unit Trusts Act 1972 and the enactment of the Unit Trusts Act 1990.

Para (*b*), by substituting VATA 1972, Sch 1 para (iv)(*b*) with effect from 1 January 1992, removes the short term letting of land or buildings in a tourist context (hotels, apartments, holiday cottages etc) from the list of exempted activities. Guesthouse accommodation, holiday home accommodation, campsite facilities etc, are included in the list of goods and service liable at 10% (new VATA 1972, Sch 3 para (vi)) with effect from 1 January 1992.

Para (*c*), by deleting VATA Sch 1 para (x), removes professional services supplied by veterinary surgeons from the list of exempted activities, with effect from 1 January 1992. This is because services supplied by veterinary surgeons became taxable at the new 12.5% rate with effect from 1 January 1992 (see s 87).

Para (*d*), by inserting VATA 1972, Sch 1 para (xi*a*) with effect from 1 January 1992, clarifies the fact that services supplied by An Post other than the public postal service, are liable to VAT (not exempt).

86 Insertion of Third Schedule to Principal Act

Notes

This section inserted a new VATA 1972, Sch 3 with effect from 1 March 1991, listing goods and services liable at 10%: building work, concrete blocks, concrete ready to pour, guesthouse accommodation, hotel accommodation, holiday home accommodation, land and buildings (developed), tour guide services, and the short term hire of boats, cars, caravans and tents. It further amended VATA 1972, Sch 3 by substituting para (vi) with effect from 1 January 1992. This latter change includes apartments and holiday cottages under the tourist accommodation heading.

87 Amendment of Sixth Schedule to Principal Act

Notes

Subs (1)(*a*) removed VATA 1972, Sch 6 paras (ii), (iii), (iv), (v) and (x) (goods and services now liable at 10% that are included in new VATA 1972, Sch 3: see s 86).

Subs (1)(*c*), by inserting VATA 1972, Sch 6 para (xii*d*) with effect from 1 July 1991, includes professional services supplied by jockeys in the list of goods and services liable at 12.5% (previously 23%).

Subs (1)(*d*), by inserting VATA 1972, Sch 6 para (xiii*j*) with effect from 1 January 1992, includes professional services supplied by veterinary surgeons in the list of goods and services liable at 12.5% (previously exempt with a right to waive that exemption: see s 78).

Subs (1)(*e*), by amending VATA 1972, Sch 6 para (xiv), removes land drainage and reclamation from the list of goods and services liable at 12.5% (now 10%: s 86).

Subs (2), by substituting VATA 1972, Sch 6 para (xii*b*), provides that the routine cleaning of land or buildings is liable at 12.5%.

PART VII
MISCELLANEOUS

124 Amendment of section 92 (tax concessions for disabled drivers, etc) of Finance Act, 1989

Notes

This section substituted "20 per cent" for "30 per cent" in FA 1989, s 92(1)(ii).

131 Care and management of taxes and duties

All taxes and duties imposed by this Act are hereby placed under the care and management of the Revenue Commissioners.

132 Short title, construction and commencement

(1) This Act may be cited as the Finance Act, 1991.

...

(4) Part III shall be construed together with the Value Added Tax Acts, 1972 to 1990, and maybe cited therewith as the Value Added Tax Acts, 1972 to 1991.

...

(9) Part III (other than sections 77 to 79, section 81, sections 83 to 85, section 86(2), paragraphs (*c*) to (*e*) of section 87(1) and section 87(2)) shall be deemed to have come into force and shall take effect as on and from the 1st day of March, 1991, paragraph (*c*) of section 87(1) shall take effect as on and from the 1st day of July, 1991, sections 77 and 78, paragraphs (*b*) to (*d*) of section 85, paragraph (*b*) of section 86(2) and paragraph (*d*) of section 87(1) shall take effect as on and from the 1st day of January, 1992.

(10) Any reference in this Act to any other enactment shall, except so far as the context otherwise requires, be construed as a reference to that enactment as amended by or under any other enactment including this Act.

(11) In this Act, a reference to a Part, section or schedule is to a Part or section of, or schedule to, this Act, unless it is indicated that reference to some other enactment is intended.

(12) In this Act, a reference to a subsection, paragraph or sub-paragraph is to the subsection, paragraph or subparagraph of the provision (including a Schedule) in which the reference occurs, unless it is indicated that reference to some other provision is intended.

FINANCE ACT 1992

(Number 9 of 1992)

ARRANGEMENT OF SECTIONS

PART III
VALUE ADDED TAX

PART VIII
MISCELLANEOUS

AN ACT TO CHARGE AND IMPOSE CERTAIN DUTIES OF CUSTOMS AND
INLAND REVENUE (INCLUDING EXCISE), TO AMEND THE LAW
RELATING TO CUSTOMS AND INLAND REVENUE (INCLUDING EXCISE)
AND TO MAKE FURTHER PROVISIONS IN CONNECTION WITH FINANCE
[28th MAY, 1992]

164 Interpretation (Part III)

In this Part —

"the Principal Act" means the Value Added Tax Act, 1972;

"the Act of 1973" means the Finance Act, 1973;

"the Act of 1976" means the Finance Act, 1976;

"the Act of 1978" means the Value Added Tax (Amendment) Act, 1978;

"the Act of 1981" means the Finance Act, 1981;

"the Act of 1982" means the Finance Act, 1982;

"the Act of 1983" means the Finance Act, 1983;

"the Act of 1984" means the Finance Act, 1984;

"the Act of 1985" means the Finance Act, 1985;

"the Act of 1986" means the Finance Act, 1986;

"the Act of 1987" means the Finance Act, 1987;

"the Act of 1990" means the Finance Act, 1990;

"the Act of 1991" means the Finance Act, 1991.

165 Amendment of section 1 (interpretation) of Principal Act

Notes

Para (*a*) amended VATA 1972, s 1 (1) as follows:

para (*a*)(i), by inserting a definition of "exportation of goods" defines the term as export to a non-EC destination;

para (*a*)(ii) deleted the definition of "harbour authority"; para (*a*)(iii), by inserting a definition of "importation of goods" defines the term as import from a non-EC location; para (*a*)(iv) inserted the definition of "intra-Community acquisition of goods" (broadly, imports and exports within the EC); para (*a*)(v) inserted the definition of "monthly control statement" with effect from 1 November 1992 (a new document to be issued by taxable persons: see s 180); para (*a*)(vi) inserted the definition of "new means of transport" (new boats, planes and vehicles); para (*a*)(vii) inserted the definition of "a person registered for value added tax" (a person registered for VAT in an EC State); para (*a*)(viii) amended definition of "taxable goods"; para (*a*)(ix) amended definition of taxable services; para (*a*)(x) inserted the definition of "vessel".

Para (*b*), by inserting VATA 1972, s 1(2A), provides that the EC territory is with effect from 1 January 1993, for the purposes of Irish VAT, the same as the EC territory detailed in the Sixth Directive Art 3.

166 Amendment of section 2 (charge of value added tax) of Principal Act

Notes

This section, by inserting VATA 1972, s 2(1A) with effect from 1 January 1993, provides that intra-Community acquisitions of goods (other than new, boats, planes and vehicles) by taxable persons are liable to VAT. A taxable person who does not carry on any exempt activities will self account for the "EC import" in both the purchases part of his VAT return and the sales part of the VAT return, with no net tax due (postponed accounting).

Intra-Community acquisitions of new boats, planes and vehicles by all persons including private individuals (not just taxable persons: VAT registered persons) are also liable to VAT.

167 Amendment of section 3 (supply of goods) of Principal Act

Notes

Para (*a*)(i) adjusts VATA 1972, s 3 (1)(*e*) (self supply to exempt activity) to provide that such a self supply may arise where goods imported VAT free from another EC State (intra-Community acquisitions of goods) are diverted to an exempt activity; para (*a*)(ii) adjusts VATA 1972, s 3 (1)(*f*)(ii) (self supply to non business use) to provide that such a self supply may arise where goods imported VAT free (intra-Community acquisition of goods) are diverted to a non business use; para (*a*)(iii), by inserting VATA 1972, s 3 (1)(*g*), provides that the transfer of goods which remain in the possession of the same legal entity (intra branch transfer) within the EC is a supply, and the goods will therefore be taxed as an intra-Community acquisition in the EC State of arrival; para (*b*) made related changes to VATA 1972, s 3 (1A); para (*c*), by substituting VATA 1972, s 3 (6), provides new rules for place of supply of dispatched goods, and turnover limits for distance sellers.

168 Intra-Community acquisition of goods

Notes

This section inserted VATA 1972, s 3A which defines the new term "Intra-Community acquisition of goods" for the transitional period of the single market.

169 Amendment of section 5 (supply of services) of Principal Act

Notes

Para (*a*) amended VATA 1972, s 5(3A) (which provides that persons must self account on certain services received from abroad) to exclude intra-EC haulage services from that subsection; para (*b*)(i), by substituting VATA 1972, s 5(6)(*b*) provides that haulage services (other than intra-EC haulage services) are deemed to be supplied where the transport takes place; para (*b*)(i), by substituting VATA 1972, s 5(6)(*c*)(ii) provides that services ancillary to haulage (loading etc) other than intra-EC haulage are deemed to take place where physically performed; and para (*c*), by substituting VATA 1972, s 5(6)(*f*)–(*h*), provides new place of supply rules for intra-EC haulage services and related loading etc service. In essence, where the recipient of such services is VAT registered, the services are deemed to be supplied in the EC State that issued the recipient's VAT number; if the recipient is not registered the haulage service is taxed in the EC State of departure, and the loading etc ancillary services are taxed where physically performed.

170 Amendment of section 8 (taxable persons) of Principal Act

Notes

Subs (1)(*a*), by substituting VATA 1972, s 8(3)(*a*), provided that a farmer is not obliged to register for VAT unless his turnover from agricultural services exceeds £15,000 in any continuous 12 month period; sub-s (1)(*b*), by inserting VATA 1972, s 8(3C) provided that the liquor license holder of a licensed premises where a dance takes place will be regarded as accountable for VAT on the dance takings.

Subs (2)(*a*) and (*b*) by amending VATA 1972, s 8(1) and inserting VATA 1972, s 8(1A), provide that persons engaging in the intra-Community acquisition of goods are taxable persons, but such persons are not obliged to register (see above) unless the value of the intra-Community acquisitions exceeds £32,000 in any continuous 12 month period; sub-s (2)(*c*) amended VATA 1972, s 8(2) to provide that intra-EC haulage services received by VAT registered persons, like Fourth Schedule services, must be "self accounted" for by the recipient; sub-s (2)(*d*) by inserting VATA 1972, s 8(2B) provided that persons who are taxable only because of an intra-Community acquisition of a new boat, plane or vehicle are not taxable unless they elect; subs (2)(*e*), by substituting VATA 1972, s 8(3), includes persons whose intra-Community acquisitions of goods do not exceed £32,000 in any continuous 12 month period in the list of persons who are not taxable unless they elect to be taxable; subs (2)(*f*) by substituting VATA 1972, s 8(6), allows the Revenue Commissioners to cancel a VAT registration where the person is no longer taxable.

171 Amendment of section 9 (registration) of Principal Act

Notes

This section, by inserting VATA 1972, s 9(1A), obliges the Revenue Commissioners to issue a VAT number to persons they have registered for VAT.

172 Amendment of section 10 (amount on which tax is chargeable) of Principal Act

Notes

Para (*a*) by inserting VATA 1972, s 10(1A) details the taxable amount for intra-Community acquisitions; para (*b*) made a corresponding referential amendment to VATA 1972, s 10(2); para (*c*) by amending VATA 1972, s 10(2)(proviso) prevents a trade in allowance being given in computing the taxable amount of an intra-Community acquisition of goods; para (*d*), by substituting VATA 1972, s 10(3)(*a*) provides that intra-Community acquisitions of goods acquired for less than market value are taxed on their open market value; para (*e*) by amending VATA 1972, s 10(4) provides that the taxable amount on self supplied goods may include the value of an intra-Community acquisition; para (*f*) by inserting VATA 1972, s 10(4B) provides that the taxable amount on intra-EC branch transfers of goods is the open market price of the goods; para (*g*) by inserting VATA 1972, s 10(5A), allows an Irish taxable person to reduce to nil the taxable amount on an intra-Community acquisition the VAT on which has already been accounted for in another EC State (triangulation); para (*h*) by amending VATA 1972, s 10(10) includes a reference to intra-Community acquisition of goods in the definition of open market price.

173 Amendment of section 11 (rates of tax) of Principal Act

Notes

Subs (1)(*a*), by substituting VATA 1972, s 11(1)(*c*) provided that the 12.5% rate would continue to apply to goods listed in VATA 1972, Sch 6 other than those specified in VATA 1972, s 11(1)(*c*)(ii), which would be liable at the new 16% rate; subs (1)(*b*) increased the rate on livestock from 2.3% to 2.7% with effect from 1 March 1992.

Subs (2)(*a*) by substituting VATA 1972, s 11(1) provides rates of 21%, 0%, 10%, 12.5% 16% and 2.7% with effect from 28 May 1992; subs (2)(*b*) deleted VATA 1972, s 11(7) (VAT on dance takings: now taxed at 21% with the liquor license holder as the accountable person: see s 170); subs (2)(*c*) made a referential amendment to VATA 1972, s 11(8)(*a*).

Subs (3)(*a*) amended VATA 1972, s 11(1) to apply the new VAT rates to intra-Community acquisitions of goods after 1 January 1993; subs (3)(*b*) made a referential amendment in VATA 1972, s 11(1A)(*a*); subs (3)(*c*) by substituting VATA 1972, s 11(1B)(*a*)(ii), (*b*)(ii) and amending VATA 1972, s 11(1B)(*g*) allows the Revenue Commissioners to make determinations regarding the VAT rates or VAT status applicable to intra-Community acquisitions of goods and provides equivalent appeal procedures; subs (3)(*d*) by amending VATA 1972, s 11(3), includes intra-Community acquisitions of goods in the package rule. Broadly, that rule provides that if a package comprising goods and/or services chargeable at different VAT rates is sold as a unit, the package is liable at the highest VAT rate applicable to any item in the package.

174 Amendment of section 12 (deductions of tax borne or paid) of Principal Act

Notes

Para (*a*), by inserting VATA 1972, s 12(1)(*a*)(iia) allows taxable persons a purchases VAT deduction for intra-Community acquisitions of goods; para (*a*), by inserting VATA 1972, s 12(1)(*a*)(iib) allows taxable persons a purchases VAT deduction (equal to the residual VAT) for intra-EC branch transfers of goods.

Para (*b*), by amending VATA 1972, s 12(3)(*a*)(iii) and VATA 1972, s 12(3)(*a*)(iv) denies a purchases VAT deduction for intra-Community acquisitions of passenger motor vehicles other than as stock in trade.

175 Amendment of section 12A (special provisions for tax invoiced by flat-rate farmers) of Principal Act

Notes

This section increased the farmer flat-rate compensation from 2.3% to 2.7% with effect from 1 March 1992 and with effect from 1 January 1993 allows a flat-rate addition to be paid to non Irish farmers, in which case the addition should be reclaimed from the VAT authorities of the EC State in which the farmer is based. Similarly unregistered Irish farmers may take a flat-rate addition from an EC based customer. That EC based customer may then reclaim the flat-rate addition paid to the Irish farmer from the Revenue Commissioners.

176 Amendment of section 13 (remission of tax on goods exported, etc.) of Principal Act

Notes

Para (*a*) amended VATA 1972, s 13(3)(*c*) to allow the repayment an EC based customer of an Irish farmer the flat-rate addition paid to that farmer; para (*b*) by inserting VATA 1972, s 13(3A), allows the Revenue Commissioners to repay (to persons other than traders in the goods in question) the residual VAT contained in the value of a new boat, plane or vehicle that has been dispatched to another EC State.

177 Amendment of section 14 (determination of tax due by reference to cash receipts) of Principal Act

Notes

Subs (1)(*a*), by amending VATA 1972, s 14(1) and deleting VATA 1972, s 14(1)(*d*) restricts the cash basis to traders whose turnover derives as to 90% (either from goods or services) from trade with other taxable persons; subs (1)(*b*) by inserting VATA 1972, s 14(1A) provides that VAT is chargeable at the rate applicable when the goods or services were supplied and is not chargeable more than once on the same supply; subs(1)(*c*) made referential amendments to VATA 1972, s 14(2); subs (1)(*d*) by inserting VATA 1972, s 14(3) provides that the cash basis does not apply to imports.

Subs (2) amended VATA 1972, s 14(3) to provide that the cash basis does not apply to intra-Community acquisitions of goods.

178 Amendment of section 15 (charge of tax on imported goods) of Principal Act

Notes

Para (*a*) substituted VATA 1972, s 15(1) to provide that VAT on imported goods is chargeable at 0%, 2.7%, 10%, 12.5%, 16% or 21% as applicable; para (*b*) deleted VATA 1972, s 15(2); para (*c*) by inserting VATA 1972, s 11(5A) allows the Revenue Commissioners to repay VAT at imported paid on goods which are subsequently dispatched (or transported) to another EC State, provided the VAT is accounted for in that EC State as an intra-Community acquisition.

179 Amendment of section 16 (duty to keep records) of Principal Act

Notes

Para (*a*) by amending VATA 1972, s 16(2), deleted the requirement to keep copies of customs entries; para (*b*) by amended VATA 1972, s 16(3), includes monthly control statements and documents relating to intra-Community acquisitions of goods must be kept for six years.

180 Amendment of section 17 (invoices) of Principal Act

Notes

Para (*a*), by amending VATA 1972, s 17(1) provides that VAT invoices etc must be issued to persons other than individuals in other EC States; para (*b*) by substituting VATA 1972, s 17(1A)(*b*)–(*d*), provides that only Revenue authorised traders may engage in electronic invoicing; para (*c*) by inserting VATA 1972, s 17(1B) provides that taxable persons with turnover in excess of £2,000,000 from taxable supplies in any continuous 12 month period must issue their customers with monthly control statements; para (*d*) amended VATA 1972, s 17(2) to allow flat-rate farmers to issue flat-rate VAT invoices to EC customers; para (*e*) amended VATA 1972, s 17(3) to provide that VAT credit notes and supplementary VAT invoices must be issued to customers (non individuals) in other EC States; para (*f*) amended VATA 1972, s 17(4)(*b*) to allow flat-rate farmers to issue flat-rate VAT credit notes and supplementary flat-rate VAT invoices to customers in EC States; para (*g*) amended VATA 1972, s 17(8) to provide that a VAT invoice need not be issued for an advance payment received for an intra-Community supply; para (*h*) inserted VATA 1972, s 17(12)(*ai*) and amended VATA 1972, s 17(12)(*b*) to provide that flat-rate farmer must issue a flat-rate VAT invoice to EC customers on request.

181 Amendment of section 18 (inspection and removal of records) of Principal Act

Notes

Para (*a*)(i), by inserted VATA 1972, s 18(1)(*a*)(iia) gives new powers of search to authorised Revenue officers; para (*a*)(ii), by amending VATA 1972, s 18(1)(*a*)(iii), allows authorised Revenue officers to remove records and take copies and extracts from such records for the purposes of any court proceedings (not just penalty proceedings); para (*a*)(iii), by amending VATA 1972, s 18(1)(*a*)(iv) allows authorised Revenue officials to inspect goods connected with intra-Community acquisitions on a trader's premises; para (*a*)(iv), by amending VATA 1972, s 18(1)(*a*)(v) allows authorised Revenue officials to require the person carrying on the business to provide information on request.

Para (*b*), by inserting VATA 1972, s 18(1A), requires taxable persons to provide customer lists and information to an authorised Revenue officer on request; para (*b*), by inserting VATA 1972, s 18(1B), redefines "records" to include computer discs, microfilmed records etc.

182 Amendment of section 19 (tax due and payable) of Principal Act

Notes

Para (*a*), by inserting VATA 1972, s 19(1A) provides that tax chargeable on intra-Community acquisitions becomes due on the 15th day of the month following the month in which the intra-Community acquisition took place;

para (*b*), by amending VATA 1972, s 19(2) provides that, in relation to advance payments, tax becomes due at the time the payment is received, but this does not apply to advance payments in respect of intra-Community acquisitions;

para (*c*), by inserting VATA 1972, s 19(4), provides that tax on intra-Community acquisitions of motor vehicles (by persons other than motor dealers), tax is payable under the rules laid down in the Value Added Tax (Payment of Tax on Intra-Community Acquisitions of Means of Transport) Regulations 1992 (SI 412/1992).

183 Statement of intra-Community supplies

Notes

This section, by inserting VATA 1972, s 19A, provides that taxable persons with sales to other EC States must make quarterly returns (export sales listings) detailing such sales.

184 Amendment of section 20 (refund of tax of Principal Act

(1) ....

(2) Every order made under section 20(3)(*a*) of the Principal Act which is a subsisting order immediately before the commencement of this section shall, upon such commencement, continue in force as if made under the said section 20(3)(*a*) as amended by this section.

Notes

Subs (1)(*a*) and (*b*), by amending VATA 1972, s 20(1) and inserting VATA 1972, s 20(1B) allow the Revenue Commissioners to request security from a trader before making a refund; subs (1)(*c*) substituted VATA 1972, s 20(3)(*a*) which allows the Minister for Finance to make repayments to unregistered person; subs (1)(*d*), by inserting VATA 1972, s 20(5) allows the Revenue Commissioners to argue that they need not make a refund to taxpayer where that refund would "unjustly enrich" the taxpayer.

185 Amendment of section 23 (determination of tax due) of Principal Act

Notes

Para (*a*) made minor changes to VATA 1972, s 23(1) which have the effect of redefining inspector's "estimates" of tax due as "assessments" of tax due, to distinguish such assessments from automatic estimates issued where a VAT return has not been received (VATA 1972, s 22); para (*b*), by inserting VATA 1972, s 23(3), allows a taxpayer to make an advance payment in relation to an inspector's assessment that is under appeal; if the payment is 80% or more of the amount finally found to be due, no interest will accrue.

186 Security to be given by certain taxable persons

Notes

This section, by inserting VATA 1972, s 23A, allows the Revenue Commissioners to request security from certain traders.

187 Amendment of section 25 (appeals) of Principal Act

Notes

Para (*a*), by inserting VATA 1972, s 25(1)(*ab*), grants a right of appeal against a Revenue decisions to substitute any persons for a foreign trader doing business in the State; para (*b*) made referential amendments to VATA 1972, s 25(2)(*k*).

188 Amendment of section 26 (penalties generally) of Principal Act

Notes

Para (*a*)(i), by amending VATA 1972, s 26(1), provides a £1,200 penalty for failure to submit a statement of intra-Community supplies; para (*a*)(ii) increased the general penalty to £1,200 (from £800); para (*b*), by amending VATA 1972, s 26(2), increased the penalty for issue of an invoice by an unregistered person from £500 to £750; para (*c*), by amending VATA 1972, s 26(2A) increased the penalty for unauthorised issue of a flat-rate VAT invoice from £500 to £750; para (*d*), by amending VATA 1972, s 26(3), increased the corresponding penalties for a company secretary from £500 to £750; para (*e*) by amending VATA 1972, s 26(3A) increased the penalties for obstruction of an authorised officer from £800 to £1,000; para (*f*), by inserting VATA 1972, s 26(3B), provides a new penalty of £1,200 (in respect of each supply) for persons who supply taxable goods in contravention of a Revenue security request.

189 Amendment of section 27 (fraudulent returns etc) of Principal Act

Notes

Para (*a*), by amending VATA 1972, s 27(1), and substituting VATA 1972, s 27(1)(*b*), extended the fraud provisions to monthly control statements and misuse of a VAT number.

Para (*b*), by amending VATA 1972, s 27(3), allows persons who have submitted incorrect monthly control statements, or misused a VAT number to correct the error that has come to the person's notice provided the error is corrected without unreasonable delay; para (*b*), by amending VATA 1972, s 27(7), provides that a monthly control statement or VAT number submitted on behalf of a person is deemed to have been submitted by that person unless he proves it was issued without his consent.

Para (*c*) by inserting VATA 1972, s 27(9A), empowers the Revenue Commissioners to seize allegedly exported goods if the goods are found in the State after the alleged date of export; para (*d*) made referential amendments to VATA 1972, s 27(10); para (*e*) by inserting VATA 1972, s 27(11), gives authorised Revenue officers a limited power of arrest.

190 Amendment of section 28 (assisting in making incorrect returns) of Principal Act

Notes

This section by amending VATA 1972, s 28, provides a penalty for assisting in making an incorrect monthly control statement. The general penalty for assisting in making incorrect returns etc is increased from £500 to £750.

191 Amendment of section 30 (time limits) of Principal Act

Notes

This section changed reference to "estimates" to "assessments" in VATA 1972, s 30 (see s 185) and extended the meaning of "neglect" to include neglect in relation to a monthly control statement.

192 Amendment of section 32 (regulations) of Principal Act

Notes

Para (*a*) inserted VATA 1972, s 32(1)(*aa*)–(*ai*), which allow the Revenue Commissioners power to make regulations regarding: tax deductible on intra-Community acquisitions, how residual tax is to be calculated, repayment of import VAT on goods dispatched to another EC State, payment of tax on intra-Community acquisitions of boats, plane and vehicles, supplies in tax free shops and distance selling.

193   Substitution of certain persons for persons not established in the State

Notes

This section substituted VATA 1972, s 37, which allows the Revenue Commissioners to substitute an Irish trader for a foreign trader who is not established in the State.

194   Amendment of First Schedule to Principal Act

Notes

Subs (1)(*a*) by inserting VATA 1972, Sch 1 para (iv)(*b*i), excludes the provision of commercial sports facilities (now 12.5%) from the list of exempted activities; subs (1)(*b*) made a referential amendment to VATA 1972, Sch 1 para (viii); subs(1)(*c*) substituted VATA 1972, Sch 1 para (xvii) (revised definition of promotion of sporting events which excludes provision of commercial sports facilities that are taxed at 12.5%; subs(1)(*e*), by amending VATA 1972, Sch 1 para (xxiii), removed the requirement that the provision of sports facilities must, to be exempt, be supplied to the members of the non profit making organisation.

Subs (2)(*a*), by amending VATA 1972, Sch 1 para (xviii), provides that the intra-Community acquisition of human organs, blood and milk is an exempted activity; subs (2)(*b*) amended VATA 1972, Sch 1 para (xxiv) to provide that the supply of non deductible goods (cars etc), other than by way of intra-EC branch transfer, is exempt.

195   Amendment of Second Schedule to Principal Act

Notes

Subs (1)(*a*), by inserting VATA 1972, Sch 2 para (v*a*), provides that international aircraft equipment repairs are included in the list of goods and services liable at 0%; subs (1)(*b*)(i) made a referential amendment to VATA 1972, Sch 2 para (xii); subs (1)(*b*)(ii), by substituting VATA 1972, Sch 2 para (xii)(*b*) with effect from 1 November 1992, restricts the drinks liable at 0% to cocoa, coffee, coffee substitutes, egg preparations, milk, milk extracts, meat preparations ("Bovril" type drinks), tea, tea preparations, and yeast preparations: this means that bottled waters etc are liable to VAT with effect from 1 November 1992; subs (1)(*b*)(iii), by substituting VATA 1972, Sch 2 para (xii)(*c*),with effect from 1 July 1992, excludes frozen desserts etc from the list of goods and services liable at 0%: this means such goods become liable at 21%; subs (1)(*b*)(iv)(I) amended VATA 1972, Sch 2 para (xii)(*d*) with effect from 1 July 1992 to exclude confectionery and bakery products (whether cooked or uncooked) from the list of goods and services liable at 0%; subs (1)(*b*)(iv)(II) amended VATA 1972, Sch 2 para (xii)(*d*) with effect from 1 July 1992 to allow bread with a crust formed by a frying process to qualify for the 0% rate; subs (1)(*b*)(v), by substituting VATA 1972, Sch 2 para (xii)(*e*) with effect from 1 July 1992, excludes crisp like snack food products from the list of goods and services liable at 0%.

Subs (2)(*a*), by substituting VATA 1972, Sch 2 para (i)–(*ai*), includes intra-Community supplies in the list of goods and services liable at 0%; subs (2)(*b*), by amending VATA 1972, Sch 2 para (iii), provides that only goods haulage to non-EC destinations will be liable at 0% on or after 1 January 1993; subs (2)(*c*) by inserting VATA 1972, Sch 2 para (iii*a*), provides that intra-EC goods transport to or from the Azores or Madeira is liable at 0%; subs (2)(*c*) by inserting VATA 1972, Sch 2 para (iii*b*), provides that the goods may be imported from outside the EC VAT free provided the goods are consigned to another EC State; subs (2)(*d*) made referential amendments to VATA 1972, Sch 2 para (vi)(*a*), para (vi)(*b*) and para (vi)(*c*) (export agent services); and subs (2)(*c*), by substituting VATA 1972, Sch 2 para (xvi) with effect from 1 January 1993, provides that after that date repair etc work on imported goods will only be liable at 0% where the goods are temporarily arriving from a non-EC State.

196   Amendment of Third Schedule to Principal Act

Notes

Para (*a*) made a referential amendment to VATA 1972, Sch 3 para (ii); para (*b*), amended VATA 1972, Sch 3 para (vi)(*a*) with effect from 1 July 1992, to provide that commercial sports facilities provided by hotels etc would be taxable at 12.5% (Sch 6) rather than the existing rate on accommodation etc (10%).

197 Amendment of Sixth Schedule to Principal Act

Notes

Subs (2) by substituting VATA 1972, Sch 6 with effect from 28 May 1992, provides a new list of goods and services liable at 12.5%: agricultural services, cinema admissions, exhibition admissions (cultural etc), fairground entertainment services, fuel (heating), meals (restaurant etc), meals (take away etc), musical show admissions, theatre admissions, veterinary services, waste disposal services.

Subs (3)(*a*) inserted Sch 6 para (vii*a*) with effect from 1 July 1992 to provide that the commercial sports facilities is included in the list of goods and services liable at 12.5%; subs (3)(*b*), by inserting VATA 1972, Sch 6 para (xi)(ai) with effect from 1 July 1992 excludes farm advisory services liable at 16% from the 12.5% rate.

198 Insertion of Seventh Schedule in Principal Act

Notes

This section, by inserting VATA 1972, Sch 7 with effect from 28 May 1992, provides a new list of goods and services liable at 16%: adult clothes and clothing materials, adult footwear and footwear leather, art works, car gas, cleaning services (land and buildings), driving lessons, farm advisory services, jockey services, photographic goods, photographic services, photographic editing services, photographic agency services, repair services, telecommunications services.

PART VIII
MISCELLANEOUS

253 Care and management of taxes and duties

All taxes and duties imposed by this Act are hereby placed under the care and management of the Revenue Commissioners.

254 Short title, construction and commencement

(1) This Act may be cited as the Finance Act, 1992.

...

(4) Part III shall be construed together with the Value Added Tax Acts, 1972 to 1991, and maybe cited therewith as the Value Added Tax Acts, 1972 to 1992.

...

(11) In relation to Part III:

    (*a*) sections 164, 173(1), 175(1) and 197(1) shall be deemed to have come into force and shall take effect as on and from the 1st day of March, 1992;

    (*b*) subparagraph (ii) of paragraph (*a*) of section 165, paragraph (*b*) of subsection (1) and paragraph (*f*) of subsection (2) of section 170, section 171, section 173(2), paragraphs (*b*) and (*d*) of subsection (1) of section 177, paragraphs (*a*) and (*b*) of section 178, paragraph (*a*) and subparagraph (i) of paragraph (*b*) of section 179, paragraph (*b*) of section 180, subparagraphs (ii) and (iv) of paragraph (*a*) and paragraph (*b*) of section 181, paragraphs (*a*), (*b*) and (*d*) of subsection (1) of section 184, sections 185, 186 and 187, subparagraph (ii) of paragraph (*a*) and paragraphs (*b*), (*c*), (*d*), (*e*) and (*f*) of section 188, paragraph (*b*) of section 190, paragraphs (*a*) and (*b*) of section 191, section 193, paragraphs (*b*) and (*d*) of subsection (1) of section 195 and paragraph (*a*) of section 196, sections 197(2) and 198 shall have effect as on and from the date of passing of this Act;

(c) paragraph (*a*) of subsection (1) of section 170, paragraphs (*a*), (*c*) and (*e*) of subsection (1) of section 194, subparagraphs (iii), (iv) and (v) of paragraph (*b*) of subsection (1) of section 195, paragraph (*b*) of section 196 and section 197(3) shall take effect as on and from the 1st day of July, 1992;

(d) subparagraph (v) of paragraph (*a*) of section 165, subparagraphs (iii), (iv) and (v) of paragraph (*b*) of section 179, paragraph (*c*) of section 180, paragraphs (*a*) and (*b*) of section 189, paragraph (*a*) of section 190, paragraph (*c*) of section 191, paragraph (*b*) of section 192 and subparagraph (ii) of paragraph (*b*) of subsection (1) of section 195 shall take effect as on and from the 1st day of November, 1992; and

(e) the provisions of this Part, other than those specified in paragraphs (*a*) to (*d*), shall take effect as on and from the 1st day of January, 1993.

(12) Any reference in this Act to any other enactment shall, unless the context otherwise requires, be construed as a reference to that enactment as amended by or under any other enactment including this Act.

(13) In this Act, a reference to a Part, section or schedule is to a Part or section of, or schedule to, this Act, unless it is indicated that reference to some other enactment is intended.

(14) In this Act, a reference to a subsection, paragraph or sub-paragraph is to the subsection, paragraph or subparagraph of the provision (including a Schedule) in which the reference occurs, unless it is indicated that reference to some other provision is intended.

FINANCE ACT 1993

(Number 13 of 1993)

ARRANGEMENT OF SECTIONS

PART III
VALUE ADDED TAX

AN ACT TO CHARGE AND IMPOSE CERTAIN DUTIES OF CUSTOMS AND INLAND REVENUE (INCLUDING EXCISE), TO AMEND THE LAW RELATING TO CUSTOMS AND INLAND REVENUE (INCLUDING EXCISE) AND TO MAKE FURTHER PROVISIONS IN CONNECTION WITH FINANCE
[17th JUNE, 1993]

PART III
VALUE ADDED TAX

81 Interpretation (Part III)

In this Part—

"the Principal Act" means the Value Added Tax Act, 1972;

"the Act of 1973" means the Finance Act, 1973;

"the Act of 1976" means the Finance Act, 1976;

"the Act of 1978" means the Value Added Tax (Amendment) Act, 1978;

"the Act of 1981" means the Finance Act, 1981;

"the Act of 1982" means the Finance Act, 1982;

"the Act of 1991" means the Finance Act, 1991;

"the Act of 1992" means the Finance Act, 1992.

82 Amendment of section 3 (supply of goods) of Principal Act

Note

This section, by amending VATA 1972, s 3(1)(*g*) with effect from 17 June 1993, treats the intra-EC transfer of a new boat, plane or vehicle as a supply.

83 Amendment of section 3A (intra-Community acquisition of goods) of Principal Act

Note

Para (*a*), by amending VATA 1972, s 3A(1)(*a*), redefines "intra-Community acquisition of goods" to include the acquisition of goods from a person who carries on an exempted activity in an EC State. Para (*b*) substituted VATA 1972, s 3A(1)(*b*) to take account of the change made by para (*a*).

84 Alcohol products

Note

This section by inserting VATA 1972, s 3B with effect from 1 August 1993, provides that, for alcohol products under duty suspension arrangements, only the last supply is a supply for VAT purposes and the VAT is due when the excise is due.

85 Amendment of section 8 (taxable persons) of Principal Act

Note

Para (*a*) provides that a farmer or sea fisherman who is only a taxable person because of intra-Community acquisitions or services received from abroad, may elect not to be taxable in respect of intra-Community acquisitions of goods made by him (VATA 1972, s 8(1A)(*c*)); a farmer whose turnover derived from the supply of racehorse training services has exceeded £15,000 in any continuous 12 month period, who is only a taxable person because of intra-Community acquisitions or services received from abroad, may elect not to be taxable in respect of intra-Community acquisitions of goods made by him (VATA 1972, s 8(1A)(*d*)).

Para (*b*) provides that a farmer or sea fisherman who is only a taxable person because of intra-Community acquisitions or services received from abroad by him, may elect not to be taxable in respect of service received from abroad by him (VATA 1972, s 8(2)(*b*)); a farmer whose turnover derived from the supply of racehorse training services has exceeded £15,000 in any continuous 12 month period, who is only a taxable person because of intra-Community acquisitions or services received from abroad, may elect not to be taxable in respect of services received from abroad by him (VATA 1972, s 8(2)(*c*)).

Para (*c*)(i) made a referential amendment in VATA 1972, s 8(3); para (*c*)(ii) made a referential amendment in VATA 1972, s 8(3)(*c*)(ii); para (*c*)(iii) deleted VATA 1972, s 8(3)(*d*) (no longer needed because of the restructuring of the section); para (*c*)(iv) substituted VATA 1972, s 8(3)(proviso)(ii) to reflect the foregoing changes.

Para (*d*), by amending VATA 1972, s 8(3A) provides that a farmer whose turnover derived from the supply of racehorse training services has exceeded £15,000 in any continuous 12 month period will only be a taxable person in respect of such services and intra-Community acquisitions of goods or services received from abroad.

Para (*e*) amended VATA 1972, s 8(5) to provide that when a person who has elected to be a taxable person wishes to deregister, any review of the liability for the election period must take account of intra-Community acquisitions.

86 Amendment of section 10 (amount on which tax is chargeable) of principle Act

Note

VATA 1972, s 10(4A) provides that where goods in warehouse are sold to an unregistered person while "in warehouse", VAT is chargeable on the full dutiable amount. This section excludes alcohol products (VATA 1972, s 3B) from such treatment.

87 Amendment of section 11 (rates of tax) of Principal Act

Note

With effect from 1 March 1993: this section abolished the 16% VAT rate, and reduced the livestock rate from 2.7% to 2.5%.

88 Amendment of section 12 (deductions for tax borne or paid) of Principal Act

Note

Para (*a*), by inserting VATA 1972, s 12(1)(*a*)(iic), allows a purchases VAT deduction for alcohol products (in accordance with regulations); para (*b*) made a technical amendment to VATA 1972, s 12(1)(*a*)(viii); para (*c*), by inserting VATA 1972, s 12(1)(*a*)(proviso), disallows purchases VAT deductions to farmers and sea fishermen who are only taxable persons because of intra-Community acquisitions of goods or services received from abroad; this amendment also disallows purchases VAT deductions to farmers who are also racehorse trainers that are only taxable persons because of racehorse training services, intra-Community acquisitions of goods, or services received from abroad.

89 Amendment of section 12A (special provisions for tax invoiced by flat-rate farmers) of Principal Act

Note

This section reduced the flat-rate compensation for unregistered farmers from 2.7% to 2.5% with effect from 1 March 1993.

90 Supplies to, and intra-Community acquisitions and imports by, certain taxable persons

Note

This section, by inserting VATA 1972, s 13A with effect from 1 August 1993, allows authorised persons to zero rate supplies to qualifying exporters (taxable persons whose turnover is derived as to 75% or more from exports).

91 Amendment of section 17 (invoices) of Principal Act

Note

Para (*a*), by amending VATA 1972, s 17(1) provides that a taxable person making distance sales to a customer in another EC State must issue that customer with a VAT invoice.

Para (*b*), by inserting VATA 1972, s 17(3A), provides that where a person issued a VAT invoice showing a higher rate of tax than the correct rate, the invoice is nullified, and the issuer must issue a VAT credit note followed by a replacement VAT invoice.

92 Amendment of section 19 (tax due and payable) of Principal Act

Note

Para (*a*), by inserting VATA 1972, s 19(3)(*a*)(proviso) provides that the tax payable for the November December VAT period may be reduced by the amount of the advance payment (see below).

Para (*b*), by substituting VATA 1972, s 19(4), provides that tax on new vehicles is payable at the time of payment of vehicle registration tax, and the tax on intra-Community acquisitions of new boats and planes (by non taxable persons) is payable in a manner determinable by regulations.

Para (*c*), by substituting VATA 1972, s 19(5) provides that a where a person is a taxable person only because of an intra-Community acquisition of excise products, the VAT is payable in a manner determinable by regulations.

Para (*c*), by inserting VATA 1972, s 19(6) provides that taxable persons with annual VAT liability in excess of £120,000 must, on 1 December in each calendar year, make an advance payment equal to one twelfth of the VAT due for the year ended 30 June immediately preceding the 1 December payment date. The advance payment is then offset against liability shown due on the November December VAT return (which is due on or before 19 January).

93 Amendment of section 20 (refund of tax) of Principal Act

Note

This section, by inserting VATA 1972, s 20(1)(proviso), provides that if an advance payment (see s 92) was made for a November December VAT period which turns out to be a repayment VAT period, the advance payment is to be refunded with the repayment.

94 Amendment of First Schedule to principal Act

Note

This section made a referential amendment to VATA 1972, Sch 1 para (iv)(*b*).

95 Amendment of Second Schedule to Principal Act

Note

Para (*a*), by inserting VATA 1972, Sch 2 para (v*b*), provides that the fuelling and provisioning of seagoing ships and aircraft (operating for reward chiefly on international routes) is liable at 0%.

Para (*b*), by inserting VATA 1972, Sch 2 para (v*i*a), provides that the supply of qualifying goods and services by an authorised person to a qualifying exporter is liable at 0%.

96 Goods and services chargeable at the rate specified in section 11(1)(*c*) of Principal Act

Note

This section substituted VATA 1972, Sch 3, which now lists remaining goods and services liable at 10%.

97 Amendment of Sixth Schedule to Principal Act

Note

These amendments restructured VATA 1972, Sch 6, so that it lists the goods and service liable at 12.5% with effect from 1 March 1993. Those goods and services are listed alphabetically in the table at the start of this book.

98 Repeal of Seventh Schedule to Principal Act

Note

This section repealed VATA 1992, Sch 7 (goods and services that were liable at 16%) with effect from 1 March 1993.

99 Amendment of section 113 (use of electronic data processing) of Finance Act, 1986

Note

This section substituted FA 1986, s 113(1)(*c*).

142 Care and management of taxes and duties

All taxes and duties imposed by this Act are hereby placed under the care and management of the Revenue Commissioners.

143 Short title, construction and commencement

(1) This Act may be cited as the Finance Act, 1993.

(2) ...

(3) Part III shall be construed together with the Value Added Tax Acts, 1972 to 1992, and may be cited together therewith as the Value Added Tax Acts, 1972 to 1993.

(4) ...

(5) ...

(6) ...

(7) ...

(8) ...

(9) In relation to Part III:

> (*a*)   section 81, subparagraph (ii) of paragraph (*c*) of section 85, paragraphs (*a*) and (*c*) of section 87, paragraph (*a*) of section 89, sections 94 and 96, subsection (1) of section 97 and section 98 shall be deemed to have come into force and shall take effect as on and from the 1st day of March, 1993;

> (*b*)   subsection (2) of section 97 shall take effect as on and from the 1st day of July, 1993;

> (*c*)   sections 84 and 86, paragraph (*a*) of section 88, section 90 and paragraph (*b*) of section 95 shall take effect as on and from the 1st day of August 1993;

> (*d*)   paragraph (b) of section 92 shall take effect as on and from the 1st day of September, 1993; and

> (*e*)   the provisions of this Part, other than those specified in paragraphs (*a*) to (*d*), shall have effect as on and from the date of passing of this Act.

(10) Any reference in this Act to any other enactment shall, except so far as the context otherwise requires, be construed as a reference to that enactment as amended by or under any other enactment including this Act.

(11) In this Act, a reference to a Part, section or Schedule is to a Part or section of, or Schedule to, this Act, unless it is indicated that reference to some other enactment is intended.

(12) In this Act, a reference to a subsection, paragraph, subparagraph or clause is to the subsection, paragraph, subparagraph or clause of the provision (including a Schedule) in which the reference occurs, unless it is indicated that reference to some other provision is intended.

Definitions

"Income Tax Acts": TCA 1997, s 1(2); "Corporation Tax Acts": TCA 1997, s 1(2).

FINANCE ACT 1994

(Number 13 of 1994)

ARRANGEMENT OF SECTIONS

PART III
VALUE ADDED TAX

AN ACT TO CHARGE AND IMPOSE CERTAIN DUTIES OF CUSTOMS AND INLAND REVENUE (INCLUDING EXCISE), TO AMEND THE LAW RELATING TO CUSTOMS AND INLAND REVENUE (INCLUDING EXCISE) AND TO MAKE FURTHER PROVISIONS IN CONNECTION WITH FINANCE
[23rd MAY 1994]

PART III
VALUE ADDED TAX

90 Interpretation (Part III)

In this Part–

"the Principal Act" means the Value Added Tax Act, 1972;

"the Act of 1978" means the Value Added Tax (Amendment) Act, 1978;

"the Act of 1982" means the Finance Act, 1982;

"the Act of 1989" means the Finance Act, 1989;

"the Act of 1992" means the Finance Act. 1992.

91 Amendment of section 1 (interpretation) of Principal Act

Notes

Para (*a*) substituted VATA 1972, s 1 definition of "new means of transport" para (*b*)(i) with effect from 1 January 1995.

Para (*b*) substituted "6,000 kilometres" for "3,000 kilometres" in VATA 1972, s 1 definition of "new means of transport" with effect from 1 January 1995.

After 1 January 1995, a vehicle will be regarded as new if it is less than six months old or if it has not travelled more than 6,000 km.

---

92 Amendment of section 3 (supply of goods) of Principal Act

Notes

This section inserted "(v*b*)" in VATA 1972, s 3(*g*)(ii) 23 May 1994.

Intra EU branch transfers are regarded as Intra EU supplies, with several exception, for example, goods transferred to another EU State to have contract work performed on them.

This amendment provides that the transfer of goods to another EU State to be used there in fuelling or provisioning a seagoing vessel will not be regarded as an Intra EU supply.

93 Person liable to pay tax in relation to certain supplies of immovable goods

Notes

This section inserted VATA 1972, s 4A. Upon the creation of a long lease, a VAT registered lessee may agree with a VAT registered lessor that the lessee will be accountable for the VAT on the creation of the lease; the lessee will also be entitled to take a simultaneous VAT deduction in the purchases VAT return. In the case of a lessee who only carries on taxable activities, this will mean that he will be entitled to an equivalent purchases VAT deduction and he will have no net payment of VAT.

The provision is subject to EU approval.

94 Amendment of section 8 (taxable persons) of Principal Act

Notes

Para (*a*) substituted "specified in the First Schedule" for "specified in paragraph (vi), (vii), (xxii) or (xxiii) of the First Schedule" in VATA 1972, s 8, subs (1A)(*e*)(iii) with effect from 23 May 1994.

Para (*b*)(i) substituted "£20,000" for "£15,000" in VATA 1972, s 8(3)(*a*).with effect from 1 July 1994.

Para (*b*)(ii) substituted VATA 1972, s 8(3)(*b*)(ii) with effect from 1 July 1994.

Para (*b*)(iii) substituted "£40,000" for "£32,000" in VATA 1972, s 8(3)(*c*)(i) with effect from 1 July 1994.

Para (*b*)(iv) substituted "£20,000" for "£15,000" in VATA 1972, s 8(3)(*e*) with effect from 1 July 1994.

Para (*c*) substituted "£20,000" for "£15,000" in VATA 1972, s 8(3A)with effect from 1 July 1994.

Para (*d*)(i) substituted "£20,000" for "£15,000" in VATA 1972, s 8(9)(*b*)(ii) definition of "farmer" with effect from 1 July 1994.

Para (*d*)(ii) substituted VATA 1972, s 8(9)(*b*)(iii) definition of "farmer" with effect from 1 July 1994.

The net effect of these changes is to increase, with effect from 1 July 1994, the registration threshold to £40,000 for traders (deriving 90% or more of their turnover from supply of goods) in any continuous 12 month period, and to £20,000 for traders (deriving 10% or more of their turnover from supply of services) in any continuous 12 month period.

95 Amendment of section 10 (amount on which tax is chargeable) of Principal Act

Notes

This section inserted VATA 1972, s 10(3)(*c*)(proviso) with effect from 23 May 1994. Bad debt relief will not apply in the case of long-term leases of property.

96 Amendment of section 12 (deductions for tax borne or paid) of Principal Act

Notes

Para (*a*) inserted VATA 1972, s 12(1)(*a*)(iii*b*). This gives the simultaneous VAT deduction in the purchases part of a VAT return of a lessee who has opted, by agreement with his lessor, to account for the VAT on the creation of a long lease.

Para (*b*)(i) inserted VATA 1972, s 12(3)(*a*)(i*a*) with effect from 23 May 1994. Advertising-related food and drink expenditure will not be deductible in the purchases part of the VAT return.

Para (*b*)(ii) inserted VATA 1972, s 12(3)(*c*)–(*d*) with effect from 23 May 1994. Expenditure on a building, or fitting out a building that will be used for entertainment is not deductible for VAT purposes.

97 Amendment of section 14 (determination of tax due by reference to cash receipts) of Principal Act

Notes

Para (*a*) substituted VATA 1972, s 14(1) with effect from 23 May 1994.

Para (*b*)(i) deleted "paragraph (*a*) of" in VATA 1972, s 14(2) with effect from 23 May 1994. Persons with annual turnover beneath £250,000 are to be entitled to the cash basis.

Para (*b*)(ii) substituted "that subsection" for "the said paragraphs (*a*)" in VATA 1972, s 14(2) with effect from 23 May 1994. This is a consequential technical change.

98 Amendment of section 27 (fraudulent returns etc. of Principal Act

Notes

This section inserted VATA 1972, s 27(9A)(4) with effect from 23 May 1994. The declaration of an incorrect VAT number, and consequent penalties, is not restricted to a taxpayer's own VAT number. Using another person's VAT number, or a fictitious VAT number, or a fraudulently obtained VAT number, constitutes "declaration of an incorrect VAT number" for VAT purposes and may give rise to penalty proceedings etc.

99 Amendment of First Schedule to Principal Act

Notes

Para (*a*) inserted "the services of loss adjusters and excluding" in VATA 1972, Sch 1 para (ix) with effect from 1 September 1994.

Para (*b*) inserted "of bets of the kind referred to in section 89 of the Finance Act, 1994," in VATA 1972, Sch 1 para (xv) with effect from the commencement of s 89.

The services of loss adjuster, previously exempt, are liable to VAT with effect from 1 September 1994. Betting remains exempt from VAT, despite technical changes (FA 1994, s 89) which relate to betting tax.

100 Amendment of Second Schedule to Principal Act

Notes

This section substituted VATA 1972, Sch 2 para (*ia*) with effect from 23 May 1994. Only sales in Revenue-approved tax-free shops will qualify for zero rating.

101 Amendment of Sixth Schedule to Principal Act

Notes

Para (*a*) substituted VATA Sch 6 para (vii) with effect from 1 July 1994.

Para (*b*) inserted "of a kind" in VATA Sch 6 para (x) with effect from 1 July 1994.

Para (*c*) substituted "(other than farm accountancy or farm management services)" for "(not being services of the kind specified in paragraph (xxii) of the Seventh Schedule)" in VATA Sch 6 para (*ai*) with effect from 23 May 1994.

To qualify for the 12.5% rate, previously, fairground entertainment services (swings, roundabouts etc) could not be provided in the same location for more than 19 days; this generally meant that only travelling fairs could avail of the 12.5% rate. The 12.5% rate now applies to all fairground services, whether travelling or not.

Dance takings, slot machine and amusement machine takings remain liable at 21%. Circus activities remain exempt (Sch 1 para (viii) where no food or drink is provided in the course of the performance).

Veterinary technician services (veterinary services provided by a person other than a fully qualified veterinary surgeon) are liable at 12.5%.

PART VII
MISCELLANEOUS

CHAPTER II
General

165 Care and management of taxes and duties

All taxes and duties imposed by this Act are hereby placed under the care and management of the Revenue Commissioners.

166 Short title, construction and commencement

(1) This Act may be cited as the Finance Act, 1994.

....

(4) Part III shall be construed together with the Value Added Tax Acts, 1972 to 1993, and may be cited together therewith as the Value Added Tax Acts, 1972 to 1994.

....

(9) In relation to Part III:

    (*a*)   paragraphs (*b*), (*c*) and (*d*) of section 94, section 97 and paragraphs (*a*) and (*b*) of section 101 shall take effect as on and from the 1st day of July, 1994;

    (*b*)   paragraph (*a*) of section 99 shall take effect as on and from the 1st day of September, 1994;

    (*c*)   section 91 shall take effect as on and from the 1st day of January, 1995;

    (*d*)   section 93 and paragraph (*a*) of section 96 shall take effect as on and from such date as the Minister for Finance may, by order, appoint;

    (*e*)   paragraph (*b*) of section 99 shall take effect as on and from the commencement of section 89;

    (*f*)   the provisions of this Part, other than those specified in paragraphs (*a*) to (*e*), shall have effect as on and from the date of passing of this Act.

(10) Any reference in this Act to any other enactment shall, except so far as the context otherwise requires, be construed as a reference to that enactment as amended by or under any other enactment including this Act.

(11) In this Act, a reference to a Part, section or Schedule is to a Part or section of, or Schedule to, this Act, unless it is indicated that reference to some other enactment is intended.

(12) In this Act, a reference to a subsection, paragraph, subparagraph, clause or subclause is to the subsection, paragraph, subparagraph, clause or subclause of the provision (including a Schedule) in which the reference occurs, unless it is indicated that reference to some other provision is intended.

FINANCE ACT 1995

(Number 8 of 1995)

ARRANGEMENT OF SECTIONS

PART III
VALUE ADDED TAX

PART VII
MISCELLANEOUS

CHAPTER II
General

AN ACT TO CHARGE AND IMPOSE CERTAIN DUTIES OF CUSTOMS AND INLAND REVENUE (INCLUDING EXCISE), TO AMEND THE LAW RELATING TO CUSTOMS AND INLAND REVENUE (INCLUDING EXCISE) AND TO MAKE FURTHER PROVISIONS IN CONNECTION WITH FINANCE
[2nd JUNE 1995]

PART III
VALUE ADDED TAX

118 Interpretation (Part III)

In this Part —

"the Principal Act" means the Value Added Tax Act, 1972;

"the Act of 1978" means the Value Added Tax (Amendment) Act, 1978;

"the Act of 1992" means the Finance Act, 1992.

119 Amendment of section 1 (interpretation) of Principal Act

Notes

Para (*a*) inserted the definition of "antiques" in VATA 1972, s 1(1) with effect from 1 July 1995.
Para (*b*) inserted the definition of "collectors' items" in VATA 1972, s 1(1) with effect from 1 July 1995.
Para (*c*) inserted the definition of "margin scheme" in VATA 1972, s 1(1) with effect from 1 July 1995.
Para (*d*) substituted the definition of "second-hand goods" for "second-hand" in VATA 1972, s 1(1) with effect from 1 July 1995.

Para (*e*) inserted the definition of "taxable dealer" in VATA 1972, s 1(1) with effect from 1 July 1995.

Para (*f*) inserted the definition of "works of art" in VATA 1972, s 1(1) with effect from 1 July 1995.

These new definitions are required to facilitate the implementation of the Seventh Directive (94/5/EC) which has amended the Sixth Directive (77/388/EEC).

The essence of the changes is that, after 1 July 1995, certain dealers in second-hand goods, in particular antique dealers and auctioneers, need only account for VAT on the gross profit margin that arises when they sell on goods acquired from unregistered persons. Motor dealers (suppliers of means of transport) will have a separate scheme under which they will be entitled, when selling a vehicle that has been acquired from an unregistered person, to a deduction for the residual VAT included in the price.

120 Amendment of section 3 (supply of goods) of Principal Act

Notes

Para (*a*) inserted "other than the transfer of ownership of the goods to a person supplying financial services of the kind specified in subparagraph (i)(*e*) of the First Schedule, where those services are supplied as part of an agreement of the kind referred to in paragraph (*b*) in respect of those goods" in VATA 1972, s 3(1)(*a*) with effect from 2 June 1995. Interest income from the granting of credit is to remain exempt from VAT, but hire purchase transaction remain liable as supplies of goods.

Para (*b*) inserted VATA 1972, s 3(1)(*aa*) with effect from 1 July 1995. The supply by an agent or auctioneer of tangible movable goods is a supply for VAT purposes.

121 Amendment of section 3A (intra-Community acquisition of goods) of Principal Act

Notes

This section inserted VATA 1972, s 3A(1A) with effect from 1 July 1995. Second-hand goods arriving in the State from another EU State that have already been subject to the margin scheme, the special scheme for auctioneers, or the special scheme for means of transport in another EU State will not be liable to VAT in Ireland, unless resold.

122 Amendment of section 4 (special provisions in relation to the supply of immovable goods) of Principal Act

Notes

Para (*a*) substituted VATA 1972, s 4(5) with effect from 2 June 1995. VAT is chargeable on the full value, including the site value, of a new house.

Para (*b*) inserted "other than a supply of immovable goods to which the provisions of subsection (5) apply" in VATA 1972, s 4(6)(*b*) with effect from 2 June 1995. This is a technical amendment which relates to para (*a*).

123 Amendment of section 5 (supply of services) of Principal Act

Notes

This section inserted "has established his business or" after "the service" in VATA 1972, s 5(5) with effect from 2 June 1995. In general, the place of supply of services is where the supplier has established his business, or where he has his fixed establishment.

124 Amendment of section 8 (taxable persons) of Principal Act

Notes

Para (*a*) inserted VATA 1972, s 8(2A)(*a*)(proviso) with effect from 1 January 1996. Member-owned golf clubs and sports clubs will no longer be able to claim exemption on the grounds that they are not profit-making, if this results in distortion of competition. Local authority sports facilities will no longer be able to claim exemption on the basis that the State is not a taxable person, if this results in distortion of competition.

Para (*b*) inserted VATA 1972, s 8(3E) with effect from 1 January 1996. The Revenue Commissioners are empowered to determine that for example, a local authority-owned sports facility which places a similar commercially run business at a disadvantage is a taxable person. The Revenue Commissioners may also determine that, for example, a member-owned golf club, which claims to be non-profit making while operating as a commercial enterprise, is a taxable person.

125 Amendment of section 10 (amount on which tax is chargeable) of Principal Act

Notes

Para (*a*) deleted VATA 1972, s 10(2)(proviso) with effect from 1 July 1995. The old "trade-in" rule is deleted as its provisions have been superseded by the Seventh Directive (see s 119).

Para (*b*) inserted VATA 1972, s 10(4C) with effect from 1 July 1995. Where goods are sold under a hire purchase agreement, the taxable amount is the total amount received by the supplier, or the open market price of the goods, whichever is higher.

126 Margin scheme goods

Notes

This section inserted VATA 1972, s 10A with effect from 1 July 1995. Certain dealers in second-hand goods, in particular antique dealers, need only account for VAT on the gross profit margin that arises when they sell on goods acquired from unregistered persons. The margin is treated as VAT-inclusive. The dealer may opt to apply the normal VAT rules if he wishes.

127 Special scheme for auctioneers

Notes

This section inserted VATA 1972, s 10B with effect from 1 July 1995. Auctioneers need only account for VAT on the gross profit margin that arises when they sell on goods acquired from unregistered persons. The margin is treated as VAT-inclusive.

128 Amendment of section 11 (rates of tax) of Principal Act

Notes

Para (*a*) inserted VATA 1972, s 11(1AA) with effect from 1 July 1995. The 12.5% rate is to apply to works of art, antiques and collectors' items.

Para (*b*) deleted VATA 1972, s 11(5) with effect from 1 July 1995. Interest charges arising in a hire purchase or credit sale transaction are no longer liable to VAT; see ss 120, 139.

129 Amendment of section 12 (deductions for tax borne or paid) of Principal Act

Notes

Para (*a*) substituted VATA 1972, s 12(1)(*a*)(vi) with effect from 1 July 1995. Taxable dealers who supply means of transport (for example motor dealers) are entitled to deduct the residual VAT included in the price of second-hand vehicles acquired from unregistered persons.

Para (*b*) inserted VATA 1972, s 12(3A) with effect from 1 July 1995. If the margin scheme is being used by a trader, and as a result he need only account for VAT on the transaction margin, he is not entitled to a purchases VAT credit on the same transaction.

130 Special scheme for means of transport supplied by taxable dealers

Notes

This section inserted VATA 1972, s 12B with effect from 1 July 1995. Taxable dealers who supply means of transport (for example motor dealers) are entitled to deduct the residual VAT included in the price of second-hand vehicles acquired from unregistered persons. This section sets how the residual VAT is calculated.

131 Amendment of section 14 (determination of tax due by reference to cash receipts) of Principal Act

Notes

This section inserted VATA 1972, s 14(1B) with effect from 2 June 1995. Traders whose annual turnover is below the annual threshold (currently €635,000) may opt to account for VAT on the cash receipts basis. The Minister for Finance may, by order, increase this annual turnover limit.

132 Amendment of section 17 (invoices) of Principal Act

Notes

This section inserted VATA 1972, s 17(1B)(proviso) with effect from 2 June 1995. Taxable persons, the value of whose supplies to other taxable persons has not exceeded £2m in the previous 12 months, need not issue monthly control statements.

133 Amendment of section 18 (inspection and removal of records) of Principal Act

Notes

This section inserted of "and the value and description of any gifts or promotional items given by him to any person in connection with such supplies or any other payments made by him to any person in connection with such supplies" after "thereon" in VATA 1972, s 18(1A)(a) with effect from 2 June 1995.

This section is related to the previous section. With the relaxation of the requirement for certain traders to supply monthly control statements to other taxable persons, any taxable person may be required to provide full details to the inspector of taxes of promotional schemes which he uses.

134 Amendment of section 19 (tax due and payable) of Principal Act, etc

Notes

This section substituted VATA 1972, s 19(3)(aa)(i) definition of "accounting period" as on and from such day or days as the Minister for Finance may by order or orders appoint, either generally or with reference to any particular category of taxable person to whom VATA 1972, s 19(3)(aa) applies.

Traders who submit an annual VAT return may opt to align that VAT return with their annual accounts year, subject to authorisation from the Collector General.

135 Amendment of section 20 (refund of tax) of Principal Act

Notes

This section inserted VATA 1972, s 20(6) with effect from 2 June 1995. The Collector General may make VAT repayments directly into a bank or building society account nominated by the trader.

136 Amendment of section 22 (estimation of tax due for a taxable period) of Principal Act

Notes

This section inserted VATA 1972, s 22(1)(proviso) with effect from 2 June 1995. The Revenue Commissioners may reduce a section 22 estimate of tax due if they believe the initial estimate was too high.

137 Amendment of section 25 (appeals) of Principal Act

Notes

Para (a) inserted VATA 1972, s 25(1)(ac) with effect from 1 January 1996. Persons deemed taxable (see s 124), for example member-owned golf clubs, or local authority sports facilities, are entitled to appeal the Revenue decision.

Para (*b*) inserted VATA 1972, s 25(1A) with effect from 2 June 1995. If the Revenue refuse to regard a person as a taxable person, that person may appeal.

Para (*c*) inserted VATA 1972, s 25(2)(*dd*) with effect from 2 June 1995.

See *WLD Worldwide Leather Diffusion Ltd v Revenue Commissioners* [1994] ITR 165.

138 Amendment of section 32 (regulations) of Principal Act.

Notes

This section inserted VATA 1972, s 32(1)(*da*)–(*de*) with effect from 2 June 1995. The Revenue Commissioners are entitled to make regulations relating to the Seventh Directive, in relation to the conditions for the margin scheme, the method of calculation of the margin, the form of invoices and documents required to be issued, the method for calculating residual tax included in the price of second-hand vehicles, and details to be provided in relation to antiques.

139 Amendment of First Schedule to Principal Act

Notes

Para (*a*) substituted VATA 1972, Sch 1 para (i)(*e*) with effect from 2 June 1995. The net effect is that in so far as hire purchase and credit sale transactions amount to "the granting and the negotiation of credit", in other words, the interest arising on such transactions, is exempt from VAT. This section is linked to section 120 above.

Para (*b*) inserted "with the exception of facilities to which paragraph (vii*b*) or (vii*c*) of the Sixth Schedule refers" after "organisations" in VATA 1972, Sch 1 para (xxiii) with effect from 1 January 1996. Member-owned golf clubs will no longer be exempt in relation to income from non-members, for example, in relation to green fees, where that income exceeds or is likely to exceed £20,000 in any continuous 12 month period.

140 Amendment of Sixth Schedule to Principal Act

Notes

Para (*a*) inserted VATA 1972, Sch 6 paras (vii*b*)–(vii*c*) with effect from 1 January 1996. The income from member-owned golf clubs that was previously exempt, for example, in relation to green fees, will now be liable at 12.5%.

Para (*b*) substituted VATA 1972, Sch 6 para (xvi) with effect from 1 July 1995. The current definition of "work of art" is separated into works of art, and "antiques" which are transferred to the new VATA 1972, Sch 6 para (xvi*a*) (see below).

Para (*c*) inserted VATA 1972, Sch 6 para (xvi*a*) with effect from 1 July 1995. Antiques that qualify for the margin scheme or auction scheme do not qualify for the 12.5% rate.

Para (*d*) substituted "used" for "second-hand" in VATA 1972, Sch 6 para (xviii)(*b*) with effect from 1 July 1995. This is a technical amendment.

Para (*e*) inserted VATA 1972, Sch 6 para (xx*a*) with effect from 1 July 1995. Greyhound feeding stuff is now liable at 12.5% (previously 21%).

Para (*f*) inserted "but excluding the supply of such goods by a taxable dealer in accordance with the provisions of subsection (3) or (8) of section 10A or by an auctioneer within the meaning of section 10B and in accordance with the provisions of subsection (3) of section 10B" after "pour" in VATA 1972, Sch 6 para (xxxii) with effect from 1 July 1995.

Para (*g*) inserted "but excluding the supply of such goods by a taxable dealer in accordance with the provisions of subsection (3) or (8) of section 10A or by an auctioneer within the meaning of section 10B and in accordance with the provisions of subsection (3) of section 10B" after "(Irish Standard 20: Part I: 1987)" in VATA 1972, Sch 6 para (xxxiii) with effect from 1 July 1995.

Concrete ready to pour and concrete blocks that qualify for the margin scheme or auction scheme do not qualify for the 12.5% rate.

141 Addition of Eighth Schedule to Principal Act

Notes

This section inserted VATA 1972, Sch 8 with effect from 1 July 1995.

PART VII

MISCELLANEOUS

CHAPTER II
General

172 Duties of a relevant person in relation to certain revenue offences

(1) In this section—

"the Acts" means—

    (*a*)   the Customs Acts,

    (*b*)   the statutes relating to the duties of excise and to the management of those duties,

    (*c*)   the Tax Acts,

    (*d*)   the Capital Gains Tax Acts,

    (*e*)   the Value Added Tax Act, 1972, and the enactments amending or extending that Act,

    (*f*)   the Capital Acquisitions Tax Act, 1976, and the enactments amending or extending that Act,

    (*g*)   the statutes relating to stamp duty and to the management of that duty,

and any instruments made thereunder and any instruments made under any other enactment and relating to tax;

"appropriate officer" means any officer nominated by the Revenue Commissioners to be an appropriate officer for the purposes of this section;

"company" means any body corporate;

"relevant person", in relation to a company, means a person who—

    (*a*)   (i)   is an auditor to the company appointed in accordance with section 160 of the Companies Act, 1963 (as amended by the Companies Act, 1990), or

           (ii)   in the case of an industrial and provident society or a friendly society, is a public auditor to the society for the purposes of the Industrial and Provident Societies Acts, 1893 to 1978, and the Friendly Societies Acts, 1896 to 1977,

        or

    (*b*)   with a view to reward assists or advises the company in the preparation or delivery of any information, declaration, return, records, accounts or other document which he or she knows will be, or is likely to be, used for any purpose of tax:

Provided that a person who would, but for this proviso, be treated as a relevant person in relation to a company shall not be so treated if the person assists or advises the company solely in the person's capacity as an employee of the said company, and a person shall be treated as assisting or advising the company in that capacity where the person's income from assisting or advising the company consists solely of emoluments to which Chapter IV of Part V of the Income Tax Act, 1967, applies;

"relevant offence" means an offence committed by a company which consists of the company—

(*a*) knowingly or wilfully delivering any incorrect return, statement or accounts or knowingly or wilfully furnishing or causing to be furnished any incorrect information in connection with any tax,

(*b*) knowingly or wilfully claiming or obtaining relief or exemption from, or repayment of, any tax, being a relief, exemption or repayment to which there is no entitlement,

(*c*) knowingly or wilfully issuing or producing any incorrect invoice, receipt, instrument or other document in connection with any tax,

(*d*) knowingly or wilfully failing to comply with any provision of the Acts requiring the furnishing of a return of income, profits or gains, or of sources of income, profits or gains, for the purposes of any tax:

Provided that an offence under this paragraph committed by a company shall not be a relevant offence if the company has made a return of income, profits or gains to the Revenue Commissioners in respect of an accounting period falling wholly or partly into the period of 3 years immediately preceding the accounting period in respect of which the offence was committed;

"tax" means tax, duty, levy or charge under the care and management of the Revenue Commissioners.

(2) If, having regard solely to information obtained in the course of examining the accounts of a company, or in the course of assisting or advising a company in the preparation or delivery of any information, declaration, return, records, accounts or other document for the purposes of tax, as the case may be, a person who is a relevant person in relation to the company becomes aware that the company has committed, or is in the course of committing, one or more relevant offences, the person shall, if the offence or offences are material—

(*a*) communicate particulars of the offence or offences in writing to the company without undue delay and request the company to—

(i) take such action as is necessary for the purposes of rectifying the matter, or

(ii) notify an appropriate officer of the offence or offences,

not later than 6 months after the time of communication, and

(*b*) (i) unless it is established to the person's satisfaction that the necessary action has been taken or notification made, as the case may be, under paragraph (*a*), cease to act as the auditor to the company or to assist or advise the company in such preparation or delivery as is specified in paragraph (*b*) of the definition of relevant person, and

(ii)   shall not so act, assist or advise before a time which is—

(I)   3 years after the time at which the particulars were communicated under paragraph (*a*), or

(II)   the time at which it is established to the person's satisfaction that the necessary action has been taken or notification made, as the case may be, under paragraph (*a*),

whichever is the earlier:

Provided that nothing in this paragraph shall prevent a person from assisting or advising a company in preparing for, or conducting, legal proceedings, either civil or criminal, which are extant or pending at a time which is 6 months after the time of communication under paragraph (*a*).

(3) Where a person, being in relation to a company a relevant person within the meaning of paragraph (*a*) of the definition of relevant person, ceases under the provisions of this section to act as auditor to the company, then the person shall deliver—

(*a*)   a notice in writing to the company stating that he or she is so resigning, and

(*b*)   a copy of the notice to an appropriate officer not later than 14 days after he or she has delivered the notice to the company.

(4) A person shall be guilty of an offence under this section if the person—

(*a*)   fails to comply with subsection (2) or (3), or

(*b*)   knowingly or wilfully makes a communication under subsection (2) which is incorrect.

(5) Where a relevant person is found guilty of an offence under this section the person shall be liable—

(*a*)   on summary conviction to a fine of £1,000 which may be mitigated to not less than one-fourth part thereof, or

(*b*)   on conviction on indictment, to a fine not exceeding £5,000 or, at the discretion of the court, to imprisonment for a term not exceeding 2 years or to both the fine and the imprisonment.

(6) Section 13 of the Criminal Procedure Act, 1967, shall apply in relation to this section as if, in lieu of the penalties specified in subsection (3) of the said section 13, there were specified therein the penalties provided for by subsection (5)(*a*) of this section, and the reference in subsection (2)(*a*) of the said section 13 to the penalties provided for in the said subsection (3) shall be construed and have effect accordingly.

(7) Notwithstanding the provisions of any other enactment, proceedings in respect of this section may be instituted within 6 years from the time at which a person is required under subsection (2) to communicate particulars of an offence or offences in writing to a company.

(8) It shall be a good defence in a prosecution for an offence under subsection (4)(*a*) in relation to a failure to comply with subsection (2) for an accused (being a person who is

a relevant person in relation to a company) to show that he or she was, in the ordinary scope of professional engagement, assisting or advising the company in preparing for legal proceedings and would not have become aware that one or more relevant offences had been committed by the company if he or she had not been so assisting or advising.

(9) If a person who is a relevant person takes any action required by subsection (2) or (3), no duty to which the person may be subject shall be regarded as contravened and no liability or action shall lie against the person in any court for so doing.

(10) The Revenue Commissioners may nominate an officer to be an appropriate officer for the purposes of this section and the name of an officer so nominated and the address to which copies of notices under subsection (2) or (3) shall be delivered shall be published in the Iris Oifigiúil.

(11) This section shall have effect as respects a relevant offence committed by a company in respect of tax which is—

(a) assessable by reference to accounting periods, for any accounting period beginning after the 30th day of June, 1995,

(b) assessable by reference to years of assessment, for the year of assessment 1995–96 and subsequent years,

(c) payable by reference to a taxable period, for a taxable period beginning after the 30th day of June, 1995,

(d) chargeable on gifts or inheritances taken on or after the 30th day of June, 1995,

(e) chargeable on instruments executed on or after the 30th day of June, 1995, or

(f) payable in any other case, on or after the 30th day of June, 1995.

Definitions

"month": IA 2005, Sch; "person": IA 2005, s 18(c); "writing": IA 2005, Sch; "year": IA 2005, Sch; "year of assessment": TCA 1997, ss 2(1), 5(1).

Notes

With effect from 6 April 1995:
this section substituted FA 1986, s 115(1).

175 Power to obtain information

(1) For the purposes of the assessment, charge, collection and recovery of any tax or duty placed under their care and management, the Revenue Commissioners may, by notice in writing, request any Minister of the Government to provide them with such information in the possession of the Minister in relation to payments for any purposes made by the Minister, whether on his own behalf or on behalf of any other person, to such persons or classes of persons as the Revenue Commissioners may specify in the notice and a Minister so requested shall provide such information as may be specified.

(2) The Revenue Commissioners may nominate any of their officers to perform any acts and discharge any functions authorised by this section to be performed or discharged by the Revenue Commissioners.

Definitions

"person": IA 2005, s 18(c); "tax": s 1(1); "writing": IA 2005, Sch.

177 Tax clearance certificates in relation to public sector contracts

(1) In this section—

"the Acts" means—

 (*a*) the Tax Acts,

 (*b*) the Capital Gains Tax Acts,

 (*c*) the Value Added Tax Act, 1972, and the enactments amending or extending that Act,

and any instruments made thereunder;

"the scheme" means a scheme of the Department of Finance for the time being in force for requiring persons to show, by means of tax clearance certificates, compliance with the obligations imposed by the Acts in relation to the matters specified in subsection (2) before the award to them of contracts that are specified in a circular of the Department of Finance entitled "Tax Clearance Procedures — Public Sector Contracts", numbered F 49/ 24/84 and issued on the 30th day of July, 1991, or any such circular amending or replacing that circular;

"tax clearance certificate" shall be construed in accordance with subsection (2).

(2) Subject to the provisions of this section, where a person who—

 (*a*) the payment or remittance of any taxes, interest or penalties required to be paid or remitted under the Acts to the Revenue Commissioners, and

 (*b*) the delivery of any returns required to be made under the Acts,

applies to the Collector-General in that behalf for the purposes of the scheme, the Collector-General shall issue to the person a certificate (in this section referred to as "a tax clearance certificate") stating that the person is in compliance with the obligations aforesaid.

(3) A tax clearance certificate shall not be issued to a person unless—

 (*a*) the person, and any partnership of which the person is or was a member, in respect of the period of the person's membership thereof,

 (*b*) in a case where the person is a partnership, each person who is a member of the partnership, and

 (*c*) in a case where the person is a company, each person who is either the beneficial owner of, or able directly or indirectly, to control, more than 50 per cent. of the ordinary share capital of the company,

is in compliance with the obligations imposed on the person and each other person (including any partnership) by the Acts in relation to the matters specified in paragraphs (*a*) and (*b*) of subsection (2).

(4) Where a person (hereafter in this subsection referred to as **"the first-mentioned person"**) applies for a tax clearance certificate in accordance with subsection (2) and the business activity to which the application relates was previously carried on by, or

was previously carried on as part of a business activity carried on by, another person (hereafter in this subsection referred to as "the second-mentioned person") and—

(*a*) the second-mentioned person is a company which is connected within the meaning of section 16(3) of the Finance (Miscellaneous Provisions) Act, 1968, with the first-mentioned person or would have been such a company but for the fact that the company has been wound up or dissolved without being wound up, or

(*b*) the second-mentioned person is a company and the first-mentioned person is a partnership and—

(i) a member of the partnership is or was able, or

(ii) where more than one such member is a shareholder of the company, those members acting together are or were able,

directly or indirectly, either on his, her or their own, or with a connected person or connected persons within the meaning of the said section 16(3), to control more than **50 per cent** of the ordinary share capital of the company, or

(*c*) the second-mentioned person is a partnership and the first-mentioned person is a company and—

(i) a member of the partnership is or was able, or

(ii) where more than one such member is a shareholder of the company, those members acting together are or were able,

directly or indirectly, either on his, her or their own, or with a connected person or connected persons within the meaning of the said section 16(3), to control more than **50 per cent** of the ordinary share capital of the company,

then, a tax clearance certificate shall not be issued to the first-mentioned person unless, in relation to the business activity to which the application relates, the second-mentioned person is in compliance with the obligations imposed on that person by the Acts in relation to the matters specified in [paragraphs (*a*) and (*b*) of subsection (2)]:[1]

Provided that this subsection shall not apply to a business the transfer of which was effected before the 9th day of May, 1995, or a business the transfer of which is or was effected after that date if a contract for the transfer was made before that date.

(5) Subsections (4), (5) and (6) of section 242 of the Finance Act, 1992, shall, with any necessary modifications, apply to an application for a tax clearance certificate under this section as they apply to an application for a tax clearance certificate under that section.

(6) A tax clearance certificate shall be valid for the period specified therein.

(7) This section shall come into operation on the 1st day of July, 1995.

Amendments

[1] Substituted by FA 1996, s 132(1) and Sch 5 Pt I para 19 with effect from 6 April 1996.

Definitions

"business": s 1(1); "person": IA 2005, s 18(*c*); "tax": s 1(1).

---

178 Care and management of taxes and duties

All taxes and duties (except the excise duties on mechanically propelled vehicles imposed by section 117) imposed by this Act are hereby placed under the care and management of the Revenue Commissioners.

179 Short title, construction and commencement

(1) This Act may be cited as the Finance Act, 1995.

...

(4) Part III shall be construed together with the Value Added Tax Acts, 1972 to 1994, and may be cited together therewith as the Value Added Tax Acts, 1972 to 1995.

...

...

(10) In relation to Part III:

- (*a*)   section 119, paragraph (*b*) of section 120, section 121, paragraph (*a*) of section 125, sections 126 and 127, paragraph (*a*) of section 128, sections 129 and 130, paragraphs (*b*), (*c*), (*d*), (*e*), (*f*) and (*g*) of section 140 and section 141 shall take effect as on and from the 1st day of July, 1995;

- (*b*)   section 124, paragraph (*a*) of section 137, paragraph (*b*) of section 139 and paragraph (*a*) of section 140 shall take effect as on and from the 1st day of January, 1996;

- (*c*)   the provisions of this Part, other than those specified in paragraphs (*a*) and (*b*), shall have effect as on and from the date of passing of this Act.

(11) Any reference in this Act to any other enactment shall, except so far as the context otherwise requires, be construed as a reference to that enactment as amended by or under any other enactment including this Act.

(12) In this Act, a reference to a Part, section or Schedule is to a Part or section of, or Schedule to, this Act, unless it is indicated that reference to some other enactment is intended.

(13) In this Act, a reference to a subsection, paragraph, subparagraph, clause or subclause is to the subsection, paragraph, subparagraph, clause or subclause of the provision (including a Schedule) in which the reference occurs, unless it is indicated that reference to some other provision is intended.

FINANCE ACT 1996

(Number 9 of 1996)

ARRANGEMENT OF SECTIONS

PART III
VALUE ADDED TAX

PART VII
MISCELLANEOUS

AN ACT TO CHARGE AND IMPOSE CERTAIN DUTIES OF CUSTOMS AND INLAND REVENUE (INCLUDING EXCISE), TO AMEND THE LAW RELATING TO CUSTOMS AND INLAND REVENUE (INCLUDING EXCISE) AND TO MAKE FURTHER PROVISIONS IN CONNECTION WITH FINANCE
[15th MAY 1996]

PART III
VALUE ADDED TAX

87 Interpretation (Part III)

In this Part—

"the Principal Act" means the Value Added Tax Act, 1972;

"the Act of 1978" means the Value Added Tax (Amendment) Act, 1978;

"the Act of 1992" means the Finance Act, 1992;

"The Act of 1993" means the Finance Act, 1993;

"The Act of 1995" means the Finance Act, 1995.

88 Amendment of section 1 (interpretation) of Principal Act

General note

The Second Simplification Directive (Council Directive 95/7/EC of 10 April 1995) introduced changes which were initially given effect in Irish law from 1 January 1996 by the European Communities (Value Added Tax) Regulations 1995 (SI 363/ 1995). FA 1996 now confirms the changes, and repeals those regulations. The changes mean that intra EU cross border contract work on movable goods is now treated as a service — and no VAT is chargeable where the customer is VAT registered within the EU.

Notes

Para (*a*) inserted definitions of "contractor" and "contract work" in VATA 1972, s 1(1) with effect from 1 January 1996 — these definitions are needed for the for the simplified treatment of contract work.
Para (*b*), by substituting "used" for "second-hand" in the definition of "goods" in VATA 1972, s 1(1) with effect from 15 May 1996 ensures that the more restrictive definition of "second-hand" is not applied to goods that are to be the subject of contract work.

Para (*c*) substituted "the State" for "a Member State" in the definition of "importation of goods" in VATA 1972, s1(1) with effect from 15 May 1996. This is a technical amendment to facilitate the simplified procedure for contract work.

89 Amendment of section 3 (supply of goods) of Principal Act

Notes

Para (*a*)(i) substituted VATA 1972, s 3(1)(*aa*) with effect from 15 May 1996; all commission sales of movable goods by auctioneers and agents are treated as supplies of goods for VAT purposes.

Para (*a*)(ii) substituted VATA 1972, s 3(1)(*c*) with effect from 1 January 1996; contract work on movable goods is now a supply of a service, and not a supply of goods. Intra EU cross border contract work (now a service) need not be reported on the quarterly EU sales listing.

Para (*a*)(iii)(I) deleted VATA 1972, s 3(1)(*g*)(iii) with effect from 1 January 1996 — that paragraph is redundant because the contract work is no longer regarded as a supply of goods.

Para (*a*)(iii)(II) substituted VATA 1972, s 3(1)(*g*)(iii*a*) with effect from 1 January 1996; a transfer of goods from Ireland to another EU State in order to have contract work carried out on them is not a supply for VAT purposes, provided the goods are later returned to Ireland.

Para (*b*) deleted VATA 1972, s 3(3), which dealt with certain auction sales, with effect from 1 January 1996; the relevant transactions are no w included in VATA 1972, s 3(1)(*aa*).

Para (*c*) substituted VAT 1972, s 3(4) with effect from 15 May 1996. An auctioneer selling goods on a commission basis is regarded as having been supplied with the goods when he sells them — this means that the auctioneer will effectively be taxed on his commission margin, but the transaction will be regarded as a simultaneous supply of goods to, and by, the auctioneer.

90 Amendment of section 5 (supply of services) of Principal Act

Notes

Para (*a*)(i) inserted "except where the provisions of subparagraph (iv) of paragraph (*f*) apply" after "movable goods" in VATA 1972, s 5(6)(*c*)(iii) with effect from 1 January 1996; para (*a*)(ii) inserted ", including contract work, except where the provisions of subparagraph (iv) of paragraph (*f*) apply" after "movable goods" in VATA 1972, s 5(6)(*c*)(iv) with effect from 1 January 1996; these changes ensure that the place of taxation rules do not apply in the case of valuation services relating to, or work on, movable goods.

Para (*b*) inserted VATA 1972, s 5(6)(*f*)(iv) with effect from 1 January 1996. The place of taxation for intra EU cross border work on movable goods, or valuation services on movable goods, is the EU State in which the customer is VAT registered, if the goods have been sent back from the country in which the repair or valuation work was performed.

91 Amendment of section 10B (special scheme of auctioneers) of Principal Act

Notes

This section substituted "auction scheme goods" for "tangible movable goods" in VATA 1972, s 10B(9) with effect from 15 May 1996. This is a technical amendment to correct a drafting inconsistency.

92 Amendment of section 11 (rates of tax) of Principal Act

Notes

Para (*a*), by substituting "2.8 per cent" for "2.5 per cent" in VATA 1972, s 11(1)(*f*) with effect from 1 March 1996, increases the rate applicable to the supply of livestock, live greyhounds and the hire of horses.

Para (*b*), by inserting VATA 1972, s 11(1AB) with effect from 1 January 1996, provides that although contract work is now a supply of services (see s 89(*a*)(ii) above), the tax rate applicable is the rate that would apply to the supply of the finished goods.

93 Amendment of section 12 (deductions for tax borne or paid) of Principal Act

Notes

Para (*a*), by inserting VATA 1972, s 12(1)(*a*)(ia) with effect from 1 July 1996, ensures that a taxable person acquiring goods from a finance company will be entitled to a VAT deduction on the basis of the document issued by the finance company.

Para (*b*) deleted "or" at the end of VATA 1972, s 12(3)(*a*)(iii) and inserted VATA 1972, s 12(3)(*a*)(iva) with effect from 15 May 1996. This is a technical amendment to ensure that a VAT deduction does not become available to traders as a consequence of the redefining of contract work as a supply of services.

94 Amendment of section 12A (special provisions of tax invoiced by flat-rate farmers) of Principal Act

Notes

This section, by substituting "2.8 per cent" for "2.5 per cent" in VATA 1972, s 12A(1) with effect from 1 March 1996, increased the farmers' flat-rate addition.

95 Amendment of section 13A (supplies to, and intra-Community acquisitions and imports by, certain taxable persons) of Principle Act

Notes

This section inserted ", supplies of contract work where the place of supply is deemed to be a Member State other than the State and supplies of contract work made in accordance with paragraph (xvi) of the Second Schedule" after "Second Schedule" in the definition of "qualifying person" in VATA 1972, s 13A(1) with effect from 1 January 1996. This change is intended to ensure that exporting firms are not affected by the redefinition of contract work as a supply of services.

96 Amendment of section 15 (charge of tax on imported goods) of Principal Act

Notes

This section inserted ", expenses resulting from the transport of the goods to another place of destination within the Community if that destination is known at the time of the importation," after "duties" in VATA 1972, s 15(3) with effect from 1 January 1996. Where imported goods are sent to another EU State, the intra EU transport cost is to be included on the value for assessment of VAT at import.

97 Amendment of section 17 (invoices) of Principal Act

Notes

Para (*a*) added VATA 1972, s 17(1)(proviso) with effect from 1 July 1996; the person supplying goods that the subject of a finance (HP) agreement must invoice the finance company and not the person acquiring the goods.

Para (*b*) inserted VATA 1972, s 17(1AA)–(1AB) with effect from 1 July 1996; the finance company must provide VAT-invoice type details in its agreement with the person acquiring the goods. The finance company is also obliged to maintain, and make available for inspection, proper books and records.

Para (*c*) inserted VATA 1972, s 17(3AB) with effect from 1 July 1996; where a finance company that has already supplied goods to a customer under a HP agreement subsequently receives a credit note from the supplier, it must issue a corresponding credit note to its customer.

Para (*d*) inserted VATA 1972, s 17(5A) with effect from 1 July 1996; if a finance company shows a greater amount of tax on its VAT-invoice type agreement, it is liable for that amount.

Para (*e*) inserted VATA 1972, s 17(7A) with effect from 1 July 1996. The VAT-invoice type agreement must be issued on or before the 22nd of the month following the month in which the goods were supplied.

98 Amendment of Second Schedule to the Principal Act

Notes

Para (*a*) deleted "or from" after "goods to" in VATA 1972, Sch 2 para (iii) with effect from 15 May 1996; transport of imported goods is no longer zero-rated under this paragraph, but under paragraph (xvi*a*), as inserted by paragraph (*b*).

Para (*b*) substituted VATA 1972, Sch 2 para (xvi) with effect from 1 January 1997; a service consisting of work on movable goods that have been brought into the EU for the purposes of such work is zero-rated, provided the goods are subsequently re- exported from the EU.

Para (*c*) inserted VATA 1972, Sch 2 para (xvi*a*) with effect from 1 January 1996. Intra EU transport of goods imported from outside the EU is zero-rated, provided the transport costs have been included in the value for VAT at importation.

99 Amendment of Sixth Schedule to the Principal Act

Notes

This section, by inserting "contract work" after "other than" in VATA 1972, Sch 6 para (xviii)(*b*) with effect from 1 January 1996, provides that contract work will not be liable at 12.5% unless the goods subject to contract work are liable at 12.5%.

100 Revocation (Part III)

Notes

This section revoked the European Convention (Value Added Tax) Regulations 1995 (SI 363/1995).

PART VII
MISCELLANEOUS

142 Care and management of taxes and duties

All taxes and duties (except the excise duties on mechanically propelled vehicles imposed by section 86) imposed by this Act are hereby placed under the care and management of the Revenue Commissioners.

143 Short title, construction and commencement

...

(4) Part III shall be construed together with the Value Added Tax Acts, 1972 to 1995, and may be cited together therewith as the Value Added Tax Acts, 1972 to 1996.

(10) In relation to Part III:

  (*a*) section 87, paragraph (*a*) of section 88, subparagraphs (ii) and (iii) of paragraph (*a*) of section 89, section 90, paragraph (*b*) of section 92, sections 95 and 96, paragraphs (*b*) and (*c*) of section 98 and section 99 shall be deemed to have come into force and shall take effect on and from the 1st day of January, 1996;

  (*b*) paragraph (*a*) of section 92 and section 94 shall be deemed to have come into force and shall take effect as on and from the 1st day of March, 1996;

  (*c*) paragraph (*a*) of section 93 and section 97 shall take effect as on and from the 1st day of July, 1996;

(*d*) the provisions of this Part, other than those specified in paragraphs (*a*), (*b*) and (*c*), shall have effect as on and from the date of passing of this Act.

(11) Any reference in this Part to any other enactment shall, except so far as the context otherwise requires, be construed as a reference to that enactment as amended by or under any other enactment included in this Act.

(12) In this Act, a reference to a Part, section or Schedule is to a Part or section of, or Schedule to, this Act, unless it is indicated that reference to some other enactment is intended.

(13) In this Act, a reference to a subsection, paragraph, subparagraph, clause or subclause is to the subsection, paragraph, subparagraph, clause or subclause of the provision (including a Schedule) in which the reference occurs, unless it is indicated that reference to some other provision is intended.

FINANCE ACT 1997

(Number 22 of 1997)

ARRANGEMENT OF SECTIONS

PART III
VALUE ADDED TAX

PART VIII
MISCELLANEOUS

AN ACT TO CHARGE AND IMPOSE CERTAIN DUTIES OF CUSTOMS AND
INLAND REVENUE (INCLUDING EXCISE), AND TO AMEND THE LAW
RELATING TO CUSTOMS AND INLAND REVENUE (INCLUDING EXCISE)
AND TO MAKE FURTHER PROVISIONS IN CONNECTION WITH FINANCE
[10th MAY, 1997]

PART III
VALUE ADDED TAX

95 Interpretation (Part III)

In this Part—

"the Principal Act" means the Value Added Tax Act, 1972;

"the Act of 1978" means the Value Added Tax (Amendment) Act, 1978;

"the Act of 1992" means the Finance Act, 1992;

"the Act of 1993" means the Finance Act, 1993;

"the Act of 1996" means the Finance Act, 1996.

96 Amendment of section 1 (interpretation) of Principal Act

Notes

Para (*a*) inserted definition of "assignment" in VATA 1972, s 1(1) as on and from 26 March 1997.

Para (*b*) inserted definition of "surrender" in VATA 1972, s 1(1) as on and from 26 March 1997.

Para (*c*) inserted definition of "telecommunications services" in VATA 1972, s 1(1) as on and from 1 July 1997.
The definitions of "assignment" and "surrender" are used in VATA 1972, s 4 to ensure that an assignment or
surrender of a leasehold interest in property is taxed as a disposal of the lease.

The definition of "telecommunications services" is based on the agreed text of an EU derogation to be
implemented by all EU States. This is to ensure that telecommunications services provided from outside the EU
to EU-based persons are taxed on the same basis as telecommunications services provided by EU-based
providers of such services.

---

97 Amendment of section 3A (intra-Community acquisition of goods) of Principal Act

Notes

This section inserted "or by a person obliged to be registered for value added tax in a Member State" after "supplied by a person registered for value added tax in a Member State," in VATA 1972, s 3A(1)(*a*).
This is a technical amendment to ensure that Irish VAT law is identical to EU VAT law in relation to intra EU acquisitions of goods.

98 Amendment of section 4 (special provisions in relation to the supply of immovable goods) of Principal Act

Notes

Para (*a*)(i) substituted VATA 1972, s 4(1)(*b*) as on and from 26 March 1997. A property lease for less than 10 years that is capable of being extended for more 10 years is treated as an interest for VAT purposes. The disposal of such an interest may therefore be chargeable to VAT.
Para (*a*)(ii) inserted VATA 1972, s 4(1)(*c*) as on and from 26 March 1997. A property lease containing an option to extend the lease is treated as having the duration of the longest possible extension of the lease.
Para (*b*) inserted "(including by way of surrender or by way of assignment)" after "disposes" in VATA 1972, s 4(2) as on and from 26 March 1997. This means that the surrender or assignment of a property lease of more than 10 years (see (*a*)(ii) above) is treated as a disposal of a lease, and therefore as a taxable supply — *by the person to whom the lease is surrendered or assigned* — see (*d*) below.
Para (*c*) inserted VATA 1972, s 4(2A)–(2C) as on and from 26 March 1997. Where a landlord later re-disposes of a lease that has been surrendered to him, his VAT charge is restricted to the unexpired portion of the original property lease surrendered to him. Thus if a landlord disposes of a surrendered 20 years lease that was handed back after four years have expired, his VAT charge on that disposal is restricted to the residual 16 years of the surrendered lease.
If a landlord disposes of a surrendered lease for a term shorter than the original lease term, the difference — the reversionary interest — is taxable. For example if a landlord, on the surrender to him of a 20 year lease after four years have expired, disposes of a new 14 year lease, the two year reversionary interest is taxable.
If the landlord does not dispose of a surrendered lease, he is treated as having made a self supply of the property, unless he opts to waive his exemption in respect of short term letting income from property, or the disposal is not taxable because it is part of a transfer of business to another taxable person.
Para (*d*) inserted VATA 1972, s 4(8) as on and from 26 March 1997. This imposes a reverse charge on assignments and surrenders of long term property leases. The recipient of the lease must self-account for VAT on the disposal of the lease.

99 Amendment of section 5 (supply of services) of Principal Act

Notes

This section inserted VATA 1972, s 5(6)(*dd*) as on and from 1 July 1997. The supply of telecommunications services to a private individual in the State by a non-EU supplier is taxable. This means that a non-EU based supplier of such services must register for VAT in the State if its turnover from such services exceeds, or is likely to exceed, £20,000 in any continuous 12 month period.

100 Amendment of section 7 (waiver of exemption) of Principal Act

Notes

Para (*a*) inserted VATA 1972, s 7(1)(proviso) as on and from 26 March 1997. Normally a landlord who waives his exemption on income from short term letting is liable to VAT on all short term letting receipts. However, where a landlord who subsequently short term lets a property (the subject of a long term lease surrendered to him) may opt to waive his exemption in respect of that property only.
Para (*b*) substituted VATA 1972, s 7(3) as on and from 26 March 1997. If a landlord who has waived his exemption on income from short term letting later cancels that waiver, he must account for VAT on any net VAT repaid to him for the period during which the waiver had effect.

101 Amendment of section 8 (taxable persons) of Principal Act

Notes

Para (*a*) substituted VATA 1972, s 8(3)(*a*) as on and from such date as the Minister for Finance may by order appoint. A supplier of horticultural produce must register for VAT if his turnover from such supplies exceeds, or is likely to exceed, £40,000 in any continuous 12 month period. A farmer who supplies horticultural produce and also supplies agricultural services must register for VAT if his turnover from such supplies exceeds, or is likely to exceed, £20,000 in any continuous 12 month period.

Para (*b*) inserted VATA 1972, s 8(3)(proviso)(i*a*) as on and from such date as the Minister for Finance may by order appoint. A trader cannot avoid VAT by subdividing his business into units, each of which is below the VAT registration limit.

102 Amendment of section 10 (amount on which tax is chargeable) of Principal Act

Notes

Para (*a*) inserted VATA 1972, s 10(3)(*d*). A taxable person cannot reduce the taxable amount by means of a discount unless he issues a proper VAT credit not in respect of that discount.

Para (*b*) inserted VATA 1972, s 10(4)(proviso) as on and from 26 March 1997. Where a tenant of a property, leased to him for more than 10 years, reclaims VAT on the acquisition of the lease and later diverts the leased property to private or non-business use, he is taxed on the full capitalised value of the lease as acquired by him. In other words, the VAT originally reclaimed by him on the acquisition of the lease is clawed back.

Para (*c*)(i) inserted "subject to subsection (7A)," before "supplies" in VATA 1972, s 10(7)(*c*). See para (*d*).

Para (*c*)(ii) deleted VATA 1972, s 10(7)(*d*). See para (*d*).

Para (*d*) inserted VATA 1972, s 10(7A). In *Argos Distributors Ltd v C & E Commissioners*, [1996] STC 359, ECJ 288/94, the European Court of Justice held that where a trader issues vouchers, the taxable amount (Sixth Directive Art 11A) is the net amount received by the trader — regardless of the vouchers' face value. The new subs (10A) amends Irish VAT law to reflect this decision.

Para (*e*) inserted VATA 1972, s 10(9)(*b*)(proviso) as on and from 26 March 1997. Where a long term property lease is surrendered or assigned, it is taxed as if it were the creation of a new lease.

Para (*f*) substituted VATA 1972, s 10(10) as on and from 26 March 1997. This ensures that a surrendered or assigned lease is taxed on the basis of its open market price — effectively the capitalised value of the future unencumbered rental income from the leased property. This is the present value of future inflows of rent charged on an arm's length basis.

103 Amendment of section 11 (rates of tax) of Principal Act

Notes

Para (*a*) substituted "3.3 per cent" for "2.8 per cent" in VATA 1972, s 11(1) as on and from 1 March 1997. This increases the rate of VAT on the supply of live cattle, deer, goats, sheep, pigs, greyhounds and horses from 2.8% to 3.3% with effect from 1 March 1997.

Para (*b*) substituted "25 pence" for "5 pence" in VATA 1972, s 11(3)(proviso). A package containing several items attracting different VAT rates will not be taxed at the highest of those rates where the price of the package does not exceed 25 pence.

104 Amendment of section 12 (deduction for tax borne or paid) of Principal Act

Notes

This section inserted VATA 1972, s 12(1)(iic)–(iid) as on and from 26 March 1997. The normal input credit deduction rules apply to a tenant surrendering or assigning a long lease — and to the landlord who later disposes of the surrendered or assigned lease.

105 Amendment of section 12A (special provisions for tax invoiced by flat-rate farmers) of Principal Act

Notes

This section substituted "3.3 per cent" for "2.8 per cent" in VATA 1972, s 12A(1) as on and from 1 March 1997. This increases the flat-rate addition for unregistered farmers with effect from 2.8% to 3.3% from 1 March 1997.

106 Amendment of section 13 (remission of tax on goods exported, etc.) of Principal Act

Notes

Para (*a*) inserted VATA 1972, s 13(1A) as on and from 1 July 1997. If a sale to a non EU based tourist is to qualify for the 0% rate, a retailer using a commercial VAT refund agent must inform the tourist of the commission being charged on, and the exchange rate being applied to, the transaction.

Para (*b*) inserted VATA 1972, s 13(3B)–(3C) as on and from 1 July 1997.

The Revenue Commissioners may introduce an authorisation procedure for retailers who wish to charge the 0% rate to non EU based tourists.

A VAT refunding agent is entitled to deduct any VAT charged to him on supplies of goods made to non EU tourists.

The Revenue Commissioners may delegate any of their powers in this regard.

107 Amendment of section 19 (tax due and payable) of Principal Act

Notes

Para (*a*) inserted VATA 1972, s 19(2A) as on and from 1 July 1997. After 1 July 1997, telecommunications services supplied from outside the EU are liable to VAT. In the absence of legislation, a payment for such services made before 1 July 1997 would not be taxable. Such prepayments are taxable if they relate to services supplied after 1 July 1997.

Para (*b*) deleted VATA 1972, s 19(3)(*a*)(proviso) as on and from 7 November 1996. See para (*c*).

Para (*c*) deleted VATA 1972, s 19(6) as on and from 7 November 1996. Traders with substantial VAT liabilities were required to make an advance VAT payment in December of each calendar year. This requirement is abolished with effect from 7 November 1996 — no advance VAT payment is needed for 1996 (or later years).

108 Amendment of section 20 (refund of tax) of Principal Act

Notes

This section deleted VATA 1972, s 20(1)(proviso) as on and from 7 November 1996. This is no longer needed following abolition of advance payment of VAT.

109 Amendment of section 25 (appeals) of Principal Act

Notes

This section inserted VATA 1972, s 25(1)(*ad*) as on and from 1 July 1997. A trader who is refused a Revenue authorisation (VATA 1972, s 13B(1B)) to operate a 0% retail export scheme may appeal against such a refusal.

110 Amendment of First Schedule to Principal Act

Notes

Para (*a*) inserted "children or young people's education," before "school" in VATA 1972, Sch 1 para (ii) as on and from 1 May 1997.

Para (*b*) inserted "and the supply of services for the protection or care of children and young persons, and the provision of goods closely related thereto, provided by persons whose activities may be regulated by regulations made under Part VII of the Child Care Act, 1991;" after "profit" in VATA 1972, Sch 1 para (vi) as on and from 1 May 1997.

This exempts the provision of creche facilities that also provide some element of education.

111 Amendment of Second Schedule to Principal Act

Notes

Para (*a*)(i) substituted VATA 1972, Sch 2 para (i)(*a*)(I) as on and from 1 July 1997.

Para (*a*)(ii) inserted VATA 1972, Sch 2 para (i)(*f*) as on and from 1 July 1997.

Goods sold under an authorised retail export scheme may be charged at 0%.

Para (*b*) inserted VATA 1972, Sch 2 para (vi*b*) as on and from 1 July 1997.

Related services supplied under an authorised retail export scheme may be charged at 0%.

112 Amendment of Fourth Schedule to Principal Act

Notes

This section inserted VATA 1972, Sch 4 para (iii*a*) as on and from 1 July 1997.

Telecommunications services are, from 1 July 1997, to be treated as taxed where received.

This means that the recipient of such services must self-account for VAT on the value of the service received. In the case of a taxable person, there will be no net VAT liability, as the trader will simultaneously account for and deduct the VAT on the value of the service. A non taxable person (for example, a bank or insurance company) must self account on the value of the service received, without any entitlement to input VAT on the service.

113 Amendment of Sixth Schedule to Principal Act

Notes

This section inserted VATA 1972, Sch 6 para (xi*a*) as on and from such date as the Minister for Finance may by order appoint. Non food-producing plants, shrubs and flowers are to be liable to VAT at 12.5% (instead of 21%).

114 Revocation (Part III)

Notes

This section revoked the European Communities (Value Added Tax) Regulations 1993 (SI 345/1993), and the Value Added Tax (Threshold for Advance Payment)(Amendment)(Order) 1994 (SI 342/1994) — with effect from 7 November 1996.

These are no longer needed, as advance payment of VAT has been abolished (see s 107).

PART VIII
Miscellaneous

158 Amendment of section 23 (publication of names of defaulters) of Finance Act, 1983

Notes

This section substituted FA 1983, s 23(2)(3) for 1997 and later years.

159 Evidence of authorisation

(1) In this section, except where the context otherwise requires—

"the Acts" means—

    (*a*) (i) the Customs Acts,

(ii)   the statutes relating to the duties of excise and to the management of those duties,

(iii)   the Tax Acts,

(iv)   the Capital Gains Tax Acts,

(v)   the Value Added Tax Act, 1972, and the enactments amending or extending that Act,

(vi)   the Capital Acquisitions Tax Act, 1976, and the enactments amending or extending that Act,

(vii)   the statutes relating to stamp duty and to the management of that duty,

and any instruments made thereunder or under any other enactment and relating to tax, and

(*b*)   the European Communities (Intrastat) Regulations, 1993 (SI No 136 of 1993);

"authorised officer" means an officer of the Revenue Commissioners who is authorised, nominated or appointed under any provision of the Acts, to exercise or perform any functions under any of the specified provisions, and **"authorised"** and **"authorisation"** shall be construed accordingly;

"functions" includes powers and duties;

"identity card", in relation to an authorised officer, means a card which is issued to the officer by the Revenue Commissioners and which contains—

(*a*)   a statement to the effect that the officer—

(i)   is an officer of the Revenue Commissioners, and

(ii)   is an authorised officer for the purposes of the specified provisions,

(*b*)   a photograph and signature of the officer,

(*c*)   a hologram showing the logo of the Office of the Revenue Commissioners,

(*d*)   the facsimile signature of a Revenue Commissioner, and

(*e*)   particulars of the specified provisions under which the officer is authorised;

"specified provisions", in relation to an authorised officer, means either or both the provisions of the Acts under which the authorised officer—

(*a*)   is authorised and which are specified on his or her identity card, and

(*b*)   exercises or performs functions under the Customs Acts or any statutes relating to the duties of excise and to the management of those duties;

"tax" means any tax, duty, levy, charge under the care and management of the Revenue Commissioners.

(2) Where, in the exercise or performance of any functions under any of the specified provisions in relation to him or her, an authorised officer is requested to produce or

show his or her authorisation for the purposes of that provision, the production by the authorised officer of his or her identity card—

(a) shall be taken as evidence of authorisation under that provision, and

(b) shall satisfy any obligation under that provision which requires the authorised officer to produce such authorisation on request.

(3) This section shall come into operation on such day as the Minister for Finance may appoint by order.

165 Care and management of taxes and duties

All taxes and duties imposed by this Act are hereby placed under the care and management of the Revenue Commissioners.

166 Short title, construction and commencement

(1) This Act may be cited as the Finance Act, 1997.

...

(4) Part III shall be construed together with the Value Added Tax Acts, 1972 to 1996, and may be cited together therewith as the Value Added Tax Acts, 1972 to 1997.

...

(10) In relation to Part III:

(a) section 95, paragraphs (b) and (c) of section 107, section 108 and section 114 shall be deemed to have come into force and shall take effect as on and from the 7th day of November, 1996;

(b) paragraph (a) of section 103 and section 105 shall be deemed to have come into force and shall take effect as on and from the 1st day of March, 1997;

(c) paragraphs (a) and (b) of section 96, section 98, section 100, paragraphs (b), (e) and (f) of section 102 and section 104 shall be deemed to have come into force and shall take effect as on and from the 26th day of March, 1997;

(d) section 110 shall be deemed to have come into force and shall take effect as on and from the 1st day of May, 1997;

(e) paragraph (c) of section 96, section 99, section 106, paragraph (a) of section 107, section 109, section 111 and section 112 shall take effect as on and from the 1st day of July, 1997;

(f) sections 101 and 113 shall take effect as on and from such date as the Minister for Finance may by order, appoint;

(g) the provisions of this Part, other than those specified in paragraphs (a), (b), (c), (d), (e) and (f), shall have effect as on and from the date of passing of this Act.

(11) Any reference in this Act to any other enactment shall, except so far as the context otherwise requires, be construed as a reference to that enactment as amended by or under any other enactment including this Act.

(12) In this Act, a reference to a Part, section or Schedule is to a Part or section of, or Schedule to, this Act, unless it is indicated that reference to some other enactment is intended.

(13) In this Act, a reference to a subsection, paragraph, subparagraph, clause or subclause is to the subsection, paragraph, subparagraph, clause or subclause of the provision (including a Schedule) in which the reference occurs, unless it is indicated that reference to some other provision is intended.

TAXES CONSOLIDATION ACT 1997

(No 39 of 1997)

ARRANGEMENT OF SECTIONS

INTERPRETATION AND BASIC CHARGING PROVISIONS

PART 1
INTERPRETATION

PART 39
ASSESSMENTS

CHAPTER 1
Income tax and corporation tax

PART 42
COLLECTION AND RECOVERY

CHAPTER 5
Miscellaneous provisions

PART 47
PENALTIES, REVENUE OFFENCES, INTEREST ON OVERDUE TAX AND OTHER SANCTIONS

CHAPTER 4
Revenue offences

CHAPTER 6
Other sanctions

PART 48
MISCELLANEOUS AND SUPPLEMENTAL

PART 49
COMMENCEMENT, REPEALS, TRANSITIONAL PROVISIONS, ETC

SCHEDULE 31

7 Application to certain taxing statutes of Age of Majority Act, 1985

(1) Notwithstanding subsection (4) of section 2 of the Age of Majority Act, 1985 (in this section referred to as **"the Act of 1985"**), subsections (2) and (3) of that section shall, subject to subsection (2), apply for the purposes of the Income Tax Acts and any other statutory provision (within the meaning of the Act of 1985) dealing with the imposition, repeal, remission, alteration or regulation of any tax or other duty under the care and management of the Revenue Commissioners, and accordingly section 2(4)(*b*)(vii) of the Act of 1985 shall cease to apply.

(2) Nothing in subsection (1) shall affect a claimant's entitlement to [relief]¹ under section 462 or 465.

Amendments
¹   Substituted by FA 2000, s 14 and Sch 1 para 2 with effect from 6 April 2000; previously "a deduction".

Cross-references
This section to be construed together with the Customs Acts, in so far as relating to customs, and with the statutes which relate to excise duty, in so far as relating to that duty: s 1104(2).
This section to be construed together with the Value Added Tax Acts 1972–1997, in so far as relating to value added tax: s 1104(3).
This section to be construed together with the Stamp Act 1891 and the enactments amending or extending that Act, in so far as relating to stamp duties: s 1104(4).
This section to be construed together with the Capital Acquisitions Tax Act 1976, and the enactments amending or extending that Act, in so far as relating to capital acquisitions tax: s 1104(5).
This section to be construed together with FA 1983, Pt VI and the enactments amending or extending that Part, in so far as relating to residential property tax. s 1104(6).

Definitions
Income Tax Acts: s 1(2).

Former enactments
FA 1986, s 112(1)–(2).

PART 33
ANTI-AVOIDANCE

CHAPTER 2
Miscellaneous

811 Transactions to avoid liability to tax

(1) (*a*)   [In this section and section 811A—]¹—

    "the Acts" means—

      (i)   the Tax Acts,

     (ii)   the Capital Gains Tax Acts,

    (iii)   the Value-Added Tax Act, 1972, and the enactments amending or extending that Act,

(iv) the [Capital Acquisitions Tax Consolidation Act 2003],[2] and the enactments amending or extending that Act,

(v) Part VI of the Finance Act, 1983, and the enactments amending or extending that Part, and

(vi) the statutes relating to stamp duty,

and any instruments made thereunder;

"business" means any trade, profession or vocation;

"notice of opinion" means a notice given by the Revenue Commissioners under subsection (6);

"tax" means any tax, duty, levy or charge which in accordance with the Acts is placed under the care and management of the Revenue Commissioners and any interest, penalty or other amount payable pursuant to the Acts;

"tax advantage" means—

(i) a reduction, avoidance or deferral of any charge or assessment to tax, including any potential or prospective charge or assessment, or

(ii) a refund of or a payment of an amount of tax, or an increase in an amount of tax, refundable or otherwise payable to a person, including any potential or prospective amount so refundable or payable,

arising out of or by reason of a transaction, including a transaction where another transaction would not have been undertaken or arranged to achieve the results, or any part of the results, achieved or intended to be achieved by the transaction;

"tax avoidance transaction" has the meaning assigned to it by subsection (2);

"tax consequences", in relation to a tax avoidance transaction, means such adjustments and acts as may be made and done by the Revenue Commissioners pursuant to subsection (5) in order to withdraw or deny the tax advantage resulting from the tax avoidance transaction;

"transaction" means—

(i) any transaction, action, course of action, course of conduct, scheme, plan or proposal,

(ii) any agreement, arrangement, understanding, promise or undertaking, whether express or implied and whether or not enforceable or intended to be enforceable by legal proceedings, and

(iii) any series of or combination of the circumstances referred to in paragraphs (i) and (ii),

whether entered into or arranged by one person or by 2 or more persons—

(I) whether acting in concert or not,

(II) whether or not entered into or arranged wholly or partly outside the State, or

(III) whether or not entered into or arranged as part of a larger transaction or in conjunction with any other transaction or transactions.

(*b*) In subsections (2) and (3), for the purposes of the hearing or rehearing under subsection (8) of an appeal made under subsection (7) or for the purposes of the determination of a question of law arising on the statement of a case for the opinion of the High Court, the references to the Revenue Commissioners shall, subject to any necessary modifications, be construed as references to the

Appeal Commissioners or to a judge of the Circuit Court or, to the extent necessary, to a judge of the High Court, as appropriate.

[(c) For the purposes of this section and section 811A, all appeals made under section 811(7) by, or on behalf of, a person against any matter or matters specified or described in the notice of opinion of the Revenue Commissioners that a transaction is a tax avoidance transaction, if they have not otherwise been so determined, shall be deemed to have been finally determined when—

    (i) there is a written agreement, between that person and an officer of the Revenue Commissioners, that the notice of opinion is to stand or is to be amended in a particular manner,

    (ii) (I) the terms of such an agreement that was not made in writing have been confirmed by notice in writing given by the person to the officer of the Revenue Commissioners with whom the agreement was made, or by such officer to the person, and

        (II) 21 days have elapsed since the giving of the notice without the person to whom it was given giving notice in writing to the person by whom it was given that the first-mentioned person desires to repudiate or withdraw from the agreement, or

    (iii) the person gives notice in writing to an officer of the Revenue Commissioners that the person desires not to proceed with an appeal against the notice of opinion.][3]

(2) For the purposes of this section and subject to subsection (3), a transaction shall be a **"tax avoidance transaction"** if having regard to any one or more of the following—

    (*a*) the results of the transaction,

    (*b*) its use as a means of achieving those results, and

    (*c*) any other means by which the results or any part of the results could have been achieved,

the Revenue Commissioners form the opinion that—

    (i) the transaction gives rise to, or but for this section would give rise to, a tax advantage, and

    (ii) the transaction was not undertaken or arranged primarily for purposes other than to give rise to a tax advantage,

and references in this section to the Revenue Commissioners forming an opinion that a transaction is a tax avoidance transaction shall be construed as references to the Revenue Commissioners forming an opinion with regard to the transaction in accordance with this subsection.

(3) (*a*) Without prejudice to the generality of subsection (2), in forming an opinion in accordance with that subsection and subsection (4) as to whether or not a transaction is a tax avoidance transaction, the Revenue Commissioners shall not regard the transaction as being a tax avoidance transaction if they are satisfied that—

    (i) notwithstanding that the purpose or purposes of the transaction could have been achieved by some other transaction which would have given rise to a greater amount of tax being payable by the person, the transaction—

        (I) was undertaken or arranged by a person with a view, directly or indirectly, to the realisation of profits in the course of the business activities of a business carried on by the person, and

        (II) was not undertaken or arranged primarily to give rise to a tax advantage, or

  (ii)   the transaction was undertaken or arranged for the purpose of obtaining the benefit of any relief, allowance or other abatement provided by any provision of the Acts and that the transaction would not result directly or indirectly in a misuse of the provision or an abuse of the provision having regard to the purposes for which it was provided.

  (*b*)   In forming an opinion referred to in paragraph (*a*) in relation to any transaction, the Revenue Commissioners shall have regard to—

     (i)   the form of that transaction,

    (ii)   the substance of that transaction,

   (iii)   the substance of any other transaction or transactions which that transaction may reasonably be regarded as being directly or indirectly related to or connected with, and

   (iv)   the final outcome and result of that transaction and any combination of those other transactions which are so related or connected.

(4) Subject to this section, the Revenue Commissioners as respects any transaction may at any time—

  (*a*)   form the opinion that the transaction is a tax avoidance transaction,

  (*b*)   calculate the tax advantage which they consider arises, or which but for this section would arise, from the transaction,

  (*c*)   determine the tax consequences which they consider would arise in respect of the transaction if their opinion were to become final and conclusive in accordance with subsection (5)(*e*), and

  (*d*)   calculate the amount of any relief from double taxation which they would propose to give to any person in accordance with subsection (5)(*c*).

(5) (*a*)   Where the opinion of the Revenue Commissioners that a transaction is a tax avoidance transaction becomes final and conclusive, they may, notwithstanding any other provision of the Acts, make all such adjustments and do all such acts as are just and reasonable (in so far as those adjustments and acts have been specified or described in a notice of opinion given under subsection (6) and subject to the manner in which any appeal made under subsection (7) against any matter specified or described in the notice of opinion has been finally determined, including any adjustments and acts not so specified or described in the notice of opinion but which form part of a final determination of any such appeal) in order that the tax advantage resulting from a tax avoidance transaction shall be withdrawn from or denied to any person concerned.

  (*b*)   Subject to but without prejudice to the generality of paragraph (*a*), the Revenue Commissioners may—

     (i)   allow or disallow in whole or in part any deduction or other amount which is relevant in computing tax payable, or any part of such deduction or other amount,

    (ii)   allocate or deny to any person any deduction, loss, abatement, relief, allowance, exemption, income or other amount, or any part thereof, or

   (iii)   recharacterize for tax purposes the nature of any payment or other amount.

  (*c*)   Where the Revenue Commissioners make any adjustment or do any act for the purposes of paragraph (*a*), they shall afford relief from any double taxation which they consider would but for this paragraph arise by virtue of any adjustment made or act done by them pursuant to paragraphs (*a*) and (*b*).

    (*d*) Notwithstanding any other provision of the Acts, where—

        (i) pursuant to subsection (4)(*c*), the Revenue Commissioners determine the tax consequences which they consider would arise in respect of a transaction if their opinion that the transaction is a tax avoidance transaction were to become final and conclusive, and

        (ii) pursuant to that determination, they specify or describe in a notice of opinion any adjustment or act which they consider would be, or be part of, those tax consequences,

then, in so far as any right of appeal lay under subsection (7) against any such adjustment or act so specified or described, no right or further right of appeal shall lie under the Acts against that adjustment or act when it is made or done in accordance with this subsection, or against any adjustment or act so made or done that is not so specified or described in the notice of opinion but which forms part of the final determination of any appeal made under subsection (7) against any matter specified or described in the notice of opinion.

    (*e*) For the purposes of this subsection, an opinion of the Revenue Commissioners that a transaction is a tax avoidance transaction shall be final and conclusive—

        (i) if within the time limited no appeal is made under subsection (7) against any matter or matters specified or described in a notice or notices of opinion given pursuant to that opinion, or

        (ii) as and when all appeals made under subsection (7) against any such matter or matters have been finally determined and none of the appeals has been so determined by an order directing that the opinion of the Revenue Commissioners to the effect that the transaction is a tax avoidance transaction is void.

(6) (*a*) Where pursuant to subsections (2) and (4) the Revenue Commissioners form the opinion that a transaction is a tax avoidance transaction, they shall immediately on forming such an opinion give notice in writing of the opinion to any person from whom a tax advantage would be withdrawn or to whom a tax advantage would be denied or to whom relief from double taxation would be given if the opinion became final and conclusive, and the notice shall specify or describe—

        (i) the transaction which in the opinion of the Revenue Commissioners is a tax avoidance transaction,

        (ii) the tax advantage or part of the tax advantage, calculated by the Revenue Commissioners which would be withdrawn from or denied to the person to whom the notice is given,

        (iii) the tax consequences of the transaction determined by the Revenue Commissioners in so far as they would refer to the person, and

        (iv) the amount of any relief from double taxation calculated by the Revenue Commissioners which they would propose to give to the person in accordance with subsection (5)(*c*).

    (*b*) Section 869 shall, with any necessary modifications, apply for the purposes of a notice given under this subsection or subsection (10) as if it were a notice given under the Income Tax Acts.

(7) Any person aggrieved by an opinion formed or, in so far as it refers to the person, a calculation or determination made by the Revenue Commissioners pursuant to subsection (4) may, by notice in writing given to the Revenue Commissioners within 30 days of the date of the notice of opinion, appeal to the Appeal Commissioners on the

grounds and, notwithstanding any other provision of the Acts, only on the grounds that, having regard to all of the circumstances, including any fact or matter which was not known to the Revenue Commissioners when they formed their opinion or made their calculation or determination, and to this section—

(a) the transaction specified or described in the notice of opinion is not a tax avoidance transaction,

(b) the amount of the tax advantage or the part of the tax advantage, specified or described in the notice of opinion which would be withdrawn from or denied to the person is incorrect,

(c) the tax consequences specified or described in the notice of opinion, or such part of those consequences as shall be specified or described by the appellant in the notice of appeal, would not be just and reasonable in order to withdraw or to deny the tax advantage or part of the tax advantage specified or described in the notice of opinion, or

(d) the amount of relief from double taxation which the Revenue Commissioners propose to give to the person is insufficient or incorrect.

(8) The Appeal Commissioners shall hear and determine an appeal made to them under subsection (7) as if it were an appeal against an assessment to income tax and, subject to subsection (9), the provisions of the Income Tax Acts relating to the rehearing of an appeal and to the statement of a case for the opinion of the High Court on a point of law shall apply accordingly with any necessary modifications; but on the hearing or rehearing of the appeal—

(a) it shall not be lawful to enquire into any grounds of appeal other than those specified in subsection (7), and

(b) at the request of the appellants, 2 or more appeals made by 2 or more persons pursuant to the same opinion, calculation or determination formed or made by the Revenue Commissioners pursuant to subsection (4) may be heard or reheard together.

(9) (a) On the hearing of an appeal made under subsection (7), the Appeal Commissioners shall have regard to all matters to which the Revenue Commissioners may or are required to have regard under this section, and—

(i) in relation to an appeal made on the grounds referred to in subsection (7)(a), the Appeal Commissioners shall determine the appeal, in so far as it is made on those grounds, by ordering, if they or a majority of them—

(I) consider that the transaction specified or described in the notice of opinion or any part of that transaction is a tax avoidance transaction, that the opinion or the opinion in so far as it relates to that part is to stand,

(II) consider that, subject to such amendment or addition thereto as the Appeal Commissioners or the majority of them deem necessary and as they shall specify or describe, the transaction, or any part of it, specified or described in the notice of opinion, is a tax avoidance transaction, that the transaction or that part of it be so amended or added to and that, subject to the amendment or addition, the opinion or the opinion in so far as it relates to that part is to stand, or

(III) do not so consider as referred to in clause (I) or (II), that the opinion is void,

(ii) in relation to an appeal made on the grounds referred to in subsection (7)(b), they shall determine the appeal, in so far as it is made on those grounds, by ordering that the amount of the tax advantage or the part of the tax advantage specified or described in the notice of opinion be increased or reduced by such amount as they shall direct or that it shall stand,

(iii) in relation to an appeal made on the grounds referred to in subsection (7)(*c*), they shall determine the appeal, in so far as it is made on those grounds, by ordering that the tax consequences specified or described in the notice of opinion shall be altered or added to in such manner as they shall direct or that they shall stand, or

(iv) in relation to an appeal made on the grounds referred to in subsection (7)(*d*), they shall determine the appeal, in so far as it is made on those grounds, by ordering that the amount of the relief from double taxation specified or described in the notice of opinion shall be increased or reduced by such amount as they shall direct or that it shall stand.

(*b*) This subsection shall, subject to any necessary modifications, apply to the rehearing of an appeal by a judge of the Circuit Court and, to the extent necessary, to the determination by the High Court of any question or questions of law arising on the statement of a case for the opinion of the High Court.

(10) The Revenue Commissioners may at any time amend, add to or withdraw any matter specified or described in a notice of opinion by giving notice (in this subsection referred to as **"the notice of amendment"**) in writing of the amendment, addition or withdrawal to each and every person affected thereby, in so far as the person is so affected, and subsections (1) to (9) shall apply in all respects as if the notice of amendment were a notice of opinion and any matter specified or described in the notice of amendment were specified or described in a notice of opinion; but no such amendment, addition or withdrawal may be made so as to set aside or alter any matter which has become final and conclusive on the determination of an appeal made with regard to that matter under subsection (7).

(11) Where pursuant to subsections (2) and (4) the Revenue Commissioners form the opinion that a transaction is a tax avoidance transaction and pursuant to that opinion notices are to be given under subsection (6) to 2 or more persons, any obligation on the Revenue Commissioners to maintain secrecy or any other restriction on the disclosure of information by the Revenue Commissioners shall not apply with respect to the giving of those notices or to the performance of any acts or the discharge of any functions authorised by this section to be performed or discharged by them or to the performance of any act or the discharge of any functions, including any act or function in relation to an appeal made under subsection (7), which is directly or indirectly related to the acts or functions so authorised.

(12) The Revenue Commissioners may nominate any of their officers to perform any acts and discharge any functions, including the forming of an opinion, authorised by this section to be performed or discharged by the Revenue Commissioners, and references in this section to the Revenue Commissioners shall with any necessary modifications be construed as including references to an officer so nominated.

(13) This section shall apply as respects any transaction where the whole or any part of the transaction is undertaken or arranged on or after the 25th day of January, 1989, and as respects any transaction undertaken or arranged wholly before that date in so far as it gives rise to, or would but for this section give rise to—

(*a*) a reduction, avoidance or deferral of any charge or assessment to tax, or part thereof, where the charge or assessment arises by virtue of any other transaction carried out wholly on or after a date, or

(b) a refund or a payment of an amount, or of an increase in an amount, of tax, or part thereof, refundable or otherwise payable to a person where that amount or increase in the amount would otherwise become first so refundable or otherwise payable to the person on a date,

which could not fall earlier than the 25th day of January, 1989.

Amendments

1 Substituted by FA 2006, s 126(*a*)(i) with effect from 31 March 2006; previously "In this section—".
2 Substituted by CATCA 2003, s 119 and Sch 3 with effect from 21 February 2003; previously "Capital Acquisitions Tax Act 1976".
3 Subs (1)(*c*) inserted by FA 2006, s 126(*a*)(ii) with effect from 31 March 2006.

Cross-references

Meaning of "the Acts" applied: Asset Covered Securities Act 2001, s 81(2).

Shipping tonnage tax, requirement not to enter into tax avoidance arrangements, meaning of "tax advantage" applied: s 697F(2)(*a*).

This section to be construed together with the Value Added Tax Acts 1972–1997, in so far as relating to value added tax: s 1104(3).

This section to be construed together with the Stamp Act 1891 and the enactments amending or extending that Act, in so far as relating to stamp duties: s 1104(4).

This section to be construed together with the Capital Acquisitions Tax Act 1976, and the enactments amending or extending that Act, in so far as relating to capital acquisitions tax: s 1104(5).

This section to be construed together with FA 1983, Pt VI and the enactments amending or extending that Part, in so far as relating to residential property tax: s 1104(6).

Transactions to avoid liability to tax, surcharge, interest and protective notification: s 811A(1)(*c*), (3)(*c*)(ii)(I), (iii)(I), (II), (7)(*b*); subs (5): s 811A(2); subs (6)(*a*): s 811A(2)(*b*), (6)(*c*); subs (7): s 811A(1)(*b*), (4)(*b*); subs (8)(*a*): s 811A(4)(*b*).

Caselaw relating to the corresponding UK provision

Bona fide commercial motives: *Marwood Homes Ltd v IRC* [1996] STI 51.

Expenditure on plant funded by non-recourse borrowings allowable: *Airspace Investments Ltd v Moore* (High Court, Lynch J, 15 April 1994) Contrast *Ensign Tankers (Leasing) Ltd v Stokes* [1992] STC 226.

Meaning of "tax advantage": *IRC v Universities Superannuation Scheme* [1997] STC 1.

Trustees of Omega Group Pension Scheme v IRC [2001] STC 121.

IRC v Trustees of the Sema Group Pension Scheme [2002] STC 276.

Definitions

Appeal Commissioners: ss 2(1), 5(1); Circuit Court: IA 2005, Sch; High Court: IA 2005, Sch; person: IA 2005, s 18(*c*); profession: ss 2(1), 5(1); profits: s 4(1); Tax Acts: s 1(2); trade: s 3(1); writing: IA 2005, Sch.

Former enactments

FA 1989, s 86.

Corresponding UK tax provision

Income and Corporation Taxes Act 1988, s 703.

MANAGEMENT PROVISIONS

PART 37
ADMINISTRATION

858 Evidence of authorisation

(1) In this section, except where the context otherwise requires—

"the Acts" means—

    (*a*) (i) the Customs Acts,

        (ii) the statutes relating to the duties of excise and to the management of those duties,

        (iii) the Tax Acts,

(iv)   the Capital Gains Tax Acts,

(v)   the Value Added Tax Act, 1972, and the enactments amending or extending that Act,

(vi)   the [Capital Acquisitions Tax Consolidation Act 2003],[1] and the enactments amending or extending that Act,

(vii)   the statutes relating to stamp duty and to the management of that duty,

and any instruments made thereunder or under any other enactment and relating to tax, and

(b)   the European Communities (Intrastat) Regulations, 1993 (SI No 136 of 1993);

"authorised officer" means an officer of the Revenue Commissioners who is authorised, nominated or appointed under any provision of the Acts to exercise or perform any functions under any of the specified provisions, and **"authorised"** and **"authorisation"** shall be construed accordingly;

"functions" includes powers and duties;

"identity card", in relation to an authorised officer, means a card which is issued to the officer by the Revenue Commissioners and which contains—

(a)   a statement to the effect that the officer—

(i)   is an officer of the Revenue Commissioners, and

(ii)   is an authorised officer for the purposes of the specified provisions,

(b)   a photograph and signature of the officer,

(c)   a hologram showing the logo of the Office of the Revenue Commissioners,

(d)   the facsimile signature of a Revenue Commissioner, and

(e)   particulars of the specified provisions under which the officer is authorised;

"specified provisions", in relation to an authorised officer, means either or both the provisions of the Acts under which the authorised officer—

(a)   is authorised and which are specified on his or her identity card, and

(b)   exercises or performs functions under the Customs Acts or any statutes relating to the duties of excise and to the management of those duties;

"tax" means any tax, duty, levy or charge under the care and management of the Revenue Commissioners.

(2) Where, in the exercise or performance of any functions under any of the specified provisions in relation to him or her, an authorised officer is requested to produce or show his or her authorisation for the purposes of that provision, the production by the authorised officer of his or her identity card—

(a)   shall be taken as evidence of authorisation under that provision, and

(b)   shall satisfy any obligation under that provision which requires the authorised officer to produce such authorisation on request.

(3) This section shall come into operation on such day as the Minister for Finance may appoint by order.

Amendments

[1]   Substituted by CATCA 2003, s 119 and Sch 3 with effect from 21 February 2003; previously "Capital Acquisitions Tax Act 1976".

Operative Date

The section came into operation from 1 July 1998 — Taxes Consolidation Act, 1997 (Section 858) (Commencement) Order, SI 212/1998, refers.

Cross-references

This section to be construed together with the Customs Acts, in so far as relating to customs: s 1104(2).

This section to be construed together with the Value Added Tax Acts 1972–1997, in so far as relating to value added tax: s 1104(3).

This section to be construed together with the Stamp Act 1891 and the enactments amending or extending that Act, in so far as relating to stamp duties: s 1104(4).

This section to be construed together with the Capital Acquisitions Tax Act 1976, and the enactments amending or extending that Act, in so far as relating to capital acquisitions tax: s 1104(5).

Former enactments

FA 1997, s 159.

859 Anonymity of authorised officers in relation to certain matters

(1) In this section—

"authorised officer" means an officer of the Revenue Commissioners nominated by them to be a member of the staff of the body;

"the body" has the meaning assigned to it by section 58;

"proceedings" includes any hearing before the Appeal Commissioners (within the meaning of the Revenue Acts);

"the Revenue Acts" means—

- (*a*)   the Customs Acts,
- (*b*)   the statutes relating to the duties of excise and to the management of those duties,
- (*c*)   the Tax Acts,
- (*d*)   the Capital Gains Tax Acts,
- (*e*)   the Value Added Tax Act, 1972, and the enactments amending or extending that Act,
- (*f*)   the [Capital Acquisitions Tax Consolidation Act 2003],[1] and the enactments amending or extending that Act,
- (*g*)   the statutes relating to stamp duty and the management of that duty,
- (*h*)   Chapter IV of Part II of the Finance Act, 1992, and
- (*i*)   Part VI of the Finance Act, 1983,

and any instruments made thereunder or under any other enactment and relating to tax;

"tax" means any tax, duty, levy or charge under the care and management of the Revenue Commissioners.

(2) Notwithstanding any requirement made by or under any enactment or any other requirement in administrative and operational procedures, including internal procedures, all reasonable care shall be taken to ensure that the identity of an authorised officer shall not be revealed.

(3) In particular and without prejudice to the generality of subsection (2):

- (*a*)   where, for the purposes of exercising or performing his or her powers or duties under the Revenue Acts in pursuance of the functions of the body, an authorised officer may apart from this section be required to produce or show

(*a*) provides a reliable assurance as to the integrity of the record from the time when it was first generated in its final form by such electronic, photographic or other process,

(*b*) permits the record to be displayed in intelligible form and produced in an intelligible printed format,

(*c*) permits the record to be readily accessible for subsequent reference in accordance with paragraph (*b*), and

(*d*) conforms to the information technology and procedural requirements drawn up and published by the Revenue Commissioners in accordance with subsection (3).

(3) The Revenue Commissioners shall from time to time draw up and publish in Iris Oifigiúil the information technology and procedural requirements to which any electronic, photographic or other process used by a person for the storage, maintenance, transmission, reproduction and communication of any record shall conform.

(4) The authority conferred on the Revenue Commissioners by this section to draw up and publish requirements shall be construed as including the authority exercisable in a like manner to revoke and replace or to amend any such requirements.

(5) (*a*) Every person who preserves records by any electronic, photographic or other process, when required to do so by a notice in writing from the Revenue Commissioners, shall, within such period as is specified in the notice, not being less than 21 days from the date of service of the notice, supply to the Revenue Commissioners full particulars relating to the process used by that person, including full particulars relating to software (within the meaning of section 912).

(*b*) A person who fails or refuses to comply with a notice served on the person under paragraph (*a*) shall be liable to a penalty of [€1,265].[2]

(6) (*a*) Subject to paragraph (*b*), where records are kept by a person (being a person who is obliged by the Acts to keep such records) by any electronic, photographic or other process which does not conform with the requirements referred to in paragraphs (*a*) to (*d*) of subsection (2), then the person shall be deemed to have failed to comply with that obligation and that person shall be liable to the same penalties as the person would be liable to if the person had failed to comply with any obligation under the Acts in relation to the keeping of records.

(*b*) Paragraph (*a*) shall not apply where the person referred to in that paragraph complies with any obligation under the Acts in relation to the keeping of records other than in accordance with the provisions of subsection (2).

(7) Where records are preserved by any electronic, photographic or other process, information contained in a document produced by any such process shall, subject to the rules of court, be admissible in evidence in any proceedings, whether civil or criminal, to the same extent as the records themselves.

(8) The Revenue Commissioners may nominate any of their officers to discharge any function authorised by this section to be discharged by the Revenue Commissioners.][3]

Amendments

¹   Substituted by CATCA 2003, s 119 and Sch 3 with effect from 21 February 2003; previously "Capital Acquisitions Tax Act 1976".

²   Substituted by FA 2001, s 232(3)(*a*)(i) with effect from 1 January 2002; previously "£1,000".

³   Substituted by FA 2001, s 232(1)(*a*) with effect from 15 February 2001 (as a result of FA 2002, s 138 and Sch 6 paras 5(*f*) and 6(*e*)(i)).

Cross-references

Capital acquisitions tax, obligation to retain certain records, subs (2): CATCA 2003, s 45A(3)(*b*).

Obligation to keep records, subs (2): s 886(3)(*b*).

Power of inspection, PAYE: s 903(1)("records").

This section to be construed together with the Value Added Tax Acts 1972–1997, in so far as relating to value added tax: s 1104(3).

This section to be construed together with the Capital Acquisitions Tax Act 1976, and the enactments amending or extending that Act, in so far as relating to capital acquisitions tax: s 1104(5).

This section to be construed together with FA 1983, Pt VI and the enactments amending or extending that Part, in so far as relating to residential property tax: s 1104(6).

Tax Briefing

TB46 Dec 2001 pp 24–25 — Electronic Storage — Retention of Tax Records in Electronic Format.

Definitions

Capital Gains Tax Acts: s 1(2); person: IA 2005, s 18(*c*); rules of court: IA 2005, Sch; Tax Acts: s 1(2); writing: IA 2005, Sch.

Former enactments

FA 1986, s 113(1)–(3); FA 1993, s 99.

Corresponding UK tax provision

Taxes Management Act 1970, s 115A.

PART 38
RETURNS OF INCOME AND GAINS, OTHER OBLIGATIONS AND RETURNS, AND REVENUE POWERS

CHAPTER 4
Revenue powers

905 Inspection of documents and records

(1) In this section—

"authorised officer" means an officer of the Revenue Commissioners authorised by them in writing to exercise the powers conferred by this section;

"property" means any asset relating to a tax liability;

[**"records"** means any document or any other written or printed material in any form, and includes any information stored, maintained or preserved by means of any mechanical or electronic device, whether or not stored, maintained or preserved in a legible form—

    (i)   which relates to a business carried on by a person, or

    (ii)   which a person is obliged by any provision relating to tax to keep, retain, issue or produce for inspection or which may be inspected under any provision relating to tax;]¹

"tax" means any tax, duty, levy or charge under the care and management of the Revenue Commissioners;

"tax liability" means any existing liability to tax or further liability to tax which may be established by an authorised officer following the exercise or performance of his or her powers or duties under this section.

(2) (*a*) An authorised officer may at all reasonable times enter any premises or place where the authorised officer has reason to believe that—

(i) any trade, profession or other activity, the profits or gains of which are chargeable to tax, is or has been carried on,

(ii) anything is or has been done in connection with any trade, profession or other activity the profits or gains of which are chargeable to tax,

(iii) any records relating to—

(I) any trade, profession, other source of profits or gains or chargeable gains,

(II) any tax liability, or

(III) any repayments of tax in regard to any person,

are or may be kept, or

(iv) any property is or has been located,

and the authorised officer may—

(A) require any person who is on those premises or in that place, other than a person who is there to purchase goods or to receive a service, to produce any records or property,

(B) if the authorised officer has reason to believe that any of the records or property which he or she has required to be produced to him or her under this subsection have not been produced, search on those premises or in that place for those records or property,

(C) examine any records or property and take copies of or extracts from any records,

(D) remove any records and retain them for a reasonable time for the purposes of their further examination or for the purposes of any legal proceedings instituted by an officer of the Revenue Commissioners or for the purposes of any criminal proceedings, and

(E) examine property listed in any records.

(*b*) An authorised officer may in the exercise or performance of his or her powers or duties under this section require any person whom he or she has reason to believe—

(i) is or was carrying on any trade, profession or other activity the profits or gains of which are chargeable to tax,

(ii) is or was liable to any tax, or

(iii) has information relating to any tax liability,

to give the authorised officer all reasonable assistance, including providing information and explanations or furnishing documents and making available for inspection property as required by the authorised officer in relation to any tax liability or any repayment of tax in regard to any person.

(*c*) Nothing in this subsection shall be construed as requiring any person carrying on a profession, or any person employed by any person carrying on a profession, to produce to an authorised officer any documents relating to a client, other than such documents—

(i)   as pertain to the payment of fees to the person carrying on the profession or to other financial transactions of the person carrying on the profession,

(ii) as are otherwise material to the tax liability of the person carrying on the profession, or

(iii) as are already required to be provided following a request issued under [section 128 of the Stamp Duties Consolidation Act, 1999],[2]

and in particular that person shall not be required to disclose any information or professional advice of a confidential nature given to a client.

...[3]

(*e*) An authorised officer shall not, without the consent of the occupier, enter any premises, or that portion of any premises, which is occupied wholly and exclusively as a private residence, except on production by such officer of a warrant issued by a Judge of the District Court expressly authorising the authorised officer to so enter.

(*f*) A Judge of the District Court may issue a warrant under paragraph (*e*) if satisfied by information on oath that it is proper to do so for the purposes of this section.

[(2A)(*a*) In this subsection **"the Acts"** has the meaning assigned to it by section 1078(1).

(*b*) Without prejudice to any power conferred by subsection (2), if a Judge of the District Court is satisfied by information on oath that there are reasonable grounds for suspecting—

(i)   that a person may have failed or may fail to comply with any provision of the Acts,

(ii) that any such failure is likely to have led or to lead to serious prejudice to the proper assessment or collection of tax (having regard to the amount of any tax liability that arises or might arise from such failure), and

(iii) that records, which are material to the proper assessment or collection of tax are likely to be kept or concealed at any premises or place,

the Judge may issue a search warrant.

(*c*) A search warrant issued under this subsection shall be expressed and shall operate to authorise an authorised officer accompanied by such other named officers of the Revenue Commissioners and such other named persons as the authorised officer considers necessary, at any time or times within one month of the date of issue of the warrant, to enter (if need be by force) the premises or other place named or specified in the warrant, to search such premises or other place, to examine anything found there, to inspect any records found there and, if there are reasonable grounds for suspecting that any records found there are material to the proper assessment or collection of tax, or that the records may be required for the purpose of any legal proceedings instituted by an officer of the Revenue Commissioners or for the purpose of any criminal proceedings, remove such records and retain them for so long as they are reasonably required for the purpose aforesaid.][4]

(3) A person who does not comply with any requirement of an authorised officer in the exercise or performance of the authorised officer's powers or duties under this section shall be liable to a penalty of [€1,265][5].

(4) An authorised officer when exercising or performing his or her powers or duties under this section shall on request show his or her authorisation for the purposes of this section.

Amendments

1 Definition of "records" substituted by FA 2002, s 132(*d*) with effect from 25 March 2002.
2 Substituted by SDCA 1999, s 162 and Sch 4 with effect from 15 December 1999; previously "section 16 of the Stamp Act, 1891".
3 Subs (2)(*d*) deleted by FA 1999, s 207(*f*)(i) with effect from 25 March 1999.
4 Subs (2A) inserted by FA 1999, s 207(*f*)(ii) with effect from 25 March 1999.
5 Substituted by FA 2001, s 240(1) and (2)(*k*) and Sch 5 Pt 1 as respects any act or omission which takes place or begins on or after 1 January 2002; previously "£1,000".

Cross-references

Authorised officers and Garda Síochána: s 906.
This section to be construed together with the Customs Acts, in so far as relating to customs: s 1104(2).
This section to be construed together with the Value Added Tax Acts 1972–1997, in so far as relating to value added tax: s 1104(3).
This section to be construed together with the Stamp Act 1891 and the enactments amending or extending that Act, in so far as relating to stamp duties: s 1104(4).
This section to be construed together with the Capital Acquisitions Tax Act 1976, and the enactments amending or extending that Act, in so far as relating to capital acquisitions tax: s 1104(5).
This section to be construed together with FA 1983, Pt VI and the enactments amending or extending that Part, in so far as relating to residential property tax: s 1104(6).

Revenue information

Information leaflet IT32 — Revenue Audit — Guide for Small Businesses.
Finance Act 1999 — Revenue Powers: Guidance Notes and Instructions, May 1999.
Code of Practice for Revenue Auditors — August 2002 (may be downloaded from Revenue's website at www.revenue.ie).

Statement of Practice

Revenue powers: SP GEN/1/94 (revised February 2006).
Revenue Powers (Finance Act 1999). SP GEN/1/99.
Revenue Internal Review Procedures — Audit and Use of Powers: SP GEN/2/99 (revised January 2005).

Tax Briefing

TB49 Aug 2002 pp 6–13 — Code of Practice Revenue Audits.
TB 59 Apr 2005 p 21 — Clarification on Code of Practice for Revenue Audits — Second Qualifying Disclosure and Mitigation of Penalties.

Case law

Held was a clear implication that the time and place for such inspection set by the taxpayer had to be reasonable: *Johnson v IRC* [1996] STI 270.

Definitions

oath: IA 2005, Sch; person: IA 2005, s 18(*c*); profession: ss 2(1), 5(1); trade: ss 3(1), 4(1), 5(1).

Former enactments

FA 1976, s 34; FA 1992, s 232.

---

906 Authorised officers and Garda Síochána

Where an authorised officer (within the meaning of section 903, 904 or 905, as the case may be) in accordance with section 903, 904 or 905 enters any premises or place, the authorised officer may be accompanied by a member or members of the Garda Síochána, and any such member may arrest without warrant any person who obstructs or interferes with the authorised officer in the exercise or performance of his or her powers or duties under any of those sections.

910 Power to obtain information from Minister of the Government

[(1) For the purposes of the assessment, charge, collection and recovery of any tax or duty placed under their care and management, the Revenue Commissioners may, by notice in writing, request any Minister of the Government or any body established by or under statute to provide them with such information in the possession of that Minister or body in relation to payments for any purposes made by that Minister or by that body, whether on that Minister's or that body's own behalf or on behalf of any other person, to such persons or classes of persons as the Revenue Commissioners may specify in the notice and a Minister of the Government or body of whom or of which such a request is made shall provide such information as may be so specified.]¹

(2) The Revenue Commissioners may nominate any of their officers to perform any acts and discharge any functions authorised by this section to be performed or discharged by the Revenue Commissioners.

Definitions

person: IA 2005, s 18(*c*); tax: s 3(1); writing: IA 2005, Sch.

Former enactments

FA 1995, s 175.

912 Computer documents and records

(1) In this section—

"the Acts" means—

    (*a*) the Customs Acts,

    (*b*) the statutes relating to the duties of excise and to the management of those duties,

    (*c*) the Tax Acts,

    (*d*) the Capital Gains Tax Acts,

    (*e*) the Value Added Tax Act, 1972, and the enactments amending or extending that Act,

    (*f*) the [Capital Acquisitions Tax Consolidation Act 2003],[1] and the enactments amending or extending that Act, and

    (*g*) Part VI of the Finance Act, 1983,

and any instruments made thereunder;

"data" means information in a form in which it can be processed;

"data equipment" means any electronic, photographic, magnetic, optical or other equipment for processing data;

"processing" means performing automatically logical or arithmetical operations on data, or the storing, maintenance, transmission, reproduction or communication of data;

"records" means documents which a person is obliged by any provision of the Acts to keep, issue or produce for inspection, and any other written or printed material;

"software" means any sequence of instructions used in conjunction with data equipment for the purpose of processing data or controlling the operation of the data equipment.

(2) Any provision under the Acts which—

    (*a*) requires a person to keep, retain, issue or produce any records or cause any records to be kept, retained, issued or produced, or

    (*b*) permits an officer of the Revenue Commissioners—

        (i) to inspect any records,

        (ii) to enter premises and search for any records, or

        (iii) to take extracts from or copies of or remove any records,

shall, where the records are processed by data equipment, apply to the data equipment together with any associated software, data, apparatus or material as it applies to the records.

(3) An officer of the Revenue Commissioners may in the exercise or performance of his or her powers or duties require—

(*a*) the person by or on whose behalf the data equipment is or has been used, or

(*b*) any person having charge of, or otherwise concerned with the operation of, the data equipment or any associated apparatus or material,

to afford him or her all reasonable assistance in relation to the exercise or performance of those powers or duties.

Amendments

¹   Substituted by CATCA 2003, s 119 and Sch 3 with effect from 21 February 2003; previously "Capital Acquisitions Tax Act 1976".

Cross-references

This section to be construed together with the Customs Acts, in so far as relating to customs: s 1104(2).

This section to be construed together with the Value Added Tax Acts 1972–1997, in so far as relating to value added tax: s 1104(3).

This section to be construed together with the Capital Acquisitions Tax Act 1976, and the enactments amending or extending that Act, in so far as relating to capital acquisitions tax: s 1104(5).

This section to be construed together with FA 1983, Pt VI and the enactments amending or extending that Part, in so far as relating to residential property tax: s 1104(6).

Use of electronic data processing, meaning of "software" applied: s 887(5)(*a*).

Revenue information

Code of Practice for Revenue Auditors — August 2002 (may be downloaded from Revenue's website at www.revenue.ie).

Statement of Practice

Revenue Powers: SP GEN/1/94 (revised February 2006).

Revenue Internal Review Procedures — Audit and Use of Powers: SP GEN/2/99 (revised January 2005).

Tax Briefing

TB49 Aug 2002 pp 6–13 — Code of Practice Revenue Audits.

TB 59 Apr 2005 p 21 — Clarification on Code of Practice for Revenue Audits — Second Qualifying Disclosure and Mitigation of Penalties.

Definitions

Tax Acts: s 1(2); person: IA 2005, s 18(*c*).

Former enactments

FA 1992, s 237.

[CHAPTER 6
Electronic transmission of returns of income, profits, etc.,
and of other Revenue returns]¹

Amendments

¹   Inserted by FA 1999, s209.

917D Interpretation (Chapter 6)

[(1) In this Chapter—

"the Acts" means—

(*a*) the statutes relating to the duties of excise and to the management of those duties,

(*b*) the Tax Acts,

(c)   the Capital Gains Tax Acts,

(d)   the Value-Added Tax Act, 1972, and the enactments amending or extending that Act,

(e)   the [Capital Acquisitions Tax Consolidation Act 2003][1], and the enactments amending or extending that Act, and

(f)   the Stamp Act, 1891, and the enactments amending or extending that Act,

and any instruments made under any of the statutes and enactments referred to in paragraphs (a) to (f);

"approved person" shall be construed in accordance with section 917G;

"approved transmission" shall be construed in accordance with section 917H;

"authorised person" has the meaning assigned to it by section 917G(3)(b);

[**"digital signature"**, in relation to a person, means an advanced electronic signature (within the meaning of the Electronic Commerce Act, 2000) provided to the person by the Revenue Commissioners solely for the purpose of making an electronic transmission of information which is required to be included in a return to which this Chapter applies and for no other purpose and a qualified certificate (within the meaning of that Act) provided to the person by the Revenue Commissioners or a person appointed in that behalf by the Revenue Commissioners;][2]

[**"electronic identifier"**, in relation to a person, means—

(a)   the person's digital signature, or

(b)   such other means of electronic identification as may be specified or authorised by the Revenue Commissioners for the purposes of this Chapter;][3]

"hard copy", in relation to information held electronically, means a printed out version of that information;

[**"return"** means any return, claim, application, notification, election, declaration, nomination, statement, list, registration, particulars or other information which a person is or may be required by the Acts to give to the Revenue Commissioners or any Revenue officer;][4]

"revenue officer" means the Collector-General, an inspector or other officer of the Revenue Commissioners (including an inspector or other officer who is authorised under any provision of the Acts (however expressed) to receive a return or to require a return to be prepared and delivered);

"tax" means any income tax, corporation tax, capital gains tax, value-added tax, gift tax, inheritance tax, excise duty or stamp duty.

...[5]

(3) Any references in this Chapter to the making of a return include references in any provision of the Acts to—

(a)   the preparing and delivering of a return;

(b)   the sending of a return;

(c)   the furnishing of a return or of particulars;

(d)   the delivering of a return;

(*e*)   the presentation of a return;

(*f*)   the rendering of a return;

(*g*)   the giving of particulars or of any information specified in any provision; and

(*h*)   any other means whereby a return is forwarded, however expressed.][6]

Amendments

[1]   Substituted by CATCA 2003, s 119 and Sch 3 with effect from 21 February 2003; previously "Capital Acquisitions Tax Act 1976".

[2]   Definition of "digital signature" substituted by FA 2001, s 235(*a*)(i)(I) with effect from 15 February 2001.

[3]   Definition of "electronic identifier" inserted by FA 2005, s 22(*a*) with effect from 25 March 2005.

[4]   Definition of "return" substituted by FA 2001, s 235(*a*)(i)(II) with effect from 15 February 2001.

[5]   Subs (2) deleted by FA 2001, s 235(*a*)(ii) with effect from 15 February 2001.

[6]   Section 917D inserted by FA 1999, s 209 with effect from 25 March 1999.

Cross-references

Mandatory electronic filing and payment of tax: s 917EA(2).

Definitions

Collector-General: ss 2(1), 851; person: IA 2005, s 18(*c*).

917E Application

[This Chapter shall apply to a return if—

(*a*)   the provision of the Acts under which the return is made is specified for the purpose of this Chapter by order made by the Revenue Commissioners, and

(*b*)   the return is required to be made after the day appointed by such order in relation to returns to be made under the provision so specified.][1]

Amendments

[1]   Section 917E inserted by FA 1999, s 209 with effect from 25 March 1999.

Notes

The Taxes (Electronic Transmission of Certain Revenue Returns) (Specified Provisions and Appointed Day) Order 2000 (SI 289/2000) specified the following provisions for the purposes of this Chapter:

>   Value Added Tax Act 1972, s 19(3)(*a*) [VAT3]

>   Value Added Tax Act 1972, s 19(3)(*aa*) [VAT3]

>   Income Tax (Employments) Regulations 1960 (SI 28/1960), r 22(1) [P45]

>   Income Tax (Employments) Regulations 1960 (SI 28/1960), r 25(6) [P45]

>   Income Tax (Employments) Regulations 1960 (SI 28/1960), r 31 [P30]

>   Income Tax (Employments) Regulations 1960 (SI 28/1960), r 31A [P30]

and appointed 28 September 2000 as the appointed day in relation to returns to be made under each of those provisions.

The Taxes (Electronic Transmission of Certain Revenue Returns) (Specified Provision and Appointed Day) Order 2001 (SI 112/2001) specified Income Tax (Employments) Regulations 1960 (SI 28/1960), r 35 [P35 and P35L] for the purposes of this Chapter and appointed 5 April 2001 as the appointed day in relation to returns to be made under that provision.

The Taxes (Electronic Transmission of Income Tax and Capital Gains Tax Returns under Self Assessment) (Specified Provision and Appointed Day) Order 2001 (SI 441/2001) specified TCA 1997, s 951(1) other than paragraph (*b*) thereof, for the purposes of this Chapter, and appointed 30 September 2001 as the appointed day in relation to the return (income tax and capital gains tax returns under self assessment) to be made under that section.

The Taxes (Electronic Transmission of Corporation Tax Returns under Self Assessment) (Specified Provision and Appointed Day) Order 2001 (SI 522/2001) specified TCA 1997, s 951(1), for the purposes of this Chapter (in so far as that section had not already been so specified, and appointed 23 November 2001 as the appointed day in relation to the returns (corporation tax returns under self assessment) to be made under that section.

The Taxes (Electronic Transmission of Certain Revenue Returns) (Specified Provisions and Appointed Day) Order 2002 (SI 194/2002) specified TCA 1997, ss 172K(1) (dividend withholding tax), 258(2) (deposit interest retention tax), 525(2) (professional services withholding tax), 730G(2) (life assurance exit tax), 739F(2) (investment undertaking exit tax), 848P (special savings incentive accounts relevant tax — monthly returns) and 848Q (special savings incentive accounts relevant tax — annual returns) for the purposes of this Chapter, and appointed 10 May 2002 as the appointed day in relation to the returns to be made under those sections.

The Taxes (Electronic Transmission of Vehicle Registration Returns) (Specified Provisions and Appointed Day) Order 2002 (SI 464/2002) specified section 131(2)(*a*) of the Finance Act 1992, section 133(2)(*a*) of the Finance Act 1992, Regulation 13(2) of the Vehicle Registration and Taxation Regulations 1992 (SI 318/1992) and Regulation 15 of the Vehicle Registration and Taxation Regulations for the purposes of this Chapter, and appointed 4 October 2002 as the appointed day in relation to returns to be made under those sections and regulations.

The Taxes (Electronic Transmission of Relevant Contracts Returns) (Specified Provisions and Appointed Day) Order 2003 (SI 127/2003) specified TCA 1997, s 531(3A)(*a*) [RCT 30] for the purposes of this Chapter, and appointed 12 April 2003 as the appointed day in relation to returns to be made under that section.

The Taxes (Electronic Transmission of Capital Acquisitions Tax Returns) (Specified Provisions and Appointed Day) Order 2003 (SI 443/2003) specified section section 46 of the Capital Acquisitions Tax Consolidation Act 2003, apart from subsections (3), (7), (13) and (15) thereof, for the purposes of this Chapter, and appointed 28 September 2003 as the appointed day in relation to returns to be made under that section.

The Taxes (Electronic Transmission of Betting Duty Returns) (Specified Provisions and Appointed Day) Order 2004 (SI 803/2004) specified section 70 of the Finance Act 2002 and Paragraphs (1) and (3) of Regulation 5 of the Betting Duty Regulations 2004 for the purposes of this Chapter, and appointed 31 December 2004 as the appointed day in relation to returns to be made under those provisions.

Cross-references

mandatory electronic filing and payment of tax: s 917EA(3)(*a*).

Definitions

the Acts: s 917D; return: s 917D.

917EA Mandatory electronic filing and payment of tax

[(1) In this section—

"electronic means" includes electrical, digital, magnetic, optical, electromagnetic, biometric, photonic means of transmission of data and other forms of related technology by means of which data is transmitted;

"repayment of tax" includes any amount relating to tax which is to be paid or repaid by the Revenue Commissioners;

"specified person" means any person, group of persons or class of persons specified in regulations made under this section for the purposes of either or both paragraphs (*a*) and (*b*) of subsection (3);

"specified return" means a return specified in regulations made under this section;

"specified tax liabilities" means liabilities to tax including interest on unpaid tax specified in regulations made under this section.

(2) Section 917D shall apply for the purposes of regulations made under this section in the same way as it applies for the purposes of this Chapter.

(3) The Revenue Commissioners may make regulations—

    (*a*) requiring the delivery by specified persons of a specified return by electronic means where an order under section 917E has been made in respect of that return,

(b) requiring the payment by electronic means of specified tax liabilities by specified persons, and

(c) for the repayment of any tax specified in the regulations to be made by electronic means.

(4) Regulations made under this section shall include provision for the exclusion of a person from the requirements of regulations made under this section where the Revenue Commissioners are satisfied that the person could not reasonably be expected to have the capacity to make a specified return or to pay the specified tax liabilities by electronic means, and allowing a person, aggrieved by a failure to exclude such person, to appeal that failure to the Appeal Commissioners.

(5) Regulations made under this section may, in particular and without prejudice to the generality of subsection (3), include provision for—

(a) the electronic means to be used to pay or repay tax,

(b) the conditions to be complied with in relation to the electronic payment or repayment of tax,

(c) determining the time when tax paid or repaid using electronic means is to be taken as having been paid or repaid,

(d) the manner of proving, for any purpose, the time of payment or repayment of any tax paid or repaid using electronic means, including provision for the application of any conclusive or other presumptions,

(e) notifying persons that they are specified persons, including the manner by which such notification may be made, and

(f) such supplemental and incidental matters as appear to the Revenue Commissioners to be necessary.

(6) The Revenue Commissioners may nominate any of their officers to perform any acts and discharge any functions authorised by regulation made under this section to be performed or discharged by the Revenue Commissioners.

(7) Where a specified person—

(a) makes a return which is a specified return for the purposes of regulations made under this section, or

(b) makes a payment of tax which is specified tax liabilities for the purposes of regulations made under this section,

in a form other than that required by any such regulation, the specified person shall be liable to a penalty of €1,520 and, for the purposes of the recovery of a penalty under this subsection, section 1061 applies in the same manner as it applies for the purposes of the recovery of a penalty under any of the sections referred to in that section.

(8) Every regulation made under this section shall be laid before Dáil Éireann as soon as may be after it is made and, if a resolution annulling the regulation is passed by Dáil Éireann within the next 21 days on which Dáil Éireann has sat after the regulation is laid before it, the regulation shall be annulled accordingly but without prejudice to the validity of anything previously done under the regulation.][1]

Amendments

[1] Section 917EA inserted by FA 2003, s 164(1)(a) with effect from such day as the Minister for Finance may appoint by order.

Cross-references

Surcharge for late returns: s 1084(1)(*b*)(i*a*).

Definitions

Appeal Commissioners: s 2(1); person: IA 2005, s 18(*c*); return: s 917D; tax: s 917D.

917F Electronic transmission of returns

[(1) Notwithstanding any other provision of the Acts, the obligation of any person to make a return to which this Chapter applies shall be treated as fulfilled by that person if information is transmitted electronically in compliance with that obligation, but only if—

   (*a*)   the transmission is made by an approved person or an authorised person,

   (*b*)   the transmission is an approved transmission,

   [(*c*)   the transmission bears the electronic identifier of that person, and]¹

   (*d*)   the receipt of the transmission is acknowledged in accordance with section 917J.

(2) In subsection (1), the reference to the information which is required to be included in the return includes any requirement on a person to—

   (*a*)   make any statement,

   (*b*)   include any particulars, or

   (*c*)   make or attach any claim.

(3) Where the obligation of any person to make a return to which this Chapter applies is treated as fulfilled in accordance with subsection (1) then, any provision of the Acts which—

   (*a*)   requires that the return include or be accompanied by any description of declaration whatever by the person making the return, apart from a declaration of an amount,

   (*b*)   requires that the return be signed or accompanied by a certificate,

   (*c*)   requires that the return be in writing,

   (*d*)   authorises the return to be signed by a person acting under the authority of the person obliged to make the return,

   (*e*)   authorises the Revenue Commissioners to prescribe the form of a return or which requires a return to be in or on any prescribed form, or

   (*f*)   for the purposes of any claim for exemption or for any allowance, deduction or repayment of tax under the Acts which is required to be made with the return, authorises the Revenue Commissioners to prescribe the form of a claim,

shall not apply.

(4) Where the obligation of any person to make a return to which this Chapter applies is treated as fulfilled in accordance with subsection (1) then, the time at which any requirement under the Acts to make a return is fulfilled shall be the day on which the receipt of the information referred to in that subsection is acknowledged in accordance with section 917J.

[(5) Where an approved transmission is made by—

   (*a*)   an approved person on behalf of another person, or

(*b*) an authorised person on behalf of another person (not being the person who authorised that person),

a hard copy of the information shall be made and authenticated in accordance with section 917K.]²

(6) (*a*) Where the obligation of any person to make a return to which this Chapter applies is treated as fulfilled in accordance with subsection (1) then, any requirement that—

    (i) the return or any claim which is to be made with or attached to the return should be accompanied by any document (in this subsection referred to as a "supporting document") other than the return or the claim, and

    (ii) the supporting document be delivered with the return or the claim,

shall be treated as fulfilled by the person subject to the requirement if the person or the approved person referred to in subsection (1)(*a*) retains the document for inspection on request by a revenue officer.

(*b*) Any person subject to the requirement referred to in paragraph (*a*) shall produce any supporting documents requested by a revenue officer within 30 days of that request.

(*c*) The references in this subsection to a document include references to any accounts, certificate, evidence, receipts, reports or statements.]³

Amendments

¹   Subs (1)(*c*) substituted by FA 2005, s 22(*b*) with effect from 25 March 2005.

²   Subs (5) substituted by FA 2001, s 235(*b*)(ii) with effect from 15 February 2001.

³   Section 917F inserted by FA 1999, s 209 with effect from 25 March 1999.

Cross-references

Electronic claims, PAYE, subs (1): s 864A(9).

Exercise of powers, subs (1): s 917L(1), (3).

Hard copies, subs (1): s 917K(1)(*a*); subs (3): s 917K(2).

Proceedings, subs (1): s 917M(1), (3), (4).

Definitions

the Acts: s 917D(1); approved transmission: s 917D(1); approved person: s 917D(1); authorised person: s 917D(1); digital signature: s 917D(1); hard copy: s 917D(1); person: IA 2005, s 18(*c*); return: s 917D(1); writing: IA 2005, Sch.

917G Approved persons

[(1) A person shall be an approved person for the purposes of this Chapter if the person is approved by the Revenue Commissioners for the purposes of transmitting electronically information which is required to be included in a return to which this Chapter applies (in this section referred to as **"the transmission"**) and [complies with the condition specified in subsection (3)(*a*) in relation to authorised persons and the condition specified in subsection (3)(*b*) in relation to the making of transmissions and the use of [electronic identifiers]¹].²

(2) A person seeking to be approved under this section shall make application in that behalf to the Revenue Commissioners [by such means as the Revenue Commissioners may determine]³ for the purposes of this section.

[(3) The conditions referred to in subsection (1) are that—

(*a*) the person notifies the Revenue Commissioners in a manner to be determined by the Revenue Commissioners of the persons (each of whom is referred to in this section as an **"authorised person"**), in addition to the person, who are authorised to make the transmission, and

(*b*) the person and each person who is an authorised person in relation to that person in making the transmission complies with the requirements referred to in subsections (2) and (3) of section 917H.][4]

(4) A person seeking to be approved under this section shall be given notice by the Revenue Commissioners of the grant or refusal by them of the approval and, in the case of a refusal, of the reason for the refusal.

(5) An approval under this section may be withdrawn by the Revenue Commissioners by notice in writing or by such other means as the Revenue Commissioners may decide with effect from such date as may be specified in the notice.

(6) (*a*) A notice withdrawing an approval under the section shall state the grounds for the withdrawal.

(*b*) No approval under this section may be withdrawn unless an approved person or an authorised person has failed to comply with one or more of the requirements referred to in section 917H(2).

(7) A person who is refused approval under this section or whose approval under this section is withdrawn may appeal to the Appeal Commissioners against the refusal or withdrawal.

(8) The appeal under subsection (7) shall be made by notice to the Revenue Commissioners before the end of the period of 30 days beginning with the day on which notice of the refusal or withdrawal was given to the person.

(9) The Appeal Commissioners shall hear and determine an appeal made to them under subsection (7) as if it were an appeal against an assessment to income tax, and the provisions of the Tax Acts relating to appeals shall apply accordingly.][5]

Amendments

[1]   Substituted by FA 2005, s 22(*c*) with effect from 25 March 2005; previously "digital signatures".

[2]   Substituted by FA 2001, s 235(*c*)(i) with effect from 15 February 2001; previously "complies with the provisions of this section and, in particular, with the conditions specified in subsection (3)".

[3]   Subs (3) substituted by FA 2001, s 235(*c*)(ii) with effect from 15 February 2001; previously "in writing or by such other means as may be approved by the Revenue Commissioners".

[4]   Subs (3) substituted by FA 2001, s 235(*c*)(iii) with effect from 15 February 2001.

[5]   Section 917G inserted by FA 1999, s 209.

Cross-references

Interpretation, meaning of "approved person" and "authorised person" applied for Chapter: s 917D(1).

Definitions

Appeal Commissioners: ss 2(1), 850; approved person: s 917D(1); authorised person: s 917D(1); person: IA 2005, s 18(*c*); Tax Acts: s 1(2); writing: IA 2005, Sch.

917H Approved transmissions

[(1) Where an approved person transmits electronically information which is required to be included in a return to which this Chapter applies the transmission shall not be an approved transmission unless it complies with the requirements of this section.

[(2) The Revenue Commissioners shall publish and make known to each approved person and each authorised person any requirement for the time being determined by them as being applicable to—

    (*a*) the manner in which information which is required to be included in a return to which this Chapter applies is to be transmitted electronically, and

    (*b*) the use of a person's [electronic identifier][1].

(3) The requirements referred to in subsection (2) include—

    (*a*) requirements as to the software or type of software to be used to make a transmission,

    (*b*) the terms and conditions under which a person may make a transmission, and

    (*c*) the terms and conditions under which a person may use that person's [electronic identifier][1].][2]][3]

[(4) For the purposes of subsection (3), the Revenue Commissioners may determine different terms and conditions in relation to different returns or categories of a return, different categories of persons and different returns or categories of a return made by different categories of persons.][4]

Amendments

[1]   Substituted by FA 2005, s 22(*d*)(i) with effect from 25 March 2005; previously "digital signature".
[2]   Subss (2)–(3) substituted by FA 2001, s 235(*d*) with effect from 15 February 2001.
[3]   Section 917H inserted by FA 1999, s 209 with effect from 25 March 1999.
[4]   Subs (4) inserted by FA 2005, s 22(*d*)(ii) with effect from 25 March 2005.

Cross-references

Approved person, subs (2): s 917G(3)(*b*), (6)(*b*); subs (3): s 917G(3)(*b*).
Interpretation, meaning of "approved transmission" applied for Chapter: s 917A(1).

Definitions

approved person: s 917D(1); authorised person: s 917D(1); digital signature: s 917D(1); return: s 917D(1).

917I Digital signatures

Amendments

Section 917I deleted by FA 2001, s 235(*e*) with effect from 15 February 2001.

917J Acknowledgement of electronic transmissions

[For the purposes of this Chapter, where an electronic transmission of information which is required to be included in a return to which this Chapter applies is received by the Revenue Commissioners, the Revenue Commissioners shall send an electronic acknowledgement of receipt of that transmission to the person from whom it was received.][1]

Amendments

[1]   Section 917J inserted by FA 1999, s 209 with effect from 25 March 1999.

Cross-references

Electronic transmission of returns: s 917F(1)(*d*), (4).

Definitions

person: IA 2005, s 18(*c*); return: s 917D(1).

917K Hard copies

[(1) A hard copy shall be made in accordance with this subsection only if—

(*a*) the hard copy is made under processes and procedures which are designed to ensure that the information contained in the hard copy shall only be the information [transmitted or to be transmitted][1] in accordance with section 917F(1),

(*b*) the hard copy is in a form approved by the Revenue Commissioners which is appropriate to the information so transmitted, and

(*c*) the hard copy is authenticated in accordance with subsection (2).

(2) For the purposes of this Chapter, a hard copy made in accordance with subsection (1) shall be authenticated only if the hard copy is signed by the person who would have been required to make the declaration, sign the return or furnish the certificate, as the case may be, but for paragraph (*a*), (*b*) or (*d*) of section 917F(3).][2]

Amendments

1   Substituted by FA 2001, s 235(*f*) with effect from 15 February 2001; previously "to be transmitted".

2   Section 917K inserted by FA 1999, s 209 with effect from 25 March 1999.

Cross-references

Electronic transmission of returns: s 917F(5).

Definitions

person: IA 2005, s 18(*c*); return: s 917D(1).

917L Exercise of powers

[(1) This section shall apply where the obligation of any person to make a return to which this Chapter applies is treated as fulfilled in accordance with section 917F(1).

(2) Where this section applies the Revenue Commissioners and a revenue officer shall have all the powers and duties in relation to the information contained in the transmission as they or that officer would have had if the information had been contained in a return made by post.

(3) Where this section applies the person whose obligation to make a return to which this Chapter applies is treated as fulfilled in accordance with section 917F(1) shall have all the rights and duties in relation to the information contained in the transmission as the person would have had if that information had been contained in a return made by post.][1]

Amendments

1   Section 917L inserted by FA 1999, s 209 with effect from 25 March 1999.

Definitions

person: IA 2005, s 18(3); return: s 917D(1); Revenue officer: s 917D(1).

917M Proceedings

[(1) This section shall apply where the obligation of any person to make a return to which this Chapter applies is treated as fulfilled in accordance with section 917F(1).

(2) In this section, **"proceedings"** means civil and criminal proceedings, and includes proceedings before the Appeal Commissioners or any other tribunal having jurisdiction by virtue of any provision of the Acts.

(3) Where this section applies a hard copy certified by a revenue officer to be a true copy of the information transmitted electronically in accordance with section 917F(1) shall be treated [for the purposes of the Acts][1] as if the hard copy—

    (*a*)   were a return or, as the case may be, a claim made by post, and

    (*b*)   contained any declaration, certificate or signature required by the Acts on such a return or, as the case may be, such a claim.

(4) For the purposes of any proceedings under the Acts, unless a Judge or any other person before whom proceedings are taken determines at the time of the proceedings that it is unjust in the circumstances to apply this provision, any rule of law restricting the admissibility or use of hearsay evidence shall not apply to a representation contained in a document recording information which has been transmitted in accordance with section 917F(1) in so far as the representation is a representation as to—

    (*a*)   the information so transmitted,

    (*b*)   the date on which, or the time at which, the information was so transmitted, or

    (*c*)   the identity of the person by whom or on whose behalf the information was so transmitted.][2]

Amendments

[1]   Substituted by FA 2001, s 235(*g*) with effect from 15 February 2001; previously "for the purposes of any proceedings in relation to which the certificate is given".

[2]   Section 917M inserted by FA 1999, s 209 with effect from 25 March 1999.

Cross-references

Electronic claims, PAYE, application of this section in respect of proceedings in relation to s 864A in the same manner as this section applies in respect of proceedings in relation to Chapter 6 of Part 38, subject to any necessary modifications including substituting in this section a reference to s 864A for a reference to s 917F(1) in each place where it occurs: s 864A(9).

Definitions

the Acts: s 917D(1); Appeal Commissioners: ss 2(1), 850; hard copy: s 917D(1); person: IA 2005, s 18(*c*); return: s 917D(1); Revenue officer: s 917D(1).

917N Miscellaneous

[The Revenue Commissioners may nominate any of their officers to perform any acts and discharge any functions authorised by this Chapter to be performed or discharged by the Revenue Commissioners.][1]

Amendments

[1]   Section 917N inserted by FA 1999, s 209 with effect from 25 March 1999.

PART 39
ASSESSMENTS

Cross-references
Rectification of excessive set off etc, of tax credit: s 927(1).

CHAPTER 1
Income tax and corporation tax

928 Transmission to Collector-General of particulars of sums to be collected

(1) After assessments to income tax and corporation tax have been made, the inspectors shall transmit particulars of the sums to be collected to the Collector-General for collection.

(2) The entering by an inspector or other authorised officer of details of an assessment to income tax or corporation tax and of the tax charged in such an assessment in an electronic, photographic or other record from which the Collector-General may extract such details by electronic, photographic or other process shall constitute transmission of such details by the inspector or other authorised officer to the Collector-General.

(3) Subsection (2) shall apply for the purposes of Value Added tax as it applies for the purposes of income tax or corporation tax with the substitution of "Value Added tax" for "income tax or corporation tax".

Cross-references
Capital acquisitions tax, application of certain income tax provisions in relation to collection and recovery of, subs (1): CATCA 2003, s 64(3).
Capital gains tax, applied by: s 931(3).
Collection of capital gains tax: s 976(1).
Collector-General: s 851(2).
Corporation tax, subs (1): s 973.
Evidence of electronic transmission of particulars of income tax to be collected in proceedings for recovery of tax, subs (2): s 967.
Generation of estimates by electronic, photographic or other process. s 990A(*b*).
Income Tax (Relevant Contracts) Regulations 2000, SI No 71 of 2000: ITRCR 2000 Reg 15(2).
Subss (2)–(3) to be construed together with the Value Added Tax Acts 1972–1997, in so far as relating to value added tax: s 1104(3).
Definitions
inspector: ss 2(1), 5(1), 852.
Former enactments
ITA 1967, s 187(1); FA 1974, s 86 and Sch 2 Pt I; CTA 1976, s 147(1)–(2); FA 1986, s 113(5); FA 1996, s 132(2) and Sch 5 Pt II.

PART 42
COLLECTION AND RECOVERY

CHAPTER 5
Miscellaneous provisions

1001 Liability to tax, etc of holder of fixed charge on book debts of company

(1) In this section, **"relevant amount"** means any amount which the company is liable to remit under—
  (*a*)   Chapter 4 of this Part, and
  (*b*)   the Value Added Tax Act, 1972.

(2) Subject to this section, where a person holds a fixed charge (being a fixed charge created on or after the 27th day of May, 1986) on the book debts of a company (within the meaning of the Companies Act, 1963), such person shall, if the company fails to pay any relevant amount for which it is liable, become liable to pay such relevant amount on due demand, and on neglect or refusal of payment may be proceeded against in the like manner as any other defaulter.

(3) This section shall not apply—

(a) unless the holder of the fixed charge has been notified in writing by the Revenue Commissioners that a company has failed to pay a relevant amount for which it is liable and that by virtue of this section the holder of the fixed charge—

(i) may become liable for payment of any relevant amount which the company subsequently fails to pay, and

(ii) where paragraph (c) does not apply, has become liable for the payment of the relevant amount which the company has failed to pay,

(b) to any amounts received by the holder of the fixed charge from the company before the date on which the holder is notified in writing by the Revenue Commissioners in accordance with paragraph (a), and

(c) where, within the period from the 2nd day of June, 1995, to the 22nd day of June, 1995, or within 21 days of the creation of the fixed charge, whichever is the later, the holder of the fixed charge furnishes to the Revenue Commissioners a copy of the prescribed particulars of the charge delivered or to be delivered to the registrar of companies in accordance with section 99 of the Companies Act, 1963, to any relevant amount which the company was liable to pay before the date on which the holder is notified in writing by the Revenue Commissioners in accordance with paragraph (a).

(4) The amount or aggregate amount which a person shall be liable to pay in relation to a company in accordance with this section shall not exceed the amount or aggregate amount which the person has, while the fixed charge on book debts in relation to the company is in existence, received directly or indirectly from that company in payment or in part payment of any debts due by the company to the person.

(5) The Revenue Commissioners may, at any time and by notice in writing given to the holder of the fixed charge, withdraw with effect from a date specified in the notice a notification issued by them in accordance with subsection (3); but such withdrawal shall not—

(a) affect in any way any liability of the holder of the fixed charge under this section which arose before such withdrawal, or

(b) preclude the issue under subsection (3) of a subsequent notice to the holder of the fixed charge.

(6) The Revenue Commissioners may nominate any of their officers to perform any acts and discharge any functions authorised by this section to be performed or discharged by the Revenue Commissioners.

Cross-references

This section to be construed together with the Value Added Tax Acts 1972–1997, in so far as relating to value added tax: s 1104(3).

Definitions

company: ss 4(1), 5(1); person: IA 2005, s 18(*c*); writing: IA 2005, Sch.

Former enactments

FA 1986, s 115; FA 1995, s 174.

1002 Deduction from payments due to defaulters of amounts due in relation to tax

(1) (*a*)   In this section, except where the context otherwise requires—

"**the Acts**" means—

(i)   the Customs Acts,

(ii)   the statutes relating to the duties of excise and to the management of those duties,

(iii)   the Tax Acts,

(iv)   the Capital Gains Tax Acts,

(v)   the Value Added Tax Act, 1972, and the enactments amending or extending that Act,

(vi)   the [Capital Acquisitions Tax Consolidation Act 2003],[1] and the enactments amending or extending that Act, and

(vii)   the [Stamp Duties Consolidation Act, 1999],[2] and the enactments amending or extending that Act,

and any instruments made thereunder;

"**additional debt**", in relation to a relevant person who has received a notice of attachment in respect of a taxpayer, means any amount which, at any time after the time of the receipt by the relevant person of the notice of attachment but before the end of the relevant period in relation to the notice, would be a debt due by the relevant person to the taxpayer if a notice of attachment were received by the relevant person at that time;

"**debt**", in relation to a notice of attachment given to a relevant person in respect of a taxpayer and in relation to that relevant person and taxpayer, means, subject to paragraphs (*b*) to (*e*), the amount or aggregate amount of any money which, at the time the notice of attachment is received by the relevant person, is due by the relevant person (whether on that person's own account or as an agent or trustee) to the taxpayer, irrespective of whether the taxpayer has applied for the payment (to the taxpayer or any other person) or for the withdrawal of all or part of the money;

"**deposit**" means a sum of money paid to a financial institution on terms under which it will be repaid with or without interest and either on demand or at a time or in circumstances agreed by or on behalf of the person making the payment and the financial institution to which it is made;

"**emoluments**" means anything assessable to income tax under Schedule E;

"**financial institution**" means a holder of a licence issued under section 9 of the Central Bank Act, 1971, or a person referred to in section 7(4) of that Act, and includes a branch of a financial institution which records deposits in its books as liabilities of the branch;

"further return" means a return made by a relevant person under subsection (4);

"interest on unpaid tax", in relation to a specified amount specified in a notice of attachment, means interest that has accrued to the date on which the notice of attachment is given under any provision of the Acts providing for the charging of interest in respect of the unpaid tax, including interest on an undercharge of tax which is attributable to fraud or neglect, specified in the notice of attachment;

"notice of attachment" means a notice under subsection (2);

"notice of revocation" means a notice under subsection (10);

"penalty" means a monetary penalty imposed on a taxpayer under a provision of the Acts;

"relevant period", in relation to a notice of attachment, means, as respects the relevant person to whom the notice of attachment is given, the period commencing at the time at which the notice is received by the relevant person and ending on the earliest of—

(i) the date on which the relevant person completes the payment to the Revenue Commissioners out of the debt, or the aggregate of the debt and any additional debt, due by the relevant person to the taxpayer named in the notice, of an amount equal to the specified amount in relation to the taxpayer,

(ii) the date on which the relevant person receives a notice of revocation of the notice of attachment, and

(iii) where the relevant person or the taxpayer named in the notice—

    (I) is declared bankrupt, the date the relevant person or the taxpayer is so declared, or

    (II) is a company which commences to be wound up, the relevant date within the meaning of section 285 of the Companies Act, 1963, in relation to the winding up;

"relevant person", in relation to a taxpayer, means a person whom the Revenue Commissioners have reason to believe may have, at the time a notice of attachment is received by such person in respect of a taxpayer, a debt due to the taxpayer;

"return" means a return made by a relevant person under subsection (2)(*a*)(iii);

"specified amount" has the meaning assigned to it by subsection (2)(*a*)(ii);

"tax" means any tax, duty, levy or charge which in accordance with any provision of the Acts is placed under the care and management of the Revenue Commissioners;

"taxpayer" means a person who is liable to pay, remit or account for tax to the Revenue Commissioners under the Acts.

(*b*) Where a relevant person is a financial institution, any amount or aggregate amount of money, including interest on that money, which at the time the notice of attachment is received by the relevant person is a deposit held by the relevant person—

   (i) to the credit of the taxpayer for the taxpayer's sole benefit, or

   (ii) to the credit of the taxpayer and any other person or persons for their joint benefit,

   shall be regarded as a debt due by the relevant person to the taxpayer at that time.

(*c*) Any amount of money due by the relevant person to the taxpayer as emoluments under a contract of service shall not be regarded as a debt due to the taxpayer.

(*d*) Where there is a dispute as to an amount of money which is due by the relevant person to the taxpayer, the amount in dispute shall be disregarded for the purposes of determining the amount of the debt.

(*e*) In the case referred to in paragraph (*b*), a deposit held by a relevant person which is a financial institution to the credit of the taxpayer and any other person or persons (in this paragraph referred to as **"the other party or parties"**) for their joint benefit shall be deemed (unless evidence to the contrary is produced to the satisfaction of the relevant person within 10 days of the giving of the notices specified in subsection (2)(*e*)) to be held to the benefit of the taxpayer and the other party or parties to the deposit equally, and accordingly only the portion of the deposit so deemed shall be regarded as a debt due by the relevant person to the taxpayer at the time the notice of attachment is received by the relevant person and, where such evidence is produced within the specified time, only so much of the deposit as is shown to be held to the benefit of the taxpayer shall be regarded as a debt due by the relevant person to the taxpayer at that time.

(2) (*a*) Subject to subsection (3), where a taxpayer has made default whether before or after the passing of this Act in paying, remitting or accounting for any tax, interest on unpaid tax, or penalty to the Revenue Commissioners, the Revenue Commissioners may, if the taxpayer has not made good the default, give to a relevant person in relation to the taxpayer a notice in writing (in this section referred to as **"the notice of attachment"**) in which is entered—

   (i) the taxpayer's name and address,

   (ii) (I) the amount or aggregate amount, or

      (II) in a case where more than one notice of attachment is given to a relevant person or relevant persons in respect of a taxpayer, a portion of the amount or aggregate amount,

   of the taxes, interest on unpaid taxes and penalties in respect of which the taxpayer is in default at the time of the giving of the notice or notices of attachment (the amount, aggregate amount, or portion of the amount or aggregate amount, as the case may be, being referred to in this section as **"the specified amount"**), and

    (iii)   a direction to the relevant person—

        (I)   subject to paragraphs (*b*) and (*c*), to deliver to the Revenue Commissioners, within the period of 10 days from the time at which the notice of attachment is received by the relevant person, a return in writing specifying whether or not any debt is due by the relevant person to the taxpayer at the time the notice is received by the relevant person and, if any debt is so due, specifying the amount of the debt, and

        (II)   if the amount of any debt is so specified, to pay to the Revenue Commissioners within the period referred to in clause (I) a sum equal to the amount of the debt so specified.

(*b*)   Where the amount of the debt due by the relevant person to the taxpayer is equal to or greater than the specified amount in relation to the taxpayer, the amount of the debt specified in the return shall be an amount equal to the specified amount.

(*c*)   Where the relevant person is a financial institution and the debt due by the relevant person to the taxpayer is part of a deposit held to the credit of the taxpayer and any other person or persons to their joint benefit, the return shall be made within a period of 10 days from—

    (i)   the expiry of the period specified in the notices to be given under paragraph (*e*), or

    (ii)   the production of the evidence referred to in paragraph (*e*)(II).

(*d*)   A relevant person to whom a notice of attachment has been given shall comply with the direction in the notice.

(*e*)   Where a relevant person which is a financial institution is given a notice of attachment and the debt due by the relevant person to the taxpayer is part of a deposit held by the relevant person to the credit of the taxpayer and any other person or persons (in this paragraph referred to as **"the other party or parties"**) for their joint benefit, the relevant person shall on receipt of the notice of attachment give to the taxpayer and the other party or parties to the deposit a notice in writing in which is entered—

    (i)   the taxpayer's name and address,

    (ii)   the name and address of the person to whom a notice under this paragraph is given,

    (iii)   the name and address of the relevant person, and

    (iv)   the specified amount,

    and which states that—

    (I)   a notice of attachment under this section has been received in respect of the taxpayer,

    (II)   under this section a deposit is deemed (unless evidence to the contrary is produced to the satisfaction of the relevant person within 10 days of the giving of the notice under this paragraph) to be held to the benefit of the taxpayer and the other party or parties to the deposit equally, and

(III)   unless such evidence is produced within the period specified in the notice given under this paragraph—

(A)   a sum equal to the amount of the deposit so deemed to be held to the benefit of the taxpayer (and accordingly regarded as a debt due to the taxpayer by the relevant person) shall be paid to the Revenue Commissioners, where that amount is equal to or less than the specified amount, and

(B)   where the amount of the deposit so deemed to be held to the benefit of the taxpayer (and accordingly regarded as a debt due to the taxpayer by the relevant person) is greater than the specified amount, a sum equal to the specified amount shall be paid to the Revenue Commissioners.

(3) An amount in respect of tax, interest on unpaid tax or a penalty, as respects which a taxpayer is in default as specified in subsection (2), shall not be entered in a notice of attachment unless—

(*a*)   a period of [14 days]³ has expired from the date on which such default commenced, and

(*b*)   the Revenue Commissioners have given the taxpayer a notice in writing (whether or not the document containing the notice also contains other information being communicated by the Revenue Commissioners to the taxpayer), not later than 7 days before the date of the receipt by the relevant person or relevant persons concerned of a notice of attachment, stating that if the amount is not paid it may be specified in a notice or notices of attachment and recovered under this section from a relevant person or relevant persons in relation to the taxpayer.

(4) If, when a relevant person receives a notice of attachment, the amount of the debt due by the relevant person to the taxpayer named in the notice is less than the specified amount in relation to the taxpayer or no debt is so due and, at any time after the receipt of the notice and before the end of the relevant period in relation to the notice, an additional debt becomes due by the relevant person to the taxpayer, the relevant person shall within 10 days of that time—

(*a*)   if the aggregate of the amount of any debt so due and the additional debt so due is equal to or less than the specified amount in relation to the taxpayer—

(i)   deliver a further return to the Revenue Commissioners specifying the additional debt, and

(ii)   pay to the Revenue Commissioners the amount of the additional debt,

and so on for each subsequent occasion during the relevant period in relation to the notice of attachment on which an additional debt becomes due by the relevant person to the taxpayer until—

(I)   the aggregate amount of the debt and the additional debt or debts so due equals the specified amount in relation to the taxpayer, or

(II)   paragraph (*b*) applies in relation to an additional debt, and

(b) if the aggregate amount of any debt and the additional debt or debts so due to the taxpayer is greater than the specified amount in relation to the taxpayer—

    (i) deliver a further return to the Revenue Commissioners specifying such portion of the latest additional debt as when added to the aggregate of the debt and any earlier additional debts is equal to the specified amount in relation to the taxpayer, and

    (ii) pay to the Revenue Commissioners that portion of the additional debt.

(5) Where a relevant person delivers, either fraudulently or negligently, an incorrect return or further return that purports to be a return or further return made in accordance with this section, the relevant person shall be deemed to be guilty of an offence under section 1078.

(6) (a) Where a notice of attachment has been given to a relevant person in respect of a taxpayer, the relevant person shall not, during the relevant period in relation to the notice, make any disbursements out of the debt, or out of any additional debt, due by the relevant person to the taxpayer except to the extent that any such disbursement—

    (i) will not reduce the debt or the aggregate of the debt and any additional debts so due to an amount that is less than the specified amount in relation to the taxpayer, or

    (ii) is made pursuant to an order of a court.

(b) For the purposes of this section, a disbursement made by a relevant person contrary to paragraph (a) shall be deemed not to reduce the amount of the debt or any additional debts due by the relevant person to the taxpayer.

(7) (a) Sections 1052 and 1054 shall apply to a failure by a relevant person to deliver a return required by a notice of attachment within the time specified in the notice or to deliver a further return within the time specified in subsection (4) as they apply to a failure to deliver a return referred to in section 1052.

(b) A certificate signed by an officer of the Revenue Commissioners which certifies that he or she has examined the relevant records and that it appears from those records that during a specified period a specified return was not received from a relevant person shall be evidence until the contrary is proved that the relevant person did not deliver the return during that period.

(c) A certificate certifying as provided by paragraph (b) and purporting to be signed by an officer of the Revenue Commissioners may be tendered in evidence without proof and shall be deemed until the contrary is proved to have been so signed.

(8) Where a relevant person to whom a notice of attachment in respect of a taxpayer has been given—

(a) delivers the return required to be delivered by that notice but fails to pay to the Revenue Commissioners within the time specified in the notice the amount specified in the return or any part of that amount, or

(b) delivers a further return under subsection (4) but fails to pay to the Revenue Commissioners within the time specified in that subsection the amount specified in the further return or any part of that amount, the amount specified in the return or further return or the part of that amount, as the case may be, which the relevant person has failed to pay to the Revenue Commissioners may, if the notice of attachment has not been revoked by a notice of revocation, be sued for and recovered by action or other appropriate proceedings at the suit of an officer of the Revenue Commissioners in any court of competent jurisdiction.

(9) Nothing in this section shall be construed as rendering any failure by a relevant person to make a return or further return required by this section, or to pay to the Revenue Commissioners the amount or amounts required by this section to be paid by the relevant person, liable to be treated as a failure to which section 1078 applies.

(10)(*a*)   A notice of attachment given to a relevant person in respect of a taxpayer may be revoked by the Revenue Commissioners at any time by notice in writing given to the relevant person and shall be revoked forthwith if the taxpayer has paid the specified amount to the Revenue Commissioners.

 (*b*)   Where in pursuance of this section a relevant person pays any amount to the Revenue Commissioners out of a debt or an additional debt due by the relevant person to the taxpayer and, at the time of the receipt by the Revenue Commissioners of that amount, the taxpayer has paid to the Revenue Commissioners the amount or aggregate amount of the taxes, interest on unpaid taxes and penalties in respect of which the taxpayer is in default at the time of the giving of the notice or notices of attachment, the first-mentioned amount shall be refunded by the Revenue Commissioners forthwith to the taxpayer.

(11) Where a notice of attachment or a notice of revocation is given to a relevant person in relation to a taxpayer, a copy of such notice shall be given by the Revenue Commissioners to the taxpayer forthwith.

(12)(*a*)   Where in pursuance of this section any amount is paid to the Revenue Commissioners by a relevant person, the relevant person shall forthwith give the taxpayer concerned a notice in writing specifying the payment, its amount and the reason for which it was made.

 (*b*)   On the receipt by the Revenue Commissioners of an amount paid in pursuance of this section, the Revenue Commissioners shall forthwith notify the taxpayer and the relevant person in writing of such receipt.

(13) Where in pursuance of this section a relevant person pays to the Revenue Commissioners the whole or part of the amount of a debt or an additional debt due by the relevant person to a taxpayer, or any portion of such an amount, the taxpayer shall allow such payment and the relevant person shall be acquitted and discharged of the amount of the payment as if it had been paid to the taxpayer.

(14) Where in pursuance of this section a relevant person is prohibited from making any disbursement out of a debt or an additional debt due to a taxpayer, no action shall lie against the relevant person in any court by reason of a failure to make any such disbursement.

(15) Any obligation on the Revenue Commissioners to maintain secrecy or any other restriction on the disclosure of information by the Revenue Commissioners shall not apply in relation to information contained in a notice of attachment.

(16) A notice of attachment in respect of a taxpayer shall not be given to a relevant person at a time when the relevant person or the taxpayer is an undischarged bankrupt or a company being wound up.

(17) The Revenue Commissioners may nominate any of their officers to perform any acts and discharge any functions authorised by this section to be performed or discharged by the Revenue Commissioners.

Amendments

1   Substituted by CATCA 2003, s 119 and Sch 3 with effect from 21 February 2003; previously "Capital Acquisitions Tax Act 1976".

2   Substituted by SDCA 1999, s 162 and Sch 4 with effect from 15 December 1999; previously "Stamp Act, 1891".

3   Substituted by FA 2001, s 238 with effect from 6 April 2001; previously "one month".

Cross-references

Taxes (Offset of Repayments) Regulations 2002, SI 471/2002, reg 2(1) (interpretation — liability at enforcement" para (*c*)).

This section to be construed together with the Customs Acts, in so far as relating to customs: s 1104(2).

This section to be construed together with the Value Added Tax Acts 1972–1997, in so far as relating to value added tax: s 1104(3).

This section to be construed together with the Stamp Act 1891 and the enactments amending or extending that Act, in so far as relating to stamp duties: s 1104(4).

This section to be construed together with the Capital Acquisitions Tax Act 1976, and the enactments amending or extending that Act, in so far as relating to capital acquisitions tax: s 1104(5).

Penalty, subss (2)(*a*)(iii)(I), (*c*), (4)(*a*)(i), (*b*)(i): Sch 29 column 1.

Definitions

company: ss 4(1), 5(1); person: IA 2005, s 18(*c*); Tax Acts: s 1(2); writing: IA 2005, Sch.

Former enactments

FA 1988, s 73(1)(*b*)–(16) and (18); FA 1992, s 241(*a*)–(*d*).

1006 Poundage and certain other fees due to sheriffs or county registrars

(1) In this section—

"the Acts" means—

    (*a*)   the Tax Acts,

    (*b*)   the Capital Gains Tax Acts,

    (*c*)   the Value Added Tax Act, 1972, and the enactments amending or extending that Act,

    (*d*)   the [Capital Acquisitions Tax Consolidation Act 2003],[1] and the enactments amending or extending that Act, and

    (*e*)   Part VI of the Finance Act, 1983, and the enactments amending or extending that Part,

and any instruments made thereunder;

"certificate" means a certificate issued under section 962;

"county registrar" means a person appointed to be a county registrar under section 35 of the Court Officers Act, 1926;

"defaulter" means a person specified or certified in an execution order or certificate on whom a relevant amount specified or certified in the order or certificate is leviable;

"**execution order**" has the same meaning as in the Enforcement of Court Orders Act, 1926;

"**fees**" means the fees known as poundage fees payable under section 14(1) of the Enforcement of Court Orders Act, 1926, and orders made under that section for services in or about the execution of an execution order directing or authorising the execution of an order of a court by the seizure and sale of a person's property or, as may be appropriate, the fees corresponding to those fees payable under section 962 for the execution of a certificate;

"**interest on unpaid tax**" means interest which has accrued under any provision of the Acts providing for the charging of interest in respect of unpaid tax, including interest on an undercharge of tax which is attributable to fraud or neglect;

"**relevant amount**" means an amount of tax or interest on unpaid tax;

"**tax**" means any tax, duty, levy or charge which, in accordance with any provision of the Acts, is placed under the care and management of the Revenue Commissioners;

references, as respects an execution order, to a relevant amount include references to any amount of costs specified in the order.

(2) Where—

    (*a*) an execution order or certificate specifying or certifying a defaulter and relating to a relevant amount is lodged with the appropriate sheriff or county registrar for execution,

    (*b*) the sheriff or, as the case may be, the county registrar gives notice to the defaulter of the lodgment or of his or her intention to execute the execution order or certificate by seizure of the property of the defaulter to which it relates, or demands payment by the defaulter of the relevant amount, and

    (*c*) the whole or part of the relevant amount is paid to the sheriff or, as the case may be, the county registrar or to the Collector-General, after the giving of that notice or the making of that demand,

then, for the purpose of the liability of the defaulter for the payment of fees and of the exercise of any rights or powers in relation to the collection of fees for the time being vested by law in sheriffs and county registrars—

    (i) the sheriff or, as the case may be, the county registrar shall be deemed to have entered, in the execution of the execution order or certificate, into possession of the property referred to in paragraph (*b*), and

    (ii) the payment mentioned in paragraph (*c*) shall be deemed to have been levied, in the execution of the execution order or certificate, by the sheriff or, as the case may be, the county registrar,

and fees shall be payable by the defaulter to such sheriff or, as the case may be, country registrar accordingly in respect of the payment mentioned in paragraph (*c*).

Amendments

1   Substituted by CATCA 2003, s 119 and Sch 3 with effect from 21 February 2003; previously "Capital Acquisitions Tax Act, 1976".

Cross-references

This section to be construed together with the Value Added Tax Acts 1972–1997, in so far as relating to value added tax: s 1104(3).

This section to be construed together with the Capital Acquisitions Tax Act 1976, and the enactments amending or extending that Act, in so far as relating to capital acquisitions tax: s 1104(5).

This section to be construed together with FA 1983, Pt VI and the enactments amending or extending that Part, in so far as relating to residential property tax: s 1104(6).

Definitions

person: IA 2005, s 18(*c*); Tax Acts: s 1(2).

Former enactments

FA 1988, s 71(1)–(2)(*a*).

1006A Offset between taxes

[(1) In this section—

"**Acts**" means

  (*a*) the Tax Acts,

  (*b*) the Capital Gains Tax Acts,

  (*c*) the Value Added Tax Act, 1972, and the enactments amending or extending that Act,

  (*d*) the statutes relating to the duties of excise and to the management of those duties,

  (*e*) the [Capital Acquisitions Tax Consolidation Act 2003],¹ and the enactments amending or extending that Act,

  (*f*) the Stamp Duties Consolidation Act, 1999,

  (*g*) Part VI of the Finance Act, 1983, and the enactments amending or extending that Part,

  (*h*) Chapter IV of Part II of the Finance Act, 1992,

and any instrument made thereunder;

[**"claim"** means a claim that gives rise to either or both a repayment of tax and a payment of interest payable in respect of such a repayment under any of the Acts and includes part of such a claim;]²

[**"liability"** means any tax due or estimated to be due under the Acts for any period or in respect of any event, as may be appropriate in the circumstances, and includes any interest due under the Acts in respect of that tax;]³

"overpayment" means a payment or remittance under the Acts (including part of such a payment or remittance) which is in excess of the amount of the liability against which it is [credited;]⁴

[**"tax"** means any tax, duty, levy or other charge under any of the Acts.]⁵

[(2) Notwithstanding any other provision of the Acts, where the Revenue Commissioners are satisfied that a person has not complied with the obligations imposed on the person by the Acts, in relation to either or both—

  (*a*) the payment of a liability required to be paid, and

(*b*) the delivery of returns required to be made,

they may, in a case where a repayment is due to the person in respect of a claim or overpayment—

(i) where paragraph (*a*) applies, or where paragraphs (*a*) and (*b*) apply, instead of making the repayment set the amount of the claim or overpayment against any liability due under the Acts, and

(ii) where paragraph (*b*) only applies, withhold making the repayment until such time as the returns required to be delivered have been delivered.

(2A) Where the Revenue Commissioners have set or withheld a repayment by virtue of subsection (2), they shall give notice in writing to that effect to the person concerned and, where subsection (2)(ii) applies, interest shall not be payable under any provision of the Acts from the date of such notice in respect of any repayment so withheld.][6]

(3) The Revenue Commissioners shall make regulations for the purpose of giving effect to this section and, without prejudice to the generality of the foregoing, such regulations shall provide for the order of priority of liabilities due under the Acts against which any claim or overpayment is to be set in accordance with subsection (2).

(4) Every regulation made under this section shall be laid before Dáil Éireann as soon as may be after it is made and, if a resolution annulling the regulation is passed by Dáil Éireann within the next 21 days on which Dáil Éireann has sat after the regulation is laid before it, the regulation shall be annulled accordingly, but without prejudice to the validity of anything previously done thereunder.

[(5) Any act to be performed or function to be discharged (other than the making of regulations) by the Revenue Commissioners which is authorised by this section may be performed or discharged by any of their officers acting under their authority.][7]][8]

Amendments

[1] Substituted by CATCA 2003, s 119 and Sch 3 with effect from 21 February 2003; previously "Capital Acquisitions Tax Act 1976".

[2] Definition of "claim" substituted by FA 2002, s 125(*a*)(i)(I) with effect from 25 March 2002.

[3] Definition of "liability" substituted by FA 2002, s 125(*a*)(i)(II) with effect from 25 March 2002.

[4] Substituted by FA 2002, s 125(*a*)(i)(III) with effect from 25 March 2002; previously "credited.".

[5] Definition of "tax" substituted by FA 2002, s 125(*a*)(i)(IV) with effect from 25 March 2002.

[6] Subs (2) substituted and subs (2A) inserted by FA 2001, s 239(*b*) with effect from 6 April 2001.

[7] Subs (5) inserted by FA 2002, s 125(*a*)(ii) with effect from 25 March 2002.

[8] Section 1006A inserted by FA 2000, s 164 with effect from 23 March 2000.

Cross-references

Capital acquisitions tax, overpayments, subs (2A): CATCA 2003, s 57(6).

Excise duty, interest on repayments, subs (2A): FA 2001, s 105D(2), (3) (inserted by FA 2003, s 98).

Interest on repayments, subs (2A): s 865A(1), (2).

Relief on retirement for certain income of certain sportsperson: s 480A(2).

Stamp duty, interest on repayments, subs (2A): SDCA 1999, s 159B(1).

Value-added tax, interest on refunds, subs (2A): VATA 1972, s 21A(2), (3).

Regulations

Taxes (Offset of Repayments) Regulations 2002, SI No 471 of 2002.

Tax Briefing

TB45 Oct 2001 pp 10–11 — Offset of Repayment Regulations.

Definitions

Dáil Éireann: IA 2005, Sch; person: IA 2005, s 18(*c*); writing: IA 2005, Sch.

1006B Appropriation of payments

[(1) In this section—

"Acts" means—

(*a*) the Tax Acts,

(*b*) the Capital Gains Tax Acts,

(*c*) the Value Added Tax Act, 1972, and the enactments amending or extending that Act,

and any instruments made thereunder;

"payment" means a payment or a remittance of a liability under the Acts and includes part of such a payment or remittance;

"liability" means any tax or charge due under the Acts for a taxable period, income tax month, income tax year or chargeable period, as appropriate.

(2) Notwithstanding any other provision of the Acts, where a payment is received by the Revenue Commissioners from a person and it cannot reasonably be determined by the Revenue Commissioners from the instructions, if any, which accompanied the payment which liabilities the person wishes the payment to be set against, the Revenue Commissioners may set the payment against any liability due by the person under the Acts.

(3) The Revenue Commissioners shall make regulations for the purpose of giving effect to this section and, without prejudice to the generality of the foregoing, such regulations shall provide for the order of priority of liabilities due under the Acts against which a payment is to be set in accordance with subsection (2).

(4) Every regulation made under this section shall be laid before Dáil Éireann as soon as may be after it is made and, if a resolution annulling the regulation is passed by Dáil Éireann within the next 21 days on which Dáil Éireann has sat after the regulation is laid before it, the regulation shall be annulled accordingly, but without prejudice to the validity of anything previously done thereunder.

[(5) Any act to be performed or function to be discharged (other than the making of regulations) by the Revenue Commissioners which is authorised by this section may be performed or discharged by any of their officers acting under their authority.][1][2]

Amendments

[1]   Subs (5) inserted by FA 2002, s 125(*b*) with effect from 25 March 2002.

[2]   Section 1006B inserted by FA 2000, s 164 with effect from 23 March 2000.

Definitions

Dáil Éireann: IA 2005, Sch; person: IA 2005, s 18(*c*).

PART 47

PENALTIES, REVENUE OFFENCES, INTEREST ON OVERDUE TAX AND OTHER
SANCTIONS

CHAPTER 4
Revenue offences

1078 Revenue offences

(1) In this Part—

"the Acts" means—

- (*a*) the Customs Acts,
- (*b*) the statutes relating to the duties of excise and to the management of those duties,
- (*c*) the Tax Acts,
- (*d*) the Capital Gains Tax Acts,
- (*e*) the Value-Added Tax Act, 1972, and the enactments amending or extending that Act,
- (*f*) the [Capital Acquisitions Tax Consolidation Act 2003][1], and the enactments amending or extending that Act,
- (*g*) the statutes relating to stamp duty and to the management of that duty, and
- (*h*) Part VI of the Finance Act, 1983,

and any instruments made thereunder and any instruments made under any other enactment and relating to tax;

"authorised officer" means an officer of the Revenue Commissioners authorised by them in writing to exercise any of the powers conferred by the Acts;

"tax" means any tax, duty, levy or charge under the care and management of the Revenue Commissioners.
[(1A)(*a*) In this subsection—

"**facilitating**" means aiding, abetting, assisting, inciting or inducing;

"**fraudulent evasion of tax by a person**" means the person—
- (*a*) evading or attempting to evade any payment or deduction of tax required under the Acts to be paid by the person or, as the case may be, required under the Acts to be deducted from amounts due to the person, or
- (*b*) claiming or obtaining, or attempting to claim or obtain, relief or exemption from, or payment or repayment of, any tax, being relief, exemption, payment or repayment, to which the person is not entitled under the Acts,

where, for those purposes, the person deceives, omits, conceals or uses any other dishonest means including—
- (i) providing false, incomplete or misleading information, or
- (ii) failing to furnish information,

to the Revenue Commissioners or to any other person.
- (*b*) For the purposes of this subsection and subsection (5) a person (in this paragraph referred to as the "**first-mentioned person**") is reckless as to whether or not he or she is concerned in facilitating—
  - (i) the fraudulent evasion of tax by a person, being another person, or

415

      (ii)   the commission of an offence under subsection (2) by a person, being another person,

if the first-mentioned person disregards a substantial risk that he or she is so concerned, and for those purposes **"substantial risk"** means a risk of such a nature and degree that, having regard to all the circumstances and the extent of the information available to the first-mentioned person, its disregard by that person involves culpability of a high degree.

  (*c*)   A person shall, without prejudice to any other penalty to which the person may be liable, be guilty of an offence under this section if the person—

      (i)   is knowingly concerned in the fraudulent evasion of tax by the person or any other person,

      (ii)   is knowingly concerned in, or is reckless as to whether or not the person is concerned in, facilitating—

         (I)   the fraudulent evasion of tax, or

         (II)   the commission of an offence under subsection (2) (other than an offence under paragraph (*b*) of that subsection),

         by any other person, or

     (iii)   is knowingly concerned in the fraudulent evasion or attempted fraudulent evasion of any prohibition or restriction on importation for the time being in force, or the removal of any goods from the State, in contravention of any provision of the Acts.][2]

(2) A person shall, without prejudice to any other penalty to which the person may be liable, be guilty of an offence under this section if the person—

  (*a*)   knowingly or wilfully delivers any incorrect return, statement or accounts or knowingly or wilfully furnishes any incorrect information in connection with any tax,

  (*b*)   knowingly aids, abets, assists, incites or induces another person to make or deliver knowingly or wilfully any incorrect return, statement or accounts in connection with any tax,

  (*c*)   claims or obtains relief or exemption from, or repayment of, any tax, being a relief, exemption or repayment to which, to the person's knowledge, the person is not entitled,

  (*d*)   knowingly or wilfully issues or produces any incorrect invoice, receipt, instrument or other document in connection with any tax,

 [(*dd*) (i)   fails to make any deduction of dividend withholding tax (within the meaning of Chapter 8A of Part 6) required to be made by the person under section 172B(1),

      (ii)   fails, having made that deduction, to pay the sum deducted to the Collector-General within the time specified in that behalf in section 172K(2),

     (iii)   fails to make any reduction required to be made by the person under section 172B(2),

     (iv)   fails, having made that reduction, to pay to the Collector-General the amount referred to in section 172B(2)(*d*), which amount is treated under that section as if it were a deduction of dividend withholding tax (within the meaning of Chapter 8A of Part 6), within the time specified in that behalf in section 172K(2), or

(v) fails to pay to the Collector-General, within the time specified in that behalf in section 172K(2), an amount referred to in section 172B(3)(*a*) which is required to be paid by the person to the Collector-General and which is treated under that section as if it were a deduction of dividend withholding tax (within the meaning of Chapter 8A of Part 6),]³

(*e*) (i) fails to make any deduction required to be made by the person under section 257(1),

(ii) fails, having made the deduction, to pay the sum deducted to the Collector-General within the time specified in that behalf in section 258(3), or

(iii) fails to pay to the Collector-General an amount on account of appropriate tax (within the meaning of Chapter 4 of Part 8) within the time specified in that behalf in section 258(4),

[(*f*) fails to pay to the Collector-General appropriate tax (within the meaning of section 739E) within the time specified in that behalf in section 739F,]⁴

(*g*) [fails without reasonable excuse]⁵ to comply with any provision of the Acts requiring—

(i) the furnishing of a return of income, profits or gains, or of sources of income, profits or gains, for the purposes of any tax,

(ii) the furnishing of any other return, certificate, notification, particulars, or any statement or evidence, for the purposes of any tax,

(iii) the keeping or retention of books, records, accounts or other documents for the purposes of any tax, or

(iv) the production of books, records, accounts or other documents, when so requested, for the purposes of any tax,

(*h*) knowingly or wilfully, and within the time limits specified for their retention, destroys, defaces or conceals from an authorised officer—

(i) any documents, or

(ii) any other written or printed material in any form, including any information stored, maintained or preserved by means of any mechanical or electronic device, whether or not stored, maintained or preserved in a legible form, which a person is obliged by any provision of the Acts to keep, to issue or to produce for inspection,

[(*hh*) knowingly or wilfully falsifies, conceals, destroys or otherwise disposes of, or causes or permits the falsification, concealment, destruction or disposal of, any books, records or other document—

(i) which the person has been given the opportunity to deliver, or as the case may be, to make available in accordance with section 900(3), or

(ii) which the person has been required to deliver or, as the case may be, to make available in accordance with a notice served under section 900, 902, 906A or 907, or an order made under section 901, 902A or 908.]⁶

(*i*) fails to remit any income tax payable pursuant to Chapter 4 of Part 42, and the regulations under that Chapter, or value-added tax within the time specified in that behalf in relation to income tax or value-added tax, as the case may be, [by the Acts,]⁷ [(*ii*) (i) fails to deduct tax required to be deducted by the person under section 531(1), or

(ii) fails, having made that deduction, to pay the sum deducted to the Collector-General within the time specified in that behalf in section 531(3A),

or][8]

(*j*) obstructs or interferes with any officer of the Revenue Commissioners, or any other person, in the exercise or performance of powers or duties under the Acts for the purposes of any tax.

(3) A person convicted of an offence under this section shall be liable—

(*a*) on summary conviction to a fine of [€3,000][9] which may be mitigated to not less than one fourth part of such fine or, at the discretion of the court, to imprisonment for a term not exceeding 12 months or to both the fine and the imprisonment, or

(*b*) on conviction on indictment, to a fine not exceeding [€126,970][10] or, at the discretion of the court, to imprisonment for a term not exceeding 5 years or to both the fine and the imprisonment.

[(3A) Where a person has been convicted of an offence referred to in subparagraph (i), (ii) or (iv) of subsection (2)(*g*), then, if an application is made, or caused to be made to the court in that regard, the court may make an order requiring the person concerned to comply with any provision of the Acts relating to the requirements specified in the said subparagraph (i), (ii) or (iv), as the case may be.][11]

[(3B) A person shall, without prejudice to any other penalty to which the person may be liable, be guilty of an offence under this section if the person fails or refuses to comply with an order referred to in subsection (3A).][12]

(4) Section 13 of the Criminal Procedure Act, 1967, shall apply in relation to an offence under this section as if, in place of the penalties specified in subsection (3) of that section, there were specified in that subsection the penalties provided for by subsection (3)(*a*), and the reference in subsection (2)(*a*) of section 13 of the Criminal Procedure Act, 1967, to the penalties provided for in subsection (3) of that section shall be construed and apply accordingly.

(5) Where an offence under this section is committed by a body corporate and the offence is shown [to have been committed with the consent or connivance of or to be attributable to any recklessness (as provided for by subsection (1A)(*b*)) on the part of][13] any person who, when the offence was committed, was a director, manager, secretary or other officer of the body corporate, or a member of the committee of management or other controlling authority of the body corporate, that person shall also be deemed to be guilty of the offence and may be proceeded against and punished accordingly.

(6) In any proceedings under this section, a return or statement delivered to an inspector or other officer of the Revenue Commissioners under any provision of the Acts and purporting to be signed by any person shall be deemed until the contrary is proved to have been so delivered and to have been signed by that person.

(7) Notwithstanding any other enactment, proceedings in respect of an offence under this section may be instituted within 10 years from the date of the commission of the offence or incurring of the penalty, as the case may be.

(8) Section 1 of the Probation of Offenders Act, 1907, shall not apply in relation to offences under this section.

(9) Sections 987(4) and 1052(4), subsections (3) and (7) of section 1053, and sections 1068 and 1069 and sections 26(6) and 27(7) of the Value-Added Tax Act, 1972, shall, with any necessary modifications, apply for the purposes of this section as they apply for the purposes of those sections, including, in the case of such of those sections as are applied by the Capital Gains Tax Acts, the Corporation Tax Acts, or Part VI of the Finance Act, 1983, the purposes of those sections as so applied.

Amendments

1. Substituted by CATCA 2003, s 119 and Sch 3 with effect from 21 February 2003; previously "Capital Acquisitions Tax Act, 1976".
2. Subs (1A) inserted by FA 2005, s 142(*a*) with effect from 25 March 2005.
3. Subs (2)(*dd*) inserted by FA 1999, s 27(*b*) with effect from 6 April 1999.
4. Subs (2)(*f*) inserted by FA 2005, s 142(*b*)(i) with effect from 25 March 2005.
5. Substituted by FA 2002, s 133(*a*) with effect from 25 March 2002; previously "knowingly or wilfully fails".
6. Subs (2)(*hh*) inserted by FA 1999, s 211(*a*) with effect from 25 March 1999.
7. Substituted by FA 2005, s 142(*b*)(ii) with effect from 25 March 2005; previously "by the Acts, or".
8. Subs (2)(*ii*) inserted by FA 2005, s 142(*b*)(iii) with effect from 25 March 2005.
9. Substituted by FA 2003, s 160(1) as respects an offence committed on or after 28 March 2003; previously "€1,900".
10. Substituted by FA 2001, s 240(1) and (2)(*k*) and Sch 5 Pt 1 as respects any act or omission which takes place or begins on or after 1 January 2002; previously "£100,000".
11. Subs (3A) inserted by FA 1999, s 211(*c*) with effect from 25 March 1999.
12. Subs (3B) inserted by FA 2002, s 133(*b*) with effect from 25 March 2002.
13. Substituted by FA 2005, s 142(*c*) with effect from 25 March 2005; previously "to have been committed with the consent or connivance of".

Cross-references

Application to High Court: information from third party, meaning of "the Acts" applied: s 902A(1).
Application to High Court seeking order requiring information: associated institutions, meaning of "the Acts" applied: s 908B(1).
Company law, subs (1): Companies Act 1990, s 21(1)(*a*)(i)(V).
Deduction from payments due to defaulters: s 1002(5), (9).
Information to be furnished by financial institutions, meaning of "the Acts" applied: s 906A(1).
Information to be furnished by third party: request of an authorised officer: s 902(11).
Inspection of documents and records, meaning of "the Acts" applied: s 905(2A)(*a*).
Penalty for false statement made to obtain allowance, subss (4), (6)–(8): s 1056(4).
Revenue offence: power to obtain information from financial institutions, meaning of "offence" applied: s 908A(1); subs (1): s 908A(1) ("the Acts").
Stamp duty, new dwelling houses and apartments with, and with no, floor area compliance certificate: Stamp Duties Consolidation Act 1999, s 91A(8); s 92(3).
This section to be construed together with the Customs Acts, in so far as relating to customs: s 1104(2).
This section to be construed together with the Value Added Tax Acts 1972–1997, in so far as relating to value added tax: s 1104(3).
This section to be construed together with the Stamp Act 1891 and the enactments amending or extending that Act, in so far as relating to stamp duties: s 1104(4).
This section to be construed together with the Capital Acquisitions Tax Act 1976, and the enactments amending or extending that Act, in so far as relating to capital acquisitions tax: s 1104(5).
This section to be construed together with FA 1983, Pt VI and the enactments amending or extending that Part, in so far as relating to residential property tax: s 1104(6).

Case law

Meaning of "criminal matter": *Director of Public Prosecutions v Seamus Boyle* (IV) ITR (395).

Subs (2)(*e*): District Justice not entitled to conclude, on basis of Revenue certificate, that taxpayer had "knowingly and wilfully" failed to submit return of income; taxpayer not present at District Court hearing and was entitled to defend himself: *O'Callaghan v Clifford and others* (IV) ITR (478).

Tax Briefing

TB36 June 1999 pp 3–4 — Revenue's Prosecution Policy.

TB38 Dec 1999 pp 10–11 — Criminal Proceedings.

Definitions

Collector-General: ss 2(1), 851; inspector: ss 2(1), 5(1), 852; month: IA 2005, Sch; person: IA 2005, s 18(*c*); profits: s 4(1); Tax Acts: s 1(2).

Former enactments

FA 1983, s 94; FA 1986, s 40(2); FA 1989, s 18 and Sch 1 para 3(2); FA 1992, s 243; FA 1996, s 132(1)–(2) and Sch 5 Pt I para 13(2) and Pt II.

1078A Concealing facts disclosed by documents

[(1) Any person who—

    (*a*) knows or suspects that an investigation by an officer of the Revenue Commissioners into an offence under the Acts or the Waiver of Certain Tax, Interest and Penalties Act 1993 is being, or is likely to be, carried out, and

    (*b*) falsifies, conceals, destroys or otherwise disposes of material which the person knows or suspects is or would be relevant to the investigation or causes or permits its falsification, concealment, destruction or disposal,

is guilty of an offence.

(2) Where a person—

    (*a*) falsifies, conceals, destroys or otherwise disposes of material, or

    (*b*) causes or permits its falsification, concealment, destruction or disposal,

in such circumstances that it is reasonable to conclude that the person knew or suspected—

    (i) that an investigation by an officer of the Revenue Commissioners into an offence under the Acts or the Waiver of Certain Tax, Interest and Penalties Act 1993 was being, or was likely to be, carried out, and

    (ii) that the material was or would be relevant to the investigation,

the person shall be taken, for the purposes of this section, to have so known or suspected, unless the court or the jury, as the case may be, is satisfied having regard to all the evidence that there is a reasonable doubt as to whether the person so knew or suspected.

(3) A person guilty of an offence under this section is liable—

    (*a*) on summary conviction to a fine not exceeding €3,000, or at the discretion of the court, to imprisonment for a term not exceeding 6 months or to both the fine and the imprisonment, or

    (*b*) on conviction on indictment, to a fine not exceeding €127,000 or, at the discretion of the court, to imprisonment for a term not exceeding 5 years or to both the fine and the imprisonment.][1]

Amendments

¹   Section 1078A inserted by FA 2003, s 161 with effect from 28 March 2003.

Definitions

person: IA 2005, s 18(*c*).

1078B Presumptions

[(1) In this section—

"return, statement or declaration" means any return, statement or declaration which a person is required to make under the Acts or the Waiver of Certain Tax, Interest and Penalties Act 1993.

(2) The presumptions specified in this section apply in any proceedings, whether civil or criminal, under any provision of the Acts or the Waiver of Certain Tax, Interest and Penalties Act 1993.

(3) Where a document purports to have been created by a person it shall be presumed, unless the contrary is shown, that the document was created by that person and that any statement contained therein, unless the document expressly attributes its making to some other person, was made by that person.

(4) Where a document purports to have been created by a person and addressed and sent to a second person, it shall be presumed, unless the contrary is shown, that the document was created and sent by the first person and received by the second person and that any statement contained therein—

　　(*a*)　unless the document expressly attributes its making to some other person, was made by the first person, and

　　(*b*)　came to the notice of the second person.

(5) Where a document is retrieved from an electronic storage and retrieval system, it shall be presumed unless the contrary is shown, that the author of the document is the person who ordinarily uses that electronic storage and retrieval system in the course of his or her business.

(6) Where an authorised officer in the exercise of his or her powers under subsection (2A) of section 905 has removed records (within the meaning of that section) from any place, gives evidence in proceedings that to the best of the authorised officer's knowledge and belief, the records are the property of any person, the records shall be presumed unless the contrary is proved, to be the property of that person.

(7) Where in accordance with subsection (6) records are presumed in proceedings to be the property of a person and the authorised officer gives evidence that, to the best of the authorised officer's knowledge and belief, the records are records which relate to any trade, profession, or, as the case may be, other activity, carried on by that person, the records shall be presumed unless the contrary is proved, to be records which relate to that trade, profession, or, as the case may be, other activity, carried on by that person.

(8) In proceedings, a certificate signed by an inspector or other officer of the Revenue Commissioners certifying that a return, statement or declaration to which the certificate refers is in the possession of the Revenue Commissioners in such circumstances as to

lead the officer to conclude that, to the best of his or her knowledge and belief it was delivered to an inspector or other officer of the Revenue Commissioners, it shall be presumed unless the contrary is proved, to be evidence that the said return, statement, or declaration was so delivered.

(9) In proceedings, a certificate, certifying the fact or facts referred to in subsection (8) and purporting to be signed as specified in that subsection, may be tendered in evidence without proof and shall be deemed until the contrary is proved to have been signed by a person holding, at the time of the signature, the office or position indicated in the certificate as the office or position of the person signing.

(10) References in this section to a document are references to a document in written, mechanical or electronic format and, for this purpose "written" includes any form of notation or code whether by hand or otherwise and regardless of the method by which, or the medium in or on which, the document concerned is recorded.]¹

Amendments

¹   Section 1078B inserted by FA 2003, s 161 with effect from 28 March 2003.

Definitions

inspector: s 2(1); person: IA 2005, s 18(*c*); profession: s 2(1); trade: ss 3(1), 4(1).

1078C Provision of information to juries

[(1) In a trial on indictment of an offence under the Acts or the Waiver of Certain Tax, Interest and Penalties Act 1993, the trial judge may order that copies of any or all of the following documents shall be given to the jury in any form that the judge considers appropriate:

   (*a*)   any document admitted in evidence at the trial,

   (*b*)   the transcript of the opening speeches of counsel,

   (*c*)   any charts, diagrams, graphics, schedules or agreed summaries of evidence produced at the trial,

   (*d*)   the transcript of the whole or any part of the evidence given at the trial,

   (*e*)   the transcript of the closing speeches of counsel,

   (*f*)   the transcript of the trial judge's charge to the jury,

   (*g*)   any other document that in the opinion of the trial judge would be of assistance to the jury in its deliberations including, where appropriate, an affidavit by an accountant or other suitably qualified person, summarising, in a form which is likely to be comprehended by the jury, any transactions by the accused or other persons which are relevant to the offence.

(2) If the prosecutor proposes to apply to the trial judge for an order that a document mentioned in subsection (1)(*g*) shall be given to the jury, the prosecutor shall give a copy of the document to the accused in advance of the trial and, on the hearing of the application, the trial judge shall take into account any representations made by or on behalf of the accused in relation to it.

(3) Where the trial judge has made an order that an affidavit by an accountant or other person mentioned in subsection (1)(*g*) shall be given to the jury, the accountant, or as the case may be, the other person so mentioned—

(*a*) shall be summoned by the prosecution to attend at the trial as an expert witness, and

(*b*) may be required by the trial judge, in an appropriate case, to give evidence in regard to any relevant procedures or principles within his or her area of expertise.]¹

Amendments

¹ Section 1078C inserted by FA 2003, s 161 with effect from 28 March 2003.

Definitions

affidavit: IA 2005, Sch; person: IA 2005, s 18(*c*).

1079 Duties of relevant person in relation to certain revenue offences

(1) In this section—

"the Acts" means—

(*a*) the Customs Acts,

(*b*) the statutes relating to the duties of excise and to the management of those duties,

(*c*) the Tax Acts,

(*d*) the Capital Gains Tax Acts,

(*e*) the Value Added Tax Act, 1972, and the enactments amending or extending that Act,

(*f*) the [Capital Acquisitions Tax Consolidation Act 2003],¹ and the enactments amending or extending that Act,

(*g*) the statutes relating to stamp duty and to the management of that duty,

and any instruments made thereunder and any instruments made under any other enactment and relating to tax;

"appropriate officer" means any officer nominated by the Revenue Commissioners to be an appropriate officer for the purposes of this section;

"company" means any body corporate;

"relevant person", in relation to a company and subject to subsection (2), means a person who—

(*a*) (i) is an auditor to the company appointed in accordance with section 160 of the Companies Act, 1963 (as amended by the Companies Act, 1990), or

(ii) in the case of an industrial and provident society or a friendly society, is a public auditor to the society for the purposes of the Industrial and Provident Societies Acts, 1893 to 1978, and the Friendly Societies Acts, 1896 to 1977,

or

(*b*) with a view to reward, assists or advises the company in the preparation or delivery of any information, declaration, return, records, accounts or other document which he or she knows will be or is likely to be used for any purpose of tax;

"relevant offence" means an offence committed by a company which consists of the company—

(a) knowingly or wilfully delivering any incorrect return, statement or accounts or knowingly or wilfully furnishing or causing to be furnished any incorrect information in connection with any tax,

(b) knowingly or wilfully claiming or obtaining relief or exemption from, or repayment of, any tax, being a relief, exemption or repayment to which there is no entitlement,

(c) knowingly or wilfully issuing or producing any incorrect invoice, receipt, instrument or other document in connection with any tax, or

(d) knowingly or wilfully failing to comply with any provision of the Acts requiring the furnishing of a return of income, profits or gains, or of sources of income, profits or gains, for the purposes of any tax, but an offence under this paragraph committed by a company shall not be a relevant offence if the company has made a return of income, profits or gains to the Revenue Commissioners in respect of an accounting period falling wholly or partly in the period of 3 years preceding the accounting period in respect of which the offence was committed;

"tax" means any tax, duty, levy or charge under the care and management of the Revenue Commissioners.

(2) For the purposes of paragraph (b) of the definition of **"relevant person"**, a person who but for this subsection would be treated as a relevant person in relation to a company shall not be so treated if the person assists or advises the company solely in the person's capacity as an employee of the company, and a person shall be treated as assisting or advising the company in that capacity where the person's income from assisting or advising the company consists solely of emoluments to which Chapter 4 of Part 42 applies.

(3) If, having regard solely to information obtained in the course of examining the accounts of a company, or in the course of assisting or advising a company in the preparation or delivery of any information, declaration, return, records, accounts or other document for the purposes of tax, as the case may be, a person who is a relevant person in relation to the company becomes aware that the company has committed, or is in the course of committing, one or more relevant offences, the person shall, if the offence or offences are material—

(a) communicate particulars of the offence or offences in writing to the company without undue delay and request the company to—

(i) take such action as is necessary for the purposes of rectifying the matter, or

(ii) notify an appropriate officer of the offence or offences,

not later than 6 months after the time of communication, and

(b) (i) unless it is established to the person's satisfaction that the necessary action has been taken or notification made, as the case may be, under paragraph (*a*), cease to act as the auditor to the company or to assist or advise the company in such preparation or delivery as is specified in paragraph (*b*) of the definition of **"relevant person"**, and

(ii)   shall not so act, assist or advise before a time which is the earlier of—

(I)   3 years after the time at which the particulars were communicated under paragraph (*a*), and

(II)   the time at which it is established to the person's satisfaction that the necessary action has been taken or notification made, as the case may be, under paragraph (*a*).

(4) Nothing in paragraph (*b*) of subsection (3) shall prevent a person from assisting or advising a company in preparing for, or conducting, legal proceedings, either civil or criminal, which are extant or pending at a time which is 6 months after the time of communication under paragraph (*a*) of that subsection.

(5) Where a person, being in relation to a company a relevant person within the meaning of paragraph (*a*) of the definition of **"relevant person"**, ceases under this section to act as auditor to the company, then, the person shall deliver—

(*a*)   a notice in writing to the company stating that he or she is so resigning, and

(*b*)   a copy of the notice to an appropriate officer not later than 14 days after he or she has delivered the notice to the company.

(6) A person shall be guilty of an offence under this section if the person—

(*a*)   fails to comply with subsection (3) or (5), or

(*b*)   knowingly or wilfully makes a communication under subsection (3) which is incorrect.

(7) Where a relevant person is convicted of an offence under this section, the person shall be liable—

(*a*)   on summary conviction, to a fine of [€1,265][2] which may be mitigated to not less than one-fourth part of such fine, or

(*b*)   on conviction on indictment, to a fine not exceeding [€6,345][3] or, at the discretion of the court, to imprisonment for a term not exceeding 2 years or to both the fine and the imprisonment.

(8) Section 13 of the Criminal Procedure Act, 1967, shall apply in relation to this section as if, in place of the penalties specified in subsection (3) of that section, there were specified in that subsection the penalties provided for by subsection (7)(*a*), and the reference in subsection (2)(*a*) of section 13 of the Criminal Procedure Act, 1967, to the penalties provided for in subsection (3) of that section shall be construed and apply accordingly.

(9) Notwithstanding any other enactment, proceedings in respect of this section may be instituted within 6 years from the time at which a person is required under subsection (3) to communicate particulars of an offence or offences in writing to a company.

(10) It shall be a good defence in a prosecution for an offence under subsection (6)(*a*) in relation to a failure to comply with subsection (3) for an accused (being a person who is a relevant person in relation to a company) to show that he or she was in the ordinary

scope of professional engagement assisting or advising the company in preparing for legal proceedings and would not have become aware that one or more relevant offences had been committed by the company if he or she had not been so assisting or advising.

(11) Where a person who is a relevant person takes any action required by subsection (3) or (5), no duty to which the person may be subject shall be regarded as having been contravened and no liability or action shall lie against the person in any court for having taken such action.

(12) The Revenue Commissioners may nominate an officer to be an appropriate officer for the purposes of this section, and the name of an officer so nominated and the address to which copies of notices under subsection (3) or (5) shall be delivered shall be published in Iris Oifigiúil.

(13) This section shall apply as respects a relevant offence committed by a company in respect of tax which is—

(a) assessable by reference to accounting periods, for any accounting period beginning after the 30th day of June, 1995,

(b) assessable by reference to years of assessment, for the year 1995–96 and subsequent years of assessment,

(c) payable by reference to a taxable period, for a taxable period beginning after the 30th day of June, 1995,

(d) chargeable on gifts or inheritances taken on or after the 30th day of June, 1995,

(e) chargeable on instruments executed on or after the 30th day of June, 1995, or

(f) payable in any other case, on or after the 30th day of June, 1995.

Amendments

1   Substituted by CATCA 2003, s 119 and Sch 3 with effect from 21 February 2003; previously "Capital Acquisitions Tax Act 1976".

2   Substituted by FA 2001, s 240(1) and (2)(k) and Sch 5 Pt 1 as respects any act or omission which takes place or begins on or after 1 January 2002; previously "£1,000".

3   Substituted by FA 2001, s 240(1) and (2)(k) and Sch 5 Pt 1 as respects any act or omission which takes place or begins on or after 1 January 2002; previously "£5,000".

Cross-references

This section to be construed together with the Customs Acts, in so far as relating to customs: s 1104(2).

This section to be construed together with the Value Added Tax Acts 1972–1997, in so far as relating to value added tax: s 1104(3).

This section to be construed together with the Stamp Act 1891 and the enactments amending or extending that Act, in so far as relating to stamp duties: s 1104(4).

This section to be construed together with the Capital Acquisitions Tax Act 1976, and the enactments amending or extending that Act, in so far as relating to capital acquisitions tax: s 1104(5).

Definitions

month: IA 2005, Sch; person: IA 2005, s 18(c); writing: IA 2005, Sch; year: IA 2005, Sch; year of assessment: ss 2(1), 5(1).

Former enactments

FA 1995, s 172.

CHAPTER 6

Other sanctions

1086 Publication of names of tax defaulters

(1) In this section—

"the Acts" means—

- (*a*) the Tax Acts,
- (*b*) the Capital Gains Tax Acts,
- (*c*) the Value-Added Tax Act, 1972, and the enactments amending or extending that Act,
- (*d*) the [Capital Acquisitions Tax Consolidation Act 2003],[1] and the enactments amending or extending that Act,
- [(*e*) the Stamp Duties Consolidation Act, 1999, and the enactments amending or extending that Act][2]
- (*f*) Part VI of the Finance Act, 1983,
- [(*g*) the Customs Acts,
- (*h*) the statutes relating to the duties of excise and to the management of those duties,][3]

and any instruments made thereunder;

["**tax**" means any tax, duty, levy or charge under the care and management of the Revenue Commissioners.][4]

(2) The Revenue Commissioners shall, as respects each relevant period (being the period beginning on the 1st day of January, 1997, and ending on the 30th day of June, 1997, and each subsequent period of 3 months beginning with the period ending on the 30th day of September, 1997), compile a list of the names and addresses and the occupations or descriptions of every person—

- (*a*) on whom a fine or other penalty was imposed by a court under any of the Acts during that relevant period,
- (*b*) on whom a fine or other penalty was otherwise imposed by a court during that relevant period in respect of an act or omission by the person in relation to [tax,][5]
- (*c*) in whose case the Revenue Commissioners, pursuant to an agreement made with the person in that relevant period, refrained from initiating proceedings for the recovery of any fine or penalty of the kind mentioned in paragraphs (*a*) and (*b*) and, in place of initiating such proceedings, accepted or undertook to accept a specified sum of money in settlement of any claim by the Revenue Commissioners in respect of any specified liability of the person under any of the Acts for—
  - (i) payment of any tax,
  - [(ii) except in the case of tax due by virtue of paragraphs (*g*) and (*h*) of the definition of "the Acts", payment of interest on that tax, and
  - (iii) a fine or other monetary penalty in respect of that tax including penalties in respect of the failure to deliver any return, statement, declaration, list or other document in connection with the tax, or][6]

[(*d*) in whose case the Revenue Commissioners, having initiated proceedings for the recovery of any fine or penalty of the kind mentioned in paragraphs (*a*) and (*b*), and whether or not a fine or penalty of the kind mentioned in those paragraphs has been imposed by a court, accepted or undertook to accept, in that relevant period, a specified sum of money in settlement of any claim by the Revenue Commissioners in respect of any specified liability of the person under any of the Acts for—

  (i) payment of any tax,
  [(ii) except in the case of tax due by virtue of paragraphs (*g*) and (*h*) of the definition of "the Acts", payment of interest on that tax, and
  (iii) a fine or other monetary penalty in respect of that tax including penalties in respect of the failure to deliver any return, statement, declaration, list or other document in connection with the tax.]⁷]⁸

[(2A) For the purposes of subsection (2), the reference to a specified sum in paragraphs (*c*) and (*d*) of that subsection includes a reference to a sum which is the full amount of the claim by the Revenue Commissioners in respect of the specified liability referred to in those paragraphs.]⁹

(3) Notwithstanding any obligation as to secrecy imposed on them by the Acts or the Official Secrets Act, 1963—

  (*a*) the Revenue Commissioners shall, before the expiration of 3 months from the end of each relevant period, cause each such list referred to in subsection (2) in relation to that period to be published in Iris Oifigiúil, and

  [(*b*) the Revenue Commissioners may, at any time after each such list referred to in subsection (2) has been published as provided for in paragraph (*a*), cause any such list to be publicised or reproduced, or both, in whole or in part, in such manner, form or format as they consider appropriate.]¹⁰

(4) [Paragraph (*c*) and (*d*)]¹¹ of subsection (2) shall not apply in relation to a person in whose case—

  (*a*) the Revenue Commissioners are satisfied that, before any investigation or inquiry had been commenced by them or by any of their officers into any matter occasioning a liability referred to in [those paragraphs]¹² of the person, the person had voluntarily furnished to them complete information in relation to and full particulars of that matter,

  (*b*) section 72 of the Finance Act, 1988, or section 3 of the Waiver of Certain Tax, Interest and Penalties Act, 1993, [applied,]¹³

  (*c*) the specified sum referred to in [paragraph (*c*) or (*d*), as the case may be,]¹⁴ of subsection (2) does not exceed [[€30,000]¹⁵, or]¹⁶

  [(*d*) the amount of fine or other penalty included in the specified sum referred to in paragraph (*c*) or (*d*), as the case may be, of subsection (2) does not exceed 15 per cent of the amount of tax included in that specified sum.]¹⁷

[(4A)(*a*) In this subsection—

  "the consumer price index number" means the All Items Consumer Price Index Number compiled by the Central Statistics Office;

"**the consumer price index number relevant to a year**" means the consumer price index number at the mid-December before the commencement of that year expressed on the basis that the consumer price index at mid-December 2001 was 100;

"**the Minister**" means the Minister for Finance.

(*b*) The Minister shall, in the year 2010 and in every fifth year thereafter, by order provide, in accordance with paragraph (*c*), an amount in lieu of the amount referred to in subsection (4)(*c*), or where such an order has been made previously, in lieu of the amount specified in the last order so made.

(*c*) For the purposes of paragraph (*b*) the amount referred to in subsection (4)(*c*) or in the last previous order made under the said paragraph (*b*), as the case may be, shall be adjusted by—

   (i) multiplying that amount by the consumer price index number relevant to the year in which the adjustment is made and dividing the product by the consumer price index number relevant to the year in which the amount was previously provided for, and

   (ii) rounding the resulting amount up to the next €1,000.

(*d*) An order made under this subsection shall specify that the amount provided for by the order—

   (i) takes effect from a specified date, being 1 January in the year in which the order is made, and

   (ii) does not apply to any case in which the specified liability referred to in paragraphs (*c*) and (*d*) of subsection (2) includes tax, the liability in respect of which arose before, or which relates to periods which commenced before, that specified date.][18]

(5) Any list referred to in subsection (2) shall specify in respect of each person named in the list such particulars as the Revenue Commissioners think fit—

(*a*) of the matter occasioning the fine or penalty of the kind referred to in subsection (2) imposed on the person or, as the case may be, the liability of that kind to which the person was subject, and

(*b*) of any interest, fine or other monetary penalty, and of any other penalty or sanction, to which that person was liable, or which was imposed on that person by a court, and which was occasioned by the matter referred to in paragraph (*a*).

[(5A) Without prejudice to the generality of paragraph (*a*) of subsection (5), such particulars as are referred to in that paragraph may include—

(*a*) in a case to which paragraph (*a*) or (*b*) of subsection (2) applies, a description, in such summary form as the Revenue Commissioners may think fit, of the act, omission or offence (which may also include the circumstances in which the act or omission arose or the offence was committed) in respect of which the fine or penalty referred to in those paragraphs was imposed, and

(*b*) in a case to which paragraph (*c*) or (*d*) of subsection (2) applies, a description, in such summary form as the Revenue Commissioners may think fit, of the matter occasioning the specified liability (which may also include the circumstances in which that liability arose) in respect of which the Revenue

Commissioners accepted, or undertook to accept, a settlement, in accordance with those paragraphs.][19]

Amendments

1   Substituted by CATCA 2003, s 119 and Sch 3 with effect from 21 February 2003; previously "Capital Acquisitions Tax Act 1976".

2   Definition of "the Acts" para (*e*) substituted by FA 2002, s 126(1)(*a*)(i)(I) as respects fines or other penalties, as are referred to in s 1086(2)(*a*) and (*b*), which are imposed by a court, and as respects specified sums, as are referred to in s 1086(2)(*c*) and (*d*), which the Revenue Commissioners accepted, or undertook to accept, in settlement of a specified liability, on or after 25 March 2002.

3   Definition of "the Acts" paras (*g*) and (*h*) inserted by FA 2002, s 126(1)(*a*)(i)(II) as respects fines or other penalties, as are referred to in s 1086(2)(*a*) and (*b*), which are imposed by a court, and as respects specified sums, as are referred to in s 1086(2)(*c*) and (*d*), which the Revenue Commissioners accepted, or undertook to accept, in settlement of a specified liability, on or after 25 March 2002.

4   Definition of "tax" substituted by FA 2002, s 126(1)(*a*)(ii) as respects fines or other penalties, as are referred to in s 1086(2)(*a*) and (*b*), which are imposed by a court, and as respects specified sums, as are referred to in s 1086(2)(*c*) and (*d*), which the Revenue Commissioners accepted, or undertook to accept, in settlement of a specified liability, on or after 25 March 2002.

5   Substituted by FA 2000, s 162(1)(*a*)(i) as respects fines or other penalties, as are referred to in s 1086(2)(*a*)–(*b*), which are imposed by a court, and as respects specified sums, as are referred to in s 1086(2)(*c*)–(*d*), which the Revenue Commissioners accepted, or undertook to accept, in settlement of a specified liability, on or after 23 March 2000; previously "tax, or".

6   Subs (2)(*c*)(ii)–(iii) substituted by FA 2002, s 126(1)(*b*)(i) as respects fines or other penalties, as are referred to in s 1086(2)(*a*) and (*b*), which are imposed by a court, and as respects specified sums, as are referred to in s 1086(2)(*c*) and (*d*), which the Revenue Commissioners accepted, or undertook to accept, in settlement of a specified liability, on or after 25 March 2002.

7   Subs (2)(*d*)(ii)–(iii) substituted by FA 2002, s 126(1)(*b*)(ii) as respects fines or other penalties, as are referred to in s 1086(2)(*a*) and (*b*), which are imposed by a court, and as respects specified sums, as are referred to in s 1086(2)(*c*) and (*d*), which the Revenue Commissioners accepted, or undertook to accept, in settlement of a specified liability, on or after 25 March 2002.

8   Subs (2)(*d*) inserted by FA 2000, s 162(1)(*a*)(ii) as respects fines or other penalties, as are referred to in s 1086(2)(*a*)–(*b*), which are imposed by a court, and as respects specified sums, as are referred to in s 1086(2)(*c*)–(*d*), which the Revenue Commissioners accepted, or undertook to accept, in settlement of a specified liability, on or after 23 March 2000.

9   Subs (2A) inserted by FA 2000, s 162(1)(*b*) as respects fines or other penalties, as are referred to in s 1086(2)(*a*)–(*b*), which are imposed by a court, and as respects specified sums, as are referred to in s 1086(2)(*c*)–(*d*), which the Revenue Commissioners accepted, or undertook to accept, in settlement of a specified liability, on or after 23 March 2000.

10   Subs (3)(*b*) substituted by FA 2002, s 126(1)(*c*) as respects fines or other penalties, as are referred to in s 1086(2)(*a*) and (*b*), which are imposed by a court, and as respects specified sums, as are referred to in s 1086(2)(*c*) and (*d*), which the Revenue Commissioners accepted, or undertook to accept, in settlement of a specified liability, on or after 25 March 2002.

11   Substituted by FA 2000, s 162(1)(*c*)(i) as respects fines or other penalties, as are referred to in s 1086(2)(*a*)–(*b*), which are imposed by a court, and as respects specified sums, as are referred to in s 1086(2)(*c*)–(*d*), which the Revenue Commissioners accepted, or undertook to accept, in settlement of a specified liability, on or after 23 March 2000; previously "Paragraph (c)".

12   Substituted by FA 2002, s 126(1)(*d*)(i) as respects fines or other penalties, as are referred to in s 1086(2)(*a*) and (*b*), which are imposed by a court, and as respects specified sums, as are referred to in s 1086(2)(*c*) and (*d*), which the Revenue Commissioners accepted, or undertook to accept, in settlement of a specified liability, on or after 25 March 2002; previously "that paragraph".

13   Substituted by FA 2002, s 126(1)(*d*)(ii) as respects fines or other penalties, as are referred to in s 1086(2)(*a*) and (*b*), which are imposed by a court, and as respects specified sums, as are referred to in s 1086(2)(*c*) and (*d*), which the Revenue Commissioners accepted, or undertook to accept, in settlement of a specified liability, on or after 25 March 2002; previously "applied, or".

14   Substituted by FA 2000, s 162(1)(*c*)(ii) as respects fines or other penalties, as are referred to in s 1086(2)(*a*)–(*b*), which are imposed by a court, and as respects specified sums, as are referred to in

s 1086(2)(*c*)–(*d*), which the Revenue Commissioners accepted, or undertook to accept, in settlement of a specified liability, on or after 23 March 2000; previously "paragraph (*c*)".

15 Substituted by FA 2005, s 143(1)(*a*) with effect from 25 March 2005, but does not apply where the specified liability referred to in TCA 1997, s 1086(2)(*c*)–(*d*) includes tax, the liability in respect of which arose before, or which relates to periods which commenced before, 1 January 2005; previously "€12,700".

16 Substituted by FA 2002, s 126(1)(*d*)(iii) as respects fines or other penalties, as are referred to in s 1086(2)(*a*) and (*b*), which are imposed by a court, and as respects specified sums, as are referred to in s 1086(2)(*c*) and (*d*), which the Revenue Commissioners accepted, or undertook to accept, in settlement of a specified liability, on or after 25 March 2002; previously "€12,700, or".

17 Subs (4)(*d*) inserted by FA 2002, s 126(1)(*d*)(iv) as respects fines or other penalties, as are referred to in s 1086(2)(*a*) and (*b*), which are imposed by a court, and as respects specified sums, as are referred to in s 1086(2)(*c*) and (*d*), which the Revenue Commissioners accepted, or undertook to accept, in settlement of a specified liability, on or after 25 March 2002.

18 Subs (4A) inserted by FA 2005, s 143(1)(*b*) with effect from 25 March 2005.

19 Subs (5A) inserted by FA 2000, s 162(1)(*d*) as respects fines or other penalties, as are referred to in s 1086(2)(*a*)–(*b*), which are imposed by a court, and as respects specified sums, as are referred to in s 1086(2)(*c*)–(*d*), which the Revenue Commissioners accepted, or undertook to accept, in settlement of a specified liability, on or after 23 March 2000.

Cross-references

Social Welfare Consolidation Act 2005, s 17(4)(*c*), payment of contributions and keeping of records; s 23(3)(*c*), regulations providing for collection of self-employment contributions.

This section to be construed together with the Value Added Tax Acts 1972–1997, in so far as relating to value added tax: s 1104(3).

This section to be construed together with the Stamp Act 1891 and the enactments amending or extending that Act, in so far as relating to stamp duties: s 1104(4).

This section to be construed together with the Capital Acquisitions Tax Act 1976, and the enactments amending or extending that Act, in so far as relating to capital acquisitions tax: s 1104(5).

This section to be construed together with FA 1983, Pt VI and the enactments amending or extending that Part, in so far as relating to residential property tax: s 1104(6).

Health Contributions Act 1979, s 10(3)(*a*)(i), power to make regulatons and to recover health contributions.

National Training Fund Act 2000, s 5(6), collection of levy.

Definitions

Tax Acts: s 1(2); year: IA 2005, Sch.

Former enactments

FA 1983, s 23, FA 1992, s 240, WCTIPA 1993, s 3(7), FA 1997, s 158.

PART 48
MISCELLANEOUS AND SUPPLEMENTAL

1093 Disclosure of information to Ombudsman

Any obligation to maintain secrecy or other restriction on the disclosure or production of information (including documents) obtained by or furnished to the Revenue Commissioners, or any person on their behalf, for taxation purposes, shall not apply to the disclosure or production of information (including documents) to the Ombudsman for the purposes of an examination or investigation by the Ombudsman under the Ombudsman Act, 1980, of any action (within the meaning of that Act) taken by or on behalf of the Revenue Commissioners, being such an action taken in the performance of administrative functions in respect of any tax or duty under the care and management of the Revenue Commissioners.

Cross-references

This section to be construed together with the Customs Acts, in so far as relating to customs: s 1104(2).

This section to be construed together with the Value Added Tax Acts 1972–1997, in so far as relating to value added tax: s 1104(3).

This section to be construed together with the Stamp Act 1891 and the enactments amending or extending that Act, in so far as relating to stamp duties: s 1104(4).

This section to be construed together with the Capital Acquisitions Tax Act 1976, and the enactments amending or extending that Act, in so far as relating to capital acquisitions tax: s 1104(5).

This section to be construed together with FA 1983, Pt VI and the enactments amending or extending that Part, in so far as relating to residential property tax: s 1104(6).

Definitions

person: IA 2005, s 18(*c*).

Former enactments

FA 1992, s 242; FA 1993, s 140; FA 1997, s 160(1).

1094 Tax clearance certificates in relation to certain licences

(1) In this section—

"the Acts" means—

    (*a*) the Tax Acts,

    (*b*) the Capital Gains Tax Acts, and

    (*c*) the Value Added Tax Act, 1972, and the enactments amending or extending that Act,

and any instruments made thereunder;

"beneficial holder of a licence" means the person who conducts the activities under the licence and, in relation to a licence issued under the Auctioneers and House Agents Act, 1947, includes the authorised individual referred to in section 8(4), or the nominated individual referred to in section 9(1), of that Act;

"licence" [means a licence, permit or authorisation][1], as the case may be, of the kind referred to in—

    (*a*) the proviso (inserted by section 156 of the Finance Act, 1992) to section 49(1) of the Finance (1909–1910) Act, 1910,

    (*b*) the further proviso (inserted by section 79(1) of the Finance Act, 1993) to section 49(1) of the Finance (1909–1910) Act, 1910,

    (*c*) the proviso (inserted by section 79(2) of the Finance Act, 1993) to section 7(3) of the Betting Act, 1931,

    (*d*) the proviso (inserted by section 79(3) of the Finance Act, 1993) to section 19 of the Gaming and Lotteries Act, 1956,

    (*e*) the proviso (inserted by section 79(4)(*a*) of the Finance Act, 1993) to subsection (1) of section 8 of the Auctioneers and House Agents Act, 1947,

    (*f*) the proviso (inserted by section 79(4)(*b*) of the Finance Act, 1993) to subsection (1) of section 9 of the Auctioneers and House Agents Act, 1947 (an auction permit under that section being deemed for the purposes of this section to be a licence),

    (*g*) the proviso (inserted by section 79(4)(*c*) of the Finance Act, 1993) to subsection (1) of section 10 of the Auctioneers and House Agents Act, 1947,

    [(*h*) section 101 of the Finance Act, 1999[,][2]][3]

    (*j*) section 93, 116 or 144 of the Consumer Credit Act, 1995[,][2]

    [(*k*) subsection (2A) (inserted by section 106 of the Finance Act, 2000) of section 62 of the National Cultural Institutions Act, 1997[,][2]][4] [(*l*) subsection (1A) (inserted by section 172 of the Finance Act, 2001) of section 2 of the Intoxicating Liquor (National Concert Hall) Act, 1983[,]²]⁵

[(*m*) subsection (3) (inserted by the Finance Act, 2002) of section 122 of the Finance Act, [1992,]⁶

(*n*) subsection (1A) (inserted by the Finance Act, 2002) of the Finance (1909–10) Act, [1910, and]⁷]⁸

[(*o*) section 21 of the Intoxicating Liquor Act 2003;]⁹

["**market value**", in relation to any property, means the price which such property might reasonably be expected to fetch on a sale in the open market on the date on which the property is to be valued;]¹⁰

"**specified date**" means the date of commencement of a licence sought to be granted under any of the provisions referred to in [paragraphs (*a*) to [(*o*)]¹¹]¹² of the definition of "**licence**" as specified for the purposes of a tax clearance certificate under subsection (2);

"**tax clearance certificate**" shall be construed in accordance with subsection (2).

(2) Subject to subsection (3), the Collector-General shall, on an application to him or her by the person who will be the beneficial holder of a licence due to commence on a specified date, issue a certificate (in this section referred to as a "**tax clearance certificate**") for the purposes of the grant of a licence if—

(*a*) that person and, in respect of the period of that person's membership, any partnership of which that person is or was a partner,

(*b*) in a case where that person is a partnership, each partner,

(*c*) in a case where that person is a company, each person who is either the beneficial owner of, or able directly or indirectly to control, more than 50 per cent of the ordinary share capital of the company,

has or have complied with all the obligations imposed on that person or on them by the Acts in relation to—

(i) the payment or remittance of the taxes, interest and penalties required to be paid or remitted under the Acts, and

(ii) the delivery of returns.

(3) Subject to subsection (4), where a person (in this section referred to as "**the first-mentioned person**") will be the beneficial holder of a licence due to commence on a specified date and another person (in this section referred to as "**the second-mentioned person**") was the beneficial holder of the licence at any time during the year ending on that date, and—

(*a*) the second-mentioned person is a company connected (within the meaning of section 10 as it applies for the purposes of the Tax Acts) with the first-mentioned person or would have been such a company but for the fact that the company has been wound up or dissolved without being wound up,

(b) the second-mentioned person is a company and the first-mentioned person is a partnership in which—

   (i)   a partner is or was able, or

   (ii) where more than one partner is a shareholder, those partners together are or were able,

   directly or indirectly, whether with or without a connected person or connected persons (within the meaning of section 10 as it applies for the purposes of the Tax Acts), to control more than 50 per cent of the ordinary share capital of the company, or

(c) the second-mentioned person is a partnership and the first-mentioned person is a company in which—

   (i)   a partner is or was able, or

   (ii) where more than one partner is a shareholder, those partners together are or were able,

   directly or indirectly, whether with or without a connected person or connected persons (within the meaning of section 10 as it applies for the purposes of the Tax Acts), to control more than 50 per cent of the ordinary share capital of the company,

then, a tax clearance certificate shall not be issued by the Collector-General under subsection (2) unless, in relation to the activities conducted under the licence, the second-mentioned person has complied with the second-mentioned person's obligations under the Acts as specified in subsection (2).

[(3A) Where—

(a) the first-mentioned person will be the beneficial holder of a licence due to commence on a specified date on foot of a certificate granted or to be granted under section 2(1) (as amended by section 23 of the Intoxicating Liquor Act, 1960) of the Licensing (Ireland) Act, 1902,

(b) the second-mentioned person was the beneficial holder of the last licence issued prior to the specified date in respect of the premises for which the certificate referred to in paragraph (a) was granted, and

(c) the acquisition of the premises by the said first-mentioned person was for a consideration of less than market value at the date of such acquisition,

then, subsection (3) shall apply as if—

   (i)   the reference to the year ending on that date were a reference to 5 years ending on that date, and

   (ii) the reference to the activities conducted under the licence was a reference to the activities conducted by the second-mentioned person under the last licence held by the said person prior to the specified date.][13]

(4) Subsection (3) shall not apply to a transfer of a licence effected before the 24th day of April, 1992, or to such transfer effected after that date where a contract for the sale or lease of the premises to which the licence relates was signed before that date.

[(5) An application for a tax clearance certificate under this section shall be made to the Collector-General in a form prescribed by the Revenue Commissioners or in such other manner as the Revenue Commissioners may allow.]¹⁴

(6) Where an application for a tax clearance certificate under this section is refused by the Collector-General, he or she shall as soon as is practicable communicate in writing such refusal and the grounds for such refusal to the person concerned.

(7) (*a*)　Where an application under this section to the Collector-General for a tax clearance certificate is refused, the person aggrieved by the refusal may, by notice in writing given to the Collector-General within 30 days of the refusal, apply to have such person's application heard and determined by the Appeal Commissioners; but no right of appeal shall exist by virtue of this section in relation to any amount of tax or interest due under the Acts.

(*b*)　A notice under paragraph (*a*) shall be valid only if—

(i)　that notice specifies—

(I)　the matter or matters with which the person is aggrieved, and

(II)　the grounds in detail of the person's appeal as respects each such matter,

and

(ii)　any amount under the Acts which is due to be remitted or paid, and which is not in dispute, is duly remitted or paid.

(*c*)　The Appeal Commissioners shall hear and determine an appeal made to them under this subsection as if it were an appeal against an assessment to income tax and, subject to paragraph (*d*), the provisions of the Income Tax Acts relating to such an appeal (including the provisions relating to the rehearing of an appeal and to the statement of a case for the opinion of the High Court on a point of law) shall apply accordingly with any necessary modifications.

(*d*)　On the hearing of an appeal made under this subsection, the Appeal Commissioners shall have regard to all matters to which the Collector-General is required to have regard under this section.

[(8) A tax clearance certificate to be issued by the Collector-General under this section may—

(*a*)　be issued in electronic format, and

(*b*)　with the agreement in writing of the applicant, be published in a secure electronic medium and be accessed by persons authorised by the applicant to do so.

(9) A tax clearance certificate shall be valid for the period specified in the certificate.]¹⁵

Amendments

¹　Substituted by FA 2002, s 127(*a*)(i)(I)(A) with effect from 25 March 2002; previously "means a licence or authorisation".

²　Substituted by FA 2002, s 127(*a*)(i)(I)(B) with effect from 25 March 2002; previously ";".

³　Definition of "licence" paras (*h*)–(*i*) substituted by FA 1999, s 212(*a*)(i) with effect from 25 March 1999.

⁴　Definition of "licence" para (*k*) inserted by FA 2000, s 163 with effect from 23 March 2000.

⁵　Definition of "licence" para (*l*) inserted by FA 2001, s 234 with effect from 6 April 2001.

[6] Substituted by Intoxicating Liquor Act 2003, s 21(7)(*a*)(i) with effect from 18 August 2003; previously "1992, and".

[7] Substituted by Intoxicating Liquor Act 2003, s 21(7)(*a*)(i), with effect from 18 August 2003; previously "1910;".

[8] Definition of "licence" paras (1)(*m*)–(*n*) inserted by FA 2002, s 127(*a*)(i)(I)(C) with effect from 25 March 2002.

[9] Definition of "licence" para (*o*) inserted by Intoxicating Liquor Act 2003, s 21(7)(*a*)(ii) with effect from 18 August 2003.

[10] Definition of "market value" inserted by FA 1999, s 212(*a*)(ii) with effect from 25 March 1999.

[11] Substituted by Intoxicating Liquor Act 2003, s 21(7)(*b*) with effect from 18 August 2003; previously "(*n*)".

[12] Substituted by FA 2002, s 127(*a*)(i)(II) with effect from 25 March 2002; previously "paragraphs (*a*) to (*j*)".

[13] Subs (3A) inserted by FA 1999, s 212(*b*) with effect from 25 March 1999.

[14] Subs (5) substituted by FA 2002, s 127(*a*)(ii) with effect from 25 March 2002.

[15] Subss (8)–(9) inserted by FA 2002, s 127(*a*)(iii) with effect from 25 March 2002.

Cross-references

This section to be construed together with the Value Added Tax Acts 1972–1997, in so far as relating to value added tax: s 1104(3).

Deduction from consideration on disposal of certain assets, meaning of "tax clearance certificate" applied: s 980(8A)(*a*)(ii).

Donations to certain sports bodies, tax clearance certificates in respect of, subs (5) to (9) applied: s 847A(3)(*b*).

Intoxicating Liquor Act 2003, s 21(6) and (7), licences to national sporting arenas.

Private Security Services Act 2004, s 24(3), (5), (7) (tax clearance) — references to subs (7) of this section.

Tax clearance certificates for purposes of the Standards in Public Offices Act 2001, subs (6) and (7) applied: Standards in Public Offices Act 2001, s 25(3), (4)(*b*).

Tax clearance certificates, general scheme, meaning of "licence" applied: s 1095(1), subss (5) to (9) applied: s 1095(6).

Case law

Collector of Customs and Excise did not have power to renew a liquor license that had expired six years earlier, although trading had continued for that period: *Connolly v Collector of Customs and Excise* (IV) ITR (419).

Revenue information

Information leaflet CG1 — Tax Clearance Scheme.

Tax Briefing

TB47 April 2002 pp 23–24 — Tax Clearance — Finance Act 2002.

eBrief

eBrief no 7–2004 — From 8 March 2004, applications for most categories of Tax Clearance Certificates should be sent directly to the taxpayer's local Revenue District. Non-residents' applications, and applications under the Standards in Public Offices Act 2001 (which sets out the tax clearance requirements for members of the Dáil and Seanad, senior public officials and candidates for appointment to the judiciary), should continue to apply to the Collector-General's Division, Sarsfield House, Limerick.

eBrief 30–2005 — Customers, who require a tax clearance certificate and have outstanding tax issues, are advised to make arrangements to bring their tax affairs up to date in good time to allow for issue of the certificate.

Customers are reminded that for security reasons tax clearance certificates are now being printed and issued from a secure central facility. Therefore, it is not possible to collect a tax clearance certificate at a local Revenue office.

Definitions

Appeal Commissioners: s 2(1); Collector-General: s 2(1); company: ss 4(1), 5(1); ordinary share capital: s 2(1); person: IA 2005, s 18(*c*); Tax Acts: s 1(2); year: IA 2005, Sch.

Former enactments

FA 1992, s 242; FA 1993, s 140; FA 1997, s 160(1).

1095 Tax clearance certificates: general scheme

[(1) In this section—

"the Acts" means—

(*a*)   the Tax Acts,

(*b*)   the Capital Gains Tax Acts, and

(*c*)   the Value Added Tax Act, 1972, and the enactments amending or extending that Act,

and any instruments made thereunder;

"licence" has the same meaning as in section 1094;

"tax clearance certificate" shall be construed in accordance with subsection (3).

(2) The provisions of this section shall apply in relation to every application by a person to the Collector-General for a tax clearance certificate other than an application for such a certificate made—

(*a*)   in relation to a licence, or

(*b*)   pursuant to the requirements of—

(i)   section 847A (inserted by the Finance Act, 2002),

(ii)   the Standards in Public Office Act, 2001, or

(iii)   Regulation 6 of the Criminal Justice (Legal Aid) (Tax Clearance Certificate) Regulations 1999 (SI No 135 of 1999).

(3) Subject to this section, where a person who is in compliance with the obligations imposed on the person by the Acts in relation to—

(*a*)   the payment or remittance of any taxes, interest or penalties required to be paid or remitted under the Acts, and

(*b*)   the delivery of any returns to be made under the Acts,

applies to the Collector-General in that behalf the Collector-General shall issue to the person a certificate (in this section referred to as a "tax clearance certificate") stating that the person is in compliance with those obligations.

(4) A tax clearance certificate shall not be issued to a person unless—

(*a*)   that person and, in respect of the period of that person's membership, any partnership of which that person is or was a partner,

(*b*)   in a case where that person is a partnership, each partner, and

(*c*)   in a case where that person is a company, each person who is either the beneficial owner of, or able directly or indirectly to control, more than 50 per cent of the ordinary share capital of the company,

is in compliance with the obligations imposed on the person and each other person (including any partnership) by the Acts in relation to the matters specified in paragraphs (*a*) and (*b*) of subsection (3).

(5) Where a person who applies for a tax clearance certificate in accordance with subsection (3) (in this section referred to as "the first-mentioned person") carries on a business activity which was previously carried on by, or was previously carried on as

part of a business activity by, another person (in this section referred to as "the second-mentioned person") and—

(*a*) the second-mentioned person is a company connected (within the meaning of section 10 as it applies for the purposes of the Tax Acts) with the first-mentioned person or would have been such a company but for the fact that the company has been wound up or dissolved without being wound up,

(*b*) the second-mentioned person is a company and the first-mentioned person is a partnership in which—

　(i) a partner is or was able, or

　(ii) where more than one partner is a shareholder, those partners together are or were able,

directly or indirectly, whether with or without a connected person or connected persons (within the meaning of section 10 as it applies for the purposes of the Tax Acts), to control more than 50 per cent of the ordinary share capital of the company, or

(*c*) the second-mentioned person is a partnership and the first-mentioned person is a company in which—

　(i) a partner is or was able, or

　(ii) where more than one partner is a shareholder, those partners together are or were able,

directly or indirectly, whether with or without a connected person or connected persons (within the meaning of section 10 as it applies for the purposes of the Tax Acts), to control more than 50 per cent of the ordinary share capital of the company,

then, a tax clearance certificate shall not be issued by the Collector-General under subsection (3) to the first-mentioned person unless, in relation to that business activity, the second-mentioned person is in compliance with the obligations imposed on that person by the Acts in relation to the matters specified in paragraphs *(a)* and *(b)* of subsection (3).

(6) Subsections (5) to (9) of section 1094 shall apply to an application for a tax clearance certificate under this section as they apply to an application for a tax clearance certificate under that section.]¹

Amendments

¹　Section 1095 substituted by FA 2002, s 127(*b*) with effect from 25 March 2002.

Cross-references

This section to be construed together with the Value Added Tax Acts 1972–1997, in so far as relating to value added tax: s 1104(3).

Deduction from consideration on disposal of certain assets, meaning of "tax clearance certificate" applied: s 980(8A)(*a*)(ii); s 980(8A)(*b*).

Taxi Regulation Act 2003, s 37(1), tax clearance certification requirements for licence applicants.

Private Security Services Act 2004, s 24 (tax clearance), meaning of "tax clearance certificate" applied; reference to subs (6) of TCA 1997, s 1095.

Public Service Management (Recruitment and Appointment) Act 2004, s 26.

Revenue precedents

Issue: Whether Local Authority obliged to operate Tax Clearance when completing a compulsory purchase of land.

Decision: Not obliged to operate tax clearance, since the Local Authority is not entering into a contract with the landowner. It is exercising its powers under a statutory scheme for land acquisition. This applies whether the price paid for the land has been agreed between the Local Authority and the land owner or has been fixed by arbitration. Where the Local authority enters into a contract with a landowner for purchase of land it would be obliged to operate Tax Clearance, even though it could compulsorily acquire the land.

Issue: Do individuals and companies need to produce a Tax Clearance Certificate in circumstances where rent in excess of £5,000 per annum is payable out of public funds.

Decision: Yes.

Issue: Do the Tax Clearance requirements of Department of Finance Circular F49/13/87 apply to payments made by the Department of Agriculture under the Forest Premium Scheme?

Decision: Yes.

Revenue information

Information leaflet CG1 — Tax Clearance Scheme.

eBrief

eBrief no 7–2004 — From 8 March 2004, applications for most categories of Tax Clearance Certificates should be sent directly to the taxpayer's local Revenue District. Non-residents' applications, and applications under the Standards in Public Offices Act 2001 (which sets out the tax clearance requirements for members of the Dáil and Seanad, senior public officials and candidates for appointment to the judiciary), should continue to apply to the Collector-General's Division, Sarsfield House, Limerick.

eBrief 30–2005 — Customers, who require a tax clearance certificate and have outstanding tax issues, are advised to make arrangements to bring their tax affairs up to date in good time to allow for issue of the certificate.

Customers are reminded that for security reasons tax clearance certificates are now being printed and issued from a secure central facility. Therefore, it is not possible to collect a tax clearance certificate at a local Revenue office.

Tax Briefing

TB47 April 2002 pp 23–24 — Tax Clearance — Finance Act 2002.

Definitions

Capital Gains Tax Acts: s 1(2); Collector-General: s 2(1); company: ss 4(1), 5(1); ordinary share capital: s 2(1); person: IA 2005, s 18(*c*); Tax Acts: s 1(2).

Former enactments

FA 1995, s 177(1)–(6); FA 1996, s 132(1) and Sch 5 Pt I para 19.

1096B Evidence of computer stored records in court proceedings etc

[(1) In this section—

"copy record" means any copy of an original record or a copy of that copy made in accordance with either of the methods referred to in subsection (2) and accompanied by the certificate referred to in subsection (4), which original record or copy of an original record is in the possession of the Revenue Commissioners;

"original record" means any document, record or record of an entry in a document or record or information stored by means of any storage equipment, whether or not in a legible form, made or stored by the Revenue Commissioners for the purposes of or in connection with tax, and which is in the possession of the Revenue Commissioners;

"provable record" means an original record or a copy record and, in the case of an original record or a copy record stored in any storage equipment, whether or not in a legible form, includes the production or reproduction of the record in a legible form;

"storage equipment" means any electronic, magnetic, mechanical, photographic, optical or other device used for storing information;

"tax" means any tax, duty, levy or charge under the care and management of the Revenue Commissioners.

(2) Where by reason of—

    (*a*)   the deterioration of,

    (*b*)   the inconvenience in storing, or

    (*c*)   the technical obsolescence in the manner of retaining or storing,

any original record or any copy record, the Revenue Commissioners may—

    (i)   make a legible copy of that record, or

    (ii)   store information concerning that record otherwise than in a legible form so that the information is capable of being used to make a legible copy of that record,

and, they may, thereupon destroy that original record or that copy record.

(3) The legible copy of—

    (*a*)   a record made, or

    (*b*)   the information concerning such record stored,

in accordance with subsection (2) shall be deemed to be an original record for the purposes of this section.

(4) In any proceedings a certificate signed by an officer of the Revenue Commissioners stating that a copy record has been made in accordance with the provisions of subsection (2) shall be evidence of the fact of the making of such a copy record and that it is a true copy, unless the contrary is shown.

(5) In any proceedings a document purporting to be a certificate signed by an officer of the Revenue Commissioners, referred to in subsection (4), shall for the purposes of this section be deemed to be such a certificate and to be so signed unless the contrary is shown.

(6) A provable record shall be admissible in evidence in any proceedings and shall be evidence of any fact stated in it or event recorded by it unless the contrary is shown, or unless the court is not satisfied as to the reliability of the system used to make or compile—

    (*a*)   in the case of an original record, that record, and

    (*b*)   in the case of a copy record, the original on which it was based.

(7) In any proceedings a certificate signed by an officer of the Revenue Commissioners, stating that a full and detailed search has been made for a record of any event in every place where such records are kept and that no such record has been found, shall be evidence that the event did not happen unless the contrary is shown or unless the court is not satisfied—

    (*a*)   as to the reliability of the system used to compile or make or keep such records,

    (*b*)   that, if the event had happened, a record would have been made of it, and

    (*c*)   that the system is such that the only reasonable explanation for the absence of such record is that the event did not happen.

(8) For the purposes of this section, and subject to the direction and control of the Revenue Commissioners, any power, function or duty conferred or imposed on them

may be exercised or performed on their behalf by an officer of the Revenue Commissioners.]¹

Amendments

¹   Section 1096B inserted by FA 2002, s 135 with effect from 25 March 2002.

PART 49

COMMENCEMENT, REPEALS, TRANSITIONAL PROVISIONS, ETC

1100 Consequential amendments to other enactments

Schedule 31, which provides for amendments to other enactments consequential on the passing of this Act, shall apply for the purposes of this Act.

1104 Short title and construction

(1) This Act may be cited as the Taxes Consolidation Act, 1997.

...

(3) Sections 7, 811, 858, 859, 872(1), 887, 905, 906, 910 and 912, subsections (2) and (3) of section 928, and sections 1001, 1002, 1006, 1078, 1079, 1086, 1093, 1094 and 1095 (in so far as relating to Value Added tax) shall be construed together with the Value Added Tax Acts, 1972 to 1997.

...

SCHEDULE 31
Consequential amendments

Section 1100

In the enactments specified in Column (1) of the following Table for the words set out or referred to in Column (2) there shall be substituted the words set out in the corresponding entry in Column (3).

Enactment amended (1)	Words to be replaced (2)	Words to be substituted (3)
... The Value Added Tax Act, 1972: section 1, in the definition of "Appeal Commissioners"	section 156 of the Income Tax Act, 1967	section 850 of the Taxes Consolidation Act, 1997
section 1, in the definition of "Collector-General"	section 162 of the Income Tax Act, 1967	section 851 of the Taxes Consolidation Act, 1997
section 1, in the definition of "inspector of taxes"	section 161 of the Income Tax Act, 1967	section 852 of the Taxes Consolidation Act, 1997
section 1, in the definition of "secretary"	section 207(2) of the Income Tax Act, 1967	section 1044(2) of the Taxes Consolidation Act, 1997
section 1(2)(*bb*)	section 73 of the Finance Act, 1988	section 1002 of the Taxes Consolidation Act, 1997

Enactment amended (1)	Words to be replaced (2)	Words to be substituted (3)
section 1(2)(*c*)(i)	Chapter III of Part I of the Finance Act, 1987	Chapter 1 of Part 18 of the Taxes Consolidation Act, 1997
section 1(2)(*c*)(ii)	section 17 of the Finance Act, 1970	Chapter 2 of Part 18 of the Taxes Consolidation Act, 1997
section 18(1)(*a*)(ii*a*)	section 94 (as amended by section 243 of the Finance Act, 1992) of the Finance Act, 1983	section 1078 of the Taxes Consolidation Act, 1997
section 24(1)(*b*)	sections 480, 485, 486, 487, 488 and 491 of the Income Tax Act, 1967	sections 962, 963, 964(1), 966, 967 and 998 of the Taxes Consolidation Act, 1997
section 24(5)	under section 485 of the Income Tax Act, 1967	under section 962 of the Taxes Consolidation Act, 1997
	section 485	section 962
section 27(11)	section 94 (as amended by section 243 of the Finance Act, 1992) of the Finance Act, 1983	section 1078 of the Taxes Consolidation Act, 1997
section 31	section 512 of the Income Tax Act, 1967	section 1065 of the Taxes Consolidation Act, 1997
First Schedule, in paragraph (i)(*g*)	section 18 of the Finance Act, 1989	section 734 of the Taxes Consolidation Act, 1997
...		
The Value Added Tax Regulations, 1979 (SI 63/ 1979):		
Regulation 15, in paragraph (2)	Section 485 of the Income Tax Act, 1967	Section 962 of the Taxes Consolidation Act, 1997
	the words from "modifications in subsection (1)" to the end of the paragraph	modification in subsection (1), namely, the words "any sum which may be levied on that person in respect of income tax" shall be construed as referring to Value Added tax payable by the person concerned
Regulation 15, in paragraph (3)	Section 486 of the Income Tax Act, 1967	Section 963 of the Taxes Consolidation Act, 1997
Regulation 15, in paragraph (3)(*a*)	income tax or sur-tax	income tax
Regulation 15, in paragraph (3)(*b*)	the Collector or other officer of the Revenue Commissioners, duly authorised to collect the said tax	the Collector-General or other officer of the Revenue Commissioners duly authorised to collect the tax

Enactment amended (1)	Words to be replaced (2)	Words to be substituted (3)
	the Collector or other officer under this section	the Collector-General or other officer under this section
Regulation 15, in paragraph (4)	Section 487 of the Income Tax Act, 1967	Section 964(1) of the Taxes Consolidation Act, 1997
Regulation 15, in paragraph (5)	Section 488 of the Income Tax Act, 1967	Section 966 of the Taxes Consolidation Act, 1997
Regulation 15, in paragraph (5)(*a*)	income tax or sur-tax	income tax
Regulation 15, in paragraph (5)(*b*)	references to an inspector and to the Collector	references to an inspector and to the Collector-General
Regulation 15, in paragraph (6)	Section 491 of the Income Tax Act, 1967	Section 998 of the Taxes Consolidation Act, 1997
	income tax or sur tax	income tax
...		

FINANCE ACT 1998

ARRANGEMENT OF SECTIONS

PART 3
VALUE ADDED TAX

AN ACT TO CHARGE AND IMPOSE CERTAIN DUTIES OF CUSTOMS AND INLAND REVENUE (INCLUDING EXCISE), TO AMEND THE LAW RELATING TO CUSTOMS AND INLAND REVENUE (INCLUDING EXCISE) AND TO MAKE FURTHER PROVISIONS IN CONNECTION WITH FINANCE. BE IT ENACTED BY THE OIREACHTAS AS FOLLOWS:

PART 3
VALUE ADDED TAX

104 Interpretation (Part 3)

In this Part —

"the Principal Act" means the Value Added Tax Act, 1972;

"**the Act of 1992**" means the Finance Act, 1992:

"**the Act of 1997**" means the Finance Act, 1997.

105 Amendment of section 3 (supply of goods) of Principal Act

Notes
This section substituted VATA 1972, s 3(1)(*f*) with effect from 27 March 1998.

106 Amendment of section 4 (special provisions in relation to the supply of immovable goods) of Principal Act

Notes
This section inserted VATA 1972, s 4(9)–(10) with effect from 27 March 1998.

107 Amendment of section 5 (supply of services) of Principal Act

Notes
Para (*a*)(i) inserted ", or a telephone card as defined in subsection (6A)," after "a telecommunications service" in VATA 1972, s 5(6)(*dd*) with effect from 1 May 1998.
Para (*a*)(ii) inserted VATA 1972, s 5(6)(*ddd*) with effect from 1 May 1998.
Para (*a*)(iii) inserted "with the exception of the supply of services referred to in paragraphs (*ddd*) and (*ee*) in the circumstances specified in those paragraphs respectively and" after "specified in the Fourth Schedule" in VATA 1972, s 5(6)(*e*) with effect from 1 May 1998.
Para (*a*)(iv) inserted VATA 1972, s 5(6)(*ee*) with effect from 1 May 1998.
Para (*b*) inserted VATA 1972, s 5(6A) with effect from 1 May 1998.

108 Amendment of section 8 (taxable persons) of Principal Act

Notes
Para (*a*)(i) inserted VATA 1972, s 8(3)(*a*)(i*a*) with effect from 1 July 1998.
Para (*a*)(ii) substituted "services specified in subparagraph (i) and either or both of goods of the type specified in subparagraph (i*a*) and goods of the type specified in subparagraph (ii) supplied in the circumstances set out in that subparagraph" for "services and goods specified in subparagraph (i) and (ii)" in VATA 1972, s 8(3)(*a*)(iii) with effect from 1 July 1998.
Para (*a*)(iii) inserted "or" at the end of VATA 1972, s 8(3)(*a*)(iii) with effect from 1 July 1998.
Para (*a*)(iv) inserted VATA 1972, s 8(3)(*a*)(iv) with effect from 1 July 1998.
Para (*b*) inserted ", (*a*)(i*a*)" after "paragraph (*a*)(i)" in VATA 1972, s 8(3)(*a*)(proviso)(i*a*) with effect from 1 July 1998.

109 Amendment of section 10 (amount on which tax is chargeable) of Principal Act

Notes
This section inserted ", other than telecommunications services," after "goods or services" in VATA 1972, s 10(6) with effect from 1 May 1998.

110 Amendment of section 11 (rates of tax) of Principal Act

Notes
This section substituted "3.6 per cent" for "3.3 per cent" in VATA 1972, s 11(1)(*f*) with effect from 1 March 1998.

111 Amendment of section 12 (deduction for tax borne or paid) of Principal Act

Notes

Para (*a*) inserted ", other than services consisting of the hiring out of motor vehicles (as defined in subsection (3)(*b*)) for utilisation in the State," after "outside the State" in VATA 1972, s 12(1)(*b*)(iii) with effect from 27 March 1998.

Para (*b*) substituted "sections 20(1A) and 20(5)" for "section 20(1A)" in VATA 1972, s 12(2) with effect from 27 March 1998.

112 Amendment of section 12A (special provisions for tax invoiced by flat-rate farmers) of Principal Act

Notes

This section substituted "3.6 per cent" for "3.3 per cent" in VATA 1972, s 12A(1) with effect from 1 March 1998.

113 Amendment of section 13 (remission of tax on goods exported, etc.) of Principal Act

Notes

This section substituted "or in respect of motor vehicles (as defined in section 12(3)(*b*))" for "or in respect of means of transport" in VATA 1972, s 13(3)(*c*) with effect from 27 March 1998.

114 Amendment of section 20 (refund of tax) of Principal Act

Notes

Para (*a*) substituted VATA 1972, s 20(4) with effect from 27 March 1998.

Para (*b*) substituted VATA 1972, s 20(5) with effect from 27 March 1998.

115 Amendment of section 30 (time limits) of Principal Act

Notes

This section substituted VATA 1972, s 30(4)(*a*) with effect from 27 March 1998.

116 Amendment of Second Schedule to Principal Act

Notes

Para (*a*) inserted VATA 1972, Sch 2 para (v*c*) with effect from 27 March 1998.

Para (*b*) substituted VATA 1972, Sch 2 para (xv*a*) with effect from 1 May 1998.

117 Amendment of Sixth Schedule to Principal Act

Notes

Para (*a*) inserted VATA 1972, Sch 6 paras (xi*b*)–(xi*c*) with effect from 1 July 1998 and para (xi*d*) with effect from 1 May 1998.

Para (*b*) substituted VATA 1972, Sch 6 para (xii) with effect from 1 May 1998.

PART 6
MISCELLANEOUS

133 Interest on unpaid or overpaid taxes

...

(6) This section shall apply as respects interest chargeable or payable under —

    (i)   sections 240, 531, 953, 991 and 1080 of the Taxes Consolidation Act, 1997,

   (ii)   sections 105 and 107 of the Finance Act, 1983,

  (iii)   sections 41 and 46 of the Capital Acquisitions Tax Act, 1976,

  (iv)   sections 18 and 22 of the Wealth Tax Act, 1975, and

   (v)   section 21 of the Value Added Tax Act, 1972,

for any month, or any part of a month, commencing on or after the date of the passing of this Act, in respect of an amount due to be paid or remitted or an amount due to be repaid or retained, as the case may be, whether before, on or after that date in accordance with those provisions.

Notes

Subs (3) repealed FA 1978, s 46 for any month or part of, commencing on or after 27 March 1998 in respect of an amount due to be paid or remitted, or repaid or retained before, on or after that date.

---

134 Appeals

Notes

Subs (2) inserted VATA 1972, s 25(2)(*ee*) as respects appeals determined by the Appeal Commissioners after 27 March 1998.

---

137 Care and management of taxes and duties

All taxes and duties imposed by this Act are hereby placed under the care and management of the Revenue Commissioners.

138 Short title, construction and commencement

(1) This Act may be cited as the Finance Act, 1998.

...

(4) Part 3 shall be construed together with the Value Added Tax Acts, 1972 to 1997, and may be cited together therewith as the Value Added Tax Acts, 1972 to 1998.

...

(7) Part 6 (so far as relating to income tax) shall be construed together with the Income Tax Acts and (so far as relating to corporation tax) shall be construed together with the Corporation Tax Acts and (so far as relating to capital gains tax) shall be construed together with the Capital Gains Tax Acts and (so far as relating to Value Added tax) shall be construed together with the Value Added Tax Acts, 1972 to 1998, and (so far as relating to residential property tax) shall be construed together with Part VI of the Finance Act, 1983, and the enactments amending or extending that Part and (so far as relating to gift tax or inheritance tax) shall be construed together with the Capital Acquisitions Tax Act, 1976, and the enactments amending or extending that Act and (so

far as relating to wealth tax) shall be construed together with the Wealth Tax Act, 1975, and the enactments amending or extending that Act.

...

(9) In relation to Part 3:

(*a*) sections 104, 110 and 112 and paragraph (*a*) of section 116 shall be deemed to have come into force and shall take effect as on and from the 1st day of March, 1998;

(*b*) sections 107 and 109, paragraph (*b*) of section 116, paragraph (xi*d*) of the Sixth Schedule to the Value Added Tax Act, 1972, as inserted by paragraph (*a*) of section 117 and paragraph (*b*) of section 117 shall take effect as on and from the 1st day of May, 1998;

(*c*) section 108 and paragraphs (xi*b*) and (xi*c*) of the Sixth Schedule to the Value-Added Tax Act, 1972, as inserted by paragraph (*a*) of section 117 shall take effect as on and from the 1st day of July, 1998;

(*d*) the provisions of this Part, other than those specified in paragraphs (*a*), (*b*) and (*c*), shall have effect as on and from the date of passing of this Act.

(10) Any reference in this Act to any other enactment shall, except so far as the context otherwise requires, be construed as a reference to that enactment as amended by or under any other enactment including this Act.

(11) In this Act, a reference to a Part, section or Schedule is to a Part or section of, or Schedule to, this Act, unless it is indicated that reference to some other enactment is intended.

(12) In this Act, a reference to a subsection, paragraph, subparagraph, clause or subclause is to the subsection, paragraph, subparagraph, clause or subclause of the provision (including a Schedule) in which the reference occurs, unless it is indicated that reference to some other provision is intended.

FINANCE ACT 1999

(No 2 of 1999)

ARRANGEMENT OF SECTIONS

PART 3
VALUE ADDED TAX

PART 7
MISCELLANEOUS

AN ACT TO CHARGE AND IMPOSE CERTAIN DUTIES OF CUSTOMS AND
INLAND REVENUE (INCLUDING EXCISE), TO AMEND THE LAW RELATING
TO CUSTOMS AND INLAND REVENUE (INCLUDING EXCISE) AND TO
MAKE FURTHER PROVISIONS IN CONNECTION WITH FINANCE.

PART 3
VALUE ADDED TAX

119 Interpretation (Part 3)

In this Part—

"the Principal Act" means the Value Added Tax Act, 1972;

"the Act of 1978" means the Value Added Tax (Amendment) Act, 1978;

"the Act of 1992" means the Finance Act, 1992;

"the Act of 1995" means the Finance Act, 1995;

"the Act of 1997" means the Finance Act, 1997;

"the Act of 1998" means the Finance Act, 1998.

120 Amendment of section 3 (supply of goods) of Principal Act

---

Notes

Para (*a*) substituted VATA 1972, s 3(1)(*g*)(ii) with effect from 25 March 1999.
Para (*b*) inserted VATA 1972, s 3(5)(*c*) with effect from 25 March 1999.
Para (*c*) substituted "£27,565" for "£27,000" in VATA 1972, s 3(6)(*d*)(proviso)(A) with effect from 25 March 1999.

121 Amendment of section 5 (supply of services) of Principal Act

---

Notes

Section 121 inserted VATA 1972, s 5(6)(*dddd*) with effect from 25 March 1999.

122 Special scheme for investment gold

Notes

Section 122 inserted VATA 1972, s 6A with effect from 1 January 2000.

123 Amendment of section 8 (taxable persons) of Principal Act

---

Notes

Section 123 substituted "bovine" for "livestock" in VATA 1972, s 8(3)(*a*)(ia) with effect from 25 March 1999.

124 Amendment of section 10 (amount on which tax is chargeable) of Principal Act

Notes

Section 124 substituted "cost of the goods to the person making the supply or, in the absence of such a cost, the cost price of similar goods in the State, and where an intra-Community acquisition occurs in the State following a supply of goods in another Member State which, if such supply was carried out in similar circumstances in the State would be a supply of goods in accordance with section 3(1)(g), then the amount on which tax is chargeable in respect of that intra-Community acquisition shall be the cost to the person making the supply in that Member State or, in the absence of a cost to that person, the cost price of similar goods in that other Member State" for "open market price" in VATA 1972, s 10(4B) with effect from 25 March 1999.

125 Amendment of section 10A (margin scheme goods) of Principal Act

Notes

Para (*a*) substituted VATA 1972, s 10A(1) definition of "margin scheme goods" with effect from 1 September 1999.
Para (*b*) inserted "agricultural machinery (within the meaning of section 12C)," in VATA 1972, s 10A(1) definition of "second-hand goods" with effect from 1 September 1999.

126 Amendment of section 10B (special scheme for auctioneers) of Principal Act

Notes

Section 126 inserted VATA 1972, s 10B(1)(*aa*) with effect from 25 March 1999.

127 Amendment of section 11 (rates of tax) of Principal Act

Notes

Section 127 substituted "4 per cent" for "3.6 per cent" in VATA 1972, s 11(1)(*f*) with effect from 1 March 1999.

128 Amendment of section 12 (deduction for tax borne or paid) of Principal Act

Notes

Para (*a*) inserted VATA 1972, s 12(1)(*a*)(iiie) with effect from 1 January 2000.
Para (*b*) inserted VATA 1972, s 12(1)(*a*)(vi*a*) with effect from 1 September 1999.

129 Amendment of section 12A (special provisions for tax invoiced by flat-rate farmers) of Principal Act

Notes

Section 129 substituted "4 per cent" for "3.6 per cent" in VATA 1972, s 12A(1) with effect from 1 March 1999.

130 Amendment of section 12B (special scheme for means of transport supplied by taxable dealers) of Principal Act

Notes

Para (*a*)(i) inserted "(other than in the circumstances where an owner as referred to in paragraph (*c*) of subsection (5) of section 3, enforces such owner's right to recover possession of a means of transport)" in VATA 1972, s 12B(2) with effect from 25 March 1999.
Para (*a*)(ii) inserted VATA 1972, s 12B(2)(*aa*) with effect from 25 March 1999.

Para (*b*) inserted "agricultural machinery (within the meaning of section 12C), and" in VATA 1972, s 12B(3) with effect from 1 September 1999.

131 Special scheme for agricultural machinery

Notes

Section 131 inserted VATA 1972, s 12C with effect from 1 September 1999.

132 Amendment of section 13 (remission of tax on goods exported, etc.) of Principal Act

Notes

Section 132 inserted "and where an amount so notified is expressed in terms of a percentage or a fraction, such percentage or fraction shall relate to the tax remitted or repayable under this subsection," in VATA 1972, s 13(1A)(iii) with effect from 1 May 1999.

133 Amendment of section 16 (duty to keep records) of Principal Act

Notes

Section 133 inserted VATA 1972, s 16(1A) with effect from 1 January 2000.

134 Amendment of section 17 (invoices) of Principal Act

Notes

Section 134 inserted VATA 1972, s 17(2A) with effect from 1 September 1999.

135 Amendment of section 19 (tax due and payable) of Principal Act

Notes

Section 135 inserted "or, if section 131 of the Finance Act, 1992, does not provide for registration of the vehicle, at a time not later than the time when the tax is due in accordance with subsection (1A)" in VATA 1972, s 19(4)(*a*)(i)(I) with effect from 25 March 1999.

136 Generation of estimates and assessments by electronic, photographic or other process

Notes

Section 136 inserted VATA 1972, s 22A with effect from 25 March 1999.

137 Amendment of section 32 (regulations) of Principal Act

Notes

Section 137 inserted VATA 1972, s 32(1)(h*a*)–(h*d*) with effect from 25 March 1999.

138 Amendment of First Schedule to Principal Act

Notes

Para (*a*) inserted VATA 1972, Sch 1 para (i)(*g*)(I*a*) with effect from 25 March 1999.
Para (*b*) inserted VATA 1972, Sch 1 paras (xviii*a*)–(xviii*b*) with effect from 1 January 2000.

139 Amendment of Second Schedule to Principal Act

Notes

Section 139 inserted VATA 1972, Sch 2 para (i)(*aa*) with effect from 1 July 1999.

PART 7
MISCELLANEOUS

207 Amendment of Chapter 4 (revenue powers) of Part 18 of Taxes Consolidation Act, 1997

...

Notes

Para (*f*)(i) deleted TCA 1997, s 905(2)(*d*).
Para (*f*)(ii) inserted TCA 1997, s 905(2A).

208 Power to obtain information from a Minister of the Government or public body

Notes

Section 208 substituted TCA 1997, s 910(1).

209 Electronic filing of tax returns

Notes

Section 209 inserted TCA 1997, Pt 38 Ch 6 (ss 917D–917N).

211 Amendment of section 1078 (revenue offences) of Taxes Consolidation Act, 1997

Notes

Para (*a*) inserted TCA 1997, s 1078(2)(*hh*).
Para (*b*) substituted "£10,000" for "£10,000" in TCA 1997, s 1078(3)(*b*).
Para (*c*) inserted TCA 1997, s 1078(3A).

212 Amendment of section 1094 (tax clearance in relation to certain licences) of Taxes Consolidation Act, 1997

Notes

Para (*a*)(i) substituted TCA 1997, s 1094(1) definition of "licence" (*h*)–(*i*).
Para (*a*)(ii) inserted TCA 1997, s 1094(1) definition of "market value".
Para (*b*) inserted TCA 1997, s 1094(3A).

216 Care and management of taxes and duties

All taxes and duties imposed by this Act are hereby placed under the care and management of the Revenue Commissioners.

217 Short title, construction and commencement

(1) This Act may be cited as the Finance Act, 1999.

...

(4) Part 3 shall be construed together with the Value Added Tax Acts, 1972 to 1998, and may be cited together therewith as the Value Added Tax Acts, 1972 to 1999.

...

(8) Part 7 (so far as relating to income tax) shall be construed together with the Income Tax Acts and (so far as relating to corporation tax) shall be construed together with the Corporation Tax Acts and (so far as relating to capital gains tax) shall be construed together with the Capital Gains Tax Acts and (so far as relating to customs) shall be construed together with the Custom Acts and (so far as relating to duties of excise) shall be construed together with the statutes which relate to duties of excise and the management of those duties and (so far as relating to Value Added tax) shall be construed together with the Value Added Tax Acts, 1972 to 1999, and (so far as relating to stamp duty) shall be construed together with the Stamp Act, 1891, and the enactments amending or extending that Act and (so far as relating to residential property tax) shall be construed together with Part VI of the Finance Act, 1983, and the enactments amending or extending that Part and (so far as relating to gift tax or inheritance tax) shall be construed together with the Capital Acquisitions Tax Act, 1976, and the enactments amending or extending that Act.

...

(11) Any reference in this Act to any other enactment shall, except so far as the context otherwise requires, be construed as a reference to that enactment as amended by or under any other enactment including this Act.

(12) In this Act, a reference to a Part, section or Schedule is to a Part or section of, or Schedule to, this Act, unless it is indicated that reference to some other enactment is intended.

(13) In this Act, a reference to a subsection, paragraph, subparagraph, clause or subclause is to the subsection, paragraph, subparagraph, clause or subclause of the provision (including a Schedule) in which the reference occurs, unless it is indicated that reference to some other provision is intended.

FINANCE ACT 2000

(No 3 of 2000)

ARRANGEMENT OF SECTIONS

PART 3
VALUE ADDED TAX

PART 7
MISCELLANEOUS

AN ACT TO CHARGE AND IMPOSE CERTAIN DUTIES OF CUSTOMS AND
INLAND REVENUE (INCLUDING EXCISE), TO AMEND THE LAW

RELATING TO CUSTOMS AND INLAND REVENUE (INCLUDING EXCISE)
AND TO MAKE FURTHER PROVISIONS IN CONNECTION WITH FINANCE.
[23rd MARCH 2000]

BE IT ENACTED BY THE OIREACHTAS AS FOLLOWS:

PART 3
VALUE ADDED TAX

107 Interpretation (Part 3)

In this Part—

"the Principal Act" means the Value Added Tax Act, 1972;

"the Act of 1978" means the Value Added Tax (Amendment) Act, 1978;

"the Act of 1992" means the Finance Act, 1992;

"the Act of 1999" means the Finance Act, 1999.

108 Amendment of section 1 (interpretation) of Principal Act

Notes

Section 108 substituted VATA 1972, s 1 (definition of "telecommunications services") with effect from 23 March 2000.

109 Amendment of section 6A (special scheme for investment gold) of Principal Act

Notes

Para (*a*) substituted "investment gold, including investment gold which is represented by securities" for "investment gold which is represented by securities" by FA 2000, s 109(*a*) with effect from 23 March 2000.

Para (*b*) inserted VATA 1972, s 6A(9) with effect from 23 March 2000.

110 Amendment of section 8 (taxable persons) of Principal Act

Notes

Para (*a*)(i) substituted "goods or services, other than services of the kind referred to in paragraph (xiii) of the Sixth Schedule," for "such goods or services" in VATA 1972, s 8(5) with effect from 23 March 2000.

Para (*a*)(ii) substituted "goods or services, other than services of the kind referred to in paragraph (xiii) of the Sixth Schedule." for "goods or services." in VATA 1972, s 8(5) with effect from 23 March 2000.

Para (*b*) inserted VATA 1972, s 8(5A) with effect from 23 March 2000.

Para (*c*) inserted "or subsection (5A)" after "subsection (5)" in VATA 1972, s 8(6) with effect from 23 March 2000.

111 Amendment of section 11 (rates of tax) of Principal Act

Notes

Section 111 substituted "4.2 per cent" for "4 per cent" in VATA 1972, s 11(1)(*f*) with effect from 1 March 2000.

112 Amendment of section 12 (deduction for tax borne or paid) of Principal Act

Notes

Para (*a*) inserted VATA 1972, s 12(1)(*a*)(vi*b*) with effect from 23 March 2000.

Para (*b*) substituted VATA 1972, s 12(4) with effect from 23 March 2000.

113 Amendment of section 12A (special provisions for tax invoiced by flat-rate farmers) of Principal Act

Notes

Section 113 substituted "4.2 per cent" for "4 per cent" in VATA 1972, s 12A(1) with effect from 1 March 2000.

114 Amendment of section 12C (special scheme for agricultural machinery) of Principal Act

Notes

Section 114 inserted VATA 1972, s 12C(1A)–(1B) with effect from 23 March 2000.

115 Amendment of section 17 (invoices) of Principal Act

Notes

Section 115 inserted "or section 12C(1B)" after "subsection (1AA)" in VATA 1972, s 17(1AB) with effect from 23 March 2000.

116 Amendment of section 20 (refund of tax) of Principal Act

Notes

Para (*a*) inserted VATA 1972, s 20(3)(*bb*) with effect from 23 March 2000.

Para (*b*) substituted VATA 1972, s 20(5)(*a*) with effect from 23 March 2000.

Para (*c*) substituted "a loss of demand for those goods or services, for the period for which the claim is being made" for "a loss of turnover" in VATA 1972, s 20(5)(*d*)(i) with effect from 23 March 2000.

Para (*d*) substituted "loss of demand" for "loss of turnover" in VATA 1972, s 20(5)(*d*)(iii) with effect from 23 March 2000.

117 Amendment of section 22 (estimation of tax due for taxable period) of Principal Act

Notes

Section 117 substituted "period" for "taxable period" where it occurs in VATA 1972, s 22(1)–(2) with effect from 23 March 2000.

118 Amendment of section 23 (assessment of tax due for any period) due for any period) of Principal Act

Notes

Para (*a*) deleted "consisting of one taxable period or of two or more consecutive taxable periods" from VATA 1972, s 23(1) with effect from 23 March 2000.

Para (*b*) deleted "the taxable period or periods comprised in" from VATA 1972, s 23(1) with effect from 23 March 2000.

119 Amendment of section 25 (appeals) of Principal Act

Notes

Section 119 substituted "periods" for "taxable periods" in VATA 1972, s 25(2)(i) with effect from 23 March 2000.

120 Amendment of section 27 (fraudulent returns, etc) of Principal Act

Notes

Section 120 deleted VATA 1972, s 120(8) with effect from 23 March 2000.

121 Amendment of section 32 (regulations) of Principal Act

Notes

Section 121 deleted "by tax-free shops" from VATA 1972, s 32(1)(*ag*) with effect from 1 July 1999.

122 Amendment of First Schedule to Principal Act

Notes

Section 122 inserted "of bets of the kind referred to in section 75 of the Finance Act, 1997" after "Finance Act, 1994" in VATA 1972, Sch 1 para (xv) with effect from 23 March 2000.

123 Amendment of Second Schedule to Principal Act

Notes

Para (*a*) substituted VATA 1972, Sch 2 para (*ia*) with effect from 1 July 1999.

Para (*b*) inserted "but not including goods for supply on board such vessels or aircraft to passengers for the purpose of those goods being carried off such vessels or aircraft" after "paragraph (v)" in VATA 1972, Sch 2 para (*vb*) with effect from 1 July 1999.

Para (*c*) inserted ", directories" after "catalogues" in VATA 1972, Sch 2 para (xva)(*a*) with effect from 23 March 2000.

124 Revocation (Part 3)

Notes

Section 124 revoked the European Communities (Value Added Tax) Regulations, 1999 (SI 196/1999) with effect from 1 July 1999.

PART 7
MISCELLANEOUS

154 Interpretation (Part 7)

In this Part **"Principal Act"** means the Taxes Consolidation Act, 1997.

162 Amendment of section 1086 (publication of names of tax defaulters) of Principal Act

Notes

Subs (1)(*a*)(i) substituted "tax," for "tax, or" in TCA 1997, s 1086(2)(*b*) and "tax, or" for "tax." in TCA 1997, s 1086(2)(*c*)(iii) as respects fines or other penalties, as are referred to in s 1086(2)(*a*)–(*b*), which are imposed by a court, and as respects specified sums, as are referred to in s 1086(2)(*c*)–(*d*), which the Revenue

Commissioners accepted, or undertook to accept, in settlement of a specified liability, on or after 23 March 2000.

Subs (1)(*a*)(ii) inserted TCA 1997, s 1086(2)(*d*) as respects fines or other penalties, as are referred to in s 1086(2)(*a*)–(*b*), which are imposed by a court, and as respects specified sums, as are referred to in s 1086(2)(*c*)–(*d*), which the Revenue Commissioners accepted, or undertook to accept, in settlement of a specified liability, on or after 23 March 2000.

Subs (1)(*b*) inserted TCA 1997, s 1086(2A) as respects fines or other penalties, as are referred to in s 1086(2)(*a*)–(*b*), which are imposed by a court, and as respects specified sums, as are referred to in s 1086(2)(*c*)–(*d*), which the Revenue Commissioners accepted, or undertook to accept, in settlement of a specified liability, on or after 23 March 2000.

Subs (1)(*c*)(i) substituted "Paragraph (*c*) and (*d*)" for "Paragraph (*c*)" in TCA 1997, s 1086(4) as respects fines or other penalties, as are referred to in s 1086(2)(*a*)–(*b*), which are imposed by a court, and as respects specified sums, as are referred to in s 1086(2)(*c*)–(*d*), which the Revenue Commissioners accepted, or undertook to accept, in settlement of a specified liability, on or after 23 March 2000.

Subs (1)(*c*)(ii) substituted "paragraph (*c*) or (*d*), as the case may be," for "paragraph (*c*)" in TCA 1997, s 1086(4)(*c*) as respects fines or other penalties, as are referred to in s 1086(2)(*a*)–(*b*), which are imposed by a court, and as respects specified sums, as are referred to in s 1086(2)(*c*)–(*d*), which the Revenue Commissioners accepted, or undertook to accept, in settlement of a specified liability, on or after 23 March 2000.

Subs (1)(*d*) inserted TCA 1997, s 1086(5A) as respects fines or other penalties, as are referred to in s 1086(2)(*a*)–(*b*), which are imposed by a court, and as respects specified sums, as are referred to in s 1086(2)(*c*)–(*d*), which the Revenue Commissioners accepted, or undertook to accept, in settlement of a specified liability, on or after 23 March 2000.

163 Amendment of section 1094 (tax clearance in relation to certain licences) of Principal Act

Notes

This section inserted para (*k*) in the definition of "licence" in TCA 1997, s 1094(1) with effect from 23 March 2000.

164 Amendment of Chapter 5 (miscellaneous provisions) of Part 42 (collection and recovery) of Principal Act

Notes

This section inserted TCA 1997, ss 1006A–1006B with effect from 23 March 2000.

165 Care and management of taxes and duties

All taxes and duties imposed by this Act are by virtue of this section placed under the care and management of the Revenue Commissioners.

166 Short title, construction and commencement

(1) This Act may be cited as the Finance Act, 2000.

...

(4) Part 3 shall be construed together with the Value Added Tax Acts, 1972 to 1999, and may be cited together with those Acts as the Value Added Tax Acts, 1972 to 2000.

...

(8) Part 7 (so far as relating to income tax) shall be construed together with the Income Tax Acts and (so far as relating to corporation tax) shall be construed together with the Corporation Tax Acts and (so far as relating to capital gains tax) shall be construed

together with the Capital Gains Tax Acts and (so far as relating to customs) shall be construed with the Customs Acts and (so far as relating to duties of excise) shall be construed together with the statutes which relate to duties of excise and the management of those duties and (so far as relating to Value Added tax) shall be construed together with the Value Added Tax Acts, 1972 to 2000, and (so far as relating to stamp duty) shall be construed together with the Stamp Duties Consolidation Act, 1999, and (so far as relating to residential property tax) shall be construed together with Part VI of the Finance Act, 1983, and the enactments amending or extending that Part and (so far as relating to gift tax or inheritance tax) shall be construed together with the Capital Acquisitions Tax Act, 1976, and the enactments amending or extending that Act.

...

(10) In relation to Part 3:

(a)   sections 107 and 121 and paragraphs (a) and (b) of section 123 shall be deemed to have come into force and shall take effect as on and from the 1 July 1999;

(b)   sections 111 and 113 shall be deemed to have come into force and shall take effect as on and from the 1 March 2000;

(c)   the provisions of this Part, other than those specified in paragraphs (a) and (b), shall have effect as on and from the date of passing of this Act.

(11) Any reference in this Act to any other enactment shall, except so far as the context otherwise requires, be construed as a reference to that enactment as amended by or under any other enactment including this Act.

(12) In this Act, a reference to a Part, section or Schedule is to a Part or section of, or Schedule to, this Act, unless it is indicated that reference to some other enactment is intended.

(13) In this Act, a reference to a subsection, paragraph, subparagraph, clause or subclause is to the subsection, paragraph, subparagraph, clause or subclause of the provision (including a Schedule) in which the reference occurs, unless it is indicated that reference to some other provision is intended.

ELECTRONIC COMMERCE ACT 2000

Number 27 of 2000

ARRANGEMENT OF SECTIONS

PART 1

PRELIMINARY AND GENERAL

Section

PART 2

LEGAL RECOGNITION AND NON-DISCRIMINATION IN RESPECT OF ELECTRONIC SIGNATURES, ORIGINALS, CONTRACTS AND RELATED MATTERS LEGAL RECOGNITION OF ELECTRONIC COMMUNICATIONS AND INFORMATION IN ELECTRONIC FORM

GENERAL

AN ACT TO PROVIDE FOR THE LEGAL RECOGNITION OF ELECTRONIC CONTRACTS, ELECTRONIC WRITING, ELECTRONIC SIGNATURES AND ORIGINAL INFORMATION IN ELECTRONIC FORM IN RELATION TO COMMERCIAL AND NON-COMMERCIAL TRANSACTIONS AND DEALINGS AND OTHER MATTERS, THE ADMISSIBILITY OF EVIDENCE IN RELATION TO SUCH MATTERS, THE ACCREDITATION, SUPERVISION AND LIABILITY OF CERTIFICATION SERVICE PROVIDERS AND THE REGISTRATION OF DOMAIN NAMES, AND TO PROVIDE FOR RELATED MATTERS. [10th JULY, 2000]

BE IT ENACTED BY THE OIREACHTAS AS FOLLOWS:

PART 1

PRELIMINARY AND GENERAL

1 Short title and commencement

(1) This Act may be cited as the Electronic Commerce Act, 2000.

(2) This Act shall come into operation on such day or days as the Minister, after consultation with the Minister for Enterprise, Trade and Employment, may appoint by order or orders, either generally or with reference to any particular purpose or provision, and different days may be so appointed for different purposes or different provisions.

2 Interpretation

(1) In this Act, unless the context otherwise requires—

"accreditation" means an accreditation under section 29(2);

"addressee", in relation to an electronic communication, means a person or public body intended by the originator to receive the electronic communication, but does not include a person or public body acting as a service provider in relation to the processing, receiving or storing of the electronic communication or the provision of other services in relation to it;

"advanced electronic signature" means an electronic signature—

    (*a*)   uniquely linked to the signatory,

    (*b*)   capable of identifying the signatory,

    (*c*)   created using means that are capable of being maintained by the signatory under his, her or its sole control, and

    (*d*)   linked to the data to which it relates in such a manner that any subsequent change of the data is detectable;

"certificate" means an electronic attestation which links signature verification data to a person or public body, and confirms the identity of the person or public body;

"certification service provider" means a person or public body who issues certificates or provides other services related to electronic signatures;

"Directive" means the European Parliament and Council Directive 1999/93/EC of 13 December, 1999 (OJ No L13/12 of 19/1/2000, p 13);

"electronic" includes electrical, digital, magnetic, optical, electro-magnetic, biometric, photonic and any other form of related technology;

"electronic communication" means information communicated or intended to be communicated to a person or public body, other than its originator, that is generated, communicated, processed, sent, received, recorded, stored or displayed by electronic means or in electronic form, but does not include information communicated in the form of speech unless the speech is processed at its destination by an automatic voice recognition system;

"electronic contract" means a contract concluded wholly or partly by means of an electronic communication;

"electronic signature" means data in electronic form attached to, incorporated in or logically associated with other electronic data and which serves as a method of authenticating the purported originator, and includes an advanced electronic signature;

"excluded law" means a law referred to in section 10;

"information" includes data, all forms of writing and other text, images (including maps and cartographic material), sound, codes, computer programmes, software, databases and speech;

"information system" means a system for generating, communicating, processing, sending, receiving, recording, storing or displaying information by electronic means;

"legal proceedings" means civil or criminal proceedings, and includes proceedings before a court, tribunal, appellate body of competent jurisdiction or any other body or individual charged with determining legal rights or obligations;

"Minister" means the Minister for Public Enterprise;

"originator", in relation to an electronic communication, means the person or public body by whom or on whose behalf the electronic communication purports to have been sent or generated before storage, as the case may be, but does not include a person or public body acting as a service provider in relation to the generation, processing, sending or storing of that electronic communication or providing other services in relation to it;

"person" does not include a public body;

"prescribed" means prescribed by regulations made under section 3;

"public body" means—

    (*a*)   a Minister of the Government or a Minister of State,

    (*b*)   a body (including a Department of State but not including a non-government organisation) wholly or partly funded out of the Central Fund or out of moneys provided by the Oireachtas or moneys raised by local taxation or charges, or

    (*c*)   a commission, tribunal, board or body established by an Act or by arrangement of the Government, a Minister of the Government or a Minister of State for a non-commercial public service or purpose;

"qualified certificate" means a certificate which meets the requirements set out in Annex I and is provided by a certification service provider who fulfils the requirements set out in Annex II;

"secure signature creation device" means a signature creation device which meets the requirements set out in Annex III;

"signatory" means a person who, or public body which, holds a signature creation device and acts in the application of a signature by use of the device either on his, her or its own behalf or on behalf of a person or public body he, she or it represents;

"signature creation data" means unique data, such as codes, pass-words, algorithms or private cryptographic keys, used by a signatory or other source of the data in generating an electronic signature;

"signature creation device" means a device, such as configured software or hardware used to generate signature creation data;

"signature verification data" means data, such as codes, passwords, algorithms or public cryptographic keys, used for the purposes of verifying an electronic signature;

"signature verification device" means a device, such as configured software or hardware used to generate signature verification data.

(2) In the application of this Act, **"writing"**, where used in any other Act or instrument under an Act (and whether or not qualified by reference to it being or being required to be under the hand of the writer or similar expression) shall be construed as including electronic modes of representing or reproducing words in visible form, and cognate words shall be similarly construed.

(3) In this Act—

    (*a*)   a reference to a section is a reference to a section of this Act, unless it is indicated that a reference to some other enactment is intended, (*b*)   a reference to a subsection, paragraph or subparagraph is a reference to a subsection, paragraph or subparagraph of the provision in which the reference is made, unless it is indicated that a reference to some other provision is intended,

(*c*)   a reference to an enactment shall, except to the extent that the context otherwise requires, be construed as a reference to that enactment as amended by or under any other enactment, and

(*d*)   a reference to an Annex by number is a reference to the Annex so numbered to the Directive and included in the Schedule to this Act.

(4) Where in any legal proceedings the question of whether—

(*a*)   a body is a non-government organisation, or

(*b*)   a body, commission, tribunal or board is or was established by an Act or by arrangement of the Government, a Minister of the Government or a Minister of State for a non-commercial service or purpose,

is in issue then, for the purpose of establishing whether it is or is not a public body as defined in subsection (1), a document signed by the Minister, a Minister of the Government or a Minister of State declaring that—

(i)   he or she is the appropriate Minister for determining whether the body is or is not a non-government organisation, and that in fact it is or is not such an organisation, or

(ii)   he or she is the appropriate Minister for determining whether the body, commission, tribunal or board was or was not so established for a non-commercial service or purpose, and that in fact it was or was not so established,

is sufficient evidence of those facts, until the contrary is shown, and the Minister, Minister of the Government or Minister of State may make such a declaration.

3 Regulations

(1) The Minister may make regulations prescribing any matter or thing referred to in this Act as prescribed or to be prescribed, or in relation to any matter referred to in this Act as the subject of regulation.

(2) Regulations under this section may contain such incidental, supplementary and consequential provisions as appear to the Minister to be necessary or expedient for the purposes of the regulations or for giving full effect to this Act.

4 Laying of orders and regulations before Houses of Oireachtas

Every order (other than an order made under section 1(2)) or regulation made by the Minister under section 3 shall be laid before each House of the Oireachtas as soon as may be after it is made and, if a resolution annulling the order or regulation is passed by either such House within the next subsequent 21 days on which that House has sat after the order or regulation is laid before it, the order or regulation shall be annulled accordingly but without prejudice to the validity of anything previously done under it.

5 Expenses of Minister

Expenses incurred by the Minister in the administration of this Act shall, to such extent as may be sanctioned by the Minister for Finance, be paid out of moneys provided by the Oireachtas.

6 Prosecution of offences

(1) Summary proceedings for offences under this Act or a regulation made under section 3 may be brought and prosecuted by the Minister or a person or public body prescribed by the Minister for that purpose.

(2) Notwithstanding section 10(4) of the Petty Sessions (Ireland) Act, 1851, summary proceedings for an offence under this Act or a regulation made under section 3 may be commenced at any time within 12 months from the date on which evidence that, in the opinion of the person or public body by whom the proceedings are brought, is sufficient to justify the bringing of the proceedings, comes to that person's or public body's knowledge.

(3) For the purpose of subsection (2), a document signed by or on behalf of the person or public body bringing the proceedings as to the date on which the evidence referred to in that subsection came to his, her or its knowledge is prima facie evidence thereof and in those or any other legal proceedings a document purporting to be issued for the purpose of this subsection and to be so signed is taken to be so signed and shall be admitted as evidence without further proof of the signature of the person or public body purporting to sign it.

7 Offences by bodies corporate

Where an offence under this Act has been committed by a body corporate and is proved to have been committed with the consent or connivance of, or to be attributable to any neglect on the part of, a person being a director, shadow director (as defined in section 3(1) of the Companies Act, 1990), manager, secretary or other officer of the body corporate, or a person who was purporting to act in any such capacity, that person, as well as the body corporate, shall be guilty of an offence and be liable to be proceeded against and punished as if he or she were guilty of the first-mentioned offence.

8 Penalties

A person or public body guilty of an offence under this Act for which no penalty other than by this section is provided shall be liable—

(*a*) on summary conviction, to a fine not exceeding £1,500 or, at the discretion of the court, to imprisonment for a term not exceeding 12 months, or to both the fine and the imprisonment, or

(*b*) on conviction on indictment, to a fine not exceeding £500,000 or, at the discretion of the court, to imprisonment for a term not exceeding 5 years, or to both the fine and the imprisonment.

PART 2
LEGAL RECOGNITION AND NON-DISCRIMINATION IN RESPECT OF ELECTRONIC SIGNATURES, ORIGINALS, CONTRACTS AND RELATED MATTERS

LEGAL RECOGNITION OF ELECTRONIC COMMUNICATIONS AND INFORMATION IN ELECTRONIC FORM

9 Electronic form not to affect legal validity or enforceability

Information (including information incorporated by reference) shall not be denied legal effect, validity or enforceability solely on the grounds that it is wholly or partly in electronic form, whether as an electronic communication or otherwise.

10 Excluded laws

(1) Sections 12 to 23 are without prejudice to—

(*a*) the law governing the creation, execution, amendment, variation or revocation of—

(i) a will, codicil or any other testamentary instrument to which the Succession Act, 1965, applies,

(ii) a trust, or

(iii) an enduring power of attorney,

(*b*) the law governing the manner in which an interest in real property (including a leasehold interest in such property) may be created, acquired, disposed of or registered, other than contracts (whether or not under seal) for the creation, acquisition or disposal of such interests,

(*c*) the law governing the making of an affidavit or a statutory or sworn declaration, or requiring or permitting the use of one for any purpose, or

(*d*) the rules, practices or procedures of a court or tribunal,

except to the extent that regulations under section 3 may from time to time prescribe.

(2) Where the Minister is of the opinion that—

(*a*) technology has advanced to such an extent, and access to it is so widely available, or

(*b*) adequate procedures and practices have developed in public registration or other services, so as to warrant such action, or

(*c*) the public interest so requires,

he or she may, after consultation with such Minister or Ministers as in the Minister's opinion has or have a sufficient interest or responsibility in relation to the matter, by regulations made under section 3, for the purpose of encouraging the efficient use of electronic communication facilities and services in commerce and the community generally while at the same time protecting the public interest, extend the application of this Act or a provision of this Act to or in relation to a matter specified in subsection (1) (including a particular aspect of such a matter) subject to such conditions as he or she thinks fit, and the Act as so extended shall apply accordingly.

(3) Without prejudice to the generality of subsection (2), the regulations may apply to a particular area or subject, or for a particular time, in the nature of a trial of technology and procedures.

11 Certain laws not to be affected

Nothing in this Act shall prejudice the operation of—

(a) any law relating to the imposition, collection or recovery of taxation or other Government imposts, including fees, fines and penalties,

(b) the Companies Act, 1990 (Uncertificated Securities) Regulations, 1996 (SI No 68 of 1996) or any regulations made in substitution for those regulations,

(c) the Criminal Evidence Act, 1992, or

(d) the Consumer Credit Act, 1995, or any regulations made thereunder and the European Communities (Unfair Terms in Consumer Contracts) Regulations, 1995 (SI No 27 of 1995).

12 Writing

(1) If by law or otherwise a person or public body is required (whether the requirement is in the form of an obligation or con-sequences flow from the information not being in writing) or permitted to give information in writing (whether or not in a form prescribed by law), then, subject to subsection (2), the person or public body may give the information in electronic form, whether as an electronic communication or otherwise.

(2) Information may be given as provided in subsection (1) only—

(a) if at the time the information was given it was reasonable to expect that it would be readily accessible to the person or public body to whom it was directed, for subsequent reference,

(b) where the information is required or permitted to be given to a public body or to a person acting on behalf of a public body and the public body consents to the giving of the information in electronic form, whether as an electronic communication or otherwise, but requires—

(i) the information to be given in accordance with particular information technology and procedural requirements, or

(ii) that a particular action be taken by way of verifying the receipt of the information,

if the public body's requirements have been met and those requirements have been made public and are objective, transparent, proportionate and non-discriminatory, and

(c) where the information is required or permitted to be given to a person who is neither a public body nor acting on behalf of a public body— if the person to whom the information is required or permitted to be given consents to the information being given in that form.

(3) Subsections (1) and (2) are without prejudice to any other law requiring or permitting information to be given—

    (*a*) in accordance with particular information technology and procedural requirements,

    (*b*) on a particular kind of data storage device, or

    (*c*) by means of a particular kind of electronic communication.

(4) This section applies to a requirement or permission to give information whether the word **"give"**, **"send"**, **"forward"**, **"deliver"**, **"serve"** or similar word or expression is used.

(5) In this section, **"give information"** includes but is not limited to—

    (*a*) make an application,

    (*b*) make or lodge a claim,

    (*c*) make or lodge a return,

    (*d*) make a request,

    (*e*) make an unsworn declaration,

    (*f*) lodge or issue a certificate,

    (*g*) make, vary or cancel an election,

    (*h*) lodge an objection,

    (*i*) give a statement of reasons,

    (*j*) record and disseminate a court order,

    (*k*) give, send or serve a notification.

13 Signatures

(1) If by law or otherwise the signature of a person or public body is required (whether the requirement is in the form of an obligation or consequences flow from there being no signature) or permitted, then, subject to subsection (2), an electronic signature may be used.

(2) An electronic signature may be used as provided in subsection (1) only—

    (*a*) where the signature is required or permitted to be given to a public body or to a person acting on behalf of a public body and the public body consents to the use of an electronic signature but requires that it be in accordance with particular information technology and procedural requirements (including that it be an advanced electronic signature, that it be based on a qualified certificate, that it be issued by an accredited certification service provider or that it be created by a secure signature creation device)— if the public body's requirements have been met and those requirements have been made public and are objective, transparent, proportionate and non-discriminatory, and

    (*b*) where the signature is required or permitted to be given to a person who is neither a public body nor acting on behalf of a public body— if the person to whom the signature is required or permitted to be given consents to the use of an electronic signature.

(3) Subsections (1) and (2) are without prejudice to any other provision of this Act or law requiring or permitting an electronic communication to contain an electronic signature, an advanced electronic signature, an electronic signature based on a qualified certificate, an electronic signature created by a secure signature creation device or other technological requirements relating to an electronic signature.

14 Signatures required to be witnessed.

(1) If by law or otherwise a signature to a document is required to be witnessed (whether the requirement is in the form of an obligation or consequences flow from the signature not being witnessed) that requirement is taken to have been met if—

> (*a*) the signature to be witnessed is an advanced electronic signature, based on a qualified certificate, of the person or public body by whom the document is required to be signed,

> (*b*) the document contains an indication that the signature of that person or public body is required to be witnessed, and

> (*c*) the signature of the person purporting to witness the signature to be witnessed is an advanced electronic signature, based on a qualified certificate.

(2) An advanced electronic signature based on a qualified certificate may be used as provided in subsection (1) only—

> (*a*) where the signature required or permitted to be witnessed is on a document to be given to a public body or to a person acting on behalf of a public body and the public body consents to the use of an electronic signature of both the person attesting the document and witnessing the signature but requires that the document and signatures be in accordance with particular information technology and procedural requirements (including that a qualified certificate on which the signature or signatures are based be issued by an accredited certification service provider)— if the public body's requirements are met and those requirements have been made public and are objective, transparent, proportionate and non-discriminatory, and

> (*b*) where the document on or in respect of which the signature is to be witnessed is required or permitted to be given to a person who is neither a public body nor acting on behalf of a public body— if the person to whom it is required or permitted to be given consents to the use of an advanced electronic signature based on a qualified certificate for that purpose.

15 Consumer law to apply

All electronic contracts within the State shall be subject to all existing consumer law and the role of the Director of Consumer Affairs in such legislation shall apply equally to consumer transactions, whether conducted electronically or non-electronically.

16 Documents under seal

(1) If by law or otherwise a seal is required to be affixed to a document (whether the requirement is in the form of an obligation or consequences flow from a seal not being affixed) then, subject to subsection (2), that requirement is taken to have been met if the document indicates that it is required to be under seal and it includes an advanced electronic signature, based on a qualified certificate, of the person or public body by whom it is required to be sealed.

(2) An advanced electronic signature based on a qualified certificate may be used as provided in subsection (1) only—

(*a*) where the document to be under seal is required or permitted to be given to a public body or to a person acting on behalf of a public body and the public body consents to the use of an electronic signature but requires that it be in accordance with particular information technology and procedural requirements (including that a qualified certificate on which it is based be issued by an accredited certification service provider) — if the public body's requirements have been met and those requirements have been made public and are objective, transparent, proportionate and non-discriminatory, and

(*b*) where the document to be under seal is required or permitted to be given to a person who is neither a public body nor acting on behalf of a public body— if the person to whom it is required or permitted to be given consents to the use of an advanced electronic signature based on a qualified certificate.

17 Electronic originals

(1) If by law or otherwise a person or public body is required (whether the requirement is in the form of an obligation or con-sequences flow from the information not being presented or retained in its original form) or permitted to present or retain information in its original form, then, subject to subsection (2), the information may be presented or retained, as the case may be, in electronic form, whether as an electronic communication or otherwise.

(2) Information may be presented or retained as provided in sub-section (1) only—

(*a*) if there exists a reliable assurance as to the integrity of the information from the time when it was first generated in its final form, whether as an electronic communication or otherwise,

(*b*) where it is required or permitted that the information be presented— if the information is capable of being displayed in intelligible form to a person or public body to whom it is to be presented,

(*c*) if, at the time the information was generated in its final form, it was reasonable to expect that it would be readily accessible so as to be useable for subsequent reference,

(*d*) where the information is required or permitted to be presented to or retained for a public body or for a person acting on behalf of a public body, and the public body consents to the information being presented or retained in electronic form, whether as an electronic communication or otherwise, but requires that it be presented or retained in accordance with particular information technology and procedural requirements — if the public body's requirements have been met and those requirements have been made public and are objective, transparent, proportionate and non-discriminatory, and

(*e*) where the information is required or permitted to be presented to or retained for a person who is neither a public body nor acting on behalf of a public body— if the person to whom the information is required or permitted to be presented or for whom it is required or permitted to be retained consents to the information being presented or retained in that form.

(3) Subsections (1) and (2) are without prejudice to any other law requiring or permitting information to be presented or retained—

(*a*) in accordance with particular information technology and procedural requirements,

(*b*) on a particular kind of data storage device, or

(*c*) by means of a particular kind of electronic communication.

(4) For the purposes of subsections (1) and (2)—

(*a*) the criteria for assessing integrity is whether the information has remained complete and unaltered, apart from the addition of any endorsement or change which arises in the normal course of generating, communicating, processing, sending, receiving, recording, storing or displaying, and

(*b*) the standard of reliability shall be assessed in the light of the purpose for which and the circumstances in which the information was generated.

18 Retention and production

(1) If by law or otherwise a person or public body is required (whether the requirement is in the form of an obligation or consequences flow from the information not being retained or produced in its original form) or permitted to retain for a particular period or produce a document that is in the form of paper or other material on which information may be recorded in written form, then, subject to subsection (2), the person or public body may retain throughout the relevant period or, as the case may be, produce, the document in electronic form, whether as an electronic communication or otherwise.

(2) A document may be retained throughout the period, or produced, by the person or public body as provided in subsection (1) only—

(*a*) if there exists a reliable assurance as to the integrity of the information from the time when it was first generated in its final form as an electronic communication,

(*b*) in the case of a document to be produced— if the information is capable of being displayed in intelligible form to the person or public body to whom it is to be produced,

(*c*) in the case of a document to be retained— if, at the time of the generation of the final electronic form of the document, it was reasonable to expect that the information contained in the electronic form of the document would be readily accessible so as to be useable for subsequent reference,

(*d*) where the document is required or permitted to be retained for or produced to a public body or for or to a person acting on behalf of a public body, and the public body consents to the document being retained or produced in electronic form, whether as an electronic communication or otherwise, but requires that the electronic form of the document be retained or produced in accordance with particular information technology and procedural requirements— if the public body's requirements have been met and those requirements have been made public and are objective, transparent, proportionate and non-discriminatory, and

(*e*) where the document is required or permitted to be retained for or produced to a person who is neither a public body nor acting on behalf of a public body— if the person for or to whom the document is required or permitted to be retained or produced consents to it being retained or produced in that form.

(3) Subsections (1) and (2) are without prejudice to any other law requiring or permitting documents in the form of paper or other material to be retained or produced—

(*a*) in accordance with particular information technology and procedural requirements,

(*b*) on a particular kind of data storage device, or

(*c*) by means of a particular kind of electronic communication.

(4) For the purposes of subsections (1) and (2)—

(*a*) the criteria for assessing integrity is whether the information has remained complete and unaltered, apart from the addition of any endorsement or change which arises in the normal course of generating, communicating, processing, sending, receiving, recording, storing or displaying, and

(*b*) the standard of reliability shall be assessed in the light of the purpose for which the information was generated and the circumstances in which it was generated.

19 Contracts

(1) An electronic contract shall not be denied legal effect, validity or enforceability solely on the grounds that it is wholly or partly in electronic form, or has been concluded wholly or partly by way of an electronic communication.

(2) In the formation of a contract, an offer, acceptance of an offer or any related communication (including any subsequent amendment, cancellation or revocation of the offer or acceptance of the offer) may, unless otherwise agreed by the parties, be communicated by means of an electronic communication.

20 Acknowledgement of receipt of electronic communications

(1) Subject to any other law, where the originator of an electronic communication indicates that receipt of the electronic communication is required to be acknowledged but does not indicate a particular form or method of acknowledgement, then, unless the originator and the addressee of the electronic communication agree otherwise, the acknowledgement shall be given by way of an electronic communication or any other communication (including any conduct of the addressee) sufficient to indicate to the originator that the electronic communication has been received.

(2) Where the originator of an electronic communication indicates that receipt of the electronic communication is required to be acknowledged, the electronic communication, in relation to the establishing of legal rights and obligations between parties, shall, until the acknowledgement is received by the originator and unless the parties otherwise agree, be treated as if it had never been sent.

(3) Where the originator of an electronic communication has indicated that receipt of the electronic communication is required to be acknowledged but has not stated that the electronic communication is conditional on the receipt of acknowledgement and the acknowledgement has not been received by the originator within the time specified or agreed or, if no time has been specified or agreed, within a reasonable time, then the electronic communication, in relation to the establishing of legal rights and obligations between parties, shall, unless the parties otherwise agree, be treated as if it had never been sent.

21 Time and place of dispatch and receipt of electronic communications

(1) Where an electronic communication enters an information system, or the first information system, outside the control of the originator, then, unless otherwise agreed between the originator and the addressee, it is taken to have been sent when it enters such information system or first information system.

(2) Where the addressee of an electronic communication has designated an information system for the purpose of receiving electronic communications, then, unless otherwise agreed between the originator and the addressee or the law otherwise provides, the electronic communication is taken to have been received when it enters that information system.

(3) Where the addressee of an electronic communication has not designated an information system for the purpose of receiving electronic communications, then, unless otherwise agreed between the originator and the addressee, the electronic communication is taken to have been received when it comes to the attention of the addressee.

(4) Subsections (1), (2) and (3) apply notwithstanding that the place where the relevant information system is located may be different from the place where the electronic communication is taken to have been sent or received, as the case may be, under those sub-sections.

(5) Unless otherwise agreed between the originator and the addressee of an electronic communication, the electronic communication is taken to have been sent from and

received at, respectively, the place where the originator and the addressee have their places of business.

(6) For the purposes of subsection (5), but subject to subsection (7)—

(*a*)   if the originator or addressee has more than one place of business, the place of business is the place that has the closest relationship to the underlying transaction or, if there is no underlying transaction, the principal place of business, and

(*b*)   if the originator or addressee does not have a place of business, the place of business is taken to be the place where he or she ordinarily resides.

(7) If an electronic communication is or is in connection with a notification or other communication required or permitted by or under an Act to be sent or given to, or served on, a company at its registered office, the registered office is taken to be the place of business of the company in connection with that electronic communication for the purpose of subsection (5).

22 Admissibility

In any legal proceedings, nothing in the application of the rules of evidence shall apply so as to deny the admissibility in evidence of—

(*a*)   an electronic communication, an electronic form of a document, an electronic contract, or writing in electronic form—

(i)   on the sole ground that it is an electronic communication, an electronic form of a document, an electronic contract, or writing in electronic form, or

(ii)   if it is the best evidence that the person or public body adducing it could reasonably be expected to obtain, on the grounds that it is not in its original form,

or

(*b*)   an electronic signature—

(i)   on the sole ground that the signature is in electronic form, or is not an advanced electronic signature, or is not based on a qualified certificate, or is not based on a qualified certificate issued by an accredited certification service provider, or is not created by a secure signature creation device, or

(ii)   if it is the best evidence that the person or public body adducing it could reasonably be expected to obtain, on the grounds that it is not in its original form.

23 Defamation law to apply

All provisions of existing defamation law shall apply to all electronic communications within the State, including the retention of information electronically.

GENERAL

24 Electronic form not required

Nothing in this Act shall be construed as—

(a) requiring a person or public body to generate, communicate, produce, process, send, receive, record, retain, store or display any information, document or signature by or in electronic form, or

(b) prohibiting a person or public body engaging in an electronic transaction from establishing reasonable requirements about the manner in which the person will accept electronic communications, electronic signatures or electronic forms of documents.

25 Prohibition of fraud and misuse of electronic signatures and signature creation devices

A person or public body who or which—

(a) knowingly accesses, copies or otherwise obtains possession of, or recreates, the signature creation device of another person or a public body, without the authorisation of that other person or public body, for the purpose of creating or allowing, or causing another person or public body to create, an unauthorised electronic signature using the signature creation device,

(b) knowingly alters, discloses or uses the signature creation device of another person or a public body, without the authorisation of that other person or public body or in excess of lawful authorisation, for the purpose of creating or allowing, or causing another person or public body to create, an unauthorised electronic signature using the signature creation device,

(c) knowingly creates, publishes, alters or otherwise uses a certificate or an electronic signature for a fraudulent or other unlawful purpose,

(d) knowingly misrepresents the person's or public body's identity or authorisation in requesting or accepting a certificate or in requesting suspension or revocation of a certificate,

(e) knowingly accesses, alters, discloses or uses the signature creation device of a certification service provider used to issue certificates, without the authorisation of the certification service provider or in excess of lawful authorisation, for the purpose of creating, or allowing or causing another person or a public body to create, an unauthorised electronic signature using the signature creation device, or

(f) knowingly publishes a certificate, or otherwise knowingly makes it available to anyone likely to rely on the certificate or on an electronic signature that is verifiable with reference to data such as codes, passwords, algorithms, public cryptographic keys or other data which are used for the purposes of verifying an electronic signature, listed in the certificate, if the person or public body knows that—

(i) the certification service provider listed in the certificate has not issued it,

(ii) the subscriber listed in the certificate has not accepted it, or

(iii)   the certificate has been revoked or suspended, unless its publication is for the purpose of verifying an electronic signature created before such revocation or suspension, or giving notice of revocation or suspension,

is guilty of an offence.

26 Activities partly outside the State

The provisions of section 25 extend to activities that took place partly outside the State.

27 Investigative procedures

(1) Where, on the sworn information of an officer of the Minister or a member of the Garda Síochána not below the rank of Inspector, a judge of the District Court is satisfied that there are reasonable grounds for suspecting that evidence of or relating to an offence under this Act is to be found at a place specified in the information, the judge may issue a warrant for the search of that place and any persons found at that place.

(2) A warrant issued under this section shall authorise a named officer of the Minister or member of the Garda Síochána, alone or accompanied by such member or other members of the Garda Síochána and such other persons as may be necessary—

(a)   to enter, within 7 days from the date of the warrant, and if necessary by the use of reasonable force, the place named in the warrant,

(b)   to search the place and any person reasonably suspected of being connected with any activities of the place found thereon, and

(c)   to seize anything found there, or anything found in the possession of a person present there at the time of the search, which that officer or member reasonably believes to be evidence of or relating to an offence under this Act and, where the thing seized is or contains information or an electronic communication that cannot readily be accessed or put into intelligible form, to require the disclosure of the information or electronic communication in intelligible form.

(3) An officer of the Minister or member of the Garda Síochána acting in accordance with a warrant issued under this section may require any person found at the place where the search is carried out to give the officer or member the person's name and address.

(4) A person who or public body which—

(a)   obstructs or attempts to obstruct an officer of the Minister or member of the Garda Síochána acting in accordance with a warrant issued under subsection (1),

(b)   fails or refuses to comply with a requirement under this section, or

(c)   gives a name or address which is false or misleading, is guilty of a summary offence.

(5) An officer of the Minister or member of the Garda Síochána may retain anything seized under subsection (2)(c) which he or she has reasonable grounds for believing to be evidence of an offence under this Act, for use as evidence in relation to proceedings in relation to any such offence, for such period as is reasonable or, if proceedings are

commenced in which the thing is required to be used in evidence, until the conclusion of the proceedings.

(6) In this section, **"place"** includes any dwelling, any building or part of a building and any vehicle, vessel or structure.

28 Confidentiality of deciphering data

Nothing in this Act shall be construed as requiring the disclosure or enabling the seizure of unique data, such as codes, passwords, algorithms, private cryptographic keys, or other data, that may be necessary to render information or an electronic communication intelligible.

PART 3
CERTIFICATION SERVICES

29 Accreditation and supervision of certification service providers

(1) A person or public body is not required to obtain the prior authority of any other person or public body to provide certification or other services relating to electronic signatures.

(2) (*a*)   The Minister, after consultation with the Minister for Enterprise, Trade and Employment, may by regulations made under section 3 establish a scheme of voluntary accreditation of certification service providers for the purpose of the Directive and to enhance levels of certification service provision in the State, and may designate accreditation authorities and prescribe such matters relating to their designation as the Minister thinks appropriate for the purpose.

(*b*)   A person or public body who or which provides certification or other services in the State relating to electronic signatures may apply as prescribed to the accreditation authority designated under paragraph (a) to participate in any scheme of voluntary accreditation established pursuant to that paragraph.

(*c*)   The regulations may prescribe—

(i)   the rights and obligations specific to the provision of certification services of participants in a scheme of voluntary accreditation, and

(ii)   the manner in which the accreditation authority designated under paragraph (a) shall elaborate and supervise compliance with those rights and obligations in accordance with the Directive and, in particular, Annex II.

(*d*)   A participant in a scheme referred to in paragraph (*a*) shall not exercise a right under the scheme without the prior permission of the accreditation authority.

(3) The Minister shall prescribe a scheme of supervision of certification service providers established in the State who issue qualified certificates to the public.

(4) (*a*)   The Minister may, after consultation with the Minister for Enterprise, Trade and Employment, by order, designate persons or public bodies for the purposes

of determining whether secure signature creation devices conform with the requirements of Annex III.

(b)   The Minister may, by order, amend or revoke an order under this subsection, including an order under this paragraph.

(5) No civil action shall lie or be maintained against a person or public body designated under or for the purposes of subsection (2), (3) or (4) in respect of any determination made or thing done by the person or public body, in good faith, in the performance or purported performance of a function under a scheme referred to in subsection (2) or (3) or for which he, she or it is designated under subsection (4).

30 Liability of certification service providers

(1) A certification service provider who provides a service to the public of issuing certificates and who as a part of that service issues a certificate as a qualified certificate or guarantees such a certificate, shall be liable for any damage caused to a person who, or public body which, reasonably relies on the certificate unless the certification service provider proves that he, she or it has not acted negligently.

(2) It shall be the duty of every certification service provider who provides to the public a service of issuing certificates and who issues a certificate as a qualified certificate or guarantees such a certificate, to take reasonable steps to ensure—

(a)   the accuracy of all information in the qualified certificate as at the time of issue and that the certificate contains all the details required by Annex I to be so contained in a qualified certificate,

(b)   that, at the time of the issue of the certificate, the signatory identified in the certificate held the signature creation device corresponding to the signature verification device given or identified in the certificate, and

(c)   that the signature creation device and the signature verification device act together in a complementary manner, in cases where the certification service provider generates both.

(3) A certification service provider who provides a service to the public of issuing certificates and who as a part of that service issues a certificate as a qualified certificate, or guarantees such a certificate, is liable for any damage caused to a person who, or public body which, reasonably relies on the certificate, for the certification service provider's failure to register or publish notice of the revocation or suspension of the certificate as prescribed, unless the certification service provider proves that he, she or it has not acted negligently.

(4) A certification service provider who provides a service to the public of issuing certificates and who as a part of that service issues a certificate as a qualified certificate, or guarantees such a certificate, may indicate in the qualified certificate limits on the uses of the certificate (including a limit on the value of transactions for which the certificate can be used) and, if the limits are clear and readily identifiable as limitations, the certification service provider shall not be liable for damages arising from a contrary use of a qualified certificate which includes such limits on its uses.

PART 4
DOMAIN NAME REGISTRATION

31 Registration of domain names

(1) The Minister may, by regulations made for the purpose of easy comprehension, fairness, transparency, avoidance of deception, promotion of fair competition and public confidence under section 3 after consultation with the Minister for Enterprise, Trade and Employment and such other persons and public bodies, if any, as the Minister thinks fit, including the body known as the Internet Corporation for Assigned Names and Numbers, authorise, prohibit or regulate the registration and use of the ie domain name in the State.

(2) Without prejudice to the generality of subsection (1), the regulations may prescribe—

- (*a*) designated registration authorities,
- (*b*) the form of registration,
- (*c*) the period during which registration continues in force,
- (*d*) the manner in which, the terms on which and the period or periods for which registration may be renewed,
- (*e*) the circumstances and manner in which registrations may be granted, renewed or refused by the registration authorities,
- (*f*) the right of appeal and appeal processes,
- (*g*) the fees, if any, to be paid on the grant or renewal of registration and the time and manner in which such fees are to be paid,
- (*h*) such other matters relating to registration as appear to the Minister to be necessary or desirable to prescribe.

(3) A person who contravenes or fails to comply with a regulation made pursuant to this section is liable on summary conviction to a fine not exceeding £500.

(4) In this section, "ie domain name" means the top level of the global domain name system assigned to Ireland according to the two-letter code in the International Standard ISO 3166–1 (Codes for Representation of Names of Countries and their Subdivision) of the International Organisation for Standardisation.

SCHEDULE
Annexes to Directive of the European Parliament and of the Council on a Community Framework for Electronic Signatures

[Section 2(3)(d)]

ANNEX I
REQUIREMENTS FOR QUALIFIED CERTIFICATES

[Section 30(2)(a)]

Qualified certificates must contain:

- (*a*) an indication that the certificate is issued as a qualified certificate;
- (*b*) the identification of the certification-service-provider and the State in which it is established;

(*c*) the name of the signatory or a pseudonym, which shall be identified as such;

(*d*) provision for a specific attribute of the signatory to be included if relevant, depending on the purpose for which the certificate is intended;

(*e*) signature-verification data which correspond to signature-creation data under the control of the signatory;

(*f*) an indication of the beginning and end of the period of validity of the certificate;

(*g*) the identity code of the certificate;

(*h*) the advanced electronic signature of the certification-service-provider issuing it;

(*i*) limitations on the scope of use of the certificate, if applicable; and

(*j*) limits on the value of transactions for which the certificate can be used, if applicable.

ANNEX II
REQUIREMENTS FOR CERTIFICATION-SERVICE-PROVIDERS ISSUING QUALIFIED CERTIFICATES

[Section 29(2)(c)(ii)]

Certification-service-providers must:

(*a*) demonstrate the reliability necessary for providing certification services;

(*b*) ensure the operation of a prompt and secure directory and a secure and immediate revocation service;

(*c*) ensure that the date and time when a certificate is issued or revoked can be determined precisely;

(*d*) verify, by appropriate means in accordance with national law, the identity and, if applicable, any specific attributes of the person to which a qualified certificate is issued;

(*e*) employ personnel who possess the expert knowledge, experience and qualifications necessary for the services provided, in particular competence at managerial level, expertise in electronic signature technology and familiarity with proper security procedures; they must also apply administrative and managerial procedures which are adequate and correspond to recognised standards;

(*f*) use trustworthy systems and products which are protected against modification and ensure the technical and cryptographic security of the processes supported by them;

(*g*) take measures against forgery of certificates, and, in cases where the certification-service-provider generates signature-creation data, guarantee confidentiality during the process of generating such data;

(*h*) maintain sufficient financial resources to operate in conformity with the requirements laid down in the Directive, in particular to bear the risk of liability for damages, for example by obtaining appropriate insurance;

(*i*) record all relevant information concerning a qualified certificate for an appropriate period of time, in particular for the purpose of providing evidence of certification for the purposes of legal proceedings. Such recording may be done electronically;

(*j*) not store or copy signature-creation data of the person to whom the certification-service-provider provides key management services;

(*k*) before entering into a contractual relationship with a person seeking a certificate to support his electronic signature, inform that person by a durable means of communication of the precise terms and conditions regarding the use of the certificate, including any limitations on its use, the experience of a voluntary accreditation scheme and procedures for complaints and dispute settlement. Such information, which may be transmitted electronically, must be in writing and in readily understandable language. Relevant parts of this information must also be made available on request to third-parties relying on the certificate;

(*l*) use trustworthy systems to store certificates in a verifiable form so that:

— only authorised persons can make entries and changes,

— Information can be checked for authenticity,

— certificates are publicly available for retrieval in only those cases for which the certificate-holder's consent has been obtained, and

— any technical changes comprising these security requirements are apparent to the operator.

ANNEX III
REQUIREMENTS FOR SECURE SIGNATURE-CREATION DEVICES

[Section 29(4)]

1 Secure signature-creation devices must, by appropriate technical and procedural means, ensure at the least that:

(*a*) the signature-creation-data used for signature generation can practically occur only once, and that their secrecy is reasonably assured;

(*b*) the signature-creation-data used for signature generation cannot, with reasonable assurance, be derived and the signature is protected against forgery using currently available technology;

(*c*) the signature-creation-data used for signature generation can be reliably protected by the legitimate signatory against the use of others.

2 Secure signature-creation devices must not alter the data to be signed or prevent such data from being presented to the signatory prior to the signature process.

FINANCE ACT 2001

(No 7 of 2001)

ARRANGEMENT OF SECTIONS

PART 4
VALUE ADDED TAX

PART 8
MISCELLANEOUS

SCHEDULE 5
AMENDMENT OF ENACTMENTS CONSEQUENT ON CHANGEOVER TO EURO

AN ACT TO PROVIDE FOR THE IMPOSITION, REPEAL, REMISSION, ALTERATION AND REGULATION OF TAXATION, OF STAMP DUTIES AND OF DUTIES RELATING TO EXCISE AND OTHERWISE TO MAKE FURTHER PROVISION IN CONNECTION WITH FINANCE INCLUDING THE REGULATION OF CUSTOMS [30th MARCH 2001]

PART 4
VALUE ADDED TAX

181 Interpretation (Part 4)

In this Part—

"Principal Act" means the Value Added Tax Act, 1972;

"Act of 1978" means the Value Added Tax (Amendment) Act, 1978;

"Act of 1995" means the Finance Act, 1995;

"Act of 1999" means the Finance Act, 1999;

"Act of 2000" means the Finance Act, 2000.

182 Amendment of section 3 (supply of goods) of Principal Act

---

Notes

Para (*a*) inserted "even if that business or that part thereof had ceased trading" to VATA 1972, s 3(5)(*b*)(iii) with effect from 6 April 2001.
Para (*b*) inserted VATA 1972, s 3(5)(*d*) with effect from 6 April 2001.

---

183 Amendment of section 5 (supply of services) of Principal Act

---

Notes

Para (*a*) inserted VATA 1972, s 5(6)(*e*)(iii*a*) with effect from 6 April 2001.
Para (*b*) substituted VATA 1972, s 5(8) with effect from 6 April 2001.

---

184 Amendment of section 8 (taxable persons) of Principal Act

---

Notes

This section inserted ", (iii*a*)" to VATA 1972, s 8(2)(*a*) with effect from 6 April 2001.

---

185 Amendment of section 10A (margin scheme goods) of Principal Act

Notes

This section substituted "paragraphs (*c*) and (*d*) of subsection (5) of section 3" for "section 3(5)(*c*)" in VATA 1972, s 10A(1) definition of "margin scheme goods" with effect from 6 April 2001.

186 Amendment of section 10B (special scheme for auctioneers) of Principal Act

Notes

This section inserted VATA 1972, s 10B(*aaa*) with effect from 6 April 2001.

187 Amendment of section 11 (rates of tax) of Principal Act

Notes

Para (*a*) substituted "20 per cent" for "21 per cent" in VATA 1972, s 11(1)(*a*) with effect from 1 January 2001.

188 Amendment of section 12 (deduction for tax borne or paid) of Principal Act

Notes

Para (*a*) inserted ", subject to making any adjustment required in accordance with section 12D," to VATA 1972, s 12(1)(*a*) with effect from 6 April 2001.

Para (*b*) inserted VATA 1972, s 12(*b*)(*ib*) with effect from 8 January 2001.

Para (*c*) substituted "shall" for "may" in VATA 1972, s 12(4)(*f*) with effect from 6 April 2001.

189 Amendment of section 12A (special provisions for tax invoiced by flat-rate farmers) of Principal Act

Notes

This section substituted "4.3 per cent" for "4.2 per cent" in VATA 1972, s 12A(1) with effect from 1 January 2001.

190 Amendment of section 12B (special scheme for means of transport supplied by taxable dealers) of Principal Act

Notes

This section substituted "paragraphs (*c*) and (*d*) of subsection (5) of section 3" for "section 3(5)(*c*)" in VATA 1972, s 12B(2)(*aa*) with effect from 6 April 2001.

191 Adjustment of tax deductible in certain circumstances

Notes

This section inserted VATA 1972, s 12D with effect from 6 April 2001.

192 Amendment of section 13A (supplies to, and intra-Community acquisitions and imports by, certain taxable persons) of Principal Act

Notes

This section substituted "subparagraphs (*a*)(I), (*aa*), or (*b*)" for "subparagraph (*a*)(I) or (*b*)" in VATA 1972, s 13A(1) definition of "qualifying person" with effect from 6 April 2001.

193 Amendment of section 17 (invoices) of Principal Act

Notes

Para (*a*) substituted VATA 1972, s 17(1A) with effect from 6 April 2001.

Para (*b*) inserted VATA 1972, s 17(1AAA) with effect from 1 July 2001.

Para (*c*) substituted "subsections (1AA), (1AAA)" for "subsection (1AA)" in VATA 1972, s 17(1AB) with effect from 1 July 2001.

194 Amendment of section 19 (tax due and payable) of Principal Act

Notes

Para (*a*) inserted "and, in the case of an authorised person referred to in subparagraph (iv)(III) that amount shall be the balance of tax remaining to be paid, if any, after deducting from it, the amount of tax paid by him by direct debit in respect of his accounting period," to VATA 1972, s 19(3)(*aa*)(ii)(II) with effect from 6 April 2001.

Para (*b*) inserted VATA 1972, s 19(3)(*aa*)(iv)(III) with effect from 6 April 2001.

195 Amendment of section 21 (interest) of Principal Act

Notes

This section inserted VATA 1972, s 21(1A) with effect from 6 April 2001.

196 Amendment of section 22 (estimation of tax due for a taxable period) of Principal Act

Notes

This section substituted "fourteen" for "twenty-one" in VATA 1972, s 22(2)(*a*) with effect from 6 April 2001.

197 Amendment of section 27 (fraudulent returns, etc) of Principal Act

Notes

Para (*a*) inserted VATA 1972, s 27(4A) with effect from 6 April 2001.

Para (*b*)(i) substituted "For the purposes of this section" for "For the purposes of subparagraph (*b*) of paragraph (1)" in VATA 1972, s 27(9A)(4) with effect from 6 April 2001.

Para (*b*)(ii) inserted VATA 1972, s 27(9A)(4)(*bb*) with effect from 6 April 2001.

198 Repeal of section 37 (substitution of agent, etc, for person not resident in State) of Principal Act

Notes

This section repealed VATA 1972, s 37 with effect from 1 January 2002.

199 Amendment of First Schedule to Principal Act

Notes

Para (*a*) inserted ", other than the supply of research services" in VATA 1972, Sch 1 para (ii) with effect from 1 September 2001.

Para (*b*) inserted "(which does not include the service of allowing a person use a toll road or a toll bridge)" to VATA 1972, Sch 1 para (iv) with effect from 1 September 2001.

Para (*c*) inserted "and" to VATA 1972, Sch 1 para (ix)(*a*) with effect from 1 May 2001.

Para (*d*)(i) deleted VATA 1972, Sch 1 para (ix)(*b*) with effect from 1 May 2001.

Para (*d*)(ii) deleted VATA 1972, Sch 1 para (ix)(*c*) with effect from 1 May 2001.

Para (*d*)(iii) deleted "the services of loss adjusters and excluding" from VATA 1972, Sch 1 para (ix) with effect from 1 May 2001.

Para (*e*) substituted VATA 1972, Sch 1 para (xi) with effect from 1 May 2001.

200 Amendment of Second Schedule to Principal Act

Notes

This section inserted VATA 1972, Sch 1 para (v*aa*) with effect from 6 April 2001.

PART 8
MISCELLANEOUS

231 Interpretation (Part 8)

In this Part **"Principal Act"** means the Taxes Consolidation Act, 1997.

232 Amendment of Chapter 3 (other obligations and returns) of Part 38 of Principal Act

...

[(2) (*a*) In paragraph (*b*) chargeable period has the same meaning as in section 321(2) of the Principal Act.

(*b*) Paragraphs (*b*), (*c*) and (*d*) of subsection (1) shall apply as respects any chargeable period commencing on or after 15 February 2001.

(*c*) Paragraphs (*a*) and (*e*) of subsection (1) shall apply as on and from 15 February 2001.][1]

Notes

Subs (1)(*a*) substituted TCA 1997, s 887 [with effect on or after 15 February 2001][1].

Subs (3)(*a*)(i) substituted "€1,265" for "£1,000" in TCA 1997, s 887(5)(*b*) with effect from 1 January 2002.

Amendments

[1] Substituted by subs (2)(*c*) which was substituted by FA 2002, s 138 and Sch 6 para 5(*f*) with effect on and from 30 March 2001; previously "as respects any chargeable period (within the meaning of s 321(2)) commencing on or after 15 February 2001".

233 Amendment of section 1078 (revenue offences) of Principal Act

Notes

Subs (1) substituted "£1,500" for "£1,000" in TCA 1997, s 1078(3)(*a*) with effect from 6 April 2001.

Subs (2)(*a*) substituted "€1,900" for "£1,500" in TCA 1997, s 1078(3)(*a*) with effect from 1 January 2002.

234 Amendment of section 1094 (tax clearance in relation to certain licences) of Principal Act

Notes

This section inserted TCA 1997, s 1094(1) definition of "licence" para (*l*) with effect from 6 April 2001.

235 Amendment of Chapter 6 (electronic transmission of returns of income, profits, etc, and of other Revenue returns) of Part 38 of Principal Act

Notes

Para (a)(i)(I) substituted TCA 1997, s 917D(1) definition of "digital signature" with effect from 6 April 2001.

Para (a)(i)(II) substituted TCA 1997, s 917D(1) definition of "return" with effect from 6 April 2001.

Para (a)(ii) deleted TCA 1997, s 917D(2) with effect from 6 April 2001.

Para (b)(i) substituted "the approved person's or the authorised person's digital signature" for "the approved person's digital signature" in TCA 1997, s 917F(1)(c) with effect from 6 April 2001.

Para (b)(ii) substituted TCA 1997, s 917F(5) with effect from 6 April 2001.

Para (c)(i) substituted "complies with the condition specified in subsection (3)(a) in relation to authorised persons and the condition specified in subsection (3)(b) in relation to the making of transmissions and the use of digital signatures" for "complies with the provisions of this section and, in particular, with the conditions specified in subsection (3)" in TCA 1997, s 917G(1) with effect from 6 April 2001.

Para (c)(ii) substituted "by such means as the Revenue Commissioners may determine" for "in writing or by such other means as may be approved by the Revenue Commissioners" in TCA 1997, s 917G(2) with effect from 6 April 2001.

Para (c)(iii) substituted TCA 1997, s 917G(3) with effect from 6 April 2001.

Para (d) substituted TCA 1997, s 917H(2)–(3) with effect from 6 April 2001.

Para (e) deleted TCA 1997, s 917I with effect from 6 April 2001.

Para (f) substituted "transmitted or to be transmitted" for "to be transmitted" in TCA 1997, s 917K(1)(a) with effect from 6 April 2001.

Para (g) substituted "for the purposes of the Acts" for "for the purposes of any proceedings in relation to which the certificate is given" in TCA 1997, s 917M(3) with effect from 6 April 2001.

236 Certificates in court proceedings

Notes

Para (a)(i) substituted TCA 1997, s 966(5) with effect from 30 March 2001.

Para (a)(ii) substituted TCA 1997, s 967 with effect from 30 March 2001.

Para (b) substituted TCA 1997, s 1080(4) with effect from 30 March 2001.

237 Amendment of Chapter 4 (collection and recovery of income tax on certain emoluments (PAYE system)) of Part 42 of Principal Act

Notes

Para (a)(i) inserted TCA 1997, s 990(1A) with effect from 6 April 2001.

Para (a)(ii) inserted "and prior to such service the employer had sent to the Collector-General the return required by Regulation 35 of the Income Tax (Employment) Regulations 1960 (SI 28/1960)" to TCA 1997, s 990(2) with effect from 6 April 2001.

Para (b) inserted TCA 1997, s 991(1A)–(1B) with effect from 6 April 2001.

Para (c) inserted TCA 1997, s 991A with effect from 6 April 2001.

238 Amendment of section 1002 (deduction from payments due to defaulters of amounts due in relation to tax) of Principal Act

Notes

This section substituted "14 days" for "one month" in TCA 1997, s 1002(3)(a).

239 Amendment of section 1006A (offset between taxes) of Principal Act

Notes

Para (*a*) inserted ", and includes any interest due under the Acts in relation to such tax, duty, levy or other charge" in TCA 1997, s 1006A(1) definition of "liability" with effect from 6 April 2001.
Para (*b*) substituted TCA 1997, s 1006A(2) with effect from 6 April 2001.

240 Amendment of enactments consequent on changeover to Euro

(1) (*a*) Subject to subsection (2), in each provision specified in column (1) of Schedule 5 for the words or amount set out in column (2) of that Schedule at that entry there shall be substituted the words or amount set out at the corresponding entry in column (3) of that Schedule.

(*b*) Where words are or an amount is mentioned more than once in a provision specified in column (1) of Schedule 5, then the substitution provided for by paragraph (*a*) shall apply as respects those words or that amount to each mention of those words or that amount in that provision.

(2) Subsection (1) shall apply—

(*a*) to the extent that the amendments relate to income tax and related matters, other than the amendments relating to such matters referred to in subparagraphs (ii), (iii), (iv), (v) and (vi) of paragraph (*m*), as respects the year of assessment 2002 and subsequent years of assessment,

(*b*) to the extent that the amendments relate to capital gains tax and related matters, other than the amendments relating to such matters referred to in paragraph (*m*)(vii),as respects the year of assessment 2002 and subsequent years of assessment,

(*c*) to the extent that the amendments relate to corporation tax and related matters, other than the amendments relating to such matters referred to in subparagraphs (i), (iii) and (iv) of paragraph (*l*), for accounting periods ending on or after 1 January 2002,

...

(i) to the extent that section 1086 of the Taxes Consolidation Act, 1997 is amended, as respects specified sums such as are referred to in paragraphs (*c*) and (*d*) of section 1086(2) of that Act which the Revenue Commissioners accept or undertake to accept on or after 1 January 2002,

...

(*k*) to the extent that the enactment amended imposes any fine, forfeiture, penalty or punishment for any act or omission, as respects any act or omission which takes place or begins on or after 1 January 2002,

and

(*l*) to the extent that—

(i) section 110 of the Taxes Consolidation Act, 1997 (in this paragraph referred to as the **"Act of 1997"**) is amended, as respects a company acquiring qualifying assets on or after 1 January 2002,

(ii)   sections 201 and 202 of the Act of 1997 and Schedule 3 to that Act are amended, as respects payments made on or after 1 January 2002,

(iii)   section 404(6) of the Act of 1997 is amended, as respects a lease entered into on or after 1 January 2002,

(iv)   section 481(2)(*c*) of the Act of 1997 is amended, as respects a certificate issued under subsection (2)(*a*)(i) of that section on or after 1 January 2002,

(v)   section 491 of the Act of 1997 is amended, as respects eligible shares (within the meaning of TCA 1997 s 488) issued on or after 1 January 2002,

(vi)   section 494(1) of the Act of 1997 is amended, as respects a relevant investment (within the meaning of section 488 of that Act) being an individual's first such investment made on or after 1 January 2002, and sections 494(5) and 494(6)(*b*) of that Act are amended, as respects a subscription for eligible shares (within the meaning of section 488 of that Act) where the specified date (within the meaning of section 494 of that Act) in relation to that subscription is a date on or after 1 January 2002,

(vii)   sections 598 and 602 of the Act of 1997 are amended, as respects disposals made on or after 1 January 2002,

...

242 Care and management of taxes and duties

All the taxes and duties imposed by this Act are placed under the care and management of the Revenue Commissioners.

243 Short title, construction and commencement

(1) This Act may be cited as the Finance Act, 2001.

...

(4) Part 4 shall be construed together with the Value Added Tax Acts, 1972 to 2000, and may be cited together therewith as the Value Added Tax Acts, 1972 to 2001.

...

(8) Part 8 (so far as relating to income tax) shall be construed together with the Income Tax Acts and (so far as relating to corporation tax) shall be construed together with the Corporation Tax Acts and (so far as relating to capital gains tax) shall be construed together with the Capital Gains Tax Acts and (so far as relating to Value Added tax) shall be construed together with the Value Added Tax Acts, 1972 to 2001 and (so far as relating to residential property tax) shall be construed together with Part VI of the Finance Act, 1983, and the enactments amending or extending that Part and (so far as relating to gift tax or inheritance tax) shall be construed together with the Capital Acquisitions Tax Act, 1976, and the enactments amending or extending that Act.

...

(10) In relation to Part 4:

(*a*)   sections 181, 187 and 189 shall be deemed to have come into force and shall take effect as on and from 1 January 2001;

(*b*) paragraph (*a*) of section 188 shall be deemed to have come into force and shall take effect as on and from 8 January 2001;

(*c*) paragraphs (*c*), (*d*) and (*e*) of section 199, and section 200, shall have effect as on and from 1 May 2001;

(*d*) paragraphs (*b*) and (*c*) of section 177 and paragraph (*b*) of section 193 shall have effect as on and from 1 July 2001;

(*e*) paragraphs (*a*) and (*b*) of section 199 shall have effect as on and from 1 September 2001;

(*f*) section 198 shall have effect as on and from 1 January 2002;

(*g*) the provisions of this Part, other than those specified in paragraphs (*a*) to (f) shall have effect as on and from the date of passing of this Act.

(11) Any reference in this Act to any other enactment shall, except so far as the context otherwise requires, be construed as a reference to that enactment as amended by or under any other enactment including this Act.

(12) In this Act, a reference to a Part, section or Schedule is to a Part or section of, or Schedule to, this Act, unless it is indicated that reference to some other enactment is intended.

(13) In this Act, a reference to a subsection, paragraph, subparagraph, clause or subclause is to the subsection, paragraph, subparagraph, clause or subclause of the provision (including a Schedule) in which the reference occurs, unless it is indicated that reference to some other provision is intended.

SCHEDULE 5
AMENDMENT OF ENACTMENTS CONSEQUENT ON CHANGEOVER TO EURO

[Section 240]

PART 4
Value Added Tax and related matters

Notes

Sch 5 Part 4 amended the following with effect from 1 January 2002:

Value Added Tax Act 1972:

s 3(6)(*d*)(A): £27,565 substituted by €35,000; s 4A(4): £X substituted by €X; s 8(1A)(*b*): £32,000 substituted by €41,000; s 8(3)(*a*)(i): £20,000 substituted by €25,500; s 8(3)(*a*)(i*a*): £40,000 substituted by 51,000; s 8(3)(*a*)(ii): £40,000 substituted by €51,000; s 8(3)(*a*)(iii): £20,000 substituted by €25,500; s 8(3)(*a*)(iv): £40,000 substituted by €51,000; s 8(3)(*c*)(i): £40,000 substituted by €51,000; s 8(3)(*e*): £20,000 substituted by €25,500; s 8(3A): £20,000 substituted by €25,500; s 8(9)(*b*)(ii): £20,000 substituted by €25,500; s 10A(8)(*b*): £500 substituted by €635; s 10A(8)(*c*): £500 substituted by €635; s 11(3): 25 pence substituted by 40 cents; s 14(1)(*b*): £500,000 substituted by €635,000; s 15A(3)(*c*): £100 substituted by €130; s 21(1): £5 substituted by €6; s 26(1): £1,200 substituted by €1,520; s 26(2): £750 substituted by €950; s 26(2A): £750 substituted by €950; s 26(3): £750 substituted by €950; s 26(3A): £1,000 substituted by €1,265; s 26(3B): £1,200 substituted by €1,520; s 27(1)(*a*): £100 substituted by €125; s 27(2)(*a*): £100 substituted by €125; s 27(2)(*a*): £500 substituted by €630; s 27(2)(*a*): £1,000 substituted by €1,265; s 27(2)(*b*): £100 substituted by €125; s 27(2)(*b*): £200 substituted by €250; s 27(4): £500 substituted by €630; s 27(4A): £500 substituted by €630; s 27(5)(*b*)(i): £100 substituted by €125; s 28: £750 substituted by €950; Sixth Schedule para (vii*b*): £20,000 substituted by €25,500; Sixth Schedule para (viic): £20,000 substituted by €25,500.

Value Added Tax Regulations 1979 (SI 83/1979):

r 18: £15 substituted by €20; r 24(2): £500 substituted by €635; r 31: £15 substituted by €20.

European Communities (Exemption from Value Added Tax on the Permanent Importation of Certain Goods) Regulations 1985 (SI 183/1985):

r 5(2)(*b*): 200 ECU substituted by €200; r 5(2)(*c*): 200 ECU substituted by €200; r 5(2)(*c*): 1,000 ECU substituted by €1,000; r 8: 10 ECU substituted by €10; r 31: £500 substituted by €630.

Value Added Tax (Statement of Intra-Community Supplies) Regulations 1993:

r 9(1): £60,000 substituted by €85,000; r 9(1): £12,000 substituted by €15,000; r 9(2): £150,000 substituted by €200,000; Reg 9(2): £12,000 substituted by €15,000.

European Communities (Intrastat) Regulations 1993 (SI 136/1993):

r 11(2): £1,000 substituted by €1,265; r 11(3): £50 substituted by €60.

Value Added Tax (Refund of Tax) (No 23) Order 1992 (SI 58/1992):

para 2(*a*): £20,000 substituted by €25,390;

Value Added Tax (Refund of Tax) (No 25) Order 1993 (SI 266/1993):

para 8: £100 substituted by €125.

Value Added Tax (Refund of Tax) (No 27) Order 1995 (SI 38/1995):

para 2 definition of "qualifying goods" sub-para (*a*): £20,000 substituted by €25,390.

Value Added Tax (Refund of Tax) (No 29) Order 1996 (SI 334/1996):

para 9: £250 substituted by €315; para 13: £100 substituted by €125.

FINANCE ACT 2002

(2002 Number 5)

ARRANGEMENT OF SECTIONS

PART 3
VALUE ADDED TAX

PART 6
MISCELLANEOUS

SCHEDULE 6
MISCELLANEOUS TECHNICAL AMENDMENTS IN RELATION TO TAX

AN ACT TO PROVIDE FOR THE IMPOSITION, REPEAL, REMISSION, ALTERATION AND REGULATION OF TAXATION OF STAMP DUTIES AND

OF DUTIES RELATING TO EXCISE AND OTHERWISE TO MAKE FURTHER
PROVISION IN CONNECTION WITH FINANCE INCLUDING THE
REGULATION OF CUSTOMS [*25th MARCH 2002*]

PART 3
VALUE ADDED TAX

98 Interpretation (Part 3)

In this Part "the Principal Act" means the Value Added Tax Act 1972.

99 Amendment of section 4 (special provisions in relation to the supply of immovable goods) of Principal Act

---

Notes

Section 99 inserted VATA 1972, s 4(3A) with effect from 25 March 2002.

100 Amendment of section 7 (waiver of exemption) of Principal Act

---

Notes

Para (*a*) renumbered VATA 1972, s 7(1) as VATA 1972, s 7(1)(*a*) with effect from 25 March 2002.
Para (*b*) inserted VATA 1972, s 7(1)(*b*) with effect from 25 March 2002.

101 Amendment of section 8 (taxable persons) of Principal Act

---

Notes

Para (*a*) inserted ", but a person not established in the State who supplies a service in the State in the circumstances set out in subsection (2)(*aa*) shall not be a taxable person and shall not be accountable for or liable to pay the tax chargeable in respect of such supply" in VATA 1972, s 8(1) with effect from 25 March 2002.
Para (*b*)(i) inserted VATA 1972, s 8(2)(*aa*)–(*ab*) with effect from 25 March 2002.
Para (*b*)(ii) inserted VATA 1972, s 8(2)(*d*) with effect from 25 March 2002.
Para (*c*)(i) inserted "and the persons so notified shall be regarded as being in a group for as long as this paragraph applies to them," in VATA 1972, s 8(8)(*a*)(i) with effect from 25 March 2002.
Para (*c*)(ii) inserted VATA 1972, s 8(8)(*d*) with effect from 25 March 2002.

102 Amendment of section 10 (amount on which tax is chargeable) of Principal Act

---

Notes

Para (*a*) substituted "Subject to subsection (6A), where" for "Where" in VATA 1972, s 10(6) with effect from 25 March 2002.
Para (*b*) inserted VATA 1972, s 10(6A) with effect from 25 March 2002.
Para (*c*) inserted "(6A) or" after "subject to subsection" in VATA 1972, s 10(7)(*c*) with effect from 25 March 2002.

103 Amendment of section 11 (rates of tax) of Principal Act

Notes

Section 103 substituted "21 per cent" for "20 per cent" in VATA 1972, s 11(1)(*a*) with effect from 1 March 2002.

104 Amendment of section 12D (adjustment of tax deductible in certain circumstances) of Principal Act

Notes

Section 104 substituted "calculate an amount which shall be payable as if it were tax due by that person in accordance with section 19 for the taxable period within which the transfer was made, and that amount shall be calculated" for "reduce the amount of tax deductible by that person, for the purposes of section 12, for the period within which the transfer was made, by an amount calculated" in VATA 1972, s 12D(4) with effect on and from 1 September 2002.

105 Amendment of section 13 (remission of tax on goods exported, etc) of Principal Act

Notes

Section 105 inserted "other than services for which in accordance with section 8(2) the person who receives them is solely liable for the tax chargeable" after "in the State" in VATA 1972, s 13(3)(*b*) with effect from 25 March 2002.

106 Amendment of section 19 (tax due and payable) of Principal Act

Notes

Para (*a*) inserted "However this subsection does not apply to the tax chargeable in respect of supplies of goods or services where tax is due in accordance with paragraph *(a)* or (*b*) of subsection (1) by a taxable person who is not authorised under section 14 to account for tax due by reference to the amount of the moneys received during a taxable period or part thereof." after "at the time of such receipt." in VATA 1972, s 19(2) with effect from 1 May 2002.

Para (*b*) inserted VATA 1972, s 19(3)(*d*) with effect from 25 March 2002.

107 Letter of expression of doubt

Notes

Section 107 inserted VATA 1972, s 19B with effect from 25 March 2002.

108 Amendment of section 21 (interest) of Principal Act

Notes

Section 108 inserted VATA 1972, s 21(1) with effect from 1 September 2002.

109 Amendment of section 25 (appeals) of Principal Act

Notes

Para (*a*) deleted VATA 1972, s 25(1)(*ab*) with effect from 25 March 2002.

Para (*b*) inserted VATA 1972, s 25(1)(*ae*)–(*af*) with effect from 25 March 2002.

110 Amendment of the First Schedule to Principal Act

Notes

Section 110 inserted VATA 1972, Sch 1 para (xv*a*) with effect from 25 March 2002.

PART 6
MISCELLANEOUS

123 Interpretation (Part 6)

In this Part "Principal Act" means the Taxes Consolidation Act 1997.

125 Amendment of Chapter 5 (miscellaneous provisions) of Part 42 of Principal Act

---

Notes

Para (*a*)(i)(I) substituted TCA 1997, s 1006A(1) definition of "claim" with effect from 25 March 2002.

Para (*a*)(i)(II) substituted TCA 1997, s 1006A(1) definition of "liability" with effect from 25 March 2002.

Para (*a*)(i)(III) substituted "credited;" for "credited." In TCA 1997, s 1006A(1) definition of "overpayment" with effect from 25 March 2002.

Para (*a*)(i)(IV) inserted TCA 1997, s 1006A(1) definition of "tax" with effect from 25 March 2002.

Para (*a*)(ii) inserted TCA 1997, s 1006A(5) with effect from 25 March 2002.

Para (*b*) inserted TCA 1997, s 1006B(5) with effect from 25 March 2002.

---

126 Amendment of section 1086 (publication of names of tax defaulters) of Principal Act

---

Notes

Subs (1)(*a*)(i)(I) substituted TCA 1997, s 1086(1) definition of "the Acts" para (*e*) as respects fines or other penalties, as are referred to in TCA 1997, s 1086(2)(*a*)–(*b*), which are imposed by a court, and as respects specified sums, as are referred to in TCA 1997, s 1086(2)(*c*)–(*d*), which the Revenue Commissioners accepted, or undertook to accept, in settlement of a specified liability, on or after 25 March 2002.

Subs (1)(*a*)(i)(II) inserted TCA 1997, s 1086(1) definition of "the Acts" paras (*g*)–(*h*) as respects fines or other penalties, as are referred to in TCA 1997, s 1086(2)(*a*)–(*b*), which are imposed by a court, and as respects specified sums, as are referred to in TCA 1997, s 1086(2)(*c*)–(*d*), which the Revenue Commissioners accepted, or undertook to accept, in settlement of a specified liability, on or after 25 March 2002.

Subs (1)(*a*)(ii) substituted TCA 1997, s 1086(1) definition of "tax" as respects fines or other penalties, as are referred to in TCA 1997, s 1086(2)(*a*)–(*b*), which are imposed by a court, and as respects specified sums, as are referred to in TCA 1997, s 1086(2)(*c*)–(*d*), which the Revenue Commissioners accepted, or undertook to accept, in settlement of a specified liability, on or after 25 March 2002.

Subs (1)(*b*)(i) substituted TCA 1997, s 1086(2)(*c*)(ii)–(iii) as respects fines or other penalties, as are referred to in TCA 1997, s 1086(2)(*a*)–(*b*), which are imposed by a court, and as respects specified sums, as are referred to in TCA 1997, s 1086(2)(*c*)–(*d*), which the Revenue Commissioners accepted, or undertook to accept, in settlement of a specified liability, on or after 25 March 2002.

Subs (1)(*b*)(ii) substituted TCA 1997, s 1086(2)(*d*)(ii)–(iii) as respects fines or other penalties, as are referred to in TCA 1997, s 1086(2)(*a*)–(*b*), which are imposed by a court, and as respects specified sums, as are referred to in TCA 1997, s 1086(2)(*c*)–(*d*), which the Revenue Commissioners accepted, or undertook to accept, in settlement of a specified liability, on or after 25 March 2002.

Subs (1)(*c*) substituted TCA 1997, s 1086(3)(*b*) as respects fines or other penalties, as are referred to in TCA 1997, s 1086(2)(*a*)–(*b*), which are imposed by a court, and as respects specified sums, as are referred to in TCA 1997, s 1086(2)(*c*)–(*d*), which the Revenue Commissioners accepted, or undertook to accept, in settlement of a specified liability, on or after 25 March 2002.

Subs (1)(*d*)(i) substituted "those paragraphs" for "that paragraph" in TCA 1997, s 1086(4)(*a*) as respects fines or other penalties, as are referred to in TCA 1997, s 1086(2)(*a*)–(*b*), which are imposed by a court, and as respects specified sums, as are referred to in TCA 1997, s 1086(2)(*c*)–(*d*), which the Revenue Commissioners accepted, or undertook to accept, in settlement of a specified liability, on or after 25 March 2002.

Subs (1)(*d*)(ii) substituted "applied," for "applied, or" in TCA 1997, s 1086(4)(*b*) as respects fines or other penalties, as are referred to in TCA 1997, s 1086(2)(*a*)–(*b*), which are imposed by a court, and as respects specified sums, as are referred to in TCA 1997, s 1086(2)(*c*)–(*d*), which the Revenue Commissioners accepted, or undertook to accept, in settlement of a specified liability, on or after 25 March 2002.

Subs (1)(*d*)(iii) substituted "€12,700, or" for "€12,700." in TCA 1997, s 1086(4)(*c*) as respects fines or other penalties, as are referred to in TCA 1997, s 1086(2)(*a*)–(*b*), which are imposed by a court, and as respects specified sums, as are referred to in TCA 1997, s 1086(2)(*c*)–(*d*), which the Revenue Commissioners accepted, or undertook to accept, in settlement of a specified liability, on or after 25 March 2002.

Subs (1)(*d*)(iii) inserted TCA 1997, s 1086(4)(*d*) as respects fines or other penalties, as are referred to in TCA 1997, s 1086(2)(*a*)–(*b*), which are imposed by a court, and as respects specified sums, as are referred to in TCA 1997, s 1086(2)(*c*)–(*d*), which the Revenue Commissioners accepted, or undertook to accept, in settlement of a specified liability, on or after 25 March 2002.

127 Tax clearance

Notes

Para (*a*)(i)(I)(A) substituted "means a licence, permit or authorisation" for "means a licence or authorisation" in TCA 1997, s 1094(1) definition of "licence" with effect from 25 March 2002.

Para (*a*)(i)(I)(B) substituted "," for ";" in TCA 1997, s 1094(1) definition of "licence" paras (*h*), (*j*), (*k*) and (*l*) with effect from 25 March 2002.

Para (*a*)(i)(I)(C) inserted TCA 1997, s 1094(1) definition of "licence" paras (*m*)–(*n*) with effect from 25 March 2002.

Para (*a*)(i)(II) substituted "paragraphs (*a*) to (*n*)" for "paragraphs (*a*) to (*j*)" in TCA 1997, s 1094(1) definition of "specified date" with effect from 25 March 2002.

Para (*a*)(ii) substituted TCA 1997, s 1094(5) with effect from 25 March 2002.

Para (*a*)(iii) inserted TCA 1997, s 1094(8)–(9) with effect from 25 March 2002.

Para (*b*) substituted TCA 1997, s 1095 with effect from 25 March 2002.

132 Amendment of Chapter 4 (revenue powers) of Part 38 of Principal Act

Notes

Para (*d*) inserted TCA 1997, s 905(1) definition of "records" with effect from 25 March 2002.

133 Amendment of section 1078 (revenue offences) of Principal Act

Notes

Para (*a*) substituted "fails without reasonable excuse" for "knowingly or wilfully fails" in TCA 1997, s 1078(2)(*g*) with effect from 25 March 2002.

Para (*b*) inserted TCA 1997, s 1078(3B) with effect from 25 March 2002.

135 Amendment of Part 48 (miscellaneous and supplemental) of Principal Act

Notes

Section 135 inserted TCA 1997, s 1096B with effect from 1 January 2002.

138 Miscellaneous technical amendments in relation to tax

The enactments specified in Schedule 6 are amended to the extent and in the manner specified in that Schedule.

139 Amendment of Provisional Collection of Taxes Act 1927

Notes

Para (*a*) substituted Provisional Collection of Taxes 1927, s 1 definition of "new tax" with effect from 25 March 2002.

Para (*b*) substituted "immediately before the date on which the resolution is expressed to take effect or, where no such date is expressed, the passing of the resolution by Dáil Éireann" for "immediately before the end of the previous financial year" in Provisional Collection of Taxes 1927, ss 2–3 with effect from 25 March 2002.

140 Care and management of taxes and duties

All taxes and duties imposed by this Act are placed under the care and management of the Revenue Commissioners.

141 Short title, construction and commencement

(1) This Act may be cited as the Finance Act 2002.

...

(4) Part 3 shall be construed together with the Value Added Tax Acts 1972 to 2001 and may be cited together with those acts as the Value Added Tax Acts 1972 to 2002.

...

(7) Part 6 (so far as relating to income tax) shall be construed together with the Income Tax Acts and (so far as relating to corporation tax) shall be construed together with the Corporation Tax Acts and (so far as relating to capital gains tax) shall be construed together with the Capital Gains Tax Acts and (so far as relating to Value Added tax) shall be construed together with the Value Added Tax Acts 1972 to 2002 and (so far as relating to residential property tax) shall be construed together with Part VI of the Finance Act 1983, and the enactments amending or extending that Part and (so far as relating to gift tax or inheritance tax) shall be construed together with the Capital Acquisitions Tax Act 1976, and the enactments amending or extending that Act.

...

(9) In relation to Part 3:

    (*a*)   sections (98) and (103) shall be taken to have come into force and shall take effect as on and from 1 March 2002;

    (*b*)   paragraph (*a*) of section (106) comes into force and takes effect as on and from 1 May 2002;

    (*c*)   section (108) comes into force and takes effect as on and from 1 September 2002;

    (*d*)   the provisions of this *Part*, other than those specified in paragraphs (*a*), (*b*), and (*c*) have effect as on and from the date of passing of this Act.

(10) Any reference in this Act to any other enactment shall, except so far as the context otherwise requires, be construed as a reference to that enactment as amended by or under any other enactment including this Act.

(11) In this Act, a reference to a Part, section or Schedule is to a Part or section of, or Schedule to, this Act, unless it is indicated that reference to some other enactment is intended.

(12) In this Act, a reference to a subsection, paragraph, subparagraph, clause or subclause is to the subsection, paragraph, subparagraph, clause or subclause of the

provision (including a Schedule) in which the reference occurs, unless it is indicated that reference to some other provision is intended.

SCHEDULE 6

MISCELLANEOUS TECHNICAL AMENDMENTS IN RELATION TO TAX

Notes

Para 1(*a*) substituted "40 cent" for "40 cents" in VATA 1972, s 11(3) with effect from 1 January 2002.

Para 1(*b*) deleted "(*b*), (*c*) or" in VATA 1972, s 12(1)(*b*)(ii) with effect from 1 January 2002.

Para 1(*c*) substituted "3(5)(*c*) or (*d*)" for "3(5)(*c*)" in VATA 1972, s 12C(1A), (1B) and (1B)(*f*) with effect from 1 January 2002.

Para 1(*d*) substituted "fourteen" for "twenty-one" in VATA 1972, s 19(3)(*aa*)(vii) with effect from 1 January 2002.

Para 1(*e*) substituted VATA 1972, Sch 1 para (i)(*g*)(I) with effect from 1 January 2002.

FINANCE ACT 2003

(2003 Number 3)

ARRANGEMENT OF SECTIONS

PART 3
VALUE ADDED TAX

SCHEDULE 6
Miscellaneous Technical Amendments in Relation to Tax

AN ACT TO PROVIDE FOR THE IMPOSITION, REPEAL, REMISSION, ALTERATION AND REGULATION OF TAXATION, OF STAMP DUTIES AND OF DUTIES RELATING TO EXCISE AND OTHERWISE TO MAKE FURTHER PROVISION IN CONNECTION WITH FINANCE INCLUDING THE REGULATION OF CUSTOMS. BE IT ENACTED BY THE OIREACHTAS AS FOLLOWS:

PART 3
Value Added Tax

112 Interpretation (Part 3)

In this Part **"Principal Act"** means the Value Added Tax Act 1972.

113 Amendment of section 1 (interpretation) of Principal Act

Notes

This section inserted VATA 1972, s 1(1) definition of "electronically supplied services" with effect from 1 July 2003.

---

114 Amendment of section 4 (special provisions in relation to the supply of immovable goods) of Principal Act

---

Notes

Para (*a*) substituted "the total amount on which tax was chargeable" for "the amount on which tax was chargeable" in VATA 1972, s 4(3A)(*d*) with effect from 28 March 2003.

Para (*b*) substituted "in respect of or in relation to" for "in respect of" where it occurs in VATA 1972, s 4(3A)(*d*) with effect from 28 March 2003.

---

115 Amendment of section 5 (supply of services) of Principal Act

---

Notes

Para (*a*) inserted "or a radio or television broadcasting service," to VATA 1972, s 5(6)(*dd*) with effect from 1 July 2003.

Para (*b*) substituted "paragraphs (*ddd*), (*ee*) and (*eee*)" for "paragraphs (*ddd*) and (*ee*)" in VATA 1972, s 5(6)(*e*) with effect from 1 July 2003.

Para (*c*) inserted VATA 1972, s 5(6)(*eee*) with effect from 1 July 2003.

---

116 Special scheme for electronic services

Notes

This section inserted VATA 1972, s 5A with effect from 1 July 2003.

---

117 Amendment of section 7 (waiver of exemption) of Principal Act

---

Notes

This section inserted VATA 1972, s 7(3)(*aa*) with effect from 28 March 2003.

---

118 Amendment of section 8 (taxable persons) of Principal Act

Notes

Para (*a*) substituted "goods in the State in the circumstances set out in subsection (1A)(*f*) or supplies a service in the State in the circumstances set out in subsection (2)(*aa*)," for "a service in the State in the circumstances set out in subsection (2)(*aa*)" VATA 1972, s 8(1) with effect from 28 March 2003.

Para (*b*) inserted "goods in the State in the circumstances set out in subsection (1A)(*f*) or supplies a service in the State in the circumstances set out in subsection (2)(*aa*)," for "a service in the State in the circumstances set out in subsection (2)(*aa*)" in VATA 1972, s 8(1A)(*f*) with effect from 28 March 2003.

119 Amendment of section 11 (rates of tax) of Principal Act

Notes

This section substituted "13.5 per cent" for "12.5 per cent" in VATA 1972, s 11(1)(*d*) with effect from 1 January 2003.

120 Amendment of section 12B (special scheme for means of transport supplied by taxable dealers) of Principal Act

Notes

Para (*a*) deleted "and" from VATA 1972, s 12B(10)(*a*), substituted "of that motor vehicle to that person, and" for "of that motor vehicle to that person." in VATA 1972, s 12B(10)(*b*) and inserted VATA 1972, s 12B(10)(*c*) with effect from 1 May 2003.

Para (*b*) inserted VATA 1972, s 12B(11) with effect from 1 May 2003.

121 Amendment of section 16 (duty to keep records) of Principal Act

Notes

Para (*a*) inserted ", subject to subsection (4)," to VATA 1972, s 16(3) with effect from 28 March 2003.

Para (*b*) inserted VATA 1972, s 16(4) with effect from 28 March 2003.

122 Amendment of section 17 (invoices) of Principal Act

Notes

Para (*a*) inserted "or to a Department of State or local authority or to a body established by statute or to a person who carries on an exempted activity" to VATA 1972, s 17(1) with effect from 1 January 2004.

Para (*b*) deleted "goods or services are supplied to a registered person by another registered person or" from VATA 1972, s 17(10)(*a*) with effect from 1 January 2004.

Para (*c*) substituted "agricultural produce" for "goods" in VATA 1972, s 17(10)(*b*) with effect from 1 January 2004.

Para (*d*) inserted VATA 1972, s 17(14) and (15) with effect from 1 January 2004.

123 Amendment of section 19 (tax due and payable) of Principal Act

Notes

This section inserted VATA 1972, s 19(6) with effect from 1 July 2003.

124 Amendment of section 20 (refund of tax) of Principal Act

Notes

Para (*a*)(i) substituted "1 May 2003" for "the 1st day of May, 1998" in VATA 1972, s 20(4)(*a*) with effect from 1 November 2003 (Finance Act 2003 (Commencement of Sections 124,125,129 and 130(*b*)) Order 2003).

Para (*a*)(ii) substituted "six years" for "ten years" in VATA 1972, s 20(4)(*a*) with effect from 1 November 2003 (Finance Act 2003 (Commencement of Sections 124,125,129 and 130(*b*)) Order 2003).

Para (*b*)(i) substituted "1 May 2003" for "the 1st day of May, 1998" in VATA 1972, s 20(4)(*b*) with effect from 1 November 2003 (Finance Act 2003 (Commencement of Sections 124,125,129 and 130(*b*)) Order 2003).

Para (*b*)(ii) substituted "1 January 2005" for "the 1st day of May, 1999," in VATA 1972, s 20(4)(*b*) with effect from 1 November 2003 (Finance Act 2003 (Commencement of Sections 124,125,129 and 130(*b*)) Order 2003).

Para (*b*)(iii) substituted "four years" for "six years" in VATA 1972, s 20(4)(*b*) with effect from 1 November 2003 (Finance Act 2003 (Commencement of Sections 124,125,129 and 130(*b*)) Order 2003).

Para (*c*) inserted "together with any interest payable in accordance with section 21A" in VATA 1972, s 20(5)(*e*) with effect from 1 November 2003 (Finance Act 2003 (Commencement of Sections 124,125,129 and 130(*b*)) Order 2003).

Para (*d*) inserted VATA 1972, s 20(7) with effect from 1 November 2003 (Finance Act 2003 (Commencement of Sections 124,125,129 and 130(*b*)) Order 2003).

125 Interest on refunds of tax

Notes

This section inserted VATA 1972, s 21A with effect from 1 November 2003 (Finance Act 2003 (Commencement of Sections 124,125,129 and 130(*b*)) Order 2003).

126 Amendment of section 22 (estimation of tax due for a taxable period) of Principal Act

Notes

This section substituted VATA 1972, s 22(1)(proviso) with effect from 28 March 2003.

127 Amendment of section 27 (fraudulent returns, etc) of Principal Act

Notes

Para (*a*) inserted VATA 1972, s 27(1A) with effect from 28 March 2003.

Para (*b*)(i) substituted "subsection (1) or (1A)" for "the foregoing subsection" in VATA 1972, s 27(2) with effect from 28 March 2003.

Para (*b*)(ii) substituted "any reference in those subsections" for "the reference in paragraph (*a*) of that subsection" in VATA 1972, s 27(2)(*a*) with effect from 28 March 2003.

128 Amendment of section 29 (recovery of penalties) of Principal Act

Notes

Para (*a*) substituted "for the recovery of the penalty in any court of competent jurisdiction as a liquidated sum, and, where appropriate, section 94 of the Courts of Justice Act, 1924 shall apply accordingly." for "for the recovery of the penalty in the High Court as a liquidated sum and the provisions of section 94 of the Courts of Justice Act, 1924, shall apply accordingly." in VATA 1972, s 29(1) with effect from 28 March 2003.

Para (*b*) substituted "the rules of court" for "the rules of the High Court" in VATA 1972, s 29(6) with effect from 28 March 2003.

129 Amendment of section 30 (time limits) of Principal Act

Notes

Para (*a*)(i) substituted "1 May 2003" for "the 1st day of May, 1998" in VATA 1972, s 30(4)(*a*)(i) with effect from 1 November 2003 (Finance Act 2003 (Commencement of Sections 124,125,129 and 130(*b*)) Order 2003).

Para (*a*)(ii) substituted "six years" for "ten years" in VATA 1972, s 30(4)(*a*)(i) with effect from 1 November 2003 (Finance Act 2003 (Commencement of Sections 124,125,129 and 130(*b*)) Order 2003).

Para (*b*)(i) substituted "1 May 2003" for "the 1st day of May, 1998" in VATA 1972, s 30(4)(*a*)(ii) with effect from 1 November 2003 (Finance Act 2003 (Commencement of Sections 124,125,129 and 130(*b*)) Order 2003).
Para (*b*)(ii) substituted "1 January 2005" for "the 1st day of May, 1999," in VATA 1972, s 30(4)(*a*)(ii) with effect from 1 November 2003 (Finance Act 2003 (Commencement of Sections 124,125,129 and 130(*b*)) Order 2003).
Para (*b*)(iii) substituted "four years" for "six years" in VATA 1972, s 30(4)(*a*)(ii) with effect from 1 November 2003 (Finance Act 2003 (Commencement of Sections 124,125,129 and 130(*b*)) Order 2003).

130 Amendment of section 32 (regulations) of Principal Act

Notes

Para (*a*) inserted VATA 1972, s 32(1)(*ba*) with effect from 1 July 2003.
Para (*b*) inserted VATA 1972, s 32(1)(*ma*) with effect from 1 November 2003 (Finance Act 2003 (Commencement of Sections 124,125,129 and 130(*b*)) Order 2003).

131 Amendment of Fourth Schedule to Principal Act

Notes

This section inserted VATA 1972, Sch 4 paras (*iiib*) and (*iiic*) with effect from 1 July 2003.

PART 7
MISCELLANEOUS

156 Interpretation (Part 6)

In this Part **"Principal Act"** means the Taxes Consolidation Act 1997.

160 Amendment of section 1078 (revenue offences) of Principal Act

Notes

Subs (1) substituted "€3,000" for "€1,900" in TCA 1997, s 1078(3)(*a*) as respects an offence committed on or after 28 March 2003.

161 Amendment of Chapter 4 (revenue offences) of Part 47 of Principal Act

Notes

This section inserted TCA 1997, ss 1078A–1078C with effect from 1 January 2003.

163 Miscellaneous technical amendments in relation to tax

The enactments specified in Schedule 6 are amended to the extent and in the manner specified in that Schedule.

164 Mandatory electronic filing and payment of tax

Notes

Subs (1)(*a*) inserted TCA 1997, s 917EA with effect from such day as the Minister for Finance may appoint by order.

170 Care and management of taxes and duties

All taxes and duties imposed by this Act are placed under the care and management of the Revenue Commissioners.

171 Short title, construction and commencement

(1) This Act may be cited as the Finance Act 2003.

...

(4) Part 3 shall be construed together with the Value Added Tax Acts 1972 to 2002 and may be cited together with those Acts as the Value Added Tax Acts 1972 to 2003.

...

(8) Part 7 shall be construed together with—

    (*d*) in so far as it relates to Value Added tax, the Value Added Tax Acts 1972 to 2003,

(10) In relation to Part 3:

    (*a*) section 119 shall be taken to have come into force and shall take effect as on and from 1 January 2003;

    (*b*) section 120 comes into force and takes effect as on and from 1 May 2003;

    (c) sections 113, 115, 116, 123, paragraph (a) of section 130, and section 127 come into force and take effect as on and from 1 July 2003;

    (*d*) section 122 comes into force and takes effect as on and from 1 January 2004;

    (*e*) sections 124, 125, 129 and paragraph (*b*) of section 130 shall take effect as on and from such day or days as the Minister for Finance may, by order or orders, appoint;

    (*f*) the provisions of this Part, other than those specified in paragraphs (*a*) to (*e*), have effect as on and from the date of passing of this Act.

(11) Any reference in this Act to any other enactment shall, except in so far as the context otherwise requires, be construed as a reference to that enactment as amended by or under any other enactment including this Act.

(12) In this Act, a reference to a Part, section or Schedule is to a Part or section of, or Schedule to, this Act, unless it is indicated that reference to some other enactment is intended.

(13) In this Act, a reference to a subsection, paragraph, subparagraph, clause or subclause is to the subsection, paragraph, subparagraph, clause or subclause of the provision (including a Schedule) in which the reference occurs, unless it is indicated that reference to some other provision is intended.

SCHEDULE 6

Miscellaneous Technical Amendments in Relation to Tax

[Section 148]

Notes

Para 2 substituted "Part VII or Part VIII of the Child Care Act 1991" for "Part VII of the Child Care Act 1991" in VATA 1972, Sch 1 para (vi) with effect from 28 March 2003.

FINANCE ACT 2004

(2004 Number 8)

ARRANGEMENT OF SECTIONS

PART 3
VALUE ADDED TAX

Section

PART 3
Value Added Tax

PART 6
MISCELLANEOUS

AN ACT TO PROVIDE FOR THE IMPOSITION, REPEAL, REMISSION, ALTERATION AND REGULATION OF TAXATION, OF STAMP DUTIES AND OF DUTIES RELATING TO EXCISE AND OTHERWISE TO MAKE FURTHER PROVISION IN CONNECTION WITH FINANCE INCLUDING THE REGULATION OF CUSTOMS.

PART 3
VALUE ADDED TAX

54 Interpretation (Part 3)

In this Part—

"Act of 1978" means the Value Added Tax (Amendment) Act 1978;

"Act of 2001" means the Finance Act 2001;

"Principal Act" means the Value Added Tax Act 1972.

55 Amendment of section 1 (interpretation) of Principal Act

Notes

Section 55 substituted VATA 1972, s 1(1)(definition of "taxable dealer"); para (*a*) with effect on and from 1 January 2005; paras (*b*) and (*c*) with effect from 25 March 2004.

56 Amendment of section 3 (supply of goods) of Principal Act

Notes

Para (*a*) substituted "such supplies," for "such supplies." in VATA 1972, s 3(6)(*d*)(proviso) and inserted VATA 1972, s 3(6)(*e*) and (*f*) with effect on and from 1 January 2005.
Para (*b*) inserted VATA 1972, s 3(6A) with effect on and from 1 January 2005.

57 Amendment of section 4 (special provisions in relation to the supply of immovable goods) of Principal Act

Notes

Section 57 substituted VATA 1972, s 3(6) with effect on and from 4 December 2003.

58 Amendment of section 8 (taxable persons) of Principal Act

Notes

Para (*a*) substituted "in paragraph (*f*) or (*g*) of subsection (1A)" for "in subsection (1A)(*f*)" in VATA 1972, s 8(1) with effect on and from 1 January 2005.
Para (*b*) inserted VATA 1972, s 8(1A)(*g*) with effect on and from 1 January 2005.

59 Amendment of section 11 (rates of tax) of Principal Act

Notes

Section 59 substituted "4.4 per cent" for "4.3 per cent" in VATA 1972, s 11(1)(*f*) with effect on and from 1 January 2004.

60 Amendment of section 12 (deduction for tax borne or paid) of Principal Act

Notes

Section 60 inserted VATA 1972, s 12(1)(*a*)(v*a*) and (v*b*) with effect from 25 March 2004.

61 Amendment of section 12A (special provisions for tax invoiced by flat-rate farmers) of Principal Act

Notes

Section 61 substituted "4.4 per cent" for "4.3 per cent" in VATA 1972, s 12A(1) with effect on and from 1 January 2004.

62 Amendment of section 15B (goods in transit (additional provisions)) of Principal Act

Notes

Para (*a*) substituted "before the date of accession" for "on or before the 31st day of December, 1994" in each place where it occurs in VATA 1972, s 15B with effect on and from 1 May 2004.

Para (*b*) substituted "date of accession" for "1st day of January, 1995" in each place where it occurs in VATA 1972, s 15B with effect on and from 1 May 2004.

Para (*c*) deleted VATA 1972, s 15B(5)(*c*)(proviso) with effect on and from 1 May 2004.

Para (*d*) inserted VATA 1972, s 15B(5A) with effect on and from 1 May 2004.

Para (*e*)(i) inserted VATA 1972, s 15B(7)(*a*)(definition of "date of accession") with effect on and from 1 May 2004.

Para (*e*)(ii) substituted VATA 1972, s 15B(7)(*a*)(definition of "new Member State") with effect on and from 1 May 2004.

63 Amendment of section 17 (invoices) of Principal Act

Notes

Section 63 inserted "or who supplies goods or services to a person in another Member State who is liable to pay Value Added tax pursuant to Council Directive No 77/388/EEC of 17 May 1977 on such supply," to VATA 1972, s 17(1) with effect from 25 March 2004.

64 Amendment of First Schedule to Principal Act

Notes

Para (*a*)(i) substituted "the management of an undertaking specified in one of the following clauses, and such management may comprise any of the three functions listed in Annex II to Directive 2001/107/EC of the European Parliament and Council (being the functions included in the activity of collective portfolio management) where those functions are supplied by the person with responsibility for the provision of the functions concerned in respect of the undertaking, and which is—" for "the management of an undertaking which is—" in VATA 1972, Sch 1 para (i)(*g*) with effect from 25 March 2004.

Para (*a*)(ii) substituted "this subparagraph apply, or" for "this subparagraph apply;" in VATA 1972, Sch 1 para (i)(*g*)(IV) with effect from 25 March 2004.

Para (*a*)(iii) inserted VATA 1972, Sch 1 para (i)(*g*)(V) with effect from 25 March 2004.

Para (*b*) substituted "the school;" for "the school." in VATA 1972, Sch 1 para (xxv)(*b*) with effect from 25 March 2004.

Para (*c*) inserted VATA 1972, Sch 1 para (xxvi) with effect from 25 March 2004.

65 Amendment of Fourth Schedule to Principal Act

Notes

Para (*a*) inserted VATA 1972, Sch 4 para (iii*d*) with effect on and from 1 January 2005.

Para (*b*) inserted "and financial fund management functions" to VATA 1972, Sch 4 para (v) with effect from 25 March 2004.

PART 6

MISCELLANEOUS

80 Interpretation (Part 6)

In this Part **"Principal Act"** means the Taxes Consolidation Act 1997.

89 Miscellaneous technical amendments in relation to tax

The enactments specified in Schedule 3 are amended to the extent and in the manner specified in that Schedule.

93 Care and management of taxes and duties

All taxes and duties imposed by this Act are placed under the care and management of the Revenue Commissioners.

94 Short title, construction and commencement

(1) This Act may be cited as the Finance Act 2004.

...

(4) Part 3 shall be construed together with the Value Added Tax Acts 1972 to 2003 and may be cited together with those Acts as the Value Added Tax Acts 1972 to 2004.

...

(7) Part 6 in so far as it relates to—

...

    (*f*)   Value Added tax, shall be construed together with the Value Added Tax Acts 1972 to 2004,

...

(9) In relation to Part 3:

    (*a*)   Section 57 shall be taken to have come into force and shall take effect as on and from 4 December 2003;

    (*b*)   Sections 59 and 61 shall be taken to have come into force and shall take effect as on and from 1 January 2004;

    (*c*)   Section 62 comes into force and takes effect as on and from 1 May 2004;

    (*d*)   paragraph (*a*) of Section 55, Sections 56, 58, Section 60 (in so far as it relates to the insertion of subparagraph (*vb*) into section 12 of the Value Added Tax Act 1972), paragraphs (*b*) and (*c*) of Section 64 and paragraph (*a*) of Section 65 come into force and take effect as on and from 1 January 2005;

    (*e*)   the provisions of this Part, other than those specified in paragraphs (*a*) to (*d*) have effect as on and from the 25 March 2004.

(10) Except where otherwise expressly provided for, where a provision of this Act is to come into operation on the making of an order by the Minister for Finance, that provision shall come into operation on such day or days as the Minister for Finance shall appoint either generally or with reference to any particular purpose or provision and different days may be so appointed for different purposes or different provisions.

(11) Any reference in this Act to any other enactment shall, except in so far as the context otherwise requires, be construed as a reference to that enactment as amended by or under any other enactment including this Act.

(12) In this Act, a reference to a Part, section or Schedule is to a Part or section of, or Schedule to, this Act, unless it is indicated that reference to some other enactment is intended.

(13) In this Act, a reference to a subsection, paragraph, subparagraph, clause or subclause is to the subsection, paragraph, subparagraph, clause or subclause of the provision (including a Schedule) in which the reference occurs, unless it is indicated that reference to some other provision is intended.

FINANCE ACT 2005

(2005 Number 5)
(Date of passing: 25 March 2005)

ARRANGEMENT OF SECTIONS

PART 3
VALUE-ADDED TAX

AN ACT TO PROVIDE FOR THE IMPOSITION, REPEAL, REMISSION, ALTERATION AND REGULATION OF TAXATION, OF STAMP DUTIES AND OF DUTIES RELATING TO EXCISE AND OTHERWISE TO MAKE FURTHER PROVISION IN CONNECTION WITH FINANCE INCLUDING THE REGULATION OF CUSTOMS.

PART 3
VALUE ADDED TAX

98 Interpretation (Part 3)

In this Part—

"Act of 2004" means the Finance Act 2004;

"Principal Act" means the Value-Added Tax Act 1972.

99 Amendment of section 3 (supply of goods) of Principal Act

Notes

Section 99 substituted VATA 1972, s 3(5)(*b*)(iii) with effect from 25 March 2005.

100 Amendment of section 4 (special provisions in relation to the supply of immovable goods) of Principal Act

Notes

Para (*a*) substituted "Subject to paragraphs (*aa*) and (*b*)" for "Subject to paragraph (*b*)" in VATA 1972, s 4(3)(*a*) with effect from such day as the Minister for Finance may, by order, appoint. By virtue of SI 225/2005, 1 May 2005 appointed as start date.

Para (*b*) inserted VATA 1972, s 4(3)(*aa*)–(*ab*) with effect from such day as the Minister for Finance may, by order, appoint. By virtue of SI 225/2005, 1 May 2005 appointed as start date.

Para (*c*) substituted VATA 1972, s 4(6)(*a*) with effect from 25 March 2005.

Para (*d*) substituted VATA 1972, s 4(8) and (9) with effect from 25 March 2005.

101 Amendment of section 5 (supply of services) of Principal Act

Notes

Para (*a*)(i) inserted VATA 1972, s 5(6)(*eea*) with effect from 25 March 2005.

Para (*a*)(ii) deleted "and has not also an establishment in the Community" from VATA 1972, s 5(6)(*eee*) with effect from 25 March 2005.

Para (*b*) inserted "or in connection with a transfer of ownership of goods in accordance with section 3(5)(*b*)(iii)" in VATA 1972, s 5(8)(*a*) with effect from 25 March 2005.

102 Amendment of section 10 (amount on which tax is chargeable) of Principal Act

Notes

Section 102 inserted VATA 1972, s 10(9)(*c*)–(*d*) with effect from 25 March 2005.

103 Amendment of section 11 (rates of tax) of Principal Act

Notes

Section 103 substituted "4.8 per cent" for "4.4 per cent" in VATA 1972, s 11(1)(*f*) with effect from 25 March 2005.

104 Amendment of section 12 (deduction for tax borne or paid) of Principal Act

Notes

Para (*a*)(i) substituted VATA 1972, s 12(1)(*a*)(iii*c*) with effect from 25 March 2005.

Para (*a*)(ii) deleted VATA 1972, s 12(1)(*a*)(iii*d*) with effect from 25 March 2005.

Para (*b*) inserted VATA 1972, s 12(5) with effect from such a day as the Minister for Finance may, by order, appoint. By virtue of SI 225/2005, 1 May 2005 appointed as start date.

105 Amendment of section 12A (special provisions for tax invoiced by flat-rate farmers) of Principal Act

Notes

Section 105 substituted "4.8 per cent" for "4.4 per cent" in VATA 1972, s 12A(1) with effect from 1 January 2005.

106 Amendment of section 19 (tax due and payable) of Principal Act

Notes

Para (*a*)(i) deleted "and" from VATA 1972, s 19(1)(*b*) with effect from 25 March 2005.

Para (*a*)(ii) inserted VATA 1972, s 19(1)(*bb*) with effect from 25 March 2005.

Para (*b*) substituted "paragraph (*a*), (*b*) or (*bb*)" for "paragraph (*a*) or (*b*)" in VATA 1972, s 19(2) with effect from 25 March 2005.

107 Amendment of section 19A (statement of intra-Community supplies) of Principal Act

Notes

Section 107 substituted VATA 1972, s 19A(6) with effect from 25 March 2005.

108 Amendment of section 24 (recovery of tax) of Principal Act

...

(2) Notwithstanding subsection (1)(*b*) regulations made under the Principal Act and to which section 24(1)(*c*) of that Act related shall continue in force and may be amended or revoked accordingly.

Notes

Subs (1)(*a*) substituted VATA 1972, s 24(1)(*a*) with effect from 25 March 2005.

Subs (1)(*b*) deleted VATA 1972, s 24(1)(*c*) with effect from 25 March 2005.

109 Amendment of section 26 (penalties generally) of Principal Act

Notes

Section 109 inserted VATA 1972, s 26(3AA) with effect from 25 March 2005.

110 Amendment of section 27 (fraudulent returns, etc.) of Principal Act

Notes

Para (*a*) deleted ", or in the case of fraud, twice the amount" from VATA 1972, s 27(1)(*b*) with effect from 25 March 2005.

Para (*b*) deleted ", or in the case of fraud twice the amount," in VATA 1972, s 27(1A)(*b*) with effect from 25 March 2005.

Para (*c*) deleted ", or, in the case of fraud, twice the amount" in VATA 1972, s 27(5)(ii) with effect from 25 March 2005.

111 Amendment of section 32 (regulations) of Principal Act

Notes

Para (*a*) inserted VATA 1972, s 32(1)(*ta*) with effect from 25 March 2005.

Para (*b*) inserted VATA 1972, s 32(1)(*www*) with effect from 25 March 2005.

Para (*c*) substituted "paragraph (*w*), (*ww*) or (*www*) of subsection (1)" for "subsection (1)(*w*) or (1)(*ww*)" in VATA 1972, s 32(2A) with effect from 25 March 2005.

112 Amendment of First Schedule to Principal Act

Notes

Para (*a*) substituted VATA 1972, Sch 1 para (xv) with effect from 25 March 2005.
Para (*b*) deleted VATA 1972, Sch 1 para (xv*a*) with effect from 25 March 2005.
Para (*c*) inserted "a supply of immovable goods to which section 3(1)(*c*) or 4 relates, or" in VATA 1972, Sch 1 para (xxiv) with effect from 25 March 2005.

113 Amendment of Sixth Schedule to Principal Act

Notes

Para (*a*)(i) inserted "(other than bread as defined in subparagraph (*d*), of paragraph (xii) of the Second Schedule" after "the supply of food" in VATA 1972, Sch 6 para (iv) with effect from 25 March 2005.
Para (*a*)(ii) substituted "heated, enabling" for "heated for the purpose of enabling" in VATA 1972, Sch 6 para (iv)(*a*) with effect from 25 March 2005.
Para (*a*)(iii) substituted "heated after cooking, enabling" for "heated after cooking for the purpose of enabling" in VATA 1972, Sch 6 para (iv)(*b*) with effect from 25 March 2005.
Para (*a*)(iv) deleted "for the purpose of" from VATA 1972, Sch 6 para (iv)(*c*) with effect from 25 March 2005.
Para (*a*)(v) substituted "at the time it is provided to the customer" for "at the time of supply" in VATA 1972, Sch 6 para (iv) with effect from 25 March 2005.
Para (*b*) substituted VATA 1972, Sch 6 para (xiii) with effect from 1 July 2005.

INTERPRETATION ACT 2005

ARRANGEMENT OF SECTIONS

PART 1
PRELIMINARY AND GENERAL

PART 2
MISCELLANEOUS RULES

PART 3
CITATION AND OPERATION OF ENACTMENTS

PART 4
MEANING AND CONSTRUCTION OF WORDS AND EXPRESSIONS

PART 5
POWERS AND DUTIES

PART 6
AMENDMENT OF ENACTMENTS, ETC

SCHEDULE
INTERPRETATION OF PARTICULAR WORDS AND EXPRESSIONS

PART 1

PART 2

AN ACT RESPECTING THE INTERPRETATION AND APPLICATION OF ACTS AND OF STATUTORY INSTRUMENTS MADE UNDER ACTS AND PROVIDING FOR THE REPEAL OF CERTAIN ENACTMENTS RELATING TO THOSE MATTERS. [*17th OCTOBER, 2005*]

BE IT ENACTED BY THE OIREACHTAS AS FOLLOWS:

PART 1
PRELIMINARY AND GENERAL

1   Short title and commencement

(1) This Act may be cited as the Interpretation Act 2005.

(2) This Act comes into operation on 1 January 2006.

2   Interpretation

(1) In this Act—

"Act" means—

(*a*)   an Act of the Oireachtas, and

(*b*)   a statute which was in force in Saorstát Éireann immediately before the date of the coming into operation of the Constitution and which continued in force by virtue of Article 50 of the Constitution;

"enactment" means an Act or a statutory instrument or any portion of an Act or statutory instrument;

"repeal" includes revoke, rescind, abrogate or cancel;

"statutory instrument" means an order, regulation, rule, bye-law, warrant, licence, certificate, direction, notice, guideline or other like document made, issued, granted or otherwise created by or under an Act and references, in relation to a statutory instrument, to **"made"** or to **"made under"** include references to made, issued, granted or otherwise created by or under such instrument.

(2) For the purposes of this Act, an enactment which has been replaced or has expired, lapsed or otherwise ceased to have effect is deemed to have been repealed.

Definitions

Constitution: Sch Pt 1; Oireachtas: Sch Pt 1.

---

3 Repeals and savings

(1) The following Acts are repealed:

(*a*)   the Interpretation Act 1889;

(*b*)   the Interpretation Act 1923;

(*c*)   the Interpretation Act 1937;

(*d*)   the Interpretation (Amendment) Act 1993.

(2) (*a*)   The repeal by this Act of an Act which assigns a meaning to a word or expression in another enactment does not affect the meaning so assigned if—

(i)   in the absence of that meaning in this Act, or

(ii)   by the application to the other enactment of the meaning assigned by this Act to the same or a similar word or expression,

the other enactment would be changed in intent or become unclear or absurd.

(*b*)   The repeal by this Act of an Act which provides for any matter (other than a matter to which paragraph (*a*) relates) in another enactment does not affect the matter so provided for if—

(i)   in the absence of that matter being provided for in this Act, or

(ii)   by the application to the other enactment of a matter provided for by this Act which corresponds to a matter provided for in the repealed Act concerned,

the other enactment would be changed in intent or become unclear or absurd.

Definitions

Act: s 2(1); enactment: s 2(1).

---

4 Application

(1) A provision of this Act applies to an enactment except in so far as the contrary intention appears in this Act, in the enactment itself or, where relevant, in the Act under which the enactment is made.

(2) The provisions of this Act which relate to other Acts also apply to this Act unless the contrary intention appears in this Act.

Definitions

Act: s 2(1); enactment: s 2(1).

PART 2
MISCELLANEOUS RULES

5 Construing ambiguous or obscure provisions, etc

(1) In construing a provision of any Act (other than a provision that relates to the imposition of a penal or other sanction)—

(*a*)   that is obscure or ambiguous, or

(b) that on a literal interpretation would be absurd or would fail to reflect the plain intention of—

    (i) in the case of an Act to which paragraph (a) of the definition of "Act" in section 2(1) relates, the Oireachtas, or

    (ii) in the case of an Act to which paragraph (b) of that definition relates, the parliament concerned,

the provision shall be given a construction that reflects the plain intention of the Oireachtas or parliament concerned, as the case may be, where that intention can be ascertained from the Act as a whole.

(2) In construing a provision of a statutory instrument (other than a provision that relates to the imposition of a penal or other sanction)—

(a) that is obscure or ambiguous, or

(b) that on a literal interpretation would be absurd or would fail to reflect the plain intention of the instrument as a whole in the context of the enactment (including the Act) under which it was made,

the provision shall be given a construction that reflects the plain intention of the maker of the instrument where that intention can be ascertained from the instrument as a whole in the context of that enactment.

Definitions

Act: s 2(1); enactment: s 2(1); statutory instrument: s 2(1).

---

6 Construing provisions in changing circumstances

In construing a provision of any Act or statutory instrument, a court may make allowances for any changes in the law, social conditions, technology, the meaning of words used in that Act or statutory instrument and other relevant matters, which have occurred since the date of the passing of that Act or the making of that statutory instrument, but only in so far as its text, purpose and context permit.

Definitions

Act: s 2(1); statutory instrument: s 2(1).

---

7 Supplemental provision to sections 5 and 6

(1) In construing a provision of an Act for the purposes of section 5 or 6, a court may, notwithstanding section 18(g), make use of all matters that accompany and are set out in—

(a) in the case of an Act of the Oireachtas, the signed text of such law as enrolled for record in the Office of the Registrar of the Supreme Court pursuant to Article 25.4.5° of the Constitution,

(b) in the case of an Act of the Oireachtas of Saorstát Éireann, the signed text of such law as enrolled for record in the office of such officer of the Supreme Court of Saorstát Éireann as Dáil Éireann determined pursuant to Article 42 of the Constitution of the Irish Free State (Saorstát Éireann),

(c) in the case of any other Act, such text of that Act as corresponds to the text of the Act enrolled in the manner referred to in paragraph (a) or (b).

(2) For the purposes of subsection (1), it shall be presumed, until the contrary is shown, that a copy of the text of an Act that is required to be judicially noticed is a copy of the text to which subsection (1) relates.

Definitions
Act: s 2(1); Constitution: Sch Pt 1; Oireachtas: Sch Pt 1.

8 Reading provisions together as one and summary proceedings for offences

Where—

    (*a*)   an Act or portion of an Act (whenever passed)—

        (i) provides that summary proceedings for offences under it may be prosecuted by a specified person, and

        (ii) is subsequently read together as one with any provision of another Act, and

    (*b*)   an offence is created under that provision which can be prosecuted in a summary manner but no express power is given to the specified person to so prosecute,

then, the specified person may bring summary proceedings for an offence under that other provision unless some other person is authorised by that other Act to bring such proceedings.

Definitions
Act: s 2(1).

9 References in enactments to Parts, etc

(1) A reference in an enactment to a Part, Chapter, section, Schedule or other division, by whatever name called, shall be read as a reference to a Part, Chapter, section, Schedule or other division of the enactment in which the reference occurs.

(2) A reference in an enactment to a subsection, paragraph, subparagraph, clause, subclause, article, subarticle or other division, by whatever name called, shall be read as a reference to a subsection, paragraph, subparagraph, clause, subclause, article, subarticle or other division of the provision in which the reference occurs.

Definitions
enactment: s 2(1).

10 Enactment always speaking

An enactment continues to have effect and may be applied from time to time as occasion requires.

Definition
enactment: s 2(1).

11 References in enactments to examples

If under the heading—

    (*a*)   in the Irish language "Sampla" or "Samplaí", or

    (*b*)   in the English language "Example" or "Examples",

an enactment includes at the end of a provision or in a schedule relating to such provision an example of the operation of the provision, then the example—

    (i)   is not to be read as exhaustive of the provision, and

    (ii) may extend, but does not limit, the meaning of the provision.

Definition

enactment: s 2(1).

12 Deviation from form

Where a form is prescribed in or under an enactment, a deviation from the form which does not materially affect the substance of the form or is not misleading in content or effect does not invalidate the form used.

Cross-references

Prescribing of forms, etc, provision not to be read as restricting this section: FA 2006, s 123.

Definition

enactment: s 2(1).

PART 3
CITATION AND OPERATION OF ENACTMENTS

13 Judicial notice

An Act is a public document and shall be judicially noticed.

Definition

Act: s 2(1).

14 Citation and references to amended enactments

(1) An Act may be cited in any enactment or other document—

    (*a*) by the long title or short title of the Act,

    (*b*) where appropriate, by the consecutive number of the Act in the calendar year and by the calendar year in which it was passed, or

    (*c*) where the Act was passed prior to the enactment of the Constitution of the Irish Free State (Saorstát Éireann) Act 1922, by its regnal year and chapter number and, where there was more than one parliamentary session in the same regnal year, by reference to the session concerned.

(2) A citation of or a reference to an enactment shall be read as a citation of or reference to the enactment as amended (including as amended by way of extension, application, adaptation or other modification of the enactment), whether the amendment is made before, on or after the date on which the provision containing the citation or reference came into operation.

(3) In citing—

    (*a*) an Act by its short title, or

    (*b*) any other enactment by its citation (if any),

a comma immediately before a reference to a year and a comma immediately after such a reference that is not required for the purpose of punctuation may be omitted.

Definitions

Act: s 2(1); enactment: s 2(1).

15 Date of passing of Acts of Oireachtas

(1) The date of the passing of an Act of the Oireachtas is the date of the day on which the Bill for the Act is signed by the President.

(2) Immediately after the Bill for an Act of the Oireachtas is signed by the President, the Clerk of Dáil Éireann shall endorse on the Act immediately after the long title the date of the passing of the Act, and that date shall be taken to be part of the Act.

Definitions

Act: s 2(1); Dáil Éireann: Sch Pt 1; Oireachtas: Sch Pt 1; President: Sch Pt 1.

16 Commencement

(1) Subject to subsection (2), every provision of an Act comes into operation on the date of its passing.

(2) Where an Act or a provision of an Act is expressed to come into operation on a particular day (whether the day is before or after the date of the passing of the Act and whether the day is named in the Act or is to be fixed or ascertained in a particular manner), the Act or provision comes into operation at the end of the day before the particular day.

(3) Subject to subsection (4), every provision of a statutory instrument comes into operation at the end of the day before the day on which the statutory instrument is made.

(4) Where a statutory instrument or a provision of a statutory instrument is expressed to come into operation on a particular day (whether the day is before or after the date of the making of the statutory instrument and whether the day is named in the instrument or is to be fixed or ascertained in a particular manner), the statutory instrument or provision comes into operation at the end of the day before the particular day.

Definitions

Act: s 2(1); statutory instrument: s 2(1).

17 Exercise of statutory powers before commencement of Act

Where an Act or a provision of an Act is expressed to come into operation on a day subsequent to the date of the passing of the Act, the following provisions apply:

   (*a*) if the day on which the Act or the provision comes into operation is to be fixed or ascertained in a particular manner, the statutory instrument, act or thing whereby the day is fixed or ascertained may, subject to any restriction imposed by the Act, be made or done at any time after the passing of the Act;

   (*b*) if, for the purposes of the Act or the provision, the Act confers a power to make a statutory instrument or do any act or thing, the making or doing of which is necessary or expedient to enable the Act or provision to have full force and effect immediately on its coming into operation, the power may, subject to any restriction imposed by the Act, be exercised at any time after the passing of the Act.

Definitions

Act: s 2(1); statutory instrument: s 2(1).

PART 4

MEANING AND CONSTRUCTION OF WORDS AND EXPRESSIONS

18 General rules of construction

The following provisions apply to the construction of an enactment:

(*a*) *Singular and plural.* A word importing the singular shall be read as also importing the plural, and a word importing the plural shall be read as also importing the singular;

(*b*) *Gender.*

    (i) A word importing the masculine gender shall be read as also importing the feminine gender;

    (ii) In an Act passed on or after 22 December 1993, and in a statutory instrument made after that date, a word importing the feminine gender shall be read as also importing the masculine gender;

(*c*) *Person.* "Person" shall be read as importing a body corporate (whether a corporation aggregate or a corporation sole) and an unincorporated body of persons, as well as an individual, and the subsequent use of any pronoun in place of a further use of "person" shall be read accordingly;

(*d*) *Adopted child.* A reference, however expressed, to a child of a person shall be read as including—

    (i) in an Act passed after the passing of the Adoption Act 1976 a reference to a child adopted by the person under the Adoption Acts 1952 to 1998 and every other enactment which is to be construed together with any of those Acts, or

    (ii) in an Act passed on or after 14 January 1988 (the commencement of section 3 of the Status of Children Act 1987), a child to whom subparagraph (i) relates or a child adopted outside the State whose adoption is recognised by virtue of the law for the time being in force in the State;

(*e*) *Distance.* A word or expression relating to the distance between two points and every reference to the distance from or to a point shall be read as relating or referring to such distance measured in a straight line on a horizontal plane;

(*f*) *Series description.* Where a consecutive series is described by reference to the first and last in the series, the description shall be read as including the first and the last in the series;

(*g*) *Marginal and shoulder notes, etc.* Subject to *section 7*, none of the following shall be taken to be part of the enactment or be construed or judicially noticed in relation to the construction or interpretation of the enactment:

    (i) a marginal note placed at the side, or a shoulder note placed at the beginning, of a section or other provision to indicate the subject, contents or effect of the section or provision,

    (ii) a heading or cross-line placed in or at the head of or at the beginning of a Part, Chapter, section, or other provision or group of sections or provisions to indicate the subject, contents or effect of the Part, Chapter, section, provision or group;

(*h*) *Periods of time.* Where a period of time is expressed to begin on or be reckoned from a particular day, that day shall be deemed to be included in the period and, where a period of time is expressed to end on or be reckoned to a particular day, that day shall be deemed to be included in the period;

(*i*) *Time.* Where time is expressed by reference to a specified hour or to a time before or after a specified hour, that time shall be determined by reference to the Standard Time (Amendment) Act 1971;

(*j*) *Offences by corporations.* A reference to a person in relation to an offence (whether punishable on indictment or on summary conviction) shall be read as including a reference to a body corporate.

Definitions

Act: s 2(1); enactment: s 2(1); statutory instrument: s 2(1).

19 Construction of statutory instruments

A word or expression used in a statutory instrument has the same meaning in the statutory instrument as it has in the enactment under which the instrument is made.

Definition

statutory instrument: s 2(1).

20 Interpretation provisions

(1) Where an enactment contains a definition or other interpretation provision, the provision shall be read as being applicable except in so far as the contrary intention appears in—

(*a*) the enactment itself, or

(*b*) the Act under which the enactment is made.

(2) Where an enactment defines or otherwise interprets a word or expression, other parts of speech and grammatical forms of the word or expression have a corresponding meaning.

Definitions

Act: s 2(1); enactment: s 2(1).

21 Interpretation of words and expressions in Schedule

(1) In an enactment, a word or expression to which a particular meaning, construction or effect is assigned in Part 1 of the Schedule has the meaning, construction or effect so assigned to it.

(2) In an enactment which comes into operation after the commencement of this Act, a word or expression to which a particular meaning, construction or effect is assigned in Part 2 of the Schedule has the meaning, construction or effect so assigned to it.

Definitions

Act: s 2(1); enactment: s 2(1).

PART 5
Powers and Duties

22 Powers under enactments

(1) A power conferred by an enactment may be exercised from time to time as occasion requires.

(2) A power conferred by an enactment on the holder of an office as that holder shall be deemed to be conferred on, and may accordingly be exercised by, the holder for the time being of that office.

(3) A power conferred by an enactment to make a statutory instrument shall be read as including a power, exercisable in the like manner and subject to the like consent and conditions (if any), to repeal or amend a statutory instrument made under that power and (where required) to make another statutory instrument in place of the one so repealed.

Definitions
enactment: s 2(1); repeal: s 2(1); statutory instrument: s 2(1).

23 Duties under enactments

(1) A duty imposed by an enactment shall be performed from time to time as occasion requires.

(2) A duty imposed by an enactment on the holder of an office as that holder shall be deemed to be imposed on, and shall accordingly be performed by, the holder for the time being of that office.

Definition
enactment: s 2(1).

24 Rules of court

Where an enactment confers a new jurisdiction on a court or extends or varies an existing jurisdiction of a court, the authority having for the time being power to make rules or orders regulating the practice and procedure of the court has, and may at any time exercise, power to make rules or orders for regulating the practice and procedure of that court in the exercise of the jurisdiction so conferred, extended or varied.

Definition
enactment: s 2(1).

25 Service by post

Where an enactment authorises or requires a document to be served by post, by using the word "serve", "give", "deliver", "send" or any other word or expression, the service of the document may be effected by properly addressing, prepaying (where required) and posting a letter containing the document, and in that case the service of the document is deemed, unless the contrary is proved, to have been effected at the time at which the letter would be delivered in the ordinary course of post.

Definition
enactment: s 2(1).

PART 6
AMENDMENT OF ENACTMENTS, ETC

26 Repeals and substitutions

(1) Where an enactment repeals another enactment and substitutes other provisions for the enactment so repealed, the enactment so repealed continues in force until the substituted provisions come into operation.

(2) Where an enactment ("former enactment") is repealed and re-enacted, with or without modification, by another enactment ("new enactment"), the following provisions apply:

(*a*)   a person appointed under the former enactment shall continue to act for the remainder of the period for which the person was appointed as if appointed under the new enactment;

(*b*)   a bond, guarantee or other security of a continuing nature given by a person under the former enactment remains in force, and data, books, papers, forms and things prepared or used under the former enactment may continue to be used as before the repeal;

(*c*)   proceedings taken under the former enactment may, subject to section 27(1), be continued under and in conformity with the new enactment in so far as that may be done consistently with the new enactment;

(*d*)   if after the commencement of this Act—

  (i)   any provision of a former enactment, that provided for the making of a statutory instrument, is repealed and re-enacted, with or without modification, as a new provision, and

  (ii) such statutory instrument is in force immediately before such repeal and re-enactment,

  then the statutory instrument shall be deemed to have been made under the new provision to the extent that it is not inconsistent with the new enactment, and remains in force until it is repealed or otherwise ceases to have effect;

(*e*)   to the extent that the provisions of the new enactment express the same idea in a different form of words but are in substance the same as those of the former enactment, the idea in the new enactment shall not be taken to be different merely because a different form of words is used;

(*f*)   a reference in any other enactment to the former enactment shall, with respect to a subsequent transaction, matter or thing, be read as a reference to the provisions of the new enactment relating to the same subject-matter as that of the former enactment, but where there are no provisions in the new enactment relating to the same subject-matter, the former enactment shall be disregarded in so far as is necessary to maintain or give effect to that other enactment.

Definitions

Act: s 2(1); enactment: s 2(1); person: s 18(*c*); statutory instrument: s 2(1).

27 Effect of repeal of enactment

(1) Where an enactment is repealed, the repeal does not—

(*a*)   revive anything not in force or not existing immediately before the repeal,

(*b*)   affect the previous operation of the enactment or anything duly done or suffered under the enactment, (*c*) affect any right, privilege, obligation or liability acquired, accrued or incurred under the enactment,

(*d*) affect any penalty, forfeiture or punishment incurred in respect of any offence against or contravention of the enactment which was committed before the repeal, or

(*e*) prejudice or affect any legal proceedings (civil or criminal) pending at the time of the repeal in respect of any such right, privilege, obligation, liability, offence or contravention.

(2) Where an enactment is repealed, any legal proceedings (civil or criminal) in respect of a right, privilege, obligation or liability acquired, accrued or incurred under, or an offence against or contravention of, the enactment may be instituted, continued or enforced, and any penalty, forfeiture or punishment in respect of such offence or contravention may be imposed and carried out, as if the enactment had not been repealed.

Definitions

enactment: s 2(1); repeal: s 2(1).

SCHEDULE
Interpretation of Particular Words and Expressions

PART 1

"affidavit", in the case of a person for the time being allowed by law to declare instead of swearing, includes declaration;

"British statute" means an Act of the Parliament of the former United Kingdom of Great Britain and Ireland;

"Circuit Court" means the Circuit Court as established and for the time being maintained by law;

"commencement", when used in relation to an enactment, means the time at which the enactment comes into operation;

"Constitution" means the Constitution of Ireland enacted by the people on 1 July 1937, as amended;

"Dáil Éireann" means the House of the Oireachtas to which that name is given by section 1 of Article 15 of the Constitution;

"District Court" means the District Court as established and for the time being maintained by law;

"financial year", in relation to an exchequer financial year, means the period which is coextensive with a calendar year;

"Government" means the Government mentioned in Article 28 of the Constitution;

"Great Britain" does not include the Channel Islands or the Isle of Man;

"High Court" means the High Court as established and for the time being maintained by law pursuant to Article 34 of the Constitution;

"land" includes tenements, hereditaments, houses and buildings, land covered by water and any estate, right or interest in or over land;

"local financial year" means a period which is coextensive with a calendar year;

"midnight" means, in relation to a particular day, the point of time at which the day ends;

"Minister of the Government" means a member of the Government having charge of a Department of State;

"month" means a calendar month;

"oath", in the case of a person for the time being allowed by law to affirm or declare instead of swearing, includes affirmation or declaration;

"Oireachtas" means the National Parliament provided for by Article 15 of the Constitution;

"ordnance map" means a map made under the powers conferred by the Survey (Ireland) Acts 1825 to 1870;

"President" means the President of Ireland or any Commission, or other body or authority, for the time being lawfully exercising the powers and performing the duties of the President;

"pre-union Irish statute" means an Act passed by a Parliament sitting in Ireland at any time before the coming into force on 1 January 1801 of the Act entitled "An Act for the Union of Great Britain and Ireland";

"rateable valuation" means the valuation under the Valuation Act 2001 of the property concerned;

"rules of court" means rules made by the authority for the time being having power to make rules regulating the practice and procedure of the court concerned;

"Saorstát Éireann statute" means an Act of the Oireachtas of Saorstát Éireann;

"Seanad Éireann" means the House of the Oireachtas to which that name is given by section 1 of Article 15 of the Constitution;

"statutory declaration" means a declaration made under the Statutory Declarations Act 1938;

"Supreme Court" means the Supreme Court as established and for the time being maintained by law pursuant to Article 34 of the Constitution;

"swear", in the case of a person for the time being allowed by law to affirm or declare instead of swearing, includes affirm and declare;

"week" means the period between midnight on any Saturday and midnight on the following Saturday;

"week-day" means a day which is not a Sunday;

"writing" includes printing, typewriting, lithography, photography, and other modes of representing or reproducing words in visible form and any information kept in a non-legible form, whether stored electronically or otherwise, which is capable by any means of being reproduced in a legible form;

"year", when used without qualification, means a period of 12 months beginning on the 1st day of January in any year.

PART 2

"Companies Acts" means the Companies Acts 1963 to 2001 and every other enactment which is to be read together with any of those Acts;

"full age", in relation to a person, means the time when the person attains the age of 18 years or sooner marries, or any time after either event;

"functions" includes powers and duties, and references to the performance of functions include, with respect to powers and duties, references to the exercise of the powers and the carrying out of the duties;

"Member State" means, where the context so admits, a Member State of the European Communities or of the European Union;

"Minister of State" means a person appointed under section 1 of the Ministers and Secretaries (Amendment) (No. 2) Act 1977 to be a Minister of State;

"public holiday" means a public holiday determined in accordance with the Organisation of Working Time Act 1997;

"Social Welfare Acts" means the Social Welfare (Consolidation) Act 1993 and every other enactment which is to be read together with that Act;

"working day" means a day which is not a Saturday, Sunday or public holiday.

FINANCE ACT 2006

No 6 of 2006

ARRANGEMENT OF SECTIONS

Section

PART 3
VALUE-ADDED TAX

PART 6
MISCELLANEOUS

SECOND SCHEDULE
Miscellaneous Technical Amendments in Relation to Tax

AN ACT TO PROVIDE FOR THE IMPOSITION, REPEAL, REMISSION, ALTERATION AND REGULATION OF TAXATION, OF STAMP DUTIES AND OF DUTIES RELATING TO EXCISE AND OTHERWISE TO MAKE FURTHER PROVISION IN CONNECTION WITH FINANCE INCLUDING THE REGULATION OF CUSTOMS.

BE IT ENACTED BY THE OIREACHTAS AS FOLLOWS:

PART 3
VALUE-ADDED TAX

92 Interpretation (Part 3)

In this Part "Principal Act" means the Value-Added Tax 25 Act 1972.

93 Amendment of section 1 (interpretation) of Principal Act

Notes

Subs (1)(*a*) inserted VATA 1972, s 1(1) definition of "ancillary supply" with effect from such day as the Minister for Finance may appoint.

Subs (1)(*b*) inserted VATA 1972, s 1(1) definition of "composite supply" with effect from such day as the Minister for Finance may appoint.

Subs (1)(*c*) inserted VATA 1972, s 1(1) definition of "individual supply" with effect from such day as the Minister for Finance may appoint.

Subs (1)(*d*) inserted VATA 1972, s 1(1) definition of "multiple supply" with effect from such day as the Minister for Finance may appoint.

Subs (1)(*e*) inserted VATA 1972, s 1(1) definition of "principal supply" with effect from such day as the Minister for Finance may appoint.

94 Amendment of section 5 (supply of services) of Principal Act

Notes

Section 94 substituted VATA 1972, s 5(3)(*a*)-(*d*) with effect from 31 March 2006.

95 Amendment of section 8 (taxable persons) of Principal Act

Notes

Para (*a*) substituted "€27,500" for "€25,500" and "€55,000" for "€51,000" where it occurs in VATA 1972, s 8(3), (3A) and (9) with effect from 1 May 2006.

Para (*b*) substituted "where it seems necessary or appropriate to them for the purpose of efficient and effective administration, including collection, of the tax" for "that it would be expedient in the interest of efficient administration of the tax" in VATA 1972, s 8(8)(*a*) with effect from 31 March 2006.

96 Amendment of section 10 (amount on which tax is chargeable) of Principal Act

Notes

Para (*a*) substituted "for the purposes of paragraph (*a*) or (*b*) of section 5(3)" for "for the purposes of section 5(3)" in VATA 1972, s 10(4) with effect from 31 March 2006.

Para (*b*) inserting ", and the amount on which tax is chargeable in relation to a supply of services by virtue of regulations made for the purposes of section 5(3)(*c*) shall be the open market price of the services supplied" after "as the case may be" in VATA 1972, s 10(4) with effect from 31 March 2006.

97 Amendment of section 11 (rates of tax) of Principal Act

Notes

Subs (1)(*a*) substituted VATA 1972, s 11(1B)(*c*) with effect from 31 March 2006.

Subs (1)(*b*) substituted VATA 1972, s 11(3) with effect from such day as the Minister for Finance may appoint by order.

98 Amendment of section 12 (deduction for tax borne or paid) of Principal Act

Notes

Para (*a*) substituted "the Community," for "the Community, and" in VATA 1972, s 12(1)(*b*)(ii)(II) with effect from 31 March 2006.

Para (*b*) inserted VATA 1972, s 12(1)(*b*)(ii*a*) with effect from 31 March 2006.

99 Amendment of section 32 (regulations) of Principal Act

Notes

Subs (1)(*a*) substituted VATA 1972, s 32(1)(*e*) with effect from such day as the Minister for Finance may appoint by order.

Subs (1)(*b*) inserted VATA 1972, s 32(2B) with effect from 31 March 2006.

100 Amendment of First Schedule to Principal Act

Notes

Para (*a*) inserted "other than the issue of new stocks, new shares, new debentures or new securities made to raise capital, the" after "the issue," in VATA 1972, Sch 1 para (i)(*a*) with effect from 31 March 2006.

Para (*b*) substituted "of stocks, shares, debentures and other securities, other than documents establishing title to goods," for "specified in subparagraph (*a*)," in VATA 1972, Sch 1 para (i)(*b*) with effect from 31 March 2006.

101 Amendment of Sixth Schedule to Principal Act

Notes

Section 101 substituted "€27,500" for "€25,500" in VATA 1972, Sch 6 paras (vii*b*) and (vii*c*) with effect from 31 March 2006.

PART 6
MISCELLANEOUS

120 Interpretation (Part 6)

In this Part **"Principal Act"** means the Taxes Consolidation Act 1997.

127 Miscellaneous technical amendments in relation to tax

The enactments specified in Schedule 2 —

    (*a*)   are amended to the extent and in the manner specified in paragraphs 1 to 8 of that Schedule, and

    (*b*)   apply and come into operation in accordance with paragraph 9 of that Schedule.

129 Care and management of taxes and duties

All taxes and duties imposed by this Act are placed under the care and management of the Revenue Commissioners.

130 Short title, construction and commencement

...

(4) Part 3 shall be construed together with the Value-Added Tax Acts 1972 to 2005 and may be cited together with those Acts as the Value-Added Tax Acts 1972 to 2006.

(7) Part 6 in so far as it relates to—

    ...

    (*f*)   value-added tax, shall be construed together with the Value-Added Tax Acts 1972 to 2006,

...

(9) Except where otherwise expressly provided for, where a provision of this Act is to come into operation on the making of an order by the Minister for Finance, that provision shall come into operation on such day or days as the Minister for Finance shall appoint either generally or with reference to any particular purpose or provision and different days may be so appointed for different purposes or different provisions.

SCHEDULE 2
Miscellaneous Technical Amendments in Relation to Tax

Section 127

...

Notes
Para 8 and s 127(*a*) substituted "by the taxable person" for "to the taxable person" in VATA 1972, ss 17(12)(*a*)(i) and 17(12)(*a*)(iii) with effect from 31 March 2006.

REGULATIONS

Repealed Regulations are shown in *italics*.

VALUE ADDED TAX REGULATIONS 1979

(SI No 63 of 1979)

Regulation

Short title and commencement

1 (1) These Regulations may be cited as the Value Added Tax Regulations, 1979.

(2) These Regulations shall come into operation on the 1st day of March, 1979.

Cross-reference
VATA 1972, s 32.

Notes
These regulations which came into effect on 1 March 1979 prescribe the manner in which VAT is to be operated in respect of elections for taxability, waiver of exemptions and the treatment of two or more taxable persons as

a single taxable person; registration and cancellation; cash receipts basis; accounts to be kept, invoices credit notes etc; returns, payments, apportionments, estimates etc; refunds and remissions of tax; valuation of interests in immovable goods; dances; relief for stock in trade held at commencement of taxability; determination of tax; supply of certain services; treatment of certain gifts and trading stamps exchanged for goods.

Interpretation

2 (1) In these Regulations—

"the Act" means the Value Added Tax Act, 1972;

"taxable turnover", in relation to any period, means the total of the amounts on which tax is chargeable for that period at any of the rates specified in section 11(1) of the Act;

"turnover", in relation to any period, means the amount on which tax would be chargeable for that period in accordance with section 10 of the Act if section 6 of the Act were disregarded.

(2) In these Regulations—

(*a*)   a reference to a regulation is to a regulation of these Regulations, and

(*b*)   a reference to a paragraph, subparagraph or clause is to a paragraph, subparagraph or clause of the regulation in which the reference occurs,

unless it is indicated that reference to some other provision is intended.

Election to be a taxable person

3 (1) A person who, in accordance with section 8(3) of the Act is not a taxable person but who desires to elect to be such a person shall furnish to the Revenue Commissioners the particulars for registration specified in Regulation 6.

(2) The furnishing of the particulars referred to in paragraph (1) shall constitute an election to be a taxable person and such election shall have effect as from the end of the taxable period during which such particulars are received by the Revenue Commissioners, or, by agreement between the person and the Revenue Commissioners, as from the end of the next preceding taxable period, until the date on which the person permanently ceases to supply taxable goods or services in the course or furtherance of business or until the date on which his election is cancelled in accordance with paragraph (3), whichever date is the earlier.

(3) A person who is a taxable person by reason only of an election in that behalf made in accordance with paragraphs (1) and (2) shall be entitled to have such election cancelled and to be treated, as from the date specified in paragraph (4), as a person who had not made such an election provided he fulfils all of the following conditions; and a person who satisfies the Revenue Commissioners in regard to his turnover in accordance with section 8(6)(*a*) of the Act may be treated as a person who is not a taxable person provided he fulfils similar conditions:

(*a*)   he shall notify the Revenue Commissioners in writing that he desires to have his election cancelled or that he desires to be treated as a person who is not a taxable person;

(*b*)   he shall furnish to the Revenue Commissioners particulars of—

   (i)   the total amount of tax paid by him in accordance with section 19(3) of the Act in respect of whichever of the following periods is the lesser:

   (I)   all the taxable periods comprised in the period commencing with the beginning of the first taxable period for which his election had effect or he was treated as a taxable person and ending with the termination of the taxable period immediately preceding that during which he notifies the Revenue Commissioners that he wishes to have his election cancelled or be treated as a person who is not a taxable person, or

   (II)   the eighteen consecutive taxable periods next before the taxable period during which he so notifies the Revenue Commissioners,

   and

   (ii)   the total amount of tax refunded to him in accordance with section 20(1) of the Act in respect of whichever of the periods referred to in clause (i) is appropriate;

(*c*)   he shall pay to the Collector-General an amount equal to the excess (if any) of the total amount referred to in clause (ii) of the preceding subparagraph over the total amount referred to in clause (i) of that subparagraph.

(4) If the conditions specified in the preceding paragraph have been fulfilled to the satisfaction of the Revenue Commissioners, they shall so notify the person concerned in writing and, on receipt by the person of such notice, his election shall be cancelled or he shall be treated as a person who is not a taxable person with effect as on and from the end of the taxable period during which the conditions have been so fulfilled; and as on and from the end of such taxable period, the person shall be treated as a person who had not elected to be a taxable person or as a person who is not a taxable person.

(5) A person who notifies the Revenue Commissioners during any taxable period (in this paragraph referred to as the final taxable period) of his desire to have his election cancelled or to be treated as a person who is not a taxable person shall not be entitled, under section 20(1) of the Act to any refund of tax, other than a refund referable solely to an error or mistake made by him, in excess of whichever of the following amounts is appropriate —

(*a*)   in a case in which there is an excess of the amount referred to in paragraph (3)(*b*)(i) over the amount referred to in paragraph (3)(*b*)(ii), an amount for the final taxable period and for any subsequent taxable period consisting of the amount of such excess, increased by the amounts paid under section 19(3) of the Act, for the final taxable period and any subsequent taxable periods up to and including the taxable period to which the claim relates and reduced by the total of the refunds under Section 20(1) of the Act previously made for any of those taxable periods, and

(*b*)   in any other case, an amount for the final taxable period or for any subsequent taxable period consisting of the excess of the total of the amounts paid under section 19(3) of the Act for the final and all subsequent taxable periods up to and including the taxable period to which the claim relates reduced by the total of the refunds under section 20(1) of the Act previously made for any of those taxable periods.

(6) In the case of a person who, in the absence of an election to be a taxable person, would (in accordance with section 8(3)(*a*) of the Act) not be such a person, paragraph (3)(*b*) shall apply as if —

(i)   the amount of tax paid by him in accordance with section 19(3) of the Act in respect of each of the taxable periods comprised in whichever of the periods referred to in clause (i) is appropriate were increased by an amount equal to 1 per cent. of the consideration on which tax was chargeable for each of those taxable periods in respect of transactions specified in section 8(9) of the Act other than in paragraph (*d*) of the definition of farmer, and

(ii)   the total amount of tax refunded to him in respect of all the taxable periods comprised in the period referred to in clause (ii) were reduced by the total amount of tax which qualified for deduction under section 12 of the Act in respect of those taxable periods and which, in accordance with any order made under section 20(3) of the Act would fall to be refunded to him if he were not a taxable person.

Waiver of exemption

4.

Amendments

Regulation 4 revoked by Value Added Tax (Waiver of Exemption) (Letting of Immovable Goods) Regulations 2003 (SI 504/2003), reg 4.

Treatment of two or more taxable persons as a single taxable person

5 (1) If two or more taxable persons desire that all the business activities carried on by each of them shall, in accordance with section 8(8) of the Act be deemed, for the purposes of the Act to be carried on by any one of those persons, each of them shall furnish the following particulars in writing to the Revenue Commissioners:—

(*a*)   his name, address and registration number;

(*b*)   the nature of the business activities carried on by him;

(*c*)   in case the person desires that all the business activities carried on by him should be deemed to be carried on by another person, the name, address and registration number of that other person;

(*d*)   in case the person desires that all the business activities carried on by another person or two or more other persons should be deemed to be carried on by the first-mentioned person, the name, address and registration number of that other person or of each of those other persons; and

(*e*)   such other information about the business activities of the person or about the business or financial relationship between him and each of the other persons carrying on the business activities aforesaid as the Revenue Commissioners may, by notice in writing, require.

(2) The Revenue Commissioners shall, in their absolute discretion, determine—

    (*a*)   whether all the business activities carried on by two or more persons who have furnished the particulars specified in paragraph (1) shall be deemed to be carried on by any one of those persons;

    (*b*)   in case all the business activities referred to in subparagraph (*a*) are deemed to be carried on by any one of the persons referred to in the said subparagraph (*a*):—

        (i)   the person by whom the said activities are deemed to be carried on;

        (ii)   the person or each of the persons all of whose business activities are deemed to be carried on by the person referred to in clause (i);

    (*c*)   the date, not being earlier than the commencement of the taxable period during which the particulars referred to in paragraph (1) are furnished, as from which all of the business activities of the person or persons concerned are deemed to be carried on by one of them, and shall notify each of the persons concerned in writing of the matters so determined.

(3) Upon the issue of a notification to a person in accordance with paragraph (2) of a determination that all the business activities referred to in the determination are deemed to be carried on by one person, the following provisions shall apply from the date specified in the notification pursuant to paragraph (2)(*c*) until the notification is cancelled in accordance with paragraph (5):

    (*a*)   in case the person to whom the notification is issued is the person by whom all the business activities referred to in the notification are deemed to be carried on, the provisions of the Act shall, subject to paragraph (4), apply to the person as if all transactions by or between himself and the other person or persons carrying on the said business activities were transactions by himself, and all other rights and obligations under the Act shall be determined accordingly,

    (*b*)   in case the person to whom the notification is issued is not the person by whom all the business activities referred to in the notification are deemed to be carried on, the provisions of the Act shall, subject to paragraph (4), apply to him as if all transactions by or between himself and the person by whom the said business activities are deemed to be carried on (in this subparagraph referred to as the last-mentioned person) were transactions by the last-mentioned person, but the person shall be jointly liable with the last-mentioned person and any other person specified in the notification to comply with all the provisions of the Act and regulations (including the provisions requiring payment of tax) that apply to him and the last-mentioned person and any other person so specified and shall be subject to the penalties under the Act to which he and the last-mentioned person and any other person so specified would be liable if they were liable to pay to the Revenue Commissioners the whole of the tax chargeable, apart from this Regulation, in respect of himself and the last-mentioned person and any other person so specified.

(4) Notwithstanding anything in paragraph (3), each of the persons all of whose business activities are during any period deemed, in accordance with this Regulation, to be carried on by one of them shall be deemed to be a registered person during the whole of

that period, and the provisions of section 17 of the Act shall apply to each of those persons as if a notification under paragraph (3) had not been issued.

(5) The Revenue Commissioners may, in their absolute discretion, by notice in writing addressed to each of a group of persons all of whose business activities are, by virtue of a notification issued in accordance with paragraph (2), deemed to be carried on by one of those persons, and as on and from the date specified in the notice (which shall not be earlier than the date of the notice) cancel the notification under the said paragraph (2); and as on and from the date specified in the said notice the provisions of the Act and Regulations shall apply to all the persons aforesaid as if a notification under the said paragraph (2) had not been issued, but without prejudice to the liability of any of the persons for tax or penalties in respect of anything done or not done during the period for which the said notification was in force.

Registration

6 ...

Notes

Revoked by Value Added Tax (Registration) Regulations 1993, r 7 (SI 30/1993).

Determination of tax due by reference to cash receipts

7 ...

Notes

Revoked by Value Added Tax (Determination of Tax Due by Reference to Moneys Received) Regulations 1986, r 4 (SI 298/ 1986).

Adjustments for returned goods, discounts, and price alterations

8 Where, in a case in which section 10(3)(c) of the Act applies and section 17(9) of the Act does not apply, by reason of the return of goods, the allowance of discount, a reduction in price or the default of a debtor, the consideration exclusive of tax actually received by a taxable person in respect of the supply by him of any goods or services is less than the amount on which tax has become chargeable in respect of such supply, or no consideration is actually received, the following provisions shall apply:

(a) the amount of the deficiency in respect of any supply shall be ascertained by deducting from the amount of consideration actually chargeable with tax, the amount exclusive of tax, or where a percentage only of the consideration is actually chargeable with tax, a corresponding percentage of the amount actually received, in respect of such supply,

(b) the sum of the deficiencies, ascertained in accordance with subparagraph (a), incurred in each taxable period and relating to consideration chargeable at each of the various rates of tax (including the zero rate) specified in section 11(1) of the Act shall be deducted from the amounts ascertained in accordance with section 10 of the Act which would otherwise be chargeable with tax at each of those rates and the net amounts as so ascertained shall be the amounts on which tax is chargeable for the taxable period:

Provided that if the sum of the deficiencies as ascertained in accordance with subparagraph (*b*) in relation to tax chargeable at any of the rates so specified exceeds the amount on which but for this Regulation tax would be chargeable at that rate, or no tax is chargeable at that rate, the tax appropriate to the excess or to the sum of the deficiencies, if no tax is chargeable, shall be treated as tax deductible in accordance with section 12 of the Act,

(*c*) the taxable person to whom a credit note is, in accordance with section 17 of the Act, issued by another taxable person in respect of an adjustment under this Regulation shall reduce the amount which would otherwise be deductible under section 12 of the Act for the taxable period during which the credit note is issued (in this Regulation referred to as the tax deduction) by the amount of tax shown thereon or by the amount of tax appropriate to the amount of the reduction of consideration shown thereon whichever is the greater (in this subparagraph referred to as the appropriate tax reduction) and if the appropriate tax reduction exceeds the tax deduction the excess shall be carried forward and deducted from the tax deduction for the next taxable period and so on until the appropriate tax reduction is exhausted.

(2) Where, in accordance with section 17(4)(*b*) of the Act a farmer credit note is issued by a flat-rate farmer, the taxable person to whom the credit note is issued shall reduce the amount which would otherwise be deductible under section 12(1)(f) of the Act for the taxable period during which the farmer credit note is issued (in this Regulation referred to as the flat-rate deduction) by the amount of the flat-rate addition shown thereon (in this subparagraph referred to as the appropriate flat-rate reduction) and, if the appropriate flat-rate reduction exceeds the flat-rate deduction, the excess shall be carried forward and deducted from the flat-rate deduction for the next taxable period and so on until the appropriate flat-rate reduction is exhausted.

Accounts

9 (1) Every taxable person shall keep full and true accounts entered up to date of—

(*a*) in relation to consideration receivable from registered persons, the amount receivable from each such person in respect of each transaction for which an invoice is required to be issued under section 17 of the Act together with a cross-reference to the copy of the relevant invoice,

(*b*) in relation to consideration receivable from unregistered persons, a daily total of the consideration receivable from all such persons together with a cross-reference to the relevant counter books, copies of sales dockets, cash register tally rolls or other documents which are in use for the purposes of the business,

(*c*) in relation to importations, a description of the goods imported together with particulars of the value thereof as determined in accordance with section 15 of the Act, the amount of the consideration relating to the purchase of the goods if purchased in connection with the importation, the amount of tax, if any, paid on importation and a cross-reference to the invoices and customs documents used in connection with the importation,

(*d*) in relation to goods, being goods developed, constructed, assembled, manufactured, produced, extracted, purchased or imported by the taxable person or by another person on his behalf and applied by him (otherwise than by way of disposal to another person) for the purposes of any business carried on by him, a description of the goods in question and the cost excluding tax, to the taxable person of acquiring or producing them except where tax chargeable in relation to the application of the goods would, if it were charged, be wholly deductible under section 12 of the Act,

(*e*)   in relation to goods, being goods which were appropriated by a taxable person for any purpose other than the purpose of his business or disposed of free of charge, where tax chargeable in relation to the goods, upon their acquisition by the taxable person, if they had been so acquired, or upon their development, construction, assembly, manufacture, production, extraction, importation or application in accordance with paragraph (*d*), as the case may be, was wholly or partly deductible under section 12 of the Act, a description of the goods in question and the cost, excluding tax, to the taxable person, of acquiring or producing them,

(*f*)   in relation to services regarded in accordance with section 5(3) of the Act as supplied by a person in the course or furtherance of business, a description of the services in question together with particulars of the cost, excluding tax, to the taxable person of supplying the services and of the consideration, if any, receivable by him in respect of the supply,

(*g*)   in relation to services referred to in section 5(6)(*e*)(ii) of the Act in respect of which a person is liable to pay tax in accordance with section 8(2) of the Act, a description of the services in question together with particulars of the cost to the person of acquiring the service,

(*h*)   in the case of services deemed, in accordance with clause (i) or (ii) of subparagraph 5(6)(*e*) of the Act to be supplied at places outside the State, the name and address of the person to whom the service is supplied, the nature of the service and the amount of the consideration receivable in respect of the supply,

(*i*)   in relation to discounts allowed or price reductions made to a registered person subsequent to the issue of an invoice to such person, the amount credited to such person and, except in a case in which section 17(9)(*a*) of the Act applies, a cross-reference to the corresponding credit note,

(*j*)   in relation to discounts allowed or price reductions made to unregistered persons, a daily total of the amount so allowed together with a cross-reference to the goods returned book, cash book or other record used in connection with the matter,

(*k*)   in relation to bad debts written off, particulars of the name and address of the debtor, the nature of the goods or services to which the debt relates and the date or dates upon which the debt was incurred,

(*l*)   in relation to goods and services supplied to the taxable person by another taxable person, the amount of the consideration, the corresponding tax invoiced by the other taxable person and a cross-reference to the corresponding invoice, (*m*) in relation to goods and services supplied by unregistered persons, other than goods and services in respect of which flat-rate farmers are required, in accordance with section 12A (1) of the Act to issue invoices, a daily total of the consideration payable to such persons and a cross-reference to the purchases book, cash book, purchases dockets or other records which are in use in connection with the business,

(*n*) in relation to goods and services supplied by flat-rate farmers but in respect of which such persons are required, in accordance with section 12A(1) of the Act, to issue invoices, the amount of the consideration (exclusive of the flat- rate addition) and of the flat-rate addition invoiced by each such person and a cross-reference to the corresponding invoice,

(*o*) in relation to discounts or price reductions received from registered persons, subsequent to the receipt of invoices from such persons, except in a case in which section 17(9)(*a*) of the Act applies, the amount of the discount or price reduction and the corresponding tax received from each such person and a cross-reference to the corresponding credit note,

(*p*) in relation to discounts or price reductions in relation to goods and services referred to in subparagraph (*n*), the amount of the discount or price reduction (exclusive of the flat-rate addition) and of the flat-rate addition and a cross-reference to the invoice issued in connection with the goods and services in question,

(*q*) in relation to discounts or price reductions received other than those referred to in subparagraphs (*o*) and (*p*), a daily total of the amounts so received and a cross-reference to the cash book or other record used in connection with such matters,

(*r*) in relation to dances—

    (i) the date upon which each dance was held and the address of the place at which it was held,

    (ii) the charge for admission to each dance,

    (iii) the number of persons admitted to each dance,

    (iv) the total amount of money received or receivable from the persons admitted to each dance in respect of admission, and

    (v) where goods or services are supplied in connection with a dance and payment of the consideration therefor is a condition of admission to the dance, the amount of such consideration in respect of each dance,

(*s*) in respect of supplies of goods specified in paragraph (i) of the Second Schedule to the Act, the name and address of the person to whom the goods are supplied, a description of the goods supplied, the amount of the consideration, a cross-reference to the copy of the relevant invoice and a cross-reference to the relevant Customs and transport documents, and

(*t*) in the case of the supply of services in circumstances that, by virtue of any of the provisions of section 5 of the Act, are deemed to be supplied outside the State, the name and address of the person to whom the services are supplied, the amount of the consideration and a cross-reference to the copy of the relevant invoice or other document.

(2) The accounts kept in accordance with paragraph (1) shall set out separately, the consideration, discounts, price reductions, bad debts and values at importation under separate headings in relation to—

(*a*) exempted activities,

(*b*) goods and services chargeable at each rate of tax, including the zero rate, and

(*c*) goods and services a percentage only of the consideration for the supply of which is chargeable to tax.

(3) (*a*) In relation to a person for the time being authorised in accordance with section 14(1)(*a*) of the Act to determine the amount of tax which becomes due by him by reference to the amount of moneys which he receives, references in this Regulation to consideration in respect of the supply of goods or services shall be construed as references to the moneys received in respect of such supply, whether made before, on or after the specified day.

(*b*) In relation to a person for the time being authorised, in accordance with section 14(1)(*b*) of the Act, to determine the amount of tax referable to taxable services which becomes due by him by reference to the amount of moneys which he receives in respect of such supply, references in this Regulation to consideration in respect of the supply of services shall be construed as references to the moneys received in respect of such supply, whether made before, on or after the specified day.

(4) Where the Revenue Commissioners are satisfied that the accounts of a taxable person are kept in such a form as to enable his liability to tax to be computed accurately and verified by them, they may, by notice in writing given to the taxable person, dispense him from keeping accounts in the form prescribed by paragraphs (1) and (2), and any such dispensation may be cancelled by them by notice in writing given to the taxable person.

Revenue publication

Purchase records: Tax Briefing, Issue 24.

Invoices and other documents

10

Notes

Revoked with effect from 1 January 1993 by Value Added Tax (Invoices and other Documents) Regulations 1992, r 6 (SI 275/ 1992).

Time limits for issuing certain documents

11

Notes

Revoked with effect from 1 January 1993 by Value Added Tax (Time Limits for Issuing Certain Documents) Regulations 1992, r 7 (SI 276/1992).

Returns

12

Notes

Revoked by Value Added Tax (Returns) Regulations 1993 (SI 247/1993), r 5.

Acceptance of estimates

13 (1) The Revenue Commissioners may, if they so think proper and until they otherwise decide, accept estimates, based on procedures approved of by them, of the tax for any taxable period which a person is required to pay by reference to a return furnished in accordance with section 19(3) of the Act and may impose in relation to any such acceptance the condition (which shall be fulfilled by the person) that the person shall, within such period as may be specified, furnish a return in accordance with the said section 19(3) or furnish such further particulars as may be specified to enable the estimates to be reviewed.

(2) Where an estimate of the tax payable for any taxable period has been accepted in accordance with paragraph (1), the estimate may be reviewed by reference to the return or other particulars furnished in accordance with the arrangement and any necessary adjustment may be made by way of additional charge of tax or repayment of tax as the circumstances may require.

(3) If a person in respect of whom an estimate of the tax payable by him has been accepted for any taxable period fails to furnish the return or other particulars the furnishing of which is a condition of acceptance of the estimate in accordance with paragraph (1), or fails to pay any additional tax found to be payable as a result of a review of an estimate for any taxable period made in accordance with paragraph (2), any additional tax which the Revenue Commissioners have reason to believe may be due may be included in an estimate of tax made in accordance with section 23 of the Act.

(4) The provisions of section 21 of the Act shall not apply to any additional charge of tax arising out of a review made in accordance with paragraph (2) if the return or other particulars referred to in that paragraph are furnished within the time specified in the condition governing the acceptance of the estimate and payment of the additional tax is made not later than the end of the time so specified.

(5) A review in accordance with paragraph (2) may extend to a period consisting of two or more consecutive taxable periods and any additional tax or repayment of tax arising out of such review shall be regarded as referable to the latest taxable period in such period.

Estimation of tax due

14

Notes

Revoked with effect from 1 January 1993 by Value Added Tax (Estimation and Assessment of Tax Due) Regulations 1992 (SI 277/1992), r 6 .

Modification of certain provisions

15 (1) Section 480 of the Income Tax Act, 1967 (No. 6 of 1967), as applied by section 24 of the Act shall so apply subject to the following modifications:

(*a*)   in subsection (1)—

(i)   the expression "the sum charged" shall be construed as referring to value added tax payable by the person concerned,

(ii)   the expression "the Collector" shall be construed as referring to the Collector-General,

(iii)   the words "in accordance with the assessments and warrants delivered to him" shall be disregarded,

(iv)   the words "the warrant delivered to him on his appointment" shall be construed as referring to the nomination given to the Collector-General on his being nominated by the Revenue Commissioners as the Collector-General,

(*b*) in subsection (4) the words "a distress levied by the Collector" shall be construed as referring to a distress levied by the Collector-General or by a person nominated by the Collector-General to represent him at the execution,

(*c*)   in subsection (5) references to the Collector or his deputy shall be construed as references to the Collector-General or to a person nominated by him for the purpose of the subsection and the requirement of appraisal of the distress shall be disregarded.

(2) [Section 962 of the Taxes Consolidation Act, 1997],[1] as applied by section 24 of the Act shall so apply subject to the following [modification in subsection (1), namely, the words "any sum which may be levied on that person in respect of income tax" shall be construed as referring to Value Added tax payable by the person concerned].[2]

(3) [Section 963 of the Taxes Consolidation Act, 1997],[3] as applied by section 24 of the Act shall so apply subject to the following modifications:

(*a*)   the words "[income tax]"[4] in subsection (1) shall be construed as referring to value added tax,

(*b*)   the expression "[the Collector-General or other officer of the Revenue Commissioners duly authorised to collect the tax]"[5] in subsections (1) and (2) and "[the Collector-General or other officer under this section]"[6] in subsection (3) shall each be construed as referring to the Collector-General.

(4) [Section 964(1) of the Taxes Consolidation Act, 1997],[7] as applied by section 24 of the Act shall so apply subject to the modification that the references to income tax shall be construed as references to value added tax.

(5) [Section 966 of the Taxes Consolidation Act, 1997],[8] as applied by section 24 of the Act shall so apply subject to the following modifications:

(*a*)   the references in subsections (1) and (5) to [income tax][9] shall be construed as references to value added tax, (*b*) in subsection (5) the [references to an inspector and to the Collector-General][10] shall each be construed as a reference to the Collector-General and the words "under an assessment which has become final and conclusive" shall be disregarded.

(6) [Section 998 of the Taxes Consolidation Act, 1997],[11] as applied by section 24 of the Act shall so apply subject to the modification that the expression "[income tax]"[12] shall be construed as referring to value added tax.

Amendments

[1] Substituted by TCA 1997, s 1100 and Sch 31; previously "Section 485 of the Income Tax Act, 1967".

[2] Substituted by TCA 1997, s 1100 and Sch 31; previously "modifications in subsection (1):
   (*a*) the words 'any sum which may be levied on him in respect of income tax' shall be construed as referring to value added tax payable by the person concerned,
   (*b*) the expression 'the Collector' shall be construed as referring to the Collector-General."

[3] Substituted by TCA 1997, s 1100 and Sch 31; previously "Section 486 of the Income Tax Act, 1967".

[4] Substituted by TCA 1997, s 1100 and Sch 31; previously "income tax or sur-tax".

[5] Substituted by TCA 1997, s 1100 and Sch 31; previously "the Collector or other officer of the Revenue Commissioners, duly authorised to collect the said tax".

[6] Substituted by TCA 1997, s 1100 and Sch 31; previously "the Collector or other officer under this section".

[7] Substituted by TCA 1997, s 1100 and Sch 31; previously "Section 487 of the Income Tax Act, 1967".

[8] Substituted by TCA 1997, s 1100 and Sch 31; previously "Section 488 of the Income Tax Act, 1967".

[9] Substituted by TCA 1997, s 1100 and Sch 31; previously "income tax or sur-tax".

[10] Substituted by TCA 1997, s 1100 and Sch 31; previously "references to an inspector and to the Collector".

[11] Substituted by TCA 1997, s 1100 and Sch 31; previously "Section 491 of the Income Tax Act, 1967".

[12] Substituted by TCA 1997, s 1100 and Sch 31; previously "income tax or sur-tax".

Apportionment of amounts

16

Notes

Reg 16 repealed by Value Added Tax (Apportionment) Regulations 2000 (SI 254/2000), r 8 with effect as on and from 1 September, 2000.

Refund of tax

17 A claim for refund of tax shall be furnished in writing to the Revenue Commissioners and shall—

(*a*) set out the grounds on which the refund is claimed,

(*b*) contain a computation of the amount of the refund claimed, and

(*c*) if so required by the Revenue Commissioners, be vouched by the receipts for tax paid and such other documents as may be necessary to prove the entitlement to a refund of the amount claimed.

Remission of small amounts of tax

18 The Revenue Commissioners may, at their discretion, remit the amount of tax, together with interest thereon, payable by a person in respect of goods and services supplied by him during any taxable period, if the total amount of the tax, exclusive of any interest chargeable thereon does not exceed [€20]¹.

Amendments

¹   Substituted by FA 2001, s 240 and Sch 5 Part 4 with effect from 1 January 2002; previously "£15".

Valuation of interests in immovable goods

19 (1) Where —

(a)   it is necessary to value an interest in immovable goods for the purposes of section 10(9) of the Act,

(b)   the disposal of such interest consists of or includes the creation of an interest, [and]¹

(c)   a rent is payable in respect of the interest so created, ...²

...³

the value of such rent to be included in the consideration for the purpose of ascertaining the open market price of the interest disposed of shall, in the absence of other evidence of the amount of that price, be—

(i)   three-quarters of the annual amount of the rent multiplied by the number of complete years for which the rent has been created, or

(ii)   the annual amount of the rent multiplied by the fraction of which the numerator is 100 and the denominator is the rate of interest (before deduction of income tax, if any) on the security of the Government which was issued last before the date of the creation of the rent for subscription in the State, and which is redeemable not less than five years after the date of issue (allowance having been made in calculating the interest for any profit or loss which will occur on the redemption of the security) ...⁴.

[However, where the rent payable in respect of the interest so created is less than the unencumbered rent in respect of that interest, the value of the rent to be included in the consideration for the purpose of ascertaining the open market price of the interest disposed of shall be calculated using the unencumbered rent.]⁵

(2) Where a person having an interest in immovable goods (in this paragraph referred to as "the disponor") disposes as regards the whole or any part of those goods of an interest which derives from that interest in such circumstances that he retains the reversion on the interest disposed of (in this paragraph referred to as the reversionary interest), the following provisions shall apply:

(a)   the value of the reversionary interest shall be ascertained by deducting the value of the interest disposed of from the value of the full interest which the disponor had in the goods or the part thereof disposed of at the time the disposition was made, and

[(b)   if under the terms of the disposition, the interest disposed of is for a period of twenty years or more, or is deemed to be for a period of twenty years or more, the value of the reversionary interest shall be disregarded.]⁶

Amendments

1   Inserted by Value Added Tax (Amendment) (Property Transactions) Regs 2002, r 4(*a*) with effect from 25 March 2002.

2   Deleted by Value Added Tax (Amendment) (Property Transactions) Regs 2002, r 4(*b*) with effect from 25 March 2002 previously "and".

3   Subpara (*d*) deleted by Value Added Tax (Amendment) (Property Transactions) Regs 2002, r 4(*c*) with effect from 25 March 2002.

4   Deleted by Value Added Tax (Amendment) (Property Transactions) Regs 2002, r 4(*d*) with effect from 25 March 2002 previously ", whichever is the lower".

5   Substituted by Value Added Tax (Amendment) (Property Transactions) Regs 2002, r 4(*e*) with effect from 25 March 2002.

6   Substituted by Value Added Tax (Valuation of Interests in Immovable Goods) (Amendment) Regulations 1998, r 3(*b*).

Procedures regarding dances

20 (1) Every person who intends to promote a dance (other than a dance to which the number of persons to be admitted is limited to one hundred and the consideration for admission to which does not exceed twenty pence), or a series of such dances, shall, not later than fourteen days before the date on which the dance, or the first dance of the series, as the case may be, is to be held, send to the Collector-General a notification in writing containing the following particulars:

(*a*)   the name and address of the person,

(*b*)   the address of the premises in which the dance or dances is or are to be held,

(*c*)   the name and address of the proprietor of the premises mentioned in subparagraph (*b*),

(*d*)   as respects the dance or each of the series of dances, the date and time of the dance or of each dance within the series of dances and the proposed admission charge, and

(*e*)   where the person promoting the dance or dances is a body of persons other than a body corporate, the name and address of the individual who will be responsible for payment of the tax.

(2) On receipt of a notification in accordance with paragraph (1), the Collector-General shall forthwith acknowledge it and shall at the same time send a notice in writing to the proprietor of the premises mentioned in the notification, specifying the dance or dances so mentioned and stating that notification in respect thereof has been received in accordance with this Regulation.

(3) The proprietor of any premises shall not promote a dance therein, or allow a dance to be promoted therein by any other person, unless he has received notice from the Revenue Commissioners that they have been notified in accordance with section 11(7)(*c*) of the Act.

(4) If any alteration is made or occurs as respects any of the particulars contained in a notification sent to the Collector-General under paragraph (1), the person responsible for sending the notification under that paragraph shall immediately notify the Collector-General in writing of the alteration.

Notes

This regulation is effectively inapplicable following repeal of VATA 1972, s 11(7) by FA 1992, s 173(2).

Relief for stock-in trade held on 1st November 1972

21 A claim for deduction under section 34(1) of the Act in respect of stock-in-trade held at the commencement of the 1st day of November, 1972, shall be supported by a statement in writing of all stock-in-trade held at that time setting out details of the stock-in-trade so held under the following headings—

(*a*)   stocks which have borne turnover tax and wholesale tax on purchase or importation other than—

    (i)   second-hand goods;

    (ii)   newspapers and periodicals;

    (iii)   motor vehicles designed and constructed for the conveyance of persons by road, and sports motor vehicles, estate cars, station wagons, motor cycles, motor scooters, mopeds and auto cycles, whether or not designed and constructed for the purpose aforesaid, excluding vehicles designed and constructed for the carriage of more than sixteen persons (inclusive of the driver), invalid carriages and other vehicles of a type designed for use by invalids or infirm persons;

    (iv)   radio receiving sets and television receiving sets which are of the domestic or portable type or which are of a kind suitable for use in road vehicles;

    (v)   gramophones, radiogramophones, record reproducers;

    (vi)   gramophone records,

(*b*)   stocks which have borne wholesale tax only on purchase, other than goods of a kind specified in clauses (i) to (vi) of subparagraph (*a*),

(*c*)   (i)   goods which suffered turnover tax only on purchase,

    (ii)   second-hand goods which were purchased from persons accountable for turnover tax and on which turnover tax was borne on purchase,

    (iii)   goods of a kind specified at (iii), (iv), (v) and (vi) of subparagraphs (*a*) and (*b*),

    (iv)   newspapers and periodicals which suffered turnover tax on purchase, and

(*d*)   stocks which do not qualify for relief.

Relief for stock-in-trade held at commencement of taxability

22 (1) A claim by a taxable person for a deduction under section 12(1) of the Act of an amount authorised to be so deducted by section 12(1A) of the Act shall be made to the Collector General and shall be supported by a statement in writing of all stock-in-trade held by him at the commencement of the first taxable period for which he is deemed to be a taxable person (in this Regulation referred to as the relevant day) setting out details of stock-in-trade so held by him under the following headings:

(*a*) stocks supplied to him by taxable persons and in respect of which, if supplied immediately before the relevant day, tax would be chargeable on the full amount of the consideration at the rate specified in section 11(1)(*a*) of the Act;

(*b*) stocks supplied to him by taxable persons and in respect of which, if supplied immediately before the relevant day, tax would be chargeable on the full amount of the consideration at the rate specified in section 11(1)(*c*) of the Act;

(*c*) stocks supplied to him by taxable persons and in respect of which, if supplied immediately before the relevant day, tax would be chargeable on the percentage of the total consideration specified in section 11(2)(*a*) of the Act at the rate specified in section 11(1)(*a*) of the Act;

(*d*) agricultural produce supplied by flat-rate farmers; and

(*e*) stocks, other than stocks referred to in subparagraph (d), in respect of which, if supplied immediately before the relevant day, tax would not be chargeable or would be chargeable at the zero rate.

(2) (*a*) The deduction in respect of stocks specified in subparagraph (*a*) or (*b*) of paragraph (1) shall be ascertained in the following manner:

    (i) the stocks shall be valued at cost inclusive of tax, or market value, whichever is the lower,

    (ii) there shall be deducted from the total value of stocks ascertained in accordance with clause (i) the value of any stocks included therein in respect of which an invoice issued in accordance with subsection (1), (2), (3) or (4) of section 17 of the Act has been or is likely to be received on or after the relevant day,

    (iii) the amount of the deduction shall be the amount of tax which would be chargeable if the stocks were supplied immediately before the relevant day by a taxable person in the course or furtherance of business for a consideration inclusive of tax equal to the amount of their value after making the deduction specified in clause (ii) and the tax fell due on the date of supply;

(*b*) the deduction in respect of stocks specified in subparagraph (*c*) or (*d*) of paragraph (1) shall be ascertained in the following manner:

    (i) the stocks shall be valued at cost inclusive of tax, or market value, whichever is the lower,

    (ii) there shall be deducted from the total value of stocks ascertained in accordance with clause (i) the value of any stocks included therein in respect of which an invoice issued in accordance with subsection (1), (2), (3) or (4) of section 17 of the Act has been or is likely to be received on or after the relevant day,

    (iii) the amount of the deduction shall be **1 per cent** of their value after making the deduction specified in clause (ii).

(3) Relief claimed in accordance with this Regulation shall be distinguished if included in a return made in accordance with section 19(3) of the Act.

Determination in regard to tax

23

Notes

Revoked with effect from 1 January 1993 by Value Added Tax (Determination in Relation to Tax Due) Regulations 1992 (SI 278/1992), r 6.

Supply of certain services

24 (1) Subject to paragraph (2) and in accordance with section 5(3)(*c*) of the Act, the following services shall be deemed to be a supply of services by a person for consideration in the course or furtherance of his business, that is to say, the supply of catering services for his own private or personal use or that of his staff for the supply of which he provides materials or facilities or towards the cost of which he contributes in whole or in part.

(2) This Regulation shall not apply to any such supplies as are referred to in paragraph (1) if the total cost of providing them has not exceeded and is not likely to exceed [€635][1] in any taxable period.

Amendments

[1]   Substituted by FA 2001, s 240 and Sch 5 Part 4 with effect from 1 January 2002; previously "£500".

Postponement of payment of tax on goods supplied while warehoused

25 (1) Where goods chargeable with a duty of excise on their manufacture or production are supplied while warehoused to a registered person for the purposes of his business, they may, in accordance with section 13(5) of the Act be removed from warehouse without payment of the tax chargeable on the supply.

(2) Where goods have been supplied while warehoused to a registered person without payment of the tax chargeable on the supply in accordance with paragraph (1), the tax chargeable in accordance with section 13(5)(*b*) of the Act in relation to the said supply shall be accounted for by that person together with any tax chargeable on the supply of goods or services by him in a return furnished by him in accordance with these Regulations for the taxable period during which the goods were removed from warehouse.

(3) Where goods have been supplied while warehoused to a registered person without payment of the tax chargeable on the supply in accordance with paragraph (1) and the tax is not accounted for in a return lodged for the period in question in accordance with paragraph (2), or the person fails to lodge a return due for that period, the tax chargeable in respect of the supply shall become due.

(4) Where—

    (*a*)   tax due by a person in accordance with paragraph (2) has not been accounted for, or

    (*b*)   tax due by a person in accordance with paragraph (3) has not been paid or accounted for, the said Commissioners may direct that as from a specified date paragraph (1) shall not apply to that person.

Postponement of payment of tax on goods imported by registered persons

26

Notes

Repealed by FA 1982, s 84 with effect from 1 September 1982.

Repayment of tax on certain importations of goods

27

Notes

Revoked with effect from 25 October 1985 by Value Added Tax (Remission and Repayment of Tax on Certain Exportations) Regulations 1985 (SI 344/1985).

Limitation of application of customs law to imported goods

28

Notes

Revoked with effect from 1 September 1982 by Value Added Tax (Imported Goods) Regulations 1983 (SI 279/1982).

Remission or repayment of tax on fishing vessels and equipment

29 (1) Tax is, in accordance with section 13(1)(*c*) of the Act, hereby remitted in respect of the supply or importation of fishing nets, and sections thereof, of a kind used by commercial sea fishermen for the purposes of their occupation and not commonly used for any other purpose.

(2) A person who establishes to the satisfaction of the Revenue Commissioners that he has borne or paid tax on—

(*a*)   the supply or hire to him, the importation by him or the maintenance or repair for him of a commercial sea fishing vessel of a gross tonnage of not more than 15 tons, on the acquisition of which he received from An Bord Iascaigh Mhara a grant or loan of money, or

(*b*)   the supply or hire to him, the importation by him or the repair, modification or maintenance for him of goods specified in the Schedule to this Regulation for use exclusively in the operation by him of a commercial sea fishing vessel of a gross tonnage of not more than 15 tons, on the acquisition of which he received from An Bord Iascaigh Mhara a grant or loan of money, or

(*c*)   the hire to him, or the repair or maintenance for him of goods specified in the Schedule to this Regulation for use exclusively in the operation by him of a commercial sea fishing vessel of a gross tonnage of more than 15 tons, whether or not the subject of a grant or loan of money from An Bord Iascaigh Mhara, or

(*d*)   the repair or maintenance for him of a fishing net specified in paragraph (1) for use exclusively in the course of a commercial sea fishing business carried on by him, and who fulfils to the satisfaction of the said Commissioners the conditions specified in paragraph (3) shall be entitled to be repaid the tax borne or paid.

(3) The conditions to be fulfilled by a person specified in paragraph (2) are—

(*a*) he shall claim a refund of tax by completing such claim form as may be provided for the purpose by the Revenue Commissioners and he shall certify the particulars shown on such claim form to be correct,

(*b*) he shall, by production of sufficient documentary evidence, establish that the outlay in relation to which his claim for a refund of tax arises was incurred in the operation by him of a vessel specified in paragraph (2) for the purposes of a commercial sea fishing business,

(*c*) he shall, by production of an invoice provided in accordance with section 17(12)(*a*)(ii) of the Act or by the production of a receipt for tax paid on goods imported, establish the amount of tax borne or paid in relation to the outlay referred to in paragraph (2),

(*d*) he shall, by the production of a certificate from An Bord Iascaigh Mhara or such other documentary evidence as may be acceptable to the Revenue Commissioners, establish where appropriate that the outlay in relation to which his claim for a refund of tax arises relates to a commercial sea fishing vessel in respect of which he qualified for financial assistance by grant or loan from An Bord Iascaigh Mhara,

(*e*) he shall establish that he is not a person registered in the register maintained under section 9 of the Act nor a person required under the provisions of that section to furnish the particulars specified for registration.

SCHEDULE

Anchors, autopilots, bilge and deck pumps, buoys and floats, compasses, cranes, echo graphs, echo sounders, electrical generating sets, fish boxes, fish finders, fishing baskets, life boats and life rafts, marine lights, marine engines, net drums, net haulers, net sounders, radar apparatus, radio navigational aid apparatus, radio telephones, refrigeration plant, trawl doors, trawl gallows, winches.

Refund to foreign traders

30 (1) A person who establishes to the satisfaction of the Revenue Commissioners that he carries on a business outside the State and that he supplies no goods or services in the State shall, subject to paragraph (2), be entitled, in accordance with section 13(3) of the Act, to be repaid tax borne by him on the purchase of goods or services or in respect of goods imported by him if he fulfils to the satisfaction of the said Commissioners the following conditions, that is to say:

(*a*) he shall claim a refund by completing such claim form as may be provided for the purpose by the Revenue Commissioners and he shall certify the particulars shown on such claim form to be correct;

(*b*) he shall, by the production of invoices or import documents, establish the amount of tax borne;

(c)   in the case of a person having an establishment in another Member State of the Community he shall produce a certificate from the relevant official department of that State that he is a person subject, under the laws of that State, to value added tax referred to in Council Directive No. 77/388/EEC of 17 May, 1977 [OJ No. L145/1 of 13.6.1977]; and

(d)   he shall establish that he is not entitled to repayment of the tax under any other provision of the Act or Regulations or of any other Act or instrument made under statute administered by the Revenue Commissioners.

(2) No repayment of tax under this Regulation shall be made in respect of—

(a)   the provision of food or drink, or accommodation or other personal services,

(b)   entertainment expenses,

(c)   the acquisition (including hiring) of motor vehicles,

(d)   the purchase of petrol,

(e)   the acquisition of goods for supply within the State or for hiring out for utilisation within the State, or

(f)   goods or services acquired or goods imported in connection with an activity which, if it took place within the State, would be an exempted activity.

(3) For the purposes of this Regulation the services specified in paragraph (iii) of the Second Schedule to the Act shall be deemed to be not supplied in the State.

Exemption of certain business gifts

31 For the purposes of section 3(1A)(a) of the Act a gift of goods made in the course or furtherance of business (otherwise than as one forming part of a series or succession of gifts made to the same person) the cost of which to the donor does not exceed [€20][1] exclusive of tax shall not be deemed to have been effected for consideration.

Amendments

[1]   Substituted by FA 2001, s 240 and Sch 5 Part 4 with effect from 1 January 2002; previously "£15".

Supplies of stamps, coupons, tokens and vouchers

32 The amount on which tax is chargeable by virtue of section 2(1)(a) of the Act in relation to supplies of stamps, coupons, tokens or vouchers specified in section 10(7)(b) of the Act shall be nil where the supplies are made by a person in relation to the operation of a business consisting mainly of the supply of goods or services in exchange for the stamps, coupons, tokens or vouchers, and the goods or services are of a kind which the person to whom the stamps, coupons, tokens or vouchers are surrendered does not supply except in relation to the operation of such a scheme.

Supplies of goods or services in exchange for stamps, coupons, tokens or vouchers

33 The amount on which tax is chargeable by virtue of section 2(1)(a) of the Act in relation to supplies of goods or services to which section 10(7)(c) of the Act relates shall be the cost, excluding tax, to the supplier of producing or acquiring the goods or providing the services, as the case may be, increased by such amount as is reasonable having regard to the open market value of similar goods or services.

Apportionment of consideration

34 For the purposes of section 11(3) of the Act—

(*a*) the consideration in respect of the provision of board and lodging, otherwise than in the course of carrying on a hotel business, shall be apportioned as to the amount which relates to the supply of services under section 5(2)(*c*) of the Act and the amount which relates to the letting of immovable goods specified in paragraph (iv) of the First Schedule to the Act;

(*b*) where a service consisting of the transport of passengers and the provision of hotel accommodation is supplied for a single consideration, such consideration shall be apportioned as to the amounts which relate to such transport of passengers and such provision of accommodation, respectively.

Disclosure of information to the Revenue Commissioners

35 Any person engaged in the supply of goods or services in the course or furtherance of business shall, when required to do so by notice in writing served on him by the Revenue Commissioners, disclose to the Revenue Commissioners such particulars of any goods or services supplied to him as may be required by such notice.

Death or incapacity of taxable person

36 If a taxable person dies, becomes bankrupt, or, being a body corporate, goes into liquidation, anything which he would have been liable to do under the Act or these Regulations shall be done by his personal representative, assignee, trustee, committee or liquidator, as the case may be.

Service of notices

37 Any notice, notification or requirement which is authorised or required to be given, served, made, sent or issued under the Act or under these Regulations may be sent by post.

Nomination of officers

38 The Revenue Commissioners may nominate any of their officers to perform any acts and discharge any functions authorised by the Act to be performed or discharged by the Revenue Commissioners.

Revocation

39 The Value Added Tax Regulations, 1972 (S.I. No. 177 of 1972), and the Value Added Tax Regulations, 1973 (S.I. No. 254 of 1973), are hereby revoked.

EUROPEAN COMMUNITIES (VALUE ADDED TAX)(MUTUAL ASSISTANCE AS REGARDS THE RECOVERY OF CLAIMS) REGULATIONS 1980

(SI No 406 of 1980)

Note

Repealed by European Communities (Mutual Assistance for the Recovery of Claims relating to Certain Levies, Duties, Taxes and Other Measures) Regulations 2002, reg 12.

EUROPEAN COMMUNITIES (MUTUAL ASSISTANCE IN THE FIELD OF VALUE ADDED TAX) REGULATIONS 1980

(SI No 407 of 1980)

Note

Repealed by European Communities (Mutual Assistance in the Field of Direct Taxation, Certain Excise Duties and Taxation of Insurance Premiums) Regulations 2003, reg 4(2).

VALUE ADDED TAX (IMPORTED GOODS) REGULATIONS 1982

(SI No 279 of 1982)

Amendments

Revoked by Value Added Tax (Imported Goods)(No 2) Regulations 1992 (SI 440/1992) with effect from 1 January 1993.

Notes

These regulations which came into effect on 1 September 1982 modified or excluded for VAT purposes various customs provisions which applied to the payment of VAT on imported goods by registered persons.

VALUE ADDED TAX (IMPORTED GOODS) REGULATIONS 1983

(SI No 129 of 1983)

Amendments

Revoked by Value Added Tax (Imported Goods) Regulations 1992 (SI 439/1992) with effect from 1 January 1993.

Notes

These regulations, which came into effect on 1 April 1983, dealt with relief from payment of VAT at importation on raw materials and components for certain manufacturers. To qualify for relief an importer must (*a*) have been registered for VAT, (*b*) have been in the business of manufacturing goods in the State and (*c*) have exported at least 75 per cent in value of his total manufactured output.

EUROPEAN COMMUNITIES (EXEMPTION FROM IMPORT CHARGES OF CERTAIN VEHICLES ETC, TEMPORARILY IMPORTED) REGULATIONS, 1983

(SI No 422 of 1983)

Cross-references

VATA 1972, s 32.

Notes

These regulations, which came into force on 1 January 1984, implemented in Ireland EC Council Directive 83/182/EEC of 28 March 1983 which provided relief from import charges for certain vehicles temporarily imported from another Member State of the EC. Importations of vehicles not covered by these regulations continue to be governed by Motor Vehicles (Temporary Importation) Regulations 1970 (SI 54/1970).

Council Directive 83/182/EEC of 28 March 1983 ceased to have effect on 31 December 1992 as regards its provisions on VAT: Council Directive 91/680/EEC of 16 December 1991 Art 2(2).

Case law

Temporary importation of car: whether for private use, taxable amount: *Keller v Revenue Commissioners, Ireland and Attorney General*, unreported, HC, Murphy J, 22 June 1993.

EUROPEAN COMMUNITIES (EXEMPTION FROM IMPORT CHARGES OF CERTAIN PERSONAL PROPERTY) REGULATIONS 1983

(SI No 423 of 1983)

Notes

These regulations, which came into force on 1 January 1984, implemented in Ireland EC Council Directive 83/183 of 28 March 1983 which provides relief from imported charges for personal property imported in connection with: a transfer of normal residence; the furnishing or relinquishing of a secondary residence; a marriage and an inheritance where property is permanently imported from another Member State of the EC. The appropriate exemptions are now contained in the European Communities (Exemption from Value Added Tax on the Permanent Importation of Certain Goods) Regulations 1985 (SI 183/185).

Council Directive 83/183/EEC of 28 March 1983 ceased to have effect on 31 December 1992 as regards its provisions on VAT: Council Directive 91/680/EEC of 16 December 1991 Art 2(2).

VALUE ADDED TAX (EXPORTED GOODS) REGULATIONS 1984

(SI No 230 of 1984)

Amendments

Revoked by Value Added Tax (Exported Goods) Regulations 1992 (SI 438/1992) with effect from 1 January 1993.

Notes

These regulations, which had effect as from 1 March 1984, provided for relief from VAT on certain supplies of goods to foreign visitors and to Irish residents departing the State for more than a year. The relevant goods had to have been shipped out of the State on board an aircraft or ship (other than private aircraft or vessels).

VALUE ADDED TAX (GOODS EXPORTED IN BAGGAGE) REGULATIONS 1984

(SI No 231 of 1984)

Amendments

Revoked by Value Added Tax (Exported Goods) Regulations 1992 (SI 438/1992) with effect from 1 January 1993.

Notes

These regulations, which had effect as from 1 March 1984, provided for relief from VAT on certain supplies of goods to foreign visitors and to Irish residents departing the State for more than a year. The relevant goods had to have been exported as personal baggage of the purchaser.

EUROPEAN COMMUNITIES (EXEMPTION FROM VALUE ADDED TAX ON THE PERMANENT IMPORTATION OF CERTAIN GOODS) REGULATIONS 1985

(SI No 183 of 1985)

1 (1) These Regulations may be cited as the European Communities (Exemption from Value Added Tax on the Permanent Importation of Certain Goods) Regulations, 1985.

Cross-reference

VATA 1972, s 32.

Notes

These regulations which came into force on 1 July 1984, give effect to the Council Directive of 28 March 1983 (83/181/EEC) and provide, subject to certain conditions, for exemption from VAT of certain importations of personal property from outside the Community. Also included are importations of scholastic materials and household effects of students coming to study on a full time basis, imports of certain goods on the transfer of undertakings to the State, imports of certain agricultural and medical products, laboratory animals, certain goods for charitable organisations or the promotion of trade and goods imported for examination, analysis or test purposes and a number of other miscellaneous exemptions.

---

(2) These Regulations shall be construed together with the Act and the Customs Acts (other than the provisions thereof specified in Regulation 30 of these Regulations) and any instrument relating to the customs made under statute (other than the instrument specified in the said Regulation 30).

2 These Regulations shall be deemed to have come into operation on the 1st day of July, 1984.

3 (1) In these Regulations—

"the Act" means the Value Added Tax Act, 1972 (No. 22 of 1972);

"the Community" means the territory of the Member States where Council Directive No. 77/388/EEC of 17 May 1977 (OJ L 145, 13.6.77, p1), applies;

"ECU" means the unit of account as defined in Council Regulation No. 3180/78 of 18 December, 1978 (OJ L 379, 30.12.78, p1);

"importation", in relation to goods, has the meaning assigned to it by Article 7 of the Council Directive No. 77/388/EEC of 17 May, 1977, and cognate words shall be construed accordingly;

"Member State" means Member State of the European Economic Community;

"tax" means value added tax.

(2) In Regulations 4, 5 and 6 of these Regulations—

"alcoholic products" means products (beer, wine, aperitifs with a wine or alcohol base, brandies, liqueurs and spirituous beverages, etc.) falling within headings 22.03 to 22.09 of the Common Customs Tariff;

"**household effects**" means personal effects, household linen and furnishings and items of equipment intended for the personal use of the persons concerned or for meeting their household needs;

"**personal property**" means any property intended for the personal use of the persons concerned or for meeting their household needs, and includes—

   (*a*) household effects,

   (*b*) cycles and motor-cycles, private motor vehicles and their trailers, camping caravans, pleasure craft and private aeroplanes,

   (*c*) household provisions appropriate to normal family requirements, household pets and saddle animals,

   (*d*) portable instruments of the applied or liberal arts required by the person concerned for the pursuit of his trade or profession, but does not include property whose nature or quantity reflects a commercial interest or property intended for an economic activity within the meaning of Article 4 of Council Directive No. 77/388/EEC of 17 May, 1977;

"**value for the purposes of tax chargeable at importation**" means the value of imported goods for the purposes of section 15 of the Act as specified in subsections (3) and (4) of that section.

(3) A word or expression that is used in these Regulations and is also used in Council Directive No. 83/181/EEC of 28 March, 1983, shall, unless the context otherwise requires, have the meaning in these Regulations that it has in that Directive.

4 (1) Subject to paragraphs (2) to (8) of this Regulation, tax shall not be charged on goods, being the personal property of any person, other than—

   (*a*) alcoholic products,

   (*b*) tobacco and tobacco products,

   (*c*) commercial means of transport,

   (*d*) articles for use in the exercise of a trade or profession, excluding portable instruments of the applied or liberal arts,

   imported from a country outside the Community by a natural person transferring his normal place of residence to the State and which—

   (i) except in special cases justified by the circumstances, have been in the possession of, and, in the case of durable goods, used by that person for a minimum period of six months before the date on which he ceases to have his normal place of residence outside the Community;

   (ii) are intended to be used at his normal place of residence in the State for the purpose for which they were used immediately before such importation;

   (iii) have borne either in the country of origin or in the country from which he is departing any customs or fiscal charges to which they are normally liable and are not the subject, on the grounds of exportation, of any exemption from or refund of such charges;

(iv)   are the personal property of that person, being a person whose normal place of residence has been outside the Community for a continuous period of at least 12 months, or who shows to the satisfaction of the Revenue Commissioners that his intention was to reside outside the Community for a continuous period of at least 12 months;

(v)   except in special cases justified by the circumstances, are entered for customs purposes, for permanent importation within 12 months of the date of establishment in the State by that person of his normal place of residence.

(2) In the case of goods which are—

(a)   supplied under diplomatic or consular arrangements,

or

(b)   supplied to international organisations, recognised as such by the public authorities in the State, or to members of such organisations within the limits and under the conditions laid down by the international conventions establishing the organisations or by headquarters agreements,

the reference in subparagraph (i) of paragraph (1) of this Regulation to six months shall be construed as a reference to twelve months, and the conditions specified in subparagraph (iii), of the said paragraph shall be deemed to have been complied with.

(3) Goods the subject of relief under paragraphs (1) or (2) of this Regulation may be imported in several separate consignments within the period specified in subparagraph (v) of the said paragraph (1).

(4) Until 12 months have elapsed from the date of the declaration for their final importation, goods which have been imported tax-free under this Regulation may not be lent, given as security, hired out or transferred, whether for a consideration or free of charge, except in circumstances duly justified to the satisfaction of, and with the prior sanction of the Revenue Commissioners.

(5) Any lending, giving as security, hiring out or transfer before the expiry of the period referred to in paragraph (4) of this Regulation shall entail payment of the relevant tax on the goods concerned, at the rate applying on the date of such loan, giving as security, hiring out or transfer, on the basis of the type of goods and the value for the purposes of tax chargeable at importation as ascertained or accepted on that date by the Revenue Commissioners.

(6) (a)   Relief under this Regulation shall also apply in respect of personal property permanently imported before the person concerned establishes his normal place of residence in the State, provided that he gives an undertaking in writing to the Revenue Commissioners that he will actually establish his normal place of residence in the State within a period of 6 months after the importation. Such undertaking shall be accompanied by security, the form and amount of which shall be determined by the Revenue Commissioners.

(b)   For the purpose of subparagraph (a) of this paragraph the period specified in paragraph (1)(i) of this Regulation shall be calculated from the date of the importation of the personal property into the State.

(7) (*a*)   Subject to subparagraphs (*b*) and (*c*) of this paragraph, where the person concerned leaves the country situated outside the Community where he had his normal place of residence and, because of occupational commitments, does not simultaneously establish his normal place of residence in the State, although having the intention of ultimately doing so, relief under this Regulation shall apply in respect of the personal property which he transfers into the State for this purpose.

  (*b*)   Relief in respect of the personal property referred to in subparagraph (1)(*a*) of this paragraph shall be granted in accordance with the conditions laid down in this Regulation on the basis that:

    (i)   the periods specified in paragraphs (1)(i) and (v) of this Regulation shall be calculated from the date of importation;

    (ii)   the period specified in paragraph (4) of this Regulation shall be calculated from the date when the person concerned actually established his normal place of residence in the State.

  (*c*)   Relief under this paragraph shall not be given unless the person concerned gives an undertaking in writing to the Revenue Commissioners that he will actually establish his normal place of residence in the State within such period as may be specified by the Revenue Commissioners having regard to the circumstances. Such undertaking shall, if the Revenue Commissioners so require, be accompanied by security, the form and amount of which shall be determined by the Revenue Commissioners.

(8) Where, owing to exceptional political circumstances, a person has to transfer his normal place of residence from a country situated outside the Community to the State, the Revenue Commissioners may in their absolute discretion waive or modify the requirements of paragraph (1) of this Regulation, in so far as it refers to use of the goods prior to and subsequent to importation, subparagraph (*b*) of that paragraph, the conditions of the said paragraph relating to commercial means of transport and to articles for use in the exercise of a trade or profession and the requirements of paragraph (4) of this Regulation.

5 (1) Subject to paragraphs (3) to (7) of this Regulation, tax shall not be charged on the importation of trousseaux and household effects, whether or not new, belonging to a person transferring his or her normal place of residence from a country outside the Community to the State on the occasion of his or her marriage.

(2) (*a*)   Subject to subparagraphs (*b*) and (*c*) of this paragraph, relief under this Regulation shall also apply to presents customarily given on the occasion of a marriage which are sent to a person fulfilling the conditions laid down in paragraph (1) of this Regulation by persons having their normal place of residence in a country situated outside the Community.

  (*b*)   The exemption shall apply to presents of a unit value not exceeding [€200][1].

  (*c*)   However, where the value of a present is more than [€200][1], but less than [€1,000][2], the Revenue Commissioners may, in their absolute discretion, grant the exemption.

(3) Relief in respect of the goods referred to in paragraph (1) of this Regulation shall be conditional on the goods having borne, either in the country of origin or in the country from which the person concerned is departing, any customs or fiscal charges to which they are normally liable.

(4) Relief under this Regulation shall apply only to a person:

(*a*)   whose normal place of residence has been outside the Community for a continuous period of at least twelve months, or where it is shown to the satisfaction of the Revenue Commissioners that the intention of the person concerned was clearly to reside outside the Community for a continuous period of at least 12 months, and

(*b*)   who produces evidence of the marriage.

(5) Relief under this Regulation shall not apply to alcoholic products, tobacco or tobacco products.

(6) Save in exceptional cases justified by the circumstances, relief under this Regulation shall be granted only in respect of goods permanently imported—

(*a*)   not earlier than two months before the date fixed for the wedding; in such case the Revenue Commissioners may make the granting of relief dependent on the provision of security in such form and of such amount as the Revenue Commissioners may determine, and

(*b*)   not later than four months after the date of the wedding.

(7) Goods the subject of relief under this Regulation may be imported in several separate consignments within the period specified in paragraph (6) of this Regulation.

(8) Until 12 months have elapsed from the date of the declaration for their final importation, goods which have been imported tax-free under this Regulation may not be lend, given as security, hired out or transferred, whether for a consideration or free of charge, except in circumstances duly justified to the satisfaction of, and with the prior sanction of the Revenue Commissioners.

(9) Any lending, giving as security, hiring out or transfer before the expiry of the period referred to in paragraph (8) of this Regulation shall entail payment of the relevant tax on the goods concerned, at the rate applying on the date of such loan, giving as security, hiring out or transfer, on the basis of the type of goods and the value for the purposes of tax chargeable at importation ascertained or accepted on that date by the Revenue Commissioners.

Amendments

1   Substituted by FA 2001, s 240 and Sch 5 Part 4 with effect from 1 January 2002; previously "200 ECU".

2   Substituted by FA 2001, s 240 and Sch 5 Part 4 with effect from 1 January 2002; previously "1,000 ECU".

---

6 (1) Subject to paragraphs (2) and (3) of this Regulation, tax shall not be charged on personal property of a deceased person imported from a country outside the Community by a person, being an individual resident in the State who either has acquired by inheritance (*causa mortis*) the ownership or the beneficial ownership of such property or who is the personal representative of such deceased person, if—

> (*a*) such individual or personal representative provides the Revenue Commissioners with a statutory declaration or a corresponding declaration made under the laws of the country of exportation that the property he is importing was acquired by inheritance or that he is the personal representative of the deceased person, as the case may be,

> (*b*) the property is imported not more than two years, or such longer period, in special cases, as the Revenue Commissioners may determine, after the date on which such individual enters into possession of the property or such personal representative takes control of the property, and

> (*c*) the property is personal property other than

>> (i) alcoholic products,

>> (ii) tobacco or tobacco products,

>> (iii) commercial means of transport,

>> (iv) articles for use in the exercise of a trade or profession, other than portable instruments of the applied or liberal arts, which were required for the exercise of the trade or profession of the deceased,

>> (v) stocks of raw materials and finished or semi-finished products,

>> (vi) livestock and stocks of agricultural products exceeding the quantities appropriate to normal family requirements.

(2) Goods the subject of relief under this Regulation may be imported in several separate consignments within the period provided for in subparagraph (*b*) of paragraph (1) of this Regulation.

(3) Paragraph (1) of this Regulation shall apply *mutatis mutandis* to personal property acquired by inheritance by a body of persons engaged in a non-profit making activity and established in the State.

7 Tax shall not be charged on articles of clothing, scholastic materials or household effects imported for their personal use during the period of their studies by persons not normally resident in the State who are enrolled in an educational establishment in the State in order to attend full-time educational courses.

8 Tax shall not be charged on the importation of goods (other than alcoholic products, perfumes, toilet waters, tobacco and tobacco products) not exceeding a total value of [€10][1] which —

> (*a*) are delivered to a consignee by letter or parcel post in a single postal delivery,

> (*b*) are despatched to him by a single consignor, and

> (*c*) do not form part of grouped consignments from the same consignor to the same consignee.

Amendments

[1]   Substituted by FA 2001, s 240 and Sch 5 Part 4 with effect from 1 January 2002; previously "10 ECU".

---

9 (1) Subject to paragraph (2) to (5) of this Regulation tax shall not be charged on—

    (*a*) machinery, plant or equipment imported by a person on cessation of his business activity abroad in order to carry on a similar activity within the State:

        Provided that the following conditions are complied with in relation to the goods, namely, the goods have been used in his business for a period of at least 12 months or such shorter period as the Revenue Commissioners consider reasonable prior to the date on which the business ceased to operate in the country of departure, are intended for the same purposes after transfer and are for use in the State in an agricultural activity or in an activity in respect of which he would be a taxable person in accordance with section 8 of the Act; or

    (*b*) livestock imported by a farmer on the transfer to the State of an activity carried on in an agricultural holding:

        Provided that the following conditions are complied with in relation to livestock, namely, the livestock are owned by the farmer for at least 12 months or such shorter period as the Revenue Commissioners consider reasonable prior to the importation and are intended to be used for farming after importation and their number is appropriate to the nature and size of the farming enterprise undertaken by the person in the State.

(2) Paragraph (1) of this Regulation shall not apply to importations by persons established outside the State the transfer of whose business to the State is consequent upon or is for the purpose of merging with, or being absorbed by, a person or persons in the State in circumstances in which a new activity is not, or is not intended to be, commenced.

(3) Notwithstanding the provisions of paragraph (1) of this Regulation, relief may be granted in respect of machinery, plant or equipment imported from another Member State by charitable or philanthropic organisations at the time of the transfer of their principal place of business to the State if the goods were not exempt under Article 15 (12) of Council Directive No. 77/388/EEC of 17 May, 1977.

(4) Relief under this Regulation shall not apply to—

    (*a*) means of transport which are not used in the production process of the business concerned nor, in the case of a service business, used directly in the provision of the service;

    (*b*) food supplies intended for human consumption or for animal feed;

    (*c*) fuel and stocks of raw materials or finished or semi-finished products;

    (*d*) livestock in the possession of dealers.

(5) Except in special cases justified by the circumstances, relief under this Regulation shall be granted only in respect of machinery, plant or equipment imported before the expiry of a period of 12 months from the date when the importer ceased his activities in the country of departure.

(6) Where the Revenue Commissioners are satisfied that there are special circumstances justifying it, they may grant relief under this Regulation notwithstanding that the

conditions specified in paragraph (1) or (2), as may be appropriate, of this Regulation are not complied with.

10 (1) Subject to paragraphs (2) to (6) of this Regulation tax shall not be charged on the importation of agricultural, stock-farming, bee-keeping, horticultural or forestry products from land situated in Northern Ireland and occupied and operated by farmers having their principal farms in the State adjacent to the land frontier of the State.

(2) Subject to paragraph (1) of this Regulation **"stock-farming products"** means such products obtained from animals reared or acquired in the State or imported in accordance with the general tax arrangements applicable in the State.

(3) Relief under this Regulation shall also apply to purebred horses of not more than 6 months of age and born outside the State of an animal covered in the State and then exported temporarily to give birth.

(4) Relief under this Regulation shall apply only to products which have not undergone any treatment other than that which normally follows their harvesting or production.

(5) Relief under this Regulation shall apply only in respect of products imported by the farmer concerned or expressly on his behalf.

(6) Relief under this Regulation shall apply, *mutatis mutandis*, to the products of fishing or fish-farming activities carried out in the lakes or waterways bordering or crossing the land frontier of the State by persons established in the State, and to the products of hunting activities carried out on such lakes or waterways by persons established in the State.

11 (1) Subject to paragraph (2) of this Regulation, tax shall not be charged on the importation from Northern Ireland of seeds, fertilizers and products for the treatment of soil and crops and intended for use on land situated in the State and operated by farmers having their principal farms in Northern Ireland adjacent to the land frontier of the State.

(2) Relief under this Regulation shall apply only to the quantities of seeds, fertilisers or other products—

(*a*)   required for the purpose of operating the land concerned;

(*b*)   imported directly into the State by the farmer or expressly on his behalf.

12 (1) Subject to the provisions of this Regulation, tax shall not be charged on the importation of the following goods:

(*a*)   live animals specially prepared and sent free of charge for laboratory use;

(*b*)   biological or chemical substances—

(i)   which are imported free of charge from another Member State, or

(ii)   which are imported from countries outside the Community subject to the limits and conditions laid down in Article 60(1)(*b*) of Council Regulation No. 918/83/EEC of 28 March 1983 (OJ l105, 23.4.1983, p1), setting up a Community system of reliefs from customs duty;

(*c*)   therapeutic substances of human origin, being human blood and its derivatives (whole human blood, dried human plasma, human albumin and fixed solutions of human plasma protein, human immunoglobulin and human fibrinogen);

(*d*)   blood-grouping reagents whether of human, animal, plant or other origin used for blood-type grouping and for the detection of blood incompatibilities;

(*e*)   tissue-typing reagents whether of human, animal plant or other origin used for the determination of human tissue-types;

(*f*)   pharmaceutical products for human or veterinary medical use by persons or animals participating in international sports events, within the limits necessary to meet their requirements during their stay in the State.

(2) (*a*)   Relief under subparagraphs (*a*) or (*b*) of paragraph (1) of this Regulation shall apply only to animals and biological and chemical substances intended for—

  (i)   public establishments, or departments of public establishments, principally engaged in education or scientific research, or

  (ii)   private establishments principally engaged in education or scientific research and approved by the Revenue Commissioners for the purposes of this Regulation.

(*b*)   Relief under subparagraphs (*c*), (*d*) or (*e*) of paragraph (1) of this Regulation shall apply only to—

  (i)   goods that—

    (I)   are intended for institutions or laboratories approved by the Revenue Commissioners for the purposes of this Regulation for use exclusively for non-commercial medical or scientific purposes,

    (II)   are accompanied by a certificate of conformity of a duly authorised body in the country of departure, and

    (III)   are in containers bearing a special label identifying them,

    and

  (ii)   special packaging essential for the transport of therapeutic substances of human origin or blood-grouping or tissue-typing reagents, and

  (iii)   solvents and accessories needed for their use and included in consignments of the goods.

13 (1) Subject to paragraphs (2) to (7) of this Regulation, and to any limit as to quantity or value that the Revenue Commissioners may impose in order to remedy any abuse and to combat major distortions of competition tax shall not be charged on the importation of—

(*a*)   basic human necessities obtained free of charge by State organisations or by charitable or philanthropic organisations approved by the Revenue Commissioners for distribution free of charge to needy persons,

(*b*)   goods sent free of charge by a person or organisation established abroad, and without any commercial intent on the part of the sender, to State organisations or charitable or philanthropic organisations approved by the Revenue

Commissioners, for the purpose of fund-raising at occasional charity events for the benefit of needy persons,

(c) equipment and office materials sent free of charge by a person or organisation established abroad, and without any commercial intent on the part of the sender, to charitable or philanthropic organisations approved by the Revenue Commissioners, for use solely for the purpose of meeting their operating needs or carrying out their stated charitable or philanthropic aims.

(2) Relief under this Regulation shall not apply to—

(a) alcoholic products,

(b) tobacco or tobacco products,

(c) motor vehicles other than ambulances.

(3) Relief under this Regulation shall be granted only to organisations the accounting procedures of which enable the Revenue Commissioners to supervise their operations and which provide such guarantees as the Revenue Commissioners may consider necessary.

(4) (a) Goods the subject of relief under paragraph (1) of this Regulation shall not be lent, hired out or otherwise disposed of, whether for consideration or free of charge, for purposes other than those laid down in the said paragraph except in circumstances duly justified to the satisfaction of and with the prior sanction of the Revenue Commissioners.

(b) Goods and equipment may be lent, hired out or transferred to an organisation entitled to benefit from relief under paragraph (1) of this Regulation where the latter body uses the goods and equipment for purposes specified in subparagraphs (a) and (b) of the said paragraph.

(c) Goods the subject of relief under this Regulation which are lent, hired out or transferred otherwise than in accordance with subparagraph (a) or (b) of this paragraph shall be subject to payment of tax at the rate applying on the date of the loan, hiring out or transfer, on the basis of the type of goods and equipment and the value for the purposes of tax chargeable at importation ascertained or accepted on that date by the Revenue Commissioners.

(5) Organisations referred to in paragraph (1) of this Regulation which cease to fulfil the conditions giving entitlement to relief under that paragraph, or which propose to use goods and equipment imported without payment of tax for purposes other than those provided for by the said paragraph (1), shall so inform the Revenue Commissioners.

(6) Goods remaining in the possession of organisations which cease to fulfil the conditions giving entitlement to relief under this Regulation shall be liable to the relevant tax payable on importation at the rate applying on the date on which those conditions cease to be fulfilled, on the basis of the type of goods and equipment and the value for the purposes of tax chargeable at importation as ascertained or accepted on that date by the Revenue Commissioners.

(7) Goods used by an organisation benefiting from relief under this Regulation for purposes other than those provided for in paragraph (1) of this Regulation shall be liable

to the relevant tax payable on importation at the rate applying on the date on which they are put to such other use on the basis of the type of goods and equipment and the value for the purposes of tax chargeable at importation ascertained on that date by the Revenue Commissioners.

14 (1) Subject to paragraphs (2) to (6) of this Regulation, tax shall not be charged on the importation of—

(*a*) articles specially designed for the education, employment or social advancement of blind or other physically or mentally handicapped persons which are—

 (i) imported by institutions or organisations principally engaged in the education of or the provision of assistance to handicapped persons, and approved by the Revenue Commissioners for the purposes of this Regulation, and

 (ii) donated to such institutions or organisations free of charge and with no commercial intent on the part of the donor;

(*b*) specific spare parts, components or accessories specifically for such articles as aforesaid and tools for use for the maintenance, checking, calibration and repair of the said articles:

Provided that such spare parts, components, accessories or tools are imported at the same time as the said articles or, if imported subsequently, that they can be identified as being intended for articles previously imported tax-free or which would be eligible for tax-free importation at the time when such entry is requested for the said spare parts, components or accessories and tools.

(2) Goods the subject of relief under this Regulation shall not be used for purposes other than the education, employment or social advancement of blind or other physically or mentally handicapped persons.

(3) (*a*) Goods the subject of relief under paragraph (1) of this Regulation may be lent, hired out or transferred, whether for a consideration or free of charge, by the institutions or organisations referred to in the said paragraph on a non-profit making basis to other such institutions or organisations with whom they are associated.

(*b*) No loan, hiring out or transfer of goods the subject of relief under this Regulation may be effected under conditions other than those provided for in subparagraph (*a*) except in special cases justified by the circumstances and with the prior sanction of the Revenue Commissioners:

Provided that—

 (i) goods may be lent, hired out or transferred to an institution or organisation itself entitled to benefit from relief under this Regulation where the latter body uses the article for purposes specified in paragraph (1) of this Regulation,

 (ii) goods the subject of relief under this Regulation which are lent, hired out or transferred otherwise than in accordance with the preceding provision of this subparagraph shall be subject to payment of tax, at the rate applying on the date of the loan, hiring out or transfer, on the basis of the type of goods and the value for the purposes of tax chargeable at importation ascertained or accepted on that date by the Revenue Commissioners.

(4) Institutions or organisation referred to in paragraph (1) of this Regulation which cease to fulfil the conditions giving entitlement to relief under the said paragraph or which propose to use such goods for purposes other than those provided for by the said paragraph shall so inform the Revenue Commissioners.

(5) Goods remaining in the possession of institutions or organisations which cease to fulfil the conditions giving entitlement to relief under paragraph (1) of this Regulation shall be liable to tax at the rate applying on the date on which those conditions cease to be fulfilled, on the basis of the type of goods and the value for the purposes of tax chargeable at importation ascertained or accepted on that date by he Revenue Commissioners.

(6) Goods used by an institution or organisation benefiting from relief under this Regulation for purposes other than those provided for in paragraph (1) of this Regulation shall be liable to tax payable on importation at the rate applying on the date on which they are put to such other use on the basis of the type of goods and the value for the purposes of tax chargeable at importation ascertained or accepted on that date by the Revenue Commissioners.

15 (1) Subject to paragraphs (2) to (8) of this Regulation, tax shall not be charged on—

    (*a*)   goods, other than building materials or equipment intended for rebuilding disaster areas, imported by State organisations, or charitable or philanthropic organisations, approved of by the Revenue Commissioners for the purposes of this Regulation—

        (i)   for distribution free of charge to victims of natural disasters affecting the territory of any Member State of the Community, or

        (ii)   for making available free of charge to the victims of such disasters, while remaining the property of the importer,

    or

    (*b*)   goods imported by disaster-relief agencies in order to meet their needs during the period of their activity in connection with such disasters.

(2) The granting of relief under paragraph (1) of this Regulation shall be subject to a decision by the Commission of the European Communities, acting at the request of the State or other Member States concerned in accordance with an emergency procedure entailing the consultation of the other Member States:

Provided that, pending notification of the Commission's decision, the Revenue Commissioners may grant relief under paragraph (1) subject to an undertaking by the organisation concerned to pay the relevant tax if relief is not granted.

(3) Entitlement to relief under this Regulation may be granted only to disaster-relief organisations the accounting procedures of which enable the Revenue Commissioners to supervise their operations and which provide such security as the Revenue Commissioners may consider necessary.

(4) The organisations benefiting from relief under paragraph (1) of this Regulation shall not lend, hire out or transfer, whether for a consideration or free of charge, the goods referred to in that paragraph under conditions other than those laid down in that paragraph except in special cases justified by the circumstances and with the prior sanction of the Revenue Commissioners:

Provided that—

  (*a*) goods may be lent, hired out or transferred to an organisation itself entitled to benefit from relief under this Regulation where the latter body uses the goods for purposes specified in paragraph (1) of this Regulation, and

  (*b*) goods the subject of relief under this Regulation which are lent, hired out or transferred otherwise than in accordance with the preceding provisions of this subparagraph shall be subject to prior payment of tax, at the rate applying on the date of the loan, hiring out or transfer, on the basis of the type of goods and the value for the purposes of tax chargeable at importation ascertained or accepted on that date by the Revenue Commissioners.

(5) The goods referred to in paragraph (1)(*a*)(ii) of this Regulation, after they cease to be used by disaster victims, may not be lent, hired out or transferred, whether for a consideration or free of charge, except in special cases justified by the circumstances and with the prior sanction of the Revenue Commissioners:

Provided that—

  (*a*) goods may be lent, hired out or transferred to an organisation itself entitled to benefit from relief pursuant to the said paragraph (1) or, if appropriate, to an organisation entitled to benefit from relief pursuant to Regulation 13(1)(*a*) of these Regulations where such organisations use them for purposes specified in the said paragraph (1) or Regulation 13(1)(*a*),

  (*b*) goods the subject of loan, hiring out or transfer otherwise than in accordance with subparagraph (i) of this proviso shall be subject to payment of tax, at the rate applying on the date of the loan, hiring out or transfer, on the basis of the type of goods and the value for the purposes of tax chargeable at importation ascertained or accepted on that date by the Revenue Commissioners.

(6) Organisations referred to in paragraph (1) of this Regulation which cease to fulfil the conditions giving entitlement to relief or which propose to use such goods for purposes other than those provided for by that paragraph shall so inform the Revenue Commissioners.

(7) In the case of goods remaining in the possession of organisations which cease to fulfil the conditions giving entitlement to relief under this Regulation when these are transferred to an organisation itself entitled to benefit from relief pursuant to this Regulation or, if appropriate, to an organisation entitled to relief pursuant to Regulation 13 of these Regulations, the appropriate relief shall be granted, if the organisation uses the goods in question for purposes which confer the right to such relief. In other cases, the goods shall be liable to the relevant tax at the rate applying on the date on which those conditions cease to be fulfilled, on the basis of the type of goods and the value for

the purposes of tax chargeable at importation ascertained or accepted on that date by the Revenue Commissioners.

(8) Goods used by an organisation benefiting from relief under this Regulation for purposes other than those provided for in paragraph (1) of this Regulation shall be liable to the relevant tax at the rate applying on the date on which they are put to such other use, on the basis of the type of goods and the value for the purposes of tax chargeable at importation ascertained or accepted on that date by the Revenue Commissioners.

16 (1) Tax shall not be charged on the importation of—

    (*a*) decorations conferred by foreign governments on persons normally resident in the State,

    (*b*) cups, medals and similar articles of an essentially symbolic nature awarded in a foreign country to persons normally resident in the State in connection with their activities in fields such as the arts, science, sport, the public service, or in recognition of merit at a particular event and imported by such persons, or

    (*c*) cups, medals and similar articles of an essentially symbolic nature awarded in a foreign country to or other persons established in a foreign country for presentation in the State for the same purposes as those specified in subparagraph (*b*) of this paragraph:

Provided that satisfactory evidence as the facts is produced to the Revenue Commissioners by the importer and the operations involved are not in any way of a commercial character.

(2) (*a*) Without prejudice, where relevant, to the provisions applicable to the international movement of travellers, tax shall not be charged on the importation of—

    (i) goods imported by

        (I) persons normally resident in the State, being goods presented to them as gifts by the host authorities, during the course of an official visit paid in a foreign country, or

        (II) persons not normally resident in and paying an official visit in the State, being goods intended to be offered as gifts on that occasion to the host authorities; or

    (ii) goods sent as gifts, in token of friendship or goodwill, by an official body, public authority or group carrying on an activity in the public interest which is located in another country, to an official body, public authority or group carrying on an activity in the public interest which is located in the State and approved by the Revenue Commissioners for the purposes of this Regulation to receive such goods free of tax.

    (*b*) Relief under subparagraph (*a*) of this paragraph shall apply only to goods, other than alcoholic products, tobacco and tobacco products, which

    (i) are offered on an occasional basis,

    (ii) do not, by their nature, value or quantity, reflect any commercial interest, and

    (iii) are not used for commercial purposes.

(3) (*a*) Within the limits and subject to the conditions laid down by the Revenue Commissioners tax shall not be charged on the importation of—

  (i)   gifts to reigning monarchs and heads of State, or

  (ii) goods to be used or consumed by reigning monarchs and foreign heads of State, or by persons officially representing them, during their official stay in the State.

(*b*) Subparagraph (*a*) of this paragraph shall apply also to persons enjoying prerogatives at international level analogous to those enjoyed by reigning monarchs or heads of State.

17 (1) Without prejudice to Regulation 19(1)(*a*)(i) of these Regulations and subject to paragraphs (2) and (3) of this Regulation, tax shall not be charged on the importation of samples of goods of negligible value which can be used only to solicit orders for goods of the type they represent.

(2) The Revenue Commissioners may, if they think fit, require that, in order to qualify for relief, articles be rendered permanently unusable by being torn, perforated, or clearly and indelibly marked, or by any other process, provided such operation does not destroy their character as samples.

(3) In this Regulation **"samples of goods"** means any article representing a type of goods whose manner of presentation and quantity for goods of the same type or quality, rule out its use for any purpose other than that of seeking orders.

18 (1)(*a*)Subject to subparagraph (*b*) of this paragraph, tax shall not be charged on the importation of printed advertising matter such as catalogues, price lists, directions for use or brochures relating to—

  (i)   goods for sale or hire, or

  (ii) transport, commercial insurance or banking services offered, by a person established outside the State.

(*b*) Relief under subparagraph (*a*) of this paragraph shall apply only to printed advertisement which fulfil the following conditions:

  (i)   printed matter shall clearly display the name of the undertaking which produces, sells or hires out the goods, or which offers the services, to which it refers,

  (ii) each consignment shall contain no more than one document or a single copy of each document if it is made up of several documents; however, tax shall not be charged on the importation of consignments comprising several copies of the same document if their total gross weight does not exceed 1 kilogram, and

  (iii) printed matter shall not be the subject of grouped consignments from the same consignor to the same consignee.

(2) Tax shall not be charged on the importation of articles for advertising purposes, of no intrinsic commercial value, sent free of charge by suppliers to their customers which, apart from their advertising function, are not capable of being used.

19 (1)(*a*)Subject to paragraphs (2) to (5), tax shall not be charged on the importation of—

(i) small representative samples of goods intended for a trade fair or similar event,

(ii) goods imported solely in order to be demonstrated or in order to demonstrate machines and apparatus displayed at a trade fair or similar event,

(iii) materials such as paints, varnishes and wallpaper, of such value and quantity as are appropriate for the purposes of building, fitting-out and decorating of a temporary stand at a trade fair or similar event, and which are incapable of further use, or

(iv) printed matter, catalogues, prospectuses, price lists, advertising posters, calendars, whether or not illustrated, unframed photographs and other article supplied free of charge in order to advertise goods displayed at a trade fair or similar event.

(*b*) In subparagraph (*a*) of this paragraph **"trade fair or similar event"** means:

(i) exhibitions, fairs, shows and similar events connected with trade, industry, agriculture or handicrafts;

(ii) exhibitions and events held mainly for charitable purposes;

(iii) exhibitions and events held mainly for scientific, technical, handicraft, artistic, educational or cultural or sporting purposes, for religious reasons or for reasons of worship, trade union activity or tourism, or in order to promote international understanding,

(iv) meetings of representatives of international organisations or collective bodies, and

(v) official or commemorative ceremonies and gatherings,

but not exhibitions staged for private purposes in commercial stores or premises to sell goods.

(2) Paragraph (1)(*a*)(i) of this Regulation shall apply only to samples which:

(*a*) are imported free of charge as such or are obtained at the exhibition from goods imported in bulk;

(*b*) are used only for distribution free of charge to the public at the exhibition for use or consumption by the persons to whom they are offered;

(*c*) are identifiable as advertising samples of low unitary value;

(*d*) are not readily marketable and, where appropriate, are packaged in such a way that the quantity of the item involved is less than the smallest quantity of the same item normally sold on the market;

(*e*) in the case of foodstuffs and beverages not packaged in the manner specified in subparagraph (*d*) of this paragraph, are intended for consumption during the exhibition;

(*f*)   in their total value and quantity, are appropriate to the nature of the exhibition, the number of visitors, and the extent of the exhibitor's participation.

(3) Paragraph (1)(*a*)(ii) of this Regulation shall apply only to goods which are:

(*a*)   consumed or destroyed during the exhibition, and

(*b*)   appropriate, in their total value and quantity, to the nature of the exhibition, the number of visitors, and the extent of the exhibitor's participation.

(4) Paragraph (1)(*a*)(iv) of this Regulation shall apply only to printed matter and articles for advertising purposes which:

(*a*)   are intended solely for distribution free of charge to the public at the exhibition;

(*b*)   in their total value and quantity, are appropriate to the nature of the exhibition, the number of visitors, and the extent of the exhibitor's participation.

(5) Clauses (i) and (ii) of paragraph (1)(*a*) of the Regulation shall not apply to—

(*a*)   alcoholic products,

(*b*)   tobacco or tobacco products, or

(*c*)   fuels, whether solid, liquid or gaseous.

20 (1) Subject to paragraphs (2) to (7) of this Regulation, tax shall not be charged on the importation of goods imported for examination, analysis or tests to determine their composition, quality or other technical characteristics for purposes of information or industrial or commercial research.

(2) Subject to the provisions of paragraph (5) of this Regulation, paragraph (1) of this Regulation shall apply to goods only if they are completely used up or destroyed in the course of the examination, analysis or test for which they are imported.

(3) This Regulation shall not apply to goods used in examinations, analysis or tests which in themselves constitute sales promotion operations.

(4) This Regulation shall apply only to the quantities of goods which are strictly necessary for the purpose for which they are imported. These quantities shall in each case be determined by the Revenue Commissioners, taking into account the said purpose.

(5) (*a*)   This regulation shall apply to goods which are not completely used up or destroyed during examination, analysis or testing if the products remaining are, with the agreement and under the supervision of the Revenue Commissioners:

(i)   completely destroyed or rendered commercially valueless on completion of the examination, analysis or testing concerned,

(ii)   surrendered to the State without causing it any expense and comply with such other conditions (if any) as the Revenue Commissioners may determine, or

(iii)   in duly justified circumstances, exported.

(*b*)   In subparagraph (*a*) of this paragraph **"products remaining"** means products resulting from the examinations, analyses or tests or goods not actually used.

(6) Save where paragraph (5)(*a*) applies, products remaining at the end of the examinations, analyses or tests referred to in paragraph (1) shall be subject to the relevant tax, at the rate applying on the date of completion of the examinations, analyses or tests concerned, on the basis of the type of goods and the value for the purposes of tax chargeable at importation ascertained or accepted on that date by the Revenue Commissioners; however, the person concerned may, with the agreement and under the supervision of the Revenue Commissioners, convert products remaining to waste or scrap, in which case the appropriate amount of tax shall be that applying to such waste or scrap at the time of conversion.

(7) The period within which the examinations, analyses or tests referred to in this Regulation are to be carried out and the administrative formalities completed in order to ensure the use of the goods concerned for the purposes intended shall be determined in each case by the Revenue Commissioners.

21 Tax shall not be charged on the importation of trademarks, patterns or designs or their supporting documents or on applications for patents for invention or the like for submission to the bodies competent to deal with the protection of copyrights or the protection of industrial or commercial patent rights.

22 Tax shall not be charged on the importation of:

(*a*) documentation, being leaflets, brochures, books, magazines, guidebooks, posters, whether or not framed, unframed photographs and photographic enlargements, maps, whether or not illustrated, window transparencies and illustrated calendars for distribution free of charge whose principal purpose is to encourage the public to visit foreign countries, in particular in order to attend cultural, tourist, sporting, religious or trade or professional meetings or events and which contain not more than **25 per cent** of private commercial advertising and the general nature of whose promotional aims is evident.

(*b*) foreign hotel lists and yearbooks published by official tourist agencies, or under their auspices, and timetables for foreign transport services that are for distribution free of charge and contain not more than **25 per cent** of private commercial advertising, or

(*c*) reference material supplied to accredited representatives or correspondents appointed by official national tourist agencies and not intended for distribution such as yearbooks, lists of telephone or telex numbers, hotel lists, fairs catalogues, specimens, of craft goods of negligible value, and literature on museums, universities, spas or other similar establishments.

23 Tax shall not be charged on the importation of—

(*a*) documents sent free of charge to the public service of the State,

(*b*) publications of foreign governments and publications of official international bodies for distribution free of charge,

(*c*) ballot papers for elections organised by bodies set up outside the State,

(*d*) objects to be submitted as evidence or for like purposes to the courts or other official agencies of the State, (*e*) specimen signatures and printed circulars concerning signatures sent as part of customary exchanges of information between public services or banking establishments,

(*f*) official printed matter sent to the Central Bank of Ireland,

(*g*) reports, statements, notes, prospectuses, application forms and other documents drawn up by companies whose headquarters are outside the State and sent to the bearers or subscribers of securities issued by such companies,

(*h*) recorded media, such as punched cards, sound recordings, microfilms and the like, which contain information sent free of charge to the addressee where such relief does not give rise to abuses or to major distortion of competition,

(*i*) files, archives, printed forms and other documents to be used in international meetings, conferences or congresses, and reports on such gatherings,

(*j*) plans, technical drawings, traced designs, descriptions and other similar documents imported with a view to obtaining or fulfilling orders outside the State or to participating in a competition held in the State,

(*k*) documents to be used in examinations held in the State by institutions set up outside the State,

(*l*) printed forms to be used as official documents in the international movement of vehicles or goods, within the framework of international conventions,

(*m*) printed forms, labels, tickets and similar documents sent by transport undertakings or by undertakings of the hotel industry located outside the State to travel agencies set up in the State,

(*n*) printed forms and tickets, bills of lading, way-bills and other commercial or office documents which have been used,

(*o*) official printed forms from national or international authorities and printed matter conforming to international standards sent for distribution by associations of another country to corresponding associations located in the State,

(*p*) photographs, slides and stereotype mats for photographs, whether or not captioned, sent to press agencies or newspaper or magazine publishers,

(*q*) visual and auditory materials of an educational, scientific or cultural character specified in the Schedule to these Regulations which are produced by the United Nations or one of its specialised agencies, whatever the use for which they are intended,

(*r*) collectors' pieces and works of art of an educational scientific or cultural character which are not intended for sale and which are imported by museums, galleries and other institutions approved of by the Revenue Commissioners for the purposes of this Regulation and on condition that the articles in question are imported free of charge or, if they are imported against payment, are not supplied by a taxable person.

24 Tax shall not be charged on the importation of—

(*a*) material such as rope, straw, cloth, paper, cardboard, wood and plastics used in the stowage and protection, including heat protection, of imported goods during their transportation to the State, where such materials are not normally re-usable and where the consideration for their supply forms part of the taxable amount as defined in Article 11 of the Sixth Council Directive No. 77/ 388/ EEC of 17 May 1977,

(*b*) litter, fodder and feeding stuffs put on board means of transport used to convey animals to the territory of the State for distribution to the said animals during the journey.

25 (1) Subject to paragraphs (2) to (4) of this Regulation, tax shall not be charged on the importation of—

(*a*) fuel contained in the standard tanks of private and commercial motor vehicles, including motor cycles,

(*b*) fuel contained in portable tanks carried by private motor vehicles and motor cycles, with a maximum of 10 litres per vehicle,

(*c*) lubricants carried in motor vehicles and required for their normal operation during the journey in question.

(2) In paragraph (1) of this Regulation—

"commercial motor vehicle" means any motorised road vehicle which by its type of construction and equipment is designed for and capable of transporting, whether for payment or not:

(*a*) more than nine persons including the driver, or

(*b*) goods,

and any road vehicle for a special purpose other than transport as such;

"private motor vehicle" means any motor vehicle not covered by the definition in (*a*);

"standard tanks" means the tanks permanently fixed by the manufacturer to all motor vehicles of the same type as the vehicle in question and whose permanent fitting enables fuel to be used directly, both for the purposes of propulsion and, where appropriate, for the operation of a refrigeration system;

gas tanks fitted to motor vehicles designed for the direct use of gas as a fuel shall also be considered to be standard tanks.

(3) Fuel the subject of relief under paragraph (1) of this Regulation shall not be used in a vehicle other than that in which it was imported nor be removed from that vehicle and stored, except during necessary repairs to that vehicle, or transferred for a consideration or free of charge by the importer.

(4) Non-compliance with the provisions of paragraph (3) shall give rise to application of tax on the goods at the rate in force on the date of such non-compliance, on the basis of the type of goods and the value for the purposes of tax chargeable at importation ascertained or accepted on that date by the Revenue Commissioners.

26 Tax shall not be charged on the importation of—

(*a*) goods for use by organisations approved by the Revenue Commissioners for the purposes of this Regulation for construction, upkeep or ornamentation of cemeteries and tombs of, and memorials to, war victims of a foreign country who are buried in the State,

(*b*) coffins containing bodies and urns containing the ashes of deceased persons, and flowers, funeral wreaths and other ornamental objects normally accompanying them, or

(*c*) flowers, wreaths and other ornamental objects imported by persons resident in another Member State of the Community attending a funeral in or visiting the state to decorate graves if such importations do not reflect, either by their nature or their quantity, any commercial intent.

27 (1) The value in Irish currency of the ECU to be applied in each year for the purposes of these Regulations shall be calculated by reference to the official rate of exchange between the currencies obtaining on the first working day of October of the previous year.

(2) The amounts in Irish currency arrived at by converting the amounts of ECU shall be rounded off to the nearest IR£.

(3) The said value applying in a particular year shall continue in force in the following year, if, without taking into account the rounding off aforesaid, the difference between the values applicable to those years is less than **5 per cent** of the earlier year's value.

28 Nothing in these Regulations shall be construed as affecting—

(*a*) the privileges and immunities granted under cultural, scientific or technical cooperation agreements concluded between the State and other countries;

(*b*) the special exemptions justified by the nature of frontier traffic which are granted under frontier arrangements concluded between the State and other countries.

29 Nothing in these Regulations shall be construed as exempting an importer from compliance with any legal requirement, obligation, restriction or prohibition other than the requirement of payment of tax on goods which, but for these Regulations, would be chargeable to tax on importation.

30 The following provisions shall not apply in relation to goods relieved from tax by virtue of these Regulations:

section 17 of the Finance Act, 1936 (No 31 of 1936), as amended by section 13 of the Finance Act, 1957 (No 20 of 1957),

paragraphs (*a*),(*b*),(*d*) and (*e*) of section 18 of the Finance Act, 1936 (No 31 of 1936),

section 18 of the Finance Act, 1938 (No 25 of 1938),

section 17 of the Finance Act, 1946 (No. 15 of 1946),

Relief from Customs Duties (Fairs, Exhibitions, and Similar Events) Order, 1965 (S.I. No 143 of 1965),

section 76 of the Finance Act, 1974 (No 27 of 1974),

Council Regulation No. 918/83/EEC of 28 March, 1983.

31 A person who, after the date of the making of these Regulations, contravenes a provision thereof, shall be guilty of an offence and shall, without prejudice to any other penalty to which he may be liable, be liable, on summary conviction, to a fine not exceeding [€630][1].

Amendments

[1]   Substituted by FA 2001, s 240 and Sch 5 Part 4 with effect from 1 January 2002; previously "£500".

SCHEDULE
GOODS REFERRED TO IN REGULATION 23(Q)

VISUAL AND AUDITORY MATERIALS OF AN EDUCATIONAL, SCIENTIFIC OR CULTURAL CHARACTER

Common Custom Tariff Heading Number	Description
37.04	Sensitized plates and film, exposed but not developed, negative or positive:
	A. Cinematograph film:
	ex II. Other positives, of an educational, scientific or cultural character
3x 37.05	Plates, unperforated film and perforated film (other than cinematograph film), exposed and developed, negative or positive, of an educational, scientific or cultural character
37.07	Cinematograph film, exposed and developed, whether or not incorporating sound track or consisting only of sound track, negative or positive:
	B. II. Other positives:
	ex A. Newsreels (with or without sound track) depicting events of current news value at the time of importation, and imported up to a limit of two copies of each subject for copying purposes.
	ex B. Other:
	—Archival film material (with or without sound track) intended for use in connection with newsreel films
	—Recreational films particularly suited for children and young people
	—Other films of an educational, scientific or cultural character
49.11	Other printed matter including printed pictures and photographs:
	ex B. Other:
	—Microcards or other information storage media required in computerized information and documentation services, of an educational scientific or cultural character.
	—Wall charts designed solely for demonstration and education

Common Custom Tariff Heading Number

Description

ex 90.21 Instruments, apparatus or models, designed solely for demonstrational purposes (for example, in education or exhibition), unsuitable for other uses:

—Patterns, models and wall charts of an educational, scientific or cultural character, designed solely for demonstration and education

—Mock-ups or visualisations of abstract concepts such as molecular structures or mathematical formulae

92.12   Gramophone records and other sound or similar recordings, matrices for the production of records, prepared record blanks, film for mechanical sound recordings, prepared tapes, wires, strips and like articles of a kind commonly used for sound or similar recording

ex B.

Recorded

—Of an educational, scientific or cultural character

Various

—Holograms for laser projection

—Multi-media kits

—Materials for programmed instruction, including materials in kit form, with the corresponding printed materials.

VALUE ADDED TAX (PLACE OF SUPPLY OF CERTAIN SERVICES) REGULATIONS 1985

(SI No 343 of 1985)

Notes

Revoked with effect from 27 May 1986 by VATA 1972, s 5(6)(*d*) (inserted by FA 1986, s 81(*b*)(i)).

VALUE ADDED TAX (REMISSION AND REPAYMENT OF TAX ON CERTAIN IMPORTATIONS) REGULATIONS 1985

(SI No 344 of 1985)

Notes

Prior to the implementation of the single market (1 January 1993), these regulations (with effect from 25 October 1985) provided relief from VAT on (*a*) goods re-imported after undergoing work in another EC Member State and (*b*) goods imported on hire, lease or loan, or for use in connection with the supply of taxable services where the goods are subsequently exported.

Where goods in (*a*) exported by a non-taxable person to another EC State for repair, maintenance etc exclusively in that State were subject to non-recoverable VAT in that other EC State, the reimportation of the goods to Ireland was be exempt from VAT at importation.

Where goods in (*b*) were imported by a non-taxable person the excess (if any) of VAT paid at importation over the VAT attributable to the hiring or leasing of the goods or their use for the supply of taxable services was repayable.

EUROPEAN COMMUNITIES (VALUE ADDED TAX) (EXEMPTION ON TEMPORARY IMPORTATIONS OF CERTAIN GOODS) REGULATIONS 1986

(SI No 264 of 1986)

Cross-reference

VATA 1972, s 32.

Notes

These regulations, which come into operation on 1 January 1986, gave effect in Ireland to the Seventeenth Council Directive (85/362/EEC) of 16 July 1985. They provided for relief from VAT for most goods, other than consumable goods and means of transport, temporarily imported into Ireland from anther EC State.

The Seventeenth Council Directive (85/362/EEC) of 16 July 1985 ceased to have effect on 31 December 1992 as regards relations between Member States: Council Directive 91/680/EEC of 16 December 1991 Art 2(1).

VALUE ADDED TAX (DETERMINATION OF TAX DUE BY REFERENCE TO MONEYS RECEIVED) REGULATIONS 1986

(SI No 298 of 1986)

Amendments

Revoked by Value Added Tax (Determination of Tax Due by Reference to Moneys Received) Regulations 1992, r 13 (SI 306/ 92).

Notes

These regulations, which come into force on 2 September 1986, amended the terms and conditions, formerly contained in VATR 1979, r 7 relating to the operation of the cash received basis of accounting for VAT. The regulations extended the definition of "connected persons" (transactions between such persons do not qualify for the cash received basis). They also gave the inspector power to withdraw the cash received basis where he was satisfied that it did not provide a reliable measure of the true liability.

VALUE ADDED TAX (FREE PORTS) REGULATIONS 1987

(SI No 275 of 1987)

1 These Regulations may be cited as the Value Added Tax (Free Ports) Regulations, 1987.

Cross-references

VATA 1972, s 32.

Notes

These regulations, which came into force on 24 July 1987, deal with relief from payment of VAT at importation of goods for use in a free port established in accordance with the Free Ports Act 1986. To qualify for relief an importer must be registered for VAT, licensed to carry on business in the free port and import the goods for the purposes of his business in the free port. Relief is not given for imports of food, drink, motor vehicles or petrol unless VAT on such imports would be deductible in normal circumstances. Relief may be withdrawn if the regulations are not complied with.

---

2 These Regulations shall be deemed to have come into operation on the 24th day of July, 1987.

3 In these Regulations—

"the Act" means the Value Added Tax Act, 1972;

"control" has the meaning ascribed to it by section 8(3B) (inserted by the Finance Act, 1984 (No. 9 of 1984)) of the Act.

4 (1) Subject to paragraph (2) of this Regulation, goods that are imported by a registered person may be delivered, or removed, directly to a free port without payment of the tax chargeable on the importation if that person complies with—

(*a*) the condition that he show to the satisfaction of the Revenue Commissioners that—

    (i) he is a person who has, under section 4 of the Free Ports Act, 1986 (No. 6 of 1986), been granted a licence authorising him to carry on within that free port any trade, business or manufacture and

    (ii) the goods are being imported for the purposes of his trade, business or manufacture in that free port,

    and

(*b*) such other conditions as the Revenue Commissioners may impose.

(2) This Regulation shall not apply to the importation of food, drink, motor vehicles or petrol except where tax on the importation of those goods would, if it were paid, be wholly deductible under section 12 of the Act.

5 (1) Without prejudice to paragraph (2) of this Regulation, goods, which have been imported by a registered person without payment of the tax chargeable on the importation in accordance with Regulation 4 of these Regulations, may not be removed from the free port concerned to any other part of the State (other than into another free port or the customs-free airport), in circumstances in which such removal is not in relation to a supply of those goods or, if it is in relation to a supply of those goods, is in relation to a supply to a person who exercises control over the registered person, or over whom the registered person exercises control, or over whom and the registered person another person exercises control.

(2) (*a*)   The removal of goods, precluded by paragraph (1) of this Regulation, may be allowed, with the prior agreement in writing of the Revenue Commissioners, in such exceptional cases as may be determined by them in their absolute discretion.

    (*b*)   Where, by virtue of this paragraph, the removal of goods is allowed, tax which would, but for these Regulations, have been payable on the importation of the goods, shall be payable at the time of the removal by the registered person specified in paragraph (1) of this Regulation.

6 Where goods have been imported by a registered person without payment of the tax chargeable on the importation in accordance with Regulation 4 of these Regulations, details of the goods, including the value by reference to each rate of tax (including the zero rate) shall, if so required, be included in the return for the taxable period during which the importation took place required to be furnished by that person under section 19 of the Act and the regulations made thereunder.

7 Where, in the opinion of the Revenue Commissioners, a person does not, or has ceased to, satisfy a condition referred to, or specified, in Regulation 4 of these Regulations, or has failed to comply with Regulation 5 or 6 of these Regulations, the Revenue Commissioners shall send to such person by post notification of their opinion and the relief provided for by the said Regulation 4 shall not apply in relation to goods imported by that person during the period from the date on which such notification would be delivered in the ordinary course of post until the time when the person concerned shows to the satisfaction of the Revenue Commissioners that he intends to comply with the conditions referred to, or specified, in the said Regulation 4 and with the said Regulations 5 and 6.

VALUE ADDED TAX (SECOND-HAND MOTOR VEHICLES) REGULATIONS 1988

(SI No 121 of 1988)

Notes

These regulations were revoked by the Value Added Tax (Special Scheme for Means of Transport: Documentation) Regulations 1996 (SI 201/1996), r 9 with effect from 1 July 1996. They provided for VAT relief in case of the acquisition for resale of certain second hand road motor vehicles by taxable persons from non-taxable persons.

VALUE ADDED TAX (FURNITURE, SILVER, GLASS AND PORCELAIN) REGULATIONS 1989

(SI No 304 of 1989)

1 These Regulations may be cited as the Value Added Tax (Furniture, Silver, Glass and Porcelain) Regulations, 1989.

Notes

These regulations, which came into effect on 1 November 1989, provide, subject to conditions, for the reduction from 21% to 12.5% in the rate of VAT applicable to the supply and importation of certain articles of furniture, silver, glass and porcelain more than 100 years old.

Cross-reference

Enabling legislation: VATA 1972, s 32, Sch 6 para (xvi)(*d*).
With effect from 1 January 1993, "importation" means importation from a non-EC country and "exportation" means exportation to a non-EC country: VATA 1972, s 1(1).

---

2 (1) In these Regulations—

"the Act" means the Value Added Tax Act, 1972;

"qualifying goods" means articles of the kind specified in Regulation 3 which are more than 100 years old, where such evidence, as specified in Regulation 4, is produced which satisfies the Revenue Commissioners that the articles concerned are more than 100 years old.

(2) In these Regulations a reference to a Regulation is to a Regulation of these Regulations.

3 (1) Paragraph (i*a*)(*d*) (inserted by the Finance Act, 1989 (No. 10 of 1989)) of the Sixth Schedule to the Act shall have effect subject to and in accordance with these Regulations.

(2) For the purposes of giving effect by these Regulations to the said paragraph (i*a*)(*d*), the following articles of furniture, silver, glass and porcelain are hereby specified to be the articles to which the said paragraph (i*a*)(*d*) of these Regulations apply, that is to say:

(*a*) in the case of furniture, any article being movable goods which have been manufactured wholly or mainly from wood, metal (other than silver), marble or other stone, or any combination thereof, and which were designed for use as furnishings, fitments or decoration for private, commercial or public buildings, or for gardens, and to which subparagraphs (*a*), (*b*) and (*c*) of paragraph (i*a*) of the Sixth Schedule to the Act do not relate;

(*b*) in the case of silver, any article manufactured wholly or mainly from silver, not being jewellery, coins, medals, ingots or bars;

(*c*) in the case of glass, any article manufactured wholly or mainly from glass, including mirrors, chandeliers and leaded or stained glass windows;

(*d*) in the case of porcelain, any article being a cup, saucer, bowl, plate, dish, jug, vase, pot, urn or similar goods, or a statue or statuary other than an article to which paragraph (i*a*)(*c*) of the Sixth Schedule to the Act relates), manufactured wholly or mainly from porcelain, china, terracotta, clay, ceramics or similar materials, or any combination thereof.

4 Evidence that qualifying goods are more than 100 years old shall consist of—

    (*a*)   a certificate issued by a member of the association known as the Irish Antique Dealers' Association, or of an equivalent trade association recognised by the Revenue Commissioners for the purpose of issuing such a certificate, or

    (*b*)   a certificate issued on behalf of the National Museum of Ireland, or

    (*c*)   a statutory declaration by a person recognised, for the purpose of making such a declaration, as a connoisseur by the Revenue Commissioners in respect of articles of the type concerned, or

    (*d*)   in the case of imported goods, a certificate, declaration or other document made under the laws of the country of exportation which in the opinion of the Revenue Commissioners correspond to any of the foregoing provisions of this Regulation, or

    (*e*)   an invoice issued in accordance with Regulation 6 or a certification made in accordance with Regulation 7.

5 A non-taxable person who supplies qualifying goods to a taxable person who is acquiring such goods for resale shall on the date of such supply, or within the ten days next following that date, issue to the taxable person who acquires the goods an invoice in respect of that supply, which sets out the following particulars:

    (*a*)   the name and address of the person who is supplying the goods to which the invoice relates,

    (*b*)   the name, address and tax registration number of the said taxable person,

    (*c*)   the date upon which the invoice is issued,

    (*d*)   the date upon which the goods to which the invoice relates are supplied,

    (*e*)   a description of the goods including details of the quantity, type, apparent material of construction, possible origin and identifying features,

    (*f*)   the consideration for the supply, and

    (*g*)   the signature or acknowledgement of the person by whom the invoice is issued,

and the taxable person to whom the qualifying goods are supplied shall provide the form for the purpose of the said invoice, enter the appropriate particulars thereon, and give a copy of the invoice to the supplier of the goods.

6 A taxable person who supplies qualifying goods to another taxable person shall include on the invoice concerned, which he is required to issue in accordance with section 17 (1) of the Act, a declaration to the effect that the goods are more than 100 years old.

7 A taxable person who supplies qualifying goods to a non-taxable person shall, for the purposes of Regulation 8, certify in writing in respect of each such supply that the said goods are more than 100 years old.

8 Every taxable person shall, in relation to qualifying goods which he has acquired or supplied, keep full and true records, entered up to date, of the acquisition and resale of such goods, together with cross-references between all such records, the relevant invoices issued in accordance with Regulations 5 and 6, and the certification made in accordance with Regulation 7.

DISABLED DRIVERS (TAX CONCESSIONS) REGULATIONS 1989

(SI No 340 of 1989)

Notes

Revoked by Disabled Drivers and Disabled Passengers (Tax Concessions) Regulations 1994 (SI 353/1994), r 19 with effect from 1 December 1994.

VALUE ADDED TAX (DETERMINATION OF TAX DUE BY REFERENCE TO MONEYS RECEIVED) (AMENDMENT) REGULATIONS 1992

(SI No 93 of 1992)

Amendments

Revoked by Value Added Tax (Determination of Tax Due by Reference to Moneys Received) Regulations 1992, r 13 (SI 306/ 1992) with effect from 28 October 1992.

Cross-references

VATA 1972, ss 14 and 32.

Notes

These regulations provided that an adjustment to take account of an increase in debtors during the period of use of the moneys received basis must be made in all cases (previously only required where moneys received basis was in use for six years). The adjustment was to be calculated by reference to the debtors position at the time of authorisation to use the moneys received basis or the position six years previous to the change of basis, whichever was the later. No adjustment was required if the cessation of use of the moneys received basis results from the death of the taxable person.

2 ....

Notes

These regulations substituted Value Added Tax (Determination of Tax Due by Reference to Moneys Received) Regulations 1986, r 3(10) (SI 298/1986) with effect from 16 April 1992.

VALUE ADDED TAX (MONTHLY CONTROL STATEMENT) REGULATIONS 1992

(SI No 230 of 1992)

1 These regulations may be cited as the Value Added Tax (Monthly Control Statement) Regulations, 1992.

2 These regulations shall come into operation on the 1st day of November, 1992.

Notes

These regulations (which came into effect on 1 November 1992) specify the details required to be shown in the monthly control statement that must be issued by suppliers (whose annual turnover from the supply of taxable goods exceeds £2m) to their customers. The regulations also specify the time limits within which the monthly control statement must be issued, and provide that each supplier must retain a copy of any monthly control statements he has issued.

---

3 In these regulations—

"the Act" means the Value Added Tax Act, 1972;

"monthly control statement" means the monthly control statement which is required to be issued in accordance with section 17(1B) of the Act.

4 Every monthly control statement issued by a taxable person shall set out the following particulars:

(*a*) the name, address and registration number of the person by whom the goods referred to in the statement were supplied,

(*b*) the name and address of the person to whom the goods referred to in the statement were supplied,

(*c*) the date of issue of the statement,

(*d*) the calendar month to which the statement refers,

(*e*) in relation to supplies of goods for which an invoice, credit note, debit note or settlement voucher was issued in accordance with section 17 of the Act, the total amount of the consideration inclusive of tax shown on each of those documents,

(*f*) in relation to supplies of goods for which an invoice, credit note, debit note or settlement voucher was not issued,
  (i) the date of each such supply,
  (ii) a description of the goods supplied,
  (iii) the consideration, exclusive of tax, for each supply,
  (iv) the rate or rates of tax and amount of tax at each rate chargeable to the person who has supplied the goods,

(*g*) in relation to any adjustment of the consideration for the supplies referred to in paragraph (*e*) or (*f*) agreed between the supplier of the goods and the taxable person and for which a credit note was not issued under section 17 of the Act,
  (i) the amount of such adjustment,
  (ii) the date of such adjustment,

(*h*) where, in respect of the supply referred to in paragraph (*e*) or (*f*), any payment has been or will be made by the person by whom the goods were supplied,

  (i)   the amount of such payment or payments

  (ii) the date or dates when such payment or payments were or will be made

  (iii) the person or persons to whom such payment or payments have been or will be made

and

(*i*) in relation to any gifts or promotional items given in connection with the supplies referred to in paragraph (*e*) or (*f*),

  (i)   a description of such gifts or promotional items

  (ii) the value of such gifts or promotional items

  (iii) the date of provision of such gifts or promotional items.

5 A monthly control statement required to be issued in accordance with section 17(1B) of the Act shall be issued not later than the last day of the month following the month during which goods are supplied.

6 Every person issuing a monthly control statement shall keep a copy thereof and references in these regulations to any such statement, other than references to its issue, shall include references to a copy thereof.

VALUE ADDED TAX (ELECTRONIC DATA EXCHANGE AND STORAGE) REGULATIONS 1992

(SI No 269 of 1992)

Amendments

Repealed by Value Added Tax (Electronic Invoicing and Storage) Regulations 2002, r 5.

VALUE ADDED TAX (INVOICES AND OTHER DOCUMENTS) REGULATIONS 1992

(SI No 275 of 1992)

1 (1) These Regulations may be cited as the Value Added Tax (Invoices and other Documents) Regulations, 1992.

(2) These Regulations shall come into operation on the 1st day of January, 1993.

Notes

These regulations specify the details which must be shown on VAT invoices, credit notes etc for those documents to be valid.

---

2 In these Regulations—

"the Act" means the Value Added Tax Act, 1972;

"registration number", in relation to a person, means the number assigned to the person for the purpose of registration under section 9 of the Act;

"value added tax registration number in another Member State" means the registration number issued to a person by the authorities of another Member State of the Community for the purposes of value added tax referred to in Council Directive No 77/388/EEC of 17 May, 1977.

[**2A** Where an amount or consideration is specified for the purposes of these Regulations, then such amount or consideration shall be expressed in a denomination of the currency of the State and be identified by the use of the symbol appropriate to the denomination so expressed.][1]

Amendments

[1]   Inserted by Value Added Tax (Invoices and Other Documents) (Amendment) Regulations 1998, r 2 with effect from 1 January 1999.

---

3   [(*a*)   Every invoice issued by a taxable person in accordance with section 17(1) of the Act shall set out the following particulars:
   (i)   the date of issue of the invoice,
   (ii)   a sequential number, based on one or more series, which uniquely identifies the invoice,
   (iii)   the full name, address and the registration number of the person who supplied the goods or services to which the invoice relates,
   (iv)   the full name and address of the person to whom the goods or services have been supplied,
   (v)   in the case of a reverse charge supply, being a supply of goods or services to a person in another Member State who is liable to pay value-added tax under Council Directive No 77/388/EEC of 17 May 1977 (OJ No L 145, 13.6.1977, p 1) on such supply, the value-added tax identification number of that person in that Member State and an indication that a reverse charge applies,

(vi)   in the case of a supply of goods, other than a reverse charge supply, to a person registered for value-added tax in another Member State, the person's value-added tax identification number in that Member State and an indication that the invoice relates to an intra-Community supply of goods,

(vii)   the quantity and nature of the goods supplied or the extent and nature of the services rendered,

(viii)   the date on which the goods or services were supplied or, in the case of supplies specified in section 17(8) of the Act, the date on which the payment on account was made, insofar as that date can be determined and differs from the date of issue of the invoice,

(ix)   in respect of the goods or services supplied:

     (I)   the unit price exclusive of tax,

     (II)   any discounts or price reductions not included in the unit price, and

     (III)   the consideration exclusive of tax,

(x)   in respect of goods or services supplied, other than reverse charge supplies,

     (I)   the consideration exclusive of tax per rate of tax, and

     (II)   the rate of tax chargeable,

(xi)   the tax payable in respect of the supply of the goods or services, except in the case of a reverse charge supply or where section 10A(9), 10B(5) or 12B(5) of the Act applies, and

(xii)   in the case where a tax representative is liable to pay the value-added tax in another Member State, the full name and address and the value-added tax identification number of that representative.][1]

(*b*)   Every invoice issued by a flat-rate farmer in accordance with section 17(2) of the Act shall be signed or acknowledged by him and shall set out the following particulars:

(i)   the name and address of the person who supplied the goods or services to which the invoice relates,

(ii)   the name address and registration number of the person to whom the goods or services were supplied,

(iii)   in the case of a supply of goods to a person registered for value added tax in another Member State the name, address and value added tax registration number in that Member State of the person to whom the goods or services have been supplied,

(iv)   the date of issue of the invoice,

(v)   the date on which the goods or services were supplied,

(vi)   a description of the goods or services supplied,

(vii)   the quantity or volume of the goods supplied,

(viii)   the consideration, exclusive of the flat-rate addition, for the supply, and

(ix)   the rate and amount of the flat-rate addition.

(*c*) Every invoice issued by a taxable person in accordance with section 17(3) of the Act shall set out the following particulars:

 (i) the name, address and registration number of the person who supplied the goods or services to which the invoice relates,

 (ii) the name and address of the person to whom the goods or services were supplied,

 (iii) in the case of a supply of goods to a person, other than an individual who does not engage in the supply of goods or services in the course or furtherance of business, in another Member State:

  (I) the name,

  (II) the address, and

  (III) where the person is a person registered for value added tax in that other Member State, the value added tax registration number in that Member State,

  of the person to whom the goods or services have been supplied,

 (iv) the date of issue of the invoice,

 (v) the amount, exclusive of tax, of the increase in consideration for the supply,

 (vi) the rate or rates of tax and amount of tax at each rate, appropriate to the increase in consideration chargeable in respect of the supply of goods or services, and

 (ix) a cross-reference to every other invoice issued by the taxable person in respect of the total consideration for the supply of the goods or services.

(*d*) Every invoice issued by a flat-rate farmer in accordance with section 17(4) of the Act shall be signed or acknowledged by him and shall set out the following particulars:

 (i) the name and address of the person who supplied the goods or services to which the invoice relates,

 (ii) the name, address and registration number of the person to whom the goods or services were supplied,

 (iii) in the case of a supply of goods to a person registered for value added tax in another Member State the name, address and value added tax registration number in that Member State of the person to whom the goods or services have been supplied,

 (iv) the date of issue of the invoice,

 (v) the amount, exclusive of the flat-rate addition, of the increase in consideration for the supply of goods or services,

 (vi) the rate and amount of the flat-rate addition,

 (vii) a cross-reference to every other invoice issued by the flat-rate farmer in respect of the total consideration for the supply of goods or services.

(*e*) Every credit note issued by a taxable person in accordance with section 17(3) of the Act shall set out the following particulars:

(i) the name, address and registration of the person issuing the credit note,

(ii) the name and address of the person to whom the credit note is issued,

(iii) in the case of a supply of goods to a person, other than an individual who does not engage in the supply of goods or services in the course or furtherance of business, in another Member State:

(I) the name,

(II) the address, and

(III) where the person is a person registered for value added tax in that other Member State, the value added tax registration number in that Member State,

of the person to whom the goods or services have been supplied,

(iv) the date of issue of the credit note,

(v) the reason why the credit note is being issued and a cross-reference to the corresponding invoice,

(vi) the amount of the consideration, exclusive of tax, in respect of which the credit note is being issued, and

(vii) the relevant rate or rates of tax, current on the date upon which the credit note is issued, and the amount of tax at each rate appropriate to the consideration for which credit is being given.

(*f*) Every farmer credit note issued in accordance with section 17(4) of the Act shall set out the following particulars:

(i) the name and address of the person issuing the credit note,

(ii) the name, address and registration number of the person to whom the credit note is being issued,

(iii) in the case of a supply of goods to a person registered for value added tax in another Member State the name, address and value added tax registration number in that Member State of the person to whom the goods or services have been supplied,

(iv) the date of issue of the credit note,

(v) the reason why the credit note is being issued and a cross-reference to the corresponding invoice,

(vi) the amount of the consideration exclusive of the flat-rate addition in respect of which the credit note is being issued, and

(vii) the rate and amount of the flat-rate addition.

[(*g*) Every invoice issued by a customer in accordance with section 17(14) of the Act in respect of goods or services supplied to that customer shall set out the details specified in Regulation 3(*a*).][2]

(*h*) Every settlement voucher issued in accordance with section 17(10) of the Act in respect of agricultural produce or agricultural services supplied to a registered person by flat-rate farmer shall be signed or acknowledged by the flat-rate farmer and shall set out the following particulars:

(i) the name and address of the person who supplied the goods or services to which the settlement voucher relates,

(ii) the name, address and registration number of the person to whom the goods or services have been supplied,

(iii) the date of issue of the settlement voucher,

(iv) the date on which the goods or services were supplied,

(v) a description of the goods or services supplied,

(vi) the quantity or volume of goods supplied,

(vii) the amount of the consideration, exclusive of the flat-rate addition, for the supply and

(viii) the rate and amount of the flat-rate addition.

(*i*) Every debit note issued in accordance with section 17(11) of the Act shall set out the following particulars:

(i) the name, address and registration number of the person issuing the debit note,

(ii) the name, address, and registration number, of the person to whom the debit note is being issued,

(iii) the date of issue of the debit note,

(iv) the reason why the debit note is being issued and a cross-reference to the corresponding invoice or settlement voucher,

(v) the amount of the consideration, exclusive of tax, in respect of which the debit note is being issued, and

(vi) the relevant rate or rates of tax and the amount of tax at each rate appropriate to the consideration shown on the debit note.

(*j*) Every farmer debit note issued in accordance with section 17(11A) of the Act shall be signed or acknowledged by the flat-rate farmer and shall set out the following particulars:

(i) the name, address and registration number of the person issuing the debit note,

(ii) the name and address of the person to whom the debit note is being issued,

(iii) the date of issue of the debit note,

(iv) the reason why the debit note is being issued and a cross-reference to the corresponding invoice or settlement voucher,

(v) the amount of the consideration, exclusive of the flat-rate addition, in respect of which the debit note is being issued, and

(vi)   the rate and the amount of the flat-rate addition appropriate to the consideration shown on the debit note.

[(*k*)   A person, other than a flat-rate farmer, issuing an invoice in accordance with section 17(3) of the Act or a credit note, settlement voucher or debit note in accordance with section 17 of the Act shall also comply with the following conditions in respect of every invoice, credit note, settlement voucher or debit note so issued:

(i)   it shall be identified by a sequential number, based on one or more series, which uniquely identifies it,

(ii)   in the case of a reverse charge supply, it shall show the Value Added tax identification number of the person who is liable to pay the Value Added tax, and an indication that a reverse charge applies,

(iii)   in respect of goods or services supplied, it shall show the unit price exclusive of tax and any discounts or price reductions not included in the unit price, and

(iv)   in respect of goods or services supplied, other than reverse charge supplies, it shall show the consideration exclusive of tax per rate of tax, and the rate of tax applicable.][3]

Amendments

1   Para 3(*a*) substituted by Value Added Tax (Invoices and Other Documents)(Amendment) Regulations 2003, r 3(*a*).

2   Reg 3(*g*) substituted by Value Added Tax (Invoices and Other Documents)(Amendment) Regulations 2003, r 3(*b*).

3   Reg 3(*k*) inserted by Value Added Tax (Invoices and Other Documents)(Amendment) Regulations 2003, r 3(*c*).

3A.   [An invoice, credit note, settlement voucher or debit note issued by a taxable person in accordance with section 17 of the Act relating to an intra-Community supply of a new means of transport (within the meaning given by section 1 of the Act) shall set out details necessary to identify the goods as a new means of transport.][1]

Amendments

1   Reg 3A inserted by Value Added Tax (Invoices and Other Documents)(Amendment) Regulations 2003, r 4.

3B.   [Every invoice issued by a taxable person in accordance with section 10A(9) or 10B(5) of the Act shall indicate that the margin scheme or auction scheme has been applied.][1]

Amendments

1   Reg 3B inserted by Value Added Tax (Invoices and Other Documents)(Amendment) Regulations 2003, r 4.

3C.   [The amount of tax included on an invoice or other document issued in accordance with section 17 of the Act shall be expressed in euro. **3D.** (1) Notwithstanding these Regulations, the Revenue Commissioners may allow invoices, credit notes, settlement vouchers or debit notes to be issued under simplified arrangements in accordance with

Article 22(9)(d) of Council Directive No 77/388/EEC of 17 May 1977 but only if they include the following particulars:

(*a*)　the date of issue,

(*b*)　identification of the supplier,

(*c*)　identification of the type of goods or services supplied,

(*d*)　the tax due or the information needed to calculate it, and

(*e*)　such other details as the Revenue Commissioners may require and to which paragraph (2) of this Regulation relates.

(2) The Revenue Commissioners shall publish in the *Iris Oifigiúil* the details to be included in the documents referred to in paragraph (1) of this Regulation and the circumstances under which they qualify for the simplified arrangements.][1]

Amendments

1　Reg 3C inserted by Value Added Tax (Invoices and Other Documents)(Amendment) Regulations 2003, r 4.

4 Any person issuing in accordance with section 17 of the Act an invoice, credit note, settlement voucher or debit note shall keep an exact copy thereof and references in these Regulations to any such document include references to a copy thereof.

5 ...[1]

Amendments

1　Reg 5 revoked Value Added Tax (Invoices and Other Documents)(Amendment) Regulations 2003, reg 5.

6 Regulation 10 of the Value Added Tax Regulations, 1979 (SI No 63 of 1979) is hereby revoked.

VALUE ADDED TAX (TIME LIMITS FOR ISSUING CERTAIN DOCUMENTS) REGULATIONS 1992

(SI No 276 of 1992)

1 (1) These Regulations may be cited as the Value Added Tax (Time Limits for Issuing Certain Documents) Regulations, 1992.

(2) These Regulations shall come into operation on the 1st day of January, 1993.

Notes

These regulations specify the time limits within which VAT invoices, credit notes etc must be issued.

---

2 In these Regulations **"the Act"** means the Value Added Tax Act, 1972.

3 An invoice, required to be issued in accordance with sections 12A or 17(1) of the Act, shall be issued within fifteen days next following the month during which the goods or services were supplied.

4 An invoice, required to be issued in accordance with sections 17(3)(*a*) or 17(4)(*a*) of the Act, shall be issued within fifteen days next following the day upon which the increased consideration is paid or the increase in consideration is agreed between the parties, whichever day is the earlier.

5 A credit note, required to be issued in accordance with sections 17(3)(*b*) or 17(4)(*b*) of the Act, shall be issued—

    (*a*)   in the case of a decrease because of an allowance of a discount, within fifteen days of the date of receipt of the money to which the discount relates, or

    (*b*)   in any other case, within fifteen days next following the day on which the decrease in consideration is agreed between the parties.

6 An invoice, required pursuant to section 17(8) of the Act, to be issued in respect of a payment for supply of goods or services before the supply is completed shall to be issued within fifteen days next following the month during which the payment was received.

7 Regulation 11 of the Value Added Tax Regulations, 1979 (SI No 63 of 1979) is hereby revoked.

VALUE ADDED TAX (ESTIMATION AND ASSESSMENT OF TAX DUE) REGULATIONS 1992

(SI No 277 of 1992)

Amendments

Repealed by Value Added Tax (Estimation and Assessment of Tax Payable and Assessment of Tax Payable or Refundable) Regs 2000, r 6.

VALUE ADDED TAX (DETERMINATION IN REGARD TO TAX) REGULATIONS 1992

(SI No 278 of 1992)

1 These Regulations may be cited as the Value Added Tax (Determination in Regard to Tax) Regulations, 1992.

Notes

These regulations specify the form and contents of a declaration (of the VAT rate applicable to a particular supply of goods or services) made by the Revenue Commissioners under VATA 1972, s 11(1B).

---

2 These Regulations shall come into operation on the 1st day of January, 1993.

3 In these Regulations —

"the Act" means the Value Added Tax Act, 1972;

"a determination" means a determination made for the purposes of section 11(1B) of the Act.

4 A determination shall be in writing, shall contain the particulars of the determination, shall be signed by the officer making the determination and shall bear the date upon which it is so signed.

5 Determinations concerning two or more matters may be included in the same document.

6 Regulation 23 of the Value Added Tax Regulations, 1979 (SI No 63 of 1979) is hereby revoked.

VALUE ADDED TAX (DETERMINATION OF TAX DUE BY REFERENCE TO MONEYS RECEIVED) REGULATIONS 1992

(SI No 306 of 1992)

1 These Regulations may be cited as the Value Added Tax (Determination of Tax Due by Reference to Moneys Received) Regulations, 1992.

Notes

These regulations specify the requirements to be met by a trader who wishes to account for VAT on the cash receipts basis (VATA 1972, s 14).

---

2 (1) In these Regulations —

"the Act" means the Value Added Tax Act, 1972;

"moneys received basis of accounting" means the method of determining, in accordance with section 14(1) of the Act, the amount of tax which becomes due by a taxable person;

"turnover from taxable supplies", in relation to any period, means the total of the amounts on which tax is chargeable for that period at any of the rates specified in section 11(1) of the Act.

(2) In these Regulations —

    (*a*)   a reference to a regulation is to a regulation of these Regulations, and

    (*b*)   a reference to a paragraph or subparagraph is to a paragraph or subparagraph of the provision in which it occurs, unless it is indicated that reference to some other provision is intended.

3 For the purposes of [section 14(1)(*a*)][1] of the Act and for the purposes of these Regulations supplies to [persons who are not registered persons][2] shall be deemed to include any supplies to a taxable person where the said taxable person is not entitled to claim, under section 12 of the Act, a full deduction of the tax chargeable in relation to the said supply.

Amendments

[1]   Substituted by Value Added Tax (Determination of Tax Due by Reference to Moneys Received) Regulations 1994 (SI 259/ 1994), para 3; previously "section 14(1)".

[2]   Substituted by Value Added Tax (Determination of Tax Due by Reference to Moneys Received) Regulations 1994 (SI 259/ 1994), para 3; previously "unregistered persons".

[4 (1) An application by a taxable person (hereafter referred to in this Regulation as the "applicant") for authorisation to use the moneys received basis of accounting shall be made in writing to the Revenue Commissioners and shall include(

    (*a*)   the applicant's name and address;

    (*b*)   the number assigned, if any, to the applicant for the purposes of registration under section 9 of the Act (the VAT registration number);

    (*c*)   the nature of the business activities carried on by the applicant.

(2) An applicant who claims eligibility under section 14(1)(*a*) of the Act shall include in any application made in accordance with this Regulation particulars of—

  (*a*)   the percentage of the applicant's turnover from taxable supplies, if any, which related to supplies to persons who are not registered persons—

    (i)   in the period of 12 months ended on the last day of the taxable period prior to the application, or

    (ii)   in the period from the commencement of his business activities to the last day of the taxable period referred to in clause (i) of this subparagraph,

    whichever is the shorter; and,

  (*b*)   the applicant's estimate of the percentage of the said applicant's turnover from taxable supplies which will relate to supplies to persons who are not registered persons in the period of 12 months commencing with the beginning of the taxable period during which the application is made.

(3) An applicant who claims eligibility under section 14(1)(*b*) of the Act shall include in any application made in accordance with this Regulation particulars of—

  (*a*)   the amount of the applicant's turnover from taxable supplies in the period of 12 months ended on the last day of the taxable period prior to the application; and

  (*b*)   the applicant's estimate of the said applicant's turnover from taxable supplies in the period of 12 months commencing with the beginning of the taxable period during which the application is made.]¹

Amendments

¹   Para 4 substituted by Value Added Tax (Determination of Tax Due by Reference to Moneys Received) Regulations 1994 (SI 259/1994), para 4.

---

5 (1) The Revenue Commissioners shall, if they consider that a person satisfies the requirements of section 14(1) of the Act, authorise the person, by notice in writing, to use the moneys received basis of accounting.

(2) An authorisation given under paragraph (1) shall have effect from the commencement of the taxable period during which it is given or from such other date as may be specified in the authorisation.

6 An authorisation to use the moneys received basis of accounting given by the Revenue Commissioners before the coming into force of these Regulations shall be deemed to have been issued in accordance with Regulation 5.

7 (1) An authorisation under Regulation 5 shall not apply to tax chargeable on any supply where the person to whom or to whose order the supply is made is a connected person.

(2) For the purposes of this Regulation any question of whether a person is connected with another person shall be determined in accordance with the following provisions:

  (*a*)   a person is connected with an individual if that person is the individual's husband or wife, or is a relative, or the husband or wife of a relative, of the individual or of the individual's husband or wife;

(b)   a person is connected with any person with whom he is in partnership, and with the husband or wife or a relative of any individual with whom he is in partnership;

(c)   subject to subparagraphs (d) and (e), a person is connected with another person if he has control over that other person, or if the other person has control over the first-mentioned person, or if both persons are controlled by another person or persons;

(d)   a body corporate is connected with another person if that person, or persons connected with him, have control of it, or the person and persons connected with him together have control of it;

(e)   a body corporate is connected with another body corporate —

   (i)   if a person has control of one and persons connected with him or he and persons connected with him have control of the other, or

   (ii)   if a group of two or more persons has control of each body corporate and the groups either consist of the same persons or could be regarded as consisting of the same persons by treating (in one or more cases) a member of either group as replaced by a person with whom he is connected;

(f)   in this paragraph **"relative"** means brother, sister, ancestor or lineal descendant.

(3) In this Regulation **"control"**, in relation to a body corporate or in relation to a partnership, has the meaning assigned to it by section 8(3B) of the Act.

8 An authorisation under Regulation 5 shall not affect the amount on which tax is chargeable in any of the circumstances referred to in subsections (2) to (9) of section 10 of the Act or tax chargeable on supplies referred to in Regulation 7.

9 [(1) A taxable person authorised in accordance with Regulation 5 shall notify the Revenue Commissioners in writing whenever, for any period of four consecutive calendar months during the validity of such authorisation, the following occurs:

(a)   the percentage of the taxable person's turnover from taxable supplies to persons who are not registered persons is less than 90 per cent; and

(b)   the taxable person's turnover from taxable supplies is such that in the twelve months immediately following such four months period it is likely to exceed £250,000,

and notification in accordance with this Regulation shall be made within 30 days of the end of such four month period.]¹

(2) Where a taxable person fails to notify the Revenue Commissioners in accordance with paragraph (1), the authorisation under Regulation 5 shall be deemed to be cancelled in accordance with Regulation 10. Such cancellation shall have effect for the purposes of section 14 of the Act from the commencement of the taxable period during which the taxable person should have notified the Revenue Commissioners in accordance with paragraph (1).

Amendments

1   Para 9(1) substituted by Value Added Tax (Determination of Tax Due by Reference to Moneys Received) Regulations 1994 (SI 259/1994), para 5.

10 (1) The Revenue Commissioners shall cancel an authorisation under Regulation 5:

(*a*)   if the person so authorised requests the cancellation by notice in writing given to the Revenue Commissioners, or

(*b*)   they consider that the person no longer satisfies the requirements of section 14(1) of the Act.

(2) An authorisation under Regulation 5 shall be cancelled by notice in writing given by the Revenue Commissioners to the person who was the subject of the authorisation. Without prejudice to Regulation 9, such cancellation shall have effect for the purposes of section 14 of the Act from the commencement of the taxable period during which notice is given or from the commencement of such later taxable period as may be specified in the notice.

11 (1)(*a*)Where a person, who for any period is authorised under Regulation 5 and such authorisation was issued prior to 28 May, 1992, ceases to be so authorised or ceased to be a taxable person, the tax payable by him for the taxable period during which such cessation occurs shall be adjusted in accordance subparagraphs (*b*) and (*c*).

(*b*)   An amount shall be established and apportioned between each rate of tax specified in section 11(1) of the Act in accordance with the following formula—

$$(A \quad B) \times \frac{C}{D}$$

where —

A is the total amount due to the person at the beginning of the authorised period for goods and services supplied by him,

B is the total amount due to the person at the end of the authorised period for goods and services supplied by him,

C is the chargeable amount in respect of taxable supplies at each such rate of tax in the 12 months prior to the date of cessation or in the authorised period, whichever is the shorter, and

D is the chargeable amount in respect of total taxable supplies in the 12 months prior to the date of cessation or in the authorised period, whichever is the shorter:

Provided that —

(i)   no adjustment of liability shall be made where A is greater than B, and

(ii)   the apportionment between the various rates of tax may be made in accordance with any other basis which may be agreed between the taxable person and the Revenue Commissioners.

(c) The amount so apportioned at each rate shall be a tax-inclusive amount and the tax therein shall be payable during the taxable period in which the cessation occurs.

(2) (a) Where a person, who for any period is authorised under Regulation 5 and such authorisation was issued on or after 28 May, 1992, ceases to be so authorised or ceases to be a taxable person, the tax payable by him for the taxable period during which the cessation occurs shall be adjusted in accordance with subparagraphs (b) and (c).

(b) The total amount due to the person at the end of the authorised period for goods and services supplied by him shall be apportioned between each rate of tax specified in section 11(1) of the Act in accordance with the following formula —

$$B \times \frac{C}{D}$$

where B, C and D have the same meaning as in subparagraph (b) of paragraph (1):

Provided that the apportionment between the various rates of tax may be made in accordance with any other basis which may be agreed between the taxable person and the Revenue Commissioners.

(c) The amount so apportioned at each rate shall be a tax-inclusive amount and the tax therein shall be payable during the taxable period in which the cessation occurs.

(3) No adjustment of liability as provided for in this Regulation shall be made if the cessation referred to in subparagraph 11(1)(a) or 11(2)(a) was occasioned by the death of the taxable person.

(4) For the purposes of this Regulation —

(a) **"the authorised period"** means the period during which the person was authorised to apply the moneys received basis of accounting:

Provided that where the person was authorised to apply the moneys received basis of accounting for more than six years the authorised period shall be deemed to be for a period of six years ending on the date on which the cancellation of the authorisation has effect.

(b) **"the tax therein"** shall be established at the rates specified in section 11(1) of the Act

(i) applicable on the date the authorised period ends or,

(ii) applicable at the time the relevant goods and services were supplied where such details can be established to the satisfaction of the Revenue Commissioners.

12 For the purposes of these Regulations and subject to the direction and control of the Revenue Commissioners, any power, function or duty conferred or imposed on the Revenue Commissioners may be exercised or performed on their behalf by an officer of the Revenue Commissioners.

13 The Value Added Tax (Determination of Tax due by reference to Moneys Received) Regulations, 1986 (SI No 298 of 1986) and the Value Added Tax (Determination of Tax Due by Reference to Moneys Received)(Amendment) Regulations, 1992 (SI No 93 of 1992) are hereby revoked.

VALUE ADDED TAX (PAYMENT OF TAX ON INTRA-COMMUNITY ACQUISITIONS OF MEANS OF TRANSPORT) REGULATIONS 1992

(SI No 412 of 1992)

Notes

Revoked with effect from 1 September 1993 by Value Added Tax (Payment of Tax on Intra-Community Acquisition of Certain New Means of Transport) Regulations 1993 (SI 248/1993), r 5.

EUROPEAN COMMUNITIES (VALUE ADDED TAX) REGULATIONS 1992

(SI No 413 of 1992)

1 (1) These Regulation may be cited as the European Communities (Value Added Tax) Regulations, 1992.

(2) These Regulations shall be construed together with the Value Added Tax Acts 1972 to 1992.

2 These Regulations shall come into operation on the 1st day of January, 1993.

3 In these Regulations—

"the Principal Act" means the Value Added Tax Act, 1972;

"the Act of 1978" means the Value Added Tax (Amendment) Act, 1978;

"the Act of 1992" means the Finance Act, 1992.

4

...

Note

This para amended VATA 1972, s 1(1)(*a*).

5

Note

This para amended VATA 1972, s 3 (1)(*g*)(i), inserted VATA 1972, s 3(1)(*g*)(iii*a*), (6)(*a*)(proviso) and (6)(*cc*), amended VATA 1972, s 3(6)(*d*)(ii), substituted VATA 1972, s 3(6)(*d*)(proviso), and added VATA 1972, s 3(8).

6

Note

This para amended VATA 1972, s 3A(1)(*a*), inserted VATA 1972, s 3A(3)(*aa*), (*ab*) and added VATA 1972, s 3A(5).

7

Note

This para amended VATA 1972, s 8(1A), substituted VATA 1972, s 8(2B), inserted VATA 1972, s 8(3D) and inserted VATA 1972, s 8(8)(*a*)(IA)–(IB).

8

Note

This para inserted VATA 1972, s 10(9A).

9

Note

This para amended VATA 1972, s 11(1)(*b*).

10

Note

This para inserted VATA 1972, s 12(1)(*b*)(i*a*) and amended VATA 1972, s 12(1)(*b*)(iii).

11

Note

This para inserted VATA 1972, s 15A.

12

Note

This para amended VATA 1972, s 17(1).

13

Note

This para inserted VATA 1972, s 19(5).

14

Note

This para inserted VATA 1972, Sch 2 para (i)(*cc*).

VALUE ADDED TAX (EXPORTED GOODS) REGULATIONS 1992

(SI No 438 of 1992)

Notes

Revoked by Value Added Tax (Retail Export Scheme) Regulations 1998 (SI 32/1998) with effect from 4 February 1998.

VALUE ADDED TAX (IMPORTED GOODS) REGULATIONS 1992

(SI No 439 of 1992)

1 These Regulations may be cited as the Value Added Tax (Imported Goods) Regulations, 1992.

Notes

These regulations allow manufacturers whose exports (including exports to EC States: intra-Community supplies) represent at least 75% in value of their total manufacturing output to import raw materials etc VAT free (from non-EC countries).

2 These Regulations shall come into operation on the 1st day of January, 1993.

3 (1) In these Regulations—

"the Act" means the Value Added Tax Act, 1972.

"qualifying goods" means goods imported and entered for the purpose of undergoing a process of manufacture or for the purpose of being incorporated with other goods as a part or ingredient of a manufactured product.

(2) In these Regulations a reference to a Regulation is to a Regulation of these Regulations, unless it is indicated that reference to some other provision is intended.

4 Qualifying goods that are imported by a registered person may, subject to compliance with the requirement of these Regulations, be delivered or removed without payment of the tax chargeable on the importation where the person shows to the satisfaction of the Revenue Commissioners—

(*a*) that he is in the business of manufacturing goods in the State,

(*b*) that the goods are being imported for the purposes of the business, and

(*c*) that the consideration relating to supplies specified in subparagraphs (i)(*a*)(1), (i)(*b*) or (i)(*c*) of the Second Schedule to the Act made by him of goods manufactured by him in the State, taking one taxable period with another, amounts to and is likely to continue to amount to not less than **75 per cent** of the consideration, excluding tax, relating to the total of his supplies of goods manufactured by him.

5 A person who wishes to import qualifying goods without payment of the tax chargeable on their importation, in accordance with Regulation 4, shall apply in writing to the Revenue Commissioners for authorisation to do so. He shall complete such form as is provided for that purpose by the Revenue Commissioners and he shall certify the particulars shown on such form to be correct. He shall in addition provide such further documentation in support of the application as the Revenue Commissioners may request.

6 Where they consider that a person satisfies the requirements of Regulation 4, the Revenue Commissioners shall authorise that person, by notice in writing, to have qualifying goods delivered or removed without payment of the tax chargeable on the importation of those goods.

7 Registered persons who, before the coming into force of these Regulations, have been authorised by the Revenue Commissioners to deliver or remove goods without payment of the tax chargeable on the importation in accordance with the Value Added Tax (Imported Goods) Regulations, 1983 (SI No 129 of 1983) shall be deemed to have been authorised in accordance with Regulation 6.

8 In relation to each consignment of goods to be imported by a person authorised under Regulation 6 without payment of the tax chargeable on the importation, the following conditions shall be complied with—

(*a*) the authorisation or, by agreement with a customs officer in the State, a copy thereof shall be produced with the relevant customs entry, and

(*b*) the relevant customs entry shall incorporate

(i) a declaration by the authorised person, or by his representative duly authorised by him in writing for this purpose, that the goods are raw materials and components for use in the authorised person's manufacturing business, and

(ii) a claim for VAT-free importation.

9 Where goods have been imported by a person without payment of the tax chargeable on the importation in accordance with these Regulations, the tax so chargeable shall be accounted for by the authorised person in the return required to be furnished by him under section 19 of the Act for the taxable period during which the importation took place.

10 (1) A person authorised in accordance with Regulation 6 shall notify the Revenue Commissioners in writing where he no longer satisfies the requirements of Regulation 4. Such notification shall be made within 30 days of the person no longer satisfying the requirements of Regulation 4.

(2) Where a person fails to notify the Revenue Commissioners in accordance with paragraph (1) of this Regulation, the authorisation under Regulation 6 shall be deemed to be cancelled in accordance with Regulation 11. Such cancellation shall have effect from the date on which the person no longer satisfies the requirements of Regulation 4.

11 (1) The Revenue Commissioners shall cancel an authorisation under Regulation 6 where they consider that the person no longer satisfies the requirements of Regulation 4.

(2) An authorisation under Regulation 6 shall be cancelled by notice in writing given by the Revenue Commissioners to the person who was the subject of the authorisation. Such cancellation shall have effect from the date of the notice or from such later date as may be specified in the notice.

12 The Value Added Tax (Imported Goods) Regulations, 1983 (SI No 129 of 1983) are hereby revoked.

VALUE ADDED TAX (IMPORTED GOODS) (NO 2) REGULATIONS 1992

(SI No 440 of 1992)

1 These Regulations may be cited as the Value Added Tax (Imported Goods) (No 2) Regulations, 1992.

Notes

These regulations modify the application of customs law as regards VAT at importation:

(*a*) on goods imported for warehousing (or for processing or re-export);

(*b*) on goods reimported by the person who exported them;

(*c*) in relation to customs drawback and repayments;

(*d*) on goods brought from the Shannon customs free airport into other parts of the State;

(*e*) in relation to the deferred payment of VAT at import;

(*f*) in relation to the application of EC customs law to VAT at import.

---

2 These Regulations shall come into operation on the 1st day of January, 1993.

3 In these Regulations—

    (*a*)   a reference to a Regulation is to a Regulation of these Regulations, and

    (*b*)   a reference to a paragraph is to a paragraph of the provision in which it occurs,

unless it is indicated that reference to some other provision is intended.

4 Without prejudice to Regulation 9, the provisions of the Customs Consolidation Act, 1876 as amended relating to the warehousing of imported goods, section 11 of the Finance (Miscellaneous Provisions) Act, 1958 (No 28 of 1958), and section 38 of the Finance Act, 1932 (No 20 of 1932), as amended by section 17 of the Finance Act, 1965 (No 22 of 1965), and the European Communities (Customs) Regulations, 1972 (SI No 334 of 1972), shall not apply to tax chargeable at importation.

5 Section 6 of the Customs and Inland Revenue Act, 1879, and section 25(2) of the Finance Act, 1933 (No 15 of 1933), shall, insofar as they apply to tax, have effect in relation to goods which are being re-imported into the State after exportation therefrom only if they are re-imported into the State by the person who exported them from the State.

6 Section 24 and 28 of the Finance Act, 1933 (No 15 of 1933), shall apply to tax chargeable at importation only insofar as the tax is not deductible under section 12 of the Act.

7 Without prejudice to Regulation 9, section 5(1) of the Customs-Free Airport Act, 1947 (No 5 of 1947), shall not, insofar as it applies to tax, have effect in relation to goods brought from the Customs-free airport (within the meaning of that Act) into any other part of the State where it is established to the satisfaction of the Revenue Commissioners that the goods are Community goods or that the tax has already been borne or paid on the goods.

8 Section 29(7) of the Finance Act, 1978 (No 21 of 1978), shall apply in relation to tax payable at importation with the modification that the reference to goods entered for home use shall be deemed to include a reference to imported goods entered for free circulation ...[1].

Amendments

[1]   Deleted by Value Added Tax (Imported Goods) (Amendment) Regs 2001, r 4 with effect from the date of consent of the Minister for Finance previously "or for processing under customs control".

9 Legislation relating to customs adopted by the European Communities concerning the placing of goods under—

     (*a*)   arrangements for temporary importation with total exemption from customs duty,

     (*b*)   external transit arrangements,

     (*c*)   temporary storage arrangements,

     (*d*)   free zone or free warehouse arrangements,

     (*e*)   customs warehousing arrangements,

     (*f*)   inward processing (suspension) arrangements, ...[1]

     (*g*)   arrangements for the admission of goods into territorial waters in connection with drilling or production platforms, [or

     (*h*)   arrangements for processing under customs control,][2]

shall only apply in relation to tax chargeable at importation where, and for such time as, goods are held under those arrangements for the purpose of compliance with and implementation of the Community rules relating to customs.

Amendments

[1]   Deleted by Value Added Tax (Imported Goods) (Amendment) Regs 2001, r 5(*a*) with effect from the date of consent of the Minister for Finance.

[2]   Inserted by Value Added Tax (Imported Goods) (Amendment) Regs 2001, r 5(*b*) with effect from the date of consent of the Minister for Finance.

10 Without prejudice to Regulation 9, legislation relating to customs adopted by the European Community concerning suspension of customs duties, reduction in customs duties, or repayment or remission of customs duties shall not apply to tax chargeable at importation.

11 The Value Added Tax (Imported Goods) Regulations, 1982 (SI No 279 of 1982) are hereby revoked.

VALUE ADDED TAX (REGISTRATION) REGULATIONS 1993

(SI No 30 of 1993)

1 These Regulations may be cited as the Value Added Tax (Registration) Regulations, 1993.

Notes

These regulations set out the details to be supplied (and the procedures to be followed) when registering (or deregistering) for VAT.

---

2 In these Regulations **"the Act"** means the Value Added Tax Act, 1972.

3 A taxable person, or a person who in accordance with section 8(3) of the Act desires to elect to be a taxable person, shall register for tax by completing such form as is provided for that purpose by the Revenue Commissioners and he shall certify the particulars shown on such form to be correct.

4 Where a change occurs in any of the particulars furnished in the form referred to in Regulation 3 of these Regulations -

    (*a*)   the registered person,

    (*b*)   if the registered person is dead, his personal representative, or

    (*c*)   if the registered person is a body of persons which is in liquidation or is otherwise being wound up, the liquidator or any other person who is carrying on business during such liquidation or, as the case may be, winding up,

shall, within thirty days immediately following the date of the change, furnish to the Revenue Commissioners particulars of the change.

5 A person who is registered in accordance with section 9 of the Act and who ceases—

    (*a*)   to supply taxable goods or services, and

    (*b*)   to make intra-Community acquisitions,

in the State shall notify the Revenue Commissioners in writing of such cessation. Such written notification must be furnished by the end of the taxable period following that in which the cessation occurred.

6 The Revenue Commissioners may, by notice in writing, cancel the registration of a person who does not become, or who ceases to be, a taxable person, and such cancellation shall have effect as on and from the date of the notice, or as on and from such date as may be specified in the notice.

7 Regulation 6 of the Value Added Tax Regulations 1979 (S.I. No. 63 of 1979) is hereby revoked.

VALUE ADDED TAX (STATEMENT OF INTRA-COMMUNITY SUPPLIES) REGULATIONS 1993

(SI No 54 of 1993)

1 These Regulations may be cited as the Value Added Tax (Statement of Intra-Community Supplies) Regulations, 1993.

Notes

These regulations set out the details to be shown on the EC export sales listing (VAT Information Exchange System return — VIES return — officially described as the statement of intra-Community supplies) that must be submitted by taxable persons. The regulations also specify how such statements may sent to the Revenue Commissioners and the frequency of such returns.

2 These Regulations shall be deemed to have come into operation on the 1st day of January, 1993.

3 (1)In these Regulations–

"the Act" means the Value Added Tax Act 1972;

"correction statement" means a statement of corrective details furnished in relation to a statement previously supplied;

"intra-Community supplies" has the meaning assigned to it by section 19A(6) of the Act;

"statement" means a statement of intra-Community supplies required to be furnished to the Revenue Commissioners by a taxable person in accordance with section 19A of the Act;

"working day" means a day other than–

    (*a*)   a Saturday or Sunday,

    (*b*)   a day that is a public holiday (within the meaning of the Holidays (Employees) Act, 1973 (No. 25 of 1973)), or

    (*c*)   any other day when the offices of the Revenue Commissioners are closed to the public.

(2) In these Regulations–

    (*a*)   a reference to a Regulation is to a Regulation of these Regulations, and

    (*b*)   a reference to a paragraph or subparagraph is to a paragraph or subparagraph of the provision in which it occurs,

unless it is indicated that reference to some other provision is intended.

4 (1) Subject to Regulation 5 a taxable person who is required in accordance with section 19A of the Act to furnish a statement of intra-Community supplies shall complete to the satisfaction of the Revenue Commissioners such forms as are provided for that purpose by them.

(2) Where for any reason a taxable person becomes aware of an error in a statement furnished in accordance with paragraph (1) he shall, within five working days, furnish a correction statement on the form provided for that purpose by the Revenue Commissioners.

5 (1) Notwithstanding the provisions of Regulation 4, a taxable person may, on written application to the Revenue Commissioners, be authorised by them to furnish a statement or correction statement on a document or in a manner other than by use of the forms referred to in Regulation 4.

(2) Where a taxable person is authorised in accordance with paragraph (1), the statement or correction statement shall be furnished in a format specified by the Revenue Commissioners and shall include all the particulars that would have been provided had the person completed the relevant form referred to in Regulation 4.

6 In furnishing a statement or correction statement in accordance with Regulation 4 or 5 a taxable person shall, in respect of the period covered by the statement–

- (*a*)   make a separate entry in respect of his intra-Community supplies to each person registered for Value Added tax in another Member State,

- (*b*)   include in each entry referred to in subparagraph (*a*) the indicator "P" where the intra-Community supplies include–

    - (i)   goods which have been returned by him to that person having undergone contract work in the State, or

    - (ii)   goods dispatched or transported by him to that person for the purposes of having contract work carried out on the goods,

- (*c*)   in the case of intra-Community supplies referred to in paragraph (*b*)(ii), omit in the entry any indication of the value of the goods and

- (*d*)   make a separate entry including the indicator "T" in respect of any supplies of the type referred to in section 3A(5)(iii) of the Act to each person registered for Value Added tax in another Member State,

and shall also furnish such other particulars of his intra-Community supplies as are requested on the appropriate form.

7 (1)

- (*a*)   A statement or correction statement may be prepared and furnished to the Revenue Commissioners by a person other than the taxable person where that person has been authorised by the taxable person to act on his behalf in that regard.

- (*b*)   Where a statement or correction statement is prepared and furnished to the Revenue Commissioners by virtue of subparagraph (*a*), the provisions of the Act shall apply as if it had been prepared and furnished to the Revenue Commissioners by the taxable person.

(2) A statement or correction statement purporting to be prepared and furnished to the Revenue Commissioners by or on behalf of any taxable person shall, for all the purposes of the Act, be deemed to have been prepared and furnished to the Revenue

Commissioners by that taxable person, or by his authority, as the case may be, unless the contrary is proved.

(3) A taxable person who authorises another person in accordance with paragraph (1) shall notify the Revenue Commissioners in writing of such authorisation.

(4) A taxable person shall, on cancelling an authorisation referred to in paragraph (1), advise the Revenue Commissioners in writing of the cancellation within five working days of such cancellation.

(5) The Revenue Commissioners may by notice in writing exclude a taxable person from the provisions of this Regulation.

8 (1) Subject to paragraph (2) and save as may be otherwise permitted by the Revenue Commissioners under these Regulations, every statement and correction statement shall be completed otherwise than in handwriting by means of typing or other similar process.

(2) Every statement and correction statement shall be signed and dated by the taxable person or the person authorised by him in accordance with paragraph (1) of Regulation 7.

(3) Where a taxable person has been authorised in accordance with Regulation 5 to furnish a statement or correction statement by electronic means or through magnetic media, any such statement shall have the same effect as if it were a signed statement or correction statement, as the case may be.

9 (1) A taxable person may, on written application to the Revenue Commissioners, be authorised by the Commissioners to submit an annual statement in accordance with section 19A(3) of the Act where the taxable person's supplies of goods and services do not exceed or are not likely to exceed [€85,000][1] in a calendar year, and his intra-Community supplies do not exceed or are not likely to exceed [€15,000][2] in that calendar year and provided such intra-Community supplies do not include the supply of new means of transport.

(2) A taxable person authorised to submit a return in accordance with section 19(3)(*aa*) of the Act may, on written application to the Revenue Commissioners, be authorised by the Commissioners to submit an annual statement in accordance with section 19A(3) of the Act where the taxable person's supplies of goods and services do not exceed or are not likely to exceed [€200,000][3] in a calendar year, and his intra-Community supplies do not exceed or are not likely to exceed [€15,000][4] in that calendar year and provided such intra- Community supplies do not include the supply of new means of transport.

Amendments

[1]   Substituted by FA 2001, s 240 and Sch 5 Part 4 with effect from 1 January 2002; previously "£60,000".

[2]   Substituted by FA 2001, s 240 and Sch 5 Part 4 with effect from 1 January 2002; previously "£12,000".

[3]   Substituted by FA 2001, s 240 and Sch 5 Part 4 with effect from 1 January 2002; previously "£200,000".

[4]   Substituted by FA 2001, s 240 and Sch 5 Part 4 with effect from 1 January 2002; previously "£12,000".

10 An authorisation under subsection (2) or (3) of section 19A of the Act shall be cancelled by notice in writing given by the Revenue Commissioners to the person who was the subject of the authorisation and any such cancellation shall have effect from the date of the notice or from such later date as may be specified in the notice.

11 The provisions of Regulations 4, 5, 6, 7 and 8 shall apply to a statement or correction statement furnished on a monthly or annual basis as the case may be: Provided that the taxable person referred to in paragraph (1) of Regulation 9 shall not be obliged to furnish details of the value of his intra-Community supplies or to comply with subparagraphs (*b*) or (*d*) of paragraph (1) of Regulation 6.

EUROPEAN COMMUNITIES (INTRASTAT)
REGULATIONS 1993

(SI No 136 of 1993)

1 These Regulations may be cited as the European Communities (Intrastat) Regulations, 1993.

2 These Regulations shall come into operation on the 22 day of May, 1993.

3 (1) In these Regulations—

"authorised officer" means an officer of the Revenue Commissioners authorised by them in writing to exercise the powers of an authorised officer referred to in these Regulations;

"the basic Regulation" means Council Regulation (EEC) No 3330/91 of 7 November, 1991;

"the Community Regulations" means the basic Regulation, Commission Regulation (EEC) No 3046/92 of 22 October 1992 and Commission Regulation (EEC) No 2256/92 of 31 July 1992 and Commission Regulation (EEC) No 3590/92 of 11 December 1992;

"the Intrastat system" means the Intrastat system referred to in the basic Regulation in so far as that system applies to trade between Member States pursuant to Articles 17 to 28 of that Regulation;

"Member State" means a Member State of the European Economic Community;

"officer of statistics" has the meaning assigned to it by the Statistics Act, 1926 (No 12 of 1926);

"records" means any document or other written or printed material in any form as well as information (including statistical information) stored, maintained or preserved by means of any mechanical or electronic device, whether or not stored, maintained or preserved in a legible form;

"trader" means a person referred in Article 20(5) of the basic Regulation of Article 4 of Commission Regulation (EEC) No 3046/92 of 22 October 1992.

Subject to paragraph (1) of this Regulation, a word or expression that is used in these Regulations and is also used in the Community Regulations shall, unless the context otherwise requires, have the same meaning in these Regulations that it has in those Regulations.

4 (1) The statistical information required by the Intrastat system which a trader is responsible for providing in respect of each month in accordance with the provisions of the Community Regulations shall be furnished to the Revenue Commissioners, on forms provided by them for that purpose, by or on behalf of that trader not later than the 10th working day immediately following the end of the month concerned and the said forms shall be completed in accordance with, as appropriate:—

(*a*) the terms of the manual entitled "VIES and INTRASTAT Traders Manual" published by the Revenue Commissioners in October, 1992, (hereafter in this

Regulation referred to as the "relevant manual") and any document published by them for the time being amending the relevant manual,

(*b*) the terms of any subsequent edition of the relevant manual published by the Revenue Commissioners that is the current such edition (hereafter in this Regulation referred to as a "replacement manual") and any document published by them for the time being amending the replacement manual.

(2) A document referred to in subparagraph (*a*) or (*b*) of paragraph (1) of this Regulation is referred to hereafter in this Regulation as a "supplement".

(3) The Revenue Commissioners may, on written application being made to them by a trader, authorise the furnishing of the statistical information referred to in paragraph (1) of this Regulation by or on behalf of that trader in a manner other than by use of the forms referred to in the said paragraph (1) and the manner to be so authorised shall be one that is specified in the relevant manual, a replacement manual or a supplement.

(4) A trader to whom on authorisation as aforesaid has been given shall furnish or cause to be furnished on his behalf the statistical information referred to in paragraph (1) of this Regulation to the Revenue Commissioners in the manner specified in the authorisation not later than the 10th working day immediately following the end of the month concerned and the information so furnished shall include all the particulars that would have been provided had the trader, or the person acting on his behalf, completed the forms referred to in the said paragraph (1).

(5) The furnishing of statistical information in accordance with paragraph (4) of this Regulation shall have the same effect as if the statistical information was furnished on the forms referred to in paragraph (1) of this Regulation.

(6) A trader who fails to comply with paragraph (1) or (4) of this Regulation shall be guilty of an offence under these Regulations.

(7) *Prima facie* evidence of the relevant manual, a replacement manual or a supplement may be given in proceedings for an offence under these Regulations by the production of a copy of the relevant manual, replacement manual or supplement purporting to be published by the Revenue Commissioners together with a certificate purporting to be signed by an officer of the Revenue Commissioners certifying that the relevant manual, replacement manual or supplement, as the case may be, contains the relevant matters as respects the obligations of the trader concerned (who shall be named in the certificate) under paragraph (1) or (4), as the case may be, of this Regulation.

(8) In proceedings for an offence under these Regulations:—

(*a*) it shall be presumed until the contrary is proved that no authorisation has been given by the Revenue Commissioners under paragraph (3) of this Regulation, and

(*b*) *prima facie* evidence of such an authorisation may be given by the production of a document purporting to be a written application by the trader concerned for the authorisation and of a document purporting to be a copy of the authorisation granted by the Revenue Commissioners.

(9) A certificate referred to in paragraph (7) of this Regulation shall:—

    (*a*) indicate the rank or position in the Office of the Revenue Commissioners of the officer who has signed it.

    (*b*) be admitted in evidence without proof of the signature of that officer.

(10)(*a*) Notice of the publication of the relevant manual shall be published in the Irish Oifigiúil as soon as may be after the commencement of these Regulations.

    (*b*) Notice of the publication of a replacement manual or a supplement shall be published in the Irish Oifigiúil as soon as may be after the publication of the replacement manual or supplement, as the case may be.

    (*c*) A notice under this paragraph shall indicate that a member of the public shall be entitled to be supplied by the Revenue Commissioners free of charge with a copy of the relevant manual, replacement manual or supplement, as the case may be, on request being made by him therefor.

    (*d*) *Prima facie* evidence of the publication of a notice under this paragraph may be given in proceedings for an offence under these Regulations by the production of a copy of the Irish Oifigiúil purporting to contain the notice.

(11) The Revenue Commissioners shall supply to a member of the public, free of charge, a copy of the relevant manual, replacement manual or supplement on request being made by him therefor.

5 (1) The Taoiseach shall specify from time to time assimilation thresholds for the purposes of Article 28 of the basic Regulation.

    (*a*) A specification by the Taoiseach of assimilation thresholds for the purposes of aforesaid shall be published in the Irish Oifigiúil as soon as may be after it is made.

    (*b*) *Prima facie* evidence of a specification as aforesaid may be given in proceedings for an offence under these Regulations by the production of a copy of the Iris Oifigiúil purporting to contain the specification.

6 A trader who, in purported compliance with Regulation 4 of these Regulations, furnishes or causes or permits to be furnished to the Revenue Commissioners information which is false, misleading or incomplete in any respect shall be guilty of an offence under these Regulations.

7 (1) An authorised officer may at all reasonable times enter any premises or place where he reasonably believes records relating to goods to which the intrastat system applies are kept and may require any person on those premises or in that place to produce to him the said records or such of them as he specifies and may search for, inspect and take copies, or extracts from, the said records and may remove the said records from those premises or that place for further inspection.

(2) A person who obstructs, hinders or interferes with an authorised officer in the exercise of the powers conferred on him by paragraph (1) of this Regulation or who refuses without lawful excuse to produce to such an officer records which he is required by such an officer to produce under the said paragraph shall be guilty of an offence under these Regulations.

8 (1) All records received or kept by a trader relating to goods in respect of which he is responsible for furnishing statistical information to the Revenue Commissioners under Regulation 4 of these Regulations shall be preserved by him for a period of not less than 2 years from the end of the month to which they relate.

(2) A trader shall produce or cause to be produced to an authorised officer upon request by that officer the records referred to in paragraph (1) of this Regulation or such of them as that officer specifies.

(3) A trader who fails to comply with paragraph (1) of this Regulation or with a request under paragraph (2) of this Regulation shall be guilty of an offence under these Regulations.

9 An officer of statistics shall:—

(*a*) have access to, and, on request, be given by the Revenue Commissioners copies of, the statistical information furnished to the Revenue Commissioners by or on behalf of traders under Regulation 4 of these Regulations,

(*b*) on request, be given such information by the Revenue Commissioners as they deem fit to give relating to goods to which the Intrastat system applies and which has come into their possession through the exercise by an authorised officer of his powers under Regulation 7 or 8 of these Regulations.

10 (1) Statistical information furnished by or on behalf of a trader under Regulation 4 of these Regulations shall not, save with the consent of that trader or for the purposes of a prosecution under these Regulations, be shown or communicated to any person other than an officer of the Revenue Commissioners or an officer of statistics in the course of his official duties.

(2) As far as practicable statistics derived from statistical information furnished by or on behalf of a trader under Regulation 4 of these Regulations shall not be published or disseminated in a manner that would result directly or indirectly in the disclosure of details relating to any business of that trader but nothing in this paragraph shall be held to impose a duty owed to a trader to avoid such a disclosure.

11 (1) A trader who by act or omission fails to comply with a provision of the Community Regulations shall be guilty of an offence under these Regulations.

(2) A person who is guilty of an offence under these Regulations shall be liable on summary conviction to a fine of [€1,265][1].

(3) Where a trader is convicted of an offence under Regulation 4 of these Regulations he shall, if the failure in respect of which he is convicted of the offence is continued after conviction, be guilty of a further offence on every day on which the failure continues and for each such offence he shall be liable on summary conviction to a fine of [€60][2].

(4) Proceedings for an offence under these Regulations may be brought and prosecuted by the Revenue Commissioners.

Amendments

[1] Substituted by FA 2001, s 240 and Sch 5 Part 4 with effect from 1 January 2002; previously "£1,000".

[2] Substituted by FA 2001, s 240 and Sch 5 Part 4 with effect from 1 January 2002; previously "£50".

12 (1) Where an offence under these Regulations is committed by a body corporate and is proved to have been committed with the consent or connivance of or be attributable to any neglect on the part of a person being a director, manager, secretary or other similar officer of the body corporate, or a person who was purporting to act in any such capacity, that person as well as the body corporate shall be guilty of an offence and shall be liable to be proceeded against and punished as if he were guilty of the first-mentioned offence.

(2) Where the affairs of a body corporate are managed by its members, paragraph (1) of this Regulation shall apply in relation to the acts and defaults of a member in connection with his functions of management as if he were a director of the body corporate.

13 (1) Subject to the provisions of this Regulation, in proceedings for an offence under these Regulations a certificates signed by an officer of the Revenue Commissioners which certifies that he has inspected the relevant records of the Revenue Commissioners and that it appears from them that the trader concerned (who shall be named in the certificate):—

(*a*) was required under Regulation 4 of these Regulations to provided statistical information of a kind and at a time or times specified in the certificate, and failed to do so, or

(*b*) failed, in a manner specified in the certificate, to do a stated act or furnish stated records or particulars in accordance with any of the provisions of these Regulations, shall be *prima facie* evidence that the trader concerned was so required to provide statistical information as aforesaid or, as the case may be, failed to do a stated act or furnish stated records or particulars as aforesaid.

(2) A certificate referred to in paragraph (1) of this Regulation shall:—

(*a*) indicate the rank or position in the Office of the Revenue Commissioners of the officer who has signed it,

(*b*) be admitted in evidence without proof of the signature of that officer.

(3) If in proceedings against a person for an offence under these Regulations it is proposed to tender in evidence a certificate referred to in paragraph (1) of this Regulation the prosecution shall cause to be served on the person not less than 21 days after the commencement of the trial of the offence a copy of the certificate together with a notice informing the person:—

(*a*) that it is proposed to tender the certificate in evidence in the proceedings,

(*b*) that the certificate shall not, without the leave of the Court, be admitted in evidence if the person serves on the solicitor for the prosecution not later than 7 days before the commencement of the trial of the offence a notice objecting to the admissibility of the certificate.

(*c*) that if the person serves a notice as aforesaid and the facts stated in the certificate are required to be proved, wholly or partly, by oral evidence at the trial of the offence the person shall be liable to pay to the prosecution the costs and witness expenses incurred in so proving the said facts unless, in the opinion of the Court, the person had good grounds for serving the said notice.

(4) (*a*) A certificate referred to in paragraph (1) of this Regulation shall not, without the leave of the Court, be admitted in evidence if the defendant concerned has served on the solicitor for the prosecution a notice referred to in paragraph (3)(*b*) of this Regulation within the period mentioned in that provision.

(*b*) If the defendant concerned has served a notice as aforesaid and the facts stated in the certificate are required to be proved, wholly or partly, by oral evidence at the trial of the offence in question the Court shall, unless it is of the opinion that the defendant had good grounds for serving the said notice, order him to pay to the prosecution the costs and witness expenses incurred in so proving the said facts.

14 The Revenue Commissioners may, in their discretion, mitigate any fine incurred under these Regulations, or stay or compound any proceedings for recovery thereof, and may also, after judgement, further mitigate or entirely remit such a fine.

VALUE ADDED TAX (RETURNS) REGULATIONS 1993

(SI No 247 of 1993)

Amendments

Revoked by Value Added Tax (Returns) Regulations 1996 (SI 294/1996), r 5.

VALUE ADDED TAX (PAYMENT OF TAX ON INTRA-COMMUNITY ACQUISITION OF CERTAIN NEW MEANS OF TRANSPORT) REGULATIONS 1993

(SI No 248 of 1993)

The Revenue Commissioners, in exercise of the powers conferred on them by sections 19(4) and 32 of the Value Added Tax Act, 1972 (No 22 of 1972), hereby make the following Regulations:

1 These Regulation may be cited as the Value Added Tax (Payment of Tax on Intra-Community Acquisitions of Certain New Means of Transport) Regulations, 1993.

2 These Regulations shall come into operation on the 1st day of September, 1993.

3 In these Regulations—

"the Act" means the Value Added Tax Act, 1972;

"new aircraft" means a new means of transport other than a motorised land vehicle or a vessel;

"new vessel" means a new means of transport other than a motorised land vehicle or an aircraft.

4 Where a person makes an intra-Community acquisition of a new aircraft or a new vessel, in respect of which he is not entitled to a deduction of tax under section 12 of the Act, the person shall—

(*a*) complete such form as may be provided by the Revenue Commissioners for the purpose of this Regulation,

(*b*) provide such further documentation in support of the details provided on the form as the Revenue Commissioners may request,

(*c*) certify that the particulars and documentation provided are true and accurate,

(*d*) not later than three days after the due date furnish, to the Collector of Customs and Excise for the area in which he is resident, the completed form and supporting documentation referred to in paragraph (*a*) and (*b*) of this Regulation and at the same time pay to that Collector the amount of tax due,

(*e*) if requested to do so, make the new aircraft or the new vessel, as appropriate, available for inspection in the State by an officer of the Revenue Commissioners.

5 The Value Added Tax (Payment of Tax on Intra-Community Acquisitions of Means of Transport) Regulations, 1992 (SI No 412 of 1992), are hereby revoked.

EUROPEAN COMMUNITIES (VALUE ADDED TAX) REGULATIONS 1993

(SI No 345 of 1993)

1 (1) These Regulations may be cited as the European Communities (Value Added Tax) Regulations, 1993.

(2) These Regulations shall be construed together with the Value Added Tax Acts 1972 to 1993.

2 In these Regulations—

"advance payment" means the advance payment referred to in section 19(6) of the Principal Act;

"due date" means the due date referred to in section 19(6) of the Principal Act;

"November liability" means—

    (*a*) the amount of tax which would be payable in accordance with section 19(3) of the Principal Act, or

    (*b*) nil, where an amount of tax would be repayable in accordance with section 20(1) of the Principal Act,

if the November period were to be treated as a taxable period;

"November period" means the month of November immediately preceding a due date;

"the Principal Act" means the Value Added Tax Act, 1972.

3 Notwithstanding the provisions of section 19(6) of the Principal Act, for the purposes of the application of the said section 19(6) and of these Regulations, all references in the said section 19(6) to the 1st day of December shall be construed as references to the 10th day of December.

4 Subject to his complying with Regulation 5, a taxable person who is liable to pay an advance payment in accordance with section 19(6) of the Principal Act may opt, as an alternative, to pay his November liability and in such circumstances all the provisions of the said section 19(6) shall apply to the November liability as if it were advance payment.

5 Where a taxable person desires to avail of the option provided for in Regulation 4, he shall, by the due date, notify the Collector-General accordingly in writing and declare his November liability to the Collector-General in writing.

VALUE ADDED TAX (DETERMINATION OF TAX DUE BY REFERENCE TO MONEYS RECEIVED) (AMENDMENT) REGULATIONS 1994

(SI No 259 of 1994)

1 (1) These Regulations may be cited as the Value Added Tax (Determination of Tax Due by Reference to Moneys Received) (Amendment) Regulations, 1994.

(2) The Principal Regulations and these Regulations shall be construed together as one and may be cited together as the Value Added Tax (Determination of Tax Due by Reference to Moneys Received) Regulations, 1992 and 1994.

2 In these Regulations—

"the Act" means the Value Added Tax Act, 1972;

"the Principal Regulations" means the Value Added Tax (Determination of Tax Due by Reference to Moneys Received) Regulations 1992 (SI No 306 of 1992).

3

Note

Para 3 substituted "section 14(1)(*a*)" for "section 14(1)" and "persons who are not registered persons" for "unregistered persons" in Value Added Tax (Determination of Tax Due by Reference to Moneys Received) Regulations 1992 (SI 306/1992), para 3.

This regulation is made to take account of the fact that traders with annual turnover below £250,000 may now avail of the cash receipts basis of accounting for VAT.

4

Notes

Para 4 substituted Value Added Tax (Determination of Tax Due by Reference to Moneys Received) Regulations 1992 (SI 306/ 1992), para 4.

5

Notes

Para 5 substituted Value Added Tax (Determination of Tax Due by Reference to Moneys Received) Regulations 1992 (SI 306/ 1992), para 9(1).

DISABLED DRIVERS AND DISABLED PASSENGERS (TAX CONCESSIONS) REGULATIONS 1994

(SI No 353 of 1994)

1 These Regulations may be cited as the Disabled Drivers and Disabled Passengers (Tax Concessions) Regulations, 1994, and shall come into operation on the 1st day of December, 1994.

Cross-references

FA 1989, s 92.

Notes

These regulations, which came into force on 1 December 1994, set out the medical criteria, certification procedures, repayment limits and other matters necessary to give effect to FA 1989, s 92 which provides for tax concessions for disabled drivers and disabled passengers.

---

2 (1) In these Regulations —

"adapted", in relation to a vehicle, does not include adaptations of production line models which are available from the manufacturer or assembler thereof as an optional extra, and "adaptation" shall be construed accordingly;

"authorised person" means a person authorised under section 136 of the Finance Act, 1992 (No 9 of 1992);

"Board medical certificate" means a certificate duly completed in the form prescribed in the Second Schedule and issued by the Disabled Drivers Medical Board of Appeal or a certificate duty completed in the form prescribed in the Second Schedule to the Disabled Drivers (Tax Concessions) Regulations, 1989 (S.I. No 340 of 1989), and so issued under those regulations;

"conversion" has the meaning assigned to it in section 130 of the Finance Act, 1992;

"disabled driver" means a severely and permanently disabled person who possesses a certificate of the kind referred to in paragraph (*a*) or (*b*) of Regulation 4 and whose disablement is of such a nature that the person concerned could not drive a vehicle unless it is specially constructed or adapted to take account of that disablement;

"disabled passenger" means a severely and permanently disabled person who possesses a certificate of the kind referred to in paragraph (*a*) or (*b*) of Regulation 4 and for whom a vehicle has been specially constructed or adapted to the extent prescribed in Regulation 10 (1)(*a*), to take account of that passenger's disablement;

"disabled person" means a person who is severely and permanently disabled, fulfilling one or more of the medical criteria set out in Regulation 3;

"licensing authority" has the meaning assigned to it in section 130 of the Finance Act, 1992;

"purchased" does not include any form of lease arrangement;

"qualifying organisation" means a philanthropic organisation which is not funded primarily by—

(*a*)   the State,

(*b*)   any board established by statute, or

(*c*)   any public or local authority,

which organisation is chiefly engaged, in a voluntary capacity on a non-commercial basis, in the care and transport of severely and permanently disabled persons and which is recognised as such, for the purposes of these Regulations, by the Revenue Commissioner;

"registered" has the meaning assigned to it in section 130 of the Finance Act, 1992;

"residual value added tax" means an amount determined by the Revenue Commissioners as being equivalent to the amount of Value Added tax which would be included in the open market selling price of a vehicle if it were sold by an authorised person at the time specified in these Regulations;

"residual vehicle registration tax" means an amount determined by the Revenue Commissioners as being equivalent to the amount of vehicle registration tax which would be chargeable if that vehicle were liable for such tax at the time specified in these Regulations;

"vehicle" has the meaning assigned to it in section 130 of the Finance Act, 1992.

(2) In these Regulations a reference to a Regulation or Schedule is to a Regulation of, or Schedule to, these Regulations and a reference to a paragraph or subparagraph is to a paragraph or subparagraph of the provision in which the reference occurs.

Medical criteria

3 For the purposes of section 92(2)(*a*) of the Finance Act, 1989, the eligibility on medical ground of disabled persons who are severely and permanently disabled shall be assessed by reference to any one or more of the following medical criteria:

(*a*)   persons who are wholly or almost wholly without the use of both legs;

(*b*)   persons wholly without the use of one of their legs and almost wholly without the use of the other leg such that they are severely restricted as to movement of their lower limbs;

(*c*)   persons without both hands or without both arms;

(*d*)   persons without one or both legs;

(*e*)   persons wholly or almost wholly without the use of both hands or arms and wholly or almost wholly without the use of one leg;

(*f*)   persons having the medical condition of dwarfism and who have serious difficulties of movement of the lower limbs.

4 Without prejudice to Regulation 5, a claim for repayment or remission under these Regulations shall be allowed only where the person who makes the claim, or in connection with whom the claim is made, is in possession of either —

(*a*)   a primary medical certificate duly completed in the form prescribed in the First Schedule as evidence of qualifying disablement, signed, dated and endorsed with the official stamp by the appropriate Director of Community Care and Medical Officer of Health, or

(*b*)   a Board medical certificate duly completed in the form prescribed in the Second Schedule as evidence of qualifying disablement, signed and dated by a member of the Disabled Drivers Medical Board of Appeal:

Provided that compliance with this Regulation may be waived by the Revenue Commissioners in the case of a claim made by a qualifying organisation.

5 Any person who is deemed, by virtue of section 92(3)(*b*) of the Finance Act, 1989, to be a person who possesses a primary medical certificate shall be deemed to have satisfied the Revenue Commissioners and the licensing authority concerned that that person is a disabled driver or a disabled passenger as the case may be.

Medical Board of Appeal

6 (1) Subject to Regulation 19(3), on the nomination of the Minister for Health the Minister for Finance shall appoint, for a period in each case of 4 years, three medical practitioners to the Disabled Drivers Medical Board of Appeal (in these Regulations referred to as "the Board") and any such practitioner may be reappointed by the Minister for Finance on the nomination of the Minister for Health for a further such period or periods.

(2) Every vacancy on the Board shall be filled by the appointment by the Minister for Finance of a medical practitioner, nominated for that purpose by the Minister for Health, for the remainder of the period to which the former member's appointment to the Board had related.

(3) Whenever the Minister for Health so requests, the Minister for Finance shall remove any named person from the Board.

(4) A person who is dissatisfied by a decision of a Director of Community Care and Medical Officer of Health in respect of primary medical certification may appeal to the Board within 28 days, or such longer period as it may allow, of the person first being informed of that decision.

(5) Where the Board adjudicates in favour of the disabled driver or disabled passenger concerned, as the case may be, it shall issue a Board medical certificate.

7 Where a licensing authority or the Revenue Commissioners have reason to believe that the person named on a primary medical certificate or a Board medical certificate or who was deemed to have satisfied the said authority or Commissioners under the terms of Regulation 5, does not fulfil any one of the criteria set out in Regulation 3, they shall refer such person to the Board who shall cancel the primary medical certificate or Board medical certificate in question, if they consider it appropriate to do so.

Reliefs for disabled drivers

8 (1) Where a person satisfied the Revenue Commissioners that that person is a disabled driver and has borne or paid Value Added tax, vehicle registration tax or residual vehicle registration tax in respect of a vehicle or in respect of the adaptation of a vehicle which —

(*a*)   is specially constructed or adapted to take account of that person's disablement,

(*b*)   is purchased by that person,

(*c*)   is registered in the name of that person, and

(*d*)   is fitted with an engine whose capacity is not greater than 2,000 cubic centimetres,

that person shall be entitled to be repaid the said amounts of tax and residual vehicle registration tax, subject to the limit specified in Regulation 9 for the purposes of this Regulation:

Provided that the Revenue Commissioners shall repay residual vehicle registration tax only where the person concerned has purchased the vehicle in question from an authorised person.

(2) Where at the time of registration of a vehicle in the name of a person who satisfies the Revenue Commissioners that that person is a disabled driver and the vehicle in question complies with the provisions set out at subparagraphs (*a*) (*b*) and (*d*) of paragraph (1), the Revenue Commissioners shall remit the vehicle registration tax payable, subject to the limit specified in Regulation 9 for the purposes of this Regulation.

(3) Where, after these Regulations come into force, a person becomes a severely and permanently disabled person who fulfils one of the medical criteria set out in Regulation 3 after that person has purchased a vehicle which complies with the provisions set out at subparagraphs (*c*) and (*d*) of paragraph (1), and the vehicle is specially adapted to take account of that person's disablement, that person shall be entitled to be repaid —

(*a*)   the amount of residual Value Added tax and residual vehicle registration tax appropriate to the vehicle at the time such person lodges a claim with the Revenue Commissioners, and

(*b*)   the Value Added tax charged in respect of the adaptation of that vehicle,

subject to the limit specified in Regulation 9 for the purposes of this Regulation.

(4) Where a person receives a repayment or remission under paragraph (1) or (2), that person shall undertake —

(*a*)   to use the vehicle in question for a period of 2 years from the date of purchase, and to inform the Revenue Commissioners immediately if any circumstances arise during that period where the vehicle is sold or otherwise disposed of by that person, and

(*b*)   to abide by the provisions of Regulation 15.

(5) Where a person receives a repayment or remission under paragraph (3), that person shall undertake —

(*a*)   to use the vehicle in question for a period of 2 years from the date on which the Revenue Commissioners receive the application for the repayment, and to inform the Revenue Commissioners immediately if any circumstances arise during that period where the vehicle is sold or otherwise disposed of by that person, and

(*b*)   to abide by the provisions of Regulation 15.

9 The total amount to be repaid and remitted under Regulation 8 or under paragraph (3) and, in so far as it relates to that paragraph, paragraph (4) of Regulation 12 shall not exceed £7,500 in respect of any vehicle.

Reliefs for disabled passengers

10 (1) Where a person satisfies the Revenue Commissioners that that person is a severely and permanently disabled passenger or a family member of such a disabled passenger residing with and responsible for the transportation of that disabled passenger and such person has borne or paid Value Added tax, vehicle registration tax or residual vehicle registration tax in respect of a vehicle or in respect of the adaptation of a vehicle which —

(*a*)   has been specially constructed or adapted for use by that disabled passenger, and where the vehicle is so adapted, the cost of such adaptation excluding Value Added tax consists of not less than the amount specified for the purpose in section 92(1) of the Finance Act, 1989:

Provided that in calculating the cost of adaptation of such vehicle, if the Revenue Commissioners so approve, there shall be included —

(i)   the cost of conversion of that vehicle, excluding the additional vehicle registration tax incurred in such conversion, and

(ii)   the purchase cost excluding Value Added tax of any adaptations previously fitted to another vehicle adapted for use by that disabled passenger, and refitted to the vehicle in question,

(*b*)   has been purchased by the disabled passenger or by the said family member of that disabled passenger for the purpose of transporting that person, and

(*c*)   is fitted with an engine whose capacity is not greater than 4,000 cubic centimetres,

the person who has borne or paid the said amounts of tax and residual vehicle registration tax shall be entitled to be repaid same, subject to the limit specified in Regulation 11 for the purposes of this Regulation:

Provided that the Revenue Commissioners shall repay residual vehicle registration tax only where the said person has purchased the vehicle in question from an authorised person.

(2) Where at the time of registration of a vehicle by a severely and permanently disabled passenger or by a family member of a severely and permanently disabled passenger residing with the responsible for the transportation of that disabled person and the vehicle in question complies with the provisions set out at subparagraphs (*a*),(*b*) and (*c*) of paragraph (1), the Revenue Commissioners shall remit the vehicle registration tax

payable, subject to the limit specified in Regulation 11 for the purposes of this Regulation.

(3) Where, after these Regulations come into force, a person becomes a severely and permanently disabled person who fulfils one of the medical criteria set out in Regulation 3 after that person or a family member of that person residing with and responsible for the transportation of that person has purchased a vehicle which complies with the provision set out at paragraph (1)(*c*) and the vehicle is adapted to the extent outlined in paragraph (1)(*a*) for the disabled person's use as a passenger, the person who has purchased the vehicle shall be entitled to be repaid —

> (*a*)   the amount of residual Value Added tax and residual vehicle registration tax appropriate to the vehicle at the time such person lodges a claim with the Revenue Commissioners, and
>
> (*b*)   the Value Added tax charged in respect of the adaptation of that vehicle,

subject to the limit specified in Regulation 11 for the purposes of this Regulation.

> (4) (*a*)   Where a person receives a repayment or remission under paragraph (1) or (2) of this Regulation that person shall undertake —
>
> > (i)   to use the vehicle in question for the transportation of the disabled passenger in question, for a period of 2 years from the date of purchase, and to inform the Revenue Commissioners immediately if any circumstances arise during that period where the vehicle is sold or otherwise disposed of by that person, and
> >
> > (ii)   to abide by the provisions of Regulation 15.
>
> (*b*)   Where a person receives a repayment or remission under paragraph (3) that person shall undertake —
>
> > (i)   to use the vehicle in question for the transportation of the disabled passenger in question, for a period of 2 years from the date on which the Revenue Commissioners receive the application for repayment, and to inform the Revenue Commissioners immediately if any circumstances arise during that period where the vehicle is sold or otherwise disposed of by that person, and
> >
> > (ii)   to abide by the provisions of Regulation 15.
>
> (*c*)   Where the Revenue Commissioners accept a claim under this Regulation in respect of the transport of a disabled passenger, they shall not accept a claim (other than in the circumstances to which Regulation 15 applies) relating to any further vehicle in respect of the transport of the same passenger for a period of 2 years from the date of purchase of the vehicle for which the claim was accepted where such claim was made under the provisions of paragraph (1) or (2), and a period of 2 years from the date of receipt of the application by the Revenue Commissioners, where such application was made under the provisions of paragraph (3).
>
> (*d*)   Where the Revenue Commissioners have accepted a claim for repayment of vehicle registration tax in respect of the transport of a disabled person as passenger under the Disabled Drivers (Tax Concessions) Regulations, 1989,

they shall not accept a claim relating to any further vehicle in respect of the transport of the same passenger for a period of 2 years from the date of purchase of the vehicle for which the claim was accepted:

Provided that the Revenue Commissioners may waive this provision in exceptional circumstances subject to the refund of a portion of the repayment, calculated in accordance with the formula set out in Regulation 15 (1).

(5) (*a*) In exceptional circumstances, the Revenue Commissioners may waive the condition concerning residency of a claimant under Regulation 10.

(*b*) The Revenue Commissioners shall waive the conditions concerning both family membership and residency of a claimant under Regulation 10 in the case of a claim lodged by a person appointed by the President of the High Court to act on behalf of a disabled passenger who is a Ward of Court.

11 The total amount to be repaid and remitted under Regulation 10 shall not exceed £12,500 in respect of any vehicle.

Reliefs for qualifying organisations

12 (1) Where a qualifying organisation satisfied the Revenue Commissioners that it has borne or paid Value Added tax, vehicle registration tax or residual vehicle registration tax in respect of a vehicle or in respect of the adaptation of a vehicle which, subject to paragraph (2)—

(*a*) is specially constructed or adapted for the transport of disabled persons, and where the vehicle is so adapted the cost of such adaptation, excluding value-added tax, consists of not less than the amount specified for the purpose in subsection 92 (1) of the Finance Act, 1989:

Provided that in calculating the cost of adaptation of such vehicle, if the Revenue Commissioners so approve, there shall be included —

(i) the cost of conversion of that vehicle, excluding the additional vehicle registration tax incurred in such conversion, and

(ii) the purchase cost excluding Value Added tax of any adaptations previously fitted to another vehicle adapted for use by that qualifying organisation, and refitted to the vehicle in question,

(*b*) is purchased by that organisation,

(*c*) is registered in the name of that organisation, and

(*d*) is fitted with an engine whose capacity is not greater than 4,000 cubic centimetres,

that organisation shall be entitled to be repaid the said amounts of tax and residual vehicle registration tax, subject to the limit specified in Regulation 13 for the purposes of this paragraph:

Provided that the Revenue Commissioners shall repay residual vehicle registration tax only where the said organisation has purchased the vehicle in question from an authorised person.

(2) Where the vehicle referred to in paragraph (1) has been specially constructed or adapted for the transport of 5 or more disabled persons, the provisions of subparagraph (1)(*d*) and of Regulation 13 shall not apply where the seating capacity in the vehicle for passengers who are not disabled persons is not greater than twice the seating capacity for disabled passengers.

(3) Where a qualifying organisation satisfies the Revenue Commissioners that it has borne or paid Value Added tax, vehicle registration tax or residual vehicle registration tax in respect of a vehicle or in respect of the adaptation of a vehicle which —

(*a*) is specially constructed or adapted to take account of the disablement of a disabled person as driver,

(*b*) is purchased by that organisation,

(*c*) is registered in the name of that organisation, and

(*d*) is fitted with an engine whose capacity is not greater then 2,000 cubic centimetres,

that organisation shall be entitled to be repaid the said amounts of tax and residual vehicle registration tax, subject to the limit specified in Regulation 9 for the purposes of this paragraph:

Provided that the Revenue Commissioners shall repay residual vehicle registration tax only where the said organisation has purchased the vehicle in question from an authorised person.

(4) Where, at the time of registration of a vehicle by a qualifying organisation, the Revenue Commissioners are satisfied that the vehicle in question complies with the provisions set out at subparagraphs (*a*), (*b*) and (*d*) of paragraph (1) or set out at subparagraphs (*a*), (*b*) and (*d*) of paragraph (3), as appropriate, they shall remit the vehicle registration tax payable.

(5) The Revenue Commissioners shall give a repayment of remission under this Regulation only where they are satisfied that the vehicle in question is a reasonable requirement of the organisation making the claim, having regard, inter alia, to the number of disabled persons being transported by that organisation, and the number and capacity of vehicles already owned by that organisation.

(6) Where an organisation receives a repayment or remission under paragraph (1) or (3) that organisation shall undertake —

(*a*) to use the vehicle in question for a period of 2 years from the date of purchase, and to inform the Revenue Commissioners immediately if any circumstances arise during that period where the vehicle is sold or otherwise disposed of by that organisation, and

(*b*) to abide by the provisions of Regulation 15.

(7) The Revenue Commissioners shall consult the National Rehabilitation Board in respect of each organisation which applies to them under these Regulations.

(8) Where the Revenue Commissioners have reasonable cause to believe that a qualifying organisation should no longer be entitled to the benefit of these Regulations,

they shall consult the National Rehabilitation Board and may withdraw the concessions from such organisation.

13 The total amount to be repaid and remitted under paragraph (1) and, in so far as it relates to that paragraph, paragraph (4) of Regulation 12 shall not exceed £12,500 in respect of any vehicle.

Passenger vehicles qualifying more than once

14 Where a repayment or remission has been granted under Regulation 10 or 12 in respect of a vehicle which is subsequently purchased for the transport of a different disabled passenger or by a different qualifying organisation, and the adaptations remain in the vehicle at the time of such subsequent purchase, the requirements set out at Regulation 10(1)(*a*) or 12(1)(*a*), as the case may be, shall be deemed to be fulfilled.

Refunds to the Revenue Commissioners

15 (1) Where a beneficiary of a repayment or remission under Regulation 8 or 10 in respect of a vehicle (in this Regulation referred to as "the first-mentioned vehicle")—

(*a*) sells it or otherwise disposes of it within 2 years of the date of purchase or, in the case of a person referred to in Regulation 8(3) or 10(3), within 2 years of the date on which the Revenue Commissioners receive the application for repayment, or

(*b*) claims a repayment or remission under the same Regulation in respect of a subsequent vehicle purchased by that person within 2 years of purchasing the first-mentioned vehicle, or, in the case of a person referred to in Regulation 8(3) or 10(3), within 2 years of the date on which the Revenue Commissioners receive the application for repayment,

such person shall refund to the Revenue Commissioners a portion of the amount which was either or both repaid and remitted on the first-mentioned vehicle, calculated by the Revenue Commissioners according to the following formula:

$$A \times \frac{B}{(C + D)}$$

where:

A   is the open market selling price of the first-mentioned vehicle on the date of its sale or disposal or on the date of purchase of the subsequent vehicle, whichever is applicable,

B   is the total amount repaid or remitted in respect of the first-mentioned vehicle and any adaptations thereto,

C   is the open market selling price of the first-mentioned vehicle at the time of its purchase by the beneficiary, and

D   is the cost including Value Added tax of any adaptations to the first-mentioned vehicle on which repayment was claimed by the beneficiary.

(2) The refund referred to in paragraph (1) shall be paid to the Revenue Commissioners within one month of the sale or disposal of the first-mentioned vehicle, but where the

circumstances referred to at paragraph (1)(*b*) apply, not later than the time of the repayment or remission of any tax in respect of the subsequent vehicle.

(3) Where a qualifying organisation which receives a repayment or remission under Regulation 12 in respect of a vehicle sells it or otherwise disposes of it within 2 years of the date of purchase such organisation shall refund to the Revenue Commissioners a portion of the amount which was either or both repaid and remitted on the vehicle, calculated by the Revenue Commissioners according to the following formula:

$$A \times \frac{B}{(C+D)}$$

where:

A   is the open market selling price of the vehicle on the date of its sale or disposal,

B   is the total amount repaid or remitted in respect of the vehicle and any adaptations thereto,

C   is the open market selling price of the vehicle at the time of its purchase by the organisation, and

D   is the cost including Value Added tax of any adaptations to the vehicle on which repayment was claimed by the organisation.

(4) The refund referred to in paragraph (3) shall be paid to the Revenue Commissioners within one month of the sale or disposal of the vehicle in question.

(5) The Revenue Commissioners shall not repay or remit any tax or residual vehicle registration tax under Regulation 8, 10 or 12 in respect of any vehicle unless the provisions of paragraph (2) or (4), as the case may be, have been fulfilled.

(6) In exceptional cases, and subject to such conditions as they consider necessary in each such case, the Revenue Commissioners may reduce the amount of the refund required under this Regulation.

Fuel repayments

16 (1) The excise duty paid on any fuel used for combustion in the engine of a vehicle on which repayment or remission of tax, or residual vehicle registration tax has been granted in accordance with these Regulations shall be repaid by the Revenue Commissioners where the use of the fuel was related to the transportation of the disabled person or persons concerned whether as driver or passenger.

(2) Where the repayment or remission of tax or residual vehicle registration tax was made under Regulation 8 or 10, the repayment of excise duty on fuel referred to in paragraph (1) shall be limited to the duty on an annual maximum of 600 gallons per beneficiary.

(3) Where the repayment or remission of tax or residual vehicle registration tax was made under Regulation 12, the repayment of excise duty on fuel referred to in paragraph (1) shall be limited to the duty on an annual maximum of 900 gallons per vehicle.

(4) The excise duty paid on any fuel used for combustion in the engine of a vehicle which would have qualified for repayment or remission of Value Added tax, vehicle

registration tax or residual vehicle registration tax in accordance with these Regulations but for the fact that the vehicle was purchased prior to the coming into effect of these Regulations, shall be repaid by the Revenue Commissioners where the use of the fuel was related to the transportation of the disabled person or persons concerned whether as driver or passenger, and the provisions of paragraphs (2) and (3) shall apply with any necessary modifications.

Road Tax

17 The licensing authority shall remit the excise duty which would, but for this provision, be payable under section 1 of the Finance (Excise Duties) (Vehicles) Act, 1952 (No 24 of 1952) (being the duty known as road tax), on any vehicle which qualifies for relief under regulation 8, 10 or 12.

General

18 (1) A person or organisation wishing to avail of the provisions of Regulation 8, 10 or 12 shall complete the Declaration in the Third Schedule in respect of each vehicle involved, and such claim form as may be provided for the purpose by the Revenue Commissioners and present them to the Revenue Commissioners, together with such documentary evidence as they shall require.

(2) A person or organisation wishing to avail of the provisions of Regulation 17 shall apply to the appropriate licensing authority and produce to it evidence that the vehicle has qualified for relief under Regulation 8, 10 or 12, and, in the case of an applicant who has qualified for relief under Regulation 8, a valid current driving licence.

REVOCATION AND TRANSITIONAL PROVISIONS, ETC

19 (1) The Disabled Drivers (Tax Concessions) Regulations, 1989 (SI No 340 of 1989), are hereby revoked.

(2) Any primary medical certificate or other certificate issued under the Regulations revoked by paragraph (1) shall be deemed to be a valid certificate for the purposes of these Regulations, and such certificate and person named thereon shall be subject to the provisions of Regulation 7.

(3) Notwithstanding paragraph (1), the Board appointed under Regulation 6 of the Disabled Drivers (Tax Concessions) Regulations, 1989, shall continue for the period of its appointment as if appointed under these Regulations and Regulation 6(1) of these Regulations shall be construed accordingly.

Regulation 4(a)

FIRST SCHEDULE
PRIMARY MEDICAL CERTIFICATE

Issued for the purposes of section 92 of the Finance Act, 1989, and the Disabled Drivers and Disabled Passengers (Tax Concessions) Regulations, 1994.

Name of applicant: Mr./Mrs./Miss/Ms *...

Normal Address: ....

....

....

I, ..., Director of Community Care and Medical Officer of Health for the .... Health Board area, hereby certify that in my opinion the person named above is a severely and permanently disabled person who meets one or more of the medical criteria set out in the Disabled Drivers and Disabled Passengers (Tax Concessions) Regulations, 1994.

Particulars of the applicant's disablement are as follows:**

(*a*)   the applicant is wholly or almost wholly without the use of both legs;

(*b*)   the applicant is wholly without the use of one leg and almost wholly without the use of the other leg such that the applicant is severely restricted as to movement of the lower limbs;

(*c*)   the applicant is without both hands or without both arms;

(*d*)   the applicant is without one or both legs;

(*e*)   the applicant is wholly or almost wholly without the use of both hands or arms and wholly or almost wholly without the use of one leg;

(*f*)   the applicant has the medical condition of dwarfism and has serious difficulties of movement of the lower limbs.

Date: ....

....(Signature)

Director of Community Care and Medical Officer of Health,

....Health Board.

Official Stamp

*Delete as appropriate.

**Tick as appropriate and cross out particulars that do not apply.

Regulation 4(b)

SECOND SCHEDULE

BOARD MEDICAL CERTIFICATE

Issued, on appeal, for the purposes of section 92 of the Finance Act, 1989, and the Disabled Drivers and Disabled Passengers (Tax Concessions) Regulations, 1994.

Name of applicant: Mr./Mrs./Miss/Ms * ....

Normal Address: ....

....

....

The Disabled Drivers Medical Board of Appeal hereby certifies that in its opinion the person named above is a severely and permanently disabled person who meets one or more of the medical criteria set out in the Disabled Drivers and Disabled Passengers (Tax Concessions) Regulations, 1994.

Particulars of the applicant's disablement are as follows:**

(*a*☐)   the applicant is wholly or almost wholly without the use of both legs;

(*b*☐)   the applicant is wholly without the use of one leg and almost wholly with-out the use of the other leg such that the applicant is severely restricted as to movement of the lower limbs;

(*c*☐)   the applicant is without both hands or without both arms;

(*d*☐)   the applicant is without one or both legs;

(*e*☐)   the applicant is wholly or almost wholly without the use of both hands or arms and wholly or almost wholly without the use of one leg;

(*f*☐)   the applicant has the medical condition of dwarfism and has serious difficulties of movement of the lower limbs.

Date: ....

....(Signature)

For and on behalf of the Disabled Drivers Medical Board of Appeal and a member of that Board.

*Delete as appropriate.

**Tick as appropriate and cross out particulars that do not apply.

Regulation 18

THIRD SCHEDULE

DISABLED DRIVERS AND DISABLED PASSENGERS (TAX CONCESSIONS) REGULATIONS, 1994.

(Every applicant must complete Part I, II or III, as appropriate)

Part I

DECLARATION BY DISABLED DRIVER.

NAME OF DISABLED DRIVER * ....

ADDRESS ....

....

....

I hereby declare as follows:

Vehicle, registration number (if available) ....

engine number .... and

chassis number ....,

is registered or about to be registered in my name, is intended for my personal use as driver and has been specially constructed or adapted to take account of my disablement. I am unable to drive any vehicle not specially adapted for my use. I am the holder of a valid current driving licence for the class to which the vehicle belongs.

Signed: . ... (applicant)

Date: . ...

WARNING: ANY PERSON WHO MAKES A FALSE DECLARATION WILL INCUR SEVERE PENALTIES.

PART II

DECLARATION BY OR ON BEHALF OF A DISABLED PASSENGER

NAME OF DISABLED PASSENGER * ....

ADDRESS ....

....

....

Where a family member is applying in respect of the transport of the above-mentioned person:

NAME OF FAMILY MEMBER APPLYING ....

ADDRESS ....

....

....

I hereby declare as follows:

Vehicle, registration number (if available) ....

engine number .... and

chassis number ....,

has been specially constructed or adapted to take account of the disablement of the passenger mentioned above and has been purchased for the purpose of transporting the passenger in question.

Signed: .... (applicant)

Date: . ...

WARNING: ANY PERSON WHO MAKES A FALSE DECLARATION WILL INCUR SEVERE PENALTIES.

PART III

DECLARATION ON BEHALF OF A QUALIFYING ORGANISATION

NAME OF ORGANISATION...

ADDRESS ....

....

....

I hereby declare as follows:

Vehicle, registration number (if available) ....

engine number .... and

chassis number ....,

either

has been specially constructed or adapted to take account of the disablement of .... (specify the number) severely and permanently disabled passengers, being cared for and transported by this organisation   *

or

has been specially constructed or adapted for the use of a disabled person as driver   *

Signed: .... (applicant)

Position in organisation (e.g. Chairman, Secretary etc.) ....

Date: ....

WARNING: ANY PERSON WHO MAKES A FALSE DECLARATION WILL INCUR SEVERE PENALTIES.

*Tick whichever is appropriate.

EUROPEAN COMMUNITIES (VALUE ADDED TAX) REGULATIONS 1994

(SI No 448 of 1994)

1 (1) These Regulation may be cited as the European Communities (Value Added Tax) Regulations, 1994.

(2) These Regulations shall be construed together with the Value Added Tax Acts 1972 to 1994.

2 These Regulations shall come into operation on the 1st day of January, 1995.

3 In these Regulations **"the Principal Act"** means the Value Added Tax Act, 1972.

4

Note

This para inserted VATA 1972, s 15B. This new section provides transitional arrangements for the taxation of trade with Austria, Finland, and Sweden, all of whom became EU Member States on 1 January 1995. Goods dispatched prior to 1 January 1995 from those States, to Ireland, remain liable to VAT at point of import if such goods were placed under a tax suspension regime on importation, and remain uncleared on 1 January 1995.

EUROPEAN COMMUNITIES (VALUE ADDED TAX) REGULATIONS 1995

(SI No 363 of 1995)

General note

The Second Simplification Directive (Council Directive 95/7/EC of 10 April 1995) introduced changes which were initially given effect in Irish law from 1 January 1996 by these regulations. The changes mean that intra EU cross border contract work on movable goods is now treated as a service — and no VAT is chargeable where the customer is VAT registered within the EU. These regulations were revoked by FA 1996, s 100, as the necessary changes were replicated in FA 1996, Pt III.

VALUE ADDED TAX (SPECIAL SCHEME FOR MEANS OF TRANSPORT; DOCUMENTATION) REGULATIONS 1996

(SI No 201 of 1996)

1 These Regulations may be cited as the Value Added Tax (Special Scheme for Means of Transport: Documentation) Regulations, 1996.

2 These Regulations shall come into operation on the 1st day of July, 1996.

3 In these Regulations—

"the Act of 1995" means the Finance Act, 1995 (No 8 of 1995);

"taxable dealer" has the meaning assigned to it by section 12B(3) (inserted by the act of 1995) of the Principal Act;

"means of transport" has the meaning assigned to it by section 12B(3) (inserted by the Act of 1995) of the Principal Act;

"the Principal Act" means the Value Added Tax Act, 1972;

"residual tax" has the meaning assigned to it by section 12B(4) (inserted by the Act of 1995) of the Principal Act.

4 (1) A taxable dealer shall deduct residual tax in accordance with section 12(1)(*a*)(vi) of the Principal Act in respect of the acquisition or purchase of a means of transport from a person specified in paragraph (*a*) or (*b*) of subsection (2) of section 12B of that Act, subject to the following conditions:

    (*a*) that the dealer prepares a document which sets out all the particulars specified in paragraph (2) of this Regulation, in respect of the transaction in question,

    (*b*) that the document referred to at subparagraph (*a*) of this paragraph is signed and dated by the person who is supplying the means of transport concerned, acknowledging the accuracy of the details therein and declaring that that person is a person of the type referred to in either paragraph (*a*) or (*b*) of subsection (2) of section 12B of the Principal Act, and

    (*c*) that the dealer gives to the person who is supplying the means of transport concerned a copy of the completed document referred to at subparagraphs (*a*) and (*b*) of this paragraph within 15 days of the date of the acquisition or purchase of that means of transport.

(2) The particulars in respect of the means of transport concerned which are to be included in the document referred to in paragraph (1) of this Regulation are as follows:

    (*a*) the name and address of the person who is supplying that means of transport;

    (*b*) the name and address of the taxable dealer who is purchasing or acquiring that means of transport;

    (*c*) the date upon which the supply of that means of transport takes place;

    (*d*) a description of that means of transport, including details of the make, model, engine number, registration number and year of manufacture; and

    (*e*) the total consideration for the supply of that means of transport.

5 A taxable dealer shall deduct residual tax in accordance with section 12(1)(*a*)(vi) of the Principal Act in respect of the acquisition or purchase of a means of transport from a person specified in paragraph (*c*) of subsection (2) of section 12B of that Act, subject to the condition that such dealer shall be in possession of an invoice issued by that person in accordance with the provisions of sections 12B(5) and 17(1) of that Act.

6 A taxable dealer shall deduct residual tax in accordance with section 12(1)(*a*)(vi) of the Principal Act in respect of the acquisition or purchase of a means of transport from a person specified in paragraph (*d*) of subsection (2) of section 12B of that Act, subject to the condition that such dealer shall be in possession of an invoice issued by that person which indicates that the supply by that person was subject to value added tax in accordance with the provisions implementing Article 26*a* or 28*o* of Council Directive 77/ 388/EEC of 17 May 1977 (OJ No L145, 13 June 1977, p 1) in the Member State in which the supply took place.

7 An invoice issued in accordance with the provisions of sections 12B(5) and 17(1) of the Principal Act shall show the following endorsement:

"Special Scheme — this invoice does not give the right to an imput credit of VAT".

8 A taxable dealer shall keep full and true records, entered up to date, of the acquisition and disposal of a means of transport, in respect of which that dealer has deducted residual tax in accordance with section 12(1)(*a*)(vi) of the Principal Act, together with appropriate cross-references between all such records.

9 The Value Added Tax (Second-hand Motor Vehicles) Regulations 1988 (SI No 121 of 1988) are hereby revoked.

VALUE ADDED TAX (RETURNS) REGULATIONS 1996

(SI No 294 of 1996)

Amendments

Repealed by Value Added Tax (Returns) Regs 2002, r 5.

VALUE ADDED TAX (RETAIL EXPORT SCHEME) REGULATIONS 1998

(SI No 34 of 1998)

1 (1) These Regulations may be cited as the Value Added Tax (Retail Export Scheme) Regulations, 1998.

(2) These Regulations shall come into operation on the first day of March, 1998.

2 (1) In these Regulations—

"the Act" means the Value Added Tax Act, 1972;

"traveller" and **"traveller's qualifying goods"** have the meanings assigned to them, respectively, by subsection 13(3B) (inserted by the Finance Act, 1997 (No 22 of 1997)) of the Act.

(2) In these Regulations—

(*a*)   a reference to a Regulation is to a Regulation of these Regulations, and

(*b*)   a reference to a paragraph or subparagraph is to a paragraph or subparagraph of the Regulation in which the reference occurs,

unless it is indicated that reference to some other Regulation is intended.

3 The application of the rate of zero per cent, specified in subsection 11(1)(*b*) of the Act, to a supply of goods or services specified in subsection 13(1A) of the Act shall be subject to the following conditions:

(*a*)   that the supplier keeps a record of the details of documentary proof inspected by him or her confirming that the purchaser was a traveller;

(*b*)   that at the time of supply, the supplier issues an invoice to the traveller showing the following details—

    (i)   the name, address and tax registration number of the supplier,

    (ii)   the name and address of the traveller,

    (iii)   the date upon which the invoice is issued,

    (iv)   a description of the goods supplied,

    (v)   the amount payable by the traveller at the time of the sale of the goods,

    (vi)   the tax charged, if any, and

    (vii)   the exchange rate or method to be used in determining the exchange rate, if repayment of the tax is to be made to the traveller,

by the supplier in a currency other than the currency of the State;

(*c*)   the notification of the charges made by the supplier, referred to in subsection 13(1A)(iii) of the Act, is made at the latest—

    (i)   where the goods are exported by the traveller, at the time of the handing over of the goods in question to the traveller,

(ii) where the goods are exported on behalf of the traveller, at the time when the goods in question are supplied to the traveller,

and which an amount is charged to the traveller for procuring a repayment of tax or arranging for the zero-rating of the supply, such amount does not exceed the amount notified in accordance with the said subsection 13(1A)(iii);

(*e*) that the time limit for making a repayment to the traveller, referred to in subsection 13(1)(ii) of the Act, is not later than the twenty-fifth working day following the receipt by the supplier of the traveller's claim to repayment;

(*f*) that the supplier keeps a copy of the invoice issued in accordance with subparagraph (*b*), duly signed by the traveller, and keeps a record in relation to each invoice of—

(i) the net amount (being the amount of tax charged to the traveller minus any commission or fee charged by the supplier to the traveller in respect of the transaction in question) repaid by the supplier to the traveller in respect of the supply in question, expressed in the currency in which the repayment was made,

(ii) where appropriate, the exchange rate used,

(iii) the date and method of such repayment, and

(iv) proof in accordance with Regulation 4, that the goods were exported by or on behalf of the traveller.

4 (1) In the case where the goods are exported by the traveller, the proof of export of the goods required shall be the invoice issued in accordance with Regulation 3(*b*) in respect of that supply, duly certified—

(*a*) by an officer of the Revenue Commissioners assigned to a customs office in the State, or

(*b*) where the goods have been exported via another Member State of the Community, by a customs officer in that Member State, or

(*c*) in such other manner as the Revenue Commissioners may deem acceptable for the purpose.

(2) In the case where the goods are exported on behalf of the traveller, the proof of export of the goods shall take the form of documentary evidence of export, duly certified by an officer of the Revenue Commissioners assigned to a customs office in the State, or, in the case where the goods are exported from another Member State of the Community, duly certified by a customs officer in that Member State.

5 The Value Added Tax (Exported Goods) Regulations, 1992 (SI No 438 of 1992), are hereby revoked.

Notes

These Regulations provide the conditions for granting relief from VAT on goods bought by visiting (non-EU) tourists or by Irish residents who are departing the EU with the intention of taking up residence outside the EU. The goods must be exported in the purchaser's personal luggage or put on board a ship or aircraft which is travelling to a non-EU destination, by the end of the third month following the month of purchase. The purchaser must get the benefit of the relief by 25 working days after lodging a valid claim, at the latest, and he/she must be made aware of the specified details concerning the transaction.

VALUE ADDED TAX (WAIVER OF EXEMPTION) (AMENDMENT) REGULATIONS 1998

(SI No 228 of 1998)

Revenue publication

Waiver of Exemption Regulations 1998: Tax Briefing, Issue 33.

---

1 These Regulations may be cited as the Value Added Tax (Waiver of Exemption) (Amendment) Regulations, 1998.

2 These Regulations shall be deemed to have come into effect on the 26th day of March, 1997.

3

Notes

Para (*a*) inserted Value Added Tax Regulations 1979, r 4(2A)–(2H) with effect from 26 March 1997.

Para (*b*) substituted "the total of the amounts of tax referred to at paragraphs (*a*), (*b*) and (*c*) of subsection (3) of section 7 of the Act" for "the total amount of tax refunded to him in accordance with section 20(1) of the Act" in Value Added Tax Regulations 1979, r 4(3)(*b*)(ii) with effect from 26 March 1997.

VALUE ADDED TAX (VALUATION OF INTERESTS IN IMMOVABLE GOODS) (AMENDMENT) REGULATIONS 1998

(SI No 482 of 1998)

1 These Regulations may be cited as the Value Added Tax (Valuation of Interests in Immovable Goods) (Amendment) Regulations, 1998.

2 In these Regulations "unencumbered rent" has the meaning assigned to it by subsection (10) (as amended by section 102 of the Finance Act, 1998 (No 22 of 1997)) of section 10 of the Value Added Tax Act, 1972 (No 22 of 1972).

3

Notes

Para (*a*) inserted Value Added Tax Regulations 1979, r 19(1)(proviso).
Para (*b*) substituted Value Added Tax Regulations 1979, r 19(2)(*b*).

VALUE ADDED TAX (ELECTRONIC DATA EXCHANGE AND STORAGE) (AMENDMENT) REGULATIONS 1998

(SI No 488 of 1998)

1 (1) These Regulations may be cited as the Value Added Tax (Electronic Data Exchange and Storage) (Amendment) Regulations, 1998.

(2) These Regulations shall come into operation on the 1st day of January, 1999.

2

Notes

This regulation inserted Value Added Tax (Electronic Data Exchange and Storage) Regulations, 1992, r 2A with effect from 1 January 1999.

VALUE ADDED TAX (INVOICES AND OTHER DOCUMENTS) (AMENDMENTS) REGULATIONS 1998

(SI No 489 of 1998)

1 (1) These Regulations may be cited as the Value Added Tax (Invoices and Other Documents) (Amendment) Regulations, 1998.

(2) These Regulations shall come into operation on the 1st day of January, 1999.

2

Notes

This regulation inserted Value Added Tax (Invoices and Other Documents) Regulations, 1992 (SI 275/1992), r 2A with effect from 1 January 1999.

EUROPEAN COMMUNITIES (VALUE ADDED TAX) REGULATIONS 1999

(SI No 196 of 1999)

Notes

Revoked by FA 2000, s 124 with effect from 1 July 1999.

VALUE ADDED TAX (SUPPLY OF FOOD, DRINK AND TOBACCO PRODUCTS ON BOARD VESSELS OR AIRCRAFT FOR ONBOARD CONSUMPTION) REGULATIONS 1999

(SI No 197 of 1999)

The Revenue Commissioners, in exercise of the powers conferred on them by paragraph (i*a*) of the Second Schedule to, and section 32 of, the Value Added Tax Act, 1972 (No 22 of 1972) (as amended by the European Communities (Value Added Tax) Regulations, 1999), hereby make the following Regulations:

1 These Regulations may be cited as the Value Added Tax (Supply of Food, Drink and Tobacco Products on board Vessels or Aircraft for onboard Consumption) Regulations, 1999.

2 These Regulations shall come into operation on the 1st day of July, 1999.

3 In these Regulations—

"the Principal Act" means the Value Added Tax Act, 1972;

"the Act of 1992" means the Finance Act, 1992 (No 9 of 1992);

"excisable products" has the meaning assigned to it by—

- (*a*) paragraphs (*a*) to (*e*) and (*i*),

  or

- (*b*) on and from the commencement of section 112 of the Finance Act, 1999 (No 2 of 1999), paragraphs (*a*) to (*f*),

of section 104 of the Act of 1992.

4 The conditions which apply for the purposes of paragraph (i*a*) of the Second Schedule to the Principal Act are that the food, drink and tobacco products shall be supplied—

- (*a*) in the case of excisable products, in such form, manner and quantities as may be permitted by the Revenue Commissioners in respect of relief from excise duty, and

- (*b*) in the case of food and drink other than drink to which paragraph (*a*) applies—

  - (i) from outlets, on board vessels or aircraft, approved by the Revenue Commissioners, and

  - (ii) in such form and quantity as renders it suitable to be consumed by passengers while on board such vessels or aircraft.

VALUE ADDED TAX (WAIVER OF EXEMPTION ON SUPPLIES OF, AND SUPPLIES RELATING TO INVESTMENT GOLD) REGULATIONS 1999

(SI No 440 of 1999)

The Revenue Commissioners, in exercise of the powers conferred on them by subsections (3) and (4) of section 6A (inserted by section 122 of the Finance Act, 1999 (No 2 of 1999)), and section 32, of the Value Added Tax Act, 1972 (No 22 of 1972), hereby make the following Regulations:

1 (1) These Regulations may be cited as the Value Added Tax (Waiver of Exemption on Supplies of, and Supplies relating to, Investment Gold) Regulations, 1999.

(2) These Regulations shall come into operation on the 1st day of January, 2000.

2 In these Regulations—

"Act of 1999" means the Finance Act, 1999 (No 2 of 1999);

"Principal Act" means the Value Added Tax Act, 1972, (No 22 of 1972);

"registration number", in relation to a person, means the number assigned to the person for the purposes of registration under section 9 of the Principal Act;

"Value Added tax registration number in another Member State" means the registration number issued to a person by the authorities of another Member State of the Community for the purposes of Value Added tax referred to in Council Directive No 77/388/EEC of 17 May, 1977 (OJ L 145, 13.5.1977, p 1).

3 A person who produces investment gold or transforms any gold into investment gold and who, in accordance with section 6A(3) of the Principal Act, wishes to waive his or her right to exemption from tax on supplies of investment gold to another person who is engaged in the supply of goods and services in the course or furtherance of business, shall apply to the Revenue Commissioners for authorisation to do so and shall furnish to them the following particulars—

    (*a*)   his or her name, address and registration number (if any), and

    (*b*)   a declaration stating that he or she produces investment gold or transforms any gold into investment gold and that he or she supplies or intends to supply investment gold to other persons engaged in the supply of goods and services in the course or furtherance of business.

4 Where they are satisfied that it is appropriate to do so for the proper administration of the tax, the Revenue Commissioners shall, within three weeks of receipt of the application for authorisation, authorise the applicant to waive, where he or she so wishes and in accordance with section 6A(3) of the Principal Act, his or her right to exemption from tax on a supply of investment gold.

5 A person, authorised in accordance with Regulation 4, who waives, in accordance with section 6A(3) of the Principal Act, his or her right to exemption from tax in respect of a supply of investment gold to another person shall, in relation to that supply, issue to that other person an invoice showing the following particulars—

(*a*)   his or her name, address and registration number,

(*b*)   the name, address and registration number (if any) of the person to whom the investment gold is being supplied,

(*c*)   in the case of a supply of investment gold to—

    (i)   a person in another Member State, that person's Value Added tax registration number (if any) in that Member State,

    (ii)   a person outside the Community, an indication of the type of business being carried on by that person,

(*d*)   the date of issue of the invoice,

(*e*)   the date of supply of the investment gold,

(*f*)   a description of the investment gold including, where applicable, form, weight, quantity, purity and any other distinguishing features,

(*g*)   the total consideration, exclusive of tax, receivable in respect of the supply,

(*h*)   the rate or rates of tax and the amount of tax at each rate chargeable in respect of the supply of the investment gold,

(*i*)   an endorsement stating "The right to exemption from tax has been waived in respect of this supply and the person to whom the investment gold is being supplied is liable for the tax chargeable on the supply in accordance with section 6A(5) of the Value Added Tax Act 1972" or words to the like effect.

6 Where a person is authorised to waive, in accordance with Regulation 4, his or her right to exemption from tax on supplies of investment gold, an intermediary, who supplies services in respect of those supplies of investment gold and who wishes to waive his or her right to exemption from tax in respect of those services, shall apply to the Revenue Commissioners for authorisation to do so and shall furnish to them the following particulars—

(*a*)   his or her name, address and registration number (if any), and

(*b*)   a declaration stating that he or she supplies services in respect of the supply of investment gold.

7 Where they are satisfied that it is appropriate to do so for the proper administration of the tax, the Revenue Commissioners shall, within three weeks of receipt of the application for authorisation, authorise the intermediary referred to in Regulation 6, to waive, in accordance with section 6A(4) of the Principal Act, his or her right to exemption from tax, on the supply of a service in respect of the supply of investment gold for which the supplier of such investment gold has waived his or her right to exemption from tax in accordance with section 6A(3) of the Principal Act.

8 An intermediary, authorised in accordance with Regulation 7, who waives, in accordance with section 6A(4) of the Principal Act, his or her right to exemption from tax on the supply of a service in respect of the supply of investment gold to another person shall, in relation to that supply, issue to that other person an invoice showing the following particulars—

(*a*) his or her name, address and registration number,

(*b*) the name, address and registration number (if any) of the person on whose name and account he or she is acting in respect of the supply of investment gold, and where that person is in another Member State, that person's Value Added tax registration number (if any) in that Member State,

(*c*) the date of issue of the invoice,

(*d*) the date of the supply of the services,

(*e*) the total consideration, exclusive of tax, receivable in respect of the supply of the services,

(*f*) the rate or rates of tax and the amount of tax at each rate chargeable in respect of the supply of the services,

(*g*) a description of the services being supplied in respect of the supply of investment gold, and

(*h*) an endorsement stating "The right to exemption from tax has been waived in respect of this supply" or words to the like effect.

9 Where the right to exemption from tax has been waived, in respect of a supply of investment gold or the supply of services relating to the supply of investment gold, that waiver shall be irrevocable for that supply.

10 The Revenue Commissioners may revoke any authorisation referred to in Regulation 4 or 7 where it appears necessary for them to do so for the proper administration of the tax and, accordingly, such authorisation shall cease to have effect from such date as may be notified by them to the holder of the authorisation.

VALUE ADDED TAX (REFUND OF TAX TO PERSONS MAKING EXEMPT SUPPLIES OF INVESTMENT GOLD) REGULATIONS 1999

(SI No 441 of 1999)

The Revenue Commissioners, in exercise of the powers conferred on them by subsections (6)(*b*), (7)(*b*) and (8)(*b*) of section 6A (inserted by section 122 of the Finance Act, 1999 (No. 2 of 1999)), and section 32 of the Value Added Tax Act, 1972 (No 22 of 1972), hereby make the following Regulations:

1 (1) These Regulations may be cited as the Value Added Tax (Refund of Tax to Persons making Exempt Supplies of Investment Gold) Regulations, 1999.

(2) These Regulations shall come into operation on the 1st day of January, 2000.

2 In these Regulations Principal Act means the Value Added Tax Act, 1972, (No 22 of 1972).

3 A person who is entitled, in accordance with subsection (6)(*b*), (7)(*b*) or (8)(*b*) of section 6A of the Principal Act, to claim a refund of the tax charged, paid or deferred in the circumstances specified in those subsections, shall claim such refund of tax—

(*a*) by completing such claim form as may be provided for that purpose by the Revenue Commissioners and certifying that the particulars shown on such claim form are correct,

(*b*) by establishing the amount of tax borne by production, where requested to do so by the Revenue Commissioners, of invoices or import documents, and

(*c*) by establishing that such person is not entitled to repayment of the tax under any other provision of the Principal Act, any Regulations made thereunder or of any other Act or instrument made under statute administered by the Revenue Commissioners.

VALUE ADDED TAX (AGRICULTURAL MACHINERY) (DOCUMENTATION) REGULATIONS 1999

(SI No 443 of 1999)

The Revenue Commissioners, in exercise of the powers conferred on them by section 32 of the Value Added Tax Act, 1972 (No. 22 of 1972), hereby make the following regulations:

1 (1) These Regulations may be cited as the Value Added Tax (Agricultural Machinery) (Documentation) Regulations, 1999.

(2) These Regulations shall come into operation on the 1st day of March, 2000.

2 In these Regulations—

"the Principal Act" means the Value Added Tax Act, 1972 (No 22 of 1972);

"the Act of 1999" means the Finance Act, 1999 (No 2 of 1999);

"agricultural machinery" has the meaning assigned to it by section 12C (inserted by the Act of 1999) of the Principal Act;

"flat-rate farmer" has the meaning assigned to it by section 12A as amended (inserted by section 11 of the Value Added Tax (Amendment) Act, 1978 (No 34 of 1978)) of the Principal Act;

"taxable dealer" has the meaning assigned to it by the said section 12C.

3 Each invoice issued by a flat-rate farmer in accordance with section 17(2A) (inserted by the Act of 1999) of the Principal Act shall be signed by him and shall include the following, that is to say:

    (*a*) his name and address;

    (*h*) the name and address of the taxable dealer to whom the agricultural machinery was supplied and the registration number assigned to him under subsection (1A) (inserted by section 171 of the Finance Act, 1992 (No 9 of 1992)) of section 9 of the Principal Act;

    (*c*) the date on which the supply of the agricultural machinery took place;

    (*d*) the date of issue of the invoice;

    (*e*) a description of the agricultural machinery, including details of the make, model and, where appropriate, the year of manufacture, the engine number and registration number thereof;

    (*f*) the consideration for the supply of the agricultural machinery, and

    (*g*) a declaration that the agricultural machinery was used by him for the purposes of his farming activities.

4 (1) Each invoice issued by a flat-rate farmer in accordance with section 17(2A) (inserted by the Act of 1999) of the Principal Act shall be issued within the period of fifteen days immediately following the month in which the agricultural machinery was supplied.

(2) A flat-rate farmer shall keep copies of all invoices to which paragraph (1) applies.

5 A taxable dealer shall keep—

    (*a*)   a full and proper record of all acquisitions and disposals of agricultural machinery by him, the entries in relation to which shall be made at the time of any such acquisition or disposal, or as soon as may be thereafter, and

    (*b*)   all invoices received in respect of agricultural machinery acquired by him and copies of all invoices in respect of agricultural machinery disposed of by him.

VALUE ADDED TAX (CANCELLATION OF ELECTION OF REGISTRATION IN RESPECT OF SIXTH SCHEDULE ACCOMMODATION) REGULATIONS 2000

(SI No 253 of 2000)

The Revenue Commissioners, in exercise of the powers conferred on them by sections 8 and 32 of the Value Added Tax Act, 1972 (No 22 of 1972), make the following Regulations:

1 (1) These Regulations may be cited as the Value Added Tax (Cancellation of Election of Registration in respect of Sixth Schedule Accommodation) Regulations, 2000.

(2) These Regulations shall come into operation on 1 September, 2000.

2 In these Regulations **"Principal Act"** means the Value Added Tax Act, 1972.

3 In these Regulations—

    (*a*) a reference to a Regulation is to a Regulation of these Regulations, and

    (*b*) a reference to a paragraph is to a paragraph of the Regulation in which the reference occurs,

unless it is indicated that reference to some other provision is intended.

4 A person who requests the cancellation of an election made by him or her under section 8 of the Principal Act and who supplies services of the kind referred to in paragraph (xiii) of the Sixth Schedule to that Act shall notify the Revenue Commissioners in writing that he or she wishes to have his or her election cancelled and shall furnish to the Revenue Commissioners any further details as may be required by them.

5 (1) A person shall be treated as a person who had not elected to be a taxable person with effect from the end of a taxable period as specified by the Revenue Commissioners which shall be no earlier than the end of the taxable period in which the notification in accordance with Regulation 4 was submitted, and the Revenue Commissioners shall so notify the person concerned accordingly.

(2) The person referred to in paragraph (1) shall furnish a return in accordance with section 19(3) of the Principal Act, and remit any tax payable, in respect of the taxable period in which the cancellation comes into effect and at the same time pay to the Revenue Commissioners in addition to any amount payable in accordance with section 8(5) of that Act, the cancellation amount provided for in section 8(5A) of that Act as if it were tax due in accordance with section 19 of that Act.

6 Regulation 3 of the Value Added Tax Regulations, 1979 (SI No 63 of 1979), is amended by the insertion of the following paragraph after paragraph 3 of that Regulation:

    "(3A) A person who requests the cancellation of an election made by him or her under section 8 of the Act and who supplies services of the kind referred to in paragraph (xiii) of the Sixth Schedule to the Act is required to fulfil the conditions specified in the Value Added Tax (Cancellation of Election of Registration in respect of Sixth Schedule Accommodation) Regulations, 2000 and, where applicable, the conditions specified in these Regulations, in order to have such election cancelled.".

VALUE ADDED TAX (APPORTIONMENT) REGULATIONS 2000

(SI No 254 of 2000)

The Revenue Commissioners, in exercise of the powers conferred on them by sections 12 and 32 of the Value Added Tax Act, 1972 (No. 22 of 1972), make the following Regulations:

1 These Regulations may be cited as the Value Added Tax (Apportionment) Regulations, 2000.

2 These Regulations shall come into operation on 1 September 2000.

3 In these Regulations—

"Principal Act" means the Value Added Tax Act, 1972;

"accounting period" means a period of 12 months ending on 31 December 2000 and on each 31 December thereafter, but if a taxable person customarily makes up accounts for periods of 12 months ending on another fixed date, an accounting period is a period of 12 months ending on that fixed date;

"authorised officer" means a person authorised for the purposes of section 18 of the Principal Act;

"final accounting period" means the period from the end of the previous accounting period to the date that a person ceases to be a taxable person;

"review period" means a period consisting of all the taxable periods which end during an accounting period.

4 In these Regulations -

    (*a*) a reference to a Regulation is to a Regulation of these Regulations, and

    (*b*) a reference to a paragraph is to a paragraph of the Regulation in which the reference occurs,

unless it is indicated that reference to some other provision is intended.

5 (1) Where a taxable person deducts, in accordance with subsections (1) and (4) of section 12 of the Principal Act, a proportion of the tax borne or payable on the taxable person's acquisition of dual-use inputs for a taxable period that proportion of tax deductible by that person for a taxable period shall be—

    (*a*) the proportion which—

        (i) correctly reflects the extent to which the dual-use inputs are used for the purposes of that person's deductible supplies or activities, and

        (ii) has due regard to the range of that person's total supplies and activities,

        for that taxable period,

    (*b*) the proportion which was calculated as being the proportion of tax deductible for the review period immediately preceding the taxable period in question, (*c*)   the proportion which that person estimates will—

    (i)   correctly reflect the extent to which the dual-use inputs will be used for the purposes of that person's deductible supplies or activities, and

    (ii)   have due regard to the range of that person's total supplies and activities,

    for the review period in which that taxable period ends, or

(*d*)   any other proportion of tax deductible which is arrived at in accordance with paragraph (3) of this Regulation.

(2) Where a taxable person estimates a proportion of tax deductible for a taxable period in accordance with paragraph (1)(*c*), then the taxable person shall submit, at the same time as the return required to be furnished in accordance with section 19(3) of the Principal Act for the taxable period in question, details setting out the basis for that estimate to the office of the Revenue Commissioners which would normally deal with the examination of the records kept by that person in accordance with section 16 of the Principal Act.

(3) If an authorised officer is satisfied that the proportion of tax deductible estimated in accordance with paragraph (1)(*c*) does not correctly reflect the extent to which the dual-use inputs will be used for the purposes of the taxable person's deductible supplies or activities and does not have due regard to the range of that person's total supplies and activities for the review period in which the taxable period ends, then that officer may direct that taxable person to use a proportion of tax deductible in accordance with subparagraph (*a*) or (*b*) of paragraph (1) or any other appropriate proportion which that officer agrees with that person.

6 (1) A taxable person who deducts, in accordance with subsections (1) and (4) of section 12 of the Principal Act, a proportion of the tax borne or payable on the taxable person's acquisition of dual-use inputs shall, at the end of each review period, calculate the proportion of tax deductible for that review period and shall, if necessary, in accordance with paragraph (2), adjust the amount of tax deducted in that review period to ensure that it correctly reflects the extent to which the dual-use inputs were used for the purposes of that person's deductible supplies or activities and had due regard to the range of that person's total supplies and activities for that review period.

(2) Any necessary adjustment under paragraph (1) shall be made by way of an increase or decrease, as the circumstances may require, in the amount of tax deductible by the taxable person, for -

(*a*)   the taxable period next following the end of the review period, or

(*b*)   such later taxable period which is agreed between the taxable person and an authorised officer,

but if the adjustment relates to that person's final accounting period any necessary adjustment shall be made by way of an increase or decrease in the amount of tax deductible for the taxable period in which that final accounting period ends.

(3) Any adjustment in accordance with paragraph (2) shall be made in the return required to be furnished in accordance with section 19(3) of the Principal Act for—

(*a*)   the taxable period next following the end of the review period, or

(*b*)   such later taxable period which is agreed between the taxable person and an authorised officer,

but if the adjustment relates to that person's final accounting period any necessary adjustment shall be made in the return required to be furnished in accordance with section 19(3) of the Principal Act for the taxable period in which that final accounting period ends.

(4) Any increase or decrease in the amount of tax deductible resulting from an adjustment of tax deductible made in accordance with this Regulation, shall be disregarded in calculating the proportion of tax deductible for the review period in which that adjustment was made.

7 Where a taxable person adjusts, in accordance with Regulation 6, the amount of tax deductible for a review period and subsequent to that adjustment it is established that that adjustment was incorrect, then the provisions of section 21 of the Principal Act shall not apply to any additional liability for tax arising out of the correction of that adjustment but only if —

(*a*)   that person, or any person acting on his or her behalf, did not act fraudulently or negligently in relation to that adjustment,

(*b*)   that person submitted, by the due date for submission of the return referred to in Regulation 6(3), details setting out the basis on which the adjustment was made to the office of the Revenue Commissioners which would normally deal with the examination of the records kept by that person in accordance with section 16 of the Principal Act, and

(*c*)   that additional liability is not the subject of an assessment of tax under section 23 of the Principal Act.

8 Regulation 16 of the Value Added Tax Regulations, 1979 (SI No 63 of 1979), is hereby revoked with effect as on and from 1 September, 2000.

VALUE ADDED TAX (ESTIMATION OF TAX PAYABLE AND ASSESSMENT OF TAX PAYABLE OR REFUNDABLE) REGULATIONS 2000

(SI No 295 of 2000)

THE REVENUE COMMISSIONERS, IN EXERCISE OF THE POWERS CONFERRED ON THEM BY SECTIONS 22, 23 AND 32 OF THE VALUE ADDED TAX ACT, 1972 (NO 22 OF 1972), MAKE THE FOLLOWING REGULATIONS:

1 These Regulations may be cited as the Value Added Tax (Estimation of Tax Payable and Assessment of Tax Payable or Refundable) Regulations, 2000.

2 These Regulations shall come into operation on 25 September 2000.

3 In these Regulations **"Principal Act"** means the Value Added Tax Act, 1972.

4 (1) An estimation of tax payable for a period for the purposes of section 22 of the Principal Act may be made by an officer of the Revenue Commissioners authorised by them in that behalf.

(2) A notice served in accordance with section 22 of the Principal Act shall contain the following particulars—

- (*a*) the name, address and registration number of the person in respect of whom an estimate is made,
- (*b*) the period to which the estimate relates, and
- (*c*) the amount of tax estimated to be payable in respect of the period referred to in subparagraph (*b*) of this paragraph.

5 (1) An assessment of tax payable or refundable for a period for the purposes of section 23 of the Principal Act may be made by an inspector of taxes or such other officer as the Revenue Commissioners may authorise in that behalf.

(2) A notice served in accordance with section 23 of the Principal Act shall contain the following particulars—

- (*a*) the name, address and registration number of the person in respect of whom an assessment is made,
- (*b*) the period to which the assessment relates,
- (*c*) the total amount of tax which it is assessed should have been paid or the total amount of tax (including, where appropriate, a nil amount) which in accordance with section 20(1) of the Principal Act should have been refunded, as the case may be, in respect of the period referred to in subparagraph (*b*) of this paragraph,
- (*d*) the total amount of tax (including, where appropriate, a nil amount) paid by the person or refunded to the person, as the case may be, in respect of the period concerned, and
- (*e*) the net amount due in respect of the period referred to in subparagraph (*b*) of this paragraph.

6

Notes

Value Added Tax (Estimation and Assessment of Tax Due) Regulations 1992 (SI 277/1992), are revoked.

7 (1) All officers who immediately before the commencement of these Regulations stood authorised for the purposes of any provision of the Regulations revoked by Regulation 6 of these Regulations shall be deemed to be authorised for the purposes of the corresponding provision of these Regulations.

(2) All estimates or assessments of tax and notices of estimation or assessment of tax made or issued under the Regulations revoked by Regulation 6 of these Regulations and in force immediately before the commencement of these Regulations shall continue in force as if made or issued under these Regulations.

TAXES (OFFSET OF REPAYMENTS) REGULATIONS 2001

(SI No 399 of 2001)

ARRANGEMENT OF REGULATIONS

PART 1
GENERAL

1. Citation and commencement.

2. Interpretation.

PART 2
OFFSETTING

3. Order of priority of offset against tax liabilities.

4. Special arrangements regarding corporation tax, income tax and capital gains tax.

5. Chronological order of priority of liabilities.

6. Nomination of liabilities by taxpayer.

7. Offset of interest.

The Revenue Commissioners, in exercise of the powers conferred on them by section 1006A of the Taxes Consolidation Act, 1997 (No 39 of 1997), make the following Regulations:

PART 1
GENERAL

Citation and commencement

1 (1) These Regulations may be cited as the Taxes (Offset of Repayments) Regulations, 2001.

(2) These Regulations shall come into operation on 14 September 2001.

Interpretation

2 (1) In these Regulations, unless the context otherwise requires—

"Acts", **"claim"**, **"liability"** and **"overpayment"** have each the same meaning as they have, respectively, in the principal section;

"Collector-General" means the person appointed under section 851 of the Principal Act;

"estimate" means an estimate of tax made in accordance with the provisions of—
(a) section 989 of the Principal Act,
(b) Regulation 13 of the Income Tax (Relevant Contracts) Regulations, 2000 (SI No 71 of 2000), or
(c) section 22 of the Value-Added Tax Act, 1972 (No 22 of 1972);

"current estimate", in relation to any particular time, means an estimate in respect of either an income tax month or a taxable period, as the case may be, the due date for which is immediately prior to that time or the income tax month or taxable period immediately preceding that month or period;

"due date", in relation to a liability, means the date on which the liability is due and payable under the appropriate provision of the Acts and, in relation to an estimate, the date on which the period for the payment of the tax for the income tax month or taxable period, as the case may be, expires;

"liability at enforcement" means a liability which, at the time at which the repayment is to be made in respect of the claim or overpayment—

    (*a*) was certified in a certificate issued, and not withdrawn, under section 962 of the Principal Act,

    (*b*) was the subject of proceedings initiated, and not withdrawn, as a debt due to the Minister for Finance, in any court of competent jurisdiction, or

    (*c*) was entered as a specified amount in a notice of attachment issued, and not revoked, under section 1002 of the Principal Act;

"Principal Act" means the Taxes Consolidation Act, 1997 (No 39 of 1997);

"principal section" means section 1006A of the Principal Act;

"taxhead" means—

    (*a*) tax deductible under Chapter 2 of Part 18 of the Principal Act and any regulations made under it,

    (*b*) income tax deductible under Chapter 4 of Part 42 of the Principal Act and any regulations made under it,

    (*c*) corporation tax,

    (*d*) income tax (other than that referred to in paragraph (b) of this definition),

    (*e*) capital gains tax,

    (*f*) value-added tax,

    (*g*) inheritance tax and gift tax,

    (*h*) stamp duties,

    (*i*) residential property tax,

    (*j*) vehicle registration tax, or

    (*k*) excise duties,

as the case may be.

(2) In these Regulations—

    (*a*) A reference to a Regulation is to a Regulation of these Regulations, unless it appears that reference to some other provision is intended;

    (*b*) a reference to a paragraph is to the paragraph of the provision in which the reference occurs, unless it appears that reference to some other provision is intended.

(3) Subject to paragraph (1), a word or expression that is used in these Regulations and is also used in any provision of the Acts has, except where the context otherwise requires, the same meaning in these Regulations as it has in that provision.

PART 2
OFFSETTING

Order of priority of set-off against liabilities

3 Subject to Regulations 4, 5, 6 and 7, the amount of any repayment in respect of a claim or overpayment made by any person, which is, by virtue of subsection (2) of the principal section, to be set against any liability of that person, shall be set against—

(*a*) firstly, any liability, other than a current estimate or a liability at enforcement, in the following sequence:

  (i) a liability arising under the same taxhead in respect of which the claim or overpayment is made,

  (ii) a liability arising under the Value-Added Tax Act, 1972, and the enactments amending or extending that Act,

  (iii) a liability arising under Chapter 4 of Part 42 of the Principal Act and the regulations made under it,

  (iv) a liability arising under Chapter 2 of Part 18 of the Principle Act and the regulations made under it,

  (v) a liability arising under the Corporation Tax Acts,

  (vi) a liability arising under any provision (other than Chapter 4 of Part 42 of the Principal Act) of the Income Tax Acts,

  (vii) a liability arising under the Capital Gains Tax Acts,

  (viii) a liability arising under Part VI of the Finance Act, 1983 (No 15 of 1983), and the enactments amending or extending that Part,

  (ix) a liability arising under the Capital Acquisitions Tax Act, 1976 (No 8 of 1976), and the enactments amending or extending that Act,

  (x) a liability arising under the Stamp Duties Consolidation Act, 1999 (No 31 of 1999), and the enactments amending or extending that Act,

  (xi) a liability arising under Chapter IV of Part II of the Finance Act, 1992 (No 9 of 1992),

  (xii) a liability arising under the statues relating to the duties of excise and to the management of those duties,

  and

(*b*) secondly, any liability, being a liability at enforcement, in the sequence set out in paragraph (a).

Special arrangements regarding corporation tax, income tax and capital gains tax

4 Notwithstanding Regulation 3 but subject to Regulations 5, 6 and 7, in any case where a repayment in respect of a claim or overpayment made by any person, is under a taxhead referred to in paragraph (*c*), (*d*) or (*e*) of the definition of "taxhead", the amount of the repayment, which is, by virtue of subsection (2) of the principal section, to be set against any liability of that person, shall be set against—

(*a*) firstly, any liability, other than a current estimate or a liability at enforcement, in the following sequence:

  (i) a liability arising under the same taxhead in respect of which the claim or overpayment is made,

  (ii) a liability arising under the Corporation Tax Acts,

  (iii) a liability arising under any provision (other than Chapter 4 of Part 42 of the Principal Act) of the Income Tax Acts,

  (iv) a liability arising under the Capital Gains Tax Acts,

  (v) a liability arising under the Value-Added Tax Act, 1972, and the enactments amending or extending that Act,

  (vi) a liability arising under Chapter 4 of Part 42 of the Principal Act and the regulations made under it,

  (vii) a liability arising under Chapter 2 of Part 18 of the Principle Act and the regulations made under it,

  (viii) a liability arising under Part VI of the Finance Act, 1983, and the enactments amending or extending that Part,

  (ix) a liability arising under the Capital Acquisitions Tax Act, 1976, and the enactments amending or extending that Act,

  (x) a liability arising under the Stamp Duties Consolidation Act, 1999, and the enactments amending or extending that Act,

  (xi) a liability arising under Chapter IV of Part II of the Finance Act, 1992,

  (xii) a liability arising under the statues relating to the duties of excise and to the management of those duties,

  and

 (b) secondly, any liability, being a liability at enforcement, in the sequence set out in paragraph (a).

Chronological order of priority of liabilities

5 For the purposes of Regulation 3 or 4, where, at any time, a repayment is to be set against more than one liability arising under a taxhead, it shall be set against any liability due for an earlier period or event in priority to a later period or event, as the case may be.

Nomination of liabilities by taxpayer.

6 Notwithstanding Regulation 3 or 4, a person may, at any time but not later than 30 days after the issue of a notice to him or her under subsection (2A) of the principal section, by notice in writing to the Collector-General request that the repayment concerned be set against liabilities in an order nominated by the person and the Collector-General shall arrange accordingly.

Offset of interest

7 For the purposes of these regulations, interest due and payable in relation to any liability to tax, duty, levy or other charge arising under the Acts in respect of any period or event, shall be deemed to be due and payable in respect of that period or event, as the case may be.

VALUE ADDED TAX (IMPORTED GOODS) (AMENDMENT) REGULATIONS 2001

(SI No 628 of 2001)

THE REVENUE COMMISSIONERS, IN EXERCISE OF THE POWERS CONFERRED ON THEM BY SECTIONS 15 AND 32 OF THE VALUE ADDED TAX ACT, 1972 (NO 22 OF 1972), AND WITH THE CONSENT OF THE MINISTER FOR FINANCE, MAKE THE FOLLOWING REGULATIONS:

1 These Regulations may be cited as the Value Added Tax (Imported Goods) (Amendment) Regulations, 2001.

2 These Regulations shall come into operation on the date of consent of the Minister for Finance.

3 In these Regulations "Regulations of 1992" means the Value Added Tax (Imported Goods) (No 2) Regulations, 1992 (SI No 440 of 1992).

4

Notes

Reg 4 deleted "or for processing under customs control" from Value Added Tax (Imported Goods) (No 2) Regs 1992, r 8.

5

Notes

Para (*a*) deleted "or" from Value Added Tax (Imported Goods) (No 2) Regs 1992, r 9;
Para (*b*) inserted "or (*h*) arrangements for processing under customs control," after Value Added Tax (Imported Goods) (No 2) Regs 1992, r 9(*g*).

---

6 These Regulations shall not apply to goods which, on the date when these Regulations come into operation, are under arrangements for processing under customs control and on the importation of which tax chargeable has been paid.

VALUE ADDED TAX (AMENDMENT) (PROPERTY TRANSACTIONS) REGULATIONS 2002

(SI No 219 of 2002)

THE REVENUE COMMISSIONERS, IN EXERCISE OF THE POWERS CONFERRED ON THEM BY SECTION 32 OF THE VALUE ADDED TAX ACT 1972 (NO 22 OF 1972) MAKE THE FOLLOWING REGULATIONS:

1 These Regulations may be cited as the Value Added Tax (Amendment) (Property Transactions) Regulations 2002.

2 In these Regulations the **"Regulations of 1979"** means the Value Added Tax Regulations 1979 (SI No 63 of 1979).

3

Notes

Para (*a*)(i) deleted "or (x)" from Value Added Tax Regulations 1979 (SI 63/1979), r 4(1).

Para (*a*)(ii) inserted "and" in Value Added Tax Regulations 1979 (SI 63/1979), r 4(1)(*b*).

Para (*a*)(iii) deleted Value Added Tax Regulations 1979 (SI 63/1979), r 4(1)(*c*).

Para (*a*)(iv) renumbered Value Added Tax Regulations 1979 (SI 63/979), r 4(1)(*d*).

Para (*b*)(i) substitute "(*c*)" for "(*d*)" in Value Added Tax Regulations 1979 (SI 63/1979), r 4(2).

Para (*b*)(ii) substituted "paragraph (iv) of the First Schedule" for "the paragraph or paragraphs referred to in subparagraph (*c*) of the said preceding paragraph" in Value Added Tax Regulations 1979 (SI 63/1979), r 4(2).

Para (*b*)(iii) substituted "paragraph (iv) of the First Schedule were not so specified" for "the paragraph or paragraphs referred to in paragraph (1)(*c*) were not specified in the said First Schedule" in Value Added Tax Regulations 1979 (SI 63/1979), r 4(2).

Para (*c*) substituted "subparagraph (*c*) of paragraph (1). However, no application under this paragraph may be made in respect of any disposal of an interest in immovable goods which is deemed to be a letting of immovable goods to which paragraph (iv) of the First Schedule applies by virtue of section 4(3A)(*a*)(ii) of the Act." for "subparagraph (*d*) of paragraph (1)." in Value Added Tax Regulations 1979 (SI 63/1979), r 4(2A)(1)(*c*).

Para (*d*) substituted "(*c*)" for "(*d*)" in Value Added Tax Regulations 1979 (SI 63/1979), r 4(2H).

Para (*e*)(i) deleted "or (x)" in Value Added Tax Regulations 1979 (SI 63/1979), r 4(3).

Para (*e*)(ii) substituted Value Added Tax Regulations 1979 (SI 63/1979), r 4(3)(*a*).

Para (*e*)(iii) substituted Value Added Tax Regulations 1979 (SI 63/1979), r 4(3)(*b*)(i).

Para (*e*)(iv)(I) inserted "deducted or deductible by him" in Value Added Tax Regulations 1979 (SI 63/1979), r 4(3)(*b*)(ii).

Para (*e*)(iv)(II) deleted ", or in case such total amount is referable partly to services specified in the paragraphs referred to in the notification aforesaid and partly to the supply of goods or other services, the amount included in such total amount which is referable to the services specified" in Value Added Tax Regulations 1979 (SI 63/1979), r 4(3)(*b*)(ii).

Para (*e*)(v) substituted Value Added Tax Regulations 1979 (SI 63/1979), r 4(3)(*c*).

Para (*f*) deleted "specified in the paragraph or paragraphs" in Value Added Tax Regulations 1979 (SI 63/1979), r 4(4).

Para (*g*) deleted "Value Added Tax Regulations 1979 (SI 63/1979), r 6 with effect from 1 November 2002.

4

Notes

Para (*a*) inserted "and" in Value Added Tax Regulations 1979 (SI 63/1979), r 19(1)(*b*) with effect from 25 March 2002;

Para (*b*) deleted "and" from Value Added Tax Regulations 1979 (SI 63/1979), r 19(1)(*c*) with effect from 25 March 2002.

Para (*c*) deleted Value Added Tax Regulations 1979 (SI 63/1979), r 19(1)(*d*) with effect from 25 March 2002.

Para (*d*) deleted ", whichever is the lower" from Value Added Tax Regulations 1979 (SI 63/1979), r 19(1) with effect from 25 March 2002.

Para (*e*) substituted Value Added Tax Regulations 1979 (SI 63/1979), r 19 (proviso) with effect from 25 March 2002.

VALUE ADDED TAX (RETURNS) REGULATIONS 2002

(SI No 267 of 2002)

THE REVENUE COMMISSIONERS, IN EXERCISE OF THE POWERS CONFERRED ON THEM BY SECTIONS 19 AND 32 OF THE VALUE ADDED TAX ACT 1972 (NO 22 OF 1972), HEREBY MAKE THE FOLLOWING REGULATIONS:

1 (1) These Regulations may be cited as the Value Added Tax (Returns) Regulations 2002.

(2) These Regulations are deemed to have come into operation on the 25 March 2002.

2 In these Regulations **"Principal Act"** means the Value Added Tax Act 1972 (No 22 of 1972).

3 Where a taxable person is required to furnish a return in accordance with paragraph (*a*) or (*b*) (inserted by section 84 of the Finance Act 1983) of section 19(3) of the Principal Act, then that person, or another person acting under that person's authority, shall complete such form as is issued for that purpose by the Collector-General in respect of the taxable period concerned and either the taxable person or the other person acting under that person's authority, as appropriate, shall sign a declaration on the form to the effect that the particulars shown on it are correct, and if that form provides for the inclusion of supplementary trading details in respect of any period, those details shall be deemed to be part of the return in respect of the taxable period concerned.

4 Where a taxable person is authorised to furnish a return in accordance with section 19(3)(*aa*) (inserted by section 58 of the Finance Act 1989) of the Principal Act, then that person, or another person acting under that taxable person's authority, shall complete such form as is issued for that purpose by the Collector-General and either that taxable person or another person acting under that person's authority, as appropriate, shall sign a declaration on the form to the effect that the particulars shown on it are correct.

5

Notes

Value Added Tax (Returns) Regulations 1996 (SI 294/1996) are revoked.

EUROPEAN COMMUNITIES (MUTUAL ASSISTANCE FOR THE RECOVERY OF CLAIMS RELATING TO CERTAIN LEVIES, DUTIES, TAXES AND OTHER MEASURES) REGULATIONS 2002

(SI No 462 of 2002)

I, CHARLIE McCREEVY, Minister for Finance, in exercise of the powers conferred on me by section 3 of the European Communities Act 1972 (No 27 of 1972) and for the purpose of giving effect to Council Directive No 76/308/EEC of 15 March 1976 (OJ No L73 of 19 March, 1976, p 18), as amended by Council Directive No 79/1071/EEC of 6 December 1979 (OJ No L331 of 27 December, 1979, p 10), Council Directive No 92/12/EEC of 25 February 1992 (OJ No L076 of 23 march, 1992, p 1), and Council Directive No 2001/44/EC of 15 June 2001 (OJ No L175 of 28 June, 2001, p 17), hereby make the following regulations:

Citation

1 These Regulations may be cited as the European Communities (Mutual Assistance for the Recovery of Claims relating to Certain Levies, Duties, Taxes and Other Measures) Regulations 2002.

Interpretation

2 (1) In these Regulations—

"claim" means any of the claims to which Regulation 3 applies;

"claimant" means the competent authority of a Member State which makes a request for assistance concerning a claim;

[**"Commission Directive"** means Commission Directive No 2002/94/EC of 9 December 2002;][1]

"Council Directive" means Council Directive No 76/308/EEC of 15 March 1976 as amended by Council Directive No 79/1071/EEC of 6 December 1979, Council Directive No 92/12/EEC of 25 February 1992, and Council Directive No 2001/44/EC of 15 June 2001;

"excise duties" means any excise duty in a Member State on—

    (*a*)   manufactured tobacco,

    (*b*)   alcohol and alcoholic beverages, or

    (*c*)   mineral oils;

"export duties" means—

    (*a*)   customs duties and charges having equivalent effect on exports, and

    (*b*)   export charges laid down within the framework of—

        (i)   the common agricultural policy, or

        (ii) specific arrangements applicable to certain goods resulting from the processing of agricultural products,

    which are imposed by, or apply within, a Member State;

"import duties" means—
- (*a*) customs duties and charges having equivalent effect on imports, and
- (*b*) import charges laid down within the framework of—
  - (i) the common agricultural policy, or
  - (ii) specific arrangements applicable to certain goods resulting from the processing of agricultural products,

  which are imposed by, or apply within, a Member State;

"Member State" means a Member State of the European Communities other than the State;

"taxes on income and capital" means those taxes set out in Article 1(3) of Council Directive 77/799/EEC of 19 December 1977 (OJ No L336/15 of 27 December 1977, p 15) (as amended by the 1994 Act of Accession (OJ No C241, 29 August 1994, p 21), in so far as it relates to Member States) read in conjunction with article 1(4) of that Directive which are imposed by, or apply within, a Member State;

"taxes on insurance premiums" means those taxes set out in the sixth indent to Article 3 of the Council Directive, read in conjunction with the seventh indent of the Council Directive, which are imposed by, or apply within, a Member State;

"value-added tax", in relation to a Member State, means the tax referred to in Council Directive No 77/388/EEC of 17 May 1977 (OJ No L145 of 13 June 1977, p 1).

(2) A word or expression that is used in these Regulations and is also used in the Council Directive has, unless the contrary intention appears, the meaning in these Regulations that it has in the Council Directive.

(3) A word or expression that is used in these Regulations and is also used in the Tax Acts has, subject to paragraph (2) and unless the contrary intention appears, the meaning in these Regulations that it has in the Tax Acts.

(4) In these Regulations—
- (*a*) a reference to a Regulation is to a Regulation of these Regulations, and
- (*b*) a reference to a paragraph or subparagraph is to the paragraph or subparagraph of the provision in which the reference occurs,

unless it is indicated that reference to some other provision is intended.

Amendments

1   Definition of "Commission Directive" substituted by European Communities (Mutual Assistance for the Recovery of Claims relating to Certain Levies, Duties, Taxes and Other Measures) (Amendment) Regulations 2003, reg 2(*a*).

Claims covered

3 This Regulation applies to a claim made by a claimant relating to—
- (*a*) refunds, interventions and other measures forming part of the system of total or partial financing of the European Agricultural Guidance and Guarantee Fund (EAGGF), including sums to be collected in connection with these actions;

(*b*)   levies and other duties provided for under the common organisation of the market for the sugar sector;

(*c*)   import duties;

(*d*)   export duties;

(*e*)   value added tax;

(*f*)   excise duties;

(*g*)   taxes on income and capital;

(*h*)   taxes on insurance premiums;

(*i*)   interest, administrative penalties and fines, and costs incidental to a claim referred to in paragraphs (*a*) to (*h*), with the exclusion of any fine or penalty in respect of which the act or commission giving rise to the fine or penalty if committed in the State would have been of a criminal nature.

Exchange of information

4 (1) In this Regulation "relevant authority", in relation to a request for information under this Regulation, means—

(*a*)   the Minister for Agriculture and Food, in the case of claims to which Regulation 3 applies which are referred to in paragraph (*a*) or (*b*), or, in so far as relates to any claim referred to in either of those paragraphs, paragraph (i), of that Regulation, and

(*b*)   the Revenue Commissioners, in the case of any other claim to which Regulation 3 applies.

(2) Subject to paragraph (3), a relevant authority may, at the request of a competent authority of a Member State, disclose to the competent authority any information in relation to a claim which is required to be disclosed by virtue of the Council Directive.

(3) (*a*)   A relevant authority shall not disclose any information for the purposes of the Council Directive which would, in the opinion of the relevant authority, be liable to prejudice the security of the State or be contrary to public policy.

(*b*)   A relevant authority shall not be obliged to disclose any information for the purposes of the Council Directive —

(i)   that the relevant authority concerned would not be able to obtain for the purposes of recovering a similar claim in the State, or

(ii)   that would, in the opinion of the relevant authority, be materially detrimental to any commercial, industrial or professional secrets.

(4) In obtaining the information referred to in paragraph (2), it shall be lawful for the relevant authority concerned to make use of the provisions of any enactment or instrument made under statute relating to the recovery of a similar claim in the State.

(5) Nothing in this Regulation shall permit the relevant authority concerned to authorise the use of information disclosed by virtue of the Council Directive to the competent authorities of a Member State other than for the purposes of the recovery of a claim or to facilitate legal proceedings in relation to the recovery of such a claim.

Recovery of claims

5 (1) The Collector-General shall, in accordance with the provisions of these Regulations, collect the amount of a claim specified in any request duly made in accordance with the Council Directive by a claimant.

(2) When the Collector-General duly receives a request from a claimant for the recovery of a claim, the Collector-General shall make demand in writing of the amount stated in the claim made by the claimant from the person against whom the claim is made.

(3) For the purposes of these Regulations, the amount of any claim made by a claimant shall be deemed due and payable not later than 7 days from the date on which the Collector-General makes demand of the amount in accordance with paragraph (2).

(4) The provisions of any enactment relating to the collection or recovery of income tax (other than sections 960, 961, 970, 971, 1000, 1003, 1004 and 1006B, and Chapter 4 of Part 42, of the Taxes Consolidation Act 1997) and the provisions of any rule of court so relating for those purposes shall, with any necessary modifications, apply in relation to the recovery of a claim referred to in paragraph (1) as they apply in relation to income tax, and for this purpose the amount of the claim shall be deemed to be an amount of income tax.

(5) For the purposes of these Regulations, the amount of the claim referred to in paragraph (1) shall be regarded as a debt due to the Minister for Finance, by the person against whom the claim is made by the claimant, in respect of a tax or duty under the care and management of the Revenue Commissioners.

(6) Any reference in this Regulation to the amount of the claim shall include any interest payable in respect of that claim under Regulation 6.

(7) The amount of any claim payable to the Collector-General under these Regulations—

 (*a*) shall be payable without any deduction of income tax, and

 (*b*) shall not be allowed as a deduction in computing any income, profits or losses for any of the purposes of the Tax Acts (except in so far as any relief is due in respect of the amount of the claim under Part 35 of the Taxes Consolidation Act 1997).

(8) On payment of an amount under these Regulations, the Collector-General shall furnish the person concerned with a receipt in respect of that payment.

Interest

6 (1) The amount of any claim payable in accordance with Regulation 5(1) shall carry interest at the rate of 0.0322 per cent for each day or part of a day from the date when the amount of the claim becomes due and payable in accordance with Regulation 5(3) until payment, and, accordingly, that date is the date on which the instrument permitting enforcement of the recovery of the claim is recognised for the purposes of the second subparagraph of Article 9.2 of the Council Directive.

(2) Subsections (2) to (4) of section 1080 of the Taxes Consolidation Act 1997 shall apply in relation to interest payable in relation to the claim referred to in paragraph (1)

as they apply in relation to interest payable under section 1080 of that Act in relation to tax charged by any assessment.

Application of rules

7 The rules laid down in Articles 4 to 12 and 14 to 17 of the Council Directive (to the extent that they are not otherwise given effect to by these Regulations) and [Articles 2 to 21 of the Commission Directive][1] shall apply in relation to claims made by claimants and which are the subject of recovery in accordance with these Regulations.

Amendments

[1] Substituted by European Communities (Mutual Assistance for the Recovery of Claims relating to Certain Levies, Duties, Taxes and Other Measures) (Amendment) Regulations 2003, reg 2(*b*); previously "Articles 2 to 28 of the Commission Directive".

Stay on proceedings

8 (1) Subject to paragraph (5), any action taken by the Revenue Commissioners or the Collector-General to recover the amount of any claim, whether by way of legal proceedings or other action, shall be stayed if—

    (*a*)   in the case of court proceedings, the defendant satisfies the court that court proceedings relevant to that person's liability on the claim to which the proceedings so instituted relate are pending before a court, tribunal or other competent body in a Member State, or

    (*b*)   in any other case, the person against whom the other action is being taken satisfies the Revenue Commissioners that court proceedings relevant to that person's liability on the claim to which the action relates are pending before a court, tribunal or other competent body in a Member State.

(2) In any legal proceedings instituted under these Regulations it shall be a defence for the defendant to show that a final decision on the claim to which the proceedings relate has been given in the defendant's favour by a court, tribunal or other body of competent jurisdiction in a Member State, and, in relation to any part of a claim to which such legal proceedings relate, it shall be a defence for the defendant to show that such a decision has been given in relation to that part of the claim.

(3) No question shall be raised in any legal proceedings instituted in pursuance of these Regulations as to the liability on the claim to which the proceedings relate of the person against whom the claim is made, [except as provided in paragraph (2)][1].

(4) For the purposes of this Regulation, legal proceedings shall be regarded as pending so long as an appeal may be brought against any decision in the proceedings; and for these purposes a decision against which no appeal lies, or against which an appeal lies within a period which has expired without an appeal having been brought, shall be regarded as a final decision.

(5) Paragraph (1) shall not apply where a claimant in accordance with the Council Directive so requests, and where the claimant so requests no action shall lie against the State (including the Revenue Commissioners, the Collector-General, any officer of the Revenue Commissioners and any agent of the Revenue Commissioners) in any court by reason of the Revenue Commissioners, the Collector-General or any such officer or

agent recovering, or taking any action to recover, the amount of, or part of the amount of, any claim the subject of such a request.

Amendments

¹ Substituted by European Communities (Mutual Assistance for the Recovery of Claims relating to Certain Levies, Duties, Taxes and Other Measures) (Amendment) Regulations 2003, reg 2(*c*); previously "except as provided in paragraph (3)".

Remittance of claims

9 Any amount recovered under these Regulations on foot of a claim made by a claimant under the Council Directive (including any interest under Regulation 6) shall be remitted to that claimant.

Application of Council Directive to certain Irish tax, etc due

10 (1) In this Regulation—

"tax" means any tax, duty, levy or charge referred to in Article 2 of the Council Directive which is under the care and management of the Revenue Commissioners;

"agricultural levy" means any levy or other measure referred to in Article 2 of the Council Directive for which the Minister for Agriculture and Food is responsible;

"interest on unpaid tax", in relation to an amount of unpaid tax, means the amount of interest that has accrued to the date on which a certificate under this Regulation is signed in respect of the unpaid tax under any provision whatever providing for the charging of interest in respect of that tax, including interest on an undercharge of tax which is attributable to fraud or neglect, as specified in the certificate.

(2) For the purpose of the Council Directive and for the avoidance of doubt, a demand by the Revenue Commissioners or the Minister for Agriculture and Food, as the case may be, for payment of an amount of tax (including, where appropriate, interest on unpaid tax) or agricultural levy where the amount demanded remains unpaid after expiration of the period for payment set out in the demand shall be an instrument permitting enforcement of the debt.

Delegation of powers and functions

11 (1) The Minister for Agriculture and Food may nominate, in writing, any of his or her officers to perform any acts and discharge any functions authorised by these Regulations to be performed or discharged by the Minister.

(2) The Revenue Commissioners may nominate, in writing, any of their officers to perform any acts and discharge any functions authorised by these Regulations to be performed or discharged by them.

(3) The Revenue Commissioners may nominate, in writing, any of their officers to perform any acts and discharge any functions authorised by these Regulations to be performed or discharged by the Collector-General.

Repeal and revocations

12 (1) Section 108 of the Finance Act 2001 is repealed.

(2) The European Communities (Agriculture and Customs) (Mutual Assistance as regards the Recovery of Claims) Regulations 1980 (SI No 73 of 1980) and the European Communities (Value-Added Tax) (Mutual Assistance as regards the Recovery of Claims) Regulations 1980 (SI No 406 of 1980) are revoked.

TAXES (OFFSET OF REPAYMENTS) REGULATIONS 2002

(SI No 471 of 2002)

ARRANGEMENT OF REGULATIONS

THE REVENUE COMMISSIONERS, IN EXERCISE OF THE POWERS CONFERRED ON THEM BY SECTION 1006A OF THE TAXES CONSOLIDATION ACT 1997 (NO 39 OF 1997), MAKE THE FOLLOWING REGULATIONS:

PART 1
GENERAL

1 Citation

These Regulations may be cited as the Taxes (Offset of Repayments) Regulations 2002.

2 Interpretation

(1) In these Regulations, unless the context otherwise requires—

"Acts", **"claim"**, **"liability"**, **"overpayment"** and **"tax"** have each the same meaning as they have, respectively, in the principal section;

"Collector-General" means the person appointed under section 851 of the Principal Act;

"estimate" means an estimate of tax made in accordance with the provisions of—

    (*a*)   section 989 of the Principal Act,

    (*b*)   Regulation 13 of the Income Tax (Relevant Contracts) Regulations 2000 (SI No 71 of 2000), or

    (*c*)   section 22 of the Value Added Tax Act 1972 (No 22 of 1972);

"current estimate", in relation to any particular time, means an estimate in respect of either an income tax month or a taxable period, as the case may be, the due date for which is immediately prior to that time or the income tax month or taxable period immediately preceding that month or period;

"due date", in relation to a liability, means the date on which the liability is due and payable under the appropriate provision of the Acts and, in relation to an estimate, the date on which the period for the payment of the tax for the income tax month or taxable period, as the case may be, expires;

"liability at enforcement" means a liability which, at the time at which the repayment is to be made in respect of the claim or overpayment —

    (*a*)   was certified in a certificate issued, and not withdrawn, under section 962 of the Principal Act,

    (*b*)   was the subject of proceedings initiated, and not withdrawn, as a debt due to the Minister for Finance, in any court of competent jurisdiction, or

    (*c*)   was entered as a specified amount in a notice of attachment issued, and not revoked, under section 1002 of the Principal Act;

"Principal Act" means the Taxes Consolidation Act 1997 (No 39 of 1997);

"principal section" means section 1006A of the Principal Act;

"taxhead" means—

    (*a*)   tax deductible under Chapter 2 of Part 18 of the Principal Act and any regulations made under it,

    (*b*)   income tax deductible under Chapter 4 of Part 42 of the Principal Act and any regulations made under it,

    (*c*)   corporation tax,

    (*d*)   an amount to be collected as income tax by the Collector-General in accordance with the provisions of the European Communities (Mutual Assistance for the Recovery of Claims relating to Certain Levies, Duties, Taxes and Other Measures) Regulations 2002 (SI No 462 of 2002),

    (*e*)   income tax (other than that referred to in paragraphs (*b*) and (*d*) of this definition),

    (*f*)   capital gains tax,

    (*g*)   Value Added tax,

    (*h*)   inheritance tax and gift tax,

    (*i*)   stamp duties,

    (*j*)   residential property tax,

    (*k*)   vehicle registration tax, or

    (*l*)   excise duties,

as the case may be.

(2) In these Regulations —

(*a*) a reference to a Regulation is to a Regulation of these Regulations, unless it appears that reference to some other provision is intended;

(*b*) a reference to a paragraph is to the paragraph of the provision in which the reference occurs, unless it appears that reference to some other provision is intended.

(3) Subject to paragraph (1), a word or expression that is used in these Regulations and is also used in any provision of the Acts has, except where the context otherwise requires, the same meaning in these Regulations as it has in that provision.

PART 2
OFFSETTING

3 Order of priority of offset against liabilities

Subject to Regulations 4, 5, 6 and 7, the amount of any repayment in respect of a claim or overpayment made by any person, which is, by virtue of subsection (2) of the principal section, to be set against any liability of that person, shall be set against—

(*a*) firstly, any liability, other than a current estimate or a liability at enforcement, in the following sequence:

(i) a liability arising under the same taxhead in respect of which the claim or overpayment is made,

(ii) a liability arising under the Value Added Tax Act 1972 and the enactments amending or extending that Act,

(iii) a liability arising under Chapter 4 of Part 42 of the Principal Act and the regulations made under it,

(iv) a liability arising under Chapter 2 of Part 18 of the Principal Act and the regulations made under it,

(v) a liability arising under the Corporation Tax Acts,

(vi) a liability arising under any provision (other than Chapter 4 of Part 42 of the Principal Act) of the Income Tax Acts,

(vii) a liability arising under the Capital Gains Tax Acts,

(viii) a liability arising under Part VI of the Finance Act 1983 (No 15 of 1983) and the enactments amending or extending that Part,

(ix) a liability arising under the Capital Acquisitions Tax Act 1976 (No 8 of 1976) and the enactments amending or extending that Act,

(x) a liability arising under the Stamp Duties Consolidation Act 1999 (No 31 of 1999) and the enactments amending or extending that Act,

(xi) a liability arising under Chapter IV of Part II of the Finance Act 1992 (No 9 of 1992),

(xii) a liability arising under the statutes relating to the duties of excise and to the management of those duties,

(*b*) secondly, any liability, being a liability at enforcement, in the sequence set out in paragraph (*a*), and

(*c*) finally, against any amount referred to in paragraph (*d*) of the definition of **"taxhead"**.

4 Special arrangements regarding corporation tax, income tax and capital gains tax

Notwithstanding Regulation 3 but subject to Regulations 5, 6 and 7, in any case where a repayment in respect of a claim or overpayment made by any person, is under a taxhead referred to in paragraph (c), (e) or (f) of the definition of "taxhead", the amount of the repayment, which is, by virtue of subsection (2) of the principal section, to be set against any liability of that person, shall be set against—

(a)   firstly, any liability, other than a current estimate or a liability at enforcement, in the following sequence:

    (i)   a liability arising under the same taxhead in respect of which the claim or overpayment is made,

    (ii)   a liability arising under the Corporation Tax Acts,

    (iii)   a liability arising under any provision (other than Chapter 4 of Part 42 of the Principal Act) of the Income Tax Acts,

    (iv)   a liability arising under the Capital Gains Tax Acts,

    (v)   a liability arising under the Value Added Tax Act 1972 and the enactments amending or extending that Act,

    (vi)   a liability arising under Chapter 4 of Part 42 of the Principal Act and the regulations made under it,

    (vii)   a liability arising under Chapter 2 of Part 18 of the Principal Act and the regulations made under it,

    (viii)   a liability arising under Part VI of the Finance Act 1983 and the enactments amending or extending that Part,

    (ix)   a liability arising under the Capital Acquisitions Tax Act 1976 and the enactments amending or extending that Act,

    (x)   a liability arising under the Stamp Duties Consolidation Act 1999 and the enactments amending or extending that Act,

    (xi)   a liability arising under Chapter IV of Part II of the Finance Act 1992,

    (xii)   a liability arising under the statutes relating to the duties of excise and to the management of those duties,

(b)   secondly, any liability, being a liability at enforcement, in the sequence set out in paragraph (a), and

(c)   finally, against any amount referred to in paragraph (d) of the definition of "taxhead".

5 Chronological order of priority of

For the purposes of Regulation 3 or 4, where, at any time, a repayment is to be set against more than one liability arising liabilities. under a taxhead, it shall be set against any liability due for an earlier period or event in priority to a later period or event, as the case may be.

6 Nomination of liabilities by taxpayer

Notwithstanding Regulation 3 or 4, a person may, at any time but not later than 30 days after the issue of a notice to him or her under subsection (2A) of the principal section, by notice in writing to the Collector-General request that the repayment concerned be set against liabilities (other than any amount referred to in paragraph (*d*) of the definition of **"taxhead"**) in an order nominated by the person and the Collector-General shall arrange accordingly.

7 Offset of interest

For the purposes of these Regulations, interest due and payable in relation to any liability to tax in respect of any period or event shall be deemed to be due and payable at the same time as the tax in respect of that period or event, as the case may be.

PART 3
MISCELLANEOUS

8 Revocation

The Taxes (Offset of Repayments) Regulations 2001 (SI No 399 of 2001) are revoked.

VALUE ADDED TAX (ELECTRONIC INVOICING AND STORAGE) REGULATIONS 2002

(SI No 504 of 2002)

THE REVENUE COMMISSIONERS, IN EXERCISE OF THE POWERS CONFERRED ON THEM BY SECTIONS 17 AND 32 OF THE VALUE ADDED TAX ACT 1972 (NO 22 OF 1972) HEREBY MAKE THE FOLLOWING REGULATIONS:

1 These Regulations may be cited as the Value Added Tax (Electronic Invoicing and Storage) Regulations 2002.

2 (1) In these Regulations—

"Act" means the Value Added Tax Act 1972 (No 22 of 1972);

"Electronic Commerce Act" means the Electronic Commerce Act 2000 (No 27 of 2000);

"advanced electronic signature" means an electronic signature which is—

- (*a*) uniquely linked to the signatory,
- (*b*) capable of identifying the signatory,
- (*c*) created using means that are capable of being maintained by the signatory under his or her sole control, and
- (*d*) linked to the data to which it relates in such a manner that any subsequent change of the data is detectable;

"electronic signature" means data in electronic form which are attached to or logically associated with a message and which serve as a method of authentication;

"electronic data interchange" means the electronic transfer, from computer to computer, of commercial and administrative data using an agreed standard to structure a message;

"electronic record" means a record required to be kept for the purposes of section 16 of the Act which is generated, transmitted and stored electronically;

"message" means an invoice, credit note, debit note, settlement voucher or document issued or received in accordance with section 17 of the Act and which is transmitted electronically;

"registration number" in relation to a person, means the number assigned to the person for the purposes of registration under section 9 of the Act;

"trading partners" means any two persons engaged by prior agreement in the electronic exchange of messages;

"transmission" means the transfer or making available of a message to a trading partner by electronic means;

"**unique identification number**" means a sequential number which is based on one or more series and which uniquely identifies a message transmitted between trading partners.

(2) In these Regulations "**signatory**", "**signature-creation data**", "**signature-creation device**", "**signature-verification-data**", and "**signature-verification device**" have the meanings assigned to them by the Electronic Commerce Act.

(3) In these Regulations—

(*a*)   a reference to a Regulation is to a Regulation of these Regulations, and

(*b*)   a reference to a paragraph, subparagraph or clause is to a paragraph, subparagraph or clause of the provision in which the reference occurs,

unless it is indicated that reference to some other provision is intended.

3 (1) A message issued or received by electronic means by a taxable person shall be deemed to be so issued or received for the purposes of section 17(1A) of the Act if each such message—

(*a*)   is transmitted between trading partners using an electronic data interchange system which satisfies the requirements specified in paragraphs (2) and (3), or

(*b*)   is transmitted between trading partners using an advanced electronic signature and an associated system which satisfy the requirements specified in paragraphs (2) and (3).

(2) The electronic data interchange system or the advanced electronic signature and associated system used by the taxable person referred to in paragraph (1) shall be capable of—

(*a*)   producing, retaining and storing, and making available to an officer of the Revenue Commissioners on request, electronic records and messages in such form and containing such particulars as may be required in accordance with sections 16 and 17 of the Act and Regulations made under the Act,

(*b*)   causing to be reproduced on paper any electronic record or message required to be produced, retained or stored in accordance with sections 16 and 17 of the Act and Regulations made under the Act,

(*c*)   allocating a unique identification number for each message transmitted, and

(*d*)   maintaining electronic records in such manner as will allow their retrieval by reference to the name of a trading partner or the date or the unique identification number, of the message.

(3) The electronic data interchange system or the advanced electronic signature and associated system used by the taxable person referred to in paragraph (1) shall—

(*a*)   preclude the repeated transmission of a message,

(*b*)   preclude the omission of any message from the electronic record,

(*c*)   verify the origin or receipt of a message by a trading partner, and

(*d*)   guarantee the integrity of the contents of a message, or of an electronic record related to that message, during transmission and during the period provided for in section 16 for the retention of records, invoices or any other documents specified in the Act or in Regulations made under the Act.

(4) (*a*)　A taxable person who issues or receives messages by electronic means in accordance with paragraph 3(1) shall retain and store such messages or copies of such messages as appropriate and electronic records related to those messages and in addition shall retain and store electronically the following data:

　　(i)　details of the form of encryption, electronic signature, signature creation data or device, signature verification data or device, or any other method used to ensure the integrity of the records and messages transmitted, retained and stored and the authenticity of their origin,

　　(ii)　details of where and in what format the information required in accordance with clause (i) is stored and how it can be accessed.

　(*b*)　A taxable person who issues or receives messages by electronic means shall—

　　(i)　provide details on request to an officer of the Revenue Commissioners on where and how an electronic record or message is stored on that taxpayer's system and how it can be accessed by that officer,

　　(ii)　allow such access to electronic records or messages for inspection by an officer of the Revenue Commissioners at all reasonable times, and

　　(iii)　reproduce any such electronic record or message on paper on request by an officer of the Revenue Commissioners including details required to be retained and stored under subparagraph (*a*).

4 A taxable person may transmit messages by means other than those referred to in Regulation 3(1) where—

　(*a*)　he or she is satisfied that such messages are recorded, retained and transmitted in accordance with section 17(1A) of the Act,

　(*b*)　the requirements of paragraphs (2), (3) and (4) of Regulation 3 are met, and

　(*c*)　he or she notifies the Revenue Commissioners accordingly, and until 31 December 2005 such notification shall be made prior to the commencement of the transmission of such messages.

5

Notes

Value Added Tax (Electronic Data Exchange and Storage) Regulations 1992 (SI 269/1992) are revoked.

EUROPEAN COMMUNITIES (MUTUAL ASSISTANCE FOR THE RECOVERY OF CLAIMS RELATING TO CERTAIN LEVIES, DUTIES, TAXES AND OTHER MEASURES) (AMENDMENT) REGULATIONS 2003

(SI No 344 of 2003)

I, CHARLIE McCREEVY, Minister for Finance, in exercise of the powers conferred on me by section 3 of the European Communities Act 1972 (No 27 of 1972) and for the purposes of giving effect to Commission Directive 2002/94/EC of 9 December 2002 (OJ No L337 of 13 December 2002, p 41), hereby make the following regulations:

1. These Regulations may be cited as the European Communities (Mutual Assistance for the Recovery of Claims relating to Certain Levies, Duties, Taxes and Other Measures)(Amendment) Regulations 2003.

Notes

Reg 2(*a*) substituted The European Communities (Mutual Assistance for the Recovery of Claims relating to Certain Levies, Duties, Taxes and Other Measures) Regulations 2002, reg 2(1) definition of "Commission Directive".

Reg (2)(*b*) substituted "Articles 2 to 28 of the Commission Directive" for "Articles 2 to 21 of the Commission Directive" in The European Communities (Mutual Assistance for the Recovery of Claims relating to Certain Levies, Duties, Taxes and Other Measures) Regulations 2002, reg 7.

Reg (2)(*c*) substituted "except as provided in paragraph (2)" for "except as provided in paragraph (3)" in The European Communities (Mutual Assistance for the Recovery of Claims relating to Certain Levies, Duties, Taxes and Other Measures) Regulations 2002, reg 8(3).

VALUE ADDED TAX (WAIVER OF EXEMPTION)(LETTING OF IMMOVABLE GOODS) REGULATIONS 2003

(SI No 504 of 2003)

The Revenue Commissioners, in exercise of the powers conferred on them by sections 7 and 32(1)(*a*) of the Value Added Tax Act 1972 (No 22 of 1972), hereby make the following regulations:

1. These Regulations may be cited as the Value Added Tax (Waiver of Exemption) (Letting of Immovable Goods) Regulations 2003.

2. (1) In these Regulations—

"Act" means the Value Added Tax Act 1972 (No 22 of 1972);

"back-dating" in relation to a waiver, means the waiving of a right to exemption from tax in respect of an exempt letting of immovable goods to which paragraph (iv) of the First Schedule to the Act refers, from a date earlier than the current taxable period referred to in Regulation 3(1)(*c*), and cognate words shall be construed accordingly;

"cancellation request period" means the taxable period during which a request for the cancellation of a waiver is made in accordance with Regulation 3(7);

"registration number" in relation to a person, means the number assigned to the person for the purposes of registration under section 9 of the Act;

"specified letting" means an exempt letting of immovable goods to which paragraph (iv) of the First Schedule to the Act applies;

"waiver" means the waiver by a person of his or her right to exemption from tax on a specified letting.

(2) In these Regulations—

    (*a*) a reference to a Regulation is to a Regulation of these Regulations, unless it is indicated that reference to some other Regulations is intended,

    (*b*) a reference to a paragraph or subparagraph is a reference to a paragraph or subparagraph of the provision in which the reference occurs, unless it is indicated that reference to some other provision is intended.

3 (1) A person who, in accordance with section 7(1) of the Act wishes to waive his or her right to exemption from tax on the supply of a specified letting, shall furnish in writing to the Revenue Commissioners the following particulars—

    (*a*) his or her name and address,

    (*b*) his or her registration number (if any), and

    (*c*) the taxable period, from the commencement of which he or she desires that the waiver should have effect, not being earlier than the current taxable period.

(2) The Revenue Commissioners shall acknowledge receipt of the particulars referred to in paragraph (1) and shall specify the taxable period (in this paragraph referred to as the **"start period"**) not being earlier than the taxable period referred to in paragraph (1)(*c*), from the commencement of which the waiver of exemption has effect. From the start

period to the date on which the person permanently ceases to supply taxable goods or services (including services to which the waiver of exemption applies), or until his or her waiver is cancelled in accordance with paragraph (8), the Act applies to him or her as if the specified letting were not an exempt activity.

(3) Where a taxable person makes a specified letting and the immovable goods which are the subject of the letting were acquired or developed by him or her for the purpose of his or her taxable supplies, then, notwithstanding paragraph (2), that person may apply to the Revenue Commissioners to backdate the waiver of his or her right to exemption in respect of that letting. However, no application under this paragraph may be made in respect of any disposal of an interest in immovable goods which is deemed to be a letting of immovable goods to which paragraph (iv) of the First Schedule to the Act applies by virtue of section 4(3A)(*a*)(ii) of the Act.

(4) An application under paragraph (3) shall be made in writing to the Revenue Commissioners and shall include the following—

     (*a*)   the name, address and registration number of the taxable person making the application,

     (*b*)   the tenant's name, address and registration number,

     (*c*)   details of the letting agreement, and

     (*d*)   the date from which the taxable person desires that the waiver shall have effect.

(5) A waiver of exemption shall be backdated only where the tenant would have been entitled to deduct, in accordance with section 12 of the Act, all the tax that would have been chargeable in respect of the letting if the waiver had applied from the date specified in accordance with paragraph (6)(*a*)(i) to the date notified in accordance with paragraph (6)(*a*)(ii).

(6) Where the Revenue Commissioners are satisfied that an applicant has complied with paragraph (4) and that paragraph (5) applies—

     (*a*)   they shall notify the applicant—

         (i)   that the waiver may be back-dated in respect of the letting for which back-dating of a waiver was sought specifying the date to which the waiver shall be back-dated being a date not earlier than 26 March 1997, and

         (ii)   of the date from which he or she is deemed, for the purposes of the Act, to have waived his or her right to exemption in respect of all specified lettings which he or she supplies, such date not being earlier than the commencement of the taxable period during which the notification issued, and

     (*b*)   any tax chargeable on the letting of immovable goods resulting from the back-dating of a waiver prior to the date notified under subparagraph (*a*)(ii) is deemed to have been due and paid by the taxable person in accordance with section 19 of the Act and deducted by the tenant in accordance with section 12 of the Act.

(7) A person who, in accordance with paragraph (1), waives his or her right to exemption in respect of a specified letting shall be entitled to have such waiver cancelled

and to be treated, as from the date specified in paragraph (8), as a person who had not so waived provided he or she—

(*a*)   applies to the Revenue Commissioners in writing to have the waiver of his or her right to exemption cancelled,

(*b*)   furnishes particulars to the Revenue Commissioners of—

(i)   the tax paid by him or her in accordance with section 19(3) of the Act in respect of or in relation to the supply of services by him or her to which the waiver applied for all taxable periods comprised in the period commencing with the beginning of the start period and ending with the termination of the taxable period immediately preceding the cancellation request period, and

(ii)   the total amount of tax deducted or deductible by him or her referred to in paragraphs (*a*), (*b*) and (*c*) of subsection (3) (inserted by section 100 of the Finance Act 1997 (No 22 of 1997)) of section 7 of the Act in respect of all of the taxable periods comprised in the period referred to in clause (i), together with the total amount of tax deducted by him or her referred to in paragraph (*aa*) (inserted by section 117 of the Finance Act 2003 (No 3 of 2003)) of the said subsection (3),

and

(*c*)   pays to the Collector-General an amount equal to the excess (if any) of the tax referred to in subparagraph (*b*)(ii) over the tax referred to in subparagraph (*b*)(i).

(8) Where a person wishing to have his or her waiver cancelled, complies with paragraph (7) to the satisfaction of the Revenue Commissioners, they shall so notify the person in writing. On receipt by the person of the notification, his or her waiver shall be cancelled with effect from the end of the taxable period during which he or she is so notified and from the end of that taxable period the person shall be treated as a person who had not waived his or her right to exemption.

(9) A person who applies for the cancellation of his or her waiver in accordance with paragraph (7) is not entitled, under section 20(1) of the Act, to any refund of tax (other than a refund referable solely to some error or mistake made by him or her) for the cancellation request period or any subsequent taxable periods, in relation to the letting to which the waiver relates, in excess of an amount calculated in accordance with the following sum:

$$A + B$$

where—

A   is the excess of the amount referred to in paragraph 7(*b*)(i) over the amount referred to in paragraph 7(*b*)(ii), but where there is no such excess A is equal to zero,

and

B   is the sum of the amounts of tax paid under section 19(3) of the Act, in relation to the letting to which the waiver relates, for the cancellation request period and any subsequent taxable periods until the waiver is cancelled.

4 Regulation 4 of the Value Added Tax Regulations 1979 (SI No 63 of 1979) is revoked.

EUROPEAN COMMUNITIES (MUTUAL ASSISTANCE IN THE FIELD OF DIRECT TAXATION, CERTAIN EXCISE DUTIES AND TAXATION OF INSURANCE PREMIUMS) REGULATIONS 2003

(SI No 711 of 2003)

I, CHARLIE Mc CREEVY, Minster for Finance, in exercise of the powers conferred on me by section 3 of the European Communities Act 1972 (No 27 of 1972) and for the purpose of giving effect to Council Directive 77/799/EEC of 19 December 1977 (OJ No L336, of 27 December 1977, p 15), as amended by Council Directive No 79/1070/EEC of 6 December 1979 (OJ No L331, of 27 December 1979, p 8), Council Directive No 92/12/EEC of 25 February 1992 (OJ No L76, of 23 March 1992, p 1) and Council Directive 2003/93/EC of 7 October 2003 (OJ No L264, of 15 October 2003, p 23), hereby make the following regulations:

1. (1) These Regulations may be cited as the European Communities (Mutual Assistance in the Field of Direct Taxation, Certain Excise Duties and Taxation of Insurance Premiums) Regulations 2003.

(2) These Regulations come into operation on 31 December 2003.

2. In these Regulations -

"authorised officer" means an officer of the Revenue Commissioners authorised in writing by the Revenue Commissioners for the purpose of these Regulations;

"the Council Directive" means Council Directive 77/799/EEC of 19 December 1977 (OJ No L336, of 27 December 1977, p 15), as amended by Council Directive No 79/1070/EEC of 6 December 1979 (OJ No L331, of 27 December 1979, p 8), Council Directive No 92/12/EEC of 25 February 1992 (OJ No L76, of 23 March 1992, p 1) and Council Directive 2003/93/EC of 7 October 2003 (OJ No L264, of 15 October 2003, p 23).

3. (1) The Revenue Commissioners and authorised officers of those Commissioners may disclose to the competent authorities of another Member State any information required to be to be so disclosed by virtue of the Council Directive.

(2) Neither the Revenue Commissioners nor an authorised officer of those Commissioners shall disclose any information in pursuance of the Council Directive unless satisfied that the competent authorities of the other Member State concerned are bound by, or have undertaken to observe, rules of confidentiality with respect to the information which are not less strict than those applying to it in the State.

(3) Nothing in this Regulation permits the Revenue Commissioners or an authorised officer of those Commissioners to authorise the use of information disclosed by virtue of the Council Directive to the competent authority of another Member State other than for the purposes of taxation or to facilitate legal proceedings for failure to observe the tax laws of that State.

4. (1) Section 107 of the Finance Act 2001 is repealed.

(2) The European Communities (Mutual Assistance in the Field of Direct Taxation) Regulations 1978 (SI No 334 of 1978) and the European Communities (Mutual Assistance in the Field of Value-Added Tax) Regulations 1980 (SI No 407 of 1980) are revoked.

VALUE ADDED TAX (INVOICES AND OTHER DOCUMENTS) (AMENDMENT) REGULATIONS 2003

SI No 723 of 2003

The Revenue Commissioners, in exercise of the powers conferred on them by sections 17 and 32 of the Value Added Tax Act 1972 (No 22 of 1972), and for the purpose of giving further effect to Council Directive 2001/115/EC of 20 December 2001 (OJ No L 15, 17.1. 2002, p 24), make the following regulations:

1. (1) These Regulations may be cited as the Value Added Tax (Invoices and Other Documents)(Amendment) Regulations 2003.

(2) These Regulations come into operation on 1 January 2004.

2. In these Regulations "Principal Regulations" means the Value Added Tax (Invoices and Other Documents) Regulations 1992 (SI No 275 of 1992).

3.

Notes

Para (*a*) substituted Value Added Tax (Invoices and Other Documents) Regulations 1992, r 3(*a*).
Para (*b*) substituted Value Added Tax (Invoices and Other Documents) Regulations 1992, r 3(*g*).
Para (*c*) inserted Value Added Tax (Invoices and Other Documents) Regulations 1992, r 3(*k*).

4.

Notes

Reg 4 substituted Value Added Tax (Invoices and Other Documents) Regulations 1992, rs 3A–3C.

5.

Notes

Reg 5 revoked Value Added Tax (Invoices and Other Documents) Regulations 1992, r 5.

VALUE-ADDED TAX (SHORT-TERM GUEST SECTOR OR HOLIDAY SECTOR) REGULATIONS 2005

SI No 321 of 2005

The Revenue Commissioners, in exercise of the powers conferred on them by section 32 and the Sixth Schedule to the Value-Added Tax Act 1972 (No 22 of 1972), and with the consent of the Minister for Finance, hereby make the following regulations:

1 (1) These Regulations may be cited as the Value-Added Tax (Short-Term Guest Sector or Holiday Sector) Regulations 2005.

(2) These Regulations come into operation on 1 July 2005.

2 A letting which constitutes a letting which is provided in the short-term guest sector or holiday sector for the purposes of paragraph (xiii)(a)(II) of the Sixth Schedule to the Value-Added Tax Act 1972 (No 22 of 1972) is a letting of all or part of a house, apartment or other similar establishment to a tourist, holidaymaker or other visitor for a period which does not exceed or is unlikely to exceed 8 consecutive weeks, but is not a letting —

(*a*) governed by the Housing (Rent Books) Regulations 1993 (SI No146 of 1993),

(*b*) of a dwelling to which Part II of the Housing (Private Rented Dwellings) Act 1982 (No 6 of 1982) applies, or

(*c*) of accommodation which is provided as a temporary dwelling for emergency residential purposes.

ORDERS

Repealed Orders are shown in *italics*.

VALUE ADDED TAX (SPECIFIED DAY) ORDER 1972

Date of imposition of the tax

(SI No 180 of 1972)

1. This Order may be cited as the Value Added Tax (Specified Day) Order, 1972.

Cross-references

VATA 1972, s 1(1).

Notes

This order appointed 1 November 1972 as the day on which VAT came into operation in place of turnover tax and wholesale tax.

---

2. The 1st day of November, 1972, is hereby appointed to be the specified day for the purposes of the Value Added Tax Act, 1972.

VALUE ADDED TAX (APPOINTED DAY) ORDER 1972

Date for registration

(SI No 192 of 1972)

1. This order may be cited as the Value Added Tax (Appointed Day) Order, 1972.

Cross-references

VATA 1972, s 9(4).

Notes

This Order appointed 1 September 1972 as the date from which taxable persons may register for VAT.

2. The 1st day of September, 1972, is hereby appointed to be the appointed day for the purpose of section 9 of the Value Added Tax Act, 1972.

VALUE ADDED TAX (REFUND OF TAX) (NO 1) ORDER 1972

(SI No 267 of 1972)

Notes

Revoked by Value Added Tax (Refund of Tax) (No 25) Order 1993 (SI 266/1993), r 9.

VALUE ADDED TAX (REDUCTION OF RATE) (NO 1) ORDER 1972

(SI No 268 of 1972)

Amendments

Revoked by FA 1973, s 80(*f*) with effect from 3 September 1973.

Notes

Where the rate of tax chargeable on the delivery of goods was 16.37%, that rate also applied to the hire of such goods. This order reduced the VAT rate applicable to the hire of such goods to 5.26%. The reduction in rate only applied where the goods were in the possession of the person (to whom the goods were hired) on 1 November 1972.

VALUE ADDED TAX (REFUND OF TAX) (NO 2) ORDER 1972

(SI No 269 of 1972)

Notes

Revoked by Value Added Tax (Refund of Tax) (Revocation) Order 1979 (SI 232/1979) with effect from 1 March 1979.

VALUE ADDED TAX (REDUCTION OF RATE) (NO 2) ORDER 1972

(SI No 326 of 1972)

Amendments

Revoked by FA 1973, s 80(*f*) with effect from 3 September 1973.

Notes

This order enabled unregistered sea fishermen to reclaim VAT on fishing boats the purchase of which had been grant aided (or loan financed) by Bord Iascaigh Mhara.

VALUE ADDED TAX (REFUND OF TAXING) (NO 3) ORDER 1972

(SI No 327 of 1972)

Amendments

Revoked by Value Added Tax (Refund of Tax)(No 12) Order 1980 (SI 262/1980) with effect from 1 March 1979.

Notes

This order enabled the Revenue Commissioners to repay VAT (in excess of the 3% rate applicable to fixed buildings) to the purchaser of a mobile home or similar structure where the mobile home etc was used (or provided for use by a local authority) as a residence.

VALUE ADDED TAX (REFUND OF TAX) (NO 4) ORDER 1972

(SI No 328 of 1972)

Amendments

Revoked by Value Added Tax (Refund of Tax) (No 13) Order (SI 263/1980).

Notes

This order enabled the Revenue Commissioners to repay VAT paid on specially constructed or adapted motor vehicles for use by disabled drivers.

PRICES AND CHARGES (TAX-INCLUSIVE STATEMENTS) ORDER 1973

(SI No 9 of 1973)

1. This Order may be cited as the Prices and Charges (Tax-inclusive Statements) Order, 1973.

2. This Order shall come into operation on the 1st day of February, 1973.

3. Where, for the purposes of or in connection with the sale by retail by a person of a commodity, the retail price of the commodity is stated orally by the person or by a servant or agent of the person or is stated on the commodity or on any container or wrapper in which the commodity is packed or on a ticket or label attached to the commodity or to such container or wrapper or in a catalogue or advertisement or in a notice or other document (other than an invoice), the price so stated shall be stated as a single amount inclusive of any charge made by the person for any tax payable in respect of the commodity.

4. Where, for purposes of or in connection with the rendering of a service by a person, the charge for the service is stated orally by the person or by a servant or agent of the person or is stated in any catalogue or advertisement or in a notice or other document (other than an invoice), the charge so stated shall be stated as a single amount inclusive of any charge made by the person for any tax payable in respect of the service.

VALUE ADDED TAX (REDUCTION OF RATE) (NO 3) ORDER 1973

(SI No 69 of 1973)

Amendments

Revoked by FA 1973, s 80(*f*) with effect from 3 September 1973.

Notes

With effect from 1 November 1972, this order applied the 0% rate to life saving services provided by the Royal National Lifeboat Institution.

VALUE ADDED TAX (REFUND OF TAX) (NO 5) ORDER 1973

(SI No 70 of 1973)

Amendments

Revoked by Value Added Tax (Refund of Tax) (No 14) Order 1980 (SI 264/1980) with effect from 1 March 1979.

Notes

With effect from 1 November 1972, this order allowed the repayment of VAT paid (in excess of 5.26%) on medical and laboratory appliances bought by hospitals, colleges etc.

VALUE ADDED TAX (REFUND OF TAX) (NO 6) ORDER 1973

(SI No 238 of 1973)

Notes

This order made consequential amendments to existing Orders arising out of changes in the rates of tax made by FA 1973. Para 2 substituted Value Added Tax (Refund of Tax)(No 3) Order 1972, r 5 (SI 327/1972); para 3(*a*) amended Value Added Tax (Refund of Tax)(No 4) Order 1972, r 4 (*c*)(i)(I) and substituted r 5 (*a*)(iii)(SI 328/1972); para 4(*a*) amended Value Added Tax (Refund of Tax)(No 5) Order 1973, r 4 and substituted r 6 (SI 70/1973).

VALUE ADDED TAX (REFUND OF TAX) (NO 7) ORDER 1974

(SI No 290 of 1974)

Eurocontrol purchases

1. This Order may be cited as the Value Added Tax (Refund of Tax) (No 7) Order, 1974.

Cross-references

VATA 1972, s 20(3).

Notes

This Order enables repayment of VAT on purchases of goods by Eurocontrol to be made subject to certain conditions.

---

2. This Order shall be deemed to have come into operation on the 1st day of November, 1972.

3. In this Order **"the Organisation"** means the European Organisation for the Safety of Air Navigation (Eurocontrol) established by the International Convention relating to Cooperation for the Safety of Air Navigation signed at Brussels on the 13th day of December, 1960, and references to the Organisation include references to the Permanent Commission for the Safety of Air Navigation comprised in the Organisation and to the Air Traffic Services Agency comprised in the Organisation.

4. Where the Organisation establishes to the satisfaction of the Revenue Commissioners that, in connection with its official activities it has borne tax on the delivery to it of goods or on the rendering to it of services, and those goods or services are of substantial value, and fulfils to the satisfaction of the said Commissioners all the conditions which are specified in paragraph 5 of this Order it shall be entitled to be repaid the tax so established as having been borne or paid.

5. (*a*) The Organisation shall claim a refund of the tax by completing such claim form as may be provided for the purpose by the Revenue Commissioners and it shall certify the particulars shown on such claim form to be correct.

(*b*) The Organisation shall, by the production of an invoice provided in accordance with section 17(12)(*a*)(i) of the Value Added Tax Act, 1972, establish the amount of tax borne in relation to such delivery or rendering.

VALUE ADDED TAX (REFUND OF TAX) (NO 8) ORDER 1978

(SI No 145 of 1978)

Notes

Revoked by Value Added Tax (Refund of Tax) (No 25) Order 1993 (SI 266/1993), r 9.

VALUE ADDED TAX (REDUCTION OF RATE) (NO 4) ORDER 1978

(SI No 146 of 1978)

Candles

1. (1) This Order may be cited as the Value Added Tax (Reduction of Rate) (No 4) Order, 1978.

(2) This Order shall come into operation on the 1st day of July, 1978.

Cross-references

VATA 1972, s 11(8).

2.

Notes

This Order, by inserting VATA 1972, Sch 2 para (xx)(*cc*) adds plain white candles and night lights to the list of zero rated goods.

VALUE ADDED TAX (AMENDMENT) ACT, 1978 (COMMENCEMENT) ORDER 1979

(SI No 8 of 1979)

Date of implementation of Value Added Tax (Amendment) Act, 1978

1. This Order may be cited as the Value Added Tax (Amendment) Act, 1978 (Commencement) Order, 1979.

Cross reference

VATAA 1978, s 32(3).

Notes

This Order brought VAT(A)A 1978 into operation on 1 March 1979.

2. The 1st day of March, 1979, is hereby appointed as the day on which sections 1 to 28 and 30 to 32 of the Value Added Tax (Amendment) Act, 1978, shall come into operation.

VALUE ADDED TAX (REFUND OF TAX) (NO 9) ORDER 1979

(SI No 59 of 1979)

Stocks of radios and record players

1. This Order may be cited as the Value Added Tax (Refund of Tax) (No 9) Order, 1979.

Cross-references

VATA 1972, s 20(3).

Notes

This Order allowed traders in radio receivers and record players (other than manufacturers) to claim a refund of VAT on stocks purchased before 1 March 1979 and held for resale on that date.

---

2. This Order shall come into operation on the 1st day of March, 1979.

3. Where a person, other than a manufacturer of goods of the kind in question, registered in accordance with section 9 of the Value Added Tax Act, 1972 (No 22 of 1972), establishes to the satisfaction of the Revenue Commissioners that—

(*a*) he holds at the commencement of the 1st day of March, 1979, a stock of radio receiving sets that are of the domestic or portable type or of a type suitable for use in road vehicles; or a stock of gramophones, radiogramophones or record players, for supply in the course of a business carried on by him, and

(*b*) he has purchased or imported the goods in question prior to the 1st day of March, 1979, in such circumstances that tax at the rate specified in section 11(1)(*c*)(ii) of the said Act was borne or paid on the goods either by him or by a previous purchaser or importer of the goods and that the tax did not qualify for deduction under subsection (1) of section 12 of the Act except to the extent specified in the proviso to that subsection,

he shall, subject to the conditions specified in Article 4 of this Order, be entitled to be repaid such of the following amounts as are appropriate:

(i) in a case where the goods in questions were imported by or delivered to the person in such circumstances that tax at the rate specified in section 11(1)(*c*)(ii) of the said Act was charged on the importation or delivery, an amount equal to **30 per cent** of the amount on which tax was so charged, and

(ii) in any other case, the amount of tax which the Revenue Commissioners are satisfied has been borne on the acquisition of the goods and which does not qualify for deduction under section 12(1)(*a*) of the Act.

4. The conditions referred to in Article 3 of this Order are:

(*a*) the person concerned shall claim a refund of the tax by completing such form as may be provided for the purpose by the Revenue Commissioners showing, if requested, the total number of items of each description of goods, the number of different makes and models within each description, the name of the supplier and the number and date of invoice in relation to each item or group of

803

items and the relative amounts of consideration or value at importation and he shall certify the particulars shown on such claim form to be correct,

(*b*) the person concerned shall, if requested by the Revenue Commissioners, by the production of invoices issued in accordance with section 17(1) of the Act or by the production of customs documents, establish to them the amount of the consideration or the value at importation, as the case may be, in relation to which a refund is claimed.

VALUE ADDED TAX (REFUND OF TAX) (REVOCATION) ORDER 1979

(SI No 232 of 1979)

Revocation of SI No 269 of 1972

1. (1) This Order may be cited as the Value Added Tax (Refund of Tax) (Revocation) Order, 1979.

(2) This Order shall be deemed to have come into operation on the 1st day of March, 1979.

Cross-reference

VATA 1972, s 20(3).

Notes

This Order revoked Value Added Tax (Refund of Tax) (No 2) Order 1972 (SI 269/1972) which enabled commercial sea fishermen who were not registered for VAT to reclaim VAT on fishing boats for which they received a grant or loan from An Bord Iascaigh Mhara. This relief is now given by VATR 1979, r 29.

---

2. The Value Added Tax (Refund of Tax) (No 2) Order, 1972 (SI No 269 of 1972), is hereby revoked.

VALUE ADDED TAX (REFUND OF TAX) (NO 10) ORDER 1979

(SI No 275 of 1979)

Vehicles for disabled persons

Amendments

Revoked by Value Added Tax (Refund of Tax) (Revocation) Order 1989 (SI 351/1989).

Notes

This order enabled the Revenue Commissioners to repay VAT paid on the purchase or importation of vehicles built (or adapted) to carry disabled persons.

VALUE ADDED TAX (REFUND OF TAX) (NO 11) ORDER 1980

(SI No 239 of 1980)

European Space Agency

1. This Order may be cited as the Value Added Tax (Refund of Tax) (No 11) Order, 1980.

Cross-references

VATA 1972, s 20(3).

Notes

This Order permits repayment of VAT on purchase of goods and services by the European Space Agency subject to certain conditions. The Order came into operation on 29 November 1976.

---

2. This Order shall be deemed to have come into operation on the 29th day of November, 1976.

3. In this Order **"the Agency"** means the European Space Agency established by the Convention for the Establishment of a European Space Agency signed at Paris on the 30th day of May, 1975.

4. Where the Agency establishes to the satisfaction of the Revenue Commissioners that it has borne tax on the supply to it of goods or services of substantial value which are strictly necessary for the exercise of its official activities and fulfils to the satisfaction of the said Commissioners all the conditions which are specified in paragraph 5 of this Order it shall be entitled to be repaid the tax so established as having been borne.

5. (*a*) The agency shall claim a refund of the tax by completing such claim form as may be provided for the purpose by the Revenue Commissioners and it shall certify the particulars shown on such claim form to be correct.

(*b*) The agency shall, by the production of an invoice, provided in accordance with section 17(12)(*a*)(i) of the Value Added Tax Act, 1972, establish the amount of tax borne in relation to such supply.

VALUE ADDED TAX (REFUND OF TAX) (NO 12) ORDER 1980

(SI No 262 of 1980)

Mobile homes

1. (1) This Order may be cited as the Value Added Tax (Refund of Tax) (No 12) Order, 1980.

(2) This Order shall be deemed to have come into operation on the 1st day of March, 1979.

Cross-references

VATA 1972, s 20(2).

Notes

This Order, which came into operation on 1 March 1979, enables repayment of VAT to be made in respect of caravans, mobile homes or similar structures purchased by a person (or local authority) for use as a residence. The refund will be such as to adjust the rate of VAT to the same effective rate as applies to the construction of permanent buildings. It is a condition for repayment that the caravan or mobile home be rated.
This Order revokes Value Added Tax (Refund of Tax) (No 3) Order 1972 (SI 327/1972) with effect from 1 March 1979.

---

2. (1) In this Order **"the Act"** means the Value Added Tax Act, 1972 (No 22 of 1972).

(2) A reference in this Order to a caravan includes a reference to a mobile home or any similar structure designed primarily for residential purposes.

3. A person who establishes to the satisfaction of the Revenue Commissioners that he has borne or paid tax in relation to the supply to or importation by him of a caravan and who fulfils to the satisfaction of the said Commissioners the conditions which are specified in paragraph 4 of this Order shall be entitled to be repaid so much of such tax as is specified in paragraph 5 of this Order.

4. The conditions to be fulfilled by a person referred to in paragraph 3 of this Order are—

    (*a*)   he shall claim a refund of the tax by completing such claim form as may be provided for the purpose by the Revenue Commissioners and he shall certify the particulars shown in such claim form to be correct;

    (*b*)   he shall establish that the caravan in relation to which a claim for a refund of the tax arises—

        (i)   is used by him as a permanent residence for himself and that neither he nor (if he is a married man having his spouse living with him) his spouse has any other place of abode within the State available for his occupation, or

        (ii)   is, in the case of a local authority, occupied as a residence by a tenant of the local authority;

    (*c*)   he shall, in the case of a person other than a local authority, by the production of a certificate from the appropriate local authority or such other documentary evidence as may be acceptable to the Revenue Commissioners, establish that the caravan has been rated under the Valuation Acts;

(*d*) he shall, by the production of invoices, provided in accordance with section 17(12)(*a*)(i) of the Act, or by the production of receipts for tax paid on importation, establish the amount of tax borne or paid by him in relation to the caravan excluding any amount referable to articles of furniture or equipment which would not be regarded as fixtures if the caravan were regarded as immovable goods at the time of its supply or importation;

(*e*) he shall establish the net tax-exclusive amount of the consideration for the supply to him of the caravan, or, if the caravan was imported by him, its net tax-exclusive value, exclusive, in either case, of the amount, if any, included in such consideration or value for the supply or importation of such articles as are referred to in subparagraph (*d*) of this paragraph;

(*f*) he shall establish that he is not entitled to a deduction under section 12 of the Act for any portion of the tax specified in subparagraph (*d*) of this paragraph.

5. The amount of tax to be repaid to a person referred to in paragraph 3 of this Order shall be so much of the amount of tax specified in paragraph 4(*d*) of this Order as the person shows to the satisfaction of the Revenue Commissioners to be in excess of the amount which would have been borne or paid by him if the rate and percentage for the time being referred to in section 11(2)(*b*) of the Act had applied to the supply or importation in question.

Cross-references

FA 1985, s 43(*b*).

---

6. The Value Added Tax (Refund of Tax) (No 3) Order, 1972 (S.I. No 327 of 1972), is hereby revoked with effect as on and from the 1st day of March 1979.

VALUE ADDED TAX (REFUND OF TAX) (NO 13) ORDER 1980

(SI No 263 of 1980)

Disabled drivers' vehicles

Notes

This Order, which revoked and replaced Value Added Tax (Refund of Tax) (No 4) Order 1972 (SI 328/1972), was itself revoked by the Value Added Tax (Refund of Tax) (Revocation) Order 1989 (SI 351/1989). Refunds of tax and excise duty to disabled drivers are now governed by the Disabled Drivers (Tax Concessions) Regulations 1989 (SI 340/1989).

VALUE ADDED TAX (REFUND OF TAX) (NO 14) ORDER 1980

(SI No 264 of 1980)

Certain hospital equipment

1. (1) This Order may be cited as the Value Added Tax (Refund of Tax) (No 14) Order, 1980.

(2) This Order shall be deemed to have come into operation on the 1st day of March, 1979.

Cross-references

VATA 1972, s 20(3).

Notes

This Order, which came into force on 1 March 1979, provides for a refund of the excess of VAT paid over the low rate on medical or research equipment by hospitals, universities, colleges, schools or similar educational bodies operating medical research laboratories (including veterinary research). This Order revokes the Value Added Tax (Refund of Tax) (No 5) Order 1973 (SI 70/1973).

With effect from 1 January 1993, "importation" means importation from a non-EC country: VATA 1972, s 1(1).

---

2. In this Order **"the Act"** means the Value Added Tax Act, 1972.

3. This Order applies to the following persons:

> (*a*) a body of persons in its capacity as a person operating a hospital;

> (*b*) a university, college, school or similar educational body in its capacity as a person operating a medical research laboratory;

> (*c*) a research institution in its capacity as a person operating a medical research laboratory.

4. A person to whom this Order applies who establishes to the satisfaction of the Revenue Commissioners that he has borne or paid tax at a rate in excess of the rate per cent. for the time being specified in section 11(1)(*a*) of the Act in relation to the supply to or importation by him of any instrument or appliance of a kind commonly used to make a diagnosis, to prevent or treat an illness, to carry out a surgical operation or to carry out scientific research and who fulfils to the satisfaction of the Revenue Commissioners the conditions which are specified in paragraph 5 of this Order shall be entitled to be repaid so much of such tax as is specified in paragraph 6 of this Order.

5. The conditions to be fulfilled by a person referred to in paragraph 4 of this Order are—

> (*a*) he shall claim a refund of the tax by completing such claim form as may be provided for the purpose by the Revenue Commissioners and he shall certify the particulars shown on such form to be correct;

> (*b*) he shall establish that he is a person to whom this Order applies and that the instruments or appliances on the supply or importation of which the tax was borne or paid by him were used by him in the capacity in relation to which this Order applies to him;

(*c*) he shall establish, by the production of invoices, provided in accordance with section 17(12)(*a*)(i) of the Act, or by the production of receipts for tax paid on imported goods, the amount of tax borne or paid by him in relation to the goods specified in paragraph 4 of this Order;

(*d*) he shall establish that he is not entitled to a deduction under section 12 of the Act for any portion of the tax specified in subparagraph (*c*) of this paragraph.

6. The amount of tax to be repaid to the claimant shall be so much of the amount of tax specified in paragraph 5(c) of this Order as the person shows to the satisfaction of the Revenue Commissioners to be in excess of the amount of tax which would have been borne or paid by him if the rate specified in section 11(1)(*a*) of the Act had applied to the supply or importation in question.

7. The Value Added Tax (Refund of Tax) (No 5) Order, 1973 (S.I. No 70 of 1973) is hereby revoked with effect as on and from the 1st day of March, 1979.

VALUE ADDED TAX (REDUCTION OF RATE) (NO 5) ORDER 1981

(SI No 53 of 1981)

Certain medical goods used by disabled persons

1. (1) This Order may be cited as the Value Added Tax (Reduction of Rate) (No 5) Order, 1981.

Cross-references

VATA 1972, s 11(8).

Notes

This Order, which came into effect on 1 March 1981, applies the zero rate of VAT to a variety of medical goods used by disabled or infirm people.

(2) This Order shall come into operation on the 1st day of March, 1981.

2.

Notes

This para inserted VATA 1972, Sch 2 para (xix*a*).

3.

Notes

This para deleted VATA 1972, Sch 3 para (xvii)(*c*) and substituted VATA 1972, Sch 3 para (xvii)(*f*).

VALUE ADDED TAX (REFUND OF TAX) (NO 15) ORDER 1981

(SI No 428 of 1981)

Certain goods for use by disabled persons

1. This Order may be cited as the Value Added Tax (Refund of Tax)(No 15) Order, 1981.

Cross-references

VATA 1972, s 20(3).

Notes

This Order provides for repayment of VAT on certain goods and applications which assist disabled people where such goods are purchased after 1 March 1981.

---

2. In this Order—

"the Act" means the Value Added Tax Act, 1972;

"disabled person" means a person who, as a result of an injury, disease, congenital deformity or physical or mental illness, or defect, suffers from a loss of physical or mental faculty resulting in a specified degree of disablement; and cognate words shall be construed accordingly;

"qualified goods" means goods other than mechanically propelled road vehicles which are aids or appliances, including parts and accessories, specially constructed or adapted for use by a disabled person and includes goods which, although not so specially constructed or adapted, are of such a kind as might reasonably be treated as so constructed or adapted having regard to the particular disablement of that person;

"specified degree of disablement" means, as regards a disablement to which the provisions of the Social Welfare (Occupational Injuries) Regulations, 1967 (No 77 of 1967), apply, a degree of disablement which, if assessed in accordance with those provisions, would be not less than **30 per cent**, and, as regards any other disablement, a degree of disablement of equivalent extent.

3. Where a person establishes to the satisfaction of the Revenue Commissioners that—

    (*a*) he has borne or paid tax which became chargeable on or after the 1st day of March, 1981, in respect of the supply to or importation by him of qualifying goods, and

    (*b*) he fulfils the conditions which are specified in paragraph 4 of this Order, and such other conditions as the said Commissioners may impose, he shall be entitled to repayment of the amount of tax so borne or paid.

4. The conditions to be fulfilled by a person referred to in paragraph 3 of this Order are—

    (*a*) he shall claim a refund of the tax by completing such claim form as may be provided for the purpose by the Revenue Commissioners and he shall certify the particulars shown on such claim form to be correct;

    (*b*) (i)   in case he is the person for whose use the goods referred to in paragraph 3 of this Order were supplied or imported, he shall, by the production of such evidence as may be acceptable to the said Commissioners, establish that he is a disabled person and that the goods are for the purpose of assisting him to overcome his disability in the performance of essential daily functions or in the exercise of a vocation, and that the goods are so used by him;

         (ii)   in case he is not the person for whose use the said goods were supplied or imported, he shall, by the production of such evidence as may be acceptable to the said Commissioners, establish that the goods were supplied by him, other than in the course of business, to a particular person who is a disabled person for the purpose of assisting that person to overcome his disability in the performance of essential daily functions or in the exercise of a vocation, and that the goods are so used by that other person;

    (*c*)   he shall by the production of invoices, provided in accordance with section 17(12)(*a*)(i) of the Act, or by the production of receipts for tax paid on goods imported, establish the amount of tax borne or paid to which the claim relates;

    (*d*)   he shall establish that he is not entitled to a deduction under section 12 of the Act or a repayment under section 20(2) of the Act or under a regulation or order, other than this Order, made under the Act in respect of any portion of the tax specified in subparagraph (*c*) of this paragraph;

    (*e*)   he shall establish that the tax specified in subparagraph (*c*) of this paragraph does not form any part of expenditure incurred by him which has been or will be met, directly or indirectly, by the State, by any board established by statute, or by any public or local authority.

VALUE ADDED TAX (REFUND OF TAX) (NO 16) ORDER 1983

(SI No 324 of 1983)

1. (1) This Order may be cited as the Value Added Tax (Refund of Tax) (No 16) Order, 1983.

(2) This Order shall be deemed to have come into operation on the 1st day of May, 1983.

Cross-references

VATA 1972, s 20(3).

Notes

This Order, which came into operation on 1 May 1983, enables sea-fishermen to reclaim VAT on importation of marine diesel for use on a registered sea-fishing vessel.

---

2. In this Order—

    (*a*) **"the Act"** means the Value Added Tax Act, 1972;

    (*b*) **"sea-fishing vessel"** means a sea-fishing boat which —

        (i) is registered in accordance with the Merchant Shipping (Registry, Lettering and Numbering of Fishing Boats) (Regulations) Order, 1927 (S.R. & O., No 105 of 1927),

        and

        (ii) is registered under the Mercantile Marine Act, 1955 (No 29 of 1955);

    (*c*) **"hydrocarbon oil"** means hydrocarbon oil of a kind specified in paragraph (i)(*c*) of the Sixth Schedule to the Act.

3. A person who establishes to the satisfaction of the Revenue Commissioners that he has borne or paid tax on the supply to or importation by him of hydrocarbon oil used for combustion in the engine of a sea-fishing vessel in the course of a sea-fishing business carried on by him and who fulfils to the satisfaction of the said Commissioners the conditions which are specified in paragraph 4 of this Order, shall be entitled to be repaid the amount of tax so borne or paid.

4. The conditions to be fulfilled by a person referred to in paragraph 3 of this Order are—

    (*a*) he shall claim a refund of the tax concerned by completing such claim form as may be provided for the purpose by the Revenue Commissioners and he shall certify the particulars shown on such claim form to be correct;

    (*b*) he shall, by the production of invoices, provided in accordance with section 17(12)(*a*)(i) of the Act, or by the production of receipts for tax paid on goods imported, establish the amount of tax borne or paid to which the claim relates;

    (*c*) he shall establish that he is not a person who is registered in the register maintained under section 9 of the Act, nor a person required under the provisions of that section to furnish the particulars specified for registration;

(*d*) except where the Revenue Commissioners otherwise allow, the claim for a refund of tax shall be made in respect of hydrocarbon oil used within a period or periods of three months.

VALUE ADDED TAX (REFUND OF TAX) (NO 17) ORDER 1984

(SI No 249 of 1984)

Notes

Revoked by Value Added Tax (Refund of Tax) (No 25) Order 1993 (SI 266/1993), r 9.

VALUE ADDED TAX (REFUND OF TAX) (NO 18) ORDER 1985

(SI No 192 of 1985)

1. (1) This Order may be cited as the Value Added Tax (Refund of Tax) (No 18) Order, 1985.

(2) This Order shall be deemed to have come into operation on the 1st day of January, 1979.

Notes

This Order, which has effect from 1 January 1979, enables VAT on certain small reserve craft, ancillary equipment and special boat buildings to be repaid to qualifying sea rescue groups subject to certain conditions. The Order is retrospective.

With effect from 1 January 1993, "importation" means importation from a non-EC country: VATA 1972, s 1(1).

---

2. In this Order —

"the Act" means the Value Added Tax Act, 1972, (No 22 of 1972);

"the Irish Water Safety Association" means the body established under the Irish Water Safety Association (Establishment) Order, 1980 (S.I. No 244 of 1980).

3. A body of persons which establishes to the satisfaction of the Revenue Commissioners that it has borne or paid tax in relation to the supply or hire to it, the importation by it or the repair, modification or maintenance for it of a boat or similar craft of a gross tonnage of 15 tons or less, designed and constructed, or adapted, for the purpose of rescue or assistance at sea, of equipment for use in or in conjunction with any such boat or craft, or of a building or structure for housing or operating such boat, craft or equipment, and which fulfils to the satisfaction of the said Commissioners the conditions specified in paragraph 4 of this Order shall be entitled to be repaid such tax.

4. The conditions to be fulfilled by a body of persons referred to in paragraph 3 of this Order are:

    (*a*) it shall claim a refund of the tax by completing such form as may be provided for the purpose by the Revenue Commissioners and shall certify the particulars shown on such form to be correct;

    (*b*) it shall, by the production of documentary evidence establish that the outlay in relation to which the claim for a refund of tax arises was incurred in respect of the supply or hire to it, the importation by it or the repair, modification or maintenance for it of a boat or similar craft of a gross tonnage of 15 tons or less designed and constructed, or adapted, for the purpose of rescue or assistance at sea, of equipment for use in or in conjunction with such boat or craft, or of a building or structure for housing or operating such boat, craft or equipment;

    (*c*) it shall, by the production of invoices provided in accordance with section 17(12)(*a*)(i) of the Act, or by the production of a receipt for tax paid on importation, establish the amount of tax borne or paid in relation to the outlay referred to in subparagraph (*b*) of this paragraph;

(*d*)   subject to paragraph 5 of this Order, it shall, by the production of documentary evidence from the Irish Water Safety Association, establish to the satisfaction of the Revenue Commissioners that it provides services of rescue or assistance at sea and that the nature and extent of such services meet the requirements of the said Association in relation to the organisation and functioning of bodies of persons providing services of rescue or assistance at sea;

(*e*)   it shall establish to the satisfaction of the Revenue Commissioners that the boat or craft, the equipment, and the building or structure specified in paragraph 3 of this Order are not used for any purpose other than in relation to rescue or assistance at sea or the training of persons in connection therewith;

(*f*)   it shall establish that it is not a person who is registered in the register maintained under section 9 of the Act, nor a person required under the provisions of that section to furnish the particulars specified for registration;

(*g*)   except where the Revenue Commissioners otherwise allow, the claim for a refund of tax shall be made only in respect of outlay incurred within a period of twelve months or more.

5. The provisions of this Order, other than paragraph 4(*d*), shall apply to claims for refund of tax made by the Irish Water Safety Association.

6. The secretary, or other officer acting as secretary for the time being, of a body of persons which makes a claim for refund of tax under this Order shall be answerable in addition to the body for doing all such acts as are required to be done by the body in relation to the making of such a claim.

VALUE ADDED TAX (EXEMPTED ACTIVITIES) (NO 1) ORDER 1985

(SI No 430 of 1985)

1. This Order may be cited as the Value Added Tax (Exempted Activities) (No 1) Order, 1985.

Cross-references

VATA 1972, s 6(2).

Notes

This Order exempts from VAT the reimbursement by credit card companies of traders for goods and services supplied to card holders.

2.

...

Notes

This para inserted VATA 1972, Sch 1 para (xi*a*).

VALUE ADDED TAX (REFUND OF TAX) (NO 19) ORDER 1986

(SI No 68 of 1986)

1. (1) This Order may be cited as the Value Added Tax (Refund of Tax) (No 19) Order, 1986.

(2) This Order shall be deemed to have come into operation on the 1st day of March, 1986.

Cross-references

VATA 1972, s 20(3).

Notes

This Order, which came into operation on 1 March 1986, enables VAT in excess of the low rate on certain touring coaches to be repaid subject to certain conditions.

---

2. In this Order **"the Act"** means the Value Added Tax Act, 1972.

[3. A person who establishes to the satisfaction of the Revenue Commissioners that he had borne or paid tax in relation to the acquisition, including the hiring (other than the hiring for a period of less than 6 consecutive months), by him of a passenger road motor vehicle not more than 24 months old, being—

(*a*) a single-deck touring coach having dimensions as designated by the manufacturer of not less than 3,350 millimetres in height, not less than 10,000 millimetres in length and not less than 1,400 millimetres in floor height, or

(*b*) a double-deck touring coach having dimensions as designated by the manufacturer of not more than 4,300 millimetres in height and not less than 10,000 millimetres in length, for use by him for the purposes of the business referred to in subparagraph (*b*) of paragraph 4 of this Order, and who fulfils to the satisfaction of the said Commissioners the conditions that are specified in the said paragraph 4 and such other conditions as the said Commissioners may impose, shall be entitled to be repaid so much of such tax as is specified in paragraph 5 of this Order.][1]

Amendments

[1] Para 3 substituted by Value Added Tax (Refund of Tax) (No 22) Order 1988 (SI 262/1988).

---

4. The conditions to be fulfilled by a person referred to in paragraph 3 of this Order are:—

(*a*) he shall claim a refund of the tax by completing such claim form as may be provided for the purpose by the Revenue Commissioners and he shall certify the particulars shown on such form to be correct;

(*b*) he shall, by the production of such evidence as the Revenue Commissioners may require, establish that he is engaged in the business of carriage of persons, including tourists, by road under contracts for group transport;

(*c*) he shall, by the production of invoices, provided in accordance with section 17(12)(*a*)(i) of the Act, or by the production of receipts for the tax paid on importation of the vehicle, establish the amount of tax borne or paid by him in relation to the acquisition by him of the vehicle;

(*d*) he shall establish that he is not entitled to a deduction under section 12 of the Act in respect of any portion of the tax specified in subparagraph (*c*) of this paragraph.

5. The amount of tax to be repaid under this Order shall be so much of the amount of tax specified in paragraph 4(*c*) of this Order as is shown to the satisfaction of the Revenue Commissioners to be in excess of the amount which would have been borne or paid if the rate and percentage for the time being specified in section 11(1)(*c*) of the Act had applied in relation to the acquisition in question.

IMPOSITION OF DUTIES (NO 283) (VALUE ADDED TAX) ORDER 1986

(SI No 412 of 1986)

Amendments

Revoked by FA 1987, s 39(*b*) with effect from 9 July 1987.

Notes

This order, which came into effect on 1 January 1987, by including "deer" in the definition of livestock in VATA 1972, s 1, provided that the VAT rate on the supply of live deer was reduced from 25% to 2.4%.

VALUE ADDED TAX (REFUND OF TAX) (NO 20) ORDER 1987

(SI No 10 of 1987)

Notes

Revoked with effect from 29 January 1992, by Value Added Tax (Refund of Tax) (No 23) Order 1992 (SI 58/ 1992).

VALUE ADDED TAX (REFUND OF TAX) (NO 21) ORDER 1987

(SI No 308 of 1987)

1. (1) This Order may be cited as the Value Added Tax (Refund of Tax) (No 21) Order, 1987.

(2) This Order shall be deemed to have come into operation on the 1st day of July, 1987.

Cross-references

VATA 1972, s 20(3).

Notes

This Order, which has effect from 1 July 1987, provides relief from tax for goods purchased for export by philanthropic organisations for use in their activities abroad.

With effect from 1 January 1993, "exportation" means exportation to a non-EC country: VATA 1972, s 1(1).

---

2. In this Order—

    (*a*) **"the Act"** means the Value Added Tax Act, 1972;

    (*b*) **"qualifying body"** means any non-profit making body of persons with aims of a philanthropic nature, engaged in humanitarian, charitable or teaching activities abroad;

    (*c*) **"qualifying goods"** means goods which, within four months of their supply in, or importation into, the State, have been exported, by or on behalf of a qualifying body, for use in its humanitarian, charitable or teaching activities abroad.

3. A person, who establishes to the satisfaction of the Revenue Commissioners that—

    (*a*) he is a qualifying body, or that he is acting on behalf of a qualifying body,

    (*b*) the goods to which the claim relates are qualifying goods,

    (*c*) he has borne or paid tax on the supply to, or importation by, him of those qualifying goods,

and who fulfils, to the satisfaction of the said Commissioners, the conditions specified in paragraph 4 of this Order, shall be entitled to be repaid such tax.

4. The conditions to be fulfilled by a person referred to in paragraph 3 of this Order are that he shall—

    (*a*) claim a refund of the tax by completing such claim form as may be provided for the purpose by the Revenue Commissioners, and certify the particulars shown on such claim form to be correct;

    (*b*) establish the amount of tax borne or paid to which the claim relates by the production of invoice or other documents, provided in accordance with section 17(12)(*a*)(i) of the Act, or by the production of receipts for tax paid on goods imported;

    (*c*) establish that he is not entitled to remission, repayment or deduction of the tax under any other provision of the Act, or under any instrument made under statute administered by the Revenue Commissioners in respect of the supply or importation of the qualifying goods.

VALUE ADDED TAX (REFUND OF TAX) (NO 22) ORDER 1988

(SI No 262 of 1988)

1. (1) This Order may be cited as the Value Added Tax (Refund of Tax) (No 22) Order, 1988.

(2) This Order shall be deemed to have come into operation on the 1st day of October, 1988.

Cross-references

VATA 1972, s 20(3).

Notes

This Order extends the existing VAT refund scheme to luxury touring coaches.

2.

...

Note

Para 2 substituted Value Added Tax (Refund of Tax) (No 19) Order 1986 (SI 68/1986), para 3.

VALUE ADDED TAX (REFUND OF TAX) (REVOCATION) ORDER 1989

(SI No 351 of 1989)

1. (1) This Order may be cited as the Value Added Tax (Refund of Tax) (Revocation) Order, 1989.

(2) This Order shall come into operation on the 21st day of December 1989.

2. The Value Added Tax (Refund of Tax) (No 10) Order, 1979, (SI No 275 1979) and the Value Added Tax (Refund of Tax) (No 13) Order, 1980 (SI No 263 of 1980), are hereby revoked.

Notes

These orders are revoked as the Disabled Drivers (Tax Concessions) Regulations (SI 340/1989) now provides equivalent relief.

VALUE ADDED TAX (REFUND OF TAX) (NO 23) ORDER 1992

(SI No 58 of 1992)

1. (1) This Order may be cited as the Value Added Tax (Refund of Tax) (No 23) Order, 1992.

(2) This Order shall be deemed to have come into operation on the 29th day of January, 1992.

Cross-references

VATA 1972, s 20(3).

Notes

This Order, which came into operation on 29 January 1992, provides for a full refund of VAT paid on qualifying medical equipment purchased through voluntary donations. It replaces and revokes the Value Added Tax (Refund of Tax) (No 20) Order 1987 (SI 10/1987).

---

2. In this Order—

"the Act" means the Value Added Tax Act, 1972 (No 22 of 1972), and every enactment which is to be construed together with that Act;

"qualifying goods" means any new instrument or new appliance, excluding means of transport—

- (*a*) in relation to which the amount on which tax is chargeable by virtue of the Act is [€25,390][1] or more,

- (*b*) which has been designed and manufactured for use solely in medical research or in diagnosis, prevention, or treatment of illness,

- (*c*) which has been the subject of a recommendation by the Minister for Health that, having regard to the requirements of the health services in the State, a refund of tax under this Order would be appropriate;

"qualifying body" means any body of persons engaged in the operation of a hospital.

Amendments

[1]   Substituted by FA 2001, s 240 and Sch 5 Part 4 with effect from 1 January 2002; previously "£20,000".

---

3. Where a person establishes to the satisfaction of the Revenue Commissioners that—

- (*a*) he has borne or paid tax which became chargeable on or after the 29th day of January, 1992, in respect of the supply to, or the importation by, him of qualifying goods,

- (*b*) he is a qualifying body or, if he is not such a body, the qualifying goods have been, or are to be, donated by him to a qualifying body,

- (*c*) no part of the funds used, or to be used, in the purchase of the qualifying goods was, or is to be, provided, directly or indirectly, by the State, or by any board established by or under statute, or by any public or local authority, or by the qualifying body which has purchased the qualifying goods or to which they have been, or are to be, donated, or by any body of persons associated with such qualifying body in the operation of a hospital, or by any body of persons operating a hospital, and

(*d*) in respect of the supply or importation of qualifying goods, he is not entitled to repayment of the tax under any provision of the Act or under any instrument other than this Order made under statute administered by the Revenue Commissioners,

and the person completes such claim form as may be provided for the purpose by the Revenue Commissioners and certifies the particulars shown on such claim form to be correct, he shall be entitled to be repaid the full tax so borne or paid.

(4) The Value Added Tax (Refund of Tax) (No 20) Order, 1987 (SI No 10 of 1987), is hereby revoked.

VALUE ADDED TAX (REFUND OF TAX) (NO 24) ORDER 1993

(SI No 134 of 1993)

Amendments

Revoked by Value Added Tax (Refund of Tax) (No 26) Order 1994 (SI 165/1994), para 6.

VALUE ADDED TAX (REFUND OF TAX) (NO 25) ORDER 1993

(SI No 266 of 1993)

1. This Order may be cited as the Value Added Tax (Refund of Tax) (No 25) Order, 1993.

2. (1) In this Order—

"the Act" means the Value Added Tax Act, 1972;

"flat-rate farmer" has the meaning assigned to it by section 12A(2) of the Act,

"qualifying person" means a flat-rate farmer who has borne or paid tax in relation to outlay on the construction, extension, alteration or reconstruction of any building or structure which is designed for use solely or mainly for the purpose of a farming business, or on the fencing, drainage or reclamation of any land intended for use for the purposes of such a business;

"registered person" means a flat-rate farmer who is a taxable person referred to in subsection (1A)(*c*) or (2)(*b*) of section 8 of the Act and who is included on the register of taxable persons maintained by the Revenue Commissioners pursuant to section 9 of the Act;

"structure" includes a farmyard, a farm road and a concrete path adjacent to farm buildings;

"unregistered person" means a flat-rate farmer other than a registered person.

(2) In this Order a reference to a paragraph is to a paragraph of this Order, unless it is indicated that reference to some other provision is intended.

3. An unregistered person who establishes to the satisfaction of the Revenue Commissioners that he is a qualifying person, and who fulfils to the satisfaction of the said Commissioners the conditions which are specified in paragraph 4, shall be entitled to be repaid so much of such tax as is specified in paragraph 7.

4. The conditions to be fulfilled by an unregistered person are as follows:

 (*a*) he shall claim a repayment of the tax by completing such claim form as may be provided for that purpose by the Revenue Commissioners and he shall certify the particulars shown on such claim form to be correct;

 (*b*) he shall produce—

  (i) the invoices or other documents, issued or given to him for the purposes of section 17 of the Act, or

  (ii) the receipts for tax paid on goods imported,
  showing the tax borne or paid by him which is the subject of the refund claim;

 (*c*) he shall, if requested to do so by the Revenue Commissioners, produce the plans, specifications or other documentary evidence in relation to—

(i)   the construction, extension, alteration or reconstruction of a building or structure which is designed for use solely or mainly for the purposes of a farming business, or

(ii)   the fencing, drainage of reclamation of any land intended for use for the purposes of such a business,

in respect of which his claim for a refund of tax is being made; and

(*d*)   he shall have complied with all the obligations imposed on him by the Act, the Income Tax Acts, the Corporation Tax Acts or the Capital Gains Tax Act, and any instruments made thereunder, in relation to—

(i)   the payment or remittance of the taxes, interest and penalties required to be paid or remitted thereunder, and

(ii)   the delivery of returns.

5. A registered person who is a qualifying person shall, subject to the conditions which are specified in paragraph 6, be entitled to reclaim so much of such tax as is specified in paragraph 7 as if such tax were deductible tax under section 12 of the Act.

6. The conditions to be fulfilled by a registered person are as follows:

(*a*)   he shall reclaim the tax in the return which he is obliged to furnish in accordance with section 19(3) of the Act and he shall certify the particulars shown on the relevant return form to be correct;

(*b*)   he shall retain all the documents referred to in subparagraphs (*b*) and (*c*) of paragraph 4 which are relevant to his claim as if they were records to be kept in accordance with section 16 of the Act; and

(*c*)   he shall have compiled with all the obligations imposed on him by the Act, the Income Tax Acts, the Corporation Tax Acts or the Capital Gains Tax Act, and any instruments made thereunder, in relation to—

(i)   the payment or remittance of the taxes, interest and penalties required to be paid or remitted thereunder, and

(ii)   the delivery of returns.

7. The amount of tax to be repaid in accordance with paragraph 3 or reclaimed in accordance with paragraph 5 shall, subject to paragraph 8, be the tax borne or paid which the qualifying person shows to the satisfaction of the Revenue Commissioners to be referable solely to outlay which relates to—

(*a*)   the construction, extension, alteration or reconstruction of that part of the building or structure which was designed solely for the purposes of a farming business and has actually been put to use in such a business carried on by him, or

(*b*)   the fencing, drainage or reclamation of any land which has actually been put to use in such a business carried on by him.

8. A claim for repayment of tax under subparagraph (*a*) of paragraph 4 shall be made only in respect of outlay involving a total amount of tax of more than [€125][1].

9. The Value Added Tax (Refund of Tax) (No 1) Order, 1972 (SI 267 of 1972), the Value Added Tax (Refund of Tax) (No 8) Order, 1978 (SI 145 of 1978) and the Value Added Tax (Refund of Tax) (No 17) Order, 1984 (SI 249 of 1984), are hereby revoked.

Amendments

[1]   Substituted by FA 2001, s 240 and Sch 5 Part 4 with effect from 1 January 2002; previously "£100".

VALUE ADDED TAX (THRESHOLD FOR ADVANCE PAYMENT) ORDER 1993

(SI No 303 of 1993)

1. This Order may be cited as the Value Added Tax (Threshold for Advance Payment) Order, 1993.

2. In this Order—

"the Act" means the Value Added Tax Act, 1972 (No 22 of 1972);

"threshold" means a threshold for the purposes of section 19(6) of the Act;

"due date" means a due date for the purposes of section 19(6) of the Act.

3. The threshold to be applied for the purposes of section 19(6) of the Act to the due date which is the 1st day of December, 1993, and to each successive due date thereafter, shall be £300,000.

VALUE ADDED TAX (REFUND OF TAX) (NO 26) ORDER 1994

(SI No 165 of 1994)

Amendments

Revoked by Value Added Tax (Refund of Tax) (No 28) Order 1996 (SI 98/1996), r 6.

VALUE ADDED TAX (THRESHOLD FOR ADVANCE PAYMENT) (AMENDMENT) ORDER 1994

(SI No 342 of 1994)

Amendments

Revoked by FA 1997, s 114 from 7 November 1996.

VALUE ADDED TAX (REFUND OF TAX) (NO 27) ORDER 1995

(SI No 38 of 1995)

1. (1) This Order may be cited as the Value Added Tax (Refund of Tax) (No 27) Order, 1995.

(2) This Order shall be deemed to have come into operation on the 27th day of January, 1994.

2. In this Order—

"the Act" means the Value Added Tax Act, 1972 (No 22 of 1972), and every enactment which is to be construed together with that Act;

"qualifying body" means—

    (*a*) a research institution, or

    (*b*) a university, college, school or similar educational body,

which conducts medical research in a laboratory;

"qualifying goods" means any new instrument or new appliance, excluding means of transport—

    (*a*) in relation to which the amount on which tax is chargeable by virtue of the Act is [€25,390][1] or more,

    (*b*) which has been designed and manufactured for use in medical research, and

    (*c*) which has been the subject of a recommendation by the Health Research Board that, having regard to the requirements of medical research in the State, a refund of tax under this Order would be appropriate.

Amendments

[1]   Substituted by FA 2001, s 240 and Sch 5 Part 4 with effect from 1 January 2002; previously "£20,000".

---

3. Where a person establishes to the satisfaction of the Revenue Commissioners that—

    (*a*) such person has borne or paid tax which became chargeable on or after the 27th day of January, 1994, in respect of the supply of goods to, the intra-Community acquisition of goods by, or the importation of goods by, such person where such goods are qualifying goods,

    (*b*) such person is a qualifying body or, if such person is not a qualifying body, the qualifying goods have been, or are to be, donated by such person to a qualifying body,

    (*c*) no part of the funds used, or to be used, in the purchase of the qualifying goods was, or is to be, provided, directly or indirectly, by the State, or by any board established by or under statute, or by any public or local authority, or by the qualifying body which has purchased the qualifying goods or to which they have been, or are to be, donated, or by any body or persons associated with such qualifying body in the operation of a medical research laboratory or by any other body of persons operating a medical research laboratory, and (*d*) such person is not entitled, under any provision of the Act or under any instrument other than this Order made under statute administered by the Revenue Commissioners, to a deduction or repayment of the tax borne or paid in respect of the supply of goods to, the intra-Community acquisition of goods by or the importation of goods by such person where such goods are qualifying goods,

and the person completes such claim form as may be provided for the purpose by the Revenue Commissioners and certifies the particulars shown on such claim form to be correct, such person shall be entitled to be repaid the full tax so borne or paid.

FINANCE ACT 1994 (COMMENCEMENT OF SECTIONS 93 AND 96(*A*)) ORDER 1995

(SI No 184 of 1995)

1. This Order may be cited as the Finance Act, 1994 (Commencement of Sections 93 and 96(*a*)) Order, 1995.

2. The 7th day of July, 1995 is hereby appointed as the date on which section 93 and 96(*a*) of the Finance Act, 1994 (No 13 of 1994), shall take effect.

VALUE ADDED TAX (REFUND OF TAX) (NO 28) ORDER 1996

(SI No 98 of 1996)

1. (1) This Order may be cited as the Value Added Tax (Refund of Tax) (No 28) Order, 1996.

(2) This Order shall be deemed to have came into operation on the 23rd day of January, 1996.

Notes

The Order provides for a full repayment of VAT to exempt coach operators, subject to certain conditions, in respect of the tax paid on touring coaches of certain age and dimensions.

---

2. (1) In this Order—

"the Act" means the Value Added Tax Act, 1972 (No 22 of 1972);

"qualifying person" means a person who—

(a) is engaged in the business of carriage for reward of tourists by road under contracts for group transport, and

(b) has complied with all the obligations imposed on the person by the Act, the Income Tax Acts, the Corporation Tax Acts or the Capital Gains Tax Acts, and any instruments made thereunder, in relation to

    (i) the payment or remittance of taxes, interest the penalties required to be paid or remitted thereunder, and

    (ii) the delivery of returns;

"qualifying vehicle" means

(a) a single-deck touring coach having dimensions as designated by the manufacturer of not less than [2,700 millimetres in height][1], not less than 8,000 millimetres in length, not less than [950 millimetres in floor height][2] and with an underfloor luggage capacity of not less than 3 cubic metres, or

(b) a double-deck touring coach having dimensions as designated by the manufacturer of not more than 4,300 millimetres in height and not less than 10,000 millimetres in length.

(2) In this Order a reference to a paragraph or subparagraph is to a paragraph or subparagraph of this Order, unless it is indicated that reference to some other provision is intended.

Amendments

[1] Substituted by Value Added Tax (Refund of Tax) (Amendment) Order 1999 para 1 with effect from 1 April 1999; previously "3,000 millimetres in height".

[2] Substituted by Value Added Tax (Refund of Tax) (Amendment) Order 1999 para 1 with effect from 1 April 1999; previously "1,000 millimetres in floor height".

---

3. (1) Unless the provisions in subparagraph (2) are applied, a qualifying person who has bone or paid tax on—

(*a*)   the supply to such person or the hiring or leasing (other than hiring or leasing for a period of less than six consecutive months) to such person, or

(*b*)   the intra-Community acquisition or importation by such person,

of a qualifying vehicle which is for use by such person in the State in the business of the carriage for reward of tourists by road under contracts for group transport shall, subject to the conditions specified in paragraph 4, be repaid the full tax so borne or paid provided that—

(i)   the supply, intra-Community acquisition or importation of the vehicle which gave rise to such tax occurred when the vehicle was not more than two years old, or

(ii)   the hiring or leasing of the vehicle (other than hiring or leasing for a period of less than six consecutive months) which gave rise to such tax was on the basis of a contract for such hire or lease first entered into when the vehicle was not more than two years old.

(2) A qualifying person who is a taxable person and who becomes liable for tax in the State in respect of the intra-Community acquisition of a qualifying vehicle may, in lieu of claiming repayment under subparagraph (1), elect to deduct the tax chargeable in respect of that acquisition in the return which such person is obliged to furnish, concerning that acquisition, in accordance with section 19(3) (inserted by section 84 of the Finance Act, 1983 (No 15 of 1983)) of the Act.

(3) The provisions of this paragraph shall apply only where—

(*a*)   the supply, hire, lease, intra-Community acquisition or importation, as the case may be, referred to in subparagraph (1) or (2) occurred on or after the date specified in paragraph 1(2), and

(*b*)   the qualifying person is not entitled to a deduction or repayment—

(i)   by any other provision of the Act or regulations made thereunder, or

(ii)   under any other enactment administered by the Revenue Commissioners,

of any portion of the tax paid or payable in respect of the qualifying vehicle.

4. The conditions to be fulfilled by a person in order to obtain a repayment of tax under this Order in accordance with subparagraph (1) of paragraph 3 are that the person shall:

(*a*)   complete such form as is provided for that purpose by the Revenue Commissioners, and shall certify the particulars shown on such form to be correct;

(*b*)   establish to the satisfaction of the Revenue Commissioners that that person is a qualifying person;

(*c*)   produce—

(i)   in the case of a supply to that person of a qualifying vehicle, an invoice, issued to that person in accordance with section 17(12)(*a*)(i) (amended by section 30(2) of, and the Second Schedule to, the Value Added Tax

(Amendment) Act, 1978 (No 34 of 1978)) of the Act, establishing the amount of tax borne by that person on that supply,

(ii) in the case of the hire or lease of a qualifying vehicle, a copy of the hiring agreement or leasing agreement, as may be appropriate, and, in respect of each repayment claim, an invoice, issued to that person in accordance with the said section 17(12)(*a*)(i) establishing the amount of tax borne by that person,

(iii) in the case of an intra-Community acquisition of a qualifying vehicle, an official receipt or other document establishing the amount of tax paid by that person in respect of the intra-Community acquisition, together with the invoice issued to that person by the supplier in the Member State of supply, or

(iv) in the case of an importation of a qualifying vehicle, an official receipt or other document establishing the amount of tax paid by that person on the importation and indicating the number of the relevant customs entry.

5. This Order shall not apply to vehicles used or intended to be used primarily for the provision of public transport services.

6. The Value Added Tax (Refund of Tax) (No 26) Order, 1994 (SI No 165 of 1994) is hereby revoked.

FINANCE ACT 1995 (SECTION 134(1)) (COMMENCEMENT) ORDER 1996

(SI No 231 of 1996)

Revenue publications

Reliefs for Diplomats: Tax Briefing, 25.

1. This Order may be cited as the Finance Act, 1995 (Section 134(1)) (Commencement) Order, 1996.

2. The 1st day of September, 1996 is hereby appointed as the day on which section 134(1) of the Finance Act, 1995 (No. 8 of 1995) shall take effect.

VALUE ADDED TAX (REFUND OF TAX) (NO 29) ORDER 1996

(SI No 334 of 1996)

1. This Order may be cited as the Value Added Tax (Refund of Tax) (No 29) Order, 1996.

2. This Order shall come into operation on the 1st day of December, 1996.

3. (1) In this Order—

(a) **"the Act of 1967"** means the Diplomatic Relations and Immunities Act, 1967 (No 8 of 1967);

(b) **"the Act"** means the Value Added Tax Act, 1972 (No 22 of 1972);

(c) **"the Act of 1992"** means the Finance Act, 1992 (No 9 of 1992);

(d) **"excisable products"** has the meaning assigned to it by section 104 of the Act of 1992;

(e) **"qualifying person"** means—

    (i) the head of a diplomatic mission of a sending State, as defined in Article 1(a) of the First Schedule to the Act of 1967,

    (ii) a member of the diplomatic staff of a diplomatic mission, as defined in Article 1(d) of the First Schedule to the Act of 1967,

    (iii) a member of the administrative and technical staff of a diplomatic mission, as defined in Article 1(f) of the First Schedule to the Act of 1967,

    (iv) the head of a consular post, as defined in Article 1(1)(c) of the Second Schedule to the Act of 1967,

    (v) a consular officer, as defined in Article 1(1)(d) of the Second Schedule to the Act of 1967, or

    (vi) a consular employee as defined in Article 1(1)(e) of the Second Schedule to the Act of 1967,

who is not a national of, or permanently resident in, the State and who is accepted by the Minister for Foreign Affairs as being entitled to privileges and immunities under the Act of 1967.

(2) In this Order a reference to a paragraph is to a paragraph of this Order and a reference to a subparagraph is to a subparagraph of the provision in which the reference occurs, unless it is indicated that reference to some other provision is intended.

4. The provisions of this Order shall apply only where the Minister for Foreign Affairs is satisfied that—

(a) the sending State of the qualifying person extends a satisfactory level of reciprocal relief to corresponding personnel representing Ireland in that State,

(b) the supply of goods and services for which relief is claimed under this Order is reasonable and appropriate to the circumstances of each case, and (*c*) the person claiming relief under this Order has respected the laws and regulations of the State.

5. A qualifying person who is a person specified in paragraph 3(1)(*e*)(i) or 3(1)(*e*)(iv) shall, subject to the conditions specified in paragraph 8, be repaid the tax borne or paid by such person on—

(*a*) the purchase or lease of the premises of a diplomatic mission as defined in Article 1(i) of the First Schedule to the Act of 1967 or a consular premises as defined in Article 1(1)(*j*) of the Second Schedule to the Act of 1967, including construction work, alteration, decoration and work of maintenance and repair carried out thereto,

(*b*) the purchase or lease of a principal residential premises, including construction work, alteration, decoration and work of maintenance and repair carried out thereto,

(*c*) the supply of, and repair to, household goods being non-perishable goods relating to the running of the premises referred to in subparagraph (*a*) and (*b*) and used at or in such premises,

(*d*) the supply of, and repair to, business goods being goods other than those specified elsewhere in this paragraph which are necessary for the purposes of carrying out the official duties of such qualifying person,

(*e*) the supply of a motor vehicle which qualifies for a refund or remission of Vehicle Registration Tax under section 134(1)*(g)* of the Act of 1992 and the supply of a bicycle:

Provided that in the case of a motor vehicle if the qualifying person intends to dispose of such motor vehicle by sale or otherwise within two years of the date of purchase, that person shall notify the Minister for Foreign Affairs of such intention, and, where so instructed by that Minister, shall refund to the Revenue Commissioners an amount determined by them deemed to be the amount of tax included in the open market selling price of the vehicle at the time of such determination,

(*f*) the hire of a motor vehicle which is necessary for the purpose of carrying out the official duties of such qualifying person,

(*g*) the hire, transport and storage of the goods, specified in subparagraphs (*c*) and (*d*),

(*h*) the supply of excisable products which qualify for a refund or remission of excise duty under section 113 of the Act of 1992,

(*i*) the supply of electricity and of gas to the premises referred to in subparagraphs (*a*) and (*b*), and of goods and services directly related to those supplies, and the supply of telecommunication services provided to the premises referred to in subparagraphs (*a*) and (*b*) and of goods and services directly related to those supplies.

6. A qualifying person who is a person specified in paragraph 3(1)(*e*)(ii) or 3(1)(*e*)(v) shall, subject to the conditions specified in paragraph 8, be repaid the tax borne or paid by such person on—

(*a*) the purchase or lease of a principal residential premises, including construction work, alteration, decoration and work of maintenance and repair carried out hereto,

(*b*) the supply of, and repair to, household goods being non-perishable goods relating to the running of the premises referred to in subparagraph (*a*) and used at or in such premises,

(*c*) the supply of, and repair to, business goods being goods which are necessary for the purposes of carrying out the official duties of such qualifying person, other than goods specified elsewhere in this paragraph or the supply of electricity, gas and telecommunication services and goods and services directly related thereto,

(*d*) the supply of a motor vehicle which qualifies for a refund or remission of Vehicle Registration Tax under section 134(1)(*g*) of the Act of 1992 and the supply of a bicycle:

Provided that in the case of a motor vehicle if the qualifying person intends to dispose of such motor vehicle by sale or otherwise within two years of the date of purchase, that person shall notify the Minister for Foreign Affairs of such intention, and, where so instructed by that Minister, shall refund to the Revenue Commissioners an amount determined by them deemed to be the amount of tax included in the open market selling price of the vehicle at the time of such determination,

(*e*) the hire of a motor vehicle which is necessary for the purpose of carrying out the official duties of such qualifying person,

(*f*) the hire, transport and storage of the goods specified in subparagraphs (*b*) and (*c*),

(*h*) the supply of excisable products which qualify for a refund or remission of excise duty under section 113 of the Act of 1992.

7. A qualifying person who is a person specified in paragraph 3(1)(*e*)(iii) or 3(1)(*e*)(vi) shall, subject to the conditions specified in paragraph 8, be repaid the tax borne or paid by such person on—

(*a*) the purchase or lease of a principal residential premises, including construction work, alteration, decoration and work of maintenance and repair carried out thereto,

(*b*) the supply of, and repair to, household goods being non-perishable goods relating to the running of the premises referred to in subparagraph (*a*) and used at or in such premises,

(*c*) the supply of, and repair to, business goods being goods which are necessary for the purposes of carrying out the official duties of such qualifying person, other than goods specified elsewhere in this paragraph or the supply of electricity, gas and telecommunication services and goods and services directly related thereto,

(*d*) the supply of a motor vehicle which qualifies for a refund or remission of Vehicle Registration Tax under section 134(1)(*g*) of the Act of 1992 and the supply of a bicycle:

Provided that in the case of a motor vehicle if the qualifying person intends to dispose of such motor vehicle by sale or otherwise within two years of the date of purchase, that person shall notify the Minister for Foreign Affairs of such intention, and, where so instructed by that Minister, shall refund to the Revenue Commissioners an amount determined by them deemed to be the amount of tax included in the open market selling price of the vehicle at the time of such determination,

(*e*) the hire of a motor vehicle which is necessary for the purposes of carrying out the official duties of such qualifying person, and

(*f*) the hire, transport and storage of the goods specified in subparagraphs (*b*) and (*c*).

8. The conditions to be fulfilled by a qualifying person in order to obtain a repayment of tax under this Order are as follows:

(*a*) the person shall complete such claim form as may be provided for the purpose by the Revenue Commissioners and shall certify the particulars shown on such claim form to be correct,

(*b*) the person shall establish the amount of tax borne or paid by such person by the production of invoices or other documents, provided in accordance with section 17(12)(*a*)(i) of the Act.

9. Where the total of the tax chargeable and the amount on which tax is chargeable in relation to a supply of any individual good or service referred to in this Order is [€315][1] or more, the amount of tax chargeable may be remitted in accordance with paragraph 10.

Amendments

[1] Substituted by FA 2001, s 240 and Sch 5 Part 4 with effect from 1 January 2002; previously "£250".

---

10. A qualifying person shall apply for remission of tax in accordance with paragraph 9 by completing such application form as may be provided for the purpose by the Revenue Commissioners and shall certify the particulars shown on such application form to be correct.

11. Where a qualifying person satisfies the requirements for remission of tax under this Order in respect of a supply of goods or services the Revenue Commissioners shall authorise that supply without payment of the tax chargeable and notify the applicant accordingly and such notification shall be valid for three months from the date of the its issue.

12. The notification referred to in paragraph 11 shall be:

(*a*) tendered by the qualifying person to the supplier of the goods or services, and (*b*)   retained by the supplier as:

    (i)   the authority under which such supplier may supply the goods or services of the qualifying person free of tax and

    (ii)   a record to be kept in accordance with section 16 of the Act.

13. A repayment of tax under this Order shall be made only in respect of claims involving a total amount of tax of more than [€125][1]:

Provided that the Revenue Commissioners may, at their discretion, waive application of this paragraph in the particular circumstances of a case.

Amendments

[1]   Substituted by FA 2001, s 240 and Sch 5 Part 4 with effect from 1 January 2002; previously "£100".

---

14. Nothing in this Order shall apply so as to affect a right to relief of tax prescribed in any other enactment.

FINANCE ACT 1997 (COMMENCEMENT OF SECTIONS 101 AND 113) ORDER, 1997

(SI No 313 of 1997)

1. This Order may be cited as the Finance Act, 1997 (Commencement of Sections 101 and 113) Order, 1997.

2. The 1st day of September, 1997, is hereby appointed as the date on which sections 101 and 113 of the Finance Act, 1997 (No 22 of 1997), shall take effect.

Notes

This Order appoints 1 September 1997 as the date for coming into operation of sections 101 and 113 of the Finance Act 1997. Section 101 amends VATA 1972, s 8(3)(*a*) to provide that a farmer whose supplies of horticultural products to final consumers exceed or are likely to exceed £40,000 per annum, or whose supplies of a combination of retail agricultural products and agricultural services exceed or are likely to exceed £20,000 per annum is obliged to register and account for VAT on such supplies. It also amends VATA 1972, s 8(3) proviso to prevent farmers engaged in the supply of retail horticultural products or agricultural services from separating these activities into smaller units in order to remain under the VAT registration limit. Section 113 amends VATA 1972, Sch 6 to provide for the application of the 12.5 per cent rate of VAT to certain horticultural products.

VALUE ADDED TAX (ELIGIBILITY TO DETERMINE TAX DUE BY REFERENCE TO MONEYS RECEIVED) ORDER 1997

(SI No 316 of 1997)

1. This Order may be cited as the Value Added Tax (Eligibility to Determine Tax Due by Reference to Moneys Received) Order, 1997.

2. The amount specified in section 14(1)(*b*) (inserted by section 97(*a*) of the Finance Act, 1994 (No 13 of 1994)) of the Value Added Tax Act, 1972 (No 22 of 1972), is hereby increased to £500,000.

Notes

VATA 1972, s 14(1)(*b*) allows a taxable person with a turnover of not more than £250,000 to use the moneys received basis of accounting for VAT. The Order increases that turnover to £500,000.

VALUE ADDED TAX (REFUND OF TAX) (AMENDMENT) ORDER 1999

(SI No 305 of 1999)

1. This Order may be cited as the Value Added Tax (Refund of Tax) (Amendment) Order, 1999.

This Order shall be deemed to have come into operation on the 1st day of April, 1999.

Notes

Para 2 substituted "2,700 millimetres in height" for "3,000 millimetres in height" and "950 millimetres in floor height" for "1,000 millimetres in floor height" in Value Added Tax (Refund of Tax) (No 28) Order 1996 (SI 98/1996), para 2(1) definition of "qualifying vehicle".

TAXES (ELECTRONIC TRANSMISSION OF CERTAIN REVENUE RETURNS) (SPECIFIED PROVISIONS AND APPOINTED DAY) ORDER 2000

(SI No 289 of 2000)

COMMISSIONERS IN EXERCISE OF THE POWERS CONFERRED ON THEM BY SECTION 917E (INSERTED BY SECTION 209 OF THE FINANCE ACT, 1999 (NO 2 OF 1999)) OF THE TAXES CONSOLIDATION ACT, 1997 (NO 39 OF 1997), ORDER AS FOLLOWS:

1. This Order may be cited as the Taxes (Electronic Transmission of Certain Revenue Returns) (Specified Provisions and Appointed Day) Order, 2000.

2. Each of the provisions set out in the Schedule to this Order is specified for the purpose of Chapter 6 of Part 38 of the Taxes Consolidation Act, 1997.

3. The 28th day of September 2000 is appointed as the day appointed by this Order in relation to returns to be made under each of the provisions specified in accordance with paragraph 2.

SCHEDULE

Section 19(3)(*a*) (as amended by the Finance Act, 1983 (No 15 of 1983)) of the Value Added Tax Act, 1972 (No 22 of 1972).

Section 19(3)(*aa*) (inserted by the Finance Act, 1989 (No 10 of 1989)) of the Value Added Tax Act, 1972.

Regulation 22(1) of the Income Tax (Employments) Regulations, 1960 (SI No 28 of 1960).

Regulation 25(6) of the Income Tax (Employments) Regulations, 1960.

Regulation 31 of the Income Tax (Employments) Regulations, 1960.

Regulation 31A (inserted by the Income Tax (Employments) Regulations, 1989 (SI No 58 of 1989) of the Income Tax (Employments) Regulations, 1960.

FINANCE ACT 2003 (COMMENCEMENT OF SECTIONS 124, 125, 129 AND 130(*b*)) ORDER 2003

(SI No 512 of 2003)

I, Charlie McCreevy, Minister for Finance, in exercise of the powers conferred on me by section 171(10)(*e*) of the Finance Act 2003 (No 3 of 2003), hereby order as follows:

1. This Order may be cited as the Finance Act 2003 (Commencement of Sections 124, 125, 129 and 130(*b*)) Order 2003.

2. The 1st day of November 2003 is appointed as the day on which sections 124, 125, 129 and 130(*b*) of section 130 of the Finance Act 2003 shall take effect.

STATEMENTS OF PRACTICE

LIABILITY OF RECIPIENTS ON CERTAIN SERVICES RECEIVED FROM ABROAD

1. Introduction

1.1. Under VAT law the place of supply is an important factor in determining who is liable for the payment of the tax. For many services the place of supply is the place where the person supplying the service is established and the supplier is legally responsible for the payment of the tax. However, there are certain categories of services which are an exception to this general rule. These exceptions include:

(i) specified services which are received for business purposes tax free from abroad by persons established in Ireland,

(ii) services, where if VAT is payable in another country (usually a Member State of the European Community) the Irish-based recipient would be entitled to a refund of VAT by the tax authorities in the country where the supplier has his fixed place of business and where if Irish VAT were chargeable it would not be wholly deductible by the recipient, and

(iii) specified services received tax free from abroad by Government Departments, local authorities, public and other statutory bodies, and organisations such as schools, colleges and hospitals which would not normally be registered for VAT.

1.2. In these instances, the place of supply is deemed under certain conditions to be in Ireland and, subject to certain threshold limits (and other exceptions in the case of taxable persons), the recipient is liable for payment of VAT. This provision means that persons engaged in "VAT-exempt" activities eg insurance, banking, stockbroking and bookmaking, who are not registered for VAT in respect of their normal supplies are obliged to do so in respect of certain services received from abroad.

2. Liability for Tax — General

2.1. For the purposes of determining the tax liability of recipients in respect of taxable services received from abroad it is convenient to classify these services into two categories:

(i) A specified group of services listed in the Fourth Schedule to the VAT Act. A full list is given in the attached Appendix. These services are referred to as Fourth Schedule services.

(ii) Other taxable services received from abroad in respect of which VAT is not payable in another Member State of the European Community, or if VAT were so payable, the recipient would be entitled to a refund by the tax authorities in the other Member State and Irish VAT if chargeable would not be wholly deductible. In practice, this second category relates mainly to the hiring and leasing of passenger vehicles and other means of transport.

2.2. All persons, including exempt bodies, public sector organisations and charitable organisations, irrespective of whether or not they are already registered for VAT, who receive taxable Fourth Schedule services from abroad, are liable, subject to threshold limitations, to pay Irish VAT on these services. An individual receiving Fourth Schedule services for his or her private non-business purposes is not obliged to register or to pay Irish VAT in respect of the receipt of those services.

2.3. All business persons, whether or not they are already registered for VAT, may be liable in certain circumstances to pay Irish VAT on other (ie non-Fourth Schedule) services received from abroad. The circumstances under which such liabilities would arise are described in paragraphs 5.1 to 5.3.

3. Taxable Fourth Schedule Services received from Abroad by Unregistered Persons

3.1. Persons who are not already VAT registered and who, for business purposes, receive from abroad any of the taxable services listed in the Appendix, are obliged, whether or not they are engaged in exempt activities, to register for and pay VAT on the services, if their expenditure on such taxable services exceeds £15,000 a year. They have no liability if their annual expenditure on these services is under £15,000. Applications for registration should be made to the local tax office. The rate of VAT is generally the standard rate (currently at 23%) but exceptions to this general rule are listed in paragraph 6.1. The amount which is liable to Irish VAT is the amount payable to the foreign supplier converted to Irish currency at the rate of exchange applicable on the date of the invoice.

3.2. A person (other than a person who has his business establishment here and supplies Fourth Schedule services wholly abroad) who is registered for VAT in respect of received services only is not entitled to any VAT deduction or refund in respect of the tax he is liable to pay on these services or, indeed, in respect of any other VAT which he may be charged direct by suppliers in the State or VAT paid at the point of import into the State.

4. Taxable Fourth Schedule Services Received from Abroad by VAT Registered Persons

4.1. Persons receiving any of the specified Fourth Schedule services from abroad who are already registered for VAT are liable for VAT on the receipt of such services, irrespective of the value of, or their expenditure on, the services. The amount which is liable is the amount payable to the foreign supplier converted to Irish currency at the rate of exchange applicable on the date of the invoice. The rate of VAT is generally the standard rate (currently 23%) but exceptions to this general rule are listed in paragraph 6.1.

4.2. If the recipient is a business person who is liable to VAT on the entire supplies made by him, and the received services are used exclusively for the purposes of his taxable business he is entitled to a deduction equal to the amount of his liability on the received services in addition to any other deduction due under the VAT Act 1972. In effect the liability on services received from abroad is cancelled but the transaction must nevertheless be declared in his VAT returns.

4.3. Where the received services are used for non-business purposes no part of the VAT payable on the received services is deductible.

4.4. If the recipient is a business person some of whose activities are liable to VAT and some are not, only that part of the VAT on a received service which is referable to the taxable part of the business may be deducted. Where there is any doubt the matter should be settled by agreement with the Inspector of Taxes.

5. Other (Non-Fourth Schedule) Taxable Services Received from Abroad

5.1. In practice these services consist, mainly, of the hiring out and leasing of means of transport (motor vehicles, boats, aircraft, etc).

5.2. Business persons who are registered for VAT and who receive any non-Fourth Schedule taxable services from abroad are liable to pay Irish VAT on these services (generally at the standard rate (currently 23%) but exceptions are listed in paragraph 6.1) if:

   (*a*) in the case of supplies from another Member State of the European Community, VAT is not payable in the country in which the supplier has his fixed place of business; or if payable is refundable to the recipient by the tax authorities in the other Member State, and

   (*b*) Irish VAT on the received services would not be wholly deductible by the recipient.

5.3. Persons who are in business and who are not registered for VAT (because their turnover is below the registration threshold or their activities are exempt) are obliged to register for, and pay VAT, generally at the standard rate, on non-Fourth Schedule taxable services received from abroad subject to the following:

   (*a*) that their expenditure on such services exceeds £15,000 a year, and

   (*b*) in the case of supplies from another Member State of the European Community, VAT is not payable in the country in which the supplier has his fixed place of business; or if payable is refundable to the recipient by the tax authorities in the other Member State.

Where the recipient is liable for tax on received services the amount which is chargeable to Irish VAT is the amount payable to the foreign supplier converted to Irish currency at the exchange rate applicable on the date of the invoice.

5.4. A person who is registered for VAT in respect of received services only is not entitled to any VAT deduction or refund in respect of the tax he is liable to pay on these services or, indeed, in respect of any other VAT which he may be charged direct by suppliers in the State or VAT paid at the point of import into the State.

6. Rates of Irish VAT on Services Received from Abroad

6.1. While the standard (currently 23%) rate applies to services generally, there are activities to which, or circumstances in which, a different rate, or exemption, applies. These include the following:

(i)	banking, financial and insurance services	exempt
(ii)	farm accountancy	10%
(iii)	customs clearance and import/export services	0%
(iv)	international goods transport	0%

(v)	ships, boats, and aircraft: repair, maintenance, hiring	0%, 10%, 23% according to size and function
(vi)	cars, boats, caravans, etc — short-term hire	10%
(vii)	services of lawyers, accountants, auctioneers, or estate agents relating to the supply of agricultural land	10%

7. Enquiries

7.1. Further information may be obtained from the Office of the Revenue Commissioners, Indirect Taxes Branch, Dublin Castle, Dublin 2. (Tel. 01–6792777 Extns 2440, 2441, 2442, 2443) or from local tax offices.

The Fourth Schedule services

APPENDIX

The specified Fourth Schedule services include exempt as well as taxable services. Liability to Irish VAT will not, of course, arise in the case of exempt services received from abroad for example, banking, financial and insurance services and certain agency services relating thereto (see heads (*f*) and (*h*) below).

The complete list of Fourth Schedule services is as follows:

(*a*) Transfers and assignments of copyright, patents, licences, trade marks and similar rights;

(*b*) hiring out of movable goods other than means of transport (but see Note hereunder);

(*c*) advertising services;

(*d*) services of consultants, engineers, consultancy bureaux, lawyers, accountants and other similar services, data processing and provision of information (but excluding services connected with immovable goods);

(*e*) acceptance of any obligation to refrain from pursuing or exercising in whole or in part, any business activity or any such rights as are referred to in paragraph (*a*);

(*f*) banking, financial and insurance services (including reinsurance, but not including the provision of safe deposit facilities);

(*g*) the provision of staff;

(*h*) the services of agents who act in the name and for the account of a principal when procuring for him any of the foregoing services.

NOTE: Subparagraph (*b*) does not apply to movable goods hired out by lessors established outside the European Community. These are excluded by a specific provision of VAT Law which, in effect, makes such lessors accountable for VAT in Ireland in the normal way.

DEDUCTIBLE TAX

(Input Credit)

1. At a recent meeting of the EC VAT Committee in Brussels, it was agreed that any expenses incurred in relation to buying or selling shares relate to an exempt activity and therefore do not qualify for input credit.

2. Accordingly no input credit may be allowed in respect of any costs directly attributable to the buying or the selling of shares.

3. No change in practice is envisaged in relation to:

    (*a*)   supplies to non EC customers (sections 12(1) and 13(3) of VAT Act 1972, as amended), or

    (*b*)   transfer of a business or part thereof (Section 3(5)(*b*)(iii) of VAT Act 1972, as amended).

LIVE HORSES

General

1. With effect from 1 January 1991, the supply (sale), importation and leasing of horses will become liable to VAT at the rate of 2.3%. This means that the exemption which live horses have enjoyed since September 1973, will come to an end, and horses will be treated in the same way for VAT purposes as cattle, goats, sheep, pigs and deer. In effect the breeding and rearing of horses will be regarded as a farming activity and VAT at 2.3% will be applied to the sale price of horses.

2. While all imports of horses will become liable to VAT at 2.3% from 1 January 1991, (see paragraphs 7, 18 and 23), insofar as transactions within the State are concerned, only supplies and leasings of horses which are made by a taxable person, in the course or furtherance of business, will come within the scope of the tax. For example, a taxable person who sells his child's riding pony will not be regarded as making a supply in the course of business, whereas a VAT registered breeder of children's ponies would. Likewise VAT payable on the purchase or importation of horses by taxable persons for non-business use may not be offset against output tax.

3. The term "live horses" has not been defined but it may be taken to cover all horses, including thoroughbreds, draught horses, foals, ponies, asses, mules and hinnies. In the practical administration of the tax the Revenue Commissioners will be prepared to regard the sale of nominations in stallions and part-ownership and shares in stallions and mares as supplies (sales) of horses also.

4. The existing treatment of dead animals will not be affected by the change. Dead horses will continue to qualify for the zero rate, although the separate supply of hides, skins and horsehair will remain liable at 23%. The sale of live horses for slaughter will not qualify for the zero rate unless, of course, sold for export by the supplier.

5. Horses will not be regarded as "means of transport" for the purpose of determining the place of supply of horse leasing services (see paragraph 16).

6. The Taxable Amount: Supplies (sales) within the State

The amount on which VAT is chargeable is "...the total consideration which the person supplying goods or services becomes entitled to receive in respect of or in relation to such supply of goods or services, including all taxes, commissions, costs and charges whatsoever, but not including value added tax, chargeable in respect of the supply". It is emphasised that the amount which is taxable is the amount excluding VAT which a taxable person becomes entitled to receive. If an auctioneer knocks down a horse to a bidder for £9,600 and adds, say £500 for commission and, say, a further £400 for other fees, giving a total of £10,500 excluding VAT he will have a liability of £241.50 (2.3% of £10,500). The amount actually payable to the Revenue will be the difference between this liability and the credits or deductions allowable (see paragraphs 8, 9 and Appendix II).

Although the auctioneer is the person responsible for paying the tax to the Revenue, in practice he will pass the tax on to the buyer.

7. The Taxable Amount: Imports

For the purposes of assessing the VAT payable at importation the value of the imported horses will be their value for customs purposes, determined on a delivery-to-State basis together with any taxes, duties or other charges levied outside or inside the State (excluding VAT — see paragraphs 12.5 and 12.11 of "Guide to the Value Added Tax").

As a general rule where the horse has been recently purchased prior to import, VAT will be payable on the purchase price. Horses imported for sale by auction in cases where the auctioneer is acting as importer for that auction will be valued at the average value for that particular sale the previous year. For horses imported in other circumstances the importer will be required to furnish a declared value which should reflect the open market value of the animal. It is a requirement of law that the cost of transport and insurance of the horses be included in all cases. (Inquiries concerning the question of valuations at importation should be made to C & E Division 6, Castle House).

8. Relief from VAT on Purchases and Imports

A taxable person who is registered and accounting for VAT is entitled to claim a deduction (or credit) in his next following VAT return in respect of most goods and services purchased or imported for the purposes of the business for which he is taxable once he is in possession of a proper VAT invoice or a stamped copy of the customs entry, as appropriate. The invoice does not have to be paid before claiming the deduction. The only tax for which a deduction may not be taken is tax relating to expenditure on hotel, etc expenses, entertainment expenses, the purchase or hire of cars and other passenger vehicles and petrol and on goods or services for exempt or private activities. No deduction is allowable in respect of purchases relating to exempted activities. Where a person has both taxable and exempt supplies his input tax will have to be apportioned, usually, on the basis of the ratio which taxable turnover bears to total turnover. Horse-racing, hunting etc are not regarded as business activities, therefore, VAT incurred on training, racing, etc expenses is not deductible.

9. Farmers (Including Stud Farmers)

For VAT purposes a farmer is a person who engages in agricultural production on land which he owns or occupies, and who does not engage in non-agricultural activities except on a moderate scale (ie from which he derives annual turnover of less than £15,000 — see Chapter 20 of VAT Guide). A farmer is not obliged to register for VAT but may elect to do so. Farmers who elect to register are subject to the normal requirements of the VAT system, and are obliged to keep records and submit returns in the same way as other registered persons. With effect from 1 January 1991, a VAT registered farmer who sells or leases horses will be obliged to account for VAT on the transactions at 2.3%. A stud farmer is a farmer for VAT purposes.

The effect of treating the breeding, rearing and supply (sale) of horses as a farming activity means that:

(1) persons engaged in these activities will be treated as farmers for VAT purposes, subject to the above requirements;

(2) sales of horses by unregistered farmers to VAT registered purchasers will qualify for the 2.3% flat-rate addition to prices.

The VAT element in expenditure incurred by unregistered farmers in the erection or alteration of farm buildings or in the draining or reclamation of land may be reclaimed subject to conditions (see paragraphs 19.4/19.6 of VAT Guide).

10. Sales of Horses by Unregistered Farmers

A farmer who does not elect to register for VAT is entitled under the VAT system to a flat- rate addition (at present 2.3%) to the prices at which he sells his produce to VAT registered purchasers. This flat-rate addition (together with the scheme of refund of VAT on expenditure relating to farm buildings and land reclamation — see paragraph 9 above) is intended to compensate the unregistered farmer for VAT borne on most of his purchases. With effect from 1 January 1991, horses will come within the scope of the flat-rate addition system which works as follows:

	£
An unregistered farmer sells a horse to a VAT registered breeder for, say,	10,000
The flat-rate addition at 2.3% is	230
The price paid to the farmer is	10,230

The breeder provided he is in possession of an invoice which he must prepare showing separately the purchase price and the 2.3% addition may claim back £230 in his next VAT return.

11. Sales of Horses by VAT Registered Farmers

Farmers who elect to register for VAT although under no obligation to do so will be liable for VAT at 2.3% on their sales or leasings of horses as from 1 January 1991. The flat-rate addition will not apply to sales by registered farmers. Purchases of horses made by them from unregistered farmers will be subject to the treatment described in paragraph 10.

See Appendix I for the rates of VAT applicable to a range of goods and services appropriate to the industry.

12. Sales of Horses through Auctioneers and Bloodstock Agents

The sale of horses through auctioneers and other agents will be treated from 1 January 1991, in the same way as the sale of other livestock, ie cattle, sheep, pigs, goats and deer. The horses for sale will be treated as being simultaneously bought and sold by the auctioneer or agent. The effect will be to cause the commission and other fees receivable by the auctioneer or agent in respect of such sale to be treated as taxable at the same rate as the sale of horse, that is at 2.3%.

If the seller is an unregistered farmer the auctioneer or agent will be entitled to set off against his own VAT liability a deduction equal to the flat-rate addition, that is 2.3% of the VAT exclusive purchase price. An example of how the arrangement works is given in Appendix II.

If the seller is a VAT registered farmer the auctioneer or agent will be entitled to claim against the tax payable on the sale the 2.3% invoiced to him by such farmer.

Auctioneers and bloodstock agents will be obliged to register if their annual turnover exceeds £32,000.

13. Syndicates

Sales of nominations in stallions and sales of shares and part-ownership in stallions and mares will be treated in the same way as sales of horses, that is, VAT will be chargeable at the 2.3% rate on the amount receivable by a taxable person. A stallion syndicate will not itself be regarded as a taxable person for VAT purposes and VAT incurred in connection with the administration of a syndicate will not be recoverable by the syndicate or its members. Members of the syndicates as co-owners of the stallions will be treated for VAT purposes in accordance with each member's individual VAT status as regards any sales of nominations. For example:

(1) An unregistered farmer will have no liability on sale of his nomination, but would be entitled to the flat-rate addition to the sale price where the nomination is sold to a taxable breeder;

(2) A taxable person will be liable at 2.3% on his receipts from sale of nominations.

14. Horses Applied to Non-Business Use

Where a taxable owner or breeder transfers to racing, show-jumping, hunting etc horses which he has bred, purchased or imported in connection with his taxable business, such transfers will be deemed to be taxable supplies and will attract liability to VAT on the basis of the cost of the animals, excluding VAT, to the supplier. VAT incurred thereafter on training and racing expenses is not deductible. Once a horse has been transferred to training for racing etc, and VAT accounted for, any further transactions will not give rise to a VAT liability unless the animal is re-applied to business use by a taxable person as a stallion or brood-mare or sold at auction.

15. Racehorse Training

The training of horses for racing is already liable to VAT at the rate of 23%. The amount on which tax is chargeable is that part of the total fee which relates to training only, ie, normally 10% of the trainer's gross fee. Racehorse training services are treated for VAT purposes as being in effect a separate business from farming. This position will not be affected by the new provisions. (See VAT Guide — paragraphs 20.22/20.24 and leaflet entitled "Racehorse Trainers").

16. Leasing of Horses: Services Received from Abroad

Leasing of horses will be liable at 2.3%.

This service, although supplied from Ireland, will, in certain circumstances, be treated as supplied abroad and not subject to Irish VAT if the lessee is resident or established outside the State.

Conversely, this service, although supplied from abroad, will be treated as supplied in Ireland an subject to Irish VAT if the lessee is resident or established in Ireland and the service is received for business purposes. In these circumstances the lessee will be responsible for paying over the tax.

A "flat-rate" farmer, obliged to register for VAT solely on account of his liability on services received from abroad (leasing, advertising, consultancy etc), may retain his "flat-rate" farmer status insofar as his farming activities are concerned, as described in paragraph 9. The matter is explained in greater detail in a leaflet entitled "Liability of Recipients on certain Services received from Abroad".

17. Sales of Horses by Foreign Farmers

The flat-rate addition will not apply to sales by farmers from outside the State to VAT registered persons in the State. Therefore in the case of horses imported for sale at the bloodstock auction sales there can be no question of a flat-rate addition to the purchase price. The import of such horses will be liable at 2.3% (but see next paragraph).

18. Horses imported for Sale by Auction

Horses imported for sale in the State will be liable to VAT in the usual way. VAT will be payable at time of importation unless the importer has been approved under the scheme for Deferred Payment under which payment may be deferred until the fifteenth day of the month following the month in which payment became due (see paragraph 22).

Where horses are imported for sale by auction, VAT registered auctioneers may avail themselves of the deferred payment scheme and undertake such importation without payment of VAT at time of importation using deferred payment facilities. The auctioneer by special arrangement undertakes liability for the VAT payable at importation which he may in due course offset against his VAT liability. The auctioneer must account for VAT at 2.3% on the ultimate sale of the horse unless of course, the horse is sold for export when the zero rate will apply. If the horse is not sold at auction the auctioneer must account for VAT at 2.3% unless the horse is re-exported.

19. Exports

Horses sold for export are liable to VAT at the zero rate. In order to qualify for the zero rate it is a requirement that the horses be transported outside the State directly by or on behalf of the seller who is required to retain proof of export, that is, a stamped copy of the Single Administrative Document (SAD — see Chapter 13 of VAT Guide).

20. Horses sold by approved Auctioneers to Overseas Purchasers

Under an arrangement peculiar to the bloodstock industry a sale to an overseas purchaser can be zero rated even though the horse may not be exported immediately. The arrangement may be operated by auctioneers who have been approved by the Revenue Commissioners for that purpose and who have undertaken responsibility for its administration. Under the arrangement a horse sold with an export undertaking may be zero rated provided the horse is exported within 24 months of the date of supply or, in the case of yearlings purchased after 1 September of any year, is exported within 28 months of purchase. If the horse is subsequently sold in the State or not exported within the required time limits VAT will have to be accounted for by the original vendor (ie the auctioneer).

Auctioneers wishing to participate in the scheme should apply to their local tax office and must be prepared to abide by the conditions imposed by the Revenue Commissioners.

21. Relief from Import VAT for Certain Permanent Importers of Horses

A horse acquired by a private (non-taxable) person whether as a gift or otherwise from a private (non-taxable) person in another Member State of the E.C., may qualify for relief at importation in respect of the residual part of the value added tax paid in the exporting Member State. (Inquiries on this and other matters concerning permanent importations and certain re-importations — see paragraph 26 — should be made to C & E Division 4, Castle House.)

There is provision for relief from VAT at importation in the case of pure-bred foals of not more than six months of age born outside the State of an animal covered in the State and then exported temporarily to give birth.

(Inquiries on this relief should be made to C & E Division 1, Dublin Castle.)

22. Deferred Payment of Import VAT

Provision exists for deferment of payment of VAT at importation to the 15 day of the month following the month of importation. The essential feature of the scheme is that Collectors of Customs and Excise, with the authority of the importer or his agent, initiate payment by the issue of a direct debit voucher drawn on the importer's or agent's bank. Details are contained in Public Notice 1183D (Rev 1) which is available from any Custom House.

Importers or agents who are not approved for deferred payment or who do not fulfil all the conditions of the scheme will be required to pay VAT at the time of importation.

23. Temporary Importation of Horses

The various reliefs from payment of VAT, subject to conditions, for horses temporarily imported into the State are as follows:

Circumstances of importation	Period of relief	Security required	Documentary requirement
(1) EC Carnet Racehorses only	6 months	No	Carnet Entry Sheet
Other horses	2 years	No	Carnet Entry Sheet
(2) ATA Carnet for exhibition at, or participation	1 year in an event	No	Importation counterfoil
(3) Horses for exhibition at, or participation in an event.	2 years	Yes	Form No. 1047
(4) Horses imported for dressage, training or breeding purposes, or for veterinary treatment.	2 years	Yes	Form No. 1047
(5) Horses imported for grazing purposes.	2 years	No	Oral declaration plus inventory
(6) Second-hand horses imported for sale by auction.	6 months	Yes	Form No. 1047

With the exception of imports under cover of the ATA Carnet (see (2) above) relief from import VAT is available for horses in free circulation owned by non-State residents which are imported, for any purpose, from other Member States provided the horses were acquired under the normal VAT provisions of the Member State of exportation and did not benefit from relief by virtue of exportation.

VAT relief is also available for horses owned by either State or non-State residents imported in the circumstances set out in (2) to (5) above from EEC or non EEC countries. However, in cases (3) to (5), relief is not available for horses imported from another Member State which are owned by State residents who are not taxable persons or, if taxable, are not entitled to deduction of tax in full, where (i) the horses are in free circulation and (ii) the horses were not acquired under the normal VAT provisions of the Member States of exportation or benefited for VAT relief by virtue of exportation.

Second-hand horses should be taken to mean "horses which had been applied for racing or other non-business use which usage has now come to an end". These animals may be temporarily imported for sale by auction only where ownership remains outside the State.

In relation to (3) to (5) above the Revenue Commissioners may, in exceptional circumstances and at their absolute discretion, on application of the person to whom relief has been granted, extend the time limit allowed from 2 years to 2 years and 8 months.

In relation to (1) above, the Revenue Commissioners may, at the request of the beneficiary, extend the period of validity of the E.C. Movement Carnet on the basis of the expected duration and nature of the operation planned. (Inquiries concerning temporary importations should be made to C & E Division 1, Dublin Castle.)

24. Re-Importation of Horses

Horses which are re-imported after having been temporarily abroad may be re-imported by the person who exported them without payment of VAT provided they have not been subjected to any process while abroad. For example, a colt sent to Epsom to run in the Derby would not be subject to VAT on its return. However, a mare sent for service to a stallion in the U.K. on its return in foal would be liable to VAT on the basis of the cost of nomination, insurance, transport, etc.

25. Foreign Breeders suffering Irish VAT

The position regarding foreign breeders suffering Irish VAT is no different from that of foreign business persons generally. Such person may, subject to conditions, claim repayment of Irish VAT on most goods and services purchased in Ireland (see Chapter 19.24 of VAT Guide). It should, however, be noted that foreign racehorse owners would not, as a general rule, be entitled to relief for Irish VAT on expenditure connected with their horse racing activities since these would not normally be regarded as business activities.

26. Registration for VAT

Applications for registration should be made to the local tax office (see VAT Guide for addresses and telephone numbers).

APPENDIX I

Rates of VAT

(This list is not exhaustive)

Accommodation of horses	if letting only of paddocks, stables — letting, minding etc supplied	exempt
	by unregistered farmers	not taxable
	letting, minding etc supplied by others	23%
Boxes, horse		23%
Bridles		23%
Exports of horses		zero
Farriers' services	repair and maintenance of hooves	10%
	supply and fitting of shoes	23%
Feeding and keeping of horses	by unregistered farmers	not taxable
	other	23%
Groom's services	by unregistered farmers	not taxable
	other	10%
Horses	supply of live horses by unregistered farmers	not taxable
	other	23%
	hiring/leasing by unregistered farmers	not taxable
	other	23%
	exports	zero
	dead horses	zero
	hides	23%
	horsehair	23%
Imports of horses	permanent	23%
	temporary	see para
Insurance and agency services relating thereto	Intra EC	exempt
	outside EC	zero
Jockeys' services		23%
Livery	see feeding and keeping	
Nominations	by unregistered farmers	not taxable
	other	23%
	mares in the ownership of foreigners imported for service by stallions owned by taxable persons and afterwards exported	zero
Pedigree Research		23%
Pony Trekking		23%
Prize money		not taxable
Racing admissions		exempt

Racehorse training		23%
Repair services		10%
Riding schools		exempt
Show jumping admissions		exempt
Stabling of horses		
Stables, Erection of	see Accommodation	10%
Swimming pools for horses	lettings	exempt
Tack		23%
Transport	within the State	23%
	international	zero
Valets' services		23%

APPENDIX II

Sale of a horse by an unregistered farmer through an auctioneer (or bloodstock agent) to another unregistered farmer.

The accepted bid price excluding VAT, is 10,000 guineas (£10,500).

The auctioneer's commission is 5% which is charged entirely to the vendor.

	£
The auctioneer is deemed to have bought the horse from the farmer for	9,600.00
Flat-rate addition at 2.3%	220.80
The auctioneer is deemed to have sold the horse for	10,500.00
VAT at 2.3%	241.20
The auctioneer's liability is 2.3% of £10,500 less £9,600 (ie 2.3% of £900)	20.70

The purchasing farmer pays the auctioneer £10,741.50 that is £10,500 plus 2.3%

The selling farmer is paid £9,820.80 that is £9,600 plus 2.3.%.

RATES OF VAT ON SERVICES FROM 1 MARCH 1991

General

1. On and from 1 March 1991 the rate of VAT on most goods and services at present liable at 10% and 23% will become 12.5% and 21% respectively. The goods and services in question are:

(*a*) admissions to certain exhibitions,

(*b*) adult clothing and footwear including materials for their manufacture,

(*c*) agricultural services,

(*d*) cabaret admissions,

(*e*) car driving instructions,

(*f*) care of the human body; hairdressing, health studio services,

(*g*) cinema admissions,

(*h*) fuel for power and heating; coal, peat, timber, electricity, gas,

(*i*) heating oil,

(*j*) general repair and maintenance services of movable goods,

(*k*) photographic services,

(*l*) restaurant/hotel meals,

(*m*) spectacles and contact lenses,

(*n*) telephone services,

(*o*) waste disposal,

(*p*) works of art; literary manuscripts, most antiques

2. A number of supplies will continue to be liable at the 10% rate. These include buildings and building work, concrete blocks, ready mix concrete, newspapers, hotel lettings, short-term hiring of cars, boats, caravans and tour guide services.

List of Services

3. All illustrative list is attached of the principal services which will be affected together with examples of those which will not and an indication of the rate of VAT which will apply on and from 1 March 1991. The list is NOT comprehensive. Information concerning the VAT rating of unlisted services and other information may be obtained from the Revenue Commissioners, Indirect Taxes Branch, Dublin Castle, Dublin 2 (Tel. 01–6792777 Ext. 2440, 2441, 2442, 2443) or from local tax offices.

Rates of VAT on Certain Services on and from 1 March 1991

Subject to 2/3rds rule — see paragraph 15.11 of "Guide to Value Added Tax"

(This list is NOT comprehensive)

	%
Accommodation (letting of rooms, etc)	
by hotels, as defined	10
Accountants (see also para 20.21 of "Guide")	21
Actuaries	21
Addressing envelopes	21
Advertising	21
Agents, commission	21
Agricultural contracting (see paras 20.19, 20.20 of "Guide")	
Agricultural machinery	
hire (and sale)	21
repair, maintenance (excl. supply of accessories and tyres, tubes, batteries)	12.5
Alarms	
in buildings (supply and fit or fit only)	10
in vehicles (supply, supply and fit, or fit only)	21
other (supply, supply and fit, or fit only)	21
Alterations (to secondhand goods)	12.5
Amusements (see Entertainment)	
Anodising	21
Arcades, amusement	21
Architects	21
Artists' services (eg portrait painting)	12.5
Batteries, including supply in the course of repair	21
Battery charging and battery repair	12.5
Beauty salon services	12.5
on sales of cosmetics etc	21
Bed & breakfast	
by hotels, as defined (sleeping accommodation only),	10
meals	12.5
Biscuits	
with meal	12.5
other (including vending machines)	21
Bicycle	
repairs	12.5
long-term hire and sale	21
short-term hire	10
Blinds and curtain making	21

Boiler cleaning	10
Book binding	0, 21
Building services	10
Boning/de-boning meat	0
Cable TV	21
Cafes	
on alcohol and soft drinks	12.5, 21
Canteens (see paras 21.11–21.16 of "Guide")	12.5
Car accessories, supply, supply and fit, or fit only of phones, alarms, batteries, tyres etc	21
Caravans	
short-term hire	10
other hire and sale (new and used)	21
repair	12.5
Car hire	
long	21
short	10
Car parking	21
Car phones (supply, supply and fit, or fit only)	21
Car repair and maintenance	12.5
Car wash	12.5
Carpet cleaning	10, 12.5
Carpet laying (see Alterations and also para 15.7 of "Guide")	10, 21
Catering	12.5
(on alcohol and soft drinks — see Chapter 21 of "Guide")	21
Chimney cleaning	10
Chips (cooked)	12.5
Chiropody	Exempt
Cinema admissions	12.5
Circus admissions	Exempt
Cleaning	
immovable goods	10
other	12.5
Coin or token operated machines	
launderettes	12.5
car park	21
car wash	12.5
juke boxes	21
weighing scales	21
amusement machines	21
video games	21

food and drink vending machines (see Chapter 21 of "Guide")	12.5, 21
other vending machines	21
Cold storage	21
Communal TV charges	21
Computer programmes	21
Confectionery	
with meals	12.5
hot take aways	12.5
other	21
Consultancy (see para 20.21 of "Guide")	21
Couriers	21
Contract cleaning	
immovable goods	10
other	12.5
Curing (animal skins)	21
Curtain cleaning	12.5
Curtain making	21
Cutting to shape (timber, mirrors)	21
Dances (see para 5.16 of "Guide")	21
Dental technicians	Exempt
Design services	21
Driving lessons (vehicles less than 1.5 tonnes)	12.5
otherwise exempt	
De-boning	0
Dry cleaning	12.5
Drying (eg timber) manufacture	21
Dyeing	12.5
Ear piercing	12.5
Electricity	12.5
Electroplating	21
Employment agencies	21
Engraving	21
Entertainment	
cabaret type including shows with which food and drink are supplied	12.5
(supplies of alcohol and soft drinks)	21
cinema admissions	12.5
circus admissions	Exempt
dances	21
admission to sporting events	Exempt

theatre admissions	Exempt
amusement machines	21
exhibition admissions	12.5
fairground entertainment	12.5 (some exempt and 21)
juke boxes	21
Etching	21
original work of art	12.5
Farm accountancy	12.5
Farm management	12.5
Film processing	12.5
Fitting services	21
Food and drink	0, 12.5, 21
(see separate leaflet)	
French polishing (of used goods)	12.5
Fruit juices	
freshly squeezed juices (non manufactured)	0
with meal	12.5
other	21
Furniture	
hire and sale	21
repair, restoration	12.5
upholstering	21 (new); 12.5 (old)
Gas conversion (vehicles)	12.5
Galvanising (new goods)	21
Glazing	10
Goods transport	21
Grain drying and storage	21
Grain grinding, mixing	21
Guest houses (see Chapter 21 of "Guide")	
Hairdressing	12.5
Haulage	21
Health studio	12.5
Hire of goods	2.3, 10, 21
Hotels (see Chapter 21 of "Guide")	
Inspection services	21
Installation services	
movable goods	21
immovable goods	10

Reconditioning	12.5
Recording studios	21
Refrigeration services	21
Repairs	
movable goods	12.5
immovable goods	10
Restaurants (see Chapter 21 of "Guide")	
Restoration services	10, 12.5
Re-surfacing	10, 12.5
Re-upholstering	12.5
Rustproofing	
old goods	10, 12.5
new goods	21
Sand blasting (of buildings)	10
Sauna service	
hotel	10
elsewhere	Exempt
Security services	21
Self-operating services (see Coin operated machines)	
Sharpening services	12.5
Shoe repairs	12.5
Signwriting	21
on fixtures	12.5
Snooker (Spectators and competition admissions exempt)	21
Soft drinks	21
Solicitors	21
Some services	12.5
Stamping (eg of precious metals)	21
Storage	21
Storage and drying of grain	21
Surveyors	21 (12.5 and some activities exempt)
Take aways (see Chapter 21 of "Guide")	
Tents	
long-term hire and sale	21
short-term hire	10
Testing	21
Tanning (hides)	21
Telecommunication services	12.5

AUTOMATED ENTRY PROCESSING FOR IMPORTS/EXPORTS

1. The Automated Entry Processing system (AEP) for the processing of Customs entries came into effect on 1 April 1991. Under the new system, Customs entries may now be made directly into the Customs computer network. This means that the information formerly inscribed on the Single Administrative Document (SAD) may now be transmitted electronically to Customs.

2. As a consequence of the new system, certified SADs will no longer be available to support claims for deduction or refund of VAT paid on imports or, for the purposes of verifying exportation of goods. Instead, the following arrangements will apply:

    (*a*) Imports

        In relation to claims for deduction or refund of VAT paid on imports traders must have evidence of payment of the VAT, ie

        — Monthly Customs & Excise statement for traders who are on the Deferred Payment/FACT Schemes (traders should claim input credits/ refunds strictly in accordance with the net VAT amount on the deferred statements, ie the amount of VAT which has been debited to their bank accounts), or

        — Official receipt issued by Customs & Excise where payment is made direct to Customs & Excise by the trader other than by the Deferred Payment/ FACT Schemes, or

        — Invoice from Customs Clearance Agent. This should show clearly the entry number and the amount and rate of VAT paid on behalf of the trader. Alternatively, a copy of the SAD showing the entry no. may be attached to the invoice.

        Each claim for deduction or refund of VAT paid on imports must also be supported by the suppliers' invoice(s) which must be cross referenced to the appropriate debit(s), on the monthly C&E statement, or to the C&E receipt etc Normal commercial documentation eg delivery dockets, proof of payment to supplier etc, where appropriate, should also be retained.

        In addition, traders/customs clearance agents may attach copy SADs showing the entry nos. to their deferred statements, receipts or invoices.

    (*b*) Exports

        With regard to exports each transaction must be supported by the sales invoice cross referenced to the normal commercial documents (delivery dockets, bills of lading, proof of payment from customer etc).

        Where necessary traders may be required to support their claim that goods have been exported, by production of documentation from the Customs Authorities of the country to which the goods were exported.

Further information concerning the trader's VAT accounting as affected by the new arrangements is available from the Revenue Commissioners, Indirect Taxes Branch, Dublin Castle, Dublin 2 (Tel. 01–6792777 Ext. 2440, 2441, 2442, 2443) or from local tax offices.

VETERINARY SERVICES

Introduction

1. With effect from 1 January 1992, services supplied by veterinary surgeons in the course of their profession will become liable to VAT at 12.5%. Services supplied by vets have hitherto been exempt from VAT, with an option for vets to elect to register if they so wished. This leaflet sets out the general implications of applying VAT to these services.

General

2. A person who supplies taxable goods or services in the course or furtherance of business in excess of specified limits (£15,000 in the case of veterinary services) is a taxable person and is required to register for VAT (see Chapter 4 of the VAT Guide).

3. A taxable person is liable to pay VAT at the appropriate rate on taxable goods and services supplied by him. A taxable person determines his VAT liability for each two-monthly taxable period (January/February, March/April, etc) by calculating the total tax due on his sales of goods or services for the period and subtracting the deductible tax invoiced to him or paid on imports in the period — the difference is the amount which he pays. If the deductible tax exceeds the tax chargeable the difference is refunded (see Chapter 7 of the VAT Guide).

4. The net effect is that a taxable person pays tax on his value added; and he does not normally bear the tax because he includes it in the price charged to his customer. The person who ultimately bears the tax is the unregistered purchaser, who is not entitled to any deduction for tax charged to him. If the customer is VAT registered he will be entitled to a deduction (ie a set-off against his own liability) of most VAT properly invoiced to him.

Which Vets Have to Register for VAT?

5. All independent vets, that is, vets who are not employees, are obliged to register for VAT if their annual turnover exceeds or is likely to exceed £15,000. Vets who are members of partnerships, or who operate as members of veterinary practices, are not regarded as independent persons for VAT purposes. In these circumstances the combined receipts of all persons contributing to the partnership or practice, are aggregated and where the combined receipts in a 12 month period exceed, or are likely to exceed £15,000 registration is obligatory. Whether a vet is operating independently or as a member of a practice or partnership is a matter which will be clear from the facts of each case.

Vets operating as employees of the State (ie subject to PAYE) are not obliged to register in respect of their activities as such, but they are obliged to register if their annual turnover from independent activities exceeds, or is likely to exceed, £15,000 (£32,000 in the case of sales of goods).

Applications for registration should be made on form VAT 1, which is available, on request, from local tax offices (see page vi of the VAT Guide for addresses and telephone numbers), or from VAT Branch (see paragraph 21 below).

Vets Carrying on Farming or Other Businesses

6. A vet who is registered, or obliged to register, because of the supply of veterinary services, and who is also engaged in other business activities, for example, farming or racehorse training, is liable to VAT in respect of all his activities. As a general rule a farmer is not obliged to register although he may opt to do so (see Chapter 20 of the VAT Guide). However, when taxable activities other than racehorse training, the annual receipts from which exceed £15,000, are carried on in addition to the farming activities, the turnover from all of the activities including farming then becomes taxable (see paragraphs 20.22 and 20.23 of VAT Guide for further information concerning persons engaged in farming, racehorse training and other activities).

Obligations of VAT Registered Persons

7. VAT registered persons are obliged to:

- (*a*) keep records which are sufficiently detailed to enable their liability as declared by themselves to be confirmed (see Chapter 11 of the VAT Guide);

- (*b*) issue invoices containing specified particulars (see Chapter 10 of the VAT Guide) in respect of taxable supplies to other taxable persons. If the consideration shown on an invoice is subsequently reduced and a tax adjustment is actually made, a credit note must be issued where the customer is a VAT registered person showing the amount of tax by which the liability has been reduced (see Chapter 5.15 of the VAT Guide);

- (*c*) submit a return on the prescribed form every two months* (see Appendix G of the VAT Guide) of their supplies and taxable purchases together with a remittance of tax due. This form is issued to registered persons before the end of each taxable period.

(*Note: Certain traders may be allowed to make returns on an annual basis. Persons who qualify will be notified in due course by the Collector-General; advance application may not be made.)

Accounting for VAT

8. The normal basis of accounting for VAT is the invoice or sales basis. However, a vet may, subject to conditions (see paragraph 10) account for VAT on the "moneys received" basis.

Invoice basis

9. A VAT registered vet using the invoice or sales basis of accounting will be liable to pay VAT by reference to his supplies as follows:-

- — in the case of transactions with persons who are not registered for VAT he is liable at the rate in force at the time of supply;

- — in the case of transactions with other VAT registered persons he is obliged to issue invoices and is liable to VAT at the rate of tax in force at the time he issues or ought to issue an invoice. (See Chapter 10 of the VAT Guide.)

In the case of vets accounting for VAT on the sales or invoice basis, VAT is not chargeable on services which are completed before 1 January 1992, no matter when the relevant invoice is issued. Services which are not completed before 1 January 1992, will not be chargeable to VAT to the extent that they are paid for (that is to the extent that the vet's office account has been credited) before 1 January 1992.

Moneys received Basis of Accounting for Tax

10. Certain registered persons, as follows, may use the moneys received basis of accounting instead of the usual sales basis:

(*a*) persons engaged in the supply of taxable services, and

(*b*) persons selling goods almost exclusively (at least 90% to unregistered persons).

(Transactions between connected persons, and property transactions, are excluded from the moneys received basis of accounting.)

This facility is available to vets but they must specify this on Form VAT 1 when applying for VAT registration.

A person opting to account for VAT on the moneys received basis is liable for tax, at the rate current at the time of receipt, on all moneys received in a taxable period. This is so even if, at the time of sale or supply of service, a different rate of tax or, indeed, no tax was in force. Vets who are registered, or obliged to register, from 1 January 1992, will be liable to VAT on all moneys received after 1 January 1992. Liability is based on the total consideration a person receives including all taxes (other than VAT), commissions, costs and charges whatsoever. In cases where money is received through agents, the taxable amount would include any amount which may be withheld by agents to cover their fees, expenses etc. A person accounting for VAT on the moneys received basis has no authority to recover from his customers any additional tax for which he may become accountable as a result of his decision to use this basis of accounting. (See Chapter 9 of the VAT Guide.)

Where payments on account are received in respect of supplies of goods and services liable at different rates, care should be taken to ensure such payments are attributed correctly at each rate of VAT (see paragraphs 16, 17, 18 below).

Taxable Amount

11. The amount on which a vet is liable, is the total amount which he is entitled to receive including commissions, costs and charges, and all taxes (other than VAT). As stated above (paragraph 5), in relation to determination of the taxable turnover for the purposes of registration, the taxable person (ie the individual, practice, partnership or other body of persons as the case may be) is the person who is accountable for VAT on the combined receipts from all supplies by or on behalf of that taxable person. This includes supplies made on the person's behalf by fellow members of the practice or partnership, assistants, locums, sub-contractors etc. As a general rule, locums (who are not employees) or sub- contractors who are independent persons must register and account for VAT if their turnover including the services supplied to the practice exceeds the taxable threshold. Such VAT would qualify for deduction by the registered practice subject to the usual rules (see paragraphs 13 and 14 below).

Withholding Tax

12. Income Tax withheld from payments to a vet which cover taxable supplies is deemed for VAT purposes to have been received by the vet. If, for example, in the case of his taxable supplies, payment of an amount due to a vet is reduced from £112.50 (£100 + £12.50 VAT) to £83.50 (£29 withheld for Income Tax) the vet is for VAT purposes deemed to have received £112.50 (£100 + £12.50) and is liable for the VAT element therein.

Example

	£
Veterinary fees	100.00
VAT at 12.5%	12.50
	112.50
Calculation of withholding tax	
VAT exclusive sum	100.00
Withholding tax at 29%	29.00
Net	71.00
VAT on the £100 fees	12.50
Total receivable by vet	83.50
Amount payable to Collector-General by the vet in respect of VAT	12.50

Deduction for VAT Charged on Purchases

13. A VAT registered vet is entitled to take a credit or deduction (ie set off against his liability) for most VAT properly invoiced to him by his suppliers or paid on imports. He is not required to pay the supplier before taking the credit.

14. The only expenditure, in respect of which a credit or deduction may not be taken, is expenditure relating to:

(*a*) the provision of food, drink, accommodation or other personal services for the person, his agents or employees (for example, hotel costs);

(*b*) entertainment expenses;

(*c*) purchase or hire of cars or other road passenger vehicles;

(*d*) purchase of petrol;

(*e*) an exempt (for example, letting of premises) or non-business activity, and

(*f*) VAT borne prior to registration (see paragraph 20).

Where a person carries on both taxable activities and other activities (for example, inspection of meat in factories as a State employee) only the expenses appropriate to his taxable activities qualify as deductible. How the deductible VAT is to be calculated in these circumstances is prescribed in regulations and may be in the ratio of the taxable turnover to the total turnover of the practice or on some other basis which may be agreed with the local inspector.

15. A credit or deduction may be taken in respect of diesel, car repairs and maintenance, and car parts (for example, a set of tyres), subject to the condition that they are used for the purposes of a taxable business.

Rates of VAT

16. The following are examples of the rates of VAT applicable to supplies made by vets. The list is not exhaustive.

A.I. Services	12.5%
	(subject to the 2/3rds rule
	— see paragraph 18)
Attendance at track meetings	12.5%
Consultancy	12.5%
Greyhounds (supply of)	2.3%
Livestock (live cattle, sheep, goats, horses,	
pigs and deer — supply of)	2.3%
Other live animals (supply of)	21%
Treatment of illness or disease	12.5%
	(subject to the 2/3rds rule)
TB testing	12.5%
Supply only of medicine	
oral	0%
non oral	21%

Supply of Goods in Addition to Supply of Services

17. Veterinary surgeons who supply medicines or other products as part of the veterinary service are liable to VAT at 12.5%, subject to the two-thirds rule (see paragraph 18). This is so even if the goods are, separately, liable at 21% or 0%. On the other hand if goods are left by the vet to be administered by the client and separate charges are made and recorded for the separate supplies, this is regarded as a separate supply of goods, taxable at the rate applicable to the goods — 21% or 0% as appropriate.

The Two-Thirds Rule

18. The rate of tax applying to all services, including veterinary services, is determined by the "two-thirds rule". This provides that a transaction is liable to VAT as a sale of goods at the appropriate rate and not as a service if the value of the goods (that is, their cost, excluding VAT, to the supplier) administered in providing the service exceeds two-thirds of the total charge to the customer, for example:

(1)	Total charge to client	£100
	Cost of non oral medicines administered	£70

(this exceeds 2/3rds of £100)

Vet is liable on this transaction at 21% (the rate applicable to a supply of non oral medicines).

(2)	Total charge to client	£200
	Cost of oral medicines administered	£150
	(this exceeds 2/3rds of £200)	

Vet is liable on this transaction at 0% (the rate applicable to a supply of oral medicines).

Supplies Liable at Different Rates

19. Where goods or goods and services liable at different rates are supplied as a unit for a composite charge tax is payable on the entire amount at the rate applicable to the highest rated item included in the supply, for example:

— a vet carries out T.B. testing on the entire herd — 12.5% supply;

— in addition he supplies oral medicine for administration by the farmer to other sick animals — 0% supply;

— he charges £200 for the entire operation;

— the vet will be liable to VAT at 12.5% on the entire charge.

If the amounts are separately charged say £150 for the testing, £50 for the oral medicine, only the £150 would attract the 12.5% rate. The £50 charge would qualify for the 0% rate.

Stock on Hands on 1 January 1992

20. No relief from VAT is available to persons supplying services in respect of tax on goods purchased prior to registration (including medicines administered in the course of providing the veterinary treatment). However vets who are registered, or are required to register, for VAT with effect from 1 January 1992, may claim a credit for the tax content of the stock-in-trade, that is goods held by them for supply only, without any element of service, on that date. The assistance of the local inspector of taxes may be sought in relation to the determination of such relief.

For the purposes of relief the stock is valued at the VAT inclusive cost or at market value, whichever is the lower. The relief may be set against a vet's tax liability for the first taxable period. Relief is allowed by reference to the rates actually charged at the time of purchase.

Enquiries

21. Inquiries should be made to the Revenue Commissioners, Indirect Taxes Branch, Dublin Castle, Dublin 2, (Tel. 01–6792777, Ext. 2440, 2441, 2442, 2443) or to inspectors of taxes.

RATES OF VAT ON SERVICES FROM 1 MARCH 1992

General

1. (i) On and from 1 March 1992 the rate of VAT on certain goods and services at present liable at 12.5% will become 16%.

The good and services in question are:

— adult clothing and footwear including materials for their manufacture,

— auto LPG,

— car driving instruction,

— hairdressing and certain other personal services,

— farm auctioneering and solicitor services relating to sales of agricultural land,

— farm accountancy and farm management services,

— general repair and maintenance services (other than building work), including car repairs,

— photographic services,

— services of jockeys,

— corrective spectacles and contact lenses,

— telecommunications,

— works of art; literary manuscripts; most antiques.

(ii) A number of supplies will continue to be liable at the 10% and 12.5% rates.

The 10% supplies include buildings and building work, concrete blocks, ready mix concrete, newspapers, hotel lettings, short-term hiring of cars, boats, caravans and tour guide services.

The 12.5% supplies include fuel for power and heating, electricity, restaurant and hotel meals, cinema admissions, certain live entertainment, admissions to certain exhibitions, waste disposal, general agricultural services and veterinary services.

List of Services

2. An illustrative list is attached of the principal services which will be affected together with those which will be liable at other rates from 1 March 1992. The list is NOT comprehensive. Information concerning the VAT rating of unlisted services and other information may be obtained from the Revenue Commissioners, Indirect Taxes Branch, Dublin Castle, Dublin 2 (Tel. 01–6792777 Ext. 2440, 2441, 2442, 2443) or from local tax offices.

Rates of VAT on Certain Services on and from 1 March 1992

Subject to 2/3rds rule — see para 15.11 of "Guide to Value Added Tax"

(This list is NOT comprehensive)

	%
Accommodation (letting of rooms, etc)	10
hotels, guest houses and similar establishments	10
accommodation which is held out as being holiday accommodation or accommodation for visitors or travellers	10
Accountants	21
farm accountancy	16
Actuaries	21
Addressing envelopes	21
Advertising	21
Agents, commission	21
Agricultural contracting	0, 12.5, 21
Agricultural machinery	
hire (and sale)	21
repair, maintenance (excl. supply of accessories and tyres, tubes, batteries)	16
Alarms	
in buildings (supply and fit or fit only)	10
in vehicles (supply, supply and fit, or fit only)	21
other (supply, supply and fit, or fit only)	21
Alterations (to secondhand goods)	16
Amusements (see Entertainment)	
Anodising	21
Arcades, amusement	21
Archaeologists	16, 21
Architects	21
Artists services (eg portrait painting)	16
Auctioneers	21
vegetables, fruit, eggs, dead poultry	0
live cattle, horses, greyhounds, sheep, goats, pigs and deer	2.7
farm auctioneering	16
Batteries, all, including supply in the course of repair	21
Battery charging and battery repair	16
Beauty salon services	16
(on sales of cosmetics)	21

Bed & Breakfast	
by hotels, guest houses etc (see Accommodation)	10
meals	12.5
Biscuits	
with meal	12.5
other (including vending machines)	21
Bicycle	
repairs	16
long-term hire and sale	21
short-term hire	10
Blinds and curtain making	21
Boiler maintenance	10
Book Binding	0, 21
Building services	10
Boning/de-boning meat	0
Cable TV	21
Cafes	12.5 (21% on alcohol and soft drinks)
Camp sites (lettings)	10
Canteens	12.5 (see para 21.11 21.16 of "Guide")
Car Accessories, supply, supply and fit or fit only of phones, alarms, batteries, tyres etc	21
Caravans	
short-term hire	10
other hire and sale (new and used)	21
repair	16
Caravan parks (lettings)	10
Car hire	
long	21
short	10
Car parking	21
Car phones (supply, supply and fit, or fit only)	21
Car repair and maintenance	16
Car wash	16
Carpet cleaning	16
Carpet laying (see Alterations and also para 15.7 of "Guide")	10, 21
Catering	12.5
(on alcohol and soft drinks see Chapter 21 of "Guide")	21
Chimney cleaning	10
Chips (cooked)	12.5

Chiropody	Exempt
Cinema admissions	12.5
Circus admissions	Exempt
Cleaning	
contract	16
immovable goods	10
Coin or token operated machines	
launderettes	16
car park	21
car wash	16
juke boxes	21
weighing scales	21
amusement machines	21
video games	21
food and drink vending machines	12.5
(see Chapter 21 of Guide")	21
other vending machines	21
Cold storage	21
Communal TV charges	21
Computer programmes	21
Confectionery	
with meals	12.5
hot take aways	12.5
other	21
Consultancy (see para 20.21 of "Guide")	21
Couriers	21
Contract cleaning (routine)	16
Curing (animal skins)	21
Curtain cleaning	16
Curtain making	21
Cutting to shape (timber, mirrors)	21
Dances	21
Dental technicians	Exempt
Design services	21
Digging and excavating (other than development)	16
Driving lessons (vehicles less than 1.5 tonnes)	16
otherwise exempt	
De-boning	0
Dry cleaning	16
Drying (eg timber)	21
Dyeing	16
Ear piercing	16

Electricity	12.5
Electroplating	21
Employment agencies	21
Engraving	21
Entertainment	
cabaret type including shows with which food and drink are supplied (supplies of alcohol and soft drinks 21%)	12.5
cinema admissions	12.5
circus admissions	Exempt
dances	21
admission to sporting events	Exempt
theatre admissions	Exempt
amusement machines	21
exhibition admissions	12.5
fairground entertainment	12.5, 21
juke boxes	21
Etching	21
original work of art	16
Farm accountancy	16
Farm management	16
Farmhouse accommodation	10
Film processing	16
Fitting services	21
Food and drink (see separate leaflet)	0, 12.5, 21
French polishing (of used goods)	16
Fruit juices	
freshly squeezed juices (non manufactured)	0
with meal	12.5
other	21
Furniture	
hire and sale	21
repair, restoration	16
upholstering	21 (new); 16 (old)
Gas conversion (vehicles)	16
Galvanising (new goods)	21
Glazing	10
Goods transport	21
for international	0
Grain drying and storage	21
Grain grinding, mixing	21

Guest houses (accommodation)	10
meals	12.5
Hairdressing	16
Haulage	21
(for international)	0
Health studio	16, 21
Hire of goods	2.7, 10, 21
Holiday cottages	10
Hotels (accommodation)	10
meals	12.5
Inspection Services	21
Installation Services	
movable goods	21
immovable goods	10
Jockeys	16
Juke boxes (to play)	21
Key cutting	21
Laminating	21
Landscaping and land reclamation and drainage	10
Laundering	16
Law searchers	21
Linen hire	21
Mailing services (addressing and distributing envelopes etc)	21
Management services (see para 20.21 of "Guide")	21
Manicuring	16
Massage	16
Meals (see Chapter 21 of "Guide")	
Microfilming	16
Motels	10
Mounting (coins onto rings)	21
Office, factory cleaning (routine)	16
other	10
Packaging services (wrapping, strapping)	21
Patents	21
Painting	
of fixtures	10
of portraits, etc	16
fittings (free-standing goods)	16, 21
Pest control	10, 16, 21
Photocopying	21
Photography	16

Polishing	
fixtures	10
second hand goods	16
new goods (eg furniture)	21
Printing	
books	0, 21
magazines	10, 21
newspapers — most daily, weekly, fortnightly	10
other	21
Picture framing	21
Puncture repairs	16
Reconditioning	16
Recording studios	21
Refrigeration services	21
Repairs	
movable goods	16
immovable goods	10
Restaurants (see Chapter 21 of "Guide")	
Restoration services	10, 16
Re-surfacing	10, 16
Re-upholstering	16
Rustproofing	
old goods	10, 16
new goods	10, 21
Sand blasting (of buildings)	10
Sanitary services (waste disposal)	12.5
Security services	21
Self-operating services (see Coin operated machines)	
Sharpening services	16
Shoe repairs	16
Signwriting	21
on fixtures	16
repair and maintenance	10, 16
Snooker	21
(spectators and competition admissions exempt)	
Soft drinks	21
Solicitors	21
some services	16
Stamping (eg of precious metals)	21
Storage	21
Storage and drying of grain	21
Surveyors	16, 21

CHANGES RELATING TO THE MONEYS RECEIVED BASIS OF ACCOUNTING

1. The Value Added Tax (Determination of Tax Due by Reference to Moneys Received) (Amendment) Regulations 1992, which were made by the Revenue Commissioners on 16 April 1992, amended the existing regulation as regards the adjustment of liability following a change in the basis of accounting for VAT.

2. Previously, where persons ceased to account for VAT on the moneys received (or "cash receipts") basis of accounting, they were required to adjust their liability for VAT to take account of any increase in their debtors during the period for which they accounted on that basis. However, where they had been accounting on the moneys received basis for longer than six years no such adjustment was required.

3. From 16 April 1992 this adjustment will be required in all cases of cessation regardless of the period of time involved. However, persons who have been accounting on the moneys received basis for longer than six years will be required to adjust their liability to take account of any increase in their debtors only in relation to the six years prior to the change.

4. There will be no change in the position where the cessation of use of the moneys received basis results from the death of the taxable person. No adjustment is required in such cases.

ADVERTISING SERVICES

1. General

The supply of advertising services in the State is a taxable activity liable to VAT at the rate of 21%. Persons who supply advertising services in the course or furtherance of business and whose annual turnover in a 12 month period exceeds, or is likely to exceed, £15,000 are obliged to register and account for VAT (see Chapter 4 of "Guide to the Value Added Tax").

2. Scope

The scope of the term "advertising services" has not been defined in VAT law. However, as a matter of practice, advertising services include all services actually carried out by advertising agencies which have the aim of promoting a product, a business or a person, for example, media publicity, promotional launches and other publicity events.

3. Place of Supply

As a general rule the place of supply of services is the place where the person supplying the services has established his business. However, as an exception to this general rule and in common with other services listed in the Fourth Schedule to the VAT Act, the place of supply of advertising services is determined by the status and location of the recipient of the services.

Advertising services supplied by an advertising agent established in Ireland to any person in Ireland or to any non-business person within the EC are deemed to be supplied in Ireland and are liable to Irish VAT. Services supplied by Irish suppliers to business persons (whether they are registered for VAT or not) outside Ireland are deemed to be supplied at the place where the customer has his business establishment. Similarly, services received in Ireland by Irish business persons (whether they are registered for VAT or not) from overseas suppliers are deemed to be supplied in Ireland and are liable to Irish VAT (see separate leaflet concerning "Services received from abroad").

4. Taxable Amount

The amount chargeable to VAT is the total consideration paid by the client in respect of the total service supplied.

Credit or deduction for advertising services is allowable except for expenditure relating to:

(a) the provision of food, drink, accommodation or other personal services for the taxable person, his agents or employees (for example, hotel costs);

(b) entertainment expenses;

(c) purchase or hire of cars or other road passenger vehicles;

(d) purchase of petrol;

(e) expenditure relating to exempt or non-business activities.

SPORTS FACILITIES

1. General

The coming in to effect of the provisions of the Finance Act 1992 will bring about fundamental changes in the treatment for VAT purposes of facilities provided for taking part in sporting activities. Up to now many of the providers of such facilities, for example, golf courses, driving ranges, tennis courts, ten-pin bowling alleys etc were regarded as exempt. With effect from 1 July 1992, the provision by a person other than a non-profit making organisation, of facilities for taking part in sporting activities will be taxable and liable to VAT at the rate of 12.5%.

2. Persons Liable

Only those persons providing sporting facilities on a commercial basis will be liable to tax. The provision of such facilities by non-profit making organisations will continue to be exempt. In deciding what is a non-profit making organisation the Revenue Commissioners will have regard, for example, to the organisation's constitution or articles of association as to whether or not it is precluded from distributing profits. In practice, most private member golf, tennis or similar clubs will continue to qualify for exemption insofar as the provision of sporting facilities for members and non-members is concerned.

3. Promotion of and Admissions to Sporting Events

The change in VAT liability affects only charges made for facilities for participation in sporting activities. There is no change insofar as spectators are concerned. Admission to sporting events, as well as receipts arising from promotion of sporting events by non-profit making organisations, will continue to qualify for exemption.

4. What are Sports Facilities?

"Sports facilities" means any grounds or premises designed or adapted for playing sport. This includes bowling alleys, driving ranges, gymnasia, golf courses, lands let for fishing or shooting, snooker halls, skating rinks, squash courts, swimming pools and tennis courts. Leisure complexes which normally comprise a gymnasium or swimming pool, together with ancillary facilities such as jacuzzi, sauna or steam room are also included.

"Sporting facilities" does not include:

(a) facilities provided for activities which do not amount to a sport, for example, board or card games, computer or video games or amusement machines;

(b) provision of equipment only, for example, the hire of golf clubs as a charge separate from green fees. In these circumstances the rate of VAT appropriate to the hire of equipment will apply. However, where hire of equipment is incidental to the provision of the sports facilities without separate charge, for example, shoes provided for persons using indoor bowling facilities, the charge will be deemed to relate to the sporting facilities and so qualify for the 12.5% rate.

5. Taxable Persons

Persons (other than non-profit making organisations) engaged in the provision of sports facilities in the course or furtherance of business will be obliged to register and account for tax where annual turnover exceeds, or is likely to exceed, £15,000. Application for registration should be made on form VAT 1 which is available on request from local VAT offices.

6. Rate of VAT

From 1 July 1992, the rate of VAT applicable to the provision of facilities for taking part in sporting activities is 12.5%. In this regard it should be noted that in some cases the provision of facilities which formerly attracted VAT at 16% or 21% may now qualify for 12.5%, for example, the rate applicable to use of gymnasia will be reduced from 16 to 12.5% while the rate applicable to provision of snooker facilities will be reduced from 21% to 12.5%.

THE MONTHLY CONTROL STATEMENT

General

1. Section 17(1B) of the Value Added Tax Act 1972 obliges a taxable person to issue a monthly control statement to each taxable person to whom he or she supplies goods. The obligation only applies where a person's taxable turnover in respect of supplies of goods to other taxable persons exceeds £2 million in the previous period of twelve months. Where the grouping provisions of section 8(8) are applicable, the £2 million threshold will apply to the supplies of the group as a whole.

Operative Date

2. The obligation to issue a monthly control statement applies in relation to goods supplied after 1 November 1992. The Revenue Commissioners will exercise flexibility in relation to the commencement date where traders need additional time to clarify the implications of the new requirement and to install and test new reporting systems (see paragraph 10).

Details to be Included on the Monthly Control Statement

3. The details to be included in the monthly control statement are set out in the Value Added Tax (Monthly Control Statement) Regulations (SI No 230 of 1992) which were made by the Revenue Commissioners on 13 August 1992.

The details are:

(*a*) the name, address and registration number of the person by whom the goods referred to in the statement were supplied;

(*b*) the name and address of the person to whom the goods referred to in the statement were supplied;

(*c*) the date of issue of the statement;

(*d*) the calendar month to which the statement refers;

(*e*) in relation to supplies of goods for which an invoice, credit note, debit note or settlement voucher was issued in accordance with section 17 of the VAT Act, the total amount of the consideration inclusive of tax shown on each of those document;

(*f*) in relation to supplies of goods for which an invoice, credit note, debit note or settlement voucher was not issued,

    (i) the date of each such supply,

    (ii) a description of the goods supplied,

    (iii) the consideration, exclusive of tax, for each supply,

    (iv) the rate or rates of tax and amount of tax at each rate chargeable to the person who has supplied the goods;

(*g*) in relation to any adjustment of the consideration for the supplies referred to in paragraph (*e*) or (*f*) agreed between the supplier of the goods and the taxable person and for which a credit note was not issued under section 17 of the VAT Act,

    (i)   the amount of such adjustment,

    (ii) the date of such adjustment;

(*h*)   where, in respect of the supply referred to in paragraph (*e*) or (*f*), any payment has been or will be made by the person issuing the monthly control statement,

    (i)   the amount of such payment or payments,

    (ii) the date or dates when such payment or payments were or will be made,

    (iii) the person or persons to whom such payment or payments have been or will be made;

    and

(*i*)   in relation to any gifts or promotional items given in connection with the supplies referred to in paragraph (*e*) or (*f*),

    (i)   a description of such gifts or promotional items,

    (ii) the value of such gifts or promotional items,

    (iii) the date of provision of such gifts or promotional items.

Time Limit for Issuing the Monthly Control Statement

4. The monthly control statement must be issued not later than the last day of the month following the month during which the goods were supplied.

Document to be Retained

5. Every person who receives a monthly control statement is obliged to retain the document for six years. The person issuing a monthly control statement is obliged to retain an exact copy of the statement for a similar period. Subject to agreement with the local tax office copies of the monthly control statements can be stored on non-paper media such as microfiche or computer tape or disc.

Use of Commercial Statements

6.1. Where a trader issues a statement to his or her customers for commercial reasons this statement will be accepted by the Revenue Commissioners as fulfilling the legal requirement of the monthly control statement, provided the commercial statement includes the required details as set out in paragraph 3 above. If the commercial statement contains details additional to those indicated in paragraph 3 (eg details of payments received from customers) it can still serve as the monthly control statement.

6.2. While the legislation requires a monthly statement, traders who use a different accounting period eg a four week cycle, can issue the statement based on this period.

6.3. Where the commercial statement contains some, but not all, of the required details, the Revenue Commissioners will accept the listing of additional details on a separate document provided that the commercial statement contains a specific cross reference to the separate documentation in the following or similar terms: "For the purpose of complying with section 17(1B) of the VAT Act additional details are contained in: Document Number .... Date......."

All Supplies to be Included

7.1. The monthly control statement must include details of all supplies made to the taxable person to whom the statement is being issued. Thus both credit sales and cash sales must be recorded on the statement.

7.2. Where a trader carries on a cash business eg where a large number of customers are supplied on a regular basis by a van sales person who issues the VAT invoice, this invoice may substitute for the monthly control statement provided it is clearly indicated that this invoice covers all supplies (irrespective of whether they are being charged for or not). Where more than one supply is made to a particular customer in any month, each invoice issued must state clearly that it is in respect of all supplies to that customer since the date of the last invoice.

All Payments to be Included

8. The monthly control statement should include details of any amounts paid by the person issuing the monthly control statement in relation to the supplies referred to on that statement (see paragraph 3(h) above). Such payments could take the form for example of payments under long term agreements, discounts, "hello money" etc. Where the person issuing the statement makes a payment which relates to supplies over a number of periods the payment may be included in the statement for the month during which the payment was made.

Gift and Promotional Items

9.1. The statement should include details of gifts and promotional items given by the supplier to the trader or any other person in respect of the supplies. The statement should show a description, value and date of:

— goods for resale supplied free, details of which have not been included in an invoice;

— capital or expense items supplied without charge eg a cold room or a freezer;

— gifts or benefits given to the trader, (including an employee of the trader or any other person) in respect of the goods supplied eg televisions, holidays etc. (However, details of these gifts need not be sent with the statement. They may be kept in a separate list provided that they are available for inspection by the local VAT inspector and that a reference to the existence of such a list is made on the monthly statement). Details of gifts of goods the aggregate cost of which in a given twelve month period does not exceed £600, need not be included in the statement. If, however, a trader does not wish to keep such details on a twelve month basis, he may opt for a monthly basis. In those cases, details of gifts which do not exceed £50 in any one month need not be included in the statement.

9.2. Items which are given for advertising purposes by the supplier and are used on the purchaser's premises eg beer mats, ash trays, etc need not be included on the statement. Similarly details of sponsorship of sporting events and sponsorship of prizes, with the exception of the provision of goods for resale, need not be included in the statement.

Modifications

10. Any trader who wishes to present the information in a format or manner different to that outlined in the Regulations and described in paragraphs 3 and 4 of this Statement of Practice, or who wishes to seek a deferral of the implementation date should apply to the local office. Revenue officers will be designated in each tax office. Revenue officers will be designated in each tax office to deal with applications and Inquiries in relation to the monthly control statement.

APPLICATION OF THE ZERO RATE TO SALES AND DELIVERIES OF GOODS TO OTHER EC MEMBER STATES AFTER 1 JANUARY 1993

General

1. Currently exports of goods to destinations outside the State qualify for the zero rate of VAT. The existing procedures will continue to apply for exports to countries outside the EC after 1 January 1993. However, under the new European Community (EC) VAT arrangements applicable from that date revised arrangements will be introduced in relation to the zero rating of goods supplied to other Member States of the EC. This Statement of Practice outlines the new requirements to enable such supplies to be zero rated.

Essential Conditions for Zero Rating

2. An Irish trader, registered for VAT may zero rate the supply of goods to a customer in another Member State provided that:

   (i)   the customer is registered for VAT in another Member State,

  (ii) the customer's VAT registration number is obtained and retained in the supplier's records (see paragraph 7),

 (iii) this number, together with the supplier's VAT registration number, is quoted on the sales invoice,

 (iv) the goods are despatched or transported to another EC Member State.

If these four conditions are not met the seller will be accountable for VAT at the appropriate Irish rate. If a supplier is not able to satisfy the Revenue Commissioners that particular consignments of goods have been sold and delivered to a VAT registered person in another Member State, the supplier will be liable for the payment of Irish VAT on the transaction.

Evidence of Despatch to Another Member State and of Removal of the Goods from the State

3. The precise commercial documentation required to confirm despatch and removal of the goods from the State will depend on the particular circumstances involved.

4. In many cases the supplier will arrange transportation of the goods and the normal commercial documentation related to the supply and transportation of the goods will be available (eg order document, delivery docket, supplier's invoice, transport document/ bill of lading, evidence of transfer of foreign currency for payment, etc). In such cases the trader should retain this documentation.

5. Where transport of the goods is arranged by the customer, or the goods are taken away by the customer using his or her own transport, the seller will need to be satisfied that the goods are dispatched or transported to another Member State. The normal documentary evidence should be retained in relation to the sale itself but, in addition, the supplier should obtain and retain documentary evidence from the customer that the goods were received in another Member State. The type of documentation acceptable will include transport documents, copies of warehouse receipts, delivery dockets, etc. It might also be prudent for the supplier to record details (eg vehicle registration nos) of the means of transport used by the customer.

6. Special care should be taken by the supplier to ensure that the four conditions outlined in paragraph 2 will be met for sales and deliveries of goods to other Member States. Examples of where a doubt could arise include:

— customer is not previously known to the supplier,

— customer will arrange to collect and transport the goods,

— customer's transport arrives at supplier's premises without advance notice or correspondence,

— payment in cash,

— type or quantity of goods being purchased are not consistent with commercial practice bearing in mind the purported destination of the goods.

Cases where one or more of these various factors combine together must be treated with particular caution. Where a doubt arises, the supplier should charge Irish VAT. If the conditions for zero rating are subsequently established the customer will be entitled to recover the VAT paid from the supplier.

Verification of Customers' VAT numbers

7. For zero rating to apply there must be a supply of goods to a person registered in another Member State. The fiscal authorities in each Member State are arranging to put in place a computerised system that will make it possible for traders to verify the VAT numbers of their customers in other Member States. However, use of the verification system is not obligatory and traders who are familiar with their customers, and are aware of their bona fides from trading with them over a period of time, will not be expected or required to use the verification system. Instead they are advised to contact their EC customers and ask them to confirm in writing their VAT registration numbers. (An example of the type of form that might be used for this purpose is attached as Appendix I.)

8. An Irish trader who has doubts about the validity of a VAT number quoted will be able to use the verification system to establish whether a particular number is valid. The system is primarily intended to be used in such circumstances and is not intended for routine checks. Pending the establishment of the VIES/INTRASTAT Office in Dundalk (probably in December 1992), verification queries will be dealt with by the VIMA Office in Dublin, Telephone (01) 6792777, Ext. 2334, 2373, 2357 or Fax (01) 6792636.

Requirement to Take all Reasonable Steps

9. Any supplier who takes all reasonable steps to confirm that the conditions for zero rating are met will not be penalised if it subsequently transpires that a problem has arisen in connection with particular consignments. However, the tax due will be demanded from the supplier in any case where he or she has failed to do so.

Fraudulent Claims for Zero Rating

10. There are severe penalties for making fraudulent claims for zero rating:

(i)   seizure and forfeiture of zero rated goods which have not been despatched or transported outside the State (subsections (9A) and (10) of section 27 of the VAT Act),

(ii) arrest of a person suspected of a criminal offence who is not established in the State, or whom an authorised Revenue Officer or a Garda has reason to believe may leave the State (subsection (11) of section 27 of the VAT Act),

(iii) civil and criminal penalties, ranging from £1,200 to £10,000 and imprisonment for a period of up to five years (sections 26, 27 and 28 of the VAT Act and section 94 of the Finance Act 1983).

APPENDIX I

Dear Customer,

VAT/TVA/IVA/MWSt/BTW

To comply with new EC regulations, we will, from January 1993, have to show your VAT/ Sales Tax Number on our invoices.

To help us with this, could you please fill in the box below with your VAT/Sales Tax Number and return it to us as soon as possible. Please ensure that the country prefix is included.

N.B. If you are not registered for VAT, please tick

In addition, to help us update our records, please forward your:

Telephone No. ....

Fax No. ....

Thank you.

Yours faithfully,

ELECTRONIC INVOICING (EDI)

General

1. A taxable person who supplies goods and services to another taxable person must issue to that other taxable person a VAT invoice. Up to now this requirement could be satisfied only by issue of a paper invoice. However the Revenue Commissioners have recently made regulations which provide for the issue of invoices, credit notes, debit notes and settlement vouchers by electronic means.

Authorisation

2. A taxable person proposing to issue or receive invoices/credit notes, etc acceptable for the purposes of the VAT system by electronic means must be authorised by the local VAT inspector to do so and must meet the following requirements:

Each taxable person must:

(*a*) apply in writing to the local VAT office for authorisation to issue or receive messages by electronic means at least one month in advance of the intended start up date stating -

    (i) his or her name, address and registration number,

    (ii) the name, address and registration number of each taxable person to whom or from whom he or she will be issuing or receiving messages electronically,

    (iii) the date from which he or she intends to issue or receive messages being not later than one month after the date of application,

    and

(*b*) make a declaration in writing that the EDI system to be used is capable of meeting the criteria which have been laid down by law (see next paragraph).

Capacity of the System

3. The system must be capable of:

    (i) producing, retaining and storing a record of the messages transmitted or received in such form and containing such particulars as are required by the VAT Act and Regulations. For the purposes of the EDI regulation "message" means an invoice, credit note, debit note or settlement voucher required to be issued in accordance with section 17 of the VAT Act (see Chapter 10 of the Guide to the Value Added Tax),

    (ii) reproducing on paper a record of any messages transmitted by or stored in the system,

    (iii) generating a sequential series of numbers unique to each two trading partners who are engaged in the electronic exchange of messages. Each batch of messages from the sender must carry a unique number which must be verified by the recipient as the next logical number from that sender. The system must have in-built safeguards to preclude the possibility of the same number issuing twice or the omission of any particular number in the sequence of numbers,

(iv) maintaining records required to be retained or stored in accordance with paragraph 4 below in such manner as will allow their retrieval by reference either to the date or the transmission sequence number of the batch of messages.

Keeping of Records

4. On receipt of authorisation the taxable person can proceed to transmit or receive messages by electronic means. The existing provisions of VAT law as regards issue, retention and storage of records apply to electronic records in the same way as they apply to paper records. However a taxable person who is authorised to issue or receive messages by electronic means must also issue, or, in the case of the recipient construct, retain and store the following additional documents:

(*a*) a batch control record (that is a summary of all the messages included in each transmission) containing the following particulars:

  (i) the name, address and registration number of the issuer,

  (ii) the name, address and registration number of the recipient,

  (iii) the date of preparation of the message,

  (iv) the transmission sequence number, and

  (v) for each type of message in the transmission the following particulars:

  (I) the total number of messages,

  (II) the total consideration, exclusive of tax, in respect of which the messages were issued or received,

  (III) the amount of the consideration liable to tax at each rate including the zero rate,

  (IV) the amount of tax appropriate to the consideration at each rate, and

  (V) the total consideration for exempt supplies, if any;

(*b*) *a summary document produced at the end of each month by both issuer and recipient containing the following particulars:

  (i) the name, address and registration number of the issuer,

  (ii) the name, address and registration number of the recipient,

  (iii) the calendar month to which the document relates, and

  (iv) in respect of that month the following particulars:

  (I) each transmission sequence number,

  (II) the total consideration, exclusive of tax, to which the document relates,

  (III) the amount of the consideration liable at each rate of tax including the zero rate,

  (IV) the amount of tax appropriate to the said consideration at each rate,

(V)   the total consideration for exempt supplies, if any, and

(v)   in the case of the authorised issuer, the sequence numbers of faulty or failed transmissions;

(c)   in the case of an authorised recipient, a document produced by him and issued to a trading partner giving details of any discrepancy between the batch control document issued by the sender and that constructed by the recipient;

(d)   in all cases, a transmission log ie a record of transmission sequence numbers between each trading partner.

*NOTE:Section 17(1B) of the Value Added Tax Act 1972, obliges a taxable person to issue a monthly control statement to each taxable person to whom he or she supplies goods. The monthly summary document referred to above may not be accepted as a monthly control statement for the purposes of section 17(1B) unless all the details required by the VAT (Monthly Control Statement) Regulations 1992, are included in that document. A separate Statement of Practice on the monthly control statement is now available.

Receipt of Transmitted Messages

5. On receipt of a transmission the recipient should

—   verify that the transmission is from an authorised sender,

—   verify that the sequence number is the next logical number from that sender,

—   recalculate the message totals and VAT liability for each rate of VAT (including zero rate)

—   compare the calculated values with the batch control record.

In the event of discrepancies between the control documents, a discrepancy report must be sent to the issuer and, after correction as necessary, the entire transmission must be reissued with a new sequence number. Discrepancy reports must be retained as part of both the issuer's and recipient's business records.

In the event of a transmission being corrupted in any way, or in the event of the receiver being unable to read the transmission, the supplier must repeat the transmission.

The received messages must be retained in the sequence in which they have been transmitted and must be kept in strict numerical order.

Acceptance of an Invoice

6. Acceptance of a transmission does not necessarily indicate acceptance of an invoice within the transmission. When received, invoices are normally validated against the original order or contract. An invalid invoice in the transmission may result in the invoice being rejected. Where correction of an invoice results in rejection of the invoice, a credit note must be transmitted by the sender followed by a re-issue of the corrected invoice, etc in a subsequent transmission.

New Trading Partners

7. Where a taxable person, already authorised to issue or receive messages by electronic means, wishes to take on a new partner, he or she should write to the local VAT office giving the name, address and registration number of the proposed new partner. That partner should, at the same time, formally apply in accordance with paragraph 2 for the appropriate authorisation.

Changes in Conditions

8. Where any change occurs in the particulars furnished by a taxable person at the time of the application for authorisation, details of the change must be notified to the local VAT office within 30 days of the change.

Withdrawal of Authorisation

9. An authorisation to issue or receive messages by electronic means may be withdrawn where the conditions in paragraphs 3, 4 and 5 above are not being fulfilled or where it is considered that it is no longer expedient to allow an authorisation to continue.

RATES OF VAT ON FOODS AND DRINK FROM 1 NOVEMBER 1992

General

1. Most food and drink sold by retail shops is chargeable to VAT at the zero rate. This includes most basic foodstuffs, for example, bread, butter, tea, sugar, meat, milk, vegetables etc (see Appendix E of Guide to the Value Added Tax for a more comprehensive list). Certain items of foods and drink are specifically excluded from the scope of the zero range. These are taxable at the rate of 21%. Food and drink liable at the 21% rate includes biscuits, sweets, chocolates, cakes, confectionery, crisps, ice-cream and soft drinks. Recent additions to this category (that is food and drink liable at the 21% rate) are:

— frozen desserts, frozen yoghurts and similar frozen products, and prepared mixes and powders for making any such product or similar products;

— uncooked confectionery and

— savoury snack products made from cereal or grain, fried bread segments, pork scratchings, and similar products.

Food and Drink Supplied in the Course of Operating a Catering Business

2. Food and drink normally chargeable to VAT at the zero rate becomes liable to VAT at 12.5% when supplied in the course of operating specified classes of business or by means of vending machines. The specified classes of business are hotels, restaurants, cafes, canteens, public houses, caterers and other similar businesses.

Food and drink normally liable to VAT at the rate of 21% becomes liable at 12.5% when supplied in the course of provision of a meal by any of the specified classes of business (see preceding paragraph) excluding alcohol and soft drinks.

3. Alcohol and soft drinks and, with effect from 1 November 1992, bottled waters and health drinks are liable to VAT at 21% in all circumstances.

4. All hot take-away food is liable at 12.5% irrespective of the rate which would apply if it were supplied otherwise (but see paragraph 9). (If, exceptionally, alcohol, bottled waters, soft drinks or fruit juices are supplied hot for taking away they will be liable at 21%.) See paragraphs 18 — 21 for further information.

5. Vending machine sales of zero rated food and drink are liable at 12.5%. Food and drink other than zero rated food and drink sold by means of a vending machine is taxable at 21%.

6. Zero rated food and drink remains free of VAT so long as it is not supplied by means of a vending machine or in the course of operating any of the specified classes of business (see paragraph 2 above).

7. Cold take-away food and drink supplied by supermarkets, etc is liable at zero or 21%, as appropriate (see paragraph 9).

Summary

8. The rates of VAT appropriate to the supply of food and drink through the various outlets are set out below. A tabular summary is attached (Appendix I).

Retail Shops Including Supermarkets

9. Food and drink supplied by retail shops is liable at the zero or 21% rate, as appropriate. Food which may have retained some heat after cooking and which is supplied in the course of a grocery business is liable at the rate appropriate to the same food when cold (for example, hot bread supplied by a grocer is liable at 0%).

10. Supermarkets which operate restaurants are generally regarded as carrying on a separate restaurant business. Food and drink supplied in the course of the restaurant business is liable at 12.5%. This includes fruit juices, ice cream, biscuits, cakes and confectionery supplied in the course of the provision of a meal (but the supply of such foods for taking away is liable at 21%). As already stated alcohol, <u>bottled waters and soft drinks</u> other than fruit juices are always liable at 21%.

11. Food and drink sold by means of vending machines is liable at 12.5% or 21%, as appropriate. The zero rate never applies and food and drink which might otherwise be zero rated is liable at 12.5% when sold by means of vending machines.

Hotels, Restaurants, Cafes, Canteens, Public Houses, Caterers And Similar Businesses

12. Food and drink, including fruit juices, supplied with a meal, but excluding alcohol, bottled waters and soft drinks, is liable at 12.5%. This is so even if the food or drink would have been liable at 21% if supplied otherwise (for example, fruit juice, ice cream, biscuits or cakes, normally liable at 21%, are liable at 12.5% when supplied in the course of the provision of a meal).

13. Food and drink supplied through a shop or vending machine is liable at 12.5% or 21%, as appropriate, as is food or drink supplied for taking away (see also paragraph 21).

14. Alcohol, bottled waters and soft drinks are liable at 21% in all circumstances.

15. Although service charges are generally regarded as not liable to VAT there are circumstances in which they are liable (see paragraph 21.8 of "Guide to the Value Added Tax"). Where they are liable, the rate of liability may be taken to be 12.5% even if the bill which is the subject of the service charge includes alcohol or soft drinks.

16. Staff meals, when taxable, are liable at 12.5% (see paragraph 21.9 of "Guide").

17. Receipts from admissions to dinner dances are liable at 21% including the dinner element in the charge. If there are separate charges for the dinner and the dance and payment of the charge for dinner is not a condition of admission to the dance the dinner charge is liable at 12.5% and the charge for admission to the dance is liable at 21% (see separate Statement of Practice on "Dances").

Take-Aways: Traders whose Business Consists Entirely of Take-Aways

18. Food and drink supplied will be liable as follows:

Hot take-away food	12.5%
Cold take-away food and drink	0%
(sandwich/cold milk) or (cold apple tart/chocolate bar) as appropriate	21%
Alcohol, bottled waters and soft drinks (hot and cold)	21%

19. If cold take-away zero rated food or drink is supplied with hot take-away food for an inclusive price (for example, coleslaw with hot chicken) the entire charge is liable at 12.5%. Soft drinks supplied with hot take-away food for an inclusive price are liable at 21%. It will be open to the proprietor of a take-away business to charge separately for the different constituents of a take-away meal and to pay tax accordingly.

20. The term hot take-away food and drink should be understood as including cooked food which is supplied while hot for the purpose of consumption while hot, that is, at a temperature above the ambient air temperature. It includes items such as burgers which consist of hot meat enclosed in a cold bun and similar food. The term does not include such food as freshly baked bread which may be hot at the time of purchase.

Take-Aways: Traders Whose Business does not Consist Entirely of Take-Aways

21. Although, strictly, zero rated food and drink supplied in the course of operating any of the specified classes of business (see paragraph 1 above) is liable at 12.5%, application may be made to the local VAT inspector to have the take-away activities treated concessionally as a separate activity and, to the extent that the take-aways consist of zero rated food and drink, relieved accordingly.

Waste Food

22. Waste food of all kind which is sold as animal food may be regarded as qualifying for the zero rate of VAT.

Location Catering

23. This service is liable at 12.5% but alcohol, bottled waters and soft drinks supplied are liable at 21%.

Catering on Off-Shore Oil Rigs outside Territorial Waters and on Foreign-Going Ships and Aircraft

24. The zero rate effectively, applies.

Catering in Schools and Hospitals

25. Catering services supplied

(*a*) to <u>patients</u> of a hospital or nursing home in the hospital or nursing home; and

(*b*) to <u>students</u> of a school in the school

are exempt. The exemption does not extend to catering for hospital or school staff.

Fruit Juices

26. For the purposes of this leaflet the term "fruit juices" means fruit and vegetable juices which in the opinion of the Revenue Commissioners have not lost their original character through the addition of water or of other substances for sweetening, preservative or other purpose.

APPENDIX I

Food and drink: rates of VAT

Type of food and drink	With meals in hotels, restaurants, canteens, pubs etc	By hotel other than with meals (see also para 27)	By means of vending machines	By retail stores (see note)	By "take-away only "businesses (see also para 27)
	(a)	(b)	(c)	(d)	(e)
	%	%	%	%	%
1. All food and drink except alcohol and soft drinks	12.5	12.5, 21	12.5, 21	0, 21	0, 12.5 (hot), 21
2. Zero rated food	12.5	12.5	12.5	0	0, (cold), 12.5 (hot)
3. Biscuits, cakes, chocolates, confectionery (cooked & uncooked) crisps, ice cream, sweets, frozen desserts, frozen yoghurts and the like, savoury snack products fried bread segments, pork scratchings and similar products	12.5	21	21	21	21
4. Alcohol, bottled waters and soft drinks including health drinks	21	21	21	21	21
5. Fruit Juices including freshly squeezed juices	12.5	21	21	21	21
6. "Take Aways" -					
- hot	---	12.5	---	---	12.5 (but see para 4)
- cold	---	12.5, 21	---	---	0, 21
- hot and cold for inclusive price	---	12.5, 21	---	---	12.5, 21
7. Chips (cooked)	12.5	12.5	12.5	12.5	12.5
8. Dinner Dances	21 (see para 17)	---	---	---	---
9. Service Charges	12.5 (see para 15) of leaflet and Ch 21.8 of "Guide")	---	---	---	---
10. Staff Meals	12.5 (see Ch 21.9 of "Guide")	---	---	---	---

NOTE: Re. Retail Stores with restaurants — see paragraph 10 of leaflet.

ZERO RATING OF GOODS AND SERVICES IN ACCORDANCE WITH SECTION 13A OF THE VAT ACT

Introduction

1. The Finance Act 1993, inserted a new section 13A and paragraph (via) of the Second Schedule in the VAT Act. These provisions provide for the zero rating in most cases of supplies of goods and services to, and intra-Community acquisitions and imports by, taxable persons who are primarily engaged in making zero rated intra-Community supplies of goods or exports. This new zero rating facility takes effect from 1 August 1993.

Qualifying Persons

2. A qualifying person under section 13A is a taxable person whose turnover from zero rated intra-Community supplies of goods or exports exceeds, or is likely to exceed, 75% of his total annual turnover. Total annual turnover comprises turnover from the supply of all goods and services, including exempt supplies. However, sale and lease-back transactions are excluded from annual turnover for the purposes of determining whether a taxable person qualifies for the scheme.

3. The previous paragraph sets out the criteria that an existing taxable person must meet if he is to qualify for the zero rating facility. In certain cases it may also be possible for a taxable person in a start-up situation to qualify for the facility on an interim basis. In such a case it will be necessary to establish, to the satisfaction of the relevant Inspector of Taxes, that the company's turnover from zero rated intra-Community supplies of goods or exports will exceed 75% of its total turnover in its first year of trading. In these cases the application for authorisation should be supported by a statement from the IDA or similar State agency giving details of the company's anticipated annual turnover and zero rated intra-Community supplies and exports.

Group Registrations

4. A VAT registered group (ie where a number of companies are treated as a single taxable person for VAT purposes) can only be authorised under section 13A if at least 75% of the group's total annual turnover is derived from zero rated intra-Community supplies of goods or exports. Individual members of VAT groups cannot obtain authorisations unless the group as a whole is a qualifying person.

Authorisation Procedure

5. Applications for authorisation should be made on form VAT 13A, which is available from the local Inspector of Taxes. The Inspector of Taxes will issue an authorisation where he is satisfied that the applicant is a qualifying person.

6. The authorisation will take effect two weeks after the date of its issue. This is to allow the authorised person sufficient time to forward copies of the authorisation to his suppliers. Accordingly, a qualifying person should apply in good time before the desired date of effect of the authorisation.

7. If an authorised person ceases to be a qualifying person under the scheme he must notify his local Inspector of Taxes immediately.

PURCHASES WITHIN THE STATE

Authorised Person

8. On receipt of the authorisation, the authorised person is obliged to send a copy of the authorisation to all persons in the State making supplies to him. It should be noted in particular that, apart from the exception mentioned in paragraph 9 below, once a person has been authorised the zero rating facility must be used in the case of all qualifying supplies, intra-Community acquisitions or imports. If a supplier charges VAT incorrectly, the authorised person is not entitled to claim the amount through his VAT return. Any such charge is a matter between the authorised person and the supplier. The original invoice should be cancelled by a credit note and a proper invoice should then be issued by the supplier.

9. It is recognised that it may be inconvenient to operate the zero rating facility in relation to petty cash or other minor purchases. Accordingly, an exception may be made to the position outlined at paragraph 8 above where the VAT on the individual transaction is less than £20.

Supplier to an Authorised Person

10. A supplier, once he has received a copy of an authorisation from an authorised person, must zero rate all qualifying supplies (see paragraph 14 below) to the authorised person and must quote the authorisation number on the VAT invoice issued in respect of the supply. If there is any doubt in relation to an authorisation, the Inspector of Taxes who issued the authorisation should be contacted to confirm its validity. When making zero rated supplies under the scheme, the supplier should ensure that the supply is in fact made to the person named on the authorisation. Particular attention should also be paid to the expiry date of the authorisation as zero rating can only apply during its period of validity.

Intra-Community Acquisitions

11. The normal Single Market VAT rules continue to apply to intra-Community acquisitions from other Member States. To obtain goods without payment of VAT in another Member State, the VAT registration number (not the authorisation number) must continue to be quoted to the foreign supplier. The section 13A authorisation means that the authorised person must account for VAT on the intra-Community acquisition at the zero rate.

Imports

12. In order to import (ie goods from outside the Community) qualifying goods at the zero rate, the authorised person should make a declaration on the relevant customs entry (SAD) that he is an authorised person under section 13A of the VAT Act and quote his authorisation number. When requested by a Customs official, a copy of the authorisation should be produced in support of the declaration.

Alcohol Products

13. Where an authorised person is accounting for VAT on supplies, intra-Community acquisitions or imports of alcohol products in accordance with section 3B of the VAT Act, the authorised person should make a declaration on the relevant excise form that he is an authorised person under section 13A of the VAT Act and quote his authorisation number. The zero rate then applies. When requested by a Customs official, a copy of the authorisation should be produced in support of the declaration.

Qualifying Goods and Services

14. The new zero rating procedure applies to all goods and services, with the following exceptions:

— the supply or hire or any passenger motor vehicle,

— the supply of petrol,

— the provision of food, drink, accommodation, entertainment and other personal services.

Self Supplies or Exempt Use

15. If an authorised person applies qualifying goods or services, which he has obtained at the zero rate, to an exempt or non-business use, he must, in respect of such application, account for and pay VAT on the cost price to him of those goods or services. Therefore, if an authorised person purchases goods for, say, £10,000 at the zero rate and the supply of these goods is normally liable at the 21% rate, he must, if he applies the goods to a non- business use, pay VAT of £2,100 with his VAT return. The authorised person has no entitlement to claim an input credit in respect of such VAT.

VAT 67 Authorisation

16. Since 1983 a scheme has existed whereby certain taxable persons can import raw materials and components VAT free. Authorisations under this scheme will be cancelled when a person is authorised under the new section 13A.

Further Information

17. Any additional queries should be addressed to your local Inspector of Taxes.

PAYMENT OF VAT ON ALCOHOL PRODUCTS AT TIME OF PAYMENT OF EXCISE DUTY

Introduction

1. New rules are being introduced from 1 August 1993 with regard to the payment of VAT on alcohol products in certain circumstances. The effect of the new rules is that, in many cases, VAT will be payable on alcohol products at the same time as the excise duty is payable, on a value inclusive of the duty.

Scope

2. The alcohol products affected are spirits, wine, made wine, beer, cider and perry which, on or after 1 August 1993, are supplied while held under a duty suspension arrangement or which have been the subject of an intra-Community acquisition or importation into the State.

3. Stocks of alcohol products held in the State under a duty suspension arrangement at the close of business on 31 July 1993 are not affected by the new VAT arrangements unless the goods are subsequently supplied while held under a duty suspension arrangement on or after 1 August 1993 (see paragraph 7).

4. Supplies of alcohol products outside a duty suspension arrangement (ie goods supplied after excise duty has been paid) continue to be dealt with under the normal VAT arrangements and are not affected by the new provisions outlined in this Statement of Practice.

Alcohol Products Supplied while Held under Duty Suspension Arrangements

5. In the case of alcohol products from any source (imports, intra-Community acquisitions or home produced) which are supplied while held under a duty suspension arrangement, only the last such supply will form the basis for VAT liability and any previous supply, intra-Community acquisition or importation will be disregarded. The VAT due on the last supply will be payable with the excise duty at the time of the removal of the goods from duty suspension. Accordingly, where alcohol products are supplied while held under a duty suspension arrangement, VAT should not be charged by the supplier or shown on any invoice issued by him in respect of the supply.

6. Where alcohol products are supplied while held under a duty suspension arrangement and the goods leave the State as a result of such a supply, the normal VAT rules will continue to apply. For example if the goods are sold to a VAT registered trader in another Member State the supply will be zero rated and no VAT will be payable under these new arrangements.

7. VAT will not be payable on removal from bonded warehouse of home manufactured alcohol products which have not been the subject of a supply while under bond. It should be noted in this context that the removal of alcohol products from one bonded warehouse to another without a transfer of ownership taking place does not constitute a supply of the goods for VAT purposes.

8. Where a company supplies a consignment of alcohol products to a company with which it is grouped for VAT purposes that supply, and any subsequent similar supplies between members of that VAT group, is disregarded for VAT purposes. The companies concerned will be required to produce, to the warehouse officer, a letter from their local VAT Inspector confirming the grouping arrangement and sales within the group will then be disregarded for the purpose of these new arrangements. Note, however, that VAT will still be payable on removal from duty suspension if there has been a prior import, intra- Community acquisition or supply to the group in relation to the goods.

Intra-Community Acquisitions of Alcohol Products

9. Under the new arrangements VAT chargeable on the intra-Community acquisition of alcohol products is payable at the same time as the excise duty is paid. It should be noted that in this case the VAT is not accounted for under the postponed accounting arrangements that apply to intra-Community acquisitions generally. If, following an intra-Community acquisition, the alcohol products in question are supplied while held under a duty suspension arrangement the rules set out in paragraphs 5 to 8 above apply and the intra-Community acquisition should be disregarded for VAT purposes.

Importations of Alcohol Products from Outside the EC

10. Under the new arrangements VAT at point of entry will no longer be chargeable on imported alcohol products being entered for an excise duty suspension arrangement (bonded warehousing). Instead the VAT due on the import will be payable with the excise duty on removal of the goods from bond. If, following importation, the alcohol products in question are supplied while held under a duty suspension arrangement the rules set out in paragraphs 5 to 8 above apply and the importation should be disregarded for VAT purposes.

Taxable Amount

11. In relation to intra-Community acquisitions and supplies, the amount on which VAT is chargeable is the invoice price of the goods increased by the amount of the excise duty payable. In the case of importations, the taxable amount is the value for customs purposes increased by the amount of customs duty and excise duty payable.

Deferred Payment

12. The legislation relating to the collection of excise duty also applies to the collection of VAT under the new arrangements. Inter alia this means that where a trader has the facility to defer payment of excise duty, payment of VAT can also be deferred to the same date. The deferred payment guarantee must be increased to reflect the additional liability at risk.

Persons Authorised under Section 13A of the VAT Act

13. Persons authorised to receive goods at the zero rate of VAT in accordance with section 13A of the VAT Act will not be required to pay the VAT due on removals by them of alcohol products from bonded warehouse or other duty suspension arrangements. This does not affect their liability to pay excise duty. A detailed Statement of Practice on the 13A authorisation procedure is available from your local VAT office (SP VAT 1/93).

Forms to be Used

14. The following forms should be used for payment of the excise duties and VAT:

(*a*) excise duty entry (C&E 1087) for intra-Community acquisitions where the excise duty and VAT is being paid on arrival in the State;

(*b*) SAD (import entry) for imports where the excise duty and VAT is being paid on arrival in the State;

(*c*) home consumption warrant (C&E 493 ABC) in respect of deliveries from warehouse for home consumption.

In connection with point (*c*) it should be noted in particular that it will no longer be permitted for warehouse keepers to produce single bulk warrants on behalf of a number of owners of goods — a separate warrant for each owner must be presented. The warrant form will be amended shortly to cater for the revised VAT position. Meantime the existing version, suitably amended, should be used.

Deductibility for VAT Return

15. Subject to the normal rules governing VAT deductibility, a trader is entitled to deduct the VAT charged under these new arrangements in the VAT return for the period in which the liability arises (ie similar to the existing arrangements for VAT paid on imports). The evidence that the trader must retain in support of his claims to deductibility is as follows:

(*a*) in the cases referred to in paragraphs 14(*a*) and (*b*) above:

— a monthly customs and excise statement where the trader uses the deferred payment/FACT schemes, or

— an official receipt in other cases;

(*b*) in the case referred to in paragraph 14(*c*) above, a copy of the home consumption warrant signed and stamped by the warehouse officer.

Further Information

16. Further inquiries in relation to the new arrangements should be addressed to the relevant warehouse officer.

RETAIL EXPORT SCHEME

1. Introduction

Subject to certain restrictions and limitations, relief from VAT is allowed in respect of purchases in the State of goods which are exported from the European Union by visitors from outside the EU. Relief applies to goods taken away by the purchaser at the time of sale, and exported from the EU in his personal baggage. It applies also to goods which are placed by, or on behalf of the purchaser on board a ship or aircraft for transportation out of the EU. The goods in question must be exported within three months from the end of the month in which they are purchased. For example goods sold during the month of January must be exported by 30 April. Relief is not allowed on services (e g. hotel accommodation, meals, car hire etc).

2. Visitors from Other Member States

The Retail Export Scheme does not apply to visitors from other Member States of the European Union. Following the abolition of fiscal frontiers on I January, 1993, VAT is no longer payable at the point of entry into the Member States of the European Union on goods which have been acquired by private individuals in other Member States. This means that EU visitors to Ireland do not have a VAT liability in their own Member States on goods which they have purchased in Ireland. Accordingly, relief is not available in respect of purchases in the State by EU visitors. Subject to paragraph 3, relief is available only in respect of goods which are leaving the European Union.

3. Residents of the EU Leaving the Community

As a concession, the Commission of the EU has decided that relief from VAT can also be given to EU residents, including therefore Irish residents, who are going to live in a non- EU country for at least a year. Satisfactory evidence of this must, however, be furnished.

4. How Relief is Granted

The granting of relief by an individual trader is optional. A trader is not obliged to participate in the scheme but may do so if he wishes. A participating trader may choose between the methods of relief at (a) (b) and (c) below. If the trader uses methods (a) or (b) he must have documentary proof of the export of the goods. Lacking such documentary proof, he himself will be liable for the VAT.

(a) The trader need not charge the VAT to the purchaser. He must then rely on the purchaser to send back documentary proof of export, otherwise, the trader will be liable to VAT on the sale in question,

(b) The trader may charge VAT to the purchaser and subsequently refund it to him when he receives from the purchaser documentary proof of export.

(c) The trader may operate the relief scheme through one of the VAT refunding agencies (see paragraph 7).

5. Obligations of Participating Traders

A participating trader is required to satisfy himself that the person to whom the goods are being supplied is entitled to relief from VAT. This can be by means of inspection of the customer's passports, travel tickets etc.

The trader must also issue to the purchaser an invoice which shows the following particulars:

— trader's name, address and VAT number;

— the name and address of the customer;

— the date of issue;

— a description of and the quantity of the goods;

— the purchase price;

— an indication of the basis on which the trader satisfied himself of the person's entitlement to relief, including details of the relevant documents inspected;

— the trader's signature.

The trader must keep a copy of this invoice together with the documentary proof that the goods have been exported from the EU.

6. Obligations of Purchasers

A purchaser of goods under the relief scheme must provide the supplier with documentary evidence that the goods have in fact been exported. Normally this proof will be the purchase invoice stamped by Customs authorities of the EU Member State from which the goods eventually leave the EU. For example, a visitor who purchases goods in Ireland and then travels to the UK before leaving the EU must have the relevant invoices stamped by the UK Customs authorities. The Irish Customs authorities will stamp invoices only for visitors who are leaving the EU directly from Ireland.

If, however, the purchaser is either unable to have the invoice stamped by the relevant Member State Customs authorities, or does not avail himself of the services of a VAT-refunding agency (see paragraph 7), he should have the documentation stamped in his own country by any person of official status — for example, by Customs, the Police, or a Notary Public — before returning it to the trader.

7. VAT Refunding Agencies

Many retailers choose to operate this relief scheme through one of the agencies which undertake to make refunds to purchasers in respect of the VAT paid. Invoices for total purchases up to a value of £200 may be lodged with these agencies which are usually located at the main departure points from the State (these invoices may be for a single item costing up to £200 or a number of items whose total value does not exceed £200). Purchasers may, of course, present such invoices direct to Customs for stamping, if so desired. Details of the agencies and of the terms and conditions under which they operate are available from the retailers concerned.

Supplies of second-hand goods, works of art, collectors' items or antiques sold under the special margin scheme may only benefit from this relief using the methods outlined at paragraphs 4(a) and (b). Because the margin scheme does not permit the issue of invoices showing VAT separately goods sold under the margin scheme will not attract refunds through the refund agencies. Traders operating through the refunding agencies must therefore charge VAT on the full sales price, which can subsequently be recouped by the visitor on departure.

The VAT refunding agencies are independent entities. The Revenue Commissioners make no endorsement of any such agencies and cannot accept any responsibility for problems encountered by traders or purchasers in dealings with them. Persons who experience delays in receiving their refunds or who are unhappy with the conditions applied by the agencies should write to the trader or to the VAT refunding agency concerned.

8. Purchases over £200

Invoices for purchases over £200 and all purchases not processed through a VAT refunding agency must be presented to the relevant Customs authorities for stamping. If so required by the Customs authorities the goods in question must be produced for inspection. If it is not possible to obtain the necessary Customs certification one of the arrangements listed in paragraph 6 may be applied.

9. Exports by Trader

The arrangements under which the zero rate of VAT applies to purchases which are exported or posted out of the EU by the trader, continue to apply.

10. Enquiries

Trader enquiries concerning the operation of the relief should be made to the local VAT Office, details of which are given in Appendix I.

BOOKS, NEWSPAPERS, PERIODICALS ETC

1. Introduction

Books, newspapers, catalogues etc are liable for VAT at different rates. This can give rise to problems of definition, for example, how does a book which qualifies for zero VAT rating or a newspaper or periodical at the 12.5 per cent rate differ from similarly described products which attract VAT at the standard rate, at present 21 per cent?

The purpose of this statement of practice is to clarify, for VAT purposes, the various distinctions between the different types of printed matter.

2. Scope of the Zero Rate

The zero rate of VAT applies to printed books and booklets including atlases. It does not include newspapers, periodicals, brochures, catalogues, programmes, books of stationery, cheque books, diaries, planners, albums, books of stamps, of tickets or of coupons.

A book or booklet qualifies for the zero rate if it consists essentially of textual or pictorial matter and it meets the following general requirements;

    (i)   it must have a distinctive cover, that is, at least the outside of the front cover must be devoid of the text,

   (ii)   it must comprise not less than four leaves (eight pages) exclusive of the cover, and

  (iii)   it must be bound (loose-leaf or otherwise), or stitched or stapled.

3. Scope of the 12.5 per cent Rate

The 12.5 per cent rate applies to newspapers and periodicals, normally published at least fortnightly, whose quantity of printed matter consists wholly or mainly of information on the principal current events and topics of general public interest. It does not apply to newspapers and periodicals concerned primarily with sectoral interests (for example, sport).

This rate also applies to literary manuscripts certified by the Director of the National Library as being of major national importance.

4. Scope of the 21 per cent Rate

Publications not qualifying for the zero or the 12.5 per cent rate are liable at 21 per cent. Such publications include magazines, periodicals of sectoral interest, brochures, catalogues, programmes, books of stationery, cheque books, diaries, albums, (see also paragraph 6 and Appendix 1).

5. Printing

Printing includes all forms of reproduction, ie lithography; off-set; heliography; photogravure; engraving; duplicating; embossing; photography etc in letters of any alphabet, figures, shorthand or other symbols, braille characters, musical notations, pictures or diagrams, generally on to paper.

Printing is regarded as a supply of goods for VAT purposes and the rate chargeable depends on the product being supplied. For example the printing of books qualifies for the zero rate while the printing of newspapers and periodicals referred to at paragraph 3 attracts VAT at 12.5 per cent, and the printing of magazines or brochures etc is subject to 21 per cent.

6. Exclusions from Zero and 12.5 per cent Rates

Various publications, some of which might otherwise qualify as printed books or booklets under the definitions in paragraph 2 or periodicals defined in paragraph 3, are specifically excluded and liable at the standard rate of VAT. The exclusions are set out below.

(A) PERIODICALS

Periodicals other than those referred to in paragraph 3 are liable at the standard (21 per cent) rate of VAT.

The distinguishing features of "periodicals" which are liable at the standard rate are that they constitute one issue in a continuous series under the same title and that they are published at regular intervals more frequently than annually, each issue being dated (even by merely indicating the period of the year eg Spring 1995) and frequently numbered.

Parts of large works published over a limited and predetermined period including a related binder supplied free of charge are not regarded as periodicals, and provided they qualify as printed books or booklets or will qualify as such when the series is completed, they will be zero rated.

(B) BROCHURES. CATALOGUES, PROGRAMMES

These are liable at the standard (21 per cent) rate of VAT. The term "brochures" includes holiday brochures and similar commercial literature, instruction notices, hymn sheets, price lists, information pamphlets, etc.

Certain tourist literature distributed free by official tourism agencies may be zero rated. However, the circumstances under which this is allowed are quite restrictive and such literature should be submitted to the local Inspector of Taxes for a ruling.

The term "catalogues" means any classified list of names, pictures, goods, etc such as library and trade catalogues. They may be illustrated and/or accompanied by descriptions of the items, brief explanations and comments for the information of prospective customers, visitors, etc.

The term "programmes" means descriptive notices of events such as study courses, concerts, entertainment, sporting activities and the like.

(C) BOOKS OF STATIONERY, CHEQUE BOOKS. DIARIES, ALBUMS, BOOKS OF STAMPS, TICKETS OR COUPONS

These terms are self-explanatory.

Combined diary/yearbooks are liable at 21 per cent unless the yearbook portion represents more than 75 per cent of the content of the publication. In that event the publication will qualify for the zero rate.

Combined diary/organiser/planner publications are also liable at 21 per cent.

7. Determinations and Appeals

A taxable person who disagrees with a VAT rating applied to his product has the right of appeal to the Appeal Commissioners, who are separate from and independent of the Revenue Commissioners. The determination and appeal procedures are explained in paragraphs 15.12–15.14 of the current (1994) "Guide to Value Added Tax".

8. Acquisitions from Other Member States of the EU and Imports

The rates which apply to publications within the State apply similarly to publications acquired from other Member States of the EU and to those imported from outside the EU.

Individuals purchasing publications for private use from other Member States of the EU will not be liable for Irish VAT as VAT will already have been charged in the supplying Member State.

9. Types of Publications: VAT Rates

A list in alphabetical order of the VAT ratings of the various types of publications is given at Appendix 1.

10. Enquiries

In any case where the rate of VAT is not clear, or is disputed, the publisher or importer should submit a copy of the publication for consideration to VAT Administration Branch, Indirect Taxes Division, Revenue Commissioners, Stamping Building, Dublin Castle, Dublin 2. (Tel 01–6792777 Exts 4858, 4859, 4861, 4862).

All other enquiries may be made at the local Inspector of Taxes.

APPENDIX 1
TYPES OF PUBLICATIONS, VAT RATES

Rate

Account Books	21%
Albums	21%
Amendment sheets for zero rated reference books	0%
Annual Reports	0%
Annuals	0% B
Atlases	0% B
Audio Cassette Books	21%
Bingo books	21%
Books, booklets (other than catalogues) including books consisting wholly or mainly of reproductions of paintings	0% B
Bookmarks, etc (included with books)	0%
Bookmarks etc (not included with books)	21%
Braille Books	0%
Brochures	21%
Calendars	21%
Catalogues	21%
Charts excluding maps	21%
Cheque Books	21%
Children's Drawing 8: Painting Books	0% B
Children's Picture Books including "cut out" and "stand up" types	0% B
Comics.	21%
Commercial promotional literature.	21%
Computer manuals	0%
Coupons, books of	21%
Diaries	21%
Diary/Organiser	21%
Dictionaries	0%
* Directories.	21%
Dust Covers (included with books)	0%
Encyclopaedias.	0%
Exercise Books.	21%
Fixture Lists	21%
Globes	21%
Greeting Cards.	21%
Hymn Books	0% B
Hymn sheets	21%
Invitation Cards	21%
Journals	21%

Leaflets 21%

Magazines — (Current events of general interest) 12 5%

Magazines — (Sectoral Interests) 21%

Maps 21%

Missals 0%

Missalettes (Mass Leaflets) 21%

Music Books. ....0% B

Newspapers — certain (current events of general interest) 12.5%

others (sectorial interest) 21%

Note Books 21%

Novels 0%

Parts of large works published over pre-determined period including
related binder supplied free of charge ....0% B

Picture Books ie books of pictures (other than catalogues) ....0% B

Periodicals — Current Affairs 12.5%

Periodicals — Sectoral Interest (eg sport). 21%

Photocopying 21%

Posters 21%

Postcards including books of postcards 21%

Prayer Books ....0% B

Price lists.. 21%

Printing

– of 0% publications 0%

– of 12.5% publications 12. 5%

– of 21% publications 21%

Programmes 21%

Puzzle books excluding periodicals ....0% B

Promotional Literature 21%

Sheet Music 21%

Stationery 21%

Stamps, Books of postal .... exempt

Telephone Directories 21%

Tickets, Books of 21%

Timetables 21%

Trade Catalogues/Promotional Literature. 21%

*The term "directories" is regarded as covering items such as lists of telephone subscribers and numbers, inhabitants and streets in a locality, members of a profession etc with various details, companies with statistical business details, etc.

The suffix B denotes that the rating indicated applies only if the publication qualifies as a printed book or booklet.

GOLF AND OTHER SPORTING ACTIVITIES

CHANGES IN THE VAT TREATMENT OF GOLF AND OTHER SPORTING ACTIVITIES — FINANCE ACT, 1995

1. Introduction.

The 1995 Finance Act made certain non-member golf turnover liable for VAT, such as, income from green fees of member-owned golf clubs and local authority golf courses.

Annual subscriptions from members continue to be exempt, as also do capital levies paid by members.

The Act also enables the Revenue Commissioners in certain limited circumstances to review the exemption from VAT of other sports and physical education activities.

This Statement of Practice should be read in conjunction with SP VAT/4/92 dealing with the VAT treatment of sporting facilities.

2. Golf

Where the total annual taxable income (ie green fee and other golf turnover) from the provision of facilities for taking part in Golf in a member-owned or local authority golf course exceeds or is likely to exceed £20,000, it will become liable for VAT at the 12.5% rate with effect from 1 January, 1996. The provision of golfing facilities includes driving ranges and par 3 golf but not pitch and putt, which is unaffected by these changes.

Taxable income includes green fees, other pay-as-you-play income, short term membership subscriptions and corporate subscriptions. The excess in competition fees paid by a non-member over the amount paid by a member is regarded as a green-fee and is therefore also taxable.

Individual membership subscriptions for member-owned golf clubs continue to be exempt from VAT as also do the fees charged to Pavilion or Social members.

For VAT purposes a member is defined as a person who, having paid his annual subscriptions, is entitled to play golf on the course without further payment for at least 200 days per year. If a member makes an additional payment which entitles him to a further benefit eg the right to play on days not covered by the terms of his membership, that payment is of course liable for VAT.

Where a golf club is already registered for VAT in respect of its non-golf activities, for example, bar, restaurant, shop, etc and its annual non-member golf turnover exceeds or is likely to exceed £20,000 it should account for VAT from 1 January 1996 on such turnover in addition to the turnover from its non-golf activities.

A golf club can elect to account for VAT in respect of its non-member golf turnover if it is below the £20,000 threshold. An application for such an election should be submitted to the appropriate Tax Office (see Appendix II).

State or local authority owned golf courses are also required to register and account for VAT from 1 January, 1996 if their annual golf turnover exceeds or is likely to exceed

£20,000. If a local authority operates a number of courses this threshold relates to the combined golf turnover of all its courses. While one VAT registration will cover all golf courses operated by a local authority, the body in question may opt for separate registration for each course if this is more convenient.

Where a golf club is made taxable in respect of its non-member golf income it may deduct VAT on its inputs. As the expenditure on the golf course and club-house will be used for both taxable (eg bar, restaurant etc) and exempt activities (eg membership fees, changing rooms etc) the input credit will have to be apportioned by agreement with the local Tax Office. As is the normal practice, expenses directly related to taxable activities will be allowed full deductibility of VAT, while expenses directly related to exempt activities will not be allowed any deductibility. Apportionment will arise therefore only where activities with an element of both taxable and exempt are involved.

The apportionment figure is calculated on the ratio of taxable turnover to total turnover. Those clubs which are already registered for their non-golf activities will be familiar with this procedure. Clubs now registering for the first time may wish to contact their local Tax Office, if in any doubt about what apportionment figure should be applied.

Examples illustrating the changes in relation to registration and accounting for VAT by member-owned golf clubs are given at Appendix I.

3. Other Sports

The provision of facilities for taking part in other sports and services closely related thereto by non-profit making organisations is exempt from VAT. However, the Finance Act 1995 enables an Inspector of Taxes to determine that the provision of such facilities by the State, a local authority or a non-profit making organisation is liable for VAT at 12.5% where the annual turnover for such activities exceeds or is likely to exceed £20,000, if:

— the exemption of those services creates or is likely to create a distortion of competition which puts a commercial supplier of similar services at a disadvantage, or

— the service is actually a commercial enterprise.

Where the Inspector of Taxes is satisfied that such conditions apply he will issue a determination in writing to the body concerned giving notice of his decision. That body may appeal such a determination within 21 days from the date of issue to the Appeal Commissioners.

Where a determination of liability for VAT is made, it will specify the date on which taxation of turnover is to commence. That date may not be earlier than the start of the next bi-monthly VAT period.

APPENDIX I

SUMMARY OF VAT POSITION IN THE CASE OF MEMBER-OWNED GOLF CLUBS

(Assume non-golf turnover = A, and non-member golf turnover = B)

1. Already registered for VAT in respect of its turnover from non-golf activities:

— if its non-member golf turnover exceeds or is likely to exceed £20,000 it must account for VAT at 12.5% on such turnover, in addition to accounting for VAT on its turnover from non-golf activities.

Example:
Already registered for A, and B exceeds £20,000; VAT on B must be accounted for in addition to A.
It is not obliged to account for VAT on its non-member golf turnover if less than £20,000 but it must continue to account for VAT on its non-golf turnover,

Example:
Already registered for A, and B less than £20,000; not obliged to account for VAT on B. but must account for VAT on A.

2. Not already registered for VAT, in respect of its turnover from non-golf activities, because that turnover is below the threshold for registration:

— if its non-member golf turnover exceeds or is likely to exceed £20,000, it must register and account for VAT on both its non-golf turnover and its non-member golf turnover,

Example:
Not registered for A, and B exceeds £20,000; must register, and account for VAT on both A and B.

— if its non-member golf turnover is less than the threshold, it is not required to register, even though the combined total of non-golf and non-member golf turnover exceeds £20,000.

Example:
Not registered for A, and B less than £20,000; not required to register, even if A + B exceeds £20,000.

ABOLITION OF DUTY-FREE SALES TO TRAVELLERS ON INTRA-COMMUNITY JOURNEYS

1. Introduction

As and from 30 June, 1999, duty-free[1] sales to travellers on intra-Community journeys[2] will be abolished. This means that such travellers will no longer be able to purchase goods free of excise duty and VAT. Such purchases — with the exception of food, drink and tobacco products for on-board consumption — will now be subject to normal rates of excise duty and VAT. Duty-free sales will, however, continue for passengers travelling to destinations outside the EU.

The information contained in this Statement of Practice is primarily aimed at economic operators engaged in the supply of, or retail selling of, goods to intra-Community travellers in airports and on board ships and aircraft, but it will also inform travellers regarding the new arrangements.

[1] "Duty-free" includes VAT-free.

[2] An "Intra-Community journey" means a journey which begins in one EU Member State and ends in another. The current 15 E.U. Member States are Austria, Belgium, Denmark, Finland, France, Germany, Greece, Ireland, Italy, Luxembourg, the Netherlands, Portugal, Spain, Sweden and the United Kingdom.

2(a) What goods may no longer qualify as duty-free?

* All goods sold or supplied in airports to travellers embarking on intra-Community journeys.

* All goods sold or supplied to passengers or crew members on intra-Community journeys, other than food, drink and tobacco products for on-board consumption during the journey.

* Supplies of provisions and merchandise to ships and aircraft intended for "take-away" sale or supply to passengers or crew.

2(b) What goods may continue to be sold duty-free?

* All goods sold or supplied to passengers travelling to destinations outside the EU.

* Small quantities of food, drink and tobacco products sold or supplied to passengers on intra-Community journeys for consumption on board. (*See also paragraph 5.*)

3. What journeys will be affected by the change?

All direct intra-Community journeys will be affected by the change.

The fact that the vessel or aircraft passes through international waters/airspace or through the territorial waters or airspace of another EU Member State or non-EU country does not affect the tax liability, provided that the route is a direct one between two EU ports/ airports.

However, if the vessel or aircraft stops off in a non-EU country or an area outside the EU fiscal area to enable passengers to embark or disembark, the route is deemed to be one to or from a non-EU country. The present rules on duty-free sales to passengers travelling to countries outside the EU will continue to apply to such routes.

4. Who will be affected by the change?

* Passengers and crews on intra-Community journeys buying goods for take-away.

* Operators of "duty-free" outlets, both land-based and on ships and aircraft.

* Suppliers of dutiable and taxable products to ships and aircraft for sale on board for take-away.

As and from 1 July, 1999, the traditional duty-free crew allowances relating to goods for take-away (or bringing ashore) will be discontinued. The on-board consumption of duty-free goods available to passengers on intra-Community journeys can, from a Revenue viewpoint, be equally availed of by crew members under the same general limitations and conditions.

5. What can be sold duty-free for consumption on board?

Food, drink and tobacco products sold or provided for consumption on board vessels or aircraft during an intra-Community journey can be supplied duty-free from a bar, restaurant or kiosk or from a bar trolley in the case of aircraft. The number of such on-board sales outlets and their location and operation will be subject to Revenue prior approval. However, sales of food, drink and tobacco products from other shops (eg supermarkets) or vending machines will not be duty-free.

To avoid abuse, the duty-free sale of goods for consumption on board will be subject to certain conditions, as follows:

i. *Alcoholic beverages* are to be served in approved outlets, with sales being restricted as follows:

* Spirits may only be sold as poured drinks or in miniature bottles; poured measures of duty-free spirits must be dispensed from a different size bottle (ie 1.125 litre) to that sold on board duty-paid (namely, 70 cl or 1 litre).

* Wine may be sold in full bottles, half-bottles or quarter bottles; however, full bottles and half-bottles must be opened (ie uncorked) before being landed over the customer.

* Beer must be sold as poured drinks or in opened cans or bottles.

ii. *Tobacco products* are to be sold in approved outlets, with sales being restricted to the following quantities to any one customer:
Cigarettes: in a single packet of 20 or smaller,
or
Cigars: in a single packet of 5 or less,
or
Cigarillos: in a single packet of 10 or less,
or
Tobacco: in a single packet of 25 gms or less.

* Note: All sales of tobacco products on board aircraft operating a no-smoking policy will be regarded as not for consumption on board and must always be duty-paid.

iii. *Other food and drink* are to be sold in quantities and in a manner suitable for immediate consumption on board, eg meals served in a restaurant and fruit, bars of chocolate, snacks, cans of soft drinks, etc sold from an approved outlet.

6. Treatment of take-away sales on intra-Community journeys

(a) Excise Duty

All take-away sales of excisable products must be duty-paid. The EU rules which apply to the charging of excise duty specify that the duty rate to be applied will be the rate in force in the Member State where the goods are released for consumption (in practice, initially, at the place and time of loading). In the case of excisable products loaded in the Member State of departure of a ferry or airline on an intra-Community journey, sales of such goods will continue to bear these rates up to the point of arrival in the territorial waters or airspace of the Member State of destination. Sales beyond this point will attract excise duty liability in the Member State of destination and will have to be accounted for to the tax authorities of that Member State. Provision exists for the reimbursement of the excise duty originally borne on the goods concerned in the Member State of departure.

In the case of sea traffic between Ireland, UK and France, the limit of territorial waters commences 12 nautical miles from the coastline. In the case of air traffic, the limit will be deemed to be 20 minutes prior to landing of the aircraft.

In practical terms, a fundamental decision for operators is whether or not to close shops/outlets for business within the territorial limits of the Member State of destination. If the decision is made to close shops, liability to excise duty on stocks, already duty-paid at the rates of the Member State of loading/departure, will not arise in the Member State of destination throughout the journey across the sea/air territory of the latter State, on both the outward and return journeys. For example in the case of a ferry, Irish duty-paid excisable goods loaded at Dunlaoghaire may be sold at the Irish duty rate up to 12 nautical miles from the UK coastline on the outward journey. If the shop is closed at this point and no further sales of these goods take place on both the outward and return journeys through UK territorial waters, liability to UK excise duty will not be incurred. Sales of this stock may re-commence at Irish duty rates without incurring UK duty liability once the ferry proceeds beyond the UK 12-mile limit on its return voyage to Dunlaoghaire.

If, on the other hand, sales of this Irish duty-paid stock take place within the 12-mile outward or return journeys across UK territorial waters, liability to UK excise duty arises and must be accounted for to the UK authorities. In this case, the UK duty liability will apply in respect of sales made up to the Irish 12 nautical miles limit.

(b) VAT

VAT is chargeable and must be accounted for in the Member State of departure. For example, goods sold on board a vessel or aircraft on a journey from Ireland to the UK will be subject to Irish VAT. On the return journey from the UK to Ireland, goods sold on board will be subject to UK VAT. The territorial limit rules for excise duty do not apply for VAT.

In the case of travel by air, each flight is regarded for VAT purposes as a separate journey. However, in cases where an aircraft has a short stopover in one Member State en route to another, and the flight number remains unchanged for both legs of the journey, the stopover will be disregarded and the VAT regime will be that of the Member State of the first place of departure. *(See paragraph 9 as regards air passengers transiting through a Member State en route to a destination outside the EU.)*

7. When can sales on board vessels or aircraft take place?

There is no Revenue restriction on when sales from on-board shops, bars, restaurants or kiosks can take place once the voyage or flight has commenced. However, attention is again drawn to the special rules applicable to sales of excisable goods within the territorial sea or air limits of the country of destination as outlined in paragraph 6(a).

8. What happens if ships or aircraft stop-off at a non-EU country during an intra-Community journey?

Take-away sales of duty-free products will be allowed on journeys where vessels or aircraft stop-off at a non-EU country or a place outside the Community's fiscal territory (eg Channel Islands, Canary Islands) provided passengers have the opportunity to disembark and make purchases during such stop-offs.

Passengers finally disembarking in Ireland following such a stop-off are restricted to the normal travellers' allowances for passengers arriving from outside the EU and must pass through normal Customs controls on arrival, ie the Red or Green Channel as appropriate.

9. Treatment of airline passengers transiting through a second EU airport en route to a final non-EU destination

Passengers on such routes in possession of a single through ticket are regarded as being on an extra-Community journey, as far as Revenue are concerned. They may avail of duty-free shopping either at the first Community airport of departure or at the final airport of departure from the Community, (eg on a through ticket from Dublin via Frankfurt to Sydney the passenger may purchase duty-free at Dublin, and at Frankfurt if the local airport authorities so permit).

10. What will be the main effect on the operation of duty-free shops at airports?

Shops in airports handling both intra- and extra-Community flights will need to distinguish, in sales and accounting, between sales to passengers travelling to destinations outside the EU (duty-free) and sales to passengers travelling to other Member States (not duty-free). The determination of whether a sale is duty-free or not will be made at the point of payment (ie at the check-out), where the passenger's ticket will provide evidence of duty-free entitlement.

These shops will be approved as tax warehouses with special approval conditions to take account of this trade.

Accounting for the excise duty and VAT will be on the basis of the total dutiable/ VATable sales over the appropriate accounting period. Deferment of the excise duty will be available, subject to provision of the usual security.

11. Treatment of duty-free stocks held on changeover

From the end of business on 30 June, 1999, arrangements will be made for the assessment of excise duty liable on stocks of goods held in shops on board ferries and at regional airports dealing only with intra-Community sales, as these will have changed in status from duty free to duty-paid on 1 July, 1999. This assessment of excise duty will not apply to airport shops handling both intra- and extra-Community traffic, since the liability in the latter shops will be determined at the point of payment at the check-outs.

In the case of ferries, the duty liability will apply to stocks held on vessels in Irish ports and arriving in Irish territorial waters on 1 July, 1999 which have not been otherwise accounted for.

12. Registration with Revenue

(a) Excise

Revenue will require all commercial operators who sell or supply excisable goods for take-away on intra-Community journeys to be registered as Registered Excise Traders (RET). Applications to register and any associated accounting enquiries should be addressed to the local Collector of Customs & Excise. Where an operator or carrier does not have an Irish business address or residence, he or she will be required to appoint a fiscal representative as agent in handling these tax matters.

(b) VAT

A trader who is not established in the State, who sells goods for take-away to passengers on board aircraft or vessels during an intra-Community journey departing from the State, will have to register for VAT in the State. There is no registration threshold applicable to such traders. They should contact the Taxes Central Registration Office, Aras Brugha, 9/15 Upper O'Connell Street, Dublin 1 and complete the appropriate registration form (TR1 or TR2).

An Irish trader who sells goods for take-away to passengers on board aircraft or vessels during intra-Community journeys departing from other Member States may have to register for VAT in each of those Member States, subject to the registration thresholds, if any, applicable in the Member States concerned. VAT must be accounted for in the Member State of departure of the transport.

13. Documentation required

Under EU law (Council Directive 92/12/EEC), excise duty-paid goods loaded on a ship or aircraft on an intra-Community journey and intended for sale to passengers for take-away are required to be covered by a prescribed Accompanying Document.

A simplified procedure, based on the use of commercial documentation, may however, apply. The main condition in granting this simplification is an undertaking from the operator that goods loaded duty-paid in one Member State will not be sold within the territorial limits of another Member State. Under such an undertaking, goods remaining intact on board while within territorial limits will be treated as "in transit" subject to Customs control. This simplified procedure cannot apply where such goods are sold within the territorial limits of another Member State.

14. Stock accounts of excisable goods to be maintained

Revenue will require periodic returns of stock positions of excisable goods in respect of each airport shop, ferry and airline bar stores, distinguishing between duty-paid and duty-free goods, showing receipts, disposals and balances as necessary. Normally, the standard stock reports used by the operators will be adequate for verification or checking purposes. Such accounts must be made available to Revenue officers on demand at all reasonable times. Officers must also be permitted to carry out physical stock checks in duty-free shops or other locations stocking duty-free goods at all reasonable time.

15. VAT transfers

Goods transferred by a person from his business in the State, for the purposes of onward supply to passengers on board a vessel or aircraft during an intra-Community journey, are not regarded as supplies of goods. Accordingly such transfers do not trigger an intra-Community supply from the State. VIES and Intrastat declarations need not be completed in the circumstances.

16. VAT position of unsold stocks

A person who holds a stock of unsold goods on arrival in one Member State, from another Member State, will not have to make an intra-Community acquisition for VAT purposes in that Member State for arrival, provided that such stock is subsequently used by that person for supply to passengers for take-away on intra-Community journeys.

17. VAT treatment in relation to provisioning

From 1 July, 1999, VAT at the appropriate rate is chargeable on the supply of provisions or merchandise to traders involved in the onward supply of those goods to airline or ferry passengers for take-away. However, in the case of supplies of food, drink and tobacco products which are for consumption on board during an international journey, the zero rate of VAT may apply. Suppliers who wish to supply such goods for on-board consumption to airlines and ferries at the zero rate must have sufficient records to substantiate the application of the zero rate.

18. Contact points for further help in relation to VAT and Excise.

Any queries on this Statement of Practice should be addressed to:

VAT	EXCISE
VAT Administration Branch,	Excise Procedures Branch B,
3rd Floor,	Room 317, 3rd Floor,
Stamping Building,	Castle House,
Dublin Castle,	South Great George's Street,
Dublin, 2	Dublin, 2
Phone (01) 6748859, (01) 6748858,	Phone (01) 6748351 or (01) 6748744.
(01) 6748861 or (01) 6748862.	

INFORMATION LEAFLETS

VAT ON PROPERTY

Claims for repayment of VAT arising out of the Supreme Court judgment in the case of Erin Executor and Trustee Company Limited, for periods prior to 27 March, 1998.

Introduction

1. The Supreme Court in the Erin Executor and Trustee Company Ltd. case held that section 4(4) of the VAT Act does not take a property out of the VAT net and that a landlord is, therefore, entitled to deduct VAT on post-letting expenses. Section 106 of the Finance Act 1998 amended section 4 of the VAT Act to take account of this judgment. There is a separate information leaflet dealing with the new legislation which has effect from 27 March, 1998.

2. This information leaflet sets out how claims for repayment of VAT on post-letting expenses arising out of the judgment for periods prior to 27 March, 1998 should be dealt with. It should be noted that this right to deductibility has been qualified in the Finance Act, 1998 and the separate information leaflet *VAT on Property — Post-letting expenses, VAT Information Leaflet No. 4 1998*, should be consulted in respect of periods from 27 March, 1998 onwards.

What is deductible?

3. The questions before the Court were —

"(1) Whether we [the Appeal Commissioners] were correct in law upon the above facts in holding that the appellant was not entitled to input credit by way of deduction under section 12 of the Value Added Tax Act, 1972 in respect of tax paid on expenses incurred by it either as general overheads or administrative costs of its business or in the maintenance, further development and management of specific properties where the same were incurred subsequent to the creation of the long-term lettings?

(2) Whether we [the Appeal Commissioners] were correct in law upon the above facts in holding that the appellant was not entitled to input credit by way of deduction under section 12 of the Value Added Tax Act, 1972 in respect of tax paid on expenses incurred by it either as general overheads or administrative costs of its business or in the maintenance or further development and management of specific properties which were required (sic) by IPFPUT [Erin] with sitting tenants and which have subsequently been partly developed?

(3) Whether we [the Appeal Commissioners] were correct in law upon the above facts in holding that the appellant was not entitled to input credit by way of deduction under section 12 of the Value Added Tax Act, 1972 in respect of tax paid on expenses incurred by it either as general overheads or administrative costs of the business or in the maintenance and management of specific properties which the appellant had acquired with sitting tenants and in respect of which no subsequent development has been carried out?

(4) Whether we [the Appeal Commissioners] were correct in law in holding that section 4(4) of the said Act of 1972 as is construed and applied by the respondent was not incompatible with or ultra vires the provisions of the said Council Directive 77/388/EEC?"

4. The answer to the first three questions was no and question 4 was not considered by the Court. The extent to which additional tax is now deductible must be considered in the context of the Supreme Court's decision concerning the first three questions. The judgment also implied that a subsequent supply of a property was chargeable to tax. The new legislation effective from 27 March, 1998 provides that such subsequent supplies are generally exempt. Revenue has decided that it will not retrospectively seek to treat such supplies as taxable. Consequently, Revenue will not refund VAT on expenses incurred in connection with such supplies. Nevertheless, as the implication of the judgment is that such supplies were taxable, a landlord could insist on claiming deductibility on expenses relating to such supplies. Where a landlord insists on deductibility, Revenue will require payment of VAT on the appropriate supply. However, while Revenue will not normally treat such supplies as taxable, they reserve the right to do so in cases where avoidance schemes are evident.

5. In accordance with the Supreme Court judgment VAT on post-letting expenses incurred by a landlord in respect of a property following a taxable supply of an interest in that property may now be deducted, subject to paragraphs 8 and 9 below, for periods prior to 27 March, 1998. Deductible expenses would include costs relating to rent reviews and rent collection, maintenance of the property and general overheads such as accountancy and office expenses. Expenses directly related to a subsequent disposal of the landlord's interest in the property, (such as the sale of the freehold with sitting tenants) are not deductible as these expenses related to a non-taxable disposal. Similarly, if the tenant surrendered his or her interest in the property and the landlord created a new interest in the property under the VAT rules applicable prior to 26 March, 1997, VAT on expenses relating to the subsequent disposal is not deductible as that disposal was not chargeable to VAT.

6. A landlord who acquired a property with sitting tenants is also affected by the judgment. Although this type of landlord has not made a taxable supply of the property, the Court has held that he or she is entitled to deduct VAT on post-letting expenses, where the creation of the lease was chargeable to VAT. Again, input tax will be allowed on expenses the landlord incurred in relation to the lease to the original tenants. General overheads will also be deductible, but see paragraph 8 below. If any of the sitting tenants was not party to the original taxable supply, input tax will not be deductible in relation to expenses relating to the letting to those tenants. This could have arisen if the original tenant surrendered his or her interest in the property and the landlord created a new interest in the property under the VAT rules applicable prior to 26 March 1997.

7. VAT on expenses relating to the acquisition of a property with sitting tenants will be allowed to the extent that the creation of the tenants' interest was subject to VAT. Therefore, in a situation where part of the property is occupied by tenants who acquired their interest as a result of a taxable supply and part of the property is not, then apportionment of the input credit will be required.

Apportionment

8. Where a landlord paid VAT on general overheads and administrative costs he or she will be entitled to deduct VAT to the extent that these costs relate to taxable supplies. In most cases affected by the Erin judgment the landlord will have both deductible and non-deductible VAT. Some apportionment of VAT on general overheads or administrative costs will be required in these cases. The most common apportionment method is based on taxable turnover over total turnover. The turnover method will be unlikely to give a fair result in relation to post letting expenses having regard to the effect of the capitalised value in the first year of the lease with no taxable turnover in the following years. A more equitable result would be one based on a break-down of the rent roll or of the area of the properties let, between those lettings which were subject to a taxable supply and those lettings which were not. Agreement on apportionment should be reached with the appropriate tax office (see Appendix). However, whatever method is used this method must be applied for all periods.

Claims

9. Any claim for a repayment of VAT on post-letting expenses following the Erin judgment should be submitted to the appropriate tax office. Claims should be prepared on an annual basis by way of a supplementary VAT return. Claims may be made for periods up to ten years prior to the date of submission of the claim. It should be noted that the 1998 Finance Act reduces from ten years to six years the time limit within which a claim for a refund of VAT generally may be made. However, as an interim measure anyone claiming a refund for taxable periods prior to 1 May, 1998 can still avail themselves of the ten year limit up to 1 May, 1999. Claims must be supported by proper VAT invoices and computations of the make-up of the claim. These supporting documents should be retained and may be subject to examination. While the provisions of section 20(5) with regard to unjust enrichment could apply to the repayment of VAT on post-letting expenses, Revenue will not invoke these provisions in regard to claims arising out of the Erin judgment.

Direct taxes

10. To the extent that this VAT has already been claimed as a deduction in the landlord's accounts adjustments will need to be made to his or her direct tax liability for the years/ periods in question.

Queries

11. Any queries about claims for repayment of VAT arising out of the judgment in the case of Erin Executor and Trustee Company Ltd. should be addressed to the appropriate tax office (see Appendix).

Revenue Commissioners.
May, 1998.

Contact addresses can be found in Revenue Addresses at start of book

VAT ON PROPERTY

VAT treatment of post-letting expenses incurred on or after 27 March, 1998

Introduction

1. The Supreme Court, in the case of Erin Executor and Trustee Company Ltd., held that a landlord was entitled to deduct VAT on post-letting expenses incurred in relation to a property which had been the subject of a taxable supply of immovable goods for VAT purposes. Section 106 of the Finance Act 1998 amends section 4 of the VAT Act to provide for the effects of the judgment. This information leaflet explains the changes to section 4 of the VAT Act and sets out the circumstances in which VAT on post-letting expenses is deductible with effect from 27 March, 1998.

2. This leaflet deals with situations that arise following the creation of a taxable leasehold interest in developed property. The creation of the interest is taxable on the capitalised value of the lease. The landlord is also liable to VAT on a self-supply of the reversionary interest on that lease in accordance with section 4(4) of the VAT Act. Where the lease created is for a period of twenty years or more the value of the reversionary interest is disregarded. The Supreme Court held that the application of section 4(4) to the reversionary interest did not take the property out of the VAT net and accordingly a landlord was entitled to VAT deductibility on post-letting expenses in relation to that property.

3. Following the Supreme Court judgment, the law has been amended to provide for the treatment of subsequent supplies of an interest in property (see paragraphs 4 to 8 of this leaflet). In general, subsequent supplies will be exempt from VAT unless the property has been redeveloped. In addition, the law now specifies the circumstances in which post-letting expenses are deductible for VAT purposes. Two situations are dealt with in this leaflet. What happens when the landlord is the person who created the taxable interest? (see paragraphs 9 and 10 of this leaflet). What happens when the landlord acquired the property after the taxable interest was created? (see paragraph 11 of the leaflet).

Post-letting expenses are defined in paragraphs 13 to 19 of this leaflet.

Subsequent supplies

4. Prior to the judgment it was the view of Revenue that where the creation of an interest in immovable goods was taxable, section 4(4) took the property out of the VAT net. This meant that subsequent supplies of an interest in that property by the landlord were generally outside the scope of VAT. However, if the property was redeveloped or was subject to a taxable surrender of that interest, a subsequent supply of an interest in that property was taxable.

5. As the Supreme Court has held that a self-supply under section 4(4) does not take the property out of the VAT net, it is necessary to provide for the VAT treatment of subsequent supplies of the property. The new section 4(9) provides for the exemption of these supplies. There are essentially two types of supply involved. The first involves the transfer of the reversionary interest, say by the sale of the freehold, during the term of the taxable interest and the second involves the disposal of an interest in the property following the expiry of the term of the lease. The changes in section 4(9) provide that, if the property concerned has not been developed since the creation of the taxable interest, subsequent supplies of the property are exempt in both situations just outlined.

6. The first case can best be illustrated by an example:

Example 1

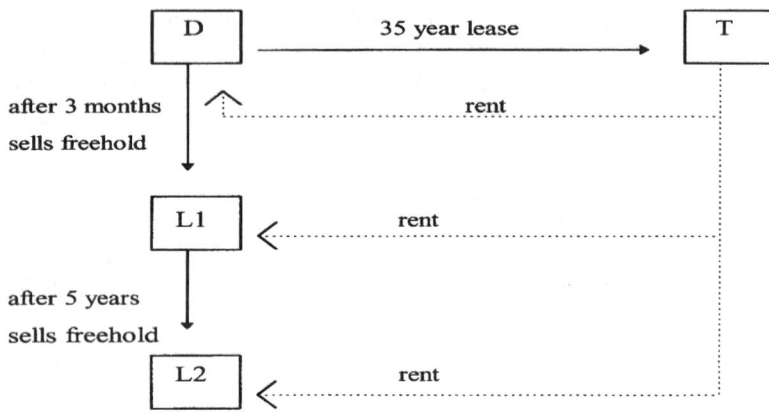

In this example D, the property developer, develops the property and creates a 35 year lease in favour of T, the tenant. The value of the lease is capitalised and VAT is accounted for. As the lease is for 35 years the value of the reversionary interest is disregarded. After 3 months D sells the freehold to L1, an investor. This sale is exempt from VAT. After 5 years L1 sells the freehold to L2, again this sale is exempt from VAT. As both sales of the freehold are exempt from VAT, any costs connected to these sales are not deductible (see, however, paragraph 11 regarding the treatment of post-letting expenses).

7. The second category involves supplies following the expiry of the term of the interest. This can be illustrated as follows:

Example 2

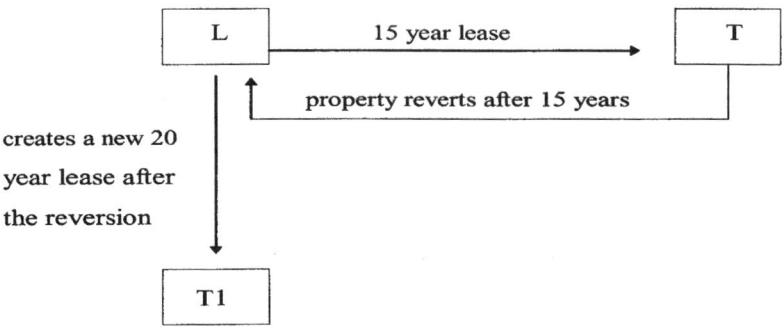

In this example L creates a fifteen year lease in favour of T. VAT is accounted for on the supply of the interest and the self-supply of the reversion. After fifteen years the property reverts to L. Following the reversion L creates a subsequent lease for twenty years to T1. This subsequent lease is exempt provided, of course, the property has not been developed since the first lease was created. As a consequence, VAT incurred on any costs associated with the new 20 year lease to T1 is not deductible.

8. Section 4(9), therefore, clarifies the treatment of subsequent supplies by the landlord after the creation of a taxable interest. It should be borne in mind that this subsection does not deal with subsequent supplies of an interest in the property following a surrender of that interest by the tenant. The VAT treatment of those transactions was amended in the Finance Act, 1997 and is explained in the booklet called *VAT on Property — Finance Act 1997 Changes — A Revenue Guide,* which is available from local tax offices.

VAT treatment of post-letting expenses from 27 March, 1998

9. The new subsection 4(10) of the VAT Act provides for the deductibility of VAT on post-letting expenses. It ensures that where the creation of an interest in immovable goods was subject to tax, the landlord is entitled to deduct VAT on post-letting expenses as defined (see paragraphs 13 to 19) over the term of the interest. The subsection specifically provides that where the landlord did not create the taxable interest, (L1 or L2 in example 1), he or she shall be deemed to be a taxable person in respect of the post-letting expenses even though he or she was not the person who made the taxable supply of the immovable goods.

The subsection also defines the post-letting expenses that are deductible.

10. Section 4(10)(a) deals with two categories of landlord. The first category is the landlord who creates the taxable interest and who in accordance with the Supreme Court judgment remains a taxable person in respect of that property. This subsection provides that the landlord is a taxable person in relation to that property in respect of:

(*a*)   taxable supplies of that property, for example, a taxable disposal of an interest in the property or a self-supply of the property,

(*b*)   taxable supplies of other goods and services effected for consideration, for example, the painting by the landlord of the building as part of a separate contract, or

(*c*)   post-letting expenses as defined (see paragraphs 13–19 below).

The subsection confirms that the landlord is entitled to deduct VAT on expenses relating to the property, which was subject to the taxable supply, only where the VAT relates to:

(i)   a taxable supply of the property other than a self-supply under section 4(4),

(ii)   a taxable supply of other goods and services effected for consideration, or

(iii) post letting expenses as defined (see paragraphs 13–19 below).

This subsection, therefore, limits the circumstances in which VAT is deductible in relation to a property which was the subject of a taxable supply. It confirms the basic principles of VAT law which provide that a taxable person is entitled to claim only input tax which directly relates to a taxable supply. Therefore, VAT on expenses such as legal fees in relation to, say, the sale of a freehold by D to L1 in example 1, is not deductible as these expenses directly relate to an exempt supply.

11. The second category of landlord dealt with in section 4(10)(a) is the landlord who acquires the property with sitting tenants. This case can best be illustrated by an example:

Example 3

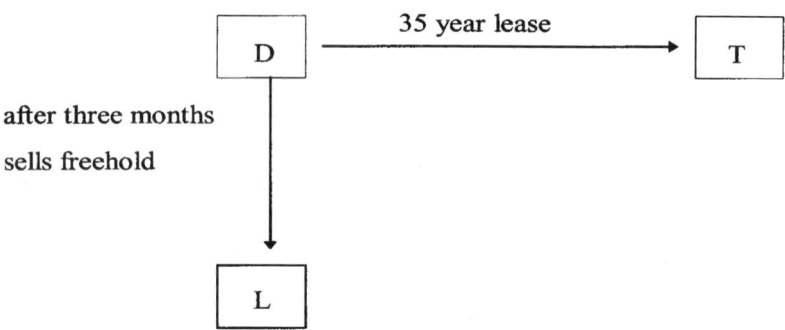

In this example, the developer (D) creates a 35 year lease in favour of the tenant (T). The value of the lease is capitalised and VAT accounted for. As the lease is for 35 years the value of the reversionary interest is disregarded. After three months D sells the freehold to L, the landlord. This supply is exempt and VAT is not deductible on expenses relating to the supply. The landlord takes on the developer's rights and obligations under the contract. The tenant will now pay the rent to the landlord.

In this example the landlord (L) has not made any taxable supply and would not normally be entitled to claim back VAT on expenses incurred. However, as VAT has been accounted for on the value of the lease on its creation, this subsection deems the landlord to be a taxable person and entitled to deduct VAT in respect of post-letting expenses as defined.

12. Where a landlord is deemed to be a taxable person in the circumstances outlined above, he or she should contact the appropriate tax office to register for VAT. If the landlord is already a taxable person because he or she makes taxable supplies and is registered for VAT, the VAT on post-letting expenses can be claimed under his or her VAT return.

Definition of post-letting expenses

13. Paragraph (b) of subsection 4(10) defines post-letting expenses in relation to a taxable lease. There are essentially two categories of deductible post-letting expenses. The first are expenses which the landlord incurs in carrying out services which he or she is obliged to carry out under the terms and conditions of the lease. In effect, these expenses directly relate to the taxable supply of the interest to the tenant. However, to qualify for deduction, the value of these obligations must have been reflected in the value of the lease for VAT purposes. This will normally be the case as the level of the rent will reflect the terms and conditions of the lease and the value of the supply for VAT purposes will therefore reflect this.

14. While section 4(10)(b)(i) refers to expenses incurred in carrying out **services,** Revenue will allow deductibility on the provision of supplies of **goods** of the type specified in section 3(1B) of the VAT Act, ie the supply of electricity, gas, and any form of power, heat, refrigeration or ventilation. To qualify for deductibility those supplies must, of course, be provided under the terms and conditions of the lease.

15. VAT on expenses that the landlord incurs which he or she is obliged to carry out under the terms of the lease but which are not reflected in the rent charged is not deductible under the provisions of this section. However, under "the landlord's concession", which has been in place since 1985, landlords have been able to deduct the VAT on these expenses and pass on a VAT credit to their taxable tenants. Where expenses such as cleaning, security, electricity, etc are provided by the landlord on a reimbursement basis from the tenants, the landlord's concession can still apply to these expenses. However, as the landlord will now be a taxable person in respect of post-letting expenses, the landlord's concession can be processed through the landlord's VAT return and a separate VAT registration is not required. Where reimbursable expenses are passed through the landlord, he or she should issue to each tenant, once a year, an invoice showing VAT charged to the tenant on these services. The VAT deductible and payable by the landlord should be incorporated in the appropriate VAT return.

16. Of course, where a landlord is actually supplying such services directly and for consideration, he or she is a taxable person in the normal way. VAT is chargeable on such service charges and the expenses which the landlord incurs in supplying those services is deductible subject to the normal rules.

17. The second category of deductible post-letting expenses are expenses which the landlord incurs in:

   (*a*)   collecting the rent payable by the tenant,

   (*b*)   carrying out a rent review,

   (*c*)   the exercise of an option to extend the term of the lease or the exercise of a break clause to terminate the lease.

General overheads

18. Revenue have decided, following consultation with trade interests, to allow deductibility on a landlord's general overheads. Under this concessional treatment the following category of expenses will also be treated as post-letting expenses:

> "general overheads of a landlord's business to the extent that the landlord's letting of immovable property was taxable as a supply of immovable goods under section 4 of the VAT Act"

These expenses will include items such as office expenses and audit fees. For the purpose of this concession general overheads do not include any goods or services which are provided by the landlord to the tenant. Effectively general overheads are expenses that the landlord incurs in relation to his or her own business. Where the landlord's entire lettings of immovable property was taxable as a supply of goods all general overheads relating to the lettings are deductible.

19. However, the concession does not extend to expenses a landlord incurs in relation to an exempt supply of property. Where a landlord acquires a property with sitting tenants, where the lease to these tenants was taxable, expenses relating to the acquisition of the property are not treated as general overheads for the purpose of this concession. Therefore VAT on expenses, such as legal fees, relating to such acquisition are not deductible.

Apportionment

20. Where a landlord has a mixed portfolio of lettings, some which were taxable as a supply of goods and some which were not, apportionment of VAT on general overheads will be required. Apportionment of input credit is usually based on the proportion of taxable turnover to total turnover. However, given the nature of property transactions a more appropriate method may be one based on a break-down of the rent roll between lettings which were subject to a taxable supply and those that were not. Any apportionment method should be agreed with the relevant tax office

Date of effect

21. These changes have effect as on and from 27 March 1998.

Queries

22. Any queries about this issue should be addressed to the appropriate tax office. See Appendix attached.

Revenue Commissioners.

August, 1998.

Contact addresses can be found in Revenue Addresses at start of book

VAT TREATMENT OF AUCTIONEERS, AND AUCTION AND AGENCY SALES

1 Introduction

The Seventh VAT Directive came into effect on 1 January, 1995. It introduced common rules in relation to the VAT treatment, within the EU, of second-hand movable goods, works of art, collectors' items and antiques. It also provided for the VAT treatment of auctioneers dealing in those goods.

The provisions of the Seventh Directive were transposed into Irish VAT law by the 1995 Finance Act. This Information Leaflet deals with the implementation of that law and the VAT treatment of all other sales made by Auctioneers as well as Auction and Agency sales. A separate Information Leaflet (entitled The Margin Scheme) deals with the VAT treatment of second-hand goods; works of art, collectors' items and antiques and should be read in conjunction with this Leaflet.

2 The principal change in relation to sales of movable goods

The principal provision is that those auctioneers selling movable goods who up to 1 July, 1995 had been treated as selling goods on behalf of their principals, and, in effect, as having supplied services, are now regarded as buying and selling the goods simultaneously and are, therefore, principals in their own right. Accordingly with effect from 1 July, 1995, all auctioneers of movable goods are treated in the same way as auctioneers of agricultural produce including livestock, and greyhounds. Sales of such goods are governed by the normal VAT rules ie the auctioneer is obliged to register if the annual turnover from sales of taxable goods exceeds or is likely to exceed £40,000 and the usual rules relating to the issue of invoices/settlement vouchers apply. (See Chapter 9 of Guide to Value Added Tax.)

Auctioneers selling immovable goods continue to be regarded as supplying a service.

The effect of these rules on the different categories of auctioneers is described below.

3 Special auction scheme (Seventh VAT Directive)

The Seventh VAT Directive provides for the application of a scheme to certain works of art, collectors' items, antiques or movable second-hand goods which are sold by an auctioneer at a public auction. This scheme provides that where those goods are sold by an auctioneer, the auctioneer is liable for VAT on the profit margin. The arrangement is referred to as the "auction scheme" and the goods concerned are referred to as "auction scheme goods".

3.1 Auction Scheme goods

The auction scheme applies to works of art, collectors' items, antiques or movable second-hand goods passed to an auctioneer for sale by public auction by a person who is:—

    (i)   a private individual,

       or

(ii)   an exempt person, (eg bank, insurance company, etc) or a taxable person who was **not** entitled to any input credit for the VAT on his/her purchase of the goods

or

(iii) a taxable dealer who has already applied the margin scheme to his or her supply of the goods (as described in Information Leaflet on The Margin Scheme).

Effectively, this means that neither the person who passed the goods to the auctioneer nor the auctioneer him/herself was entitled to claim a VAT input credit on the transaction. The auctioneer should take reasonable precautions to ensure that the goods qualify as auction scheme goods, as at (i) to (iii) above.

3.2 Auctioneer's margin

The auctioneer's margin is the difference between what the auctioneer receives from the purchaser and what he/she pays to the person who passed the goods to him/her for sale, and it is tax inclusive. For example, the auctioneer receives £525 from the purchaser on sale of the goods and passes £500 to the seller. The auctioneer's margin in this instance is £25 tax inclusive.

3.3 Taxable amount

The taxable amount is the auctioneer's margin less the amount of VAT included in that margin. The following examples illustrate the position, assuming that

"A" is the seller of the goods,

"B" is the auctioneer, and

"C" is the purchaser of the goods from the auctioneer.

		£
(*a*)	Sale proceeds (gross) from C => B =	525
	less commission — charged to seller A =	25
	Seller's net proceeds — A =	500
	Auctioneer's margin including tax at 21% =	25
	Tax included in the margin (at 21%) =	$\frac{25 \times 21}{121} = 4.33$

Taxable Amount = £25 less £4.33
                = £20.67

Example (a) above reflects normal practice. However, there may be situations where an auctioneer charges commission to both the seller and the purchaser. Where this occurs, the auctioneer's margin and the taxable amount are calculated as follows:—

			£
(*b*)	Sale proceeds (gross) from C => B	=	550
	less commission — charged to seller A	=	25
		=	525

less commission — charged to buyer C	=	25
Seller's net proceeds — A	=	500
Margin, including tax at 21%	=	50
Tax included in the margin (at 21%)	=	$\underline{50} \times 21 = 8.67$
		121
Taxable Amount	=	£50 less £8.67
	=	£41.33

3.4 VAT rates

Generally, the normal VAT rules apply. The rate applicable is the rate applying to a sale of goods as new but there are some exceptions under the auction scheme. The exceptions are works of art and antiques, which are normally liable at the rate of 12.5 per cent but which become liable at the 21 per cent rate when sold under the auction/margin scheme. For technical reasons to do with the wording of the VAT Act "concrete, ready to pour" and "concrete blocks" also fall into this category and would become liable at 21% in the unlikely event of an auction sale of these products. (See Appendix 1.)

3.5 Time of supply

For VAT accounting purposes, where the goods are passed to an auctioneer for sale, the time of supply to the auctioneer is regarded as having taken place when the auctioneer **sells** the goods to a purchaser at a public auction.

The auctioneer is obliged to issue both to the purchaser and the vendor written details of the transaction.

3.6 Invoices

An auctioneer should not show on the invoice issued by him/her to the purchaser, the amount of VAT for which he/she is accountable in respect of auction scheme goods. Any such invoice should be clearly endorsed — **"Auction Scheme — this invoice does not give the right to an input credit of VAT"**.

If the principal is required under normal VAT rules to issue an invoice, the invoice issued by the auctioneer to the purchaser will fulfill this requirement.

3.7 Supply of goods to other EU Member States

Where an auctioneer supplies auction scheme goods to a VAT registered person in another EU Member State, the supply cannot be zero-rated as an intra-Community supply. Irish VAT included in the margin must be accounted for as if it was an auction scheme sale within the State. In this connection, the Member State of dispatch is deemed to be the legal place of supply. The foreign purchaser is not entitled to a repayment of such VAT.

3.8 Future taxation

Auction scheme goods purchased from an auctioneer by a taxable person in connection with his or her business activities are treated in the same way as the other assets of his or her business and are fully liable to VAT on disposal.

4 Agricultural produce (including fish) — These are not generally margin scheme or auction scheme goods.

4.1 Live cattle, sheep, goats, pigs and deer

These animals are generally sold through livestock marts, or by auctioneers or livestock dealers. Sales by marts, auctioneers or dealers are liable to VAT at the livestock rate. This rate is currently of 3.6 per cent and is chargeable on the final accepted VAT exclusive bid or selling price plus such commissions or fees, if any, as are charged to the purchaser. Marts, auctioneers or dealers are obliged to register for VAT if their annual turnover exceeds or is likely to exceed £40,000.

Unregistered Farmers If a farmer is not registered for VAT, the auctioneer can pay him or her an amount called a flat-rate addition currently equal to 3.6 per cent of the VAT exclusive sale price. The auctioneer is entitled to set off against his or her own VAT liability a deduction equal to 3.6 per cent of the final accepted VAT exclusive bid or selling price less such commissions or fees, if any, as are charged to the farmer.

Example:—

Sale price of livestock — Net	£10,000
Flat-rate addition (3.6%)	£360
Total payable to farmer (unregistered)	£10,360

Auctioneer claims back the flat-rate addition of £360 in his/her VAT return.

In order to qualify for the flat-rate addition, the farmer must sign a once-off declaration to the effect that he/she is not registered for VAT. (Appendix II.) That declaration must be retained by the auctioneer. If the farmer does not sign the declaration, he or she will be required instead to sign a settlement voucher or invoice made out by the auctioneer in respect of each separate sale, before the 3.6 per cent addition can be paid.

To claim the 3.6 per cent deduction, the auctioneer must be in possession of that invoice, which must show details of the transaction and separately show the purchase price and the 3.6 per cent addition.

Registered farmers

In the case of livestock sold on behalf of registered farmers the auctioneer is entitled to claim the 3.6 per cent VAT invoiced to him/her by such farmers against the tax payable by him/her on the sale. Livestock is liable to VAT at the rate of 3.6 per cent.

Foreign buyers

Livestock sold within the State to export companies is taxable in the same way as livestock sold to other buyers.

Sales of livestock to persons registered for VAT in other EU Member States and which are despatched or transported from this State are zero rated provided that the essential conditions for zero-rating are met. (See SOP 8/92 Application of the Zero Rate to Sales and Deliveries of Goods to Other EU Member States after 1 January, 1993.)

Livestock purchased within the State by non-EU buyers, including non-EU farmers, from a VAT-registered person, for example, a VAT-registered mart or export company, is taxable but the tax is refundable to the foreign buyer, subject to conditions. Claims for repayment should be made to VAT Repayments (Unregistered) Section, Office of the Accountant General of Revenue, Kilrush Road, Ennis, Co. Clare. The flat-rate addition which applies to supplies of agricultural produce and services within the State also applies to supplies made to VAT-registered traders in other Member States with effect from 1 January 1993. (See SOP 2/93,Flat-Rate Farmers and the Single Market.)

4.2 Vegetables, fruit, eggs and dead poultry

These goods qualify for the zero rate of VAT and the auctioneer has a VAT liability on his or her commission or other charges albeit at the zero rate. He or she is entitled to claim the 3.6 per cent VAT input credit in respect of sales made on behalf of unregistered farmers, as outlined at 4.1 above.

4.3. Fish

Dead fish are liable at the zero rate of VAT and the auctioneer has a VAT liability on his or her commission or other charges at the zero rate.

The rules outlined at 4.1 above apply, also, to sales of fish sold on behalf of unregistered fish farmers and unregistered fresh water fisherman, as well as VAT registered sea-fishermen.

4.4 Live Poultry and Live Ostriches

Live poultry and live ostriches are liable at 12.5 per cent with effect from the 1 May, 1998.

The rules outlined at 4.1 above apply, also, to sales of poultry and ostriches sold on behalf of farmers.

4.5 Flowers

Flowers are liable at 12.5 per cent (see SOP–1/97 Horticultural Retailers) and the auctioneer is liable to pay VAT at this rate on the final accepted bid plus any commission or fees charged to the purchaser. The rules outlined at 4.1 above apply, also, to sales of flowers sold on behalf of farmers.

4.6 Taxable consideration

Auctioneers selling agricultural produce are generally obliged to register for VAT if their annual turnover exceeds or is likely to exceed £40,000. VAT is chargeable on "the total consideration which the person supplying the goods or services becomes entitled to receive in respect of or in relation to such supply of goods or services, including all taxes, commissions, costs and charges whatsoever, but not including Value Added tax chargeable in respect of the supply".

5 Bloodstock, ie live horses

Horses are treated similarly to other livestock in so far as the sale by auctioneers and the flat-rate addition are concerned.

However other special rules apply, as follows:—

5.1 Horses imported for sale by auction

Where horses are imported for sale by auction, VAT-registered auctioneers may avail of the deferred payment scheme and undertake such importation without payment of VAT at the time of importation using deferred payment facilities.

The auctioneer, by special arrangement, undertakes liability for the VAT payable at importation. This however may in due course be disregarded provided the auctioneer accounts for VAT at 3.6 per cent on the ultimate sale of the horse, unless of course, the horse is sold for export or to a VAT registered person in another Member State of the EU and the horse is in fact despatched or transported from the State.

If the horse is not sold at auction the auctioneer must account for VAT at 3.6 per cent on the import value unless, again, the horse is re-exported.

5.2 Horses sold by Approved Auctioneers to Overseas Purchasers

Under a special arrangement for the bloodstock industry, a sale to an overseas purchaser can be zero-rated even though the horse may not immediately be exported or dispatched to a registered person in another Member State. The arrangement may be operated by auctioneers who have been approved by the Revenue Commissioners for that purpose and who have undertaken responsibility for its administration. Under the arrangement a horse sold with an export undertaking or under a similar intra-Community arrangement may be zero-rated provided the horse is exported or despatched from the State within 24 months of the date of supply or, in the case of yearlings purchased after 1 September of any year, is exported within 28 months of purchase. If the horse is subsequently sold in the State or not exported or dispatched from the State within the required time limits, VAT will have to be accounted for by the original vendor (ie the auctioneer).

5.3 Auctioneers wishing to participate in the scheme should apply to their local Tax Office and must be prepared to abide by the conditions set down by the Revenue Commissioners.

6 Motor vehicles

A special scheme applies to auction sales of motor vehicles. This is detailed in a separate Information Leaflet. (VAT Treatment of Second-hand Vehicles.)

7 Property (immovable goods)

Auctioneers dealing with immovable goods continue to be regarded as supplying a service, and are liable for VAT on their commissions plus charges at the standard rate. The auctioneer who charges a commission or fee, exclusive of VAT, of say, £500 in respect of the sale of a house is liable for VAT on this amount at 21 per cent. If in addition, he or she is entitled to recover an amount to cover expenses eg subsistence, travel, telephone, this amount forms part of the taxable consideration and is taxable at the same rate.

8 Enquiries

Appendix III gives details of the various Revenue Offices which should be contacted for further information.

Revenue Commissioners,

Dublin Castle November, 1998

Appendix I

Goods currently taxed at the lower rate which must be taxed at the standard rate (21%) when sold under the auction scheme or margin scheme.

(i) a work of art being —

    (*a*) a painting, drawing or pastel, or any combination thereof, executed entirely by hand,

    (*b*) an original lithograph, engraving or print, or any combination thereof, produced directly from lithographic stones, plates or other engraved surfaces, which are executed entirely by hand, or

    (*c*) an original sculpture or statuary, excluding mass-produced reproductions and works of craftsmanship of a commercial character.

(ii) antiques, being articles of furniture, silver, glass or porcelain, whether hand-decorated or not, which are shown to be more than 100 years old.

(iii) concrete ready to pour.

(iv) blocks of concrete of a kind which comply with the specification contained in the Standard Specification (Concrete Building Blocks, Part I, Normal Density Blocks) Declaration, 1987 (Irish Standard 20: Part 1, 1987).

Appendix II
SALE OF LIVESTOCK BY FLAT-RATE FARMERS

1. flat-rate farmers — ie farmers who are not registered for VAT — receive a flat addition of 3.6 (new rate with effect from 1 March 1998) on the price received by them when they sell livestock to VAT registered persons such as marts, factories or exporters.

2. Under new VAT arrangements a flat-rate farmer must sign a once off declaration so that the outlet can include in the sellers cheque the flat-rate addition of 3.6%.

3. The outlet cannot pay the flat-rate addition unless a declaration has been completed.

IF YOU ARE A FLAT-RATE FARMER ENTITLED TO THE 3.6% ADDITION PLEASE COMPLETE THE FOLLOWING AND RETURN TO YOUR OUTLET AS SOON AS POSSIBLE.

DECLARATION

TO: (Name of outlet) [   ]

I hereby declare that I am a flat-rate farmer as defined by the VAT Act 1972 (as amended) and that, as such, I am entitled to obtain the flat-rate addition as referred to in section 12A of the Act. I agree to notify you of any change in circumstances which would effect my entitlement to the flat-rate addition.

NAME (Block Capitals) [   ]

SIGNED [   ]

ADDRESS [   ]

DATE [   ]

WITNESS [   ]

SIGNED [   ]

ADDRESS [   ]

This completed declaration will be retained by your outlet and will entitle you to continue to receive the flat-rate addition of 3.6% on all sales by you as a flat-rate farmer through this outlet.

Contact addresses can be found in Revenue Addresses at start of book

VAT ON TELECOMMUNICATIONS SERVICES

General

1. Several provisions in the 1997 and 1998 Finance Acts relate to changes in the VAT rules concerning international telecommunications services.

2. Prior to 1 July, 1997, the place where telecommunications services were deemed to be supplied was the place where the supplier had established his/her business. Therefore, a supply of telecommunications services from a supplier in, say, the US to a customer in the EU escaped VAT altogether because the place of liability to tax was outside the scope of EU VAT. This meant that although such services were entirely consumed within the EU, they were not subject to EU VAT. The opposite case also applied as EU suppliers of telecommunications services to customers outside the EU were obliged to account for VAT on those services, even though they were entirely consumed outside the EU. This resulted in distortion of competition to the disadvantage of the EU suppliers. To combat this, all Member States have sought and received identical derogations from Article 9(1) of the Sixth VAT Directive.

3. The arrangements set out in this leaflet explain how the derogation is applied in Ireland. The new rules deal primarily with international telecommunications suppliers.

4. Under the terms of the derogation, as from 1 July, 1997, VAT is chargeable on supplies of telecommunications services used within the EU, even if the supplier is established outside the EU. There are various rules which determine where and by whom this VAT must be accounted for. Also, certain supplies by EU suppliers to non-EU established customers are now taken out of the VAT net.

5. The main features of Irish VAT law and practice can now be summarised as follows:

the term "telecommunications service" has been defined for VAT purposes (see paragraph 8);

— telecommunications services have been added to the Fourth Schedule of the VAT Act (see Statement of Practice SP — VAT 5/94-Fourth Schedule Services) with the result that a customer in the State, other than a private individual, who buys telecommunications services from outside the EU or from another Member State must self-account for and pay the VAT on those services and

a service provider established in the State whose customers are business persons outside the State may supply those customers without VAT;

— an EU service provider who supplies a service to a private individual in another Member State must account for the VAT in his/her own Member State;

— a non-EU service provider who supplies a service to private individuals in this State must register and account for the VAT here;

> — a service provider established here must account for VAT here on services which he/she provides to private individuals who, although resident outside the EU, use the services while they are here. Such a service provider is not liable for VAT on the services which the non-EU resident uses outside the EU.

6. The derogation includes certain anti-avoidance rules concerning pre-payments, which have the effect of applying the new rules to payments made prior to 1 July, 1997, in respect of services supplied after that date.

7. The following chart (Chart A) illustrates how the new rules are being operated throughout the EU.

Chart A

Liability to VAT on supplies of telecommunications services.

	Status and place of establishment or residence of customer	Supplier in Ireland	Supplier in OMS	Supplier outside EU
1	business customer in Ireland	Supplier accounts for Irish VAT	Customer accounts for Irish VAT	Customer accounts for Irish VAT
2	private individual in Ireland	Supplier accounts for Irish VAT	Supplier accounts for OMS VAT	Supplier must register and account for Irish VAT
3	business customer in OMS	Customer accounts for OMS VAT	Supplier/ customer accounts for OMS VAT[1]	Customer accounts for OMS VAT
4	private individual in OMS	Supplier accounts for Irish VAT	Supplier accounts for OMS VAT[2]	Supplier must register and account for OMS VAT
5	outside EU, whether business customer or private individual	Outside the scope of Irish VAT — No VAT payable (but see column 6)	Outside the scope of Irish VAT	Outside the scope of EU VAT
6	private individual resident outside EU but avails of service while in Ireland	Supplier accounts for Irish VAT	Outside the scope of Irish VAT	Outside the scope of Irish VAT when mobile services, cards etc are involved

OMS = other Member State of the EU

[1] If supplier and customer in the same Member State, supplier pays VAT.
   If supplier and customer in different Member States, customer pays VAT in his/her Member State.

[2] Supplier pays VAT in his/her Member State, even if customer in a different State.

Scope of the tax

8. The scope of the term "telecommunications services" has been defined in the VAT Act as:

> "services relating to the transmission, emission or reception of signals, writing, images and sounds or information of any nature by wire, radio, optical or other electromagnetic systems, including the transfer or assignment of the right to use capacity for such transmission, emission or reception".

9. In general, the services concerned are those which consist of making available the means of telecommunication. The types of service covered by the definition include the following:

— telephone calls, telephone calls delivered by cellular phones, paging, the transmission element of Electronic Data Interchange, teleconferencing and call-back services;

— switching, completion of another provider's calls, the provision of leased lines and circuits or global networks;

— telex, facsimile, multi-messaging;

— e-mail and access to the internet;

— satellite transmission services, covering transponder rental/hire and both space segments and earth segments, which includes uplinks and downlinks via land earth stations, coastal stations, outside broadcasting units, or similar.

Added value services, for which the customer pays a charge in addition to the telecommunications service access charge, are not included in the definition. Each added value service is to be treated according to the VAT rules appropriate to the service in question eg advertising service (see SP VAT 3/92 — Advertising Services).

It should be noted that, by common agreement among all Member States, the definition does not cover the service of broadcasting, which remains taxable by reference to the place where the supplier has established his/her business or has a fixed establishment.

Who is liable?

10. Persons who are liable to pay VAT in the State in respect of telecommunications services are the following:

(i) telecommunications suppliers established in the State (see para 13) whose customers are

— established or resident in the State, (whether business customers or other) or

— private individuals in another Member State of the EU, or

— private individuals resident outside the EU and are availing of the service while in the State, on or after 1 May 1998

if the annual turnover of the supplier exceeds or is likely to exceed £20,000;

(ii) telecommunications suppliers established outside the EU whose customers are private individuals in the State, regardless of the size of the supplier's turnover;

(iii) business customers, who receive telecommunications supplies from outside the State (either from another Member State or from outside the EU), regardless of the value of the supply received.

The categories mentioned in subparagraphs (ii) and (iii) above are liable for the VAT involved in respect of supplies made/received on or after 1 July 1997. Persons who are not already registered for VAT, and who now find themselves obliged to register and account for VAT on telecommunications services should contact the Central Registration Information Office at Arus Brugha, 9/15 Upper O'Connell Street, Dublin 2 for the appropriate form and information about the registration procedure. A list of Offices to which enquiries may be made is attached at Appendix I.

11. Where a telecommunications supplier established in another Member State supplies services to private individuals in this State, that supplier is liable to VAT on those services in the Member State where he or she is established.

12. Where a telecommunications supplier is established in the State and all the customers are either established outside the EU (and using the service outside the EU), or are business customers in another Member State, the supplier is deemed not to be supplying taxable services here. Therefore, unless that supplier is registered for VAT in respect of other activities, he or she would not normally be in a position to register for VAT here. However, such a supplier can recover VAT paid on the business inputs by applying to VAT Repayments Section, Ennis (see Statement of Practice SP — VAT/2/94 -Repayments to Unregistered Persons).

The Supplier

13. The place of establishment of a supplier is the place where the supplier has established the business or has an establishment, or, if he or she has more than one establishment, the one which is most concerned with the supply in question. If the supplier has established the business in several countries, and there is doubt about which establishment is most concerned with a particular supply, he or she should consult the local Inspector of Taxes (see Appendix I). In general terms, a supplier is regarded as making supplies from the location where he or she has the technical and staff resources sufficient to make those supplies. (However, a supplier whose establishment is outside the EU but who supplies private individuals within the State must register here and account for the VAT on those supplies.)

The customer

14. The status and place of establishment or residence of the customer and, in certain circumstances, the place of use and enjoyment must be taken into account in deciding where the service is to be taxed.

As regards status, the customer is either a private individual, a business customer or a public body. Farmers who are not registered for VAT are treated as business customers in respect of telecommunications services they receive from abroad for the purpose of their farming activities. Although they must register and account for VAT on these telecommunications services, they are entitled to retain their unregistered status for their farming activities. Public bodies ie Government Departments, local authorities and other statutory bodies must self-account for VAT in respect of telecommunication services received from suppliers outside the State where EU VAT has not been charged.

The Member State or country of establishment or residence of the customer can be identified in several ways, for example

— the country where the customer uses the service (eg a fixed line in a particular location)

— the country where the customer is billed for the service.

Normally it will be possible to identify which country is the appropriate one for the purposes of deciding where an international telecommunications service should be taxed (or if tax is due at all). However, if there is a doubt, for example if a business customer received a fixed line service or a mobile phone service in one country but is invoiced for it at an establishment in another country, the parties concerned should contact their local Inspector of Taxes to confirm whether, and where, tax is payable.

Effect of the rules on certain services

15. (a) Mobile phone services

Irish suppliers of mobile phone services are liable to VAT on services provided to business and private customers established or resident in the State, for their usage of the service anywhere in the world.

If an Irish supplier of mobile phone services makes supplies to business customers established in another Member State of the EU, those services are not subject to Irish VAT but the customers are liable to VAT in the Member State where they are established.

Similarly, any business customers who are established here and supplied with mobile phone services in Ireland from suppliers outside the State and who use their mobile phones for business purposes must account for the VAT on those services here. They are entitled to deductibility of that VAT under the normal deductibility rules.

(b) Phone cards

There are several variations of cards which can be used to procure telecommunications services, and the VAT treatment can vary, depending on the transaction involved. The following paragraphs indicate the VAT treatment of the cards currently available. Suppliers marketing new cards are advised to check on the correct VAT treatment in advance.

(i) Pre-paid phone cards

Pre-paid phone cards are specifically legislated for in the Finance Act, 1998. The following rules apply in the case of

— physical cards denominated in terms of units of service;

— physical cards denominated in money amounts;

— other tokens including personal identification numbers (PINs) which give the customer a right to access a telecom network without incurring a further charge at the time when that network is accessed (note — in this case it is possible that the customer may not receive a physical card or token at the time of sale — merely an allocation of a PIN, for which the payment is made).

For the purpose of clarity, the term 'pre-paid phone card' will be used to cover all the above possibilities.

The place and time of taxation are, respectively, the place and time of supply of the pre-paid phone card itself. Pre-paid phone cards sold in Ireland attract VAT at 21%. The Finance Act 1998 contains a provision to ensure there is not double taxation when a telecom service is provided on foot of a pre-paid phone card on which the VAT has already been accounted for. A company which sells pre-paid phone cards either as a wholesaler or retailer is normally liable to VAT on those sales as if it was in the business of supplying any taxable fourth schedule service (see Statement of Practice SP — VAT 5/94 — Fourth Schedule Services). However, the Revenue are prepared to accept arrangements whereby a company which supplies pre-paid phone cards to retailers within the State can account for VAT by reference to the full retail value of the card so no liability attaches to the retailer. Retailers should not, however, assume this arrangement applies in the case of all pre-paid phone card sales and should check with their suppliers. Any telecommunications supplier wishing to avail of this arrangement should apply to the local Inspector of Taxes. The Finance Act, 1998, makes provision for the repayment of VAT to a taxable person who, in the course of business, sells pre-paid phone cards *which are subsequently used outside the EU* to access a telecommunications network. (The repayment does not apply to cards used within the EU.) The repayment is allowed *to the extent that* the card is used outside the EU. This means that, in the case where a customer uses the same card both in the EU and also outside it, part of the VAT which was accounted for at the time of the sale of the card can be refunded to the taxable person, to the extent that the card was used outside the EU. The taxable person (telecommunications supplier or retailer) can make the appropriate adjustment in the VAT 3 return for the period in which the telecommunications supplier's records of the place of use of the card become available.

The formula for calculating the VAT deduction is as follows:

$$(A-B) \times \frac{C}{C + 100}$$

where

A   equals the tax inclusive price charged *by* the company (telecommunications supplier or retailer) which sold the card for that part of the value of the card which was used up in accessing the telecommunications service in a country outside the EU, and

B   equals the tax inclusive price charged *to* the company which sold the card for that part of the value of the card which was used up in accessing the telecommunications service in a country outside the EU, and

C   is the percentage rate of tax chargeable on the supply of the card at the time of that supply by that supplier (currently 21).

Where pre-paid phone cards are supplied through a number of suppliers eg a telecommunications supplier and a retailer each supplier can claim a VAT refund based on the formula **provided** the appropriate proof of use outside the EU is available.

The following examples illustrate how a VAT refund may be calculated in various circumstances:—

1) retail selling price of phone card = IR£10.00

2) records/accounts show that IR£2.5 in value of phone calls (ie 25 per cent) accessed outside EU

3) retailer has a 10 per cent mark-up.

Example 1   **- Supplier to retailer to final consumer**

Supplier   - Formula

$$(A - B) \times \frac{C}{C + 100} = (2.3 - \text{nil}) \times \frac{21}{21 + 100} = 39\,p$$

VAT refund to Supplier = 39p

Retailer   Formula

$$(A - B) \times \frac{C}{C + 100} = (2.5 - 2.3) \times \frac{21}{21 + 100} = 4p$$

VAT refund to Retailer = 4p

The combined refunds of 43p equals VAT at 21 per cent included in the value of IR£2.50 which reflects the value of the card accessed outside the EU.

Example 2   - Supply of pre-paid phone card by a company which supplies to retailers but which accounts for VAT on the full retail value of the card and no VAT liability is attached to the retailer.

Supplier   - Formula

$$(A - B) \times \frac{C}{C + 100} = (2.5 - \text{nil}) \times \frac{21}{21 + 100} = 43\,p$$

VAT refund to Supplier = 43p

As in the previous example the VAT refund equals the VAT at 21 per cent included in the value of IR£2.50. (ie value of card accessed outside EU) but the full refund is made to the supplier of the pre-paid phone card who is accounting on the gross retail value of the card.

Repayment is also available to taxable or exempt bodies who incur VAT under the reverse-charge mechanism on purchases of pre-paid phone cards from abroad, if the subsequent use of the cards takes place outside the EU. This can be claimed as a deduction on the VAT 3 return in the period when the record of the use of the cards becomes available.

Example 3

Retailer who accounts for VAT under the reverse — charge mechanism on purchase of pre-paid phone cards from abroad.

	IR£
Price to retailer from foreign supplier	7.5 0
- self accounts for VAT at 21 per cent in this State	1.60
VAT incl. price	9.10
Retailer sells (assuming 10 per cent mark-up)	8.30
-VAT at 21 per cent	1.7 0
VAT incl. price	10.00
Retailer entitled to refund of VAT to the extent that phone card was used outside EU (ie 25 per cent of 1.7)	= 43p

Example 4

Exempt body which accounts for VAT under the reverse — charge mechanism on purchase of pre-paid phone cards from abroad.

	IR£
Price to exempt body from foreign supplier	7.50
-self accounts for VAT at 21 per cent in this State	1.60
VAT incl. price	9.10
Exempt body uses card outside EU (for business purposes or not), to the extent of 25 per cent.	
Exempt body entitled to refund of VAT to the extent of 25 per cent (ie 25 per cent of 1.6)	= 40p

It is emphasised that a person claiming repayment of VAT for the non-EU use of a pre-paid phone card must have the appropriate proof that the card was used outside the EU and the extent of such use. This must be retained in the records and may be required for inspection.

(ii)   Telephone charge cards or post-paid PIN cards

These are cards which are sold to customers for telephone use in advance of payment. The charge card operates on the basis of a PIN which is keyed in as part of the dialling sequence. The customer is subsequently invoiced in respect of the use of the card, frequently by incorporating the appropriate amount into the normal telephone bill covering the telephone services to his or her establishment or residence. While these cards are marketed as a convenience for persons travelling abroad, they can also be used within the State. When the card is used abroad, the customer dials a free-phone number allocated to the country where he or she is making the call, and this puts him or her in contact with the network which issued the card and which will later issue the invoice. That network then connects the customer to the required number.

For VAT purposes these transactions are treated as telecommunications services supplied to the customer at the location of the customer's establishment or residence, regardless of where the customer is physically located when using the card. The VAT treatment is the same as that for other invoiced telecom services, as outlined in this leaflet.

(c) Internet

Access to the Internet is regarded as a telecommunications service for VAT purposes. Therefore, a person who supplies access to the Internet in return for subscription or fee by the customer is treated as a supplier of telecommunications services. If the customer is charged for access to specialised services *via* the Internet, these extra charges are not regarded as part of the charge for the telecommunications service. The VAT treatment of such extra charges follows the normal VAT rules regarding supplies of services, ie the nature of the service supplied dictates which VAT rule applies.

(d) Leased Lines

The provision of access to lines or networks is treated as a telecommunications service, including access under long or short-term lease arrangements.

Further Information

Any additional queries should be addressed to your local Inspector of Taxes.

Contact addresses can be found in Revenue Addresses at start of book

VAT RETAIL EXPORT SCHEME

What is the retail export scheme?

Value Added Tax (VAT) is a retail sales tax and the retail export scheme is a scheme whereby visitors from outside the European Union can purchase goods to take home with them and benefit from tax relief. Relief is not allowed on services (for instance, hotel accommodation, meals, car hire etc).

How does it work?

The scheme operates in two principal ways. Either the tourist pays the tax when making purchases and subsequently gets a refund from the relevant retailer or refund agency, or, in certain retail outlets, the goods are sold tax free at the point of sale. This will be explained in greater detail below.

In effect this means a reduction of 17.36% on the normal sale price.

Are there conditions attached to the relief?

— Yes. The goods must be exported out of the European Union within three months from the end of the month in which they are purchased. For instance, goods purchased during the month of January must be exported by 30th April.

— The tourist must provide documentary proof that the goods have been exported.

How exactly is the tax refunded?

— The retailer need not charge the VAT to the tourist. He must then rely on the tourist to send back documentary proof of export, otherwise, the retailer himself will be liable to VAT on the sale in question.

— The retailer may charge VAT to the tourist and subsequently refund it to him when he receives documentary proof of export.

— The retailer may operate the scheme through one of the VAT refunding agencies (see below).

What kind of proof of export is needed?

Normally proof of export will be the purchase invoice stamped by Customs at the last point of departure from the European Union. For example, a tourist who purchased goods in Ireland and then travels to the UK before leaving the EU must have the relevant invoices stamped by the UK Customs authorities. The Irish Customs authorities will only stamp invoices for tourists who are leaving the EU directly from Ireland.

If, for any reason, the tourist is unable to have the invoice stamped by the relevant Customs authorities at the point of departure, or does not avail himself of the services of a VAT-refunding agency (see below), he can still have the documentation stamped in his own country by a person of official status (for example, by Customs, the Police, or a Notary Public) before returning it to the retailer in Ireland.

VAT refund agencies

Many retailers operate the refund scheme using refund agencies which arrange for the tourist or visitor to benefit from the tax concession. These agencies operate independently of the tax authorities.

There are three variations in how these agencies operate;

— goods can be sold tax free at the point of sale;

— tax is paid at the point of sale and subsequently refunded to the tourist at the airport when leaving;

— tax is paid at the point of sale and subsequently refunded by the Agency to the tourist, either by post or by credit card transfer.

Individual invoices for purchases of a value up to and including £200 may be lodged directly with the refund booths at Dublin and Shannon airports without a Customs stamp. (This is for the convenience of the tourists. The agency itself will subsequently get these invoices stamped by Customs). However, invoices for purchases over £200 in value must always be presented by the tourist to Customs for stamping. In the event that the agency booths are closed a Customs stamp will always be required.

In the case of agents which operate as a (1) above the tourist will subsequently be obliged to pay the tax due, by credit card transaction, if the voucher is not handed in at the airport or subsequently returned.

It is important for tourists to retain their own copy of the invoice received from the retailer, for future reference, if necessary. If mailing an invoice back for refund it would be advisable to keep a photocopy.

Is the full tax refundable?

In order to cover administration costs retailers and refund agencies usually charge an administration fee. All agencies are obliged to clearly indicate the level of this fee. Similarly, agencies making refunds in foreign currency are obliged to indicate the exchange rate used.

What if I don't receive my refund?

The retailer or agency is obliged to make the refund at the latest within five weeks after receipt of the tourist's invoice. If a refund is not received the tourist should contact the retailer or agency concerned.

In the event of any difficulty experienced by the tourist in this regard, he may contact the Revenue Commissioners, VAT Administration Branch, Dublin Castle, Dublin 2. It should be noted however that the Revenue Commissioners do not make refunds directly to tourists, under this scheme.

Can EU residents ever benefit?

Yes. As a special concession tax relief can also be given to European Union residents, including Irish residents, who are going to live outside the European Union for a period of at least a year. Naturally, evidence to back this up will be required.

Goods exported directly by retailers

Apart from the scheme described above, retailers also send directly to the tourists homes (outside the EU only) goods ordered or purchased by them. Where this occurs, no tax is payable by the tourist.

Issued by the Revenue Commissioners

April 1998

PLANT AND MACHINERY

The Revenue Commissioners are prepared to accept that the provision <u>with an operator</u> of any of the machines specified below is chargeable to VAT at the 12.5 per cent rate.

Excavators/Traxcavators/Diggers	Verge Trimmers
Trench cutters with loader attachment	Hedge Cutters
Bulldozers	Sludge disposal units
Graders	Sludge pumps/tankers
Scrapers	Excavators with rock breaker
Road Rollers	Kango hammers
Vibrating Rollers	Compactors
Hand Vibrating Rollers	Tar spraying machines
Macadam laying and spreading machines	

The provision with an operator of other items of plant and machinery is chargeable at the standard rate.

THE HIRE WITHOUT AN OPERATOR OF ANY MACHINE WILL CONTINUE TO BE CHARGEABLE TO VAT AT THE RATE APPROPRIATE TO A SALE OF THE MACHINE WHEN NEW.

FOREIGN FIRMS DOING BUSINESS IN IRELAND

1. Introduction

Firms not established in Ireland are frequently involved in supplying goods or services here. Such firms may also be involved in the purchase here of goods and services for their own business and end up paying Irish VAT on their purchases.

The VAT treatment of such traders differs in certain ways from that applicable to traders established in the State and the purpose of this leaflet is to clarify the various issues affecting such non-established firms.

2 Foreign firms supplying goods/services in Ireland

All foreign traders supplying taxable goods or services here are obliged to register and account for Irish VAT. The turnover thresholds for VAT registration which apply to Irish firms do not apply and such foreign firms not established in the State must register regardless of the level of sales.

Applications for registration should be made on forms TR1 (sole traders/partnerships) or TR2 (companies) to the **Taxes Central Registration Office, Arus Brugha, 9/15 Upper O'Connell Street, Dublin 1. (tel. 01–8746821)**

The Revenue Commissioners may request persons supplying taxable goods or services to provide a security for the tax which becomes due as a result of sales made in the State. The security may be in the form of a bond issued by a bank licensed to carry on a banking business in the State or, alternatively, may be in cash/bank draft/money order form. The Revenue may where it appears requisite for them to do so for the protection of the revenue, deem an agent acting on behalf of a foreign trader, or on whose premises the foreign trader makes his sales, to have made such supplies and to be accountable for the VAT due. Thus, for example, the organisers of a trade fair may be held liable for the VAT due by foreign traders making sales at the trade fair in question. Similarly, an Irish concert promoter may be held liable for VAT in respect of performances by non-resident artistes, bands, etc. Where this is felt necessary notice will be served on the Irish agent and he will only be liable from the date of service of this notice.

3 Obligations of foreign traders to keep records

A foreign firm which supplies taxable goods or services in this country and which is registered for Irish VAT is subject to the same obligations as an Irish firm in relation to maintaining in this country the appropriate accounts and records required for the purposes of the tax and producing them at its place of business in this country to an authorised officer when requested. Where the records are normally kept outside the country and their maintenance in this country would create serious difficulties, the Inspectors of Taxes will be prepared, subject to appropriate safeguards, to consider applications for the relaxation of certain of the requirements. There will be no relaxation of the requirement that the foreign firm must produce the records for examination in this country.

4 VAT returns

Foreign firms registered for Irish VAT are required to make their returns in Irish pounds or Euros. VAT returns are due by the 19th day of the month following the end of a taxable period.

5 Foreign firms making distance sales to Ireland

Distance sales covers mail order sales and phone or tele sales made to persons in the State who are not registered for VAT by a supplier registered in another Member State where such supplier is responsible for delivery of the goods.

Where the value of distance sales to the State by a supplier in another Member State exceeds or is likely to exceed IR £27,565 in a year, (£35,000) that supplier must register for VAT in the State and must account for VAT at the appropriate Irish rates. If the threshold is not exceeded, the supplier may, nevertheless, opt to register and account for VAT in the State on his or her distance sales. Alternatively, the supplier may apply to Revenue to have a fiscal representative appointed to act in relation to his or her VAT obligations in the State.

Foreign firms making distance sales of excisable goods (spirits, tobacco etc) are obliged to register for VAT irrespective of the level of turnover.

6 Agents

In many cases, foreign firms have agents or representatives in this country who take orders and transmit them to their principals abroad. In some cases the principals send back the orders directly to the customer and, in other cases, to the agent or representative for distribution.

Where orders are sent to its agent or representative for distribution the foreign firm must register even if the agent holds only a small stock of goods and irrespective of the level turnover. Agents or representatives of foreign firms ought normally to be registered on their own account. Such agents should not quote their own VAT numbers in connection with the importation of goods by their principals nor account for VAT in respect of the intra-Community acquisition of such goods.

7 Fiscal Representatives

Where a trader is established in another EU Member State but is making taxable supplies or intra-Community acquisitions in Ireland he or she may appoint, or the Revenue Commissioners may appoint, a fiscal representative. The fiscal representative thus appointed becomes jointly and severally liable with the foreign based trader. The fiscal representative will normally also act on behalf of the trader insofar as other aspects of VAT are concerned (eg completion of the VAT return).

8 Stock supplied from another Member State and held in Ireland for onward supply to a customer in the State.

Where a foreign firm sends consignment stock from another Member State to Ireland for the use of customers then the foreign firm is not obliged to register for VAT. The VAT will be accounted for by means of intra-Community acquisition by the customer when the stock is drawn off. The warehouse keeper must in all cases be independent of, that is not an employee or agent of, the supplier.

9 Building Sub-contractors

Foreign building sub-contractors carrying out work in the State may have Relevant Contracts Tax (known as withholding tax) deducted from their payments. Application for repayment of this tax can be made to the Revenue Commissioners, Nenagh. However, before such repayment will be made verification that VAT has been correctly accounted for will be carried out.

Further details regarding this tax can be obtained by contacting the **Revenue Commissioners Office, Nenagh, Co. Tipperary (telephone 067–33533).**

10 Supply and installation/assembly

Foreign firms which consign goods direct to Irish customers and subsequently supply the service of installation or assembly are liable to VAT on the full consideration received including the amount for the goods themselves. Such traders are obliged to register and account for VAT in Ireland.

11 Goods consigned from outside the EU by foreign firms direct to Irish customers

In the case of goods consigned by foreign firms direct to Irish customers from outside the EU including postal packets exceeding IR £500 (£634.87) in value it is primarily a matter for the importer or his agent (usually the shipping company or a customs clearance firm) to present the necessary entry documents to the Customs. Any VAT (or duty) payable is a matter for the importer.

In the case of parcel post importation's exceeding IR £200 (£253.95) but not exceeding IR £500 (£634.87) in value the goods are assessed by Customs and any VAT payable is collected from the consignee by An Post.

In the case of parcel post importations not exceeding IR £200 (£253.95) in value, if the consignee is registered for Irish VAT his registration number should be shown on the Customs declarations form affixed to or accompanying the parcel. This declarations form must show the nature and value of the goods enclosed in the parcel.

The VAT due in respect of the importation of these goods will be deferred but must be accounted for in the VAT return for the period.

12 Foreign firms purchasing goods/services in the State

The general position is that a person who is engaged in business outside the State and who is not engaged in business in the State may claim repayment of Irish VAT on most business purchases in Ireland. The main conditions governing repayment are:

(*a*) the claimant must produce a certificate that he is VAT-registered in another Member State of the EU (this condition does, not, of course, apply to claimants from outside the EU);

(*b*) the goods/services giving rise to the claim must be goods/services in respect of which tax would be deductible if the claimant's business was carried on in Ireland and must not include goods for supply within the State or *certain motor vehicles for hiring out for utilisation within the State;

(*c*) the business for which the goods/services were purchased must be a business which would be taxable if carried on in Ireland.

*certain motor vehicles in this context means motor vehicles designed and constructed for the conveyance of persons by road and sports motor vehicles, estate cars, station wagons, motor cycles, motor scooters, mopeds and auto cycles, whether our not designed and constructed for the purpose aforesaid, excluding vehicles designed and constructed for the carriage of more than 16 persons (inclusive of the driver), invalid carriages and other vehicles of a type designed for use by invalids or infirm persons.

All enquiries relating to repayments to foreign firms not registered for VAT in the State should be made to the **Accountant-General, Revenue Commissioners, Kilrush Road, Ennis, Co. Clare (telephone 065–41200).** Similarly, claim forms can be obtained from that office.

13 Zero rating of services supplied to foreign traders (VAT 60A Procedure)

Foreign traders in receipt of taxable services from Irish traders **on a regular and continuous basis** may apply to have those services concessionally relieved from VAT. In this way, the necessity of applying to the Revenue Commissioners for VAT repayments is avoided.

Application for relief is made by way of Form VAT 60A. Traders established in EU Member States must submit a certificate of taxable status with their applications. Form VAT 60A is available from the **Office of the Accountant General, Revenue Commissioners, Kilrush Road, Ennis, Co. Clare.**

The relief is subject to periodic review, is valid for two years, but may be renewed on application. **The relief does not apply to supplies of taxable goods.**

14 Payment of tax by foreign sender (F.D.D.)

Under the system known internationally as Franc de Droits (F.D.D.) it may be possible for a sender in a non EU country to pay the tax and duty on goods imported by post into this country to the postal authorities in the country of despatch. The VAT will be transferred to the Customs authorities in this country through An Post to whom enquiries in the matter should be made.

15 Other taxes (Income Tax Corporation Tax. P.A.Y.E., P.R.S.I., etc)

Information about the other taxes for which a foreign trader may become liable can be obtained from **Taxes Central Registration Office, Arus Brugha, 9/15 Upper O'Connell St., Dublin 1. (Tel. 01–8746821).**

16 Further Information

Any additional queries should be addressed to the local Inspector of Taxes (Appendix).
Revenue Commissioners
March 1999

Contact addresses can be found in Revenue Addresses at start of book

VAT TREATMENT OF BUILDING AND ASSOCIATED SERVICES

Introduction

1. Contractors operating in the building industry have the same obligation to comply with VAT law as other VAT-registered traders.

This Information Leaflet describes how VAT is applied to the various goods and services associated with the industry.

Building and other contractors

2. All contractors operating in the building industry, including building contractors themselves, as well as electrical, plumbing, plastering, heating, painting, roofing and flooring contractors, carry on a taxable business and are therefore obliged to register for VAT if their annual turnover exceeds or is likely to exceed £20,000 (£25,394).

This limit does not apply to non-established contractors operating in the State, irrespective of their turnover.

VAT-registered contractors are entitled, in the same way as other taxable persons are, to deduct the VAT properly invoiced to them by their suppliers, and where this results in an excess over VAT payable by them in a particular VAT period, they may claim a repayment on the VAT 3 return form.

Application of the 12.5 per cent rate

3. The 12.5 per cent rate of VAT applies to most activities carried on by building contractors and other contractors operating in the building sector. It normally applies, therefore, to house building and construction work generally; to building renovation and demolition; to building maintenance and repair; to the installation of plumbing, heating and electrical services; and to the supply, installation, maintenance and repair of fixtures. The 12.5 per cent rate applies also to the supply and placing in a fixed position of garden sheds, greenhouses and similar structures, subject to certain conditions.

The 12.5 per cent rate does not apply to the supply only of any building materials other than ready to pour concrete and concrete blocks, nor does it apply to the supply and fitting, or fitting only, of fittings, as distinct from fixtures.

Fixtures

4. Fixtures are goods which have become attached to buildings in such a way that they cannot be removed without substantial damage being caused to the goods themselves or to the building to which they are attached. In the case of houses, fixtures could, as a general rule, be said to include the basic structural items normally to be found in a new, unfurnished, standard house. Fixtures would not however include carpets and other floor coverings, cookers, hobs, gas and electric fires and the like.

It is important to note that, apart from ready to pour concrete and concrete blocks, the supply only of goods does not qualify for the 12.5 per cent rate of VAT even though the goods may ultimately become fixtures. For example, the supply only of kitchen units to a builder is chargeable at 21 per cent even though the units, when installed in a building by the builder, may be chargeable at 12.5 per cent (see paragraph 8 below on the two-thirds rule). The builder, of course, is entitled to full deduction for the tax charged to him or her on the unit, subject to the usual conditions. The installation only or the maintenance and repair of fixtures is normally taxable at 12.5 per cent, unless the two-thirds rule applies.

Examples are at paragraph 5 below.

Fixtures which qualify for the 12.5 per cent rate

5. The following are examples of goods which are regarded as qualifying for the 12.5 per cent rate of VAT *once they have been permanently installed as fixtures* and subject, of course, to the two-thirds rule.

Advertising hoardings

Air-conditioning equipment

Airdomes

Attic insulation

Attic ladders

Baths Blinds — certain types, for example where rail is countersunk into the ceiling or parapet

Burglar alarms

Canopies (at filling stations)

Central heating systems

Cold rooms (excluding free-standing type)

Counters (excluding free-standing type)

Curtain rails (fixed)

Double glazing

Electrical wiring down to and including lampholders, power points and fuse boards

Fencing posts

Fire escapes

Fireplaces

Built-in kitchen units

Built-in wardrobes and presses

Floor covering stuck down over its entire surface

Foam insulation (injected into cavity walls)

Gates

Generators

Headstones (fixed)

Immersion heaters

Lifts and associated machinery

Milking parlour equipment

Mirrored tiles and similar fixed wall-coverings

PABX telephone systems

Partitioning

Pelmets (fixed)

Prefabricated buildings (subject to conditions)

Recessed lighting (excluding light tubes and lamps)

Roller shutters

Sewage treatment plants

Sinks

Sliding door equipment

Slurry tanks (fixed)

Storage heaters/radiators

Storage tanks for oil or water for heating etc systems

Strong room (in banks)

Switch equipment

Traffic signalling equipment

Weighbridges

Window cleaning rails (for cradle)

Window guards (wire mesh)

Fittings

6. As distinct from fixtures, fittings are goods which, though often attached to buildings, can be removed without substantial damage being caused to the goods themselves or to the building to which they are attached. They are therefore subject to the 21 per cent rate.

Examples are as follows:

Blinds — most types

Clocks including time clocks such as flexitime equipment

Cooker hoods

Curtains

Electric and gas fires

Exhibition stands

Fitted carpets and lino, other than floor covering stuck down over its entire surface

Free-standing shop counters

Kitchen cookers

Lighting other than recessed lighting

Mirrors

Most shelving

Refrigeration units, including deep freezes

Safes (certain)

Seating, including cinema and church seating whether or not secured to the floor

Snooker tables and other games tables

Washing machines and dishwashers, including plumbed-in machines.

The supply, or supply and fitting for a single inclusive charge, of these goods is chargeable to VAT at 21 per cent. For example the supply and fitting of a kitchen cooker for an inclusive charge is liable at 21 per cent. If, however, it was necessary to re-wire for a power supply point and a separate charge was raised for such work, the 12.5 per cent rate would apply to that separate charge. The connection only of the cooker to an existing power supply would however be subject to 21 per cent.

VAT on a typical building job

7. The following sets out in very general terms how VAT applies at the various stages of building contracts. The rate of VAT on building jobs is generally 12.5 per cent. The rate of VAT on fittings is 21 per cent.

Sequence of Events	VAT Liability
(i) Tender	Not governed by VAT law. Obviously the contractor, in his or her own interest, should make it clear whether his or her tender price is inclusive or exclusive of VAT. The customer, especially if not registered for VAT, will probably wish to know how much, in total, he or she is being quoted and accordingly it may be advisable to give the rate and amount of VAT if tendering on a tax-exclusive basis. While the rate of VAT will generally be 12.5 per cent there are circumstances where this is not so.
(ii) Award of contract	Not governed by VAT law.
(iii) Deposit (or payment in advance)	Tax payable by reference to taxable period within which payment is received, whether the contractor is on the sales or the moneys received basis. A VAT invoice in respect of payments received must be issued within the required time limit to customers who are registered for VAT. It does not have to be issued to unregistered customers but may be if it suits the contractor's business convenience.

(iv) Contractor's progress account	Tax not payable at time of issue. Account does not rank as VAT invoice.
(v) Progress payment to contractor	Tax payable by reference to taxable period within which payment is received, whether the contractor is on the sales or moneys received basis. A VAT invoice must be issued as at (iii) above.
(vi) Certificate from architect, engineer, etc	Certificate does not rank as a VAT invoice.
(vii) Final payment to contractor (excluding retention money)	Tax payable by reference to taxable period within which payment is received, whether the contractor is on the sales or moneys received basis. A VAT invoice must be issued as at (iii) and (v) above and must show VAT on the final payment only and not on the full consideration.
(viii) Retention money	(b) Tax payable by reference to the taxable period within which money is received if contractor is on the moneys received basis. A VAT invoice must be issued when guarantee period expires if customer is registered for VAT.
	(b) Tax payable by reference to the taxable period within which money is received if contractor is on the moneys received basis. A VAT invoice must be issued when guarantee period expires if customer is registered for VAT.

The two-thirds rule

8. The rate of VAT applying to services, including building services, depends on the two-thirds rule. This provides that a transaction is liable to VAT as a sale of goods at the appropriate rate, and not as a service, if the value of the goods used in providing the service (that is, their cost, excluding VAT, to the service contractor) exceeds two-thirds of the total VAT exclusive charge to the customer.

The two-thirds rule does not usually affect building services in which the labour element is substantial. It would be likely to come into operation in the case of a service consisting of the supply and installation of, say, a transformer or a strong room. The possibility of its application should never

be overlooked and contractors should consult their local Inspector of Taxes if there is any doubt about the correct liability to VAT. Sub-contractors, in particular, may find that the 21 per cent rate may apply to their portion of a main contract even though the main contract may itself be liable at the 12.5 per cent rate.

Do-it-yourself (DIY)

9. Building materials, with the exception of ready to pour concrete and concrete blocks to which the 12.5 per cent rate applies, are liable at 21 per cent. There is no provision for the repayment to private individuals who do their own building work of any excess of tax charged on building materials over the 12.5 per cent rate which would be chargeable if the work was done by a contractor registered for VAT.

Property transactions

10. VAT on dealings in land and buildings (property) is the subject of separate booklets and leaflets which may be obtained from any local Tax Office, as listed.

As a general rule property does not attract a liability to VAT unless all the following conditions are satisfied:—

(a) the property must have been developed in whole or in part after 31 October, 1972;

(b) the vendor must have a taxable interest in the property;

(c) the vendor must have disposed of a taxable interest in the property;

(d) the disposal must have been made in the course or furtherance of business; and

(e) the circumstances must have been such that the person disposing of the interest was entitled to a tax credit for any tax suffered in relation to the development or the acquisition of his or her interest.

All these matters and others, including the valuation of interests, together with assignments and surrenders are discussed in booklets entitled "Property Transactions" and "VAT on Property — Finance Act, 1997 Changes" which should always be consulted.

In addition, two Information Leaflets namely VAT on Property — claims for repayment for periods prior to 27 March 1998 (No. 3/98) and VAT on Property — VAT treatment of post-letting expenses for periods on or after 27 March 1998 (No. 4/98) are available.

Enquiries

11. Enquiries should be made to the appropriate local Tax Office. See list at Appendix attached.
Revenue Commissioners
September, 1999.

INFORMATION LEAFLET NO 3/99

VAT TREATMENT OF INTERNATIONAL LEASING
OF MEANS OF TRANSPORT

1 Introduction

This leaflet sets out the VAT treatment of international leasing of means of transport. It outlines the changes in the VAT treatment of such leasing services having regard to the European Court of Justice judgment in the case of ARO Lease BV against Inspector der Belastingdienst Grote Ondernemingen Amsterdam (Case C–190/95) referred to as the "ARO" case. It outlines the changes in relation to leasing in the Finance Acts of 1998 and 1999, resulting from the judgment.

The information leaflet clarifies the meaning of "established" in the context of the ARO case and sets out the VAT treatment of the leasing of cars and other means of transport supplied by a lessor established in one country to a customer in another.

2 The ARO judgment

The judgment dealt with car leasing from the Netherlands into Belgium. The lessor (ARO Lease BV) was established in the Netherlands. It had no administrative or physical presence in Belgium but it had 800 (out of 6,800) of its vehicles leased to customers in Belgium. Both the Dutch and the Belgian tax authorities sought to collect VAT on the leases to Belgian customers.

The ECJ held that

> "a leasing company established in one Member State does not supply services from a fixed establishment in another Member State if it makes passenger cars available in the second State under leasing agreements to customers established there, if its customers have entered into contact with it through self-employed intermediaries established in the second State, if they have chosen their cars from dealers established in the second State, if the leasing company has acquired the cars in the second State, in which they are registered, and has made them available to its customers under leasing agreements drawn up and signed at its main place of business, and if the customers bear maintenance costs and pay road tax in the second State, but the leasing company does not have an office or any premises on which to store the cars there".

In short, the judgment describes the precise circumstances of the ARO case and says that in those circumstances, the place of supply and of taxation is the Member State of the lessor.

The question of whether the hire or lease of vehicles by an undertaking in one Member State to customers in another Member State constituted a "fixed establishment" was further addressed in the ECJ case of Lease Plan Luxembourg SA and the Belgian State (Case C–390/96). On this point the Court ruled......

> "that an undertaking established in one Member State which hires out or leases a number of vehicles to clients established in another Member State **does not**

possess a fixed establishment in that other State merely by engaging in that hiring out or leasing".

3 Implications for Ireland

Prior to the ARO judgment Revenue took the view that a lessor in one Member State which hired out means of transport to customers in another Member State had established its business in the State in which the vehicles and customers were located. Accordingly, liability to VAT arose in the second Member State. To comply with the principle enunciated in the ARO and Lease Plan judgments, Revenue has revised its treatment of cross-border leasing transactions. The principle established by the rulings of the ECJ is that where a lessor in one Member State hires or leases vehicles to customers in another Member State the place of supply is the Member State where the lessor has established its business.

4 Meaning of Establishment.

The Sixth VAT Directive does not define "established" or "establishment" but establishment has been defined for the purposes of Irish VAT law.

"Establishment" means

> "any fixed place of business, but does not include a place of business of an agent of a person unless the agent has and habitually exercises general authority to negotiate the terms of and makes agreements on behalf of the person or has a stock of goods with which he regularly fulfils on behalf of the person agreements for the supply of goods".

The question of determining the place of establishment will depend on the facts of each case. Neither ARO nor Lease Plan was deemed to have an establishment in the Member State in which the vehicles were hired out. The Court found that independent garages which facilitated the leasing company's customers in arranging provision of the leased vehicles did not constitute an establishment of the lessor. However, the relationship between the supplier of the goods, any agent who acts on behalf of the lessor and the lessor will have to be examined in order to determine whether the lessor is established in the State.

Accordingly, where Revenue is satisfied that:

— the leasing arrangements are entered into by a lessor established in another Member State by means of agreements drawn up and signed, and management decisions taken in that Member State in which it has established its business,

— the vehicles are made available under those leasing arrangements to customers in the State and

— the lessor has no staff, or fixed establishment or a structure adequate, in terms of human and technical resources, to supply the services in the State,

the leasing services will be regarded as supplied in the other Member State.

Where a lessor established in another Member State leases vehicles to customers here and has either an establishment here or a structure adequate, in terms of human and technical resources, to supply the services in question, the services are regarded as supplied in the State and the lessor will be liable for Irish VAT.

5 How the effects of the judgment apply in practice.

The practical effect of the application of the ARO judgment to leasing of means of transport involving domestic and international suppliers is best demonstrated in a series of charts, as follows:—

Chart A — describes the treatment of leasing of cars.

Chart B — describes the treatment of leasing of deductible means of transport to VAT registered lessees.

Chart C — describes the leasing of rail-cars, buses, aircraft etc to passenger transport undertakings.

These Charts are at Appendix I.

6 What are Means of Transport?

Although "new means of transport" is defined in section 1 of the Value Added Tax Act, 1972 and "means of transport" is defined for the purposes of the special scheme for second-hand cars in section 12B, in general terms, including for the purposes of a leasing transaction a broader definition is applied. "Means of transport" is taken to mean motor vehicles and other equipment and devices, which might be pulled or drawn by such vehicles, and are normally used for carrying out a transport contract, as well, of course, as vessels and aircraft.

7 Deductibility

One of the consequences of the change in the treatment of cross-border leasing of means of transport was a review of our deductibility rules. Prior to the passing of the Finance Act 1998, Section 13 (3) of the Value Added Tax Act prohibited the refund of VAT to foreign leasing companies which purchased vehicles (either commercial vehicles or passenger cars) for hiring out in the State. Section 13 (3) was amended in the Finance Act, 1998, to provide that a lessor established outside the State will be able to get a VAT refund on means of transport (apart from motor cars — see definition at Appendix II) purchased here for the purpose of leasing out to customers here.

The revised position is reflected in Charts A, B and C.

A taxable person in another Member State, which has leasing services supplied to it by a lessor established in the State on an ongoing basis and which is entitled to reclaim the VAT chargeable on those leasing services under the 8th Directive, may apply to the Revenue Commissioners to have the services treated as subject to the zero rate under the VAT 60A procedure. Any relief so granted is subject to periodic review. The relief does not apply to supplies of goods. (Application Form VAT 60A is available from VAT Repayments Section, Government Buildings, Ennis, Co. Clare).

8 Leasing to a passenger transport undertaking

At present, Revenue concessionally allows the place of supply in relation to certain leasing services to be outside the State. Essentially this concession relates to leasing of means of transport by lessors established in the State to passenger transport undertakings in other Member States. Following a review of the implications of the judgment this concession will no longer apply from 1 November 1999. Where a leasing agreement started while the concession applied, leasing services relating to the period from 1 November should operate under the new rules.

However, as indicated in Chart C, Revenue will allow a refund of VAT in relation to the leasing of means of transport to passenger transport undertakings in other Member States on the basis that the undertakings are engaged in passenger transport outside the State (ie transport effected entirely outside Ireland or transport between Ireland and another country) and provided they meet the 8th Directive requirements. The 60A procedure referred to at paragraph 7 above may apply.

9 Leasing to lessees outside the European Community

Section 121 of the Finance Act, 1999 inserted a new paragraph (*dddd*) into section 5 (6) of the VAT Act, 1972. This paragraph provides that the place of supply of the leasing of means of transport by a lessor in the State is outside the European Community where the means of transport are to be effectively used and enjoyed outside the Community. This means that the leasing of, for example, railway rolling stock for use in the United States by a lessor established in Ireland is not subject to Irish VAT. The lessor is of course entitled to deduction of his or her inputs relating to this activity in the normal way or to a refund under the 13th Directive.

10 Effective use and enjoyment

Effective use and enjoyment is not defined in the VAT Act. This provision is based on Article 9.3 of the Sixth Directive. The purpose of this provision is to allow Member States to treat services which are consumed outside the European Community as outside the scope of EU VAT.

If there is any doubt about whether the use and enjoyment takes place outside the Community a lessor should charge VAT. In addition while the use and enjoyment of a means of transport at the start of the leasing agreement may be outside the Community, a lessor is responsible for ensuring that the correct VAT treatment is applied to the leasing service for the full period of the lease. Therefore, if during the period of the lease agreement the lessee transfers the means of transport to a Member State, VAT should be charged on the leasing service when the conditions of section 5 (6) (*dddd*) no longer apply.

11 Further Information

Further information can be obtained from the local Tax Office (see Appendix III).

Revenue Commissioners,

Dublin Castle.

July, 1999.

APPENDIX I

Chart A

Leasing of Means of Transport

Motor Vehicles (Cars, motor cycles and other vehicles as defined in section 12 (3)(b) of the Value Added Tax Act, 1972).[1]

VAT Treatment

	Place of establishment of Lessor	Lessee established or resident in	Place of taxation of Leasing Services	Deductibility		
				On acquisition of the Vehicle by the Lessor		On Lease rental charged to VAT — registered lessee
				Sourced in Ireland	Sourced in OMS	
1	Ireland	OMS	Ireland	Yes[2]	OMS/8th Directive rules apply	No
2	OMS	Ireland	OMS	No. Section 13(3)(c) of VAT Act	OMS/8th Directive rules apply on purchase of car in OMS ICA on arrival in the State. VAT payable not deductible.(Section 13 (3) (c)) OMS rules apply on purchase of car in OMS. ICA on arrival in the State. Deductible	OMS rules apply
3	Outside the EU	Ireland	Ireland [3]	Yes (lessor is obliged to register for VAT in the State)		No.
4	Ireland	Outside the EU	Outside EU. Section 5(6)(dddd)[4]	Yes	OMS/8th Directive rules apply. ICA on arrival in the State. Deductible	N/A

OMS = Other Member State

ICA = Intra-Community acquisition.

[1] "motor vehicles" means motor vehicles designed and constructed for the conveyance of persons by road and sports motor vehicles, estate cars, station wagons, motor cycles, motor scooters, mopeds and auto cycles, whether or not designed and constructed for the purpose aforesaid, excluding vehicles designed and constructed for the carriage of more than 16 persons (inclusive of the driver), invalid carriages and other vehicles of a type designed for use by invalids or infirm persons.

[2] OMS rules apply on intra-Community acquisition of the vehicle in the OMS.

[3] or if effectively used outside the State, the place where the vehicles are effectively used.

[4] Section 5(6)(dddd) introduced in Finance Act, 1999 (see paragraph 9) if effectively used and enjoyed outside the EU.

Chart B					
Leasing of Means of Transport					
Leasing of deductible Means of Transport (Vans/lorries etc to VAT-Registered persons).					
VAT Treatment					
	Place of establishment of Lessor	Lessee established or resident in	Place of Taxation of Leasing Service	Deductibility		
				On acquisition by the Lessor		On Lease rental charged to VAT — registered lessee
				Sourced in Ireland	Sourced in OMS	
1	Ireland	OMS	Ireland	Yes[1]	OMS/8th Directive rules apply.	Yes (8th Directive)
2	OMS	Ireland	OMS	Yes under 8th Directive rules	OMS/8th Directive rules apply. ICA on arrival in the State. VAT payable is deductible (Section 13(3)(c)).	OMS rules apply
3	Outside the EU	Ireland	Ireland[2]	Yes (lessor is obliged to register for VAT in the State)	OMS rules apply on purchase in OMS. ICA on arrival in the State. Deductible.	Yes
4	Ireland	Outside the EU	Outside EU Section 5(6)(dddd)[3]	Yes	OMS/8th Directive rules apply. ICA on arrival in the State. Deductible.	N/A

OMS = Other Member State

ICA = Intra-Community acquisition

[1] OMS rules apply on intra-Community acquisition in the OMS.

[2] or if effectively used outside the State, the place where effectively used.

[3] Section 5(6)(*dddd*) introduced in Finance Act, 1999 (see paragraph 9) if effectively used and enjoyed outside the EU.

Chart C
Leasing of Means of Transport
Leasing of Means of Transport to Passenger Transport Undertakings (rail — cars, buses, aircraft etc).
VAT Treatment

	Place of establishment of Lessor	Lessee established or resident in	Place of Taxation of Leasing Service	Deductibility		
				On acquisition by the Lessor		On Lease rental charged to lessee (ie the passenger transport undertaking)
				Sourced in Ireland	Sourced in OMS	
1	Ireland	OMS	Ireland	Yes[1]	OMS/8th Directive rules apply	Yes[2]
2	OMS	Ireland	OMS	Yes under 8th Directive rules	OMS/8th Directive rules on purchase. ICA on arrival in the State. Deductible.	OMS/8th Directive rules
3	Outside the EU	Ireland	Ireland	Yes (lessor is obliged to register for VAT in the State)	OMS/8th Directive rules on purchase. ICA on arrival in the State. Deductible.	No[2]
4	Ireland	Outside the EU	Outside EU. Section 5 (6) (*dddd*)[4]	Yes	N/A	

OMS = Other Member State
ICA = Intra-Community acquisition.

[1]   OMS rules apply on intra-Community acquisition in OMS
[2]   Deductible to the extent that the lessee is an undertaking engaged in passenger transport services outside the State (see paragraph 8).
[3]   Or if effectively used outside the State the place where the goods are effectively used.
[4]   Section 5(6)(dddd) introduced in Finance Act 1999 (see paragraph 9) if effectively used and enjoyed outside the EU.

Appendix II
Value Added Tax Act, 1972
Section 12 (3)(b)

"Motor vehicles" means motor vehicles designed and constructed for the conveyance of persons by road and sports motor vehicles, estate cars, station wagons, motor cycles, motor scooters, mopeds and auto cycles, whether or not designed and constructed for the purpose aforesaid, excluding vehicles designed and constructed for the carriage of more than 16 persons (inclusive of the driver), invalid carriages and other vehicles of a type designed for use by invalids or infirm persons.

Contact addresses can be found in Revenue Addresses at start of book

EXPLANATORY LEAFLET ON VALUE ADDED TAX IN THE CASE OF CHARITIES

PART 1

Does Value Added Tax (VAT) Apply to Charities?

Yes, there is **no** general exemption in respect of Value Added Tax for organisations which have been granted charitable tax exemption. *There are, however, specific reliefs from VAT in certain circumstances and, where appropriate, such reliefs may also be availed of by charities (see Part 2 of this leaflet).*

Must a Charity register and account for VAT?

Charities are not, in the normal course, regarded as supplying goods or services in the course or furtherance of a business and as such are neither obliged nor entitled to register and account for VAT on their income. They are not therefore entitled to a repayment of VAT incurred on their purchases other than in the specific circumstances provided for in Part 2 of this leaflet. Charities carrying on a trade eg the sale of publications, operating a restaurant etc are however obliged to register for VAT in respect of such trading activities subject to the threshold for registration, currently £40,000 for the sale of goods, being exceeded.

It should be noted that a Charity or any other group engaged in non-commercial activity which acquires or is likely to acquire more than £32,000 worth of goods from another EU Member State in any period of twelve months is obliged to register and account for VAT in respect of such intra-Community acquisition(s). Registration does not give VAT deduction rights to the charity. Similarly, a charity is obliged to register and account for VAT on certain services received from abroad irrespective of the level of expenditure involved. These services are typically the services of consultants, lawyers, accountants etc. Further details in this regard can be obtained from your local tax office.

If, as a charity, you are required to register for VAT you must complete form STR (in the case of an unincorporated body) or form TR2 (in the case of a limited company) which is obtainable from the Taxes Central Registration Office, Arus Brugha, 9/15 Upper O'Connell St, Dublin 1 Tel: 01–8746821 or from your local tax office.

PART 2

Specific reliefs from VAT and which may relate to charitable activities

1. Organisations involved in the transport of severely and permanently physically disabled persons

Repayment of VAT paid may be claimed in relation to the purchase and adaptation of vehicles for use by organisations for the transport of severely and permanently disabled persons. A qualifying organisation means a philanthropic organisation which is not funded primarily by the State, by any board established by statute, or by any public or local authority. The organisation must be chiefly engaged, in a voluntary capacity and on a non-commercial basis, in the care and transport of severely and permanently physically disabled persons and is recognised as such by the Revenue Commissioners.

There is provision for the repayment or reduction of Vehicle Registration Tax (VRT) under this heading also.

2. Radios for the blind

Section 20(2) VAT Act 1972 provides for repayment of VAT paid in respect of radio broadcasting reception apparatus intended for use by blind persons. The repayment is only made to the institution/society if it shows to the satisfaction of the Revenue Commissioners that:

— its primary object is the amelioration of the lot of blind persons; and,

— the goods in question are intended for the use of blind persons.

Repayment claim form VAT 59 refers.

3. Appliances for use by Disabled Persons

Statutory Instrument No. 428/81 provides for repayment of VAT on certain aids and appliances purchased by or on behalf of a disabled person which assist that disabled person in the performance of essential daily functions or in the exercise of a vocation eg stair-lifts.

Repayment claim form VAT 61A refers.

4. Sea rescue craft and equipment

Statutory Instrument No. 192/85 enables VAT on certain small reserve craft (15 tons gross tonnage or less), ancillary equipment and special boat buildings and also on the hire, repair and maintenance of these craft, to be repaid to qualifying sea rescue groups.

Repayment claim form VAT 70 refers.

5. Humanitarian Goods for Export

Statutory Instrument No. 308/87 provides relief from VAT for goods purchased for exportation by philanthropic organisations for humanitarian, charitable or teaching activities abroad eg Apostolic Societies, Chernobyl Children Projects etc.

Repayment claim form VAT 73 refers.

6. Donated medical equipment

Statutory Instrument No. 58/92 provides for repayment of VAT suffered by a hospital or a donor on the purchase of new medical instruments and appliances (excluding means of transport) which are funded by voluntary donations. The VAT refund may be claimed by whomever suffers the tax ie the hospital or the donor, as appropriate, but not, of course, both. The principal conditions are that the instrument or appliance must:

— cost £20,000 or more (exclusive of VAT);

— be designed and manufactured for use solely in medical research or in diagnosis, prevention or treatment of illness;

— not have been part-funded by the State, and

— be the subject of a recommendation by the Minister for Health that, having regard to the requirements of the health services in the State, a refund of the VAT would be appropriate.

Repayment claim form VAT 72 refers.

7. Donated Research Equipment

Statutory Instrument No. 38/95 provides for repayment of VAT, incurred in the purchase or importation of any new instrument or appliance (excluding means of transport) through voluntary donations, to a research institution or a university, school or similar educational body engaged in medical research in a laboratory. The principal conditions are that the instrument or appliance must:

— cost £20,000 or more (exclusive of VAT);

— be designed and manufactured for use in medical research;

— not have been part-funded by the State, and

— be the subject of a recommendation by the Health Research Board that, having regard to the requirements of medical research in the State, a refund of the VAT would be appropriate.

Repayment claim form VAT 72A refers.

Addresses for further Contact

Repayment of VAT	Claim Form	Contact Address
1. Vehicle purchased by an organisation for the transport of severely and permanently disabled persons	DDO	Central Repayments Office Revenue Commissioners Coolshannagh Monaghan Tel: 047–82800 Fax: 047–82782
2. Radios for the Blind	VAT 59	VAT Repayments (Unregistered Section) Accountant General's Office Revenue Commissioners Government Offices Kilrush Road Ennis Tel: 065–6841200 Fax: 065–6840394
3. Appliances for use by disabled persons	VAT 61A	
4. Sea rescue craft and equipment	VAT 70	
5. Humanitarian Goods for Export	VAT 73	
6. Donated Medical Equipment	VAT 72	
7. Donated Research Equipment	VAT 72A	

Further Information:

You can obtain further information, should you require it, by contacting your local tax office.

Issued June, 1999 - Office of the Revenue Commissioners,
Charities Section,
Government Offices,
Nenagh,
Co. Tipperary.

Tel: 067–33533 or 6774211 for callers from Dublin Fax: 067–32916

While every effort is made to ensure that the information given in this leaflet is accurate, it is not a legal document. Responsibility cannot be accepted for any liability incurred or loss suffered as a consequence of relying on any matter published herein.

VAT — CLAIMS AND PAYMENTS

HELP US TO HELP YOU MAKING A CORRECT VAT 3 RETURN

Delays in processing VAT returns are often caused by simple clerical errors in preparing the return.

It is in your interest that your return is correct whether you are making a claim or a payment.

Do not submit invoices with your return.

You should retain these for examination by the Inspector of Taxes.

VAT 3 CHECKLIST

Is your correct name and VAT number on the VAT 3?

Have you used an original VAT form?

- a photocopy MUST NOT be used.

If you did not receive or have lost the original form, phone us and we will immediately supply a new one.

Have you completed your return in ink?

- details in pencil are not acceptable.

Is the return signed?

Are all your entries on the return form legible?

Have you accounted for acquisitions from other EU countries?

Is the declaration arithmetically correct?

- if you are making a payment, use box T3

the figure in box T3 should be the T1 minus the T2 figure

- if you are making a claim, us box T4

the figure in box T4 should be the T2 minus the T1 figure

Have you supplied the Collector-General with details of your Bank/Building Society Account Number and Sort Code for repayment directly to your account?

A separate help leaflet is available on this subject

Have you completed boxes E1 & E2?

- "NIL" must be inserted if there are no entries being made

KEEP THIS CHECKLIST

Use it each time you complete your return.

By doing so, you help us to improve our service to you.

Completed VAT return forms should be sent to:—
Office of the Collector-General,

Sarsfield House,

Francis Street,

Limerick

Further enquiries relating to a VAT Repayment claim should be made to
The Office of the Accountant General,

Revenue Commissioners,

Kilrush Road,

Ennis,

Co. Clare.

LO Call: 1890 20 20 33

Telephone: (065) 6841200 Fax: (065) 6841366

BANK DETAILS

It is important that you supply the Collector-General with current details of your Bank/
Building Society account Number and Sort code, in order to facilitate repayment
directly to your account. You should always advise the Collector-General in the event of
you moving your account, in order that your subsequent repayments may remain
correctly credited to you

A separate leaflet on "Direct VAT Repayment" is available from all Revenue Enquiry
Offices or by telephoning the Collector-General at the number relevant to your
registration number above.

LEAFLETS AVAILABLE IN THIS RANGE

CG2: Due Dates, Payments and Returns

CG3: Payments to the Collector-General

CG4: Change of Address

CG5: VAT — Claims and Repayments

CG6: P35 End-of-Year Return

In addition, a leaflet is available on Direct.

(November 2001)

PRINTING AND PRINTED MATTER

1 Introduction

1.1. The scope of each of the three rates of VAT (zero, 12.5 and 20 per cent) in relation to the supply of printed matter is set out in detail in the following paragraphs. The general position is that books are zero rated, newspapers and periodicals are subject to 12.5 per cent and stationery and other printed matter are liable at the standard rate of 20 per cent. This information leaflet updates and replaces *Statement of Practice SP- VAT/ 10/94.*

It should be noted that the 20 per cent rate will increase to 21 per cent from 1 March, 2002.

2 Printing

2.1. Printing includes all forms of reproduction ie lithography; off-set; heliography; photogravure; engraving; duplicating; embossing; photography etc in letters of any alphabet, figures, shorthand or other symbols, braille characters, musical notations, pictures or diagrams.

2.2. The rate chargeable for printing depends on the product being printed. For example, the printing of books qualifies for the zero rate while the printing of newspapers and periodicals attracts VAT at the 12.5 per cent rate.

3 Zero-rated printed matter

3.1. The zero-rate of VAT applies to printed books and booklets including atlases. It also covers children's picture, drawing and colouring books, and books of music. Annual publications, even a periodical which is published once a year as a special edition which does **not** replace, for example, the standard monthly edition are liable to VAT at zero per cent. In order to qualify for the zero rate, a publication must meet the four requirements listed hereunder:—

   (i)   it must consist essentially of textual or pictorial matter

   (ii) it must have a distinctive cover, that is at least the outside of the front cover must be devoid of text,

   (iii) it must comprise not less than four leaves (eight pages) exclusive of the cover, and

   (iv) it must be bound (loose-leaf or otherwise), or stitched or stapled.

3.2. Parts of large works published over a limited and pre-determined period including a related binder supplied free of charge are **not** regarded as periodicals, and provided they qualify as printed books or booklets or will qualify as such when the series is completed, are zero-rated.

4 Printed matter liable at the 12.5 per cent rate

— **All newspapers and periodicals are liable at the 12.5 per cent rate.** This includes sectoral publications (sports/entertainment, fashion/health/beauty, mens/womens, computers/cars, etc).

— Holiday/tourist brochures, prospectuses, leaflets, programmes, catalogues (including directories) and similar printed matter. Similarly newspapers which deal with sectoral issues (eg sports papers) attract the lower rate.

— Maps and charts, and sheet music not in book or booklet form.

5 Printed matter liable at the standard rate of VAT

5.1. All printed matter not falling within the zero-rated or the lower-rated categories is automatically liable at the standard rate of 20 per cent (21 per cent from 1 March, 2002).

5.2. Essentially this covers all stationery and the like, advertising and other printed matter. This includes;

— books of stationery, cheque books and the like

— calendars, greeting cards, business cards

— diaries, organisers, yearbooks, planners and the like the total area of whose pages consist of 25 per cent or more of blank pages for the insertion or recording of information

— albums and the like

— books of tokens, of tickets or of coupons

— other advertising matter.

5.3. Examples of advertising material attracting the standard rate are posters, beer mats etc. A detailed list is given in Appendix 1.

5.4. It should be noted that the supply of **all** publications in other formats eg CD-ROMS and audio cassette tapes is liable to VAT at 20 per cent (21 per cent from 1 March, 2002).

6 Package Rule

6.1. In circumstances where an information pack is printed for a single consideration, the rate of VAT applicable to the pack is the rate appropriate to the highest rated item contained therein eg a pack containing a book and a CD is liable to VAT at 20% (21% from 1 March, 2002).

7 Acquisitions from other Member States of the EU and Imports

7.1. The rates which apply to publications within the State apply similarly to publications acquired by traders from other Member States of the EU and to those imported from outside the EU. In general private individuals purchasing publications from other member States of the EU are not liable for Irish VAT as VAT will already have been charged in the supplying Member State.

8 Internet

8.1. Digitised publications are text and/or images produced in an electronic form capable of being transmitted electronically, or "downloaded".

8.2. When printed matter is purchased/downloaded via the internet it is considered to be a service within the meaning of the Fourth Schedule to the VAT Act, 1972 (as amended) ie "the provision of information". The effect of this is that **all** digitised publications regardless of their rate when printed (eg a book liable at zero per cent) are treated as a supply of services rather than goods and are liable to VAT at 20 per cent (21 per cent from 1 March, 2002).

8.3. The VAT treatment of "Fourth Schedule Services" is set out in *Information Leaflet No. 9/01* which is available on request and, also on the Revenue website, at www.revenue.ie

9 Types of publications: VAT Rates

9.1. A list in alphabetical order of the VAT ratings of the various types of publications is given at Appendix I.

10 Enquiries

10.1. In any case where the rate of VAT is not clear the publisher or importer can submit a copy of the publication for consideration to his/her local Inspector of Taxes or to the VAT Administration Branch, Indirect Taxes Division, Revenue, Stamping Building, Dublin Castle, Dublin 2. (Tel. 01–6475000).

All other enquiries should be made to the local Inspector of Taxes.

10.2. A list of useful addresses, telephone, fax numbers and E-mail addresses is attached at Appendix II.

APPENDIX I

Types of Publications, VAT Rates	Rate
Account Books	20%
Albums	20%
Annual Reports	0%
Annuals	0%
Atlases	0%
Audio Cassette Books	20%
Beer Mats	20%
Bingo books	20%
Books, booklets (other than catalogues) including books consisting wholly or mainly of reproductions of paintings	0%
Bookmarks etc (included with books)	0%
Bookmarks etc (not included with books)	20%
Braille Books	0%
Brochures	12.5%

Calendars	20%
Cards eg business, greeting	20%
Catalogues	12.5%
Charts and maps	12.5%
Rate	
Cheque Books	20%
Children's Drawing & Painting Books	0%
Children's Picture Books including "cut out" and "stand up" types	0%
Comics	12.5%
Computer manuals	0%
Coupons, books of	20%
Diaries (however, see paragraph 5.2)	20%
Diaries/Organisers/Planners	20%
Dictionaries	0%
Directories	12.5%
Dust Covers (included with books)	0%
Encyclopaedias	0%
Exercise Books	20%
Fixture Lists	12.5%
Forms	20%
Globes	20%
Hymn Books	0%
Hymn sheets	12.5%
Rate	
Invitation Cards	20%
Journals (Diary)	20%
Journals (Research)*	12.5%
Leaflets including flyers	12.5%
Magazines	12.5%
Maps	12.5%
Missals	0%
Missalettes (Mass Leaflets)	12.5%
Music Books	0%
Newspapers	12.5%
Note Books	20%
Parts of large works published over pre-determined period including related binder supplied free of charge	0%
Picture Books ie books of pictures (other than catalogues)	0%
Periodicals	12.5%
Photocopying	20%

Posters	20%
Postcards including books of postcards	20%
Prayer Books	0%
Rate	
Printing —	
— of 0% publications	0%
— of 12.5% publications	12.5%
— of 20% publications	20%
Programmes	12.5%
Prospectuses	12.5%
Puzzle books excluding periodicals	0%
Sheet Music	12.5%
Stationery	20%
Stamps, Books of postal	exempt
Telephone Directories	12.5%
Tickets, Books of	20%
Timetables	12.5%
Tokens, Books of	20%
Trade Catalogues/Promotional Literature	12.5%

* Where journals are normally paid for by annual subscription, have their pages sequentially numbered by reference to the completed work and are supplied with a binder or are bound for no extra cost in book form at the end of the year, they are regarded as qualifying for the zero rate.

Note: The 20% rate of VAT will increase to 21% with effect from 1 March, 2002.

A full list of our offices countrywide can be found in the 'List of Offices' / 'Map of Ireland' sections on our website at http://www.revenue.ie/.

'EMERGENCY' ACCOMMODATION, INCLUDING ACCOMMODATION PROVIDED FOR ASYLUM SEEKERS AND HOMELESS PEOPLE, AND ANCILLARY SERVICES

1 Introduction

This information leaflet outlines the appropriate VAT treatment of the short-term letting of accommodation to State agencies such as the Directorate for Asylum Seekers Services (to be renamed the 'Reception and Integration Agency' during 2001), Local Authorities and Health Boards, for use as 'emergency' accommodation, including accommodation provided for asylum seekers and homeless people. This leaflet also outlines the appropriate VAT treatment of the provision of ancillary services, such as catering, laundry, cleaning and security.

2 Short-Term Letting of 'Emergency' Accommodation

The position in relation to the short-term letting of accommodation for use as 'emergency' accommodation, is as follows:

(a) *State-owned accommodation*

The provision of accommodation in State-owned property is outside the scope of VAT.

(b) *Self-catering accommodation (eg apartments or houses)*

Short-term letting of self-catering accommodation, let otherwise than as holiday accommodation, is VAT exempt. When let as 'emergency' accommodation, it continues to be exempt. The owner of the accommodation may choose to waive his/her exemption (see paragraph 4).

(c) *Hotel or guesthouse accommodation*

Accommodation in a hotel or guesthouse activity, provided by taxable persons,[1] is taxable (at the 12½% VAT rate). However, if the hotel or guesthouse is contracted to a State agency as being provided exclusively as 'emergency' accommodation and it is not available for letting to the general public, the owner has the option either:

(i)   to continue to treat the property as a hotel or guesthouse (this means that the activity continues to be taxable), or

(ii) to elect to treat the provision of accommodation as a letting of immovable goods other than by a hotel or guesthouse, but as 'emergency accommodation' (Revenue accepts that this means that the activity is VAT exempt).

If the owner elects to change the status of his/her supplies from taxable to exempt, as outlined at (ii) above, and if first, the property has been developed since 1 November 1972 and second, the owner was entitled to recover VAT on the acquisition or development of the property, the change in status of the supplies from taxable to exempt constitutes a self-supply. The effect of this is that the owner must account for VAT on the cost of acquiring or developing the property. In practice, Revenue deals with this by clawing back the VAT claimed by the owner on the acquisition or development of the property.

If the status of the supplies is changed from taxable to exempt, as outlined at (ii) above, and they subsequently revert to being taxable (as could happen if, say, the accommodation ceases to be provided exclusively for asylum seekers/ homeless people), there is no mechanism to undo the self-supply provisions. This means that any VAT clawed back by Revenue is not recoverable by the hotel or guesthouse owner when he/she again becomes liable to account for VAT on the provision of accommodation.

If only a part of the hotel or guesthouse accommodation is provided as 'emergency' accommodation and the remaining part is available for letting to the general public, all of the lettings, whether for the general public or for 'emergency' cases, are taxable (at the 12½% VAT rate).

Footnote

[1] For VAT purposes, a 'taxable person' is a person who is liable to account for VAT. Generally speaking, a person becomes a 'taxable person' when his/her annual turnover from the sale of taxable goods or the supply of taxable services in the course or furtherance of business, exceeds certain thresholds. The threshold in relation to the provision of accommodation is £20,000 (€25,394.76).

Further details are available in the Revenue publication '*Guide to Value Added Tax*', paragraph 2.2. This publication is available on the Revenue web-site at *www.revenue.ie/pdf/vatbook.pdf*.

3 Ancillary Services

Ancillary services such as catering, laundry, cleaning and security, provided by taxable persons[2] are liable to VAT at the appropriate rate. For example, catering, laundry and routine cleaning services are liable to VAT at 12½% while security services are liable at 20%.

Where a hotel or guesthouse owner has elected to treat his/her supply of accommodation as exempt 'emergency accommodation', the supply of ancillary services in connection with the provision of that accommodation would only become liable to VAT if the annual taxable turnover from such services exceeds £20,000 (assuming, of course, that this person makes no other taxable supplies). All suppliers of exempt 'emergency accommodation' should keep a breakdown in their income and expenditure records between amounts relating to the exempt supply of accommodation and those relating to the supply of ancillary services.

Footnote

[2] For an explanation of 'taxable person', see footnote 1. The annual taxable turnover threshold in relation to the supply of services such as catering, laundry, cleaning and security, is £20,000 (€25,394.76).

4 Waiver of Exemption

A property owner who is engaged in exempt lettings may apply to the Revenue Commissioners to waive his/her right to exemption, in accordance with the relevant VAT legislation.

By waiving the right to exemption, the property owner must charge VAT, at 20%, on all of his/her short-term property lettings. He/she is however allowed VAT credit, at the appropriate rate, on inputs but only during the period for which he/she is registered for VAT.

The application to waive the entitlement to exemption must be in writing and must include the following:

(a)   the property owner's name, address and VAT registration number;

(b)   details of the letting agreement;

(c)   the date from which the property owner wishes the waiver to take effect which, in circumstances such as this, cannot be earlier than the commencement of the period in which the application is made.

5 Cancellation of Waiver of Exemption

A property owner who is engaged in exempt lettings and who has waived his/her right to exemption, may subsequently cancel the waiver of exemption, in accordance with the relevant VAT legislation. If the property owner cancels the waiver of exemption, he/she is obliged to repay any excess of VAT input credits received over VAT payments made during the period of the waiver, or the previous ten years, whichever is the shorter.

6 Further Information

Further information on this issue may be obtained from your local Inspector of Taxes, for whom contact details are provided on the attached Appendix, or from:

VAT Administration Branch

Indirect Taxes — Policy & Legislation Division
Stamping Building
Dublin Castle
Dublin 2
tel: 01–6745000   fax: 01–6795236   e-mail: vat@revenue.ie

Revenue Website: www.revenue.ie

VAT Information on Revenue Website: **www.revenue.ie/services/tax€info/ taxes8.htm**

Issued by the Office of the Revenue Commissioners
Dublin Castle
Dublin 2
February 2001

Contact addresses can be found in Revenue Addresses at start of book

RESEARCH SERVICES CARRIED OUT BY THIRD LEVEL EDUCATIONAL BODIES

1 Introduction

1.1. Section 199 of the Finance Act 2001 amended the First Schedule to the VAT Act, which deals with exempt supplies. The effect of the amendment is that from 1 September 2001 the supply of research services by educational bodies is no longer an entirely exempt activity, but, in certain circumstances, is subject to VAT. Where VAT applies, it is normally chargeable at the standard rate, apart from supplies to the European Commission under the EU Commission Framework programmes, which are entitled to the zero rate.

1.2. Following the Finance Act 2001 amendment, paragraph (ii) of the First Schedule to the VAT Act now exempts "school or university education....... including the supply of goods or services incidental thereto, *other than the supply of research services*". Prior to the insertion of the words in italics, all research carried out by educational bodies was treated as exempt because it was regarded as incidental to their primary function of education. Therefore, such bodies did not charge VAT on any of their research activities and they were not entitled to deduct VAT on their inputs in relation to such activities.

2 The purpose of this leaflet

2.1. This leaflet explains the impact of this change on the various types of research carried out by educational bodies. It gives guidance on how an educational body can go about determining what constitutes the supply of taxable research and what remains exempt as a purely educational activity.

2.2. Attention is drawn to the transitional arrangements, as set out in paragraph 7 below, which apply to the new provisions.

2.3. Should doubt or difficulty arise in relation to the taxable status of any particular case or activity, individual organisations should contact their local Inspector of Taxes for advice.

3 The effect of the amendment

3.1. With the introduction of these new provisions, educational bodies who engage in research activities and receive payment associated with those activities must consider the VAT implications of the transaction. To come within the charge for VAT according to the VAT Act, 1972, there must be a *'supply of services for consideration'*. There are various principles derived from European Court of Justice decisions that define what is a supply for consideration, and these are outlined briefly in Appendix 1. The key principles are:

— there must be a direct link between the goods or services supplied and the payment received,

— there must be a legal relationship between the supplier and the recipient,

— the service must be "consumed" by an identifiable customer or customers.

3.2. Various activities which are often carried out by third level educational bodies cannot be considered as part of their educational function and are, hence, never covered by the exemption applying to "school or university education......including the supply of goods or services incidental thereto". These activities are taxable when supplied for consideration by a third level educational body. Examples of such activities may be:

— management consultancy and business efficiency advice;

— collection and recording of statistics, with or without accompanying collation, analysis and interpretation,

— market research and opinion polling; writing computer programmes;

— routine testing and analysis of materials, components and processes.

3.3. Any other research activities carried out by a third level educational body which comply with the three key principles outlined by the European Court of Justice will generally be taxable.

3.4. Where a third level educational body carries out a research activity which is not subject to VAT, any subsequent commercial exploitation of the results of such research by the third level body would be a separate taxable activity.

4 Types of funding

4.1. The type of funding for research is a key determination of whether a transaction constitutes a supply for consideration. The funding received by third level educational bodies for research can be categorised as follows for VAT purposes:

— Funding from the European Commission under their Framework Programmes

— Fees for contract work for a client which produces a specific result.

— Funding for non-specific research in a particular area of study.

5 The application of VAT to various types of funding for research

5.1. Supplies of research to the European Commission under the Fifth and any following Framework Programmes are taxable from 1 September 2001. The decision concerning the taxable status of transactions under the Framework Programme was issued by the Commission, and applies throughout the EU. The reasons given by the Commission to explain why research contracts issued under this programme are taxable are shown in Appendix 2. However, the rate applied in this particular case is the zero rate because, under EU law, any taxable supply of a good or service to the European Commission is zero-rated. In general, taxable supplies of research are normally subject to the standard rate (currently 20 per cent.).

5.2. Research funded from national sources which constitutes a supply for consideration is taxable at the standard rate. This could include research carried out on a consultancy, outsourcing, or contract basis for State agencies.

5.3. Research funded from various national sources where it falls into the third category in paragraph 4, ie, funding that is not directly linked to the supply of specific research, should, in general, remain outside the VAT net.

6 Pointers to help to determine VAT status of research carried out by educational institutions:

The usefulness of the following questions is to assist in deciding whether a research activity constitutes a supply for consideration:

— Is there a direct link between the service provided and the consideration received? An indicator of a direct link could be the use of a contract rather than grant of a subsidy, a donation or a letter of agreement for funding. If no direct link exists, then there is no supply for consideration, and hence no VAT liability.

— Is there a legal relationship between the supplier and the recipient pursuant to which there is reciprocal performance and remuneration received by the supplier of the service (which constitutes the value actually given in return for the service supplied to the recipient)? Such a relationship is a strong indicator that a supply for consideration has taken place.

— What type of research is being carried out? Is it the type of research known as 'basic research', ie, research that is carried out for the purpose of creating, improving of enhancing knowledge or information about a particular discipline or activity, the output of which is available to a reasonably wide range of groups or individuals and is not produced solely for the benefit of whoever funds the research? Or, is it the type of research known as 'applied research'? This tends to take the results of basic research which have a commercial potential and further refine them to realise that potential. Its purpose is to produce results which can be commercially exploited, usually by whoever commissions and funds the research. Applied research is more likely than basic research to be a supply for consideration.

— What is the objective of the educational body in carrying out the research? Is it only to improve its standing in the research world or improve knowledge in a particular field? If so, it is likely that the results of the research would not be handed back to the funding body. The primary motivation could be educational.

— What is the objective of the funding body in funding each piece of research? Is it the production of specific results or deliverables, which could be commercially exploited, or the generation of knowledge in a general area of study or in the public interest?

— If the research produces specific results, who gets ownership rights of these? If they remain with the third level educational body which carried out the research, there is no supply to the funding body. However, if the third level body were to commercially exploit such results, such exploitation would be taxable.

7 Transitional arrangements

7.1. Special arrangements apply to contracts in place prior to the date the amendment comes into force (1 September 2001):

— Supplies of research under contracts entered into prior 1 July 2001 may continue to be treated as exempt. In order for the exemption to apply, a signed written contract must be in place prior to 1 July 2001, with supporting documentation (eg, tendering documents, etc) available for inspection.

— Supplies of research under contracts entered into post–1 July 2001 are taxable from 1 September 2001.

7.2. Where a contract contains an 'option to renew' clause, a new contract shall be deemed to be created upon exercise of this option. Accordingly, the VAT implications must be considered for any contract renewal after 30 June 2001.

8 Apportionment of input tax

8.1. Educational bodies will be entitled to reclaim VAT on any inputs relating to their taxable research business. However, as many of the inputs, for example, capital equipment, premises, and information technology, will be used both for their taxable supplies and their educational activities, VAT on inputs must be apportioned between deductible and non-deductible VAT, under Section 12(4) of the VAT Act. Those bodies should have appropriate recording systems to allow them comply with the VAT system in relation to this issue.

8.2. Revenue will shortly publish a separate guide to the apportionment of input tax which will be of information to educational bodies who make taxable supplies of research in addition to their exempt activities.

9 Place of supply

9.1. A taxable research activity is a consultancy service and under the third paragraph of the Fourth Schedule to the VAT Act, 1972, is taxable where received. A separate Statement of Practice (SP-VAT/5/94) on Fourth Schedule services is available and should be consulted where appropriate.

10 The application of Section 13A of the VAT Act

10.1. The normal Section 13A rules apply to supplies of taxable research services to companies authorised under that Section. Again, a separate Statement of Practice is available (SP-VAT/1/93 – Zero-rating of goods and services in accordance with section 13A of the VAT Act), and should be consulted where appropriate.

11 Enquiries

For further information please contact your local Inspector of Taxes, or VAT Administration, Stamping Building, Dublin Castle, Dublin 2. (Tel: 01–6475000 Extns. 48858, 48859, 48861. 48862, Fax: 01–6795236, E–mail: vat@revenue.ie).

Revenue

August, 2001.

Appendix 1
Principles derived from European Court of Justice decisions that define what constitute a supply for consideration

— There must be a direct link between the goods or services supplied and the consideration received. Any benefits arising from the supply must be conferred directly onto the person providing the consideration. It is not a supply for consideration if the person providing the consideration only indirectly receives the benefit, eg if the benefits actually accrue to the industry or group as a whole. (*Apple and Pear Development Council Case 102/86*). The link between the goods or services supplied and the fee paid must be such that a relationship can be established between the level of the benefits which the recipient obtains from the services provided and the amount of consideration. (*Tolsma Case 16/93*).

— There must be a 'legal relationship between the provider of the service and the recipient pursuant to which there is reciprocal performance, the remuneration received by the provider of the service constituting the value actually given in return for the service supplied to the recipient'. (*Tolsma Case 16/93*).

— There must be consumption of a service in order for the consideration to be subject to VAT. VAT is a tax on consumption of goods or services — there must be a supply of a good or service for consumption by identifiable customers or the provision of a benefit capable of being regarded as a cost component of the activity of another person in the commercial chain (*Mohr Case 215/94 and Landboden-Agrardienste GmbH Case 384/95*).

Appendix 2

In 1997 the European Commission provided the following list of reasons to explain why the Commission now regard research under the Framework Programmes as constituting a taxable supply of services:

— Call for tender: With the intention to build up know-how in certain fields of technology, the Commission publishes programme particulars in the Official Journal and calls on interested parties to submit a tender for a project that could achieve the specified results. Apparently many participants in research projects design their activities and projects in anticipation of a likely tender.

— Selection: The Commission never funds all eligible projects. Depending on the programme particulars only one or a certain number of projects are chosen, usually those which are likely to produce the intended research results (patents, know-how, etc). With view to the funding there is actually competition between the bids.

— Legal Form: The winning joint-venture signs a contract with the Commission. The Commission has opted for a contract as a legal instrument governing the research project as it allows for much tighter control than a grant of a subsidy.

— Activity: The contract obliges the participant to undertake a detailed research project, with a view to obtain specified results, to protect the research results and to either exploit the results commercially themselves or to grant licenses.

— Consideration: The Commission undertakes to cover, subject to the maximum amount fixed in the contract, 50% of the expenses incurred by the contractor in execution of its contractual obligation.[1]

— Termination: If it turns out, at any time in the execution of the project, that the project will not produce the intended results, the Commission has the right to terminate the contract.

— The property: Each of the contractors will keep the property rights on its own research results (single or joint ownership). They are, however, obliged to grant to each other royalty free licenses for commercial exploitation.

— Royalty free licenses for the Commission: The Commission's own joint research centres may ask for a royalty free license on all research results obtained in execution of the contract. They may use the licenses even in their own commercial operations. It is understood that the remuneration paid by the Commission covers for this aspect as well.

— Transfer of Property: Provided that a contracting party fails to protect and to exploit intellectual and commercial property derived from the project, the property will pass on to the Commission.

— Publication and Publicity: The contractors have to provide project reports and other useful material to the Commission. The Commission may publish the reports or disseminate data on exploitable results. The contractor is obliged to participate, on the request of the Commission, in trade fairs and to give presentations.

Footnote

[1]   It should be noted that other methods are also used to calculate Commission funding under Framework contracts.

(November 2001)

INTRA-COMMUNITY ACQUISITIONS AND POSTPONED ACCOUNTING

1 Single Market

1.1. Following the introduction of the Single Market on 1 January, 1993, the way in which VAT was charged on goods moving between Member States of the EU was changed. The concept of import and export was abolished for such trade and replaced by a system of intra-Community supply and acquisition of goods. This Information Leaflet sets out the VAT treatment of intra-Community acquisitions and the postponed accounting system for such acquisitions. It updates and replaces *Statement of Practice SPVAT/15/92.*

2 Acquisitions from other Member States

2.1. Under this system—

   (i)   the taxable person becomes liable for VAT on the acquisition of goods from another Member State of the EU,

  (ii)   the taxable person declares a liability for VAT in the VAT return

 (iii)   if the taxable person is entitled to full deductibility (input credit), the VAT payable on the intra-Community acquisition is deducted in the same VAT period, thus effectively cancelling out the VAT liability, and

  (iv)   the taxable person accounts for VAT on any subsequent supply of the goods in the appropriate VAT return.

2.2. Postponed accounting is the mechanism by which a taxable person in the State accounts for the VAT charge which arises in respect of goods acquired from another Member State.

2.3. The Collector-General's Division operates a bi-monthly VAT 3 return and an annual return of trading details. The VAT 3 return requires the taxable person to declare summary VAT details. In addition two statistical boxes in respect of intra-Community transactions have to be completed (E1 and E2). The annual return of trading is a more detailed form which requires a breakdown of the annual trading figures by VAT rate. A copy of the VAT 3 return is attached at Appendix II. A separate leaflet on completion of the VAT 3 return is available from the Collector-General's Division. (See contact details at Appendix III.)

3 Postponed Accounting with full deductibility

3.1. A person registered for VAT in the State can buy goods in another Member State at the zero rate provided the goods are dispatched or transferred to another Member State. The taxable person is required to account for VAT on any intra-Community acquisition of the goods on arrival in the State, at the appropriate Irish VAT rate, in Box T1 of the VAT3 return for the period in which the goods are acquired. Where the taxable person is entitled to full deductibility, a simultaneous input credit may be taken in Box T2 of the same VAT3 return, thus cancelling the liability (see Appendix I — example 1). The treatment of taxable persons who are not entitled to full deductibility is dealt with in paragraphs 6 to 7 below.

3.2. If the goods acquired are subsequently supplied, liability on that supply will arise in the normal way in the period in which the supply is made (see Appendix I – example 1).

4 Partially exempt persons

4.1. As outlined above taxable persons with full deductibility can take a simultaneous credit for any VAT liability on intra-Community acquisitions. However a number of taxable persons are registered for VAT but do not have full input tax deductibility eg a bank which is primarily involved in exempt activities but also carries on a taxable activity such as leasing of movable goods. Where such persons acquire goods in another Member State, they are liable to VAT on the acquisition of these goods but they may not be entitled to a simultaneous deduction. The making of intra-Community acquisitions does not affect the person's existing input tax deductibility entitlements. The taxable person is required to account for VAT on any intra-Community acquisition, at the appropriate Irish VAT rate, in Box T1 of the VAT3 return, for the period in which the goods were acquired. However the extent to which this VAT may be simultaneously deducted (Box T2 on the VAT3 return) varies.

4.2. A full deduction of the VAT on the intra-Community acquisition arises if the goods are wholly attributable to a person's taxable activities. No deduction of the VAT is allowable if the intra-Community acquisition relates to a person's exempt activities. If the intra-Community acquisition is used for both types of activity ie dual use inputs, the tax should be deducted in accordance with the taxable person's existing apportionment arrangements (see Appendix I — example 2).

5 Persons required to register solely because of intra-Community acquisitions

5.1. (*a*) Wholly exempt bodies (eg insurance companies and building societies) and

(*b*) non-taxable entities (eg public authorities and universities) are required to register for VAT if their intra-Community acquisitions exceed £32,000 (€40,631.62) (€41,000 from 1 January 2002) per annum. Bodies which exceed this limit must account for VAT on their intra-Community acquisitions, through their VAT return, (Box T1), at the rate applicable to the supply of such goods within the State. They are not entitled to any deduction in relation to the intra-Community acquisitions or indeed any other VAT that they have borne on purchases or imports (see Appendix I — example 3).

6 Intra-Community acquisitions by farmers

6.1. Farmers are also obliged to register for VAT where their intra-Community acquisitions exceed **or are likely to exceed** £32,000 (€40,631.62)(€41,000 from 1 January 2002) per annum. However, farmers registered in respect of their acquisitions may opt to retain their flat-rate status for the purpose of obtaining the 4.3 per cent flat-rate addition on their agricultural supplies to registered persons.

7 Racehorse trainers

7.1. Similarly, a flat-rate farmer who is registered for VAT in respect of racehorse training, who is obliged to account for VAT on intra-Community acquisitions may retain flat-rate farmer status for all agricultural purposes, other than racehorse training.

8 Retail Schemes

8.1. Traders who calculate their VAT liability by reference to a retail scheme should specifically ensure that goods for resale acquired in another Member State are always accounted for at the correct rate and that they include the intra-Community acquisition at the correct VAT rate in the scheme as purchases for resale. The VAT rate applicable to an intra-Community acquisition is always that which applies to the supply of the same goods here.

9 How to calculate the VAT due on intra-Community acquisitions

9.1. VAT becomes due on the date of issue of the invoice or, if no invoice issues, on the fifteenth of the month following the acquisition. The rate of VAT applicable is the rate that applies to the supply of the same goods in the State. The VAT is assessed on the price charged for the goods. If the supplier's invoice is in foreign currency, the rate of exchange applicable when the tax becomes due should be used. Tax is payable by the 19th day of the month following the period during which the tax became due. The following example serves to illustrate the arrangements:—

Example:

A local authority acquires a computer from a German company. The supply in Germany is zero-rated because the local authority has provided its VAT registration number to the German company and the goods have been despatched or transported to Ireland.

Computer delivered 29.4.01. Invoice issued 12.5.01. Invoiced amount €200,000. VAT on acquisition at 20% € 40,000. No input credit allowed. VAT (€40,000) payable to Collector-General (with May/June VAT return) by 19 July 2001.

10 Intra-Community acquisitions of new means of transport

10.1. The purchase of new means of transport in other Member States by private individuals and taxable persons is subject to VAT in the country of destination.

10.2. In the case of private individuals and taxable persons who are not entitled to a VAT deduction, VAT on the acquisition of a new means of transport is normally payable with the Vehicle Registration Tax (VRT) or, if no VRT is payable, at the time of registration of the vehicle. In the case of new vessels and aircraft, VAT becomes payable to the relevant Collector of Customs and Excise not later than three days after the date of arrival in the State.

10.3. Taxable persons who are entitled to a VAT deduction on the acquisition of a new means of transport must account for the VAT through their VAT return.

11 Intra-Community transport of goods

11.1. The special arrangements relating to the intra-Community transport of goods are dealt with in Information Leaflet No. 16/01.

12 INTRASTAT returns

12.1. Traders acquiring more than £150,000 (€190,460.71) (€190,500 from 1 January 2002) worth of goods per annum from other Member States are also obliged to submit a periodic INTRASTAT return.

13 Branch to branch transfers

13.1. For VAT purposes, branch to branch (with some exceptions) and similar transfers of goods between business persons in different EU Member States are also treated as being intra-Community supplies and acquisitions.

14 Certain transfers not supplies

14.1. For VAT purposes certain transfers to other Member states are not treated as intra-Community supplies/acquisitions.

14.2. These include goods for installation or assembly by the supplier, (in this case the supplier is obliged to register and account for VAT in the State.) transfers for the purposes of having contract work carried out on them and transfers with a view to their temporary use in another Member State.

15 Further Inquiries

15.1. Further information may be obtained from VAT Administration, Stamping Building, Dublin Castle, Dublin 2 (Tel. 6745000, Extns. 48858, 48859, 48861, 48862 or from local inspectors of taxes.

15.2. A list of useful address, telephone, fax numbers and E-mail addresses is attached at Appendix III.

Example 1
Appendix I

A company with full deductibility acquires a computer in the UK for €80,000. Supply is zero-rated in the UK The company sells the computer in the State during the same taxable period for €100,000 plus VAT. These are the only transactions in the period.

Acquisition of computer	€80,000 @ 20%	€16,000 include in Box	T1	of VAT 3
Simultaneous input credit	€80,000 @ 20%	€16,000 " " "	T2	" " "
Supply of computer in the State	€100,000 @ 20%	€20,000 " " "	T1	" " "
Net VAT payable		€20,000 " " "	T3	" " "

Example 2

An Irish bank (60% taxable/40% exempt activities) acquires a computer in the UK which is a dual use input to be used for both its taxable and exempt activities in the UK for €80,000. Supply is zero-rated in the UK.

Acquisition of computer	€80,000 @ 20%	€16,000 include in Box	T1	of VAT 3
Simultaneous input credit	€80,000 @ 60%	€ 9,600 " " "	T2	" " "
Net VAT payable		€6,400 " " "	T3	" " "

Example 3

Acquisition of computer	€80,000 @ 20%	€16,000 include in Box	T1	of VAT 3
No input credit		_____		
Net VAT payable		€16,000 " " "	T3	" " "

An insurance company or university acquires a computer in the UK for €80,000. Supply is zero-rated in the UK.

Contact addresses can be found in Revenue Addresses at start of book

VALUE ADDED TAX INFORMATION LEAFLET NO 8/01

DISTANCE SALES IN THE SINGLE MARKET

(November 2001)

1 What are distance sales?

1.1. Distance selling in the EU occurs when a supplier in one EU Member State sells goods to a person in another Member State who is not registered for VAT and the supplier is responsible for the delivery of the goods. It includes mail order sales, phone or tele-sales or physical goods ordered over the internet.

This information leaflet replaces *Statement of Practice SP-VAT/14/92.*

1.2. Under the distance selling arrangements, sales to customers in other Member States who are not registered for VAT are liable to VAT in the Member State of the supplier provided that the threshold appropriate to the Member State of the customer is not breached (see paragraph 4.1). Where sales exceed the threshold in any particular Member State, the supplier must register and account for VAT in that Member State.

2 Distance sales to the State

2.1. Where the value of distance sales to persons in the State by a supplier in another Member State exceeds or is likely to exceed IR£27,565 (€35,000) in a calendar year, that supplier must register for VAT in the State and must account for VAT at the appropriate Irish rates. If the threshold is not exceeded, the supplier may, nevertheless, opt to register and account for VAT in the State on his or her distance sales.

3 Distance sales from the State

3.1. An Irish supplier who makes distance sales to customers in other Member States who are not registered for VAT, is liable to Irish VAT on such sales until the value of the sales reaches the threshold applying in that other Member State (see paragraph 4.1). Once the value of the supplier's sales exceeds that threshold in the other Member State, the supplier is obliged to register in that Member State and account for VAT at the rates applicable there. If the appropriate threshold is not exceeded, the supplier may, nevertheless, opt to account for VAT in the Member State to which the distance sales are made.

3.2. It should be noted that a supplier who is engaged in distance sales to several Member States is required to register in each Member State in which the value of his or her distance sales exceeds the appropriate threshold.

4 Thresholds

4.1. Under the EU VAT arrangements, Member States were required to adopt a distance sales threshold of either IR£27,565 (€35,000) or IR£78,756 (€100,000).

The turnover limits applicable in the various Member States are as follows:—

€35,000 IR £27,565	€100,000 IR £78,756
Belgium	Austria
Denmark	France

Finland	Germany
Greece	Luxembourg
Ireland	Netherlands
Italy	United Kingdom
Portugal	
Spain	
Sweden	

4.2. The value of distance sales of excisable goods should not be taken into account for the purposes of determining whether or not the threshold has been exceeded. If the threshold, excluding the value of excisable goods, is not exceeded the supplier may continue to account for VAT in the Member State from which s/he makes his or her supplies.

4.3. Any supplier who makes distance sales of excisable goods eg alcohol, tobacco and oil to another Member State must register and account for VAT in that Member State, since distance sales of excisable goods are always subject to VAT in the Member State to which they are dispatched.

5 Goods excluded from the distance selling arrangements

5.1. Sales of new means of transport are excluded from the distance selling arrangements. These sales are always intra-Community acquisitions and the person acquiring the new means of transport must pay VAT in the Member State of destination.

6 Obligations of traders

6.1. If a foreign supplier is obliged to register for VAT in the State because the annual value of his or her distance sales to the State exceeds or is likely to exceed £27,565 (€35,000) s/he must complete the appropriate registration form (TR1 or TR2) and submit it to the Inspector of Taxes, at the Taxes Central Registration Office (TCRO) (see Appendix II for contact details). Once registered for VAT the distance seller will be obliged to;

— calculate VAT due on the value of his or her distance sales,

— complete the periodic VAT 3 return, showing the VAT liability,

— send the completed return to the Collector-General, together with payment of any VAT due, within the prescribed time limit,

— keep proper records so as to enable the VAT liability to be determined,

— make those records available for inspection by Revenue on request.

6.2. Advice on how to complete the VAT 3 return, is available from the Collector-General's Division (see contact details at Appendix II).

6.3. If an Irish supplier is obliged to register for VAT in another Member State because the value of his or her distance sales to that Member State exceeds the relevant threshold, s/he should contact the fiscal authority of the Member State concerned who will provide details of the requirements for registration. Contact details for these fiscal authorities are provided at Appendix I.

7 INTRASTAT — distance sales from the State

7.1. A supplier who is registered for VAT in the State and also registered in another Member State because of his or her distance sales to that Member State must include the value of such sales in the INTRASTAT Box E1 of the Irish VAT 3 return. However, a person who is registered for VAT in Ireland should **not** include the value of distance sales to other Member States in Box E1 where s/he is not registered for VAT in those Member States.

8 INTRASTAST — distance sales to the State

8.1. A supplier, registered in another Member State who is also registered in the State because of his or her distance sales to the State, should include the value of such sales in the INTRASTAT Box E2 of the Irish VAT return.

9 Internet

9.1. Sales of goods ordered via the internet but physically supplied are considered to be distance sales for VAT purposes. However digitised goods, that is goods for downloading by the customer via the internet are considered to be services, within the meaning of the Fourth Schedule for VAT purposes.

10 Further information

10.1. The addresses of the VAT Authorities in other EU Member States are set out in Appendix I.

10.2. Further information can be obtained from the inspector of taxes, Dublin Audit District 6. For this address and other useful addresses, telephone fax and E-mail addresses see Appendix II.

APPENDIX I

Fiscal Authority	Address
Austria	UID-Búro des Bundesministerium fur Finanzen
	Erdbergerstrabe 192–196 A–1034 Wien.
Belgium	Ministere des Finances,
	Administration des douanes et accises,
	Cité administrative de l'Etat,
	Tour Finances – Boite 37,
	Boulevard de Jardin Botanique 50,
	1010 Brussels.
Denmark	Ministry of Taxation,
	Central Customs and Tax Administration,
	Amaliegada 44,
	DK – 1256 Copenhagen.
France	Direction generale des douanes et droits indirects,
	Ministere de l'Economie, des Finances
	Et du Budget,
	23 bis rue de l'Universite,
	75700 Paris.

Finland	Provincial Tax Office of Uusimaa, Finland.
Germany	Bundesministerium der Finanzen, Postfach 13 08, 5300 Bonn 1.
Greece	Ministry of Finance, General Directorate of Taxation and Public Property, Division 14 VAT and Special Taxes, Sina 2–4, 104 72 Athens.
Ireland	Office of the Revenue Commissioners, VAT Administration Branch, New Stamping Building, Dublin Castle, Dublin 2.
Italy	Ministero delle Finanze, Dipartmento dello Dogane e delle Imposte indirette, 11 Capo delle Circoscrizione reggente, Rome.
Luxembourg	Administration des Douanes, L–2010 Luxembourg.
The Netherlands	Directoraat-Generaal der Belastingen, Korte Voorhout 7, Postadres Postbus 20201, 2500 EE'S-Gravenhage.
Portugal	Ministerio dos Financas, Divisao de Impostos sobre o Consumo, Rua da Alfandegas 5, 1194 Lisbon.
Spain	Direccion General de Aduanas e, Impuestos Especiales, Ministerio de Economia y Hacienda, Guzman El Bueno 137, 28003 Madrid.
Sweden	Skattemyndighetem 1 Stolkholm Ian, Skattekantor riks, 10661 Stockholm, Sweden.
United Kingdom	H.M. Customs and Excise, New King's Beam House, 22 Upper Ground, London SE1 9PJ.

Contact addresses can be found in Revenue Addresses at start of book

(November 2001)

GOVERNMENT DEPARTMENTS, LOCAL AUTHORITIES, HEALTH BOARDS, HOSPITALS, EDUCATIONAL BODIES, AND OTHER NON-TAXABLE ENTITIES ACQUIRING GOODS FROM OTHER EU MEMBER STATES

1 General

1.1. Government Departments, local authorities, health boards, public hospitals, educational establishments and other similar bodies are treated as non-taxable entities for VAT purposes. This means that they may pay VAT on any goods purchased or imported but generally speaking, they cannot recover these VAT payments. They are not required to register for VAT in respect of supplies of goods by them but may be required to register and account for VAT in respect of goods received from other Member States of the EU.

This information leaflet updates and replaces *Statement of Practice SP-VAT/11/92.*

2 "Non-Taxable entities" — Who is affected?

2.1. "Non-taxable entities" include State bodies (such as Government Departments, local authorities, health boards, etc), educational establishments (such as schools, universities, VECs, etc), public hospitals, charities, sports bodies and church bodies — in fact all groups of persons (other than private individuals) engaged in any type of non-commercial activity.

3 Obligations of non-taxable entities to register for VAT

3.1. A non-taxable entity that acquires, or is likely to acquire, more than £32,000 (€40,631.62) (€41,000 from 1 January, 2002) worth of goods from other EU Member States in any period of 12 months is obliged to register for VAT in respect of those acquisitions. Such a non-taxable entity should register for VAT by completing form TR1 or TR2 which can be obtained from, and which should be returned to the Taxes Central Registration Office (TCRO). For contact details please refer to Appendix I.

3.2. Registration is not required where the £32,000 (€40,631.62) threshold for acquisitions is not exceeded or likely to be exceeded. In these cases goods acquired from other Member States are charged the VAT applicable in the supplier's Member State but are not charged Irish VAT when the goods enter the State. Non-taxable entities below the threshold may, however, elect to register if they so wish.

4 Special rules for certain goods

4.1. It should be noted that intra-Community acquisitions of new means of transport, (ie motor vehicles, boats and planes) are always subject to VAT when they are brought into the State, even when the annual threshold is not exceeded. There are special rules for paying VAT on these items and, in certain cases, on excisable goods also.

5 VAT registration number

5.1. On registration, the local Inspector of Taxes will issue a VAT number to the non-taxable entity. This number should be made available to all suppliers in other Member States to enable those suppliers to zero rate their supplies on despatch to Ireland.

6 Obligations when registered

6.1. All VAT registered persons are obliged:

— to calculate VAT due on their intra-Community acquisitions of goods,

— to complete the periodic VAT return showing their VAT liability,

— to send the completed return to the Collector-General, together with the tax due, within the prescribed time limit,

— to keep proper records of their acquisitions from other Member States so as to enable their VAT liability to be determined,

— to make these records available for inspection by Revenue, on request.

A separate leaflet, which explains how to complete the VAT 3 return, is available from the Collector-General's Division (for contact details see Appendix I).

7 Invoices

7.1. Non-taxable persons, once registered for VAT who acquire goods from taxable persons in other Member States should be issued with an invoice by their supplier. This invoice will form the basis for determining the VAT due on the acquisition.

8 How to calculate the VAT due on intra-Community acquisitions

8.1. VAT becomes due on the date of issue of the invoice or, if no invoice issues, on the fifteenth of the month following the acquisition. The rate of VAT applicable is the rate that applies to the supply of the same goods in Ireland. The VAT is assessed on the price charged for the goods. The following example serves to illustrate the arrangement.

8.2. Example:

Local authority acquires a computer from a German company. The supply in Germany is zero-rated because the local authority has provided its VAT registration number to the German company and the goods have been despatched or transported to Ireland.

Computer delivered	29.4.01
Invoice issued	10.5.01
Invoiced amount	€200,000
VAT on acquisition at 20%	€40,000

No entitlement to recover the VAT

VAT (€40,000) payable to Collector-General (with May/June VAT return) by 19.07.01.

9 Rate of Exchange

9.1. Where acquiring goods from a country, which is not part of the Euro zone the rate of exchange to be used for VAT purposes is the rate applicable when the tax becomes due.

10 No entitlement to recover VAT paid

10.1. Non-taxable entities which are required to register for VAT in respect of intra-Community acquisitions are not entitled to recover VAT paid on those acquisitions. This is similar to the situation where the non-taxable entity pays VAT on goods purchased in the State or at point of entry, without entitlement to deduction.

11 Received services

11.1. Non-taxable entities are required to account for VAT in respect of certain services received by them VAT free from abroad. There is no threshold for registration purposes. The services affected include advertising, consultancy services and hiring of goods other than means of transport. (A detailed information leaflet No. 9/01 entitled *Fourth Schedule services* on this subject is available on request). Non-taxable entities, already registered for VAT because they receive such services, are, regardless of the level of their intra-Community acquisitions of goods, liable to Irish VAT on those acquisitions.

12 Intrastat

12.1. Non-taxable entities which acquire more than £150,000 (€190,460.71) (€190,500 from 1 January 2002) worth of goods per annum from other Member States are required to make a monthly statistical return in respect of these acquisitions. Details of this requirement are contained in the VIES and Intrastat Traders Manual, which is available from the VIMA Office (see contact details at Appendix I).

13 Imports from Non-EU countries

13.1. VAT on imports of goods from outside the EU is payable at point of entry and Customs documentation is required. Non-taxable entities should note that the imports of goods from outside the EU are not to be included when calculating the £32,000 (€40,631.62) (€41,000 from 1 January, 2002) registration threshold (referred to in paragraph 4 above) — this threshold relates only to goods acquired from other Member States. Customs documentation in relation to imports from outside the EU is required.

14 Further information

14.1. Further information may be obtained from VAT Administration, Stamping Building, Dublin Castle, Dublin 2 (Tel 67485000, Extns 48858, 48859, 48861, 48862 or from local Inspectors of Taxes.

14.2. A list of useful addresses, telephone, fax numbers and E-mail addresses is attached at Appendix I.

Contact addresses can be found in Revenue Addresses at start of book

(November 2001)

FARMERS AND INTRA-EU TRANSACTIONS

1 Introduction

1.1. This Information Leaflet sets out the VAT arrangements that apply to intra-EU transactions insofar as farmers are concerned. It updates and replaces Statement of Practice SP-VAT/2/93.

2 Definition of farmer for VAT purposes

2.1. For VAT purposes a farmer means a person who engages in at least one of the agricultural production activities in the State listed in Appendix I and—

- (*a*) whose supplies consist exclusively of agricultural produce (other than bovine semen and nursery stock, see paragraph 3.2 (*b*)) and/or agricultural services (other than agricultural contracting services, see paragraph 3.2 (*a*))

- (*b*) whose supplies consist exclusively of agricultural produce (but see (*a*) above) and/or agricultural services (but see (*a*) above) and one or more of the following:—

  - (i) machinery, plant or equipment which s/he has used for his/her farming activity;

  - (ii) racehorse training services for which the annual turnover does not exceed and is not likely to exceed €25,500;

  - (iii) goods, other than those referred to above, for which the annual turnover does not exceed and is not likely to exceed €51,000 or services, other than those referred to above, for which the annual turnover does not exceed and is not likely to exceed €25,500.

2.2. In brief therefore, a person who engages in agricultural production, and whose turnover from non-agricultural activities does not exceed the appropriate annual threshold, is a flat-rate farmer ie a farmer who is not obliged to register for VAT in respect of his/her farming activities.

3 Obligation to register

3.1. A farmer is obliged to register where:—

- (*a*) his/her annual turnover from agricultural contracting activities other than insemination services, stock minding and stock rearing exceeds or is likely to exceed €25,500

- (*b*) his/her annual turnover from sales of bovine semen other than to other farmers licensed as an A.I. centre or supplies to a person over whom the farmer exercises control, exceeds or is likely to exceed €51,000

- (*c*) his/her annual turnover from retail sales of horticultural products exceeds or is likely to exceed €51,000 (*d*)   his/her annual turnover from supplies of agricultural services and either or both bovine semen or nursery stock exceeds or is likely to exceed €25,500

(*e*)   s/he is in receipt of Fourth Schedule services from abroad (see Appendix III)

(*f*)   his/her annual turnover from sales of bovine semen and nursery stock exceeds or is likely to exceed €51,000

(*g*)   his/her annual turnover from intra-Community acquisitions exceeds or is likely to exceed €41,000

(*h*)   his/her annual turnover from taxable goods or services, other than any exclusions mentioned above exceeds or is likely to exceed the appropriate thresholds.

4 Option to register

4.1. A farmer who is not obliged to register may elect to do so.

4.2. If a farmer is obliged to register under paragraph 3.1 (*e*) or (*g*) above such registration is effectively "ring fenced" to the intra-Community acquisitions or the Fourth Schedule services. S/he is not obliged to register in respect of his/her farming activities.

4.3. Where s/he registers in respect of racehorse training this registration may also be isolated and s/he is not required to register in respect of his/her farming activities. In general Revenue will accept that where a racehorse trainer is also a farmer, that the training element is only 10 per cent of the total turnover.

5 Flat-rate farmers

5.1. A flat-rate farmer is a farmer who is not registered for VAT in respect of his/her farming activities. In order to compensate for VAT paid on supplies to him/her, such a farmer is entitled to a flat-rate addition (at present 4.3%) to the prices at which his/her agricultural produce or agricultural services are supplied to VAT-registered persons including marts, agricultural co-operatives and meat factories. A flat-rate farmer is also entitled to reclaim VAT incurred in respect of the construction, extension, alteration or reconstruction of farm buildings, and land drainage, from the VAT Repayment (Unregistered) Section (see Appendix IV for contact details).

5.2. Flat-rate farmers have no Irish VAT liability in respect of purchases in other Member States provided the €41,000 threshold is not exceeded. Instead, VAT is charged in the Member State of purchase at the rate applicable there. Farmers who exceed the acquisitions threshold are liable to Irish VAT regardless of whether or not they have paid VAT in the Member State of purchase. Therefore, to avoid double taxation, farmers whose purchases in other Member States exceed or are likely to exceed €41,000 per annum must register for VAT here.

6 Sales of agricultural produce by flat-rate farmers to persons who are registered for VAT in other Member States

6.1. The flat-rate addition which applies to supplies of agricultural produce within the State also applies to supplies made to VAT-registered traders in other Member States.

6.2. The VAT-registered person in the other Member State who buys the goods should, in order to obtain a refund of the flat-rate addition, be in possession of an invoice showing separately the purchase price of the goods and the flat-rate addition. This invoice, which is normally prepared by the purchaser, must be signed by the flat-rate farmer who must retain a copy of the invoice. A flat-rate farmer who is registered in respect of intra-Community acquisitions and/or because of Fourth Schedule services received from abroad only (see paragraph 4.2) should treat such sales in the same way and should not include his/her VAT number on the invoice. The purchaser of the goods in the other Member State may reclaim the flat-rate addition from Revenue, VAT Repayments (Unregistered) Section (see Appendix IV for contact details) by completing the appropriate claim form (VAT 60 EU) and by submitting it together with a certificate of taxable status and the supporting invoice.

7 "Distance sales"

7.1. Special rules obtain in the case of "distance sales". Distance sales are where a supplier in one EU Member State sells goods to a person in another Member State who is unregistered for VAT and the supplier is responsible for the delivery of the goods. Farmers should be aware of these rules because the practical effect is that they may have to register for VAT in another Member State.

7.2. *Information Leaflet No. 8/01* is available on this subject. Briefly, the position is that a flat-rate farmer who makes distance sales in excess of an annual threshold to another Member State is obliged to register for and charge VAT in that other Member State. The Member States apply the following thresholds:

€35,000	€100,000
Belgium	Austria
Denmark	France
Finland	Germany
Greece	Luxembourg
Ireland	Netherlands
Italy	United Kingdom
Portugal	
Spain	
Sweden	

8 Purchases by flat-rate farmers of goods from other Member States

8.1. A flat-rate farmer who is obliged to register for and pay VAT in respect of intra-Community acquisitions (and certain services received from abroad, if any — see paragraph 9) can, (unless s/he elects to be taxable in respect of all his/her activities) nevertheless retain flat-rate farmer status in all other respects. Even if his/her acquisitions do not exceed the €41,000 threshold a farmer may opt to register in respect of intra-Community acquisitions (see paragraph 4.2).

8.2. A flat-rate farmer who is registered in respect of intra-Community acquisitions may purchase goods in other Member States free of VAT, subject to the normal Single

Market rules, by quoting his/her VAT number to the supplier. The farmer is obliged to pay Irish VAT on such acquisitions through the periodic VAT return. A farmer registered in this way will not have any entitlement to recovery of VAT paid (but see paragraphs 5.1 and 10.1).

9 Certain services received from abroad

9.1. A flat-rate farmer receiving certain services from abroad is also required to register for VAT in respect of these services regardless of their cost to him/her. There is no threshold in respect of such services.

9.2. The services concerned include hire of equipment and machinery, accountancy and legal services, and consultancy services. A full list of the services concerned is contained in Appendix III. A farmer who is obliged to register for and pay VAT because of the receipt of these services must also account for VAT on all his/her intra-Community acquisitions, regardless of their value, but can, (unless s/he elects to be taxable in respect of all his/her activities) nevertheless, retain his/her flat-rate farmer status in all other respects. A farmer registered in this way will not have an entitlement to recovery of VAT paid (but see paragraphs 5.1 and 10.1). The requirement to register in respect of such services does not affect the farmer's flat-rate status but it does make him/her liable to VAT in respect of intra-Community acquisitions of goods, even if the €41,000 threshold is not exceeded (see paragraphs 8.1 and 8.2).

10 Refunds on farm building work, etc

10.1. Under an existing Refund Order, a flat-rate farmer may recover the VAT paid by him/her in respect of farm buildings and land drainage by completing claim form VAT 58 and returning it, with the supporting invoices, to VAT Repayments Section (see Appendix IV for contact details). Where a flat-rate farmer is registered for VAT in respect of intra-Community acquisitions and/or certain services received from abroad (see paragraphs 8 and 9) s/he is still entitled to a refund under the Order. However this refund must be claimed as a deduction through periodic VAT returns.

11 Livestock brought into the State from another Member State

11.1. Temporary importation schemes apply in relation to imports from non-Community countries but livestock brought into the State from other Member States are normally treated as intra-Community acquisitions which are liable to VAT in the State once the threshold is exceeded (see paragraphs 8.1 and 8.2). This will not be the case, however, in the circumstances set out in paragraph 11.2.

11.2. Where livestock are brought into the State from another Member State for the purpose of having a service or treatment carried out on them (eg veterinary services) an intra-Community acquisition does not arise. Instead the service is liable to Irish VAT. In addition, an intra-Community acquisition does not arise in relation to livestock brought into the State where the livestock would qualify for temporary importation without payment of VAT if they were imported into the State from outside the EU. This normally means that transfer of ownership does not take place and that the livestock remain in the State for less than two years.

12 Livestock sent from the State temporarily to another Member State

12.1. The principles set down in paragraphs 11.1 and 11.2 apply in reverse with regard to livestock sent temporarily from the State to another Member State. In the case of such temporary transfers, the person who dispatches the livestock from the State must maintain a record showing details of the goods and the name, address and VAT number (if any) of the person to whom they are sent.

13 Intra-Community goods transport services

13.1. The VAT treatment of intra-Community goods transport services (ie transport of goods from one Member State of the EU to another) is explained in detail in *Information Leaflet No. 16/01*. Farmers who regularly receive such services may wish to study that information leaflet.

13.2. In general, a farmer who is not registered for VAT will be charged VAT by the haulage company at the appropriate rate, in the Member State of departure of the transport. For example, Irish VAT at the 20% rate (21% from 1 March 2002) will apply if goods are being transported from Ireland to France. No entitlement to recovery of such VAT arises for the farmer (but see paragraph 5.1).

13.3. If the farmer is registered for VAT only in respect of intra-Community acquisitions or received services s/he will not be entitled to any recovery of VAT charged by the haulier (but see paragraph 5.1). If the transport service is being received from a haulier in another Member State the farmer should ensure that his/her VAT number is made available to that haulier so as to avoid double taxation. The farmer must then pay VAT in respect of the service as if it were s/he who supplied the service in the same way as s/he accounts for VAT on received services (see paragraph 9). Again there is no entitlement to recovery of this VAT for the farmer (but see paragraph 5.1).

14 New means of transport

14.1. There are special rules concerning the intra-Community acquisition of new means of transport. The person acquiring the new means of transport must always account for VAT in the Member State of destination of the goods.

14.2. The following table gives details of what is regarded as being a new means of transport for VAT purposes.

Means of Transport	*Specification*	*"New"*
Motor Vehicle	over 48 cc	6 months old or less
	or	or
	over 7.2. kw power	travelled 6,000 km or less
Boat	over 7.5 metres in length	3months old or less
		or
		sailed for 100 hrs. or less
Aircraft	over 1,550 kg take-off weight	3 months old or less
		or
		flown for 40 hrs. or less

14.3. If a flat-rate farmer acquires a new motor vehicle in another Member State, VAT must be paid on this vehicle at the time of its registration in the State. In the case of intra-Community acquisitions of new boats and aircraft, the VAT due must be paid to the local Collector of Customs & Excise on arrival of the boat or aircraft in the State. However, the acquisition of a new means of transport will not affect the flat-rate status of the farmer and the value of the new means of transport will not be included in the value of intra-Community acquisitions for the purpose of determining whether a farmer is required to register for VAT in respect of those acquisitions.

14.4. Agricultural plant and machinery, including tractors, are not regarded as a new means of transport for VAT purposes and are taxed under the normal rules for intra-Community transactions ie acquisitions of plant and machinery are treated as intra-Community acquisitions for the purpose of determining whether a farmer must register (see paragraph 8).

15 Further Information

15.1. Further information may be obtained from VAT Administration, Stamping Building, Dublin Castle, Dublin 2 (Tel 67485000), or from local Inspectors of Taxes.

15.2. A list of useful addresses, telephone, fax numbers and E-mail addresses is attached at Appendix IV.

APPENDIX I

Annex A of Council Directive No. 77/388/EEC of 17 May, 1997

List of agricultural production activities

   I. CROP PRODUCTION

      1.   General agriculture, including viticulture

      2.   Growing of fruit (including olives) and of vegetables, flowers and ornamental plants, both in the open and under glass

      3.   Production of mushrooms, spices, seeds and propagating materials; nurseries

   II. STOCK FARMING TOGETHER WITH CULTIVATION

      1.   General stock farming

      2.   Poultry farming

      3.   Rabbit farming

      4.   Beekeeping

      5.   Silkworm farming

      6.   Snail farming

  III. FORESTRY

  IV. FISHERIES

      1.   Fresh-water fishing

      2.   Fish farming

3. Breeding of mussels, oysters and other molluscs and crustaceans

4. Frog farming

V. Where a farmer, processes, using means normally employed in an agricultural, forestry or fisheries undertaking, products deriving essentially from his agricultural production, such processing shall also be regarded as agricultural production.

APPENDIX II
Annex B of Council Directive No. 77/388/EEC of 17 May, 1977
List of agricultural services

Supplies of agricultural services which normally play a part in agricultural production shall be considered the supply of agricultural services, and include the following in particular:

— field work, reaping and mowing, threshing, baling, collecting, harvesting, sowing and planting

— packing and preparation for market, for example drying, cleaning, grinding, disinfecting and ensilage of agricultural products

— storage of agricultural products

— stock minding, rearing and fattening

— hiring out, for agricultural purposes, of equipment normally used in agricultural, forestry or fisheries undertakings

— technical assistance

— destruction of weeds and pests, dusting and spraying crops and land

— operation of irrigation and drainage equipment

— lopping, tree felling and other forestry services.

APPENDIX III

The complete list of the services referred to in paragraph 9 is as follows:—

(a) transfers and assignments of copyright, patents, licences, trade marks and similar rights;

(b) hiring out of movable goods other than means of transport (but see Note hereunder);

(c) advertising services;

(d) services of consultants, engineers, consultancy bureaux, lawyers, accountants and other similar services, data processing and provision of information (but excluding services connected with immovable goods);

(e) telecommunications services;

(f) acceptance of any obligation to refrain from pursuing or exercising in whole or in part, any business activity or any such rights as are referred to in paragraph (a);

(g) banking, financial and insurance services (including reinsurance, but not including the provision of safe deposit facilities);

(h)   the provision of staff;

(i)   the services of agents who act in the name and for the account of a principal when procuring for him any services specified in paragraphs (a) to (h).

NOTE   Subparagraph (b) does not apply to movable goods hired out by lessors established outside the European Union. These are excluded by a specific provision of VAT Law which, in effect, makes such lessors accountable for VAT in Ireland in the normal way.

Contact addresses can be found in Revenue Addresses at start of book

FINANCIAL INSTITUTIONS, INSURANCE COMPANIES, THEATRES, PROVIDERS OF PASSENGER TRANSPORT AND OTHER EXEMPT PERSONS ACQUIRING GOODS FROM OTHER EU MEMBER STATES

(November 2001)

1 General

1.1. Financial institutions, insurance companies, theatres, providers of passenger transport and other persons engaged in exempt activities are not liable to VAT insofar as their exempted activities are concerned. This means that they pay VAT on any goods purchased or imported but are not required to register in respect of exempt supplies made by them.

1.2. Since the abolition of fiscal frontiers on 1 January, 1993, VAT is no longer payable on goods brought in from other EU Member States. Instead revised arrangements were introduced to deal with such goods. This information leaflet outlines these arrangements insofar as they apply to exempt persons.

2 Exempt Persons — Who is affected?

2.1. "Exempt persons" are those persons who supply exempt goods and services. Typically these include bodies such as financial institutions, insurance companies and persons who supply educational, medical and welfare services as well as funeral undertakers, theatrical and certain sports promoters. A more detailed list may be found in Appendix A of the *"Guide to the Value Added Tax 1999"*.

3 Obligations of exempt persons to register for VAT

3.1. Where an exempt person acquires or is likely to acquire more than £32,000 (€40,631.62) (€41,000 from 1 January, 2002) worth of goods (other than new means of transport or excisable goods) from other EU Member States in any period of 12 months, that person is obliged to register for VAT in respect of those intra-Community acquisitions. The exempt person should register for VAT by completing form TR1 or TR2 which can be obtained from, and which should be returned to, the Taxes Central Registration Office (T.C.R.O). 9/15 Upper O'Connell St., Dublin 1 (see contact details at Appendix I).

3.2. Registration is not required where the €40,631.62 threshold for intra-Community acquisitions is not exceeded. In those cases, goods acquired from other Member States will be chargeable to VAT in the supplier's Member State but will not be charged Irish VAT when the goods enter the State. Exempt persons below the threshold may, however, elect to register if they so wish.

4 Special rules for certain goods

4.1. Intra-Community acquisitions of new means of transport, ie new motor vehicles, boats and planes, are always liable to Irish VAT, even when the annual threshold is not exceeded. There are special rules for paying VAT on these goods and, in certain cases, on excisable goods also.

5 VAT registration number

5.1. On registration, the local Inspector of Taxes issues a VAT number to the exempt person. This number should be made available by the exempt person to all his or her suppliers of goods in other Member States to enable those suppliers to zero rate their supplies on despatch to the State.

6 Obligations when registered

6.1. Exempt persons, once registered for VAT, are obliged

— to calculate VAT due on their intra-Community acquisitions of goods,

— to complete the periodic VAT return showing their VAT liability,

— to send the completed return to the Collector-General, together with any tax payable, within the prescribed time limit,

— to keep proper records of their acquisitions from other Member States to enable their VAT liability to be determined,

— to make those records available for inspection by Revenue on request.

Advice on how to complete the VAT 3 return, is available from the Collector-General's Division (see contact details at Appendix I).

7 Invoices

7.1. Once registered for VAT exempt persons who acquire goods from taxable persons in other Member States should be issued with an invoice by their supplier. This invoice will form the basis for determining the VAT due on the acquisition.

8 How to calculate the VAT due on intra-Community acquisitions

8.1. VAT becomes due on the date of issue of the invoice or, if no invoice issues, on the fifteenth day of the month following the month in which the acquisition is made. The rate of VAT applicable is the rate that applies to the supply of the same goods in the State. The VAT is calculated on the price charged for the goods. The following example illustrates the arrangements:—

8.2. Example:

An insurance company in the State acquires a computer from a German company. The supply in Germany is zero-rated because the insurance company has provided its VAT registration number to the German company and the goods have been transported to the State.

Computer delivered	29.4.01
Invoice issued	12.5.01
Invoiced amount	€100,000
VAT on acquisition at 20%	€20,000

No input credit allowed.

VAT (€20,000) payable to Collector-General (with May/June VAT return) by 19.07.01.

9 Rate of Exchange

9.1. Where acquiring goods from a country, which is not part of the Euro zone the rate of exchange to be used is the rate applicable when the tax becomes due.

10 Deductibility

10.1. Where exempt persons are required to register solely because of their intra-Community acquisitions, they are not entitled to a deduction in respect of VAT paid on those acquisitions. Exempt persons already registered for VAT because they engage in both taxable and exempt activities are entitled to deductibility in respect of inputs relating to those taxable activities, eg a bank which is primarily involved in exempt activities but which also carries on a taxable activity such as leasing of movable goods. Such persons may also be entitled to full or partial deductibility in respect of VAT due on intra-Community acquisitions. A full deduction of the VAT on the intra-Community acquisitions will arise if the acquisitions are wholly attributable to the person's taxable activities. No input credit is allowable if the intra-Community acquisitions relate solely to the person's exempt activities. If the intra-Community acquisitions are common to both types of activity ie dual use inputs, the input credit should be apportioned in accordance with the persons current apportionment arrangements.

11 Inter-company transfers

11.1. A transfer of goods from one branch of a business to another within the State is not a supply for VAT purposes. However, under the Single Market VAT arrangements, a transfer of goods from a business in one Member State to another Member State for the purposes of the business, is deemed to be an intra-Community supply in the Member State of despatch and an intra-Community acquisition in the Member State of arrival. The rules relating to intra-Community acquisitions apply in such cases in the same way as if the goods had been purchased.

11.2. Where, for example, the UK head office of a wholly exempt insurance company transfers a computer to its Irish branch, the transfer is a supply in the UK and an intra-Community acquisition in the State. If the Irish branch's acquisitions exceed or are likely to exceed £32,000 (€40,631.62) (€41,000 from 1 January 2002) in any period of 12 months, it is obliged to register and account for VAT in the State at the standard rate on the current market value of the computer. If the threshold is not exceeded and the Irish branch has not elected to register, the supply is liable to VAT in the UK.

11.3. In the converse case of a transfer of a computer from an Irish branch to the UK head office, the same rules apply in determining where the charge of VAT will arise. In that case, the Irish branch, being an exempt person, will have borne VAT on the purchase of the computer with no right of deduction. In order to avoid double taxation, the Irish branch will be allowed to take an appropriate VAT deduction at the time of the transfer of the computer. The amount of the tax which may be deducted will not be the amount paid on the original purchase of the computer but the amount of tax contained in the value of the computer at the time of transfer known as the "residual tax". The following example shows the calculation of the residual tax:

(a) Assume computer purchased in Ireland in 1999 for €500,000 plus 21% VAT ie a total of €605,000. The VAT paid at that stage was not deductible.

(b) At time of transfer assume the open market value of the computer is €200,000 and VAT rate applying is 20%.

(c) The residual tax contained in the market value of the computer is calculated as follows:

$$\frac{€200,000 \times 100}{120} = €166,666 @ 20\%$$

This residual VAT of €33,333 will be allowed as a deduction to the Irish branch.

12 Fourth Schedule services

12.1. Exempt persons are required to account for VAT in respect of certain services received by them from abroad for business purposes regardless of their value. The services affected include advertising, consultancy and financial services. (An information leaflet No. 09/01 entitled *Fourth Schedule Services* is available. (see contact details at Appendix I) Exempt persons already registered for VAT because they receive such services, are, regardless of the level of their intra-Community acquisitions of goods, liable to Irish VAT on those acquisitions.

13 INTRASTAT

13.1. Persons, including exempt persons, who acquire more than £150,000 (€190,460.71) (€190,500 from 1 January 2002) worth of goods per annum from other Member States will also be required to make a monthly statistical return in respect of those acquisitions. Details of this requirement are contained in the VIES and INTRASTAT Traders Manual, which is available from the VIMA Office (address on list attached).

14 Imports from non-EU countries

14.1. Exempt persons should note that the imports of goods from outside the EU are not to be included when calculating the £32,000 (€40,631.62) registration threshold. This threshold relates only to goods acquired from other Member States. Such imports of goods from outside the EU are liable to Irish VAT at the point of importation and customs documentation continues to be required.

15 Further Information

15.1. Further information may be obtained from VAT Administration, Stamping Building, Dublin Castle, Dublin 2 (Tel 6745000, Extns 48858, 48859, 48861, 48862 or from local Inspectors of Taxes.

15.2. A list of useful addresses, telephone, fax numbers and e-mail addresses is attached at Appendix I.

Contact addresses can be found in Revenue Addresses at start of book

(November 2001)

VAT AND GIFTS

1 Introduction

1.1. As well as dealing with the VAT treatment of gifts, this information leaflet also covers self-supplies, industrial samples, replacement goods, promotional schemes, gift vouchers and tokens etc.

It updates and replaces *Statement of Practice SP-VAT/3/94* and an Information Note of January 1998 on ECJ decisions relating to promotional schemes.

2 Gifts

2.1. As a general rule gifts of taxable goods made in the course or furtherance of a business are liable to VAT unless their cost to the donor, excluding VAT, is £15 (€19.05) (€20 from 1 January, 2002) or less. Where gifts are taxable the chargeable amount is their cost to the donor, excluding VAT. In the case of gifts costing more than €19.05 no allowance can be made for the amount below which gifts are not taxable. Accordingly the person who makes a gift of goods costing €19.05 excluding VAT, has no liability, while the same person making a gift of goods costing €21, excluding VAT, has a liability for tax on €21. The rate of tax depends on the goods involved. Goods given "free" with purchases of other goods (for example, clocks with purchases of heating oil) are regarded as qualifying for the same treatment as gifts.

2.2. A VAT-registered person is generally entitled to an input credit or deduction in his/her VAT return for VAT charged to him/her in respect of the importation, purchase or intra-Community acquisition of goods given away as gifts, subject to the usual conditions. In the case of goods on the acquisition of which only certain persons are entitled to a deduction (petrol, cars etc) only those persons entitled to deduction have a liability to pay VAT on such goods when they are given away as gifts. If, for example, a supermarket was to give away a car as a gift it would not be liable to pay VAT on such a gift since it would not have been entitled to a deduction in respect of the acquisition of the car.

2.3. The gifts concession does not apply if the gift forms part of a series or succession of gifts made to the same person (for example, the gift to a person each week or month of a piece of crockery consisting of a part of a complete china set).

3 "Money-off" Schemes

3.1. These are schemes under which a manufacturer (or a distributor or wholesaler) redeems a money-off voucher, issued in his/her name, which has been accepted by a retailer as part payment for a sale. Reimbursement made by the manufacturer to the retailer on redemption of the money-off coupon from the retailer reduces the taxable amount on which the manufacturer must account for VAT. Accordingly the manufacturer is entitled to deduct the amount reimbursed for the voucher from his/her taxable amount.

This reimbursement to the retailer by the manufacturer should be treated as "third party consideration" forming part of the total consideration for the supply and taxed accordingly in the hands of the retailer. The Sixth VAT Directive (Article 11 (A) (1) (a)) provides that third party consideration is taxable. Section 10 (1) of the VAT Act provides that the amount on which tax is chargeable is "the total consideration which the person supplying goods becomes entitled to receive" in respect of a supply. This includes third party consideration.

4 "Cash-back" Schemes

4.1. These are schemes under which a manufacturer (or a distributor or wholesaler) undertakes to refund cash to a retail customer. The customer sends a voucher back to the manufacturer (with proof of a qualifying purchase) and the manufacturer sends money to the value of the voucher directly back to the customer.

4.2. The manufacturer's taxable amount is reduced by the amount reimbursed to the retail customer. In cash-back cases only the manufacturer's taxable amount should be reduced provided the manufacturer retains adequate records of refunds made and keeps them available for inspection.

5 Goods paid for by vouchers

5.1. These are schemes under which a supplier of goods sells vouchers at a discount to companies who purchase them to distribute them to their staff or to resell to the public at below face value.

The supplier undertakes to accept a voucher at its face value in full or part payment of goods purchased by a customer who was not the buyer of the voucher.

5.2. Subject to the conditions set out below the taxable amount attributable to a voucher in the circumstances outlined is the sum of money obtained by the supplier of the goods from the sale of the voucher and not the face value of that voucher.

5.3. A trader operating such a scheme must be able to demonstrate to his/her local inspector of taxes that s/he has a system in place which enables him/her, when a voucher is being redeemed, to clearly identify the original purchaser of that voucher and to determine the amount of any discount granted to that original purchaser.

5.4. The initial transaction involving the sale of the voucher is not a taxable transaction. VAT becomes chargeable only when the voucher is presented in exchange for goods. For this reason, this relief is allowed only in cases where a proper audit trail is maintained by the trader to the satisfaction of his/her local inspector of taxes.

6 Advertising goods

6.1. Gifts in the nature of advertising, such as trophies bearing the name of the donor, or gifts to employees for long service, outstanding sales and the like, are treated in the same way as other gifts.

6.2. Certain goods given free of charge for business use to trade customers may continue to be supplied tax free even though in excess of €19.05 in value. Examples are advertising mirrors, glasses or beer mats, bearing the donor's name, supplied to a hotel or public house, display stands supplied to a grocer or a showcase supplied to a jeweller.

7 Industrial samples

7.1. The gift, in reasonable quantity, to an actual or potential customer of industrial samples in a form not ordinarily available for sale to the public is not taxable in any circumstances, regardless of the value of the goods.

8 Replacement goods

8.1. Replacement goods supplied free of charge in accordance with warranties or guarantees on original goods are not taxable.

9 Self-Supplies of Goods and Services

9.1. Gifts are to be distinguished from self-supplies. A trader who supplies himself/ herself or his/her family with goods from stock (eg where a record dealer takes one of his CDs for his/her own use) is not entitled to the benefit of the gifts relief.

9.2. All self-supplies of goods are liable to VAT on the basis of cost, excluding VAT, to the supplier.

9.3. The only self-service at present taxable is a catering self-service (see next paragraph). Although other self-services are not at present taxable, tax must be accounted for on goods used in supplying such self-services. For example, the garage-owner who uses business goods to repair his/her private car is liable for tax on the cost to him/her of the goods used in the repairs. There is no liability on the value of the labour supplied.

10 Staff Catering in hotels etc

10.1. Meals provided to catering staff free of charge by hotels and other catering establishments are liable to VAT if the actual cost to the hotel, etc of providing them exceeds £20,000 (€25,394.76) a year (€25,500 from 1 January 2002). The weekly amount liable to VAT for each employee will be the sum agreed in that respect with Revenue from time to time.

11 Gift Tokens and book tokens

11.1. The chargeable amount in the case of goods or services supplied in exchange for tokens is the amount stated on the token as well, of course, as any money paid in addition to that amount.

11.2. The sale of gift tokens, book tokens, etc is not liable to tax except where, and to the extent that, the amount charged exceeds the value shown on the tokens (for example, a combined gift token/greeting card).

12 Cash Basis

12.1. Traders who account on the cash basis and who exchange vouchers, etc for cash must include the value of such vouchers as cash in their taxable receipts.

13 Enquiries

13.1. Further information may be obtained from VAT Administration, Stamping Building, Dublin Castle, Dublin 2 (Tel: 01–6745000) or from local inspectors of taxes.

13.2. A list of useful addresses, telephone, fax numbers and e-mail addresses is attached at Appendix I.

Contact addresses can be found in Revenue Addresses at start of book

VALUE ADDED TAX INFORMATION LEAFLET NO 15/01

(November 2001)

VAT AND SOLICITORS

1 Introduction

1.1. This information leaflet sets out the treatment of solicitors in relation to VAT. It updates and replaces the information leaflet of the same title issued in April 1988.

2 Which solicitors have to register for VAT?

2.1. All independent solicitors (that is, solicitors who are not employees) are obliged to register for VAT, if their annual turnover from the supply of taxable services (see paragraphs 9.1–11.1) exceeds or is likely to exceed £20,000 (€25,394.76) (€25,500 from 1 January 2002). Applications for registration should be made on form TR1 which is available on request. "Turnover" consists of professional fees together with "... all taxes (excl. VAT), commissions, costs and charges whatsoever ..." (section 10(1) VAT Act) which a solicitor is entitled to receive. State Solicitors are not obliged to register in respect of their activities as State Solicitors but they are obliged to register if their annual turnover from other professional activities exceeds or is likely to exceed £20,000 (€25,394.76) (€25,500 from 1 January 2002).

3 Obligations of VAT-registered solicitors

3.1. VAT-registered solicitors are obliged to —

(*a*) keep sufficiently detailed records to enable their liability as declared by themselves to be confirmed (see paragraph 4.1);

(*b*) issue invoices containing specified particulars (see Appendix I) in respect of taxable services supplied to other VAT-registered persons. If the consideration shown on an invoice is reduced, a credit note must be issued if the client is a VAT-registered person. Copies of invoices and credit notes must be retained;

and

(*c*) submit every two months, returns of their outputs and purchases together with remittances for any tax due. Solicitors may have the choice of paying VAT on the basis of services supplied or moneys received subject to their annual turnover exceeding or being likely to exceed £500,000 (€634,869.04) (€635,000 from 1 January, 2002).

4 Records to be kept

4.1. Details of the records which solicitors are obliged to keep are given in Chapter 10 of the *Guide to the Value Added Tax 1999*. Essentially the records need to be in such a form and contain such information as is necessary to confirm that the values entered in a solicitor's VAT return or series of VAT returns are correct both as to amount and VAT ratings (in effect, the records the solicitor used to compile his return). Accordingly the records need to distinguish by VAT rate between taxable, exempt and non-taxable output (see paragraph 7.1) and taxable inputs (see paragraph 8.2).

5 Confidentiality

5.1. General supervision of the operation of the VAT system is exercised by means of periodic visits by Revenue officers to taxpayers' premises. In examining a solicitor's records for the purposes of VAT control the officers would wish to see only such documents as are directly relevant to the solicitor's own VAT liability. If verification of liability would not be possible from these documents, the solicitor may be requested to provide additional information. Revenue officers would not seek to breach the confidential relationship existing between solicitors and their clients. Revenue are prepared, if it suits any solicitor's convenience, to accept a code system in lieu of names for a solicitor's clients.

6 Examination of Records

6.1. Examination of records is normally carried out by the local inspector of taxes. The purpose of examination is to ensure that records are maintained in accordance with the VAT Act and Regulations and that the records systems used are adequate to give the correct VAT payable (or repayable) by the taxpayer. Examination covers both a check of the returns which have been made on forms VAT 3 against the actual records, an examination of the records kept and a check of invoices issued and received.

6.2. Inspecting officers normally include in their examination:

- (*a*) Office bank account, office bank statements and cheque payments book and returned cheques (b) Cash book
- (*c*) Copies of invoices issued
- (*d*) Purchases book and invoices received
- (*e*) Discounts or reductions granted and the appropriate credit notes
- (*f*) Credit notes received
- (*g*) Record of taxable services supplied
- (*h*) Debtors' accounts

6.3. It is accepted that a solicitor handles both his own business money (office money) and money belonging to his clients and that the rules of the Law Society require him to keep the two sets of money physically separate and to record the entries separately in his books of account. Receipts lodged to a client's bank accounts (current, deposit or specially designated accounts) are treated as monies held in trust and Revenue accepts that amounts so held do not attract liability to VAT. It is understood that, on the issue of a Bill of Costs, withdrawals from these accounts are authorised for the benefit of the solicitor's own accounts. Where a solicitor maintains a floating balance of his own monies in a client's bank account certification will be required that:

- (*a*) these monies do not arise from profit costs retained in the client's bank account or lodged direct to that account, and
- (*b*) disbursements which are part of the solicitor's service eg travelling or hotel costs, have not been paid direct from a client's bank account.

6.4. Where such certification is available it will not be necessary for Revenue officers to examine client's accounts. Ordinary office debtors' accounts ie where profit costs are charged as distinct from client's own money transactions, should normally be made available to cross check accounts issued, discounts allowed and cash received.

6.5. Profit cost accounts normally indicate the amounts in respect of a solicitor's own profit costs and also costs in respect of outlay. Where it is clearly shown that part of outlay is liable to VAT and part not liable, it will form the basis, together with receipts from small transactions (eg fees for drafting wills or for producing documents), of the solicitor's own liability to VAT.

6.6. A solicitor's receipts should be so segregated in the records as to enable returns to be made and checked under the various headings (zero, 12.5 and 20 per cent.).

7 Rates of VAT

7.1. Almost all services supplied by solicitors are liable to VAT at 20 per cent. The principal exceptions are the following:

(*a*)	collection of insurance premiums	Exempt
(*b*)	letting of solicitor's own premises (short-term)	Exempt
(*c*)	services connected with property situated outside the State (see paragraph 12.1)	0 per cent
(*d*)	Fourth Schedule services (see paragraph 13)	0 per cent
(*e*)	Directors' fees; Commissioner for Oaths fees; Notary Public fees	not taxable.

8 Taxable Amount

8.1. The amount on which a solicitor is liable, and the amount by reference to which a solicitor is or is not obliged to register, is the amount of his/her professional fees together with "all taxes (other than VAT), commissions, costs and charges whatsoever" which the solicitor is entitled to receive in respect of or in relation to the supply of his/her services. Outlays made by a solicitor on behalf of a client are not regarded as part of the solicitor's charges and are not, therefore, taxable. Expenses incurred by a solicitor in the course of, and for the purposes of, carrying out his/her professional services are regarded as part of the solicitor's charges and are taxable.

8.2. Those outlays which are not liable to VAT in the hands of a solicitor include:

Advertising

Company Registration, etc. Fees including Company Seals

Counsels' Fees (see note in paragraph 8.2)

Court Fees and Fines

Deposits (such as house deposits paid by clients)

Land Registry Fees

Photographs of Court

Exhibits

Registration of Deeds Fees

Search Fees

Stamp Duty and other duties and taxes

Surveyors' and Estate Agents' Fees

Valuation Services (by actuaries and Valuation Office)

Witnesses' Fees and Expenses.

8.3. Where it is practicable for these outlays to be invoiced direct by the supplier to the client (although transmitted through the solicitor) the solicitor would be involved hardly at all but it is most important for the solicitor to ensure that all invoices relating to such transactions are in the name of the client. If they are not, the client, if s/he is a VAT-registered person and there is an amount of VAT invoices, will not be entitled to a deduction for the tax. (NOTE re counsels' fees: When counsel has received payment of fees s/he will issue to the instructing solicitor, at the solicitor's request, a combined VAT invoice/receipt drawn up in the name of the lay client).

8.4. Those expenses which are regarded as part of a solicitor's charges for professional services and which are liable to VAT include:

Courier Fees

Hire of consultation rooms from Incorporated Law Society (exempt if charged out separately by solicitor)

Hotel costs, photocopying, postage, summons serving fees, telephone, town agent fees, travelling costs.

9 Deduction for VAT charged on purchases

9.1. A VAT-registered solicitor is entitled to take a credit or deduction (ie set off against his/her liability) for most VAT properly invoiced to him/her by his/her suppliers. S/he does not have to have paid his/her suppliers to be entitled to the credit.

9.2. The only expenditure in respect of which a tax credit may not be taken is expenditure relating to:

(*a*) the provision of food, drink, accommodation or other personal services for the solicitor, his/her agents or employees (for example, hotel costs)

(*b*) entertainment expenses

(*c*) purchase or hire of car or other road passenger vehicles

(*d*) purchase of petrol

(*e*) an exempt (for example short-term letting of premises), or non-business activity

(*f*) VAT incurred prior to registration.

9.3. A credit or deduction may be taken in respect of diesel, car repairs and maintenance, and car parts (for example, a set of tyres), subject to the condition that they are used for the purposes of a taxable business.

10 Accounting for Tax

10.1. The normal basis of accounting is the invoice or sales basis. A VAT-registered solicitor using this basis of accounting is liable to pay VAT by reference to services supplied. VAT is not chargeable on services which are completed before the date of registration no matter when the relevant invoice is issued. Services which are not completed before the date of registration will not be chargeable to VAT to the extent that they are paid for (that is, that the solicitor's office account has been credited) before that date.

11 Moneys Received Basis of Accounting

11.1. An alternative basis is the moneys received basis. This alternative basis is available to solicitors whose annual turnover exceeds or is likely to exceed £500,000, (€634,869.04) (€635,000 from 1 January 2002). To avail him/herself of the moneys received basis of accounting a solicitor needs to indicate this specifically on form TR1 when applying for VAT registration.

11.2. A solicitor who opts to be accountable for VAT on his/her moneys received is liable for tax, at the rate in force at the time the services are supplied on all moneys received in each tax period excluding moneys received in respect of exempt services such as collection of insurance premiums, short-term lettings by the solicitor of his/her own property (land and buildings), agency services in regard to the lending of money and payments on which VAT has already been accounted for if previously on the invoice basis of accounting.

Monies received in respect of services supplied during the period prior to registration are not taxable.

11.3. Moneys received by a VAT-registered person include any sums:

— credited to his/her account in a bank, building society or other financial concern,

— received by a solicitor on his/her behalf, or

— paid to Revenue by a third party to his/her account in accordance with certain provisions of the taxes acts.

A VAT-registered person is also deemed to have received money if liability in respect of a business transaction is settled by setting off against it a credit due in respect of some other transaction. Care must be taken when money is received through an agent that any amount withheld by the agent to covers fees, expenses etc, is included in the taxable amount.

11.4. Moneys received are treated as being inclusive of VAT and only the tax-exclusive content is taxable. If, for example, a solicitor accounting on the moneys received basis were to receive, say, €10,000 in a taxable period March/April 2002 his/her liability would be €1667, that is €8,333 at 20 per cent.

11.5. It may be open to a solicitor to change from one basis of accounting to the other. Details can be found in Chapter 8 of the *Guide to the Value Added Tax 1999* and *Information Leaflet No. 22/01*.

12 Withholding tax

12.1. Income Tax withheld from payments for professional services is deemed, for VAT purposes, to have been received by the taxpayer. If, for example, payment of an amount due to a solicitor is reduced from €1,200 (€1,000 + €200 VAT) to €1,000 (€200 withheld for Income Tax) the solicitor is for VAT purposes deemed to have received €1,200. The same position applies to tax withheld from payments to certain building sub-contractors.

13 Foreign services

13.1. VAT is an EU Community tax and the Sixth VAT Directive, which aims at achieving uniform application of the system throughout the EU, contains rules for determining the place of supply of services. These may be briefly summarised as follows in relation to "foreign" services supplied by a solicitor:—

    (*a*) Legal services relating to immovable property are deemed to be supplied where the property is situated. Accordingly, a solicitor acting for a client in relation to the purchase, say, of a property in Northern Ireland is not liable to Irish VAT but he may have a liability in respect of UK VAT,

    (*b*) other legal services supplied to persons not resident or not established in Ireland, will be liable to Irish VAT only if they are supplied for non-business purposes (ie to private individuals) to a client who resides anywhere in the EU.

14 Summary

14.1. All solicitors, other than employees, are, subject to the £20,000 (€25,394.76) (€25,500 from 1 January, 2002) annual turnover limit, obliged to register for, and pay VAT. (For the position of State Solicitor please see paragraph 2.1. For the position of Commissioners for Oaths and Notaries Public please see paragraph 11 (e)).

14.2. Application for registration should be made on form TR1 which, when completed, should be sent to the local Inspector of Taxes.

14.3. Virtually all activities of solicitors are taxable. Accordingly conveyancing, trust work, litigation, company formation and private work are liable to VAT. The rate of VAT is generally 20 per cent (but see paragraph 7.1).

14.4. If a solicitor should choose to pay VAT on the basis of moneys received s/he is liable at the rate in force at the time the services are supplied and not at the rate in force when payment is received, if different.

14.5. VAT-registered solicitors are entitled to a deduction for VAT properly invoiced to them on or after the date of their VAT registration in respect of purchases of most goods and services for business purposes (see paragraph 9).

14.6. VAT-registered solicitors are obliged to keep detailed records and to make returns every two months of the value of professional services supplied and goods and services purchased for business purposes (see paragraph 6.2).

15 Further information

15.1. Inquiries may be made to Revenue, VAT Administration Branch, Stamping Building, Dublin Castle, Dublin 2. (Tel. 01–6745000) or from Inspectors of Taxes (see attached Appendix II).

15.2. A list of useful addresses, telephone, fax and E-mail addresses is attached at Appendix II.

APPENDIX I
INVOICE (see note)

From		To
Smyth and Smyth,		
Solicitors,		Mr. J. Jones,
123, Litigation Street,		456, Caveat Row,
Dublin 2.		Dublin 1.
VAT No. 1234567A		Ref: No.

	€
To fees for professional (taxable) services	400
To expenses (details attached)	100
	500
VAT @ 20 per cent	100
	600
To outlays on your behalf (details attached)	210
TOTAL	810

NOTE ON INVOICES No special form of invoice is prescribed for use in relation to Value Added Tax but an invoice must contain the following details: (i) date of issue (ii) name, address and registration number of person issuing the invoice (iii) description and date of supply of services (iv) taxable consideration (v) rate and amount of VAT.

An invoice, giving these details, must be issued by every VAT-registered person in respect of every taxable transaction with another registered person. Although there is no obligation to do so, a solicitor may, if it suits his/her business convenience, issue the same type of invoice to both VAT-registered clients and VAT-unregistered clients.

VAT invoices should be issued by solicitors to their clients only and not to the parties who may be making payment, if different (for example, the losing party in an action in the Courts).

The client, if s/he is VAT-registered, is the only person who may be entitled to a deduction for the VAT charged.

A copy of the invoice must be retained by a solicitor for six years. S/he must retain the original of the purchase invoice for the same period. The Inspector of Taxes may authorise a lesser period on request.

NOTE ON SETTLEMENT VOUCHERS

A settlement voucher is an invoice in reverse, that is, it is an invoice issued to the person who has supplied goods/services by the purchaser. The only difference is that the settlement voucher must contain, in addition to the details required on an invoice, the VAT registration number of the purchaser. Once both parties agree, a settlement voucher suffices for the same purpose, and is subject to the same requirements, as an invoice.

Contact addresses can be found in Revenue Addresses at start of book

(November 2001)

VAT TREATMENT OF GOODS TRANSPORT AND ANCILLARY SERVICES BETWEEN EU COUNTRIES

1 General

1.1. Special rules apply to the transport of goods between EU Member States. These rules are set out in this information leaflet and for convenience the treatment is summarized in Appendix 1 to this leaflet.

This Information Leaflet updates and replaces *Statement of Practice SP-VAT/12/92.*

2 Intra-Community goods transport services supplied by persons registered for VAT in the State

2.1. Where a person registered for VAT in the State supplies intra-Community goods transport services, that is, the transport of goods from one Member State to another, to a customer registered for VAT in the State, the supplier is liable to Irish VAT and must account for it in the normal way (same as internal transport services).

2.2. Where a person registered for VAT in the State supplies such services to customers registered for VAT in another Member State no Irish VAT liability arises for the supplier. The customers are, however, obliged to account for VAT in their own Member States as if the customers themselves had supplied the services.

2.3. If a customer is not registered for VAT (eg a private individual) the supply of intra-Community goods transport services is taxable in the place of departure ie where the transport of the goods begins. In the case of the transport of goods on behalf of a private individual from Ireland to the UK liability to VAT arises in Ireland because that is the place of departure; in the case of haulage on behalf of a private individual from the UK to Ireland liability arises in the UK. Suppliers of intra-Community goods transport services to unregistered persons should note that if they are providing services which are taxable in another Member State they are subject to the rules relating to VAT in that other Member State.

3 Domestic transport services supplied as part of intra-Community transport services

3.1. Where a domestic goods transport service (ie where transport begins and ends in the State) is supplied to a person registered for VAT in another Member State and that service forms part of an intra-Community goods transport service, no Irish VAT liability arises for the supplier and the customer should account for VAT in his/her own Member State as if s/he had supplied the service. In effect the supplier treats the supply as if it were an intra-Community transaction.

3.2. An example of this would be where a shipping company, registered for VAT in the UK is contracted to transport goods from London to Athlone. The shipping company transports the goods from London to Dublin and then employs an Irish transporter to transport the goods from Dublin to Athlone. In this example the Irish transporter will invoice the UK shipping company free of VAT. The UK company accounts for the VAT on this transaction in the UK on the reverse charge basis.

3.3. The Irish transporter must obtain and retain for subsequent inspection documentary evidence to confirm that the service provided by him/her is part of an overall intra-Community transport service.

3.4. It should be noted that this arrangement does not apply to **wholly** domestic goods transport services, even where these are supplied to a person registered for VAT in another Member State. Neither does it apply to intra-Community goods transport services supplied to Irish VAT-registered customers by transporters registered for VAT in the State. In both these cases Irish VAT is chargeable.

4 Domestic and intra-Community transport services supplied in connection with transport of goods into and out of the Community (Imports and Exports)

4.1. Expenses incurred in the transport of imported goods to their place of destination within the EU should be included in the value for VAT at point of entry, **if known** and taxed accordingly. The effect of this is that the internal EU transport costs will attract the same rate of VAT as that chargeable on the goods at importation.

4.2. Where the costs of transport within the EU are included in the value for VAT at importation and charged with VAT accordingly the **transport service itself** is then zero-rated.

4.3. A haulier providing zero-rated transport services in these circumstance is obliged to obtain and retain for subsequent inspection, documentary evidence that the transport costs were included in the value for VAT at importation.

4.4. If the onward transport costs are **not** known at the time of importation and therefore not included in the value for tax at point of entry, then the transport service may be liable at a positive rate (see Appendix I).

4.5. Transport services supplied in connection with goods which are to be exported out of the EU are not affected by this provision. Such services will continue to be zero-rated provided, of course, that the transporter is in a position to satisfy the Inspector of Taxes that the zero-rating correctly applies and that s/he holds documentary evidence that the transportation in question is part of an export transportation service.

5 Ancillary services in Ports and Airports

5.1. Services ancillary to intra-Community goods transport (ie loading, unloading, handling etc) supplied in port areas or in airports **to meet the direct needs of ships or aeroplanes** is zero-rated. This zero-rating applies for example to loading, unloading and handling of cargo in the port or airport, limited storage in the port or airport (no more than five days) while awaiting the onward transport of the goods. A more comprehensive list of the services affected is contained in Appendix III.

5.2. The zero-rating referred to in paragraph 5.1 **does not** apply to services ancillary to intra-Community goods transport supplied beyond the direct needs of ships and aeroplanes, such as breaking down of containers, packing or repacking and similar handling services supplied in connection with the onward distribution of goods, etc. Long term storage and warehousing of goods also continues to be taxable in the normal way.

5.3. Ancillary services in connection with intra-Community goods transport supplied outside of ports and airports are taxable by reference to the normal rules applying to transport services. Where supplied to an Irish VAT-registered or to an unregistered customer they are liable to Irish VAT. Where supplied to a customer registered for VAT in another Member State VAT liability arises in that other Member State in the customer's hands.

5.4. Services ancillary to the import and export of goods into and out of the Community will continue to be zero-rated in the normal way.

6 Agency services supplied by Irish VAT-registered persons

6.1. The treatment of agency services (eg shipping agents) in connection with intra-Community goods transport and ancillary services is the same as that which applies to the services themselves. Such agency services supplied to VAT-registered persons are taxed by reference to the Member State of registration of the customer. In the case of such agency services supplied to unregistered persons, liability arises in the Member State where the transport begins or the ancillary service is carried out.

7 VAT status of immediate customer

7.1. Suppliers of goods transport services should note that it is the VAT status of the immediate customer for the haulage or ancillary service that determines the VAT treatment of the supply. For example, where a supplier of goods transport services is contracted by a freight forwarder to transport goods belonging to a third party to another Member State, it is the VAT status of the freight forwarder that determines the treatment of the supply rather than the VAT status of the owner of the goods.

8 Verification of customers' VAT numbers

8.1. As outlined above, the VAT status of the customer is the key element in determining the VAT treatment of intra-Community goods transport and ancillary services. Traders are advised to contact their EU customers and ask them to confirm in writing their VAT registration number. (An example of the type of letter that might be used for this purpose is attached in Appendix II).

8.2. The fiscal authorities in each Member State have put in place a computerised system that makes it possible, where necessary, for traders to verify the VAT numbers of their customers in other Member States. An Irish trader who has doubts about the validity of a VAT number quoted is able to use the verification system to establish whether a particular number is valid. The system is primarily intended to be used in such circumstances and is not intended for routine checks. Use of the verification system is **not** obligatory and traders who are aware of their customers' bona fides from trading with them over a period of time are not expected or required to use the verification system.

8.3. Transport operators should note that where they supply intra-Community goods transport and related ancillary services to a VAT-registered person in another Member

State the customer's VAT number must be shown on the relevant invoice. This will ensure that the Inspector of Taxes can verify that VAT liability does not arise in the State in respect of the supply in question.

9 Customers registered for VAT in the State

9.1. Customers registered for VAT in the State receiving intra-Community goods transport and related services from suppliers registered for VAT in the State are charged Irish VAT which may be deducted in accordance with the normal VAT rules relating to deductibility.

9.2. Customers registered for VAT in the State receiving such services from suppliers who are not registered in Ireland but are registered in another Member State are not charged VAT by their suppliers. However, these customers must account for Irish VAT in respect of such services as if the customers themselves had supplied the services. This is done by declaring a liability to VAT at the standard rate in the VAT return. Customers entitled to full or partial deduction of VAT charged to them simultaneously take a deduction of all or some of the tax. Customers who are not entitled to deduction in full or in part of the tax must pay the tax for which they are liable when sending the VAT return to the Collector-General.

9.3. The same procedure must be followed by customers registered for VAT in other Member States who receive intra-Community goods transport services from suppliers registered for VAT in Ireland.

10 VAT at importation; treatment of onward transport costs

10.1. Where the onward costs are known at the time of importation, whether shown separately or not, they are included in the amount which is subject to VAT at the point of entry and taxable at the rate applicable to the supply of the goods in the State. Where, for example, goods are imported into Ireland for onward movement to another Member State, or vice versa, then if the value of the haulage is included in the amount subject to VAT at the point of entry the haulage service is zero-rated.

11 Further Information

11.1. Further information may be obtained from local Inspectors of Taxes.

11.2. A list of useful addresses, telephone and fax numbers and e-mail addresses is attached at Appendix IV.

Appendix 1
INTRA-EU GOODS TRANSPORT — TREATMENT IN SINGLE MARKET

	Haulier	**Customer**	**Circumstances**	**VAT Position**
1.	Person registered for VAT in Ireland	Person registered for VAT in Ireland	Intra-EU transport	Haulier charges Irish VAT.*
2.	Person registered for VAT in Ireland	Person registered for VAT in other Member State.	Intra-EU transport	Haulier charges no Irish VAT. Customer liable to VAT in other Member State under the reverse charge rule.
3.	Person registered for VAT in Ireland	Not registered for VAT (eg private individual)	Intra-EU transport from Ireland	Haulier charges Irish VAT because the transport begins in Ireland.
4.	Person registered for VAT in Ireland	Not registered for VAT (eg private individual)	Intra-EU transport to Ireland	Liable to VAT in the other Member State because that is where the transport begins. Irish haulier must register for VAT in the other Member State subject to the VAT rules in that other Member State.
5.	Person registered for VAT in other Member State	Person registered for VAT in Ireland	Intra-EU transport to or from Ireland	Haulier does not charge any VAT. Customer must account for Irish VAT* under the reverse charge rule.
6.	Person registered for VAT in other Member State	Not registered for VAT (eg private individual)	Intra-EU transport from Ireland	Liability to Irish VAT arises because the transport begins in Ireland. Haulier must register and charge customer Irish VAT.

7.	Person registered for VAT in other Member State	Not registered for VAT (eg private individual)	Intra-EU transport to Ireland	No liability to Irish VAT. Haulier charges the customer VAT in the other Member State at the rate applicable there because that is where the transport begins.
8.	Person registered for VAT in Ireland	Registered for VAT or private individual	Import of goods to Ireland where	Where the costs of transport are included in the value for VAT at Ireland is the final importation then the transport service is destination zero-rated.
9.	Person registered for VAT in Ireland	Registered for VAT or private individual	Import of goods into another Member State where Ireland is the final destination	Intra-Community transport service. However, if the value of haulage is included in the amount subject to VAT at the point of entry, then the haulage destination service is zero-rated.
10.	Person registered for VAT in Ireland or in other Member State	Registered for VAT or private individual	Import of goods to Ireland where another Member State is the final destination	Intra-Community transport service. However, if the value of the haulage is included in the amount subject to VAT at the point of entry then the haulage service is zero-rated.

*Note: In most cases Irish VAT can be claimed as a credit by a VAT-registered trader.

Appendix II

Dear Customer,

VAT/TVA/IVA/MWSt/BTW

To comply with EU regulations, we must show your VAT/Sales Tax Number on our invoices.

To help us with this, could you please fill in the box below with your VAT/Sales Tax Number and return it to us as soon as possible. Please ensure that the country prefix is included.

N.B. If you are not registered for VAT, please tick

In addition, to help us update our records, please forward your:

Telephone No. ....

Fax No. ....

Address ....

E. mail ....

Thank you.

Yours faithfully,

Appendix III

Ancillary transport services to which the zero-rate applies when supplied in ports and airports

River and harbour pilotage Mooring and unmooring Stevedoring

Landing

Stowing

Loading

Restowing

Cranage

Tonnage dues Cargo dues

Towage

Contact addresses can be found in Revenue Addresses at start of book

(November 2001)

REPAYMENTS TO UNREGISTERED PERSONS

1 Introduction

1.1. This information leaflet sets out the various schemes for repayment of VAT to unregistered persons. It updates and replaces *Statement of Practice SP-VAT/2/94.*

2 Foreign businesses paying Irish VAT

2.1. The general position is that a person who is engaged in business outside the State and who is not engaged in business in the State may under the terms of the 8th or 13th EU VAT Directives claim repayment of Irish VAT on most business purchases in Ireland. The main conditions governing repayment are:

    (*a*) the claimant must produce a certificate that s/he is VAT-registered in another Member State of the EU (this condition does not apply to claimants from outside the EU reclaiming under the EU 13th VAT Directive);

    (*b*) the goods/services giving rise to the claim must be goods/services in respect of which tax would be deductible if the claimant's business was carried on in Ireland and must not include goods for supply within the State or motor vehicles for hiring out for utilisation within the State;

    (*c*) the business for which the goods/services were purchased must be a business which would be taxable if carried on in Ireland;

    (*d*) application is by way of form VAT 60 which is available from the VAT Repayments Section, Government Buildings, Kilrush Road, Ennis, Co. Clare.

3 Zero-rating of services supplied to foreign traders (VAT 60A Procedure)

3.1. Foreign traders in receipt of taxable services from Irish traders on a regular and continuous basis may apply to have those services relieved from VAT. In this way, the necessity of applying to Revenue for VAT repayments is avoided.

3.2. Application for relief is made by way of Form VAT 60A. Traders established in EU Member States must submit a certificate of taxable status with their applications. Form VAT 60A is available from the **Office of the Accountant General, Revenue, Kilrush Road, Ennis, Co. Clare** (see Appendix 1 for contact details).

3.3. This relief is subject to periodic review, is valid for two years, but may be renewed on application. **The relief does not apply to supplies of taxable goods.**

4 Farm buildings or structures, land drainage and land reclamation

4.1. Farmers who are not registered for VAT and who pay VAT in relation to the construction, extension, alteration or reconstruction of farm buildings and structures or on land drainage and land reclamation may reclaim this VAT (Repayment claim form VAT 58). Farmers who are registered for VAT in respect of their intra-Community acquisitions only or in respect of certain services received from abroad (see *Information*

Leaflet 12/01) are similarly entitled to repayment but must claim this refund as a deduction or input credit in their VAT return.

4.2. No refunds are allowable where the VAT invoice was issued six years or more prior to the date of the claim.

5 Sea fishing vessels and equipment

5.1. The purchase intra-Community acquisition, importation, hire, maintenance and repair of sea-fishing vessels of a gross tonnage of not more than 15 tons are liable to VAT. An unregistered fisherman may claim repayment of such VAT provided the fishing vessel concerned has been the subject of a grant or loan from An Bord Iascaigh Mhara.

5.2. An unregistered fisherman may also claim repayment of VAT on the purchase, intra-Community acquisition, importation, hire, maintenance and repair of the following specified fishing equipment:—

> Anchors, autopilots, bilge and deck pumps, buoys and floats, compasses, cranes, echo graphs, echo sounders, electrical generating sets, fish boxes, fish finders, fishing baskets, life boats and life rafts, marine lights, marine engines, net drums, net hauliers, net sounders, radar apparatus, radio navigational aid apparatus, radio telephones, refrigeration plant, trawl doors, trawl gallows and winches.

5.3. If the vessel for which the equipment is intended is not more than 15 tons (gross tonnage), it is a condition that the vessel must have been the subject of a grant or loan from An Bord Iascaigh Mhara. Repayment in respect of equipment for a vessel of more than 15 tons (gross tonnage) may be claimed whether or not the vessel was the subject of a grant or loan. (Repayment claim form VAT 58A).

5.4. Application should be made to the **Central Repayments Office, Revenue, Coolshannagh, Co. Monaghan (tel. 047–38010).**

5.5. There is no provision for relief on other equipment or on materials purchased for the carrying out of repair or maintenance work by an unregistered fisherman himself or by any other unregistered person.

5.6. There is no VAT on the supply of fishing nets of a kind used by commercial fishermen.

6 Marine diesel

6.1. An unregistered fisherman may claim repayment of VAT borne or paid on the purchase intra-Community acquisition or importation of marine diesel. Excise duty may also be reclaimed in respect of VAT-registered and unregistered fishermen. Claims for repayment should be made on a three-monthly basis. (Repayment claim form C & E No. 1007/VAT 5813 — obtainable from the local Officer of Customs and Excise).

Application should be made to the Central Repayments Office, Revenue, Coolshannagh, Co. Monaghan (tel. 047–38010).

7 VAT charged at customs

7.1. Repayment of VAT charged at import where the VAT was not legally owed eg VAT overpaid due to miscalculation, may be made by the Central Repayments office, Coolshannagh, Co. Monaghan.

7.2. Application must first be made to the local Customs offices where the VAT was charged. Claims must be made within three years.

8 Sea rescue craft, equipment, etc

8.1. Repayment may be reclaimed by qualifying groups, of VAT incurred on outlay on small sea rescue craft (15 tons gross tonnage or less), ancillary equipment and special boat buildings used exclusively in connection with rescue or assistance at sea or with the training of persons for such purposes (Repayment claim form VAT 70).

9 Disabled Persons

9.1. Repayment may be claimed on VAT paid in relation to vehicles (*a*) for use by severely and permanently disabled persons as drivers or passengers and (*b*) for use by organisations for the transport of severely and permanently disabled persons. There is also provision for the repayment of, and in certain circumstances, the remission of Vehicle Registration Tax.

9.2. Application forms and public notices are available from the Central Repayments Office, Disabled Drivers Section, Revenue, Coolshannagh, Co. Monaghan (Tel: 047 — 38010).

10 Equipment for disabled persons

10.1. Repayment may be claimed by disabled persons of the VAT paid on certain special aids and appliances. The relief is also available in certain circumstances to persons other than disabled persons who purchase such goods for handing over to a particular disabled person (Repayment claim form VAT 61A).

11 Radios for the blind

11.1. An institution or society having for its primary object the amelioration of the lot of blind persons may claim repayment of the VAT borne or paid by it on the purchase or importation of radio sets which are intended for the use of blind persons (Repayment claim form VAT 59).

12 Residential caravans and mobile homes

12.1. Repayment may be claimed of VAT in excess of 12.5% which has been borne or paid on the supply or importation of a caravan, mobile home, or similar structure purchased by a person as a residence or, in the case of a local authority, provided for letting as a residence. Where the claimant is not a local authority, repayment is conditional on the caravan, etc being rated (Repayment claim form VAT 62).

13 Documents

13.1. Repayment may be claimed of the tax charged at importation on documents imported in circumstances of a non-commercial nature where tax would not have been payable if the transaction had occurred within the State. There is no special form for claiming repayment under this heading. Details of the relief are given in Notice No. 1317, obtainable from **Revenue (Supply Branch), Wicklow House, South Great George's Street, Dublin 2 (tel. 01–6745000).**

14 Irish companies providing certain services outside the State

14.1. A person who conducts a business from within the State but who does not supply goods or services in the State may claim a refund of deductible VAT on outlay on goods or services, in certain circumstances (Form VAT 60E). For example, an Irish bank or insurance company providing services outside the EU, which are not taxable in this country, may be entitled to claim relief as a "foreign" business.

15 Touring Coaches

15.1. Repayment may be claimed by persons engaged in the business of carriage for reward of tourists, by road under contracts for group transport, of VAT incurred in expenditure on the purchase, lease/hire of touring coaches, subject to certain conditions. (Repayment claim form VAT 71).

16 Donated medical equipment

16.1. Repayment of VAT incurred in the purchase or importation of new medical instruments and appliances (excluding means of transport) purchased through voluntary donations may be claimed by hospitals or donors, as appropriate, subject to conditions. The principal conditions are that the instrument or appliance be:—

(*a*) €25,390 or more in value (exclusive of tax),

(*b*) designed and manufactured for use solely in medical research or in diagnosis, prevention or treatment of illness,

(*c*) no part of the funds used in the purchase of the goods is provided directly or indirectly by the State, and

(*d*) the subject of a recommendation by the Minister for Health that having regard to the requirements of the health services in the State, a refund of tax would be appropriate. (Repayment claim form VAT 72).

17 Donated Research Equipment

17.1. Repayment of VAT incurred in the purchase or importation of any new instrument or appliance (excluding means of transport) purchased through voluntary donations may be claimed by a research institution or a university, school or similar educational body engaged in medical research in a laboratory. The principal conditions are that the instrument or appliance be:—

(*a*) €25,390 or more in value (exclusive of tax),

(*b*) designed and manufactured for use in medical research,

(*c*) no part of the funds used in the purchase of the goods is provided, directly or indirectly, by the State, and (*d*) the subject of a recommendation by the Health Research Board that, having regard to the requirements of medical research in the State, a refund of tax would be appropriate (Repayment claim form VAT 72A).

18 Humanitarian goods

18.1. Repayment may be claimed, by philanthropic organisations, of VAT paid on the supply in, or importation into, the State of goods which are exported or re-exported for use in the organisations' humanitarian, charitable or teaching activities abroad (Repayment claim form 73).

19 Irish businesses paying foreign VAT

19.1. Traders who are registered for the purposes of Irish VAT and who pay VAT in another Member State of the EU are normally entitled to claim a repayment of tax from the relevant Member State subject to conditions. Further information is available from VAT Repayments Section (tel. 065–6841200).

20 Investment gold

20.1. Where exempt supplies of investment gold are made the VAT incurred on the supply, transformation, change of form and on the goods and services linked to the production of/transformation into investment gold may be refunded in certain circumstances (Repayment Claim Form 6A).

21 Enquiries

21.1. Except where stated otherwise in the preceding paragraphs, all enquiries relating to repayments to unregistered persons should be made to the **Office of the Accountant General, Revenue, Kilrush Road, Ennis, Co. Clare (Telephone 065–6841200).**

Similarly, all claim forms referred to, except where stated otherwise, can be obtained, on request, from that Office also.

21.2. A list of useful addresses, telephone, fax numbers and E-mail addresses is attached at Appendix I.

Contact addresses can be found in Revenue Addresses at start of book

VAT ON DANCES

(November 2001)

1 Introduction

1.1. The promotion of dances is a taxable activity liable to VAT at the rate of 20 per cent (21 per cent from 1 March, 2002). Dances are treated as an ordinary part of the activities carried on by a taxable person in the course or furtherance of business. There are special arrangements for dances held on licensed premises.

This Information Leaflet updates and replaces *Statement of Practice SP-VAT/6/92* of the same title.

2 General Rules

2.1. Where a dance is held on premises licensed for the sale of intoxicating liquor the licensee is deemed to be the promoter of the dance. The licensee is deemed to have received the total amount payable in respect of admissions (see paragraph 3.3), is liable to account for the tax chargeable and, if not already registered, is obliged to register if annual receipts from taxable activities exceed, or are likely to exceed €25,500.

2.2. Where a dance is held on premises which are not licensed for the sale of intoxicating liquor, the promoter of the dance is accountable for the VAT chargeable, subject to the normal VAT rules. The promoter is obliged to register and account for VAT where his or her annual receipts from taxable activities (including the promotion of dances) exceed or are likely to exceed €25,500.

3 DANCES IN LICENSED PREMISES

Scope

3.1. Dances which are promoted in the course or furtherance of business come within the scope of VAT liability. "Dances" includes all **public** dances, that is, functions or gatherings which include dancing, and which are open to the public on payment of an admission charge, or on pre-purchase of a ticket (for example, cabarets, supper dances, discos, socials, and dances run by sports clubs). It does not include **private** dinner dances, where admission is **not** open to the public, for example, wedding receptions. Dinner dances held for fund-raising purposes but not in the course or furtherance of business, (for example benefit dances organised by charities or clubs on an occasional basis) in hotels or other licensed premises are also outside of the scope of the provisions. In these latter cases the hotelier or licensee is not regarded as the promoter of the dance and is, therefore, liable only in respect of the receipts relating to the services supplied — for example, meals, drinks, etc.

Dances promoted by non-licensees

3.2. Where a person other than the licensee promotes public dances on the licensee's premises liability for the VAT chargeable remains with the licensee. The promoter is not the person accountable for VAT in these circumstances. Accordingly, the licensee would need to ensure that s/he takes appropriate steps to ensure that s/he is in a position to make the appropriate returns and pay over the tax chargeable to the Collector-General. In this regard, since the promoter's records are subject to examination by the Inspector, the licensee might consider agreeing with the promoter on right of access to the promoter's relevant records.

Taxable Amount

3.3. The amount on which tax is chargeable is the total consideration received in connection with the dance. This includes the amounts paid by those admitted to the dance together with any other consideration received in connection with the dance. As already mentioned the obligation to account for the tax is the responsibility of the licensee, notwithstanding that such amounts may be received or receivable by a promoter or other person.

3.4. Where persons are admitted to dances for amounts less than the face-value of the ticket or where no admission is charged (complimentary tickets) the normal VAT rules apply and only the amount actually payable will attract liability.

Deductible VAT

3.5. A VAT-registered licensee is entitled to take credit or deduction against his or her VAT liability for the VAT charged on goods and services purchased in connection with the dance. It is a requirement of the VAT system that to take credit or deduction, the VAT-registered person must be in possession of proper VAT invoices made out to him or her. Subject to this requirement the licensee would be able to take credit for VAT charged and invoiced on the printing of tickets, spot prizes, advertising, light, heat, bands or groups, and other qualifying expenditure connected with the dance.

3.6. Deductions are not allowable unless the invoices are made out in the name of the licensee. Where the expenses are incurred by and the charges are invoiced to somebody other than the licensee deduction against the licensee's liability will not be allowed.

4 Dinner Dances

4.1. Receipts from admissions to dinner dances are liable at 20 per cent (21 per cent from 1 March, 2002) including the dinner element included in the charge. If there are separate charges for the dinner and the dance and the payment of the charge for dinner is not a condition of admission to the dance, the dinner charge is liable at 12.5 per cent and the charge for admission to the dance is liable at 20 per cent (21 per cent from 1 March, 2002).

5 Further Information

5.1. Enquires should be made to the local Inspector of Taxes.

5.2. A list of useful addresses, telephone and fax numbers and E-mail addresses is attached.

Contact addresses can be found in Revenue Addresses at start of book

(November 2001)

ZERO RATING OF GOODS AND SERVICES IN ACCORDANCE WITH SECTION 13A OF THE VAT ACT

1 Introduction

1.1. Section 13A of the VAT Act provides for the zero-rating in most cases of supplies of goods and services to, and intra-Community acquisitions and imports by, taxable persons who are primarily engaged in making zero-rated intra-Community supplies of goods or exports.

2 Qualifying Persons

2.1. A qualifying person under section 13A is a taxable person whose turnover from zero-rated intra-Community supplies of goods or exports exceeds, or is likely to exceed, 75% of his total annual turnover. Total annual turnover comprises turnover from the supply of all goods and services, including exempt supplies. However, sale and lease-back transactions are excluded from annual turnover for the purposes of determining whether a taxable person qualifies for the scheme.

2.2. In certain cases it may also be possible for a taxable person in a start-up situation to qualify for the zero rating facility on an interim basis. In such a case it is necessary to establish, to the satisfaction of the relevant Inspector of Taxes, that the person's turnover from zero-rated intra-Community supplies of goods or exports will exceed 75% of its total turnover in its first year of trading. In these cases the application for authorisation should be supported by a statement from the IDA or similar State agency giving details of the person's anticipated annual turnover and zero-rated intra-Community supplies and exports.

3 Group Registrations

3.1. A VAT-registered group (ie where a number of companies are treated as a single taxable person for VAT purposes) can only be authorised under section 13A if at least 75% **of the group's** total annual turnover is derived from zero-rated intra-Community supplies of goods or exports. Sales between individual group members are ignored for this purpose. Individual members of VAT groups cannot obtain authorisations unless the group as a whole is a qualifying person.

4 Authorisation Procedure

4.1. Applications for authorisation should be made on Form VAT 13A, which is available from the local Inspector of Taxes (see contact details at Appendix I). The local Inspector will issue an authorisation where s/he is satisfied that the applicant is a qualifying person.

4.2. The authorisation will take effect two weeks after the date of its issue. This is to allow the authorised person sufficient time to forward copies of the authorisation to his/her suppliers. Accordingly, a qualifying person should apply in good time before the desired date of effect of the authorisation.

4.3. If an authorised person ceases to be a qualifying person under the scheme s/he must notify his/her local Inspector of Taxes immediately.

5 Purchases within the State

5.1. (*a*) Authorised person

On receipt of the authorisation, the authorised person is obliged to send a copy of the authorisation to **all** persons in the State making supplies to him/her. It should be noted in particular that, apart from the exception mentioned in paragraph 9 below, once a person has been authorised, the zero-rating facility must be used in the case of all qualifying supplies, intra-Community acquisitions or imports. If a supplier charges VAT incorrectly, the authorised person is **not** entitled to claim the amount through his/her VAT return. Any such charge is a matter between the authorised person and the supplier. The original invoice should be cancelled by a credit note and a proper invoice should then be issued by the supplier.

5.2. It is recognised that it may be inconvenient to operate the zero-rating facility in relation to petty cash or other minor purchases. Accordingly, an exception may be made to the position outlined at paragraph 3.1 above where the VAT on the individual transaction is less than £20 (€25.40) (€30 from 1 January 2002).

5.3. (*b*) Supplier to an authorised person

A supplier, once s/he has received a copy of an authorisation from an authorised person, must zero-rate all qualifying supplies (see paragraph 9 below) to the authorised person and must quote the authorisation number on the VAT invoice issued in respect of the supply. If there is any doubt in relation to an authorisation, the Inspector of Taxes who issued the authorisation should be contacted to confirm its validity. When making zero-rated supplies under the scheme, the supplier should ensure that the supply is in fact made to the person named on the authorisation. Particular attention should also be paid to the expiry date of the authorisation as zero-rating can only apply during its period of validity.

6 Intra-Community Acquisitions

6.1. The normal Single Market VAT rules continue to apply to intra-Community acquisitions. To obtain goods without payment of VAT in another Member State, the VAT registration number (**not** the authorisation number) must continue to be quoted to the foreign supplier. The section 13A authorization means that the authorized person must account for VAT on the intra-Community acquisition at the zero rate.

7 Imports

7.1. In order to import qualifying goods from outside the European Union, the authorised person should make a declaration on the relevant customs entry (SAD) that s/he is an authorised person under section 13A of the VAT Act and quote his/her authorisation number. When requested by a Customs official, a copy of the authorisation should be produced in support of the declaration.

8 Alcohol Products

8.1. Where an authorised person is accounting for VAT on supplies, intra-Community acquisitions or imports of alcohol products in accordance with section 3B of the VAT Act, the authorised person should make a declaration on the relevant excise form that s/he is an authorised person under section 13A of the VAT Act and quote his/her authorisation number. The zero-rate then applies. When requested by a Customs official, a copy of the authorisation should be produced in support of the declaration.

9 Qualifying goods and services

9.1. The zero-rating procedure applies to all goods and services, with the following exceptions:

— the supply or hire of any passenger motor vehicle,

— the supply of petrol,

— the provision of food, drink, accommodation, entertainment or other personal services.

10 Self-supplies or exempt use

10.1. If an authorised person applies qualifying goods or services, which have been obtained at the zero rate, to an exempt or non-business use, s/he must, in respect of such application, account for and pay VAT on the cost price to him/her of those goods or services. Therefore, if an authorised person purchases goods for, say, €10,000 at the zero rate and the supply of these goods is normally liable at the 20% rate, s/he must, if s/he applies the goods to a non-business use, pay VAT of €2,000 with his/her VAT return. The authorised person has no entitlement to claim an input credit in respect of such VAT.

11 Further Information

11.1. Further information may be obtained from Revenue, VAT Administration, Stamping Building, Dublin Castle, Dublin 2 (Tel 01–67485000 Extns 48858, 48859, 48861, 48862 or from local Inspectors of Taxes.

11.2. A list of useful addresses, telephone, fax numbers and E-mail addresses is attached at Appendix I.

Contact addresses can be found in Revenue Addresses at start of book

(November 2001)

MONEYS RECEIVED OR "CASH" BASIS OF ACCOUNTING

1 General

1.1. This Information Leaflet sets out which VAT-registered traders may opt to account for VAT on the basis of moneys received from their customers instead of the normal method based on the issue of invoices to their customers, and how such traders may apply to operate this scheme. It updates and replaces *Statement of Practice SP-VAT/16/ 92* of the same title.

2 Description of moneys received basis

2.1. VAT is normally accounted for on the invoice basis, ie VAT is payable on the total sales invoiced in the relevant period regardless of whether or not the trader has been paid for the supply in that period. However, certain traders can opt for the moneys received (cash) basis of accounting, under which the trader is not required to account for VAT until payment for the supply is actually received.

3 Traders who may opt for moneys received basis

3.1. The traders who may opt to account for VAT in this way are:—

— VAT-registered traders whose supplies of goods or services are almost exclusively (at least 90%) made to unregistered persons. This would apply in practice mainly to retail outlets, public houses, restaurants, hairdressers and any similar type of business (see paragraph 5 below), or

— VAT-registered traders whose annual turnover does not exceed or is not likely to exceed €635,000.

3.2. It should be noted that the use of this basis of accounting in no way removes from a VAT-registered trader his or her obligations as regards the issue of invoices and other documents, the maintenance of records, lodgment of returns etc.

3.3. The supply of goods and services to a person who is not entitled to **full** deduction of the VAT charged in respect of that supply may be treated as a supply to an unregistered person, for the purposes of determining whether a person qualifies to use the cash basis (ie for the purpose of the 90% rule).

3.4. Examples of such supplies are

— the supply of a car

— provision of accommodation or entertainment services

— the supply of goods to an exempt body

— the supply of goods to a person who is registered for VAT solely in respect of his intra-Community acquisitions or Fourth Schedule services.

provided that in each case the person in receipt of the supply is not entitled to a **full** deduction of the VAT charged.

4 Excluded transactions

4.1. Transactions between connected persons are excluded from the moneys received basis of accounting. VAT on any transactions between such persons must be paid by reference to the normal invoice/sales basis. VAT on property transactions must always be accounted for on the invoice basis.

5 Application and authorisation

5.1. A taxable person who wishes to account on the cash basis, should apply in writing for authorisation to his or her local Inspector of Taxes setting out the following details—

    (*a*)   name and address;

    (*b*)   VAT registration number, if any;

    (*c*)   the nature of the person's business activities;

    (*d*)   the percentage of turnover from taxable supplies, if any, which related to supplies to unregistered persons for whichever of the following periods is the shorter:

        — the period of 12 months ended on the last day of the taxable period prior to the application, or

        — the period from the commencement of business activities to the last day of the taxable period prior to the application;

    (*e*)   an estimate of the percentage of the turnover from taxable supplies to unregistered persons for the 12 months from the start of the taxable period during which the application is made;

    (*f*)   level of annual turnover, if under €635,000.

5.2. An authorization to account for VAT on the cash basis has effect from the start of the period during which it is given, or from a subsequent date if so specified.

5.3. Persons who are applying for VAT registration for the first time, and find that they are eligible for this basis of accounting should indicate in the appropriate box on the application form (STR, TR1 or TR2) whether or not they wish to use the moneys received basis.

6 VAT liability on moneys received

6.1. A trader who has opted to account on the moneys received basis is liable for VAT at the rate applicable at the time the goods or services are supplied and **not** at the rate applicable when payment is received, if a change in rate has taken place in the interim.

6.2. Moneys received by a VAT-registered trader include any sums:

    — credited to the trader's account in a bank, building society or other financial concern,

    — received by another person on the trader's behalf, or

    — paid to Revenue by a third party to the trader's account in accordance with the Commissioners' power of attachment.

6.3. A VAT-registered trader is also deemed to have received money if liability in respect of a business transaction is settled by setting off against it a credit due in respect of some other transaction. Care must be taken when money is received through an agent that any amount withheld by the agent to cover fees, expenses etc, is included in the taxable amount.

7 Withholding tax

7.1. Income Tax withheld from payments for professional services is deemed, for VAT purposes, to have been part of the consideration received by the trader. If, for example, payment of an amount due to a solicitor is reduced from €1,200 [€1,000 + €200 VAT] to €1,000 [€200 withheld for Withholding Tax] the solicitor is deemed for VAT purposes to have received €1,200 and must therefore account for VAT on the full amount of €1,200. The same position applies to tax withheld from payments to certain building sub-contractors.

8 Credit card transactions

8.1. In the case of credit card transactions the taxable amount is the marked selling price, that is, the amount actually charged to the customer by the supplier. Amounts withheld by credit card companies from their settlements with traders are part of the taxable amount and should not be disregarded.

9 Credit notes

9.1. A VAT-registered trader accounting for VAT on the basis of moneys received **must** issue to a VAT-registered customer a credit note showing VAT if there is a discount or price reduction allowed subsequent to the issue of an invoice. The effect of the credit note is to reduce the VAT deduction available to the customer on the basis of the original invoice. This has no effect on the liability of the person issuing the credit note since he or she is calculating liability by reference to the moneys actually received.

10 Review of eligibility and cancellation of authorisation

10.1. Where a taxable person is authorised to account for VAT on the moneys received basis but, for a period of four consecutive months his or her turnover from taxable supplies to unregistered persons is less than 90% of total turnover, the taxable person should notify the local Inspector of Taxes accordingly by the end of the following month and indicate the actual percentage of such supplies. If the change in the level of such supplies to unregistered persons is of a marginal or temporary nature, the authorisation may be allowed to continue.

10.2. Where a taxable person is authorised to operate the cash receipts basis because his/her annual turnover is less than €635,000 that person must apply to have that authorisation cancelled where it is clear that the turnover will exceed the limit in any continuous period of twelve months.

10.3. Cancellation of an authorisation will have effect from the start of the VAT accounting period during which the person is notified of such cancellation by the local Inspector of Taxes or from the start of a later VAT accounting period if specified in the notice. Where a taxable person fails to notify the local Inspector of Taxes as in paragraph 10.1 above, the authorisation will be deemed to have been automatically cancelled with effect from the start of the VAT accounting period within which the notification should have been made.

11 Changing from moneys received basis to invoice/sales basis

11.1. Where a trader accounting for VAT on the monies received basis changes to the invoice basis, or ceases to be a taxable person, liability for VAT at the time of the change must be assessed. Where the authorisation was issued prior to 28 May, 1992, this is done by comparing the amount of trade debts outstanding at the beginning of the period six years prior to the period in which the change takes place with the amount outstanding at the end of the period in which the change takes place. If the trade debts at the end of that period exceed those at the beginning the trader is required to pay VAT on the excess at the appropriate rate or rates.

11.2. Where the authorisation was issued on or after 28 May, 1992 then the settlement figure is ascertained by apportioning the total amount due to the person at the end of the authorised period between the various rates.

12 Changing from invoice/sales basis to moneys received basis

12.1. Where a VAT-registered trader already accounting for VAT on the invoice basis obtains permission to change to the moneys received basis, that trader is liable for VAT on any moneys received on and after the approved date of the change, excluding any payments on which VAT has already been accounted for in respect of goods and services supplied while accounting on the invoice basis.

13 Further Enquiries

13.1. Further enquiries on this subject should be made to the local Inspector of Taxes.

13.2. A list of useful addresses, fax and telephone numbers and E-mail addresses is attached at Appendix I.

Contact addresses can be found in Revenue Addresses at start of book

AGRICULTURAL SERVICES

(November 2001)

1 Introduction

1.1. This information leaflet updates and replaces *Statement of Practice SP-VAT/5/92* of the same title.

1.2. A farmer who supplies agricultural services in addition to carrying on a farming business is obliged to register and account for VAT if the receipts from such agricultural services exceed or are likely to exceed €25,500 in any 12 month period. In this context the term "agricultural services" does not include insemination services, stock-minding or stock rearing, all of which may be excluded for the purposes of calculating the €25,500 threshold. Farmers supplying agricultural services consisting **only** of insemination services, stock-minding or stock-rearing are not obliged to register for VAT but may opt to do so.

1.2. Agricultural services, as described, are treated for VAT purposes in the same way as other non-farming activities engaged in by farmers. For the purposes of determining whether or not a person is obliged to **register**, receipts from insemination services and stock-minding and stock-rearing may be disregarded. However, once a person becomes registered for VAT, **all** taxable receipts must be taken into account in determining liability, including receipts from farming and non-farming activities, (if any), in addition to receipts from the agricultural services. A list of typical agricultural services and the appropriate rates of VAT is attached at Appendix 1.

1.3. Application for registration should be made to a person's Local Inspector of Taxes (see Appendix II for addresses, telephone numbers and fax numbers and E-mail addresses). It should be noted that once registered for VAT, the farmer ceases to be a "flat-rate" farmer. Accordingly, the flat-rate addition to prices does not apply to his/her sales to other VAT-registered persons. Instead, credit for VAT borne on inputs is obtained directly in the returns which s/he becomes obliged to make in the same way as other VAT-registered persons.

2 Obligations of VAT-registered Farmers

2.1. VAT-registered farmers are obliged to—

(a) keep records which are sufficiently detailed to enable their liability as declared by themselves to be confirmed;

(b) issue invoices containing specified particulars (see Chapter 9 of the VAT Guide 1999) in respect of taxable supplies to other taxable persons. If the consideration shown on an invoice is subsequently reduced and a tax adjustment is actually made, a credit note must be issued where the customer is a VAT-registered person, showing the amount of tax by which the liability has been reduced;

(c) submit a return on the appropriate form, normally every two months, of their supplies and taxable purchases together with a remittance for any tax due. This form is issued to registered persons before the end of each taxable period.

3 Determination of Liability

3.1. A VAT-registered farmer is liable to pay VAT at the appropriate rate on taxable goods and services supplied by him/her. A VAT-registered farmer determines his/her VAT liability for each two-monthly taxable period (January/February, March/April, etc) by calculating the total tax due on his/her sales of goods or services for the period and subtracting the deductible tax invoiced to him/her or paid on imports from non EU countries in the period — the difference is the amount which s/he pays. If the deductible tax exceeds the tax chargeable the difference is refunded (see Chapter 6 of the VAT Guide 1999).

4 Taxable Amount

4.1. The amount on which a taxable person is liable, is the total amount which the person is entitled to receive for the goods or services supplied, including commissions, costs and charges, and all taxes (other than VAT).

5 Accounting for VAT

5.1. The normal basis of accounting for VAT is the invoice or sales basis. However, a person may, subject to certain conditions (see paragraph 7) account for VAT on the "moneys received" basis.

6 Invoice Basis

6.1. A VAT-registered person using the invoice or sales basis of accounting will be liable to pay VAT by reference to his/her supplies as follows:—

— in the case of transactions with persons who are not registered for VAT s/he is liable at the rate in force at the time the goods or services are supplied;

— in the case of transactions with other VAT-registered persons s/he is obliged to issue invoices and is liable to VAT at the rate of tax in force at the time s/he issues, or ought to issue an invoice.

7 Moneys received Basis

7.1. Certain registered persons, including farmers, may use the moneys received basis of accounting instead of the more usual sales/invoice basis. Persons qualifying are

(a) persons whose annual turnover does not exceed and is not likely to exceed €635,000,

(b) persons supplying goods and services almost exclusively (at least 90 per cent) to unregistered persons.

7.2. Farmers wishing to avail themselves of this facility must specify this when applying for registration.

8 Deduction for VAT charged on Purchases

8.1. A VAT-registered farmer is entitled to take a credit or deduction (ie set off against his/her liability) for VAT properly invoiced to him/her or paid on imports or intra-Community acquisitions in respect of most goods and services used in connection with his/her taxable activities. S/he is not required to pay the supplier before taking the credit.

8.2. Expenditure, in respect of which a credit or deduction may not be taken, is expenditure relating to:—

(*a*) the provision of food, drink, accommodation or other personal services for the person, his/her agents or employees (for example, hotel costs);

(*b*) entertainment expenses;

(*c*) purchase or hire of cars or other road passenger vehicles;

(*d*) purchase of petrol;

(*e*) contract work involving the handing over of goods when such goods are themselves not deductible;

(*f*) an exempt (for example, letting of premises for a period of less than 10 years) or non-business activity, and

(*g*) VAT borne prior to registration.

8.3. A credit or deduction may be taken in respect of diesel, car repairs and maintenance, and car parts (for example, a set of tyres), subject to the condition that they are used for the purposes of a taxable business.

9 Further Information

9.1. A list of useful addresses, telephone, fax numbers and E-mail addresses is attached at Appendix II.

APPENDIX I
VAT RATES ON TYPICAL AGRICULTURAL SERVICES

(The list is not exhaustive)

Supply	Rate %
Ploughing, harrowing, discing, rolling	12.5
Combined supply and sowing/planting of seeds/plants etc for the production of food, including animal feed zero other seeds, plants, etc	12.5
Sowing/planting only of all seeds/plants	12.5
Combined supply and spreading of fertilisers	zero
Spreading only of fertilisers	12.5
Spraying/dusting of crops (whether or not chemicals are supplied by contractor)	12.5
Harvesting, reaping, mowing, baling	12.5

Silage making (including supply of silage additive and polythene cover)	12.5
Transport, storage	20 (21 with effect from 1/3/02)
Stock minding and rearing	12.5
Stock-insemination	12.5
General consultancy and advisory services (including tax and general financial advisory services)	20 (21 with effect from 1/3/02)
Farm relief services	12.5
Farm management and accountancy services	20 (21 with effect from 1/3/02)
Farm advisory services	12.5
Hiring of agricultural or other equipment	20 (21 with effect from 1/3/02)
Land drainage and land reclamation including removal of weed, scrub, bracken, pests, etc and the supply and spreading of fertilisers and seeds under inclusive contract	12.5
Pruning, tree felling, hedge trimming	12.5
Landscaping (excluding architectural design services and the like)	12.5
Letting of farm buildings (short-term for period of less than 10 years) exempt	
Agricultural products — packing and preparation for market	20 (21 with effect from 1/3/02)
cleaning, grinding and disinfecting	20 (21 with effect from 1/3/02)

Where services liable at different rates are supplied for an inclusive charge the higher or highest rate involved normally applies to the entire charge.

Contact addresses can be found in Revenue Addresses at start of book

(November 2001)

HORTICULTURAL RETAILERS

1 Introduction

1.1. This Information Leaflet updates and replaces *Statement of Practice SP-VAT/1/97* of the same title.

1.2. All **retailers** of horticultural products, including garden centres and flat-rate farmers whose annual retail sales of horticultural products and other goods exceed or are likely to exceed the €51,000 VAT registration threshold, are obliged to register and account for VAT. "Horticultural products" for this purpose means non-food products of a type listed at paragraph 2.1. below. "Other goods" means goods other than agricultural products.

2 Rate

2.1. The reduced rate of 12.5 per cent applies to;

— live plants, including instant lawn turf

— live trees

— live shrubs

— bulbs, roots and the like

— seeds

— cut flowers

   ornamental foliage.

Plants, trees, bulbs, roots and seeds used for growing food are not included here. They are taxable at the zero rate. Artificial flowers, dried flowers and dried foliage are taxable at the 20 per cent rate (21 per cent from 1 March, 2002). Cut trees, for example, Christmas trees, are also liable at the standard rate.

3 Obligation to register

3.1. Farmers and garden centres, who supply horticultural products to the general public, must register and account for VAT on all their business activities subject to the €51,000 registration threshold.

3.2. A retailer of horticultural products cannot avoid registering for VAT by splitting his/her business into a number of separate smaller units, each selling less than the annual registration limit; the various units will be grouped as a single business for VAT purposes.

3.3. In addition, where a person supplies a combination of retail horticultural produce and agricultural services, the registration threshold is €25,500. This is the normal VAT registration threshold which applies where a person supplies both goods and services.

3.4. Businesses such as florists benefit from the reduced VAT rate of 12.5 per cent on the horticultural produce of a type listed at paragraph 2.1.

4 Further information

4.1. Further enquiries should be made to your local Inspector of Taxes.

4.2. A list of useful addresses, telephone, fax numbers and e-mail addresses is attached.

Contact addresses can be found in Revenue Addresses at start of book

(November 2001)

INTRA-COMMUNITY SUPPLIES

1 Single Market

1.1. Following the introduction of the Single Market on 1 January 1993, the way in which VAT was charged on goods moving between Member States of the EU was changed. The concept of import and export for such trade was abolished and replaced by a system of intra-Community supply and acquisition of goods. This information leaflet sets out the VAT treatment of intra-Community supplies.

2 Supplies of goods to other Member States

2.1. The supply of goods by a VAT-registered trader in one EU member State to a VAT-registered trader in another EU Member State, with some exceptions, qualifies as an intra-Community supply. A VAT-registered trader in the State may zero rate the supply of goods to a customer in another EU Member State if:—

— the customer is registered for VAT in that other EU Member State,

— the customer's VAT registration number (including country prefix) is obtained and retained in the supplier's records,

— this number, together with the supplier's VAT registration number, is quoted on the sales invoice,

— the goods are dispatched or transported to that other Member State.

2.2. If these four conditions are not met the supplier is liable for VAT at the appropriate Irish rate. If the supplier is not able to satisfy Revenue that particular consignments of goods have been sold and delivered to a VAT-registered person in another Member State, the supplier becomes liable for the payment of Irish VAT on the transaction. **Where any of the above four conditions are not satisfied the supplier should charge Irish VAT.** If the conditions for zero-rating are subsequently established the customer is entitled to recover the VAT paid from the supplier. The supplier can then take an adjustment in his/her VAT return for the period.

3 Evidence of despatch to another Member State and removal of the goods from the State

3.1. The precise commercial documentation required to confirm despatch and removal of the goods from the State depends on the particular circumstances involved.

3.2. In many cases a supplier arranges transportation of the goods and the normal commercial documentation related to the supply and transportation of the goods is available (eg order document, delivery docket, supplier's invoice, transport document/bill of lading, evidence of transfer of foreign currency for payment, etc). In such cases the supplier should retain this documentation.

3.3. Where transport of the goods is arranged by the customer, or the goods are taken away by the customer using his or her own transport, the supplier needs to be satisfied that the goods are dispatched or transported to another Member State. The normal documentary evidence should be retained in relation to the sale itself but, in addition, the supplier should obtain and retain documentary evidence from the customer that the goods were received in another Member State. The type of documentation acceptable includes transport documents, copies of warehouse receipts, delivery dockets, etc. It might also be prudent for the supplier to record details of the means of transport (eg vehicle registration nos.) used by the customer.

3.4. Special care should be taken by the supplier to ensure that the four conditions outlined in paragraph 2 are met for sales and deliveries of goods to other Member States. Some examples of where a doubt can arise are where:

— customer is not previously known to the supplier

— customer arranges to collect and transport the goods

— customer's transport arrives at supplier's premises without advance notice or correspondence

— payment is made in cash

— type or quantity of goods being purchased are not consistent with commercial practice bearing in mind the purported destination of the goods.

3.5. Cases where one or more of these various factors combine together must be treated with particular caution. Where a doubt arises, the supplier should charge Irish VAT. If the conditions for zero-rating are subsequently established the customer is entitled to recover the VAT paid from the supplier.

4 Verification of customers' VAT numbers

4.1. For zero-rating to apply there must be a supply of goods to a person registered for VAT in another Member State. The fiscal authorities in each Member State have put in place a computerised system that makes it possible for traders to verify the VAT numbers of their customers in other Member States. However, use of the verification system is not obligatory and traders who are familiar with their customers, and are aware of their bona fides from trading with them over a period of time, are not expected or required to use the verification system. Instead they are advised to contact their EU customers and ask them to confirm in writing their VAT registration numbers. (An example of the type of form that might be used for this purpose is attached as Appendix I).

4.2. An Irish trader who has doubts about the validity of a VAT number quoted may use the verification system to establish whether or not a particular number is valid. The system is primarily intended to be used in such circumstances and is not intended for routine checks. Verification of queries is dealt with by the VIMA (see contact details at Appendix II).

5 Requirement to take all reasonable steps

5.1. Any supplier who takes all reasonable steps to confirm that the conditions for zero-rating are met will not be penalised if it subsequently transpires that a problem has arisen in connection with particular consignments. However, the tax due will be demanded from the supplier in any case where he or she has failed to do so.

6 Fraudulent claims for zero-rating

6.1. There are severe penalties for making fraudulent claims for zero-rating:

(i) seizure and forfeiture of zero-rated goods which have not been despatched or transported outside the State (subsections (9A) and (10) of section 27 of the VAT Act).

(ii) a person who acquires goods VAT free in another Member State as a result of making a declaration of an incorrect VAT registration number shall be liable to a penalty of £500 (€634.89) (€630 from 1 January 2002) plus an amount equal to the amount of tax which would have be chargeable.

(iii) arrest of a person suspected of a criminal offence who is not established in the State, or whom an authorised Revenue Officer or a Garda has reason to believe may leave the State (subsection (11) of section 27 of the VAT Act),

(iv) civil and criminal penalties, ranging from £1,200 (€1,523.69) (€1,520 from 1 January 2002 to £100,000 (€26,973.80) (€126,970 from 1 January 2002) and imprisonment for a period of up to five years (sections 26, 27 and 28 of the VAT Act and section 94 of the Finance Act, 1983).

7 Sale of new vehicles to persons in other EU Member States

7.1. Sales of new means of transport, ie motor vehicles, boats, aircraft, etc, are always intra-Community supplies/acquisitions and any person acquiring a new means of transport must always pay VAT in the EU Member State of arrival.

7.2. For a dealer selling a new means of transport to a person registered for VAT in another EU Member State, the VAT treatment is the same as that which applies to goods generally.

7.3. In the case of the sale of a new vehicle, for example, to a private individual in another EU Member State, VAT is ultimately payable in the EU Member State of destination. If the private individual collects the vehicle in the State, VAT should be charged by the dealer. However, once the customer satisfies the dealer that VAT has been paid in his/her own EU Member State, the dealer should refund the VAT charged to the customer and adjust his/her VAT liability accordingly. The dealer should retain documentary proof. The normal level of proof required would be a copy of the receipt of VAT payment or proof of registration of the vehicle in the other EU Member State.

8 What is a new means of transport?

8.1. The following table sets out what is regarded as being a "new means of transport" for VAT purposes:

Means of Transport	Specification	"New"
Motor Vehicle	Over 48cc or over 7.2 kw power	6 months old or less or travelled 6,000 km or less
Boat	over 7.5 metres in length	3 months old or less or sailed for 100 hrs. or less
Aircraft	over 1,550 kg take-off weight	3 months old or less Or flown for 40 hrs. or less

9 Triangular transactions

9.1. Triangulation in the Single Market involves two supplies of goods between three VAT-registered traders in three different EU Member States eg where a trader in one Member State orders goods from a trader in a second Member State, to be delivered to a trader in a third Member State. To reduce the administrative and compliance burdens both on traders and the relevant revenue authorities with regard to registration and accounting, a simplification measure known as triangulation is in operation in such cases. A technical notice on the VAT treatment of triangulation in the Single Market is available on request.

10 Certain transfers are not supplies

10.1. For VAT purposes, certain transfers to other Member States are not treated as intra-Community supplies/acquisitions. These include goods for installation or assembly by the supplier, (in this case the supplier must register for VAT in the State) transfers for the purposes of having contract work carried out and transfer with a view to their temporary use in another Member State.

11 Branch to branch transfers of goods

11.1. For VAT purposes, branch to branch (with some exceptions) and similar transfers of goods between business persons in different EU Member States are treated as being intra-Community supplies and acquisitions.

12 VIES returns

12.1. When an Irish VAT-registered trader makes zero-rated supplies of goods to a trader in another EU Member State, summary details of those supplies must be returned to Revenue on a quarterly or monthly basis. This return, known as the VIES return, is to enable the authorities in each EU Member State to ensure that intra-Community transactions are properly recorded and accounted for.

13 INTRASTAT returns

13.1. Traders engaged in intra-Community trade are also obliged to make a periodic INTRASTAT return, for statistical purposes, where the value of goods acquired by them from other Member States exceeds £150,000 (€190,460.71) (€190,500 from 1 January 2002) per annum or the value of goods supplied by them to other EU Member States exceeds £500,000 (€634,869.03) (€635,000 from 1 January, 2002) per annum.

14 Further information

14.1. For further information please contact your local inspector of taxes details of which are in Appendix II. That office should also be contacted where a trader suspects that a person is attempting to obtain zero-rated goods under false pretences.

14.2. A list of useful addresses, telephone, fax numbers and E-mail addresses is attached at Appendix II.

APPENDIX I

VAT/TVA/IVA/MWSt/BTW

Dear Customer,

To comply with EU regulations, we have to show your VAT/Sales Tax Number on our invoices.

To help us with this, could you please fill in the box below with your VAT/Sales Tax Number and return it to us as soon as possible. Please ensure that the country prefix is included.

N.B. If you are not registered for VAT, please tick. ☐

In addition, to help us update our records, please forward your:

Telephone No.....................

Fax No.............................

Address ....

E-mail address ....

Thank you.

Your faithfully,

Contact addresses can be found in Revenue Addresses at start of book

VALUE ADDED TAX AND FOOTWEAR

1. Footwear other than certain children's footwear (see paragraphs 2 to 4 below), is chargeable to VAT at the 20% rate.

2. VAT law provides that the zero rate applies to articles of children's personal footwear of sizes which do not exceed the average foot size appropriate to children under 11 years of age, which are described, labelled, marked or marketed on the basis of age or size.

3. It is therefore important to note that the legal basis for the relief of certain children's footwear requires that the footwear in question is both:——

— designed specifically for the use of children and

— of a size no larger than the average size applicable to children under 11 years of age.

4. In the practical administration of the tax, baby and infant footwear, and footwear which has been specifically designed for children, in sizes up to and including size 5½ (38 continental or other equivalent) qualify for the zero rate.

Children's footwear, the sizes of which exceed 5½ (38 continental or other equivalent) and adults' footwear, irrespective of size is taxable at 20% VAT.

5. It is accepted that there may be a difficulty in respect of a small number of styles which are not designed as either adults' or children's footwear, and which are manufactured in the full range of sizes from the smallest children's size* to large adult sizes. The Revenue Commissioners are prepared, concessionally, to accept that the zero rate may apply to sizes up to and including size 5½ for these specific styles.

Footwear ranges not starting at the smallest children's size*, eg ranges starting at large size 1 or 2, will continue to be taxable at 20% in all sizes unless it can be shown that they were designed for the use of children, in which case the size 5½ cut-off will apply.

Sports leisure wear and trainer type footwear is normally designed in three separate ranges, ie for men, for women, and for children. Accordingly, men's and women's ranges are taxable in all sizes and children's ranges are zero-rated (except for any sizes exceeding 5½). Where a particular range of footwear is available in a single style common to adults and children, and where it is also available in the full range of sizes from smallest children's size* to large adult sizes, then it may also benefit from the concession outlined above.

This concession applies from 1 July, 1997.

* Smallest to be taken as the usual smallest size in non-infant children's ranges.

6. Articles of footwear which are not described, labelled, marked or marketed on the basis of age or size do not qualify for the zero rate.

7. The term "footwear" should be understood as meaning shoes, boots, slippers etc including fur footwear but not socks, stockings etc.

8. The Revenue Commissioners are prepared to continue with their concessional treatment of football boots and other sports footwear as being articles of "personal footwear" and they therefore may benefit from the concession outlined at paragraph 5 above. However roller blades, roller-skates, etc will continue to be taxable at 20% in all sizes.

9. Second-hand footwear is liable at the same rate as it would be if new, that is zero or 20%.

10. The hiring of footwear is a service and taxable at 20% VAT irrespective of the type of footwear involved.

11. The repair of footwear is taxable at 12.5% VAT.

12. Imports and intra-Community acquisitions of footwear are taxable on resale at the zero or 20% rates, as appropriate. Intra-Community acquisitions must also be shown correctly on VAT returns.

Inquiries

13. For information on the procedure to be followed in connection with registration for VAT and the general operation of the VAT system the Guide to Value Added Tax should be consulted. Inquiries may also be made on any matter concerning VAT and footwear to Inspectors of Taxes (see Appendix 1 attached), or to the Revenue Commissioners (VAT Administration Branch) Stamping Building, Dublin Castle, Dublin 2. (tel. 6792777 Ext. 48858, 48859, 48861, 48862).

TRANSFER OF A BUSINESS OR PART THEREOF

August 2002

1 Introduction

1.1 The VAT Act provides that where a transfer of ownership of goods takes place in the course of the transfer of a business or part of a business from one taxable person to another taxable person, that transfer is deemed not to be a supply for VAT purposes. Similar provisions apply as regards the transfer between qualifying entities of goodwill or other intangible assets.

1.2 These provisions are important trade facilitation measures aimed at reducing compliance costs for traders involved in this type of transaction. However, traders are advised that when they are involved in a transfer of this type, particularly as an acquirer of a business or part thereof, they should check with their local Inspector of Taxes before paying any VAT invoiced by the vendor. Where a transfer of business is involved it is important to note that any VAT paid by a purchaser to a vendor in these circumstances will not be deductible as no supply is deemed to have taken place.

2 What the law says

2.1 The precise wording of the law and the corresponding provisions in EU law are contained in Appendix I.

3 What is the transfer of a business or part thereof?

3.1 There is no definition of a transfer of a business or part thereof in VAT law. However, the component parts of the transfer of a business can normally be broken down into the transfer of some or all of the following: Staff, immovable assets, movable assets, intangible assets including goodwill and licences, stock in trade, debtors, creditors, cash on hands or in the bank.

4 Circumstances in which the transfer rules apply

4.1 The transfer, in order to qualify for the transfer of business rules, must be made to another person in circumstances where that other person intends to apply those goods or services for the purposes of a taxable business and where those goods or services constitute an amalgam of assets capable of assisting in the realisation of that business. However, it is not a requirement of Irish VAT law that the transfer must constitute a transfer of a business as a going concern.

4.2 In practice therefore, a person who transfers a business or part of a business to another person where all or part of the assets are intended to be used:—

(*a*) to carry on the same or a similar taxable business,

(*b*) for the purposes of the acquirer's own taxable business, following the cessation of the transferor's business or

(*c*) to carry on a different taxable business in the premises and use the assets acquired is not required to account for VAT on the transfer of such a business or part of a business.

4.3 Once-off sales of business assets do not qualify as VAT-free supplies. For example, the sale of an oil tanker by a garage owner who also delivers home heating oil is not a VAT-free supply under Section 3 (5) (b) (iii) of the VAT Act. However, the sale of the entire home-heating oil distribution business which also includes an oil tanker would qualify as a VAT-free sale.

4.4 It should be noted that, in relation to the transfer of goodwill and other intangible assets the term "taxable person" does not include a person registered only for the purposes of intra-Community acquisitions or received Fourth Schedule services.

4.5 Where a person acquiring a business or part of a business has applied for but has not yet received a VAT registration number, the vendor should apply the provisions of Section 3(5)(*b*)(iii).

5 Milk Quota

5.1 The transfer of intangible assets between farmers and between non-taxable persons is not chargeable to VAT. A transfer of a milk or beet quota between farmers does not give rise to a VAT liability. The transfer of business rules apply where the business has ceased trading.

6 Transfers of property as part of a transfer of a business or part thereof

6.1 The Finance Act 2001 introduced special measures to deal with transfers of business which include property or interests in property where either the transferor or transferee or both are not entitled to full deductibility on acquisition or development of the property. Section 12D of the VAT Act deals with transfers of an interest of ten years or more in property in the context of a transfer of a business where one of the parties involved is not entitled to full deductibility. The purpose of the section is to limit, by means of clawbacks, the opportunity for a taxable person who is not entitled to deduct all the VAT on his or her inputs, to obtain, using the transfer of business rules, an interest in property VAT-free. The provision also reduces the extent of any trapped VAT by means of add-backs where the transferor was not entitled to full deductibility on the acquisition. Further information on this subject is available in the VAT and Property Transactions Guide.

7 Services in relation to a transfer

7.1 Section 12(1)(*a*)(iii*a*) of the VAT Act provides that input credit is allowable in respect of services in connection with a transfer of goods in accordance with Section 3(5)(*b*)(iii). In practice, input credit may also be taken in respect of services in connection with the transfer of goodwill or other intangible assets in accordance with Section 5(8) where the parties to the transaction are taxable persons. Such credit may be taken by the transferor or transferee.

8 Enquiries

8.1 Enquiries on any case of doubt should be referred in advance to the local Inspector of Taxes.

8.2 A list of useful addresses, telephone, fax numbers and E-mail addresses is attached at Appendix II.

APPENDIX I

1. Section 3(5)(*b*)(iii) of the Value Added Tax Act, 1972 (as amended) is as follows:—

   "(*b*) The transfer of ownership of goods — …..

   (iii) in connection with the transfer of a business or part thereof to another taxable person even if that business or part thereof had ceased trading, shall be deemed, for the purposes of this Act, not to be a supply of the goods …."

2. Section 5(8)(*a*) of the VAT Act is as follows:—

   "(*a*) The transfer of goodwill or other intangible assets of a business, in connection with the transfer of the business or part thereof, even if that business or that part thereof had ceased trading, by—

   (i) a taxable person to another taxable person or a flat-rate farmer, or

   (ii) a person who is not a taxable person to another person,

   shall be deemed, for the purposes of this Act, not be a supply of services.

   (*b*) For the purposes of this subsection, 'taxable person' shall not include a person who is a taxable person solely by virtue of subsections (1A) and (2) of section 8".

3. Corresponding provisions in EU law are in Article 5.8 of the EU 6th VAT Directive as follows:—

   "In the event of a transfer, whether for consideration or not as a contribution to a company, of a totality of assets or part thereof, Member States may consider that no supply of goods has taken place and in that event the recipient shall be treated as the successor to the transferor….".

4. Article 6.5 of the Directive states that ….. "Article 5.8 shall apply in like manner to the supply of services".

Contact addresses can be found in Revenue Addresses at start of book

A LETTER OF EXPRESSION OF DOUBT

September, 2002

This VAT Information Leaflet assumes you have a knowledge of the principles of VAT as explained in the "Guide to Value Added Tax".

1. General

Section 107 of the Finance Act, 2002, inserted a new section 19B into the Value Added Tax Act, 1972. This section allows a person who is in doubt about the application of VAT law to a transaction to lodge a "letter of expression of doubt" with Revenue. If the expression of doubt is accepted by Revenue as genuine, interest will not apply to any VAT found to be due following Revenue's examination of the application of VAT law to the transaction. This provision does not affect the taxpayer's right to contact Revenue in the normal way for advice on the VAT treatment of any transaction.

It is also important to note that it is not intended that the expression of doubt facility will displace or override the normal obligations of taxable persons in regard to the VAT code. Thus, for example, in relation to section 4A, taxable persons will still be obliged to make applications in advance of the supply of property and the expression of doubt facility will not suffice to deem such applications to have been made retrospectively.

2. Operative Date

This facility can be used in respect of transactions taking place on or after 1 March 2002.

3. How does the new section work?

- A person who wishes to use this provision must submit a letter of expression of doubt (which can be in the form of electronic communication or letter) on time (see paragraph 5) to the Office of the Inspector of Taxes that normally deals with the tax affairs of the taxable person. (Details listed in Appendix 1 attached).
- The VAT return in respect of the period in which the transaction occurs must be lodged separately and on time with the Office of the Collector-General in the normal way.
- The Inspector will issue an acknowledgement of receipt of the letter of expression of doubt (see paragraph 13).
- If the expression of doubt is not accepted as genuine the person will be so advised in writing, within 14 days of its receipt, by the Office of the local Inspector of Taxes. The taxpayer then should submit a supplementary VAT return to the Collector-General with any additional VAT liability due, for the period in which the transaction took place. As interest will be payable on any additional liability in these circumstances arrangements should be made to submit the supplementary return without delay.
- If the expression of doubt is accepted as genuine the inspector will make a ruling as soon as possible as to the correct VAT treatment of the transaction.

Where additional VAT liability is identified it must be included in the VAT return for the period in which the ruling is given as if it were tax due for that period. No interest will apply in such circumstances to the VAT due on that transaction, provided that the return is submitted and VAT paid by the relevant due date.

4. Details to be included in the letter of expression of doubt

A letter of expression of doubt must be clearly identified as such and must:

- set out full details of the circumstances of the transaction in doubt,
- identify the amount of tax or deductibility in doubt in respect of the taxable period to which the expression of doubt relates (see paragraph 8 in relation to recurring transactions),
- make reference to the provisions of the law giving rise to the doubt,
- be accompanied by any relevant supporting documentation.

5. Time limit for submission of a letter of expression of doubt

A letter of expression of doubt must be submitted to the Office of the local Inspector of Taxes (see Appendix 1) at the time the VAT return, for the period in which the transaction occurred, is submitted to the Collector-General. However, an expression of doubt will not be accepted unless the VAT return is lodged by the due date (19th of the month following the end of the taxable period – see also paragraph 12).

6. What must be included in the VAT return if an expression of doubt is being lodged?

The transaction giving rise to the doubt should be included or excluded in the VAT return on the basis of the treatment which the taxable person or agent feels is correct. For example, if a taxable person is lodging an expression of doubt about a rating issue but considers that a rate lower than the standard rate applies, then he/she may account for VAT on the return at the lower rate but lodge the expression of doubt with the local Inspector of Taxes at the same time. If a taxable person has a doubt about whether a transaction is taxable at all, (or exempt from VAT), then this transaction may be excluded from the return but details should be included in the letter of expression of doubt. Again, if a taxable person considers that he/she is entitled to deductibility as regards any transaction then a VAT credit may be claimed in the return subject to a letter of expression of doubt being furnished.

7. What is the position regarding the issue of a VAT invoice?

Where a taxable person lodges an expression of doubt in relation to the tax treatment of a transaction in respect of which a VAT invoice must issue, the VAT details on the invoice must be consistent with the tax treatment that the taxpayer decides to adopt (see paragraph 6). In this regard it should be noted that the outcome of the expression of doubt could be that additional VAT is payable in respect of the transactions in questions.

8. What is the position regarding recurring transactions?

Transactions which give rise to a letter of expression of doubt can be recurring. These recurring transactions can arise in two different situations, firstly where the same type of transaction recurs during a taxable period, and secondly where the same type of transaction recurs during a taxable period subsequent to the taxable period in respect of which a letter of expression of doubt has been lodged. The second situation will only arise where Revenue has not yet given a ruling on the transaction in question. In the first instance, it is necessary only to submit one example of the documentation on the type of transaction involved with the letter of expression of doubt. However, the full amount of the VAT in doubt in the total of all the recurring transactions during that period must be mentioned in the letter of expression of doubt.

In the second instance, where sample documentation has already been submitted with the first letter of expression of doubt and Revenue's ruling is awaited, it is only necessary in the subsequent letters of expression of doubt to refer to the first letter of expression of doubt, but the amount of tax in doubt in each return must be identified in each subsequent letter.

9. Circumstances when a letter of an expression of doubt is not accepted as genuine

A letter of expression of doubt will not be accepted where —

- Revenue has issued general guidelines such as the Guide to Value Added Tax, Statements of Practice, Information Leaflets, Notes for Guidance, FOI Precedents Database or VAT Rates Database about the application of the law in similar circumstances.
- Revenue is of the opinion that the matter is sufficiently free from doubt as not to warrant an expression of doubt, or
- Revenue is of the opinion that the taxable person was acting with a view to the evasion or avoidance of tax.

Where Revenue does not accept that a letter of expression of doubt is genuine the taxable person will be informed in writing of the reason or reasons for the non acceptance of the letter by Revenue.

10. Appeal

A person aggrieved by a decision of Revenue that a letter of expression of doubt is not genuine may appeal to the Appeal Commissioners, by giving notice in writing to his/her local Inspector of Taxes (see Appendix 1), within twenty-one days from the date of the decision.

Of course, where a taxable person is aggrieved by a Revenue ruling regarding the VAT treatment of the transaction which is the subject of the letter of expression of doubt, he/she can appeal this in the normal way.

11. Interest

- Where Revenue accepts that a genuine expression of doubt has been lodged by a taxable person, interest charges will not apply to any additional liability arising from the matter in doubt provided the additional liability is included in the return for the taxable period in which Revenue's ruling on the VAT treatment of the transaction in question is issued as if it were tax due for that period.
- However, interest charges will arise in situations where Revenue does not accept an expression of doubt as genuine. Interest will apply from the day after

the due date for submission of the return for the period in which the transaction occurred, not from the date of the Revenue decision.

- Interest will also apply in situations where the Appeal Commissioners uphold a decision of Revenue that a particular letter of expression of doubt was not genuine. Interest in these situations will apply from the day after the due date for submission of the return for the period in which the transaction occurred.
- Where—
  — a genuine expression of doubt is lodged,
  — Revenue (or, where appropriate, the Appeal Commissioners) determine that VAT is due on a transaction, and
  — VAT is not paid (or accounted for) by the due date for the VAT return covering the taxable period in which the Revenue ruling is issued,

  interest will apply from the day after the due date for submission of the return for the period in which the Revenue ruling is issued.

- Where —
  — a genuine expression of doubt is lodged,
  — Revenue (or, where appropriate, the Appeal Commissioners) determine that VAT claimed by a taxpayer was not, in fact, deductible on a transaction.
  — the VAT deducted is not repaid to Revenue by the due date for the VAT return covering the taxable period in which the Revenue ruling is issued, interest will apply from the day after the due date for submission of the return for the period in which the Revenue ruling is issued.

12. Can a person not registered for VAT avail of this facility?

The legislation also provides that a person not registered for VAT who is in doubt as to whether he/she is a taxable person, may avail of the expression of doubt mechanism. In these circumstances the taxable person must lodge the letter of expression of doubt not later than the nineteenth day of the month following the taxable period in which the transaction giving rise to the doubt occurred.

13. Documents to be retained/records kept

The taxable person must keep the Revenue acknowledgement of his or her expression of doubt as part of his or her records (see paragraph 3). A letter of expression of doubt shall be deemed not to have been made unless its receipt is acknowledged by Revenue and that acknowledgement forms part of the records kept by the taxable person for the purposes of section 16 of the VAT Act. A taxable person should contact the Office of the local Inspector of Taxes in the event that an acknowledgement of the letter of expression of doubt is not received.

Contact addresses can be found in Revenue Addresses at start of book.

VAT TREATMENT OF CULTURAL, ARTISTIC AND ENTERTAINMENT SERVICES SUPPLIED BY NON-ESTABLISHED PERSONS

September 2002

Introduction

1. The purpose of this information leaflet is to outline changes to the VAT treatment of cultural, artistic and entertainment services supplied by non-established persons in the State which apply from 25 March 2002. What are 'cultural, artistic and entertainment' services?

2. The 'cultural, artistic and entertainment' services affected by the changes in VAT treatment include concerts, music recitals, theatrical performances, art exhibitions, dance exhibitions, comedy shows, and similar services. What is a 'non-established' person?

3. In practice, a non-established person is regarded as being either an individual who is not normally resident in this State or who does not have a business establishment here, or a company which does not have a business establishment here. For example, a promoter who does not have a business establishment here is regarded as being a nonestablished promoter.

4. For the purposes of this information leaflet, non-established persons supplying cultural, artistic and entertainment services will be referred to as 'non-established performers'. Changes with effect from 25 March 2002.

5. Prior to 25 March 2002, a non-established performer supplying taxable goods or services in this State was obliged to register and account for Irish VAT on his/her sales, regardless of the level of sales involved. However, Revenue could deem a person connected with the supplies (for example, the concert promoter or the owner of the concert venue) to be actually making the supplies and thus liable to account for any VAT due. Alternatively, the performer could appoint a 'fiscal representative' in the State to account for any VAT due.

6. With effect from 25 March 2002, a non-established performer is not liable for VAT on his or her taxable supplies of cultural, artistic and/or entertainment services. Instead, the promoter, agent or other person who commissions the performance or event is automatically liable for the VAT due. (However, deferral of the application of these new provisions is available in certain circumstances and under which the nonestablished performer remains liable to VAT. See paragraphs 18–19 on page 4 for details.)

7. For ease of reference in this information leaflet, the promoter, agent or other person who commissions the performance or event will be referred to as the 'promoter' and the performance or event will be referred to simply as the 'performance'.

8. The promoter must account for VAT on all supplies in respect of the performance, regardless of the level of turnover concerned. The normal turnover thresholds which apply to goods and services provided by persons who are established in this State[1] do not therefore apply.

Non-established promoter: provider of the premises may be liable

9. Where a non-established promoter arranges for the supply of cultural, artistic, entertainment or similar services, the provider of the premises in which the performance is to take place has certain obligations to Revenue.

10. For the purposes of these provisions, the 'provider of the premises' is a person who *'owns, occupies or controls'* the venue in which the performance is to take place. In a situation where a non-established promoter is engaged by the owner of a venue, the owner would be the sole provider of the premises. However, in a situation where a non-established promoter is engaged by a third party who has hired the venue from its owner, there could be two providers of the premises: first, the owner of the venue; and second, the third party, who by virtue of having hired the venue, is likely to have gained a temporary right to occupy it.

11. The provider of the premises (whether the owner or a third party, or both jointly) is obliged to give the following information to Revenue:
- the name and address of the promoter, and
- details, such as the dates, duration and venue of the performance.

[1]   In general, persons who are established in this State only become obliged to account for VAT when their turnover from sales of taxable goods is €51,000 or supplies of taxable services is €25,500.

12. The provider of the premises should send this information, not later than 14 days before the performance is scheduled to begin, to Revenue's Special Enquiry Branch, contact details for which are as follows:

Special Enquiry Branch
Chief Inspector of Taxes
Office of the Revenue Commissioners
Plaza Complex
Belgard Road
Tallaght
Dublin 24

Tel: 01–6470700
Fax: 01–6341981
e-mail: seb@revenue.ie

13. Where this information is not furnished to Revenue, the provider of the premises may be made jointly and severally liable with the non-established promoter for the VAT liability in respect of the performance. In practice, this could mean that if the nonestablished promoter fails to account for any VAT due, the provider of the premises (whether the owner or a third party, or both jointly) may become liable for the entire amount of VAT due in respect of the performance.

Non-established trader: obligation to register for Irish VAT

14. Any trader who is not established in this State but who is engaged in selling taxable goods here is obliged to register and account for Irish VAT on his/her sales. This obligation to register and account for Irish VAT exists, regardless of the level of sales made or the number of days spent here by the non-established trader in making those sales. An example of a non-established trader engaged in selling taxable goods here would be one who sells merchandise (such as souvenirs, CDs, tapes, videos etc) at a concert.

Non-established trader: provider of the premises may be liable

15. Where a provider of a premises (whether the owner or a third party) allows a nonestablished trader to supply goods for a period of less than seven consecutive days on the premises in which the performance is to be held, that provider of the premises must give the following information to Revenue:

- the name and address of the non-established trader,
- the dates on which the non-established trader intends to trade on the premises, and
- the address of the premises.

16. The provider of the premises should send this information, not later than 14 days before the performance is scheduled to begin, to Revenue's Special Enquiry Branch, contact details for which are supplied in paragraph 12 on page 3.

17. Where this information is not furnished to Revenue, the provider of the premises may be made jointly and severally liable with the non-established trader for his/her VAT liability in respect of his/her supplies of goods in the premises concerned. In practice, this could mean that if the non-established trader fails to account for any VAT due, the provider of the premises (whether the owner or a third party, or both jointly) may become liable for the entire amount of VAT due in respect of the non-established trader's sales here.

Possible deferral of the application of these new provisions

18. If a promoter has received funding from the Arts Council at any time since 25 March 1999, he/she may apply to Revenue to defer the application of the new provisions to a time not later than 1 March 2003. The effect of deferring these provisions is that it is the non-established performer, not the promoter, who remains liable for the VAT due on the supply of the services performed by him/her. However, with effect from 1 March 2003, the new provisions will apply automatically.

19. All applications for deferral of the new provisions should be sent to Revenue's Special Enquiry Branch, contact details for which are supplied in paragraph 12 on page 3. These applications must be sent to Special Enquiry Branch well in advance of the performance being held. In practice, Revenue would expect to receive such applications at least 14 days in advance of the performance date. Any applications sent after the performance has been held will not be accepted.

Legislation

20. These changes form part of a package of measures which were introduced in order to comply with Council Directive 2000/65/EC which removed the right of an EU Member State to oblige a non-established person to appoint a 'fiscal representative' in the State to account for any VAT due by that non-established person. This directive was enacted into national legislation by section 198 of Finance Act 2001 which repealed section 37 of the VAT Act, 1972, together with section 101 of Finance Act 2002 which amended section 8 of the VAT Act, 1972.

Further information

21. Further information on this matter generally may be obtained from your local Inspector of Taxes, for whom contact details are provided on the attached Appendix, or from the following:

VAT Interpretation Branch Special Enquiry Branch
Indirect Taxes – Policy & Legislation Division Chief Inspector of Taxes
Office of the Revenue Commissioners Office of the Revenue Commissioners
Stamping Building Plaza Complex
Dublin Castle Belgard Road
Dublin 2 Tallaght
Dublin 24

Tel: 01–6475000 Tel: 01–6470700
Fax: 01–6795236 Fax: 01–6341981
e-mail: vat@revenue.ie e-mail: seb@revenue.ie

22. Further information on the obligations of non-established traders is available in our VAT information leaflet *'VAT Treatment of Foreign Firms Doing Business in Ireland'*. This information leaflet was published in 1999 and is currently in the process of being updated. An up-to-date version will soon be available on our website.

Issued by the Office of the Revenue Commissioners
Dublin Castle
Dublin 2

September 2002

Contact addresses can be found in Revenue Addresses at start of book.

MULTIPLIER FOR VALUATION OF INTEREST IN IMMOVABLE GOODS, REGULATION 19(1) OF VALUE — ADDED TAX REGULATIONS 1979

The following are the details of the Government Security applicable from 20 February 2003.

Date of Issue	Title of Stock	Redemption Date	Purchase Price	Rate of Interest	Redemption Yield	Multiplier of Annual Rent $\dfrac{100}{\text{Redemption Yield}}$
20 Feb 2003	3.25% Treasury Bond 2009	18 Apr 2009	€99.315	3.25%	3.377%	29.61

It should be noted that the Operative Date for the new Multiplier will be 1 March 2003.

VAT Interpretation Branch,
Indirect Taxes Policy & Legislation Division,
Dublin Castle.
21 February 2003.

ELECTRONICALLY SUPPLIED SERVICES AND RADIO AND TELEVISION BROADCASTING SERVICES

Changes introduced by Council Directive 2002/38/EC

June 2003

Contents

1. INTRODUCTION

Background

1.1. Council Directive 2002/38/EC of 7 May 2002, regarding the value added tax arrangements applicable to radio and television broadcasting services and certain electronically supplied services, was transposed into national law in the

2003 Finance Act (No. 3 of 2003). The new measures deal with the place of supply rules for these services, and include an **optional** special scheme for non-EU suppliers supplying digital products into the EU. The measures will come into effect on 1 July 2003.

1.2. The Directive was needed because the existing VAT rules applicable to radio and television broadcasting services and to electronically supplied services were inadequate for taxing services supplied from outside the EU but consumed within the EU and for preventing the distortion of competition. In particular, the Directive sought to ensure that where these services were consumed in the EU then they should be taxed in the EU and not taxed if they were consumed outside the EU.

What the leaflet covers

1.3. This Information Leaflet explains the different measures introduced by the Directive. Parts 2, 3 and 4 deal with electronically supplied services and cover definitions (Part 2), the new place of supply rules (Part 3) and the new special scheme for non-EU suppliers (Part 4). Part 5 of the leaflet explains the new rules in connection with radio and television broadcasting services. Detailed guidelines on the interpretation of "electronically supplied services", which have been agreed unanimously by the EU VAT Committee, are reproduced in the Appendix.

2. ELECTRONICALLY SUPPLIED SERVICES

What are electronically supplied services?

2.1. An "electronically supplied service" is one that is delivered over the Internet (or an electronic network which is reliant on the Internet or similar network for its provision) and is heavily dependent on information technology for its supply – ie the service is essentially automated, involving minimal human intervention and in the absence of information technology does not have viability. An indicative list of such services is given in Annex L of the 6th VAT Directive reproduced here.

2.2. On the basis of the above definition, the EU VAT Committee, which discusses VAT technical issues, has indicated that an electronically supplied service includes:

— *Digitised products*, (such as software and changes to or upgrades of Services which provide or support a business or personal presence on an electronic network (for example, a web site);

— *Services* automatically generated from computer, via the Internet or an electronic network, in response to specific data input by the customer;

— *Other services* which are automated and dependent on the Internet or an electronic network for their provision.

2.3. In general, the use of the Internet or other electronic networks by parties to communicate with respect to transactions or to facilitate trading does not, any more than the use of a phone or fax, affect the normal VAT rules that apply. For example, where parties simply use the Internet to convey information in the course of a business transaction (eg, e-mail), this does not change the nature of that transaction. This differs from a supply that is completely dependent on the Internet in order to be carried out (eg, searching and retrieving information from a database with no human intervention).

Detailed examples of electronically supplied services

2.4.   Tables published by the VAT Committee, giving examples of transactions that are either included or excluded from the definition of "electronically supplied services", are reproduced in the Appendix to this Information Leaflet. These guidelines were agreed unanimously at the 67th meeting of the Committee in [January 2003]. While the lists are not exhaustive, they classify a wide range of supplies to provide clear examples of those that are regarded as being electronically supplied and those that are not. This should help ensure consistency of treatment of these services between Member States.

2.5.   Supplies that are regarded as being electronically supplied (Table 1 of the Appendix) are treated in accordance with the new rules laid down in the Directive and transposed into national law with effect from 1 July 2003. Supplies that are regarded as not being electronically supplied (Table 2 of the Appendix) are treated in accordance with other place of supply rules.

2.6.   Particular care should be taken where a service includes both electronic and other elements. Such composite transactions must generally be considered on a case-by-case basis.

The VAT rate

2.7.   Electronically supplied services are taxable at the standard rate in each Member State, unless an exemption applies in a Member State. For example, if the "traditional" forms of supply of gambling is exempt in a Member State, it would also be exempt in that Member State if it is supplied as an electronically supplied service.

(Please note that radio and television broadcasting services do not come within the scope of the definition of electronically supplied services – see Part 5 of this Leaflet).

3. PLACE OF SUPPLY RULES FOR ELECTRONIC SERVICES

Business to Business (B2B)

3.1.   The new "B2B" place of supply rules apply to all business-to-business supplies where the recipient is established in a Member State for electronically supplied services.

The rules provide that the place of supply will be the place where the customer has established his or her business. The reverse charge rule applies, under which the customer will account for the VAT.

Business to Consumer (B2C)

3.2.   The new "B2C" place of supply rules for electronically supplied services provides that, where a non-EU business supplies to a private consumer in any Member State, the place of supply will be the place where the consumer normally resides. For example, if a Canadian business supplies electronic services to an Irish consumer on or after 1 July 2003, the place of supply (and of taxation) is the Ireland.

3.3. This is a totally new B2C rule. Up to now, private consumers getting electronic supplies from non-EU businesses were not in the VAT net. This gave non-EU suppliers an unfair competitive advantage compared to EU businesses supplying to private customers in the EU. The main effect of the new rule is that suppliers of these services are liable to register and account for VAT in every Member State where they have private customers. **However, an optional special scheme is available which allows such non-EU businesses opt to register in one Member State only – this is covered in part 4 of the Information Leaflet.**

3.4. The "B2C" place of supply rule for electronically supplied services supplied by an EU business to a private consumer in the EU, is still the Member State in which the supplier is established.

B2B: Verification of business status

How can a supplier verify their customer's business status?

3.5. For business-to-business supplies within the EU the evidence required at the time of the transaction would normally be the customer's VAT registration number and country identification code prefix. The number must conform to the format for the registration person's Member State.

It is possible to verify Irish VAT registration numbers with the VIMA Office who can be contacted at ***vimahelp@revenue.ie***. Other Member States may have similar systems by which it is possible to check the validity of VAT registration numbers.

Under normal trading practices businesses will often know their business customers and, in such cases, they will not therefore need to routinely check all VAT numbers quoted, provided that the numbers conform to the correct country format.

If you are unable to confirm that the customer is in business or if there remains any doubt about the use of a VAT registration number, VAT should be charged as appropriate on all supplies to that customer including supplies that have already been made.

Summary table on the place of supply

The position in relation to various supplies is summarised in the table below.

Table 3.1 – place of supply rules for electronic services

From	To	Place of supply
Business in Ireland	Business in Ireland	Ireland
	Business in other MS	Other Member State
	Business outside EU	Outside EU (no VAT)
	Private consumer in Ireland	Ireland
	Private consumer in other MS	Ireland
	Private consumer outside EU	Outside EU (no VAT)
Business in OMS	Business in Ireland	Ireland
	Private consumer in Ireland	Other Member State
Business outside EU	Business in Ireland	Ireland
	Private consumer in Ireland	Ireland

4. THE SPECIAL SCHEME FOR ELECTRONIC SERVICES

4.1. The optional scheme for the VAT treatment of electronic services supplied B2C by non-EU established businesses to private consumers in the EU, comes into force on 1 July 2003. The purpose of the special scheme is to reduce the compliance burden and administrative costs for taxable persons.

Broad outline of the special scheme

4.2. The special scheme enables the non-EU supplier to choose a Member State in which to register for and pay VAT, regardless of the Member State in which the suppliers private consumer resides. Once registered the supplier makes VAT returns to that Member State, declaring the VAT due on all the on-line sales to consumers within the EU. The rate of VAT will be the standard rate in the country the consumer resides. A special on-line return form will be provided under which the supplier must provide a breakdown of all electronic supplies to customers in each Member State. Payment is to be made to a designated account in the Member State of registration. That Member State re-distributes the VAT receipts to Member States in accordance with the amounts due as declared by the supplier.

4.3. For example, an Australian business supplies on-line digital products to private B2C in Ireland, France and Germany. It opts to register for the special scheme in Ireland. It charges Irish VAT to its Irish customers, French VAT to its French customers and German VAT to its German customers. It registers electronically in Ireland, puts all the details on a single quarterly electronic return and pays all the VAT due to the Irish Revenue each quarter. The Irish Revenue will retain the Irish VAT and distribute the French and German VAT to those countries.

What businesses are eligible to use the special scheme?

4.4. A business is eligible to use the special scheme if that business·
— supplies electronically supplied services to private consumers who reside in the EU,
— is not established within the EU, and
— is not otherwise registered (or required to be registered) for VAT in any Member State.

How will the scheme operate in Ireland?

4.5. The Revenue Commissioners are setting up a register of non-EU suppliers who opt to register in this country under the scheme. Registration will only be accessible through the Revenue On-line System (ROS). Suppliers must supply certain details (specified below) to ROS in order to register under the scheme. A link will be provided on the Revenue website (***www.revenue.ie***) home page to the ROS home page where a new section, especially for non-EU customers, will facilitate applicants in the registration process.

4.6. A supplier registered under the scheme will be allocated an identification number (the special VAT number for electronic services supplies) and a digital certificate by ROS. Suppliers on the Irish register will use their digital certificates to access the system via the Revenue On-Line Service, ROS home page. Suppliers must submit special VAT returns and pay Revenue the VAT due in respect of their supplies in all Member States including Ireland within 20 days of the end of each calendar quarter. Payment must be made in euro to bank account designated by the Revenue Commissioners.

Registration – information needed and procedures

4.7. The non-EU supplier must furnish the following information to Revenue in order to register under the scheme:
   — Name and postal address,
   — Electronic addresses including website addresses,
   — National tax number, if any,
   — A statement that the supplier is not registered for VAT within the EU, and
   —The date from which the supply of electronically supplied services to EU consumers commences

4.8. The information must be supplied electronically, on the registration form available on the Revenue On-line Service ROS – see paragraph 4.6 above. When registration is confirmed, Revenue will e-mail the applicant his or her special VAT number, together with details on how the digital certificate is to be retrieved.

Must a business be making supplies before registering?

4.9. Not necessarily. On registration, the supplier must state the date from which the supply of electronically supplied services to EU consumers commences. For example, a supplier could register in August on the basis that the supplies would start from 1 September. Note however that nil returns must be submitted if there are no supplies in a calendar quarter – see paragraph [**4.11**].

Must a business make supplies in Ireland in order to register here?

4.10. No. Businesses who only make, or intend making, supplies under the special scheme to customers in other EU countries may register for the special scheme in Ireland if they so wish. The VAT due in those other Member States will be paid to the Revenue Commissioners, who will distribute it to the relevant tax authorities.

The procedure for submitting VAT returns and making payments

4.11. The special VAT returns are due for each calendar quarter (30 September, 31 December, 31 March and 30 June) and must be submitted by the 20th of the month at the end of the quarter to which the return relates. For example, the return for the calendar quarter ending on 30 September 2003 must be submitted by 20 October 2003. The VAT due in respect of supplies in all Member States must be paid at the same time as the return, into a bank account designated by the Revenue Commissioners. Payments must be made in euro. Nil returns must also be submitted.

4.12. The special VAT return must show the following information:
   — The non-EU supplier's identification number,

— For each Member State where VAT is due, the total value (excluding VAT), the applicable VAT rate and the amount of VAT due at each applicable rate in respect of electronically supplied services for the quarter, and

— The total VAT payable in all Member States

4.13. The special VAT returns must be filed electronically on the website for the special scheme. Suppliers will use their digital certificates to access the Revenue On€line Service ROS – see para [**4.5**] above. The return screen on the ROS system will include instructions on when and how payments should be made – this will be done by Electronic Funds Transfer (EFT). Suppliers should give both their VAT number and details on the relevant quarterly period to the bank when making payments. Receipts for moneys received will be issued to the supplier via the ROS system.

Supplies made in currencies other than the euro

4.14. Where transactions are carried out using currencies other than the euro, the supplier should convert the amount into euro using the conversion rate published by the European Central Bank for the last date of the relevant calendar quarter. If there is no publication on that date, the rate on the next day of publication should be used.

VAT on purchases

4.15. A person from outside the EU who makes supplies in Ireland under the scheme is not entitled to deduct input VAT using the VAT return. However, the supplier is entitled to claim a refund under the terms of the 13th Directive in respect of VAT paid on goods or services used for the purposes of taxable activities falling under the special scheme. Claims in respect of the VAT paid in Ireland should be made to the Revenue Commissioners under the standard 13th Directive procedures. For further information contact *unregvat@revenue.ie*

Records

4.16. Suppliers registered for the special scheme must keep records of all transactions affecting their VAT liability – for example, the value and date of the transaction, the customer's name and location, etc. These records must be kept for 10 years and must be made available electronically, on request, to the tax authorities in the Member State where the supplier is registered for the special scheme and to each Member State where the supplier's customers reside.

Changes in details supplied or business circumstances

4.17. Suppliers under the scheme are required to notify Revenue if there are any changes in the details provided under paragraph [**4.7**] (name and address, websites, etc) or if their taxable activity changes to the extent that they are no longer eligible to use the special scheme. For example, if the supplier begins to supply goods or services, in the EU, will be liable to register for VAT under the normal rules and will cease to be eligible for the scheme.

4.18.   Revenue may exclude from the scheme suppliers who fail to comply with the provisions of the scheme.

Suppliers not registered for the special scheme in Ireland

4.19.   Non-EU businesses who supply electronic services to consumers in Ireland and are registered for the special scheme in another Member State must pay the Irish VAT due to the tax authorities in that other Member State, under the terms of their Special Scheme. Such businesses must also keep records of the Irish (and other) transactions – see paragraph [**4.16**].

4.20.   Non-EU businesses who supply electronic services to consumers in Ireland and are not registered for the special scheme in <u>any</u> Member State must register in Ireland and account for the Irish VAT in respect of those supplies, under the normal VAT rules. These businesses must also register and account for VAT in each and every other Member State where supplies are made.

5. RADIO AND TELEVISION BROADCASTING SERVICES

The new place of supply rules

5.1.   The new place of supply rules provide that these services will be taxed in the Member State of consumption. In particular,
—   Where businesses supply radio and television broadcasting services to businesses in the EU, the place of supply will be where the customer has established his or her business. The reverse charge rule applies, under which the business customer will account for the VAT. This is similar to the B2B rule for electronic services – see **paragraph 3.1**.
—   Where non-EU businesses supply radio and television broadcasting services to private consumers in Ireland, the place of taxation is Ireland and the supplier must register and account for the VAT here. This is similar to the B2C rule for electronic services – see **paragraph 3.2**. However, there is no optional special scheme for non-EU suppliers of radio and TV broadcasting services.

Some examples

5.2.   Taxable persons — for example VAT registered pubs and clubs – who buy in broadcasting services from suppliers established in other Member States or outside the EU (by means of a satellite dish and decoder), will be taxed in Ireland under the reverse charge procedure. This is a change to the current rule, which says the place of taxation is where the supplier is established.

5.3.   Private individuals in Ireland who pay for broadcasting services supplied by non-EU suppliers (eg "pay per view") will be taxable in Ireland under the new rules. The non-EU supplier will be obliged to register and account for VAT in Ireland in respect of all his or her supplies to private individuals in the State.

APPENDIX – VAT COMMITTEE GUIDELINES

Table 1 – Examples of services regarded as being electronically supplied

Annex L Reference	Supplies covered by the legal text	Example of a service that is an electronically supplied service
Item 1	A. Web site supply, web-hosting and distance maintenance of programmes and equipment	Web-site hosting and web-page hosting Automated, on-line distance maintenance of programmes Remote systems administration On-line data warehousing (ie, where specific data is stored and retrieved electronically) On-line supply of on-demand disc space
Item 2	A. Software and updating thereof	Accessing or downloading software (eg procurement/accountancy programmes, anti-virus software) plus updates Bannerblockers (software to block banner adverts showing) Download drivers, such as software that interfaces PC with peripheral equipment (eg, printers) On-line automated installation of filters on web-sites On-line automated installation of firewalls
Item 3	A. Images	Accessing or downloading desktop themes Accessing or downloading photographic or pictorial images or screensavers
	B. Text and information	The digitised content of books and other electronic-publications Subscription to on-line newspaper and journals Weblogs and website statistics On-line news, traffic information and weather reports On-line information generated automatically by software from specific data input by the customer, such as legal and financial data (eg, continually updated stock market data) The provision of advertising space (eg, banner ads on a web site/web page)
	C. Making databases available	Use of search engines and Internet directories

Item 4	A. Music	Accessing or downloading of music onto PCs, mobile phones, etc Accessing or downloading of films
	B. Films	Accessing or downloading of jingles, excerpts, ringtones, or other sounds
	C. Broadcasts and events – political, cultural, artistic, sporting, scientific and entertainment	Web-based broadcasting that is only provided over the Internet or similar electronic network and is not simultaneously broadcast over a traditional radio or television network, as opposed to Item 4, Table 2
	D. Games, including games of chance and gambling games	Downloads of games onto PCs, mobile phones, etc Accessing automated on-line games which are dependent on the Internet, or other similar electronic networks, where players are remote from one another
Item 5	A. Distance teaching	Teaching that is automated and dependent on the Internet or similar electronic network to function, including virtual classrooms, as opposed to Item 2(b), Table 2 Workbooks completed by pupil on-line and marked automatically, without human intervention
Item 6 Other services included:	A. Those not explicitly listed in Items 1–5	On-line auction services (to the extent that they are not already considered to be web-hosting services under Item 1) that are dependent on automated databases and data input by the customer requiring little or no human intervention (eg, an on-line market place or on-line shopping portals), as opposed to Item 3(f), Table 2 Internet Service Packages (ISPs) in which the telecommunications component is an ancillary and subordinate part (ie, a package that goes beyond mere Internet access comprising various elements (eg, content pages containing news, weather, travel information; games fora; web-hosting; access to chat-lines etc))

Table 2 – Examples of services not regarded as being electronically supplied

Example of a transaction not considered to be a supply of an 'electronically supplied service'	Rationale
1) A supply of . . . a) A good, where the order and processing is done electronically b) A CD-ROM, floppy disc and similar tangible media c) Printed matter such as a book, newsletter, newspaper or journal d) A CD, audio cassette e) A Video cassette, DVD f) Games on a CD-ROM	These are supplies of goods
2) A supply of . . . a) services of lawyers and financial consultants, etc who advise clients through e-mail b) interactive teaching services where the course content is delivered by a teacher over the Internet or an electronic network (ie, via remote link)	This is a supply of service that relies on substantial human intervention and the Internet or electronic network is only used as a means of communication
3) A supply of . . . a) Physical repair services of computer equipment b) Off-line data warehousing services c) Advertising services, such as in newspapers, on posters and on television d) Telephone helpdesk services e) Teaching services involving correspondence courses such as postal courses f) Conventional auctioneers' services reliant on direct human intervention, irrespective of how bids are made (eg, in person, Internet or telephone), as opposed to Item 6(a), Table 1	These are supplies of services that are not delivered over the Internet and rely on substantial human intervention
4) A supply of a radio and television broadcasting service provided over the Internet or similar electronic network simultaneous to the same broadcast being provided over traditional radio or television network, as opposed to Item 4(c), Table 1	This is a supply of a radio and television broadcasting service, which is covered by the penultimate indent of Article 9(2)(e)
5) A supply of . . . a) Videophone services (ie, telephone services with a video component) b) Access to the Internet and World Wide Web c) Telephony (ie, telephone service provided through the Internet)	These are supplies of telecommunication services and are covered by the place of supply rules for such services under the ninth indent of Article 9(2)(e)

NEW VAT TREATMENT OF VEHICLES REGISTERED BY DISTRIBUTORS OR DEALERS PRIOR TO SALE

1. Under the terms of section 120 of the Finance Act 2003, the VAT and VRT treatment of vehicles registered by distributors or dealers in their own name will change on 1 May 2003.

Vehicles to which the new rules apply

2. The only vehicles involved are those of the type, which, outside of the motor trade, are non-deductible vehicles for VAT purposes. These are the vehicles classified for Vehicle Registration Tax (VRT) purposes as category A vehicles (cars in general) and motor cycles.

Vehicle registered on or after 1 May 2003

3. Where on or after 1 May 2003 a distributor or dealer (referred to in this statement, for convenience, as dealer) registers a category A vehicle or a motor cycle in the name of the distributorship/dealership, etc, the vehicle is treated as removed from stock in trade. This removal results in a 'self-supply' for VAT purposes. This means that a dealer who has taken deductibility for VAT on the purchase or importation of the vehicle must account for VAT on that vehicle in the VAT return for the period in which the vehicle is registered in the dealer's name as if the vehicle were sold at cost price.

Vehicle subsequently sold on

4. When the vehicle is subsequently sold to a customer, the dealer will be entitled to make a claim on the VAT 3 return for a residual input credit. This means that the vehicle is treated as if it were bought into stock from outside the trade, for sale as a second hand vehicle. The basis for calculating the residual VAT is the VAT-inclusive cost price plus VRT (see calculation at paragraph 6). *This residual VAT available for credit cannot exceed the amount of VAT due on the sale of the vehicle.*

5. As the residual input credit is only available at the time of the sale of the vehicle to a customer, both the claim for the VAT credit and the VAT on the sale of the vehicle will be accounted for in the same VAT return. The effect of this mechanism is that the residual input credit will be offset against the output VAT on the sale, and the dealer will actually pay VAT only on the difference between the cost price (inclusive of VAT and VRT) and the sale price. *However, the dealer cannot claim more residual credit than the VAT due on the sale. If the cost price (inclusive of VAT and VRT) is greater than the sale price the residual input credit is limited to an amount equal to the VAT on the sale price.*

Calculation of the amount of the residual input credit

6. The residual input credit is calculated according to the formula normally used for the calculation of residual input credit for second hand motor vehicles, with slight variation, as follows:

$$A \times \frac{B}{B + 100}$$

Where—

    A   is the cost price (inclusive of VAT and VRT) and
    B   is the percentage rate of VAT.

Example:

Assume the cost price of a vehicle qualifying for the new treatment by the dealer is as follows:

Cost of vehicle to the dealer excluding VAT and VRT	€11,465
VAT (amount of liability in respect of self supply)	2,408
VRT	5,625
Cost price (inclusive of VAT and VRT)	€19,498
Vehicle Sold for	€21,000

The Value Added Tax due on the sale is accounted for as follows:

VAT due on the sale (21,000 121) X 21 =	€3,644.62
Residual credit* due (19,498 121) X 21=	€3,383.95
Net VAT due on sale of demo vehicle	€260.67

* The residual credit cannot exceed the VAT due on the sale

VRT Refund Scheme for Vehicles in demonstration to be abolished

7. As a consequence of the changes in the Finance Act 2003 the current VRT refund scheme for demonstration vehicles will be abolished in respect of vehicles registered on or after 1 May 2003. Any vehicle which is already registered and in demonstration before that date will be treated under the old rules, ie the VRT refund will be payable under the normal conditions, but the scheme outlined above and detailed in Section 120 of the Finance Act 2003 will not apply.

VAT ON PROPERTY (MULTIPLIER)

VAT multiplier to be used when valuing an interest in immovable goods from 1990 to date.

DATE ISSUE	REDEMPTION YIELD	MULTIPLIER
21 May 1991	9.30 per cent	10.75
24 January 1992	9.11 per cent	10.98
14 June 1993	7.37 per cent	13.57
15 October 1993	6.87 per cent	14.56
17 August 1994	8.56 per cent	11.68
15 May 1995	8.52 per cent	11.74
19 April 1996	6.93 per cent	14.43(1)
17 September 1997	6.26 per cent	15.97
11 May 1999	4.26 per cent	23.47(2)
29 January 2002	5.14 per cent	19.45
1 March 2003	3.377 per cent	29.61
1 February 2004	4.702 per cent	21.27

1. The operative date for the multiplier of 14.43 is the 26 March, 1997

2. The operative date for the multiplier of 23.47 is the 30 June, 1999.

(June 2004)

SECTION 4(8) VAT ACT 1972

Circumstances where the reverse charge applies:

Where VAT is chargeable on a surrender of a leasehold interest or on an assignment of a leasehold interest **to** any of the following classes of person:

    (a)   a taxable person (for VAT purposes),

    (b)   a Department of State or a local authority, or

    (c)   a person supplying goods of a kind referred to in paragraph (a) of the definition of 'exempted activity' in section 1 of the VAT Act, 1972 [property, the supply of which is not chargeable to VAT], or

    (d)   a person supplying services of a kind referred to in paragraphs (i), (iv), (ix), (xi), (xia), (xiii) and (xiv) of the First Schedule to the VAT Act, 1972, in the course or furtherance of business[1],

then, for VAT purposes, these persons are deemed to supply those goods in the course or furtherance of business and they, rather than the person making the surrender/assignment, will be liable to pay the VAT on the surrender/assignment. They must declare the VAT liability in their VAT return and where they are taxable persons[2] they may be entitled to claim a deduction (or input credit) for the VAT, in accordance with Section 12 of the VAT Act 1972.

Example 1

Joe, a builder and taxable person, is the lessee under a 35 year lease of an office and yard (developed since 1/11/1972). He assigns the lease to Melanie, another taxable person, who operates a garden centre. In the normal course, Melanie will account for VAT on the value of the assignment, even though she is the customer in the transaction

---

Notes

[1]   See appendix A to Revenue Guide to VAT www.revenue.ie/pdf/vatguide_03pdf.

[2]   A taxable person for this purpose is a person liable to register for VAT – see Revenue Guide to Value Added Tax, Chapter 2.1 www.revenue.ie/doc/proptran.doc

---

Circumstances where the reverse charge does not apply:

The reverse charge does not apply and VAT must be applied in the normal way by the person making the supply/assignment in all other circumstances where VAT is chargeable on a surrender /assignment of a leasehold interest.

It is not possible to compile a comprehensive list of those persons who should be charged VAT on such surrenders or assignments, however, the following is a non-exhaustive list:

    (a)   Private persons

    (b)   School Bodies

    (c)   Doctors or Dentists

    (d)   Certain Hospital Authorities

    (e) Bookmakers
    (f) The National Lottery
    (g) Undertakers

Example 2

Fred, a florist and taxable person, has a 35-year lease of a unit (developed since 1/11/1972) in a Shopping Centre. He assigns his lease to Larry, a bookmaker. In this case, Fred must account for VAT on the supply. He will therefore invoice Larry.

Example 3

Suzy, an accountant and a taxable person, has a 20-year lease of a ground floor office. The property was developed since 1/11/1972. Donal, the landlord, who resides in the upper section of the property, agrees to take a surrender of the lease. He will use it to expand his residence and will not use it for business purposes. Suzy must account for VAT on the surrender.

(June 2004)

VAT AND PROPERTY — THE 10% RULE

1. INTRODUCTION

The so-called 10% rule is a simplification rule designed to assist in determining whether the creation of an interest in property is taxable. The rule provides where relatively insignificant amounts of extension, alteration or demolition work have been carried out to the property prior to its disposal the property will be regarded as not having been developed. The rule has been in place since 1973 and has been operated without difficulty in the vast majority of appropriate property transactions. It provides the necessary clarity to determine whether or not the supply of a property may be regarded as taxable.

The rule is of course merely a simplification measure and has no statutory authority. It was pointed out in a 2001 High Court case (Forbes and Tobin) that the rule cannot be relied on by a purchaser where the vendor insists that the property has been developed even though the vendor may not have incurred expenditure in excess of 10% (or the de minimis amount) of the sale value in carrying out the development of the property.

The Revenue Commissioners have reviewed the 10% rule and have decided to issue the following guidelines to bring greater clarity to the application of the rule. At the same time the maximum expenditure permitted within the rule is being increased from €100,000 to €300,000.

It should be remembered that once a property is regarded as developed after 1 November 1972 it remains developed irrespective of the amounts of expenditure incurred thereafter by its owner or subsequent owners. The taxability or otherwise of such a property depends on the normal rules for taxability and the 10% de minimis rule has no relevance as regards any further disposal of the property. (See example D).

2. Legislation

Section 1 of the VAT Act 1972 as amended defines development as

"**development**" in relation to any land, means-

(a) the construction, demolition, extension, alteration or reconstruction of any building on the land, or

(b) the carrying out of any engineering or other operation in, on, over or under the land to adapt it for materially altered use,

and "**developed**" shall be construed correspondingly

3. Meaning of Extension, Alteration or Demolition where there is no essential change of use for the purposes of the 10% Rule in determining the taxable status of a property.

1   In determining whether or not a property was developed after 31 October 1972, or subsequent to its acquisition after that date (if not already developed), relatively small and routine outlay on extensions, alterations or demolitions

carried out periodically (which did not adapt the property for materially altered use) for the purposes of the persons taxable activities may be ignored notwithstanding that a vat credit or deduction may have been claimed in relation to such outlay. In practical terms this may be taken as meaning that, where there is no essential change in the use of the property or where the expenditure was not carried out to adapt the property for such a change, such outlay may be ignored if it is reasonably clear that its cost would not exceed 10 per cent of the total amount on which tax would be chargeable if the work in question were treated as a development, or €300,000 whichever is the lesser.

2 The carrying out of any engineering or other operation in, on, over or under the land to adapt it for materially altered use, is always regarded as development and the 10 per cent rule, as outlined in (1) above, does not apply in determining whether or not a supply of immovable goods so developed is subject to Value Added Tax.

Examples

	Properties undeveloped for VAT purposes at the time of acquisition by the supplier			Property developed at time of acquisition
	Example A Retail Shop	**Example B Factory Building**	**Example C Field/Site**	**Example D Office Building**
Being sold for (or capitalised value of rent)	€1,000,000	€8,000,000	€1,500,000	€3,000,000
Outlay on alterations subsequent to acquisition by the supplier	€90,000	€700,000	€90,000	€275,000

What are the VAT implications?

Example A, a shopkeeper purchased a retail shop in 1986. The retail shop was undeveloped for VAT purposes at the time of acquisition by the shopkeeper. Since the acquisition the shopkeeper incurred outlay of €90,000 on various alterations. The retail shop is now being sold for €1,000,000.

The property which **has not** been adapted for materially altered use would be regarded as not having been developed subsequent to its acquisition by the shop-keeper, because the outlay on subsequent alteration did not exceed €300,000 and is also less than 10% of the selling price. Consequently, the supply would be regarded as outside the scope of VAT.

Example B, a manufacturing company purchased a factory building in 1996. The factory was undeveloped for VAT purposes at the time of acquisition by the manufacturing company. Since the acquisition the manufacturing company incurred outlay of €700,000 on various alterations. The factory building is now being sold for €8,000,000.

The property, which, although it **has not** been adapted for materially altered use, would be regarded as developed by the manufacturing company because the outlay (of €700,000) on subsequent alteration exceeded €300,000. Consequently, the manufacturing company is liable to tax on the supply, provided all the other requirements for taxability are satisfied. VAT would be chargeable by reference to the full supply value of €8,000,000.

Example C, an investor purchased a field in 2001. The field was undeveloped for VAT purposes at the time of acquisition by the investor. Since the acquisition the investor incurred outlay of €90,000 involving the laying of roads, sewers and service cables over the entire area of the field. The field is now being sold for €1,500,000.

The field, **has been** adapted for materially, altered use, involving the carrying out of an engineering or other operation in, on, over or under the land. Consequently, the investor making the supply would be liable to tax on its supply, provided all the other requirements for taxability are satisfied. This is so because the development involved the carrying out of an engineering or other operation in, on, over or under the land to adapt it for materially altered use and this type of development is not covered by the 10% rule as outlined in this memo. VAT would be chargeable by reference to the full supply value of €1,500,000.

Example D, an accountancy firm purchased an office building in 1999. The office building was developed in 1999 by a developer who supplied it to the accountancy firm. Since the acquisition the accountancy firm incurred outlay of €275,000 on various alterations. The office building is now being sold for €3,000,000.

The office building was developed after 1 November 1972. It remains developed for VAT purposes irrespective of the amounts of expenditure incurred thereafter by the accountancy firm. The taxability or otherwise of such a property depends on the normal rules for taxability and the 10% de minimis rule has no relevance as regards any further disposal of the property. €3,000,000.

FOURTH SCHEDULE SERVICES

Introduction

1. This information leaflet sets out the VAT treatment of what are described as "Fourth Schedule services", which means the services listed in the Fourth Schedule to the VAT Act, 1972 (as amended). [See Appendix I]. This leaflet replaces Information Leaflet No. 9/01.

What are "Fourth Schedule services"?

2. Under VAT law the place of supply is a key factor in determining who is liable for payment of the tax. The general rule in relation to the place of supply of services is that services are taxable at the place where the supplier's business is established. However, there are certain categories of services such as consultancy which are an exception to this general rule and it is those exceptions which are listed in the Fourth Schedule to the VAT Act 1972 (as amended). They are referred to as "Fourth Schedule services". The corresponding provisions of the EU 6th VAT Directive are contained in Article 9.2 (e).

3. Examples of Fourth Schedule services include:
— transfer of intangible assets e.g. patents, licences, greenhouse gas emission allowances.
— hire of plant and machinery e.g. scaffolding, cranes etc.
— supply of staff by employment agencies.
— services of a general nature provided by engineers, auctioneers, architects etc.

The following are not Fourth Schedule services; - hairdressers, repairs and services of equipment. - services relating to specific property e.g. engineers and architects.

4. The liability for tax on "Fourth Schedule services" in which both the supplier and recipient are based in the State lies with the supplier and is taxed under the General Rule (see 2)

5. When Fourth Schedule services are received for business purposes in this State from outside the State the place of supply is deemed to be in this State and it is the recipient who is liable for payment of VAT. This provision means that even persons engaged in "VAT-exempt" activities e.g. insurance, banking, stock broking and bookmaking, who are not registered for VAT in respect of their normal supplies are obliged to register and account for VAT in respect of the receipt of these services from outside the State.

6. Similarly when such services are supplied from a business in the State to a person in another Member State of the EU for the purpose of his business, Irish VAT is not chargeable on the supply. The VAT is charged in the State where the recipient is established. Services supplied for non-business purposes in another Member State do attract Irish VAT. Services supplied to non-EU countries are not liable for Irish VAT whether for business or private use.

Liability for tax on "Fourth Schedule services" received from outside the State

7. All persons, including charitable organisations and exempt bodies (e.g. banks, insurance companies), who receive taxable Fourth Schedule services for business purposes from outside the State, must register and account for Irish VAT on these services. Government Departments, Local Authorities and bodies established by statute who receive Fourth Schedule services from another EU Member State must register and account for the VAT on these services unless VAT is payable on these services in the Member State of supply. There is no threshold for registration purposes.

8. An individual receiving Fourth Schedule services for private (non-business) purposes is not obliged to register or to pay Irish VAT in respect of the receipt of those services.

Taxable "Fourth Schedule services" received from outside the State by unregistered persons for business purposes.

9. Persons who are not already registered for VAT and who, for business purposes, receive any of the taxable services listed in Appendix I from outside the State are obliged, whether or not they are engaged in exempt activities, to register for and pay VAT on those services, irrespective of their value. Flat-rate farmers, fishermen and race-horse trainers who register in respect of Fourth Schedule services are entitled to retain their unregistered status in respect of their farm or fishing activities.

Applications for registration should be made to the local Revenue District (see contact details in Appendix IV).

10. Fourth Schedule services received VAT free in another EU Member State by a person who purports to be a taxable person, are liable to Irish VAT in the State.

11. The rate of VAT for Fourth Schedule services is the same as that which applies to similar services supplied within the State (generally the standard rate which is 21 per cent). However, the receipt of banking, financial and insurance services is exempt from VAT. The amount, which is liable to Irish VAT, is the amount payable to the foreign supplier at the rate of exchange (if not in Euro) applicable on the date of the invoice.

12. A person who is registered for VAT in respect of "Fourth Schedule services" solely is not entitled to any VAT deduction or refund in respect of the tax payable on those services or, indeed, in respect of any other VAT which may be charged directly by suppliers in the State. Neither is there any entitlement to any deduction or refund of VAT paid at the point of import into the State or of VAT paid in respect of intra-Community acquisitions.

Taxable "Fourth Schedule services" received from outside the State by VAT-registered persons

13. VAT-registered persons receiving any of the specified Fourth Schedule services from outside the State are liable for VAT on the receipt of such services.

14. If the recipient is a business person whose activities are liable for VAT, a deduction equal to the amount of the liability on the Fourth Schedule services may be deducted. In effect the liability on services received from outside the State is cancelled out but the transactions must nevertheless be declared in the persons VAT returns.

15. Where the Fourth Schedule services are used for non-business purposes, no part of the VAT payable on the Fourth Schedule services is deductible.

If the recipient is a business person some of whose activities are liable for VAT and some of which are not, only that part of the VAT on a Fourth Schedule service which is referable to the taxable part of the business may be deducted. Where there is any doubt the matter should be settled by agreement with the Inspector of Taxes.

Supply of "Fourth Schedule services" outside the State by Irish businesses.

16. When an Irish business supplies a taxable Fourth Schedule service for business purposes to any person established outside the State there is no liability to Irish VAT. In such cases the place of supply is deemed to be the place of establishment of the recipient.

Where the service is supplied for business purposes to a customer in another EU Member State, the invoice issued by the supplier must record the VAT identification number of that person in that Member State and an indication that a reverse charge applies.

17. Services supplied to private individuals are liable to Irish VAT if the individuals reside in another EU Member State. However, no VAT is chargeable if supplied to private individuals living outside the European Union.

"Fourth Schedule services" - summary table

Country of establishment of supplier	Country in which customer established	Status of Customer	Place of supply	Person liable to pay Irish VAT
Ireland	Ireland	Business or Private	Ireland	Supplier
Ireland	Other EU State	Business	Other EU State	No Irish VAT
Ireland	Other EU State	Private	Ireland	Supplier
Ireland	Outside EU	Business or Private	Outside EU	No Irish VAT* **
Other EU State	Ireland	Business	Ireland	Customer
Other EU State	Ireland	Private	Other EU State	No Irish VAT
Outside EU	Ireland	Business	Ireland	Customer
Outside EU	Ireland	Private	Outside EU	No Irish VAT* **

*Telecommunications

However, where telecommunications services are supplied to a private customer and the effective use and enjoyment of these services takes place within the State, the place of taxation is Ireland and VAT registration by the supplier is required. For additional information on the special VAT treatment of these services see Information Leaflet No.32/01 entitled Telecommunications Services http://www.revenue.ie/pdf/inforno.7.pdf

** Electronically Supplied Services

The "business to consumer" place of supply rule for electronically supplied services provides that, where a non-EU business supplies to a private consumer in any Member State, the place of supply will be the place where the consumer normally resides. For example, if a Canadian business supplies electronic services to an Irish consumer, the place of supply (and of taxation) is the State. An information leaflet on the special VAT treatment of these services is available on Revenue website at: www.revenue.ie/doc/e-Info_3.doc

Property

18. Services supplied related to property are not regarded as Fourth Schedule services.

19. Property includes buildings, walls, fences, or other structures fixed permanently to the land. Machinery installed in buildings other than as a fixture is normally not regarded as land but as goods.

20. Examples of land related services:
— Services supplied in the course of construction, alteration, demolition, repair or maintenance of any building.
— Services of estate agents, auctioneers, architects, surveyors, engineers and similar professional people relating to land and buildings. This includes the management, conveyancing, survey or valuation of property by a solicitor, surveyor or loss adjuster.

21. Examples of services, which are not land related.
— Repair and maintenance of machinery, which is not installed as a fixture. This is work on goods.
— Advice or information relating to land prices or the property market in general which is not referring to a specific site or property.
— Feasibility studies assessing the potential of a business in a geographic area.

Natural Gas and Electricity

22. From 1 January 2005, the provision of access to and transportation of natural gas and electricity through distribution systems and other directly linked services will become Fourth Schedule services. This treatment also applies to charges for other directly linked services such as grid management, monitoring etc.

Financial Fund Management

23. From 1 July 2004, Financial fund management functions, which are part of the service of the management of an undertaking, are regarded for taxation purposes as Fourth Schedule services. These management services will be taxable or exempt depending on whether or not the fund in question qualifies under paragraph (i) (g) of the First Schedule to the VAT Act 1972 as amended.

24. When management services are provided to a fund in Ireland, the place of supply of the service for VAT purposes is here. Conversely, when management services are provided to a fund outside Ireland, the place of supply of the service for VAT purposes is outside Ireland.

25. Financial fund management functions are any of the three functions listed in Annexe II to Directive 2001/107/EC of the European Parliament and Council.

Enquiries

26. For further information on any VAT matter, whether a general enquiry or an enquiry relating to a specific transaction, you should contact your local Revenue district. Contact details for all Revenue districts are provided in appendix IV.

Issued by:

Indirect Taxes Division
Revenue Legislation Services
Dublin Castle
Dublin 2

APPENDIX I
Fourth Schedule to the VAT Act, 1972 (as amended).

Services that, where taxable, are taxed where received
- (i) Transfers and assignments of copyright, patents, licences, trade marks and similar rights;
- (i*a*) hiring out of movable goods other than means of transport
- (ii) advertising services;
- (iii) services of consultants, engineers, consultancy bureau, lawyers, accountants and other similar services, data processing and provision of information (but excluding services connected with immovable goods);
- (iii*a*) telecommunications services;
- (iii*b*) radio and television broadcasting services;
- (iii*c*) electronically supplied services;
- (iii*d*) the provision of access to, and of transport or transmission through, natural gas and electricity distribution systems and the provision of other directly linked services; *
- (iv) acceptance of any obligation to refrain from pursuing or exercising in whole or in part, any business activity or any such rights as are referred to in paragraph (i);
- (v) banking, financial and insurance services (including re-insurance **[and financial fund management functions]**, but not including the provision of safe deposit facilities);
- (vi) the provision of staff;
- (vii) the services of agents who act in the name and for the account of a principal when procuring for him any services specified in paragraphs (i) to (vi).
- *(iii*d*) effective from 1 January 2005

APPENDIX II

The following publications are available on the revenue website at www.revenue.ie.

Paper copies of these publications may be obtained from Revenue's forms and leaflets Services by phoning our Lo-Call number: 1890 30 67 06 (This service is available on a 24 hour basis, 7 days a week. All calls are charged at the local rates).

Advertising services
http://www.revenue.ie/pdf/vat04.92doc

VAT treatment of Auctioneers and Auction and Agency sales
http://www.revenue.ie/pdf/info5.pdf

VAT on telecommunications
http://www.revenue.ie/pdf/inforno.7.pdf

VAT treatment of Building and associated services
http://www.revenue.ie/pdf/infor299.pdf

Intra-Community Acquisitions and postponed Accounting
http://www.revenue.ie/pdf/info7_01.pdf

Research services carried out by third level Educational Bodies
http://www.revenue.ie/pdf/research.pdf
http://www.revenue.ie/pdf/research .doc

VAT and Solicitors
http://www.revenue.ie/pdf/informlea15.pdf
http://www.revenue.ie/pdf/informlea15.doc

Agricultural Services
http://www.revenue.ie/pdf/info23_01.pdf

(No. 02/03) E-Commerce:
www.revenue.ie/doc/e-Info_3.doc

Guide to Apportionment:
www.revenue.ie/doc/guideapp.doc

APPENDIX III
European Member States

AT — Austria

BE — Belgium

CY — Cyprus

Cz — Czech Republic

DE — Germany

DK — Denmark

EE — Estonia

EL — Greece

ES — Spain

FI — Finland

FR — France

GB — United Kingdom

HU — Hungary

IE — Ireland

IT — Italy

LT — Lithuania

LU — Luxembourg

LV — Latvia

MT — Malta

NL — Netherlands

PL — Poland

PT — Portugal

SE — Sweden

SL — Slovenia

SK — Slovakia

Contact addresses can be found in Revenue Addresses at start of book.

VAT TREATMENT OF INVOICING

1 Introduction

This information leaflet sets out the current rules relating to the issue of invoices, credit notes and other documents for VAT purposes, and outlines the importance of these documents in the operation of the VAT system.

2 Importance of Invoices and Credit Notes

2.1 The information given on invoices and credit notes normally establishes the VAT liability of the supplier of goods or services and the entitlement of the customer to a deduction, where applicable, for the VAT charged. It is vital, therefore, that these documents are properly drawn up and carefully retained. The checking of these documents forms a most important part of the periodic examination, which Revenue officers may make of a trader's VAT position.

2.2 VAT law contains specific requirements for the issue and retention of invoices, credit notes and related documents. Failure to comply with these requirements leaves a trader liable to penalties. Traders who issue invoices and credit notes, and persons to whom these documents are issued, should ensure that the documents accurately represent the transactions to which they refer.

3 Who must issue a VAT Invoice?

3.1 A taxable person (that is, a person registered for VAT) who supplies goods or services is obliged to issue a VAT invoice where the supply is made to any of the following:

- another taxable person,
- a Government Department,
- a local authority,
- a body established by statute,
- a person who caries on an activity which is exempt from VAT,
- a person, who is not an individual, in another EU Member State,
- a person in another EU Member State where a reverse charge applies, that is, where the VAT is not accountable for by the supplier in Ireland but is accountable for by the customer in the other EU Member State, and
- a person in another EU Member State under the distance selling rules. Distance selling occurs when a supplier in one EU Member State sells goods to a person in another EU Member State who is not registered for VAT and the supplier is responsible for the delivery of the goods. It includes mail order sales and phone or tele-sales but does not include sales of new means of transport or excisable goods. (An Information Leaflet relating to the treatment of distance sales is available on the Revenue website by clicking here.)

3.2 It should be noted that a taxable person is required, if requested in writing, to issue a VAT invoice in respect of a transaction with an unregistered person in the State who is entitled to a repayment of the VAT. A taxable person is not required to issue a VAT invoice to an unregistered person otherwise, but may do so if he or she so wishes.

4 Information required on VAT Invoice

4.1 The VAT invoice issued must show:

- the date of issue of the invoice,

- a sequential number, based on one or more series, which uniquely identifies the invoice,

- the full name, address and VAT registration number of the person who supplied the goods or services to which the invoice relates,

- the full name and address of the person to whom the goods or services were supplied,

- in the case of a reverse charge supply, the VAT identification number of the person to whom the supply was made and an indication that a reverse charge applies,

- in the case of the supply of goods, other than a reverse charge supply, to a person registered for VAT in another EU Member State, the person's VAT identification number in that Member State and an indication that the invoice relates to an intra-Community supply of goods,

- the quantity and nature of the goods supplied or the extent and nature of the services supplied,

- the date on which the goods or services were supplied or, where payment in full, or by instalments, for goods or services is made before the completion of the supply, the date on which the payment on account was made in so far as that date differs from the date of issue of the invoice.

- the unit price, exclusive of tax, of the goods or services supplied, any discounts or price reductions not included in the unit price, and the consideration for the supply exclusive of VAT,

- except where a reverse charge applies, the amount of the consideration exclusive of VAT taxable at each rate (including zero rate) of VAT and the rate of tax chargeable,

- the VAT payable in respect of the supply, except where a reverse charge applies or where the Margin Scheme, Special Scheme for Auctioneers or Special Scheme for second-hand Motor Vehicles applies (see paragraph 16), and

- in the case where a tax representative is liable to pay VAT in another EU Member Sate, the full name and address and value-added tax identification number of the representative.

4.2 As indicated in paragraph 4.1, the unit price has to be shown on an invoice. This applies to countable goods and services. For services this could be, for example, an hourly rate or a price for standard services. If the supply of a particular service cannot readily be broken down into countable elements, then, the total tax-exclusive price for the specific service will be accepted as the unit price.

4.3 An invoice issued by a taxable person relating to an Intra-Community supply of a new means of transport must include details necessary to identify the goods as a new means of transport. In the case of motor vehicles, "new" means that the vehicle has been supplied 6 months or less after the date of first entry into service or that it has travelled 6,000 kilometres or less.

4.4 Where a person is engaged in EU triangular transactions, the person must also include an explicit reference to the EU simplified triangulation arrangements on the invoice. Triangulation involves two supplies of goods between three VAT-registered traders in three different EU Member States, e.g. where a trader in one Member State orders goods from a trader in a second Member State, to be delivered to a trader in a third Member State.

5 Increase in Invoiced Amounts – Supplementary Invoices

5.1 Because the amount of VAT shown on an invoice affects the VAT liability of both the VAT-registered supplier and the VAT-registered customer, any change in the amount of VAT payable or deductible on an invoice must be properly vouched.

5.2 If, subsequent to the issue of an invoice, the amount charged is increased, the supplier must issue a supplementary invoice on which the increase in the charge and the appropriate VAT rate is shown.

6 Decrease in Invoiced Amounts – Credit Notes

6.1 Where, because of an allowance or discount or similar adjustment, the amount of VAT payable as shown on an invoice is subsequently reduced, the person who issued the invoice should issue a credit note (but see paragraph 7.1). This note should state the amount of the reduction in the price and the appropriate VAT. The supplier may then reduce, by the amount credited, his or her liability for the accounting period in which the credit note is issued, and the recipient must increase his or her liability by the same amount. All credit notes must contain a reference to the corresponding invoices.

6.2 Where the supplier is accounting for VAT on the moneys received basis, a credit note showing VAT must always be issued. No reduction in the supplier's VAT liability may be made on this account. The VAT deduction or credit available to the customer on the basis of the original invoice is reduced as a result of the issue of the credit note.

7 Where a Credit Note is not required

7.1 A VAT-registered supplier on the invoiced sales basis and a VAT-registered customer may agree in respect of a transaction not to make any change in the VAT shown on the original invoice. In such circumstances, even if the price charged is reduced subsequently, there is no obligation to issue a credit note in respect of the VAT and the amount of VAT originally invoiced is allowed to stand.

7.2 The arrangements mentioned in paragraph 7.1 above apply in the circumstances where the discount or other reduction is taken on the goods only. If the customer takes the discount or other reduction on the VAT as well as on the price, the supplier must always issue a credit note. If the supplier is accounting for VAT on the invoiced sales basis, the supplier must then adjust his or her VAT liability downwards and the customer must adjust his or her VAT liability upwards. Moreover, a VAT-registered supplier who is on the moneys received basis of accounting must always issue a credit note.

8 Incorrect Rate of VAT charged – Credit Note and Revised Invoice required

8.1 Where a person issues a VAT invoice that shows a rate of VAT, which is subsequently found to be higher than the rate correctly applicable, the person must issue a credit note cancelling the invoice and must then issue a revised invoice. This may arise, for example, in relation to an intra-Community supply where the supplier charges VAT initially (e.g. because of being unsure that the goods will leave the State) and subsequently is satisfied that the goods should have been zero-rated. However, the rule is not confined to intra-Community supplies; it is equally applicable in the case of internal supplies where tax is charged at the standard rate when a reduced rate is in fact applicable.

9 Information required on Credit Notes

The credit note must show:

- the date of issue of the note,

- a number, which uniquely identifies the note,

- the full name, address and VAT registration number of the person issuing the note,

- the full name, address and VAT registration number of the person to whom the note is being issued,

- in the case of a supply to a person who is registered for value-added tax in another EU Member State, the person's VAT identification number in that Member State,

- the reason why the note is being issued and a cross-reference to the invoice which was issued for the supply in respect of which the consideration was reduced,

- the amount of the consideration, exclusive of tax, in respect of which the note is being issued, and

- the rate or rates of tax in force when the related invoice was issued and the amount of tax at each rate as appropriate to the consideration shown on the note.

10 Settlement Vouchers and Debit Notes

Settlement vouchers and debit notes are often used in commercial transactions instead of invoices and credit notes. Settlement vouchers and debit notes must contain the VAT registration number of the person issuing them and the VAT registration number of the supplier, in addition to all the other details required to be shown by a taxable person on invoices and credit notes. It is also a condition that the supplier of goods or services is prepared to accept such documents. If accepted, the supplier is subject to the same obligations as if he or she had issued an invoice or credit note.

11 Self-billing and outsourcing arrangements

11.1 Where a person supplies goods or services to a customer who is registered for VAT, the customer may issue the required invoice provided –

- there is prior agreement between the supplier and the customer that the customer may draw up and issue the invoice,

- all conditions relating to the content or issue of the invoice are met by the customer, and

- agreed procedures are in place for the acceptance by the supplier of the validity of the invoice.

An invoice issued under these arrangements is regarded as having been issued when the supplier accepts it in accordance the agreed procedures referred to above.

11.2 A supplier may outsource the issuing of invoices. When an invoice is issued under outsourcing arrangements it is regarded as having been issued by the supplier if –

- the invoice is issued by a person who acts in the name and on behalf of the supplier, and

- all conditions relating to the content or issue of the invoice are met.

11.3 Self-billing and outsourcing can also apply to credit notes and debit notes.

12 Invoices, etc. issued in Foreign Currency

12.1 Invoices issued for VAT purposes in amounts expressed in foreign (non-Euro denominated) currency should contain the corresponding figures in Euro and must contain the actual VAT amount in euro. The copy of the invoice that has to be retained must show the same figures. This rule also applies to credit notes, debit notes and settlement vouchers.

12.2 The latest selling rate recorded by the Central Bank at the time the VAT becomes due should be used when converting foreign currency invoices. The Central Bank rates for most major currencies appear on a daily basis in the newspapers. It is possible, by agreement with Revenue, to use an alternative method of determining the exchange rate, for example, the rate determined on a calendar month basis under the monthly rate of exchange system for customs valuation purposes. Such agreements are subject to the condition that the agreed method must be used in respect of all the trader's foreign currency transactions. Traders who wish to avail of this facility should write to their local Revenue District indicating the exchange rate method they propose to use and obtain appropriate agreement.

13 Time limit for issuing VAT Invoices and Credit Notes

13.1 In general, where a VAT invoice has to be issued, it must be issued within 15 days of the end of the month in which the goods or services are supplied. In the case of a supplementary invoice, the invoice must be issued within 15 days following either the day on which the increased in consideration is paid or the day on which the increase in consideration is agreed between the parties concerned, whichever is the earlier.

13.2 Situations may arise where payment in full, or by instalments, for goods or services supplied to a VAT-registered person is made before the completion of the supply. In such cases the person receiving payment must issue an invoice within 15 days following the end of the month following that during which each payment was received. This rule does not apply in the case of intra-Community supplies of goods.

13.3 In the case of credit notes, where a decrease is due to a discount, the note must be issued within 15 days following the date of receipt of the money to which the discount relates. In any other case, the credit note must be issued within 15 days on which the decrease in consideration is agreed between the parties concerned.

13.4 Failure to issue an invoice or credit note in time leaves the person concerned liable to penalties.

14 Incorrect Amounts on VAT Invoices and Credit Notes

A VAT-registered trader who issues an invoice showing a greater amount of VAT than is correct for the transaction is nonetheless liable for the whole amount of VAT shown on the invoice. If a trader issues a credit note showing a lesser amount of VAT than is proper, the trader is liable for the deficiency. In either case the trader may also be liable to penalties.

15 Invoices issued by Unregistered Persons

Where a trader not registered for VAT issues an invoice showing an amount of VAT, that trader is liable for the VAT shown on the invoice. Such a person also leaves himself liable to penalties. This rule does not apply to an unregistered farmer who issues an invoice under the special arrangements for flat-rate farmers (see paragraph 18).

16 Margin Scheme goods / Special Scheme for Auctioneers / Special Scheme for second-hand Motor Vehicles

16.1 In so far the amount on which VAT is chargeable is concerned, special schemes operate in relation to sales by dealers and auctioneers of second-hand movable goods, works of art, collectors items and antiques. The principal feature of the schemes is that dealers and auctioneers effectively pay VAT only on their margin in certain circumstances. Where a supply of goods is made under either of these schemes, the invoice must indicate that the appropriate scheme applies.

16.2 A special scheme also operates in relation to the VAT treatment of second-hand motor vehicles. It provides for the right to deduct residual VAT in respect of the purchase of a qualifying second-hand vehicle, including by way of trade-in. A separate VAT Information Leaflet on the VAT treatment of second-hand vehicles is available.

17 Hire Purchase Transactions

17.1 In the case of goods supplied subject to a hire-purchase type arrangement, the supplier must issue the invoice to the financial institution concerned instead of to the customer. The invoice must give the name and address of the financial institution, as well as all the other details normally required on a VAT invoice.

17.2 The financial institution involved in a hire-purchase type arrangement must issue a document to the customer, which acts as a VAT invoice in the hands of the customer, for the purposes of enabling the customer to claim VAT deductibility. The document must include the name, address and VAT registration number of the supplier, the name and address of both the financial institution and the customer, and must show separately the amount of tax that appeared on the corresponding invoice received by the financial institution. The document must be issued within 22 days following the month of supply of the goods.

17.3 Where a financial institution receives a VAT credit note in a hire-purchase arrangement, after goods have been supplied and invoiced to a customer, the institution must then issue to the customer a document corresponding to that credit note. The document must contain the details required on a normal VAT credit note, and the amount shown on the document in respect of tax is the amount by which the customer's entitlement to a VAT deduction is to be reduced.

17.4 The financial institution is responsible for any excess VAT amount it inserts on the document that serves as a VAT invoice. If the amount allowed as a credit to the customer is in excess of the amount shown on the supplier's invoice, the institution is liable for the excess. The institution may also be liable to penalties.

18 Flat-rate Farmers

18.1 Flat-rate farmers supplying agricultural produce or services, or supplying agricultural machinery to a taxable dealer, are required to issue an invoice (flat-rate invoice) for these supplies in accordance with sections 12A and 12C, respectively, of the Value-Added Tax Act 1972 if:

- the issue of the invoice is requested by the purchaser,
- the purchaser provides the form for the invoice and enters the appropriate particulars on it, and
- the purchaser gives the flat-rate farmer a copy of the invoice.

A flat-rate farmer may nevertheless choose to issue the invoice even if any of these conditions are not fulfilled.

18.2 Where after the issue of a flat-rate invoice the consideration is increased or reduced, then -

- if the consideration is increased, a further invoice for the additional amount must be issued, subject to the same conditions as regards the preparation of the invoice by the purchaser, etc., and
- if the consideration is reduced, the farmer must issue a farmer credit note if the customer is a taxable person and the taxable person must make a corresponding adjustment in the amount of flat-rate credit claimed as a deduction.

18.3 If a person, other than a flat-rate farmer, issues a flat rate invoice, that person is liable for the amount of the flat-rate addition and, for the purposes of payment of the amount, is treated as a taxable person.

18.4 If a flat-rate farmer issues an invoice for a fictitious transaction or for an inflated amount for a genuine transaction, he or she is liable for the amount of the flat-rate addition or the excess amount, as appropriate. For the purposes of payment of the amount in question, the flat-rate farmer will be treated as taxable person.

18.5 If a flat-rate farmer is obliged to issue a farmer credit note but fails to do so within the relevant time limit, he or she is liable for the amount of the flat-rate addition that should have been stated on the note. If he or she issues a farmer credit stating a lesser sum of flat-rate addition than is appropriate to the reduction in consideration or discount, he or she is liable for the amount of the deficiency of the flat-rate addition. In either of these cases the flat-rate farmer is treated as a taxable person for the purposes of payment of the amount due. He or she is also liable to penalties.

19 Simplified Invoicing

19.1 Simplified arrangements for issuing invoices, credit notes, settlement vouchers or debit notes may be allowed -

- when commercial, technical or administrative practices in a particular business sector make it difficult to comply with general invoicing requirements, or

- if the amount of the invoice is minor.

19.2 Under a simplified arrangement the relevant documents must include the following details:

- the date of issue,

- the identification of the supplier, including the supplier's VAT number,

- the identification of the types of goods or services supplied, and

- the tax due or the information needed to calculate the tax due.

19.3 Revenue has agreed simplified invoicing arrangements in the Corporate Purchasing Card sector and may negotiate similar agreements in other sectors. In the case of the Corporate Purchasing Card sector, it has been agreed that:

- the Evidence for VAT Deduction Report is recognised as a VAT Invoice and contains the information necessary to form a valid invoice.

- such reports can be used as the basis for claiming input credit.

- input credit can be claimed by reference to the transaction date rather than the date of issue of the report.

- commodity codes as agreed with Revenue can be used to describe goods and services.

- such reports can be either in paper or electronic format.

19.4 Credit Card companies, which have Corporate Purchasing Card schemes, must satisfy their customers that the simplified VAT invoicing procedure in operation by the company has been approved by the Revenue Commissioners.

19.5 Applications for approval of simplified invoicing arrangements should be made to VAT Interpretation Branch, Indirect Taxes Division, Revenue Commissioners, Dublin Castle, Dublin 2 via the applicant's local Revenue District.

20 Electronic Invoicing

20.1 It is open to traders to operate an electronic invoicing system provided the particulars to be contained in such invoices or other documents are recorded, retained and transmitted electronically by a system that ensures the integrity of those particulars and the authenticity of their origin.

20.2 Invoices, etc maybe transmitted between trading partners using either an electronic data interchange (EDI) system, or an advanced electronic signature (AES) and associated system, which satisfy the requirements set out below. A taxable person may also use a different electronic system to the EDI or AES systems, provided the requirements in question are met and the person notifies the Revenue Commissioners accordingly. Until 31 December 2005, such a notification must be made prior to the commencement of the transmission of electronic invoices, etc.

20.3 The electronic system in use must be capable of –

- producing, retaining and storing, and making available to a Revenue officer on request, electronic records and messages in such form and containing such particulars as are required for VAT purposes,

- reproducing paper copies of such records or messages,

- allocating a unique identification number for each message transmitted, and

- maintaining the electronic records in such manner as allows their retrieval by reference to a trading partner or the unique identification number of the message.

20.4 The system in use must also –

- preclude the repeated transmission of a message and the omission of a message from the electronic record,

- verify the origin or receipt of a message from a trading partner, and

- guarantee the integrity of the contents of a message or an electronic record related to that message during transmission and during the period for the retention of records for VAT purposes.

21 Retention of, and Inspection of, Records

21.1 Every taxable person must retain all books, records and documents relevant to the business, including invoices, credit notes, settlement vouchers and debit notes (and copies of any such documents issued to another person). These business records must be preserved in their original form* for 6 years from the date of the latest transaction to which they refer, unless the written permission of the local Revenue District has been obtained for their retention for a shorter period. This rule applies equally to electronic records and messages. In addition, a taxable person keeping electronic records must retain and store particulars such as details of the form of encryption, electronic signature, etc used and the format in which they are stored and how they can be accessed.

*Invoices that have been issued in paper form must be retained in paper form. Electronic retention of invoices is only acceptable where they were originally issued electronically.

21.2 Authorised Revenue officers have extensive powers in regard to the inspection of records, and failure by traders or their employees or associates to co-operate with the officers is an offence. These officers will have proof of their identity. They will check the trader's VAT returns against the trader's records and will crosscheck invoices, etc, against the suppliers' and customers' records. Returns of VAT will also be checked against the trading accounts for Income Tax and Corporation Tax purposes.

22 Enquiries

Any enquiries regarding any issue contained in this Information Leaflet should be addressed to your local Revenue District. Details for all Revenue Districts can be found by clicking here.

VAT Interpretation Branch,
Indirect Taxes Division,
Dublin Castle.

LIVE THEATRICAL AND MUSICAL EVENTS

1 Definitions

In this Information Leaflet, certain terms have specific meanings assigned to them, as follows:

"Admission": The allowing of an audience into an event. Admission includes the selling of tickets and the taking of money at the entrance, so that the person who sells a ticket for an event is deemed to be providing admission, and is treated for VAT accordingly.

"Food and drink": This includes all types of food, hot or cold, and all drinks, including water, and soft drinks. By concession, Revenue is prepared to extend the exemption from VAT to include events where certain types of food and drink are available (see Appendix 1).

"Live theatrical or musical event (event)": A play, musical, concert, recital, dramatic presentation, dance presentation, cabaret, comedy act or similar event performed before a live audience.

"Performance": The time when the performers are actually on stage or otherwise providing the entertainment for the audience.

"Performer(s)": The actors, musicians, dancers and comedians etc. who entertain the audience. Also includes a group, such as a theatre company, which has the actual performers as employees.

"Premises-provider": A person who owns, occupies or controls the venue (including land in the case of an open-air outdoor event) in which an event is to take place.

"Promotion": The financing or organizing of an event, including publicizing and other ventures to increase sales or public awareness.

"Self-promoting performer": A performer who finances, organizes and publicizes the performance and/or event.

"Ticket agent/ticket seller": A person engaged by the promoter to distribute and sell tickets for an event, normally reimbursed by way of a charge to the customer included in the ticket price and/or by commission charged to the promoter.

2 Legislation - relevant sections of the VAT Act

The law provides for an exemption from VAT for the following:

"promotion of and admissions to live theatrical or musical performances, including circuses, but not including

(a) dances, or

(b) performances in conjunction with which facilities are available for the consumption of food or drink during all or part of the performance by persons attending the performance".

[Paragraph (viii) of the First Schedule to the VAT Act 1972 (as amended)]

The law further provides that the following are liable to VAT at 13.5 per cent:

" promotion of and admissions to live theatrical or musical performances, excluding

(*a*)   dances, and

(*b*)   performances specified in paragraph (viii) of the First Schedule;"

[Paragraph (vi) of the Sixth Schedule to the VAT Act 1972 (as amended)].

The promotion of and admissions to dances are liable at the standard rate of 21 per cent. Where a dance is held on licensed premises, the law also specifies who is responsible for accounting for VAT:

"The licensee of any premises (being premises in respect of which a licence for the sale of intoxicating liquor either on or off those premises was granted) shall be deemed to be the promoter of any dance held, during the subsistence of that licence, on those premises and shall be deemed to have received the total money, excluding tax, paid by those admitted to the dance together with any other consideration received or receivable in connection with the dance"

[Section 8(3C)(*a*) of the VAT Act 1972 (as amended)]

3 Summary

3.1 Background

The exemption from VAT for live theatrical and musical events was introduced in 1985. In the intervening two decades a certain amount of confusion has arisen concerning the type of events to which it applies. Following a number of requests for clarification it was decided to issue this leaflet to restate the law and provide guidance regarding its application.

This Information Leaflet sets out the VAT treatment of the different services involved in the staging of live theatrical and musical events. These services include promoting the event, distributing and selling tickets, providing security and catering, the sale of concessions within the venue, the sale of goods within the venue, the performing of the artists, and the granting of admission. Each of these subjects is dealt with in detail in the main body of the leaflet and a brief synopsis of their treatment for VAT is set out below.

3.2 Ticket prices, promoter's fees and ticket agent's commission

The law provides that promoter's fees and admission charges for a live event are liable to 13.5 per cent VAT if food or drink is available at the event (See Paragraph 5). If no food or drink is available, then promoter's fees and admission charges are exempt from VAT (See Paragraph 4). Non-resident promoters are obliged to register for and charge VAT in Ireland (See Paragraph 9). Commission fees, credit card handling charges and any other charges made by ticket selling agents form part of the price of the ticket, and are liable to VAT at the same rate (See Paragraph 11).

In conjunction with the law, a concession currently operates (See Appendix II – The Theatres' Concession) in respect of venues where food or drink is provided, and must be consumed, in a part of the venue completely separate from the performance. In addition, as a result of the consultation process undertaken for this leaflet, a new concessionary treatment is being offered by Revenue in respect of the supply of certain types of food and drink at events (See Appendix I for full details). In effect, the supply of crisps, sweets, soft drinks and water will not make an otherwise exempt event liable to VAT. Only the supply of substantial snacks, hot food or alcoholic drink will be considered when deciding if an event is exempt or liable to VAT.

3.3 Performer's fees

Any fee charged by a performer is liable to VAT at 21 per cent. A performer who is registered for VAT will issue a VAT invoice for the amount of his/her fee and charge VAT at 21 per cent on the full amount of that fee. A non-resident performer will normally not be required to register for VAT in Ireland. In the case of performances by non-resident performers, the person who hired the performer, normally the promoter, will account for the VAT (See Paragraph 9). If the actual performers are employees of a production company, then the amount received by that company is regarded as the performance fee, rather than the salary paid to the performers. Where a performer promotes his/her own performance, then the fee paid may be split as between the promotion activities and the performance (See Paragraph 10).

3.4 Security, catering and similar services

These services are all liable to VAT at the appropriate rates (See Paragraph 7). If a company supplying these services is not established in Ireland it must register and account for VAT.

3.5 Traders selling goods or services within a venue

Goods and services sold in the course of an event are liable to VAT in the usual way. Non-resident traders are obliged to register for VAT prior to trading. Concessions that permit traders to sell goods or services within a venue are liable to VAT at 21 per cent on the full amount received in respect of the granting of the concession (See Paragraph 8).

4 Events which come within the scope of the exemption from VAT

The exemption from VAT covers promotion charges and admission fees for all live events in venues where there are no facilities available for consumption of substantial snacks, hot food or alcoholic drink (see Appendix 1) during all or part of the performance by persons attending. Promotion of and admission to any indoor live theatrical or musical event will be exempt where:

- No substantial snacks, hot food or alcoholic drink are supplied to persons attending the event during any part of the performance.

- No substantial snacks, hot food or alcoholic drink are available for purchase during any part of the event in the room in which the performance is taking place.

- No substantial snacks, hot food or alcoholic drink are available for purchase at any part of the venue which can subsequently be taken by persons attending the event or on their behalf into the room in which the performance is taking place.

Indoor events to which the exemption applies generally include plays, concerts and similar events in theatres and concert halls, and any other halls or similar establishments where substantial snacks, hot food or alcoholic drink are not permitted to be consumed during all or part of the performance.

This diagram shows the VAT treatment of the supplies that go to make up an exempt event.

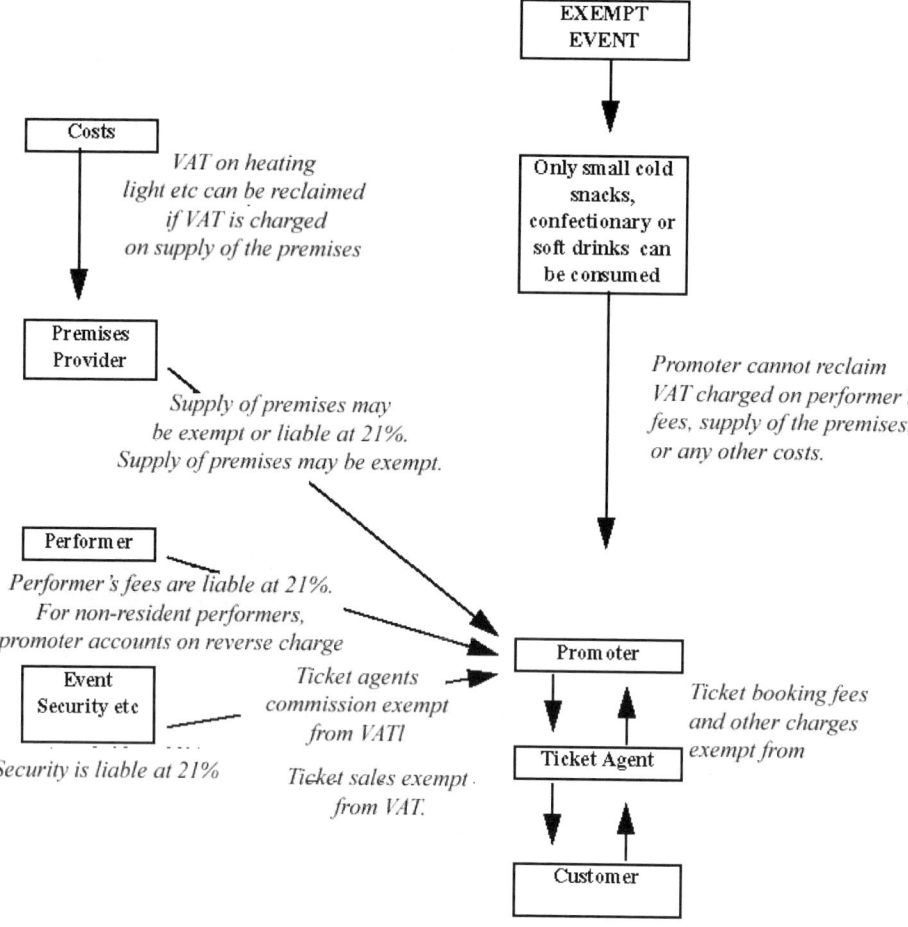

If no substantial snacks, hot food or alcoholic drink are available at the event, then the ticket sales are exempt from VAT. This means that the promoter is not able to recover VAT charged by performers, security etc. in connection with the event.

5 Events which are liable to VAT at 13.5%?

The exemption does not cover promotion of or admission to events where facilities are available for the consumption of substantial snacks, hot food or alcoholic drink during all or part of the performance by persons attending the performance. This exclusion from exemption also applies where a separate charge is made for the food and drink.

The **13.5% rate of VAT** applies to events where there are <u>facilities for the consumption</u> * of substantial snacks, hot food or alcoholic drink during the performance by persons attending the performance. VAT at this rate must be accounted for on money received for tickets, and any fee charged by the promoter in relation to these events. However, this VAT may be offset by the right of the promoter and the ticket agent to recover any VAT charged to them in connection with the staging of the event, such as VAT on the performer's fee, security, hire of equipment etc.

* The expression 'facilities for the consumption of food or drink' does not imply a formal sit-down venue. If people attending an event can obtain food or drink and consume it, then it must be accepted that facilities are available to do so.

Accordingly, VAT is chargeable at 13.5% on promotion and admission charges in respect of any live theatrical or musical event under Paragraph (vi) of the Sixth Schedule to the VAT Act 1972 (as amended) where:

- Substantial snacks, hot food or alcoholic drink are provided to persons attending the event in the room/venue in which the performance takes place as part of the admission fee.

- Substantial snacks, hot food or alcoholic drink are available for purchase by persons attending the event in the room/venue in which the performance is taking place.

- Substantial snacks, hot food or alcoholic drink are available for purchase at any part of the venue which can subsequently be taken by persons attending the event or on their behalf into the room/venue where the performance is taking place.

Events to which the reduced (13.5%) rate applies generally include:

- Cabaret and other performances where the consumption of substantial snacks, hot food or alcoholic drink are associated with the performance.

- Musical or comedy performances in theatres, public houses and other venues where substantial snacks, hot food or alcoholic drink are served during the course of the performance.

- Performances in hotels, restaurants or other establishments where substantial snacks, hot food or alcoholic drink are supplied in conjunction with the performance.

- Outdoor concerts where substantial snacks, hot food or alcoholic drink are available within the confines of the venue.

This diagram illustrates the VAT treatment of the supplies that go to make up a taxable event.

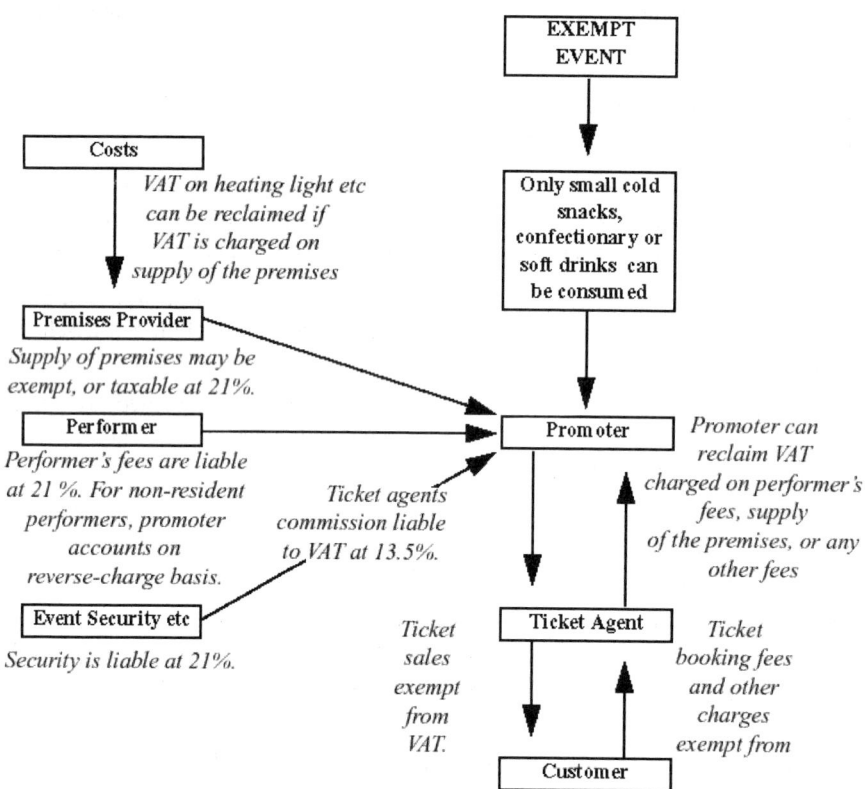

If substantial snacks, hot food or alcoholic drink are available at the event, then the ticket sales are liable to VAT at 13.5%. This allows the promoter to recover VAT charged by performers, security etc. in connection with the event. Since much of the VAT charged to the promoter is at the 21% rate, the promoter may actually be in a net VAT repayment position - ie the VAT charged to the promoter in respect of costs may exceed the VAT due on ticket sales.

6 Events which are liable to VAT at 21%?

Neither the exemption nor the reduced rate applies to the promotion of or admission to venues where the entertainment, if any, is not a live theatrical or musical performance. The standard rate of VAT applies to charges made in respect of the promotion of or admission to these venues.

Venues and events to which the standard (21%) rate applies generally include:

- Dances,
- Discotheques,

- Night-clubs and similar clubs,
- Public houses and any other such premises where there is no live musical or theatrical performance.

N.B. The 21% rate of VAT applies to dances, whether or not there is a live band. In these cases, it will be clear that people are attending the dance, rather than the performance by the band.

7 Traders operating within a venue

Where a concession, licence or right is granted to any person to sell food, drink or any merchandise, or to supply any services, in a venue, any consideration paid in respect of such a concession, licence or right is liable to VAT at the standard (21%) rate. Any traders operating such a concession, licence or right must register and account for VAT in the usual way in respect of sales made by them. However, the sale of programmes containing only details of the performance is regarded as ancillary to the performance, and liable to VAT at the same rate as the admission fee.

All traders are also responsible for ensuring that they possess all relevant permits and licences required by law or regulations. In particular, any trader selling alcoholic drinks at an event must possess a licence in his/her own name issued under the Intoxicating Liquor Licensing Acts which allows the sale of alcoholic drinks at the venue and for that event. It is illegal for a trader at an event to sell intoxicating liquor under a licence granted to any other person, including the promoter of the event.

8 VAT rates for ticket sales and other supplies associated with an event

Irish VAT law allows different rates of VAT to apply to the sale of tickets for different kinds of events. There are also different rates which apply to other services associated with events, and these rates are set out in the table below.

Examples of the services and charges associated with events	Only small cold snacks, confectionary or soft drinks can be consumed	Substantial snacks, hot food or alcoholic drink can be consumed
Ticket prices	Exempt	13.5
ticket booking fees	Exempt	13.5
ticket agent's commission	Exempt	13.5
promoter's fees	Exempt	13.5
performer's fees	21	21
security	21	21
catering	13.5	13.5
concessions *	21	21

* Where the promoter or premises-provider charges traders for the right to sell goods and services at the venue.

As can be seen, the VAT rate that applies to the admission fees for live theatrical or musical events also extends to other fees and charges connected with the issuing of tickets and promotion of the events. These include:

- The booking fees or handling fees charged for issuing a ticket;
- The commissions charged by ticket agents;
- The fees charged by promoters to performers who have hired them to organise events;
- The fees charged by promoters to venue owners for sourcing performers;

9 Treatment of non-established performers and traders

A separate information leaflet deals with the VAT treatment of cultural, artistic and entertainment services supplied by non-established persons. The provisions contained in that leaflet which refer to the supply of services by non-established performers are included below.

9.1 Relevant sections of the VAT Act

The law provides that

"where a person not established in the State supplies a cultural, artistic, entertainment or similar service in the State, then any person, other than a person acting in a private capacity, who receives that service shall

(i)   in relation to it, be a taxable person or be deemed to be a taxable person, and

(ii) be liable to pay the tax chargeable as if that taxable person had in fact supplied the service for consideration in the course or furtherance of business;

but where that service is commissioned or procured by a promoter, agent or other person not being a person acting in a private capacity, then that promoter, agent or person shall be deemed to be the person who receives the service;"

[Section 8(2)(*aa*) of the VAT Act 1972 (as amended)]

In addition Section 8(2)(d) of the VAT Act 1972 (as amended) provides that a 'premises provider' (being a person who owns, occupies or controls land) who allows non-established traders or promoters to operate on the land, has certain obligations with regard to the VAT liability of these non-established traders or promoters.

In the case of non-established traders supplying goods for a period of less than 7 consecutive days on the land, the premises provider must, not later than 14 days before the day on which the non-established trader is allowed to trade on the land, notify the local Revenue District of the name and address of the trader, the dates on which the trader intends to supply goods, and the address of the land.

In the case of non-established promoters supplying a cultural, artistic, entertainment, or similar service, the premises provider must, not later than 14 days before the day on which the service is scheduled to begin, notify the local Revenue District of the name and address of the promoter, and the dates, duration and venue of the event or performance.

Where a premises provider fails to provide true and correct information as required, then he/she may be made jointly and severally liable with the non-established trader or promoter for the VAT due in respect of the supplies made by them.

9.2 What VAT obligations have non-established traders?

Where non-established performers or any other non-established traders make sales of merchandise such as CDs, posters, t-shirts etc at a venue in the State, they are obliged to register and account for VAT on all such sales and all other supplies made by them.

9.3 Non-established traders – What liability has the provider of the premises?

Where a person who owns, occupies or controls premises (whether the owner or a third party) allows a non-established trader to supply goods for a period of less than seven consecutive days on the premises in which a performance is to be held, the provider of the premises must give the following information to Revenue:

- The name and address of the non-established trader.
- The dates on which the non-established trader intends to trade on the premises
- The address of the premises

The provider of the premises must give this information to the District Officer of the appropriate local Revenue District not later than 14 days before the performance is scheduled to begin.

Where this information is not given to Revenue as set out above, the provider of the premises may be made jointly and severally liable with the non-established trader for the VAT liability in respect of the supplies of goods in the premises concerned. In practice, this means that if the non established trader fails to register and account for any VAT due in respect of sales made in the State, the provider of the premises, whether the owner or a third party or both jointly, will become liable for the entire amount of VAT due.

9.4 Non-established performers – who accounts for VAT on performances?

A non-established performer is an individual who is not normally resident in the State or who does not have a business establishment here. It also may be a performance company which does not have a business establishment here. Section 8(2)(*aa*) of the VAT Act as set out in paragraph 9.1 above provides that a non-established performer is not obliged to register and account for VAT in respect of live theatrical or musical performances in the State. Instead, the promoter, agent or other person (including non-established promoters etc – see Paragraph 9.5) who commissions the performance or event is automatically obliged to account for the VAT due. This applies even where the turnover from the performance does not exceed registration thresholds.

9.5 What VAT obligations have non-established promoters?

Non-established promoters supplying services in Ireland must register and account for VAT on taxable supplies made by them, and also in respect of any payments made by them to non-established performers*. In practice this means that registration is required in all circumstances, except only where the non-established promoter is <u>promoting only</u> a performance by a performer registered for VAT in Ireland, and this performance features in an event which comes under the exemption from VAT. *This applies even where the payments are the subject of a separate contract covering a number of performances in different countries, or where the performer issues an invoice from an establishment outside the State in respect of the performance. If the place of supply of the performance is Ireland, then the VAT liability for payments to the performer arises in Ireland.*

9.6 Non-established promoters – what liability has the provider of premises?

Where a non-established promoter arranges for the supply of live musical or theatrical entertainment, the person who owns, occupies or controls the premises in which the performance is to take place has certain obligations to Revenue.

The provider of the premises must give the following information to Revenue:

- The name and address of the non-established promoter.

- Details such as the dates, duration and venue of the performance.

The provider of the premises must give this information to the District Officer of the appropriate local Revenue District not later than 14 days before the performance is scheduled to begin.

Where this information is not given to Revenue as set out above, the provider of the premises may be made jointly and severally liable with the non-established promoter for the VAT liability in respect of the performance. In practice, this means that if the non-established promoter fails to register and account for any VAT due, the provider of the premises, whether the owner or a third party or both jointly, will become liable for the entire amount of VAT due.

10 The withdrawal of the '50% (50/50) rule' for non-established performers

The '50% rule' was an administrative procedure whereby Revenue, on a concessional basis, allowed promoters/performers/venue owners (as appropriate) to account for VAT on performances by non-established performers as follows:

"50% of the gross income @ 21% was treated as being the amount of tax payable by the performer on his/her performance at the event. There were no input credits available against this amount. There were no further reductions available."

This was intended to simplify the application of VAT for non-established performers. However, the law was changed to remove the requirement for non-established performers to register and account for VAT, with effect from March 2002 (see Paragraph 9.4 above). This change removed the necessity for the '50% rule'. However this 'rule' continued to be applied in certain circumstances.

In order to ensure a consistent approach to the taxation of performances by non-established performers, the provisions of the legislation referred to in Paragraph 9.4 above must now apply in all circumstances. The '50% rule' therefore can no longer apply to such performances, and this concession is now withdrawn (but see Paragraph 15 for effective date).

11 Treatment of performers who promote their own performances

Where a performer promotes, either by him/herself or with others, an event in which he/she is performing, any payment received must be apportioned as between the performance and the promotion. Any such apportionment will depend on the individual circumstances, and the performer must demonstrate to the satisfaction of Revenue that the apportionment is a correct one. Where the actual performers are employees of the promoter or another company, the promoter or other company is liable for VAT on the performance.

If a performer can show evidence of real work carried out in the promotion of the event, Revenue is prepared to accept that a portion of the payment received by a self-promoting performer may be treated as being in respect of the promotion, up to a maximum of 40 per cent of the total, which is either exempt or liable to VAT according to the nature of the event. The remainder, at least 60 per cent, is treated as being in respect of the performance, and liable to VAT at the standard (21%) rate.

12 Sales of tickets by ticket agents and distributors

A promoter of an event may use a ticket agent to sell tickets for events. Promoters and ticket agents may also use a network of distributors, such as local music stores, to ensure a broad distribution of tickets. The actual sale of a ticket by a promoter, a ticket agent or distributor is the supply to the customer of the right to admission to an event.

Accordingly, for an event that does not come within the scope of the exemption, the agent or distributor who sells a ticket is liable to account for VAT on the full sale price (the face value of the ticket and all booking charges and fees whatsoever, including any commission charged to the promoter) at the rate appropriate to the event.

The agent or distributor should issue a VAT invoice for the commission on the sale. The person to whom the agent or distributor forwards the balance of the ticket price (eg another agent or the promoter) must issue a VAT invoice on receipt of the money, and account for VAT on the amount received.

The diagram below illustrates the VAT treatment of the sale of tickets for a taxable event by ticket agents and distributors.

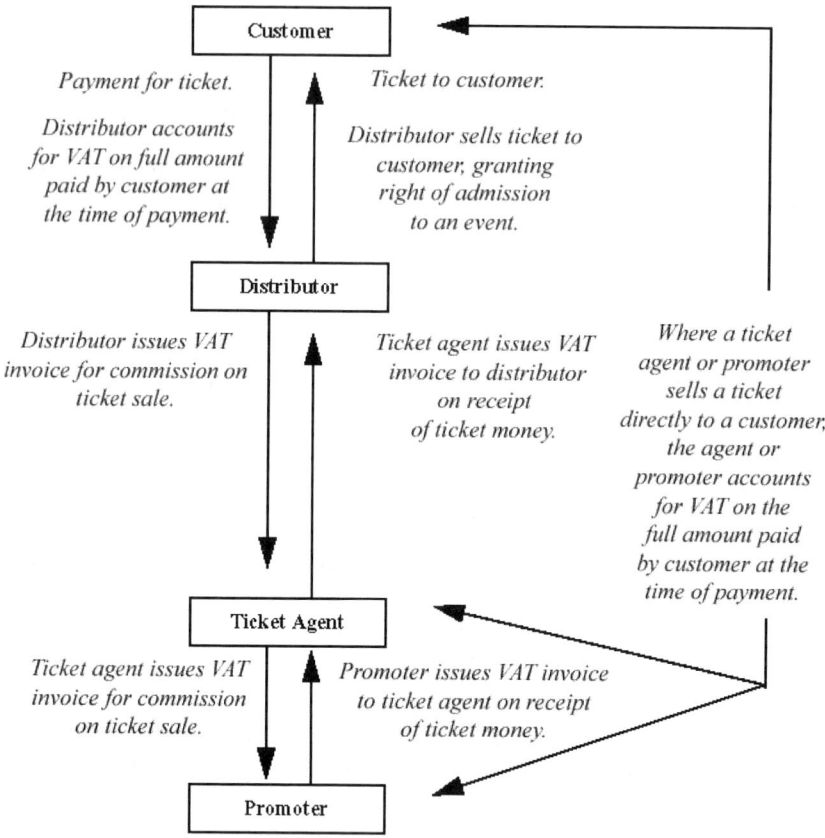

13 The treatment of advance ticket sales

Payments received in advance of the supply of goods or services are always liable to VAT at the time the payment is made. This also applies to sales of tickets for live theatrical and musical events, where these are sold prior to the date on which the event takes place (but see Paragraph 15 for effective date).

Ticket sales in advance are liable to VAT by reference to the date on which the ticket is sold and VAT must be accounted for in the taxable period in which the sale is made, and not when the event takes place. The rate of VAT that applies is always the rate current at the time of sale of the ticket.

If an event is cancelled, and the promoter, ticket-agent or distributor refunds the full amount of the ticket, including VAT, to the purchaser, a claim may be made in the next VAT return for a repayment of any VAT previously submitted.

It should be noted that advance payments by promoters to performers are also liable to VAT at the time of payment.

14 Royalties, licence fees etc. paid by promoters or performers

Certain performances consist of or contain material which is subject to copyright or similar intellectual property protection. Any fee charged by a person registered for VAT in Ireland in respect of the right to use this material is liable to VAT at 21 per cent.

Where the person who holds the copyright etc. is not established in the State, then payments made come within the scope of the Fourth Schedule to the VAT Act 1972 (as amended). This means that the promoter or performer who pays the fee must also account for the VAT on the fee as though he/she had supplied the right to use the material. If the event comes within the scope of the exemption, then this VAT may not be recovered.

15 Date from which this leaflet takes effect

This Information Leaflet is issued in order to clarify the application of VAT to live theatrical and musical events. In some cases, the treatment of certain issues as set out in the leaflet may entail changes from current practice. In recognition of difficulties that traders might encounter with a sudden implementation of these changes, Revenue is prepared to defer implementation of these to a later date.

Accordingly, the 50% or 50/50 rule (see Paragraph 10) may continue to operate until 1 January 2007. The VAT due on any events taking place on or after 1 January 2007 must be accounted for as set out in Paragraph 9 above.

Tickets sold in advance (see Paragraph 13) for events taking place before 1 January 2007 may continue to be treated in accordance with current practices. However, VAT must be accounted for on tickets sold in advance for events taking place on or after 1 January 2007 by reference to the date on which the ticket is sold.

Otherwise, the provisions contained in the leaflet should be regarded as effective from the date of the appropriate governing legislation.

16 Enquiries

For further information on any VAT matter, whether a general enquiry or an enquiry relating to a specific transaction, you should contact your local Revenue District. Details for all Revenue Districts can be found by clicking here.

VAT Interpretation Branch,
Indirect Taxes Division,
Dublin Castle.

APPENDIX I
NEW CONCESSION REGARDING THE SUPPLY OF CERTAIN KINDS OF FOOD AND DRINK

Previously, where food and/or drink were available at any event, the promotion and admission fees were in all cases liable to VAT. However, in recognition of certain practical difficulties, and to ensure consistency of treatment, Revenue is prepared to concessionally disregard the supply of certain items of food and drink when considering the VAT treatment of events.

Revenue will allow the exemption to continue to apply to events where certain cold snack foods, confectionary and soft drinks can be consumed during the performance. This means that promotion charges and the sales of tickets for these events will not now be subject to VAT, whereas previously the availability of any food and drink would have denoted a VAT liability. The items of food and drink to which this concession refers are as follows:

Food		Drink	
Confectionery:	Packets of sweets Bars (eg chocolate) Chewing gum Lollipops etc.	Soft drinks:	Carbonated (fizzy) drinks Fruit juices Milk 'Smoothies' and other milk or yoghurt based drinks 'Slushies' and similar ice drinks.
Savoury snacks:	Crisps and similar snacks Peanuts Popcorn (incl. heated)		
		Water:	Still bottled water Sparkling bottled water
Fruit			
		Hot drinks:	Tea Coffee Hot chocolate

Sales of any other kind of food and drink including sandwiches, wraps, hot snacks, meals and alcoholic drink are not included in this concession. The sale of such items would have the effect of bringing the event within the scope of VAT.

APPENDIX II
THE 'THEATRES' CONCESSION' - FOOD OR DRINK SUPPLIED IN A SEPARATE ROOM

Many theatres allow the supply of food and drink during an interval or intermission in a performance. Revenue concessionally allowed the exemption from VAT to continue to apply to these events on the following conditions:

- The food and drink was only available in a room separate from the auditorium in which the performance was taking place,

- The performance was not visible from the room where the food or drink is available,

- Patrons were not permitted to take the food or drink into the auditorium where the performance was taking place before, during or after the interval.

While this concession was originally only granted in respect of theatres, Revenue has extended it to include other types of performances in other venues. Accordingly, in the case of any event, where substantial snacks, hot food or alcoholic drink (See Appendix I above) are available to the audience at any stage during the performance, then the event remains within the exemption if it is the stated and enforced policy of the management that the following conditions are adhered to:

- Substantial snacks, hot food or alcoholic drink are only available in a separate part of the venue from that in which the performance takes place,
- The performance is not visible from the area where the substantial snacks, hot food or alcoholic drink are available,
- Patrons are not permitted to take substantial snacks, hot food or alcoholic drink into the part of the venue where the performance takes place at any time during the performance.

The availability of substantial snacks, hot food or alcoholic drink under any other circumstances would have the effect of bringing the event within the scope of VAT.

EUROPEAN UNION DIRECTIVES

The Sixth Council Directive (77/388/EEC) is the cornerstone of the harmonised system of VAT in that it introduced a common system of VAT with a uniform basis in the European Community.

It has been interpreted many times and many of these interpretations have been formulated into other Directives and Regulations (many of these are referred to in the next section of this book). It has been directly amended by the directives listed below. These amendments have been incorporated into the Sixth Directive which is reproduced in this section.

Amending Directives and Directives that are no longer valid are shown in *italic*.

FIRST COUNCIL DIRECTIVE

of 11 April 1967

67/227/EEC

on the harmonisation of legislation of Member States concerning turnover taxes
(OJ L71, 14.4.1967, p 1301)

THE COUNCIL OF THE EUROPEAN ECONOMIC COMMUNITY,

Having regard to the Treaty establishing the European Economic Community, and in particular Articles 99 and 100 thereof;

Having regard to the proposal from the Commission;

Having regard to the Opinion of the European Parliament;

Having regard to the Opinion of the Economic and Social Committee;

Whereas the main objective of the Treaty is to establish, within the framework of an economic union, a common market within which there is healthy competition and whose characteristics are similar to those of a domestic market;

Whereas the attainment of this objective presupposes the prior application in Member States of legislation concerning turnover taxes such as will not distort conditions of competition or hinder the free movement of goods and services within the common market;

Whereas the legislation at present in force does not meet these requirements; whereas it is therefore in the interest of the common market to achieve such harmonisation of legislation concerning turnover taxes as will eliminate, as far as possible, factors which may distort conditions of competition, whether at national or Community level, and make it possible subsequently to achieve the aim of abolishing the imposition of tax on importation and the remission of tax on exportation in trade between Member States;

Whereas, in the light of the studies made, it has become clear that such harmonisation must result in the abolition of cumulative multi-stage taxes and in the adoption by all Member States of a common system of value added tax;

Whereas a system of value added tax achieves the highest degree of simplicity and of neutrality when the tax is levied in as general a manner as possible and when its scope covers all stages of production and distribution and the provision of services; whereas it is therefore in the interest of the common market and of Member States to adopt a common system which shall also apply to the retail trade;

Whereas, however, the application of that tax to retail trade might in some Member States meet with practical and political difficulties; whereas, therefore, Member States should be permitted, subject to prior consultation, to apply the common system only up to and including the wholesale trade stage, and to apply, as appropriate, a separate complementary tax at the retail trade stage, or at the preceding stage;

Whereas it is necessary to proceed by stages, since the harmonisation of turnover taxes will lead in Member States to substantial alterations in tax structure and will have appreciable consequences in the budgetary, economic and social fields;

Whereas the replacement of the cumulative multi-stage tax systems in force in the majority of Member States by the common system of value added tax is bound, even if the rates and exemptions are not harmonised at the same time, to result in neutrality in competition, in that within each country similar goods bear the same tax burden, whatever the length of the production and distribution chain, and that in international trade the amount of the tax burden borne by goods is known so that an exact equalisation of that amount may be ensured; whereas, therefore, provision should be made, in the first stage, for adoption by all Member States of the common system of value added tax, without an accompanying harmonisation of rates and exemptions;

Whereas it is not possible to foresee at present how and within what period the harmonisation of turnover taxes can achieve the aim of abolishing the imposition of tax on importation and the remission of tax on exportation in trade between Member States; whereas it is therefore preferable that the second stage and the measures to be taken in respect of that stage should be determined later on the basis of proposals made by the Commission to the Council;

HAS ADOPTED THIS DIRECTIVE

Article 1

Member States shall replace their present system of turnover taxes by the common system of value added tax defined in Article 2.

In each Member State the legislation to effect this replacement shall be enacted as rapidly as possible, so that it can enter into force on a date to be fixed by the Member State in the light of the conjunctural situation; this date shall not be later than [1 January 1972][1].

From the entry into force of such legislation, the Member State shall not maintain or introduce any measure providing for flat-rate equalisation of turnover taxes on importation or exportation in trade between Member States.

Amendments

[1]   "1 January 1972" substituted for the date "1 January 1970" by Council Directive 69/463/EEC (Third Directive) Art 1; see OJ L320, 20.12.1969, p 34.

Article 2

The principle of the common system of value added tax involves the application to goods and services of a general tax on consumption exactly proportional to the price of the goods and services, whatever the number of transactions which take place in the production and distribution process before the stage at which tax is charged.

On each transaction, value added tax, calculated on the price of the goods or services at the rate applicable to such goods or services, shall be chargeable after deduction of the amount of value added tax borne directly by the various cost components.

The common system of value added tax shall be applied up to and including the retail trade stage.

...[1]

Amendments

[1] repealed by Council Directive 77/388/EEC (Sixth Directive of 17 May 1977) Art 36; see OJ L145, 13.6 1977, p 1, previously it read—

"However, until the abolition of the imposition of tax on importation and the remission of tax on exportation in trade between Member States, Member States may, subject to the consultation provided for in Article 5, apply this system only up to and including the wholesale trade stage, and may apply, as appropriate, a separate complementary tax at the retail trade stage or at the preceding stage."

Case law

Where a farmer received compensation for discontinuing milk production, there was no "consumption" within the meaning of Art 2, and therefore no supply of services: *Mohr v Finamzant Bad Segeberg*, ECJ 215/94, [1996] STC 328.

Article 3

The Council shall issue, on a proposal from the Commission, a second Directive concerning the structure of, and the procedure for applying, the common system of value added tax.

Cross references

See Council Directive 67/228/EEC (Second Directive), OJ L71, 14.4.1967, p 1303. This directive ceases to apply in member states in accordance with Art 37 of Council Directive 77/388/EEC (Sixth Directive), OJ L145, 13.6.1977, p 1.

Article 4

In order to enable the Council to discuss this, and if possible to take decisions before the end of the transitional period, the Commission shall submit to the Council, before the end of 1968, proposals as to how and within what period the harmonisation of turnover taxes can achieve the aim of abolishing the imposition of tax on importation and the remission of tax on exportation in trade between Member States, while ensuring the neutrality of those taxes as regards the origin of the goods or services.

In this connection, particular account shall be taken of the relationship between direct and indirect taxes, which differs in the various Member States; of the effects of an alteration in tax systems on the tax and budget policy of Member States; and of the influence which tax systems have on conditions of competition and on social conditions in the Community.

Article 5

Amendments

Article 5 repealed by Council Directive 77/388/EEC (Sixth Directive) Art 36; see OJ L145, 13.6.1977, p 1, previously it read—

"Article 5

Should a Member State intend to exercise the power provided for in the last paragraph of Article 2, it shall so inform the Commission in good time, having regard to Article 102 of the Treaty."

Article 6

This Directive is addressed to the Member States.

SECOND COUNCIL DIRECTIVE

of 11 April 1967

67/228/EEC

on the harmonisation of legislation of Member States concerning turnover taxes Structure and procedures for application of the common system of value added tax

THE COUNCIL OF THE EUROPEAN ECONOMIC COMMUNITY,

Having regard to the Treaty establishing the European Economic Community, and in particular Articles 99 and 100 thereof;

Having regard to the First Council Directive of 11 April 1967 (OJ No 71, 14.4.1967, p 1301) on the harmonisation of legislation of Member States concerning turnover taxes;

Having regard to the proposal from the Commission;

Having regard to the Opinion of the European Parliament;

Having regard to the Opinion of the Economic and Social Committee;

Whereas the replacement of the turnover taxes in force in Member States by a common system of value added tax is intended as a means of attaining the objectives set out in the First Directive;

Whereas, until the abolition of the imposition of tax on importation and the remission of tax on exportation, it is possible to grant Member States substantial autonomy in determining the rate or differential rates of tax;

Whereas it is also possible to accept on a transitional basis certain differences in the procedure for applying the tax in Member States; whereas it is, however, necessary to make provision for appropriate procedures to ensure neutrality in competition between Member States and to restrict progressively or to abolish the differences in question, so that national systems of value added tax may be brought into alignment, thereby preparing the way for the attainment of the objective set out in Article 4 of the First Directive;

Whereas, in order to enable the system to be applied in a simple and neutral manner, and to keep the standard rate of tax within reasonable limits, it is necessary to limit special systems and exceptional measures;

Whereas the system of value added tax makes it possible, where appropriate, for social and economic reasons, to effect reductions or increases in the tax burden on certain goods and services by means of a differentiation in the rates, but the introduction of zero rates gives rise to difficulties, so that it is highly desirable to limit strictly the number of exemptions and to make the reductions considered necessary by applying reduced rates which are high enough to permit in normal circumstances the deduction of the tax paid at the preceding stage, which moreover achieves in general the same result as that at present obtained by the application of exemptions in cumulative multi-stage systems;

Whereas it has proved possible to leave Member States themselves to make rules concerning the numerous services whose cost has no influence on the prices of goods, and the systems to be applied in the case of small undertakings, subject, as regards the latter, to prior consultation;

Whereas it has proved necessary to provide for special systems for the application of the value added tax to the agricultural sector and to request the Commission to submit to the Council, as soon as possible proposals to this effect;

Whereas it is necessary to provide for a rather large number of special provisions covering interpretation, derogations and certain detailed application procedures, and to establish a list of the services compulsorily subject to the common system; and whereas these provisions and this list should appear in the Annexes forming an integral part of this Directive;

HAS ADOPTED THIS DIRECTIVE:

Article 1

Member States shall introduce, in accordance with a common system, a tax on turnover (hereinafter called "value added tax").

The structure of, and procedures for applying this tax shall be established by Member States in accordance with the provisions of the following Articles and of Annexes A and B.

Article 2

The following shall be subject to the value added tax:

(*a*)   The supply of goods and the provision of services within the territory of the country by a taxable person against payment;

(*b*)   the importation of goods.

Article 3

"Territory of the country" means the territory in which the State concerned applies the value added tax; this territory shall, as a general rule, include the whole of, the national territory, including territorial waters.

Article 4

"Taxable person" means any person who independently and habitually engages in transactions pertaining to the activities of producers, traders or persons providing services, whether or not for gain.

Article 5

1. **"Supply of goods"** means the transfer of the right to dispose of tangible property as owner.

2. The following shall also be considered as supply within the meaning of paragraph 1:

(*a*)   the actual handing over of goods, under a contract which provides for the hiring of goods for a certain period, or the sale on deferred terms of goods, in both cases subject to a clause to the effect that ownership shall pass at the latest upon payment of the final instalment due;

(*b*) the transfer, by order of a public authority, of ownership in goods against payment of compensation;

(*c*) the transfer of goods pursuant to a contract under which commission is payable on purchase or sale;

(*d*) the delivery of moveable property produced tinder a contract for work, that is to say the handing over by a contractor to his customer of moveable property which he has made from materials and objects entrusted to him by the customer for this purpose, whether or not the contractor has provided a part of the products used;

(*e*) the delivery up of works of construction, including those in which moveable property is incorporated in immoveable property.

3. The following shall be treated as supply against payment:

(*a*) the appropriation by a taxable person, from his undertaking, of goods which he applies to his own private use or transfers free of charge;

(*b*) the use for the needs of his undertaking, by a taxable person, of goods produced or extracted by him or by another person on his behalf.

4. The place of supply shall be deemed as being:

(*a*) in cases where the goods are dispatched or transported either by the supplier or by the consignee, or by a third person: the place where the goods were at the time when the dispatch or transport to the consignee began;

(*b*) in cases where the goods are not dispatched or transported: the place where the goods were at the time of supply.

5. The chargeable event shall occur it the moment when delivery is effected. In the case, however, of supply involving payments on account before delivery, it may be provided that the chargeable event shall already have occurred at the moment of issue of the invoice or, at the latest, at the moment of receipt of the payment, in respect of the whole of the amount invoiced or received.

Article 6

1. "Provision of services" means any transaction which does not constitute a supply of goods within the meaning of Article 5.

2. The rules laid down in this Directive as regards the taxation of the provision of services shall be compulsorily applicable only to services listed in Annex B.

3. The place of the provision of service shall, is a general rule, be regarded as being the place where the services provided, the right transferred or granted, or the object hired, is used or enjoyed.

4. The chargeable event shall occur at the moment when the service is provided. In the case, however, of the provision of services of indeterminate length or exceeding a certain period or involving payments on account, it may be provided that the chargeable event shall already have occurred at the moment of issue of the invoice or, at the latest, at the moment of the receipt of the payment on account, in respect of the whole of the amount invoiced or received.

Article 7

1. "Importation of goods" means the entry of such goods into the "territory of the country" within the meaning of Article 3.

2. At importation, the chargeable event shall occur at the time of such entry. Member States may, however, link the chargeable event and the date when payment of value added tax falls due with the chargeable event and the date when payment of customs duties or other import taxes, charges and levies falls due.

The same link may be established, as regards the chargeable event and the date when payment of value added tax falls due, in respect of the supply of imported goods placed under a system of suspension of customs duties or other taxes, charges or levies.

Article 8

The basis of assessment shall be:

(*a*)   in the case of supply of goods and of the provision of services, everything which makes up the consideration for the supply of the goods or the provision of services, including all expenses and taxes except the value added tax itself;

(*b*)   in the case of the transactions referred to in Article 5(3)(*a*) and (*b*), the purchase price of the goods or of like goods or, if there is no purchase price, the cost price;

(*c*)   in the case of importation of goods, the customs value, plus all duties, taxes, charges and levies due by reason of importation, except the value added tax itself. The same basis of assessment shall apply when the goods are exempt from customs duties or are not subject to *ad valorem cus*toms duties.

In the case of importation of goods, each Member State may add to the basis of assessment the incidental expenses (picking, transport, insurance, etc.) arising up to the place of destination which have not been included in that basis.

Article 9

1. The standard rate of value added tax shall lie fixed by each Member State at a percentage of the basis of assessment which shall be the same for the supply of goods and for the provision of services.

2. In certain cases, the supply of goods and the provision of services may, however, be subject to increased rates or to reduced rates. Each reduced rate shall be determined in such a manner that the amount of value added tax resulting from the application of this rate shall normally permit the deduction of the whole of the value added tax which is deductible under Article 11.

3. The rate applicable to importation of goods shall be that which is applied in the territory of the country to the supply of like goods.

Article 10

1. The following shall be exempted from value added tax on conditions laid down by each Member State:

   (*a*)   the supply of goods consigned or transported to places outside the territory in which the State concerned applies value added tax;

   (*b*)   the provision of services relating to goods covered by (*a*) or in transit.

2. The provision of services relating to importations of goods may, subject to the consultations mentioned in Article 16, he exempted from value added tax.

3. Each Member State may, subject to the consultations mentioned in Article 16, determine the other exemptions which it considers necessary.

Article 11

1. Where goods and services are used for the purposes of his undertaking, the taxable person shall be authorised to deduct from the tax for which he is liable:

   (*a*)   the value added tax invoiced to him in respect of goods supplied to him or in respect of services rendered to him;

   (*b*)   the value added tax paid ill respect of imported goods;

   (*c*)   the value added tax which he has paid in respect of the use of goods referred to in Article 5(3)(*b*).

2. Value added tax oil goods and services used in non-taxable or exempt transactions shall not be deductible.

The taxable person shall however he authorised to make the deduction if the supply of goods or the provision of services takes place abroad or is exempt under Article 10(1) or (2).

As regards goods and services which are used both in transactions giving entitlement to deduction and in transactions which do not give entitlement to deduction, deduction shall only be allowed for that part of the value added tax which is proportional to the amount relating to the transactions giving entitlement to deduction (pro rata rule).

3. The deduction shall be made from the value added tax due for the period during which deductible tax is invoiced in the case of paragraph 1(*a*) or paid in the case of paragraph 1(*b*) and (*c*) (immediate deductions).

In the case of a partial deduction under paragraph 2 the amount of the deduction shall be provisionally determined in accordance with criteria established by each Member State and finally adjusted after the end of the year when the pro rata figure for the year of acquisition has been calculated.

As regards capital goods, the adjustment shall be effected on the basis of the variations of the pro rata figure which have occurred during a period of five years including the year during which the goods were acquired; the adjustment shall apply each year to only one-fifth of the tax borne by capital goods.

4. Certain goods and services may be excluded from the deduction system, in particular those capable of being exclusively or partially used for the private needs of the taxable person or of his staff.

Case Law

Para 4: Implication of the words "in particular" was that the power granted to Member States was a general one, not restricted to the private use items: *Royscott Leasing Ltd and Royscott Industrial Leasing Ltd, Allied Domecq, TC Harrison Group Ltd v C & E Commrs*, C305/97

Article 12

1. Every taxable person shall keep sufficiently detailed accounts to permit application of the value added tax and inspection by the tax authorities.

2. Every taxable person shall issue ail invoice ill respect of goods supplied and services provided by him to another taxable person.

3. Every taxable person shall each month lodge a declaration showing, in respect of transactions carried out during the preceding month, all the information required to calculate the tax and the deductions to be made. Every taxable person shall pay the amount of the value added tax when lodging the declaration.

Article 13

Should a Member State consider that, in exceptional cases, special measures should be adopted in order to simplify the charging procedure in respect of the tax or to prevent certain frauds, it shall so inform the Commission and the other Member States.

Should there, within one month, be objections from one or more States or from the Commission, the request for derogation shall be brought before the Council, which shall act on a proposal from the Commission within three months.

Should it appear from the conclusion of the Commission that only a simplification of the charging procedure or a measure designed to prevent fraud is involved, the Council shall act by a qualified majority on the derogation requested.

Should it appear, on the contrary, from those conclusions that the proposed measure might be prejudicial to the very principles of the system introduced by this Directive, and in particular to neutrality in competition between Member States, the Council shall act unanimously.

In either case, the Council shall act in accordance with the same procedure as regards the period of application of such measures.

The State concerned may not apply the proposed measures until the period for entering objections has expired or, where there have been objections, until after the Council's decision, if such decision is favourable.

These provisions shall cease to be applicable when the imposition of tax on importation and the remission of tax on exportation are abolished in trade between Member States.

Article 14

Each Member State may, subject to the consultation; mentioned in Article 16, apply to small undertakings whose subjection to the normal system of value added tax would meet with difficulties the special system best suited to national requirements and possibilities.

Article 15

1. The Commission shall submit to the Council, as soon as possible, proposals for Directives on common procedures for applying value added tax to transactions relating to agricultural products.

2. Until the date fixed in the Directive referred to in paragraph 1 for the application of such common procedures, each Member State may, subject to the consultations mentioned in Article 16, apply to undertakings in the agricultural sector whose subjection to the normal system of value added tax would meet with difficulties the special system best suited to national requirements and possibilities.

Article 16

Where a Member State must, in accordance with t c provisions of this Directive, enter into consultations, it shall refer the matter to the Commission in good time, having regard to the application of Article 102 of the Treaty.

Article 17

With a view to the transition from the present systems of turnover taxes to the common system of value added tax, Member Stares may:

— adopt transitional measures to levy the tax in advance;

— apply, during a certain transitional period, in respect of capital goods, the method of deduction by annual instalments (deductions *pro rata temporis);*

— exclude, in whole or in part, during a certain transitional period, capital goods from the deduction system provided for in Article 11;

and, subject to the consultations mentioned in Article 16:

— authorise (in order to grant relief, total or partial, but general in scope, from the turnover tax charged up to the time of introducing value added tax) standard deductions in respect of capital goods not yet written off and of stocks in hand at that time. Member States may, however, restrict such deductions to goods exported during a period of one year from the introduction of value added tax. in that event, such deductions shall only be allowed in respect of stocks in hand at the time referred to above and exported in an unaltered state;

— provide for reduced rates or even exemptions with refund, if appropriate, of the tax paid at the preceding stage, where the total incidence of such measures does not exceed that of the reliefs applied under the present system. Such measures may only be taken for clearly defined social reasons and for the benefit of the final consumer, and may not remain in force after the abolition of the imposition of tax on importation and the remission of tax on exportation in trade between Member States.

Article 18

The Commission shall, after consulting the Member States, submit to the Council, for the first time on 1 January 1972 and every two years thereafter, a report on the operation of the common system of value added tax in Member States.

Article 19

The Council shall, in the interest of the common market, adopt at the proper time, on a proposal from the Commission, the appropriate Directives to complete the common system of value added tax, and in particular to restrict progressively or to abolish measures adopted by Member States in derogation from this system, so that national systems of value added tax may be brought into alignment, thereby preparing the way for the attainment of the objective set out in Article 4 of the First Directive.

Article 20

The Annexes shall form an integral part of this Directive.

Article 21

This Directive is addressed to the Member States.

Done at Brussels, 11 April 1967.

For the Council

The President
R. VAN ELSLANDE

ANNEX A

1. Regarding Article 3

If a Member State intends to apply value added tax in a territory smaller than its national territory, it shall enter into the consultations mentioned in Article 16.

2. Regarding Article 4

The expression "activities of producers, traders, or persons providing services" is to be understood in a wide sense and to cover all economic activities, including, therefore, activities of the extractive industries, agriculture and the professions.

If a Member State intends not to tax certain activities, it should achieve its purpose by means of exemptions rather than by excluding from the scope of the tax persons pursuing such activities.

Member States may also consider as a "taxable person" anyone who engages occasionally in the transactions referred to in Article 4.

The expression **"independently"** is intended in particular to exclude from taxation wage-earners who are bound to their employer by a contract of service. This expression also makes it possible for each Member State not to consider as separate taxable persons, but as one single taxable person, persons who, although independent from the legal point of view, are, however, organically linked to one another by economic, financial or organisational relationships. Any Member State intending to adopt such a system shall enter into the consultations mentioned in Article 16.

States, regional and local government bodies and other public corporate bodies shall not as a general rule be considered as taxable persons in respect of activities which they pursue in their official capacity as official authorities.

If, however, they pursue activities as producers, traders, or providers of services, they may be considered as liable to tax in respect of such activities.

3. Regarding Article 5(1)

"Tangible property" means both moveable and immoveable tangible property.

The supply of electric current, gas, heat, refrigeration and the like shall be considered as supply of goods.

In case of contribution to a company of the whole or part of the contributor's assets, Member States may regard the benefiting company as the successor in title of the contributor.

4. Regarding Article 5(2)(a)

For the purposes of this Directive, the contract referred to in Article 5(2)(a) "must not be subdivided into part hire and part sale, but shall be regarded, as soon as concluded, as a contract involving a taxable supply.

5. Regarding Article 5(2)(d) and (e)

Member States which, for specifically national reasons, cannot consider the transactions referred to in Article 5(2) (*d*) and (*c*) as supply shall classify them in the category of provision of services, subjecting them to the rate which would be applicable to them if they were considered as supply.

The following, inter alia, shall be considered as "works of construction":

— the construction of buildings, bridges, roads, ports, etc., in performance of a building contract;
— earth-moving and planting of gardens;
— installation work (of central heating, for example);
— repairs to buildings, other than current maintenance.

6. Regarding Article 5(3)(a)

As regards the appropriation of goods in an unaltered state bought by a taxable person, Member States may, instead of taxing, forbid deduction or adjust it if deduction has already been effected. However, appropriation for giving gifts of small value and samples, which from the tax point of view may be classified as overhead expenses, shall not be considered as taxable supply. Moreover, the provisions of Article 11(2) shall not be applicable to such appropriations.

7. Regarding Article 5(3)(b)

This provision shall only be applied to ensure equality of taxation between, on the one hand, goods purchased and intended for the needs of the undertaking, and in respect of which there is no entitlement to immediate or complete deduction, and, on the other hand, goods produced or extracted by the taxable person or on his behalf by a third person which are also used for the same needs.

8. Regarding Article 5(5)

The "chargeable event" means the event giving rise to the tax.

9. Regarding Article 6 (1)

The definition of provision of services given in this paragraph involves classification of, inter alia, the following as provision of services:

— the assignment of intangible property;
— the carrying out of an obligation to refrain from doing something;
— the carrying out of a service rendered by order of a public authority;
— the carrying out of work on goods, if such work is not considered as supply within the meaning of Article 5(2)(*d*) and (*e*) as, for example, current maintenance work, the laundering of linen, etc.

This definition shall not prevent taxation by Member States of certain transactions engaged in by a taxable person as services "rendered to oneself" when such a measure proves necessary in order to avoid distortion of competition.

10. Regarding Article 6(2)

Member States shall refrain, is far as possible, from granting exemption from tax in respect of the provision of the services listed in Annex B.

11. Regarding Article 6(3)

The Council shall, acting unanimously on a proposal from the Commission, lay down, before 1 January 1970, special rules concerning certain services for which such rules may prove necessary, derogating where appropriate from the provisions of Article 6(3). Until those rules have been laid down, each Member State may, in order to simplify the procedure for charging the tax, derogate from the provisions of Article 6(3); it shall, however, take the necessary steps to avoid double taxation or non-taxation.

12. Regarding Article 8

Any Member State which applies value added tax only up to and including the wholesale stage may, in the case of goods sold by retail by a taxable person, reduce the basis of assessment by a certain percentage; the basis thus reduced shall not, however, be lower than the purchase or cost price plus, where appropriate, the amount of the customs duties (including levies), taxes and charges on the goods (except value added tax), even if payment thereof has been suspended.

In the case of importation of goods sold by retail, the same reduction shall be applied to the basis of assessment.

It shall be left to Member States to define, in accordance with their national concepts, the concept of "sale of goods by retail".

Each Member State may, subject to the consultations mentioned in Article 16, law down, as a measure to prevent fraud and in respect of specified goods and services, that, in derogation from Article 8, the basis of assessment shall not be lower than a minimum basis determined by its national law.

13. Regarding Article 8(a)

The expression **"consideration"** means everything received in return for the supply of goods or the provision of services, including incidental expenses (packing, transport, insurance, etc.) that is to say not only the cash amounts charged, but also, for example, the value of the goods received in exchange or, in the case of goods or services supplied by order of a public authority, the amount of the compensation received.

This provision shall not, however, prevent each Member State which considers it necessary for the achievement of greater neutrality in competition from being able to exclude from the basis of assessment in respect of supply the incidental expenses arising as from the place of supply as defined in Article 5(4) and to tax such expenses as consideration for the provision of services.

Further, the expenses paid in the name and for the account of the customer which are shown in the accounts of the supplier as transitory items shall not be included in the basis of assessment.

The customs duties and other charges, taxes, etc, paid at importation by agents and other intermediaries in customs clearance including forwarding agents, under their own name, may also he excluded from the basis of assessment corresponding to the services they have provided.

14. Regarding Article 8(c)

In intra-Community trade, Member States shall endeavour to apply to importations of goods a basis of assessment which corresponds, as far as possible, to that used for supply made within the territory of the country; this basis shall include the same components as those taken into account pursuant to Article 8(*c*).

Until the abolition of the imposition of tax on importation and the remission of tax on exportation in trade between Member States at the latest, and subject to the consultations mentioned in Article 16, each Member State may apply to importations of goods from third countries a basis of assessment which corresponds, as far as possible, to that used for supply within the territory of the country; this basis shall include the same components as those taken into account pursuant to Article 8(*c*).

15. Regarding Article 9(2)

Where this paragraph is applied to the transport services referred to in Annex B, item 5, it must be so applied as to ensure equality of treatment as between the different modes of transport.

16. Regarding Article 10(1)(a)

Relief from tax as provided for in this provision refers to the supply of goods directly exported, that is to say supply made by the exporter. Member States may, however, extend exemption to supply made at the preceding stage.

17. Regarding Article 10(1)(b)

Member States may, however, refrain from granting this exemption if relief from the value added tax charged on the provision of these services is effected in favour of the beneficiary of the services by means of deductions. Moreover, Member States may, except in the case of the provision of services relating to goods in transit, restrict such exemption to the provision of services relating to goods the supply of which inside the country is taxable.

18. Regarding Article 10(2)

This provision relates in particular to the provision of international transport services at importation and to port services.

19. Regarding Article 10(2) and (3)

Where these paragraphs are applied to the transport services referred to in Annex B, item 5, they must be so applied as to ensure equality of treatment as between the different modes of transport.

20. Regarding Article 11(1)(a)

In the cases provided for in Article 5(5), second sentence, and Article 6(4), second sentence, the deductions may he made is soon as the invoice is received, even though the goods have not yet been supplied or the services rendered.

21. Regarding Article 11(2), second subparagraph

Member States may, however, restrict the right to deduction to transactions relating to goods the supply of which inside the country is taxable,

22. Regarding Article 11(2), third subparagraph

The pro rata figure shall, in general, he determined in respect of all the transactions carried out by the taxable person (general pro rata figure). However, a taxable person may, exceptionally, obtain administrative permission to determine special pro rata figures for certain sectors of his activities.

23. Regarding Article 11(3), first subparagraph

Subject to the consultations mentioned in Article 16, each Member State may, on conjunctural grounds, partially or wholly exclude capital goods from the deduction system, or apply in respect of such goods, instead of the method immediate deductions, that of annual instalments (deductions pro rata temporis).

24. Regarding Article 11(3), third subparagraph

Member States may specify certain tolerances in order to limit the number of adjustments in the event of variations in the annual pro rata figure as compared with the initial pro rata figure which served as a basis for deductions in the case (if capital goods.

25. Regarding Article 12(2)

The invoice must show separately the price exclusive of tax and the corresponding tax for each different rate, together with any exemption.

Each Member State may, in special cases, provide for derogations from this rule and also from the obligation laid down in Article 12(2). Such derogations, however, must be strictly limited.

Notwithstanding the other measures to be taken by Member States to ensure payment of the tax and to prevent fraud, all persons, whether taxable or not, who show the value added tax on an invoice, must pay the amount thereof.

26. Regarding Article 12(3)

Each Member State may, for practical reasons, shorten the period laid down in Article 12(3) or authorise certain taxable persons to lodge the declaration quarterly, half-yearly or annually.

During the first six months of each year, the taxable person shall, where appropriate, lodge a declaration concerning all the previous year's transactions, and including all the particulars necessary for any adjustments.

Each Member State shall, as regards importation of goods, adopt measures governing the procedure in respect of the declaration and of the payment which must ensue.

27. Regarding Article 14

Where this Article is applied to the transport referred to in Annex B, item 5, it must he so applied as to ensure equality of treatment as between the different modes of transport.

28. Regarding Article 17, fourth indent

Stocks may be valued inter alia by reference to the actions carried out during preceding years by the taxable persons.

ANNEX B

List of the services referred to in Article 6(2):

1. assignments of patents, trade marks, and other similar rights. and the granting of licences in respect of. such rights;

2. work, other than that referred to in Article 5(2)(*d*), on tangible moveable property, carried out for a taxable person;

3. provision of services to prepare or co-ordinate the carrying out of works of construction, as, for example, services provided by architects and by firms providing on-site supervision of works;

4. commercial advertising services;

5. transport and storage of goods, and ancillary services;

6. hiring of tangible moveable property to a taxable person;

7. provision of staff to a taxable person;

8. services provided by consultants, engineers, planning offices and similar services, in scientific, economic or technical fields;

9. the carrying out of an obligation to refrain from exercising, in whole or in part, a business activity or a right included in this list;

10. the services of forwarding agents, brokers, business agents and other independent intermediaries, in so far as they relate to supply or importation of goods or the provision of services included in this list.

Note

This Directive has now been wholly substituted; see the Sixth Directive. However, many judgments still refer to the Second Directive and for this reason it is included in full here.

[COUNCIL DIRECTIVE

of 15 March 1976

76/308/EEC

(OJ L073, 19/03/1976 p 18–23)

on mutual assistance for the recovery of claims relating to certain levies, duties, taxes and other measures][1]

Amendments

[1]   Substituted by Council Directive 2001/44/EC of 15 June 2001, Art 1(1) with effect from 5 July 2001.

THE COUNCIL OF THE EUROPEAN COMMUNITIES,

Having regard to the Treaty establishing the European Economic Community, and in particular Article 100 thereof,

Having regard to Council Regulation (EEC) No 729/70 of 21 April 1970 on the financing of the common agricultural policy (OJ No L 94, 28.4.1970, p 13), as last amended by Regulation (EEC) No 2788/72 (OJ No L 295, 30.12.1972, p 1), and in particular Article 8(3) thereof,

Having regard to the proposal from the Commission,

Having regard to the opinion of the European Parliament (OJ No C 19, 12.4.1973, p 38),

Having regard to the opinion of the Economic and Social Committee (OJ No C 69, 28.8.1973, p 3),

Whereas it is not at present possible to enforce in one Member State a claim for recovery substantiated by a document drawn up by the authorities of another Member State;

Whereas the fact that national provisions relating to recovery are applicable only within national territories is in itself an obstacle to the establishment and functioning of the common market; whereas this situation prevents Community rules from being fully and fairly applied, particularly in the area of the common agricultural policy, and facilitates fraudulent operations;

Whereas it is therefore necessary to adopt common rules on mutual assistance for recovery;

Whereas these rules must apply both to the recovery of claims resulting from the various measures which form part of the system of total or partial financing of the European Agricultural Guidance and Guarantee Fund and to the recovery of agricultural levies and customs duties within the meaning of Article 2 of Decision 70/243/ECSC, EEC, Euratom of 21 April 1970 on the replacement of financial contributions from Member States by the Communities' own resources (OJ No L 94, 28.4.1970, p 19), and of Article 128 of the Act of Accession; whereas they must also apply to the recovery of interest and costs incidental to such claims;

Whereas mutual assistance must consist of the following: the requested authority must on the one hand supply the applicant authority with the information which the latter needs in order to recover claims arising in the Member State in which it is situated and notify the debtor of all instruments relating to such claims emanating from that Member State, and on the other hand it must recover, at the request of the applicant authority, the claims arising in the Member State in which the latter is situated;

Whereas these different forms of assistance must be afforded by the requested authority in compliance with the laws, regulations and administrative provisions governing such matters in the Member State in which it is situated;

Whereas it is necessary to lay down the conditions in accordance with which requests for assistance must be drawn up by the applicant authority and to give a limitative definition of the particular circumstances in which the requested authority may refuse assistance in any given case;

Whereas when the requested authority is required to act on behalf of the applicant authority to recover a claim, it must be able, if the provisions in force in the Member State in which it is situated so permit and with the agreement of the applicant authority, to allow the debtor time to pay or authorize payment by installment; whereas any interest charged on such payment facilities must also be remitted to the Member State in which the applicant authority is situated;

Whereas, upon a reasoned request from the applicant authority, the requested authority must also be able, in so far as the provisions in force in the Member State in which it is situated so permit, to take precautionary measures to guarantee the recovery of claims arising in the applicant Member State; whereas such claims must not however be given any preferential treatment in the Member State in which the requested authority is situated;

Whereas it is possible that during the recovery procedure in the Member State in which the requested authority is situated the claim or the instrument authorizing its enforcement issued in the Member State in which the applicant authority is situated may be contested by the person concerned; whereas it should be laid down in such cases that the person concerned must bring the action contesting the claim before the competent body of the Member State in which the applicant authority is situated and that the requested authority must suspend any enforcement proceedings which it has begun until a decision is taken by the aforementioned body;

Whereas it should be laid down that documents and information communicated in the course of mutual assistance for recovery may not be used for other purposes;

Whereas this Directive should not curtail mutual assistance between particular Member States under bilateral or multilateral agreements or arrangements;

Whereas it is necessary to ensure that mutual assistance functions smoothly and to this end to lay down a Community procedure for determining the detailed rules for the application of such assistance within an appropriate period; whereas it is necessary to set up a committee to organize close and effective collaboration between the Member States and the Commission in this area,

HAS ADOPTED THIS DIRECTIVE:

Article 1

This Directive lays down the rules to be incorporated into the laws, regulations and administrative provisions of the Member States to ensure the recovery in each Member State of the claims referred to in Article 2 which arise in another Member State.

Article 2

[This Directive shall apply to all claims relating to:

(a) refunds, interventions and other measures forming part of the system of total or partial financing of the European Agricultural Guidance and Guarantee Fund (EAGGF), including sums to be collected in connection with these actions;

(b) levies and other duties provided for under the common organisation of the market for the sugar sector;

(c) import duties;

(d) export duties;

(e) value added tax;

(f) excise duties on:

— manufactured tobacco,

— alcohol and alcoholic beverages,

— mineral oils;

(g) taxes on income and capital;

(h) taxes on insurance premiums;

(l) interest, administrative penalties and fines, and costs incidental to the claims referred to in points (a) to (h), with the exclusion of any sanction of a criminal nature as determined by the laws in force in the Member State in which the requested authority is situated.][1]

Amendments

[1] Article 2 substituted by Council Directive 2001/44/EC of 15 June 2001, Art 1(2) with effect from 5 July 2001.

Article 3

In this Directive:

— **"applicant authority"** means the competent authority of a Member State which makes a request for assistance concerning a claim referred to in Article 2;

— **"requested authority"** means the competent authority of a Member State to which a request for assistance is made;

[— **"import duties"** means customs duties and charges having equivalent effect on imports, and import charges laid down within the framework of the common agricultural policy or in that of specific arrangements applicable to certain goods resulting from the processing of agricultural products,

— **"export duties"** means customs duties and charges having equivalent effect on exports, and export charges laid down within the framework of the common agricultural policy or in that of specific arrangements applicable to certain goods resulting from the processing of agricultural products,

— **"taxes on income and capital"** means those enumerated in Article 1(3) of Directive 77/799/EEC (Council Directive 77/799/EEC of 19 December 1977 concerning mutual assistance by the competent authorities of the Member States in the field of direct taxation (OJ L 336, 27.12.1977, p 15). Directive as last amended by the 1994 Act of Accession), read in conjunction with Article 1(4) of that Directive,

— **"taxes on insurance premiums"** means:

in Austria:

(i)   Versicherungssteuer

(ii)   Feuerschutzsteuer

in Belgium:

(i) Taxe annuelle sur les contrats d'assurance

(ii) Jaarlijkse taks op de verzekeringscontracten

in Germany:

(i)   Versicherungssteuer

(ii)   Feuerschutzsteuer

in Denmark:

(i)   Afgift af lystfartøjsforsikringer

(ii)   Afgiftaf ansvarsforsikringer for motorkøretøjer m.v.

(iii)   Stempelafgift af forsikringspræmier

in Spain: Impuesto sobre la prima de seguros

in Greece:

(i)   Φςρος κύκλου εργασιών (Φ.Κ.Ε)

(ii)   Τέλη Χαρτοσήμου

in France: Taxe sur les conventions d'assurances

in Finland:

(i)   Eräistä vakuutusmaksuista suoritettava vero/skatt på vissa försäkringspremier

(ii)   Palosuojelumaksu/brandskyddsavgift

in Italy: Imposte sulle assicurazioni private ed I contratti vitalizi di cui alla legge

in Ireland: levy on insurance premiums

in Luxembourg:

(i) Impôt sur les assurances

(ii) Impôt dans l'interêt du service d'incendie

in the Netherlands: Assurantiebelasting

in Portugal: Imposto de selo sobre os prémios de seguros

in Sweden: none

in the United Kingdom: insurance premium tax (IPT)

[in Malta: *Taxxa fuq Dokumenti u Trasferimenti*

in Slovenia:

(i) *davek od prometa zavarovalnih poslov*

(ii) *pozarna taksa.*][1]

This Directive shall also apply to claims relating to identical or analogous taxes which supplement or replace the taxes on insurance premiums referred to in the sixth indent. The competent authorities of the Member States shall communicate to each other and to the Commission the dates of entry into force of such taxes.][2]

Amendments

[1]   Inserted by the Act concerning the conditions of accession of the Czech Republic, the Republic of Estonia, the Republic of Cyprus, the Republic of Latvia, the Republic of Lithuania, the Republic of Hungary, the Republic of Malta, the Republic of Poland, the Republic of Slovenia and the Slovak Republic and the adjustments to the Treaties on which the European Union is founded (OJ L 236 p 33, 23.9.2003).

[2]   Inserted by Council Directive 2001/44/EC of 15 June 2001, Art 1(3) with effect from 5 July 2001.

Article 4

1. At the request of the applicant authority, the requested authority shall provide any information which would be useful to the applicant authority in the recovery of its claim.

In order to obtain this information, the requested authority shall make use of the powers provided under the laws, regulations or administrative provisions applying to the recovery of similar claims arising in the Member State where that authority is situated.

2. The request for information shall indicate [the name, address and any other relevant information relating to the identification to which the applicant authority normally has access][1] of the person to whom the information to be provided relates and the nature and amount of the claim in respect of which the request is made.

3. The requested authority shall not be obliged to supply information:

(*a*) which it would not be able to obtain for the purpose of recovering similar claims arising in the Member State in which it is situated;

(*b*) which would disclose any commercial, industrial or professional secrets; or

(*c*) the disclosure of which would be liable to prejudice the security of or be contrary to the public policy of the State.

4. The requested authority shall inform the applicant authority of the grounds for refusing a request for information.

Amendments

¹   Substituted by Council Directive 2001/44/EC of 15 June 2001, Art 1(4) with effect from 5 July 2001; previously "the name and address".

Article 5

1. The requested authority shall, at the request of the applicant authority, and in accordance with the rules of law in force for the notification of similar instruments or decisions in the Member State in which the requested authority is situated, notify to the addressee all instruments and decisions, including those of a judicial nature, which emanate from the Member State in which the applicant authority is situated and which relate to a claim and/or to its recovery.

2. The request for notification shall indicate [the name, address and any other relevant information relating to the identification to which the applicant authority normally has access]¹ of the addressee concerned, the nature and the subject of the instrument or decision to be notified, if necessary the name and address of the debtor and the claim to which the instrument or decision relates, and any other useful information.

3. The requested authority shall promptly inform the applicant authority of the action taken on its request for notification and, more especially, of the date on which the instrument or decision was forwarded to the addressee.

Amendments

¹   Substituted by Council Directive 2001/44/EC of 15 June 2001, Art 1(5) with effect from 5 July 2001; previously "the name and address".

Article 6

1. At the request of the applicant authority, the requested authority shall, in accordance with the laws, regulations or administrative provisions applying to the recovery of similar claims arising in the Member State in which the requested authority is situated, recover claims which are the subject of an instrument permitting their enforcement.

2. For this purpose any claim in respect of which a request for recovery has been made shall be treated as a claim of the Member State in which the requested authority is situated, except where Article 12 applies.

Article 7

[**1.** The request for recovery of a claim which the applicant authority addresses to the requested authority must be accompanied by an official or certified copy of the instrument permitting its enforcement, issued in the Member State in which the applicant authority is situated and, if appropriate, by the original or a certified copy of other documents necessary for recovery.

2. The applicant authority may not make a request for recovery unless:

    (*a*) the claim and/or the instrument permitting its enforcement are not contested in the Member State in which it is situated, except in cases where the second subparagraph of Article 12(2) is applied, (*b*) it has, in the Member State in which it is situated, applied appropriate recovery procedures available to it on the basis of the instrument referred to in paragraph 1, and the measures taken will not result in the payment in full of the claim.

3. The request for recovery shall indicate:

(*a*) the name, address and any other relevant information relating to the identification of the person concerned and/or to the third party holding his or her assets;

(*b*) the name, address and any other relevant information relating to the identification of the applicant authority;

(*c*) a reference to the instrument permitting its enforcement issued in the Member State in which the applicant authority is situated;

(*d*) the nature and the amount of the claim, including the principal, the interest, and any other penalties, fines and costs due indicated in the currencies of the Member States in which both authorities are situated;

(*e*) the date of notification of the instrument to the addressee by the applicant authority and/or by the requested authority;

(*f*) the date from which and the period during which enforcement is possible under the laws in force in the Member State in which the applicant authority is situated;

(*g*) any other relevant information.

4. The request for recovery shall also contain a declaration by the applicant authority confirming that the conditions set out in paragraph 2 have been fulfilled.

5. As soon as any relevant information relating to the matter which gave rise to the request for recovery comes to the knowledge of the applicant authority it shall forward it to the requested authority.]¹

Amendments

¹   Article 7 substituted by Council Directive 2001/44/EC of 15 June 2001, Art 1(6) with effect from 5 July 2001.

Article 8

[**1.** The instrument permitting enforcement of the claim shall be directly recognised and automatically treated as an instrument permitting enforcement of a claim of the Member State in which the requested authority is situated.

2. Notwithstanding the first paragraph, the instrument permitting enforcement of the claim may, where appropriate and in accordance with the provisions in force in the Member State in which the requested authority is situated, be accepted as, recognised as, supplemented with, or replaced by an instrument authorising enforcement in the territory of that Member State.

Within three months of the date of receipt of the request for recovery, Member States shall endeavour to complete such acceptance, recognition, supplementing or replacement, except in cases where the third subparagraph is applied. They may not be refused if the instrument permitting enforcement is properly drawn up. The requested authority shall inform the applicant authority of the grounds for exceeding the period of three months.

If any of these formalities should give rise to contestation in connection with the claim and/or the instrument permitting enforcement issued by the applicant authority, Article 12 shall apply.][1]

Amendments

[1]   Article 8 substituted by Council Directive 2001/44/EC of 15 June 2001, Art 1(6) with effect from 5 July 2001.

Article 9

[1. Claims shall be recovered in the currency of the Member State in which the requested authority is situated. The entire amount of the claim that is recovered by the requested authority shall be remitted by the requested authority to the applicant authority.

2. The requested authority may, where the laws, regulations or administrative provisions in force in the Member State in which it is situated so permit, and after consultations with the applicant authority, allow the debtor time to pay or authorise payment by instalment. Any interest charged by the requested authority in respect of such extra time to pay shall also be remitted to the Member State in which the applicant authority is situated.

From the date on which the instrument permitting enforcement of recovery of the claim has been directly recognised or accepted, recognised, supplemented or replaced in accordance with Article 8, interest will be charged for late payment under the laws, regulations and administrative provisions in force in the Member State in which the requested authority is situated and shall also be remitted to the Member State in which the applicant authority is situated.][1]

Amendments

[1]   Article 9 substituted by Council Directive 2001/44/EC of 15 June 2001, Art 1(6) with effect from 5 July 2001.

Article 10

[Notwithstanding Article 6(2), the claims to be recovered shall not necessarily benefit from the privileges accorded to similar claims arising in the Member State in which the requested authority is situated.][1]

Amendments

[1]   Article 10 substituted by Council Directive 2001/44/EC of 15 June 2001, Art 1(6) with effect from 5 July 2001.

Article 11

The requested authority shall inform the applicant authority immediately of the action it has taken on the request for recovery.

Article 12

1. If, in the course of the recovery procedure, the claim and/or the instrument permitting its enforcement issued in the Member State in which the applicant authority is situated are contested by an interested party, the action shall be brought by the latter before the competent body of the Member State in which the applicant authority is situated, in accordance with the laws in force there. This action must be notified by the applicant authority to the requested authority. The party concerned may also notify the requested authority of the action.

2. As soon as the requested authority has received the notification referred to in paragraph 1 either from the applicant authority or from the interested party, it shall suspend the enforcement procedure pending the decision of the body competent in the matter [unless the applicant authority requests otherwise in accordance with the second subparagraph][1]. Should the requested authority deem it necessary, and without prejudice to Article 13, that authority may take precautionary measures to guarantee recovery in so far as the laws or regulations in force in the Member State in which it is situated allow such action for similar claims.

[Notwithstanding the first subparagraph of paragraph 2, the applicant authority may in accordance with the law, regulations and administrative practices in force in the Member State in which it is situated, request the requested authority to recover a contested claim, in so far as the relevant laws, regulations and administrative practices in force in the Member State in which the requested authority is situated allow such action. If the result of contestation is subsequently favourable to the debtor, the applicant authority shall be liable for the reimbursement of any sums recovered, together with any compensation due, in accordance with the laws in force in the Member State in which the requested authority is situated.][2]

3. Where it is the enforcement measures taken in the Member State in which the requested authority is situated that are being contested the action shall be brought before the competent body of that Member State in accordance with its laws and regulations.

4. Where the competent body before which the action has been brought in accordance with paragraph 1 is a judicial or administrative tribunal, the decision of that tribunal, in so far as it is favourable to the applicant authority and permits recovery of the claim in the Member State in which the applicant authority is situated shall constitute the "instrument permitting enforcement" within the meaning of Articles 6, 7 and 8 and the recovery of the claim shall proceed on the basis of that decision.

Amendments

[1]   Inserted by Council Directive 2001/44/EC of 15 June 2001, Art 1(7)(*a*) with effect from 5 July 2001.
[2]   Inserted by Council Directive 2001/44/EC of 15 June 2001, Art 1(7)(*b*) with effect from 5 July 2001.

Article 13

On a reasoned request by the applicant authority, the requested authority shall take precautionary measures to ensure recovery of a claim in so far as the laws or regulations in force in the Member State in which it is situated so permit.

In order to give effect to the provisions of the first paragraph, Articles 6, 7(1), (3) and (5), 8, 11, 12 and 14 shall apply mutatis mutandis.

Article 14

[The requested authority shall not be obliged:

(*a*) to grant the assistance provided for in Articles 6 to 13 if recovery of the claim would, because of the situation of the debtor, create serious economic or social difficulties in the Member State in which that authority is situated, in so far as the laws, regulations and administrative practices in force in the Member State in which the requested authority is situated allow such action for similar national claims;

(*b*) to grant the assistance provided for in Articles 4 to 13, if the initial request under Article 4, 5 or 6 applies to claims more than five years old, dating from the moment the instrument permitting the recovery is established in accordance with the laws, regulations or administrative practices in force in the Member State in which the applicant authority is situated, to the date of the request. However, in cases where the claim or the instrument is contested, the time limit begins from the moment at which the applicant State establishes that the claim or the enforcement order permitting recovery may no longer be contested.][1]

The requested authority shall inform the applicant authority of the grounds for refusing a request for assistance. Such reasoned refusal shall also be communicated to the Commission.

Amendments

[1]   Substituted by Council Directive 2001/44/EC of 15 June 2001, Art 1(8) with effect from 5 July 2001.

Article 15

1. Questions concerning periods of limitation shall be governed solely by the laws in force in the Member State in which the applicant authority is situated.

2. Steps taken in the recovery of claims by the requested authority in pursuance of a request for assistance, which, if they had been carried out by the applicant authority, would have had the effect of suspending or interrupting the period of limitation according to the laws in force in the Member State in which the applicant authority is situated, shall be deemed to have been taken in the latter State, in so far as that effect is concerned.

Article 16

Documents and information sent to the requested authority pursuant to this Directive may only be communicated by the latter to:

(*a*) the person mentioned in the request for assistance;

(*b*) those persons and authorities responsible for the recovery of the claims, and solely for that purpose;

(*c*) the judicial authorities dealing with matters concerning the recovery of the claims.

Article 17

Requests for assistance [the instrument permitting the enforcement and other relevant documents][1] shall be accompanied by a translation in the official language, or one of the official languages of the Member State in which the requested authority is situated, without prejudice to the latter authority's right to waive the translation.

Amendments

[1] Substituted by Council Directive 2001/44/EC of 15 June 2001, Art 1(9) with effect from 5 July 2001; previously "and relevant documents".

Article 15

Member States shall renounce all claims upon each other for the reimbursement of costs resulting from mutual assistance which they grant each other pursuant to this Directive.

However, the Member State in which the applicant authority is situated shall remain liable to the Member State in which the requested authority is situated for costs incurred as a result of actions held to be unfounded, as far as either the substance of the claim or the validity of the instrument issued by the applicant authority are concerned.

Article 18

[**1.** The requested authority shall recover from the person concerned and retain any costs linked to recovery which it incurs, in accordance with the laws and regulations of the Member State in which it is situated that apply to similar claims.

2. Member States shall renounce all claims on each other for the refund of costs resulting from mutual assistance which they grant each other pursuant to this Directive.

3. Where recovery poses a specific problem, concerns a very large amount in costs or relates to the fight against organised crime, the applicant and requested authorities may agree reimbursement arrangements specific to the cases in question.

4. The Member State in which the applicant authority is situated shall remain liable to the Member State in which the requested authority is situated for any costs and any losses incurred as a result of actions held to be unfounded, as far as either the substance of the claim or the validity of the instrument issued by the applicant authority are concerned.][1]

Amendments

[1] Article 19 substituted by Council Directive 2001/44/EC of 15 June 2001, Art 1(10) with effect from 5 July 2001.

Article 19

Member States shall provide each other with a list of authorities authorized to make or receive requests for assistance.

Article 20

[**1.** The Commission shall be assisted by a recovery committee (hereinafter referred to as 'the Committee'), composed of representatives of the Member States and chaired by the representative of the Commission.

2. Where reference is made to this paragraph, Articles 5 and 7 of Decision 1999/468/EC shall apply.

The period referred to in Article 5(6) of Decision 1999/468/EC shall be set at three months.

3. The Committee shall adopt its own rules of procedure.]¹

Amendments

¹   Article 20 substituted by Council Directive 2001/44/EC of 15 June 2001, Art 1(11) with effect from 5 July 2001.

Article 21

The committee may examine any matter concerning the application of this Directive raised by its chairman either on his own initiative or at the request of the representative of a Member State.

Article 22

[The detailed rules for implementing Articles 4(2) and (4), 5(2) and (3) and Articles 7, 8, 9, 11, 12(1) and (2), 14, 18(3) and 25 and for determining the means by which communications between the authorities may be transmitted, the rules on conversion, transfer of sums recovered, and the fixing of a minimum amount for claims which may give rise to a request for assistance, shall be adopted in accordance with the procedure laid down in Article 20(2).]¹

Amendments

¹   Article 22 substituted by Council Directive 2001/44/EC of 15 June 2001, Art 1(12) with effect from 5 July 2001.

Article 23

The provisions of this Directive shall not prevent a greater measure of mutual assistance being afforded either now or in the future by particular Member States under any agreements or arrangements, including those for the notification of legal or extra legal acts.

Article 24

Member States shall bring into force the measures necessary to comply with this Directive not later than 1 January 1978.

Article 25

Each Member State shall inform the Commission of the measures which it has adopted to implement this Directive. The Commission shall forward this information to the other Member States.

[Each Member State shall inform the Commission annually of the number of requests for information, notification and recovery sent and received each year, the amount of the claims involved and the amounts recovered. The Commission shall report biennially to the European Parliament and the Council on the use made of these arrangements and on the results achieved.]¹

Amendments

[1]   Inserted by Council Directive 2001/44/EC of 15 June 2001, Art 1(13) with effect from 5 July 2001.

Article 26

This Directive is addressed to the Member States.

SIXTH COUNCIL DIRECTIVE

of 17 May 1977

77/388/EEC

On the harmonization of the laws of the Member States relating to turnover taxes — Common system of value added tax: uniform basis of assessment

(OJ L145, 13.6.1977, p 1)

THE COUNCIL OF THE EUROPEAN COMMUNITIES,

Having regard to the Treaty establishing the European Economic Community, and in particular Articles 99 and 100 thereof,

Having regard to the proposal from the Commission,

Having regard to the opinion of the European Parliament, (OJ C40, 8.4.74, p 25)

Having regard to the opinion of the Economic and Social Committee, (OJ C 139, 12.11.74, p 15)

Whereas all Member States have adopted a system of value added tax in accordance with the first and second Council Directives of 11 April 1967 on the harmonization of the laws of the Member States relating to turnover taxes, (OJ 71, 14.4.67, pp 1301–1367)

Whereas the Decision of 21 April 1970 on the replacement of financial contributions from Member States by the Communities' own resources (OJ L94, 28.4.70, p 19) provides that the budget of the Communities shall, irrespective of other revenue, be financed entirely from the Communities' own resources; whereas these resources are to include those accruing from value added tax and obtained by applying a common rate of tax on a basis of assessment determined in a uniform manner according to Community rules;

Whereas further progress should be made in the effective removal of restrictions on the movement of persons, goods, services and capital and the integration of national economies;

Whereas account should be taken of the objective of abolishing the imposition of tax on the importation and the remission of tax on exportation in trade between Member States; whereas it should be ensured that the common system of turnover taxes is non-discriminatory as regards the origin of goods and services, so that a common market permitting fair competition and resembling a real internal market may ultimately be achieved;

Whereas, to enhance the non-discriminatory nature of the tax, the term "taxable person" must be clarified to enable the Member States to extend it to cover persons who occasionally carry out certain transactions;

Whereas the term "taxable transaction" has led to difficulties, in particular as regards transactions treated as taxable transactions; whereas these concepts must be clarified;

Whereas the determination of the place where taxable transactions are effected has been the subject of conflicts concerning jurisdiction as between Member States, in particular as regards supplies of goods for assembly and the supply of services; whereas although the place where a supply of services is effected should in principle be defined as the place where the person supplying the services has his principal place of business, that place should be defined as being in the country of the person to whom the services are supplied, in particular in the case of certain services supplied between taxable persons where the cost of the services is included in the price of the goods;

Whereas the concepts of chargeable event and of the charge to tax must be harmonized if the introduction and any subsequent alterations of the Community rate are to become operative at the same time in all Member States;

Whereas the taxable base must be harmonized so that the application of the Community rate to taxable transactions leads to comparable results in all the Member States;

Whereas the rates applied by Member States must be such as to allow the normal deduction of the tax applied at the preceding stage;

Whereas a common list of exemptions should be drawn up so that the Communities' own resources may be collected in a uniform manner in all the Member States;

Whereas the rules governing deductions should be harmonized to the extent that they affect the actual amounts collected; whereas the deductible proportion should be calculated in a similar manner in all the Member States;

Whereas it should be specified which persons are liable to pay tax, in particular as regards services supplied by a person established in another country;

Whereas the obligations of taxpayers must be harmonized as far as possible so as to ensure the necessary safeguards for the collection of taxes in a uniform manner in all the Member States; whereas taxpayers should, in particular, make a periodic aggregate return of their transactions, relating to both inputs and outputs where this appears necessary for establishing and monitoring the basis of assessment of own resources;

Whereas Member States should nevertheless be able to retain their special schemes for small undertakings, in accordance with common provisions, and with a view to closer harmonization; whereas Member States should remain free to apply a special scheme involving flat rate rebates of input value added tax to farmers not covered by normal schemes; whereas the basic principles of this scheme should be established and a common method adopted for calculating the value added of these farmers for the purposes of collecting own resources;

Whereas the uniform application of the provisions of this Directive should be ensured; whereas to this end a Community procedure for consultation should be laid down; whereas the setting up of a Value Added Tax Committee would enable the Member States and the Commission to cooperate closely;

Whereas Member States should be able, within certain limits and subject to certain conditions, to take or retain special measures derogating from this Directive in order to simplify the levying of tax or to avoid fraud or tax avoidance;

Whereas it might appear appropriate to authorize Member States to conclude with non-member countries or international organizations agreements containing derogations from this Directive;

Whereas it is vital to provide for a transitional period to allow national laws in specified fields to be gradually adapted,

HAS ADOPTED THIS DIRECTIVE:

TITLE I
INTRODUCTORY PROVISIONS

Article 1

Member States shall modify their present value added tax systems in accordance with the following Articles.

They shall adopt the necessary laws, regulations and administrative provisions so that the systems as modified enter into force at the earliest opportunity and by 1 January 1978 at the latest.

TITLE II
SCOPE

Article 2

The following shall be subject to value added tax:

1. the supply of goods or services effected for consideration within the territory   s 2(1)(A)
of the country by a taxable person acting as such;

2. the importation of goods.   s 2(1)(B)

Cross-references

Intra-Community acquisition of goods and new means of transport: Art 28a.

Case law

Subject	Case	Case reference
Busking, non-quantifiable amounts of voluntary donations, not a supply of services effected for consideration	*Tolsma v Inspecteur der Omzet-belasting Leeuwarden*	[1994] STI 324, ECJ 16/93
Greek arrangements whereby petrol was charged to VAT once only on importation (and not along the supply chain) were held to be in breach of Art 2	*BP Soupergas Aronimos Etairia Geniki Emporiki Viomichaniki kai Antiprossopeion v Greece*	[1995] STC 805, ECJ 62/93
Person who habitually supplies free services not taxable	*Staatssecretaris van Financiën v Hong Kong Trade Development Council*	[1982] ECR 1277, [1983] 1 CMLR 73, ECJ 89/81
Services for which no definite subjective consideration received not taxable	*Staatssecretaris van Financiën v Cooperatieve Aardappelen Bewaarplaats GA*	ECJ 154/80

No rule requiring Member States to tax transport services beyond the territorial limits in international waters	*EC Commission v France*	[1991] STI 455, ECJ 30/89
Illegality of sales does not prevent VAT being due. Sales of counterfeit perfume are liable to VAT	*Regina v Goodwin & Unstead*	4 June 1998, C–3/97
Renting out of space in a coffee shop for the sale of narcotic drugs falls within the scope of the 6th Directive	*Staatssecretaris van Financien v Coffeeshop "Siberië" vof*	29 June 1999, C–158/98
The mere acquisition of ownership in and the holding of bonds and the receipt of income therefrom cannot be regarded as economic activities within meaning of Art 4(2)	*Finanzamt Augsburg-Stadt v Markegemeinde Welden*	6 February 1997, C–247/95
Factoring company purchasing debts and assuming the risk of debtors	*MKG-Kraftfahrzeuge Factoring Gmbh v Finanzamp Gross-Gerau*	26 June 2003, C–305/01

Illegal activities

No VAT liability on illegal supplies of drugs	*Mol v Inspecteur der Invoerrechten en Accijnzen*	ECJ 269/86
No VAT liability on illegal supplies of drugs	*Vereniging Happy Family v Inspecteur der Omzetbelastin*	[1989] 3 CMLR 729, ECJ 289/86
No VAT liability on illegal imports of drugs	*Einberger v Hauptzollamt Freiburg (No 2)*	[1984] ECR 1177, (1985) 1 CMLR 765, ECJ 294/82
No VAT liability on illegal import of counterfeit money	*Witzemann v Hauptzollamt Munchen-Mitte*	[1991] STI 60, ECJ 343/89
By exempting certain professional services, Spain had not complied with Art 2	*EC Commission v Spain*	(1991) OJ C297/07, ECJ 35/90
Research activities of public-sector higher-education establishments	*Commission v Germany*	20 June 2002, C–287/00
Admission of a member to a partnership in consideration of payment of a contribution in kind	*KapHag Renditefonds v Finannzamt Charlottenburg*	26 June 2003, C–442/01
Abuse of rights	*Halifax Plc v Commissioners of Customs & Excise*	21 February 2006, C–255/02
Abuse of rights	*University of Huddersfield Higher Education Corporation v Commissioners of Customs & Excise*	21 February 2006, C–233/02
Abuse of rights	*BUPA Hospitals Ltd v Commissioners of Customs & Excise*	21 February 2006, C–419/02

TITLE III
TERRITORIAL APPLICATION

Article 3

[1. For the purposes of this Directive,   s 1(2A)

— **"territory of a Member State"** shall mean the territory of the country as defined in respect of each Member State in paragraphs 2 and 3,

— **"Community"** and **"territory of the Community"** shall mean the territory of the Member States as defined in respect of each Member State in paragraphs 2 and 3,

— **"third territory"** and **"third country"** shall mean any territory other than those defined in paragraphs 2 and 3 as the territory of a Member State.

2. For the purposes of this Directive, the **"territory of the country"** shall be the area of application of the Treaty establishing the European Economic Community as defined in respect of each Member State in Article 227.

3. The following territories of individual Member States shall be excluded from the territory of the country:

— Federal Republic of Germany:
the Island of Heligoland,
the territory of Büsingen,
Kingdom of Spain:
Ceuta,
Melilla,

— Republic of Italy:
Livigno,
Campione d'Italia,
the Italian waters of Lake Lugano.

The following territories of individual Member States shall also be excluded from the territory of the country:

— Kingdom of Spain:
the Canary Islands,

— French Republic:
the overseas departments,

— Hellenic Republic
Agio Oroz

[**4.** By way of derogation from paragraph 1, in view of the conventions and treaties which they have concluded respectively with the French Republic and the United Kingdom of Great Britain and Northern Ireland, the Principality of Monaco and the Isle of Man shall not be treated for the purposes of the application of this Directive as third territories.

Member States shall take the measures necessary to ensure that transactions originating in or intended for:

— the Principality of Monaco are treated as transactions originating in or intended for the French Republic,

— the Isle of Man are treated as transactions originating in or intended for the United Kingdom of Great Britain and Northern Ireland.[1]

5. If the Commission considers that the provisions laid down in paragraphs 3 and 4 are no longer justified, particularly in terms of fair competition or own resources, it shall submit appropriate proposals to the Council.] [2]

Amendments

[1]   Para (4) substituted by Council Directive 92/111/EEC of 14 December 1992 Art 1(1).

[2]   Art 3 substituted by Council Directive 91/680/EEC of 16 December 1991, Art 1(1) with effect from 1 January 1993.

Case law

Subject	Case	Case reference
Transport via international waters from a point in an EC State to a point in the same EC State taxable	*Trans Tirreno Express SpA v Ufficio Provinciale IVA, Sassari*	[1986] 2 CMLR 100, ECJ 283/84
Services supplied on board ships over which a member state has jurisdiction taxable even if outside the member State's territorial jurisdiction	*Berkholz v Finanzampt Hamburg-Mitte-Altstadt*	[1985] 3 CMLR 667, ECJ 168/84

TITLE IV
TAXABLE PERSONS

Article 4

Revenue publications

Addresses for foreign traders: Tax Briefing, Issue 30.

s 8

1. **"Taxable person"** shall mean any person who independently carries out in any place any economic activity specified in paragraph 2, whatever the purpose or results of that activity.

2. The economic activities referred to in paragraph 1 shall comprise all activities of producers, traders and persons supplying services including mining and agricultural activities and activities of the professions. The exploitation of tangible or intangible property for the purpose of obtaining income therefrom on a continuing basis shall also be considered an economic activity.

3. Member States may also treat as a taxable person anyone who carries out, on an occasional basis, a transaction relating to the activities referred to in paragraph 2 and in particular one of the following:

(*a*) the supply before first occupation of buildings or parts of buildings and the land on which they stand; Member States may determine the conditions of application of this criterion to transformations of buildings and the land on which they stand.

Member States may apply criteria other than that of first occupation, such as the period elapsing between the date of completion of the building and the date of first supply or the period elapsing between the date of first occupation and the date of subsequent supply, provided that these periods do not exceed five years and two years respectively.

"A building" shall be taken to mean any structure fixed to or in the ground;

(*b*) the supply of building land.

"Building land" shall mean any unimproved or improved land defined as such by the Member States.

4. The use of the word "independently" in paragraph 1 shall exclude employed and other persons from the tax in so far as they are bound to an employer by a contract of employment or by any other legal ties creating the relationship of employer and employee as regards working conditions, remuneration and the employer's liability. _{s 8(1)}

Subject to the consultations provided for in Article 29, each Member State may treat as a single taxable person persons established in the territory of the country who, while legally independent, are closely bound to one another by financial, economic and organizational links. _{s 8(8), VATR 1979 R 5}

5. States, regional and local government authorities and other bodies governed by public law shall not be considered taxable persons in respect of the activities or transactions in which they engage as public authorities, even where they collect dues, fees, contributions or payments in connection with these activities or transactions. _{s 8(2A)}

However, when they engage in such activities or transactions, they shall be considered taxable persons in respect of these activities or transactions where treatment as non-taxable persons would lead to significant distortions of competition.

In any case, these bodies shall be considered taxable persons in relation to the activities listed in Annex D, provided they are not carried out on such a small scale as to be negligible.

Member States may consider activities of these bodies which are exempt under Article 13 or 28 as activities which they engage in as public authorities.

Cross-references

Person who from time to time supplies a new means of transport: Art 28a(4).

Case law

Subject	Case	Case reference
"Economic activity" does not include activities carried out on an occasional basis but does include the hiring out of tangible property	*Enkler v Finamzamt Homburg* [1996] STC 1316, ECJ 230/94	

Interpretation	*Hamann v Finanzamt Hamburg-Eimsbüttel*	[1991] STC 193, [1990] 2 CMLR 383, ECJ 51/88; see also ECJ 283/81
Additional taxation on buildings or building land	*Kerrutt v Finanzamt Mönchengladback-Mitte*	[1987] 2 CMLR 221, ECJ 73/85
Interaction of Art 4(1) and Art 17 (deduction)	*Re VAT on leased buildings, EC Commission v France*	[1989] 1 CMLR 505, ECJ 50/87
Advocate General's opinion: "Building land" includes both prepared and unprepated sites, and land which is officially designated for building, or for which permission to build has been granted	*Gemeente Emmen v Belastingdienst Grote Ondernemingen*	[1996] STC 496, ECJ 468/93
Mere acquisition of ownership in and the holding of bonds and the receipt of income therefrom cannot be regarded as economic activities within the meaning of a 4(2)	*Finanzamt Augsbur-Stradt v Marktgemeinde Welden*	6 February 1997, C–247/95
Taxable persons		
Independent third party tax collectors	*Ayuntamiento de Sevilla v Recaudadores de las Zonas Primera y Segunda*	[1991] OJ C220/10, ECJ 202/90
Intending trader	*Rompelman and Rompelman-Van Deelen v Minister van Financiën*	ECJ 268/83
Intending trade who carries out a feasibility study	*Intercommunale voor Zeewaterontzilting v Belgian State*	ECJ 110/ 94
Notaries and bailiffs	*Re Notaries and Bailiffs: EC Commission v Netherlands*	[1988] 2 CMLR 921, ECJ 235/85
Not taxable persons		
Trustee buying and selling shares in the course of managing assets of a charitable trust	*Wellcome Trust Ltd v C & E Commissioners*	[1996] STC 945, ECJ 155/94
Person supplying services against a statutory charge	*Apple and Pear Development Council v C & E Commissioners*	[1988] STC 221, [1988] 2 CMLR 394, [1988] 2 All ER 922, ECJ 102/86
Person habitually supplying free services	*Staatssecretaris van Financiën v Hong Kong Trade Development Council*	[1982] ECR 1277, [1983] 1 CMLR 73, ECJ 89/81
Public authorities	*Ufficio Distrettuale delle Imposte Dirette di Fiorenzuola d'Arda v Comune di Carpaneto Piacentino*	[1990] 3 CLMR 153, ECJ 4/89
Public authorities	*Ufficio Provinciale Imposta sui Valore Aggiunto di Piacenza v Comune di Rivergaro*	[1990] STC 205, ECJ 231/87 and 129/88
Holding companies	*Polysar Investments Netherlands BV v Inspecteur der Invoerrechten en Accijnzen*	[1991] STI 638, ECJ 60/90

Holding companies	*Harnas & Helm CV v Staatssecretaris van Financiën*	[1997] STC 364, ECJ 80/85
Concept of taxable person — place where services are supplied — SICAV	*Banque Bruxelles Lambert SA v the Belgin State*	21 October 2004, C–8/03
Abuse of rights	*Halifax Plc v Commissioners of Customs & Excise*	21 February 2006, C–255/02
Abuse of rights	*University of Huddersfield Higher Education Corporation v Commissioners of Customs & Excise*	21 February 2006, C–233/02
Abuse of rights	*BUPA Hospitals Ltd v Commissioners of Customs & Excise*	21 February 2006, C–419/02

TITLE V
Taxable transactions

Article 5
Supply of goods

1. **"Supply of goods"** shall mean the transfer of the right to dispose of tangible s 3(1) property as owner.

2. Electric current, gas, heat, refrigeration and the like shall be considered s 3(1B) tangible property.

3. Member States may consider the following to be tangible property:

    (*a*)   certain interest in immovable property;

    (*b*)   rights *in rem* giving the holder thereof a right of user over immovable property;

    (*c*)   shares or interests equivalent to shares giving the holder thereof *de jure* or *de facto* rights of ownership or possession over immovable property or part thereof.

4. The following shall also be considered supplies within the meaning of paragraph 1:

    (*a*)   the transfer, by order made by or in the name of a public authority or in s 3(1)(D) pursuance of the law, of the ownership of property against payment of compensation;

    (*b*)   the actual handing over of goods, pursuant to a contract for the hire of s 3(1)(B) goods for a certain period or for the sale of goods on deferred ter ms, which provides that in the normal course of events ownership shall pass at the latest upon payment of the final instalment;

    (*c*)   the transfer of goods pursuant to a contract under which commission is s 3(4) pay able on purchase or sale.

s 3(1) **[5.** Member States may consider the handing over of certain works of construction to be supplies with the meaning of paragraph 1.] [1]

s 3(1)(F) **6.** The application by a taxable person of goods forming part of his business assets for his private use or that of his staff, or the disposal thereof free of charge or more generally their application for purposes other than those of his business, where the value added tax on the goods in question or the component parts thereof was wholly or partly deductible, shall be treated as supplies made for consideration. However, applications for the giving of samples or the making of gifts of small value for the purposes of the taxable person's business shall not be so treated.

s 3(1A),
VATR
1979 R 31   **7.** Member States may treat as supplies made for consideration:

s 3(1)(F)   (*a*) the application by a taxable person for the purposes of his business of goods p roduced, constructed, extracted, processed, purchased or imported in the course of such business, where the value added tax on such goods, had they been acquired from another taxable person, would not be wholly deductible;

   (*b*) the application of goods by a taxable person for the purposes of a non-taxable transaction, where the value added tax on such goods became wholly or partly deductible upon their acquisition or upon their application in accordance with subparagraph (*a*);

   (*c*) except in those cases mentioned in paragraph 8, the retention of goods by a taxable person or his successors when he ceases to carry out a taxable economic activity where the value added tax on such goods became wholly or partly deductible upon their acquisition or upon their application in accordance with subparagraph (*a*).

s 3(5)
(B)(III)   **8.** In the event of a transfer, whether for consideration or not or as a contribution to a company, of a totality of assets or part thereof, Member States may consider that no supply of goods has taken place and in that event the recipient shall be treated as the successor to the transferor. Where appropriate, Member States may take the necessary measures to prevent distortion of competition in cases where the recipient is not wholly liable to tax.

Amendments

[1] Substituted by Council Directive 95/7/EC of 10 April 1995 Art 1(1) with effect from 1 January 1996.

Cross-references

Delivery to another taxable person of contract work, and transfer by a taxable person of goods from his undertaking to another member state, regarded as supplies of goods effected for consideration: Art 28a(5).

Case law

Subject	Case	Case reference
Para (1): "capital goods", meaning	*Verbond van Nederlandse Ondernemingen v Inspecteur der Invoerrechten en Accijnzen*	[1977] ECR 113, [1977] 1 CMLR 413, ECJ 51/76
Para (3)(*b*): Supply of goods not limited to legal transfer of property	*Staatssecretaris van Financiën v Shipping and Forwarding Enterprise Safe BV*	[1991] STC 627, ECJ 320/88

"Exploitation", meaning. Rights in rem tangible property	*W M van Tiem v Staatssecretaris van Financiën*	[1991] STI 59, ECJ 186/89
Para (5)(*a*): "made" and "repair": production of goods from customer's materials, a new article is made when its has a different function from the materials provided	*Van Dijk's Boekhuis BV v Staatssecretaris van Financiën*	[1986] 2 CMLR 575, ECJ 139/84
Para (6): A builder (taxable person) who acquired land for his own use and built a house on it only taxable as regards the houses:	*P de Jong v Staatssecretaris van Financiën*	(1992) OJ C135/p 15 ECJ 20/91
Para (6): no VAT arises on disposal of asset where deduction not allowed	*H Kühne v Finanzamt München III*	[1990] STC 749, [1990] 3 CMLR 287, ECJ 50/88
Taxpayer not a taxable person with regard to sale of private dwelling where it was sold together with business premises	*Finamzamt Uelzen v Armbrecht*	[1995] STC 997
Transfer of an undertaking, meaning	*Spijkers (Josef Maria Antonius) v Gebroeders Benedik Abbatoir CV and Alfred Benedik en Zonen BV*	ECJ 24/85
	Dr Sophie Redmond Stichting [Foundation] vHendrikus Bartol and others	ECJ 29/91
Part of a business, meaning	*Commerz-Credit-Bank AG - Europartner v Finanzamt Saarbrücken*	ECJ 50/91
VAT recovery entitlement where related services relate to a transfer of a business	*Abbey National plc v Commissioners of Customs & Excise*	22 February 2001, C–408/98
Fuel management agreement	*Auto Lease Holland BV v Bundesamt für Finanzen*	6 February 2003, C–185/01
Transfer of a totality of assets	*Zita Modes SARL v Administration de l'enregistrement et des domains*	27 November 2003, C –497/01

Article 6
Supply of services

1. "Supply of services" shall mean any transaction which does not constitute a supply of goods within the meaning of Article 5.

Such transactions may include *inter alia*:

s 5(1),
VATR
1979

— assignments of intangible property whether or not it is the subject of a document establishing title,

— obligations to refrain from an act or to tolerate an act or situation,

— the performance of services in pursuance of an order made by or in the name of a public authority or in pursuance of the law.

2. The following shall be treated as supplies of services for consideration:

A 5(3),
VATR
1979 R 24

    (*a*) the use of goods forming part of the assets of a business for the private use of the taxable person or of his staff or more generally for purposes other than those of his business where the value added tax on such goods is wholly or partly deductible;

    (*b*) supplies of services carried out free of charge by the taxable person for his own private use or that of his staff or more generally for purposes other than those of his business.

Member States may derogate from the provisions of this paragraph provided that such derogation does not lead to distortion of competition.

s 5(3)   **3.** In order to prevent distortion of competition and subject to the consultations provided for in Article 29, Member States may treat as a supply of services for consideration the supply by a taxable person of a service for the purposes of his undertaking where the value added tax on such a service, had it been supplied by another taxable person, would not be wholly deductible.

s 5(4)   **4.** Where a taxable person acting in his own name but on behalf of another takes part in a supply of services, he shall be considered to have received and supplied those services himself.

s 5(8)

5. Article 5(8) shall apply in like manner to the supply of services.

Case law

Subject	Case	Case reference
Para (1): Where a farmer received compensation for discontinuing milk production, there was no "consumption" within the meaning of article 2 of the First Directive, and therefore no supply of services	*Mohr v Finamzamt Bad Segeberg*	ECJ 215/94, [1996] STC 328
Provision of restaurant meals is a service	*Faaborg Gelting Linien A/S v Finamzamt Flensburg*	[1996] STC 774, ECJ 231/94
Para (2): transport company providing transport service and cash collection service, collection charge was regarded as inseparable from and ancillary to the transport service	*NV Nederlandse Spoorwegen v Staatssecretaris van Financiën*	[1979] ECR 2041, [1980] 1 CMLR 144, ECJ 126/78
Self-supply, Private use of business-owned car, whether associated expenses part of taxable amount	*Finamzämt München v Mohsche*	[1997] STC 195, ECJ 193/91
Production of goods from customer's materials, a new article is made when its has a different function from the materials provided	*Van Dijk's Boekhuis BV v Staatssecretaris van Financiën*	[1986] 2 CMLR 575, ECJ 139/84

Article 7
Imports

s 15

[1. "Importation of goods" shall mean:

    (*a*)   the entry into the Community of goods which do not fulfil the conditions laid down in Articles 9 and 10 of the Treaty establishing the European Economic Community or, where the goods are covered by the Treaty establishing the European Coal and Steel Community, are not in free circulation;

    [(*b*) the entry into the Community of goods from a third territory, other than the goods covered by (*a*).] [1]

2. The place of import of goods shall be the Member State within the territory of which the goods are when they enter the Community.

3. Notwithstanding paragraph 2, where goods referred to in paragraph 1(*a*) are, on entry into the Community, placed under one of the arrangements referred to in Article 16(1)(B)[(*a*), (*b*), (*c*) and (*d*)] ,[2] under arrangements for temporary importation with total exemption from import duty or under external transit arrangements, the place of import of such goods shall be the Member State within the territory of which they cease to be covered by those arrangements.

[Similarly, when goods referred to in paragraph 1(*b*) are placed, on entry into the Community, under one of the procedures referred to in Article 33a(1)(*b*) or (*c*), the place of import shall be the Member State within whose territory this procedure ceases to apply.] [3] [4]

Amendments

[1]   Para (1)(*b*) substituted by Council Directive 92/111/EEC of 14 December 1992 Art 1(3), with effect from 1 January 1993.

[2]   Added by Council Directive of 14 December 1992 Art 1(2), with effect from 1 January 1993.

[3]   Substituted by Council Directive of 14 December 1992 Art 1(1), with effect from 1 January 1993.

[4]   Art 7 substituted by Council Directive 91/680/EEC of 18 December 1991 Art 1(2), with effect from 1 January 1993.

Case law

Subject	Case	Case reference
Importation into the Netherlands from the Netherlands Antilles deemed to be an importation into the EC	*Van der Kooy v Staatsecretaris van Financien*	29 January 1999, C–181/97
Imports — Removal of Goods from Customs Arrangements	*Liberexim BV v Staatssecretaris van Financiën*	11 July 2002, C–371/99

TITLE VI

PLACE OF TAXABLE TRANSACTIONS

Article 8

Supply of goods

s 3(6)(A)

1. The place of supply of goods shall be deemed to be:

s 3(6)(B)   (*a*) in the case of goods dispatched or transported either by the supplier or by the person to whom they are supplied or by a third person: the place where the goods are at the time when dispatch or transport to the person to whom they are supplied begins. Where the goods are installed or assembled, with or without a trial run, by or on behalf of the supplier, the place of supply shall be deemed to be the place where the goods are installed or assembled. In cases where the installation or assembly is carried out [in a Member State other than] [1] that of the supplier, [the Member State within the territory of which the installation or assembly is carried out] [2] shall take any necessary steps to avoid double taxation in that State;

s 3(6)(C)   (*b*) in the case of goods not dispatched or transported: the place where the goods are when the supply takes place.

s 3(6)(C)   [(*c*) in the case of goods supplied on board ships, aircraft or trains during the part of a transport of passengers effected in the Community: at the point of the departure of the transport of passengers.

For the purposes of applying this provision:

— **"part of a transport of passengers effected in the Community"** shall mean the part of the transport effected, without a stop in a third territory, between the point of departure and the point of arrival of the transport of passengers,

— **"the point of departure of the transport of passengers"** shall mean the first point of passenger embarkation foreseen within the Community, where relevant after a leg outside the Community,

— **"the point of arrival of the transport of passengers"** shall mean the last point of disembarkation of passengers foreseen within the Community of passengers who embarked in the Community, where relevant before a leg outside the Community.

In the case of a return trip, the return leg shall be considered to be a separate transport.

The Commission shall, by 30 June 1993 at the latest, submit to the Council a report accompanied, if necessary, by appropriate proposals on the place of taxation of goods supplied for consumption and services, including restaurant services, provided for passengers on board ships, aircraft or trains.

By 31 December 1993, after consulting the European Parliament, the Council shall take a unanimous decision on the Commission proposal.

Until 31 December 1993, Member States may exempt or continue to exempt goods supplied for consumption on board whose place of taxation is determined in accordance with the above provisions, with the right to deduct the value added tax paid at an earlier stage.] [3]

[(*d*) in the case of the supply of gas through the natural gas distribution system, or of electricity, to a taxable dealer: the place where that taxable dealer has established his business or has a fixed establishment for which the goods are supplied, or, in the absence of such a place of business or fixed establishment, the place where he has his permanent address or usually resides.

"Taxable dealer" for the purposes of this provision means a taxable person whose principal activity in respect of purchases of gas and electricity is reselling such products and whose own consumption of these products is negligible.

(*e*) in the case of the supply of gas through the natural gas distribution system, or of electricity, where such a supply is not covered by point (*d*): the place where the customer has effective use and consumption of the goods. Where all or part of the goods are not in fact consumed by this customer, these non consumed goods are deemed to have been used and consumed at the place where he has established his business or has a fixed establishment for which the goods are supplied. In the absence of such a place of business or fixed establishment, he is deemed to have used and consumed the goods at the place where he has his permanent address or usually resides.] [4]

[**2.** By way of derogation from paragraph 1(*a*), where the place of departure of s 3(6)(A) the consignment or transport of goods is in a third territory, the place of supply by the importer as defined in [Article 21(4)] [5] and the place of any subsequent supplies shall be deemed to be within the Member State of import of the goods.] [6]

Amendments

[1]   Substituted by Council Directive 91/680/EEC of 16 December 1991, Art 1(3) with effect from 1 January 1993.

[2]   Substituted by Council Directive 91/680/EEC of 16 December 1991, Art 1(5) with effect from 1 January 1993.

[3]   Para (1)(*c*) substituted by Council Directive 92/111/EEC of 14 December 1992 Art 1(4) with effect from 1 January 1993.

[4]   Substituted by Council Directive 2000/65/EC of 17 October 2000 (OJ L 269, 21/10/2000 p 44–46) Art 1(6) with effect from 17 October 2000; previously "Article 21(2)".

[5]   Para (1)(*d*)–(*e*) inserted by Council Directive 2003/92/EC of 7 October 2003, Art 1(1) with effect from 11 October 2003.

[6]   Para (2) substituted by Council Directive 91/680/EEC of 16 December 1991, art1(5), with effect from 1 January 1993.

Cross-references

Derogation from Art 8(1)(*a*) and (2): Art 28b(B).

Article 9
Supply of services

s 5(5)   **1.** The place where a service is supplied shall be deemed to be the place where the supplier has established his business or has a fixed establishment from which the service is supplied or, in the absence of such a place of business or fixed establishment, the place where he has his permanent address or usually resides.

2. However:

s 5(6)(A)   (*a*)   the place of the supply of services connected with immovable property, including the services of estate agents and experts, and of services for preparing and coordinating construction works, such as the services of architects and of firms providing on-site supervision, shall be the place where the property is situated;

s 5(6)(B)   (*b*)   the place where transport services are supplied shall be the place where transport takes place, having regard to the distances covered;

s 5(6)(C)   (*c*)   the place of the supply of services relating to:

— cultural, artistic, sporting, scientific, educational, entertainment or similar activities, including the activities of the organizers of such activities, and where appropriate, the supply of ancillary services,

— ancillary transport activities such as loading, unloading, handling and similar activities,

— valuations of movable tangible property,

— work on movable tangible property,

shall be the place where those services are physically carried out;

(*d*)   ...¹

s 5(6)(E),   (*e*)   the place where the following services are supplied when performed for
SCH 4   customers established outside the Community or for taxable persons established in the Community but not in the same country as the supplier, shall be the place where the customer has established his business or has a fixed establishment to which the service is supplied or, in the absence of such a place, the place where he has his permanent address or usually resides:

— transfers and assignments of copyrights, patents, licences, trade marks and similar rights,

— advertising services,

— services of consultants, engineers, consultancy bureaux, lawyers, accountants and other similar services, as well as data processing and the supplying of information,

— obligations to refrain from pursuing or exercising, in whole or in part, a business activity or a right referred to in this point (*e*),

— banking, financial and insurance transactions including reinsurance, with the exception of the hire of safes,

— the supply of staff,

— the services of agents who act in the name and for the account of another, when they procure for their principal the services referred to in this point (*e*),

[— the hiring out of movable tangible property with the exception of all forms of transport] ;²

[— the provision of access to, and of transport or transmission through, natural gas and electricity distribution systems and the provision of other directly linked services.] ³

[— Telecommunications. Telecommunications services shall be deemed to be services relating to the transmission, emission or reception of signals, writing, images and sounds or information of any nature by wire, radio, optical or other electromagnetic systems, including the related transfer or assignment of the right to use capacity for such transmission, emission or reception. Telecommunications services within the meaning of this provision shall also include provision of access to global information networks] ⁴[,

— radio and television broadcasting services,

— electronically supplied services, inter alia, those described in Annex L.] ⁵

[(*f*) the place where services referred to in the last indent of subparagraph (*e*) are supplied when performed for non-taxable persons who are established, have their permanent address or usually reside in a Member State, by a taxable person who has established his business or has a fixed establishment from which the service is supplied outside the Community or, in the absence of such a place of business or fixed establishment, has his permanent address or usually resides outside the Community, shall be the place where the non-taxable person is established, has his permanent address or usually resides.] ⁶

[3. In order to avoid double taxation, non-taxation or the distortion of competition, the Member States may, with regard to the supply of services referred to in paragraph 2(*e*), except for the services referred to in the last indent when supplied to non-taxable persons, and also with regard to the hiring out of forms of transport consider:] ⁷

(*a*) the place of supply of services, which under this Article would be situated within the territory of the country, as being situated outside the Community where the effective use and enjoyment of the services take place outside the Community;

(*b*) the place of supply of services, which under this Article would be situated outside the Community, as being within the territory of the country where the effective use and enjoyment of the services take place within the territory of the country.

[4. In the case of telecommunications services and radio and television broadcasting services referred to in paragraph 2(*e*) when performed for non-taxable persons who are established, have their permanent address or usually reside in a Member State, by a taxable person who has established his business or has a fixed establishment from which the service is supplied outside the

Community, or in the absence of such a place of business or fixed establishment, has his permanent address or usually resides outside the Community, Member States shall make use of paragraph 3(*b*).] [8]

Amendments

[1] Deleted by Council Directive 84/386/EEC (Tenth Directive) of 31 July 1984, Art 1 with effect from 1 July 1985.

[2] Inserted by Council Directive 84/386/EEC (Tenth Directive) of 31 July 1984, Art 1 with effect from 1 July 1985.

[3] Indent added by Council Directive 2003/92/EC of 7 October 2003, Art 1(2) with effect from 11 October 2003.

[4] Inserted by Council Directive 99/59/EC of 17 June 1999, Art 1 with effect from 1 January 2000.

[5] Inserted by Council Directive 2002/38/EC of 7 May 2002 (OJ L128, 15.5.2002, p 41) Art 1(1)(*a*) for a period of 3 years beginning on 1 July 2003.

[6] Inserted by Council Directive 2002/38/EC of 7 May 2002 (OJ L128, 15.5.2002, p 41) Art 1(1)(*b*) for a period of 3 years beginning on 1 July 2003.

[7] Substituted by Council Directive 2002/38/EC of 7 May 2002 (OJ L128, 15.5.2002, p 41) art 1(1)(*c*) for a period of 3 years beginning on 1 July 2003; previously "**3.** In order to avoid double taxation, non-taxation or the distortion of competition the Member States may, with regard to the supply of services referred to in 2(*e*) [and the hiring out of forms of transport] [4] consider:

    [4] Substituted by Council Directive 84/386/EEC (Tenth Directive) of 31 July 1984, Art 1 with effect from 1 July 1985.".

[8] Substituted by Council Directive 2002/38/EC of 7 May 2002 (OJ L128, 15.5.2002, p 41) art 1(1)(*d*) for a period of 3 years beginning on 1 July 2003; previously "[**4.** In the case of telecommunications services referred to in paragraph 2(*e*) supplied by a taxable person established outside the Community to non-taxable persons established inside the Community, Member States shall make use of paragraph 3(*b*).] [5]

    [5] Inserted by Council Directive 99/59/EC of 17 June 1999, Art 2 with effect from 1 January 2000.".

Cross-references

Derogation from Art 9(2)(*b*), 9(2)(*c*) and 9(1) respectively: Art 28b(C), (D), (E).

Case law

Subject	Case	Case reference
Para (1): Services (gaming machines) supplied on board ships over which a member state has jurisdiction taxable even if outside the member State's territorial jurisdiction; meaning of "fixed establishment"	*Berkholz v Finanzampt Hamburg-Mitte-Altstadt*	[1985] 3 CMLR 667, ECJ 168/84
Restaurant meals provided on ferry travelling between Denmark and Germany regarded as supplied where the ferry operator had its principal establishment	*Faaborg Gelting Linien A/S v Finamzamt Flensburg*	[1996] STC 774, ECJ 231/94
Para (1): Hire of means of transport supplied provided from hirer's establishment	*Aro Lease BV v Inspector der Belastngllienst Grote Ouderingen, Amsterdam*	ECJ 190/95
Para (2)(*c*): Sound engineering services provided at concerts and entertainment events regarded as supplied where physically performed	*Dudda v Finamzamt Bergisch Gladbach*	[1996] STC 1290, ECJ 327/94

Para (2)(*e*): Advertising services, meaning	*EC Commission v France, Luxembourg, Spain*	[1993] STI 1424, ECJ cases 68, 69 and 73/92
Place of supply of services — no fixed establishment in another Member State merely by virtue of hiring out or leasing cars to clients in that Member State	*Lease Plan Luxembourg S\A v The Belgium State*	7 May 1998, C–390/96
Place of supply of services deemed to be the place of the supplier's business or fixed establishment etc	*Maatschap MJM Lindhorst, KPPG Powels & Scheres v Inspecteur der Omzetbelastingdienst Ondermingen*	6 March 1997, C–167/95
Community definition of a lawyer. Supply of the services of an arbitrator would be where that arbitrator established his business	*Von Hoffmann v Finanzamt Trier*	September 1997, C–145/96
Place of supply — advertising services	*Design Concept SA v Flanders Expo SA*	5 June 2003, C–438/01
Concept of taxable person — place where services are supplied — SICAV	*Banque Bruxelles Lambert SA v the Belgin State*	21 October 2004, C–8/03
Transfer of softwear and related services	*Levob Verzekeringen BV v Staatssecretaris van Financiën*	27 October 2005, C–41/04

TITLE VII
CHARGEABLE EVENT AND CHARGEABILITY OF TAX

Article 10

1. (*a*) **"Chargeable event"** shall mean the occurrence by virtue of which the legal conditions necessary for tax to become chargeable are fulfilled. ss 15,19(1), 19(3)

   (*b*) The tax becomes **"chargeable"** when the tax authority becomes entitled under the law at a given moment to claim the tax from the person liable to pay, notwithstanding that the time of payment may be deferred.

2. The chargeable event shall occur and the tax shall become chargeable when the goods are delivered or the services are performed. Deliveries of goods other than those referred to in Article 5(4)(*b*) and supplies of services which give rise to successive statements of account or payments shall be regarded as being completed at the time when the periods to which such statements of account or payments pertain expire. [Member States may in certain cases provide that continuous supplies of goods and services which take place over a period of time shall be regarded as being completed at least at intervals of one year.] [1]

However, where a payment is to be made on account before the goods are delivered or the services are performed, the tax shall become chargeable on receipt of the payment and on the amount received. s 19(2)

By way of derogation from the above provisions, Member States may provide that the tax shall become chargeable, for certain transactions or for certain categories of taxable person, either:

S 14

— no later than the issue of the invoice ...[2], or

— no later than receipt of the price, or

— where an invoice ...[2] is not issued, or is issued late, within a specified period from the date of the chargeable event.

[**3.** The chargeable event shall occur and the tax shall become chargeable when the goods are imported. Where goods are placed under one of the arrangements referred to in Article 7(3) on entry into the Community, the chargeable event shall occur and the tax shall become chargeable only when the goods cease to be covered by those arrangements.

However, where imported goods are subject to customs duties, to agricultural levies or to charges having equivalent effect established under a common policy, the chargeable event shall occur and the tax shall become chargeable when the chargeable event for those Community duties occurs and those duties become chargeable.

Where imported goods are not subject to any of those Community duties, Member States shall apply the provisions in force governing customs duties as regards the occurrence of the chargeable event and the moment when the tax becomes chargeable.] [3]

Amendments

[1]   Inserted by Council Directive 2000/65/EC of 17 October 2000 (OJ L 269, 21/10/2000 p 44–46) Art 1(1) with effect from 17 October 2000.

[2]   Deleted by Council Directive 2001/111/EC of 20 December 2001 Art 4(1) with effect from 6 February 2002; previously "or of the document serving as invoice".

[3]   Para (3) substituted by Council Directive 91/680/EEC of 16 December 1991, Art 1(6) with effect from 1 January 1993.

Case law

Subject	Case	Case reference
Chargeable event occurs when goods are definitively (not temporarily) imported	*Pezullo Molini Pastifici SpA v Ministero delle Finanze*	[1996] STC 1236, ECJ 166/94
Interim payments of VAT required by Italian law precluded by articles 10 and 22(4)	*Balocchi v Ministero delle Finanze dello Stato*	[1993] STI 1348, ECJ 10/92
Italian derogation allowed receipt of price to be the chargeable event	*Ufficio IVA di Trapani v Italittica SpA*	[1995] STC 1059, ECJ
Time when service supplied not to be identified with invoice issue date or date payment on account received (if later)	*Impresa Construzioni Comm Quirino Mazzalai v Ferrovia del Renon SpA*	[1976] ECR 657, 1977 1 CMLR 105, ECJ 111/75
Stolen goods	*Les Assurances Du Crédit NV v Bowy and Decoopmann*	ECJ 205/90

TITLE VIII
TAXABLE AMOUNT

Article 11

A. Within the territory of the country

s 10

1. The taxable amount shall be:

(*a*) in respect of supplies of goods and services other than those referred to s 10(1) in (*b*), (*c*) and (*d*) below, everything which constitutes the consideration which has been or is to be obtained by the supplier from the purchaser, the customer or a third party for such supplies including subsidies directly linked to the price of such supplies;

(*b*) in respect of supplies referred to in Article 5(6) and (7), the purchase price of the goods or of similar goods or, in the absence of a purchase price, the cost price, determined at the time of supply;

(*c*) in respect of supplies referred to in Article 6(2), the full cost to the taxable person of providing the services;

(*d*) in respect of supplies referred to in Article 6(3), the open market value of the services supplied.

"Open market value" of services shall mean the amount which a customer at s 10(10) the marketing stage at which the supply takes place would have to pay to a supplier at arm's length within the territory of the country at the time of the supply under conditions of fair competition to obtain the services in question.

2. The taxable amount shall include:

(*a*) taxes, duties, levies and charges, excluding the value added tax itself;

(*b*) incidental expenses such as commission, packing, transport and insurance costs charged by the supplier to the purchaser or customer. Expenses covered by a separate agreement may be considered to be incidental expenses by the Member States.

VATR
1979 R 8

3. The taxable amount shall not include:

(*a*) price reductions by way of discount for early payment;

(*b*) price discounts and rebates allowed to the customer and accounted for at the time of the supply;

(*c*) the amounts received by a taxable person from his purchaser or customer as repayment for expenses paid out in the name and for the account of the latter and which are entered in his books in a suspense account. The taxable person must furnish proof of the actual amount of this expenditure and may not deduct any tax which may have been charged on these transactions.

[**4.** By way of derogation from paragraphs 1, 2 and 3, Member States which, on 1 January 1993, did not avail themselves of the option provided for in the third subparagraph of Article 12(3)(*a*) may, where they avail themselves of the option provided for in Title B(6), provide that, for the transactions referred to in the second subparagraph of Article 12(3)(*c*), the taxable amount shall be equal to a fraction of the amount determined in accordance with paragraphs 1, 2 and 3.

That fraction shall be determined in such a way that the value added tax thus due is, in any event, equal to at least 5% of the amount determined in accordance with paragraphs 1, 2 and 3.] [1]

B. Importation of goods

[1. The taxable amount shall be the value for customs purposes, determined in accordance with the Community provisions in force; this shall also apply for the import of goods referred to in Article 7(1)(b).] [2]

2. ...[3]

[3. The taxable amount shall include, insofar as they are not already included:

(a) taxes, duties, levies and other charges due outside the importing Member State and those due by reason of importation, excluding the value added tax to be levied;

(b) incidental expenses, such as commission, packing, transport and insurance costs, incurred up to the first place of destination within the territory of the importing Member State.

"First place of destination" shall mean the place mentioned on the consignment note or any other document by means of which the goods are imported into the importing Member State. In the absence of such an indication, the first place of destination shall be taken to be the place of the first transfer of cargo in the importing Member State.

[The incidental expenses referred to above shall also be included in the taxable amount where they result from transport to another place of destination within the territory of the Community if that place is known when the chargeable event occurs.] [4] [5]

4. The taxable amount shall not include those factors referred to in A(3)(a) and (b).

5. When goods have been temporarily exported [from the Community] [6] and are re- imported after having undergone [outside the Community] [7] repair, processing or adaptation, or after having been made up or reworked [outside the Community] [7], ...[8], Member States shall take steps to ensure that the treatment of the goods for value added tax purposes is the same as that which would have applied to the goods in question had the above operations been carried out within the territory of the country.

[6. By way of derogation from paragraphs 1 to 4, Member States which, on 1 January 1993, did not avail themselves of the option provided for in the third paragraph of Article 12(3)(a) may provide that for imports of the works of art, collectors' items and antiques defined in Article 26a(A)(a), (b) and (c), the taxable amount shall be equal to a fraction of the amount determined in accordance with paragraphs 1 to 4.

That fraction shall be determined in such a way that the value added tax thus due on the import is, in any event, equal to at least 5% of the amount determined in accordance with paragraphs 1 to 4.] [9]

C. Miscellaneous provisions

1. In the case of cancellation, refusal or total or partial non-payment, or where the s 10(3)(c) price is reduced after the supply takes place, the taxable amount shall be reduced accordingly under conditions which shall be determined by the Member States.

However, in the case of total or partial non-payment, Member States may derogate from this rule.

[**2.** Where information for determining the taxable amount on importation is expressed in a currency other than that of the Member State where assessment takes place, the exchange rate shall be determined in accordance with the Community provisions governing the calculation of the value for customs purposes.

Where information for the determination of the taxable amount of a transaction other than an import transaction is expressed in a currency other than that of the Member State where assessment takes place, the exchange rate applicable shall be the latest selling rate recorded, at the time the tax becomes chargeable, on the most representative exchange market or markets of the Member State concerned, or a rate determined by reference to that or those markets, in accordance with the procedures laid down by that Member State. However, for some of those transactions or for certain categories of taxable person, Member States may continue to apply the exchange rate determined in accordance with the Community provisions in force governing the calculation of the value for customs purposes.] [10]

3. As regards returnable packing costs, Member States may:
— either exclude them from the taxable amount and take the necessary measures to see that this amount is adjusted if the packing is not returned,
— or include them in the taxable amount and take the necessary measures to see that this amount is adjusted where the packing is in fact returned.

Amendments

[1]   Art 11A(4) inserted by Council Directive 94/5/EC of 14 February 1994 Art 1(1)(*a*) with effect from 1 January 1995.

[2]   Art 11B(1) substituted by Council Directive 92/111/EEC of 14 December 1992, Art 1(5) with effect from 1 January 1993.

[3]   Art 11B(2) deleted by Council Directive 91/680/EEC of 16 December 1991, Art 1(7)(2nd indent) with effect from 1 January 1993.

[4]   Substituted by Council Directive 95/7/EC of 10 April 1995 Art 1(2) with effect from 1 January 1996.

[5]   Art 11B(3) substituted by Council Directive 91/680/EEC of 16 December 1991, Art 1(8) with effect from 1 January 1993.

[6]   Words in Art 11B(5) added by Council Directive 91/680/EEC of 16 December 1991, Art 1(9) with effect from 1 January 1993.

[7]   Substituted by Council Directive 91/680/EEC of 16 December 1991, Art 1(9) with effect from 1 January 1993.

[8]   Deleted by Council Directive 91/680/EEC of 16 December 1991, Art 1(*a*) with effect from 1 January 1993.

[9]   Art 11B(6) inserted by Council Directive 94/5/EC of 14 February 1994 Art 1(1)(*b*) with effect from 1 January 1995.

[10]   Art 11C(2) substituted by Council Directive 91/680/EEC of 16 December 1991, Art 1(10) with effect from 1 January 1993.

Case law

Subject	Case	Case reference
Art 27: Law imposing minimum basis of assessment was not within German Art 27 derogation where consideration was at market rate and there was no tax avoidance	*Werner Skripalle*	ECJ 63/96
Credit card transaction, retailer's gross consideration (including credit card commission) is the taxable amount	*Chaussures Bally SA v Ministry of Finance (Belgium)*	[1997] STC 209, ECJ 18/92
Collection of charge for goods by person delivering them	*NV Nederlandse Spoorwegen v Staatssecretaris van Financiën*	[1979] ECR 2041, [1980] 1 CMLR 144, ECJ 126/78
Compensation received for discontinuing milk production did not constitute supply of services (art 6(1)) as there was no "consumption" within the meaning of article 2 of the First Directive, and therefore no taxable amount (11A(1)(*a*))	*Mohr v Finamzamt Bad Segeberg*	ECJ 215/94, [1996] STC 328
Gaming machine takings, taxable amount	*Glawe Spiel (HJ) und Unterhaltungsgeräte Aufstellungsgesellschaft mbH & Co KG v Finamzamt Hamburg-Barmbek-Uhlenhorst*	[1994] STC 543, ECJ 38/93
Goods supplied free of charge on introduction of new customer, taxable amount	*Empire Stores Ltd v C & E Commissioners*	[1994] STC 638, ECJ 33/93
Greek arrangements whereby petrol was charged to VAT once only on importation (and not along the supply chain) were held to be in breach of Art 11A(1), 11B(1) and (2)	*BP Soupgas Anonimos Etairia Geniki Emporiki Viomichaniki Kai Antiprossopeion v Greece*	[1995] STC 805, ECJ 62/93
No subjective consideration for services	*Staatsecretaris van Financiën v Cooperatieve Aardappelen Bewaarplaats GA*	ECJ 154/80
Interest payable prior to the payment of the full price is regarded as part of the consideration; interest payable after the date of the supply constitutes granting of credit and is exempt	*Muys' en De Winter's Bouw-en Aannwmingsbedrijf BV v Staatsecretaris van Financiën*	[1993] STI 1367, ECJ 281/91
Interest (penalty) on late payment of court judgment not taxable	*BAZ Bausystem AG v Finanzamt München für Körperschaften*	[1982] ECR 2527, [1982] 3 CMLR 688, ECJ 222/81
Vouchers, taxable amount is the net amount actually received	*Argos Distributors Ltd v C & E Commissioners*	[1996] STC 359, ECJ 288/94
Tax authorities may not receive VAT greater than paid by final consumer	*Elida Gibbs Ltd v C & E Commissioners*	[1996] STC 1388, ECJ 317/94

Refusal of C & E to refund tax where unpaid consideration is not expressed in money UK government had exceeded its authority	*Goldsmiths (Jewellers) Ltd v The Commissioners C & E*	3 July 1997, C–33-/95
Taxable status of credit card commission	*SA Chasseures Bally v The Belgium State*	25 May 1993, C–18/92
Vouchers, rebates and taxable amount. VAT taxable amount. Giving vouchers is a supply for consideration	*Kuwait Petroleum (GB) Ltd v The Commissioners C & E*	27 April 1999, C–48/97, [1999] STC 488

Open market value

Art 11A(1): Wholesaler supplying "inducement" goods to retailer	*Naturally Yours Cosmetics Ltd v C & E Commissioners*	[1988] STC [1989] CMLR 797, ECJ 230/87
Art 11A(3)(*b*): Coupons accepted in part payment, "open market value" includes the difference between normal retail price and actual sum received where retailer receives a coupon given to the customer on previous purchase a normal retail sale price	*Boots Co plc v C & E Commissioners*	[1990] STC 387, ECJ 126/88
Rounding off of amounts due	*'K' Line Air Service Europe BV v Eulaerts NV and Belgian State Taxation*	ECJ 131/91

Pre-single market (residual VAT)

Residual VAT in imported goods	*Bergeres-Becque v Chef de Service Interregional des Douanes*	[1986] 2 CMLR 143, ECJ 39/85
Used goods imported from another EC State	*Gaston Schul, Douane Expediteur BV v Inspecteur der Invoerrechten en Accijnzen*	[1982] ECR 1409, [1982] 3 CMLR 229, ECJ 15/81
Failure to comply with judgment of the Court	*Re VAT on Motor Cars, EC Commission v Belgium*	[1989] 2 CMLR 972, ECJ 391/85
Taxable amount on imported goods purchased from private individual	*Staatssecretaris van Financiën v Gaston Schul Douane Expediteur BV*	[1986] 1 CMLR 559, ECJ 47/84
Service charges	*EC Commission v France*	29 March 2001, C–404/99
Taxable amount involving credit sale of goods with credit granted by third party at no cost to customer	*Primback v Commissioners of Customs & Excise*	15 May 2001, C–34/99
Treatment of Grants	*Keeping Newcastle Warm Ltd v Commissioners of Customs & Excise*	13 June 2002, C–353/00
Taxable Amount — Reduction Coupons	*Yorkshire Co-operatives Ltd v Commissioners of Customs & Excise*	16 January 2003, C–398/99
Taxable Amount — Money Off Coupons	*Commission v Federal Republic of Germany*	15 October 2002, C–427/98

| Taxable Amount — Competition Entry Fees | *Town & County Factors Ltd v Commissioners of Customs & Excise* | 17 September 2002, C–498/99 |
| VAT Repayments — Time Limits | *Marks & Spencer plc v Commissioners of Customs & Excise* | 11 July 2002, C–62/00 |

TITLE IX
RATES

s 11

Article 12

1. The rate applicable to taxable transactions shall be that in force at the time of the chargeable event. However:

> (*a*) in the cases provided for in the second and third subparagraphs of Article 10(2), the rate to be used shall be that in force when the tax becomes chargeable;
>
> (*b*) in the cases provided for in the second and third subparagraphs of Article 10(3), the rate applicable shall be that in force at the time when the tax becomes chargeable.] [1]

ART 28.2 **2.** In the event of changes in the rates, Member States may:

> — effect adjustments in the cases provided for in paragraph 1(*a*) in order to take account of the rate applicable at the time when the goods or services were supplied,
>
> — adopt all appropriate transitional measures.

3. [(*a*) The standard rate of value added tax shall be fixed by each Member State as a percentage of the taxable amount and shall be the same for the supply of goods and for the supply of services. From 1 January 2001 to 31 December 2005, this percentage may not be less than 15%.

> On a proposal from the Commission and after consulting the European Parliament and the Economic and Social Committee, the Council shall decide unanimously on the level of the standard rate to be applied after 31 December 2005.] [2]

> Member States may also apply either one or two reduced rates. These rates shall be fixed as a percentage of the taxable amount, which may not be less than 5%, and shall apply only to supplies of the categories of goods and services specified in Annex H.] [3]

> [The third subparagraph shall not apply to the services referred to in the last indent of Article 9(2)(*e*).] [4]

> (*b*) Member States may apply a reduced rate to supplies of natural gas and electricity provided that no risk of distortion of completion exists. A Member State intending to apply such a rate must, before doing so, inform the Commission. The Commission shall give a decision on the

existence of a risk of distortion of competition. If the Commission has not taken that decision within three months of the receipt of the information a risk of distortion of competition is deemed not to exist.

[(c) Member States may provide that the reduced rate, or one of the reduced rates, which they apply in accordance with the third paragraph of (*a*) shall also apply to imports of works of art, collectors' items and antiques as referred to in Article 26a(A)(*a*), (*b*) and (*c*).

Where they avail themselves of this option, Member States may also apply the reduced rate to supplies of every work of art, within the meaning of Article 26a(A)(*a*):

— effected by their creator or his successors in title,

— effected on an occasional basis by a taxable person other than a taxable dealer, where these works of art have been imported by the taxable person himself or where they have been supplied to him by their creator or his successors in title or where they have entitled him to full deduction of value added tax.] [5]

...[6]

...[7]

Member States will take all necessary measures to combat fraud in this area from 1 January 1993. These measures may include the introduction of a system of accounting for VAT on supplies of gold between taxable persons in the same Member State which provides for the payment of tax by the buyer on behalf of the seller and a simultaneous right for the buyer to a deduction of the same amount of tax as input tax.] [8]

4. ....[9] Each reduced rate shall be so fixed that the amount of value added tax resulting from the application thereof shall be such as in the normal way to permit the deduction therefrom of the whole of the value added tax deductible under the provisions of Article 17.

[On the basis of a report from the Commission, the Council shall starting in 1994, review the scope of the reduced rates every two years. The Council, acting unanimously on a proposal from the Commission, may decide to alter the list of goods and services in Annex H.] [10]

[**5.** Subject to paragraph 3(*c*), the rate applicable on the importation of goods shall be that applied to the supply of like goods within the territory of the country.] [11]

[**6.** The Portuguese Republic may apply to transactions carried out in the autonomous regions of the Azores and Madeira and to direct imports to those regions, reduced rates in comparison to those applying on the mainland.] [12]

Amendments

[1] Para (1)(*b*) substituted by Council Directive 92/111/EEC of 14 December 1992, Art 1(6) with effect from 1 January 1993.

[2] Para (3)(*a*) first and second subparagraphs substituted by Council Directive 2001/41/EC of 19 January 2001 Art 1 with effect from 21 July 2001.

[3] Para (3)(*a*) substituted by Council Directive 99/49/EC of 25 May 1999, Art 1 with effect from 1 January 1999.

[4] Inserted by Council Directive 2002/38/EC of 7 May 2002 (OJ L128, 15.5.2002, p 41) Art 1(2) for a period of 3 years beginning on 1 July 2003.

[5] Para (3)(*b*) substituted by Council Directive 94/5/EEC of 14 February 1994, Art 1(2)(*a*) with effect from 1 January 1995.

[6] Para (3)(*d*) deleted by Council Directive 96/42/EC of 25 June 1996 with effect from 1 January 1995.

[7] Para (3) substituted by Council Directive 92/77/EEC of 19 October 1992, Art 1(1).

[8] Para (3)(*e*) deleted by Council Directive 98/80/EC of 12 October 1998 (OJ L 281, 17/10/1998 p 31–34) Art 2 with effect from 17 October 1998.

[9] Deleted by Council Directive 92/77/EEC of 19 October 1992, Art 1(3) with effect from 1 January 1993.

[10] Inserted by Council Directive 92/77/EEC of 19 October 1992, Art 1(3) with effect from 1 January 1993.

[11] Para (5) substituted by Council Directive 94/5/EC of 14 February 1994 Art 1(2)(*b*) with effect from 1 January 1995.

[12] Para (6) inserted by the Act of Accession 1985 Art 26, Annex I, Part V, point 2.

Case law

Subject	Case	Case reference
Production of goods from customer's materials, a new article is made when its has a different function from the materials provided	*Van Dijk's Boekhuis BV v Staatssecretaris van Financiën*	[1986] 2 CMLR 575, ECJ 139/84
"Clearly defined social reasons" for zero rating (VAT on electricity supplied to businesses)	*EC Commission v Ireland*	[1988] 3 CMLR 189, ECJ 415/85
	EC Commission v United Kingdom	[1988] STC 456, [1989] 1 All ER 364, [1988] 3 CMLR 169, ECJ 416/85
Discriminatory tax rates		
Imported works of art	*Krystyna Gmurzynska-Bscher v Oberfinanzdirektion Köln*	ECJ 231/89
Differential taxation	*EC Commission v Greece*	ECJ 278/83 and 200/85
Differing VAT rates (under Italian law on) different sparkling wines — the classification used was deemed to discriminate against imports	*Re Italian VAT on sparkling wines, EC Commission v Italy*	[1985] 3 CMLR 688, ECJ 278/83
See also (no discrimination)	*Re VAT on Diesel Cars, EC Commission v Italy*	[1988] 1 CMLR 97, ECJ 200/85

TITLE X

EXEMPTIONS

Article 13

Exemptions within the territory of the country

s 6(1)

A. Exemptions for certain activities in the public interest

1. Without prejudice to other Community provisions, Member States shall exempt the following under conditions which they shall lay down for the purpose of ensuring the correct and straightforward application of such exemptions and of preventing any possible evasion, avoidance or abuse:

(*a*) the supply by the public postal services of services other than passenger transport and telecommunications services, and the supply of goods incidental thereto;   Sch 1(xia)

(*b*) hospital and medical care and closely related activities undertaken by bodies governed by public law or, under social conditions comparable to those applicable to bodies governed by public law, by hospitals, centres for medical treatment or diagnosis and other duly recognized establishments of a similar nature;   Sch 1(iii)– (iiib),(v), (xxv)

(*c*) the provision of medical care in the exercise of the medical and paramedical professions as defined by the Member State concerned;   Sch 1(iii)– (iiib),(v)

(*d*) supplies of human organs, blood and milk;   Sch 1 (xviii)

(*e*) services supplied by dental technicians in their professional capacity and dental prostheses supplied by dentists and dental technicians;   Sch 1(iii)– (iiib),(v)

(*f*) services supplied by independent groups of persons whose activities are exempt from or are not subject to value added tax, for the purpose of rendering their members the services directly necessary for the exercise of their activity, where these groups merely claim from their members exact reimbursement of their share of the joint expenses, provided that such exemption is not likely to produce distortion of competition;   Sch 1 (xxiia)

(*g*) the supply of services and of goods closely linked to welfare and social security work, including those supplied by old people's homes, by bodies governed by public law or by other organizations recognized as charitable by the Member State concerned;   Sch 1(vii)

(*h*) the supply of services and of goods closely linked to the protection of children and young persons by bodies governed by public law or by other organizations recognized as charitable by the Member State concerned;   Sch 1(vi)

(*i*) children's or young people's education, school or university education, vocational training or retraining, including the supply of services and of goods closely related thereto, provided by bodies governed by public law having such as their aim or by other organizations defined by the Member State concerned as having similar objects;   Sch 1(ii), (xxv)

(*j*) tuition given privately by teachers and covering school or university education;   Sch 1(ii)

(k) certain supplies of staff by religious or philosophical institutions for the purpose of subparagraphs (*b*), (*g*), (*h*) and (*i*) of this Article and with a view to spiritual welfare;

SCH
1(XXII)

(*l*) supply of services and goods closely linked thereto for the benefit of their members in return for a subscription fixed in accordance with their rules by non-profit-making organizations with aims of a political, trade-union, religious, patriotic, philosophical, philanthropic or civic nature, provided that this exemption is not likely to cause distortion of competition;

SCH
1(XXIII)

(*m*) certain services closely linked to sport or physical education supplied by non-profit-making organizations to persons taking part in sport or physical education;

SCH
1(VIII),
(VIIIA)

(*n*) certain cultural services and goods closely linked thereto supplied by bodies governed by public law or by other cultural bodies recognized by the Member State concerned;

(*o*) the supply of services and goods by organizations whose activities are exempt under the provisions of subparagraphs (*b*), (*g*), (*h*), (*i*), (*l*), (*m*) and (*n*) above in connection with fund-raising events organized exclusively for their own benefit provided that exemption is not likely to cause distortion of competition. Member States may introduce any necessary restrictions in particular as regards the number of events or the amount of receipts which give entitlement to exemption;

(*p*) the supply of transport services for sick or injured persons in vehicles specially designed for the purpose by duly authorized bodies;

SCH 1(XIII)

(*q*) activities of public radio and television bodies other than those of a commercial nature.

2. (*a*) Member States may make the granting to bodies other than those governed by public law of each exemption provided for in (1)(*b*), (*g*), (*h*), (*i*), (*l*), (*m*) and (*n*) of this Article subject in each individual case to one or more of the following conditions:

— they shall not systematically aim to make a profit, but any profits nevertheless arising shall not be distributed but shall be assigned to the continuance or improvement of the services supplied,

— they shall be managed and administered on an essentially voluntary basis by persons who have no direct or indirect interest, either themselves or through intermediaries, in the results of the activities concerned,

— they shall charge prices approved by the public authorities or which do not exceed such approved prices or, in respect of those services not subject to approval, prices lower than those charged for similar services by commercial enterprises subject to value added tax,

— exemption of the services concerned shall not be likely to create distortions of competition such as to place at a disadvantage commercial enterprises liable to value added tax.

(*b*) The supply of services or goods shall not be granted exemption as provided for in (1)(*b*), (*g*), (*h*), (*i*), (*l*), (*m*) and (*n*) above if:

— it is not essential to the transactions exempted,

— its basic purpose is to obtain additional income for the organization by carrying out transactions which are in direct competition with those of commercial enterprises liable for value added tax.

B. Other exemptions

Without prejudice to other Community provisions, Member States shall exempt the following under conditions which they shall lay down for the purpose of ensuring the correct and straightforward application of the exemptions and of preventing any possible evasion, avoidance or abuse:

         SCH 1(IX)(B)–(C), SCH 1(XI)

(*a*) insurance and reinsurance transactions, including related services performed by insurance brokers and insurance agents;

         SCH 1(IV)

(*b*) the l easing or letting of immovable property excluding:

1. the provision of accommodation, as defined in the laws of the Member States, in the hotel sector or in sectors with a similar function, including the provision of accommodation in holiday camps or on sites developed for use as camping sites;

2. the letting of premises and sites for parking vehicles;

3. lettings of permanently installed equipment and machinery;

4. hire of safes.

Member States may apply further exclusions to the scope of this exemption;

(*c*) supplies of goods used wholly for an activity exempted under this Article or under Article 28(3)(*b*) when these goods have not given rise to the right to deduction, or of goods on the acquisition or production of which, by virtue of Article 17(6), value added tax did not become deductible;

         SCH 1(XXIV)

         SCH 1(I), (IX)(D)

(*d*) the following transactions:

1. the granting and the negotiation of credit and the management of credit by the person granting it;

2. the negotiation of or any dealings in credit guarantees or any other security for money and the management of credit guarantees by the person who is granting the credit;

3. transactions, including negotiation, concerning deposit and current accounts, payments, transfers, debts, cheques and other negotiable instruments, but excluding debt collection and factoring;

4. transactions, including negotiation, concerning currency, bank notes and coins used as legal tender, with the exception of collectors' items; "collectors' items" shall be taken to mean gold, silver or other metal coins or bank notes which are not normally used as legal tender or coins of numismatic interest;

5. transactions, including negotiation, excluding management and safekeeping, in shares, interests in companies or associations, debentures and other securities, excluding:

— documents establishing title to goods,

— the rights or securities referred to in Article 5(3);

6. management of special investment funds as defined by Member States;

(*e*) the supply at face value of postage stamps valid for use for postal services within the territory of the country, fiscal stamps, and other similar stamps;

SCH
1(XV)(XVI)
(*f*) betting, lotteries and other forms of gambling, subject to conditions and limitations laid down by each Member State;

(*g*) the supply of buildings or parts thereof, and of the land on which they stand, other than as described in Article 4(3)(*a*);

(*h*) the supply of land which has not been built on other than building land as described in Article 4(3)(*b*).

s 7

C. Options

VATR
1979

Member States may allow taxpayers a right of option for taxation in cases of:

(*a*) letting and leasing of immovable property;

(*b*) the transactions covered in B(*d*) (*g*) and (*h*) above.

Member States may restrict the scope of this right of option and shall fix the details of its use.

Cross-references

For exemptions not included in this title, see Arts 28c and 28k(1), (2).

Case law

Subject	Case	Case reference
Whether postal handling charge a customs charge	*Donner v State of the Netherlands*	[1983] ECR 19, [1983] 1 CMLR 711, ECJ 39/82
Art 13A(1)(*b*), (*g*): The terms establishments and organisations were sufficiently broad to include natural persons trading in partnerships	*Gregg & Anor v Customs & Excise Commissioners*	C–216/97 [1997] BVC 395
Art 13A(1)(*c*): meaning of "medical care", corrective spectacles not exempt	*EC Commission v United Kingdom*	[1988] STC 251, [1988] 2 All ER 557, ECJ 353/85
Art 13A(1)(*f*): did not apply to non-profit making foundation performing work for another non-profit making foundation (receiving exact reimbursement of expenses)	*Stichting Uitvoering Financiële Acties v Staatssecretaris van Financiën*	[1991] 2 CMLR 429, ECJ 348/87
Art 13A(1)(*g*): did not apply to profit making creches run by "natural persons"	*Bulthuis Griffioen v Inspector der Omzetbelasting*	[1995] STC 954, ECJ 453/93
Art 13B(*b*): Sites for parking vehicles includes covered garages	*Skatteministeriet v Henriksen*	[1990] STC 768, [1990] 3 CMLR 558, ECJ 173/88

Payment received by tenant for early surrender of lease, not taxable where grant of lease, and rent paid, were exempt	*Lubbock Fine and Co v Commissioners of Customs & Excise*	[1994] STC 101, ECJ 63/92
Art 13B(*d*): Credit card transaction, retailer's gross consideration (including credit card commission) is the taxable amount	*Chaussures Bally SA v Ministry of Finance (Belgium)*	[1993] STI 944, ECJ 18/92
Interest payable prior to the payment of the full price is regarded as part of the consideration; interest payable after the date of the supply constitutes granting of credit and is exempt	*Muys' en De Winter's Bouw- en Aannwmingsbedrijf BV v Staatsecretaris van Financiën*	[1993] STI 1367, ECJ 281/91
Transport services provided to (not by) postal services taxable	*Re VAT on Postal Transport, EC Commission v Germany*	[1986] 2 CMLR 177, ECJ 107/84
German law treating short-term accommodation as similar as hotel accommodation (standard rated). Held not to be in conflict with 6th Directive Art 13B	*Blasi v Finanzamt Munchen*	12 February 1998, C–346/95
Application of a supplementary tax on use of gaming machines not in breach of Art 33	*Careda SA, Femra & FACOMARE v Administration General del Estado (Ministerio de Economia y Hacienda)*	26 June 1997, C–370/95, 371/95, 372/95
Denial of right to deduct VAT on means of passenger transport constituting tools of trade not in breach of 6th Directive	*EC Commission v France*	18 June 1999, C–43/96
Failure to fulfil obligations under the 6th Directive by treating supplies of goods on which input tax could not be deducted as outside the scope of VAT rather than exempt	*EC Commission v Italy, 25 June 1997*	C–45/95
Exemption available to sporting bodies. Limitation held to contravene EU law (6th Dir Art 13A)	*EC Commission v Spain*	7 May 1998, C–124/96
Unlicensed gambling. Competition with licensed gambling. Unlawful gambling entited to VAT exemption as legal gambling	*Karl Heinz Fischer v Finanzamt Donaueschingen*	11 June 1998, C–283/95
Any foreign exchange transaction by any kind of business is a supply and is liable to VAT	*The Commissioners C & E v The First National Bank of Chicago*	July 1997, C–172/96
Definition of a trade union deemed to include employees' organisations	*The Institute of the Motor Industry v The Commissioners C & E*	12 November 1999–07–06, C–149/97
Supplies by insurance intermediaries, restriction of exemption	*Card Protection Plan v The Commissioners C & E*	25 February 1999, C–349/96, [1999] BTC 5121, [1999] BVC 155
Exemption for medical care provided in the exercise of the medical and para-medical professions — expert medical report	*Margarete Unterpertinger v Pensionsvarsicherungsanstalt der Arbeiter*	20 November 2003, C–212/01

Letting of immovable property — cigarette vending machine installed in commercial premises	*Sinclair Collins v Commissioners of Customs and Excise*	12 June 2003, C–275/01
Phychotherapeutic treatment given in an out-patient facility provided by a foundation governed by private law	*Christoph-Dornier-Stiftung fur Klinische Psychologie v finanzamt Giesen*	6 November 2003, C–45/01
Medical care provided in the exercise of the medical and paramedical professions	*Dr Peter L d'Ambremunil, Dispute Resolution Services Ltd v Customs and Excise*	20 November 2003, C–307/01

Direct effect of Directives

Member States were to adopt the Sixth Directive by 1 January 1978, but it was not implemented in Germany until 1 January 1980. Nevertheless its exemptions could be relied upon with effect from 1 January 1979 (Ninth Directive)	*R A Grendel GmbH v Finanzamt für Körperschaften, Hamburg*	[1982] ECR 2301, [1983] 1 CMLR 379, ECJ 255/81
but not before 1 January 1979	*Kloppenburg v Finanzamt Leer*	[1984] ECR 1075, [1985] 1 CMLR 205, ECJ 70/83
A credit negotiator who had covertly passed on VAT in 1978 and 1979 could not afterwards claim exemption	*Weissgerber v Finanzamt Neustadt an der WeinstraBe*	[1991] STC 589, ECJ 207/87
See also	*EC Commission v Italy*	ECJ 104/86
	Bianco and Girard	331/85, 376/85, 378/85
Whether provision of "call centre" services considered as exempt transactions in securities	*CSC Financial Services Ltd v Commissioners of Customs & Excise*	13 December 2001, C–235/00
Reverse premium in relation to lease	*Mirror Group plc v Commissioners of Customs & Excise*	9 October 2001, C–409/98
Inducement payment in relation to the assignment of a lease	*Cantor Fitzgerald International v Commissioners of Customs & Excise*	9 October 2001, C–108/99
Member States entitlement regarding treatment of "low value" leases of property as supplies of goods	*Stichting "Goed Wonen" v Staatssecretaris van Financien*	4 October 2001, C–326/99
Treatment of toll roads	*Commission of the European Communities v Ireland*	12 September 2000, C–358/97
Meaning of "non profit making organisations"	*Kennemer Golf & Country Club v Staatsecretaris va Financien*	21 March 2002, C–174/00
Research activities of public-sector higher-education establishments	*Commission v Germany*	20 June 2002, C–287/00
Exemption of care provided by capital companies	*Ambulanter Pfegedienst Kügler GmbH v Finanzamt für Körperschaften I in Berlin*	10 September 2002, C–141/00
Cultural Services by a Soloist	*Matthias Hoffman v Bundesgerichtshof (Germany)*	3 April 2003, C–144/00
Letting of Immovable Property (Prefabricated Building)	*Rudolf Maierhofer v Finanzamt Augsburg-Land*	16 January 2003, C –315/00
Letting of immovable property — Licence to occupy	*Belgian State v Temco Europe SA*	18 November 2004, C–284/03

Outsourcing insurance related services	*Staatssectretaris van*	3 March 2005, C–472/03
— agency services	*Financien v Arthur Andersen*	
	& Co	
Share issues	*Kretzetchnik AG v Finanzamt*	26 May 2005, C–465/03
	Linz	

Article 14

s 15

Exemptions on importation

1. Without prejudice to other Community provisions, Member States shall exempt the following under conditions which they shall lay down for the purpose of ensuring the correct and straightforward application of such exemption and of preventing any possible evasion, avoidance or abuse:

(*a*) final importation of goods of which the supply by a taxable person would in all circumstances be exempted within the country;

(*b*) ...[1]

(*c*) ...[2]

(*d*) final importation of goods qualifying for exemption from customs duties other than as provided for in the Common Customs Tariff ...[3]. However, Member States shall have the option of not granting exemption where this would be liable to have a serious effect on conditions of competition ...[4];

[This exemption shall also apply to the import of goods, within the meaning of Article 7(1)(*b*), which would be capable of benefiting from the exemption set out above if they had been imported within the meaning of Article 7(1)(*a*);] [5]

(*e*) reimportation by the person who exported them of goods in the state in which they were exported, where they qualify for exemption from customs duties ...[6];

(*f*) ...[7];

(*g*) importations of goods:

— under diplomatic and consular arrangements, which qualify for exemption from customs duties ...[8],

— by international organizations recognized as such by the public authorities of the host country, and by members of such organizations, within the limits and under the conditions laid down by the international conventions establishing the organizations or by headquarters agreements,

— into the territory of Member States which are parties to the North Atlantic Treaty by the armed forces of other States which are parties to that Treaty for the use of such forces or the civilian staff accompanying them or for supplying their messes or canteens where such forces take part in the common defence effort;

(*h*) importation into ports by sea fishing undertakings of their catches, unprocessed or after undergoing preservation for marketing but before being supplied;

(*i*)   the supply of services, in connection with the importation of goods where the value of such services is included in the taxable amount in accordance with Article 11B(3)(*b*);

(*j*)   importation of gold by Central Banks;

[(*k*)   import of gas through the natural gas distribution system, or of electricity.] [9]

2. The Commission shall submit to the Council at the earliest opportunity proposals designed to lay down Community tax rules clarifying the scope of the exemptions referred to in paragraph 1 and detailed rules for their implementation.

Until the entry into force of these rules, Member States may:

— maintain their national provisions in force on matters related to the above provisions,

— adapt their national provisions to minimize distortion of competition and in particular the non-imposition or double imposition of value added tax within the Community,

— use whatever administrative procedures they consider most appropriate to achieve exemption.

Member States shall inform the Commission, which shall inform the other Member States, of the measures they have adopted and are adopting pursuant to the preceding provisions.

Amendments

[1]   Para (1)(*b*) deleted Council Directive 91/680/EEC of 16 December 1991, Art 1(11) with effect from 1 January 1993.

[2]   Para (1)(*c*) deleted by Council Directive 92/111/EEC of 14 December 1992, Art 1(8) with effect from 1 January 1993.

[3]   Deleted by Council Directive 91/680/EEC of 16 December 1991, Art 1(11) with effect from 1 January 1993.

[4]   Deleted by Council Directive 91/680/EEC of 16 December 1991, Art 1(11) with effect from 1 January 1993.

[5]   Added by Council Directive 92/111/EEC of 14 December 1992, Art 1(8) with effect from 1 January 1993.

[6]   Deleted by Council Directive 91/680/EEC of 16 December 1991, Art 1(11) with effect from 1 January 1993.

[7]   Para (1)(*f*) deleted by Council Directive 91/680/EEC of 16 December 1991, Art 1(11) with effect from 1 January 1993.

[8]   Deleted by Council Directive 91/680/EEC of 16 December 1991, Art 1(11) with effect from 1 January 1993.

[9]   Para (1)(*k*) inserted by Council Directive 2003/92/EC of 7 October 2003, Art 1(3) with effect from 11 October 2003.

Cross-references

Goods imported into an EC State other than that of arrival: Art 28c(D).

Directives adopted under Art 14(2): Council Directive 83/181/EEC (clarifying the scope of Art 14(1)(*d*)); Council Directive 85/362/ EEC (Seventeenth Directive) (clarifying the scope of Art 14(1)(*c*)).

Case law

Note: the following decisions are less significant following the implementation of the Single Market.

Subject	Case	Case reference
Double imposition of VAT on motor vehicles	*Ministère Publique and Ministere des Finances v Profant*	[1986] 2 CMLR 378, ECJ 249/84
"Frontier zone", meaning	*Michael Paul v Hauptzollamt Emmerich*	ECJ 54/84
National rules prohibiting use of temporarily imported motor vehicles, permissible	*Re Carciati*	[1980] ECR 2773, [1981] 2 CMLR 274, ECJ 823/79
	Abbink (Jan Gerrit, criminal proceedings)	[1984] ECR 4079, [1986] 1 CMLR 579, ECJ 134/83
"Normal residence", meaning, Danish national working in Germany	*Rigsadvokaten v N C Ryborg*	[1991] STI 501, ECJ 297/89
Temporary importation of racehorses	*R v C & E Commissioners, ex parte Tattersalls Ltd*	[1988] STC 630, [1988] 3 CMLR 113, ECJ 10/87
Travellers' allowances, Member State not upholding EEC Treaty	*Re border shopping: EC Commission v Ireland*	[1990] 3 CMLR 103, ECJ 158/88
	EC Commission v Denmark	(1991) OJ C4/2, ECJ 208/88
Temporary importation of motor vehicle	*Ministère Public des Finances du Royaume de Belgique v Ledoux*	[1991] STC 553, ECJ 127/86

Article 15

[Exemption of exports from the Community and like transactions and international transport] [1]

s 13(1), (2), SI 230/1984, SI 231/1984

Without prejudice to other Community provisions Member States shall exempt the following under conditions which they shall lay down for the purpose of ensuring the correct and straightforward application of such exemptions and of preventing any evasion, avoidance or abuse:

1. the supply of goods dispatched or transported to a destination [outside the Community] [2] by or on behalf of the vendor;

2. the supply of goods dispatched or transported to a destination [outside the Community] [2] by or on behalf of a purchaser not established within the territory of the country, with the exception of goods transported by the purchaser himself for the equipping, fuelling and provisioning of pleasure boats and private aircraft or any other means of transport for private use;

[[In the case of the supply of goods to be carried in the personal luggage of travellers, this exemption shall apply on condition that:

— the traveller is not established within the Community,

— the goods are transported to a destination outside the Community before the end of the third month following that in which the supply is effected,

— the total value of the supply, including value added tax, is more than the equivalent in national currency of ECU 175, fixed in accordance with Article 7(2) of Directive 69/169/EEC (OJ No l 133, 4.6.1969, p 6.

Directive as last amended by Directive 94/4/EC (OJ No L 60, 3.3.1994, p 14)); however, Members States may exempt a supply with a total value of less than that amount.

For the purposes of applying the second subparagraph:

— a traveller not established within the Community shall be taken to mean a traveller whose domicile or habitual residence is not situated within the Community. For the purposes of this provision, "domicile or habitual residence" shall mean the place entered as such in a passport, identity card or other identity documents which the Member State within whose territory the supply takes place recognizes as valid,

— proof of exportation shall be furnished by means of the invoice or other document in lieu thereof, endorsed by the customs office where the goods left the Community.

Each Member State shall transmit to the Commission specimens of the stamps it uses for the endorsement referred to in the second indent of the third subparagraph. The Commission shall transmit this information to the tax authorities in the other Member States.] [3] [4]

[3. The supply of services consisting of work on movable property acquired or imported for the purpose of undergoing such work within the territory of the Community, and dispatched or transported out of the Community by the person providing the services or by the customer if [not established within the territory of the country] [5] or on behalf of either of them;] [6]

4. the supply of goods for the fuelling and provisioning of vessels:

(a) used for navigation on the high seas and carrying passengers for reward or used for the purpose of commercial, industrial or fishing activities;

(b) used for rescue or assistance at sea, or for inshore fishing, with the exception, for the latter, of ships' provisions;

(c) of war, as defined in subheading 89.01 A of the Common Customs Tariff, leaving the country and bound for foreign ports or anchorages.

[The Commission shall submit to the Council as soon as possible proposals to establish Community fiscal rules specifying the scope of and practical arrangements for implementing this exemption and the exemptions provided for in (5) to (9). Until these rules come into force, Member States may limit the extent of the exemption provided for in this paragraph.] [7]

Sch 2(v)(A)(B)   5. the supply, modification, repair, maintenance, chartering and hiring of the sea-going vessels referred to in paragraph 4(a) and (b) and the supply, hiring, repair and maintenance of equipment — including fishing equipment — incorporated or used therein;

Sch 2(vB),(vA)   6. the supply, modification, repair, maintenance, chartering and hiring of aircraft used by airlines operating for reward chiefly on international routes, and the supply, hiring, repair and maintenance of equipment incorporated or used therein;

Sch 2(vB)   7. the supply of goods for the fuelling and provisioning of aircraft referred to in paragraph 6;

8. the supply of services other than those referred to in paragraph 5, to meet the direct needs of the sea-going vessels referred to in that paragraph or of their cargoes;

9. the supply of services other than those referred to in paragraph 6, to meet the Sᴄʜ 2(ᴠᴄ) direct needs of aircraft referred to in that paragraph or of their cargoes;

10. supplies of goods and services:

— under diplomatic and consular arrangements,

— to international organizations recognized as such by the public authorities of the host country, and to members of such organizations, within the limits and under the conditions laid down by the international conventions establishing the organizations or by headquarters agreements,

— effected within a Member State which is a party to the North Atlantic Treaty and intended either for the use of the forces of other States which are parties to that Treaty or of the civilian staff accompanying them, or for supplying their messes or canteens when such forces take part in the common defence effort.

[— to another Member State and intended for the forces of any Member State which is a party to the North Atlantic Treaty, other than the Member State of destination itself, for the use of those forces or of the civilian staff accompanying them, or for supplying their messes or canteens when such forces take part in the common defence effort.] [8]

This exemption shall be [subject to [limitations] [9] laid down by the host Member State] [10] until Community tax rules are adopted.

[In cases where the goods are not dispatched or transported out of the country, and in the case of services, the benefit of the exemption may be given by means of a refund of the tax.] [11]

Sᴄʜ 2(x)

11. supplies of gold to Central Banks;

12. goods supplied to approved bodies which export them [from the Community] [12] as part of their humanitarian, charitable or teaching activities [outside the Community] [13]. This exemption may be implemented by means of a refund of the tax;

[**13.** The supply of services, including transport and ancillary operations, but excluding the supply of services exempted in accordance with Article 13, where these are directly connected with the export of goods or imports of goods covered by the provisions of Article 7(3) or Article 16(1), Title A;] [14]

14. services supplied by brokers and other intermediaries, acting in the name and Sᴄʜ 2(ᴠɪ) for account of another person, where they form part of transactions specified in this Article, or of transactions carried out [outside the Community] [15].

This exemption does not apply to travel agents who supply in the name and for account of the traveller services which are supplied in other Member States.

[15. the Portuguese Republic may treat sea and air transport between the islands making up the autonomous regions of the Azores and Madeira and between those regions and the mainland in the same way as international transport.] [16]

Amendments

[1]   Substituted by Council Directive 91/680/EEC of 16 December 1991, Art 1(12) with effect from 1 January 1993.

[2]   Substituted by Council Directive 91/680/EEC of 16 December 1991, Art 1(13) with effect from 1 January 1993.

[3]   Substituted by Council Directive 95/7/EC of 10 April 1995 Art 1(3) with effect from 1 January 1996.

[4]   Inserted by Council Directive 92/111/EEC of 14 December 1992, Art 1(9) with effect from 1 January 1993.

[5]   Substituted by Council Directive 92/111/EEC of 14 December 1992, Art 1(9) with effect from 1 January 1993.

[6]   Para (3) substituted by Council Directive 91/680/EEC of 16 December 1991, Art 1(14) with effect from 1 January 1993.

[7]   Substituted by Council Directive 92/111/EEC of 14 December 1992, Art 1(9) with effect from 1 January 1993.

[8]   Inserted by Council Directive 91/680/EEC of 16 December 1991, Art 1(15) with effect from 1 January 1993.

[9]   Substituted by Council Directive 92/111/EEC of 14 December 1992, Art 1(9) with effect from 1 January 1993.

[10]   Substituted by Council Directive 91/680/EEC of 16 December 1991, Art 1(16) with effect from 1 January 1993.

[11]   Substituted by Council Directive 92/111/EEC of 14 December 1992, Art 1(9) with effect from 1 January 1993.

[12]   Inserted by Council Directive 91/680/EEC of 16 December 1991, Art 1(17) with effect from 1 January 1993.

[13]   Substituted by Council Directive 91/680/EEC of 16 December 1991, Art 1(17) with effect from 1 January 1993.

[14]   Para (13) substituted by Council Directive 92/111/EEC of 14 December 1992, Art 1(9) with effect from 1 January 1993.

[15]   Substituted by Council Directive 91/680/EEC of 16 December 1991, Art 1(19) with effect from 1 January 1993.

[16]   Para (15) inserted by the Act of Accession 1985 Art 26, Annex I, Part V, point 2.

Case law

Subject	Case	Case reference
Para (4): fuelling and provisioning, only direct supplies regarded as exempt; fuelling and provisioning need not be simultaneous	*Staatssecretaris van Financiën v Velker International Oil Co Ltd NV*	[1990] STC 640, ECJ 185/89
Meaning of "aircraft used by airlines operating chiefly on international routes"	*Cimber Air A/S v Skatteministeriet*	16 September 2004, C–382/02

Article 16

s 13(1),(2)

Special exemptions linked to international goods traffic

[**1.** Without prejudice to other Community tax provisions, Member States may, subject to the consultations provided for in Article 29, take special measures designed to exempt all or some of the following transactions, provided that they are not aimed at final use and/or consumption and that the amount of value added tax due on cessation of the arrangements on situations referred to at A to E corresponds to the amount of tax which would have been due had each of these transactions been taxed within the territory of the country:

A. imports of goods which are intended to be placed under warehousing arrangements other than customs;

B. supplies of goods which are intended to be:

   (*a*)   produced to customs and, where applicable, placed in temporary storage;

   (*b*)   placed in a free zone or in a free warehouse;

   (*c*)   placed under customs warehousing arrangements or inward processing arrangements;

   (*d*)   admitted into territorial waters:

   —   in order to be incorporated into drilling or production platforms, for purposes of the construction, repair, maintenance, alteration or fitting-out of such platforms, or to link such drilling or production platforms to the mainland,

   —   for the fuelling and provisioning of drilling or production platforms;

   (*e*)   placed, within the territory of the country, under warehousing arrangements other than customs warehousing.

   For the purposes of this Article, warehouses other than customs warehouses shall be taken to be:

   —   for products subject to excise duty, the places defined as tax warehouses for the purposes of Article 4(*b*) of Directive 92/12/ EEC,

   —   for goods other than those subject to excise duty, the places defined as such by the Member States. However, Member States may not provide for warehousing arrangements other than customs warehousing where the goods in question are intended to be supplied at the retail stage.

   Nevertheless, Member States may provide for such arrangements for goods intended for:

   —   taxable persons for the purposes of supplies effected under the conditions laid down in Article 28k,

   —   tax-free shops within the meaning of Article 28k, for the purpose of supplies to travellers taking flights or sea crossings to third countries, where those supplies are exempt pursuant to Article 15,

— taxable persons for the purposes of supplies to travellers on board aircraft or vessels during a flight or sea crossing where the place of arrival is situated outside the Community,

— taxable persons for the purposes of supplies effected free of tax pursuant to Article 15, point 10.

The places referred to in (*a*), (*b*), (*c*) and (*d*) shall be as defined by the Community customs provisions in force;

C. supplies of services relating to the supplies of goods referred to in B;

D. supplies of goods and of services carried out:

(*a*) in the places listed in B(*a*), (*b*), (*c*) and (*d*) and still subject to one of the situations specified therein;

(*b*) in the places listed in B(*e*) and still subject, within the territory of the country, to the situation specified therein.

Where they exercise the option provided for in (*a*) for transactions effected in customs warehouses, Member States shall take the measures necessary to ensure that they have defined warehousing arrangements other than customs warehousing which permit the provisions in (*b*) to be applied to the same transactions concerning goods listed in Annex J which are effected in such warehouses other than customs warehouses;

E. supplies:

— of goods referred to in Article 7(1)(*a*) still subject to arrangements for temporary importation with total exemption from import duty or to external transit arrangements,

— of goods referred to in Article 7(1)(*b*) still subject to the internal Community transit procedure provided for in Article 33a,

as well as supplies of services relating to such supplies.

By way of derogation from the first subparagraph of Article 21(1)(*a*), the person liable to pay the tax due in accordance with the first subparagraph shall be the person who causes the goods to cease to be covered by the arrangements or situations listed in this paragraph.

When the removal of goods from the arrangements or situations referred to in this paragraph gives rise to importation within the meaning of Article 7(3), the Member State of import shall take the measures necessary to avoid double taxation within the country.] [1]

[**1a.** Where they exercise the option provided for in paragraph 1, Member States shall take the measures necessary to ensure that intra-Community acquisitions of goods intended to be placed under one of the arrangements or in one of the situations referred to in paragraph 1(B) benefit from the same provisions as supplies of goods effected within the country under the same conditions.] [2]

s 13A   **2.** Subject to the consultation provided for in Article 29, Member States may opt to exempt intra-Community acquisitions of goods made by a taxable person and imports for and supplies of goods to a taxable person intending to export them [outside the Community] [3] as they are or after processing, as well as supplies of services linked with his export business, up to a maximum equal to the value of his exports during the preceding 12 months.

[When they take up this option the Member States shall, subject to the consultation provided for in Article 29, extend the benefit of this exemption to intra- Community acquisitions of goods by a taxable person, imports for and supplies of goods to a taxable person intending to supply them, as they are or after processing, under the conditions laid down in Article 28c(A), as well as supplies of services relating to such supplies, up to a maximum equal to the value of his supplies of goods effected under the conditions laid down in Article 28c(A) during the preceding twelve months.

Member States may set a common maximum amount for transactions which they exempt under the first and second subparagraphs.] [4]

3. The Commission shall submit to the Council at the earliest opportunity proposals concerning common arrangements for applying value added tax to the transactions referred to in paragraphs 1 and 2.

Amendments

[1] Para (1) substituted by Art 28c(E)(1) which was amended by Council Directive 95/7/EC of 10 April 1995 Art 1(9) with effect from 1 January 1996 (1 January 1997 for Germany and Luxembourg).

[2] Para (1a) substituted by Art 28c(E)(1) which was amended by Council Directive 95/7/EC of 10 April 1995 Art 1(9) with effect from 1 January 1996 (1 January 1997 for Germany and Luxembourg).

[3] Inserted by Art 28c(E) (inserted by Council Directive 92/111/EEC of 14 December 1992 Art 1(13)) with effect from 1 January 1993.

[4] Inserted by Art 28c(E) (inserted by Council Directive 92/111/EEC of 14 December 1992 Art 1(13)) with effect from 1 January 1993.

Cross-references

Dispatch or transport of goods to, from or between the Azores and Madeira: Arts 28c(C).
Exercise of option under Art 16(2): Art 28k(4).

TITLE XI

DEDUCTIONS

s 12

Article 17

Origin and scope of the right to deduct

1. The right to deduct shall arise at the time when deductible tax becomes chargeable.

[**2.** Insofar as the goods and services are used for the purposes of his taxable transactions, the taxable person shall be entitled to deduct from the tax which he is liable to pay:

[(*a*) value added tax due or paid within the territory of the country in respect of goods or services supplied or to be supplied to him by another taxable person;] [1]

(*b*) value added tax due or paid in respect of imported goods within the territory of the country;

(*c*) value added tax due pursuant to Articles 5(7)(*a*), (6)(3) and 28a(6);

(*d*) value added tax due pursuant to Article 28a(1)(*a*).] [2]

[**3.** Member States shall also grant every taxable person the right to the deduction or refund of the value added tax referred to in paragraph 2 insofar as the goods and services are used for the purposes of:

    (*a*)   transactions relating to the economic activities referred to in Article 4(2), carried out in another country, which would be deductible if they had been performed within the territory of the country;

   [(*b*)   transactions which are exempt pursuant to Article 14(1)(*g*) and (i), 15, 16(1) (B), (C), (D) or (E) or (2) or 28c (A) and (C).] [3]

s 12(1)(B)   (*c*)   any of the transactions exempt pursuant to Article 13B(*a*) and (*d*)(1) to (5), when the customer is established outside the Community o r when those transactions are directly linked with goods to be exported to a country outside the Community.] [4]

s 13(3)   [**4.** The refund of value added tax referred to in paragraph 3 shall be effected:

    —   to taxable persons who are not established within the territory of the country but who are established in another Member State in accordance with the detailed implementing rules laid down in Directive 79/1072/EEC (OJ L 331, 27.12.1979, p 11);

    —   to taxable persons who are not established within the territory of the Community, in accordance with the detailed implementing rules laid down in Directive 86/560/EEC (OJ L 326, 21.11.1986, p 40).

[For the purposes of applying the above:

    (*a*)   the taxable persons referred to in Article 1 of Directive 79/1072/EEC shall also be considered for the purposes of applying the said Directive as taxable persons who are not established in the country when, inside the territory of the country, they have only carried out supplies of goods and services to a person who has been designated as the person liable to pay the tax in accordance with [Article 21(1)(*a*) and (*c*)] [5];

    (*b*)   the taxable persons referred to in Article 1 of Directive 86/560/EEC shall also be considered for the purposes of applying the said Directive as taxable persons who are not established in the Community when, inside the territory of the country, they have only carried out supplies of goods and services to a person who has been designated as the person liable to pay the tax in accordance with Article 21(1)(*a*);

    (*c*)   Directives 79/1072/EEC and 86/560/EEC shall not apply to supplies of goods which are, or may be, exempted under Article 28c(A) when the goods supplied are dispatched or transported by the acquirer or for his account.] [6]] [7]

s 12(4), VATR 1979 R 16   **5.** As regards goods and services to be used by a taxable person both for transactions covered by paragraphs 2 and 3, in respect of which value added tax is deductible, and for transactions in respect of which value added tax is not deductible, only such proportion of the value added tax shall be deductible as is attributable to the former transactions.

This proportion shall be determined, in accordance with Article 19, for all the transactions carried out by the taxable person.

However, Member States may:

(a) authorize the taxable person to determine a proportion for each sector of his business, provided that separate accounts are kept for each sector;

(b) compel the taxable person to determine a proportion for each sector of his business and to keep separate accounts for each sector;

(c) authorize or compel the taxable person to make the deduction on the basis of the use of all or part of the goods and services;

(d) authorize or compel the taxable person to make the deduction in accordance with the rule laid down in the first subparagraph, in respect of all goods and services used for all transactions referred to therein;

(e) provide that where the value added tax which is not deductible by the taxable person is insignificant it shall be treated as nil.

6. Before a period of four years at the latest has elapsed from the date of entry into force of this Directive, the Council, acting unanimously on a proposal from the Commission, shall decide what expenditure shall not be eligible for a deduction of value added tax. Value added tax shall in no circumstances be deductible on expenditure which is not strictly business expenditure, such as that on luxuries, amusements or entertainment.

Until the above rules come into force, Member States may retain all the exclusions provided for under their national laws when this Directive comes into force.

7. Subject to the consultation provided for in Article 29, each Member State may, for cyclical economic reasons, totally or partly exclude all or some capital goods or other goods from the system of deductions. To maintain identical conditions of competition, Member States may, instead of refusing deduction, tax the goods manufactured by the taxable person himself or which he has purchased in the country or imported, in such a way that the tax does not exceed the value added tax which would have been charged on the acquisition of similar goods.

Amendments

¹ Para (2)(*a*) substituted by Art 28*f*(1) which was amended by Council Directive 95/7/EC of 10 April 1995 Art 1(10) with effect from 25 May 1995.

² Para (2) substituted by Art 28*f*(1) which was inserted by Council Directive 91/680/EEC of 16 December 1991, Art 1(22) with effect from 1 January 1993 for the transitional period specified in Art 28l first para.

³ Para (3)(*b*) substituted by Art 28f(1) (as amended by Council Directive 2004/66/EC Annex V para (1)(*c*) of 26 April 2004) with effect from 1 May 2004.

⁴ Para (3) substituted by Art 28*f*(1) which was inserted by Council Directive 91/680/EEC of 16 December 1991, Art 1(22) with effect from 1 January 1993 for the transitional period specified in Art 28l first para.

⁵ Substituted by Art 28*f*(1) (amended by Council Directive 2000/65/EC of 17 October 2000 (OJ L269, 21/10/2000 p 44–46) Art 1(2)) with effect from 17 October 2000; previously "Article 21(1)(*a*)".

⁶ Inserted by Council Directive 92/111/EEC of 14 December 1992, Art 1(18) with effect from 1 January 1993.

⁷ Para (4) substituted by Art 28f(1) which was inserted by Council Directive 91/680/EEC of 16 December 1991, Art 1(22) with effect from 1 January 1993 for the transitional period specified in Art 28l first para.

Cross-references

Right of deduction by person who from time to time supplies a new means of transport: Art 28a(4).
Right of deduction in relation to supplies by tax-free shops: Art 28k(3).

Case law

Subject	Case	Case reference
Right to deduct arises only in respect of goods/services which are directly and immediately linked to taxable transactions	*BLP Group v C & E Commissioners*	[1995] STC 424, ECJ 4/94
Greece held to be in breach of Art 17(1) and (2)	*BP Soupergas Anonimos Etairia Geniki Emporiki Viomichaniki v Greece*	[1995] STC 805, ECJ 62/93
Taxpayer not entitled to deduction in relation to sale of private dwelling where it was sold together with business premises	*Finamzampt Uelzen v Armbrecht*	[1995] STC 997, ECJ
Partially taxable holding company, exclusion of dividends (received from group companies) in denominator when computing input credit	*Sofitam SA (formerly Satam SA) v Minister Responsible for the Budget*	[1997] STC 226, ECJ 333/91
Para (2)(*a*): Although a deduction is only available for goods "supplied", a taxable person may claim a deduction for goods physically supplied to employees (but invoiced to the taxable trader)	*Leesportefeuille "Intiem" CV v Staatssecretaris van Financiën*	[1989] 2 CMLR 856, ECJ 165/86
Para (6): Member States entitled to retain the exclusions from the right to deduct VAT	*Royscott Leasing and Royscott Industrial Leasing Ltd, Allied Domecq, TC Harrison Group Ltd v C & E Comms*	C–305/97
Belgian lawyer (VAT exempt) not entitled to refund of Dutch VAT paid on car hire	*Debouche v Inspecteur der Invoerrechten en Accijnzen*	[1996] STC 406, ECJ 302/93
Kingdom of the Netherlands should allow employer VAT recovery in respect of employee allowance	*Commission v Netherlands*	8 November 2001, C–338/98
Expenditure incurred in connect with acquisition of shareholdings in subsidiaries is attributable to general business overheads	*Cibo Participations*	27 September 2001, C–16/00
Conditions for exercise of right to deduct input tax — requirement to hold invoice	*Finanzamt Gummersbach v Gerhard Bockemuhl*	1 April 2004, C–90/02
Right to deduct VAT incurred on expenditure relating to transfer of business	*Finanzamt Offenbach am Main-Land v Faworld Vorgrundungsgesselschaft Peter Hunninghausen und Wolfgang Klein GbR*	29 April 2004, C–137/02
Right to deduct input tax — conditions of exercise	*Terra Baubedarf-Handel GmbH v Finanzamt Osterholz-Scharmbeck*	29 April 2004, C–152/02
Share issues	*Kretzetchnik AG v Finanzamt Linz*	26 May 2005, C–465/03

Article 18
Rules governing the exercise of the right to deduct

s 12

[**1.** To exercise his right of deduction, a taxable person must:

(*a*) in respect of deductions pursuant to Article 17(2)(*a*), hold an invoice drawn up in accordance with Article 22(3);

(*b*) in respect of deductions pursuant to Article 17(2)(*b*), hold an import document specifying him as consignee or importer and stating or permitting the calculation of the amount of tax due;

(*c*) in respect of deductions pursuant to Article 17(2)(*c*), comply with the formalities established by each Member State;

(*d*) when he is required to pay the tax as a customer or purchaser where Article 21(1) applies, comply with the formalities laid down by each Member State;

(*e*) in respect of deductions pursuant to Article 17(2)(*d*), set out in the declaration provided for in Article 22(4) all the information needed for the amount of the tax due on his intra-Community acquisitions of goods to be calculated and hold an invoice in accordance with Article 22(3).][1]

2. The taxable person shall effect the deduction by subtracting from the total amount of value added tax due for a given tax period the total amount of the tax in respect of which, during the same period, the right to deduct has arisen and can be exercised under the provisions of paragraph 1.

s 3(7)

However, Member States may require that as regards taxable persons who carry out occasional transactions as defined in Article 4(3), the right to deduct shall be exercised only at the time of the supply.

3. Member States shall determine the conditions and procedures whereby a taxable person may be authorized to make a deduction which he has not made in accordance with the provisions of paragraphs 1 and 2.

[**3a.** Member States may authorise a taxable person who does not hold an invoice in accordance with Article 22(3) to make the deduction referred to in Article 17(2)(*d*); they shall determine the conditions and arrangements for applying this provision.][2]

4. Where for a given tax period the amount of authorised deductions exceeds the amount of tax due, the Member States may either make a refund or carry the excess forward to the following period according to conditions which they shall determine.

s 20(2),
VATR
1979 R 17

However, Member States may refuse to refund or carry forward if the amount of the excess is insignificant.

Amendments

[1] Para (1) substituted by Art 28f(2) which was inserted by Council Directive 91/680/EEC of 16 December 1991, Art 1(22) with effect from 1 January 1993 for the transitional period specified in Art 28l first para.

[2] Para (3a) inserted by Art 28f(3) which was inserted by Council Directive 91/680/EEC of 16 December 1991, Art 1(22) with effect from 1 January 1993 for the transitional period specified in Art 28l first para.

Case law

Subject	Case	Case reference
Advocate General opinion: input credit may be allowed if proof of purchase exists where an original invoice mislaid	*Reisdorf v Finamzamt Köln-West*	[1997] STC 180, ECJ 85/95
Possession of an invoice. A Member State must accept a copy invoice where there is no risk of fraud and no risk of further application for the same refund	*Société Generales des Grandes Sources d'Eaux Minerals v Bundesmt fur Finanzen*	June 1998, C–367/98

Article 19

s 12, VATR
1979 R 16

Calculation of the deductible proportion

1. The proportion deductible under the first subparagraph of Article 17(5) shall be made up of a fraction having:

— as numerator, the total amount, exclusive of value added tax, of turnover per year attributable to transactions in respect of which value added tax is deductible under Article 17(2) and (3),

— as denominator, the total amount, exclusive of value added tax, of turnover per year attributable to transactions included in the numerator and to transactions in respect of which value added tax is not deductible. The Member States may also include in the denominator the amount of subsidies, other than those specified in Article 11A(1)(*a*).

The proportion shall be determined on an annual basis, fixed as a percentage and rounded up to a figure not exceeding the next unit.

s 12(4)   **2.** By way of derogation from the provisions of paragraph 1, there shall be excluded from the calculation of the deductible proportion, amounts of turnover attributable to the supplies of capital goods used by the taxable person for the purposes of his business. Amounts of turnover attributable to transactions specified in Article 13B(*d*), in so far as these are incidental transactions, and to incidental real estate and financial transactions shall also be excluded. Where Member States exercise the option provided under Article 20(5) not to require adjustment in respect of capital goods, they may include disposals of capital goods in the calculation of the deductible proportion.

3. The provisional proportion for a year shall be that calculated on the basis of the preceding year's transactions. In the absence of any such transactions to refer to, or where they were insignificant in amount, the deductible proportion shall be estimated provisionally, under supervision of the tax authorities, by the taxable person from his own forecasts. However, Member States may retain their current rules.

Deductions made on the basis of such provisional proportion shall be adjusted when the final proportion is fixed during the next year.

Case law

Subject	Case	Case reference
Partially taxable holding company, exclusion of dividends (received from group companies) in denominator when computing input credit	*Satam SA v Minister Responsible for the Budget*	[1993] STI 1077, ECJ 333/91
Property management business deriving 14% of its annual receipts from interest earned on advances, required to apportion credit	*Régie Dauphinoise Cabinet A Forest SARL v Ministre du Budget*	[1996] STC 1176, ECJ 306/94.
Contrast, where the bond holder was not regarded as carrying on an economic activity.	*Harnas & Helm CV v Staatssecretariss van Financiën*	[1997] STC 364, ECJ 80/85

Article 20
Adjustments of deductions

s 12, VATR 1979

1. The initial deduction shall be adjusted according to the procedures laid down by the Member States, in particular:

- (*a*)   where that deduction was higher or lower than that to which the taxable person was entitled;
- (*b*)   where after the return is made some change occurs in the factors used to determine the amount to be deducted, in particular where purchases are cancelled or price reductions are obtained; however, adjustment shall not be made in cases of transactions remaining totally or partially unpaid and of destruction, loss or theft of property duly proved or confirmed, nor in the case of applications for the purpose of making gifts of small value and giving samples specified in Article 5(6). However, Member States may require adjustment in cases of transactions remaining totally or partially unpaid and of theft.

2. In the case of capital goods, adjustment shall be spread over five years including that in which the goods were acquired or manufactured. The annual adjustment shall be made only in respect of one fifth of the tax imposed on goods. The adjustment shall be made on the basis of the variations in the deduction entitlement in subsequent years in relation to that for the year in which the goods were acquired or manufactured.

By way of derogation from the preceding subparagraph, Member States may base the adjustment on a period of five full years starting from the time at which the goods are first used.

[In the case of immovable property acquired as capital goods, the adjustment period may be extended up to 20 years.] [1]

3. In the case of supply during the period of adjustment capital goods shall be regarded as if they had still been applied for business use by the taxable person until expiry of the period of adjustment. Such business activities are presumed to be fully taxed in cases where the delivery of the said goods is taxed; they are presumed to be fully exempt where the delivery is exempt. The adjustment shall be made only once for the whole period of adjustment still to be covered.

However, in the latter case, Member States may waive the requirement for adjustment in so far as the purchaser is a taxable person using the capital goods in question solely for transactions in respect of which value added tax is deductible.

4. For the purposes of applying the provisions of paragraphs 2 and 3, Member States may:

— define the concept of capital goods,

— indicate the amount of the tax which is to be taken into consideration for adjustment,

— adopt any suitable measures with a view to ensuring that adjustment does not involve any unjustified advantage,

— permit administrative simplifications.

s 12(4) **5.** If in any Member State the practical effect of applying paragraphs 2 and 3 would be insignificant, that Member State may subject to the consultation provided for in Article 29 forego application of these paragraphs having regard to the need to avoid distortion of competition, the overall tax effect in the Member State concerned and the need for due economy of administration.

6. Where the taxable person transfers from being taxed in the normal way to a special scheme or vice versa, Member States may take all necessary measures to ensure that the taxable person neither benefits nor is prejudiced unjustifiably.

Amendments

¹   Substituted by Council Directive 95/7/EC of 10 April 1995 Art 1(2) with effect from 1 January 1996.

Case law

Subject	Case	Case reference
Intending trader a taxable person	*Rompelman and Rompelman-Van Deelen v Minister van Financiën*	ECJ 268/83
Para (4): "capital goods", meaning	*Verbond van Nederlandse Ondernemingen v Inspecteur der Invoerrechten en Accijnzen*	[1977] ECR 113, [1977] 1 CMLR 413, ECJ 51/76
Used for business and non-business purposes	*Lennartz v Finanzamt München III*	[1991] STI 700, ECJ 97/90
Taxable person has valid right to recover input tax even if subsequently unable to make the planned taxable supplies due to circumstances beyond his control	*Belgium v Ghent Coal Termminal NV*	15 January 1998, C–37/95
Invoices		
Particulars required by authorities should not make deduction difficult	*Léa Jeunehomme and Société Anonyme d'Etude et de Gestion Immobiliére "EGI" v Belgian State*	[1988] STI 598, ECJ 123 and 330/87
Taxpayer not entitled to deduction in relation to sale of private dwelling where it was sold together with business premises	*Finamzampt Uelzen v Armbrecht*	[1995] STC 997, ECJ
VAT not deductible solely because it is stated on invoice	*Genius Holding BV v Staatssecretaris van Financiën*	[1991] STC 239, ECJ 342/87

TITLE XII
Persons liable for payment for tax

Article 21   s 8(3)

Persons liable for payment for tax

[**1.** Under the internal system, the following shall be liable to pay value added tax:

[(*a*) the taxable person carrying out the taxable supply of goods or of services, except for the cases referred to in (*b*), (*c*) and (*f*). Where the s 37 taxable supply of goods or of services is effected by a taxable person who is not established within the territory of the country, Member States may, under the conditions determined by them, lay down that the person liable to pay tax is the person for whom the taxable supply of goods or of services is carried out;] ¹

(*b*) taxable persons to whom services covered by Article 9(2)(*e*) are supplied or persons who are identified for value added tax purposes s 37, within the territory of the country to whom services covered by Article ᴬʀᵗ 28ɢ 28b(C), (D), (E) and (F) are supplied, if the services are carried out by a taxable person not established within the territory of the country;

(*c*) the person to whom the supply of goods is made when the following conditions are met:

— the taxable operation is a supply of goods made under the conditions laid down in Article 28c(E)(3),

— the person to whom the supply of goods is made is another taxable person or a non-taxable legal person identified for the purposes of value added tax within the territory of the country,

— the invoice issued by the taxable person not established within the territory of the country conforms to Article 22(3).

However, Member States may provide a derogation from this obligation, s 15 where the taxable person who is not established within the territory of the country has appointed a tax representative in that country;

(*d*) any person who mentions the value added tax on an invoice ...¹;

(*e*) any person effecting a taxable intra-Community acquisition of goods;

[(*f*) persons who are identified for value added tax purposes within the territory of the country and to whom goods are supplied under the conditions set out in Article 8(1)(d) or (e), if the supplies are carried out by a taxable person not established within the territory of the country.] ³

2. By way of derogation from the provisions of paragraph 1:

(*a*) where the person liable to pay tax in accordance with the provisions of paragraph 1 is a taxable person who is not established within the territory of the country, Member States may allow him to appoint a tax representative as the person liable to pay tax. This option shall be subject to conditions and procedures laid down by each Member State;

(*b*) where the taxable transaction is effected by a taxable person who is not established within the territory of the country and no legal instrument exists, with the country in which that taxable person is established or has his seat, relating to mutual assistance similar in scope to that laid down by Directives 76/308/EEC (OJ L 73, 19.3.1976, p. 18. Directive as last amended by the 1994 Act of Accession) and 77/799/EEC (OJ L 336, 27.12.1977, p 15. Directive as last amended by the 1994 Act of Accession) and by Council Regulation (EEC) No 218/92 of 27 January 1992 on administrative cooperation in the field of indirect taxation (VAT) (OJ L 24, 1.2.1992, p 1), Member States may take steps to provide that the person liable for payment of the tax shall be a tax representative appointed by the non-established taxable person.

3. In the situations referred to in paragraphs 1 and 2, Member States may provide that someone other than the person liable for payment of the tax shall be held jointly and severally liable for payment of the tax.

4. On importation, value added tax shall be payable by the person or persons designated or accepted as being liable by the Member State into which the goods are imported.] [4]

Note

Art 28*g* (as amended by Council Directive 2001/115/EC, Art 4(5) with effect from 6 February 2002) purported to delete "or other document serving as invoice" from para 1(*d*), however, that text appears in para 1(*c*).

Amendments

[1] Deleted by Art 28*g* (amended by Council Directive 2001/115/EC of 20 December 2001, Art 4(5)) with effect from 6 February 2001; previously "or other document serving as invoice".

[2] Para (1)(*a*) substituted by Art 28*g* (amended by Council Directive 2003/92/EC of 7 October 2003, Art 1(4)) with effect from 11 October 2003.

[3] Para (1)(*f*) inserted by Art 28*g* (amended by Council Directive 2003/92/EC of 7 October 2003, art 1(5)) with effect from 11 October 2003.

[4] Article 21 substituted by Art 28*g* (amended by Council Directive 2000/65/EC of 17 October 2000 (OJ L 269, 21/10/2000 p 44–46) Art 1(4)) with effect from 17 October 2000.

Case law

Subject	*Case*	*Case reference*
Stolen goods	*Les Assurances Du Crédit NV v Bowy and Decoopman*	ECJ 205/90

VATR
1979

TITLE XIII
OBLIGATIONS OF PERSONS LIABLE FOR PAYMENT

ss 15,
17(9)–(13)

Article 22

Obligations under the internal system

[**1.** [(*a*) Every taxable person shall state when his activity as a taxable person commences, changes or ceases. Member States shall, subject to conditions which they lay down, allow the taxable person to make such statements by electronic means, and may also require that electronic means are used.] [1]

(*b*) Without prejudice to (*a*), every taxable person referred to in Article 28(*a*)(1)(*a*), second subparagraph, shall state that he is effecting intra-Community acquisitions of goods when the conditions for application of the derogation provided for in that Article are not fulfilled.

(*c*) Member States shall take the measures necessary to identify by means of an individual number:

[— Every taxable person, with the exception of those referred to in Article 28a(4), who, within the territory of the country, effects supplies of goods or of services giving him the right of deduction, other than supplies of goods or of services for which tax is payable solely by the customer or the recipient in accordance with Article 21(1)(*a*), (*b*), (*c*) or (*f*). However, Member States need not identify certain taxable persons referred to in article 4(3),] ²

— every taxable person referred to in paragraph 1(*b*) and every taxable person who exercises the option provided for the third subparagraph of Article 28a(1)(*a*).

[— every taxable person who, within the territory of the country, effects intra-Community acquisitions of goods for the purposes of his operations relating to the economic activities referred to in Article 4(2) carried out abroad,] ³

(*d*) Each individual identification number shall have a prefix in accordance with ISO International Standard No 3166 —alpha 2 —by which the Member State of issue may be identified. [Nevertheless, the Hellenic Republic shall be authorised to use the prefix "GR".] ⁴

(*e*) Member States shall take the measures necessary to ensure that their identification systems distinguish the taxable persons referred to in (*c*) and to ensure the correct application of the transitional arrangements for the taxation of intra-Community transactions as laid down in this Title.

2 (*a*) Every taxable person shall keep accounts in sufficient detail for value added tax to be applied and inspected by the tax authorities. _{ss 16(1), 17(8)}

[(*b*) Every taxable person shall keep a register of the goods he has s 17(2)(4) dispatched or transported or which have been dispatched or transported on his behalf out of the territory defined in Article 3 but within the Community for the purposes of the transactions referred to in the fifth, sixth and seventh indents of Article 28a(5)(*b*).

Every taxable person shall keep sufficiently detailed accounts to permit the identification of goods dispatched to him from another Member State by or on behalf of a taxable person identified for purposes of value added tax in that other Member State, in connection with which a service has been provided pursuant to the third or fourth indent of Article 9(2)(*c*);] ⁵

Every taxable person shall keep a register of materials dispatched to him from another Member State by or on behalf of a taxable person identified for purposes of value added tax in that other Member State with a view to the supply to that taxable person of contract work.

s 17(1),
(4), SI 279,
1992 **[3** (*a*) Every taxable person shall ensure that an invoice is issued, either by himself or by his customer or, in his name and on his behalf, by a third party, in respect of goods or services which he has supplied or rendered to another taxable person or to a non- taxable legal person. Every taxable person shall also ensure that an invoice is issued, either by himself or by his customer or, in his name and on his behalf, by a third party, in respect of the supplies of goods referred to in Article 28b(B)(I) and in respect of goods supplied under the conditions laid down in Article 28c(A).

Every taxable person shall likewise ensure that an invoice is issued, either by himself or by his customer or, in his name and on his behalf, by a third party, in respect of any payment on account made to him before any supplies of goods referred to in the first subparagraph and in respect of any payment on account made to him by another taxable person or non-taxable legal person before the provision of services is completed.

Member States may impose on taxable persons an obligation to issue an invoice in respect of goods or services other than those referred to in the preceding subparagraphs which they have supplied or rendered on their territory. When they do so, Member States may impose fewer obligations in respect of these invoices than those listed under points (*b*), (*c*) and (*d*).

The Member States may release taxable persons from the obligation to issue an invoice in respect of goods or services which they have supplied or rendered in their territory and which are exempt, with or without refund of the tax paid at the preceding stage, pursuant to Article 13, Article 28(2)(*a*) and Article 28(3)(*b*).

Any document or message that amends and refers specifically and unambiguously to the initial invoice is to be treated as an invoice. Member States in whose territory goods or services are supplied or rendered may allow some of the obligatory details to be left out of such documents or messages.

Member States may impose time limits for the issue of invoices on taxable persons supplying goods and services in their territory.

Under conditions to be laid down by the Member States in whose territory goods or services are supplied or rendered, a summary invoice may be drawn up for several separate supplies of goods or services.

Invoices may be drawn up by the customer of a taxable person in respect of goods or services supplied or rendered to him by that taxable person, on condition that there is at the outset an agreement between the two parties, and on condition that a procedure exists for the acceptance of each invoice by the taxable person supplying the goods or services. The

Member States in whose territory the goods or services are supplied or rendered shall determine the terms and conditions of the agreement and of the acceptance procedures between the taxable person and his customer.

Member States may impose further conditions on the issue of invoices by the customers of taxable persons supplying goods or services on their territory. For example, they may require that such invoices be issued in the name and on behalf of the taxable person. Such conditions must always be the same wherever the customer is established.

Member States may also lay down specific conditions for taxable persons supplying goods or services in their territory in cases where the third party, or the customer, who issues invoices is established in a country with which no legal instrument exists relating to mutual assistance similar in scope to that laid down by Council Directive 76/308/EEC of 15 March 1976 on mutual assistance for the recovery of claims relating to certain levies, duties, taxes and other measures (OJ L 73, 19.3.1976, p 18. Directive as last amended by Directive 2001/44/EC (OJ L 175, 28.6.2001, p 17)), Council Directive 77/799/EEC of 19 December 1977 concerning mutual assistance by the competent authorities of the Member States in the field of direct and indirect taxation (OJ L 336, 27.12.1977, p 15. Directive as last amended by the 1994 Act of Accession) and by Council Regulation (EEC) No 218 of 27 January 1992 on administrative cooperation in the field of indirect taxation (VAT) (OJ L 24, 1.2.1992, p 1).

(*b*)   Without prejudice to the specific arrangements laid down by this Directive, only the following details are required for VAT purposes on invoices issued under the first, second and third subparagraphs of point (*a*):

— the date of issue;

— a sequential number, based on one or more series, which uniquely identifies the invoice,

— the VAT identification number referred to in paragraph 1(c) under which the taxable person supplied the goods or services;

— where the customer is liable to pay tax on goods supplied or services rendered or has been supplied with goods as referred to in Article 28c(A), the VAT identification number as referred to in paragraph 1 (c) under which the goods were supplied or the services rendered to him;

— the full name and address of the taxable person and of his customer;

— the quantity and nature of the goods supplied or the extent and nature of the services rendered;

— the date on which the supply of goods or of services was made or completed or the date on which the payment on account referred to in the second subparagraph of point (a) was made, insofar as that a date can be determined and differs from the date of issue of the invoice;

— the taxable amount per rate or exemption, the unit price exclusive of tax and any discounts or rebates if they are not included in the unit price;

— the VAT rate applied;

— the VAT amount payable, except where a specific arrangement is applied for which this Directive excludes such a detail;

— where an exemption is involved or where the customer is liable to pay the tax, reference to the appropriate provision of this directive, to the corresponding national provision, or to any indication that the supply is exempt or subject to the reverse charge procedure;

— where the intra-Community supply of a new means of transport is involved, the particulars specified in Article 28a(2);

— where the margin scheme is applied, reference to Article 26 or 26a, to the corresponding national provisions, or to any other indication that the margin scheme has been applied;

— where the person liable to pay the tax is a tax representative within the meaning of [Article 21(4)] [6], the VAT identification number referred to in paragraph 1(*c*) of that tax representative, together with his full name and address.

Member States may require taxable persons established on their territory and supplying goods or services on their territory to indicate the VAT identification number referred to in paragraph 1(*c*) of their customer in cases other than those referred to in the fourth indent of the first subparagraph.

Member States shall not require invoices to be signed.

The amounts which appear on the invoice may be expressed in any currency, provided that the amount of tax to be paid is expressed in the national currency of the Member State where the supply of goods or services takes place, using the conversion mechanism laid down in Article 11C(2).

Where necessary for control purposes, Member States may require invoices in respect of goods supplied or services rendered in their territory and invoices received by taxable persons in their territory to be translated into their national languages.

(*c*) Invoices issued pursuant to point (*a*) may be sent either on paper or, subject to an acceptance by the customer, by electronic means.

Invoices sent by electronic means shall be accepted by Member States provided that the authenticity of the origin and integrity of the contents are guaranteed:

— by means of an advanced electronic signature within the meaning of Article 2(2) of Directive 1999/93/EC of the European Parliament and of the Council of 13 December 1999 on a Community framework for electronic signatures (OJ L 13, 19.1.2000, p 12); Member States may however ask for the advanced electronic signature to be based on a qualified certificate and created by a secure- signature-creation device, within the meaning of Article 2(6) and (10) of the aforementioned Directive;

— or by means of electronic data interchange (EDI) as defined in Article 2 of Commission Recommendation 1994/820/EC of 19 October 1994 relating to the legal aspects of electronic data interchange (OJ L 338, 28.12.1994, p 98) when the agreement relating to the exchange provides for the use of procedures guaranteeing the authenticity of the origin and integrity of the data; however Member States may, subject to conditions which they lay down, require that an additional summary document on paper is necessary.

Invoices may, however, be sent by other electronic means subject to acceptance by the Member State(s) concerned. The Commission will present, at the latest on 31 December 2008, a report, together with a proposal, if appropriate, amending the conditions on electronic invoicing in order to take account of possible future technological developments in this field.

Member States may not impose on taxable persons supplying goods or services in their territory any other obligations or formalities relating to the transmission of invoices by electronic means. However, they may provide, until 31 December 2005, that the use of such a system is to be subject to prior notification.

Member States may lay down specific conditions for invoices issued by electronic means for goods or services supplied in their territory from a country with which no legal instrument exists relating to mutual assistance similar in scope to that laid down by Directives 76/308/EEC and 77/799/EEC and by Regulation (EEC) No 218/92.

When batches containing several invoices are sent to the same recipient by electronic means, the details that are common to the individual invoices may be mentioned only once if, for each invoice, all the information is accessible.

(*d*) Every taxable person shall ensure that copies of invoices issued by himself, by his customer or, in his name and on his behalf, by a third party, and all the invoices which he has received are stored.

For the purposes of this Directive, the taxable person may decide the place of storage provided that he makes the invoices or information stored there available without undue delay to the competent authorities whenever they so request. Member States may, however, require taxable persons established in their territory to notify them of the place of storage, if it is outside their territory. Member States may, in addition, require taxable persons established in their territory to store within the country invoices issued by themselves or by their customers or, in their name and on their behalf, by a third party, as well as all the invoices which they have received, when the storage is not by electronic means guaranteeing full on-line access to the data concerned.

The authenticity of the origin and integrity of the content of the invoices, as well as their readability, must be guaranteed throughout the storage period. As regards the invoices referred to in the third subparagraph of point (*c*), the information they contain may not be altered; it must remain legible throughout the aforementioned period.

The Member States shall determine the period for which taxable persons must store invoices relating to goods or services supplied in their territory and invoices received by taxable persons established in their territory.

In order to ensure that the conditions laid down in the third subparagraph are met, Member States referred to in the fourth subparagraph may require that invoices be stored in the original form in which they were sent, whether paper or electronic. They may also require that when invoices are stored by electronic means, the data guaranteeing the authenticity of the origin and integrity of the content also be stored.

Member States referred to in the fourth subparagraph may impose specific conditions prohibiting or restricting the storage of invoices in a country with which no legal instrument exists relating to mutual assistance similar in scope to that laid down by Directives 76/308/EEC, 77/799/EEC and by Regulation (EEC) No 218/92 and to the right of access by electronic means, download and use referred to in Article 22a.

Member States may, subject to conditions which they lay down, require the storage of invoices received by non-taxable persons.

(*e*) For the purposes of points (*c*) and (*d*), transmission and storage of invoices "by electronic means" shall mean transmission or making available to the recipient and storage using electronic equipment for processing (including digital compression) and storage of data, and employing wires, radio transmission, optical technologies or other electromagnetic means.

For the purposes of this Directive, Member States shall accept documents or messages in paper or electronic form as invoices if they meet the conditions laid down in this paragraph.] [6]

4 [(*a*) Every taxable person shall submit a return by a deadline to be determined by Member States. That deadline may not be more than two months later than the end of each tax period. The tax period shall be fixed by each Member State at one month, two months or a quarter. Member States may, however, set different periods provided that they do not exceed one year. Member States shall, subject to conditions which they lay down, allow the taxable person to make such returns by electronic means, and may also require that electronic means are used.] [7]

(*b*) The return shall set out all the information needed to calculate the tax that has become chargeable and the deductions to be made including, where appropriate, and insofar as it seems necessary for the establishment of the basis of assessment, the total value of the transactions relative to such tax and deductions and the value of any exempt transactions.

(*c*)   The return shall also set out:

— on the one hand, the total value, less value added tax, of the supplies of goods referred to in Article 28c(A) on which tax has become chargeable during the period.

The following shall also be added: the total value, less value added tax, of the supplies of goods referred to in the second sentence of Article 8(1)(*a*) and in Article 28b(B)(1) effected in the territory of the country on which tax has become chargeable during the return period, where the place of departure of the dispatch or transport of the goods is situated within the territory of another Member State.

[— on the other hand, the total amount, less value added tax, of the intra-Community acquisitions of goods referred to in Article 28a(1) and (6) effected within the territory of the country on which tax has become chargeable.

The following shall also be added: the total value, less value added tax, of the supplies of goods referred to in the second sentence of Article 8(1)(*a*) and in Article 28(*b*)(B)(1) effected in the territory of the country on which tax has become chargeable during the return period, where the place of departure of the dispatch or transport of the goods is situated within the territory of another Member State, and the total amount, less value added tax, of the supplies of goods made within the territory of the country for which the taxable person has been designated as the person liable for the tax in accordance with Article 28c(E)(3) and under which the tax has become payable in the course of the period covered by the declaration,] [8]

The following shall also be added: the total value, less value added tax, of the supplies of goods referred to in the second sentence of Article 8(1)(*a*) and in Article 28b(B)(1) effected within the territory of another Member State for which tax has become chargeable during the return period, where the place of departure of the dispatch or transport of the goods is situated in the territory of the country.

5 Every taxable person shall pay the net amount of the value added tax when s 19(4) submitting the regular return. Member States may, however, set a different date for the payment of that amount or may demand an interim payment.

6 [(*a*)   Member States may require a taxable person to submit a statement, including all the particulars specified in paragraph 4, concerning all transactions carried out in the preceding year. That statement shall provide all the information necessary for any adjustments. Member States shall, subject to conditions which they lay down, allow the taxable person to make such statements by electronic means, and may also require that electronic means are used.] [9]

(*b*) [Every taxable person identified for value added tax purposes shall also submit a recapitulative statement of the acquirers identified for value added tax purposes to whom he has supplied goods under the conditions provided for in Article 28c(A)(*a*) and (*d*), and of consignees identified for value added tax purposes in the transactions referred to in the fifth subparagraph.] [10]

[The recapitulative statement shall be drawn up for each calendar quarter within a period and in accordance with procedures to be determined by the Member States, which shall take the measures necessary to ensure that the provisions concerning administrative cooperation in the field of indirect taxation are in any event complied with. Member States shall, subject to conditions which they lay down, allow the taxable person to make such statements by electronic means, and may also require that electronic means are used.] [11]

The recapitulative statement shall set out:

— the number by which the taxable person is identified for purposes of value added tax in the territory of the country and under which he effected supplies of goods in the conditions laid down in Article [28c(A)(*a*)] [12],

[— the number by which each person acquiring goods is identified for purposes of value added tax in another Member State and under which the goods were supplied to him,] [13]

— for each person acquiring goods, the total value of the supplies of goods effected by the taxable person. Those amounts shall be declared for the calendar quarter during which the tax became chargeable.

The recapitulative statements shall also set out:

— for the supplies of goods covered by Article [28c(A)(*d*)] [14], the number by means of which the taxable person is identified for purposes of value added tax in the territory of the country, the number by which he is identified in the Member State of arrival of the dispatch or transport [and the total amount of the supplies, determined in accordance with Article 28e(2).] [15],

— the amounts of adjustments made pursuant to Article 11(C)(1). Those amounts shall be declared for the calendar quarter during which the person acquiring the goods is notified of the adjustment.

...[16]

[In the cases set out in the third subparagraph of Article 28b(A)(2), the taxable person identified for value added tax purposes within the territory of the country shall mention in a clear way on the recapitulative statement:

— the number by which he is identified for value added purposes within the territory of the country and under which he carried out the intra-Community acquisition and the subsequent supply of goods,

— the number by which, within the territory of the Member State of arrival of the dispatch or transport of the goods, the consignee of the subsequent supply by the taxable person is identified,

— and, for each consignee, the total amount, less value added tax, of the supplies made by the taxable person within the territory of the Member State of arrival of the dispatch or transport of the goods. These amounts shall be declared for the calendar quarter during which the tax became chargeable.] [17]

(*c*) By way of derogation from (*b*), Member States may:

— require recapitulative statements to be filed on a monthly basis;
— require that recapitulative statements give additional particulars.

(*d*) In the case of supplies of new means of transport effected under the conditions laid down in Article 28c(A)(*b*) by a taxable person identified for purposes of value added tax to a purchaser not identified for purposes of value added tax or by a taxable person as defined in Article 28a(4), Member States shall take the measures necessary to ensure that the vendor communicates all the information necessary for value added tax to be applied and inspected by the tax authority.

(*e*) Member States may require taxable persons who in the territory of the country effect intra-Community acquisitions of goods as defined in Article 28a(1)(*a*) and (6) to submit statements giving details of such acquisitions provided, however, that such statements may not be required for a period of less than one month.

Member States may also require persons who effect the intra-Community acquisitions of new means of transport as defined to in Article 28a(1)(*b*) to provide, when submitting the return referred to in paragraph 4, all the information necessary for value added tax to be applied and inspected by the tax authority.

[7 Member States shall take the measures necessary to ensure that those persons who, in accordance with Article 21(1) and (2), are considered to be liable to pay the tax instead of a taxable person not established within the territory of the country comply with the obligations relating to declaration and payment set out in this Article; they shall also take the measures necessary to ensure that those persons who, in accordance with Article 21(3), are held to be jointly and severally liable for payment of the tax comply with the obligations relating to payment set out in this Article.] [18]

8 Member States may impose other obligations which they deem necessary for the correct collection of the tax and for the prevention of evasion, subject to the requirement of equal treatment for domestic transactions and transactions carried out between Member States by taxable persons and provided that such obligations do not, in trade between Member States, give rise to formalities connected with the crossing of frontiers.

ss 16(2), 17(5)–(7), SI 275/ 1992, SI 277/1992

[The option provided for in the first subparagraph cannot be used to impose additional obligations over and above those laid down in paragraph 3.] [19]

9 (*a*)   Member States may release from certain or all obligations:

— taxable persons carrying out only supplies of goods or of services which are exempt under Articles 13 and 15,

— taxable persons eligible for the exemption from tax provided for in Article 24 and for the derogation provided for in Article 28a(1)(*a*), second subparagraph;

— taxable persons carrying out none of the transactions referred to in paragraph 4(*c*).

[Without prejudice to the provisions laid down in point (*d*), Member States may not, however, release the taxable persons referred to in the third indent from the obligations referred to in Article 22(3).] [20]

(*b*)   Member States may release taxable persons other than those referred to in (*a*) from certain of the obligations referred to in 2(*a*).

(*c*)   Member States may release taxable persons from payment of the tax due where the amount involved is insignificant.

[(*d*)   Subject to consultation of the Committee provided for in Article 29 and under the conditions which they may lay down, Member States may provide that invoices in respect of goods supplied or services rendered in their territory do not have to fulfil some of the conditions laid down in paragraph 3(*b*) in the following cases:

— when the amount of the invoice is minor, or

— when commercial or administrative practice in the business sector concerned or the technical conditions under which the invoices are issued make it difficult to comply with all the requirements referred to in paragraph 3(*b*).

In any case, these invoices must contain the following:

— the date of issue,

— identification of the taxable person,

— identification of the type of goods supplied or services rendered,

— the tax due or the information needed to calculate it.

The simplified arrangements provided for in this point may not be applied to transactions referred to in paragraph 4(*c*).] [21]

[(*e*)   In cases where Member States make use of the option provided for in the third indent of point (*a*) to refrain from allocating a number as referred to in paragraph 1(*c*) to taxable persons who do not carry out any of the transactions referred to in paragraph 4(*c*), and where the supplier or the customer have not been allocated an identification number of this type, the invoice should feature instead another number called the tax reference number, as defined by the Member States concerned.

When the taxable person has been allocated an identification number as referred to in paragraph 1(*c*), the Member States referred to in the first subparagraph may also require the invoice to show:

— for services rendered referred to in Article 28b(C), (D), (E) and (F) and for supplies of goods referred to in Article 28c(A) and (E) point 3, the number referred to in paragraph 1(*c*) and the tax reference number of the supplier;

— for other supplies of goods and services, only the tax reference number of the supplier or only the number referred to in paragraph 1(*c*).] [22]

10 Member States shall take measures to ensure that non-taxable legal persons who are liable for the tax payable in respect of intra-Community acquisitions of goods covered by the first subparagraph of Article 28a(1)(*a*) comply with the above obligations relating to declaration and payment and that they are identified by an individual number as defined in paragraph 1(*c*), (*d*) and (*e*).

[**11** In the case of intra-Community acquisitions of products subject to excise duty referred to in Article 28a(1)(*c*) as well as] [23] In the case of intra-Community   s 19A acquisitions of new means of transport covered by Article 28a(1)(*b*), Member States shall adopt arrangements for declaration and subsequent payment.

12 Acting unanimously on a proposal from the Commission, the Council may authorise any Member State to introduce particular measures to simplify the statement obligations laid down in paragraph 6(*b*). Such simplification measures, which shall not jeopardize the proper monitoring of intra-Community transactions, may take the following forms:

(*a*) Member States may authorize taxable persons who meet the following three conditions to file one-year recapitulative statements indicating the numbers by which the persons to whom those taxable persons have supplied goods under the conditions laid down in Article 28c(A) are identified for purposes of value added tax in other Member States:

— the total annual value, less value added tax, of their supplies of goods or provisions of services, as defined in Articles 5, 6 and 28a(5), does not exceed ECU 35,000 the amount of the annual turnover which is used as a reference for application of the exemption from tax provided for in Article 24,

— the total annual value, less value added tax, of supplies of goods effected by them under the conditions laid down in Article 28c(A) does not exceed the equivalent in national currency of ECU 15 000,

— supplies of goods effected by them under the conditions laid down in Article 28c(A) are other than supplies of new means of transport;

(*b*) Member States which set at over three months the tax period for which a taxable person must submit the returns provided for in paragraph 4 may authorize such persons to submit recapitulative statements for the same period where those taxable persons meet the following three conditions:

> — the overall annual value, less value added tax, of the goods and services they supply, as defined in Articles 5, 6 and 28a(5), does not exceed the equivalent in national currency of ECU 200 000,
>
> — the total annual value, less value added tax, of supplies of goods effected by them under the conditions laid down in Article 28c(A) does not exceed the equivalent in national currency of ECU 15 000,
>
> — supplies of goods effected by them under the conditions laid down in Article 28c(A) are other than supplies of new means of transport.]
>
> [24]

Amendments

[1] Substituted by Council Directive 2002/38/EC of 7 May 2002 (OJ L128, 15.5.2002, p 41) Art 2(1) with effect from 1 July 2003; previously "(*a*) Every taxable person shall state when his activity as a taxable person commences, changes or ceases.".

[2] Para (1)(*c*) first indent substituted by Art 28h (amended by Council Directive 2003/92/EC of 7 October 2003, art 1(6)) with effect from 11 October 2003.

[3] Para (1)(*c*)(3rd indent) inserted by Council Directive 92/111/EEC of 14 December 1992, Art 1(20) with effect from 1 January 1993.

[4] Inserted by Art 28h which was amended by Council Directive 2001/115/EC, Art 2(1) with effect from 6 February 2002.

[5] Para (2)(*b*) substituted by Art 28h which was amended by Council Directive 95/7/EC of 10 April 1995, Art 1(12) with effect from 25 May 1995.

[6] Para 3 substituted by Art 28h which was amended by Council Directive 2001/115/EC, Art 2(2) with effect from 6 February 2002.

[7] Substituted by Council Directive 2002/38/EC of 7 May 2002 (OJ L128, 15.5.2002, p 41) Art 2(2) with effect from 1 July 2003; previously "(*a*) Every taxable person shall submit a return by a deadline to be determined by Member States. That deadline may not be more than two months later than the end of each tax period. The tax period shall be fixed by each Member State at one month, two months or a quarter. Member States may, however, set different periods provided that they do not exceed one year.".

[8] Para (4)(*c*)(2nd indent) substituted by Council Directive 92/111/EEC of 14 December 1992, art 1(20) with effect from 1 January 1993.

[9] Substituted by Council Directive 2002/38/EC of 7 May 2002 (OJ L128, 15.5.2002, p 41) Art 2(3) with effect from 1 July 2003; previously "(*a*) Member States may require a taxable person to submit a statement, including all the particulars specified in paragraph 4, concerning all transactions carried out in the preceding year. That statement shall provide all the information necessary for any adjustments.".

[10] Substituted by Council Directive 2002/38/EC of 7 May 2002 (OJ L128, 15.5.2002, p 41) Art 2(4) with effect from 1 July 2003; previously "he recapitulative statement shall be drawn up for each calendar quarter within a period and in accordance with procedures to be determined by the Member States, which shall take the measures necessary to ensure that the provisions concerning administrative co-operation in the field of indirect taxation are in any event complied with.".

[11] Para (6)(*b*)(1st para) substituted by Art 28h which was amended by Council Directive 95/7/EC of 10 April 1995, Art 1(12) with effect from 25 May 1995.

[12] Substituted by Council Directive 92/111/EEC of 14 December 1992, Art 1(20) with effect from 1 January 1993.

[13] Para (6)(*b*)(3rd subpara)(2nd indent) substituted by Art 28h which was amended by Council Directive 95/7/EC of 10 April 1995, Art 1(12) with effect from 25 May 1995.

[14] Substituted by Council Directive 92/111/EEC of 14 December 1992, Art 1(20) with effect from 1 January 1993.

[15] Substituted by Council Directive 92/111/EEC of 14 December 1992, Art 1(20) with effect from 1 January 1993.

16   Para (6)(*b*)(5th subpara) deleted by Art 28h which was amended by Council Directive 95/7/EC of
     10 April 1995, Art 1(12) with effect from 25 May 1995.

17   Inserted by Council Directive 92/111/EEC of 14 December 1992, Art 1(20) with effect from
     1 January 1993.

18   Para (7) substituted by Art 28h (amended by Council Directive 2000/65/EC of 17 October 2000,
     Art 1(5)(*b*)) with effect from 17 October 2000.

19   Inserted by Art 28h which was amended by Council Directive 2001/115/EC, Art 2(3) with effect
     from 6 February 2002.

20   Inserted by Art 28h which was amended by Council Directive 2001/115/EC, Art 2(4) with effect
     from 6 February 2002.

21   Para 9(*d*) inserted by Art 28h which was amended by Council Directive 2001/115/EC, Art 2(5)
     with effect from 6 February 2002.

22   Para 9(*e*) inserted by Art 28h which was amended by Council Directive 2001/115/EC, Art 2(6)
     with effect from 6 February 2002.

23   Inserted by Council Directive 92/111/EEC of 14 December 1992, Art 1(20) with effect from
     1 January 1993.

24   Art 22 substituted by Council Directive 91/680/EEC of 16 December 1991, Art 28h with effect
     from 1 January 1993 for the transitional period specified in Art 28l first para.

Case law

Subject	Case	Case reference
Interim payments of VAT required by Italian law precluded by articles 10 and 22(4)	*Balocchi v Ministero delle Finanze dello Stato*	[1993] STI 1348, ECJ 10/92
Invoices: particulars required by authorities should not make deduction difficult	*Léa Jeunehomme and Société Anonyme d'Etude et de Gestion Immobiliére "EGI" v Belgian State*	[1988] STI 598, ECJ 123 and 330/87
Advocate General opinion: imput credit allowed if proof of purchases exists where original invoice mislaid	*Reisdorf v Finamzamt Köln-West*	[1997] STC 180, ECJ 85/95
Para (8) applies only to transactions between Member States—it does not preclude a Member State from imposing stricter rules on internal transactions	*Eisman Alto Adige Srl v Ufficio IVA di Bolzano*	[1996] STC 1374, ECJ 217/94
Member State to regard credit notes as a document serving as an invoice if all necessary information included 17 September 1997	*Finanzamt Osnabuck- Land v Langhorst*	C–141/96
Member State to regard credit notes as a document serving as an invoice if all necessary information included	*Finanzamt Osnabruck — Land v Langhorst*	17 September 1997, C–141/96

Article 22a

[Right of access to invoices stored by electronic means in another Member State

When a taxable person stores invoices which he issues or receives by an
electronic means guaranteeing on-line access to the data and when the place of
storage is in a Member State other than that in which he is established, the
competent authorities in the Member State in which he is established shall have a

right, for the purpose of this directive, to access by electronic means, download and use these invoices within the limits set by the regulations of the Member State where the taxable person is established and as far as that State requires for control purposes.] [1]

Amendments

[1]   Article 22a inserted by Council Directive 2001/115/EC, Art 3 with effect from 6 February 2002.

s 15

Article 23
Obligations in respect of imports

As regards imported goods, Member States shall lay down the detailed rules for the making of the declarations and payments.

In particular, Member States may provide that the value added tax payable on importation of goods by taxable persons or persons liable to tax or certain categories of these two need not be paid at the time of importation, on condition that the tax is mentioned as such in a return to be submitted under Article 22(4).

Case law

Subject	Case	Case reference
Differing accounting and payment periods for import VAT and VAT on internal transactions are permissible	*Dansk Denkavit v Ministeriet for Skatter og Afgifter*	[1984] ECR 2649, [1985] 3 CMLR 729, ECJ 42/83
Penalties relating to import VAT should not be more severe than penalties relating to internal transactions	*The State (Italy) v Rainer Drexl*	[1989] 2 CMLR 241, ECJ 299/86

s 8(3)

TITLE XIV
SPECIAL SCHEMES

Article 24
Special scheme for small undertakings

1. Member States which might encounter difficulties in applying the normal tax scheme to small undertakings by reason of their activities or structure shall have the option, under such conditions and within such limits as they may set but subject to the consultation provided for in Article 29, of applying simplified procedures such as flat-rate schemes for charging and collecting the tax provided they do not lead to a reduction thereof.

2. Until a date to be fixed by the Council acting unanimously on a proposal from the Commission, but which shall not be later than that on which the charging of tax on imports and the remission of tax on exports in trade between the Member States are abolished:

> (*a*)   Member States which have made use of the option under Article 14 of the second Council Directive of 11 April 1967 to introduce exemptions

or graduated tax relief may retain them and the arrangements for applying them if they conform with the value added tax system.

Those Member States which apply an exemption from tax to taxable persons whose annual turnover is less than the equivalent in national currency of 5,000 European units of account at the conversion rate of the day on which this Directive is adopted, may increase this exemption up to 5,000 European units of account.

Member States which apply graduated tax relief may neither increase the ceiling of the graduated tax reliefs nor render the conditions for the granting of it more favourable;

(*b*)   Member States which have not made use of this option may grant an exemption from tax to taxable persons whose annual turnover is at the maximum equal to the equivalent in national currency of 5,000 European units of account at the conversion rate of the day on which this Directive is adopted; where appropriate, they may grant graduated tax relief to taxable persons whose annual turnover exceeds the ceiling fixed by the Member States for the application of exemption;

(*c*)   Member States which apply an exemption from tax to taxable persons whose annual turnover is equal to or higher than the equivalent in national currency of 5,000 European units of account at the conversion rate of the day on which this Directive is adopted, may increase it in order to maintain its value in real terms.

3. The concepts of exemption and graduated tax relief shall apply to the supply of goods and services by small undertakings.

Member States may exclude certain transactions from the arrangements provided for in paragraph 2. The provisions of paragraph 2 shall not, in any case, apply to the transactions referred to in Article 4(3).

[In all circumstances supplies of new means of transport effected under the conditions laid down in Article 28c(A) as well as supplies of goods and services effected by a taxable person who is not established in the territory of the country shall be excluded from the exemption from tax under paragraph 2.] [1]

4. The turnover which shall serve as a reference for the purposes of applying the provisions of paragraph 2 shall consist of the amount, exclusive of value added tax, of goods and services supplied as defined in Articles 5 and 6, to the extent that they are taxed, including transactions exempted with refund of tax previously paid in accordance with Article 28(2), and the amount of the transactions exempted pursuant to Article 15, the amount of real property transactions, the financial transactions referred to in Article 13B(*d*), and insurance services, unless these transactions are ancillary transactions.

However, disposals of tangible or intangible capital assets of an undertaking shall not be taken into account for the purposes of calculating turnover.

5. Taxable persons exempt from tax shall not be entitled to deduct tax in accordance with the provisions of Article 17, nor to show the tax on their invoices ...[2].

6. Taxable persons eligible for exemption from tax may opt either for the normal value added tax scheme or for the simplified procedures referred to in paragraph 1. In this case they shall be entitled to any graduated tax relief which may be laid down by national legislation.

7. Subject to the application of paragraph 1, taxable persons enjoying graduated relief shall be treated as taxable persons subject to the normal value added tax scheme.

8. At four-yearly intervals, and for the first time on 1 January 1982, and after consultation of the Member States, the Commission shall report to the Council on the application of the provisions of this Article. It shall as far as may be necessary, and taking into account the need to ensure the long-term convergence of national regulations, attach to this report proposals for:

    (*a*) improvements to be made to the special scheme for small undertakings;

    (*b*) the adaptation of national systems as regards exemptions and graduated value added tax relief;

    (*c*) the adaptation of the limit of 5,000 European units of account mentioned in paragraph 2.

9. The Council will decide at the appropriate time whether the realization of the objective referred to in Article 4 of the first Council Directive of 11 April 1967 requires the introduction of a special scheme for small undertakings and will, if appropriate, decide on the limits and common implementing conditions of this scheme. Until the introduction of such a scheme, Member States may retain their own special schemes which they will apply in accordance with the provisions of this Article and of subsequent acts of the Council.

Amendments

1   Inserted by Art 28i which was inserted by Council Directive 91/680/EEC of 16 December 1991, Art 1(22) with effect from 1 January 1993 for the transitional period specified in Art 28l first para, and subsequently amended by Council Directive 92/111/EEC of 14 December 1992, Art 1(21) with effect from 1 January 1993.

2   Deleted by Council Directive 2001/115/EC, Art 4(2) with effect from 6 February 2002; previously "or on any other documents serving as invoices".

Article 24a

[In implementing Article 24(2) to (6), the following Member States may grant an exemption from value added tax to taxable persons whose annual turnover is less than the equivalent in national currency at the conversion rate on the date of their accession:

    —   in the Czech Republic: EUR 35000;

    —   in Estonia: EUR 16000;

    —   in Cyprus: EUR 15600;

    —   in Latvia: EUR 17200;

    —   in Lithuania: EUR 29000;

    —   in Hungary: EUR 35000;

    —   in Malta: EUR 37000 when the economic activity consists principally in the supply of goods, EUR 24300 when the economic activity consists

principally in the supply of services with a low value added (high inputs), and EUR 14600 in other cases, namely service providers with a high value added (low inputs);
— in Poland: EUR 10000;
— in Slovenia: EUR 25000;
— in Slovakia: EUR 35000.] [1]

Amendments

[1]   Article 24 bis substituted by Council Directive 2004/66/EC of 26 April 2004 Annex V para (1)(*a*) with effect from 1 May 2004.

Article 25
Common flat-rate scheme for farmers

ss 8(3),(9), 17(9)–(13)

1. Where the application to farmers of the normal value added tax scheme, or the simplified scheme provided for in Article 24, would give rise to difficulties, Member States may apply to farmers a flat-rate scheme tending to offset the value added tax charged on purchases of goods and services made by the flat-rate farmers pursuant to this Article.

2. For the purposes of this Article, the following definitions shall apply:
— **"farmer"**: a taxable person who carries on his activity in one of the undertakings defined below,
— **"agricultural, forestry or fisheries undertakings"**: an undertaking considered to be such by each Member State within the framework of the production activities listed in Annex A,
— **"flat-rate farmer"**: a farmer subject to the flat-rate scheme provided for in paragraphs 3 et seq,
— **"agricultural products"**: goods produced by an agricultural, forestry or fisheries undertaking in each Member State as a result of the activities listed in Annex A,
— **"agricultural service"**: any service as set out in Annex B supplied by a farmer using his labour force and/or by means of the equipment normally available on the agricultural, forestry or fisheries undertaking operated by him,
— **"value added tax charge on inputs"**: the amount of the total value added tax attaching to the goods and services purchased by all agricultural, forestry and fisheries undertakings of each Member State subject to the flat-rate scheme where such tax would be deductible under Article 17 by a farmer subject to the normal value added tax scheme,
— **"flat-rate compensation percentages"**: the percentages fixed by Member States in accordance with paragraph 3 and applied by them in the cases specified in paragraph 5 to enable flat-rate farmers to offset at a fixed rate the value added tax charge on inputs,
— **"flat-rate compensation"**: the amount arrived at by applying the flat-rate compensation percentage provided for in paragraph 3 to the turnover of the flat-rate farmer in the cases referred to in paragraph 5.

3. Member States shall fix the flat-rate compensation percentages, where necessary, and shall notify the Commission before applying them. Such percentages shall be based on macro-economic statistics for flat-rate farmers alone for the preceding three years. They may not be used to obtain for flat-rate farmers refunds greater than the value added tax charges on inputs. Member States shall have the option of reducing such percentages to a nil rate. The percentage may be rounded up or down to the nearest half point.

Member States may fix varying flat-rate compensation percentages for forestry, for the different sub-divisions of agriculture and for fisheries.

4. Member States may release flat-rate farmers from the obligations imposed upon taxable persons by Article 22.

[When they exercise this option, Member States shall take the measures necessary to ensure the correct application of the transitional arrangements for the taxation of intra-Community transactions as laid down in Title XVIa.] [1]

[**5.** The flat-rate percentages provided for in paragraph 3 shall be applied to the prices, exclusive of tax, of:

(*a*) agricultural products supplied by flat-rate farmers to taxable persons other than those eligible within the territory of the country for the flat-rate scheme provided for in this Article;

(*b*) agricultural products supplied by flat-rate farmers, under the conditions laid down in Article 28c(A), to non-taxable legal persons not eligible, in the Member State of arrival of the dispatch or transport of the agricultural products thus supplied, for the derogation provided for in Article 28a(1)(*a*), second subparagraph;

(*c*) agricultural services supplied by flat-rate farmers to taxable persons other than those eligible within the territory of the country for the flat-rate scheme provided for in this Article.

ss 12A,
17(2),(4) This compensation shall exclude any other form of deduction.] [2]

[**6.** In the case of the supplies of agricultural products and of agricultural services referred to in paragraph 5, Member States shall provide for the flat-rate compensation to be paid either:

(*a*) by the purchaser or customer. In that event, the taxable purchaser or customer shall be authorized, as provided for in Article 17 and in accordance with the procedures laid down by the Member States, to deduct from the tax for which he is liable within the territory of the country the amount of the flat-rate compensation he has paid to flat-rate farmers.

Member States shall refund to the purchaser or customer the amount of the flat-rate compensation he has paid to flat-rate farmers in respect of any of the following transactions:

— supplies of agricultural products effected under the conditions laid down in Article 28c(A) to taxable persons, or to non-taxable legal persons acting as such in another Member State within which they are not eligible for the derogation provided for in the second subparagraph of Article 28a(1)(*a*);

— supplies of agricultural products effected under the conditions laid down in Article 15 and in Article 16(1)(B), (D) and (E) to taxable purchasers established outside the Community, provided that the products are used by those purchasers for the purposes of the transactions referred to in Article 17(3)(*a*) or (*b*) or for the purposes of services which are deemed to be supplied within the territory of the country and on which tax is payable solely by the customers under Article 21(1)(*b*);

— supplies of agricultural services to taxable customers established within the Community but in other Member States or to taxable customers established outside the Community, provided that the services are used by those customers for the purposes of the transactions referred to in Article 17(3)(*a*) and (*b*) or for the purposes of services which are deemed to be supplied within the territory of the country and on which tax is payable solely by the customers under Article 21(1)(*b*).

Member States shall determine the method by which the refunds are to be made; in particular, they may apply Article 17(4); or

(*b*)   by the public authorities.] [3]

7. Member States shall make all necessary provisions to check properly the payment of the flat-rate compensation to the flat-rate farmers.

8. As regards all supplies of agricultural products and agricultural services other than those covered by paragraph 5, the flat-rate compensation is deemed to be paid by the purchaser or customer.

9. Each Member State may exclude from the flat-rate scheme certain categories of farmers and farmers for whom the application of the normal value added tax scheme, or the simplified scheme provided for in Article 24(1), would not give rise to administrative difficulties.

[Whenever they exercise the option provided for in this Article, Member States shall take all measures necessary to ensure that the same method of taxation is applied to supplies of agricultural products effected under the conditions laid down in Article 28b(B)(1), whether the supply is effected by a flat-rate farmer or by a taxable person other than a flat-rate farmer.] [4]

10. Every flat-rate farmer may opt, subject to the rules and conditions to be laid down by each Member State, for application of the normal value added tax scheme or, as the case may be, the simplified scheme provided for in Article 24(1).

11. The Commission shall, before the end of the fifth year following the entry into force of this Directive, present to the Council new proposals concerning the application of the value added tax to transactions in respect of agricultural products and services.

12. When they take up the option provided for in this Article the Member States shall fix the uniform basis of assessment of the value added tax in order to apply the scheme of own resources using the common method of calculation in Annex C.

Amendments

1 Inserted by Art 28j(1) which was inserted by Council Directive 91/680/EEC of 16 December 1991, Art 1(22) with effect from 1 January 1993 for the transitional period specified in Art 28l first para.

2 Para (5) substituted by Art 28j(2) which was inserted by Council Directive 91/680/EEC of 16 December 1991, Art 1(22) with effect from 1 January 1993 for the transitional period specified in Art 28l first para.

3 Para (6) substituted by Art 28j(2) which was inserted by Council Directive 91/680/EEC of 16 December 1991, Art 1(22) with effect from 1 January 1993 for the transitional period specified in Art 28l first para.

4 Inserted by Art 28j(3) which was inserted by Council Directive 91/680/EEC of 16 December 1991, Art 1(22) with effect from 1 January 1993 for the transitional period specified in Art 28l first para.

Case law

Subject	Case	Case reference
Flat-rate farmers	*Re Flat-rate VAT for Farmers, EC Commission v Italy*	[1989] 3 CMLR 748, ECJ 3/86

Article 26
Special scheme for travel agents

1. Member States shall apply value added tax to the operations of travel agents in accordance with the provisions of this Article, where the travel agents deal with customers in their own name and use the supplies and services of other taxable persons in the provision of travel facilities. This Article shall not apply to travel agents who are acting only as intermediaries and accounting for tax in accordance with Article 11 A (3)(*c*). In this Article travel agents include tour operators.

2. All transactions performed by the travel agent in respect of a journey shall be treated as a single service supplied by the travel agent to the traveller. It shall be taxable in the Member State in which the travel agent has established his business or has a fixed establishment from which the travel agent has provided the services. The taxable amount and the price exclusive of tax, within the meaning of Article 22(3)(*b*), in respect of this service shall be the travel agent's margin, that is to say, the difference between the total amount to be paid by the traveller, exclusive of value added tax, and the actual cost to the travel agent of supplies and services provided by other taxable persons where these transactions are for the direct benefit of the traveller.

3. If transactions entrusted by the travel agent to other taxable persons are performed by such persons outside the Community, the travel agent's service shall be treated as an exempted intermediary activity under Article 15(14). Where these transactions are performed both inside and outside the Community, only that part of the travel agent's service relating to transactions outside the Community may be exempted.

4. Tax charged to the travel agent by other taxable persons on the transactions described in paragraph 2 which are for the direct benefit of the traveller, shall not be eligible for deduction or refund in any Member State.

Case law

Subject	*Case*	*Case reference*
Letting of holiday dwellings	*Beheermattschappij van Ginkel Waddinxveen BV, Reisen Passingbureau Ban Ginkel v Inspecteur der Omzetbelasting*	[1996] STC 825, ECJ 163/91
Place of supply	*C & E Commissioners v DFDS A/S*	[1997] STC 384, ECJ 280/95
Tour operators — special scheme. Article 26 applies equally to traders who effect identical transactions to travel agents or tour operators	*TP Madgett & RM Baldwin (t\a Howden Court Hotel) v The Commissioners C & E*	22 November 1998, C–308/96 & C-94/97

Article 26a

Special arrangements applicable to second-hand goods, works of art, collectors' items and antiques

A. Definitions

[For the purpose of this Article, and without prejudice to other Community provisions:

   (*a*) *works of art* shall means the objects referred to in (*a*) of Annex I.
   However, Member States shall have the option of not considering as "works of art" the items mentioned in the final three indents in (*a*) in Annex I;

   (*b*) *collectors items* shall mean the objects referred to in (*b*) of Annex I;

   (*c*) *antiques* shall mean the objects referred to in (*c*) of Annex I;

   (*d*) *second-hand goods* shall mean tangible movable property that is suitable for further use as it is or after repair, other than works of art, collectors' items or antiques and other than precious metals or precious stones as defined by the Member States;

   (*e*) *taxable dealer* shall mean a taxable person who, in the course of his economic activity, purchases or acquires for the purposes of his undertaking, or imports with a view to resale, second-hand goods and/ or works of art, collectors' items or antiques, whether that taxable person is acting for himself or on behalf of another person pursuant to a contract under which commission is payable on purchase or sale;

   (*f*) *organizer of a sale by public auction* shall mean any taxable person who, in the course of his economic activity, offers goods for sale by public auction with a view to handing them over to the highest bidder;

(g) *principal of an organizer of a sale by public auction* shall mean any person who transmits goods to an organizer of a sale by public auction under a contract under which commission is payable on a sale subject to the following provisions:

— the organizer of the sale by public auction offers the goods for sale in his own name but on behalf of his principal,

— the organizer of the sale by public auction hands over the goods, in his own name but on behalf of his principal, to the highest bidder at the public auction.

B. Special arrangements for taxable dealers

1. In respect of supplies of second-hand goods, works of art, collectors' items and antiques effected by taxable dealers, Member States shall apply special arrangements for taxing the profit margin made by the taxable dealer, in accordance with the following provisions.

2. The supplies of goods referred to in paragraph 1 shall be supplies, by a taxable dealer, of second-hand goods, works of art, collectors' items or antiques supplied to him within the Community:

— by a non-taxable person,

or

— by another taxable person, in so far as the supply of goods by that other taxable person is exempt in accordance with Article 13(B)(c),

or

— by another taxable person in so far as the supply of goods by that other taxable person qualifies for the exemption provided for in Article 24 and involves capital assets,

or

— by another taxable dealer, in so far as the supply of goods by that other taxable dealer was subject to value added tax in accordance with these special arrangements.

3. The taxable amount of the supplies of goods referred to in paragraph 2 shall be the profit margin made by the taxable dealer, less the amount of value added tax relating to the profit margin. That profit margin shall be equal to the difference between the selling price charged by the taxable dealer for the goods and the purchase price.

For the purposes of this paragraph, the following definitions shall apply:

— *selling price* shall mean everything which constitutes the consideration, which has been, or is to be, obtained by the taxable dealer from the purchaser or a third party, including subsidies directly linked to that transaction, taxes, duties, levies and charges and incidental expenses such as commission, packaging, transport and insurance costs charged by the taxable dealer to the purchaser but excluding the amounts referred to in Article 11(A)(3),

— *purchase price* shall mean everything which constitutes the consideration defined in the first indent, obtained, or to be obtained, from the taxable dealer by his supplier.

4. Member States shall entitle taxable dealers to opt for application of the special arrangements to supplies of:

    (*a*) works of art, collectors' items or antiques which they have imported themselves;

    (*b*) works of art supplied to them by their creators or their successors in title;

    (*c*) works of art supplied to them by taxable person other than a taxable dealer where the supply by that other taxable person was subject to the reduced rate pursuant to Article 12(3)(*c*).

Member States shall determine the detailed rules for exercising this option which shall in any event cover a period at least equal to two calendar years.

If the option is taken up, the taxable amount shall be determined in accordance with paragraph 3. For supplies of works of art, collectors' items or antiques which the taxable dealer has imported himself, the purchase price to be taken into account in calculating the margin shall be equal to the taxable amount on importation, determined in accordance with Article 11(B), plus the value added tax due or paid on importation.

5. Where they are effected in the conditions laid down in Article 15, the supplies of second-hand goods, works of art, collectors' item or antiques subject to the special arrangements for taxing the margin shall be exempt.

6. Taxable persons shall not be entitled to deduct from the tax for which they are liable the value added tax due or paid in respect of goods which have been, or are to be, supplied to them by a taxable dealer, in so far as the supply of those goods by the taxable dealer is subject to the special arrangements for taxing the margin.

7. In so far as goods are used for the purposes of supplies by him subject to the special arrangements for taxing the margin, the taxable dealer shall not be entitled to deduct from the tax for which he is liable;

    (*a*) the value added tax due or paid in respect of works of art, collectors' items or antiques which he has imported himself;

    (*b*) the value added tax due or paid in respect of works of art which have been, or are to be, supplied to him by their creators or their successors in title;

    (*c*) the value added tax due or paid in respect of works of art which have been, or are to be, supplied to him by a taxable person other than a taxable dealer.

8. Where he is led to apply both the normal arrangements for value added tax and the special arrangements for taxing the margin, the taxable dealer must follow separately in his accounts the transactions falling under each of these arrangements, according to rules laid down by the Member States.

9. The taxable dealer may not indicate separately on the invoices which he issues, ...[1], tax relating to supplies of goods which he makes subject to the special arrangements for taxing the margin.

10. In order to simplify the procedure for charging the tax and subject to the consultation provided for in Article 29, Member States may provide that, for certain transactions or for certain categories of taxable dealers, the taxable amount of supplies of goods subject to the special arrangements for taxing the margin shall be determined for each tax period during which the taxable dealer must submit the return referred to in Article 22(4).

In that event, the taxable amount for supplies of goods to which the same rate of value added tax is applied shall be the total margin made by the taxable dealer less the amount of value added tax relating to that margin.

The total margin shall be equal to the difference between:

— the total amount of supplies of goods subject to the special arrangements for taxing the margin effected by the taxable dealer during the period; that amount shall be equal to the total selling prices determined in accordance with paragraph 3,

and

— the total amount of purchases of goods as referred to in paragraph 2 effected, during that period, by the taxable dealer; that amount shall be equal to the total purchase prices determined in accordance with paragraph 3.

Member States shall take the necessary measures to ensure that the taxable persons concerned do not enjoy unjustified advantages or sustain unjustified loss.

11. The taxable dealer may apply the normal value added tax arrangements to any supply covered by the special arrangements pursuant to paragraph 2 or 4.

Where the taxable dealer applies the normal value added tax arrangements to:

(*a*) the supply of a work of art, collectors' item or antique which he has imported himself, he shall be entitled to deduct from his tax liability the value added tax due or paid on the import of those goods;

(*b*) the supply of a work of art supplied to him by its creator or his successors in title, he shall be entitled to deduct from his tax liability the value added tax due or paid for the work of art supplied to him;

(*c*) the supply of a work of art supplied to him by a taxable person other than a taxable dealer, he shall be entitled to deduct from his tax liability the value added tax due or paid for the work of art supplied to him.

This right to deduct shall arise at the time when the tax due for the supply in respect of which the taxable dealer opts for application of the normal value added tax arrangements become chargeable.

C. Special arrangements for sales by public auction.

1. By way of derogation from B, Member States may determine, in accordance with the following provisions, the taxable amount of supplies of second-hand goods, works of art, collectors' items or antiques effected by an organizer of sales by public auction, acting in his own name, pursuant to a contract under which commission is payable on the sale of those goods by public auction, on behalf of:

— a non-taxable person,

or

— another taxable person, in so far as the supply of goods, within the meaning of Article 5(4)(c), by that other taxable person is exempt in accordance with Article 13(B)(c),

or

— another taxable person, in so far as the supply of goods, within the meaning of Article 5(4)(c), by that other taxable person qualifies for the exemption provided for in Article 24 and involves capital assets,

or

— a taxable dealer, in so far as the supply of goods, within the meaning of Article 5(4)(c), by that other taxable dealer, is subject to tax in accordance with the special arrangements for taxing the margin provided for in B.

2. The taxable amount of each supply of goods referred to in paragraph 1 shall be the total amount invoiced in accordance with paragraph 4 to the purchaser by the organizer of the sale by public auction, less:

— the net amount paid or to be paid by the organizer of the sale by public auction to his principal, determined in accordance with paragraph 3,

and

— the amount of the tax due by the organizer of the sale by public auction in respect of his supply.

3. The net amount paid or to be paid by the organizer of the sale by public auction to his principal shall be equal to the difference between:

— the price of the goods at public auction,

and

— the amount of the commission obtained or to be obtained by the organizer of the sale by public auction from his principal, under the contract whereby commission is payable on the sale.

4. The organizer of the sale by public auction must issue to the purchaser an invoice ...[2] itemizing:

— the auction price of the goods,

— taxes, dues, levies and charges,

— incidental expenses such as commission, packing, transport and insurance costs charged by the organizer to the purchaser of the goods.

That invoice must not indicate any value added tax separately.

5. The organizer of the sale by public auction to whom the goods were transmitted under a contract whereby commission is payable on a public auction sale must issue a statement to his principal.

That statement must itemize the amount of the transaction, ie the auction price of the goods less the amount of the commission obtained or to be obtained from the principal.

A statement so drawn up shall serve as the invoice which the principal, where he is a taxable person, must issue to the organizer of the sale by public auction in accordance with Article 22(3).

6. Organizers of sales by public auction who supply goods under the conditions laid down in paragraph 1 must indicate in their accounts, in suspense accounts:

— the amounts obtained or to be obtained from the purchase of the goods,
— the amount reimbursed or to be reimbursed to the vendor of the goods.

These amounts must be fully substantiated.

7. The supply of goods to a taxable person who is an organizer of sales by public auction shall be regarded as being effected when the sale of those goods by public auction is itself effected.

D. Transitional arrangements for the taxation of trade between Member States

During the period referred to in Article 281, Member States shall apply the following provisions:

(*a*) supplies of new means of transport, within the meaning of Article 28a(2), effected within the conditions laid down in Article 28c(A) shall be excluded from the special arrangements provided for in B and C;

(*b*) by way of derogation from Article 28a(1)(*a*), intra-Community acquisition of second-hand goods, works of art, collectors' items or antiques shall not be subject to value added tax where the vendor is a taxable dealer acting as such and the goods acquired have been subject to tax in the Member State of departure of the dispatch or transport, in accordance with the special arrangements for taxing the margin provided for in B, or where the vendor is an organizer of sales by public auction acting as such and the goods acquired have been subject to tax in the Member State of departure of the dispatch or transport, in accordance with the special arrangements provided for in C;

(*c*) Articles 28b(B) and 28c(A)(*a*), (*c*) and (*d*) shall not apply to supplies of goods subject to value added tax in accordance with either of the special arrangements laid down in B and C.] [3]

Amendments

[1] Deleted by Council Directive 2001/115/EC, Art 4(2) with effect from 6 February 2002; previously "or on any other documents serving as invoices".

[2] Deleted by Council Directive 2001/115/EC, Art 4(3) with effect from 6 February 2002; previously "or a document in lieu".

[3] Article 26a inserted by Council Directive 94/5/EC of 14 February 1994 Art 1(3).

Article 26b
Special scheme for investment gold

[A. Definition

For the purposes of this Directive, and without prejudice to other Community provisions: "investment gold" shall mean:

(i) gold, in the form of a bar or a wafer of weights accepted by the bullion markets, of a purity equal to or greater than 995 thousandths, whether or not represented by securities. Member States may exclude from the scheme small bars or wafers of a weight of 1 g or less;

(ii) gold coins which:

— are of a purity equal to or greater than 900 thousandths,

— are minted after 1800,

— are or have been legal tender in the country of origin, and

— are normally sold at a price which does not exceed the open market value of the gold contained in the coins by more than 80 %.

Such coins are not, for the purpose of this Directive, considered to be sold for numismatic interest.

Each Member State shall inform the Commission before 1 July each year, starting in 1999, of the coins meeting these criteria which are traded in that Member State. The Commission shall publish a comprehensive list of these coins in the "C" series of the Official Journal of the European Communities before 1 December each year. Coins included in the published list shall be deemed to fulfil these criteria for the whole year for which the list is published.

B. Special arrangements applicable to investment gold transactions

Member States shall exempt from value added tax the supply, intra-Community acquisition and importation of investment gold, including investment gold represented by certificates for allocated or unallocated gold or traded on gold accounts and including, in particular, gold loans and swaps, involving a right of ownership or claim in respect of investment gold, as well as transactions concerning investment gold involving futures and forward contracts leading to a transfer of right of ownership or claim in respect of investment gold.

Member States shall also exempt services of agents who act in the name and for the account of another when they intervene in the supply of investment gold for their principal.

C. Option to tax

Member States shall allow taxable persons who produce investment gold or transform any gold into investment gold as defined in A a right of option for taxation of supplies of investment gold to another taxable person which would otherwise be exempt under B.

Member States may allow taxable persons, who in their trade normally supply gold for industrial purposes, a right of option for taxation of supplies of investment gold as defined in A(i) to another taxable person, which would otherwise be exempt under B. Member States may restrict the scope of this option.

Where the supplier has exercised a right of option for taxation pursuant to the first or second paragraph, Member States shall allow a right of option for taxation for the agent in respect of the services mentioned in the second paragraph of B.

Member States shall specify the details of the use of these options, and shall inform the Commission of the rules of application for the exercise of these options in that Member State.

D. Right of deduction

1. Taxable persons shall be entitled to deduct

- (*a*) tax due or paid in respect of investment gold supplied to them by a person who has exercised the right of option under C or supplied to them pursuant to the procedure laid down in G;
- (*b*) tax due or paid in respect of supply to them, or intra-Community acquisition or importation by them, of gold other than investment gold which is subsequently transformed by them or on their behalf into investment gold;
- (*c*) tax due or paid in respect of services supplied to them consisting of change of form, weight or purity of gold including investment gold,

if their subsequent supply of this gold is exempt under this Article.

2. Taxable persons who produce investment gold or transform any gold into investment gold, shall be entitled to deduct tax due or paid by them in respect of supplies, or intra-Community acquisition or importation of goods or services linked to the production or transformation of that gold as if their subsequent supply of the gold exempted under this Article were taxable.

E. Special obligations for traders in investment gold

Member States shall, as a minimum, ensure that traders in investment gold keep account of all substantial transactions in investment gold and keep the documentation to allow identification of the customer in such transactions.

Traders shall keep this information for a period of at least five years.

Member States may accept equivalent obligations under measures adopted pursuant to other Community legislation, such as Council Directive 91/308/EEC of 10 June 1991 on prevention of the use of the financial system for the purpose of money laundering (OJ L 166, 28.6.1991, p 77), to meet the requirements of the first paragraph.

Member States may lay down stricter obligations, in particular on special record keeping or special accounting requirements.

F. Reverse charge procedure

By way of derogation from Article 21(1)(*a*), as amended by Article 28*g*, in the case of supplies of gold material or semi-manufactured products of a purity of 325 thousandths or greater, or supplies of investment gold where an option referred to in C of this Article has been exercised, Member States may designate the purchaser as the person liable to pay the tax, according to the procedures and conditions which they shall lay down. When they exercise this option, Member States shall take the measures necessary to ensure that the person designated as liable for the tax due fulfils the obligations to submit a statement and to pay the tax in accordance with Article 22.

G. Procedure for transactions on a regulated gold bullion market

1. A Member State may, subject to consultation provided for under Article 29, disapply the exemption for investment gold provided for by this special scheme in respect of specific transactions, other than intra-Community supplies or exports, concerning investment gold taking place in that Member State:

(*a*) between taxable persons who are members of a bullion market regulated by the Member State concerned, and

(*b*) where the transaction is between a member of a bullion market regulated by the Member State concerned and another taxable person who is not a member of that market.

Under these circumstances, these transactions shall be taxable and the following shall apply.

2. (*a*) For transactions under 1(*a*), for the purpose of simplification, the Member State shall authorise suspension of the tax to be collected as well as dispense with the recording requirements of value added tax.

(*b*) For transactions under 1(*b*), the reverse charge procedure under F shall be applicable. Where a non-member of the bullion market would not, other than for these transactions, be liable for registration for VAT in the relevant Member State, the member shall fulfil the fiscal obligations on behalf of the non-member, according to the provisions of that Member State.] [1]

Amendments

[1]   Inserted by Council Directive 98/80/EC of 12 October 1998 (OJ L 281, 17/10/1998 P. 31–34) art 1 with effect from 17 October 1998.

Article 26c
Special scheme for non-established taxable persons supplying
electronic services to non-taxable persons

A. Definitions

[For the purposes of this Article, the following definitions shall apply without prejudice to other Community provisions:

(*a*) **"non-established taxable person"** means a taxable person who has neither established his business nor has a fixed establishment within the territory of the Community and who is not otherwise required to be identified for tax purposes under Article 22;

(*b*) **"electronic services"** and **"electronically supplied services"** means those services referred to in the last indent of Article 9(2)(*e*);

(*c*) **"Member State of identification"** means the Member State which the non-established taxable person chooses to contact to state when his activity as a taxable person within the territory of the Community commences in accordance with the provisions of this Article;

(*d*) **"Member State of consumption"** means the Member State in which the supply of the electronic services is deemed to take place according to Article 9(2)(*f*);

(*e*) **"value added tax return"** means the statement containing the information necessary to establish the amount of tax that has become chargeable in each Member State.

B. Special scheme for electronically supplied services

1. Member States shall permit a non-established taxable person supplying electronic services to a non-taxable person who is established or has his permanent address or usually resides in a Member State to use a special scheme in accordance with the following provisions. The special scheme shall apply to all those supplies within the Community.

2. The non-established taxable person shall state to the Member State of identification when his activity as a taxable person commences, ceases or changes to the extent that he no longer qualifies for the special scheme. Such a statement shall be made electronically.

The information from the non-established taxable person to the Member State of identification when his taxable activities commence shall contain the following details for the identification: name, postal address, electronic addresses, including websites, national tax number, if any, and a statement that the person is not identified for value added tax purposes within the Community. The non-established taxable person shall notify the Member State of identification of any changes in the submitted information.

3. The Member State of identification shall identify the non-established taxable person by means of an individual number. Based on the information used for this identification, Member States of consumption may keep their own identification systems.

The Member State of identification shall notify the non-established taxable person by electronic means of the identification number allocated to him.

4. The Member State of identification shall exclude the non-established taxable person from the identification register if:

(*a*) he notifies that he no longer supplies electronic services, or

(*b*) it otherwise can be assumed that his taxable activities have ended, or

(*c*) he no longer fulfils the requirements necessary to be allowed to use the special scheme, or (*d*) he persistently fails to comply with the rules concerning the special scheme.

5. The non-established taxable person shall submit by electronic means to the Member State of identification a value added tax return for each calendar quarter whether or not electronic services have been supplied. The return shall be submitted within 20 days following the end of the reporting period to which the return refers.

The value added tax return shall set out the identification number and, for each Member State of consumption where tax has become due, the total value, less value added tax, of supplies of electronic services for the reporting period and total amount of the corresponding tax. The applicable tax rates and the total tax due shall also be indicated.

6. The value added tax return shall be made in euro. Member States which have not adopted the euro may require the tax return to be made in their national currencies. If the supplies have been made in other currencies, the exchange rate valid for the last date of the reporting period shall be used when completing the value added tax return. The exchange shall be done following the exchange rates published by the European Central Bank for that day, or, if there is no publication on that day, on the next day of publication.

7. The non-established taxable person shall pay the value added tax when submitting the return. Payment shall be made to a bank account denominated in euro, designated by the Member State of identification. Member States which have not adopted the euro may require the payment to be made to a bank account denominated in their own currency.

8. Notwithstanding Article 1(1) of Directive 86/560/EEC, the non-established taxable person making use of this special scheme shall, instead of making deductions under Article 17(2) of this Directive, be granted a refund according to Directive 86/560/EEC. Articles 2(2), 2(3) and 4(2) of Directive 86/560/EEC shall not apply to the refund related to electronic supplies covered by this special scheme.

9. The non-established taxable person shall keep records of the transactions covered by this special scheme in sufficient detail to enable the tax administration of the Member State of consumption to determine that the value added tax return referred to in paragraph 5 is correct. These records should be made available electronically on request to the Member State of identification and to the Member State of consumption. These records shall be maintained for a period of 10 years from the end of the year when the transaction was carried out.

10. [Article 21(4)] [1](*b*) shall not apply to a non-established taxable person who has opted for this special scheme.] [2]

Amendments

[1]   Substituted by Council Directive 2000/65/EC of 17 October 2000 (OJ L 269, 21/10/2000 p 44–46) Art 1(6) with effect from 17 October 2000; previously "Article 21(2)".

[2]   Inserted by Council Directive 2002/38/EC of 7 May 2002 (OJ L128, 15.5.2002, p 41) Art 1(3) for a period of 3 years beginning on 1 July 2003.

TITLE XV
SIMPLIFICATION PROCEDURES

Article 27

[**1.** The Council, acting unanimously on a proposal from the Commission, may authorise any Member State to introduce special measures for derogation from the provisions of this Directive, in order to simplify the procedure for charging the tax or to prevent certain types of tax evasion or avoidance. Measures intended to simplify the procedure for charging the tax, except to a negligible extent, may not affect the overall amount of the tax revenue of the Member State collected at the stage of final consumption.

2. A Member State wishing to introduce the measure referred to in paragraph 1 shall send an application to the Commission and provide it with all the necessary information. If the Commission considers that it does not have all the necessary information, it shall contact the Member State concerned within two months of receipt of the application and specify what additional information is required. Once the Commission has all the information it considers necessary for appraisal of the request it shall within one month notify the requesting Member State accordingly and it shall transmit the request, in its original language, to the other Member States.

3. Within three months of giving the notification referred to in the last sentence of paragraph 2, the Commission shall present to the Council either an appropriate proposal or, should it object to the derogation requested, a communication setting out its objections.

4. In any event, the procedure set out in paragraphs 2 and 3 shall be completed within eight months of receipt of the application by the Commission.] [1]

5. Those Member States which apply on 1 January 1977 special measures of the type referred to in paragraph 1 above may retain them providing they notify the Commission of them before 1 January 1978 and providing that where such derogations are designed to simplify the procedure for charging tax they conform with the requirement laid down in paragraph 1 above.

Amendments

[1]   Paras (1)–(4) substituted by Council Directive 2004/7/EC of 20 January 2004 Art 1(1) with effect from 19 February 2004.

Cross-references

Art 27(1): derogations granted: Authorisation 83/333/EEC (derogations under a draft agreement between Germany and Luxembourg); Authorisation 84/468/EEC (derogations under a draft agreement between Germany and the Netherlands); Decision 89/487/EEC (authorising France to derogate from Art 17(6)); Decision 89/488/EEC (authorising France to derogate from Art 17(2)).

Case law

Subject	Case	Case reference
Para (1): "special measures": Member State which failed to inform EC Commission of "special measure" could not rely on it in the national court	*Direct Cosmetics Ltd v C & E Commissioners*	[1985] STC 479, [1985] 2 CMLR 145, ECJ 5/84

	Direct Cosmetics Ltd and	[1988] STC 540,
	Laughtons Photographs Ltd v C	ECJ 138/ 139/86
	& E Commissioners	
Tax avoidance. Derogation held not to	*Finanzamt Bergisch Glaadback*	29 May 1997, C–63/96
be valid where costs exceeded market	*v Skripalle*	
value of the supply		

TITLE XVI
TRANSITIONAL PROVISIONS

s 2(1A)

Article 28

1. Any provisions brought into force by the Member States under the provisions of the first four indents of Article 17 of the second Council Directive of 11 April 1967 shall cease to apply, in each Member State, as from the respective dates on which the provisions referred to in the second paragraph of Article 1 of this Directive come into force.

[**1a.** Until a date which may not be later than 30 June 1999, the United Kingdom of Great Britain and Northern Ireland may, for imports of works of art, collectors' items or antiques which qualified for an exemption on 1 January 1993, apply Article 11(B)(6) in such a way that the value added tax due on importation is, in any event, equal to 2,5% of the amount determined in accordance with Article 11(B)(1) to (4).] [1]

[**2.** Notwithstanding Article 12(3), the following provisions shall apply during the transitional period referred to in Article 28l.

(*a*) Exemptions with refund of the tax paid at the preceding stage and reduced rates lower than the minimum rate laid down in Article 12(3) in respect of the reduced rates, which were in force on 1 January 1991 and which are in accordance with Community law, and satisfy the conditions stated in the last indent of Article 17 of the second Council Directive of 11 April 1967, may be maintained.

Member States shall adopt the measures necessary to ensure the determination of own resources relating to these operations.

In the event that the provisions of this paragraph create for Ireland distortions of competition in the supply of energy products for heating and lighting, Ireland may, on specific request, be authorised by the Commission to apply a reduced rate to such supplies, in accordance with Article 12(3). In that case, Ireland shall submit its request to the Commission together with all necessary information. If the Commission has not taken a decision within three months of receiving the request, Ireland shall be deemed to be authorised to apply the proposed reduced rates.

(*b*) Member States which, at 1 January 1991 in accordance with Community law, applied exemptions with refund of tax paid at the preceding stage, or reduced rates lower than the minimum laid down in Article 12(3) in respect of the reduced rates, to goods and services other than those specified in Annex H, may apply the reduced rate or one of the two reduced rates provided for in Article 12(3) to any such supplies.

(c) Member States which under the terms of Article 12(3) will be obliged to increase their standard rate as applied at 1 January 1991 by more than 2%, may apply a reduced rate lower than the minimum laid down in Article 12(3) in respect of the reduced rate to supplies of categories of goods and services specified in Annex H. Furthermore, those Member States may apply such a rate to restaurant services, children's clothing, children's footwear and housing. Member States may not introduce exemptions with refund of the tax at the preceding stage on the basis of this paragraph.

(d) Member States which at 1 January 1991 applied a reduced rate to restaurant services, children's clothing, children's footwear and housing, may continue to apply such a rate to such supplies.

(e) Member States which at 1 January 1991 applied a reduced rate to supplies of goods and services other than those specified in Annex H may apply the reduced rate or one of the two reduced rates provided for in Article 12(3) to such supplies, provided that the rate is not lower than 12%.

[This provision may not apply to supplies of second-hand goods, works of art, collectors' items or antiques subject to value added tax in accordance with one of the special arrangements provided for an Article 26a(B) and (C).] [2]

(f) The Hellenic Republic may apply VAT rates up to 30% lower than the corresponding rates applied in mainland Greece in the departments of Lesbos, Chios, Samos, the Dodecanese and the Cyclades, and on the following islands in the Aegean: Thasos, Northern Sporades, Samothrace and Skiros.

(g) On the basis of a report from the Commission, the Council shall, before 31 December 1994, re-examine the provisions of subparagraphs (a) to (f) above in relation to the proper functioning of the internal market in particular. In the event of significant distortions of competition arising, the Council, acting unanimously on a proposal from the Commission, shall adopt appropriate measures.

[(h) Member States which, on 1 January 1993, were availing themselves of the option provided for in Article 5(5)(a) as in force on that date, may apply to supplies under contract to make up work the rate applicable to the goods after making up.

For the purposes of applying this provision, supplies under a contract to make up work shall be deemed to be delivery by a contractor to his customer of movable property made or assembled by the contractor from materials or objects entrusted to him by the customer for this purpose, whether or not the contractor has provided any part of the materials used.] [3]] [4]

[(i) Member States may apply a reduced rate to supplies of live plants (including bulbs, roots and the like, cut flowers and ornamental foliage) and wood for use as firewood.] [5]

[(*j*) the Republic of Austria may apply one of the two reduced rates provided for in the third subparagraph of Article 12(3)(*a*) to the letting of immovable property for residential use, provided that the rate is not lower than 10%;

(*k*) the Portuguese Republic may apply one of the two reduced rates provided for in the third subparagraph of Article 12(3)(*a*) to restaurant services, provided that the rate is not lower than 12%.] [6]

3. During the transitional period referred to in paragraph 4, Member States may:

(*a*) continue to subject to tax the transactions exempt under Article 13 or 15 set out in Annex E to this Directive;

(*b*) continue to exempt the activities set out in Annex F under conditions existing in the Member State concerned;

(*c*) grant to taxable persons the option for taxation of exempt transactions under the conditions set out in Annex G;

(*d*) continue to apply provisions derogating from the principle of immediate deduction laid down in the first paragraph of Article 18(2);

(*e*) continue to apply measures derogating from the provisions of Articles ...[7] 6(4) and 11 A(3)(*c*);

(*f*) provide that for supplies of buildings and building land purchased for the purpose of resale by a taxable person for whom tax on the purchase was not deductible, the taxable amount shall be the difference between the selling price and the purchase price;

(*g*) by way of derogation from Articles 17(3) and 26(3), continue to exempt without repayment of input tax the services of travel agents referred to in Article 26(3). This derogation shall also apply to travel agents acting in the name and on account of the traveller.

[**3a.** Pending a decision by the Council, which, under to Article 3 of Directive 89/ 465/EEC (OJ L 3.8.89, p 21), is to act on the abolition of the transitional derogations provided for in paragraph 3, Spain shall be authorized to exempt the transactions referred to in point 2 of Annex F in respect of services rendered by authors and the transactions referred to in points 23 and 25 of Annex F.] [8]

4. The transitional period shall last initially for five years as from 1 January 1978. At the latest six months before the end of this period, and subsequently as necessary, the Council shall review the situation with regard to the derogations set out in paragraph 3 on the basis of a report from the Commission and shall unanimously determine on a proposal from the Commission, whether any or all of these derogations shall be abolished.

5. At the end of the transitional period passenger transport shall be taxed in the country of departure for that part of the journey taking place within the Community according to the detailed rules of procedure to be laid down by the Council acting unanimously on a proposal from the Commission.

[**6.** The Council, acting unanimously on a proposal from the Commission, may authorise any Member State to apply for a maximum period of [six years between 1 January 2000 and 31 December 2005] [9] the reduced rates provided for in the third subparagraph of Article 12(3)(*a*) to services listed in as maximum of two of the categories set out in Annex K. In exceptional cases a Member State may be authorised to apply the reduced rate to services in three of the abovementioned categories.

The services concerned must satisfy the following requirements:

(*a*) they must be labour-intensive;

(*b*) they must be largely provided direct to final consumers;

(*c*) they must be mainly local and not likely to create distortions of competition;

(*d*) there must be a close link between the lower prices resulting from the rate reduction and the foreseeable increase in demand and employment.

The application of a reduced rate must not prejudice the smooth functioning of the internal market.

Any Member State wishing to introduce the measure provided for in the first subparagraph shall inform the Commission before 1 November 1999 and shall provide it before that date with all relevant particulars, and in particular the following:

(*a*) scope of the measure and detailed description of the services concerned;

(*b*) particulars showing that the conditions laid down in the second and third subparagraphs have been met;

(*c*) particulars showing the budgetary cost of the measure envisaged.

Those Member States authorised to apply the reduced rate referred to in the first subparagraph shall, before 1 October 2002, draw up a detailed report containing an overall assessment of the measure's effectiveness in terms notably of job creation and efficiency.

Before 31 December 2002 the Commission shall forward a global evaluation report to the Council and Parliament accompanied, if necessary, by a proposal for appropriate measures for a final decision on the VAT rate applicable to labour-intensive services.] [10]

Amendments

[1] Para (1*a*) inserted by Council Directive 94/5/EC of 14 February 1994, Art 1(4).

[2] Inserted in para (2)(*e*) by Council Directive 94/5/EC of 14 February 1994, Art 1(5).

[3] Para (2)(*h*) inserted by Council Directive 95/7/EC of 10 April 1995 Art 1(2) with effect from 25 May 1995.

[4] Para (2) substituted by Council Directive 92/77/EEC of 19 October 1992, Art 1(4) with effect from 1 January 1993.

[5] Para (2)(*i*) inserted by Council Directive 96/42/EC of 25 June 1996 with effect from 1 January 1996.

[6] Paras (2)(*k*)–(*j*) inserted by Council Directive 2000/17/EC of 30 March 2000 (OJ L 084, 5/4/2000 p 24–25) Art 1 with effect from 5 April 2000 and covers the period 1 January 1999 until the end of the transitional period referred to in Sixth VAT Directive Art 281.

[7] Deleted by Council Directive 94/5/EC of 14 February 1994 Art 1(8); previously "5(4)(*c*),".

[8] Para (3*a*) inserted by Council Directive 91/680/EEC of 16 December 1991, Art 1(21) with effect from 1 January 1993.

[9] Substituted by Council Directive 2004/15/EC of 10 February 2004, Art 1 with effect from 1 January 2004; previously "four years between 1 January 2000 and 31 December 2003".

[10] Para (6) inserted by Council Directive 99/85/EC of 22 October 1999, Art 1 with effect from 28 October 1999 (date of publishing in the Official Journal).

Cross-references

Application of Art 28(3)(*b*) to Greece: Act of Accession 1979 Art 128 and Annex VIII Part II point 2(*b*).

Case law

Subject	Case	Case reference
Sale of land exempt for VAT purposes under the provisions of transitional period	*Norbury Developments Ltd v The Commissioners C & E*	29 April 1999, C–136/97, [1999] BVC 270
Assignment of rights — motion picture exhibition. ECJ claimed that it had no jurisdiction to answer a question referred to it by the Skatterattsnamnden	*Victoria Films A/S v Skatterattsnamnden*	12 November 1999, C–134/97

TITLE XVIa
TRANSITIONAL ARRANGEMENTS FOR THE TAXATION OF TRADE BETWEEN MEMBER STATES

Amendments

[1] This title (art 28a-m) inserted by Council Directive 91/680/EEC of 16 December 1991 Art 22.

Cross-references

Period of application of this title: Art 281.

Article 28a

Scope

[**1.** The following shall also be subject to value added tax:

(*a*) intra-Community acquisitions of goods for consideration within the territory of the country by a taxable person acting as such or by a non-taxable legal person where the vendor is a taxable person acting as such who is not eligible for the tax exemption provided for in Article 24 and who is not covered by the arrangements laid down in the second sentence of Article 8(1)(*a*) or in Article 28(*b*)(B)(1).

[By way of derogation from the first subparagraph, intra-Community acquisitions of goods made under the conditions set out in paragraph 1a by a taxable person or non-taxable legal person shall not be subject to value added tax.] [1]

Member States shall grant taxable persons and non taxable legal persons eligible under the second subparagraph the right to opt for the general scheme laid down in the first subparagraph. Member States shall determine the detailed rules for the exercise of that option which shall in any case apply for two calendar years.

(*b*)   intra-Community acquisitions of new means of transport effected for consideration within the country by taxable persons or non-taxable legal persons who qualify for the derogation provided for in the second subparagraph of (*a*) or by any other non-taxable person.

[(*c*)   the intra-Community acquisition of goods which are subject to excise duties effected for consideration within the territory of the country by a taxable person or a non-taxable legal person who qualifies for the derogation referred to in the second subparagraph of point (*a*), and for which the excise duties become chargeable within the territory of the country pursuant to Directive 92/12/EEC (OJ L 76, 23.3.1992, p 1.)] ²

[1a. The following shall benefit from the derogation set out in the second subparagraph of paragraph 1(*a*):

(*a*)   intra-Community acquisitions of goods whose supply within the territory of the country would be exempt pursuant to Article 15(4) to (10);

(*b*)   intra-Community acquisitions of goods other than those at (*a*), made:

— by a taxable person for the purpose of his agricultural, forestry or fisheries undertaking, subject to the flat-rate scheme set out in Article 25, by a taxable person who carries out only supplies of goods or services in respect of which value added tax is not deductible, or by a non-taxable legal person,

s 1(1)
— for a total amount not exceeding, during the current calendar year, a threshold which the Member States shall determine but which may not be less than the equivalent in national currency of ECU 10,000, and

— provided that the total amount of intra-Community acquisitions of goods did not, during the previous calendar year, exceed the threshold referred to in the second indent.]

The threshold which serves as the reference for the application of the above shall consist of the total amount, exclusive of value added tax due or paid in the Member State from which the goods are dispatched or transported, of intra-Community acquisitions of goods other than new means of transport and other than goods subject to excise duty.] ³

2. For the purposes of this Title:

(*a*)   the following shall be considered as **"means of transport"**: vessels exceeding 7.5 metres in length, aircraft the take-off weight of which exceeds 1550 kilograms and motorised land vehicles the capacity of which exceeds 48 cubic centimetres or the power of which exceeds 7.2 kilowatts, intended for the transport of persons or goods, except for the vessels and aircraft referred to in Article 15(5) and (6);

s 3A(5)
[(*b*)   the means of transport referred to in (*a*) shall not be considered to be "new" where both of the following conditions are simultaneously fulfilled:

— they were supplied more than three months after the date of first entry into service. However, this period shall be increased to six months for the motorized land vehicles defined in (*a*),

— they have travelled more than 6,000 kilometres in the case of land vehicles, sailed for more than 100 hours in the case of vessels, or flown for more than 40 hours in the case of aircraft.

Member States shall lay down the conditions under which the above facts can be regarded as established.] [4]

3. "Intra-Community acquisition of goods" shall mean acquisition of the right s 3A(1)(A) to dispose as owner of movable tangible property dispatched or transported to the person acquiring the goods by or on behalf of the vendor or the person acquiring the goods to a Member State other than that from which the goods are dispatched or transported.

Where goods acquired by a non-taxable legal person are dispatched or transported from a third territory and imported by that non-taxable legal person into a Member State other than the Member State of arrival of the goods dispatched or transported, the goods shall be deemed to have been dispatched or transported from the Member State of import. That Member State shall grant the importer as defined in [Article 21(4)] [5] a refund of the value added tax paid in connection with the importation of the goods insofar as the importer establishes that his acquisition was subject to value added tax in the Member State of arrival of the goods dispatched or transported.

4. Any person who from time to time supplies a new means of transport under the s 3A(1)(B) conditions laid down in Article 28c(A) shall also be regarded as a taxable person.

The Member State within the territory of which the supply is effected shall grant the taxable person the right of deduction on the basis of the following provisions:

— the right of deduction shall arise and may be exercised only at the time of the supply;

— the taxable person shall be authorized to deduct the value added tax included in the purchase price or paid on the importation or intra-Community acquisition of the means of transport, up to an amount not exceeding the tax for which he would be liable if the supply were not exempt.

Member States shall lay down detailed rules for the implementation of these provisions.

5. [The following shall be treated as supplies of goods effected for consideration:] [6]

...[7]

(*b*) the transfer by a taxable person of goods from his undertaking to s 3(1)(G) another Member State.

The following shall be regarded as having been transferred to another Member State: any tangible property dispatched or transported by or on behalf of the taxable person out of the territory defined in Article 3 but within the Community for the purposes of his undertaking, other than for the purposes of one of the following transactions:

— the supply of the goods in question by the taxable person within the territory of the Member State of arrival of the dispatch or transport under the conditions laid down in the second sentence of Article 8(1)(*a*) and in Article 28b(B)(1),

— the supply of the goods in question by the taxable person under the conditions laid down in Article 8(1)(*c*),

— the supply of the goods in question by the taxable person within the territory of the country under the conditions laid down in Article 15 or in Article 28c(A),

...[8]

[— the supply of a service performed for the taxable person and involving work on the goods in question physically carried out in the Member State in which the dispatch or transport of the goods ends, provided that the goods, after being worked upon, are re-dispatched to that taxable person in the Member State from which they had initially been dispatched or transported,] [9]

— temporary use of the goods in question within the territory of the Member State of arrival of the dispatch or transport of the goods for the purposes of the supply of services by the taxable person established within the territory of the Member State of departure of the dispatch or transport of the goods,

— temporary use of the goods in question, for a period not exceeding 24 months, within the territory of another Member State in which the import of the same goods from a third country with a view to temporary use would be eligible for the arrangements for temporary importation with full exemption from import duties,

[— the supply of gas through the natural gas distribution system, or of electricity, under the conditions set out in Article 8(1)(*d*) or (*e*).] [10]

[However, when one of the conditions to which the benefit of the above is subordinated is no longer met, the goods shall be considered as having been transferred to a destination in another Member State. In this case, the transfer is carried out at the moment that the conditions is no longer met.] [11]

6. The intra-Community acquisition of goods for consideration shall include the use by a taxable person for the purposes of his undertaking of goods dispatched or transported by or on behalf of that taxable person from another Member State within the territory of which the goods were produced, extracted, processed, purchased, acquired as defined in paragraph 1 or imported by the taxable person within the framework of his undertaking into that other Member State.

[The following shall also be deemed to be an intra-Community acquisition of goods effected for consideration: the appropriation of goods by the forces of a State party to the North Atlantic Treaty, for their use or for the use of the civilian staff accompanying them, which they have not acquired subject to the general rules governing taxation on the domestic market of one of the Member States, when the importation of these goods could not benefit from the exemption set out in Article 14(1)(*g*).] [12]

7. Member States shall take measures to ensure that transactions which would have been classed as "supplies of goods" as defined in paragraph 5 or Article 5 if they had been carried out within the territory of the country by a taxable person acting as such are classed as "intra-Community acquisitions of goods".] [13]

Amendments

[1]　Substituted by Council Directive 92/111/EEC of 14 December 1992, Art 1(10) with effect from 1 January 1993.

[2]　Para (1)(*c*) inserted by Council Directive 92/111/EEC of 14 December 1992, Art 1(10) with effect from 1 January 1993.

[3]　Para (1a) inserted by Council Directive 92/111/EEC of 14 December 1992, Art 1(10) with effect from 1 January 1993.

[4]　Para (2)(*b*) substituted by Council Directive 94/5/EC of 14 February 1994 Art 1 para (6).

[5]　Substituted by Council Directive 2000/65/EC of 17 October 2000 (OJ L 269, 21/10/2000 p 44–46) Art 1(6) with effect from 17 October 2000; previously "Article 21(2)".

[6]　Substituted by Council Directive 95/7/EC of 10 April 1995 Art 1(6) with effect from 25 May 1995.

[7]　Deleted by Council Directive 95/7/EC of 10 April 1995 Art 1(6) with effect from 25 May 1995.

[8]　Deleted by Council Directive 95/7/EC of 10 April 1995 Art 1(6) with effect from 25 May 1995.

[9]　Substituted by Council Directive 95/7/EC of 10 April 1995 Art 1(6) with effect from 25 May 1995.

[10]　Indent added by Council Directive 2003/92/EC of 7 October 2003, Art 1(7) with effect from 11 October 2003.

[11]　Inserted by Council Directive 92/111/EEC of 14 December 1992, Art 1(10) with effect from 1 January 1993.

[12]　Inserted by Council Directive 92/111/EEC of 14 December 1992, Art 1(10) with effect from 1 January 1993.

[13]　Art 28a inserted by Council Directive 91/680/EEC of 16 December 1991, Art 1(22) with effect from 1 January 1993.

Cross-references

Period of application: Art 28l.

SS
3A(2)(A)
3A(2)(B)

Article 28b
Place of transactions

A. Place of the intra-Community acquisition of goods

[**1.** The place of the intra-Community acquisition of goods shall be deemed to be the place where the goods are at the time when dispatch or transport to the person acquiring them ends.

2. Without prejudice to paragraph 1, the place of the intra-Community acquisition of goods referred to in Article 28a(1)(*a*) shall, however, be deemed to be within the territory of the Member State which issued the value added tax identification number under which the person acquiring the goods made the acquisition, unless the person acquiring the goods establishes that that acquisition has been subject to tax in accordance with paragraph 1.

If, however, the acquisition is subject to tax in accordance with paragraph 1 in the Member State of arrival of the dispatch or transport of the goods after having been subject to tax in accordance with the first subparagraph, the taxable amount shall be reduced accordingly in the Member State which issued the value added tax identification number under which the person acquiring the goods made the acquisition.

[For the purposes of applying the first subparagraph, the intra-Community acquisition of goods shall be deemed to have been subject to tax in accordance with paragraph 1 when the following conditions have been met:

s 3(6)(D)
— the acquirer establishes that he has effected this intra-Community acquisition for the needs of a subsequent supply effected in the Member State referred to in paragraph 1 and for which the consignee has been designated as the person liable for the tax due in accordance with Article 28c(E)(3),
— the obligations for declaration set out in the last subparagraph of Article 22(6)(*b*) have been satisfied by the acquirer.] [1]

B. Place of the supply of goods

s 3(6)(D) **1.** By way of derogation from Article 8(1)(*a*) and (2), the place of the supply of goods dispatched or transported by or on behalf of the supplier from a Member State other than that of arrival of the dispatch or transport shall be deemed to be the place where the goods are when the dispatch or transport to the purchaser ends, where the following conditions are fulfilled:

— the supply of goods is effected for a taxable person eligible for the derogation provided for in the second subparagraph of Article 28(*a*)(1)(*a*), for a non-taxable legal person who is eligible for the same derogation or for any other non-taxable person,
— the supply is of goods other than new means of transport and other than goods supplied after assembly or installation, with or without a trial run, by or on behalf of the supplier.

Where the goods thus supplied are dispatched or transported from a third territory and imported by the supplier into a Member State other than the Member State of arrival of the goods dispatched or transported to the purchaser, they shall be regarded as having been dispatched or transported from the Member State of import.

2. However, where the supply is of goods other than products subject to excise duty, paragraph 1 shall not apply to supplies of goods dispatched or transported to the same Member State of arrival of the dispatch or transport where:

— the total value of such supplies, less value added tax, does not in one calendar year exceed the equivalent in national currency of ECU 100,000 and

s 3(6)(D)
— the total value, less value added tax, of the supplies of goods other than products subject to excise duty effected under the conditions laid down in paragraph 1 in the previous calendar year did not exceed the equivalent in national currency of ECU 100,000.

The Member State within the territory of which the goods are when dispatch or transport to the purchaser ends may limit the thresholds referred to above to the equivalent in national currency of ECU 35,000 where that Member State fears that the threshold of ECU 100,000 referred to above would lead to serious distortions of the conditions of competition. Member States which exercise this option shall take the measures necessary to inform the relevant public authorities in the Member State of dispatch or transport of the goods.

Before 31 December 1994, the Commission shall report to the Council on the operation of the special ECU 35,000 thresholds provided for in the preceding subparagraph. In that report the Commission may inform the Council that the abolition of the special thresholds will not lead to serious distortions of the conditions of competition. Until the Council takes a unanimous decision on a Commission proposal, the preceding subparagraph shall remain in force.

3. The Member State within the territory of which the goods are at the time of s 5(6)(F)– departure of the dispatch or transport shall grant those taxable persons who effect (G) supplies of goods eligible under paragraph 2 the right to choose that the place of such supplies shall be determined in accordance with paragraph 1.

The Member States concerned shall determine the detailed rules for the exercise of that option, which shall in any case apply for two calendar years.

C. Place of the supply of services in the intra-Community transport of goods

1. By way of derogation from Article 9(2)(*b*), the place of the supply of services in the intra-Community transport of goods shall be determined in accordance with paragraphs 2, 3 and 4. For the purposes of this Title the following definitions shall apply:

— **"the intra-Community transport of goods"** shall mean transport where the place of departure and the place of arrival are situated within the territories of two different Member States[.] ²

[The transport of goods where the place of departure and the place of arrival are situated within the territory of the country shall be treated as intra- Community transport of goods where such transport is directly linked to transport of goods where the place of departure and the place of arrival are situated within the territories of two different Member States;] ²

— **"the place of departure"** shall mean the place where the transport of s 5(6)(G)(I) goods actually starts, leaving aside distance actually travelled to the place where the goods are,

— **"the place of arrival"** shall mean the place where the transport of s 5(6)(F)(I) goods actually ends.

2. The place of the supply of services in the intra-Community transport of goods shall be the place of departure.

3. However, by way of derogation from paragraph 2, the place of the supply of services in the intra-Community transport of goods rendered to customers identified for purposes of value added tax in a Member State other than that of the departure of the transport shall be deemed to be within the territory of the Member State which issued the customer with the value added tax identification number under which the service was rendered to him.

s 5(6)(F)(II**4.** Member States need not apply the tax to that part of the transport corresponding to journeys made over waters which do not form part of the territory of the Community as defined in Article 3.

D. Place of the supply of services ancillary to the intra-Community transport of goods

s 5(6)(G)
(III)
By way of derogation from Article 9(2)(*c*), the place of the supply of services involving activities ancillary to the intra-Community transport of goods, rendered to customers identified for purposes of value added tax in a Member State other than that within the territory of which the services are physically performed, shall be deemed to be within the territory of the Member State which issued the customer with the value added tax identification number under which the service was rendered to him.

E. Place of the supply of services rendered by intermediaries

s 5(6)(G)(I)**1.** By way of derogation from Article 9(1), the place of the supply of services rendered by intermediaries, acting in the name and for the account of other persons, where they form part of the supply of services in the intra-Community transport of goods, shall be the place of departure.

s 5(6)(F)
(III)
However, where the customer for whom the services rendered by the intermediary are performed is identified for purposes of value added tax in a Member State other than that of the departure of the transport, the place of the supply of services rendered by an intermediary shall be deemed to be within the territory of the Member State which issued the customer with the value added tax identification number under which the service was rendered to him.

s 5(6)(G)
(II)
2. By way of derogation from Article 9(1), the place of the supply of services rendered by intermediaries acting in the name and for the account of other persons, where they form part of the supply of services the purpose of which is activities ancillary to the intra-Community transport of goods, shall be the place where the ancillary services are physically performed.

s 5(6)
(F)(II)
However, where the customer of the services rendered by the intermediary is identified for purposes of value added tax in a Member State other than that within the territory of which the ancillary service is physically performed, the place of supply of the services rendered by the intermediary shall be deemed to be within the territory of the Member State which issued the customer with the value added tax identification number under which the service was rendered to him by the intermediary.

s 5(6)
(G)(II)
3. By way of derogation from Article 9(1), the place of the supply of services rendered by intermediaries acting in the name and for the account of other persons, when such services form part of transactions other than those referred to in paragraph 1 or 2 or in Article 9(2)(*e*), shall be the place where those transactions are carried out.

s 5(6)
(F)(III)
However, where the customer is identified for purposes of value added tax in a Member State other than that within the territory of which those transactions are

carried out, the place of supply of the services rendered by the intermediary shall be deemed to be within the territory of the Member State which issued the customer with the value added tax identification number under which the service was rendered to him by the intermediary.

[F. Place of the supply of services in the case of valuations of or work on movable tangible property

By way of derogation from Article 9(2)(*c*), the place of the supply of services s 5(6) involving valuations or work on movable tangible property, provided to (F)(IV) customers identified for value added tax purposes in a Member State other than the one where those services are physically carried out, shall be deemed to be in the territory of the Member State which issued the customer with the value added tax identification number under which the service was carried out for him.

This derogation shall not apply where the goods are not dispatched or transported out of the Member State where the services were physically carried out.] [4] [5]

Amendments

[1]   Inserted by Council Directive 92/111/EEC of 14 December 1992, Art 1(11) with effect from 1 January 1993.

[2]   Substituted by Council Directive 95/7/EC of 10 April 1995 Art 1(7) with effect from 25 May 1995.

[3]   Inserted by Council Directive 95/7/EC of 10 April 1995 Art 1(7) with effect from 25 May 1995.

[4]   Art 28b(F) inserted Council Directive 95/7/EC of 10 April 1995 Art 1(7) with effect from 25 May 1995.

[5]   Art 28*b* inserted by Council Directive 91/680/EEC of 16 December 1991, Art 1(22) with effect from 1 January 1993.

Case law

Services by intermediaries — place   *Staatssectretaris van Financien*   27 May 2004, C–68/03
of supply   *v D Lipjes*

Cross-references

Period of application: Art 28l.

Article 28c
Exemptions

A. Exempt supplies of goods   Sch 2(I)(B)

[Without prejudice to other Community provisions and subject to conditions which they shall lay down for the purpose of ensuring the correct and straightforward application of the exemptions provided for below and preventing any evasion, avoidance or abuse, Member States shall exempt:

(*a*)   supplies of goods, [as defined in Article 5] [1], dispatched or transported s 3A(1)(B) by or on behalf of the vendor or the person acquiring the goods out of the territory referred to in Article 3 but within the Community, effected for another taxable person or a non-taxable legal person acting as such in a Member State other than that of the departure of the dispatch or transport of the goods.

Sch 2(1)(c)   This exemption shall not apply to supplies of goods by taxable persons exempt from tax pursuant to Article 24 or to supplies of goods effected for taxable persons or non-taxable legal persons who qualify for the derogation in the second subparagraph of Article 28a(1)(*a*);

Sch 2(1)(D)   (*b*)   supplies of new means of transport, dispatched or transported to the purchaser by or on behalf of the vendor or the purchaser out of the territory referred to in Article 3 but within the Community, effected for taxable persons or non-taxable legal persons who qualify for the derogation provided for in the second subparagraph of Article 28a(1)(*a*), or for any other non-taxable person;

Sch
2(1)(cc)   [(*c*)   the supply of goods subject to excise duty dispatched or transported or transported to the purchaser, by the vendor, by the purchaser or on his behalf, outside the territory referred to in Article 3 but inside the Community, effected for taxable persons or non-taxable legal persons who qualify for the derogation set out in the second subparagraph of Article 28a(1)(*a*), when the dispatch or transport of the goods is carried out in accordance with Article 7(4) and (5), or Article 16 of Directive 92/12/EEC.
This exemption shall not apply to supplies of goods subject to excise duty effected by taxable persons who benefit from the exemption from tax set out in Article 24;] [2]

[(*d*)   the supply of goods, within the meaning of Article 28a(5)(*b*), which benefit from the exemptions set out above if they have been made on behalf of another taxable person.] [3]

B. Exempt intra-Community acquisitions of goods

Without prejudice to other Community provisions, and subject to conditions which they shall lay down for the purpose of ensuring the correct and straightforward application of the exemptions provided for below and preventing any evasion, avoidance or abuse, Member States shall exempt:

(*a*)   the intra-Community acquisition of goods the supply of which by taxable persons would in all circumstances be exempt within the territory of the country;

(*b*)   the intra-Community acquisition of goods the importation of which would in all circumstances be exempt under Article 14(1);

Sch 2(IIIA)   (*c*)   the intra-Community acquisition of goods where, pursuant to Article 17(3) and (4), the person acquiring the goods would in all circumstances be entitled to full reimbursement of the value added tax due under Article 28a(1).

C. Exempt transport services

Sch 2(IIIB)   The Member States shall exempt the supply of intra-Community transport services involved in the dispatch or transport of goods to and from the islands making up the autonomous regions of the Azores and Madeira as well as the dispatch or transport of goods between those islands.

D. Exempt importation of goods

Where goods dispatched or transported from a third territory are imported into a Member State other than that of arrival of the dispatch or transport, Member States shall exempt such imports where the supply of such goods by the importer as defined in [Article 21(4)] [4] is exempt in accordance with paragraph A.

Member States shall lay down the conditions governing this exemption with a view to ensuring its correct and straightforward application and preventing any evasion, avoidance or abuse.

[E. Other exemptions

1. [Substitutes Art 16(1) and (1a)] [5]

2. [Amends Art 16(2)]

3. Member States shall take specific measures to ensure that value added tax is not charged on the intra-Community acquisition of goods effected, within the meaning of Article 28b(A)(1), within its territory when the following conditions are met:

— the intra-Community acquisition of goods is effected by a taxable person who is not established in the territory of the country but who is identified for value added purposes in another Member State,

— the intra-Community acquisition of goods is effected for the purposes of a subsequent supply of goods made by a taxable person in the territory of the country,

— the goods so acquired by this taxable person are directly dispatched or transported from another Member State than that in which he is identified for value added tax purposes and destined for the person for whom he effects the subsequent supply,

— the person to whom the subsequent supply is made is a taxable person or a non-taxable legal person who is identified for value added tax purposes within the territory of the country,

— the person to whom the subsequent supply is made has been designated in accordance with [Article 21(1)(c)] [6] as the person liable for the tax due on the supplies effected by the taxable person not established within the territory of the country.] [7] [8]

Amendments

[1] Substituted by Council Directive 95/7/EC of 10 April 1995, Art 1(8) with effect from 25 May 1995; previously "as defined in Articles 5 and 28a(5)(*a*)".

[2] Art 28c(A)(*c*) substituted by Council Directive 92/111/EEC of 14 December 1992, Art 1(12) with effect from 1 January 1993.

[3] Art 28c(A)(*d*) inserted by Council Directive 92/111/EEC of 14 December 1992, Art 1(12) with effect from 1 January 1993.

[4] Substituted by Council Directive 2000/65/EC of 17 October 2000 (OJ L 269, 21/10/2000 p 44–46) Art 1(6) with effect from 17 October 2000; previously "Article 21(2)".

[5] Art 28c(E)(1) substituted by Council Directive 95/7/EC of 10 April 1995 Art 1(9) with effect from 1 January 1996.

[6] Substituted by Council Directive 2000/65/EC of 17 October 2000 (OJ L 269, 21/10/2000 p 44–46) Art 1(3) with effect from 17 October 2000; previously "the third subparagraph of Article 21(1)(*a*)".

7 Art 28c(E) substituted by Council Directive 92/111/EEC of 14 December 1992, Art 1(13) with effect from 1 January 1993.

8 Art 28c originally inserted by Council Directive 91/680/EEC of 16 December 1991, Art 1(22) with effect from 1 January 1993.

Cross-references
Period of application: Art 28l.

Article 28d
Chargeable event and chargeability of tax

[**1.** The chargeable event shall occur when the intra-Community acquisition of goods is effected. The intra-Community acquisition of goods shall be regarded as being effected when the supply of similar goods is regarded as being effected within the territory of the country.

2. For the intra-Community acquisition of goods, tax shall become chargeable on the 15th day of the month following that during which the chargeable event occurs.

[**3.** By way of derogation from paragraph 2, tax shall become chargeable on the issue of the invoice ...[1] provided for in the first subparagraph of Article 22(3)(*a*) where that invoice ...[2] is issued to the person acquiring the goods before the fifteenth day of the month following that during which the taxable event occurs.]
[3]

4. By way of derogation from Article 10(2) and (3), tax shall become chargeable for supplies of goods effected under the conditions laid down in Article 28c(A) on the 15th day of the month following that during which the chargeable event occurs.

[However, tax shall become chargeable on the issue of the invoice provided for in the first subparagraph of Article 22(3)(*a*) ...[1] where that invoice ...[2] is issued before the fifteenth day of the month following that during which the taxable event occurs.] [4]] [5]

Amendments

1 Deleted by Council Directive 2001/115/EC, Art 4(4) with effect from 6 February 2002; previously "or other document serving as invoice".

2 Deleted by Council Directive 2001/115/EC, Art 4(2) with effect from 6 February 2002; previously "or document".

3 Para (3) substituted by Council Directive 92/111/EEC of 14 December 1992, Art 1(14) with effect from 1 January 1993.

4 Substituted by Council Directive 92/111/EEC of 14 December 1992, Art 1(15) with effect from 1 January 1993.

5 Art 28d inserted by Council Directive 91/680/EEC of 16 December 1991, Art 1(22) with effect from 1 January 1993.

Article 28e
Taxable amount and rate applicable

[**1.** In the case of the intra-Community acquisition of goods, the taxable amount shall be established on the basis of the same elements as those used in accordance with Article 11(A) to determine the taxable amount for supply of the same goods within the territory of the country. [In particular, in the case of the intra- Community acquisition of goods referred to in Article 28a(6), the taxable amount shall be determined in accordance with Article 11(A)(1)(*b*) and paragraphs 2 and 3.] [1]

Member States shall take the measures necessary to ensure that the excise duty due or paid by the person effecting the intra-Community acquisition of a product subject to excise duty is included in the taxable amount in accordance with Article 11(A)(2)(*a*).

[When, after the moment the intra-Community acquisition of goods was effected, the acquirer obtains the refund of excise duties paid in the Member State from which the goods were dispatched or transported, the taxable amount shall be reduced accordingly in the Member State where the intra-Community acquisition took place.] [2]

[**2.** For the supply of goods referred to in Article 28c(A)(*d*), the taxable amount shall be determined in accordance with Article 11(A)(1)(*b*) and paragraphs 2 and 3.] [3]

[**3**] . [4]The tax rate applicable to the intra-Community acquisition of goods shall be that in force when the tax becomes chargeable.

[**4**] . [4] The tax rate applicable to the intra-Community acquisition of goods shall be that applied to the supply of like goods within the territory of the country.] [5]

Amendments

[1] Substituted by Council Directive 92/111/EEC of 14 December 1992, Art 1(16) with effect from 1 January 1993.

[2] Inserted by Council Directive 92/111/EEC of 14 December 1992, Art 1(16) with effect from 1 January 1993.

[3] Inserted by Council Directive 92/111/EEC of 14 December 1992, Art 1(17) with effect from 1 January 1993.

[4] Substituted by Council Directive 92/111/EEC of 14 December 1992, Art 1(17) with effect from 1 January 1993.

[5] Art 28e inserted by Council Directive 91/680/EEC of 16 December 1991, Art 1(22) with effect from 1 January 1993.

Cross-references

Period of application: Art 28l.

Article 28f
Right of deduction

[**1.** [[Substitutes Art 17(2), [(2a)] [1], [(3)] [2], (4).] [3]]

2. [Substitutes Art 18(1).]

3. [Inserts Art 18(3a).]] [4]

Amendments

[1] Amended by Council Directive 95/7/EC of 10 April 1995 Art 1(10) with effect from 25 May 1995.

[2] Amended by Council Directive 2004/66/EC Annex V para (1)(*c*) of 26 April 2004 with effect from 1 May 2004.

[3] Amended by Council Directive 2000/65/EC of 17 October 2000 (OJ L 269, 21/10/2000 p 44–46), Art 1(2) with effect from 17 October 2000.

[4]   Art 28f inserted by Council Directive 91/680/EEC of 16 December 1991, Art 22 with effect from
    1 January 1993 and amended by Council Directive 92/111/EEC of 14 December 1992, Art 1(18)
    with effect from 1 January 1993.

Cross-references

Period of application: Art 28l.

Article 28g
Persons liable for payment of the tax

[Substitutes Art 21] [1]

Amendments

[1]   Art 28g inserted by Council Directive 91/680/EEC of 16 December 1991, Art 1(22) with effect
    from 1 January 1993 and amended by Council Directive 92/111/EEC of 14 December 1992,
    Art 1(19) with effect from 1 January 1993. Subsequently amended by Council Directive 95/7/EC
    of 10 April 1995, Art 1(10) with effect from 25 May 1995; Council Directive 2000/65/EC of 17
    October 2000 with effect from 17 October 2000; Council Directive 2001/115/EC, Art 4(5) with
    effect from 6 February 2002; Council Directive 2003/92/EC of 7 October 2003 Art 1(4)–(5) with
    effect from 11 October 2003.

Cross-references

Period of application: Art 28l.

Article 28h
Obligations of persons liable for payment

[Substitutes Art 22] [1]

Amendments

[1]   Art 28h inserted by Council Directive 91/680/EEC of 16 December 1991, Art 1(22) with effect
    from 1 January 1993 and amended by Council Directive 92/111/EEC of 14 December 1992,
    art 1(20) with effect from 1 January 1993. Subsequently amended by Council Directive 95/7/EC
    of 10 April 1995 Art 1(12) with effect from 25 May 1995; Council Directive 2000/65/EC of
    17 October 2000 Art 1(5) with effect from 17 October 2000; Council Directive 2001/115/EC
    of 20 December 2001 Art 2 with effect from 6 February 2002; Council Directive 2003/92/EC of
    7 October 2003 Art 1(6) with effect from 11 October 2003

Cross-references

Period of application: Art 28l.

Article 28i
Special scheme for small undertakings

[Amends Art 24(3)] [1]

Amendments

[1]   Art 28i inserted by Council Directive 91/680/EEC of 16 December 1991, Art 1(22) with effect
    from 1 January 1993 and amended by Council Directive 92/111/EEC of 14 December 1992,
    Art 1(21) with effect from 1 January 1993.

Cross-references

Period of application: Art 28l.

Article 28j
Common flat-rate scheme for farmers

[1. [Amends Art 25(4)]

2. [Substitutes Art 25(5), (6)]

3. [Amends Art 25(9)]] ¹

Amendments

¹ Art 28j inserted by Council Directive 91/680/EEC of 16 December 1991, Art 1(22) with effect from 1 January 1993.

Article 28k
Miscellaneous provisions

[The following provisions shall apply until 30 June 1999:

1. Member States may exempt supplies by tax-free shops of goods to be carried away in the personal luggage of travellers taking intra-Community flights or sea crossings to other Member States. For the purposes of this Article:

(*a*) **"tax-free shop"** shall mean any establishment situated within an airport or port which fulfils the conditions laid down by the competent public authorities pursuant, in particular, to paragraph 5;

(*b*) **"traveller to another Member State"** shall mean any passenger holding a transport document for air or sea travel stating that the immediate destination is an airport or port situated in another Member State;

(*c*) **"intra-Community flight or sea crossing"** shall mean any transport, by air or sea, starting within the territory of the country as defined in Article 3, where the actual place of arrival is situated within another Member State.

Supplies of goods effected by tax-free shops shall include supplies of goods effected on board aircraft or vessels during intra-Community passenger transport.

This exemption shall also apply to supplies of goods effected by tax-free shops in either of the two Channel Tunnel terminals, for passengers holding valid tickets for the journey between those two terminals.

2. Eligibility for the exemption provided for in paragraph 1 shall apply only to supplies of goods:

[(*a*) the total value of which per person per journey does not exceed ECU 90.] ¹
Where the total value of several items or of several supplies of goods, per person per journey exceeds those limits, the exemption shall be granted up to those amounts, on the understanding that the value of an item may not be split;

(*b*) involving quantities per person per journey not exceeding the limits laid down by the Community provisions in force for the movement of travellers between third countries and the Community.

The value of supplies of goods effected within the quantitative limits laid down in the previous subparagraph shall not be taken into account for the application of (*a*).

3. Member States shall grant every taxable person the right to a deduction or refund of the value added tax referred to in Article 17(2) insofar as the goods and services are used for the purposes of his supplies of goods exempt under this Article.

4. Member States which exercise the option provided for in Article 16(2) shall also grant eligibility under that provision to imports, intra-Community acquisitions and supplies of goods to a taxable person for the purposes of his supplies of goods exempt pursuant to this Article.

5. Member States shall take the measures necessary to ensure the correct and straightforward application of the exemptions provided for in this Article and to prevent any evasion, avoidance or abuse.] [2]

Amendments

[1]   Substituted by Council Directive 94/4/EC of 14 February 1994.

[2]   Art 28k inserted by Council Directive 91/680/EEC of 16 December 1991, Art 1(22) with effect from 1 January 1993.

Cross-references

Period of application: Art 28l.

Article 28l
Period of application

[The transitional arrangements provided for in this Title shall enter into force on 1 January 1993. Before 31 December 1994 the Commission shall report to the Council on the operation of the transitional arrangements and submit proposals for a definitive system.

The transitional arrangements shall be replaced by a definitive system for the taxation of trade between Member States based in principle on the taxation in the Member State of origin of the goods or services supplied. To that end, after having made a detailed examination of that report and considering that the conditions for transition to the definitive system have been fulfilled satisfactorily the Council acting unanimously on a proposal from the Commission and after consulting the European Parliament, shall decide before 31 December 1995 on the arrangements necessary for the entry into force and the operation of the definitive system.

The transitional arrangements shall enter into force for four years and shall accordingly apply until 31 December 1996. The period of application of the transitional arrangements shall be extended automatically until the date of entry into force of the definitive system and in any event until the Council has decided on the definitive system.] [1]

Amendments

[1]   Art 28l inserted by Council Directive 91/680/EEC of 16 December 1991, Art 1(2) with effect from 1 January 1993.

Cross-references

Period of application: Art 28l.

Article 28m
Rate of conversion

[To determine the equivalents in their national currencies of amounts expressed in ecus in this Title Member States shall use the rate of exchange applicable on 16 December 1991 (OJ No C 328, 17. 12. 1991, p 4).] [1]

Notes

However, the Czech Republic, Estonia, Cyprus, Latvia, Lithuania, Hungary, Malta, Poland, Slovenia and Slovakia shall use the rate of exchange applicable on the date of their accession.

Amendments

[1] Art 28m substituted by Council Directive 2004/66/EC Annex V para (1)(*b*) of 26 April 2004 with effect from 1 May 2004.

Cross-references

Period of application: Art 28l.

Article 28n
Transitional measures

[**1.** When goods:

— entered the territory of the country within the meaning of Article 3 before 1 January 1993,

and

— were placed, on entry into the territory of that country, under one of the regimes referred to in Article 14(1)(*b*) or (*c*), or Article 16(1)(A),

and

— have not left that regime before 1 January 1993, the provisions in force at the moment the goods were placed under that regime shall continue to apply for the period, as determined by those provisions, the goods remain under that regime.

2. The following shall be deemed to be an import of goods within the meaning of Article 7(1):

(*a*) the removal, including irregular removal, of goods from the regime referred to in Article 14(1)(*c*) under which the goods were placed before 1 January 1993 under the conditions set out in paragraph 1;

(*b*) the removal, including irregular removal, of goods from the regime referred to in Article 16(1)(A) under which the goods were placed before 1 January 1993 under the conditions set out in paragraph 1;

(*c*) the termination of a Community internal transit operation started before 1 January 1993 in the Community for the purpose of supply of goods for consideration made before 1 January 1993 in the Community by a taxable person acting as such;

(*d*) the termination of an external transit operation started before 1 January 1993;

(*e*) any irregularity or offence committed during an external transit operation started under the conditions set out in (*c*) or any Community external transit operation referred to in (*d*);

(*f*)   the use within the country, by a taxable or non-taxable person, of goods which have been supplied to him, before 1 January 1993, within another Member State, where the following conditions are met:

— the supply of these goods has been exempted, or was likely to be exempted, pursuant to Article 15(1) and (2),

— the goods were not imported within the country before 1 January 1993.

For the purpose of the application of (*c*), the expression **"Community internal transit operation"** shall mean the dispatch or transport of goods under the cover of the internal Community transit arrangement or under the cover of a T2 L document or the intra-Community movement carnet, or the sending of goods by post.

3. In the cases referred to in paragraph 2(*a*) to (*e*), the place of import, within the meaning of Article 7(2), shall be the Member State within whose territory the goods cease to be covered by the regime under which they were placed before 1 January 1993.

4. By way of derogation from Article 10(3), the import of the goods within the meaning of paragraph 2 of this Article shall terminate without the occurrence of a chargeable event when:

(*a*)   the imported goods are dispatched or transported outside the Community within the meaning of Article 3;

or

(*b*)   the imported goods, within the meaning of paragraph 2(*a*), are other than a means of transport and are dispatched or transported to the Member State from which they were exported and to the person who exported them;

or

(*c*)   the imported goods, within the meaning of paragraph 2(*a*), are means of transport which were acquired or imported before 1 January 1993, in accordance with the general conditions of taxation in force on the domestic market of a Member State, within the meaning of Article 3, and/or have not been subject by reason of their exportation to any exemption from or refund of value added tax.

This condition shall be deemed to be fulfilled when the date of the first use of the means of transport was before 1 January 1985 or when the amount of tax due because of the importation is insignificant.] [1]

Amendments

[1]   Art 28n inserted by Council Directive 92/111/EEC of 14 December 1992, Art 1(22) with effect from 1 January 1993.

[**TITLE XVI**B

**TRANSITIONAL PROVISIONS APPLICABLE IN THE FIELD OF SECOND-HAND
GOODS, WORKS OF ART, COLLECTORS' ITEMS AND ANTIQUES**

Article 28o

1. Member States which at 31 December 1992 were applying special tax s 12B
arrangements other than those provided for in Article 26a(B) to supplies of
second-hand means of transport effected by taxable dealers my continue to apply
those arrangements during the period referred to in Article 28l in so far as they
comply with, or are adjusted to comply with, the following conditions:

(*a*) the special arrangements shall apply only to supplies of the means of
transport referred to in Article 28a(2)(*a*) and regarded as second-hand
goods within the meaning of Article 26a(A)(*d*), effected by taxable
dealers within the meaning of Article 26a(A)(*e*), and subject to the
special tax arrangements for taxing the margin pursuant to Article
26a(B)(1) and (2). Supplies of new means of transport within the
meaning of Article 28a(2)(*b*) that are carried out under the conditions
specified in Article 28c(A) shall be excluded from these special
arrangements;

(*b*) the tax due in respect of each supply referred to in (*a*) is equal to the
amount of tax that would be due if that supply had been subject to the
normal arrangements for value added tax, less the amount of value
added tax regarded as being incorporated in the purchase price of the
means of transport by the taxable dealer;

(*c*) the tax regarded as being incorporated in the purchase price of the
means of transport by the taxable dealer shall be calculated according to
the following method:

— the purchase price to be taken into account shall be the purchase
price within the meaning of Article 26a(B)(3),

— that purchase price paid by the taxable dealer shall be deemed to
include the tax that would have been due if the taxable dealer's
supplier had subjected the supply to the normal value added tax
arrangements,

— the rate to be taken into account shall be the rate applicable within
the meaning of Article 12(1), in the Member State within which the
place of the supply to the taxable dealer, determined in accordance
with Article 8, is deemed to be situated;

(*d*) the tax due in respect of each supply as referred to in (*a*), determined in
accordance with the provisions of (*b*), may not be less than the amount
of tax that would be due if that supply had been subject to the special
arrangements for taxing the margin in accordance with Article
26a(B)(3).

For the application of the above provisions, the Member States have the
option of providing that if the supply had been subject to the special
arrangements for taxation of the margin, that margin would not have
been less then 10% of the selling price, within the meaning of B(3);

(*e*) the taxable dealer shall not be entitled to indicate separately on the invoices he issues, ...[1], tax relating to supplies which he is subjecting to the special arrangements;

(*f*) taxable persons shall not be entitled to deduct from the tax for which they are liable tax due or paid in respect of second-hand means of transport supplied to them by a taxable dealer, in so far as the supply of those goods by the taxable dealer is subject to the tax arrangements in accordance with (*a*);

(*g*) by way of derogation from Article 28a(1)(*a*), intra-Community acquisition of means of transport are not subject to value added tax where the vendor is a taxable dealer acting as such and the second-hand means of transport acquired has been subject to the tax, in the Member State of departure of the dispatch or transport, in accordance with (*a*);

(*h*) Articles 28b(B) and 28c(A)(*a*) and (*d*) shall not apply to supplies of second-hand means of transport subject to tax in accordance with (*a*).

2. By way of derogation from the first sentence of paragraph 1, the Kingdom of Denmark shall be entitled to apply the special tax arrangements laid down in paragraph 1(*a*) to (*h*) during the period referred to in Article 28l.

3. Where they apply the special arrangements for sales by public auction provided for in Article 26a(C), Member States shall also apply these special arrangement to supplies of second-hand means of transport effected by an organizer of sales by public auction acting in his own name, pursuant to a contract under which commission is payable on the sale of those goods by public auction, on behalf of a taxable dealer, in so far as the supply of the second-hand means of transport, within the meaning of Article 5(4)(*c*), by that other taxable dealer, is subject to tax in accordance with paragraphs 1 and 2.

4. For supplies by a taxable dealer of works of art, collectors' items or antiques that have been supplied to him under the conditions provided for in Article 26a(B)(2), the Federal Republic of Germany shall be entitled, until 30 June 1999, to provide for the possibility for taxable dealers to apply either the special arrangements for taxable dealers, or the normal VAT arrangements according to the following rules;

(*a*) for the application of the special arrangements for taxable dealers to these suppliers of goods, the taxable amount shall be determined in accordance with Article 11(A)(1), (2) and (3);

(*b*) in so far as the goods are used for the needs of his operations which are taxed in accordance with (*a*), the taxable dealer shall be authorized to deduct from the tax for which he is liable:

— the value added tax due or paid for works of art, collectors' items or antiques which are or will be supplied to him by another taxable dealer, where the supply by that other taxable dealer has been taxed in accordance with (*a*),

— the value added tax deemed to be included in the purchase price of the works of art, collectors' items or antiques which are or will be supplied to him by another taxable dealer, where the supply by that other taxable dealer has been subject to value added tax in accordance with the special arrangements for the taxation of the margin provided for in Article 26a(B), in the Member State within whose territory the place of that supply, determined in accordance with Article 8, is deemed to be situated.

This right to deduct shall arise at the time when the tax due for the supply taxed in accordance with (*a*) becomes chargeable;

(*c*)   for the application of the provisions laid down in the second indent of (*b*), the purchase price of the works of art, collectors' items or antiques the supply of which by a taxable dealer is taxed in accordance with (*a*) shall be determined in accordance with Article 26a(B)(3) and the tax deemed to be included in this purchase price shall be calculated according to the following method:

— the purchase price shall be deemed to include the value added tax that would have been due if the taxable margin made by the supplier had been equal to 20% of the purchase price,

— the rate to be taken into account shall be the rate applicable, within the meaning of Article 12(1), in the Member State within whose territory the place of the supply that is subject to the special arrangements for taxation of the profit margin, determined in accordance with Article 8, is deemed to be situated;

(*d*)   where he applies the normal arrangements for value added tax to the supply of a work of art, collectors' item or antique which has been supplied to him by another taxable dealer and where the goods have been taxed in accordance with (*a*), the taxable dealer shall be authorized to deduct from his tax liability the value added tax referred to in (*b*);

(*e*)   the category of rates applicable to these supplies of goods shall be that which was applicable on 1 January 1993;

(*f*)   for the application of the fourth indent of Article 26a(B)(2), the fourth indent of Article 26a(C)(1) and Article 26a(D)(*b*) and (*c*), the supplies of works of art, collectors' items or antiques, taxed in accordance with (*a*), shall be deemed by Member States to be supplies subject to value added tax in accordance with the special arrangements for taxation of the profit margin provided for in Article 26a(B);

(*g*)   where the supplies of works of art, collectors' items or antiques taxed in accordance with (*a*) are effected under the conditions provided for in Article 28c(A), the invoice issued in accordance with Article 22(3) shall contain an endorsement indicating that the special taxation arrangements for taxing the margin provided for in Article 28o(4) have been applied.] [2]

Amendments

[1]   Deleted by Council Directive 2001/115/EC, Art 4(6) with effect from 6 February 2002; previously "or on any other document in lieu".

[2]   Title XVIb and Article 28o inserted by Council Directive 94/5/EC of 14 February 1994 Art 1(7) (OJ No L 60, 3.3.1994, p 21).

[TITLE XVIc
TRANSITIONAL MEASURES APPLICABLE IN THE CONTEXT OF THE ACCESSION
TO THE EUROPEAN UNION OF AUSTRIA, FINLAND AND SWEDEN

Article 28p

1. For the purpose of applying this Article:

— **"Community"** shall mean the territory of the Community as defined in Article 3 before accession,
— **"new Member States"** shall means the territory of the Member States acceding to the European Union by the Treaty signed on 24 June 1994, as defined for each of those Member States in Article 3 of this Directive,
— **"enlarged Community"** shall mean the territory of the Community as defined in Article 3, after accession.

2. When goods:

— entered the territory of the Community or of one of the new Member States before the date of accession, and
— were placed, on entry into the territory of the Community or of one of the Member States, under a temporary admission procedure with full exemption from import duties, under one of the regimes referred to in Article 16(1)(B)(*a*) to (*d*) or under a similar regime in one of the new Member States, and
— have not left that regime before the date of accession,

the provision in force at the moment the goods were placed under that regime shall continue to apply until the goods leave this regime, after the date of accession.

3. When goods:

— were placed, before the date of accession, under the common transit procedure or under another customs transit procedure, and
— have not left that procedure before the date of accession,

the provisions in force at the moment the goods were placed under that procedure shall continue to apply until the goods leave this procedure, after the date of accession.

For the purposes of the first indent, **"common transit procedure"** shall mean the measures for the transport of goods in transit between the Community and the countries of the European Free Trade Association (EFTA) and between the EFTA countries themselves, as provided for in the Convention of 20 May 1987 on a common transit procedure (OJ No L 226, 13.8.1987, p 2).

4. The following shall be deemed to be an importation of goods within the meaning of Article 7(1) where it is shown that the goods were in free circulation in one of the new Member States or in the Community:

(*a*) the removal, including irregular removal, of goods from a temporary admission procedure under which they were placed before the date of accession under the conditions set out in paragraph 2;

(*b*) the removal, including irregular removal, of goods either from one of the regimes referred to in Article 16(1)(B)(*a*) to (*d*) or from a similar regime under which they were placed before the date of accession under the conditions set out in paragraph 2;

(*c*) the termination of one of the procedures referred to in paragraph 3 which was started before the date of accession in one of new Member States for the purposes of a supply of goods for consideration effected before that date in that Member State by a taxable person acting as such;

(*d*) any irregularity or offence committed during one of the procedures referred to in paragraph 3 under the conditions set out at (*c*).

5. The use after the date of accession within a Member State, by a taxable or non-taxable person, of goods supplied to him before the date of accession within the Community or one of the new Member States shall also be deemed to be an importation of goods within the meaning of Article 7(1) where the following conditions are met:

— the supply of those goods has been exempted, or was likely to be exempted, either under Article 15(1) and (2) or under a similar provision in the new Member States,

— the goods were not imported into one of the new Member States or into the Community before the date of accession.

6. In the cases referred to in paragraph 4, the place of import within the meaning of Article 7(3) shall be the Member State within whose territory the goods cease to be covered by the regime under which they were placed before the date of accession.

7. By way of derogation from Article 10(3), the importation of goods within the meaning of paragraphs 4 and 5 of this Article shall terminate without the occurrence of a chargeable event when:

(*a*) the imported goods are dispatched or transported outside the enlarged Community; or

(*b*) the imported goods within the meaning of paragraph 4(*a*) are other than means of transport and are redispatched or transported to the Member State from which they were exported and to the person who exported them; or

(*c*) the imported goods within the meaning of paragraph 4(*a*) are means of transport which were acquired or imported before the date of accession in accordance with the general conditions of taxation in force on the domestic market of one of the new Member States or of one of the Member States of the Community and/or have not been subject, by reason of their exportation, to any exemption from, or refund of, value added tax.

This condition shall be deemed to be fulfilled when the date of the first use of the means of transport was before 1 January 1987 or when the amount of tax due by reason of the importation is insignificant.] [1]

Amendments

[1]   Title XVIc and Article 28p inserted by Council Directive 94/76/EC of 22 December 1994 Art 1 (OJ No L 365, 31.12.94, p 53).

TITLE XVII
VALUE ADDED TAX COMMITTEE

Article 29

1. An Advisory Committee on value added tax, hereinafter called "the Committee", is hereby set up.

2. The Committee shall consist of representatives of the Member States and of the Commission.

The chairman of the Committee shall be a representative of the Commission. Secretarial services for the Committee shall be provided by the Commission.

3. The Committee shall adopt its own rules of procedure.

4. In addition to points subject to the consultation provided for under this Directive, the Committee shall examine questions raised by its chairman, on his own initiative or at the request of the representative of a Member State, which concern the application of the Community provisions on value added tax.

Article 29a
Implementing measures

[The Council, acting unanimously on a proposal from the Commission, shall adopt the measures necessary to implement this Directive.] [1]

Amendments

[1]   Article 29a inserted by Council Directive 2004/7/EC of 20 January 2004 Art 1(2) with effect from 19 February 2004.

TITLE XVIII
MISCELLANEOUS

Article 30
International Agreements

[**1.** The Council, acting unanimously on a proposal from the Commission, may authorise any Member State to conclude with a third country or an international organisation an agreement which may contain derogations from this Directive.

2. A Member State wishing to conclude such an agreement shall send an application to the Commission and provide it with all the necessary information. If the Commission considers that it does not have all the necessary information, it shall contact the Member State concerned within two months of receipt of the application and specify what additional information is required. Once the Commission has all the information it considers necessary for appraisal of the request it shall within one month notify the requesting Member State accordingly and it shall transmit the request, in its original language, to the other Member States.

3. Within three months of giving the notification referred to in the last sentence of paragraph 2, the Commission shall present to the Council either an appropriate proposal or, should it object to the derogation requested, a communication setting out its objections.

4. In any event, the procedure set out in paragraphs 2 and 3 shall be completed within eight months of receipt of the application by the Commission.] [1]

Amendments

[1]   Article 30 substituted by Council Directive 2004/7/EC of 20 January 2004 Art 1(3) with effect from 19 February 2004.

Article 31
Unit of account

1. The unit of account used in this Directive shall be the European unit of account (EUA) defined by Decision 75/250/EEC (OJ L 104, 24.4.1975, p 35).

2. When converting this unit of account into national currencies, Member States shall have the option of rounding the amounts resulting from this conversion either upwards or downwards by up to 10%.

Article 32
Second-hand goods

Amendments

Deleted by Council Directive 94/5/EC of 14 February 1994 Art 1(9).

Article 33

[**1.** Without prejudice to other Community provisions, in particular those laid down in the Community provisions in force relating to the general arrangements for the holding, movement and monitoring of products subject to excise duty, this Directive shall not prevent a Member State from maintaining or introducing taxes on insurance contracts, taxes on betting and gambling, excise duties, stamp duties and, more generally, any taxes, duties or charges which cannot be characterized as turnover taxes, provided however that those taxes, duties or charges do not, in trade between Member States, give rise to formalities connected with the crossing of frontiers.

2. Any reference in this Directive to products subject to excise duty shall apply to the following products as defined by the current Community provisions:

— mineral oils;
— alcohol and alcoholic beverages;
— manufactured tobacco.] [1]

Amendments

[1]   Art 33 substituted by Council Directive 91/680/EEC of 16 December 1991, Art 1(23); with effect from 1 January 1993.

Case law

Subject	Case	Case reference
Danish employment (market contribution) levy payable essentially on the same basis as VAT, in breach of EC Treaty	*EC Commission v Denmark*	[1994] STI 37, ECJ 234/91
Tax on gaming machines not a turnover tax because it was based on the placing of the machine at the disposal of the public	*Lambert v Directeur des Services Fiscaux de l'Orne*	(1989) OJ C92/8, ECJ 317/86; 48, 49, 285, 363–367/87, 65, 78–80/99
	Bergandi v Directeur Général des Impôts	[1991] STC 529, [1989] 2 CMLR 933, ECJ 252/86
Tax based on business annual turnover used to finance sickness etc benefits not a turnover tax	*Rousseau-Wilmot SA v Caisse de Compensation de l'Organisation Autonome Nationale de l'Industrie et du Commerce (Organic)*	[1986] 3 CMLR 677, ECJ 295/84
Stamp duty not a turnover tax	*Beaulande v Directeur des Services Fiscaux, Nantes*	[1996] STC 1111
Italian lawyers' national provident fund supplementary contributions (based on fee paid by client which has already been subject to VAT) not in breach of Art 33	*Aldo Bozzi v Cassa Naxionale di Previdenza ed Assistenza*	(1992) OJ C142/8, ECJ 347/90
25% tax on public performance in dancehalls, restaurants etc not in breach of Art 33	*Giant NV v Commune d'OVerijse*	(1991) OJ C96/8, ECJ 109/90
Fiscal charge, preliminary ruling	*Dansk Denkavit ApS and P Poulsen Trading ApS v Skatteministeriet*	(1992) OJ C107/p 3, ECJ 200/90
Consumption tax ("BVB") on passenger cars not prohibited by Art 33	*Wisselink en Co BV v Staatssecretaris van Financiën*	ECJ 93 and 94/88
Turnover taxes (6th Dir Art 33)	*Erna Pelzl & Others v Steirmäkische Landesregierung, Wiener Städische Allgemeine Versicherungs AG & Others v Tiroler Landesregierung, STUAG Bau-Aktiengellschaft v Kärtner Landesregierung*	8 June 1999, Joined Cases C–338/97, C–344/97, C–390/97
Levying of a tax on members of chambers of commerce not a turnover tax and therefore not illegal	*SPAR Osterreichische Warenhandels AG v Finanzlandesdirektion fur Salzburg*	February 1998, C–318/96

Article 33a

[**1.** Goods referred to in Article 7(1)(*b*) entering the Community from a territory which forms part of the customs territory of the Community but which is considered as a third territory for the purposes of applying this Directive shall be subject to the following provisions:

(*a*) the formalities relating to the entry of such goods into the Community shall be the same as those laid down by the Community customs provisions in force for the import of goods into the customs territory of the Community;

(*b*) when the place of arrival of the dispatch or transport of these goods is situate outside the Member State where they enter the Community, they shall circulate in the Community under the internal Community transit procedure laid down by the Community customs provisions in force, insofar as they have been the subject of a declaration placing them under this regime when the goods entered the Community;

(*c*) when at the moment of their entry into the Community the goods are found to be in one of the situations which would qualify them, if they were imported within the meaning of Article 7(1)(*a*), to benefit from one of the arrangements referred to in Article 16(1)(B)(*a*), (*b*), (*c*) and (*d*), or under a temporary arrangement in full exemption from import duties, the Member States shall take measures ensuring that the goods may remain in the Community under the same conditions as those laid down for the application of such arrangements.

2. Goods not referred to in Article 7(1)(*a*) dispatched or transported from a Member State to a destination in a territory that forms parts of the customs territory of the Community but which is considered as a third territory for the purposes of applying this Directive shall be subject to the following provisions:

(*a*) the formalities relating to the export of those goods outside the territory of the Community shall be the same as the Community customs provisions in force in relation to export of goods outside the customs territory of the Community;

(*b*) for goods which are temporarily exported outside the Community, in order to be reimported, the Member States shall take the measures necessary to ensure that, on reimportation into the Community, such goods may benefit from the same provisions as if they had been temporarily exported outside the customs territory of the Community.] [1]

Amendments

[1] Art 33a substituted by Council Directive 92/111/EEC of 14 December 1992, Art 1(24) with effect from 1 January 1993.

TITLE XIX
FINAL PROVISIONS

Article 34

For the first time on 1 January 1982 and thereafter every two years, the Commission shall, after consulting the Member States, send the Council a report on the application of the common system of value added tax in the Member States. This report shall be transmitted by the Council to the European Parliament.

Article 35

At the appropriate time the Council acting unanimously on a proposal from the Commission, after receiving the opinion of the European Parliament and of the Economic and Social Committee, and in accordance with the interests of the common market, shall adopt further Directives on the common system of value added tax, in particular to restrict progressively or to repeal measures taken by the Member States by way of derogation from the system, in order to achieve complete parallelism of the national value added tax systems and thus permit the attainment of the objective stated in Article 4 of the first Council Directive of 11 April 1967.

Article 36

The fourth paragraph of Article 2 and Article 5 of the first Council Directive of 11 April 1967 are repealed.

Article 37

Second Council Directive 67/228/EEC of 11 April 1967 on value added tax shall cease to have effect in each Member State as from the respective dates on which the provisions of this Directive are brought into application.

Article 38

This Directive is addressed to the Member States.

Done at Brussels, 17 May 1977.

SCH 5

ANNEX A
List of agricultural production activities

I. CROP PRODUCTION

1. General agriculture, including viticulture
2. Growing of fruit (including olives) and of vegetables, flowers and ornamental plants, both in the open and under glass
3. Production of mushrooms, spices, seeds and propagating materials; nurseries

II. STOCK FARMING TOGETHER WITH CULTIVATION

1. General stock farming
2. Poultry farming
3. Rabbit farming
4. Beekeeping
5. Silkworm farming
6. Snail farming

III. FORESTRY

IV. FISHERIES

1. Fresh-water fishing
2. Fish farming

3. Breeding of mussels, oysters and other molluscs and crustaceans

4. Frog farming

V. Where a farmer processes, using means normally employed in an agricultural, forestry or fisheries undertaking, products deriving essentially from his agricultural production, such processing shall also be regarded as agricultural production

ANNEX B
List of agricultural services

Supplies of agricultural services which normally play a part in agricultural production shall be considered the supply of agricultural services, and include the following in particular:

— field work, reaping and mowing, threshing, baling, collecting, harvesting, sowing and planting
— packing and preparation for market, for example drying, cleaning, grinding, disinfecting and ensilage of agricultural products
— storage of agricultural products
— stock minding, rearing and fattening
— hiring out, for agricultural purposes, of equipment normally used in agricultural, forestry or fisheries undertakings
— technical assistance
— destruction of weeds and pests, dusting and spraying of crops and land
— operation of irrigation and drainage equipment
— lopping, tree felling and other forestry services

ANNEX C
Common method of calculation

Note

This Annex, which deals with calculation of VAT own resources is not relevant for the purposes of this work.

ANNEX D
List of the activities referred to in the third paragraph of article 4(5)

1. Telecommunications

2. The supply of water, gas, electricity and steam

3. The transport of goods

4. Port and airport services

5. Passenger transport

6. Supply of new goods manufactured for sale

7. The transactions of agricultural intervention agencies in respect of agricultural products carried out pursuant to Regulations on the common organization of the market in these products

8. The running of trade fairs and exhibitions

9. Warehousing

10. The activities of commercial publicity bodies

11. The activities of travel agencies

12. The running of staff shops, cooperatives and industrial canteens and similar institutions

13. Transactions other than those specified in Article 13A(1)(*q*), of radio and television bodies.

ANNEX E
Transactions referred to in article 28(3)(a)

1. ...[1]

2. Transactions referred to in Article 13A(1)(*e*)

3. ...[1]

4. ...[1]

5. ...[1]

6. ...[1]

7. Transactions referred to in Article 13A(1)(*q*)

8. ...[1]

9. ...[1]

10. ...[1]

11. Supplies covered by Article 13B(*g*) in so far as they are made by taxable persons who were entitled to deduction of input tax on the building concerned.

12. ...[1]

13. ...[1]

14. ...[1]

15. The services of travel agents referred to in Article 26, and those of travel agents acting in the name and on account of the traveller, for journeys outside the Community.

Amendments

[1] Abolished by Council Directive 89/465/EEC (Eighteenth Directive) of 18 July 1989 Art 1(1) with effect from 1 January 1990.

ANNEX F
Transactions referred to in article 28(3)(b)

_{Sch 1(xvii)} **1.** Admission to sporting events.

2. Services supplied by authors, artists, performers, lawyers and other members of the liberal professions, other than the medical and paramedical professions, in so far as these are not services specified in Annex B to the second Council Directive of 11 April 1967.

3. ...[1]

4. ...[1]

5. Telecommunications services supplied by public postal services and supplies of goods incidental thereto.

6. Services supplied by undertakers and cremation services, together with goods Sch 1(xix) related thereto.

7. Transactions carried out by blind persons or workshops for the blind provided these exemptions do not give rise to significant distortion of competition.

8. The supply of goods and services to official bodies responsible for the construction, setting out and maintenance of cemeteries, graves and monuments commemorating war dead.

9. ...[1]

10. Transactions of hospitals not covered by Article 13 A (1)(*b*).

11. ...[1]

12. The supply of water by public authorities.

13. ...[1]

14. ...[1]

15. ...[1]

16. Supplies of those buildings and land described in Article 4(3).

17. Passenger transport.

The transport of goods such as luggage or motor vehicles accompanying passengers and the supply of services related to the transport of passengers, shall only be exempted in so far as the transport of the passengers themselves is exempt.

18. ...[1]

19. ...[1]

20. ...[1]

21. ...[1]

22. ...[1]

23. The supply, modification, repair, maintenance, chartering and hiring of aircraft, including equipment incorporated or used therein, used by State institutions.

24. ...[1]

25. The supply, modification, repair, maintenance, chartering and hiring of warships.

26. ...[2]

27. The services of travel agents referred to in Article 26, and those of travel agents acting in the name and on account of the traveller, for journeys within the Community.

Amendments

[1] Deleted by Council Directive 89/465/EEC (Eighteenth Directive) of 18 July 1989 Art 1(2) with effect from 1 January 1990.

[2] Deleted by Council Directive 98/80/EC of 12 October 1998 (OJ L 281, 17/10/1998 p 31–34) art 2 with effect from 17 October 1998; previously "Transactions concerning gold other than gold for industrial use.".

ANNEX G
Right of option

1. The right of option referred to in Article 28(3)(*c*) may be granted in the following circumstances:

(*a*) in the case of transactions specified in Annex E:
Member States which already exempt these supplies but also give right of option for taxation, may maintain this right of option

(*b*) in the case of transactions specified in Annex F:
Member States which provisionally maintain the right to exempt such supplies may grant taxable persons the right to opt for taxation

2. Member States already granting a right of option for taxation not covered by the provisions of paragraph 1 above may allow taxpayers exercising it to maintain it until at the latest the end of three years from the date the Directive comes into force.

[ANNEX H
List of supplies of goods and services which may be subject
to reduced rates of VAT

In transposing the categories below which refer to goods into national legislation, Member States may use the combined nomenclature to establish the precise coverage of the category concerned.

Category Description

1   Foodstuffs (including beverages but excluding alcoholic beverages) for human and animal consumption; live animals, seeds, plants and ingredients normally intended for use in preparation of foodstuffs; products normally intended to be used to supplement or substituted foodstuffs

2   Water supplies

3   Pharmaceutical products of a kind normally used for health care, prevention of diseases and treatment for medical and veterinary purposes, including products used for contraception and sanitary protection

4 Medical equipment, aids and other appliances normally intended to alleviate or treat disability, for the exclusive personal use of the disabled, including the repair of such goods, and children's car seats

5 Transport of passengers and their accompanying luggage

6 Supply, including on loan by libraries, of books (including brochures, leaflets and similar printed matter, children's picture, drawing or colouring books, music printed or in manuscript, maps and hydrographic or similar charts), newspapers and periodicals, other than material wholly or substantially devoted to advertising matter

7 Admissions to shows, theatres, circuses, fairs, amusement parks, concerts, museums, zoos, cinemas, exhibitions and similar cultural events and facilities

Reception of broadcasting services

8 Services supplied by or royalties due to writers, composers and performing artists

9 Supply, construction, renovation and alteration of housing provided as part of a social policy

10 Supplies of goods and services of a kind normally intended for use in agricultural production but excluding capital goods such as machinery or buildings

11 Accommodation provided by hotels and similar establishments including the provision of holiday accommodation and the letting of camping sites and caravan parks

12 Admission to sporting events

13 Use of sporting facilities

14 Supply of goods and services by organisations recognised as charities by Member States and engaged in welfare or social security work, insofar as these supplies are not exempt under Article 13

15 Services supplied by undertakers and cremation services, together with the supply of goods related thereto

16 Provision of medical and dental care as well as thermal treatment in so far as these services are not exempt under Article 13

17 Services supplied in connection with street cleaning, refuse collection and waste treatment, other than the supply of such services by bodies referred to in Article 4(5)] [1]

Amendments

[1]   Annex H inserted by Council Directive 92/77/EEC of 19 October 1992 Art 1(5) with effect from 1 January 1993.

[ANNEX I
Works of art, collectors' items and antiques

For the purposes of this Directive:

(a)   **"works of art"** shall mean:

— pictures, collages and similar decorative plaques, paintings and drawings, executed entirely by hand by the artist, other than plans and drawings for architectural, engineering, industrial, commercial, topographical or similar purposes, hand-decorated manufactured articles, theatrical scenery, studio back cloths or the like of painted canvas (CN code 9701),

— original engravings, prints and lithographs, being impressions produced in limited numbers directly in black and white or in colour of one or of several plates executed entirely by hand by the artist, irrespective of the process or of the material employed by him, but not including any mechanical or photomechanical process (CN code 9702 00 00),

— original sculptures and statuary, in any material, provided that they are executed entirely by the artist; sculpture casts the product of which is limited to eight copies and supervised by the artist or his successors in title (CN code 9703 00 00); on an exceptional basis, in cases determined by the Member States, the limit of eight copies may be exceeded for statuary casts produced before 1 January 1989,

— tapestries (CN code 5805 00 00) and wall textiles (CN code 6304 00 00) made by hand from original designs provided by artists, provided that there are not more than eight copies of each,

— individual pieces of ceramics executed entirely by the artist and signed by him,

— enamels on copper, executed entirely by hand, limited to eight numbered copies bearing the signature of the artist or the studio, excluding articles of jewellery and goldsmiths' and silversmiths' wares,

— photographs taken by the artist, printed by him or under his supervision, signed and numbered and limited to 30 copies, all sizes and mounts included;

(*b*) **"collectors' items"** shall mean:

— postage or revenue stamps, postmarks, first-day covers, pre-stamped stationery and the like, franked, or if unfranked not being of legal tender and not being intended for use as legal tender (CN code 9704 00 00),

— collections and collectors' pieces of zoological, botanical, mineralogical, anatomical, historical, archaeological, palaetological, ethnographic or numismatic interest (CN code 9705 00 00);

(*c*) **"antiques"** shall mean objects other than works of art or collectors' items, which are more than 100 years old (CN code 9706 00 00).] [1]

Amendments

[1] Annex I inserted by Council Directive 94/5/EC of 14 February 1994 Art 1(10).

[ANNEX J

Description of goods	CN code
Tin	8001
Copper	7402
	7403
	7405
	7408
Zinc	7901
Nickel	7502
Aluminium	7601
Lead	7801
Indium	ex 8112 91
	ex 8112 99
Cereals	1001 to 1005
	1006:
	unprocessed rice only
	1007 to 1008
Oil seeds and oleaginous fruit	1201 to 1207
Coconuts, Brazil nuts and cashew nuts	0801
Other nuts	0802
Olives	0711 20
Grains and seeds (including soya beans)	1201 to 1207
Coffee, no roasted	0901 11 00
	0901 12 00
Tea	0902
Cocoa beans, whole or broken, raw or roasted	1801
Raw sugar	1701 11
	1701 12
Rubber, in primary forms or in plates, sheets or strip	4001
	4002
Wool	5101
Chemicals in bulk	Chapters 28 and 29
Mineral oils (including propane and butane; also including crude petroleum oils)	2709
	2710
	2711 12
	2711 13
Silver	7106
Platinum (palladium, rhodium)	7110 11 10

	7110 21 00
	7110 31 00
Potatoes	0701

Vegetable oils and fats and their fractions, whether or not 1507 to 1515] [1]
refined, but not chemically modified

Amendments

[1]   Annex J inserted by Council Directive 95/7/EC of 10 April 1995 Art 1(13) with effect from 1
January 1996.

[ANNEX K

List of supplies of services referred to in Article 28(6)

1. Small services of repairing:

— bicycles,
— shoes and leather goods,
— clothing and household linen (including mending and alteration).

2. Renovation and repairing of private dwellings, excluding materials which form
a significant part of the value of the supply.

3. Window cleaning and cleaning in private households.

4. Domestic care services (e.g. home help and care of the young, elderly, sick or
disabled).

5. Hairdressing.] [1]

Notes

[1]   Annex K inserted by Council Directive 99/85/EC of 22 October 1999, Arts 1(2) and 3 with effect
from 28 October 1999 (date of publishing in the Official Journal).

[ANNEX L
ILLUSTRATIVE LIST OF ELECTRONICALLY SUPPLIED SERVICES
REFERRED TO IN ARTICLE 9(2)(*e*)

1. Website supply, web-hosting, distance maintenance of programmes and
equipment.

2. Supply of software and updating thereof.

3. Supply of images, text and information, and making databases available.

4. Supply of music, films and games, including games of chance and gambling
games, and of political, cultural, artistic, sporting, scientific and entertainment
broadcasts and events.

5. Supply of distance teaching.

Where the supplier of a service and his customer communicates via electronic
mail, this shall not of itself mean that the service performed is an electronic
service within the meaning of the last indent of Article 9(2)(*e*).] [1]

Amendments

[1]   Substituted by Council Directive 2002/38/EC of 7 May 2002 (OJ L128, 15.5.2002, p 41) Annex
with effect from 1 July 2003.

[COUNCIL DIRECTIVE

of 19 December 1977

77/799/EEC

(OJ L336, 27.12.1977, p 15)

concerning mutual assistance by the competent authorities of the Member States in the field of direct taxation, certain excise duties and taxation of insurance premiums][1]

THE COUNCIL OF THE EUROPEAN COMMUNITIES,

Having regard to the Treaty establishing the European Economic Community, and in particular Article 100 thereof,

Having regard to the proposal from the Commission,

Having regard to the opinion of the European Parliament (OJ No C293, 12.12.1976, p 34),

Having regard to the opinion of the Economic and Social Committee (OJ No C56, 7.3.1977, 66),

Whereas practices of tax evasion and tax avoidance extending across the frontiers of Member States lead to budget losses and violations of the principle of fair taxation and are liable to bring about distortions of capital movements and of conditions of competition; whereas they therefore affect the operation of the common market;

Whereas, for these reasons the Council adopted on 10 February 1975 a resolution on the measures to be taken by the Community in order to combat international tax evasion and avoidance (OJ No C35, 14.2.1975, p 1);

Whereas the international nature of the problem means that national measures, whose effect does not extend beyond national frontiers, are insufficient; whereas collaboration between administrations on the basis of bilateral agreements is also unable to counter new forms of tax evasion and avoidance, which are increasingly assuming a multinational character;

Whereas collaboration between tax administrations within the Community should therefore be strengthened in accordance with common principles and rules;

Whereas the Member States should, on request, exchange information concerning particular cases; whereas the State so requested should make the necessary enquiries to obtain such information;

Whereas the Member States should exchange, even without any request, any information which appears relevant for the correct assessment of taxes on income and on capital, in particular where there appears to be an artificial transfer of profits between enterprises in different Member States or where such transactions are carried out between enterprises in two Member States through a third country in order to obtain tax advantages, or where tax has been or may be evaded or avoided for any reason whatever;

1355

Whereas it is important that officials of the tax administration of one Member State be allowed to be present in the territory of another Member State if both the States concerned consider it desirable;

Whereas care must be taken to ensure that information provided in the course of such collaboration is not disclosed to unauthorised persons, so that the basic rights of citizens and enterprises are safeguarded; whereas it is therefore necessary that the Member States receiving such information should not use it, without the authorisation of the Member State supplying it, other than for the purposes of taxation or to facilitate legal proceedings for failure to observe the tax laws of the receiving State; whereas it is also necessary that the receiving States afford the information the same degree of confidentiality which it enjoyed in the State which provided it, if the latter so requires;

Whereas a Member State which is called upon to carry out enquires or to provide information shall have the right to refuse to do so where its laws or administrative practices prevent its tax administration from carrying out these enquiries or from collecting or using this information for its own purposes, or where the provision of such information would be contrary to public policy or would lead to the disclosure of a commercial, industrial or professional secret or of a commercial process, or where the Member State for which the information is intended is unable for practical or legal reasons to provide similar information.

Whereas collaboration between the Members States and the Commission is necessary for the permanent study of cooperation procedures and the pooling of experience in the fields considered, and in particular in the field of the artificial transfer of profits within groups of enterprises, with the aim of improving those procedures and of preparing appropriate Community rules,

---

Amendments

1   Title substituted by Council Directive 2003/93/EC of 7 October 2003 Art 1(1) with effect from 15 October 2003.

HAS ADOPTED THIS DIRECTIVE:

Article 1
General provisions

[**1.** In accordance with this Directive the competent authorities of the Member State shall exchange any information that may enable them to effect a correct assessment of taxes on income and capital and any information relating to the assessment of the following indirect taxes:
   [—   taxation of insurance premiums referred to in the sixth indent of Article 3 of Council Directive 76/308/EEC,][1]
   —   excise duty on mineral oils,
   —   excise duty on alcohol and alcoholic beverages,
   —   excise duty on manufactured tobacco.][2]

2. There shall be regarded as taxes on income and on capital, irrespective of the manner in which they are levied, all taxes imposed on total income, on total capital, or on elements of income or of capital, including taxes on gains from the disposal of movable or immovable property, taxes on the amounts of wages or salaries paid by enterprises, as well as taxes on capital appreciation.

3. The taxes referred to in paragraph 2 are at present, in particular:

in Belgium:

> Impôt des personnes physiques/Personenbelasting
> Impôt des sociétés/Vennootschapsbelasting
> Impôt des personnes morales/Rechtspersonenbelasting
> Impôt des non-résidents/Belasting der niet-verblijfhouders

in Denmark:

> Indkomstskaten til staten
> Selsskabsskat
> Den Kommunale indkomstskat
> Den amtskommunale indkomstskat
> Folkepensionsbidragene
> Sømandsskatten
> Den saerlige indkomstskat
> Kirkeskatten
> Formueskatten til staten
> Bidrag til dagpengefonden

in Germany:

> Einkommensteurer
> Körperschaftsteuer
> Vermögensteurer
> Gewerbesteuer
> Grundsteuer

[*in Greece:*

> Φυρυζ ει συδηματοζφυσι κων προσωπων
> Φοροζ ει συδηματοζφομι κων προσωπων
> Φοροζ κεκι νπουεερι ουσι]³

[*in Spain*:

> Impuesto sobre la Renta de las Personas Fisicas
> Impuesto sobre Sociedades
> Impuesto Extraordinario sobre el Patrimonio de las Personas Fisicas]³

in France:

> Impôt sur le revenu
> Impôt sur les sociétés
> Tax professionelle
> Taxe foncière sur les propriétés bâties
> Taxe foncière sur les propriétés non bâties

in Ireland:

> Income tax
> Corporation tax
> Capital gains tax
> Wealth tax

in Italy:

    Imposta sul reddito delle persone fisiche

    Imposta sul reddito delle persone giuridiche

    Imposta locale sui redditi

in Luxembourg:

    Impôt sur le revenu des personnes physiques

    Impôt sur le revenu de collectivés

    Impôt commercial communal

    Impôt sur la fortune

    Impôt foncier

in the Netherlands:

    Inkomstenbelasting

    Vennootschapsbelasting

    Vermogensbelasting

[*in Austria:*

    Einkommensteuer

    Körperschaftsteuer

    Grundsteuer

    Bodenwertabgabe

    Abgabe von land- und forstwirtschaftlichen Betrieben][4]

[*in Portugal:*

    Contribuicao predial

    Imposto sobre a industria agricola

    Contribuicao industrial

    Imposto de capitais

    Imposto profissional

    Imposto complementar

    Imposto de mais-valias

    Imposto sobre o rendimento do petroleo

    Os adicionais devidos sobre os impostos precedentes.][3]

[*in Finland*

    Valtion tuloverot — de statliga inkomstskatterna

    Yhteisöjen tulovero — inkomstskatten för samfund

    Kunnallisvero — kommunalskatten

    Kirkollisvero — kyrkoskatten

    Kansaneläkevakuutusmaksu — folkpensionsförsäkringspremien

    Sairausvakuutusmaksu — sjukförsäkringspremien

    Korkotulon lähdevero — källskatten på ränteinkomst

    Rajoitetusti verovelvollisen lähdevero — källskatten för begränsat skattskyldig

    Valtion varallisuusvero — den statliga förmögenhetsskatten

    Kiinteistövero — fastighetsskatten][4]

[*in Sweden*

    Den statliga inkomstskatten

    Sjömansskatten

Kupongskatten
Den särskilda inkomstskatten för utomlands bosatta
Den särskilda inkomstskatten för utomlands bosatta artister m.fl.
Den statliga fastighetsskatten
Den kommunala inkomstskatten
Förmögenhetsskatten][4]

in the United Kingdom:
Income tax
Corporation tax
Capital gains tax
Petroleum revenue tax
Development land tax

[*in the Czech Republic:*
Daně z příjmů
Daň z nemovitostí
Daň dědická, da. darovací a daň z převodu nemovitostí
Daň z přidané hodnoty
Spotřební dan.

in Estonia:
Tulumaks
Sotsiaalmaks
Maamaks

in Cyprus:
Φόρος Εισοδήματος
Έκτακτη Εισφορά για την Άμυνα της Αημοκρατίας
Φόρος Κεφαλαιουχικών Κερδών
Φόρος Ακίνητης Ιδιοκτησίας

in Latvia:
iedzīvotāju ienākuma nodoklis
nekustamā īpašuma nodoklis
uzņēmumu ienākuma nodoklis

in Lithuania:
Gyventoj. pajam. mokestis
Pelno mokestis
Įmoni. ir organizacijų nekilnojamojo turto mokestis
Žemųs mokestis
Mokestis užvalstybinius gamtos išteklius
Mokestis už aplinkos teršimą
Naftos ir dujų ištekli. mokestis
Paveldimo turto mokestis

in Hungary:
személyi jövedelemadó
társasági adó

osztalékadó
általános forgalmi adó
jövedéki adó
építményadó
telekadó

in Malta:
Taxxa fuq l-income

in Poland:
Podatek dochodowy od osób prawnych
Podatek dochodowy od osób fizycznych
Podatek od czynności cywilnopranych

in Slovenia:
Dohodnina
Davki občanov
Davek od dobička pravnihoseb
Posebni davek na bilančno vsoto bank in hranilnic

in Slovakia:
daň príjmov fyzickýchosôb
daň príjmov právnickýchosôb
daň dedi.stva
daň darovania
daň prevodu a prechodu nehnutel'ností
daň nehnutel'ností
daň pridanej hodnoty
spotrebné dane.][5]

4. Paragraph 1 shall also apply to any identical or similar taxes imposed subsequently, whether in addition to or in place of the taxes listed in paragraph 3. The competent authorities of the Member States shall inform one another and the Commission of the date of entry into force of such taxes.

5. The expression **"competent authority"** means:

in Belgium:
De minister van financiën or an authorised representative
Le ministre des finances or an authorised representative

[*in Denmark:*
Skatteministeren or an authorized representative;][6]

in Germany:
Der Bundesminister der Finanzen or an authorised representative

[*in Greece:*
Ypoyrgos Oikonomikon or an authorized representative;][6]

[*in Spain:*
El Ministro de Economia y Hacienda or an authorised representative][3]

in France:

Le ministre de l'économie or an authorised representative

in Ireland:

The Revenue Commissioners or their authorised representative

in Italy:

[il Capo del Dipartimento per le Politiche Fiscali or his authorised representatives][7]

[*in Luxembourg:*

Le ministre de finance or an authorised representative][4]

in the Netherlands:

De minister van financiën or an authorised representative

[*in Austria*

Der Bundesminister für Finanzen or an authorized representative][4]

[*in Portugal:*

O Ministro das Finanças or an authorized representative.][3]][6]

[*in Finland*

Valtiovarainministeriö or an authorised representative][4]

[*in Sweden*

[Chefen för Finansdepartementet or his authorised representative][8]][4] ·

[*in the United Kingdom:*

[The Commissioners of Customs and Excise or an authorised representative for information required concerning taxes on insurance premiums and excise duty.

The Commissioners of Inland Revenue or an authorised representative for all other information.][9]][6]

[*in the Czech Republic:*

Ministr financí or an authorised representative][5]

[*in Estonia:*

Rahandusminister or an authorised representative][5]

[*in Cyprus:*

Υπουργός Οικονομικών or an authorised representative][5]

[*in Latvia:*

Finanšu ministrs or an authorised representative][5]

[*in Lithuania:*

Finansų ministras or an authorised representative][5]

[*in Hungary:*

A pénzügyminiszter or an authorised representative][5]

[*in Malta:*

Il-Ministru responsabbli ghall-Finanzior an authorised representative][5]

[*in Poland:*
   Minister Finansów or an authorised representative][6]

[*in Slovenia:*
   Minister za finance or an authorised representative][6]

[*in Slovakia:*
   Minister financií or an authorised representative][6]

Amendments

[1]   Substituted by Council Directive 2003/93/EC of 7 October 2003, Art 1(2) with effect from 15 October 2003.

[2]   Para (1) substituted by Council Directive 92/12/EEC of 25 February 1992 Art 32(*a*).

[3]   Inserted by the Act of Accession 1985, Art 26, Annex I, Part V, Point 7.

[4]   Inserted by the Act of Accession of Austria, Sweden and Finland (OJ C241 p 21, 29.8.1994) (adapted by Council Decision 95/1/EC, Euratom, ECSC (OJ L1 p 1, 1.1.1995)).

[4]   Inserted by the Act concerning the conditions of accession of the Czech Republic, the Republic of Estonia, the Republic of Cyprus, the Republic of Latvia, the Republic of Lithuania, the Republic of Hungary, the Republic of Malta, the Republic of Poland, the Republic of Slovenia and the Slovak Republic and the adjustments to the Treaties on which the European Union is founded (OJ L 236 p 33, 23.9.2003).

[6]   Substituted by Council Directive 92/12/EEC of 25 February 1992 Art 32(*b*).

[7]   Substituted by Council Directive 2004/56/EC of 21 April 2004 Art 1(1)(*a*) with effect from 29 April 2004.

[8]   Substituted by Council Directive 2004/56/EC of 21 April 2004 Art 1(1)(*b*) with effect from 29 April 2004

[9]   Substituted by Council Directive 2003/93/EC of 7 October 2003, Art 1(2)(*a*) with effect from 15 October 2003.

Article 2
Exchange on request

1. The competent authority of a Member State may request the competent authority of another Member State to forward the information referred to in Article 1(1) in a particular case. The competent authority of the requested State need not comply with the request if it appears that the competent authority of the State making the request has not exhausted its own usual sources of information, which it could have utilised, according to the circumstances, to obtain the information requested without running the risk of endangering the attainment of the sought after result.

2. For the purpose of forwarding the information referred to in paragraph 1, the competent authority of the requested Member State shall arrange for the conduct of any enquiries necessary to obtain such information.

[In order to obtain the information sought, the requested authority or the administrative authority to which it has recourse shall proceed as though acting on its own account or at the request of another authority in its own Member State.][1]

Amendments

[1]   Inserted by Council Directive 2004/56/EC of 21 April 2004 Art 1(2) with effect from 29 April 2004.

Article 3
Automatic exchange of information

For categories of cases which they shall determine under the consultation procedure laid down in Article 9, the competent authorities of the Member States shall regularly exchange the information referred to in Article 1(1) without prior request.

Article 4
Spontaneous exchange of information

1. The competent authority of a Member State shall without prior request forward the information referred to in Article 1(1), of which it has knowledge, to the competent authority of any other Member State concerned, in the following circumstances:

   (*a*) the competent authority of the one Member State has grounds for supposing that there may be a loss of tax in the other Member State;

   (*b*) a person liable to tax obtains a reduction in or an exemption from tax in the one Member State which would give rise to an increase in tax or to liability to tax in the other Member State;

   (*c*) business dealings between a person liable to tax in a Member State and a person liable to tax in another Member State are conducted through one or more countries in such a way that a saving in tax may result in one or the other Member States or in both;

   (*d*) the competent authority of a Member State has grounds for supposing that a saving of tax may result from artificial transfers of profits within groups of enterprises;

   (*e*) information forwarded to the one Member State by the competent authority of the other Member State has enabled information to be obtained which may be relevant in assessing liability to tax in the latter Member State.

2. The competent authorities of the Member State may, under the consultation procedure laid down in Article 9, extend the exchange of information provided for in paragraph 1 to cases other than those specified therein.

3. The competent authorities of the Member States may forward to each other in any other case, without prior request, the information referred to in Article 1(1) of which they have knowledge.

Article 5
Time limit for forwarding information

The competent authority of a Member State which, under the preceding Articles, is called upon to furnish information, shall forward it as swiftly as possible. If it encounters obstacles in furnishing the information or if it refuses to furnish the information, it shall forthwith inform the requesting authority to this effect, indicating the nature of the obstacles or the reasons for its refusal.

Article 6
Collaboration by officials of the State concerned

For the purpose of applying the preceding provisions, the competent authority of the Member State providing the information and the competent authority of the Member State for which the information is intended may agree, under the consultation procedure laid down in Article 9, to authorise the presence in the first Member State of officials of the tax administration of the other Member State. The details for applying this provision shall be determined under the same procedure.

Article 7
Provisions relating to secrecy

[**1**. All information made known to a Member State under this Directive shall be kept secret in that State in the same manner as information received under its national legislation. In any case, such information:

— may be made available only to the persons directly involved in the assessment of the tax or in the administrative control of this assessment,
— may be made known only in connection with judicial proceedings or administrative proceedings involving sanctions undertaken with a view to, or relating to, the making or reviewing the tax assessment and only to persons who are directly involved in such proceedings; such information may, however, be disclosed during public hearings or in judgements if the competent authority of the Member State supplying the information raises no objection at the time when it first supplies the information,
— shall in no circumstances be used other than for taxation purposes or in connection with judicial proceedings or administrative proceedings involving sanctions undertaken with a view to, or in relation to, the making or reviewing of the tax assessment.

In addition, Member States may provide for the information referred to in the first subparagraph to be used for assessment of other levies, duties and taxes covered by Article 2 of Directive 76/308/EEC (OJ L 73, 19.3.1976, p 18).][1]

12. Paragraph 1 shall not oblige a Member State whose legislation or administrative practice lays down, for domestic purposes, narrower limits than those contained in the provisions of that paragraph, to provide information if the State concerned does not undertake to respect those narrower limits.

3. Notwithstanding paragraph 1, the competent authorities of the Member State providing the information may permit it to be used for other purposes in the requesting State, if, under the legislation of the informing State, the information could, in similar circumstances, be used in the informing State for similar purposes.

4. Where a competent authority of a Member State considers that information which it has received from the competent authority of another Member State is likely to be useful to the competent authority of a third Member State, it may transmit it to the latter competent authority with the agreement of the competent authority which supplied the information.

Amendments

¹ Para (1) substituted by Council Directive 2004/56/EC of 21 April 2004 Art 1(3) with effect from 29 April 2004.

Article 8
Limits to exchange of information

[**1.** This Directive does not impose any obligation upon a Member State from which information is requested to carry out inquiries or to communicate information, if it would be contrary to its legislation or administrative practices for the competent authority of that State to conduct such inquiries or to collect the information sought.]¹

2. The provision of information may be refused where it would lead to the disclosure of a commercial, industrial or professional secret or of a commercial process, or of information whose disclosure would be contrary to public policy.

[**3.** The competent authority of a Member State may decline transmission of information when the Member State requesting it is unable, for reasons of fact or law, to provide the same type of information.]²

Amendments

¹ Para (1) substituted by Council Directive 2004/56/EC of 21 April 2004 Art 1(4)(*a*) with effect from 29 April 2004.
² Para (3) substituted by Council Directive 2004/56/EC of 21 April 2004 Art 1(4)(*b*) with effect from 29 April 2004.

Article 8a
Notification

[**1.** At the request of the competent authority of a Member State, the competent authority of another Member State shall, in accordance with the rules governing the notification of similar instruments in the requested Member State, notify the addressee of all instruments and decisions which emanate from the administrative authorities of the requesting Member State and concern the application in its territory of legislation on taxes covered by this Directive.

2. Requests for notification shall indicate the subject of the instrument or decision to be notified and shall specify the name and address of the addressee, together with any other information which may facilitate identification of the addressee.

3. The requested authority shall inform the requesting authority immediately of its response to the request for notification and shall notify it, in particular, of the date of notification of the decision or instrument to the addressee.]¹

Amendments

¹ Article 8a inserted by Council Directive 2004/56/EC of 21 April 2004 Art 1(5) with effect from 29 April 2004.

Article 8b
Simultaneous controls

[**1.** Where the tax situation of one or more persons liable to tax is of common or complementary interest to two or more Member States, those States may agree to conduct simultaneous controls, in their own territory, with a view to exchanging the information thus obtained, whenever they would appear to be more effective than controls conducted by one Member State alone.

2. The competent authority in each Member State shall identify independently the persons liable to tax whom it intends to propose for simultaneous control. It shall notify the respective competent authorities in the other Member States concerned of the cases which, in its view, should be subject to simultaneous control. It shall give reasons for its choice, as far as possible, by providing the information which led to its decision. It shall specify the period of time during which such controls should be conducted.

3. The competent authority of each Member State concerned shall decide whether it wishes to take part in the simultaneous control. On receipt of a proposal for a simultaneous control, the competent authority shall confirm its agreement or communicate its reasoned refusal to its counterpart authority.

4. Each competent authority of the Member States concerned shall appoint a representative with responsibility for supervising and coordinating the control operation.][1]

Amendments

[1]   Article 8b inserted by Council Directive 2004/56/EC of 21 April 2004 Art 1(5) with effect from 29 April 2004.

Article 9
Consultations

1. For the purposes of the implementation of this Directive, consultations shall be held, if necessary in a Committee, between:

— the competent authorities of the Member States concerned at the request of either, in respect of bilateral questions,

— the competent authorities of all the Member States and the Commission, at the request of one of those authorities or the Commission, in so far as the matters involved are not solely of bilateral interest.

2. The competent authorities of the Member States may communicate directly with each other. The competent authorities of the Member States may by mutual agreement permit authorities designated by them to communicate directly with each other in specified cases or in certain categories of cases.

3. Where the competent authorities make arrangements on bilateral matters covered by this Directive other than as regards individual cases, they shall as soon as possible inform the Commission thereof. The Commission shall in turn notify the competent authorities of the other Member States.

Article 10
Pooling of experience

The Member States shall, together with the Commission, constantly monitor the cooperation procedure provided for in this Directive and shall pool their experience, especially in the field of transfer pricing within groups of enterprises, with a view to improving such cooperation and, where appropriate, drawing up a body of rules in the fields concerned.

Article 11
Applicability of wider-ranging provisions of assistance

The foregoing provisions shall not impede the fulfilment of any wider obligations to exchange information which might flow from other legal acts.

Article 12
Final provisions

1. Member States shall bring into force the necessary laws, regulations and administrative provisions in order to comply with this Directive not later than 1 January 1979 and shall forthwith communicate them to the Commission.

2. Member States shall communicate to the Commission the texts of any important provisions of national law which they subsequently adopt in the field covered by this Directive.

Article 13

This Directive is addressed to the Member States.

Done at Brussels, 19 December 1977

EIGHTH COUNCIL DIRECTIVE

of 6 December 1979

79/1072/EEC

(OJ L331, 6.12.1979, p 11)

Refunds to foreign traders

THE COUNCIL OF THE EUROPEAN COMMUNITIES,

Having regard to the Treaty establishing the European Economic Community,

Having regard to Sixth Council Directive 77/388/EEC of 17 May 1977 on the harmonisation of the laws of the Member States relating to turnover taxes — Common system of value added tax (uniform basis of assessment) (OJ L 145, 13.6.77, p 1) and in particular Article 17(4) thereof,

Having regard to the proposal from the Commission (OJ C26, 1.2.1978, p 5),

Having regard to the opinion of the European Parliament (OJ C39, 12.2.1979, p 14),

Having regard to the opinion of the Economic and Social Committee (OJ C269, 13.11.1978, p 51),

Whereas, pursuant to Article 17(4) of Directive 77/388/EEC, the Council is to adopt Community rules laying down the arrangements governing refunds of value added tax, referred to in paragraph 3 of the said Article, to taxable persons not established in the territory of the country;

Whereas rules are required to ensure that a taxable person established in the territory of one member country can claim for tax which has been invoiced to him in respect of supplies of goods or services in another Member State or which has been paid in respect of imports into that other Member State, thereby avoiding double taxation;

Whereas discrepancies between the arrangements currently in force in Member States, which give rise in some cases to deflection of trade and distortion of competition, should be eliminated;

Whereas the introduction of Community rules in this field will mark progress towards the effective liberalization of the movement of persons, goods and services thereby helping complete the process of economic integration;

Whereas such rules must not lead to the treatment of taxable persons differing according to the Member State in the territory of which they are established;

Whereas certain forms of tax evasion or avoidance should be prevented;

Whereas, under Article 17(4) of Directive 77/388/EEC, Member States may refuse the refund or impose supplementary conditions in the case of taxable persons not established in the territory of the Community; whereas steps should, however, also be taken to ensure that such taxable persons are not eligible for refunds on more favourable terms than those provided for in respect of Community taxable persons;

Whereas, initially, only the Community arrangements contained in this Directive should be adopted; whereas these arrangements provide, in particular, that decisions in respect of applications for refund should be notified within six months of the date on which such applications were lodged; whereas refunds should be made within the same period; whereas, for a period of one year from the final date laid down for the implementation of these arrangements, the Italian Republic should be authorized to notify the decisions taken by its competent services with regard to applications lodged by taxable persons not established within its territory and to make the relevant refunds within nine months, in order to enable the Italian Republic to reorganize the system at present in operation, with a view to applying the Community system;

Whereas further arrangements will have to be adopted by the Council to supplement the Community system; whereas, until the latter arrangements enter into force, Member States will refund the tax on the services and the purchases of goods which are not covered by this Directive, in accordance with the arrangements which they adopt pursuant to Article 17(4) of Directive 77/388/EEC,

HAS ADOPTED THIS DIRECTIVE:

Article 1
Definition of claimant

For the purposes of this Directive, 'a taxable person not established in the territory of the country' shall means a person as referred to in Article 4(1) of Directive 77/388/EEC who, during the period referred to in the first and second sentences of the first subparagraph of Article 7(1), has had in that country neither the seat of his economic activity, nor a fixed establishment from which business transactions are effected, nor, if no such seat or fixed establishment exists, his domicile or normal place of residence, and who, during the same period, has supplied no goods or services deemed to have been supplied in that country, with the exception of:

(*a*) transport services and services ancillary thereto, exempted pursuant to Article 14(1)(i), Article 15 or Article 16(1), B, C and D of Directive 77/388/EEC;

(*b*) services provided in cases where tax is payable solely by the person to whom they are supplied, pursuant to Article 21(1)(*b*) of Directive 77/388/EEC.

Article 2
Right to refund

Each Member State shall refund to any taxable person who is not established in the territory of the country but who is established in another Member State, subject to the conditions laid down below, any value added tax charged in respect of services or movable property supplied to him by other taxable persons in the territory of the country or charged in respect of the importation of goods into the country, in so far as such goods and services are used for the purposes of the transactions referred to in Article 17(3)(*a*) and (*b*) of Directive 77/388/EEC and of the provision of services referred to in Article 1(*b*).

Revenue publications

Addresses for foreign traders: Tax Briefing, Issue 30.

Article 3
Requirements— where no goods or services supplied

To qualify for refund, any taxable person as referred to in Article 2 who supplies no goods or services deemed to be supplied in the territory of the country shall:

(*a*)　submit to the competent authority referred to in the first paragraph of Article 9 an application modelled on the specimen contained in Annex A, attaching originals of invoices or import documents. Member States shall make available to applicants an explanatory notice which shall in any event contain the minimum information set out in Annex C;

(*b*)　produce evidence, in the form of a certificate issued by the official authority of the State in which he is established, that he is a taxable person for the purposes of value added tax in that State. However, where the competent authority referred to in the first paragraph of Article 9 already has such evidence in its possession, the taxable person shall not be bound to produce new evidence for a period of one year from the date of issue of the first certificate by the official authority of the State in which he is established. Member States shall not issue certificates to any taxable persons who benefit from tax exemption pursuant to Article 24(2) of Directive 77/388/EEC;

(*c*)　certify by means of a written declaration that he has supplied no goods or services deemed to have been supplied in the territory of the country during the period referred to in the first and second sentences of the first subparagraph of Article 7(1);

(*d*)　undertake to repay any sum collected in error.

Case law

Belgian lawyer (VAT exempt) not entitled to refund of Dutch VAT paid on car hire: *Debouche v Inspecteur der Invoerrechten en Accijnzen* [1996] STC 1406, ECJ 302/93.

Para (*a*): Taxpayer entitled to submit duplicate invoice where original is lost for reasons beyond his control: *Societe Generale des Grandes Sources d'Eaux Minerals Francais v Bundesamt fur Finanzen* [1999] BVC 3, C–361/96.

Article 4
Requirements — where certain services supplied

To be eligible for the refund, any taxable person as referred to in Article 2 who has supplied in the territory of the country no goods or services deemed to have been supplied in the country other than the services referred to in Article 1(*a*) and (*b*) shall:

(*a*)　satisfy the requirements laid down in Article 3(*a*), (*b*) and (*d*);

(*b*)　certify by means of a written declaration that, during the period referred to in the first and second sentences of the first subparagraph of Article 7(1), he has supplied no goods or services deemed to have been supplied in the territory of the country other than services referred to in Article 1(*a*) and (*b*).

Article 5
Qualifying goods and services

For the purposes of this Directive, goods and services in respect of which tax may be refundable shall satisfy the conditions laid down in Article 17 of Directive 77/388/EEC as applicable in the Member State of refund.

This Directive shall not apply to supplies of goods which are, or may be, exempted under item 2 of Article 15 of Directive 77/388/EEC.

Article 6
Restriction on imposition of further obligations

Member States may not impose on the taxable persons referred to in Article 2 any obligation, in addition to those referred to in Articles 3 and 4, other than the obligation to provide, in specific cases, the information necessary to determine whether the application for refund is justified.

Article 7
Miscellaneous provisions

1. The application for refund provided for in Articles 3 and 4 shall relate to invoiced purchases of goods or services or to imports made during a period of not less than three months or not more than one calendar year. Applications may, however, relate to a period of less than three months where the period represents the remainder of a calendar year. Such applications may also relate to invoices or import documents not covered by previous applications and concerning transactions completed during the calendar year in question. Applications shall be submitted to the competent authority referred to in the first paragraph of Article 9 within six months of the end of the calendar year in which the tax became chargeable.

If the application relates to a period of less than one calendar year but not less than three months, the amount for which application is made may not be less than the equivalent in national currency of 200 European units of account; if the application relates to a period of a calendar year or the remainder of a calendar year, the amount may not be less than the equivalent in national currency of 25 European units of account.

2. The European unit of account shall be that defined in the Finance Regulation of 21 December 1977. (OJ L356, 31.12.1977, p 1) as determined on 1 January of the year of the period referred to in the first and second sentences of the first subparagraph of paragraph 1. Member States may round up or down, by up to 10% the figures resulting from this conversion into national currency.

3. The competent authority referred to in the first paragraph of article 9 shall stamp each invoice and/or import document to prevent their use for further application and shall return them within one month.

4. Decisions concerning applications for refund shall be announced within six months of the date when the applications, accompanied by all the necessary documents required under this Directive for examination of the application, are submitted to the competent authority referred to in paragraph 3. Refunds shall be made before the end of the above mentioned period, at the applicant's request, in either the Member State of refund or the State in which he is established. In the latter case, the bank charges for the transfer shall be payable by the applicant.

The grounds for refusal of an application shall be stated. Appeals against such refusals may be made to the competent authorities in the Member State concerned, subject to the same conditions as to form and time limits as those governing claims for refunds made by taxable persons established in the same State.

5. Where a refund has been obtained in a fraudulent or in any other irregular manner, the competent authority referred to in paragraph 3 shall proceed directly to recover the amounts wrongly paid and any penalties imposed, in accordance with the procedure applicable in the Member State concerned, without prejudice to the provisions relating to mutual assistance in the recovery of value added tax.

In the case of fraudulent applications which cannot be made the subject of an administrative penalty, in accordance with national legislation, the Member State concerned may refuse for a maximum period of two years from the date on which the fraudulent application was submitted any further refund to the taxable person concerned. Where an administrative penalty has been imposed but has not been paid, the Member State concerned may suspend any further refund to the taxable person concerned until it has been paid.

Article 8
Non-EEC traders

... 1

Refunds may not be granted on terms more favourable than those applied in respect of taxable persons established in the territory of the Community.

Amendments

1   Deleted by Thirteenth Council Directive 86/560/EEC of 17 November 1986 Art 7.

Article 9
Competent authorities

Member States shall make known, in an appropriate manner, the competent authority to which the application referred to in Article 3(*a*) and in Article 4(*a*) are to be submitted.

The certificates referred to in Article 3(*b*) and in Article 4(*a*), establishing that the person concerned is a taxable person, shall be modelled on the specimens contained in Annex B.

Article 10
Date of implementation

Member States shall bring into force the provisions necessary to comply with this Directive no later than 1 January 1981. This Directive shall apply only to applications for refunds concerning value added tax charged on invoiced purchases or services or in imports made as from that date.

Member States shall communicate to the Commission the texts of the main provisions of national law which they adopt in the field covered by this Directive. The Commission shall inform the other Member States thereof.

Article 11
Derogation

By way of derogation from Article 7(4), the Italian Republic may, until 1 January 1982, extend the period referred to in this paragraph from six to nine months.

Article 12
Operation review

Three years after the date referred to in Article 10, the Commission shall, after consulting the Member States, submit a report to the Council on the application of this Directive, and in particular Articles 3, 4 and 7 thereof.

Article 13
Scope

This Directive is addressed to the Member States.

Done at Brussels, 6 December 1979

ELEVENTH COUNCIL DIRECTIVE

of 26 March 1980

80/368/EEC

(OJ L090, 03/04/1980 p 41–41)

on the harmonization of the laws of the Member States relating to turnover taxes —
exclusion of the French overseas departments from the scope of Directive 77/388/EEC

THE COUNCIL OF THE EUROPEAN COMMUNITIES,

Having regard to the Treaty establishing the European Economic Community, and in particular Articles 99 and 100 thereof,

Having regard to the proposal from the Commission,

Whereas the third subparagraph of Article 227(2) of the Treaty requires that the institutions of the Community should, within the framework of the procedures provided for in the Treaty, take care that the economic and social development of the French overseas departments is possible;

Whereas, in accordance with the judgment handed down by the Court of Justice on 10 October 1978 in Case 148/77, the Treaty and secondary legislation apply in the French overseas departments unless a decision is taken by the Community institutions adopting measures particularly suited to the economic and social conditions of those departments;

Whereas, for reasons connected with their geographic, economic and social situation, the French overseas departments should be excluded from the scope of the common system of value added tax as established by Council Directive 77/388/EEC (OJ No L 145, 13.6.1977, p 1);

Whereas implementation of this Directive does not involve any amendment of the laws of the Member States,

HAS ADOPTED THIS DIRECTIVE:

Article 1

The following indent shall be added to Article 3(2) of Directive 77/388/EEC:
"-   French Republic: — the overseas departments."

Article 2

This Directive shall apply with effect from 1 January 1979.

Article 3

This Directive is addressed to the Member States.

COUNCIL DIRECTIVE

of 28 March 1983

83/181/EEC

Determining the scope of Article 14(1)(d) of Directive 77/388/EEC as regards exemption from Value Added Tax on the final importation of certain goods

Note

This Directive ceases to have effect on 31 December 1992 as regards relations between Member States; see Council Directive 91/680/EEC of 16 December 1991, Art 2(1).

THE COUNCIL OF THE EUROPEAN COMMUNITIES

Having regard to the Treaty establishing the European Economic Community, and in particular Articles 99 and 100 thereof,

Having regard to the proposal from the Commission,

Having regard to the opinion of the European Parliament,

Having regard to the opinion of the Economic and Social Committee,

Whereas, pursuant to Article 14(1)(*d*) of Council Directive 77/388/EEC of 17 May 1977 on the harmonisation of the laws of the Member States relating to turnover taxes — Common system of value added tax: uniform basis of assessment (OJ No L145, 13.6.1977, p 1), Member States shall, without prejudice to other Community provisions and under conditions which they shall lay down for the purpose, *inter alia*, of preventing any possible evasion, avoidance or abuse, exempt final importation of goods qualifying for exemption from customs duties other than as provided for in the Common Customs Tariff or which would qualify therefor if they were imported from a third country;

Whereas, in accordance with Article 14(2) of the above mentioned Directive, the Commission is required to submit to the Council proposals designed to lay down Community tax rules clarifying the scope of the exemptions referred to in paragraph 1 of the said Article and detailed rules for their implementation;

Whereas, while it is deemed desirable to achieve the greatest possible degree of uniformity between the system for customs duties and that for value added tax, account should be taken, in applying the latter system of the differences as regards objective and structure between customs duties and value added tax;

Whereas arrangements for value added tax should be introduced that differ according to whether goods are imported from third countries or from other Member States and to the extent necessary to comply with the objectives of tax harmonisation; whereas the exemptions on importation can be granted only on condition that they are not liable to affect the conditions of competition on the home market;

Whereas certain reliefs at present applied in the Member States stem from conventions with third countries or with other Member States which, given their purpose, concern only the signatory Member States; whereas it is not expedient to define at Community level conditions for granting such reliefs, and whereas the Member States concerned need merely be authorised to retain them,

HAS ADOPTED THIS DIRECTIVE:

Article 1

1. The scope of the exemptions from value added tax referred to in Article 14(1)(*d*) of Directive 77/388/EEC and the rules for their implementation referred to in Article 14(2) of that Directive shall be defined by this Directive. In accordance with the aforesaid Article, the Member States shall apply the exemptions laid down in this Directive under the conditions fixed by them in order to ensure that such exemptions are correctly and simply applied and to prevent any evasion, avoidance or abuses.

2. For the purposes of this Directive:

(*a*) **"imports"** means imports as defined in Article 7 of 77/388/EEC and the entry for home use after being subject to one of the systems provided for in Article 16(1)(A) of the said Directive or a system of temporary admission or transit;

(*b*) **"personal property"** means any property intended for the personal use of the persons concerned or for meeting their household needs.

The following, in particular, shall constitute "personal property":

— household effects,
— cycles and motor-cycles, private motor vehicles and their trailers, camping caravans, pleasure craft and private aeroplanes.

Household provisions appropriate to normal family requirements, household pets and saddle animals shall also constitute "personal property".

The nature or quantity of personal property shall not reflect any commercial interest, nor shall they be intended for an economic activity within the meaning of Article 4 of Directive 77/388/EEC. However, portable instruments of the applied or liberal arts, required by the person concerned for the pursuits of his trade or profession, shall also constitute personal property;

(*c*) **"household effects"** means personal effects, household linen and furnishings and items of equipment intended for the personal use of the persons concerned or for meeting their household needs;

(*d*) **"alcoholic products"** means products (beer, wine, aperitifs with a wine or alcohol base, brandies, liqueurs and spirituous beverages, etc) falling within heading Nos [22.03 to 22.08][1] of the Common Customs Tariff;

(*e*) **"Community"** means the territory of the Member States where Directive 77/388/EEC applies.

Amendments

[1] Substituted by Commission Directive 89/219/EEC of 7 March 1989, Art 1.

TITLE I
IMPORTATION OF PERSONAL PROPERTY BELONGING TO INDIVIDUALS COMING FROM COUNTRIES SITUATED OUTSIDE THE COMMUNITY

CHAPTER I
Personal property of natural persons transferring their normal place of residence from a third country to the community

Article 2

Subject to Articles 3 to 10, exemption from VAT on importation shall be granted on personal property imported by natural persons transferring their normal place of residence from outside the Community to a Member State of the Community.

Article 3

Exemption shall be limited to personal property which:

(*a*) except in special cases justified by the circumstances, has been in the possession of and, in the case of non-consumable goods, used by the person concerned at his former normal place of residence for a minimum of six months before the date on which he ceases to have his normal place of residence outside the Community;

(*b*) is intended to be used for the same purpose at his new normal place of residence.

The Member States may in addition make exemption conditional upon such property having borne, either in the country of origin or in the country of departure, the customs and/or fiscal charges to which it is normally liable.

Article 4

Exemption may be granted only to persons whose normal place of residence has been outside the Community for a continuous period of at least 12 months.

However, the competent authorities may grant exceptions to this rule provided that the intention of the person concerned was clearly to reside outside the Community for a continuous period of at least 12 months.

Article 5

Exemption shall not be granted in respect of:

(*a*) alcoholic products;

(*b*) tobacco or tobacco products;

(*c*) commercial means of transport;

(*d*) articles for use in the exercise of a trade or profession, other than portable instruments of the applied or liberal arts.

Vehicles intended for mixed use for commercial or professional purposes may also be excluded from exemption.

Article 6

Except in special cases, exemption shall be granted only in respect of personal property entered for permanent importation within 12 months of the date of establishment, by the person concerned, of his normal place of residence in the Member State of importation.

The personal property may be imported in several separate consignments within the period referred to in the preceding paragraph.

Article 7

1. Until 12 months have elapsed from the date of the declaration for its final importation, personal property which has been imported exempt from tax may not be lent, given as security, hired out or transferred, whether for a consideration or free of charge, without prior notification to the competent authorities.

2. Any loan, giving as security, hiring out or transfer before the expiry of the period referred to in paragraph 1 shall entail payment of the relevant value added tax on the goods concerned, at the rate applying on the date of such loan, giving as security, hiring out or transfer, on the basis of the type of goods and the customs value ascertained or accepted on that date by the competent authorities.

Article 8

1. By way of derogation from the first paragraph or Article 6, exemption may be granted in respect of personal property permanently imported before the person concerned establishes his normal place of residence in the Member State of importation, provided that he undertakes actually to establish his normal place of residence there within a period of six months. Such undertaking shall be accompanied by a security, the form and amount of which shall be determined by the competent authorities.

2. Where use is made of the provisions of paragraph 1, the period laid down in Article 3 shall be calculated from the date of importation into the Member States concerned.

Article 9

1. Where, owing to occupational commitments, the person concerned leaves the country situated outside the Community where he had his normal place of residence without simultaneously establishing his normal place of residence in the territory of a Member State, although having the intention of ultimately doing so, the competent authorities may authorise exemption in respect of the personal property which he transfers into the said territory for this purpose.

2. Exemption in respect of the personal property referred to in paragraph 1 shall be granted in accordance with the conditions laid down in Articles 2 to 7, on the understanding that:

    (*a*) the periods laid down in Article 3(*a*) and the first paragraph of Article 6 shall be calculated from the date of importation;

    (*b*) the period referred to in Article 7(1) shall be calculated from the date when the person concerned actually establishes his normal place of residence in the territory of a Member State.

3. Exemption shall also be subject to an undertaking from the person concerned that he will actually establish his normal place of residence in the territory of a Member State within a period laid down by the competent authorities in keeping with the circumstances. The latter may require this undertaking to be accompanied by a security, the form and amount of which they shall determine.

Article 10

The competent authorities may derogate from Articles 3(*a*) and (*b*), 5(*c*) and (*d*) and 7 when a person has to transfer his normal place of residence from a country situated outside the Community to the territory of a Member State as a result of exceptional political circumstances.

CHAPTER II
Goods imported on the occasion of a marriage

Article 11

1. Subject to Articles 12 to 15, exemption shall be granted in respect of trousseaux and household effects, whether or not new, belonging to a person transferring his or her normal place of residence from a country outside the Community to the territory of a Member State on the occasion of his or her marriage.

[**2.** Exemption shall also be granted in respect of presents customarily given on the occasion of a marriage which are received by a person fulfilling the conditions laid down in paragraph 1 from person having their normal place of residence in a country situated outside the Community. The exemption shall apply to presents of a unit value not more than 200 ECU. Member States may, however, grant exemption for more than 200 ECU provided that the value of each exempt present does not exceed 1,000 ECU.][1]

3 The Member State may make exemption of the goods referred to in paragraph 1 conditional on their having borne, either in the country of origin or in the country of departure, the customs and/or fiscal charges to which they are normally liable.

Amendments

[1]   Substituted by Council Directive 88/331/EEC of 13 June 1988, Art 1(1).

Article 12

1. The exemption referred to in Article 11 may be granted only to persons:

   (*a*)   whose normal place of residence has been outside the Community for a continuous period of at least 12 months. However, derogations from this rule may be granted provided that the intention of the person concerned was clearly to reside outside the Community for a continuous period of at least 12 months;

   (*b*)   who produce evidence of their marriage.

Article 13

No exemption shall be granted for alcoholic products, tobacco or tobacco products.

Article 14

1. Save in exceptional circumstances, exemption shall be granted only in respect of goods permanently imported:

— not earlier than two months before the date fixed for the wedding (in this case exemption may be made subject to the lodging of appropriate security, the form and amount of which shall be determined by the competent authorities), and

— not later than four months after the date of the wedding.

2. Goods referred to in Article 11 may be imported in several separate consignments within the period referred to in paragraph 1.

Article 15

1 Until 12 months have elapsed from the date of the declaration for their final importation, goods which have been imported exempt from tax may not be lent, given as security, hired out or transferred, whether for a consideration or free of charge, without prior notification to the competent authorities.

2 Any loan, giving as security, hiring out or transfer before the expiry of the period referred to in paragraph 1 shall entail payment of the relevant value added tax on the goods concerned, at the rate applying on the date of such loan, giving as security, hiring out or transfer, on the basis of the type of goods and the value ascertained or accepted on that date by the competent authorities.

CHAPTER III
Personal property acquired by inheritance

Article 16

Subject to Articles 17 to 19, exemption shall be granted in respect of personal property acquired by inheritance by a natural person having his normal place of residence in a Member State.

Article 17

Exemption shall not be granted in respect of:

(*a*)   alcoholic products;

(*b*)   tobacco or tobacco products;

(*c*)   commercial means of transport

(*d*)   articles for use in the exercise of a trade or profession, other than portable instruments of the applied or liberal arts, which were required for the exercise of the trade or profession of the deceased;

(*e*)   stocks of raw materials and finished or semi-finished products;

(*f*)   livestock and stocks of agricultural products exceeding the quantities appropriate to normal family requirements.

Article 18

1. Exemption shall be granted only in respect of personal property permanently imported not later than two years from the date on which the person becomes entitled to the goods (final settlement of the inheritance).

However, this period may be extended by the competent authorities on special grounds.

2. The goods may be imported in several separate consignments within the period referred to in paragraph 1.

Article 19

Articles 16 to 18 shall apply *mutatis mutandis* to personal property acquired by inheritance by legal persons engaged in a non-profitmaking activity who are established in the territory of a Member state.

TITLE II
SCHOOL OUTFITS, SCHOLASTIC MATERIALS AND OTHER SCHOLASTIC HOUSEHOLD EFFECTS

Article 20

1. Exemption shall be granted in respect of outfits, scholastic materials and household effects representing the usual furnishings for a student's room and belonging to pupils or students coming to stay in a Member State for the purposes of studying there and intended for their personal use during the period of their studies.

2. For the purposes of this Article:

    (*a*)   pupil or student means any person enrolled in an educational establishment in order to attend full-time the courses offered therein;

    (*b*)   outfit means underwear and household linen as well as clothing, whether or not new;

    (*c*)   scholastic materials means articles and instruments (including calculators and type-writers) normally used by pupils or students for the purposes of their studies.

Article 21

Exemption shall be granted at least once per school year.

TITLE III
IMPORTS OF NEGLIGIBLE VALUE

Article 22

[Goods of a total value not exceeding 10 ECU shall be exempt on admission. Member States may grant exemption for imported goods of a total value of more than 10 ECU but not exceeding 22 ECU.

However, Member Sates may exclude goods which have been imported on mail order from the exemption provided for in the first sentence of the first subparagraph.][1]

Amendments

[1]   Art 22 substituted by Council Directive 88/331/EEC of 13 June 1988, Art 1(2).

Article 23

Exemption shall not apply to the following:

(*a*) alcoholic products;

(*b*) perfumes and toilet waters;

(*c*) tobacco or tobacco products.

TITLE IV
CAPITAL GOODS AND OTHER EQUIPMENT IMPORTED ON THE TRANSFER OF ACTIVITIES

Article 24

1. Without prejudice to the measures in force in the Member State with regard to industrial and commercial policy, and subject to Articles 25 to 28, Member states may allow exemption, on admission, for imports of capital goods and other equipment belonging to undertakings which definitively cease their activity in the country of departure in order to carry on a similar activity in the Member State into which the goods are imported and which, in accordance with Article 22(1) of Directive 77/388/EEC, have given advance notice to the competent authorities of the Member State of importation of the commencement of such activity.

Where the undertaking transferred is an agricultural holding, its livestock shall also be exempt on admission.

2. For the purposes of paragraph 1:

— **"activity"** means an economic activity as referred to in Article 4 of Directive 77/388/EEC,

— **"undertaking"** means an independent economic unit of production or of the service industry.

Article 25

1. The exemption referred to in Article 24 shall be limited to capital goods and equipment which:

(*a*) except in special cases justified by the circumstances, have actually been used in the undertaking for a minimum of 12 months prior to the date on which the undertaking ceased to operate in the country of departure;

(*b*) are intended to be used for the same purposes after the transfer;

(*c*) are to be used for the purposes of an activity not exempted under Article 13 of Directive 77/388/EEC;

(*d*) are appropriate to the nature and size of the undertaking in question.

2. However, Member States may exempt capital goods and equipment imported from another Member State by charitable or philanthropic organisations at the time of the transfer of their principal place of business to the Member State of importation.

Such exemption shall, however, be granted only on condition that at the time when they were acquired the capital goods and equipment in question were not exempt under Article 15(12) of Directive 77/388/EEC.

3. Pending entry into force of the common rules referred to in the first subparagraph of Article 17(6) of Directive 77/388/EEC, Member States may exclude from the exemption, in whole or in part, capital goods in respect of which they have availed themselves of the second subparagraph of that paragraph.

Article 26

No exemption shall be granted to undertakings established outside the Community and the transfer of which into the territory of a Member State is consequent upon or is for the purpose of merging with, or being absorbed by, an undertaking established in the Community, without a new activity being set up.

Article 27

No exemption shall be granted for:

(*a*) means of transport which are not of the nature of instruments of production or of the service industry;

(*b*) supplies of all kinds intended for human consumption or for animal feed;

(*c*) fuel and stocks of raw materials or finished or semi-finished products;

(*d*) livestock in the possession of dealers.

Article 28

Except in special cases justified by the circumstances, the exemption referred to in Article 24 shall be granted only in respect of capital goods and other equipment imported before the expiry of a period of 12 months from the date when the undertaking ceased its activities in the country of departure.

TITLE V
IMPORTATION OF CERTAIN AGRICULTURAL PRODUCTS AND PRODUCTS INTENDED FOR AGRICULTURAL USE

CHAPTER I
Products obtained by community farmers on properties located in a state other than the state of importation

Article 29

1. Subject to Articles 30 and 31, agricultural, stock-farming, bee-keeping, horticultural and forestry products from properties located in a country adjoining the territory of the Member State of importation which are operated by agricultural producers having their principal undertaking in that Member State and adjacent to the country concerned shall be exempt on admission.

2. To be eligible under paragraph 1, stock-farming products must be obtained from animals reared, acquired or imported in accordance with the general tax arrangements applicable in the Member State of importation.

3. Pure-bred horses, not more than six months old and born outside the Member State of importation of an animal covered in that State and then exported temporarily to give birth, shall be exempt on admission.

Article 30

Exemption shall be limited to products which have not undergone any treatment other than that which normally follows their harvest or production.

Article 31

Exemption shall be granted only in respect of products imported by the agricultural producer or on his behalf.

Article 32

This Chapter shall apply *mutatis mutandis* to the products of fishing or fish-farming activities carried out in the lakes or waterways bordering the territory of the Member State of importation by fishermen established in that Member State and to the products of hunting activities carried out on such lakes or waterways by sportsmen established in that Member State.

CHAPTER III
Seeds, fertilizers and products for the treatment of soil and crops

Article 33

Subject to Article 34, seeds, fertilizers and products for the treatment of soil and crops, intended for use on property located in a Member State adjoining a country situated outside the Community or another Member State and operated by agricultural producers having the principal undertaking in the said country situated outside the Community or Member State adjacent to the territory of the Member State of importation shall be exempt on admission.

Article 34

1. Exemption shall be limited to the quantities of seeds, fertilizers or other products required for the purpose of operating the property.

2. It shall be granted only for seeds, fertilizers or other products introduced directly into the importing Member State by the agricultural producer or on his behalf.

3. Member States may make exemption conditional upon the granting of reciprocal treatment.

TITLE VI
IMPORTATION OF THERATEUTIC SUBSTANCES, MEDICINES, LABORATORY ANIMALS AND BIOLOGICAL OR CHEMICAL SUBSTANCES

CHAPTER I

Laboratory animals and biological or chemical substances intended for research

Article 35

1. The following shall be exempt on admission:

(*a*) animals specially prepared and sent free of charge for laboratory use;

(*b*) biological or chemical substances:

— which are imported free of charge from the territory of another Member State, or

— which are imported from countries outside the Community subject to the limits and conditions laid down in [Article 60][1] of Council Regulation (EEC) No 918/83 of 28 March 1983 setting up a Community system of reliefs from customs duty.

2. The exemption referred to in paragraph 1 shall be limited to animals and biological or chemical substances which are intended for:

— either public establishments principally engaged in education or scientific research including those departments of public establishments which are principally engaged in education or scientific research,

— or private establishments principally engaged in education or scientific research and authorised by the competent authorities of the Member States to receive such articles exempt from tax.

Amendments

[1] Substituted by Council Directive 88/331/EEC of 13 June 1988, Art 1(3).

CHAPTER II

Therapeutic substances of human origin and blood-grouping and tissue-typing reagents

Article 36

1. Without prejudice to the exemption provided for in Article 14(1)(a) of Directive 77/388/EEC and subject to Article 37, the following shall be exempted:

(*a*) therapeutic substances of human origin;

(*b*) blood-grouping reagents;

(*c*) tissue-typing reagents.

2. For the purposes of paragraph 1:

— **"therapeutic substances of human origin"** means human blood and its derivatives (whole human blood, dried human plasma, human albumin and fixed solutions of human plasma protein, human immunoglobulin and human fibrinogen),

—   **"blood grouping reagents"** means all reagents, whether of human, animal, plant or other origin used for blood-type grouping and for the detection of blood incompatibilities,

—   **"tissue-typing reagents"** means all reagents whether of human, animal, plant or other origin used for the determination of human tissue-types.

Article 37

Exemption shall be limited to products which:

(*a*)   are intended for institutions or laboratories approved by the competent authorities, for use exclusively for non-commercial medical or scientific purposes;

(*b*)   are accompanied by a certificate of conformity issued by a duly authorised body in the country of departure;

(*c*)   are in containers bearing a special label identifying them.

Article 38

Exemption shall include the special packaging essential for the transport of therapeutic substances of human origin or blood-grouping or tissue-typing reagents and also any solvents and accessories needed for their use which may be included in the consignments.

[CHAPTER IIa
Reference substances for the quality control of medical products

Article 38(a)

Consignments which contain samples of reference substances approved by the World Health Organisation for the quality control of materials used in the manufacture of medicinal products and which are addressed to consignees authorised by the competent authorities of the Member States to receive such consignments free of tax shall be exempt on admission.]¹

Amendments

¹   Added by Council Directive 88/331/EEC of 13 June 1988, Art 1(4).

CHAPTER III
Pharmaceutical products used at international sports events

Article 39

Pharmaceutical products for human or veterinary medical use by persons or animals participating in international sports events shall, within the limits necessary to meet their requirements during their stay in the Member State of importation, be exempt on admission.

TITLE VII
GOODS FOR CHARITABLE OR PHILANTHROPIC ORGANISATIONS

Article 40

Member States may impose a limit on the quantity or value of the goods referred to in Articles 41 to 55, in order to remedy any abuse and to combat major distortions of competition.

CHAPTER I
Goods imported for general purposes

Article 41

1. Subject to Articles 42 to 44, the following shall be exempt on admission:

(*a*) basic necessities obtained free of charge and imported by State organisations or other charitable or philanthropic organisations approved by the competent authorities for distribution free of charge to needy persons;

(*b*) goods of every description sent free of charge, by a person or organisation established in a country other than the Member State of importation, and without any commercial intent on the part of the sender, to State organisations or other charitable or philanthropic organisations approved by the competent authorities, to be used for fund raising at occasional charity events for the benefit of needy persons;

(*c*) equipment and office materials sent free of charge, by a person or organisation established in a country other than the Member State of importation, and without any commercial intent on the part of the sender, to charitable or philanthropic organisations approved by the competent authorities, to be used solely for the purpose of meeting their operating needs or carrying out their stated charitable or philanthropic aims.

2. For the purposes of paragraph 1(*a*) **"basic necessities"** means those goods required to meet the immediate needs of human beings, eg food, medicine, clothing and bed-clothes.

Article 42

Exemption shall not be granted in respect of:

(*a*) alcoholic products;

(*b*) tobacco or tobacco products;

(*c*) coffee and tea;

(*d*) motor vehicles other than ambulances.

Article 43

Exemption shall be granted only to organisations accounting procedures of which enable the competent authorities to supervise their operations and which offer all the guarantees considered necessary.

Article 44

1. Exempt goods may not be put out by the organisation entitled to exemption for loan, hiring out or transfer, whether for a consideration or free of charge, for purposes other than those laid down in Article 41(1)(*a*) and (*b*), unless the competent authorities have been informed thereof in advance.

2. Should goods and equipment be lent, hired out or transferred to an organisation entitled to benefit from exemption pursuant to Articles 41 and 43, the exemption shall continue to be granted provided that the latter uses the goods and equipment for purposes which confer the right to such exemption.

In other cases, loan, hiring out or transfer shall be subject to prior payment of value added tax at the rate applying on the date of the loan, hiring out or transfer, on the basis of the type of goods and equipment and the value ascertained or accepted on that date by the competent authorities.

Article 45

1. Organisations referred to in Article 41 which cease to fulfil the conditions giving entitlement to exemption, or which are proposing to use goods and equipment exempt on admission for purposes other than those provided for by that Article, shall so inform the competent authorities.

2. Goods remaining in the possession of organisation which cease to fulfil the conditions giving entitlement to exemption shall be liable to the relevant import value added tax at the rate applying on the date on which those conditions cease to be fulfilled, on the basis of the type of goods and equipment and the value as ascertained or accepted on that date by the competent authorities.

3. Goods used by the organisation benefiting from the exemption for purposes other than those provided for in Article 41 shall be liable to the relevant import value added tax at the rate applying on the date on which they are put to another use on the basis of the type of goods and equipment and the value as ascertained on that date by the competent authorities.

CHAPTER II
Articles imported for the benefit of handicapped persons

Article 46

1. Articles specially designed for the education, employment or social advancement of blind or other physically or mentally handicapped persons shall be exempt on admission where:

(*a*) they are imported by institutions or organisations that are principally engaged in the education of or the provision of assistance to handicapped persons and are authorised by the competent authorities of the Member States to receive such articles exempt from tax; and

(*b*) they are donated to such institutions or organisations free of charge and with no commercial intent on the part of the donor.

2. Exemption shall apply to specific spare parts, components or accessories specifically for the articles in question and to the tools to be used for maintenance, checking, calibration and repair of the said articles, provided that such spare parts, components, accessories or tools are imported at the same time as the said articles or, if imported subsequently, that they can be identified as being intended for articles previously exempt on admission or which would be eligible to be so exempt at the time when such entry is requested for the specific spare parts, components or accessories and tools in question.

3. Articles exempt on admission may not be used for purposes other than the education, employment or social advancement of blind or other handicapped persons.

Article 47

1. Goods exempt on admission may be lent, hired out or transferred, whether for a consideration or free of charge, by the beneficiary institutions or organisations on a non-profitmaking basis to the persons referred to in Article 46 with whom they are concerned, without payment of valued added tax on importation.

2. No loan, hiring out or transfer may be effected under conditions other than those provided for in paragraph 1 unless the competent authorities have first been informed.

Should an article be lent, hired out or transferred to an institution or organisation itself entitled to benefit from this exemption, the exemption shall continue to be granted, provided the latter uses the article for purposes which confer the right to such exemption.

In other cases, loan, hiring out or transfer shall be subject to prior payment of value added tax, at the rate applying on the date of the loan, hiring out or transfer, on the basis of the type of goods and the value ascertained or accepted on that date by the competent authorities.

Article 48

1. Institutions or organisations referred to in Article 46 which cease to fulfil the conditions giving entitlement to exemption, or which are proposing to use articles exempt on admission for purposes other than those provided for by that Article shall so inform the competent authorities.

2. Articles remaining in the possession of institutions or organisations which cease to fulfil the conditions giving entitlement to exemption shall be liable to the relevant import value added tax at the rate applying on the date on which those conditions cease to be fulfilled, on the basis of the type of goods and the value ascertained or accepted on that date by the competent authorities.

3. Articles used by the institution or organisation benefiting from the exemption for purposes other than those provided for in Article 46 shall be liable to the relevant import value added tax at the rate applying on the date on which they are put to another use on the basis of the type of goods and the value ascertained or accepted on that date by the competent authorities.

CHAPTER III
Goods imported for the benefit of disaster victims

Article 49

1. Subject to Articles 50 to 55, goods imported by State organisations or other charitable or philanthropic organisations approved by the competent authorities shall be exempt on admission where they are intended:

(*a*) for distribution free of charge to victims of disaster affecting the territory of one or more Member States; or

(*b*) to be made available free of charge to the victims of such disasters, while remaining the property of the organisations in question.

2. Goods imported by disaster-relief agencies in order to meet their needs during the period of their activity shall also benefit upon admission from the exemption referred to in paragraph 1 under the same conditions.

Article 50

No exemption shall be granted for materials and equipment intended for rebuilding disaster areas.

Article 51

Granting of the exemption shall be subject to a decision by the Commission, acting at the request of the Member State or States concerned in accordance with an emergency procedure entailing the consultation of the other Member States. This decision shall, where necessary, lay down the scope and the conditions of the exemption.

Pending notification of the Commission's decision, Member States affected by a disaster may authorise the suspension of any import value added tax chargeable on goods imported for the purposes described in Article 49, subject to an undertaking by the importing organisation to pay such tax if exemption is not granted.

Article 52

Exemption shall be granted only to organisations the accounting procedures of which enable the competent authorities to supervise their operations and which offer all the guarantees considered necessary.

Article 53

1. The organisations benefiting from the exemption may not lend, hire out or transfer, whether for a consideration or free of charge, the goods referred to in Article 49(1) under conditions other than those laid down in that Article without prior notification thereof to the competent authorities.

2. Should goods be lent, hired out or transferred to an organisation itself entitled to benefit from exemption pursuant to Article 49, the exemption shall continue to be granted, provided the latter uses the goods for purposes which confer the right to such exemption.

In other cases, loan, hiring out or transfer shall be subject to prior payment of value added tax, at the rate applying on the date of the loan, hiring out or transfer, on the basis of the type of goods and the value ascertained or accepted on that date by competent authorities.

Article 54

1. The goods referred to in Article 49(1)(*b*), after they cease to be used by disaster victims, may not be lent, hired out or transferred, whether for a consideration or free of charge, unless the competent authorities are notified in advance.

2. Should goods be lent, hired out or transferred to an organisation itself entitled to benefit from exemption pursuant to Article 49 or, if appropriate, to an organisation entitled to benefit from exemption pursuant to Article 41(1)(*a*), the exemption shall continue to be granted, provided such organisations use them for purposes which confer the right to such exemption.

In other cases, loan, hiring out or transfer shall be subject to prior payment of value added tax, at the rate applying on the date of the loan, hiring out or transfer, on the basis of the type of goods and the value ascertained or accepted on that date by competent authorities.

Article 55

1. Organisations referred to in Article 49 which cease to fulfil the conditions giving entitlement to exemption, or which are proposing to use the goods exempt on admission for purposes other than those provided for by that Article shall so inform the competent authorities.

2. In the case of goods remaining in the possession of organisations which cease to fulfil the conditions giving entitlement to exemption, when these are transferred to an organisation itself entitled to benefit from exemption pursuant to this chapter or, if appropriate, to an organisation entitled to benefit from exemption pursuant to Article 41, the exemption shall continue to be granted, provided the organisation uses the goods in question for purposes which confer the right to such exemptions. In other cases, the goods shall be liable to the relevant import value added tax at the rate applying on the date on which those conditions cease to be fulfilled, on the basis of the type of goods and the value ascertained or accepted on that date by the competent authorities.

3. Goods used by the organisations benefiting from the exemption for purposes other than those provided for in this chapter shall be liable to the relevant import value added tax at the rate applying on the date on which they are put to another use, on the basis of the type of goods and the value ascertained or accepted on that date by the competent authorities.

TITLE VII
IMPORTATION IN THE CONTEXT OF CERTAIN ASPECTS OF INTERNATIONAL RELATIONS

CHAPTER I
Honorary decorations or awards

Article 56

On production of satisfactory evidence to the competent authorities by the person concerned, and provided the operations involved are not in any way of a commercial character exemption shall be granted in respect of:

(*a*) decorations conferred by the government of a country other than the Member State of importation on persons whose normal place of residence is in the latter State;

(*b*) cups, medals and similar articles of an essentially symbolic nature which, having been awarded in a country other than the Member State of importation to persons having their normal place of residence in the latter State as a tribute to their activities in fields such as the arts, the sciences, sport or the public service or in recognition of merit at a particular event, are imported by such persons themselves;

(*c*) cups, medals and similar articles of an essentially symbolic nature which are given free of charge by authorities or persons established in a country other than the Member State of importation, to be presented in the territory of the latter State for the same purposes as those referred to in (*b*).

[(*d*) Awards, trophies and souvenirs of a symbolic nature and of limited value intended for distribution free of charge to persons normally resident in a country other than that of import, at business conferences or similar international events; their nature, unitary value or other features, must not be such as might indicate that they are intended for commercial purposes.]¹

Amendments

¹   Art 56(*d*) inserted by Council Directive 88/331/EEC of 13 June 1988, Art 1(5).

CHAPTER II
Presents received in the context of international relations

Article 57

Without prejudice, where relevant, to the provisions applicable to the international movement of travellers, and subject to Articles 58 and 59, exemption shall be granted in respect of goods:

(*a*) imported by persons who have paid an official visit in a country other than that of their normal residence and who have received such goods on that occasion as gifts from the host authorities;

(*b*) imported by persons coming to pay an official visit in the Member State of importation and who intend to offer them on that occasion as gifts to the host authorities;

(c)   sent as gifts, in token of friendship or goodwill, by an official body, public authority or group carrying on an activity in the public interest which is located in a country other than the Member State of importation, to an official body, public authority or group carrying on an activity in the public interest which is located in the Member State of importation and approved by the competent authorities to receive such goods exempt from tax.

Article 58

No exemption shall be granted for alcoholic products, tobacco or tobacco products.

Article 59

Exemption shall be granted only:

— where the articles intended as gifts are offered on an occasional basis,

— where they do not, by their nature, value or quantity, reflect any commercial interest,

— if they are not used for commercial purposes.

CHAPTER III
Goods to be used by monarchs or heads of state

Article 60

Exemption from tax, within the limits and under the conditions laid down by the competent authorities, shall be granted in respect of:

(a)   gifts to reigning monarchs and heads of State;

(b)   goods to be used or consumed by reigning monarchs and heads of State of another State, or by persons officially representing them, during their official stay in the Member State of importation. However, exemption may be made subject, by the Member State of importation, to reciprocal treatment.

The provisions of the preceding subparagraph are also applicable to persons enjoying prerogatives at international level analogous to those enjoyed by the reigning monarchs or heads of State.

TITLE IX
IMPORTATION OF GOODS FOR THE PROMOTION OF TRADE

CHAPTER I
Samples of negligible value

Article 61

1. Without prejudice to Article 65(1)(a), samples of goods which are of negligible value and which can be used only to solicit orders for goods of the type they represent shall be exempt on admission.

2. The competent authorities may require that certain articles, to qualify for exemption on admission, be rendered permanently unusable by being torn, perforated, or clearly and indelibly marked, or by any other process, provided such operation does not destroy their character as samples.

For the purposes of paragraph 1, **"samples of goods"** means any article representing a type of goods whose manner of presentation and quantity, for goods of the same type or quality, rule out its use for any other purpose other than that of seeking orders.

CHAPTER II
Printed matter and advertising material

Article 62

[Subject to Article 63, printed advertising matter such as catalogues, price lists, directions for use or brochures shall be exempt on admission provided that they relate to:

(*a*) goods for sale or hire by a person established outside the Member State of import, or

(*b*) services offered by a person established in another Member State, or

(*c*) transport, commercial insurance or banking services offered by a person established in a third country.][1]

Amendments

[1]   Art 62 substituted by Council Directive 88/331/EEC of 13 June 1988, Art 1(6).

Article 63

[The exemption referred to in Article 62 shall be limited to printed advertisements which fulfil the following conditions:

(*a*) printed matter must clearly display the name of the undertaking which produces, sells or hires out the goods, or which offers the services to which it refers;

(*b*) each consignment must contain no more than one document or a single copy of each document if it is made up of several documents. Consignments comprising several copies of the same document may nevertheless be granted exemption provided their total gross weight does not exceed one kilogram;

(*c*) printed matter must not be the subject of grouped consignments from the same consignor to the same consignee.

However, the conditions under (*b*) and (*c*) shall not apply to printed matter relating to either goods for sale or hire or services offered by a person established in another Member State provided that the printed matter has been imported, and will be distributed, free of charge.][1]

Amendments

[1]   Art 63 substituted by Council Directive 88/331/EEC of 13 June 1988, Art 1(6).

Article 64

Articles for advertising purposes, of no intrinsic commercial value, sent free of charge by suppliers to their customers which, apart from their advertising function, are not capable of being used shall also be exempt on admission.

CHAPTER III
Goods used or consumed at a trade fair or similar event

Article 65

1. Subject to Articles 66 to 69, the following shall be exempt on admission:

- (*a*) small representative samples of goods intended for a trade fair or similar event;

- (*b*) goods imported solely in order to be demonstrated or in order to demonstrate machines and apparatus displayed at a trade fair or similar event;

- (*c*) various materials of little value, such as paints, varnishes and wallpaper, which are to be used in the building, fitting-out and decoration of temporary stands at a trade fair or similar event, which are destroyed by being used;

- (*d*) printed matter, catalogues, prospectuses, price lists, advertising posters, calendars, whether or not illustrated, unframed photographs and other articles supplied free of charge in order to advertise goods displayed at a trade fair or similar event.

2. For the purposes of paragraph 1, **"trade fair or similar event"** means:

- (*a*) exhibitions, fairs, shows and similar events connected with trade, industry, agriculture or handicrafts;

- (*b*) exhibitions and events held mainly for charitable reasons;

- (*c*) exhibitions and events held mainly for scientific, technical, handicraft, artistic, educational or cultural or sporting reasons, for religious reasons or for reasons of worship, trade union activity or tourism, or in order to promote international understanding;

- (*d*) meetings of representatives of international organisations or collective bodies;

- (*e*) official or commemorative ceremonies and gatherings;

but not exhibitions staged for private purposes in commercial stores or premises to sell goods.

Article 66

The exemption referred to in Article 65(1)(*a*) shall be limited to samples which:

- (*a*) are imported free of charge as such or are obtained at the exhibition from goods imported in bulk;

- (*b*) are exclusively distributed free of charge to the public at the exhibition for use or consumption by the persons to whom they have been offered;

(*c*)   are identifiable as advertising samples of low unitary value;

(*d*)   are not easily marketable and, where appropriate, are packaged in such a way that the quantity of the item involved is lower than the smallest quantity of the same item actually sold on the market;

(*e*)   in the case of foodstuffs and beverages not packaged as mentioned in (*d*), are consumed on the spot at the exhibition;

(*f*)   in their total value and quantity, are appropriate to the nature of the exhibition, the number of visitors and the extent of the exhibitor's participation.

Article 67

The exemption referred to in Article 65(1)(*b*) shall be limited to goods which are:

(*a*)   consumed or destroyed at the exhibition, and

(*b*)   are appropriate, in their total value and quantity, to the nature of the exhibition, the number of visitors and the extent of the exhibitor's participation.

Article 68

The exemption referred to in Article 65(1)(*d*) shall be limited to printed matter and articles for advertising purposes which:

(*a*)   are intended exclusively to be distributed free of charge to the public at the place where the exhibition is held;

(*b*)   in their total value and quantity, are appropriate to the nature of the exhibition, the number of visitors and the extent of the exhibitor's participation.

Article 69

The exemption referred to in Article 65(1)(*a*) and (*b*) shall not be granted for:

(*a*)   alcoholic products;

(*b*)   tobacco or tobacco products;

(*c*)   fuels, whether solid, liquid or gaseous.

TITLE X
GOODS IMPORTED FOR EXAMINATION, ANALYSIS OR TEST PURPOSES

Article 70

Subject to Articles 71 to 76, goods which are to undergo examination, analysis or tests to determine their composition, quality or other technical characteristics for purposes of information or industrial or commercial research shall be exempt on admission.

Article 71

Without prejudice to Article 74, the exemption referred to in Article 70 shall be granted only on condition that the goods to be examined, analysed or tested are completely used up or destroyed in the course of the examination, analysing or testing.

Article 72

No exemption shall be granted in respect of goods used in examination, analysis or tests which in themselves constitute sales promotion operations.

Article 73

Exemption shall be granted only in respect of the quantities of goods which are strictly necessary for the purposes for which they are imported. These quantities shall in each case be determined by the competent authorities, taking into account the said purpose.

Article 74

1. The exemption referred to in Article 70 shall cover goods which are not completely used up or destroyed during examination, analysis or testing, provided that the products remaining are, with the agreement and under the supervision of the competent authorities:

— completely destroyed or rendered commercially valueless on completion of examination, analysis or testing, or

— surrendered to the state without causing it any expense, where this is possible under national law, or

— in duly justified circumstances, exported outside the territory of the Member State of importation.

2. For the purposes of paragraph 1, **"products remaining"** means products resulting from the examinations, analyses or tests or goods not actually used.

Article 75

Save where Article 74(1) is applied, products remaining at the end of the examinations, analyses or tests referred to in Article 70 shall be subject to the relevant import value added tax, at the rate applying on the date of completion of the examinations, analyses or tests, on the basis of the type of goods and the value ascertained or accepted on that date by the competent authorities.

However, the interested party may, with the agreement and under the supervision of the competent authorities, convert products remaining to waste or scrap. In this case, the import duties shall be those applying to such waste or scrap at the time of conversion.

Article 76

The period within which the examinations, analyses or tests must be carried out and the administrative formalities to be completed in order to ensure the use of the goods for the purposes intended shall be determined by the competent authorities.

TITLE XI
MISCELLANEOUS EXEMPTIONS

CHAPTER I

*Consignments sent to organisations protecting copyrights or industrial
and commercial patent rights*

Article 77

Trademarks, patterns or designs and their supporting documents, as well as applications
for patents for invention or the like, to be submitted to the bodies competent to deal with
the protection of copyrights or the protection of industrial or commercial patent rights
shall be exempt on admission.

CHAPTER II
Tourist information literature

Article 78

The following shall be exempt on admission:

(*a*)   documentation (leaflets, brochures, books, magazines, guidebooks, posters,
whether or not framed, unframed photographs and photographic enlargements,
maps, whether or not illustrated, window transparencies, and illustrated
calendars) intended to be distributed free of charge and the principal purpose
of which is to encourage the public to visit foreign countries, in particular in
order to attend cultural, tourist, sporting, religious or trade or professional
meetings or events, provided such literature contains not more than 25% of
private commercial advertising and that the general nature of its promotional
aims is evident;

(*b*)   foreign hotel lists and yearbooks published by official tourist agencies, or
under their auspices, and timetables for foreign transport services, provided
that such literature is intended for distribution free of charge and contains not
more than 25% of private commercial advertising;

(*c*)   reference material supplied to accredited representatives or correspondents
appointed by official national tourist agencies and not intended for
distribution, i.e. yearbooks, lists of telephone or telex numbers, hotel lists, fairs
catalogues, specimens of craft goods of negligible value, and literature on
museums, universities, spas or other similar establishments.

CHAPTER III
Miscellaneous documents and articles

Article 79

The following shall be exempt on admission:

(*a*)   documents sent free of charge to the public services of Member States;

(*b*)   publications of foreign governments and publications of official international
bodies intended for distribution without charge;

(*c*) ballot papers for elections organised by bodies set up in countries other than the Member State of importation;

(*d*) objects to be submitted as evidence or for like purposes to the courts or other official agencies of the Member State;

(*e*) specimen signatures and printed circulars concerning signatures sent as part of customary exchange of information between public services or banking establishments;

(*f*) official printed matter sent to the central banks of the Member States;

(*g*) reports, statements, notes, prospectuses, application forms and other documents drawn up by companies with headquarters outside the Member States of importation and sent to the bearers or subscribers of securities issued by such companies;

(*h*) recorded media (punched cards, sound recordings, microfilms, etc) used for the transmission of information sent free of charge to the addressee, in so far as exemption does not give rise to abuses or to major distortions of competition;

(*i*) files, archives, printed forms and other documents to be used in international meetings, conferences or congresses, and reports on such gatherings;

(*j*) plans, technical drawings, traced designs, descriptions and other similar documents imported with a view to obtaining or fulfilling orders in a country other than the Member State of importation or to participating in a competition held in that State;

(*k*) documents to be used in examinations held in the Member State of importation by institutions set up in another country;

(*l*) printed forms to be used as official documents in the international movement of vehicles or goods, within the framework of international conventions;

(*m*) printed forms, labels, tickets and similar documents sent by transport undertakings or by undertakings of the hotel industry located in a country other than the Member State of importation to travel agencies set up in that State;

(*n*) printed forms and tickets, bills of lading, way-bills and other commercial or office documents which have been used;

(*o*) official printed forms from national or international authorities, and printed matter conforming to international standards sent for distribution by associations of countries other than the Member State of importation to corresponding associations located in that State;

(*p*) photographs, slides and stereotype mats for photographs, whether or not captioned, sent to press agencies to newspaper or magazine publishers;

(*q*) articles listed in the Annex to this Directive which are produced by the United Nations or one of its specialised agencies whatever the use for which they are intended:

(*r*) collectors' pieces and works of art of an educational, scientific or cultural character which are not intended for sale and which are imported by museums, galleries and other institutions approved by the competent authorities of the

Member States for the purpose of duty-free admission of these goods. The exemption is granted only on condition that the articles in question are imported free of charge or, if they are imported against payment, that they are not supplied by a taxable person.

[(s) importations of official publications issued under the authority of the country of export, international institutions, regional or local authorities and bodies under public law established in the country of export, and printed matter distributed on the occasion of elections to the European Parliament or on the occasion of national elections in the country in which the printed matter originates by foreign political organisation officially recognised as such in the Member States, insofar as such publications and printed matter have been subject to tax in the country of export and have not benefited from remission of tax on export.][1]

Amendments

[1]   Art 79(s) inserted by Council Directive 88/331/EEC of 13 June 1988, Art 1(7).

CHAPTER IV
Ancillary materials for the stowage and protection of goods during their transport

Article 80

The various materials such as rope, straw, cloth, paper and cardboard, wood and plastics which are used for the stowage and protection — including heat protection — of goods during their transport to the territory of a Member State, shall be exempt on admission, provided that:

(a)   they are not normally re-usable; and

(b)   the consideration paid for them forms part of the taxable amount as defined in Article 11 of Directive 77/388/EEC.

CHAPTER V
Litter, fodder, and feedingstuffs for animals during their transport

Article 81

Litter, fodder and feedingstuffs of any description put on board the means of transport used to convey animals to the territory of a Member State for the purpose of distribution to the said animals during the journey shall be exempt on admission.

CHAPTER VI
Fuel and lubricants present in land motor vehicles and special containers

Article 82

[1. Subject to Articles 84, 84 and 85, the following shall be exempt on admission:

(a)   fuel contained in the standard tanks of

— private and commercial motor vehicles and motor cycles;

— special containers;

(*b*)   fuel contained in portable tanks carried by private motor vehicles and motor cycles, up to a maximum of 10 litres per vehicle and without prejudice to national provisions on the holding and transport of fuel.

2.   For the purposes of paragraph 1:

(*a*)   **"commercial motor vehicle"** means any motorised road vehicle (including tractors with trailers) which, by its type of construction and equipment, is designed for, and capable of, transporting, whether for payment or not:

— more than nine persons including the drive,

— goods,

and any road vehicle for a special purpose other than transport as such;

(*b*)   **"private motor vehicles"** means any motor vehicle not covered by the definition set out in (*a*);

(*c*)   **"standard tanks"** means:

— the tanks permanently fixed by the manufacturer to all motor vehicles of the same type as the vehicle in question and whose permanent fitting enables fuel to be used directly, both for the purpose of propulsion and, where appropriate, for the operation, during transport, of refrigeration systems and other systems.

Gas tanks fitted to motor vehicles designed for the direct use of gas as a fuel and tanks fitted to ancillary systems with which the vehicle may be equipped shall also be considered to be standard tanks,

— tanks permanently fixed by the manufacturer to all containers of the same type as the container in question and whose permanent fitting enables fuel to be used directly for the operation, during transport, of refrigeration systems and other systems with which special containers are equipped;

(*d*)   **"special container"** means any container fitted with specially designed apparatus for refrigeration systems, oxygenation systems, thermal insulation systems, or other systems.][1]

Amendments

[1]   Art 82 substituted by Council Directive 88/331/EEC of 13 June 1988, Art 1(9).

Article 83

[Member States may limit the application of the exemption for fuel contained in the standard fuel tanks of commercial motor vehicles [and special containers][1]:

(*a*)   when the vehicle comes from a third country, to 200 litres per vehicle and per journey;

(*b*)   when the vehicle comes from another Member State:

— to 200 litres per vehicle and per journey in the case of vehicles designed for, and capable of, the transport, with or without remuneration, of goods;

— to 600 litres per vehicle and per journey in the case of vehicles designed for, and capable of, the transport, with or without remuneration, of more than nine persons, including the driver.

Acting in accordance with the procedures provided for by the Treaty on this point, the Council shall decide, on a proposal from the Commission, before 1 July 1986, on the increase of the quantity of fuel admitted duty-free and contained in the standard fuel tanks of the vehicles referred to in the first indent of (*b*) of the first subparagraph.

[(*c*) to 200 litres per special container and per journey.][2][3

Amendments

1   Inserted by Council Directive 88/331/EEC of 13 June 1988, Art 1(10).
2   Para (*c*) inserted by Council Directive 88/331/EEC of 13 June 1988, Art 1(10).
3   Art 83 substituted by Council Directive 85/346/EEC of 8 July 1985.

Article 84

Member States may limit the amount of fuel exempt on admission in the case of:

[(*a*) commercial motor vehicles engaged in international transport coming from third countries to their frontier zone, to a maximum depth of 25 kilometres as the crow flies, where such transport consists of journeys made by persons residing in that zone;][1]

(*b*) private motor vehicles belonging to persons residing in the frontier zone, to a maximum depth of 15 km as the crow flies, contiguous with a third country.

Amendments

1   Para (*a*) substituted by Council Directive 85/346/EEC of 8 July 1985.

Article 85

Fuel exempt on admission may not be used in a vehicle other than that in which it was imported nor be removed from that vehicle and stored, except during necessary repairs to that vehicle, or transferred for a consideration or free of charge by the person granted the exemption.

Non-compliance with the preceding paragraph shall give rise to application of the import value added tax relating to the products in question at the rate in force on the date of such non-compliance, on the basis of the type of goods and the value ascertained or accepted on that date by the competent authorities.

Article 86

The exemption referred to in Article 82 shall also apply to lubricants carried in motor vehicles and required for their normal operation during the journey in question.

CHAPTER VII
Goods for the construction, upkeep or ornamentation of memorials to, or cemeteries for, war victims

Article 87

Exemption from tax shall be granted in respect of goods imported by organisations authorised for that purpose by the competent authorities, for use in the construction, upkeep or ornamentation of cemeteries and tombs of, and memorials to, war victims of a country other than the Member State of importation who are buried in the latter State.

CHAPTER VIII
Coffins, funerary urns and ornamental funerary articles

Article 88

The following shall be exempt on admission:

(*a*) coffins containing bodies and urns containing the ashes of deceased persons, as well as the flowers, funeral wreaths and other ornamental objects normally accompanying them;

(*b*) flowers, wreaths and other ornamental objects brought by persons resident in a Member State other than that of importation, attending a funeral or coming to decorate graves in the territory of a Member State of importation provided these importations do not reflect, by either their nature or their quantity, any commercial intent.

TITLE XII
GENERAL AND FINAL PROVISIONS

Article 89

Where this Directive provides that the granting of an exemption shall be subject to the fulfilment of certain conditions, the person concerned shall, to the satisfaction of the competent authorities, furnish proof that these conditions have been met.

Article 90

1. The exchange value in national currency of the ECU to be taken into consideration for the purposes of this Directive shall be fixed once a year. The rates to be applied shall be those obtaining on the first working day in October and shall take effect on 1 January the following year.

2. Member States may round off the amounts in national currency arrived at by converting the amounts in ECU.

3. Member States may continue to apply the amounts of the exemptions in force at the time of the annual adjustment provided for in paragraph 1, if conversion of the amounts of the exemptions expressed ECU leads, before the rounding-off provided for in paragraph 2, to an alteration of less than 5% in the exemption expressed in national currency [or to a reduction in that exemption][1].

Amendments

1 Inserted by Council Directive 88/331/EEC of 13 June 1988, Art 1(11).

Article 91

No provision of this Directive shall prevent Member States from continuing to grant:

(*a*) the privileges and immunities granted by them under cultural, scientific or technical co-operation agreements concluded between them or with third countries;

(*b*) the special exemptions justified by the nature of frontier traffic which are granted by them under frontier agreements concluded between them or with countries outside the Community.

[(*c*) exemptions in the context of agreements entered into on the basis of reciprocity with third countries that are Contracting Parties to the Convention on International Civil Aviation (Chicago 1944) for the purposes of implementing Recommended Practices 4.42 and 4.44 in Annex 9 to the Convention (eighth edition, July 1980).][1]

Amendments

1 Para (*c*) inserted by Council Directive 88/331/EEC of 13 June 1988.

Article 92

Until the establishment of Community exemptions upon importation, Member States may retain the exemptions granted to:

(*a*) merchant-navy seamen;

(*b*) workers returning to their country after having resided for at least six months outside the importing Member State on account of their occupation.

Article 93

1. Member States shall bring into force the measures necessary to comply with this Directive with effect from 1 July 1984.

2. Member States shall inform the Commission of the measures which they adopt to give effect to this Directive, indicating, where the cases arise, those measures which they adopt by simple reference to identical provisions of Regulation (EEC) No 918/83.

Article 94

This Directive is addressed to the Member States.

Done at Brussels, 28 March 1983

ANNEX
Visual and auditory materials of an educational, scientific or cultural character

CN code	Description
3704 00	Photographic plates, film, paper, paperboard and textiles, exposed but not developed:
ex 3704 00 10	- Plates and film:
	- Cinematograph film, positives, of an educational, scientific or cultural character
ex 3705	Photographic plates and film, exposed and developed, other than cinematograph film:
	- Of an educational, scientific or cultural character
3706	Cinematograph film, exposed and developed, whether or not incorporating sound track or consisting only of sound track:
3706 10	- Of a width of 35 mm or more:
	— Other:
ex 3706 10 99	— Other positives:
	—— Newsreels (with or without sound track) depicting events of current news value at the time of importation, and imported up to a limit of two copies of each subject for copying purposes
	—— Archival film material (with or without soundtrack) intended for use in connection with newsreel films
	—— Recreational films particularly suited for children and young people
	—— Other films of educational, scientific or cultural character
3706 90	- Other:
	— Other.
	— Other positives:
ex 3706 90 51	—— Newsreels (with or without sound track) depicting events of current news value at the time of importation, and imported up to a limit of two copies of each subject for copying purposes
ex 3706 90 91	—— Archival film material (with or without soundtrack) intended for use in connection with newsreel films
ex 3706 90 99	—— Recreational films particularly suited for children and young people
	—— Other films of educational, scientific or cultural character:
4911	Other printed matter, including printed pictures and photographs:
	- Other:
49 11 99	— Other:
ex 4911 99 90	— Other:
	—— Microcards or other information storage media required in computerised information and documentation services of an educational, scientific or cultural character

	—— Wall charts designed solely for demonstration and education
ex 8524	Records, tapes and other recorded media for sound or other similarly recorded phenomena including matrices and masters for the production of records, but excluding products of Chapter 37:
	- Of an educational, scientific or cultural character
ex 9023 00	Instruments, apparatus and models, designed for demonstration purposes (for example, in education or exhibitions), unsuitable for other uses:
	- Patters, models and wall charts of an educational, scientific or cultural character, designed solely for demonstration and education
	- Mock-ups or visualisations of abstract concepts such a molecular structures or mathematical formulae
Various	Holograms for laser projection
	Multimedia kits
	Materials for programmed instructions, including materials in kit form with the corresponding printed materials

Amendments

[1] Annex replaced by Commission Directive 89/219/EEC of 7 March 1989, Art 1.

COUNCIL DIRECTIVE

of 28 March 1983

83/182/EEC

(OJ L105, 23.4.1983, p 53)

*On tax exemptions within the Community for certain means of transport temporarily
imported into one Member State from another*

Note

This Directive ceased to have effect on 31 December 1992 as regards its provisions on VAT; see Council
Directive 91/680/EEC of 16 December 1991, Art 2(2).

COUNCIL DIRECTIVE

of 28 March 1983

83/183/EEC

(OJ L105, 23.4.1983, p 64)

Note

This Directive ceased to have effect on 31 December 1992 as regards its provisions on VAT; see Council Directive 91/680/EEC of 16 December 1991, Art 2(2).

TENTH COUNCIL DIRECTIVE

of 31 July 1984

84/386/EEC

(OJ No. L208/58, 3.8.1984)

Hiring out of movable tangible property (other than means of transport)

THE COUNCIL OF THE EUROPEAN COMMUNITIES,

Having regard to the Treaty establishing the European Economic Community, and in particular Articles 99 and 100 thereof,

Having regard to the Sixth Council Directive 77/388/EEC of 17 May 1977 on the harmonisation of the laws of the Member States relating to turnover taxes Common system of value added tax: uniform basis of assessment,

Having regard to the proposal from the Commission,

Having regard to the opinion of the European Parliament,

Having regard to the opinion of the Economic and Social Committee,

Whereas, pursuant to Article 4(2) of the aforementioned Directive, the hiring out of movable tangible property may constitute an economic activity subject to value added tax;

Whereas application of Article 9(1) of the aforementioned Directive to the hiring out of movable tangible property may lead to substantial distortions of competition where the lessor and the lessee are established in different Member States and the rates of taxation in those States differ;

Whereas it is therefore necessary to establish that the place where a service is supplied is the place where the customer has established his business or has a fixed establishment for which the service has been supplied or, in the absence thereof, the place where he has his permanent address or usually resides;

Whereas, however, as regards the hiring out of forms of transport, Article 9(1) should, for reasons of control, be strictly applied, the place where the supplier has established his business being treated as the place of supply of such services,

HAS ADOPTED THIS DIRECTIVE

Article 1
Services affected

Notes

Para (1) deleted Sixth Directive Art 9(2)(*d*); para (2) amended Sixth Directive Art 9(2)(*e*); para (3) amended Sixth Directive Art 9(3).

Article 2
Date of implementation

1. Member States shall bring into force the measures necessary to comply with this Directive by 1 July 1985.

2. Member States shall inform the Commission of the provisions which they adopt for the purpose of applying this Directive. The Commission shall inform the other Member States thereof.

Article 3
Scope

This Directive is addressed to the Member States.

Done at Brussels, 31 July 1984.

Case law

Failure to fulfil obligations under Tenth Directive: *EC Commission v Italy* (1989) OJ C66/5, ECJ 353/87.

SEVENTEENTH COUNCIL DIRECTIVE

of 16 July 1985

85/362/EEC

(OJ L192, 24.7.1985, p 20)

*On the harmonisation of the laws of the Member States relating to turnover taxes —
exemption from value added tax on the temporary importation of goods other than
means of transport*

Note

This Directive ceased to have effect on 31 December 1992 as regards relations between Member States; see
Council Directive 91/680/EEC of 16 December 1991 Art 2(1).

THIRTEENTH COUNCIL DIRECTIVE

of 17 November 1986

86/560/EEC

(OJ L326, 21.11.1968, p 40)

*On the harmonisation of the laws of the Member States relating to turnover taxes —
arrangements for the refund of value added tax to taxable persons not established in
Community territory*

THE COUNCIL OF THE EUROPEAN COMMUNITIES,

Having regard to the Treaty establishing the European Economic Community, and in
particular Articles 99 and 100 thereof,

Having regard to Sixth Council Directive 77/388/EEC of 17 May 1977 on the
harmonisation of the laws of the Member States relating to turnover taxes — Common
system of value added tax: uniform basis of assessment (OJ L145, 13.6.1977, p 1), and
in particular Article 17(4) thereof,

Having regard to the proposal from the Commission (OJ C223, 27.8.1982, p 5 and OJ
C196, 23.7.1983, p 6),

Having regard to the opinion of the European Parliament (OJ C161, 20.6.1983, p 111),

Having regard to the opinion of the Economic and Social Committee (OJ C176,
4.7.1983, p 22),

Whereas Article 8 of Eighth Council Directive 79/1072/EEC (OJ No L331, 21.12.1979,
p 11) on the arrangements for the refund of value added tax to taxable persons not
established in the territory of the country provides that in the case of taxable persons not
established in the territory of the Community, Member States may refuse refunds or
impose special conditions;

Whereas there is a need to ensure the harmonious development of trade relations
between the Community and third countries based on the provisions of Directive 79/
1072/EEC, while taking account of the varying situations found in third countries;

Whereas certain forms of tax evasion or avoidance should be prevented,

HAS ADOPTED THIS DIRECTIVE:

Article 1

For the purposes of this Directive:

1. **"A taxable person not established in the territory of the Community"** shall mean
a taxable person as referred to in Article 4(1) of Directive 77/388/EEC who, during the
period referred to in Article 3(1) of this Directive, has had in that territory neither his
business nor a fixed establishment from which business transactions are effected, nor, if
no such business or fixed establishment exists, his permanent address or usual place of

residence, and who, during the same period, has supplied no goods or services deemed to have been supplied in the Member State referred to in Article 2, with the exception of:

(a) transport services and services ancillary thereto, exempted pursuant to Article 14(1)(i), Article 15 or Article 16(1)B, C and D of Directive 77/388/EEC;

(b) services provided in cases where tax is payable solely by the person to whom they are supplied, pursuant to Article 21(1)(b) of Directive 77/388/EEC;

2. "Territory of the Community" shall mean the territories of the Member States in which Directive 77/388/EEC is applicable.

Article 2

1. Without prejudice to the provisions of Articles 3 and 4, each Member State shall refund to any taxable person not established in the territory of the Community, subject to the conditions set out below, any value added tax charged in respect of services or movable property supplied to him in the territory of the country by other taxable persons or charged in respect of the importation of goods into the country in so far as such goods and services are used for the purposes of the transactions referred to in Article 17(3)(a) and (b) of Directive 77/388/EEC or of the provision of the services referred to in point 1(b) of Article 1 of this Directive.

2. Member States may make the refund referred to in paragraph 1 conditional upon the granting by third States of comparable advantages regarding turnover taxes.

3. Member States may require the appointment of a tax representative.

Article 3

1. The refunds referred to in Article 2(1) shall be granted upon application by the taxable person. Member States shall determine the arrangements for submitting applications, including the time limits for doing so, the period which applications should cover, the authority competent to receive them and the minimum amounts in respect of which applications may be submitted. They shall also determine the arrangements for making refunds, including the time limits for doing so. They shall impose on the applicant such obligations as are necessary to determine whether the application is justified and to prevent fraud, in particular the obligation to provide proof that he is engaged in an economic activity in accordance with Article 4(1) of Directive 77/388/EEC. The applicant must certify, in a written declaration that, during the period prescribed, he has not carried out any transaction which does not fulfil the conditions laid down in point 1 of Article 1 of this Directive.

2. Refunds may not be granted under conditions more favourable than those applied to Community taxable persons.

Article 4

1. For the purposes of this Directive, eligibility for refunds shall be determined in accordance with Article 17 of Directive 77/388/EEC, as applied in the Member State where the refund is paid.

2. Member States may, however, provide for the exclusion of certain expenditure or make refunds subject to additional conditions.

3. This Directive shall not apply to supplies of goods which are or may be exempted under point 2 of Article 15 of Directive 77/388/EEC.

Article 5

1. Member States shall bring into force the laws, regulations and administrative provisions necessary to comply with this Directive by 1 January 1988 at the latest. This Directive shall apply only to applications for refunds concerning value added tax charged on purchases of goods or services invoiced or on imports effected on or after that date.

2. Member States shall communicate to the Commission the texts of the main provisions of national law which they adopt in the field covered by this Directive and shall inform the Commission of the use they make of the option afforded by Article 2(2). The Commission shall inform the other Member States thereof.

Article 6

Within three years of the date referred to in Article 5, the Commission shall, after consulting the Member States, submit a report to the Council and to the European Parliament on the application of this Directive, particularly as regards the application of Article 2(2).

Article 7

As from the date on which this Directive is implemented and at all events by the date mentioned in Article 5, the last sentence of Article 17(4) of Directive 77/388/EEC and Article 8 of Directive 79/1072/EEC shall cease to have effect in each Member State.

Article 8

This Directive is addressed to the Member States.

EIGHTEENTH COUNCIL DIRECTIVE

of 18 July 1989

89/465/EEC

(OJ L226, 3.8.1988, p 21)

*on the harmonization of the laws of the Member States relating to turnover taxes —
Abolition of certain derogations provided for in Article 28(3) of the Sixth Directive, 77/
388/EEC*

THE COUNCIL OF THE EUROPEAN COMMUNITIES,

Having regard to the Treaty establishing the European Economic Community, and in particular Article 99 thereof,

Having regard to the proposal from the Commission (OJ C347, 29.12.1984, p 3 and OJ C183, 11.7.1987, p 9)

Having regard to the opinion of the European Parliament (OJ C125, 11.5.1987, p 27),

Having regard to the opinion of the Economic and Social Committee. (OJ C218, 29.8.1985, p 11),

Whereas Article 28(3) of the Sixth Council Directive, 77/388/EEC, of 17 May 1977 on the harmonization of the laws of the Member States relating to turnover taxes — Common system of value added tax: uniform basis of assessment, (OJ L145, 13.6.1977, p 1), as last amended by the Act of Accession of Spain and Portugal, allows Member States to apply measures derogating from the normal rules of the common system of value added tax during a transitional period; whereas that period was originally fixed at five years; whereas the Council undertook to act, on a proposal from the Commission, before the expiry of that period, on the abolition, where appropriate, of some or all of those derogations;

Whereas many of those derogations give rise, under the Communities' own resources system, to difficulties in calculating the compensation provided for in Council Regulation (EEC, Euratom) No 1553/89 of 29 May 1989 on the definitive uniform arrangements for the collection of own resources accruing from value added tax (OJ L155, 7.6.1989, p 9) whereas, in order to ensure that that system operates more efficiently, there are grounds for abolishing those derogations;

Whereas the abolition of those derogations will also contribute to greater neutrality of the value added tax system at Community level;

Whereas some of the said derogations should be abolished respectively from 1 January 1990, 1 January 1991, 1 January 1992 and 1 January 1993;

Whereas, having regard to the provisions of the Act of Accession, the Portuguese Republic may, until 1 January 1994 at the latest, postpone the abolition of the exemption of the transactions referred to in points 3 and 9 in Annex F to Directive 77/388/EEC;

Whereas it is appropriate that, before 1 January 1991, the Council should, on the basis of a Commission report, review the situation with regard to the other derogations provided for in Article 28(3) of Directive 77/388/EEC, including the one referred to in the second subparagraph of point 1 of Article 1 of this Directive, and that it should take a decision, on a proposal from the Commission, on the abolition of these derogations, bearing in mind any distortion of competition which has resulted from their application or which may arise in connection with the future completion of the internal market,

HAS ADOPTED THIS DIRECTIVE:

Article 1

Directive 77/388/EEC is hereby amended as follows:

1. With effect from 1 January 1990 the transactions referred to in points 1, 3 to 6, 8, 9, 10, 12, 13 and 14 of Annex E shall be abolished.

Those Member States which, on 1 January 1989, subjected to value added tax the transactions listed in Annex E, points 4 and 5, are authorized to apply the conditions of Article 13A(2)(*a*), final indent, also to services rendered and goods delivered, as referred to in Article 13A(1)(*m*) and (*n*), where such activities are carried out by bodies governed by public law.

2. In Annex F:

(*a*) The transactions referred to in points 3, 14 and 18 to 22 shall be abolished with effect from 1 January 1990;

(*b*) The transactions referred to in points 4, 13, 15 and 24 shall be abolished with effect from 1 January 1991;

(*c*) The transaction referred to in point 9 shall be abolished with effect from 1 January 1992;

(*d*) The transaction referred to in point 11 shall be abolished with effect from 1 January 1993.

Article 2

The Portuguese Republic may defer until 1 January 1994 at the latest the dates referred to in Article 1, point 2(*a*), for the deletion of point 3 from Annex F and in Article 1, point 2(*c*), for the deletion of point 9 from Annex F.

Article 3

By 1 January 1991 the Council, on the basis of a report from the Commission, shall review the situation with regard to the other derogations laid down in Article 28(3) of Directive 77/388/EEC, including that referred to in the second subparagraph of point 1 of Article 1 of this Directive and, acting on a Commission proposal, shall decide whether these derogations should be abolished, having regard to any distortions of competition which have resulted from their having been applied or which might arise from measures to complete the Internal Market.

Article 4

In respect of the transactions referred to in Article 1, 2 and 3, Member States may take measures concerning deduction of value added tax in order totally or partially to prevent the taxable persons concerned from deriving unwarranted advantages or sustaining unwarranted disadvantages.

Article 5

1. Member States shall take the necessary measures to comply with this Directive not later than the dates laid down in Article 1 and 2.

2. Member States shall inform the Commission of the main provisions of national law which they adopt in the field governed by this Directive.

Article 6

This Directive is addressed to the Member States.

COUNCIL DIRECTIVE

of 16 December 1991

91/680/EEC

(OJ L376, 31.12.91, p 1)

*Supplementing the common system of value added tax and amending Directive 77/388/
EEC with a view to the abolition of fiscal frontiers*

THE COUNCIL OF THE EUROPEAN COMMUNITIES,

Having regard to the Treaty establishing the European Economic Community, and in particular Article 99 thereof,

Having regard to the proposal from the Commission, (OJ C252, 22.9.1987, p 2, OJ C176, 17, 17.7.1990, p 8 and OJ C131, 22.5.1991, p 3),

Having regard to the Opinion of the European Parliament, (OJ C324, 24.12.1990, p 97),

Having regard to the Opinion of the Economic and Social Committee, (OJ C237, 12.9.1988, p 19, OJ C332, 31.12.1990, p 121),

Whereas Article 8a of the Treaty defines the internal market as an area without internal frontiers in which the free movement of goods, persons, services and capital is ensured in accordance with the provisions of the treaty;

Whereas the completion of the internal market requires the elimination of fiscal frontiers between Member States and that to that end the imposition of tax on imports and the remission of tax on exports in trade between Member States be definitively abolished;

Whereas fiscal controls at internal frontiers will be definitively abolished as from 1 January 1993 for all transactions between Member States;

Whereas the imposition of tax on imports and the remission of tax on exports must therefore apply only to transactions with territories excluded from the scope of the common system of value added tax;

Whereas, however, in view of the conventions and treaties applicable to them, transactions originating in or intended for the Principality of Monaco and the Isle of Man must be treated as transactions originating in or intended for the French Republic and the United Kingdom of Great Britain and Northern Ireland respectively;

Whereas the abolition of the principle of the imposition of tax on imports in relations between the Member States will make provisions on tax exemptions and duty-free allowances superfluous in relations between the Member States; whereas, therefore, those provisions should be repealed and the relevant Directives adapted accordingly;

Whereas the achievement of the objective referred to in Article 4 of the First Council Directive of 11 April 1967 (OJ 71, 14.4.1967, p 1301/67) as last amended by the Sixth Directive 77/388/EEC (OJ L145, 13.6.1977, p 1) requires that the taxation of trade between Member States be based on the principle of the taxation in the Member State of origin of goods and services supplied without prejudice, as regards Community trade between taxable persons, to the principle that tax revenue from the imposition of tax at the final consumption stage should accrue to the benefit of the Member State in which that final consumption takes place;

Whereas, however, the determination of the definitive system that will bring about the objectives of the common system of value added tax on goods between Member States requires conditions that cannot be completely brought about by 31 December 1992;

Whereas, therefore, provision should be made for a transitional phase, beginning on 1 January 1993 and lasting for a limited period, during which provisions intended to facilitate transition to the definitive system for the taxation of trade between Member States, which continues to be the medium-term objective, will be implemented;

Whereas during the transitional period intra-Community transactions carried out by taxable persons other than exempt taxable persons should be taxed in the Member States of destination, at those Member States' rates and under their conditions;

Whereas intra-Community acquisitions of a certain value by exempt persons or by non-taxable legal persons and certain intra-Community distance selling and supplies of new means of transport to individuals or exempt or non-taxable bodies should also be taxed, during the transitional period, in the Member States of destination, at those Member States' rates and under their conditions, insofar as such transactions would, in the absence of special provisions, be likely to cause significant distortions of competition between Member States;

Whereas the necessary pursuit of a reduction of administrative and statistical formalities for undertakings, particularly small and medium-sized undertakings, must be reconciled with the implementation of effective control measures and the need, on both economic and tax grounds, to maintain the quality of Community statistical instruments;

Whereas advantage must be taken of the transitional period of taxation of intra-Community trade to take measures necessary to deal with both the social repercussions in the sectors affected and the regional difficulties, in frontier regions in particular, that might follow the abolition of the imposition of tax on imports and of the remission of tax on exports in trade between Member States; whereas the Member States should therefore be authorised, for a period ending on 30 June 1999, to exempt supplies of goods carried out within specified limits by duty-free shops in the context of air and sea travel between Member States;

Whereas the transitional arrangements will enter into force for four years and will accordingly apply until 31 December 1996; whereas they will be replaced by a definitive system for the taxation of trade between Member States based on the principle of the taxation of goods and services supplied in the Member State of origin, so that the objective referred to in Article 4 of the First Council Directive of 11 April 1967 is achieved;

Whereas to that end the Commission will report to the Council before 31 December 1994 on the operation of the transitional arrangements and make proposals for the details of the definitive system for the taxation of trade between Member States; whereas the Council, considering that the conditions for transition to the definitive system have been fulfilled satisfactorily, will decide before 31 December 1995 on the arrangements necessary for the entry into force and the operation of the definitive system, the transitional arrangements being automatically continued until the entry into force of the definitive system and in event until the Council has decided on the definitive system;

Whereas, accordingly, Directive 77/388/EEC as last amended by Directive 89/465/EEC should be amended,

HAS ADOPTED THIS DIRECTIVE:

Article 1

Notes

Para (1) substituted Sixth Directive Art 3; para (2) substituted of Sixth Directive Art 7; para (3) amended Sixth Directive Art 8(1)(*a*); para (4) added Sixth Directive Art 8(1)(*c*); para (5) substituted Sixth Directive Art 8(2); para (6) substituted Sixth Directive Art 10(3); para (7) substituted Sixth Directive Art 11B(1) and deleted Art 11B(2); para (8) substituted of Sixth Directive Art 11B(3); para (9) amended Sixth Directive Art 11(B)(5); para (10) substituted Sixth Directive Art 11C(2); para (11) deleted Sixth Directive Art 14(1)(*b*), amended Sixth Directive Art 14(1)(*d*), (*e*), deleted Sixth Directive Art 14(1)(*f*), and amended Sixth Directive Art 14(1)(*g*); para (12) substituted Sixth Directive Art 15 heading; para (13) amended Sixth Directive Art 15(1)–(2); para (14) substituted Sixth Directive Art 15(3); paras (15)–(16) amended Sixth Directive Art 15(10); para (17) amended Sixth Directive Art 15(12); para (18) substituted Sixth Directive Art 15(13); para (19) amended Sixth Directive Art 15(14); para (20) substituted Sixth Directive Art 16(1A), substituted Sixth Directive Art 16(1B), substituted Sixth Directive Art 16(1C), substituted Sixth Directive Art 16(1D); para (21) inserted Sixth Directive Art 28(3a); para (22) inserted Sixth Directive TITLE XVIa, Arts 28*a*–28*m*; para (23) substituted Sixth Directive Art 33; para (24) inserted Sixth Directive Art 33a.

Article 2

1. The following Directives shall cease to have effect on 31 December 1992 as regards relations between Member States:

— Directive 83/181/EEC (OJ L105, 23, 1.1983, p 38), as last amended by Directive 89/219/EEC (OJ L92, 5.4.1989, p 13)

— Directive 85/362/EEC (OJ L 192, 24.7.1985).

2. The provisions on value added tax laid down in the following Directive shall cease to have effect on 31 December 1992:

— Directive 74/651/EEC (OJ L354, 30.12.1974, p 6), as last amended by Directive 88/663/EEC (OJ L382, 31.12.1988, p 40),

— Directive 83/182/EEC (OJ L105, 23.4.1983, p 59),

— Directive 83/183/EEC (OJ L105, 23.4.1983, p 64), as amended by Directive 89/604/EEC.

3. The provisions of Directive 69/169/EEC (OJ L133, 4.6.1969, p 6), as last amended by Directive 91/191/EEC (OJ L 94 16.4.1991, p 24) relating to value added tax shall cease to have effect on 31 December 1992 as regards relations between Member States.

Article 3

1. Member States shall adapt their present value added tax systems to this Directive.

They shall bring into force such laws, regulations and administrative provisions as are necessary for their arrangements thus adapted to Article 1(1) to (20) and (22) to (24) and 2 of this Directive to enter into force on 1 January 1993.

2. Member States shall inform the Commission of the provisions which they adopt to apply this Directive.

3. Member States shall communicate to the Commission the texts of the provisions of national law which they adopt in the field governed by this Directive.

4. When Member States adopt such measures they shall include a reference to this Directive or shall accompany them by such a reference on the occasion of their official publication.

The manner in which such references shall be made shall be laid down by the Member States.

Article 4

This Directive is addressed to the Member States.

Done at Brussels, 16 December 1991.

COUNCIL DIRECTIVE

of 19 October 1992

92/77/EEC

(OJ L 316, 31.10.92, p 1)

supplementing the common system of value added tax and amending Directive 77/388/ EEC (approximation of VAT rates)

THE COUNCIL OF THE EUROPEAN COMMUNITIES,

Having regard to the Treaty establishing the European Economic Community, and in particular Article 99 thereof,

Having regard to the proposal from the Commission (OJ No C 176, 17.7.1990, p 8),

Having regard to the opinion of the European Parliament (OJ No C 324, 24.12.1990, p 104),

Having regard to the opinion of the Economic and Social Committee (OJ No C 332, 31.12.1990, p 1),

Whereas completing the internal market, which is one of the fundamental objectives of the Community, requires as a first step that fiscal controls at the frontiers be abolished;

Whereas, if distortions are to be avoided, such abolition implies in the case of value added tax, not only a uniform tax base but also a number of rates and rate levels which are sufficiently close as between Member States; whereas it is therefore necessary to amend Directive 77/388/EEC (OJ No L 145, 13.6.1977, p 1. Last amended by Directive 91/680/ EEC (OJ No L 376, 31.12.1991, p 1);

Whereas, during the transitional period, certain derogations concerning number and level of rates should be possible,

HAS ADOPTED THIS DIRECTIVE:

Article 1

Notes

This article amended Directive 77/388/EEC as follows:

para 1 substituted Art 12(3);

para 2 deleted the 1st sentence of Art 12(4);

para 3 added subparagraph to Art 12(4);

para 4 substituted Art 28(2);

para 5 inserted Annex H.

Article 2

1. Member States shall bring into force the laws, regulations and administrative provisions necessary to comply with this Directive not later than 31 December 1992. They shall forthwith inform the Commission thereof.

When Member States adopt these measures, they shall contain a reference to this Directive or shall be accompanied by such reference on the occasion of their official publication. The methods of making such reference shall be laid down by the Member States.

2. Member States shall communicate to the Commission the texts of the provisions of national law which they adopt in the field governed by this Directive.

Article 3

This Directive is addressed to the Member States.

Done at Luxembourg, 19 October 1992.

COUNCIL DIRECTIVE

of 14 December 1992

92/111/EEC

(OJ L384/47, 30.12.92)

Amending Directive 77/388/EEC and introducing simplification measures with regard to value added tax

THE COUNCIL OF THE EUROPEAN COMMUNITIES,

Having regard to the Treaty establishing the European Economic Community, and in particular Article 99 thereof,

Having regard to the proposal from the Commission,

Having regard to the opinion of the European Parliament (OJ C337, 21.12.1992),

Having regard to the opinion of the Economic and Social Committee (Opinion delivered on 24 November 1992 (not yet published in the Official journal)),

Whereas Article 3 of the Council Directive 91/680/EEC of 16 December 1991 supplementing the common system of value added tax and amending Directive 77/388/ EEC with a view to the abolition of fiscal frontiers (OJ L376, 31.12.1991, p 1) sets 1 January 1993 as the date for the entry into force of these provisions in all the Member States;

Whereas in order to facilitate the application of these provisions and to introduce the simplifications needed, it is necessary to supplement the common system of value added tax, as applicable on 1 January 1993, so as to clarify how the tax shall apply to certain operations carried out with third territories and certain operations carried out inside the Community, as well to define the transitional measures between the provisions in force on 31 December 1992 and those which will enter into force as from 1 January 1993;

Whereas in order to guarantee the neutrality of the common system of turnover tax in respect of the origin of goods, the concept of a third territory and the definition of an import must be supplemented;

Whereas certain territories forming part of the Community customs territory are regarded as third territories for the purposes of applying the common system of value added tax; whereas value added tax is therefore applied to trade between the Member States and those territories according to the same principles as apply to any operation between the Community and third countries; whereas it is necessary to ensure that such trade is subject to fiscal provisions equivalent to those which would be applied to operations carried out under the same conditions with territories which are not part of the Community customs territory; whereas as a result of these provisions the Seventeenth Council Directive 85/362/EEC of 16 July 1985 on the harmonisation of the laws of the Member States relating to turnover taxes — Exemption from value added tax on the temporary importation of goods other than means of transport (OJ L192,

24.7.1985, p 20. Directive as last amended by Directive 90/237/EEC (OJ L133, 24.5.1990, p 91)), becomes null and void;

Whereas it is necessary to state exactly how the exemptions relating to certain export operations or equivalent operations will be implemented; whereas it is necessary to adapt the other Directives concerned accordingly;

Whereas it is necessary to clarify the definition of the place of taxation of certain operations carried out on board ships, aircraft or trains transporting passengers inside the Community;

Whereas the transitional arrangements for taxation for trade between the Member States must be supplemented to take account both of the Community provisions relating to excise duties and the need to clarify and simplify the detailed rules for the application of the tax of certain operations which will be carried out between the Member States as from 1 January 1993;

Whereas Council Directive 92/12/EEC of 25 February 1992 on the general arrangements of products subject to excise duty and on the holding, movement and monitoring of such products (OJ L76, 23.3.1992, p 1) lays down particular procedures and obligations in relation to declarations in the case of shipments of such products to another Member State; whereas as a result the methods of applying tax to certain supplies and intra- Community acquisitions of products liable to excise duties can be simplified to the benefit both of the persons liable to pay tax and the competent administrations;

Whereas it is necessary to define the scope of the exemptions referred to in Article 28c of Directive 77/388/EEC (OJ L145, 13.6.1977, p 1. Directive as amended by Directive 92/ 77/EEC (OJ L316, 31.10.1992, p 1); whereas it is also necessary to supplement the provisions concerning the chargeability of the tax and the methods of determining the taxable amount of certain intra-Community operations;

Whereas, for taxable operations in the domestic market linked to intra-Community trade in goods which are carried out during the period laid down in Article 28l of Directive 77/ 388/EEC by taxable persons not established in the Member State referred to in Article 28b(A)(1) of the said Directive, it is necessary to take simplification measures guaranteeing equivalent treatment in all the Member States; whereas to achieve this, the provisions concerning the taxation system and the person liable to tax in respect of such operations must be harmonised;

Whereas in order to take account of the provisions relating to the person liable to pay tax in the domestic market and to avoid certain forms of tax evasion or avoidance, it is necessary to clarify the Community provisions concerning the repayment to taxable persons not established in the country of the value added tax referred to in Article 17(3) of Directive 77/388/EEC as amended by Article 28f of the said Directive;

Whereas the abolition as from 1 January 1993 of tax on imports and tax relief on exports for trade between the Member States makes it necessary to have transitional measures in order to ensure the neutrality of the common system of value added tax and to avoid situations of double-taxation or non-taxation;

Whereas it is therefore necessary to lay down special provisions for cases where a Community procedure, started before 1 January 1993 for the purposes of a supply effected before that date by a taxable person acting as such in respect of goods dispatched or transported to another Member State, is not completed until after 31 December 1992;

Whereas such provisions should also apply to taxable operations carried out before 1 January 1993 to which particular exemptions were applied which as a result delayed the taxable event;

Whereas it is also necessary to lay down special measures for means of transport which, not having been acquired or imported subject to the general domestic tax conditions of a Member State, have benefited, by the application of national measures, from an exemption from tax because of their temporary import from another Member State;

Whereas the application of these transitional measures, both in relation trade between the Member States and to operations with third territories, presupposes supplementing the definition of the operations to be made subject to taxation as from 1 January 1993 and the clarification for such cases of the concepts of the place of taxation, the taxable event and the chargeability of the tax;

Whereas, on account of the current economic situation, the Kingdom of Spain and the Italian Republic have requested that, as a transitional measure, provisions derogating from the principle of immediate deduction laid down in the first subparagraph of Article 18(2) of Directive 77/388/EEC be applied; whereas this request should be granted for a period of two years which may not be extended;

Whereas this Directive lays down common provisions for simplifying the treatment of certain intra-Community operations; whereas, in a number of cases, it is for the Member States to determine the conditions for implementing these provisions; whereas certain Member States will not be able to complete the legislative procedure necessary to adapt their legislation on value added tax within the period laid down; whereas an additional period should therefore be allowed for the implementation of this Directive; whereas a maximum period of twelve months is sufficient for this purpose;

Whereas it is accordingly necessary to amend Directive 77/388/EEC,

Article 1

1. — 25. ....

Notes

Para (1) replaced Art 3(4);

para (2) replaced Art 7(1)(*b*);

para (3) amended Art 7(3), and added Art 7(3)(2nd subpara);

para (4) replaced Art 7(1)(*c*);

para (5) replaced Art 11(B)(1);

para (6) replaced Art 12(1)(*b*);

para (7) replaced Art 12(3)(*a*);

para (8) deleted Art 14(1)(*c*) and added para to Art 14(1)(*d*);

para (9) extended Art 15(2), amended Art 15(3), replaced Art 15(4)(2nd subpara), amended Art 15(10), replaced Art 15(1)(3rd subpara), and replaced Art 15(13);

para (10) replaced Art 28a(1)(*a*)(2nd subpara), added Art 28a(1)(*c*), inserted Art 28a(1*a*), added para to Art 28a(5)(*b*), and added para to Art 28a(*b*);

para (11) added Art 28b(1)(*a*)(2nd subpara);

para (12) replaced Art 28c(A)(*c*) and added Art 28c(A)(*d*);

para (13) replaced Art 28c(E);

para (14) replaced Art 28d(3);

para (15) replaced Art 28d(4);

para (16) amended Art 28e(1);

para (17) renumbered Art 28e(2)–(3) as Art 28e(3)–(4) and inserted a new Art 28e(2);

para (18) by amending Art 28f, added para to Art 17(4);

para (19) by amending Art 28g, substituted Art 21(1)(*a*)–(*b*);

para (20) by amending Art 28h, extended Art 22(1)(*c*), Art 22(3)(*b*), replaced Art 22(4)(*c*)(3rd indent), replaced Art 22(6)(*b*)(1st subpara), amended Art 22(6)(*b*)(3rd subpara, 1st indent), amended Art 22(6)(*b*)(4th subpara, 1st indent), added Art 22(6)(*b*)(new subpara), amended Art 22(11);

para (21) replaced Art 28i;

para (22) added Art 28n;

para (23) replaced Art 33a(1)–(2);

para (24) revoked Directive 85/362/EEC, as last amended by Directive 90/237/EEC, with effect from 31 December 1992;

para (25) revoked Directive 69/169/EEC, Directive as last amended by Directive 91/680/EEC, Art 6 with effect from 1 January 1993.

Article 2

1. As from 1 January 1993 and for a period of two years, which may not be extended, the Kingdom of Spain and the Italian Republic shall be authorised to apply provisions derogating from the principle of immediate deduction provided for in the first subparagraph of Article 18(2). These provisions may not have the effect of delaying by more than one month the time when the right to deduction, having arisen, may be exercised under Article 18(1).

However, for taxable persons who file the returns provided for in Article 22(4) for quarterly tax periods, the Kingdom of Spain and the Italian Republic shall be authorised to provide that the right to deduction which has come into being which could, under Article 18(1), be exercised in a given quarter, may not be exercised until the following quarter. This provision shall only apply where the Kingdom of Spain or the Italian Republic authorises such taxable persons to opt for the filing of monthly returns.

2. By way of derogation from the third subparagraph of Article 15(10), the Portuguese Republic, the French Republic, the Kingdom of the Netherlands and the Federal Republic of Germany shall be authorised, in regard to contracts concluded after 31 December 1992, to abolish the repayment, procedure, where it is prohibited by this Directive by 1 October 1993 at the latest.

Article 3

The Council, acting unanimously on a Commission proposal, shall adopt before 30 June, 1993, detailed rules for the taxation of chain transactions between taxable persons, so that such rules may enter into force on 1 January 1994.

Article 4

1. The Member States shall adapt their present value added tax system to the provisions of this Directive.

They shall adopt the necessary laws, regulations and administrative provisions for their adapted systems to enter into force 1 January 1993.

Member States may, however, provide that information relating to transactions referred to in the last subparagraph of Article 22(6)(*b*) for which the tax becomes payable during the first three calendar months of 1993 must appear at the latest on the summary statement signed for the second calendar quarter of 1993.

2. By way of derogation from the second subparagraph of paragraph 1, Member States shall be authorised to adopt the necessary laws, regulations and administrative provisions in order to implement by 1 January 1984 at the latest the provisions laid down in the following paragraphs of Article 1:

　　　—paragraph 11,

　　　—paragraph 13, insofar as it relates to Article 28c(E)(3);

　　　—paragraph 19, insofar as it relates to the third subparagraph of Article 21(1)(*a*),

　　　—paragraph 20, insofar as it relates to obligations in respect of the transactions referred to in the preceding indents.

Member States which, on 1 January 1993, apply measures equivalent to those mentioned above shall adopt the necessary measures to ensure that the principles laid down in Article 22(6) and in current Community provisions on administrative cooperation in the area of indirect taxation are complied with as from 1 January 1993 without fail.

3. By way of derogation from the second subparagraph of paragraph 1, the Federal Republic of Germany shall be authorised to adopt the necessary laws, regulations and administrative provisions in order to implement by 1 October 1993 at the latest the provisions laid down in Article 1(10) with regard to Article 28a(1*a*)(*a*).

4. Member States shall inform the Commission of the provisions which they adopt to apply this Directive.

5. Member States shall communicate the provisions of domestic law which they adopt in the field covered by this Directive to the Commission.

6. When Member States adopt these provisions, they shall contain a reference to this Directive or shall be accompanied by such reference on the occasion of their official publication. The methods of making such a reference shall be laid down by the Member States.

Article 5

This Directive is addressed to the Member States.

Done at Brussels, 14 December 1992.

COUNCIL DIRECTIVE

of 14 February 1994

94/4/EC

(OJ L060, 03/03/1994 p 14–15)

amending Directives 69/169/EEC and 77/388/EEC and increasing the level of allowances for travellers from third countries and the limits on tax-free purchases in intra-Community travel

THE COUNCIL OF THE EUROPEAN UNION,

Having regard to the Treaty establishing the European Community, and in particular Article 99 thereof,

Having regard to the proposal from the Commission (OJ No C 102, 14.4.1984, p 10 and OJ No C 78, 26.3.1985, p 9.),

Having regard to the opinion of the European Parliament (OJ No C 46, 18.2.1985, p 75 and opinion delivered on 20 January 1994 (not yet published in the Official Journal)),

Having regard to the opinion of the Economic and Social Committee (OJ No C 248, 17.9.1984, p 26.),

Whereas Article 1(1) of Council Directive 69/169/EEC of 28 May 1969 on the harmonization of provisions laid down by law, regulation or administrative action relating to exemption from turnover tax and excise duty on imports in international travel (OJ No L 133, 4.6.1969, p 6. Directive as last amended by Directive 92/111/EEC (OJ No L 384, 30.12.1992, p 47)) provides for allowances in respect of goods contained in the personal luggage of travellers coming from third countries on condition that such imports have no commercial character;

Whereas the total value of the goods eligible for this exemption may not exceed ECU 45 per person; whereas, in accordance with Article 1 (2) of Directive 69/169/EEC, Member States may reduce the allowance to ECU 23 for travellers under 15 years of age;

Whereas account must be taken of measures in favour of travellers recommended by specialized international organizations, in particular the measures contained in Annex F.3 to the International Convention on the Simplification and Harmonization of Customs Procedures;

Whereas these objectives could be attained by increasing the allowances;

Whereas it is necessary to provide, for a limited period, a derogation for Germany, taking into account the economic difficulties likely to be caused by the amount of the allowances, particularly as regards travellers entering the territory of that Member State by land frontiers linking Germany to countries other than Member States and the EFTA members or by means of coastal navigation coming from the said countries;

Whereas there are special links between continental Spain and the Canary Islands, Ceuta and Melilla;

Whereas it is necessary to ensure, during the period when these sales are authorized pursuant to the provisions of Article 28k of Council Directive 77/388/EEC of 17 May 1977 on the harmonization of the laws of the Member States relating to turnover taxes — Common system of value added tax: uniform basis of assessment (OJ No L 145, 13.6.1977, p 1. Directive as last amended by Directive 92//111/EEC (OJ No L 384, 30.12.1992, p 47)), that the real value of goods likely to be sold in tax-free shops to travellers on intra-Community flights or sea crossings is maintained,

HAS ADOPTED THIS DIRECTIVE:

Article 1

...

Article 2

In Article 28k of Directive 77/388/EEC, the first subparagraph of point 2(*a*) shall be replaced by the following:

"(*a*)   the total value of which per person per journey does not exceed ECU 90."

By way of derogation from Article 28m, Member States shall determine the equivalent in national currency of the above amount in accordance with Article 7(2) of Directive 69/169/EEC.'

Article 3

1. Member States shall bring into force the provisions necessary to comply with this Directive by 1 April 1994 at the latest. They shall forthwith inform the Commission thereof.

When Member States adopt these provisions, they shall contain a reference to this Directive or shall be accompanied by such reference on the occasion of their official publication. The methods of making such a reference shall be laid down by the Member States.

2. By way of derogation from paragraph 1, the Federal Republic of Germany shall be authorized to bring into force the measures necessary to comply with this Directive by 1 January 1998 at the latest for goods imported by travellers entering German territory by a land frontier linking Germany to countries other than Member States and the EFTA members or by means of coastal navigation coming from the said countries.

3. Member States shall communicate to the Commission the text of the provisions of domestic law which they adopt in the field covered by this Directive.

Article 4

This Directive shall enter into force on the day of its publication in the Official Journal of the European Communities.

Article 5

This Directive is addressed to the Member States.

COUNCIL DIRECTIVE

of 14 February 1994

94/5/EC

(OJ No L 60, 3.3.1994, p 16)

*supplementing the common system of value added tax and amending Directive 77/388/
EEC — Special arrangements applicable to second-hand goods, works of art,
collectors' items and antiques*

Revenue publication

Second Hand Directive: Tax Briefing, Issues 22, 30.

THE COUNCIL OF THE EUROPEAN UNION,

Having regard to the Treaty establishing the European Community, and in particular Article 99 thereof,

Having regard to the opinion of the European Parliament (OJ No C 323, 27.12.1989, p 120),

Having regard to the opinion of the Economic and Social Committee (OJ No C 201, 7.8.1989, p 6),

Whereas, in accordance with Article 32 of the Sixth Council Directive 77/388/EEC of 17 May 1977 on the harmonizaion of the laws of the Member States relating to turnover taxes — Common system of value added tax: uniform basis of assessment (OJ No L 145, 13.6.1977, p 1. Directive as last amended by Directive 92/11/EEC (OJ No L 384, 30.12.1992, p 47), the Council is to adopt a Community taxation system to be applied to used goods, works of art, antique and collectors' items;

Whereas the present situation, in the absence of Community legislation, continues to be marked by the application of very different systems which cause distortion of competition and deflection of trade both internally and between Members States; whereas these differences also include a lack of harmonization in the levying of the own resources of the community; whereas consequently it is necessary to bring this situation to an end as soon as possible;

Whereas the Court of Justice has, in a number of judgments, noted the need to attain a degree of harmonization which allows double taxation in intra-community trade to be avoided;

Whereas it is essential to provide, in specific areas, for transitional measures enabling legislation to be gradually adapted;

Whereas, within the internal market, the satisfactory operation of the value added tax mechanisms means that Community rules with the purpose of avoiding double taxation and distortion of competition between taxable persons must be adopted;

Whereas it is accordingly necessary to amend Directive 77/388/EEC,

Has adopted this Directive:

Article 1

Article 2

Member States may take measures concerning the right to deduct value added tax in order to avoid the taxable dealers concerned enjoying unjustified advantages or sustaining unjustified loss.

Article 3

Acting unanimously on a proposal from the Commission, the Council may authorize any Member State to introduce particular measures for the purpose of combating fraud, by providing that the tax due in application of the arrangements for taxing the profit margin provided for in Article 26a(B) cannot be less than the amount of tax which would be due if the profit margin were equal to a certain percentage of the selling price. This percentage shall be fixed taking into account the normal profit margins realized by economic operators in the sector concerned.

Article 4

1. Member States shall adapt their present value added tax system to this Directive.

They shall bring into force such laws, regulations and administrative provisions as are necessary for their system thus adapted to enter into force on 1 January 1995 at the latest.

2. Member States shall inform the Commission of the provisions which they adopt to apply this Directive.

3. Member States shall communicate to the Commission the provisions of national law which they adopt in the field covered by this Directive.

4. When Member States adopt such provisions, they shall contain a reference to this Directive or be accompanied by such reference on the occasion of their official publication. The methods of making such a reference shall be laid down by the Member States.

Article 5

This Directive is addressed to the Member States.

COUNCIL DIRECTIVE

of 22 December 1994

94/76/EC

(OJ No L 365, 31.12.94, p 53)

amending Directive 77/388/EEC by the introduction of transitional measures applicable, in the context of the enlargement of the European Union on 1 January 1995, as regards value added tax

THE COUNCIL OF THE EUROPEAN UNION

Having regard to the 1994 Accession Treaty, and in particular Articles 2 and 3 thereof, and the 1994 act of Accession, and in particular Article 169 thereof,

Having regard to the proposal from the Commission,

Whereas, subject to the special provisions set out in Chapter IX of Annex XV to the Act of Accession, the common system of value added tax is to apply to the new Member States as from the date on which the Accession Treaty enters into force;

Whereas, as a result of the abolition on that date of the imposition of tax on importation and remission of tax on exportation in trade between the Community as constituted at present and the new Member States, and between the new Member States themselves, transitional measures are necessary to safeguard the neutrality of the common system of value added tax and prevent situations of double taxation or non-taxation;

Whereas such measures must, in this respect, meet concerns akin to those that led to the measures adopted on completion of the internal market on 1 January 1993, and in particular the provisions of Article 28n of Council Directive 77/388/EEC of 17 May 1977 on the harmonization of the laws of the Member States relating to turn-over — Common system of value added tax: uniform basis of assessment (OJ No L 145, 13.6.1977, p 1. Directive as last amended by Directive 94/5/EC (OJ No 60, 3.3.1994, p 16));

Whereas, in the customs sphere, goods will be deemed to be in free circulation in the enlarged Community where it is shown that they were in free circulation in the current Community or in one of the new Member States at the time of accession; whereas conclusions should be drawn from this, particularly for Article 7(1) and (3) and Article 10(3) of Directive 77/388/EEC;

Whereas it is necessary in particular to cover situations in which goods have been placed, prior to accession, under one of the arrangements referred to in Article 16(1)(B)(a) to (d), under a temporary admission procedure with full exemption from import duties or under a similar procedure in the new Member States;

Whereas it is also necessary to lay down specific arrangements for cases where a special procedure (export or transit), initiated prior to the entry into force of the Accession Treaty in the framework of trade between the current Community and the new Member States and between those Member States for the purposes of a supply effected prior to that date by a taxable person acting as such, is not terminated until after the date of accession,

HAS ADOPTED THIS DIRECTIVE:

Article 1

Note

Article 1 inserted Directive 77/388/EEC, Title XVIc and Article 28p.

Article 2

1. Subject to the entry into force of the 1994 Accession Treaty, Member States shall bring into force the laws, regulations and administrative provisions necessary to comply with this Directive on the date of entry into force of this Directive. They shall forthwith inform the Commission thereof.

When Member States adopt those provisions, they shall contain a reference to this Directive or shall be accompanied by such reference on the occasion of their official publication. The methods of making such a reference shall be laid down by the Member States.

2. Member States shall communicate to the Commission the provisions of domestic law which they adopt in the field covered by this Directive.

Article 3

This Directive shall enter into force on the same date as the 1994 Accession Treaty.

Article 4

This Directive is addressed to the Member States.

Done at Brussels, 22 December 1994.

COUNCIL DIRECTIVE

of 10 April 1995

95/7/EC

(OJ L 102, 5.5.95, p 18)

amending Directive 77/388/EEC and introducing new simplification measures with regard to value added tax (scope of certain exemptions and practical arrangements for implementing them

Revenue publication

Second Simplification Directive: Tax Briefing, Issue 22.

THE COUNCIL OF THE EUROPEAN UNION,

Having regard to the Treaty establishing the European Community, and in particular Article 99 thereof,

Having regard to the proposal from the Commission,

Having regard to the opinion of the European Parliament,

Having regard to the opinion of the Economic and Social Committee,

Whereas the operation of the internal market can be improved by introducing common rules clarifying the scope of, and arrangements for, applying some of the exemptions provided for in Articles 14(1), 15, point 2, and 16(1) of the Sixth Council Directive 77/388/EEC of 17 May 1977 on the harmonization of the laws of the Member States relating to turnover taxes (common system of value added tax: uniform basis of assessment (OJ No L 145, 13.6.1977, p 1. Directive as last amended by Directive 94/76/EC (OJ No L 365, 31.12.1994, p 53); whereas the introduction of such common rules is provided for by the aforesaid Directive, and in particular Articles 14(2) and 16(3) thereof;

Whereas Article 3 of Council Directive 92/111/EEC of 14 December 1992 amending Directive 77/388/EEC and introducing simplification measures with regard to value added tax (OJ No 384, 30.12.1992, p 47) provides for the adoption of special rules for the taxation of chain transactions between taxable persons; whereas such rules must ensure not only compliance with the principle of neutrality of the common system of value added tax as regard the origin of goods and services but also compliance with the choices made as the principles governing value added tax and its monitoring arrangements during the transitional period;

Whereas it is appropriate to include in the taxable amount on importation all ancillary costs arising from the transport of goods to anyplace of destination in the Community since that place is known at the time the importation is carried out; whereas, as a result, the supplies of services in question enjoy the exemptions provided for in Article 14(1)(i) of Directive 77/388/EEC;

Whereas Article 15(2) of that Directive provides that the Commission shall submit to the Council proposals to establish Community tax rules specifying the scope of, and practical arrangements for implementing, the export exemptions applicable to supplies of goods carried in the personal luggage of travellers;

Whereas it is appropriate that the period serving as a basis for calculating the adjustments provided for by Article 20(2) of the said Directive should be extended up to 20 years by Member States for immovable property acquired as capital goods, bearing in mind the duration of their economic life;

Whereas Member States should be enabled to maintain the rate applicable to goods after making up work which they carried out under a contract to make up work on 1 January 1993;

Whereas the rules governing territorial application and the tax arrangements applicable in the field of intra-community goods-transport services function in a simple and satisfactory manner for both traders and the authorities in the Member States;

Whereas, by treating a transport operation with a Member State as an intra-Community goods-transport operation where it is directly linked to a transport operation between Member States, it is possible to simplify not only the principles and arrangements for taxing those domestic transport services but also the rules applicable to ancillary services and to services supplied by intermediaries involved in the supply of these various services;

Whereas the qualification of certain works on movable property as work carried out under a contract to make up work is a source of difficulty and should be eliminated;

Whereas, with a view to facilitating intra-Community trade in the field of work on movable tangible property, the tax arrangements applicable for these transactions should be modified when they are carried out for a person who is identified for value added tax purposes on a Member State other than that of their physical execution;

Whereas Article 16(1)(B) to (E) of the said Directive, taken together in particular with Article 22(9) concerning release from obligations, makes it possible to overcome the difficulties encountered by traders participating in transaction chains involving goods placed and kept under warehousing arrangements;

Whereas it is necessary in this connection to ensure that the tax treatment applied to supplies of goods and the provision of services relating to certain of the goods which may be placed under customs warehousing arrangements can also be applied to the same transactions involving goods placed under warehousing arrangements other than customs warehousing;

Whereas these transactions concern principally raw materials and other goods negotiated on international forward markets; whereas a list of the goods covered by these provisions should be drawn up;

Whereas, subject to consultation of the Committee on Value Added Tax, the Member States are responsible for defining those warehousing arrangements other than customs warehousing; whereas it is necessary nevertheless to exclude in principle from such arrangements goods that are intended to be supplied at the retail stage;

Whereas it is necessary to clarify some of the rules for applying tax when goods cease to be covered by the arrangements provided for in Article 16(1)(B) to (E) of the said Directive, particularly as regard the person liable for payment of the tax due;

Whereas it is necessary to clarify the scope of those provisions of Article 17(2)(*a*) of the said Directive that are applicable during the transitional period referred to in Article 281;

Whereas it is accordingly necessary to amend Directive 77/388/EEC,

HAS ADOPTED THIS DIRECTIVE:

Article 1

Notes

From 25 May 1995:
para (1) substituted Council Directive 77/388/EEC, Art 5(5);
para (2) substituted Council Directive 77/388/EEC, Art 11(B)(3)(*b*)(3rd subpara);
para (3) substituted Council Directive 77/388/EEC, Art 15(2)(2nd and 3rd subparas);
para (4) substituted Council Directive 77/388/EEC, Art 20(2)(last subpara);
para (5) inserted Council Directive 77/388/EEC, Art 28(2)(*h*);
para (6) substituted Council Directive 77/388/EEC, Art 28a(5)(introductory para), deleted Art 28a(5)(*a*), deleted Art 28a(5)(*b*)(2nd subpara 3rd indent);
para (7) substituted a full stop for a comma in Council Directive 77/388/EEC, Art 28h(C)(1)(1st indent) and inserted a subpara, inserted Art 28h(F);
para (8) substituted "as defined in Article 5" for "as defined in Articles 5 and 28a(5)(*a*)";
para (9) substituted Council Directive 77/388/EEC, Art 16(1) and added para (1*a*) by substituting Council Directive 77/388/EEC, Art 28c(E)(1);
para (10) substituted Council Directive 77/388/EEC, Art 17(2)(*a*) by amending Council Directive 77/388/EEC, Art 28f(1);
para 11 substituted Council Directive 77/388/EEC, Art 21(1)(*b*) by amending Council Directive 77/388/EEC, Art 28g;
para 12 substituted Council Directive 77/388/EEC, Art 22(2)(*b*), Art 22(3)(*b*)(2nd subpara)(1st indent), Art 22(6)(*b*)(1st subpara), Art 22(6)(*b*)(3rd subpara) and deleted Art 22(6)(*b*)(5th subpara);
para 13 inserted Council Directive 77/388/EEC Annex J.

Article 2

1. Member States shall bring into force the laws, regulations and administrative provisions necessary to comply with this Directive on 1 January 1996. They shall forthwith inform the Commission thereof.

When Member States adopt these measures, they shall contain a reference to this Directive or shall be accompanied by such reference on the occasion of their official publication. The methods of making such reference shall be laid down by Member States.

2. By way of derogation from the first subparagraph of paragraph 1, Member States may take measures by way of law, regulation or administrative action in order to bring the provisions in Article 1(3), (4) and (9) into force not later than 1 January 1996.

However, the Federal Republic of Germany and the Grand Duchy of Luxembourg are authorized to take measures by way of law, regulation or administrative action in order to apply the provisions in Article 1(9) not later than 1 January 1997.

3. Member States shall communicate to the Commission the text of the provisions of national law which they adopt in the field governed by this Directive.

Article 3

This Directive shall enter into force on the 20th day following its publication in the Official Journal of the European Communities.

Article 4

This Directive is addressed to the Member States.

Done at Luxembourg, 10 April 1995.

COUNCIL DIRECTIVE

of 25 June 1996

96/42/EC

(OJ L170, 9.7.1996, p 34)

amending Directive 77/388/EEC on the common system of value added tax

THE COUNCIL OF THE EUROPEAN UNION,

Having regard to the Treaty establishing the European Community, and in particular Article 99 thereof,

Having regard to the proposal from the Commission,

Having regard to the opinion of the European Parliament (OJ No C17, 22.1.1996, p 26),

Having regard to the opinion of the Economic and Social Committee (OJ No C236, 11.9.1995, p 10),

Whereas Article 12(3)(*d*) of Directive 77/388/EEC (OJ L145, 13.6.1977, p 1. Directive as last amended by Directive 95/7/EC (OJ No L102, 5.5.1995, p 18)) lays down that the rules concerning the taxation of agricultural outputs other than those falling within category 1 of Annex H are to be decided unanimously by the Council before 31 December 1994 on a proposal from the Commission; whereas, until that date, those Member States which had already been applying a reduced rate might continue to do so while those applying a standard rate could not apply a reduced rate; whereas that allowed a two-year postponement in the application of the standard rate;

Whereas experience has shown that the structural imbalance in the VAT rates applicable by Member States to agricultural outputs of the floricultural and horticultural sectors has led to reported cases of fraudulent activities; whereas that structural imbalance is a direct result of the application of Article 12(3)(*d*) and should be redressed accordingly;

Whereas the most appropriate solution would be to extend to all Member States, on a transitional basis, the option of applying a reduced rate to supplies of agricultural outputs of the floricultural and horticultural sectors and of wood used as firewood,

HAS ADOPTED THIS DIRECTIVE:

Article 1

Note

This Article amended Directive 77/388/EEC as follows:
Para 1 deleted Art 12(3)(*d*);
para 2 inserted Art 28(2)(*i*).

Article 2

Member States shall communicate to the Commission the text of the provisions of domestic law which they adopt in the field covered by this Directive.

Article 3

This Directive shall apply from 1 January 1995.

Article 4

This Directive is addressed to the Member States.

Done at Luxembourg, 25 June 1996.

COUNCIL DIRECTIVE

of 12 October 1998

98/80/EC

(OJ L 281, 17/10/1998 p 31–34)

supplementing the common system of value added tax and amending Directive 77/388/ EEC — Special scheme for investment gold

THE COUNCIL OF THE EUROPEAN UNION,

Having regard to the Treaty establishing the European Community and in particular Article 99 thereof,

Having regard to the proposal from the Commission (OJ C 302, 19.11.1992, p 9),

Having regard to the opinion of the European Parliament (OJ C 91, 28.3.1994, p 91),

Having regard to the opinion of the Economic and Social Committee (OJ C 161, 14.6.1993, p 25),

Whereas, under the sixth Council Directive 77/388/EEC of 17 May 1977 on the harmonisation of the laws of the Member States relating to turnover taxes — common system of value added tax: uniform basis of assessment (OJ L 145, 13.5.1977, p 1. Directive as last amended by Directive 96/95/EC (OJ L 338, 28.12.1996, p 89)) transactions concerning gold are in principle taxable although, on the basis of the transitional derogation provided for in Article 28(3) in conjunction with point 26 of Annex F to the said Directive, Member States may continue to exempt transactions concerning gold other than gold for industrial use; whereas the application by some Member States of that transitional derogation is the cause of a certain distortion of competition;

Whereas gold does not only serve as an input for production but is also acquired for investment purposes; whereas the application of the normal tax rules constitutes a major obstacle to its use for financial investment purposes and therefore justifies the application of a specific tax scheme for investment gold; whereas such a scheme should also enhance the international competitiveness of the Community gold market;

Whereas supplies of gold for investments purposes are similar in nature to other financial investments often exempted from tax under the current rules of the sixth Directive, and therefore exemption from tax appears to be the most appropriate tax treatment for supplies of investment gold;

Whereas the definition of investment gold should only comprise forms and weights of gold of very high purity as traded in the bullion markets and gold coins the value of which primarily reflects its gold price; whereas, in the case of gold coins, for reasons of transparency, a yearly list of qualifying coins should be drawn up providing security for the operators trading in such coins; whereas the legal security of traders demands that coins included in this list be deemed to fulfil the criteria for exemption of this Directive for the whole year for which the list is valid; whereas such list will be without prejudice to the exemption, on a case-by-case basis, of coins, including newly minted coins which are not included in the list but which meet the criteria laid down in this Directive;

Whereas since a tax exemption does, in principle, not allow for the deduction of input tax while tax on the value of the gold may be charged on previous operations, the deduction of such input tax should be allowed in order to guarantee the advantages of the special scheme and to avoid distortions of competition with regard to imported investment gold;

Whereas the possibility of using gold for both industrial and investment purposes requires the possibility for operators to opt for normal taxation where their activity consists either in the producing of investment gold or transformation of any gold into investment gold, or in the wholesale of such gold when they supply in their normal trade gold for industrial purposes;

Whereas the dual use of gold may offer new opportunities for tax fraud and tax evasion that will require effective control measures to be taken by Member States; whereas a common standard of minimum obligations in accounting and documentation to be held by the operators is therefore desirable although, where this information does already exist pursuant to other Community legislation, a Member State may consider these requirements to be met;

Whereas experience has shown that, with regard to most supplies of gold of more than a certain purity the application of a reverse charge mechanism can help to prevent tax fraud while at the same time alleviating the financing charge for the operation; whereas it is justified to allow Member States to use such mechanism; whereas for importation of gold Article 23 of the Sixth Directive allows, in a similar way, that tax is not paid at the moment of importation provided it is mentioned in the declaration pursuant to Article 22(4) of that Directive;

Whereas transactions carried out on a bullion market regulated by a Member State require further simplifications in their tax treatment because of the huge number and the speed of such operations; whereas Member States are allowed to disapply the special scheme, to suspend tax collection and to dispense with recording requirements;

Whereas since the new tax scheme will replace existing provisions under Article 12(3)(e) and point 26 of Annex F of the Sixth Directive, these provisions should be deleted,

HAS ADOPTED THIS DIRECTIVE:

Article 1

Notes

Art 1 inserted Directive 77/388/EEC, Art 26*b* with effect from 17 October 1998.

Article 2

Notes

Art 2 deleted Directive 77/388/EEC, Art 12(3)(*e*) and Annex F point 26 with effect from 17 October 1998.

Article 3

1. Member States shall bring into force the laws, regulations and administrative provisions necessary to comply with this Directive on 1 January 2000. They shall forthwith inform the Commission thereof.

When Member States adopt these measures, they shall contain a reference to this Directive or shall be accompanied by such reference on the occasion of their official publication. The methods of making such reference shall be laid down by the Member States.

2. Member States shall communicate to the Commission the text of the provisions of domestic law which they adopt in the field governed by this Directive.

Article 4

This Directive shall enter into force on the day of its publication in the Official Journal of the European Communities.

Article 5

This Directive is addressed to the Member States.

Done at Luxembourg, 12 October 1998.

COUNCIL DIRECTIVE

of 25 May 1999

99/49/EC

(OJ L139, 02/06/1999 p 27–28)

amending, with regard to the level of the standard rate, Directive 77/388/EEC on the common system of value added tax

THE COUNCIL OF THE EUROPEAN UNION,

Having regard to the Treaty establishing the European Community, and in particular Article 93 thereof,

Having regard to the proposal from the Commission (OJ C 409, 30.12.1998, p 13),

Having regard to the opinion of the European Parliament (Opinion of 23 March 1999 (not yet published in the Official Journal)),

Having regard to the opinion of the Economic and Social Committee (OJ C 101, 12.4.1999, p 73),

(1) Whereas Article 12(3)(*a*) of sixth Council Directive 77/388/EEC of 17 May 1977 on the harmonisation of the laws of the Member States relating to turnover taxes — Common system of value added tax: uniform basis of assessment (OJ L 145, 13.6.1977, p 1. Directive as last amended by Directive 98/80/EC (OJ L 281, 17.10.1998, p 31)), lays down that the Council shall decide on the level of the standard rate to be applied after 31 December 1998; whereas the standard rate of value added tax is fixed by each Member State as a percentage of the taxable amount and is the same for the supply of goods and for the supply of services; whereas from 1 January 1993 until 31 December 1998, this percentage may not be less than 15%;

(2) Whereas experience has shown that the standard rate of value added tax currently in force in the various Member States, combined with the mechanism of the transitional system, have ensured that this transitional system has functioned satisfactorily; whereas it seems therefore appropriate, with regard to the standard rate, to maintain the current level of the minimum rate for a further period of time;

(3) Whereas, however, the Commission report on rates highlighted the fact that distortions of competition exist and are likely to be accentuated by the introduction of the single currency; whereas the period of application of the standard rate should be limited to two years in order to enable the Council at a later stage to decide on the levels of both the standard rate and reduced rate or rates,

HAS ADOPTED THIS DIRECTIVE:

Article 1

Notes

This Article substituted Directive 77/388/EEC, Art 12(3)(*a*) with effect from 1 January 1999.

Article 2

1. Member States shall bring into force the laws, regulations and administrative provisions necessary to comply with this Directive by 1 January 1999 at the latest. They shall forthwith inform the Commission thereof.

When Member States adopt these measures, they shall contain a reference to this Directive or shall be accompanied by such reference at the time of their official publication. The methods of making such a reference shall be laid down by the Member States.

2. Member States shall communicate to the Commission the text of the provisions of domestic law which they adopt in the field covered by this Directive.

Article 3

This Directive shall enter into force on the day of its publication in the Official Journal of the European Communities.

It shall apply from 1 January 1999.

Article 4

This Directive is addressed to the Member States.

COUNCIL DIRECTIVE

of 17 June 1999

99/59/EC

(OJ L162, 26/06/1999 p 63–64)

amending Directive 77/388/EEC as regards the value added tax arrangements applicable to telecommunications services

THE COUNCIL OF THE EUROPEAN UNION,

Having regard to the Treaty establishing the European Community, and in particular Article 93 thereof,

Having regard to the proposal from the Commission (OJ C 78, 12.3.1997, p 22),

Having regard to the Opinion of the European Parliament (Opinion delivered on 6 May 1999 (not yet published in the Official Journal)),

Having regard to the Opinion of the Economic and Social Committee (OJ C 287, 22.9.1997, p 28),

Whereas:

(1) Article 14 of the Treaty defines the internal market as comprising an area without internal frontiers in which the free movement of goods, persons, services and capital is ensured in accordance with the provisions of the Treaty;

(2) the rules currently applicable to VAT on telecommunications services under Article 9 of the Sixth Council Directive (77/388/EEC) of 17 May 1977 on the harmonisation of the laws of the Member States relating to turnover taxes — Common system of value added tax: uniform basis of assessment (OJ L 145, 13.6.1977, p 1. Directive as last amended by Directive 1999/49/EC (OJ L 139, 2.6.1999, p 27)) are inadequate for taxing all such services consumed within the Community and for preventing distortions of competition in this area;

(3) in the interests of the proper functioning of the internal market, such distortions should be eliminated and new harmonised rules introduced for this type of activity;

(4) action should be taken to ensure, in particular, that telecommunications services used by customers established in the Community are taxed in the Community;

(5) to this end, telecommunications services supplied to taxable persons established in the Community or to recipients established in third countries should, in principle, be taxed at the place of the recipient of the services;

(6) in order to ensure uniform taxation of telecommunications services supplied by taxable persons established in third countries to non-taxable persons established in the Community which are effectively used or enjoyed in the Community, Member States should make use of the provisions of Article 9(3)(b) of Directive 77/388/EEC on changing the place of supply; whereas, however, Article 9(3) of that Directive may

remain applicable where corresponding telecommunications services are supplied to other recipients in the Community;

(7) for the purpose of establishing a special rule for determining the place of supply of telecommunications services, such services need to be defined; such definition should draw on definitions already adopted at international level, which include international telephone call routing and termination services and access to global information networks;

(8) taxation at the place of the recipient of the services also means that taxable persons will not have to have recourse to the procedures under Directives 79/1072/EEC (OJ L 331, 27.12.1979, p 11. Directive as last amended by the 1994 Act of Accession) and 86/560/EEC (OJ L 326, 21.11.1986, p 40); the new rules for determining the place of supply should not mean that foreign taxable persons have to be identified for tax purposes in another State; this will be achieved by making it compulsory for the recipient of the services to be liable for the tax, provided that recipient is a taxable person;

(9) Directive 77/388/EEC should be amended accordingly,

HAS ADOPTED THIS DIRECTIVE:

Article 1

Notes

Para 1 replaced the full stop at the end of Directive 77/388/EEC, Art 9(2)(*e*) and inserted a new indent with effect from 1 January 2000.
Para 2 inserted Directive 77/388/EEC, Art 9(4) with effect from 1 January 2000.
Para 3 substituted Directive 77/388/EEC, Art 21(1)(*b*) with effect from 1 January 2000.

Article 2

1. Member States shall adopt the laws, regulations and administrative provisions necessary to comply with this Directive by 1 January 2000. They shall inform the Commission thereof.

When Member States adopt these measures, they shall contain a reference to this Directive or shall be accompanied by such reference at the time of their official publication. The methods of making such reference shall be laid down by the Member States.

2. Member States shall communicate to the Commission the text of the provisions of domestic law which they adopt in the field covered by this Directive.

Article 3

This Directive shall enter into force on the day of its publication in the Official Journal of the European Communities.

Article 4

This Directive is addressed to the Member States.

COUNCIL DIRECTIVE

of 22 October 1999

99/85/EC

(OJ L277, 28/10/1999 p 34–36)

amending Directive 77/388/EEC as regards the possibility of applying on an experiment basis a reduced VAT rate on labour-intensive services

THE COUNCIL OF THE EUROPEAN UNION,

Having regard to the Treaty establishing the European Community, and in particular Article 93 thereof,

Having regard to the proposal from the Commission (OJ C 102, 13.4.1999, p 10),

Having regard to the opinion of the European Parliament (OJ C 279, 1.10.1999, p 105),

Having regard to the opinion of the Economic and Social Committee (OJ C 209, 22.7.1999, p 20),

Whereas:

(1) Article 12(3)(*a*) of Council Directive 77/388/EEC of 17 May 1977 on the harmonisation of the laws of the Member States relating to turnover taxes — common system of value added tax: uniform basis of assessment (OJ L 145, 13.6.1977, p 1. Directive as last amended by Directive 1999/59/EC (OJ L 162, 26.6.1999, p 63)) provides that the Member States may apply either one or two reduced rates only to supplies of goods and services of the categories specified in Annex H to Directive 77/388/EEC;

(2) however, the problem of unemployment is so serious that those Member States wishing to do so should be allowed to experiment with the operation and impact, in terms of job creation, of a reduction in the VAT rate on labour-intensive services which are not currently listed in Annex H;

(3) this reduced VAT rate is likely to reduce the incentive for the businesses concerned to join or remain in the black economy;

(4) however, the introduction of a targeted reduction in the VAT rate could have a negative impact on the smooth functioning of the internal market and on tax neutrality; provision should therefore be made for an authorisation procedure to be introduced for a full and clearly defined three-year period and for the scope of this measure to be made subject to strict conditions so that it remains verifiable and limited;

(5) in view of the experimental nature of the measure, a detailed assessment of its impact in terms of job creation and efficiency should be carried out by the Member States which implement it and by the Commission;

(6) the measure should be strictly limited in time and should end by 31 December 2002 at the latest;

(7) implementation of this Directive does not involve any amendment of the laws of the Member States,

HAS ADOPTED THIS DIRECTIVE:

Article 1

Notes

Para 1 inserted Directive 77/388/EEC, Art 28(6) with effect from 28 October 1999 (date of publishing in the Official Journal).
Para 2 inserted Directive 77/388/EEC Annex K with effect from 28 October 1999 (date of publishing in the Official Journal).

Article 2

This Directive shall enter into force on the day of its publication in the Official Journal of the European Communities.

Article 3

Notes

This Article inserted Directive 77/388/EEC Annex with effect from 28 October 1999 (date of publishing in the Official Journal).

COUNCIL DIRECTIVE

of 30 March 2000

00/17/EC

OJ L 084, 5/4/2000 p 24–25

amending Directive 77/388/EEC on the common system of value added tax —
transitional provisions granted to the Republic of Austria
and the Portuguese Republic

THE COUNCIL OF THE EUROPEAN UNION,

Having regard to the Treaty establishing the European Community, and in particular Article 93 thereof,

Having regard to the proposal from the Community,

Having regard to the opinion of the European Parliament (Opinion delivered on 15 March 2000 (not yet published in the Official Journal)),

Having regard to the opinion of the Economic and Social Committee (OJ C 75, 15.3.2000, p 21),

Whereas:

(1) Point 2(*e*) of Part IX "Taxation" of Annex XV to the 1994 Act of Accession authorised the Republic of Austria to derogate from Article 28(2) of sixth Council Directive 77/388/EEC of 17 May 1977 on the harmonisation of the laws of the Member States relating to turnover taxes — common system of value added tax: uniform basis of assessment(3), (hereinafter referred to as the "sixth VAT Directive") and to apply a reduced rate to the letting of immovable property for residential use until 31 December 1998, provided that the rate was not lower than 10%.

(2) Under Article 13(B)(*b*) of the sixth VAT Directive, the letting of immovable property for residential use in Austria has been exempt from VAT since 1 January 1999 without the right to deduct input tax. However, under Article 13(C)(*a*) of that Directive, Austria may allow taxpayers the right to opt for taxation. In that case, the normal VAT rate and the normal rules for the right to deduction apply.

(3) The Republic of Austria considers that the measure is still essential, mainly because the transitional VAT regime is still in force and the situation has not really changed since the negotiation of the 1994 Act of Accession.

(4) The Republic of Austria also considers that dispensing with the reduced rate of 10% would inevitably lead to an increase in the price of immovable property rental for the final consumer.

(5) The Portuguese Republic applied a reduced rate of 8% to restaurant services as at 1 January 1991. Under Article 28(2)(*d*) of the sixth VAT Directive, Portugal was permitted to continue applying that rate. However, after a comprehensive amendment of

the rates and for political and budgetary reasons, restaurant services were made subject to the normal rate from 1992.

(6) The Portuguese Republic wishes to reintroduce a reduced rate on these services on the basis that maintaining the normal rate had adverse consequences, in particular job losses and an increase in undeclared employment, and that application of the normal rate increased the price of restaurant services for the final consumer.

(7) As the derogations in question concern supplies of services within a single Member State, the risk of distortion of competition can be considered non-existent.

(8) In these circumstances, return to the previous situation may be considered for both the Republic of Austria and the Portuguese Republic, provided that application of the derogations is limited to the transitional period referred to in Article 281 of the sixth VAT Directive. However, the Republic of Austria must take the necessary steps to ensure that the reduced rate has no adverse effects on the European Communities' own resources accruing from VAT, the basis of assessment for which must be reconstituted in accordance with Regulation (EEC, Euratom) No 1553/89(4),

HAS ADOPTED THIS DIRECTIVE:

Article 1

Notes

Article 1 inserted Directive 77/388/EEC (Sixth VAT Directive) of 17 May 1977, Art 28(2)(*j*)–(*k*) with effect from 5 April 2000 and covers the period 1 January 1999 until the end of the transitional period referred to in Sixth VAT Directive Art 281.

Article 2

1. The Member States referred to in Article 1 shall bring into force the laws, regulations and administrative provisions necessary to comply with this Directive. They shall forthwith inform the Commission thereof.

When the Member States adopt these measures, they shall contain a reference to this Directive or shall be accompanied by such a reference on the occasion of their official publication. The methods for making such a reference shall be laid down by the Member States.

2. The Member States referred to in Article 1 shall communicate to the Commission the text of the provisions of national law which they adopt in the field governed by this Directive.

Article 3

This Directive shall enter into force on the day of its publication in the Official Journal of the European Communities.

It shall apply as from 1 January 1999 until the end of the transitional period referred to in Article 281 of the Sixth VAT Directive.

Article 4

This Directive is addressed to the Member States.

Done at Brussels, 30 March 2000.

COUNCIL DIRECTIVE

of 17 October 2000

00/65/EC

OJ L 269, 21/10/2000 p 44–46

amending Directive 77/388/EEC as regards the determination of the person liable for payment of value added tax

THE COUNCIL OF THE EUROPEAN UNION,

Having regard to the Treaty establishing the European Community, and in particular Article 93 thereof,

Having regard to the proposal from the Commission (OJ C 409, 30.12.1998, p 10),

Having regard to the opinion of the European Parliament (OJ C 219, 30.7.1999, p 91),

Having regard to the opinion of the Economic and Social Committee (OJ C 116, 28.4.1999, p 14),

Whereas:

(1) The present rules laid down by Article 21 of sixth Council Directive 77/388/EEC of 17 May 1977 on the harmonisation of the laws of the Member States relating to turnover taxes — Common system of value added tax: uniform basis of assessment (OJ L 145, 13.6.1977, p 1. Directive as last amended by Directive 2000/17/EC (OJ L 84, 5.4.2000, p 24)), as regards the determination of the person liable for payment of the tax, create serious problems for business and, in particular, for the smallest businesses.

(2) Council Directive 76/308/EEC of 15 March 1976 on mutual assistance for the recovery of claims resulting from operations forming part of the system of financing the European Agricultural Guidance and Guarantee Fund and of the agricultural levies and customs duties (OJ L 73, 19.3.1976, p 18. Directive as last amended by the 1994 Act of Accession), Council Directive 77/799/EEC of 19 December 1977 concerning mutual assistance by the competent authorities of the Member States in the field of direct taxation (OJ L 336, 27.12.1977, p 15. Directive as last amended by the 1994 Act of Accession) and Council Regulation (EEC) No 218/92 of 27 January 1992 on administrative cooperation in the field of indirect taxation (VAT)(OJ L 24, 1.2.1992, p 1) organise mutual assistance between the Member States as regards the correct establishment of VAT and its recovery.

(3) The Commission report on the second phase of the SLIM (simpler legislation for the internal market) project recommends a study of the possibilities and different ways of reforming the tax representation system laid down by Article 21 of Directive 77/388/EEC.

(4) The only change which can in fact substantially simplify the common system of VAT in general and the determination of the person liable for payment of the tax in particular is no longer to allow Member States the option of requiring the appointment of a tax representative.

(5) Therefore, the appointment of a tax representative should in future only be an option for non-established taxable persons.

(6) Under Article 22 of Directive 77/388/EEC, Member States may impose directly on non-established taxable persons the same obligations as those which apply to established taxable persons, including those which may be laid down under Article 22(8).

(7) Where non-established taxable persons are nationals of countries with which no legal instrument exists which organises mutual assistance similar to that laid down within the Community, it will be possible for the Member States to continue to require such non-established taxable persons to designate a tax representative to be the person liable for payment of the tax in their stead or to designate an agent.

(8) Member States will continue to be entirely free to designate the person liable for payment of the tax on importation.

(9) Member States may continue to provide that someone other than the person liable for payment of the tax shall be held jointly and severally liable for payment of the tax.

(10) Article 10 of Directive 77/388/EEC should also be clarified in order to prevent certain cases of tax avoidance in the case of continuous supplies.

(11) Directive 77/388/EEC should therefore be amended accordingly,

HAS ADOPTED THIS DIRECTIVE:

Article 1

Notes

Para (1) inserted "Member States may in certain cases provide that continuous supplies of goods and services which take place over a period of time shall be regarded as being completed at least at intervals of one year." in Directive 77/388/EEC (Sixth VAT Directive) of 17 May 1977 Art 10(2) with effect from 17 October 2000.

Para (2) substituted "Article 21(1)(*a*) and (*c*)" for "Article 21 (1)(*a*)" in Directive 77/388/EEC (Sixth VAT Directive) of 17 May 1977 Art 28f(1) (which amends Art 17(2)–(4)), in Art 17(4)(*a*) with effect from 17 October 2000.

Para (3) substituted "Article 21(1)(*c*)" for "the third subparagraph of Article 21(1)(*a*)" in Directive 77/388/EEC (Sixth VAT Directive) of 17 May 1977 Art 28c(E) "Other Exemptions" (3) fifth indent with effect from 17 October 2000.

Para (4) substituted Directive 77/388/EEC (Sixth VAT Directive) of 17 May 1977 Art 21 with effect from 17 October 2000.

Para (5)(*a*) substituted Directive 77/388/EEC (Sixth VAT Directive) of 17 May 1977 Art 28h (which inserts Art 22)) in Art 22(1)(*c*) first indent with effect from 17 October 2000.

Para (5)(*b*) substituted Directive 77/388/EEC (Sixth VAT Directive) of 17 May 1977 Art 28h (which inserts Art 22)) in Art 22(7) with effect from 17 October 2000.

Para (6) substituted "Article 21(4)" for "Article 21(2)" throughout the Directive 77/388/EEC (Sixth VAT Directive) of 17 May 1977 with effect from 17 October 2000.

Article 2

1. Member States shall bring into force the laws, regulations and administrative provisions necessary to comply with this Directive not later than 31 December 2001. They shall forthwith inform the Commission thereof.

When Member States adopt these measures, they shall contain a reference to this Directive or shall be accompanied by such reference on the occasion of their official publication. The methods of making such a reference shall be laid down by the Member States.

2. Member States shall communicate to the Commission the text of the provisions of national law which they adopt in the field governed by this Directive and a table correlating the provisions of this Directive with the provisions of national law.

Article 3

This Directive shall enter into force on the day of its publication in the Official Journal of the European Communities.

Article 4

This Directive is addressed to the Member States.

Done at Luxembourg, 17 October 2000.

COUNCIL DIRECTIVE

of 19 January 2001

01/41/EC

OJ L 194, 18/07/2001 p 36–37

amending the sixth Directive (77/388/EEC) on the common system of value added tax, with regard to the length of time during which the minimum standard rate is to be applied

THE COUNCIL OF THE EUROPEAN UNION,

Having regard to the Treaty establishing the European Community, and in particular Article 93 thereof,

Having regard to the proposal from the Commission,

Having regard to the opinion of the European Parliament (Opinion delivered on 14 December 2000 (not yet published in the Official Journal)),

Having regard to the opinion of the Economic and Social Committee (Opinion delivered on 29 November 2000 (not yet published in the Official Journal)),

Whereas:

(1) Article 12(3)(a) of the sixth Council Directive (77/388/EEC) of 17 May 1977 on the harmonisation of the laws of the Member States relating to turnover taxes — Common system of value added tax: uniform basis of assessment (OJ L 145, 13.6.1977, p 1. Directive as last amended by Directive 2000/65/EC (OJ L 269, 21.10.2000, p 44)), hereinafter referred to as the sixth VAT Directive, lays down that the Council is to decide on the level of the standard rate applicable after 31 December 2000.

(2) While the standard rate of value added tax currently in force in the various Member States, combined with the mechanism of the transitional system, has ensured that this system has functioned to an acceptable degree, it is nonetheless important to prevent a growing divergence in the standard rates of VAT applied by the Member States from leading to structural imbalances in the Community and distortions of competition in some sectors of activity, at least in the period in which a new VAT strategy is being implemented to simplify and modernise current Community legislation on VAT, as set out in the Commission Communication of 7 June 2000.

(3) It is therefore appropriate to maintain the current minimum standard rate at 15 % for a further period long enough to allow the strategy for simplification and modernisation to be implemented,

HAS ADOPTED THIS DIRECTIVE:

Article 1

Notes

Article 1 substituted Directive 77/388/EEC (Sixth VAT Directive) of 17 May 1977 Art 12(3)(*a*) first and second subparagraphs with effect from 21 July 2001.

Article 2

1. Member States shall bring into force the laws, regulations and administrative provisions necessary to comply with this Directive before 1 January 2001. They shall forthwith inform the Commission thereof.

When Member States adopt these measures, they shall contain a reference to this Directive or shall be accompanied by such reference on the occasion of their official publication. The methods of making such reference shall be laid down by Member States.

2. Member States shall communicate to the Commission the text of the provisions of national law which they adopt in the field covered by this Directive.

Article 3

This Directive shall enter into force on the third day following that of its publication in the Official Journal of the European Communities.

It shall apply from 1 January 2001.

Article 4

This Directive is addressed to the Member States.

Done at Brussels, 19 January 2001.

COUNCIL DIRECTIVE

of 15 June 2001

01/44/EC

OJ L 175, 28/06/2001 p 17–20

amending Directive 76/308/EEC on mutual assistance for the recovery of claims resulting from operations forming part of the system of financing the European Agricultural Guidance and Guarantee Fund, and of agricultural levies and customs duties and in respect of value added tax and certain excise duties

THE COUNCIL OF THE EUROPEAN UNION,

Having regard to the Treaty establishing the European Community, and in particular Articles 93 and 94 thereof,

Having regard to the proposal from the Commission (OJ C 269, 28.8.1998, p 16 and OJ C 179, 24.6.1999, p 6),

Having regard to the opinion of the European Parliament (OJ C 150, 28.5.1999, p 621 and opinion delivered on 16.5.2001 (not yet published in the Official Journal)),

Having regard to the opinion of the Economic and Social Committee (OJ C 101, 12.4.1999, p 26),

Whereas:

(1) The existing arrangements for mutual assistance for recovery set out in Directive 76/308/EEC (OJ L 73, 19.3.1976, p 18. Directive as last amended by the 1994 Act of Accession) should be modified to meet the threat to the financial interests of the Community and the Member States and to the internal market posed by the development of fraud.

(2) In the context of the internal market, Community and national financial interests, which are increasingly threatened by fraud, must be protected so as to safeguard better the competitiveness and fiscal neutrality of the internal market.

(3) In order to safeguard better the financial interests of the Member States and the neutrality of the internal market, claims relating to certain taxes on income and capital and taxes on insurance premiums should be added to the scope of the mutual assistance provided for by Directive 76/308/EEC.

(4) In order to permit more efficient and effective recovery of claims in respect of which a request for recovery has been made, the instrument permitting enforcement of the claim should, in principle, be treated as an instrument of the Member State in which the requested authority is situated.

(5) The use of mutual assistance for recovery cannot, save in exceptional circumstances, be based on financial benefits or an interest in the results obtained, but Member States should be able to agree the reimbursement arrangements when recovery poses a specific problem.

(6) The measures necessary for the implementation of this Directive should be adopted in accordance with Council Decision 1999/468/EC of 28 June 1999 laying down the procedures for the exercise of implementing powers conferred on the Commission (OJ L 184, 17.7.1999, p 23).

(7) Directive 76/308/EEC should therefore be amended accordingly,

HAS ADOPTED THIS DIRECTIVE:

Article 1

Notes

Para (1) substituted the title to Directive 76/308/EEC of 15 March 1976 with effect from 5 July 2001.

Para (2) substituted Directive 76/308/EEC of 15 March 1976, Art 2 with effect from 5 July 2001.

Para (3) inserted indents to Directive 76/308/EEC of 15 March 1976, Art 3 with effect from 5 July 2001.

Para (4) substituted "the name, address and any other relevant information relating to the identification to which the applicant authority normally has access" for "the name and address" in Directive 76/308/EEC of 15 March 1976, Art 4(2) with effect from 5 July 2001.

Para (5) substituted "the name, address and any other relevant information relating to the identification to which the applicant authority normally has access" for "the name and address" in Directive 76/308/EEC of 15 March 1976, Art 5(2) with effect from 5 July 2001.

Para (6) substituted Directive 76/308/EEC of 15 March 1976, Arts 7–10 with effect from 5 July 2001.

Para (7)(*a*) added "unless the applicant authority requests otherwise in accordance with the second subparagraph" to the first sentence of Directive 76/308/EEC of 15 March 1976, Art 12(2) with effect from 5 July 2001.

Para (7)(*b*) added a subparagraph to Directive 76/308/EEC of 15 March 1976, Art 12(2) with effect from 5 July 2001.

Para (8) substituted Directive 76/308/EEC of 15 March 1976, Art 14 first paragraph with effect from 5 July 2001.

Para (9) substituted "the instrument permitting the enforcement and other relevant documents" for "and relevant documents" in Directive 76/308/EEC of 15 March 1976, Art 17 with effect from 5 July 2001.

Para (10) substituted Directive 76/308/EEC of 15 March 1976, Art 18 with effect from 5 July 2001.

Para (11) substituted Directive 76/308/EEC of 15 March 1976, Art 20 with effect from 5 July 2001.

Para (12) substituted Directive 76/308/EEC of 15 March 1976, Art 22 with effect from 5 July 2001.

Para (13) added a paragraph to Directive 76/308/EEC of 15 March 1976, Art 25 with effect from 5 July 2001.

Article 2

1. Member States shall bring into force the laws, regulations and administrative provisions necessary to comply with this Directive not later than 30 June 2002. They shall forthwith inform the Commission thereof.

When Member States adopt these measures, they shall contain a reference to this Directive or shall be accompanied by such reference on the occasion of their official publication. The methods of making such reference shall be laid down by Member States.

2. Member States shall communicate to the Commission the text of the main provisions of national law which they adopt in the field covered by this Directive together with a table showing how the provisions of this Directive correspond to the national provisions adopted.

Article 3

This Directive shall enter into force on the 20th day following its publication in the Official Journal of the European Communities.

Article 4

This Directive is addressed to the Member States.

Done at Göteborg, 15 June 2001.

COUNCIL DIRECTIVE

of 20 December 2001

01/115/EC

Amending Directive 77/388/EEC with a view to simplifying, modernising and harmonising the conditions laid down for invoicing in respect of value added tax

THE COUNCIL OF THE EUROPEAN UNION,

Having regard to the Treaty establishing the European Community. and in particular Article 93 thereof,

Having regard to the proposal from the Commission (OJ C 96 E. 27.3.2001. p 145),

Having regard to the opinion of the European Parliament (Opinion delivered on 13 June 2001 (not yet published in the Official Journal)). Having regard to the opinion of the Economic and Social Committee (OJ C 193. 10.7.2001. p 53).

Whereas:

(1) The current conditions laid down for invoicing and listed under Article 22(3), in the version given in Article 28h of the Sixth Council Directive 77/388/EEC of 17 May 1977 on the harmonisation of the laws of the Member States relating to turnover taxes – Common system of value added tax: uniform basis of assessment (OJ L 145. 13.6.1977. p 1. Directive as last amended by Directive 2001/4/EC (OJ L 22. 24.1.2001. p 17)), are relatively few in number, thus leaving it to the Member States to define the most important such conditions. At the same time. the conditions are no longer appropriate given the development of new invoicing technologies and methods.

(2) The Commission report on the second phase of the SLIM exercise (Simpler Legislation for the Single Market) recommended that a study be carried out to determine what details should be required for VAT purposes when drawing up an invoice and what the legal and technical requirements are as regards electronic invoicing.

(3) The conclusions of the Ecofin Council of June 1998 underlined the fact that the development of electronic commerce has made it necessary to establish a legal framework for the use of electronic invoicing to enable tax administrations to continue to perform their controls.

(4) It is therefore necessary. in order to ensure that the internal market functions properly, to draw up a list, harmonised at Community level, of the particulars that must appear on invoices for the purposes of value added tax and to establish a number of common arrangements governing the use of electronic invoicing and the electronic storage of invoices. as well as for self-billing and the outsourcing of invoicing operations.

(5) Lastly, the storage of invoices should comply with the conditions laid down by Directive 95/46/EC of the European Parliament and of the Council of 24 October 1995 on the protection of individuals with regard to the processing of personal data and on the free movement of such data (OJ L 281, 23.11.1995, p 31).

(6) Since the introduction of the transitional VAT arrangements in 1993, Greece has adopted the prefix GR rather than the prefix GR laid down in the ISO International Standard No 3166-alpha 2 referred to in Article 22(1)(*d*). Given the consequences of amending the prefix in all the Member States, it is important to lay down an exception for Greece providing that the ISO Standard does not apply in Greece.

(7) Directive 77/388/EEC should therefore be amended accordingly,

HAS ADOPTED THIS DIRECTIVE:

Article 1

Directive 77/388/EEC is hereby amended in accordance with the following Articles.

Article 2

Notes

Para (1) amended Directive 77/388/EEC, Art 28h (which replaced Art 22) by inserting inserted "Nevertheless, the Hellenic Republic shall be authorised to use the prefix 'GR'." in the substituted Art 22(1)(*d*) with effect from 6 February 2002.

Para (2) amended Directive 77/388/EEC, Art 28h (which replaced Art 22) by substituting para 3 in the substituted Art 22 with effect from 6 February 2002.

Para (3) amended Directive 77/388/EEC, Art 28h (which replaced Art 22) by inserting "The option provided for in the first subparagraph cannot be used to impose additional obligations over and above those laid down in paragraph 3." in the substituted Art 22(8) with effect from 6 February 2002.

Para (4) amended Directive 77/388/EEC, Art 28h (which replaced Art 22) by inserting "Without prejudice to the provisions laid down in point (*d*), Member States may not, however, release the taxable persons referred to in the third indent from the obligations referred to in Article 22(3)." in the substituted Art 22(9)(*a*) with effect from 6 February 2002.

Para (5) amended Directive 77/388/EEC, Art 28h (which replaced Art 22) by inserting para (9)(*d*) in the substituted Art 22 with effect from 6 February 2002.

Para (6) amended Directive 77/388/EEC, Art 28h (which replaced Art 22) by inserting para (9)(*e*) in the substituted Art 22 with effect from 6 February 2002.

Article 3

Notes

Article 3 inserted Directive 77/388/EEC, Art 22a with effect from 6 February 2002.

Article 4

Notes

Para (1) deleted "or of the document serving as invoice" from Directive 77/388/EEC, Art 10(2) indents 1 and 3 with effect from 6 February 2002.

Para (2) deleted "or on any other documents serving as invoices" and "or on any other document serving as an invoice" from Directive 77/388/EEC, Arts 24(5) and 26a(B) point 9 with effect from 6 February 2002.

Para (3) deleted "or a document in lieu" from Directive 77/388/EEC, Art 26a(C) with effect from 6 February 2002.

Para (4) deleted "or other document serving as invoice" and "or document" from Directive 77/388/EEC, Art 28d(3) with effect from 6 February 2002.

Para (5) amended Directive 77/388/EEC, Art 28g (which replaced Art 21) by deleting "or other document serving as invoice" from the substituted Art 21(1)(*d*) with effect from 6 February 2002.

Para (6) deleted "or on any other document in lieu" from Directive 77/388/EEC, Art 28o(1)(*e*) with effect from 6 February 2002.

Article 5

Member States shall bring into force the laws, regulations and administrative provisions necessary to comply with this Directive with effect from 1 January 2004. They shall forthwith inform the Commission thereof.

When Member States adopt these measures, they shall contain a reference to this Directive or shall be accompanied by such a reference on the occasion of their official publication. The methods of making such a reference shall be laid down by the Member States.

Article 6

This Directive shall enter into force on the 20th day following that of its publication in the Official Journal of the European Communities.

Article 7

This Directive is addressed to the Member States.

COUNCIL DIRECTIVE

of 7 May 2002

02/38/EC

(OJ L128, 15.5.2002, p 41)

amending and amending temporarily Directive 77/388/EEC as regards the value added tax arrangements applicable to radio and television broadcasting services and certain electronically supplied services

THE COUNCIL OF THE EUROPEAN UNION,

Having regard to the Treaty establishing the European

Community, and in particular Article 93 thereof,

Having regard to the proposal from the Commission (OJ C 337 E, 28.11.2000, p 65),

Having regard to the opinion of the European Parliament (OJ C 232, 17.8.2001, p 202),

Having regard to the opinion of the Economic and Social Committee (OJ C 116, 20.4.2001, p 59),

Whereas:

(1) The rules currently applicable to VAT on radio and television broadcasting services and on electronically supplied services, under Article 9 of the sixth Council Directive 77/388/EEC of 17 May 1977 on the harmonisation of the laws of the Member States relating to turnover taxes — Common system of value added tax: uniform basis of assessment (OL L 145, 13.6.1977, p 1. Directive as last amended by Council Directive 2001/115/EC (OJ L 15, 17.1.2002, p. 24)), are inadequate for taxing such services consumed within the Community and for preventing distortions of competition in this area.

(2) In the interests of the proper functioning of the internal market, such distortions should be eliminated and new harmonised rules introduced for this type of activity. Action should be taken to ensure, in particular, that such services where effected for consideration and consumed by customers established in the Community are taxed in the Community and are not taxed if consumed outside the Community.

(3) To this end, radio and television broadcasting services and electronically supplied services provided from third countries to persons established in the Community or from the Community to recipients established in third countries should be taxed at the place of the recipient of the services.

(4) To define electronically supplied services, examples of such services should be included in an annex to the Directive.

(5) To facilitate compliance with fiscal obligations by operators providing electronically supplied services, who are neither established nor required to be identified for tax purposes within the Community, a special scheme should be established. In applying this scheme any operator supplying such services by electronic means to non-taxable

persons within the Community, may, if he is not otherwise identified for tax purposes within the Community, opt for identification in a single Member State.

(6) The non-established operator wishing to benefit from the special scheme should comply with the requirements laid down therein, and with any relevant existing provision in the Member State where the services are consumed.

(7) The Member State of identification must under certain conditions be able to exclude a non-established operator from the special scheme.

(8) Where the non-established operator opts for the special scheme, any input value added tax that he has paid with respect to goods and services used by him for the purpose of his taxed activities falling under the special scheme, should be refunded by the Member State where the input value added tax was paid, in accordance with the arrangements of the thirteenth Council Directive 86/560/EEC of 17 November 1986 on the harmonisation of the laws of the Member States relating to turnover taxes — arrangements for the refund of value added tax to taxable persons not established in Community territory (OJ L 326, 21.11.1986, p 40). The optional restrictions for refund in Article 2(2) and (3) and Article 4(2) of the same Directive should not be applied.

(9) Subject to conditions which they lay down, Member States should allow certain statements and returns to be made by electronic means, and may also require that electronic means are used.

(10) Those provisions pertaining to the introduction of electronic tax returns and statements should be adopted on a permanent basis. It is desirable to adopt all other provisions for a temporary period of three years which may be extended for practical reasons but should, in any event, based on experience, be reviewed within three years from 1 July 2003.

(11) Directive 77/388/EEC should therefore be amended accordingly,

HAS ADOPTED THIS DIRECTIVE:

Article 1

Notes

Para 1(*a*) replaced final full stop with a comma and inserted 2 further indents in Directive 77/388/EEC, Art 9(2)(*e*) for a period of 3 years beginning on 1 July 2003.

Para 1(*b*) inserted Directive 77/388/EEC, Art 9(2)(*f*) for a period of 3 years beginning on 1 July 2003.

Para 1(*c*) substituted Directive 77/388/EEC, Art 9(3)(introductory phrase) for a period of 3 years beginning on 1 July 2003.

Para 1(*d*) substituted Directive 77/388/EEC, Art 9(4) for a period of 3 years beginning on 1 July 2003.

Para 2 inserted a 4th subparagraph to Directive 77/388/EEC, Art 12(3)(*a*) for a period of 3 years beginning on 1 July 2003.

Para 3 inserted Directive 77/388/EEC, Art 26*c* for a period of 3 years beginning on 1 July 2003.

Article 2

Notes

Para 1 substituted Directive 77/388/EEC, Art 22(1)(*a*) (inserted by Art 28h) with effect from 1 July 2003.

Para 2 substituted Directive 77/388/EEC, Art 22(4)(*a*) (inserted by Art 28h) with effect from 1 July 2003.

Para 3 substituted Directive 77/388/EEC, Art 22(6)(*a*) (inserted by Art 28h) with effect from 1 July 2003.

Para 4 substituted Directive 77/388/EEC, Art 22(6)(*b*)(second para) (inserted by Art 28h) with effect from 1 July 2003.

Article 3

1. Member States shall bring into force the laws, regulations and administrative provisions necessary to comply with this Directive on 1 July 2003. They shall forthwith inform the Commission thereof.

When Member States adopt these measures, they shall contain a reference to this Directive or shall be accompanied by such reference on the occasion of their official publication. Member States shall determine how such reference is to be made.

2. Member States shall communicate to the Commission the text of the provisions of domestic law which they adopt in the field covered by this Directive.

Article 4

Article 1 shall apply for a period of three years starting from 1 July 2003.

Article 5

The Council, on the basis of a report from the Commission, shall review the provisions of Article 1 of this Directive before 30 June 2006 and shall either, acting in accordance with Article 93 of the Treaty, adopt measures on an appropriate electronic mechanism on a non-discriminatory basis for charging, declaring, collecting and allocating tax revenue on electronically supplied services with taxation in the place of consumption or, if considered necessary for practical reasons, acting unanimously on the basis of a proposal from the Commission, extend the period mentioned in Article 4.

Article 6

This Directive shall enter into force on the day of its publication in the Official Journal of the European Communities.

Article 7

This Directive is addressed to the Member States.

Done at Brussels, 7 May 2002.

ANNEX

Notes

This Annex inserted Directive 77/388/EEC Annex L with effect from 1 July 2003.

COUNCIL DIRECTIVE

of 3 December 2002

02/92/EC

OJ L 009, 15/01/2003 p 3–10

amending Directive 77/388/EEC to extend the facility allowing Member States to apply reduced rates of VAT to certain labour-intensive services

THE COUNCIL OF THE EUROPEAN UNION,

Having regard to the Treaty establishing the European Community, and in particular Article 93 thereof,

Having regard to the proposal from the Commission,

Having regard to the opinion of the European Parliament (Opinion delivered on 20 November 2002 (not yet published in the Official Journal)),

Having regard to the opinion of the Economic and Social Committee (Opinion delivered on 24 October 2002 (not yet published in the Official Journal)),

Whereas:

(1) Article 28(6) of Council Directive 77/388/EC of 17 May 1977 on the harmonisation of the laws of the Member States relating to turnover taxes — common system of value added tax: uniform basis of assessment (OJ L 145, 13.6.1977, p 1. Directive as last amended by Directive 2002/38/EC (OJ L 128, 15.5.2002, p 41)), allows the reduced rates provided for in the third subparagraph of Article 12(3)(a) also to be applied to the labour-intensive services listed in the categories set out in Annex K to that Directive for a maximum period of three years from 1 January 2000 to 31 December 2002.

(2) Council Decision 2000/185/EC of 28 February 2000 authorising Member States to apply a reduced rate of VAT to certain labour-intensive services in accordance with the procedure provided for in Article 28(6) of Directive 77/388/EEC (OJ L 59, 4.3.2000, p 10) authorised certain Member States to apply, up to 31 December 2002, a reduced rate of VAT to those labour-intensive services for which they had submitted an application.

(3) Based on the reports to be drawn up by 1 October 2002 by the Member States that have applied such reduced rates, the Commission is required to submit a global evaluation report to the Council and the European Parliament by 31 December 2002, accompanied if necessary by a proposal for a final decision on the rate to be applied to labour-intensive services.

(4) In view of the time needed to produce a thorough global evaluation of such reports to extend the maximum period of application set for this measure in Directive 77/388/EEC.

(5) Directive 77/388/EEC should therefore be amended accordingly,

HAS ADOPTED THIS DIRECTIVE:

Article 1

Notes

Article 1 substituted "four years between 1 January 2000 and 31 December 2003" for "three years between 1 January 2000 and 31 December 2002" in Directive 77/388/EEC (Sixth VAT Directive) of 17 May 1977, Art 28(6) with effect from 15 January 2003.

Article 2

This Directive shall enter into force on the day of its publication in the Official Journal of the European Communities.

Article 3

This Directive is addressed to the Member States.

Done at Brussels, 3 December 2002.

COMMISSION DIRECTIVE

of 9 December 2002

02/94/EC

OJ L 337, 13/12/2002 p 41–54

laying down detailed rules for implementing certain provisions of Council Directive 76/308/EEC on mutual assistance for the recovery of claims relating to certain levies, duties, taxes and other measures

THE COMMISSION OF THE EUROPEAN COMMUNITIES,

Having regard to the Treaty establishing the European Community,

Having regard to Council Directive 76/308/EEC of 15 March 1976 on mutual assistance for the recovery of claims relating to certain levies, duties, taxes and other measures (OJ L 73, 19.3.1976, p 18), as last amended by Directive 2001/44/EC (OJ L 175, 28.6.2001, p 17), and in particular Article 22 thereof,

Whereas:

(1) The system of mutual assistance between the competent authorities of Member States, as set out in Directive 76/308/EEC, has been amended as regards the information to be supplied to the applicant authority, the notification of the addressee concerning the applicable instruments and decisions, the adoption of precautionary measures, and the recovery by the requested authority of claims on behalf of the applicant authority.

(2) As regards each of those aspects, therefore, Commission Directive 77/794/EEC of 4 November 1977 laying down detailed rules for implementing certain provisions of Directive 76/308/EEC on mutual assistance for the recovery of claims resulting from operations forming part of the system of financing the European Agricultural Guidance and Guarantee Fund, and of agricultural levies and customs duties, and in respect of value added tax (OJ L 333, 24.12.1977, p 11), as last amended by Directive 86/489/EEC (OJ L 283, 4.10.1986, p 23), should be amended accordingly.

(3) Furthermore, detailed rules should be laid down concerning the means by which communications between authorities may be transmitted.

(4) In the interests of clarity, Directive 77/794/EEC should be replaced.

(5) The measures provided for in this Directive are in accordance with the opinion of the Committee on Recovery,

HAS ADOPTED THIS DIRECTIVE:

CHAPTER I
GENERAL PROVISIONS

Article 1

This Directive lays down the detailed rules for implementing Article 4(2) and (4), Article 5(2) and (3), Article 7, Article 8, Article 9, Article 11, Article 12(1) and (2), Article 14, Article 18(3) and Article 25 of Directive 76/308/EEC.

It also lays down the detailed rules on conversion, transfer of sums recovered, the fixing of a minimum amount for claims which may give rise to a request for assistance, as well as the means by which communications between authorities may be transmitted.

Article 2

For the purposes of this Directive:

1. transmission **"by electronic means"** shall mean transmission using electronic equipment for processing (including digital compression) of data and employing wires, radio transmission, optical technologies or other electromagnetic means;

2. "CCN/CSI" network shall mean the common platform based on the Common Communication Network (CCN) and Common System Interface (CSI), developed by the Community to ensure all transmissions by electronic means between competent authorities in the area of Customs and Taxation.

CHAPTER II
REQUESTS FOR INFORMATION

Article 3

The request for information referred to in Article 4 of Directive 76/308/EEC shall be made out in writing in accordance with the model in Annex I to this Directive. If the request cannot be transmitted by electronic means, it shall bear the official stamp of the applicant authority and shall be signed by an official thereof duly authorised to make such a request.

Where a similar request has been addressed to any other authority, the applicant authority shall indicate in its request for information the name of that authority.

Article 4

The request for information may relate to:

   1 the debtor;
   2 any person liable for settlement of the claim under the law in force in the Member State in which the applicant authority is situated (hereinafter "the Member State of the applicant authority");
   3 any third party holding assets belonging to one of the persons mentioned under point 1 or 2.

Article 5

1. The requested authority shall acknowledge receipt of the request for information in writing as soon as possible and in any event within seven days of such receipt.

2. Immediately upon receipt of the request the requested authority shall, where appropriate, ask the applicant authority to provide any additional information necessary. The applicant authority shall provide all additional necessary information to which it normally has access.

Article 6

1. The requested authority shall transmit each item of requested information to the applicant authority as and when it is obtained.

2. Where all or some of the requested information cannot be obtained within a reasonable time, having regard to the particular case, the requested authority shall so inform the applicant authority, indicating the reasons therefor.

In any event, at the end of six months from the date of acknowledgement of receipt of the request, the requested authority shall inform the applicant authority of the outcome of the investigations which it has conducted in order to obtain the information requested.

In the light of the information received from the requested authority, the applicant authority may request the latter to continue its investigations. That request shall be made in writing within two months of the receipt of the notification of the outcome of the investigations carried out by the requested authority, and shall be treated by the requested authority in accordance with the provisions applying to the initial request.

Article 7

If the requested authority decides not to comply with the request for information, it shall notify the applicant authority in writing of the reasons for the refusal to comply with the request, specifying the provisions of Article 4 of Directive 76/308/EEC on which it relies. Such notification shall be given by the requested authority as soon as it has taken its decision and in any event within three months of the date of the acknowledgement of the receipt of the request.

Article 8

The applicant authority may at any time withdraw the request for information which it has sent to the requested authority. The decision to withdraw shall be transmitted to the requested authority in writing.

CHAPTER III
REQUESTS FOR NOTIFICATION

Article 9

The request for notification referred to in Article 5 of Directive 76/308/EEC shall be made out in writing in duplicate in accordance with the model in Annex II to this Directive. The said request shall bear the official stamp of the applicant authority and shall be signed by an official thereof duly authorised to make such a request.

Two copies of the instrument or decision, notification of which is requested, shall be attached to the request.

Article 10

The request for notification may relate to any natural or legal person who, in accordance with the law in force in the Member State of the applicant authority, is required to be informed of any instrument or decision which concerns that person.

In so far as such is not indicated in the instrument or decision of which notification is requested, the request for notification shall refer to the rules in force in the Member State of the applicant authority governing the procedure for contestation of the claim or for its recovery.

Article 11

1. The requested authority shall acknowledge receipt of the request for notification in writing as soon as possible and in any event within seven days of such receipt.

Immediately upon receipt of the request for notification, the requested authority shall take the necessary measures to effect notification in accordance with the law in force in the Member State in which it is situated.

If necessary, but without jeopardising the final date for notification indicated in the request for notification, the requested authority shall ask the applicant authority to provide additional information.

The applicant authority shall provide all additional information to which it normally has access.

The requested authority shall in any event not question the validity of the instrument or decision of which notification is requested.

2. The requested authority shall inform the applicant authority of the date of notification as soon as this has been effected, by returning to it one of the copies of the request with the certificate on the reverse side duly completed.

CHAPTER IV
REQUESTS FOR RECOVERY OR FOR PRECAUTIONARY MEASURES

Article 12

1. Requests for recovery or for precautionary measures referred to in Articles 6 and 13 respectively of Directive 76/308/EEC shall be made out in writing in accordance with the model in Annex III to this Directive.

Such requests, which shall include a declaration that the conditions laid down in Directive 76/308/EEC for initiating the mutual assistance procedure have been fulfilled, shall bear the official stamp of the applicant authority and shall be signed by an official thereof duly authorised to make such a request.

2. The instrument permitting enforcement shall accompany the request for recovery or for precautionary measures. A single instrument may be issued in respect of several claims where they concern one and the same person.

For the purposes of Articles 13 to 20 of this Directive, all claims covered by the same instrument permitting enforcement shall be deemed to constitute a single claim.

Article 13

Requests for recovery or for precautionary measures may relate to any person referred to in Article 4.

Article 14

1. If the currency of the Member State of the requested authority is different from the currency of the Member State of the applicant authority, the applicant authority shall express the amount of the claim to be recovered in both currencies.

2. The rate of exchange to be used for the purposes of paragraph 1 shall be the latest selling rate recorded on the most representative exchange market or markets of the Member State of the applicant authority on the date when the request for recovery is signed.

Article 15

1. The requested authority shall, in writing, as soon as possible and in any event within seven days of receipt of the request for recovery or for precautionary measures:

    (*a*)   acknowledge receipt of the request;

    (*b*)   ask the applicant authority to complete the request if it does not contain the information or other particulars mentioned in Article 7 of Directive 76/308/EEC.

The applicant authority shall provide all information to which it has access.

2. If the requested authority does not take the requisite action within the three-month period laid down in Article 8 of Directive 76/308/EEC, it shall, as soon as possible and in any event within seven days of the expiry of that period, inform the applicant authority in writing of the grounds for its failure to comply with the time limit.

Article 16

Where, within a reasonable time having regard to the particular case, all or part of the claim cannot be recovered or precautionary measures cannot be taken, the requested authority shall so inform the applicant authority, indicating the reasons therefor.

No later than at the end of each six-month period following the date of acknowledgement of the receipt of the request, the requested authority shall inform the applicant authority of the state of progress or the outcome of the procedure for recovery or for precautionary measures.

In the light of the information received from the requested authority, the applicant authority may request the latter to re-open the procedure for recovery or for precautionary measures. That request shall be made in writing within two months of the receipt of the notification of the outcome of that procedure, and shall be treated by the requested authority in accordance with the provisions applying to the initial request.

Article 17

1. Any action contesting the claim or the instrument permitting its enforcement which is taken in the Member State of the applicant authority shall be notified to the requested authority in writing by the applicant authority immediately after the latter has been informed of such action.

2. If the laws, regulations and administrative practices in force in the Member State of the requested authority do not permit precautionary measures or the recovery requested under the second subparagraph of Article 12(2) of Directive 76/308/EEC, the requested authority shall notify the applicant authority to that effect as soon as possible and in any event within one month of the receipt of the notification referred to in paragraph 1.

3. Any action which is taken in the Member State of the requested authority for reimbursement of sums recovered or for compensation in relation to recovery of contested claims under the second subparagraph of Article 12(2) of Directive 76/308/ EEC shall be notified to the applicant authority in writing by the requested authority immediately after the latter has been informed of such action.

The requested authority shall as far as possible involve the applicant authority in the procedures for settling the amount to be reimbursed and the compensation due. Upon a reasoned request from the requested authority, the applicant authority shall transfer the sums reimbursed and the compensation paid within two months of the receipt of that request.

Article 18

1. If the request for recovery or for precautionary measures becomes devoid of purpose as a result of payment of the claim or of its cancellation or for any other reason, the applicant authority shall immediately inform the requested authority in writing so that the latter may stop any action which it has undertaken.

2. Where the amount of the claim which is the subject of the request for recovery or for precautionary measures is adjusted for any reason, the applicant authority shall immediately inform the requested authority in writing, and if necessary issue a new instrument permitting enforcement.

3. If the adjustment entails a reduction in the amount of the claim, the requested authority shall continue the action which it has undertaken with a view to recovery or to the taking of precautionary measures, but that action shall be limited to the amount still outstanding.

If, at the time when the requested authority is informed of the reduction in the amount of the claim, an amount exceeding the amount still outstanding has already been recovered by it but the transfer procedure referred to in Article 19 has not yet been initiated, the requested authority shall repay the amount overpaid to the person entitled thereto.

4. If the adjustment entails an increase in the amount of the claim, the applicant authority shall as soon as possible address to the requested authority an additional request for recovery or for precautionary measures.

That additional request shall, as far as possible, be dealt with by the requested authority at the same time as the original request from the applicant authority. Where, in view of the state of progress of the existing procedure, consolidation of the additional request with the original request is not possible, the requested authority shall be required to comply with the additional request only if it concerns an amount not less than that referred to in Article 25(2).

5. In order to convert the adjusted amount of the claim into the currency of the Member State of the requested authority, the applicant authority shall use the exchange rate used in its original request.

Article 19

Any sum recovered by the requested authority, including, where applicable, the interest referred to in Article 9(2) of Directive 76/308/EEC, shall be transferred to the applicant authority in the currency of the Member State of the requested authority. The transfer shall take place within one month of the date on which recovery was effected.

The competent authorities of the Member States may agree different arrangements for the transfer of amounts below the threshold referred to in Article 25(2) of this Directive.

Article 20

Irrespective of any amounts collected by the requested authority by way of the interest referred to in Article 9(2) of Directive 76/308/EEC, the claim shall be deemed to have been recovered in proportion to the recovery of the amount expressed in the national currency of the Member State of the requested authority, on the basis of the exchange rate referred to in Article 14(2) of this Directive.

CHAPTER V
TRANSMISSION OF COMMUNICATIONS

Article 21

1. All information communicated in writing pursuant to this Directive shall, as far as possible, be transmitted only by electronic means, except for:

(*a*) the request for notification referred to in Article 5 of Directive 76/308/EEC and the instrument or decision of which notification is requested;

(*b*) requests for recovery or for precautionary measures referred to in Articles 6 and 13 respectively of Directive 76/308/EEC, and the instrument permitting enforcement.

2. The competent authorities of the Member States may agree to waive the communication on paper of the requests and instruments specified in paragraph 1.

Article 22

Each Member State shall designate a central office with principal responsibility for communication by electronic means with other Member States. That office shall be connected to the CCN/CSI network.

Where several authorities are appointed in a Member State for the purpose of applying this Directive, the central office shall be responsible for the forwarding of all communication by electronic means between those authorities and the central offices of other Member States.

Article 23

1. Where the competent authorities of the Member States store information in electronic data bases and exchange such information by electronic means, they shall take all measures necessary to ensure that any information communicated in whatever form pursuant to this Directive is treated as confidential.

It shall be covered by the obligation of professional secrecy and shall enjoy the protection extended to similar information under the national law of the Member State which received it.

2. The information referred to in paragraph 1 may be made available only to the persons and authorities referred to in Article 16 of Directive 76/308/EEC.

Such information may be used in connection with judicial or administrative proceedings initiated for the recovery of levies, duties, taxes and other measures referred to in Article 2 of Directive 76/308/EEC.

Persons duly accredited by the Security Accreditation Authority of the European Commission may have access to this information only in so far as is necessary for the care, maintenance and development of the CCN/CSI network.

3. Where the competent authorities of the Member States communicate by electronic means, they shall take all measures necessary to ensure that all communications are duly authorised.

Article 24

Information and other particulars communicated by the requested authority to the applicant authority shall be conveyed in the official language or one of the official languages of the Member State of the requested authority or in another language agreed between the applicant and requested authorities.

CHAPTER VI
ELIGIBILITY AND REFUSAL OF REQUESTS FOR ASSISTANCE

Article 25

1. A request for assistance may be made by the applicant authority in respect of either a single claim or several claims where those are recoverable from one and the same person.

2. No request for assistance may be made if the total amount of the relevant claim or claims listed in Article 2 of Directive 76/308/EEC is less than EUR 1500.

Article 26

If the requested authority decides, pursuant to the first paragraph of Article 14 of Directive 76/308/EEC, to refuse a request for assistance, it shall notify the applicant authority in writing of the reasons for the refusal. Such notification shall be given by the requested authority as soon as it has taken its decision and in any event within three months of the date of receipt of the request for assistance.

CHAPTER VII
REIMBURSEMENT ARRANGEMENTS

Article 27

Each Member State shall appoint at least one official duly authorised to agree reimbursement arrangements under Article 18(3) of Directive 76/308/EEC.

Article 28

1. If the requested authority decides to request reimbursement arrangements it shall notify the applicant authority in writing of the reasons for its view that recovery of the claim poses a specific problem, entails very high costs or relates to the fight against organised crime.

The requested authority shall append a detailed estimate of the costs for which it requests reimbursement by the applicant authority.

2. The applicant authority shall acknowledge receipt of the request for reimbursement arrangements in writing as soon as possible and in any event within seven days of receipt.

Within two months of the date of acknowledgement of receipt of the said request, the applicant authority shall inform the requested authority whether and to what extent it agrees with the proposed reimbursement arrangements.

3. If no agreement is reached between the applicant and requested authority with respect to reimbursement arrangements, the requested authority shall continue recovery procedures in the normal way.

CHAPTER VIII
FINAL PROVISIONS

Article 29

Each Member State shall inform the Commission before 15 March each year, as far as possible by electronic means, of the use made of the procedures laid down in Directive 76/308/EEC and of the results achieved in the previous calendar year, in accordance with the model in Annex IV to this Directive.

Article 30

The Member States shall bring into force the laws, regulations and administrative provisions necessary to comply with this Directive by 30 April 2003 at the latest. They shall forthwith inform the Commission thereof.

When Member States adopt those provisions, they shall contain a reference to this Directive or be accompanied by such a reference on the occasion of their official publication. Member States shall determine how such reference is to be made.

Article 31

The Commission shall communicate to the other Member States the measures which each Member State takes for implementing this Directive.

Each Member State shall notify the other Member States and the Commission of the name and address of the competent authorities for the purpose of applying this Directive, as well as of the officials authorised to agree arrangements under Article 18(3) of Directive 76/308/EEC.

Article 32

Directive 77/794/EEC is hereby repealed.

References to the repealed Directive shall be construed as references to this Directive.

Article 33

This Directive shall enter into force on the 20th day following that of its publication in the Official Journal of the European Communities.

Article 34

This Directive is addressed to the Member States.

Done at Brussels, 9 December 2002.

ANNEX I

Model for the request for information referred to in Article 4 of Directive 76/308/EEC

DIRECTIVE 76/308/EEC

(Article 4)

(Description of the applicant authority, address, telephone, fax and bank account number, etc.)

(Name, e-mail address, telephone, fax and language skills of the official dealing with the request)

....
(Place and date of sending request)

....
(File reference of applicant authority)

To:

....

(Name of the authority to whom the request is sent, Post Box, place etc.)

....

....

(Space reserved for the authority to whom the request is sent)

REQUEST FOR INFORMATION

I, the undersigned .... ,
(Name and official capacity)

acting as the agent duly authorised by the applicant authority indicated above, hereby request the following information to be obtained in accordance with Article 4 of Directive 76/308/EEC:

Information relating to the person concerned (¹)		
(a) For natural persons:	Name:	
	Date and place of birth:	
For legal entities:	Legal status:	Company name:
Address (known/assumed (*)):		
Principal debtor /Co-debtor /Third party holding assets (*):		
(b) Name of the principal debtor if different from person concerned:		
Address (known/assumed (*)):		
(c) Other relevant information concerning the above persons:		

Information relating to the claim(s)
— Amount: Principal: Interests: Costs: Penalties:
— Exact nature of the claim(s):
— Final date permitting recovery:
— Other information:
Other requested authorities:
Information requested

(Signature)

(Official stamp)

(*) Delete as appropriate.
(¹) Natural or legal person.

ANNEX II

Model for the request for notification referred to in Article 5 of Directive 76/308/EEC

DIRECTIVE 76/308/EEC

(Article 5)

(Description of the applicant authority, address, telephone, fax and bank account number, etc.)

(Name, e-mail address, telephone, fax and language skills of the official dealing with the request)

....

(Place and date of sending request)

....

(File reference of applicant authority)

To: (Name of the authority to whom the request is sent, Post Box, place etc.)

....

(Space reserved for the authority to whom the request is sent)

REQUEST FOR NOTIFICATION

I, the undersigned ....

(Name and official capacity)

acting as the agent duly authorised by the applicant authority indicated above, hereby request notification, pursuant to Article 5 of Directive 76/308/EEC, of the following instrument/decision (*):

Information relating to the person concerned (¹)		
(a) For natural persons:	Name:	
	Date and place of birth:	
For legal entities:	Legal status:	Company name:
Address (known/assumed (*)):		
Principal debtor/Co-debtor /Third party holding assets (*)		
(b) Name of the principal debtor if different from person concerned:		
Address (known/assumed (*)):		
(c) Other relevant information concerning the above persons:		
Information relating to the claim(s)		
— Nature and subject of the instrument (or decision) to be notified:		
— Amount (inclusive of interest, penalties and costs):		
— Exact nature of the claim(s):		
— Final date for notification:		
— Other information:		
.... (Signature)		(Official stamp)
(*) Delete as appropriate. (¹) Natural or legal person.		

CERTIFICATE

The undersigned hereby certifies:

— that the instrument/decision (*) attached to the request overleaf has been notified to the addressee referred to in the said request dated .... The notification was made in the following manner (¹):

— that the instrument/decision (*) attached to the request overleaf was not able to be notified to the addressee referred to in the said request for the following reasons (*):

....
(Date)

....
(Signature)

(Official stamp)

———

(*) Delete as appropriate.
(¹) Indicate exactly whether the notification was made to the addressee in person or by another procedure.

ANNEX III

ANNEX III

Model for the requests for recovery or for precautionary measures referred to in Articles 6 and 13 of Directive 76/308/EEC

DIRECTIVE 76/308/EEC

(Articles 6 to 13)

(Description of the applicant authority, address, telephone, fax and bank account number, etc.)

(Name, e-mail address, telephone, fax and language skills of the official dealing with the request)

....
(Place and date of sending request)

....
(File reference of applicant authority)

To

....

(Name of the authority to whom the request is sent, Post Box, place etc.)

....

....

(Space reserved for the authority to whom the request is sent)

REQUEST FOR RECOVERY/PRECAUTIONARY MEASURES TO BE TAKEN

I, the undersigned ....,
(Name and official capacity)

acting as the agent duly authorised by the applicant authority indicated above, hereby request:

— recovery of the following claim(s) covered by the attached unit of execution pursuant to Article 7 of Directive 76/308/EEC: the conditions of Article 7(2)(a) and (b) are satisfied (*)

— precautionary measures to be taken, pursuant to Article 13 of Directive 76/308/EEC, in respect of the person mentioned below concerning the claim(s) covered by the attached unit of execution; I attach hereto a statement of the reason for this request (*).

Please remit the entire amount of the claim recovered to:

....
(Bank account number)

....
(Name and address of the account holder)

....
(Payment reference)

Payment by instalment is: acceptable without further consultation/only acceptable after consultation/not acceptable (*)

....
(Signature)

(Official stamp)

Information relating to the person concerned (^{1})		
(a) For natural persons:	Name:	
	Date and place of birth:	
For legal entities:	Legal status:	Company name:
Address (known/assumed (*)):		
Principal debtor/Co-debtor/Third party holding assets (*)		
(b) Name of the principal debtor if different from person concerned:		
Address (known/assumed (*)):		
(c) If relevant: assets of the debtor held by a third party:		
(d) Other relevant information:		
(Detailed description of all other relevant information known about the above persons)		
(*) Delete as appropriate. (^{1}) Natural or legal person.		

Information relating to the claim(s)

(Rate of exchange used:)

Exact nature of the claim(s) (Article 2 points (a) to (h) Directive 76/308/EEC)	Amount of principal (^{1}) (^{2})	Amount of administrative penalties and fines (^{1}) (^{2})	Amount of interest up to the date of signature of this document (^{1}) (^{2})	Amount of the costs up to the date of signature of this document (^{1}) (^{2})	Total amount of the claim (^{2})	Date on which enforcement becomes possible	Date of notification of the instrument to the addressee	Period of limitation	Reference to the instrument permitting the enforcement	Details of other documents attached

Other information

(^{1}) Where the unit of execution is general; indicate the amounts of the different claims.
(^{2}) Amount expressed in the currency of the requested authority and of the applicant authority.

ANNEX IV

Model for the Communication from the Member States to the Commission referred to in Article 25 of Directive 76/308/EEC

DIRECTIVE 76/308/EEC

(Article 25)

Requests for mutual assistance on recovery of claims sent and received by .... in the year ....

Member State	Requests for information		Requests for notification		Requests for recovery								
					Requests sent				Requests received				
							Amounts of the claims recovered for requests made during the year (X)				Amounts of the claims recovered for requests made during the year (X)		
	Number received	Number sent	Number received	Number sent	Number	Amount of the claims involved	Amount	Year	Number	Amount of the claims involved	Amount	Year
[Belgique/België												
Česká Republika												
Danmark												
Deutschland												
Eesti												
Ελλάδα												
España												
France												
Ireland												
Italia												
Κύπρος												
Latvija												
Lietuva												
Luxembourg												
Magyarország												
Malta												
Nederland												
Österreich												
Polska												
Portugal												
Slovenija												
Slovensko												
Finland/Suomi												
Sverige												
United Kingdom]												

Amendments

[1]   Annex IV substituted by Commission Directive 2004/79/EC of 4 March 2004 Annex with effect from 1 May 2004.

COUNCIL DIRECTIVE

of 7 October 2003

03/92/EC

OJ L 260, 11/10/2003 p 8–9

amending Directive 77/388/EEC as regards the rules on the place of supply of gas and electricity

THE COUNCIL OF THE EUROPEAN UNION,

Having regard to the Treaty establishing the European Community, and in particular Article 93 thereof,

Having regard to the proposal from the Commission (Proposal of 5 December 2002 (not yet published in the Official Journal)),

Having regard to the opinion of the European Parliament (Opinion delivered on 13.5.2003 (not yet published in the Official Journal)),

Having regard to the opinion of the European Economic and Social Committee (Opinion delivered on 26.3.2003 (not yet published in the Official Journal)),

Whereas:

(1) Increasing liberalisation of the gas and electricity sector, aimed at completing the internal market for electricity and natural gas, has revealed a need to review the current VAT rules on the place of supply of those goods, set out in the Sixth Council Directive 77/388/EEC of 17 May 1977 on the harmonisation of the laws of the Member States relating to turnover taxes — Common system of value added tax: uniform basis of assessment (OJ L 145, 13.6.1977, p 1. Directive as last amended by Directive 2002/93/EC (OJ L 331, 7.12.2002, p 27)), in order to modernise and simplify the operation of the VAT system within the context of the internal market, a strategy to which the Commission is committed.

(2) Electricity and gas are treated as goods for VAT purposes, and, accordingly, the place of their supply with respect to cross-border transactions has to be determined in accordance with Article 8 of Directive 77/388/EEC. However, since electricity and gas are difficult to track physically it is particularly difficult to determine the place of supply under the current rules.

(3) In order to attain a real internal market for electricity and gas without VAT obstacles, the place of supply of gas through the natural gas distribution system and of electricity, before the goods reach the final stage of consumption, should be determined to be the place where the customer has established his business.

(4) The supply of electricity and gas in the final stage, from traders and distributors to final consumer, should be taxed at the place where the customer has effective use and consumption of the goods, in order to ensure that taxation takes place in the country where actual consumption takes place. This is normally the place where the meter of the customer is located.

(5) Electricity and gas are supplied through distribution networks, to which network operators provide access. In order to avoid double or non-taxation, it is necessary to harmonise the rules governing the place of supply of the transmission and transportation services. Access to and use of the distribution systems and the provision of other services directly linked to these services should therefore be added to the list of specific instances set out in Article 9, paragraph 2(e) of Directive 77/388/EEC.

(6) The import of gas through the natural gas distribution system, or of electricity, should be exempted in order to avoid double taxation.

(7) Those changes in the rules governing the place of supply of gas through the natural gas distribution system, or of electricity, should be combined with a compulsory reverse charge when the customer is a person identified for VAT purposes.

(8) Directive 77/388/EEC should therefore be amended accordingly,

HAS ADOPTED THIS DIRECTIVE:

Article 1

Notes

Para (1) inserted Directive 77/388/EEC (Sixth VAT Directive) of 17 May 1977 Art 8(1)(*d*)–(*e*) with effect from 11 October 2003.
Para (2) inserted Directive 77/388/EEC (Sixth VAT Directive) of 17 May 1977 Art 9(2)(*e*) ninth indent with effect from 11 October 2003.
Para (3) inserted Directive 77/388/EEC (Sixth VAT Directive) of 17 May 1977 Art 14(1)(*k*) with effect from 11 October 2003.
Para (4) substituted Directive 77/388/EEC (Sixth VAT Directive) of 17 May 1977 Art 21(1)(*a*) (as set out in Art 28g) with effect from 11 October 2003.
Para (5) inserted Directive 77/388/EEC (Sixth VAT Directive) of 17 May 1977 Art 21(1)(*f*) (as set out in Art 28g) with effect from 11 October 2003.
Para (6) substituted Directive 77/388/EEC (Sixth VAT Directive) of 17 May 1977 Art 22(1)(*c*) first indent (as set out in Art 28h) with effect from 11 October 2003.
Para (7) inserted Directive 77/388/EEC (Sixth VAT Directive) of 17 May 1977 Art 28a(5)(*b*) additional indent with effect from 11 October 2003.

Article 3

This Directive shall enter into force on the day of its publication in the Official Journal of the European Union.

Article 4

This Directive is addressed to the Member States.

Done at Luxembourg, 7 October 2003.

COUNCIL DIRECTIVE

of 7 October 2003

03/93/EC

OJ L 264, 15/10/2003 p 23–24

amending Council Directive 77/799/EEC concerning mutual assistance by the competent authorities of the Member States in the field of direct and indirect taxation

THE COUNCIL OF THE EUROPEAN UNION,

Having regard to the Treaty establishing the European Community, and in particular Articles 93 and 94 thereof,

Having regard to the proposal from the Commission (OJ C 270, E, 25.9.2001, p 96),

Having regard to the opinion of the European Parliament (OJ C 284 E, 21.11.2002, p 121),

Having regard to the opinion of the European Economic and Social Committee (OJ C 80, 3.4.2002, p 76),

Whereas:

(1) In order to combat value added tax (VAT) evasion it is necessary to strengthen cooperation between tax administrations within the Community and between the latter and the Commission in accordance with common principles.

(2) To that end, Council Regulation (EEC) No 218/92 (OJ L 24, 1.2.1992, p 1. Regulation as last amended by Regulation (EC) No 792/2002 (OJ L 128, 15.5.2002, p 1)), which supplemented, as regards VAT, the system of cooperation established by Council Directive 77/799/EEC of 19 December 1977 concerning mutual assistance by the competent authorities of the Member States in the field of direct and indirect taxation (OJ L 336, 27.1.1977, p 15. Directive as last amended by the 1994 Act of Accession), has been replaced by Council Regulation (EC) No 1798/2003 of 7 October 2003 on administrative cooperation in the field of value added tax and repealing Regulation (EEC) No 218/92 (See page 1 of this Official Journal). The latter Regulation sets out all the provisions relating to administrative cooperation in the field of VAT, with the exception of mutual assistance as provided for by Council Directive 76/308/EEC of 15 March 1976 on mutual assistance for the recovery of claims relating to certain levies, duties, taxes and other measures (OJ L 73, 19.3.1976, p 18. Directive as last amended by Directive 2001/44/EC (OJ L 175, 28.6.2001, p 17)).

(3) The scope of mutual assistance laid down by Directive 77/799/EEC must be extended to taxation of the insurance premiums referred to in Directive 76/308/EEC so as to better protect the financial interests of the Member States and the neutrality of the internal market.

(4) Directive 77/799/EEC should therefore be amended accordingly,

HAS ADOPTED THIS DIRECTIVE:

Article 1

Directive 77/799/EEC is hereby amended as follows:

Notes

Para (1) substituted Council Directive 77/799/EEC of 19 December 1977 title with effect from 15 October 2003.
Para (2) substituted Council Directive 77/799/EEC of 19 December 1977 Art 1(1) first indent with effect from 15 October 2003.
Para (2)(*a*) substituted Council Directive 77/799/EEC of 19 December 1977 Art 1(5) wording under heading of "in the United Kingdom" with effect from 15 October 2003.
Para (2)(*b*) substituted Council Directive 77/799/EEC of 19 December 1977 Art 1(5) wording under heading of "in Italy" with effect from 15 October 2003.
Para (3) substituted Council Directive 77/799/EEC of 19 December 1977 Art 7(1) with effect from 15 October 2003.

Article 2

References made to Directive 77/799/EEC in relation to value added tax (VAT) shall be construed as references to Regulation (EC) No 1798/2003.

Article 3

1. Member States shall bring into force the laws, regulations and administrative provisions necessary to comply with this Directive on 31 December 2003. They shall forthwith inform the Commission thereof.

When Member States adopt those provisions, they shall contain a reference to this Directive or shall be accompanied by such a reference on the occasion of their official publication. Member States shall determine how such reference is to be made.

2. Member States shall communicate to the Commission the texts of the provisions of national law which they adopt in the field covered by this Directive.

Article 4

This Directive shall enter into force on the day of its publication in the Official Journal of the European Union.

Article 5

This Directive is addressed to the Member States.

Done at Luxembourg, 7 October 2003.

COUNCIL DIRECTIVE

of 20 January 2004

04/7/EC

OJ L 027 , 30/01/2004 p 44–45

amending Directive 77/388/EEC concerning the common system of value added tax, as regards conferment of implementing powers and the procedure for adopting derogations

THE COUNCIL OF THE EUROPEAN UNION,

Having regard to the Treaty establishing the European Community, and in particular Article 93 thereof,

Having regard to the proposal from the Commission,

Having regard to the opinion of the European Parliament (Opinion delivered on 16 December 2003 (not yet published in the Official Journal)),

Having regard to the opinion of the European Economic and Social Committee (Opinion delivered on 30 October 2003 (not yet published in the Official Journal)),

Whereas:

(1) Articles 27 and 30 of Council Directive 77/388/EEC of 17 May 1977 on the harmonisation of the laws of the Member States relating to turnover taxes — Common system of value added tax: uniform basis of assessment (OJ L 145, 13.6.1977, p 1. Directive as last amended by Directive 2003/92/EC (OJ L 260, 11.10.2003, p 8)), lay down procedures that may result in the tacit approval of derogations by the Council.

(2) In the interests of transparency and legal certainty, it is preferable to ensure that every derogation authorised under Article 27 or Article 30 of Directive 77/388/EEC takes the form of an explicit decision adopted by the Council acting on a proposal from the Commission.

(3) The possibility of tacit approval by the Council on the expiry of a given period should therefore be removed.

(4) In order to ensure that a Member State which has submitted a request for derogation is not left in doubt as to what action the Commission plans to take in response, time limits should be laid down within which the Commission must present to the Council either a proposal for authorisation or a communication setting out its objections.

(5) In order to enable Member States to follow more closely the processing of their requests, the Commission should be required, once it has all the information it considers necessary for appraising a request, to notify the requesting Member State accordingly and transmit the request, in its original language, to the other Member States.

(6) In the second sentence of paragraph 1 of Article 27 of Directive 77/388/EEC it is emphasised that the assessment of the negligible extent of the effect of the simplification measure on the amount of tax due at the final consumption stage is made

in a global manner by reference to macroeconomic forecasts relating to the likely impact of the measure on the Community's own resources provided from VAT.

(7) In the absence of any mechanism for the adoption of binding measures to govern the implementation of Directive 77/388/EEC, the application of rules laid down in that Directive varies from one Member State to another.

(8) In order to improve the functioning of the internal market, it is essential to ensure more uniform application of the current VAT system. The introduction of a procedure for the adoption of measures to ensure the correct implementation of existing rules would represent a major step forward in that respect.

(9) Those measures should, in particular, address the problem of double taxation of cross-border transactions which can occur as the result of divergences between Member States in the application of the provisions of Directive 77/388/EEC governing the place of supply.

(10) However, the scope of each implementing measure should remain limited since, albeit designed to clarify a provision laid down in Directive 77/388/EEC, it could never derogate from such a provision.

(11) Although the scope of the implementing measures would be limited, those measures would have a budgetary impact which for one or more Member States could be significant.

(12) The impact of such measures on the budgets of Member States justifies the Council reserving the right to exercise powers for the implementation of Directive 77/388/EEC itself.

(13) Given the restricted scope of the measures envisaged, measures implementing Directive 77/388/EEC should be adopted by the Council acting unanimously on a proposal from the Commission.

(14) Since, for those reasons, the objectives of this Directive cannot be sufficiently achieved by the Member States acting alone and can therefore be better achieved at Community level, the Community may adopt measures in accordance with the principle of subsidiarity as set out in Article 5 of the Treaty. In accordance with the principle of proportionality, as set out in that Article, this Directive does not go beyond what is necessary in order to achieve those objectives.

(15) Directive 77/388/EEC should therefore be amended accordingly,

HAS ADOPTED THIS DIRECTIVE:

Article 1

Notes

Para (1) substituted Directive 77/388/EEC of 17 May 1977 Art 27(1)–(4) with effect from 19 February 2004.

Para (2) inserted Directive 77/388/EEC of 17 May 1977 Art 29a with effect from 19 February 2004.

Para (3) substituted Directive 77/388/EEC of 17 May 1977 Art 30 with effect from 19 February 2004.

Article 2

This Directive shall enter into force on the 20th day following its publication in the Official Journal of the European Union.

Article 3

This Directive is addressed to the Member States.

Done at Brussels, 20 January 2004.

COUNCIL DIRECTIVE

of 10 February 2004

04/15/EC

Official Journal L 052, 21/02/2004 p 61–61

amending Directive 77/388/EEC to extend the facility allowing Member States to apply reduced rates of VAT to certain labour-intensive services

THE COUNCIL OF THE EUROPEAN UNION,

Having regard to the Treaty establishing the European Community, and in particular Article 93 thereof,

Having regard to the proposal from the Commission,

Having regard to the opinion of the European Parliament (Opinion delivered on 15 January 2004 (not yet published in the Official Journal)),

Having regard to the opinion of the European Economic and Social Committee (Opinion delivered on 28 January 2004 (not yet published in the Official Journal)),

Whereas:

(1) Article 28(6) of Council Directive 77/388/EEC of 17 May 1977 on the harmonisation of the laws of the Member States relating to turnover taxes — common system of value added tax: uniform basis of assessment (OJ L 145, 13.6.1977, p 1. Directive as last amended by Directive 2004/7/EC (OJ L 27, 30.1.2004, p 44)), allows the reduced rates provided for in the third subparagraph of Article 12(3)(a) also to be applied to the labour-intensive services listed in the categories set out in Annex K to that Directive for a maximum period of four years from 1 January 2000 to 31 December 2003.

(2) Council Decision 2000/185/EC of 28 February 2000 authorising Member States to apply a reduced rate of VAT to certain labour-intensive services in accordance with the procedure provided for in Article 28(6) of Directive 77/388/EEC (OJ L 59, 4.3.2000, p 10. Decision as amended by Decision 2002/954/EC (OJ L 331, 7.12.2002, p 28)), authorised certain Member States to apply a reduced rate of VAT to those labour-intensive services for which they had submitted an application up to 31 December 2003.

(3) On the basis of the assessment reports submitted by the Member States that have applied the reduced rate, the Commission submitted its global evaluation report on 2 June 2003.

(4) In line with its strategy to improve the operation of the VAT system within the context of the internal market, the Commission adopted a proposal for a general review of the reduced rates of VAT to simplify and rationalise them.

(5) Since the Council has not reached an agreement on the content of the proposal, it should be given the necessary time to do so, in order to avoid legal uncertainty from 1

January 2004 the maximum period of application set for this measure in Directive 77/388/EEC should therefore be extended.

(6) In order to ensure the continuous application of Article 28(6) of Directive 77/388/EEC, provision should be made for this Directive to apply retroactively.

(7) Implementation of this Directive in no way implies change in the legislative provisions of Member States.

(8) Decision 77/388/EEC should be amended accordingly,

HAS ADOPTED THIS DIRECTIVE:

Article 1

Notes

Article 1 substituted "six years between 1 January 2000 and 31 December 2005" for "four years between 1 January 2000 and 31 December 2003" in Directive 77/388/EC, Art 28(6) with effect from 1 January 2004.

Article 2

This Directive shall enter into force on the day of its adoption.

It shall apply from 1 January 2004.

Article 3

This Directive is addressed to the Member States.

Done at Brussels, 10 February 2004.

COUNCIL DIRECTIVE

of 21 April 2004

04/56/EC

Official Journal L 127, 29/04/2004 p 70–72

amending Directive 77/799/EEC concerning mutual assistance by the competent authorities of the Member States in the field of direct taxation, certain excise duties and taxation of insurance premiums

THE COUNCIL OF THE EUROPEAN UNION,

Having regard to the Treaty establishing the European Community, and in particular Articles 93 and 94 thereof,

Having regard to the proposal from the Commission,

Having regard to the opinion of the European Parliament (Opinion delivered on 15 January 2004 (not yet published in the Official Journal)),

Having regard to the opinion of the European Economic and Social Committee (OJ C 32, 5.2.2004, p 94),

Whereas:

(1) Council Directive 77/799/EEC of 19 December 1977 concerning mutual assistance by the competent authorities of the Member States in the field of direct taxation, certain excise duties and taxation of insurance premiums (OJ L 336, 27.12.1977, p 15. Directive as last amended by Directive 2003/93/EC (OJ L 264, 15.10.2003, p 23)) established the ground rules for administrative cooperation and the exchange of information between Member States in order to detect and prevent tax evasion and tax fraud and to enable Member States to carry out a correct tax assessment. It is essential to improve, expand and modernise those rules.

(2) When a Member State conducts enquiries in order to obtain the information necessary to respond to a request for assistance, that State should be regarded as acting on its own account; in that way, there will only be one set of rules applying to the information-gathering process and the investigation will not be undermined by delays.

(3) It is inappropriate, if the fight against tax fraud is to be effective, that a Member State which has received information from another Member State should subsequently have to request permission to disclose the information in public hearings or judgements.

(4) It should be made clear that a Member State is not under any obligation to carry out enquiries in order to obtain the information necessary to respond to a request for assistance where either its legislation or administrative practices do not permit its competent authority to conduct enquiries or to collect such information.

(5) It should be possible for the competent authority of a Member State to refuse information or assistance when the requesting Member State is not in a position to supply the same type of information, whether for reasons of fact or of law.

(6) In view of the legal requirement in certain Member States that a taxpayer be notified of decisions and instruments concerning his tax liability and of the ensuing difficulties for the tax authorities, including cases where the taxpayer has relocated to another Member State, it is desirable that, in such circumstances, the tax authorities should be able to call upon the assistance of the competent authorities of the Member State to which the taxpayer has relocated.

(7) Since the tax situation of one or more persons liable to tax established in several Member States often is of common or complementary interest, it should be made possible for simultaneous controls to be carried out to such persons by two or more Member States, by mutual agreement and on a voluntary basis, whenever such controls appear to be more effective than controls carried out by only one Member State.

(8) The Commission submitted its proposal for a Directive on the basis of Article 95 of the Treaty. The Council, taking the view that the proposal for a Directive related to the harmonisation of legislation in the field of both direct and indirect taxation and that the act should therefore be adopted on the basis of Articles 93 and 94 of the Treaty, consulted the European Parliament by letter dated 12 November 2003 informing it of the Council's intention of changing the legal basis.

(9) Directive 77/799/EEC should therefore be amended accordingly,

HAS ADOPTED THIS DIRECTIVE:

Article 1

Notes

Para (1)(*a*) substituted Directive 77/799/EEC of 19 December 1977 Art 1(5) wording under heading of "in Italy" with effect from 29 April 2004.

Para (1)(*b*) substituted Directive 77/799/EEC of 19 December 1977 Art 1(5) wording under heading of "in Sweden" with effect from 29 April 2004.

Para (2) inserted a paragraph to Directive 77/799/EEC of 19 December 1977 Art 2(2) with effect from 29 April 2004.

Para (3) substituted Directive 77/799/EEC of 19 December 1977 Art 7(1) with effect from 29 April 2004.

Para (4)(*a*) substituted Directive 77/799/EEC of 19 December 1977 Art 8(1) with effect from 29 April 2004.

Para (4)(*b*) substituted Directive 77/799/EEC of 19 December 1977 Art 8(3) with effect from 29 April 2004.

Para (5) inserted Directive 77/799/EEC of 19 December 1977 Arts 8a–8b with effect from 29 April 2004.

Article 2

Member States shall bring into force the laws, regulations and administrative provisions necessary to comply with this Directive before 1 January 2005. They shall forthwith communicate to the Commission the text of those provisions and a correlation table between those provisions and this Directive.

When Member States adopt these measures, they shall contain a reference to this Directive or shall be accompanied by such a reference on the occasion of their official publication. The methods of making such reference shall be laid down by Member States.

Article 3

This Directive shall enter into force on the day of its publication in the Official Journal of the European Union.

Article 4

This Directive is addressed to the Member States.

Done at Luxembourg, 21 April 2004.

COUNCIL DIRECTIVE

of 26 April 2004

04/66/EC

OJ L 168, 01/05/2004 p 35-67

adapting Directives 1999/45/EC, 2002/83/EC, 2003/37/EC and 2003/59/EC of the European Parliament and of the Council and Council Directives 77/388/EEC, 91/414/EEC, 96/26/EC, 2003/48/EC and 2003/49/EC, in the fields of free movement of goods, freedom to provide services, agriculture, transport policy and taxation, by reason of the accession of the Czech Republic, Estonia, Cyprus, Latvia, Lithuania, Hungary, Malta, Poland, Slovenia and Slovakia

THE COUNCIL OF THE EUROPEAN UNION,

Having regard to the Treaty establishing the European Community,

Having regard to the Treaty on the accession of the Czech Republic, the Republic of Estonia, the Republic of Cyprus, the Republic of Latvia, the Republic of Lithuania, the Republic of Hungary, the Republic of Malta, the Republic of Poland, the Republic of Slovenia and the Slovak Republic to the European Union (OJ L 236, 23.9.2003, p 17) (hereinafter referred to as the 'Treaty of Accession'), and in particular Article 2(3) thereof,

Having regard to the Act of Accession of the Czech Republic, the Republic of Estonia, the Republic of Cyprus, the Republic of Latvia, the Republic of Lithuania, the Republic of Hungary, the Republic of Malta, the Republic of Poland, the Republic of Slovenia and the Slovak Republic and the adjustments to the Treaties on which the European Union is founded (OJ L 236, 23.9.2003, p 33) (hereinafter referred to as the 'Act of Accession'), and in particular Article 57 thereof,

Having regard to the proposal from the Commission,

Whereas:

(1) For certain acts which remain valid beyond 1 May 2004 and require adaptation by reason of accession, the necessary adaptations were not provided for in the Act of Accession, or were provided for but need further adaptation. All these adaptations need to be adopted before accession so as to be applicable as from accession.

(2) Pursuant to Article 57(2) of the Act of Accession, such adaptations are to be adopted by the Council in all cases where the Council alone or jointly with the European Parliament adopted the original act.

(3) Directives 1999/45/EC (OJ L 200, 30.7.1999, p 1. Directive as last amended by Regulation (EC) No 1882/2003 (OJ L 284, 31.10.2003, p 1)), 2002/83/EC (OJ L 345, 19.12.2002, p 1), 2003/37/EC (OJ L 171, 9.7.2003, p 1) and 2003/59/EC (OJ L 226, 10.9.2003, p 4) of the European Parliament and of the Council and Council Directives 77/388/EEC (OJ L 145, 13.6.1977, p 1. Directive as last amended by Directive 2004/7/EC (OJ L 27, 30.1.2004, p 44)), 91/414/EEC (OJ L 230, 19.8.1991, p 1. Directive as last amended by Regulation (EC) No 806/2003 (OJ L 122, 16.5.2003, p 1)), 96/26/EC (OJ L

124, 23.5.1996, p 1. Directive as last amended by the Act of Accession), 2003/48/EC (OJ L 157, 26.6.2003, p 38) and 2003/49/EC (OJ L 157, 26.6.2003, p 49) should therefore be amended accordingly,

HAS ADOPTED THIS DIRECTIVE:

Article 1

Directives 1999/45/EC, 2002/83/EC, 2003/37/EC, 2003/59/EC, 77/388/EEC, 91/414/EEC, 96/26/EC, 2003/48/EC and 2003/49/EC are amended as set out in the Annex of this Directive.

Article 2

Member States shall bring into force the laws, regulations and administrative provisions necessary to comply with this Directive by the date of entry into force of the Treaty of Accession. As regards the provisions of this Directive adapting Directive 91/414/EC as amended, as well as Directives 2002/83/EC, 2003/37/EC and 2003/59/EC, the date of transposition shall be that laid down therein. Member States shall forthwith submit the text of the provisions transposing this Directive to the Commission, with a table setting out their correlation with the specific provisions of this Directive.

When Member States adopt those provisions, they shall contain a reference to this Directive or be accompanied by such a reference on the occasion of their official publication. The methods of making such reference shall be laid down by Member States.

Article 3

This Directive shall enter into force only subject to and on the date of the entry into force of the Treaty of Accession.

Article 4

This Directive is addressed to the Member States.

Done at Brussels, 26 April 2004 .

ANNEX

V. TAXATION

Notes

Para (1)(*a*) substituted Directive 77/388/EEC of 17 May 1977 Art 24 bis with effect from 1 May 2004.
Para (1)(*b*) substituted Directive 77/388/EEC of 17 May 1977 Art 28m with effect from 1 May 2004.
Para (1)(*c*) substituted Directive 77/388/EEC of 17 May 1977 Art 17(3)(*b*) (as set out in Art 28f) with effect from 1 May 2004.

COMMISSION DIRECTIVE

of 4 March 2004

04/79/EC

Official Journal L 168 , 01/05/2004 p 68–69

adapting Directive 2002/94/EC, in the field of taxation, by reason of the accession of the Czech Republic, Estonia, Cyprus, Latvia, Lithuania, Hungary, Malta, Poland, Slovenia and Slovakia

THE COMMISSION OF THE EUROPEAN COMMUNITIES,

Having regard to the Treaty of Accession of the Czech Republic, Estonia, Cyprus, Latvia, Lithuania, Hungary, Malta, Poland, Slovenia and Slovakia (OJ L 236, 23.9.2003, p 17), and in particular Article 2(3) thereof,

Having regard to the Act of Accession of the Czech Republic, Estonia, Cyprus, Latvia, Lithuania, Hungary, Malta, Poland, Slovenia and Slovakia (OJ L 236, 23.9.2003, p 33), and in particular Article 57(1) thereof,

Whereas:

(1) For certain acts which remain valid beyond 1 May 2004 , and require adaptation by reason of accession, the necessary adaptations were not provided for in the 2003 Act of Accession, or were provided for but need further adaptations. All these adaptations need to be adopted before accession so as to be applicable as from accession.

(2) Pursuant to Article 57(2) of the Act of Accession, such adaptations are to be adopted by the Commission in all cases where the Commission adopted the original act.

(3) Commission Directive 2002/94/EC (OJ L 337, 13.12.2002, p 41) should therefore be amended accordingly,

HAS ADOPTED THIS DIRECTIVE:

Article 1

Directive 2002/94/EC is amended as set out in the Annex.

Article 2

Member States shall bring into force the laws, regulations and administrative provisions necessary to comply with this Directive by the date of accession at the latest. They shall forthwith communicate to the Commission the text of those provisions and a correlation table between those provisions and this Directive.

When Member States adopt those provisions, they shall contain a reference to this Directive or be accompanied by such a reference on the occasion of their official publication. Member States shall determine how such reference is to be made.

Article 3

This Directive shall enter into force subject to, and as from the date of, the entry into force of the Treaty of Accession of the Czech Republic, Estonia, Cyprus, Latvia, Lithuania, Hungary, Malta, Poland, Slovenia and Slovakia.

Article 4

This Directive is addressed to the Member States.

Done at Brussels, 4 March 2004 .

ANNEX
TAXATION

Notes

Annex substituted Commission Directive 02/94/EC of 9 December Annex IV list with effect from 1 May 2004.

EUROPEAN UNION DECISIONS

COUNCIL DECISION

of 21 December 1992

92/617/EEC

(OJ L408, 31/12/1992 p 13–13)

*authorizing Ireland to apply particular measures in accordance with Article 22(12)(a)
and (b) of Directive 77/388/EEC*

THE COUNCIL OF THE EUROPEAN COMMUNITIES,

Having regard to the Treaty establishing the European Economic Community,

Having regard to the Sixth Council Directive, 77/388/EEC, of 17 May 1977 on the harmonization of the laws of the Member States relating to turnover taxes — Common system of value added tax: uniform basis of assessment (OJ No L 145, 13.6.1977, p 1. Directive as last amended by Directive 92/77/EEC (OJ No L 316, 31.10.1992, p 1)), and in particular Article 22 thereof Having regard to the proposal from the Commission,

Whereas, under Article 22(12) of Directive 77/388/EEC, the Council, acting unanimously on a proposal from the Commission, may authorize any Member State to introduce particular measures to simplify the statement obligations laid down in paragraph 6 (b) of Article 22; whereas Article 22(12) further stipulates that such simplification measures may not jeopardize the proper monitoring of intra-Community transactions, and may take the forms outlined in subparagraphs (a) and (b) of Article 22(12);

Whereas the Irish Government, by letter received by the Commission on 23 July 1992, has requested authorization for simplification measures which take the form laid down in subparagraphs (a) and (b) of Article 22(12);

Whereas the authorization will be temporary;

Whereas the particular measure will not affect the European Communities' own resources arising from value added tax,

HAS ADOPTED THIS DECISION:

Article 1

As provided for by Article 22(12) of Directive 77/388/EEC, Ireland is hereby authorized, with effect from 1 January 1993 until 31 December 1996 or until the end of the transitional arrangements in the unlikely event that this is later, to introduce particular measures in accordance with subparagraphs (*a*) and (*b*) of Article 22(12), to simplify the obligations laid down in paragraph 6(*b*) of Article 22 regarding recapitulative statements.

Article 2

This Decision is addressed to Ireland.

COUNCIL DECISION

of 24 July 1997

97/510/EC

(OJ L214, 06/08/1997 p 37–38)

authorizing Ireland to apply a measure derogating from Article 21 of the Sixth Directive (77/388/EEC) on the harmonization of the laws of the Member States relating to turn-over taxes

THE COUNCIL OF THE EUROPEAN UNION,

Having regard to the Treaty establishing the European Community,

Having regard to the Sixth Council Directive (77/388/EEC) of 17 May 1977 on the harmonization of the laws of the Member States relating to turnover taxes — Common system of value added tax: uniform basis of assessment (OJ No L 145, 13.6.1977, p 1. Directive as last amended by Directive 96/95/EC, OJ No L 338, 28.12.1996, p. 89), and in particular Article 27 thereof,

Having regard to the proposal from the Commission,

Whereas, under the terms of Article 27(1) of Directive 77/388/EEC, the Council, acting unanimously on a proposal from the Commission, may authorize any Member State to introduce special measures for derogation from the provisions of that Directive in order to simplify the procedure for charging the tax or to prevent certain types of tax evasion or avoidance;

Whereas, by registered letter to the Commission dated 5 February 1997, Ireland requested authorization to introduce a measure derogating from Article 21(1) of Directive 77/388/EEC;

Whereas, in accordance with Article 27(3) of Directive 77/388/EEC, the other Member States were informed on 4 March 1997 of the request made by Ireland;

Whereas Ireland operates a specific system of applying VAT to property based, on the one hand, on the option under Article 5(3) of Directive 77/388/EEC to treat the supply of certain interests (i.e. a lease of 10 years or more) in immovable property as a supply of goods and, on the other hand, on a derogation authorized under Article 27(5) to treat the granting of such an interest by a lessor as a disposal of the lessor's entire interest in the property;

Whereas Community law gives Member States a great deal of discretion in determining the VAT treatment to be applied to immovable goods, and its transposition has led to considerable variations in the national laws applied in this field;

Whereas avoidance schemes have been set up, based on the use of surrender, including by way of abandonment of a leasehold interest or assignment of a leasehold interest, which result in the avoidance of the VAT where the ultimate acquirer of the property is not entitled to a full deduction of VAT;

Whereas it is also necessary to extend the derogation to the surrender or assignment of a leasehold interest to a taxable person having full right of deduction, as the surrender or the assignment of a leasehold interest will often arise due to financial difficulties of the lessee;

Whereas the measure envisaged is a derogation from Article 21(1)(*a*) of Directive 77/388/EEC, whereby the person liable for the tax is the taxable person who carries out the taxable transaction;

Whereas the derogation provides that, where a surrender or assignment of a lease-hold interest is a taxable supply of goods, the person acquiring the interest is liable for the payment of the tax if that person is a taxable person or a non-taxable legal person;

Whereas this derogation should ensure a better functioning of the current VAT regime applied by Ireland on immovable goods;

Whereas, given the limited scope of the derogation, the special measure is proportionate to the aim pursued;

Whereas there exists a serious risk that use of the said VAT avoidance scheme will increase in the period between the request for a derogation and the authorization thereof; whereas at the latest since the publication on 26 March 1997 of the draft legislation which is the subject of the present request for a derogation, suppliers, lessors and lessees of property have no longer had a legitimate expectation of the continuation of the Irish legislation in force before that date; whereas it is therefore appropriate to authorize the derogation to take effect from 26 March 1997;

Whereas the Commission adopted on 10 July 1996 a work programme based on a step-by-step approach for progressing towards a new common system of VAT;

Whereas the tax treatment of immovable goods is an important issue to be reviewed in this programme;

Whereas the last package of proposals is to be put forward by mid-1999 and, in order to permit an evaluation of the coherence of the derogation with the global approach of the new common VAT system, the authorization is granted until 31 December 1999;

Whereas the derogation does not have a negative impact on the own resources of the European Communities accruing from VAT,

HAS ADOPTED THIS DECISION:

Article 1

By way of derogation from Article 21(1)(*a*) of Directive 77/388/EEC, Ireland is hereby authorized, from 26 March 1997 until [31 December 2007][1], to designate the person to whom the supply is made as the person liable to pay the tax where the two following conditions are met:

— a surrender or assignment of a leasehold interest is treated as a supply of goods made by a lessee,

— the person acquiring the leasehold interest is a taxable person or a non-taxable legal person.

Amendments

[1] Substituted by Council Decision 2003/857/EC of 25 November 2003 Art 1; previously "31 December 2003".

Article 2

This Decision is addressed to Ireland.

COUNCIL DECISION

of 28 February 2000

00/185/EC

OJ L 059 , 04/03/2000 p 10–11

authorising Member States to apply a reduced rate of VAT to certain labour-intensive services in accordance with the procedure provided for in Article 28(6) of Directive 77/388/EEC

THE COUNCIL OF THE EUROPEAN UNION,

Having regard to the Treaty establishing the European Community,

Having regard to Sixth Council Directive 77/388/EEC of 17 May 1977 on the harmonisation of the laws of the Member States relating to turnover taxes — common system of value added tax: uniform basis of assessment (OJ L 145, 13.6.1977, p 1. Directive as last amended by Directive 1999/85/EEC (OJ L 277, 28.10.1999, p 34)), and in particular Article 28(6) thereof,

Having regard to the proposal from the Commission,

Whereas:

(1) Under Article 28(6) of Directive 77/388/EEC, the Council, acting unanimously on a proposal from the Commission, may authorise any Member State that has submitted an application in accordance with the procedure and conditions provided for in that Article, to apply a reduced rate of VAT to certain labour-intensive services.

(2) The services concerned must meet the conditions provided for in the Directive and be included in the list in Annex K to the Directive.

(3) This is an experiment limited to a maximum period of three years running from 1 January 2000 to 31 December 2002.

(4) However, the introduction of such a targeted reduction in the VAT rate entails some risk to the proper operation of the internal market and tax neutrality; provision should therefore be made for an authorisation period for a full and clearly defined three-year period, for the measure to be on an optional basis for Member States, and for its scope to be made subject to strict conditions so that it remains verifiable and limited.

(5) In view of the experimental nature of the measure, a detailed assessment of its impact in terms of job creation and efficiency should be carried out by the Member States which implement it and by the Commission.

(6) The Member States that have submitted an application have complied with the procedure and conditions set out in Directive 77/388/EEC.

(7) Three Member States, France, Luxembourg and the Netherlands have applied for authorisation to apply a reduced rated of VAT exceptionally to a third category of the services listed in Annex K; in each case the reduction in rate in the third of the sectors selected can have only an insignificant economic impact.

(8) The United Kingdom has applied for authorisation to apply a reduced rate of VAT to dwelling-related services only in the Isle of Man; in the light of the specific territorial rules governing the status of the Isle of Man, including Article 299(6)(c) of the Treaty, the Treaty on the accession of the United Kingdom and Article 3(4) of Directive 77/388/ EEC, and in the light of the fact that the rules on the location of such services will ensure that they are taxed where the dwelling is located, applying a reduced rate of VAT carries no risk of distortion of competition; however, restricting the reduced rate to the Isle of Man is something which can be authorised only as an exceptional measure. In relation to other territories of Member States where the Treaty and Directive 77/388/ EEC are fully applicable, such a step could not be taken without jeopardising the principle of applying uniform rates in a single Member State.

(9) The other Member States have been informed about the applications for authorisation.

(10) This Decision will have no impact on the Communities' own resources derived from VAT,

HAS ADOPTED THIS DECISION:

Article 1

In accordance with Article 28(6) of Directive 77/388/EEC, the following Member States are hereby authorised to apply the reduced rates provided for in the third subparagraph of Article 12(3)(a) for a maximum of three years running from 1 January 2000 to 31 December 2002 to the services for which they have submitted applications in accordance with the required procedure, and which are listed under their names below:

1 the Kingdom of Belgium for the sectors listed at points 1 and 2 of Annex K to Directive 77/388/EEC:

— small services for repairing:

    (*a*)   bicycles;

    (*b*)   shoes and leather goods;

    (*c*)   clothing and household linen (including mending and alteration),

— renovation and repairing of private dwellings more than five years old, excluding materials which form a significant part of the value of the supply;

2 the Hellenic Republic for the sectors listed at point 1, last indent, and point 4 of Annex K to Directive 77/388/EEC:

— repairing of clothing and household linen (including mending and alteration),

— domestic care services;

3 the Kingdom of Spain for the sectors listed at points 2 and 5 of Annex K to Directive 77/388/EEC:

— bricklaying for the repair of private dwellings excluding materials which form a significant part of the value of the supply,

— hairdressing;

4 the French Republic for the sectors listed at points 2, 3 and 4 of Annex K to Directive 77/388/EEC:

— renovation and repairing of private dwellings completed more than two years ago, excluding materials which form a significant part of the value of the supply,
— domestic care services,
— window cleaning and cleaning in private households;

5 the Italian Republic for the sectors listed at points 2 and 4 of Annex K to Directive 77/388/EEC:

— renovation and repairing of private dwellings excluding materials which form a significant part of the value of the supply,
— domestic care services;

6 the Grand Duchy of Luxembourg for the sectors listed at points 1, 3 and 5 of Annex K to Directive 77/388/EEC:

— small services for repairing:

   (*a*) bicycles;
   (*b*) shoes and leather goods;
   (*c*) clothing and household linen (including mending and alteration),

— hairdressing,
— window cleaning and cleaning in private households;

7 the Kingdom of the Netherlands for the sectors listed at points 1, 2 and 5 of Annex K to Directive 77/388/EEC:

— small services for repairing:

   (*a*) bicycles;
   (*b*) shoes and leather goods;
   (*c*) clothing and household linen (including mending and alteration),

— hairdressing,
— painting and plastering services for the renovation and repairing of private dwellings more than 15 years old, excluding materials which form a significant part of the value of the supply;

8 the Portuguese Republic for the sectors listed at points 2 and 4 of Annex K to Directive 77/388/EEC:

— renovation and repairing of private dwellings, excluding materials which form a significant part of the value of the supply,
— domestic care services;

9 the United Kingdom for one sector, referred to in point 2 of Annex K to Directive 77/388/EEC, but for the Isle of Man only:

— renovation and repairing of private dwellings, excluding materials which form a significant part of the value of the supply.

Article 2

Before 1 October 2002 each of the Member States listed in Article 1 shall draw up a detailed report containing an overall assessment of the measure's effectiveness in terms of job creation and efficiency and forward it to the Commission.

Article 3

This Decision shall take effect on the day of its publication in the Official Journal of the European Communities.

It shall apply from 1 January 2000 to 31 December 2002.

Article 4

This Decision is addressed to the Member States referred to in Article 1.

Done at Brussels, 28 February 2000.

COUNCIL DECISION

of 25 November 2003

03/857/EC

OJ L 324, 11/12/2003 p 36–36

amending Decision 97/510/EC authorising Ireland to apply a measure derogating from Article 21 of the Sixth Directive (77/388/EEC) on the harmonisation of the laws of the Member States relating to turnover taxes

THE COUNCIL OF THE EUROPEAN UNION,

Having regard to the Treaty establishing the European Community,

Having regard to the Sixth Council Directive (77/388/EEC) of 17 May 1977 on the harmonisation of the laws of the Member States relating to turnover taxes — Common system of value added tax: uniform basis of assessment (OJ L 145, 13.6.1977, p 1. Directive as last amended by Directive 2003/92/EC (OJ L 260, 11.10.2003, p 8)), and in particular Article 27(1) thereof,

Having regard to the proposal from the Commission,

Whereas:

(1) By letter received by the Secretariat-General of the Commission on 4 July 2003, Ireland requested the extension of Decision 97/510/EC (OJ L 214, 6.8.1997, p 37. Decision amended by Decision 2000/435/EC (OJ L 172, 12.7.2000, p 24)) authorising it to apply a measure derogating from Article 21 of the Sixth Directive which enables it to combat tax evasion and tax fraud in the real-estate sector until 31 December 2007.

(2) The matters of law and of fact which justified the application of the special measures in question have not changed and still pertain

(3) The authorisation should therefore be extended until 31 December 2007.

(4) The derogation in question has no impact on the European Communities' own resources from valued added tax,

HAS ADOPTED THIS DECISION:

Article 1

Notes

Article 1 substituted "31 December 2007" for "31 December 2003" in Decision 97/510/EC, Art 1.

Article 2

This Decision is addressed to Ireland.

Done at Brussels, 25 November 2003.

EUROPEAN UNION REGULATIONS

Goods imported into Ireland are valued for VAT purposes in the same manner as for customs purposes (VATA 1972, s 15(3) and Sixth Directive Art 11B(2)). The valuation rules are contained in the Community Customs Code which effectively consolidated the European Union customs regulations into two regulations: Council Regulation 92/2913/EEC of 12 October 1992 established the Community Customs Code, and Commission Regulation 92/2454/EEC of 2 July 1993 provided detailed rules for the implementation of the Code.

With the introduction of the single market with effect from 1 January 1993, taxable persons are obliged to maintain more records and make additional statistical returns to the Revenue Commissioners. The relevant European Union regulations are reproduced in this section.

page

COUNCIL REGULATION

of 7 November 1991

91/3330/EEC

On the statistics relating to the trading of goods between Member States
(OJ L316, 16.11.91, P 1)

Amendment

Regulation 91/3330/EEC repealed by Parliament and Council Regulation 04/638/EC art 15 with effect from 1 January 2005, references to the repealed regulation should be construed as references to Parliament and Council Regulation 04/638/EC.

COUNCIL REGULATION

of 27 January 1992

92/218/EEC

On administrative cooperation in the field of indirect taxation (VAT)

(OJ L24, 1.2.1992, p 1)

THE COUNCIL OF THE EUROPEAN COMMUNITIES,

Having regard to the Treaty establishing the European Economic Community, and in particular Article 99 thereof,

Having regard to the proposal from the Commission,

Having regard to the opinion of the European Parliament,

Having regard to the opinion of the Economic and Social Committee,

Whereas the establishment of the internal market in accordance with Article 8a of the Treaty requires the creation of an area without internal frontiers in which the free movement of goods, persons, services and capital is ensured; whereas the internal market requires changes in the legislation on value added tax as provided in Article 99 of the Treaty;

Whereas in order to avoid tax revenue losses for Member States the tax harmonisation measures taken to complete the internal market and for the transitional period must include the establishment of a common system for the exchange of information on intra-Community transactions between the competent authorities of the Member States;

Whereas in order to permit the abolition of fiscal controls at internal frontiers in accordance with the aims set out in Article 8a of the Treaty the transitional value added tax system introduced by Directive 91/680/EEC, amending Directive 77/388/EEC, must be effectively established without the risk of fraud which might cause distortions of competition;

Whereas this Regulation provides for a common system for the exchange of information on intra-Community transactions, supplementing Directive 77/799/EEC, as last amended by Directive 79/1070/EEC, and intended to serve tax purposes;

Whereas the Member States should provide the Commission with any value added tax information which may be of interest at Community level;

Whereas the establishment of a common system of administrative cooperation may affect individuals' legal positions, in particular because of the exchange of information concerning their tax positions;

Whereas care must be taken to ensure that the provisions concerning the control of indirect taxes are in balance with administrations' needs for effective control and administrative burdens imposed on taxable persons;

Whereas the operation of such a system requires the establishment of a standing committee on administrative cooperation;

Whereas the Member States and the Commission must establish an effective system for the electronic storage and transmission of certain data for value added tax control purposes;

Whereas care must be taken to ensure that information provided in the course of such collaboration is not disclosed to unauthorised persons, so that the basic rights of citizens and undertakings are safeguarded; whereas it is therefore necessary that an authority receiving such information should not, without the authorisation of the authority supplying it, use it for purposes other than taxation or to facilitate legal proceedings for failure to comply with the tax laws of the Member States concerned; whereas the receiving authority must also accord such information the same degree of confidentiality as it enjoyed in the Member State which provided it, if the latter so requires;

Whereas the Member States and the Commission must collaborate on the continuous analysis of cooperation procedures and the pooling of the experience gained in the fields in question, with the aims of improving those procedures and drawing up appropriate Community rules,

HAS ADOPTED THIS REGULATION:

Article 1

This Regulation lays down the ways in which the administrative authorities in the Member States responsible for the application of laws on value added tax shall cooperate with each other and with the Commission to ensure compliance with those laws.

[To that end it lays down procedures for the exchange by electronic means of value added tax information on intra-Community transactions as well as on services supplied electronically in accordance with the special scheme provided for by Article 26c of Directive 77/388/EEC, and also for any subsequent exchange of information and, as far as services covered by that special scheme are concerned, for the transfer of money between Member States' competent authorities.][1]

Amendments

1   Substituted by Commission Regulation 2002/792/EC, Art 1(1). See OJ L128, 15.5.02, p 1.

Article 2

1. For the purposes of this Regulation:

— **"competent authority"** shall mean the authority appointed to act as correspondent as defined in paragraph 2,

— **"applicant authority"** shall mean the competent authority of a Member State which makes a request for assistance,

— **"requested authority"** shall mean the competent authority of a Member State to which a request for assistance is made,

— **"person"** shall mean:

— a natural person,

— a legal person or,

— where the possibility is provided for under the legislation in force, an association of persons recognised as having the capacity to perform legal acts but lacking the legal status of a legal person,

— **"to grant access"** shall mean authorising access to the relevant electronic date base and providing data by electronic means,

— **"value added tax identification number"** shall mean the number provided for in with Article 22(1)(*c*), (*d*) and (*e*) of Directive 77/388/EEC,

— **"intra-Community transactions"** shall mean the intra-Community supply of goods and the intra-Community supply of services as defined in this paragraph,

— **"intra-Community supply of goods"** shall mean any supply of goods which must be declared in the recapitulative statement provided for in Article 22(6)(*b*) of Directive 77/388/EEC,

[— **"intra-Community supply of services"** shall mean any supply of services covered by Article 28b (C), (D), (E) or (F) of Directive 77/388/EEC,][1]

— **"intra-Community acquisition of goods"** shall mean acquisition of the right to dispose as owner of movable tangible property as defined in Article 28a(3) of Directive 77/388/EEC.

2. Each Member State shall notify the other Member States and the Commission of the competent authorities appointed to act as correspondents for the purpose of applying this Regulation. In addition, each member State shall nominate a central office with principal responsibility for liaison with other Member States in the field of administrative cooperation.

3. The Commission shall publish a list of competent authorities in the *Official Journal of the European Communities* and, where necessary, update it.

Amendments

1 Substituted by Commission Regulation 2002/792/EC, Art 1(2). See OJ L128, 15.5.02, p 1.

TITLE I
EXCHANGE OF INFORMATION — GENERAL PROVISIONS

Article 3

1. The obligation to give assistance provided for in this Regulation shall not cover the provision of information or documents obtained by the administrative authorities referred to in Article 1 at the request of a judicial authority.

However, in cases of applications for assistance, such information and documents shall be provided whenever the judicial authority, to which reference must be made, gives its consent.

2. This Regulation shall not restrict the application of provisions of other agreements or instruments relating to cooperation on tax matters.

3. This Regulation shall not affect the application in the Member States of the rules on mutual assistance in criminal matters.

TITLE II
EXCHANGE OF INFORMATION RELATING TO VALUE ADDED TAX IN CONNECTION WITH INTRA-COMMUNITY TRANSACTIONS

Article 4

1. The competent authority of each Member State shall maintain an electronic data base in which it shall store and process the information that it collects in accordance with Article 22(6)(*b*) of Directive 77/388/EEC. To allow the use of this information in the procedures provided for in this Regulation the information shall be stored for at least five years after the end of the calendar year in which access to the information was to be granted. Member States shall ensure that their data bases are kept up to date, complete and accurate. Under the procedure laid down in Article 10 criteria shall be defined to determine what amendments that are not significant, material or useful need not be made.

2. From the data collected in accordance with paragraph 1, the competent authority of a Member State shall obtain directly and without delay from each Member State, or may have direct access to, the following information:

— the value added tax identification numbers issued by the Member State receiving the information, and

— the total value of all intra-Community supplies of goods made to the persons to whom those numbers were issued by all operators identified for the purposes of value added tax in the Member State; the value shall be expressed in the currency of the Member State providing the information and shall relate to calendar quarters.

3. From the data collected in accordance with paragraph 1 and solely in order to combat tax fraud, the competent authority of a Member State shall, wherever it considers it necessary for the control of intra-Community acquisitions of goods, obtain directly and without delay, or have direct access to, the following information:

— the value added tax identification numbers of all persons who have made the supplies referred to in the second indent of paragraph 2, and

— the total value of such supplies from each such person to each person to whom one of the value added tax identification numbers referred to in the first indent of paragraph 2 has been issued; the values shall be expressed in the currency of the Member State providing the information; the value shall be expressed in the currency of the Member State providing the information and shall relate to calendar quarters.

4. Where the competent authority of a Member State is obliged to grant access to information under this Article it shall, as regards the information referred to in paragraphs 2 and 3, do so within three months of the end of the calendar quarter to which the information relates. By way of derogation from this rule, where information is added to a data base in the circumstances provided for in paragraph 1, access to such additions shall be granted as quickly as possible and in any event no more than three months after the end of the quarter in which the additional information was collected; the conditions under which access to the corrected information may be granted shall be defined by means of the procedure laid down in Article 10.

5. Where, for purposes of the application of this Article, the competent authorities of the Member States keep information in electronic data bases and exchange such information by electronic means they shall take all measures necessary to ensure compliance with Article 9.

Article 5

1. Where the information provided under Article 4 is insufficient, the competent authority of a Member State may at any time and in specific cases request further information. The requested authority shall provide the information as quickly as possible and in any event no more than three months after receipt of the request.

2. In the circumstances described in paragraph 1 the requested authority shall at least provide the applicant authority with invoice numbers, dates and values in relation to individual transactions between persons in the Member States concerned.

Article 6

1. The competent authority of each Member State shall maintain an electronic data base which shall contain a register of persons to whom value added tax identification numbers have been issued in that Member State.

2. At any time the competent authority of a Member State may obtain directly or have communicated to it, from the data collected in accordance with Article 4(1), confirmation of the validity of the value added tax identification number under which a person effected or received an intra-Community supply of goods or of services. On specific request the requested authority shall also communicate the date of issue and, where appropriate, the date of cessation of the validity of the value added tax identification number.

3. Where it is so requested a competent authority shall also provide without delay the name and address of the person to whom a number has been issued, provided that such information is not stored by the applicant authority with a view to its possible use at some future time.

[4. The competent authority of each Member State shall ensure that persons involved in the intra-Community supply of goods or of services and persons supplying services referred to in the last indent of Article 9(2)*e* of Directive 77/388/EEC are allowed to obtain confirmation of the validity of the value added tax identification number of any specified person. In accordance with the procedure referred to in Article 10, Member States shall, in particular, provide such confirmation by electronic means.]¹

5. Where, for purposes of the application of this Article, the competent authorities of the Member States keep information in electronic data bases and exchange such information by electronic means they shall take all measures necessary to ensure compliance with Article 9.

Amendments

1 Para 4 substituted by Commission Regulation 2002/792/EC, Art 1(3). See OJ L128, 15.5.02, p 1.

TITLE III
CONDITIONS GOVERNING THE EXCHANGE OF INFORMATION

Article 7

1. A requested authority in one Member State shall provide an applicant authority in another Member State with the information referred to in Article 5(2) provided that:

— the number and the nature of the requests for information made by the applicant authority within a specific period of time do no impose a disproportionate administrative burden on that requested authority,

— that applicant authority exhausts the usual sources of information which it can use in the circumstances to obtain the information requested, without running the risk of jeopardising the achievement of the desired end,

— that applicant authority requests assistance only if it would be able to provide similar assistance to the applicant authority of another Member State.

In accordance with the procedure laid down in Article 10 and taking into account experience of the new administrative cooperation system during its first year of operation, the Commission shall submit general criteria for the definition of the scope of these commitments before July 1994.

2. If an applicant authority is unable to comply with the general provisions of paragraph 1 it shall notify the requested authority accordingly without delay, stating its reasons. If a requested authority considers that the general provisions of paragraph 1 are not complied with and that it is therefore not obliged to provide the information, it shall notify the applicant authority accordingly without delay, stating its reasons. The applicant authority and the requested authority shall attempt to reach agreement. If they fail to reach agreement within one month of notification either authority may request that the matter be examined under Article 11.

3. This Article shall be without prejudice to the application of Directive 77/799/EEC as regards the exchange of information referred to in Article 5(1).

Article 8

In cases of exchanges of information as defined in Article 5, where the national legislation in force in a Member State provides for notification of the person concerned of the exchange of information, those provisions may continue to apply except where their application would prejudice the investigation of tax evasion in another Member State. In the latter event, at the express request of the applicant authority, the requested authority shall refrain from such notification.

Article 9

1. Any information communicated in whatever form pursuant to this Regulation shall be of a confidential nature. It shall be covered by the obligation of professional secrecy and shall enjoy the protection extended to similar information under both the national law of the Member State which received it and the corresponding provisions applicable to Community authorities.

In any case, such information:

— may be made available only to the persons directly concerned with the basis of assessment, collection or administrative control of taxes for the purposes of the assessment of taxes, or to persons employed by Community institutions whose duties require that they have access to it,

— may in addition be used in connection with judicial or administrative proceedings that may involve sanctions, initiated as a result of infringements of tax law.

2. By way of derogation from paragraph 1, the competent authority of the Member State providing the information shall permit its use for other purposes in the Member State of the applicant authority, if, under the legislation of the Member State of the requested authority, the information could be used in the Member State of the requested authority for similar purposes.

3. Where the applicant authority considers that information which it has received from the requested authority is likely to be useful to the competent authority of a third Member State, it may transmit it to the latter with the agreement of the requested authority.

[TITLE IIIA
PROVISIONS CONCERNING THE SPECIAL SCHEME IN ARTICLE 26C
OF DIRECTIVE 77/388/EEC][1]

Amendments

1   Inserted by Commission Regulation 2002/792/EC, Art 1(4). See OJ L128, 15.5.02, p 1.

Article 9a

[The following provisions shall apply concerning the special scheme provided for in Article 26c in Directive 77/388/EEC. The definitions contained in point A of that Article shall also apply for the purpose of this Title.][1]

Amendments

1   Inserted by Commission Regulation 2002/792/EC, Art 1(4). See OJ L128, 15.5.02, p 1.

Article 9b

[**1.** The information from the non-established taxable person to the Member State of identification when his activities commences set out in the second subparagraph of Article 26c(B)(2) of Directive 77/388/EEC is to be submitted in an electronic manner.

The technical details, including a common electronic message, shall be determined in accordance with the procedure provided for in Article 10.

2. The Member State of identification shall transmit this information by electronic means to the competent authorities of the other Member States within 10 days from the end of the month during which the information was received from the non-established taxable person. In the same manner, the competent authorities of the other Member States shall be informed of the allocated identification number. The technical details, including a common electronic message, by which this information is to be transmitted shall be determined in accordance with the procedure provided for in Article 10.

3. The Member State of identification shall without delay inform by electronic means the competent authorities of the other Members States if a non-established taxable person is excluded from the identification register.]¹

Amendments

1   Inserted by Commission Regulation 2002/792/EC, Art 1(4). See OJ L128, 15.5.02, p 1.

Article 9c

[**1.** The return with the details set out in the second subparagraph of Article 26c(B)(5) of Directive 77/388/EEC is to be submitted in an electronic manner. The technical details, including a common electronic message, shall be determined in accordance with the procedure provided for in Article 10.

2. The Member State of identification shall transmit this information by electronic means to the competent authority of the Member State concerned at the latest 10 days after the end of the month that the return was received. Member States which have required the tax return to be made in a national currency other than euro shall convert the amounts into euro using the exchange rate valid for the last date of the reporting period. The exchange shall be done following the exchange rates published by the European Central Bank for that day, or, if there is no publication on that day, on the next day of publication. The technical details by which this information is to be transmitted shall be determined in accordance with the procedure provided for in Article 10.

3. The Member State of identification shall transmit by electronic means to the Member State of consumption the information needed to link each payment with a relevant quarterly tax return.]¹

Amendments

1   Inserted by Commission Regulation 2002/792/EC, Art 1(4). See OJ L128, 15.5.02, p 1.

Article 9d

[The provisions in Article 4(1) shall apply also to information collected by the Member State of identification in accordance with Article 26c(B)(2) and (5) of Directive 77/388/EEC.]¹

Amendments

1   Inserted by Commission Regulation 2002/792/EC, Art 1(4). See OJ L128, 15.5.02, p 1.

Article 9e

[The Member State of identification shall ensure that the amount the non-established taxable person has paid is transferred to the bank account denominated in euro, which has been designated by the Member State of consumption to which the payment is due. Member States which required the payments in a national currency other than euro shall convert the amounts into euro using the exchange rate valid for the last date of the reporting period. The exchange shall be done following the exchange rates published by the European Central Bank for that day, or, if there is no publication on that day, on the next day of publication. The transfer shall take place at the latest 10 days after the end of the month that the payment was received.

If the non-established taxable person does not pay the total tax due, the Member State of identification shall ensure that the payment is transferred to the Member States of consumption in proportion to the tax due in each Member State. The Member State of identification shall inform by electronic means the competent authorities of the Member States of consumption thereof.][1]

Amendments

1   Inserted by Commission Regulation 2002/792/EC, Art 1(4). See OJ L128, 15.5.02, p 1.

Article 9f

[**1.** Member States shall notify by electronic means the competent authorities of the other Member States of the relevant bank account numbers for receiving payments according to Article 9e.

2. Member States shall without delay notify by electronic means the competent authorities of the other Member States and the Commission of changes in the standard tax rate.][1]

Amendments

1   Inserted by Commission Regulation 2002/792/EC, Art 1(4). See OJ L128, 15.5.02, p 1.

TITLE IV
CONSULTATION AND COORDINATION PROCEDURES

Article 10

1. The Commission shall be assisted by a Standing Committee on Administrative Cooperation in the field of Indirect Taxation, hereinafter referred to as "the Committee". It shall consist of representatives of the Member States and have a representative of the Commission as chairman.

2. The measures required for the application of Articles 4 and 7(1) shall be adopted in accordance with the procedure laid down in paragraphs 3 and 4 of this Article.

3. The Commission representative shall submit to the Committee a draft of the measures to be adopted. The Committee shall deliver its opinion on that draft within a time limit which the chairman may lay down according to the urgency of the matter. The

Committee's opinion shall be delivered by a majority, the Member States' votes being weighted in accordance with Article 148(2) of the Treaty. The chairman shall not vote.

4. The Commission shall adopt the measures contemplated where they are in accordance with the Committee's opinion.

Where those measures are not in accordance with the Committee's opinion of if the Committee does not deliver an opinion, the Commission shall without delay submit to the Council a proposal on the measures to be adopted. The Council shall act by a qualified majority.

If within three months of the proposal's being submitted to it the Council has not acted, the proposed measures shall be adopted by the Commission, unless the Council has decided against those measures by a simple majority.

Article 11

The Member States and the Commission shall examine and evaluate the operation of the arrangements for administrative cooperation provided for in this Regulation and the Commission shall pool the Member States' experience, in particular that concerning new means of tax avoidance and evasion, with the aim of improving the operation of those arrangements. To that end the Member States shall also communicate to the Commission any value added tax information on intra-Community transactions that may be of interest at Community level.

Article 12

1. On matters of bilateral interest, the competent authorities of the Member States may communicate directly with each other. The competent authorities of the Member States may by mutual agreement permit authorities designated by them to communicate directly with each other in specified cases or categories of cases.

2. For the purpose of applying this Regulation, Member States shall take all necessary steps to:

(*a*) ensure efficient internal coordination between the competent authorities referred to in Article 1;

(*b*) establish direct cooperation between the authorities specially empowered for the purposes of such coordination;

(*c*) make suitable arrangements to ensure the smooth operation of the arrangements for the exchange of information provided for in this Regulation.

3. The Commission shall communicate to the competent authority of each Member State, as quickly as possible, any information which it receives and which it is able to supply.

TITLE V
FINAL PROVISIONS

Article 13

[1. The Commission and the Member States shall ensure that such existing or new communication and information exchange systems which are necessary to provide for the exchanges of information described in Articles 9*b* and 9*c* are operational by the date specified in Article 3(1) of Directive 2002/38/EC. The Commission will be responsible for whatever development of the common communication network/common system interface (CCN/CSI) is necessary to permit the exchange of this information between Member States. Member States will be responsible for whatever development of their systems is necessary to permit this information to be exchanged using the CCN/CSI.]¹

[2]². Member States shall waive all claims for the reimbursement of expenses incurred in applying this Regulation except, as appropriate, in respect of fees paid to experts.

Amendments

1   Inserted by Commission Regulation 2002/792/EC, Art 1(5). See OJ L128, 15.5.02, p 1.
2   Renumbered by Commission Regulation 2002/792/EC, Art 1(5). See OJ L128, 15.5.02, p 1.

Article 14

1. Every two years after the date of entry into force of this Regulation, the Commission shall report to the European Parliament and the Council on the conditions of application of this Regulation on the basis, in particular, of the continuous monitoring procedures provided for in Article 11.

2. Member States shall communicate to the Commission the texts of any provisions of national law which they adopt in the field governed by this Regulation.

Article 15

This Regulation shall enter force on the third day following it publication in the *Official Journal of the European Communities*.

No exchange of information under this Regulation shall take place before 1 January 1993.

Done at Brussels, 27 January 1992.

COMMISSION REGULATION

of 31 July 1992

92/2256/EEC

On statistical thresholds for the statistics on trade between Member States

(OJ L219, 4.8.1992, p 40)

THE COMMISSION OF THE EUROPEAN COMMUNITIES,

Having regard to the Treaty establishing the European Economic Community,

Having regard to Council Regulations (EEC) No 3330/91 of 7 November 1991 on the statistics relating to the trading of goods between Member States, and in particular Article 30 thereof,

Whereas the burden on intra-Community operators must be lightened as much as possible, either by exempting them from statistical obligations or by simplifying procedures;

Whereas this lightening of the burden must be limited only by the demands of statistics of a satisfactory quality, which must consequently be defined by common accord;

Whereas, once this quality has been defined, all the Member States must have their necessary instruments to ensure it, while taking account of their own economic and commercial structure; where it is for the Member States themselves to strike the most appropriate balance between lightening of the statistical burden and quality on the basis of the information available to them;

Whereas the information to be analysed by the Member States in order to fix their thresholds differs, particularly as regards coverage, depending on whether they are to be introduced in 1993 or to be adapted as from 1994; whereas a distinction should therefore be drawn between the rules to be followed on one single occasion, as in the first case, and those to be followed each year, as in the second case;

Whereas the obligations of the persons responsible for providing information should be defined in such a way as to take maximum account of their interests, particularly if their intra-Community transactions are expanding;

Whereas the measures provided for in this Regulation are in accordance with the opinion of the Committee on Statistics relating to the trading of goods between Member States.

HAS ADOPTED THIS REGULATION:

Article 1

The Member States shall set annually, in national currency, the assimilation and simplification thresholds referred to in Article 28 of Regulation (EEC) No 3330/91, hereinafter **"the Basic Regulation"**. They shall ensure when setting these thresholds that, first, they meet the quality requirements laid down in this Regulation and, secondly, they exploit to the full the ensuing opportunities to relieve the burden on intra-Community operators.

Article 2

For the purposes of this Regulation:

(*a*) **"error"** means the discrepancy between the results obtained with and without application of the thresholds referred to in Article 1; when a correction procedure is applied to the results obtained following application of the thresholds, the error is calculated in relation to the corrected results;

(*b*) **"total value"** means:

— for the introduction of the thresholds in 1993, the value either of the outgoing goods or of the incoming goods, accounted for by intra-Community operators over a period of twelve months,

— for the adjustment of the thresholds from 1994, the value of either of the outgoing goods or of the incoming goods accounted for by intra-Community operators over a twelve-month period, other than those who are exempt under Article 5 of the Basic Regulation;

(*c*) **"coverage"** means in relation to a given total value, the proportionate value of the outgoing goods or of the incoming goods, accounted for by the intra-Community operators who lie above the assimilation threshold.

Article 3

1. For the introduction of the assimilation thresholds in 1993, the Member States shall meet the following quality requirements:

(*a*) Results by goods category

Each Member State shall ensure that the error in annual values does not exceed 5% for 90% of the eight-digit sub-headings of the combined Nomenclature which represent 0,005% or more of the total value of its outgoing or incoming goods.

However, each Member State may raise this quality requirement up to the point that the error in annual values does not exceed 5% for 90% of the eight- digit sub-headings of the Combined Nomenclature which represent 0,001% or more of the total value of its outgoing or incoming goods.

(*b*) Results by partner country

Each Member State shall ensure that the error in the annual values of its results by partner country, excluding countries which represent less than 3% of the total value of its outgoing or incoming goods, does not exceed 1%.

(*c*) Time series

Each Member State shall ensure that:

— for 90% of the eight-digit sub-headings of the combined nomenclature which represent the percentage of the total value of its outgoing or incoming goods laid down in point (*a*), and

— for 90% of its results by partner country,

The fluctuation over time of the error in annual values will not exceed the limits (L) laid down in the Annex.

If in any Member State applying the requirement leads to an increase in the number of parties responsible for providing information who are required to submit the periodic declaration laid down in Article 13 of the Basis Regulation that is excessive in proportion to the number involved under the more stringent of the other two requirements, the Member State concerned may take steps to reduce the imbalance accordingly. It shall inform the Commission of the action taken.

2. When a Member State's share of the total value of outgoing or incoming goods in the Community is less than 3%, that Member State may depart from the quality requirements laid down in the first subparagraph of paragraph 1(*a*) and the first indent of the first subparagraph of paragraph 1(*c*). In such cases, the 90% and 0,005% shares shall be replaced by 70% and 0,01% respectively.

3. To meet the quality requirements set out in paragraphs 1 and 2, the Member States shall base the calculation of their thresholds on the results of trade with the other Member States for twelve-month periods prior to the introduction of the thresholds.

For Member States unable to make this calculation because figures are incomplete, the assimilation thresholds shall be fixed at a level not lower than the lowest, nor higher than the highest, thresholds set by the other Member States. However, this provision shall not be binding for Member States which are exempt under paragraph 2.

4. If, for certain groups of goods, the application of the thresholds calculated in accordance with the provisions of this Article yields results which, *mutatis mutandis*, fail to meet the quality requirements set out in paragraphs 1 and 2 above, and if the thresholds cannot be lowered without reducing the relief which Article 1 guarantees to intra- Community operators, appropriate measures may be taken, at the initiative of the Commission or the request of a Member State, in accordance with the procedure laid down in Article 40 of the Basic Regulation.

Article 4

For the introduction of the simplification thresholds in 1993, the Member States may set these:

— at levels above ECR 100,000 pursuant to the first subparagraph of Article 28(9) of the Basic Regulation, provided that they ensure that at least 95% of the total value of their outgoing or incoming goods is covered by periodic declarations containing all the information required under Article 23 of the Basic Regulation,

— where they are exempt under Article 3(2), at levels below ECU 100,000 pursuant to the second subparagraph of Article 28(9) of the Basic Regulation, to the extent necessary to ensure that at least 95% of the total value of their outgoing or incoming goods is covered by periodic declarations containing all the information required under Article 23 of the Basic Regulation.

Article 5

The information relating to the information of the assimilation and simplification thresholds in 1993 shall be published not later than 31 August 1992.

Article 6

1. For the adjustment of the assimilation thresholds from 1994, the quality requirements specified in Article 3 shall be regarded as met if the coverage is maintained at the level which obtained when the thresholds were introduced.

2. The condition laid down in paragraph 1 shall be met if Member States:

(*a*) calculate their thresholds for the year following the current year on the basis of the latest available results for their trade with the other Member States over a twelve-month period, and

(*b*) set their thresholds at a level which allows the same coverage for the period thus defined as for the period used as a basis for calculating their thresholds for the current year.

Member States shall notify the Commission if they use a different method to meet this condition.

3. Member States may lower their coverage provided that the quality requirements laid down in Article 3 continue to be met.

4. Member States shall calculate adjustments to their assimilation thresholds each year. The thresholds shall be adjusted if the adjustment involves a charge of at least 10% in the threshold values for the current year.

Article 7

1. For the adjustment of the simplification thresholds from 1994, the Member States which set these thresholds

— at levels higher than the values laid down in by Article 28(8) of the Basic Regulation, shall ensure that the condition laid down in the first indent of Article 4 of this Regulation is met,

— at levels below these values, since they are exempt pursuant to Article 3(2) above, shall ensure that they comply with the limit laid down in the second indent of Article 4 of this Regulation.

2. To ensure that the condition referred to in the first indent of Article 4 is met or that the limit referred to in the second indent of Article 4 is complied with, it shall be sufficient for Member States to calculate the adjustment of the simplification thresholds using the method laid down in Article 6(2) for adjusting the assimilation thresholds. Member States shall notify the Commission if they use a different method.

Article 8

The information relating to the adjustment of assimilation and simplification thresholds from 1994 shall be published not later than 31 October of the preceding year.

Article 9

1. Parties responsible for providing information shall be freed from their obligations to the extent allowed by application of the assimilation and simplification thresholds set for a given year, provided they have not exceeded these thresholds during the previous year.

2. For each statistical threshold, the provisions adopted shall apply for the whole year.

However, if the value of the intra-Community transactions carried out by a party responsible for providing information at some time during the year exceeds the threshold applicable to him, he shall provide information on his intra-Community transactions from the month in which this threshold was exceeded in accordance with the provisions applying to the threshold which becomes applicable. If this provision involves the transmission of the periodic declarations referred to in Article 13 of the Basic Regulation, the Member States shall lay down the time limit for transmitting these declarations in accordance with their particular administrative arrangements.

Article 10

The Member States shall communicate to the Commission the information regarding the thresholds they have calculated at least two weeks before publication. At the Commission's request, they shall also communicate the information required for assessing these thresholds, both for the period on which their calculation is based and for a given calendar year.

Article 11

This Regulation shall enter into force on the seventh day following its publication in the *Official Journal of the European Communities*.

This Regulation shall be binding in its entirety and directly applicable in all Member States.

Done at Brussels, 31 July 1992.

ANNEX

Notes

This Annex contains the relevant mathematical formulae used to compute the limits.

COUNCIL REGULATION

of 12 October 1992

92/2913/EEC

establishing the Community Customs Code

(OJ No L 302, 19.10.1992)

TITLE I
GENERAL PROVISIONS

TITLE II
FACTORS ON THE BASIS OF WHICH IMPORT DUTIES OR EXPORT DUTIES AND THE OTHER MEASURES PRESCRIBED IN RESPECT OF TRADE IN GOODS ARE APPLIED

TITLE III
PROVISIONS APPLICABLE TO GOODS BROUGHT INTO THE CUSTOMS TERRITORY OF THE COMMUNITY UNTIL THEY ARE ASSIGNED A CUSTOMS APPROVED TREATMENT OR USE

TITLE IV
CUSTOMS-APPROVED TREATMENT OR USE

TITLE VII
CUSTOMS DEBT

TITLE VIII
APPEALS

TITLE IX
FINAL PROVISIONS

THE COUNCIL OF THE EUROPEAN COMMUNITIES,

Having regard to the Treaty establishing the European Economic Community, and in particular Articles 28, 100a and 113 thereof,

Having regard to the proposal from the Commission (OJ No C 128, 23.5.1990, p 1),

In cooperation with the European Parliament (OJ No C 72, 18.3.1991, p 176 and Decision of 16 September 1992 (not yet published in the Official Journal),

Having regard to the opinion of the Economic and Social Committee (OJ No C 60, 8.3.1991, p 5),

Whereas the Community is based upon a customs union; whereas it is advisable, in the interests both of Community traders and the customs authorities, to assemble in a code the provisions of customs legislation that are at present contained in a large number of Community regulations and directives; whereas this task is of fundamental importance from the standpoint of the internal market;

Whereas such a Community Customs Code (hereinafter called "the Code") must incorporate current customs legislation; whereas it is, nevertheless, advisable to amend that legislation in order to make it more consistent, to simplify it and to remedy certain omissions that still exist with a view to adopting complete Community legislation in this area;

Whereas, based on the concept of an internal market, the Code must contain the general rules and procedures which ensure the implementation of the tariff and other measures introduced at Community level in connection with trade in goods between the Community and third countries; whereas it must cover, among other things, the implementation of common agricultural and commercial policy measures taking into account the requirements of these common policies;

Whereas it would appear advisable to specify that this Code is applicable without prejudice to specific provisions laid down in other fields; whereas such specific rules as may exist or be introduced in the context, *inter alia*, of legislation relating to agriculture, statistics, commercial policy or own resources;

Whereas, in order to secure a balance between the needs of the customs authorities in regard to ensuring the correct application of customs legislation, on the one hand, and the rights of traders to be treated fairly, on the other, the said authorities must be granted, *inter alia*, extensive powers of control and the said traders a right of appeal; whereas the implementation of a customs appeals system will require the United Kingdom to introduce new administrative procedures which cannot be effected before 1 January 1995;

Whereas in view of the paramount importance of external trade for the Community, customs formalities and controls should be abolished or at least kept to a minimum;

Whereas it is important to guarantee the uniform application of this Code and to provide, to that end, for a Community procedure which enables the procedures for its implementation to be adopted within a suitable time; whereas a Customs Code

Committee should be set up in order to ensure close and effective cooperation between the Member States and the Commission in this field;

Whereas in adopting the measures required to implement this Code, the utmost care must be taken to prevent any fraud or irregularity liable to affect adversely the General Budget of the European Communities,

HAS ADOPTED THIS REGULATION:

TITLE I
GENERAL PROVISIONS

CHAPTER 1
Scope and basic definitions

Article 1

Customs rules shall consist of this Code and the provisions adopted at Community level or nationally to implement them. The Code shall apply, without prejudice to special rules laid down in other fields

— to trade between the Community and third countries,

— to goods covered by the Treaty establishing the European Coal and Steel Community, the Treaty establishing the European Economic Community or the Treaty establishing the European Atomic Energy Community.

Article 2

1. Save as otherwise provided, either under international conventions or customary practices of a limited geographic and economic scope or under autonomous Community measures, Community customs rules shall apply uniformly throughout the customs territory of the Community.

2. Certain provisions of customs rules may also apply outside the customs territory of the Community within the framework of either rules governing specific fields or international conventions.

Article 3

[The customs territory of the Community shall comprise:

— the territory of the Kingdom of Belgium,

— the territory of the Kingdom of Denmark, except the Faroe Islands and Greenland,

— the territory of the Federal Republic of Germany, except the Island of Heligoland and the territory of Busingen (Treaty of 23 November 1964 between the Federal Republic of Germany and the Swiss Confederation),

— the territory of the Kingdom of Spain, except Ceuta and Melilla,

— the territory of the French Republic, except the overseas territories and "collectivites territoriales",

— the territory of the Hellenic Republic,

— the territory of Ireland,

— the territory of the Italian Republic, except the municipalities of Livigno and Campione d'Italia and the national waters of Lake Lugano which are between the bank and the political frontier of the area between Ponte Tresa and Porto Ceresio,

— the territory of the Grand Duchy of Luxembourg,

— the territory of the Kingdom of the Netherlands in Europe,

— the territory of the Republic of Austria,

— the territory of the Portuguese Republic,

— the territory of the Republic of Finland, including the Aland Islands, provided a declaration is made in accordance with Article 227 (5) of the EC Treaty,

— the territory of the Kingdom of Sweden,

— the territory of the United Kingdom of Great Britain and Northern Ireland and of the Channel Islands and the Isle of Man;][1]

2. The following territories situated outside the territory of the Member States shall, taking the conventions and treaties applicable to them into account, be considered to be part of the customs territory of the Community:

...[2]

(*b*) FRANCE

The territory of the Principality of Monaco as defined in the Customs Convention signed in Paris on 18 May 1963 (*Journal officiel* of 27 September 1963, p 8679).

(*c*) ITALY

The territory of the Republic of San Marino as defined in the Convention of 31 March 1939 (Law of 6 June 1939, no 1220).

3. The customs territory of the Community shall include the territorial waters, the inland maritime waters and the airspace of the Member States, and the territories referred to in paragraph 2, except for the territorial waters, the inland maritime waters and the airspace of those territories which are not part of the customs territory of the Community pursuant to paragraph 1.

Amendments

[1]   Substituted by the Fourth Act of Accession 1994.

[2]   Deleted by the Fourth Act of Accession 1994.

Article 4

For the purposes of this Code, the following definitions shall apply:

(1) **"Person"** means:

— a natural person,

— a legal person,

— where the possibility is provided for under the rules in force, an association of persons recognized as having the capacity to perform legal acts but lacking the legal status of a legal person.

(2) **"Persons established in the Community"** means:

— in the case of a natural person, any person who is normally resident there,

— in the case of a legal person or an association of persons, any person that has in the Community its registered office, central headquarters or a permanent business establishment.

(3) **"Customs authorities"** means the authorities responsible *inter alia* for applying customs rules.

(4) **"Customs office"** means any office at which all or some of the formalities laid down by customs rules may be completed.

(5) **"Decision"** means any official act by the customs authorities pertaining to customs rules giving a ruling on a particular case, such act having legal effects on one or more specific or identifiable persons; this term covers *inter alia* a binding tariff information within the meaning of Article 12.

(6) **"Customs status"** means the status of goods as Community or non-Community goods.

(7) **"Community goods"** means goods:

— wholly obtained or produced in the customs territory of the Community under the conditions referred to in Article 23 and not incorporating goods imported from countries or territories not forming part of the customs territory of the Community,

— imported from countries or territories not forming part of the customs territory of the Community which have been released for free circulation,

— obtained or produced in the customs territory of the Community, either from goods referred to in the second indent alone or from goods referred to in the first and second indents.

(8) **"Non-Community goods"** means goods other than those referred to in subparagraph 7. Without prejudice to Articles 163 and 164, Community goods shall lose their status as such when they are actually removed from the customs territory of the Community.

(9) **"Customs debt"** means the obligation on a person to pay the amount of the import duties (customs debt on importation) or export duties (customs debt on exportation) which apply to specific goods under the Community provisions in force.

(10) **"Import duties"** means:

— customs duties and charges having an effect equivalent to customs duties payable on the importation of goods,

— agricultural levies and other import charges introduced under the common agricultural policy or under the specific arrangements applicable to certain goods resulting from the processing of agricultural products.

(11) **"Export duties"** means:

— customs duties and charges having an effect equivalent to customs duties payable on the exportation of goods,

— agricultural levies and other export charges introduced under the common agricultural policy or under the specific arrangements applicable to certain goods resulting from the processing of agricultural products.

(12) **"Debtor"** means any person liable for payment of a customs debt.

(13) **"Supervision by the customs authorities"** means action taken in general by those authorities with a view to ensuring that customs rules and, where appropriate, other provisions applicable to goods subject to customs supervision are observed.

(14) **"Control by the customs authorities"** means the performance of specific acts such as examining goods, verifying the existence and authenticity of documents, examining the accounts of undertakings and other records, inspecting means of transport, inspecting luggage and other goods carried by or on persons and carrying out official inquiries and other similar acts with a view to ensuring that customs rules and, where appropriate, other provisions applicable to goods subject to customs supervision are observed.

(15) **"Customs-approved treatment or use of goods"** means:

(*a*) the placing of goods under a customs procedure;

(*b*) their entry into a free zone or free warehouse;

(*c*) their re-exportation from the customs territory of the Community;

(*d*) their destruction;

(*e*) their abandonment to the Exchequer.

(16) **"Customs procedure"** means:

(*a*) release for free circulation;

(*b*) transit;

(*c*) customs warehousing;

(*d*) inward processing;

(*e*) processing under customs control;

(*f*) temporary admission;

(*g*) outward processing;

(*h*) exportation.

(17) **"Customs declaration"** means the act whereby a person indicates in the prescribed form and manner the wish to place goods under a given customs procedure.

(18) **"Declarant"** means the person making the customs declaration in his own name or the person in whose name a customs declaration is made.

(19) **"Presentation of goods to customs"** means the notification to the customs authorities, in the manner laid down, of the arrival of goods at the customs office or at any other place designated or approved by the customs authorities.

(20) **"Release of goods"** means the act whereby the customs authorities make goods available for the purposes stipulated by the customs procedure under which they are placed.

(21) **"Holder of the procedure"** means the person on whose behalf the customs declaration was made or the person to whom the rights and obligations of the abovementioned person in respect of a customs procedure have been transferred.

(22) **"Holder of the authorization"** means the person to whom an authorization has been granted.

(23) **"Provisions in force"** means Community or national provisions.

(24) **"Committee procedure"** means the procedure provided for in Article 249.

CHAPTER 2
Sundry general provisions relating in particular to the rights and obligations of persons with regard to customs rules

SECTION 1
RIGHT OF REPRESENTATION

Article 5

1. Under the conditions set out in Article 64(2) and subject to the provisions adopted within the framework of Article 243(2)(*b*), any person may appoint a representative in his dealings with the customs authorities to perform the acts and formalities laid down by customs rules.

2. Such representation may be:

— direct, in which case the representative shall act in the name of and on behalf of another person, or

— indirect, in which case the representative shall act in his own name but on behalf of another person.

A Member State may restrict the right to make customs declarations:

— by direct representation, or

— by indirect representation,

so that the representative must be a customs agent carrying on his business in that country's territory.

3. Save in the cases referred to in Article 64(2)(*b*) and (3), a representative must be established within the Community.

4. A representative must state that he is acting on behalf of the person represented, specify whether the representation is direct or indirect and be empowered to act as a representative.

A person who fails to state that he is acting in the name of or on behalf of another person or who states that he is acting in the name of or on behalf of another person without being empowered to do so shall be deemed to be acting in his own name and on his own behalf.

5. The customs authorities may require any person stating that he is acting in the name of or on behalf of another person to produce evidence of his powers to act as a representative.

SECTION 2
DECISIONS RELATING TO THE APPLICATION OF CUSTOMS RULES

Article 6

1. Where a person requests that the customs authorities take a decision relating to the application of customs rules that person shall supply all the information and documents required by those authorities in order to take a decision.

2. Such decision shall be taken and notified to the applicant at the earliest opportunity.

Where a request for a decision is made in writing, the decision shall be made within a period laid down in accordance with the existing provisions, starting on the date on which the said request is received by the customs authorities. Such a decision must be notified in writing to the applicant.

However, that period may be exceeded where the customs authorities are unable to comply with it. In that case, those authorities shall so inform the applicant before the expiry of the abovementioned period, stating the grounds which justify exceeding it and indicating the further period of time which they consider necessary in order to give a ruling on the request.

3. Decisions adopted by the customs authorities in writing which either reject requests or are detrimental to the persons to whom they are addressed shall set out the grounds on which they are based. They shall refer to the right of appeal provided for in Article 243.

4. Provision may be made for the first sentence of paragraph 3 to apply likewise to other decisions.

Article 7

Save in the cases provided for in the second subparagraph of Article 244, decisions adopted shall be immediately enforceable by customs authorities.

Article 8

1. A decision favourable to the person concerned shall be annulled if it was issued on the basis of incorrect or incomplete information and:

— the applicant knew or should reasonably have known that the information was incorrect or incomplete, and

— such decision could not have been taken on the basis of correct or complete information;

2. The persons to whom the decision was addressed shall be notified of its annulment.

3. Annulment shall take effect from the date on which the annulled decision was taken.

Article 9

1. A decision favourable to the person concerned shall be revoked or amended where, in cases other than those referred to in Article 8, one or more of the conditions laid down for its issue were not or are no longer fulfilled.

2. A decision favourable to the person concerned may be revoked where the person to whom it is addressed fails to fulfil an obligation imposed on him under that decision.

3. The person to whom the decision is addressed shall be notified of its revocation or amendment.

4. The revocation or amendment of the decision shall take effect from the date of notification. However, in exceptional cases where the legitimate interests of the person to whom the decision is addressed so require, the customs authorities may defer the date when revocation or amendment takes effect.

Article 10
(annulment of decisions on grounds unconnected with customs legislation)

Articles 8 and 9 shall be without prejudice to national rules which stipulate that decisions are invalid or become null and void for reasons unconnected with customs legislation.

SECTION 3
INFORMATION

Article 11

1. Any person may request information concerning the application of customs legislation from the customs authorities.

Such a request may be refused where it does not relate to an import or export operation actually envisaged.

2. The information shall be supplied to the applicant free of charge. However, where special costs are incurred by the customs authorities, in particular as a result of analyses or expert reports on goods, or the return of the goods to the applicant, he may be charged the relevant amount.

Article 12

Note

Article 12 is outside the scope of this work.

SECTION 4
OTHER PROVISIONS

Article 13

The customs authorities may, in accordance with the conditions laid down by the provisions in force, carry out all the controls they deem necessary to ensure that customs legislation is correctly applied.

Article 14

For the purposes of applying customs legislation, any person directly or indirectly involved in the operations concerned for the purposes of trade in goods shall provide the customs authorities with all the requisite documents and information, irrespective of the medium used, and all the requisite assistance at their request and by any time limit prescribed.

Article 15

All information which is by nature confidential or which is provided on a confidential basis shall be covered by the obligation of professional secrecy. It shall not be disclosed by the customs authorities without the express permission of the person or authority providing it; the communication of information shall be permitted where the customs authorities may be obliged or authorized to do so pursuant to the provisions in force, particularly in respect of data protection, or in connection with legal proceedings.

Article 16

The persons concerned shall keep the documents referred to in Article 14 for the purposes of control by the customs authorities, for the period laid down in the provisions in force and for at least three calendar years, irrespective of the medium used. That period shall run from the end of the year in which:

(*a*) in the case of goods released for free circulation in circumstances other than those referred to in (*b*) or goods declared for export, from the end of the year in which the declarations for release for free circulation or export are accepted;

(*b*) in the case of goods released for free circulation at a reduced or zero rate of import duty on account of their end-use, from the end of the year in which they cease to be subject to customs supervision;

(*c*) in the case of goods placed under another customs procedure, from the end of the year in which the customs procedure concerned is completed;

(*d*) in the case of goods placed in a free zone or free warehouse, from the end of the year on which they leave the undertaking concerned.

Without prejudice to the provisions of Article 221(3), second sentence, where a check carried out by the customs authorities in respect of a customs debt shows that the relevant entry in the accounts has to be corrected, the documents shall be kept beyond the time limit provided for in the first paragraph for a period sufficient to permit the correction to be made and checked.

Article 17

Where a period, date or time limit is laid down pursuant to customs legislation for the purpose of applying legislation, such period shall not be extended and such date or time limit shall not be deferred unless specific provision is made in the legislation concerned.

Article 18

1. The value of the ecu in national currencies to be applied within the framework of customs legislation shall be fixed once a year. The rates to be applied shall be those obtaining on the first working day of October, with effect from January 1 of the following calendar year. If a rate is not available for a particular national currency, the rate to be applied for that currency shall be that obtaining on the last day for which a rate was published in the *Official Journal of the European Communities*.

2. However, where a change in the bilateral central rate of one or more national currencies occurs:

(*a*) during a calendar year, the amended rates shall be used for converting the ecu into national currencies for the purposes of determining the tariff classification of goods and customs duties and charges having equivalent effect. They shall take effect from the 10th day after the date on which those rates are available;

(*b*) after the first working day of October, the amended rates shall be used for converting the ecu into national currencies for the purposes of determining the tariff classification of goods and customs duties and charges having equivalent effect and shall be applicable, by way of derogation from paragraph 1, throughout the following calendar year, except where a change in the bilateral central rate occurs during that period, in which case subparagraph (*a*) shall apply.

"Amended rates" means the rates obtaining on the first day after a change in the bilateral central rate, where such rates are available for all Community currencies.

Article 19

The procedure of the Committee shall be used to determine in which cases and under which conditions the application of customs legislation may be simplified.

TITLE II

FACTORS ON THE BASIS OF WHICH IMPORT DUTIES OR EXPORT DUTIES AND THE OTHER MEASURES PRESCRIBED IN RESPECT OF TRADE IN GOODS ARE APPLIED

CHAPTER 1

Customs Tariff of the European Communities and tariff classification of goods

Articles 20–26

Note

Articles 20–26 are outside the scope of this work.

PREFERENTIAL ORIGIN OF GOODS

Article 27

The rules on preferential origin shall lay down the conditions governing acquisition of origin which goods must fulfil in order to benefit from the measures referred to in Article 20(3)(*d*) or (*e*).

Those rules shall:

(*a*) in the case of goods covered by the agreements referred to in Article 20(3)(*d*), be determined in those agreements;

(*b*) in the case of goods benefiting from the preferential tariff measures referred to in Article 20(3)(*e*), be determined in accordance with the Committee procedure.

CHAPTER 3
Value of goods for customs purposes

Article 28

The provisions of this Chapter shall determine the customs value for the purposes of applying the Customs Tariff of the European Communities and non-tariff measures laid down by Community provisions governing specific fields relating to trade in goods.

Article 29

1. The customs value of imported goods shall be the transaction value, that is, the price actually paid or payable for the goods when sold for export to the customs territory of the Community, adjusted, where necessary, in accordance with Articles 32 and 33, provided:

(*a*) that there are no restrictions as to the disposal or use of the goods by the buyer, other than restrictions which:

— are imposed or required by law or by the public authorities in the Community,

— limit the geographical area in which the goods may be resold,

or

— do not substantially affect the value of the goods;

(*b*) that the sale or price is not subject to some condition or consideration for which a value cannot be determined with respect to the goods being valued;

(*c*) that no part of the proceeds of any subsequent resale, disposal or use of the goods by the buyer will accrue directly or indirectly to the seller, unless an appropriate adjustment can be made in accordance with Article 32; and

(*d*) that the buyer and seller are not related, or, where the buyer and seller are related, that the transaction value is acceptable for customs purposes under paragraph 2.

2. (*a*) In determining whether the transaction value is acceptable for the purposes of paragraph 1, the fact that the buyer and the seller are related shall not in itself be sufficient grounds for regarding the transaction value as unacceptable. Where necessary, the circumstances surrounding the sale shall be examined and the transaction value shall be accepted provided that the relationship did not influence the price. If, in the light of information provided by the declarant or otherwise, the customs authorities have grounds for considering that the relationship influenced the price, they shall communicate their grounds to the declarant and he shall be given a reasonable opportunity to respond. If the declarant so requests, the communication of the grounds shall be in writing.

(*b*) In a sale between related persons, the transaction value shall be accepted and the goods valued in accordance with paragraph 1 wherever the declarant demonstrates that such value closely approximates to one of the following occurring at or about the same time:

(i) the transaction value in sales, between buyers and sellers who are not related in any particular case, of identical or similar goods for export to the Community;

(ii) the customs value of identical or similar goods, as determined under Article 30(2)(*c*);

(iii) the customs value of identical or similar goods, as determined under Article 30(2)(*d*).

In applying the foregoing tests, due account shall be taken of demonstrated differences in commercial levels, quantity levels, the elements enumerated in Article 32 and costs incurred by the seller in sales in which he and the buyer are not related and where such costs are not incurred by the seller in sales in which he and the buyer are related.

(*c*) The tests set forth in subparagraph (*b*) are to be used at the initiative of the declarant and only for comparison purposes. Substitute values may not be established under the said subparagraph.

3. (*a*) The price actually paid or payable is the total payment made or to be made by the buyer to or for the benefit of the seller for the imported goods and includes all payments made or to be made as a condition of sale of the imported goods by the buyer to the seller or by the buyer to a third party to satisfy an obligation of the seller. The payment need not necessarily take the form of a transfer of money. Payment may be made by way of letters of credit or negotiable instruments and may be made directly or indirectly.

(*b*) Activities, including marketing activities, undertaken by the buyer on his own account, other than those for which an adjustment is provided in Article 32, are not considered to be an indirect payment to the seller, even though they might be regarded as of benefit to the seller or have been undertaken by agreement with the seller, and their cost shall not be added to the price actually paid or payable in determining the customs value of imported goods.

Article 30

1. Where the customs value cannot be determined under Article 29, it is to be determined by proceeding sequentially through subparagraphs (*a*), (*b*), (*c*) and (*d*) of paragraph 2 to the first subparagraph under which it can be determined, subject to the proviso that the order of application of subparagraphs (*c*) and (*d*) shall be reversed if the declarant so requests; it is only when such value cannot be determined under a particular subparagraph that the provisions of the next subparagraph in a sequence established by virtue of this paragraph can be applied.

2. The customs value as determined under this Article shall be:

(*a*) the transaction value of identical goods sold for export to the Community and exported at or about the same time as the goods being valued;

(*b*) the transaction value of similar goods sold for export to the Community and exported at or about the same time as the goods being valued;

(*c*) the value based on the unit price at which the imported goods or identical or similar imported goods are sold within the Community in the greatest aggregate quantity to persons not related to the sellers;

(*d*) the computed value, consisting of the sum of:

— the cost or value of materials and fabrication or other processing employed in producing the imported goods,

— an amount for profit and general expenses equal to that usually reflected in sales of goods of the same class or kind as the goods being valued which are made by producers in the country of exportation for export to the Community,

— the cost or value of the items referred to in Article 32(1)(*e*).

3. Any further conditions and rules for the application of paragraph 2 above shall be determined in accordance with the committee procedure.

Article 31

1. Where the customs value of imported goods cannot be determined under Articles 29 or 30, it shall be determined, on the basis of data available in the Community, using reasonable means consistent with the principles and general provisions of:

— the agreement on implementation of Article VII of the General Agreement on Tariffs and Trade,

— Article VII of the General Agreement on Tariffs and Trade,

— the provisions of this Chapter.

2. No customs value shall be determined under paragraph 1 on the basis of:

(*a*) the selling price in the Community of goods produced in the Community;

(*b*) a system which provides for the acceptance for customs purposes of the higher of two alternative values;

(*c*) the price of goods on the domestic market of the country of exportation;

(*d*)   the cost of production, other than computed values which have been determined for identical or similar goods in accordance with Article 30(2)(*d*);

(*e*)   prices for export to a country not forming part of the customs territory of the Community;

(*f*)   minimum customs values; or

(*g*)   arbitrary or fictitious values.

Article 32

1. In determining the custom's value under Article 29, there shall be added to the price actually paid or payable for the imported goods:

(*a*)   the following, to the extent that they are incurred by the buyer but are not included in the price actually paid or payable for the goods:

   (i)   commissions and brokerage, except buying commissions,

   (ii)   the cost of containers which are treated as being one, for customs purposes, with the goods in question,

   (iii)   the cost of packing, whether for labour or materials;

(*b*)   the value, apportioned as appropriate, of the following goods and services where supplied directly or indirectly by the buyer free of charge or at reduced cost for use in connection with the production and sale for export of the imported goods, to the extent that such value has not been included in the price actually paid or payable:

   (i)   materials, components, parts and similar items incorporated in the imported goods,

   (ii)   tools, dies, moulds and similar items used in the production of the imported goods,

   (iii)   materials consumed in the production of the imported goods,

   (iv)   engineering, development, artwork, design work, and plans and sketches undertaken elsewhere than in the Community and necessary for the production of the imported goods;

(*c*)   royalties and licence fees related to the goods being valued that the buyer must pay, either directly or indirectly, as a condition of sale of the goods being valued, to the extent that such royalties and fees are not included in the price actually paid or payable;

(*d*)   the value of any part of the proceeds of any subsequent resale, disposal or use of the imported goods that accrues directly or indirectly to the seller;

(*e*)   (i)   the cost of transport and insurance of the imported goods, and

   (ii)   loading and handling charges associated with the transport of the imported goods

to the place of introduction into the customs territory of the Community.

2. Additions to the price actually paid or payable shall be made under this Article only on the basis of objective and quantifiable data.

3. No additions shall be made to the price actually paid or payable in determining the customs value except as provided in this Article.

4. In this Article, the term **"buying commissions"** means fees paid by an importer to his agent for the service of representing him in the purchase of the goods being valued.

5. Notwithstanding paragraph 1(*c*):

(*a*) charges for the right to reproduce the imported goods in the Community shall not be added to the price actually paid or payable for the imported goods in determining the customs value; and

(*b*) payments made by the buyer for the right to distribute or resell the imported goods shall not be added to the price actually paid or payable for the imported goods if such payments are not a condition of the sale for export to the Community of the goods.

Article 33

1. Provided that they are shown separately from the price actually paid or payable, the following shall not be included in the customs value:

(*a*) charges for the transport of goods after their arrival at the point of introduction into the customs territory of the Community;

(*b*) charges for construction, erection, assembly, maintenance or technical assistance, undertaken after importation on imported goods such as industrial plant, machinery or equipment;

(*c*) charges for interest under a financing arrangement entered into by the buyer and relating to the purchase of imported goods, irrespective of whether the finance is provided by the seller or another person, provided that the financing arrangement has been made in writing and where required, the buyer can demonstrate that:

— such goods are actually sold at the price declared as the price actually paid or payable, and

— the claimed rate of interest does not exceed the level for such transactions prevailing in the country where, and at the time when, the finance was provided;

(*d*) charges for the right to reproduce imported goods in the Community;

(*e*) buying commissions;

(*f*) import duties or other charges payable in the Community by reason of the importation or sale of the goods.

Article 34

Specific rules may be laid down in accordance with the procedure of the committee to determine the customs value of carrier media for use in data processing equipment and bearing data or instructions.

Article 35

Where factors used to determine the customs value of goods are expressed in a currency other than that of the Member State where the valuation is made, the rate of exchange to be used shall be that duly published by the competent authorities of the Member State concerned.

Such rate shall reflect as effectively as possible the current value of such currency in commercial transactions in terms of the currency of such Member State and shall apply during such period as may be determined in accordance with the procedure of the committee.

Where such a rate does not exist, the rate of exchange to be used shall be determined in accordance with the procedure of the committee.

Article 36

1. The provisions of this chapter shall be without prejudice to the specific provisions regarding the determination of the value for customs purposes of goods released for free circulation after being assigned a different customs-approved treatment or use.

2. By way of derogation from Articles 29, 30 and 31, the customs value of perishable goods usually delivered on consignment may, at the request of the declarant, be determined under simplified rules drawn up for the whole Community in accordance with the committee procedure.

TITLE III
PROVISIONS APPLICABLE TO GOODS BROUGHT INTO THE CUSTOMS TERRITORY OF THE COMMUNITY UNTIL THEY ARE ASSIGNED A CUSTOMS-APPROVED TREATMENT OR USE

CHAPTER 1
Entry of goods into the customs territory of the Community

Article 37

1. Goods brought into the customs territory of the Community shall, from the time of their entry, be subject to customs supervision. They may also be subject to control by the customs authority in accordance with the provisions in force

2. They shall remain under such supervision for as long as necessary to determine their customs status, if appropriate, and in the case of non-Community goods and without prejudice to Article 82(1), until their customs status is changed, they enter a free zone or free warehouse or they are re-exported or destroyed in accordance with Article 182.

Article 38

1. Goods brought into the customs territory of the Community shall be conveyed by the person bringing them into the Community without delay, by the route specified by the customs authorities and in accordance with their instructions, if any:

   (*a*) to the customs office designated by the customs authorities or to any other place specified or approved by those authorities; or, (*b*) to a free zone, if the goods are to be brought into that free zone direct:

— by sea or air, or

— by land without passing through another part of the customs territory of the Community, where the free zone adjoins the land frontier between a Member State and a third country.

2. Any person who assumes responsibility for the carriage of goods after they have been brought into the customs territory of the Community, *inter alia* as a result of transhipment, shall become responsible for compliance with the obligation laid down in paragraph 1.

3. Goods which, although still outside the customs territory of the Community, may be subject to the control of the customs authority of a Member State under the provisions in force, as a result of *inter alia* an agreement concluded between that Member State and a third country, shall be treated in the same way as goods brought into the customs territory of the Community.

4. Paragraph 1(*a*) shall not preclude implementation of any provisions in force with respect to tourist traffic, frontier traffic, postal traffic or traffic of negligible economic importance, on condition that customs supervision and customs control possibilities are not thereby jeopardized.

5. Paragraphs 1 to 4 and Articles 39 to 53 shall not apply to goods which have temporarily left the customs territory of the Community while moving between two points in that territory by sea or air, provided that carriage has been effected by a direct route and by regular air service or shipping line without a stop outside Community customs territory.

This provision shall not apply to goods loaded in third country ports or airports or at free ports.

6. Paragraph 1 shall not apply to goods on board vessels or aircraft crossing the territorial sea or airspace of the Member States without having as their destination a port or airport situated in those Member States.

Article 39

1. Where, by reason of unforeseeable circumstances or *force majeure*, the obligation laid down in Article 38(1) cannot be complied with, the person bound by that obligation or any other person acting in his place shall inform the customs authorities of the situation without delay. Where the unforeseeable circumstances or *force majeure* do not result in total loss of the goods, the customs authorities shall also be informed of their precise location.

2. Where, by reason of unforeseeable circumstances or *force majeure*, a vessel or aircraft covered by Article 38(6) is forced to put into port or land temporarily in the customs territory of the Community and the obligation laid down in Article 38(1) cannot be complied with, the person bringing the vessel or aircraft into the customs territory of the

Community or any other person acting in his place shall inform the customs authorities of the situation without delay.

3. The customs authorities shall determine the measures to be taken in order to permit customs supervision of the goods referred to in paragraph 1 as well as those on board a vessel or aircraft in the circumstances specified in paragraph 2 and to ensure, where appropriate, that they are subsequently conveyed to a customs office or other place designated or approved by the authorities.

CHAPTER 2
Presentation of goods to customs

Article 40

Goods which, pursuant to Article 38(1)(*a*), arrive at the customs office or other place designated or approved by the customs authorities shall be presented to customs by the person who brought the goods into the customs territory of the Community or, if appropriate, by the person who assumes responsibility for carriage of the goods following such entry.

Article 41

Article 40 shall not preclude the implementation of rules in force relating to goods:

(*a*) carried by travellers;

(*b*) placed under a customs procedure but not presented to customs.

Article 42

Goods may, once they have been presented to customs, and with the permission of the customs authorities, be examined or samples may be taken, in order that they may be assigned a customs-approved treatment or use. Such permission shall be granted, on request, to the person authorized to assign the goods such treatment or use.

CHAPTER 3
Summary declaration and unloading of goods presented to customs

Article 43

Subject to Article 45, goods presented to customs within the meaning of Article 40 shall be covered by a summary declaration.

The summary declaration shall be lodged once the goods have been presented to customs. The customs authorities may, however, allow a period for lodging the declaration which shall not extend beyond the first working day following the day on which the goods are presented to customs.

Article 44

1. The summary declaration shall be made on a form corresponding to the model prescribed by the customs authorities. However, the customs authorities may permit the use, as a summary declaration, of any commercial or official document which contains the particulars necessary for identification of the goods.

2. The summary declaration shall be lodged by:

(*a*)   the person who brought the goods into the customs territory of the Community or by any person who assumes responsibility for carriage of the goods following such entry, or

(*b*)   the person in whose name the persons referred to in subparagraph (*a*) acted.

Article 45

Without prejudice to the provisions governing goods imported by travellers and consignments by letter and parcel post, the customs authorities may waive the lodging of a summary declaration on condition that this does not jeopardize customs supervision of the goods, where, prior to the expiry of the period referred to in Article 43, the formalities necessary for the goods to be assigned a customs-approved treatment or use are carried out.

Article 46

1. Goods shall be unloaded or transhipped from the means of transport carrying them solely with the permission of the customs authorities in places designated or approved by those customs authorities.

However, such permission shall not be required in the event of the imminent danger necessitating the immediate unloading of all or part of the goods. In that case, the customs authorities shall be informed accordingly forthwith.

2. For the purpose of inspecting goods and the means of transport carrying them, the customs authorities may at any time require goods to be unloaded and unpacked.

Article 47

Goods shall not be removed from their original position without the permission of the customs authorities.

CHAPTER 4

Obligation to assign goods presented to customs a customs-approved treatment or use

Articles 48–57

Note

Articles 48–57 are outside the scope of this work.

TITLE IV
CUSTOMS-APPROVED TREATMENT OR USE

CHAPTER 1
General

Article 58

1. Save as otherwise provided, goods may at any time, under the conditions laid down, be assigned any customs-approved treatment or use irrespective of their nature or quantity, or their country of origin, consignment or destination.

2. Paragraph 1 shall not preclude the imposition of prohibitions or restrictions justified on grounds of public morality, public policy or public security, the protection of health and life of humans, animals or plants, the protection of national treasures possessing artistic, historic or archaeological value or the protection of industrial and commercial property.

CHAPTER 2
Customs procedures

SECTION 1
PLACING OF GOODS UNDER A CUSTOMS PROCEDURE

Article 59

1. All goods intended to be placed under a customs procedure shall be covered by a declaration for that customs procedure.

2. Community goods declared for an export, outward processing, transit or customs warehousing procedure shall be subject to customs supervision from the time of acceptance of the customs declaration until such time as they leave the customs territory of the Community or are destroyed or the customs declaration is invalidated.

Article 60

Insofar as Community customs legislation lays down no rules on the matter, Member States shall determine the competence of the various customs offices situated in their territory, account being taken, where applicable, of the nature of the goods and the customs procedure under which they are to be placed.

Article 61

The customs declaration shall be made:

(*a*) in writing; or

(*b*) using a data-processing technique where provided for by provisions laid down in accordance with the committee procedure or where authorized by the customs authorities; or

(*c*) by means of an oral declaration or any other act whereby the holder of the goods expresses his wish to place them under a customs procedure, where such a possibility is provided for by the rules adopted in accordance with the committee procedure.

A. Declarations in writing

I. Normal procedure

Article 62

1. Declarations in writing shall be made on a form corresponding to the official specimen prescribed for that purpose. They shall be signed and contain all the particulars necessary for implementation of the provisions governing the customs procedure for which the goods are declared.

2. The declaration shall be accompanied by all the documents required for implementation of the provisions governing the customs procedure for which the goods are declared.

Article 63

Declarations which comply with the conditions laid down in Article 62 shall be accepted by the customs authorities immediately, provided that the goods to which they refer are presented to customs.

Article 64

1. Subject to Article 5, a customs declaration may be made by any person who is able to present the goods in question or to have them presented to the competent customs authority, together with all the documents which are required to be produced for the application of the rules governing the customs procedure in respect of which the goods were declared.

2. However,

  (*a*) where acceptance of a customs declaration imposes particular obligations on a specific person, the declaration must be made by that person or on his behalf;

  (*b*) the declarant must be established in the Community.

  However, the condition regarding establishment in the Community shall not apply to persons who:

  — make a declaration for Community transit or temporary importation;

  — declare goods on an occasional basis, provided that the customs authorities consider this to be justified.

3. Paragraph 2(*b*) shall not preclude the application by the Member States of bilateral agreements concluded with third countries, or customary practices having similar effect, under which nationals of such countries may make customs declarations in the territory of the Member States in question, subject to reciprocity.

Article 65

The declarant shall, at his request, be authorized to amend one or more of the particulars of the declaration after it has been accepted by customs. The amendment shall not have the effect of rendering the declaration applicable to goods other than those it originally covered.

However, no amendment shall be permitted where authorization is requested after the customs authorities:

(*a*) have informed the declarant that they intend to examine the goods; or,

(*b*) have established that the particulars in question are incorrect; or,

(*c*) have released the goods.

Article 66

1. The customs authorities shall, at the request of the declarant, invalidate a declaration already accepted where the declarant furnishes proof that goods were declared in error for the customs procedure covered by that declaration or that, as a result of special circumstances, the placing of the goods under the customs procedure for which they were declared is no longer justified.

Nevertheless, where the customs authorities have informed the declarant of their intention to examine the goods, a request for invalidation of the declaration shall not be accepted until after the examination has taken place.

2. The declaration shall not be invalidated after the goods have been released, except in cases defined in accordance with the committee procedure.

3. Invalidation of the declaration shall be without prejudice to the application of the penal provisions in force.

Article 67

Save as otherwise expressly provided, the date to be used for the purposes of all the provisions governing the customs procedure for which the goods are declared shall be the date of acceptance of the declaration by the customs authorities.

Article 68

For the verification of declarations which they have accepted, the customs authorities may:

(*a*) examine the documents covering the declaration and the documents accompanying it. The customs authorities may require the declarant to present other documents for the purpose of verifying the accuracy of the particulars contained in the declaration;

(*b*) examine the goods and take samples for analysis or for detailed examination.

Article 69

1. Transport of the goods to the places where they are to be examined and samples are to be taken, and all the handling necessitated by such examination or taking of samples, shall be carried out by or under the responsibility of the declarant. The costs incurred shall be borne by the declarant.

2. The declarant shall be entitled to be present when the goods are examined and when samples are taken. Where they deem it appropriate, the customs authorities shall require the declarant to be present or represented when the goods are examined or samples are taken in order to provide them with the assistance necessary to facilitate such examination or taking of samples.

3. Provided that samples are taken in accordance with the provisions in force, the customs authorities shall not be liable for payment of any compensation in respect thereof but shall bear the costs of their analysis or examination.

Article 70

1. Where only part of the goods covered by a declaration are examined, the results of the partial examination shall be taken to apply to all the goods covered by that declaration.

However, the declarant may request a further examination of the goods if he considers that the results of the partial examination are not valid as regards the remainder of the goods declared.

2. For the purposes of paragraph 1, where a declaration form covers two or more items, the particulars relating to each item shall be deemed to constitute a separate declaration.

Article 71

1. The results of verifying the declaration shall be used for the purposes of applying the provisions governing the customs procedure under which the goods are placed.

2. Where the declaration is not verified, the provisions referred to in paragraph 1 shall be applied on the basis of the particulars contained in the declaration.

Article 72

1. The customs authorities shall take the measures necessary to identify the goods where identification is required in order to ensure compliance with the conditions governing the customs procedure for which the said goods have been declared.

2. Means of identification affixed to the goods or means of transport shall be removed or destroyed only by the customs authorities or with their permission unless, as a result of unforeseeable circumstances or *force majeure*, their removal or destruction is essential to ensure the protection of the goods or means of transport.

Article 73

1. Without prejudice to Article 74, where the conditions for placing the goods under the procedure in question are fulfilled and provided the goods are not subject to any prohibitive or restrictive measures, the customs authorities shall release the goods as soon as the particulars in the declaration have been verified or accepted without verification. The same shall apply where such verification cannot be completed within a reasonable period of time and the goods are no longer required to be present for verification purposes.

2. All the goods covered by the same declaration shall be released at the same time.

For the purposes of this paragraph, where a declaration form covers two or more items, the particulars relating to each item shall be deemed to constitute a separate declaration.

Article 74

1. Where acceptance of a customs declaration gives rise to a customs debt, the goods covered by the declaration shall not be released unless the customs debt has been paid or secured. However, without prejudice to paragraph 2, this provision shall not apply to the temporary importation procedure with partial relief from import duties.

2. Where, pursuant to the provisions governing the customs procedure for which the goods are declared, the customs authorities require the provision of a security, the said goods shall not be released for the customs procedure in question until such security is provided.

Article 75

Any necessary measures, including confiscation and sale, shall be taken to deal with goods which:

    (*a*)   cannot be released because:

        — it has not been possible to undertake or continue examination of the goods within the period prescribed by the customs authorities for reasons attributable to the declarant; or,

        — the documents which must be produced before the goods can be placed under the customs procedure requested have not been produced; or,

        — payments or security which should have been made or provided in respect of import duties or export duties, as the case may be, have not been made or provided within the period prescribed; or

        — they are subject to bans or restrictions;

    (*b*)   are not removed within a reasonable period after their release.

II. Simplified procedures

Article 76

1. In order to simplify completion of formalities and procedures as far as possible while ensuring that operations are conducted in a proper manner, the customs authorities shall, under conditions laid down in accordance with the committee procedure, grant permission for:

    (*a*)   the declaration referred to in Article 62 to omit certain of the particulars referred to in paragraph 1 of that Article for some of the documents referred to in paragraph 2 of that Article not to be attached thereto;

    (*b*)   a commercial or administrative document, accompanied by a request for the goods to be placed under the customs procedure in question, to be lodged in place of the declaration referred to in Article 62;

    (*c*)   the goods to be entered for the procedure in question by means of an entry in the records; in this case, the customs authorities may waive the requirement that the declarant present the goods to customs.

The simplified declaration, commercial or administrative document or entry in the records must contain at least the particulars necessary for identification of the goods. Where the goods are entered in the records, the date of such entry must be included.

2. Except in cases to be determined in accordance with the committee procedure, the declarant shall furnish a supplementary declaration which may be of a general, periodic or recapitulative nature.

3. Supplementary declarations and the simplified declarations referred to in subparagraphs 1(*a*), (*b*) and (*c*), shall be deemed to constitute a single, indivisible instrument taking effect on the date of acceptance of the simplified declarations; in the cases referred to in subparagraph 1(*c*), entry in the records shall have the same legal force as acceptance of the declaration referred to in Article 62.

4. Special simplified procedures for the Community transit procedure shall be laid down in accordance with the committee procedure.

B. Other declarations

Article 77

Where the customs declaration is made by means of a data-processing technique within the meaning of Article 61(*b*), or by an oral declaration or any other act within the meaning of Article 61(*c*), Articles 62 to 76 shall apply *mutatis mutandis* without prejudice to the principles set out therein.

C. Post-clearance examination of declarations

Article 78

1. The customs authorities may, on their own initiative or at the request of the declarant, amend the declaration after release of the goods.

2. The customs authorities may, after releasing the goods and in order to satisfy themselves as to the accuracy of the particulars contained in the declaration, inspect the commercial documents and data relating to the import or export operations in respect of the goods concerned or to subsequent commercial operations involving those goods. Such inspections may be carried out at the premises of the declarant, of any other person directly or indirectly involved in the said operations in a business capacity or of any other person in possession of the said documents and data for business purposes. Those authorities may also examine the goods where it is still possible for them to be produced.

3. Where revision of the declaration or post-clearance examination indicates that the provisions governing the customs procedure concerned have been applied on the basis of incorrect or incomplete information, the customs authorities shall, in accordance with any provisions laid down, take the measures necessary to regularize the situation, taking account of the new information available to them.

SECTION 2
RELEASE FOR FREE CIRCULATION

Article 79

Release for free circulation shall confer on non-Community goods the customs status of Community goods.

It shall entail application of commercial policy measures, completion of the other formalities laid down in respect of the importation of goods and the charging of any duties legally due.

Article 80

1. By way of derogation from Article 67, provided that the import duty chargeable on the goods is one of the duties referred to in the first indent of Article 4(10) and that the rate of duty is reduced after the date of acceptance of the declaration for release for free circulation but before the goods are released, the declarant may request application of the more favourable rate.

2. Paragraph 1 shall not apply where it has not been possible to release the goods for reasons attributable to the declarant alone.

Article 81

Where a consignment is made up of goods falling within different tariff classifications, and dealing with each of those goods in accordance with its tariff classification for the purpose of drawing up the declaration would entail a burden of work and expense disproportionate to the import duties chargeable, the customs authorities may, at the request of the declarant, agree that import duties be charged on the whole consignment on the basis of the tariff classification of the goods which are subject to the highest rate of import duty.

Article 82

1. Where goods are released for free circulation at a reduced or zero rate of duty on account of their end-use, they shall remain under customs supervision. Customs supervision shall end when the conditions laid down for granting such a reduced or zero rate of duty cease to apply, where the goods are exported or destroyed or where the use of the goods for purposes other than those laid down for the application of the reduced or zero rate of duty is permitted subject to payment of the duties due.

2. Articles 88 and 90 shall apply *mutatis mutandis* to the goods referred to in paragraph 1.

Article 83

Goods released for free circulation shall lose their customs status as Community goods where:

(*a*) the declaration for release for free circulation is invalidated after release in accordance with Article 66, or

(*b*) the imported duties payable on those goods are repaid or remitted:

— under the inward processing procedure in the form of the drawback system;

or

— in respect of defective goods or goods which fail to comply with the terms of the contract, pursuant to Article 238; or

— in situations of the type referred to in Article 239 where repayment or remission is conditional upon the goods being re-exported or being assigned an equivalent customs-approved treatment or use.

SECTION 3
SUSPENSIVE ARRANGEMENTS AND CUSTOMS PROCEDURES WITH ECONOMIC IMPACT

A. Provisions common to several procedures

Article 84

1. In Articles 85 to 90:

(*a*) where the term **"procedure"** is used, it is understood as applying, in the case of non-Community goods, to the following arrangements:

— external transit;
— customs warehousing;
— inward processing in the form of a system of suspension;
— processing under customs control;
— temporary importation;

(*b*) where the term **"customs procedure with economic impact"** is used, it is understood as applying to the following arrangements:

— customs warehousing;
— inward processing;
— processing under customs control;
— temporary importation;
— outward processing.

2. **"Import goods"** means goods placed under a suspensive arrangement and goods which, under the inward processing procedure in the form of the drawback system, have undergone the formalities for release for free circulation and the formalities provided for in Article 125.

3. **"Goods in the unaltered state"** means import goods which, under the inward processing procedure or the procedures for processing under customs control, have undergone no form of processing.

Article 85

The use of any customs procedure with economic impact shall be conditional upon authorization being issued by the customs authorities.

Article 86

Without prejudice to the additional special conditions governing the procedure in question, the authorization referred to in Article 85 and that referred to in Article 100(1) shall be granted only:

— to persons who offer every guarantee necessary for the proper conduct of the operations;

— where the customs authorities can supervise and monitor the procedure without having to introduce administrative arrangements disproportionate to the economic needs involved.

Article 87

1. The conditions under which the procedure in question is used shall be set out in the authorization.

2. The holder of the authorization shall notify the customs authorities of all factors arising after the authorization was granted which may influence its continuation or content.

Article 88

The customs authorities may make the placing of goods under a suspensive arrangement conditional upon the provision of security in order to ensure that any customs debt which may be incurred in respect of those goods will be paid.

Special provisions concerning the provision of security may be laid down in the context of a specific suspensive arrangement.

Article 89

1. A suspensive arrangement with economic impact shall be discharged when a new customs-approved treatment or use is assigned either to the goods placed under that arrangement or to compensating or processed products placed under it.

2. The customs authorities shall take all the measures necessary to regularize the position of goods in respect of which a procedure has not been discharged under the conditions prescribed.

Article 90

The rights and obligations of the holder of a customs procedure with economic impact may, on the conditions laid down by the customs authorities, be transferred successively to other persons who fulfil any conditions laid down in order to benefit from the procedure in question.

B. External transit

I. General provisions

Articles 91–200

Note

Articles 91–200 are outside the scope of this work.

CHAPTER 2
Incurrence of a customs debt

Article 201

1. A customs debt on importation shall be incurred through:

(*a*) the release for free circulation of goods liable to import duties, or

(*b*) the placing of such goods under the temporary importation procedure with partial relief from import duties.

2. A customs debt shall be incurred at the time of acceptance of the customs declaration in question.

3. The debtor shall be the declarant. In the event of indirect representation, the person on whose behalf the customs declaration is made shall also be a debtor.

Where a customs declaration in respect of one of the procedures referred to in paragraph 1 is drawn up on the basis of information which leads to all or part of the duties legally owed not being collected, the persons who provided the information required to draw up the declaration and who knew, or who ought reasonably to have known that such information was false, may also be considered debtors in accordance with the national provisions in force.

Article 202

1. A customs debt on importation shall be incurred through:

(*a*) the unlawful introduction into the customs territory of the Community of goods liable to import duties, or

(*b*) the unlawful introduction into another part of that territory of such goods located in a free zone or free warehouse.

For the purpose of this Article, unlawful introduction means any introduction in violation of the provisions of Articles 38 to 41 and the second indent of Article 177.

2. The customs debt shall be incurred at the moment when the goods are unlawfully introduced.

3. The debtors shall be:

— the person who introduced such goods unlawfully,

— any persons who participated in the unlawful introduction of the goods and who were aware or should reasonably have been aware that such introduction was unlawful, and

— any persons who acquired or held the goods in question and who were aware or should reasonably have been aware at the time of acquiring or receiving the goods that they had been introduced unlawfully.

Article 203

1. A customs debt on importation shall be incurred through:

— the unlawful removal from customs supervision of goods liable to import duties.

2. The customs debt shall be incurred at the moment when the goods are removed from customs supervision.

3. The debtors shall be:

— the person who removed the goods from customs supervision,

— any persons who participated in such removal and who were aware or should reasonably have been aware that the goods were being removed from customs supervision,

— any persons who acquired or held the goods in question and who were aware or should reasonably have been aware at the time of acquiring or receiving the goods that they had been removed from customs supervision, and

— where appropriate, the person required to fulfil the obligations arising from temporary storage of the goods or from the use of the customs procedure under which those goods are placed.

Article 204

1. A customs debt on importation shall be incurred through:

(*a*) non-fulfilment of one of the obligations arising, in respect of goods liable to import duties, from their temporary storage or from the use of the customs procedure under which they are placed, or

(*b*) non-compliance with a condition governing the placing of the goods under that procedure or the granting of a reduced or zero rate of import duty by virtue of the end-use of the goods,

in cases other than those referred to in Article 203 unless it is established that those failures have no significant effect on the correct operation of the temporary storage or customs procedure in question.

2. The customs debt shall be incurred either at the moment when the obligation whose non-fulfilment gives rise to the customs debt ceases to be met or at the moment when the goods are placed under the customs procedure concerned where it is established subsequently that a condition governing the placing of the goods under the said procedure or the granting of a reduced or zero rate of import duty by virtue of the end-use of the goods was not in fact fulfilled.

3. The debtor shall be the person who is required, according to the circumstances, either to fulfil the obligations arising, in respect of goods liable to import duties, from their temporary storage or from the use of the customs procedure under which they have been placed, or to comply with the conditions governing the placing of the goods under that procedure.

Article 205

1. A customs debt on importation shall be incurred through:

— the consumption or use, in a free zone or a free warehouse, of goods liable to import duties, under conditions other than those laid down by the legislation in force.

Where goods disappear and where their disappearance cannot be explained to the satisfaction of the customs authorities, those authorities may regard the goods as having been consumed or used in the free zone or the free warehouse.

2. The debt shall be incurred at the moment when the goods are consumed or are first used under conditions other than those laid down by the legislation in force.

3. The debtor shall be the person who consumed or used the goods and any persons who participated in such consumption or use and who were aware or should reasonably have been aware that the goods were being consumed or used under conditions other than those laid down by the legislation in force.

Where customs authorities regard goods which have disappeared as having been consumed or used in the free zone or the free warehouse and it is not possible to apply the preceding paragraph, the person liable for payment of the customs debt shall be the last person known to these authorities to have been in possession of the goods.

Article 206

1. By way of derogation from Articles 202 and 204(1)(*a*), no customs debt on importation shall be deemed to be incurred in respect of specific goods where the person concerned proves that the non-fulfilment of the obligations which arise from:

— the provisions of Articles 38 to 41 and the second indent of Article 177, or

— keeping the goods in question in temporary storage, or

— the use of the customs procedure under which the goods have been placed,

results from the total destruction or irretrievable loss of the said goods as a result of the actual nature of the goods or unforeseeable circumstances or *force majeure*, or as a consequence of authorization by the customs authorities.

For the purposes of this paragraph, goods shall be irretrievably lost when they are rendered unusable by any person.

2. Nor shall a customs debt on importation be deemed to be incurred in respect of goods released for free circulation at a reduced or zero rate of import duty by virtue of their end- use, where such goods are exported or re-exported with the permission of the customs authorities.

Article 207

Where, in accordance with Article 206(1), no customs debt is deemed to be incurred in respect of goods released for free circulation at a reduced or zero rate of import duty on account of their end-use, any scrap or waste resulting from such destruction shall be deemed to be non-Community goods.

Article 208

Where in accordance with Article 203 or 204 a customs debt is incurred in respect of goods released for free circulation at a reduced rate of import duty on account of their end-use, the amount paid when the goods were released for free circulation shall be deducted from the amount of the customs debt.

This provision shall apply *mutatis mutandis* where a customs debt is incurred in respect of scrap and waste resulting from the destruction of such goods.

Article 209

1. A customs debt on exportation shall be incurred through:

— the exportation from the customs territory of the Community, under cover of a customs declaration, of goods liable to export duties.

2. The customs debt shall be incurred at the time when such customs declaration is accepted.

3. The debtor shall be the declarant. In the event of indirect representation, the person on whose behalf the declaration is made shall also be a debtor.

Article 210

1. A customs debt on exportation shall be incurred through:

— the removal from the customs territory of the Community of goods liable to export duties without a customs declaration.

2. The customs debt shall be incurred at the time when the said goods actually leave that territory.

3. The debtor shall be:

— the person who removed the goods, and

— any persons who participated in such removal and who were aware or should reasonably have been aware that a customs declaration had not been but should have been lodged.

Article 211

1. A customs debt on exportation shall be incurred through:

— failure to comply with the conditions under which the goods were allowed to leave the customs territory of the Community with total or partial relief from export duties.

2. The debt shall be incurred at the time when the goods reach a destination other than that for which they were allowed to leave the customs territory of the Community with total or partial relief from export duties or, should the customs authorities be unable to determine that time, the expiry of the time limit set for the production of evidence that the conditions entitling the goods to such relief have been fulfilled.

3. The debtor shall be the declarant. In the event of indirect representation, the person on whose behalf the declaration is made shall also be a debtor.

Article 212

The customs debt referred to in Articles 201 to 205 and 209 to 211 shall be incurred even if it relates to goods subject to measures of prohibition or restriction on importation or exportation of any kind whatsoever. However, no customs debt shall be incurred on the unlawful introduction into the customs territory of the Community of counterfeit currency or of narcotic drugs and psychotropic substances which do not enter into the economic circuit strictly supervised by the competent authorities with a view to their use for medical and scientific purposes. For the purposes of criminal law as applicable to customs offences, the customs debt shall nevertheless be deemed to have been incurred where, under a Member State's criminal law, customs duties provide the basis for determining penalties, or the existence of a customs debt is grounds for taking criminal proceedings.

Article 213

Where several persons are liable for payment of one customs debt, they shall be jointly and severally liable for such debt.

Article 214

1. Save as otherwise expressly provided by this Code and without prejudice to paragraph 2, the amount of the import duty or export duty applicable to goods shall be determined on the basis of the rules of assessment appropriate to those goods at the time when the customs debt in respect of them is incurred.

2. Where it is not possible to determine precisely when the customs debt is incurred, the time to be taken into account in determining the rules of assessment appropriate to the goods concerned shall be the time when the customs authorities conclude that the goods are in a situation in which a customs debt is incurred.

However, where the information available to the customs authorities enables them to establish that the customs debt was incurred prior to the time when they reached that conclusion, the amount of the import duty or export duty payable on the goods in question shall be determined on the basis of the rules of assessment appropriate to the goods at the earliest time when existence of the customs debt arising from the situation may be established from the information available.

3. Compensatory interest shall be applied, in the circumstances and under the conditions to be defined in the provisions adopted under the committee procedure, in order to prevent the wrongful acquisition of a financial advantage through deferment of the date on which the customs debt was incurred or entered in the accounts.

Article 215

1. A customs debt shall be incurred at the place where the events from which it arises occur.

2. Where it is not possible to determine the place referred to in paragraph 1, the customs debt shall be deemed to have been incurred at the place where the customs authorities conclude that the goods are in a situation in which a customs debt is incurred.

3. Where a customs procedure is not discharged for goods, the customs debt shall be deemed to have been incurred at the place where the goods:

— were placed under that procedure, or

— enter the Community under that procedure.

4. Where the information available to the customs authorities enables them to establish that the customs debt was already incurred when the goods were in another place at an earlier date, the customs debt shall be deemed to have been incurred at the place which may be established as the location of the goods at the earliest time when existence of the customs debt may be established.

Article 216

1. In so far as agreements concluded between the Community and certain third countries provide for the granting on importation into those countries of preferential tariff treatment for goods originating in the Community within the meaning of such agreements, on condition that, where they have been obtained under the inward processing procedure, non-Community goods incorporated in the said originating goods are subject to payment of the import duties payable thereon, the validation of the documents necessary to enable such preferential tariff treatment to be obtained in third countries shall cause a customs debt on importation to be incurred.

2. The moment when such customs debt is incurred shall be deemed to be the moment when the customs authorities accept the export declaration relating to the goods in question.

3. The debtor shall be the declarant. In the event of indirect representation, the person on whose behalf the declaration is made shall also be a debtor.

4. The amount of the import duties corresponding to this customs debt shall be determined under the same conditions as in the case of a customs debt resulting from the acceptance, on the same date, of the declaration for release for free circulation of the goods concerned for the purpose of terminating the inward processing procedure.

CHAPTER 3
Recovery of the amount of the customs debt

SECTION 1
ENTRY IN THE ACCOUNTS AND COMMUNICATION OF THE AMOUNT OF DUTY TO THE DEBTOR

Articles 217–232

Note

Articles 217–232 are outside the scope of this work.

CHAPTER 4
Extinction of customs debt

Article 233

Without prejudice to the provisions in force relating to the time-barring of a customs debt and non-recovery of such a debt in the event of the legally established insolvency of the debtor, a customs debt shall be extinguished:

(*a*) by payment of the amount of duty;

(*b*) by remission of the amount of duty;

(c) where, in respect of goods declared for a customs procedure entailing the obligation to pay duties:
— the customs declaration is invalidated in accordance with Article 66,
— the goods, before their release, are either seized and simultaneously or subsequently confiscated, destroyed on the instructions of the customs authorities, destroyed or abandoned in accordance with Article 182 or destroyed or irretrievably lost as a result of their actual nature or of unforeseeable circumstances or *force majeure*;

(d) where goods in respect of which a customs debt is incurred in accordance with Article 202 are seized upon their unlawful introduction and are simultaneously or subsequently confiscated.

In the event of seizure and confiscation, the customs debt shall, nonetheless for the purposes of the criminal law applicable to customs offences, be deemed not to have been extinguished where, under a Member State's criminal law, customs duties provide the basis for determining penalties or the existence of a customs debt is grounds for taking criminal proceedings.

Article 234

A customs debt, as referred to in Article 216, shall also be extinguished where the formalities carried out in order to enable the preferential tariff treatment referred to in Article 216 to be granted are cancelled.

CHAPTER 5
Repayment and remission of duty

Articles 235–242

Note
Articles 235–242 are outside the scope of this work.

TITLE VIII
Appeals

Article 243

1. Any person shall have the right to appeal against decisions taken by the customs authorities which relate to the application of customs legislation, and which concern him directly and individually.

Any person who has applied to the customs authorities for a decision relating to the application of customs legislation and has not obtained a ruling on that request within the period referred to in Article 6(2) shall also be entitled to exercise the right of appeal.

The appeal must be lodged in the Member State where the decision has been taken or applied for.

2. The right of appeal may be exercised:
(a) initially, before the customs authorities designated for that purpose by the Member States;
(b) subsequently, before an independent body, which may be a judicial authority or an equivalent specialized body, according to the provisions in force in the Member States.

Article 244

The lodging of an appeal shall not cause implementation of the disputed decision to be suspended.

The customs authorities shall, however, suspend implementation of such decision in whole or in part where they have good reason to believe that the disputed decision is inconsistent with customs legislation or that irreparable damage is to be feared for the person concerned.

Where the disputed decision has the effect of causing import duties or export duties to be charged, suspension of implementation of that decision shall be subject to the existence or lodging of a security. However, such security need not be required where such a requirement would be likely, owing to the debtor's circumstances, to cause serious economic or social difficulties.

Article 245

The provisions for the implementation of the appeals procedure shall be determined by the Member States.

Article 246

This title shall not apply to appeals lodged with a view to the annulment or revision of a decision taken by the customs authorities on the basis of criminal law.

TITLE IX
FINAL PROVISIONS

CHAPTER 1
Customs Code Committee

Article 247

1. A Customs Code committee, hereinafter called "the committee", composed of representatives of the Member States with a representative of the Commission as chairman, is hereby established.

2. The committee shall adopt its rules of procedure.

Article 248

1. The committee may examine any question concerning customs legislation which is raised by its chairman, either on his own initiative or at the request of a Member State's representative.

Article 249

1. The provisions required for the implementation of this Code, including implementation of the Regulation referred to in Article 184, except for Title VIII and subject to Articles 9 and 10 of Regulation (EEC) No 2658/87 (OJ No L 256, 7.9.1987, p 1) and to paragraph 4, shall be adopted in accordance with the procedure laid down in

paragraphs 2 and 3, in compliance with the international commitments entered into by the Community.

2. The representative of the Commission shall submit to the committee a draft of the measures to be taken. The committee shall deliver its opinion on the draft within a time limit which the chairman may lay down according to the urgency of the matter. The opinion shall be delivered by the majority laid down in Article 148(2) of the Treaty in the case of decisions which the Council is required to adopt on a proposal from the Commission. The votes of the representatives of the Member States within the committee shall be weighted in the manner set out in that Article. The chairman shall not vote.

3. (*a*) The Commission shall adopt the measures envisaged if they are in accordance with the opinion of the committee.

   (*b*) If the measures envisaged are not in accordance with the opinion of the committee, or if no opinion is delivered, the Commission shall, without delay, submit to the Council a proposal relating to the provisions to be adopted. The Council shall act by a qualified majority.

   (*c*) If, on the expiry of a period of three months from the date of referral to the Council, the Council has not acted, the proposed measures shall be adopted by the Commission.

4. The provisions necessary for implementing Articles 11, 12 and 21 shall be adopted by the procedure referred to in Article 10 of Regulation (EEC) No 2658/87.

CHAPTER 2

Legal effects in a Member State of measures taken, documents issued and findings made in another Member State

Article 250

Where a customs procedure is used in several Member States,

— the decisions, identification measures taken or agreed on, and the documents issued by the customs authorities of one Member State shall have the same legal effects in other Member States as such decisions, measures taken and documents issued by the customs authorities of each of those Member States;

— the findings made at the time controls are carried out by the customs authorities of a Member State shall have the same conclusive force in the other Member State as the findings made by the customs authorities of each of those Member States;

CHAPTER 3

Other final provisions

Article 251

1. The following Regulations and Directives are hereby repealed:

— Council Regulation (EEC) No 1224/80 of 28 May 1980 on the valuation of goods for customs purposes (OJ No L 134, 31.5.1980, p 1), as last amended by Regulation (EEC) No 4046/89 (OJ No L 388, 30.12.1989, p 24);

— Council Regulation (EEC) No 2151/84 of 23 July 1984 on the customs territory of the Community (OJ No L 197, 27.7.1984, p 1), as last amended by the Act of Accession of Spain and Portugal;

Note

Repeals within the scope of this work only are mentioned: other repeals have been omitted.

Article 252

Note

Article 252 is outside the scope of this work.

Article 253

This Regulation shall enter into force on the third day following that of its publication in the *Official Journal of the European Communities.*

It shall apply from 1 January 1994.

Title VIII shall not apply to the United Kingdom until 1 January 1995.

However, Article 161 and, in so far as they concern re-exportation, Articles 182 and 183 shall apply from 1 January 1993. In so far as the said Articles make reference to provisions in this Code and until such time as such provisions enter into force, the references shall be deemed to allude to the corresponding provisions in the Regulations and Directives listed in Article 251.

Before 1 October 1993, the Council shall, on the basis of a Commission progress report on discussions regarding the consequences to be drawn from the monetary conversion rate used for the application of common agricultural policy measures, review the problem of trade in goods between the Member States in the context of the internal market. This report shall be accompanied by Commission proposals if any, on which the Council shall take a decision in accordance with the provisions of the Treaty.

Before 1 January 1998, the Council shall, on the basis of a Commission report, review this Code with a view to making such adaptations as may appear necessary taking into account in particular the achievement of the internal market. This report shall be accompanied by proposals, if any, on which the Council shall take a decision in accordance with the provisions of the Treaty.

This Regulation shall be binding in its entirety and directly applicable in all Member States.

COMMISSION REGULATION

of 22 October 1992

92/3046/EEC

Laying down provisions implementing and amending Council Regulation (EEC) No 3330/ 91 on the statistics relating to the trading of goods between Member States

(OJ L307, 23.10.1992, p 27)

THE COMMISSION OF THE EUROPEAN COMMUNITIES,

Having regard to the Treaty establishing the European Economic Community,

Having regard to Council Regulation (EEC) No 3330/91 of 7 November 1991 on the statistics relating to the trading of goods between Member States (OJ No L 316, 16.11.1991, p 1), and in particular Article 30 thereof,

Whereas, with a view to establishing the statistics relating to the trading of goods between Member States, the field of application of the Intrastat system should be precisely defined in relation to both the goods to be included and those to be excluded;

Whereas the date from which the intra-Community operator shall in practice comply with his obligations to supply information must be determined; whereas the extent of the obligations of the third party to whom the party responsible for providing the information may transfer that task should be defined;

Whereas certain of the rules to be complied with by the departments concerned must be specified in detail in particular with a view to efficient management of the registers of intra-Community operation; whereas it is useful to specify the provisions relating to certain fiscal aspects of statistical information;

Whereas there should be additions to the definition of the data to be reported and to the arrangements for reporting such data;

Whereas a list should be drawn up of the goods to be excluded from the statistical returns relating to the trading of goods;

Whereas account should be taken initially of existing simplified procedures and of the special requirements of certain sectors;

Whereas the amendments to Council Directive 77/388/EEC (OJ No L 145, 13.6.1977, p 1) by Directive 91/680/EEC require certain provisions of Regulation (EEC) No 3330/91 (OJ No L 376, 31.12.1977, p 1) to be adapted, pursuant to the first indent of Article 33 thereof;

Whereas the measures provided for in this Regulation are in accordance with the opinion of the Committee on the statistics relating to the trading of goods between Member States,

HAS ADOPTED THIS REGULATION:

Article 1

With a view to establishing the statistics relating to the trading of goods between Member States, the Community and its Member States shall apply Regulation (EEC) No 3330/91, hereinafter referred to as **the Basic Regulation**, in accordance with the rules laid down in this Regulation.

Article 2

1. In connection with trade between the Community as constituted on 31 December 1985 and Spain or Portugal, and between those two last-mentioned Member States, the Intrastat system shall also apply to goods still liable to certain customs duties and charges having equivalent effect or which remain subject to other measures laid down by the Act of Accession.

2. The Intrastat system shall apply to the products referred to in Article 3(1) of Council Directive 92/12/EEC OJ No L 76, 23.3.1992, p 1), regardless of the form and content of the document accompanying them, when they move between the territories of the Member States.

Article 3

1. The Intrastat system shall not apply:

    (*a*) to goods placed or obtained under the inward processing customs procedure (suspension system) or the procedure of processing under customs control;

    (*b*) to goods circulating between parts of the statistical territory of the Community, at least one of which is not part of the territory of the Community pursuant to Council Directive 88/388/EEC.

2. The Member States shall be responsible for collecting data on the goods referred to in paragraph 1 on the basis of the customs procedures applicable to such goods.

3. If the statistical copy of the Single Administrative Document containing the data listed in Article 23 of the Basic Regulation, with the exception of the information referred to in paragraph 2(*e*) of that Article, is not available, the customs departments shall at least once a month send the relevant statistical departments a periodic list of those same data by type of goods, in accordance with the arrangements agreed upon by the said departments.

4. Articles 2, 4, 8, 9, 12(1), (3), (4), (5), (6) and (7); 13, 14, 19, 21 and 22(3)(*a*) and (*b*), first indent, shall not apply to the goods referred to in paragraph 1.

The other provisions of this Regulation shall apply to these goods without prejudice to any customs regulations which otherwise apply.

Article 4

1. Any natural or legal person carrying out an intra-Community operation for the first time, whether the goods are arriving or being dispatched, shall become responsible for providing the required information within the meaning of Article 20(5) of the Basic Regulation.

2. The party referred to in paragraph 1 shall provide the data on his intra-Community operations via the periodic declarations referred to in Article 13 of the Basic Regulation as from the month during which the assimilation threshold is exceeded, in accordance with the provisions relating to the threshold which become applicable to him.

The Member States shall determine the deadline for transmission in line with their particular administrative organisation.

3. When the VAT registration number of a party responsible for providing the information is amended as a result of a change of ownership, name, address, legal status or similar change which does not affect his intra-Community operations to a significant extent, the rule defined in paragraph 1 need not be applied to the party in question at the time of the change. It shall remain subject to the statistical obligations to which it was subject before the change.

Article 5

1. The third party referred to in Article 9(1) of the Basic Regulation is hereinafter referred to as the declaring third party.

2. The declaring third party shall provide the competent national departments with the following information:

(*a*)   in accordance with Article 6(1), the information necessary:

— to identify himself,

— to identify each of the parties responsible for providing the information who have transferred this task to him;

(*b*)   for each of the parties responsible for providing information, the data required by the Basic Regulation and in implementation thereof.

Article 6

1. The information necessary to identify an intra-Community operator within the meaning of Article 10 of the Basic Regulation shall be the following:

— full name of the person or firm,

— full address including post code,

— under the circumstances laid down in Article 10(6) of the Basic Regulation, the VAT registration number.

However, the statistical departments referred to in Article 10(1) of the Basic Regulation may dispense with one or more of the abovementioned items of information or, under circumstances to be determined by them, exempt the intra-Community operators from providing them.

In the Member States referred to in Article 10(3) of the Basic Regulation, the information which serves to identify an intra-Community operator shall be supplied to the abovementioned statistical departments by the tax authorities referred to in the said

Article as and when it becomes available to the latter unless there is an agreement to the contrary between the departments concerned.

2. The minimum of list data to be recorded in the register of intra-Community operators, within the meaning of Article 10 of the Basic Regulation, shall contain, for each intra-Community operator, the following:

(a) the year and month of entry in the register;

(b) the information necessary to identify the operator as laid down in paragraph 1;

(c) where applicable, whether the operator is the consignor, consignee or declarant, or, as from 1 January 1993, a party responsible for providing information or declaring third party, upon either consignment or receipt; in the Member States referred to in Article 10(3) of the Basic Regulation, the information stipulated in paragraph 1 of the present Article shall show whether each operator in question is a consignor or a consignee;

(d) in the case of a consignor or consignee or, as from 1 January 1993, a party responsible for providing information, the total value of his intra-Community operations, by month and by flow, together with, as from that same date the value referred to in Article 11(3) of the Basic Regulation; however, this information need not be recorded:

— prior to 1993, in those Member States referred to in Article 10(3) of the Basic Regulation,

— if the checking of the information recorded as statistics using the information referred to in article 11(3) of the Basic Regulation and the functioning of the statistical thresholds referred to in Article 28 of the said Regulation are organised separately from the management of the register of intra-Community operators.

The competent national departments may record other data in the register in accordance with their requirements.

Article 7

With a view to implementing Article 10(6) of the Basic Regulation, the case where responsibility for the information, for given operations, lies not with the operator as a legal entity *per se* but with a constituent part of this entity, such as a branch office, a kind- of-activity unit or local unit, may be considered a justified exception.

Article 8

In the lists referred to in Article 11(1) of the Basic Regulation, the tax authorities responsible shall mention intra-Community operators who, as a result of a scission, merger or cessation of activity during the period under review will no longer appear on the said lists.

Article 9

1. The party responsible for providing information shall transmit the data required under the Basic Regulation and in implementation thereof:

(a) in accordance with the Community provision in force;

(*b*)   direct to the competent national departments or via the collection offices which the Member States have set up for this or for other statistical or administrative purposes;

(*c*)   or a given reference period, at his discretion:

—   either by means of a single declaration, within a time limit which the competent national departments shall lay down in their instructions to the parties responsible for providing information and which shall be between the fifth and the tenth working day following the end of that period,

—   or by means of several part-declarations; in this case, the competent national departments may require agreement to be reached with them on the frequency of transmission and deadlines, but the last part- declaration must be transmitted within the time limit laid down under the first indent above.

2. By way of derogation from paragraph 1, a party responsible for providing information who benefits from exemption by virtue of application of the assimilation threshold provided for in Article 28(4) of the Basic Regulation must, when transmitting the information, conform only to the regulations of the tax authorities responsible.

3. Pursuant to Article 34 of the Basic Regulation, the provisions of this Article relating to the periodicity of the declaration shall not prevent the conclusion of an agreement providing for the supply of data in real time, when the data are transmitted electronically.

4. By way of derogation to paragraph 1 above, in those Member States where the periodic statistical declaration is the same as the periodic tax declaration, the provisions relating to the transmission of the statistical declaration shall be drawn up in line with Community or national tax regulations.

Article 10

In the medium for the information, the Member States whose statistical territory is described in the nomenclature of countries annexed to Council Regulation (EEC) No 1736/75 (OJ No L 183, 14.7.1975, p 3) shall be designated by either alphabetical or numerical codes, as follows:

France:	FR	or	001,
Belgium and Luxembourg:	BL	or	002,
Netherlands:	NI	or	003,
Germany:	DE	or	004,
Italy:	IT	or	005,
United Kingdom:	GB	or	006,
Ireland:	IE	or	007,
Denmark:	DK	or	008,
Greece:	GR	or	009,
Portugal:	PT	or	010,
Spain:	ES	or	011.

Article 11

When the quantity of goods to be mentioned on the data medium is determined:

(*a*) **"net mass"** shall mean the actual mass of the good excluding all packaging; it must be given in kilograms;

(*b*) **"supplementary units"** shall mean the units measuring quantity, other than the units measuring mass expressed in kilograms; they must be mentioned in accordance with the information set out in the current version of the combined nomenclature, opposite the subheadings concerned, the list of which is published in Part I "Preliminary provisions" of the said nomenclature.

Article 12

1. The value of the goods, as referred to in Article 23(1)(*d*) of the Basic Regulation, shall be given as follows:

— by type of goods, the statistical value,

— by statistical declaration, the amount invoiced.

2. The statistical value shall be fixed:

— upon dispatch, on the basis of the taxable amount to be determined the taxation purposes in accordance with Directive 77/388/EEC for deliveries of goods specified under Section A(1)(*a*) and, where appropriate, for the operations specified under section A(1)(*b*) of Article 11 of the same Directive, minus, however, any taxes deductible because of the dispatch; it shall, on the other hand, include transport and insurance costs relating to that part of the journey which takes place on the statistical territory of the Member State of dispatch,

— on arrival, on the basis of the taxable amount to be determined for taxation purposes, in accordance with Article 28e of the Directive referred to above, for acquisition of goods, minus, however, taxes due because of the release for consumption and transport and insurance costs relating to that part of the journey which takes place on the statistical territory of the Member State of arrival.

The statistical value must be declared in accordance with the first subparagraph, even if the taxable amount does not have to be determined for taxation purposes.

For goods resulting from processing operations, the statistical value shall be established as if those goods had been produced entirely in the Member State of processing.

3. The amount invoiced shall be the total amount (excluding VAT) of invoices or documents servings as invoices relating to all the goods included in a statistical declaration.

4. The party responsible for providing information may indicate the invoiced amount broken down by type of goods.

By way of derogation to paragraph 1, the Member States may require the invoiced amount to be broken down by type of goods. In this case, they shall calculate the statistical value and exempt the party responsible for providing the statistical information from the need to mention it. However, those responsible for providing the information may be required to supply information on ancillary costs on a sample basis.

The second subparagraph shall apply either to all parties required to transmit the periodic declaration referred to in Article 13(1) of the Basic Regulation or solely to those parties who benefit from the application of simplification thresholds.

5. The Member States may exercise the option laid down in the second subparagraph of paragraph 4, even if their particular administrative organisation prevents them from taking the simplification measure which, by virtue of this subparagraph, must accompany the exercise of this option, namely, exemption from the requirement to mention the statistical value.

In the instructions relating to the statistical declaration to the parties responsible for providing information, the technical reasons why both the statistical value and the invoiced amount must be mentioned, by type of goods, shall be indicated in advance.

The Member States shall transmit a copy of these instructions to the Commission before 1 November 1992 and, thereafter, whenever they are updated.

6. In the case of work under contract, the amount invoiced shall be the amount entered in the accounts for the work, including any ancillary costs. It shall be mentioned only in the case of the dispatch and the arrival which follow the contract work.

7. "Ancillary costs" means the costs incurred in the movement of goods between the Member State of dispatch and the Member State of arrival, such as transport and insurance costs.

Article 13

1. For the purposes of this Regulation:

(*a*) **"transaction"** shall mean any operation, whether commercial or not, which leads to a movement of goods covered by statistics on the trading of goods between Member States;

(*b*) **"nature of the transaction"** shall mean all those characteristics which distinguish one transaction from another.

2. A distinction shall be made between transactions which differ in nature, in accordance with the list in Annex I.

The nature of the transaction shall be specified, on the information medium, by the code number corresponding to the appropriate category of column A in the abovementioned list.

3. Within the limits of the list referred to in paragraph 2, the Member States may prescribe the collection of data on the nature of the transaction up to the level which they use for the collection of data on trade third countries, regardless of whether they collect them in this connection as data on the nature of the transaction or as data on customs procedures.

Article 14

1. For the purposes of this Regulation, **"delivery terms"** shall mean those provisions of the sales contract which lay down the obligations of the seller and the buyer respectively, in accordance with the Incoterms of the International Chamber of Commerce listed in Annex II.

2. Within the limits of the list referred to in paragraph 1 and without prejudice to paragraph 3:

(*a*)   those Member States which apply the second subparagraph of Article 12(4) shall stipulate that data on delivery terms shall be collected on the information medium and shall give details of how they are to be mentioned;

(*b*)   the other Member States may stipulate that data on delivery terms shall be collected on the information medium up to the level at which they collect data on trade with third countries.

3. The delivery terms shall be indicated, for each type of goods, by one of the abbreviations in the list referred to in paragraph 1.

Article 15

1. **"Presumed mode of transport"** shall indicate, upon dispatch, the mode of transport determined by the active means of transport by which the goods are presumed to be going to leave the statistical territory of the Member State of dispatch and, upon arrival, the mode of transport determined by the active means of transport by which the goods are presumed to have entered the statistical territory of the Member State on arrival.

2. The modes of transport to be mentioned on the information medium are as follows:

Code	Title
1	Transport by sea
2	Transport by rail
3	Transport by road
4	Transport by air
5	Consignments by post
7	Fixed transport installations
8	Transport by inland waterway
9	Own propulsion

The mode of transport shall be designated on the said medium by the corresponding code number.

Article 16

1. **"Country of origin"** shall mean the country where the goods originate.

Goods which are entirely obtained in a country originate in that country.

An item in the production of which two or more countries are involved originates in the country where the last significant processing or working, economically justified and carried out in an enterprise equipped for this purpose and leading to the manufacture of a new product or representing an important stage of manufacture, takes place.

2. The country of origin shall be designated by the code number given to it in the current version of the country nomenclature annexed to Regulation (EEC) No 1736/75, without prejudice to the last sentence of Article 47 of the said Regulation.

Article 17

1. "Region of origin" shall mean the region of the Member State of dispatch where the goods were produced or were erected, assembled, processed, repaired or maintained; failing this, the region of origin shall be replaced either by the region where the commercial process took place or by the region where the goods were dispatched.

2. "Region of destination" shall mean the region of the Member State of arrival where the goods are to be consumed or erected, assembled, processed, repaired or maintained; failing this, the region of destination shall be replaced either by the region where the commercial process is to take place or by the region to which the goods are dispatched.

3. Each Member State exercising the option provided for in Article 23(2)(*b*) of the Basic Regulation shall draw up a list of its regions and determine the code, which shall have a maximum of two characters, by which those regions shall be indicated on the information medium.

Article 18

1. "Port or airport of loading" shall means the port or airport situated on the statistical territory of the Member State of dispatch at which the goods are loaded onto the active means of transport on or in which they are presumed to be going to leave that territory.

2. "Port or airport of unloading" shall mean the port or airport situated on the statistical territory of the Member State of arrival at which the goods are unloaded from the active means of transport on or in which they are presumed to have entered that territory.

3. Each Member State exercising the option provided for in Article 23(2)(*c*) or (*d*) of the Basic Regulation shall draw up a list of ports and airports to be mentioned on the information medium and shall fix the code by which they are to be indicated on that medium.

Article 19

1. "Statistical procedure" shall mean the category of dispatch or arrival within which a given intra-Community operation takes place and which is not adequately referred to in column A or column B of the list of transactions in Annex I.

2. Any Member State wishing to exercise the option provided for in Article 23(2)(*e*) of the Basic Regulation shall draw up a list of the statistical procedures to be mentioned on the information medium and fix the code by which they are to be indicated on that medium.

Article 20

Data relating to the goods listed in Annex III shall be excluded from compilation and, consequently, pursuant to Article 25(4) of the Basic Regulation, from collection.

Article 21

1. For the purposes of this Regulation, **"specific movements of goods"** shall mean movements of goods having specific features which have some significance for the interpretation of the information and stem either from the movement as such or from the nature of the goods or from the transaction which results in the movement of the goods or from the consignor or consignee of the goods.

2. In the absence of provisions drawn up under Article 33 of the Basic Regulation, the Member States may apply, as regards data to specific movements of goods, the simplified procedures which were applied, under Regulation (EEC) No 1736/75, prior to the date referred to in the second paragraph of Article 35 of the Basic Regulation.

3. Those Member States wishing to have more detailed information than that resulting from the application of Article 21 of the Basic Regulation may, by way of derogation from that Article, organise the collection of that information, for one or more specific product groups, provided that the party responsible for providing the information is allowed to elect to supply it in accordance with either the combined nomenclature or the additional subdivisions.

Those Member States exercising that option shall notify the Commission that they are doing so. At the same time, they shall state the reasons for their decision, supply the list of relevant combined nomenclature subheadings and describe the collection method they are using.

Article 22

[Amends references to Council Directive 77/388/EEC in Council Regulation 3330/91]

Article 23

This Regulation shall enter into force on the seventh day following its publication in the *Official Journal of the European Communities.*

Those of its provisions which relate to the Articles referred to in the second paragraph of Article 35 of the Basic Regulation shall apply from the same date as those said Articles.

This Regulation shall be binding in its entirety and directly applicable in all Member States.

Done at Brussels, 22 October 1992.

COMMISSION REGULATION

of 11 December 1992

92/3590/EEC

concerning the statistical information media for statistics on trade between Member States

(OJ L364, 12.12.1992, p 32)

Amendment

Regulation 92/3590/EEC repealed by Commission Regulation of 18 November 2004 (04/1982/EC) art 27 with effect from 1 January 2005.

COUNCIL REGULATION

of 5 April 1993

93/854/EC

on Transit Statistics Relating to the Trading of Goods between Member States

THE COUNCIL OF THE EUROPEAN COMMUNITIES

Having regard to the Treaty establishing the European Economic Community, and in particular Article 100a thereof,

Having regard to the proposal from the Commission (OJ C107, 28.4.1992, p 16),

In cooperation with the European Parliament (OJ C337, 21.12.1992, p 210; OJ C72, 15.3.1993),

Having regard to the opinion of the Economic and Social Committee (OJ C223, 31.8.1992, p 6),

Whereas the abolition of customs formalities, controls and documentation for all movements of goods across internal frontiers is necessary for the completion of the internal market;

Whereas, in the Member States, statistics on the trading of goods between Member States resulting from transit movements and movements into and out of warehouses may nevertheless still be needed;

Whereas Council Regulation (EEC) No 3330/91 of 7 November 1991 on the statistics relating to the trading of goods between Member States (OJ L316, 16.11.1991, p 1) prohibits the Member States from introducing or maintaining compulsory formalities for the purpose of keeping statistics on transit and storage; whereas it is necessary for that purpose to provide a Community legal base;

Whereas the framework in which the Member States are authorised to organise their statistical surveys on these movements must be determined in order to prevent the burden on those responsible for providing information varying excessively from one Member State to another;

Whereas, within that framework, it is necessary to determine the purpose of transit and storage statistics and the consequences for the collection of information, to ensure that responsibility for collecting that information is directed towards existing administrative sources and to make use of the competent services of the latter to fill any gaps, without increasing the burden on those responsible for providing information;

Whereas that burden must not exceed certain limits, as regards classification, data to be declared or data media;

Whereas it is important that the burden of transit and storage statistics be alleviated, particularly for small and medium-sized enterprises; whereas this should be effected by means of statistical thresholds;

Whereas the Commission must not only adopt provisions implementing this Regulation but must also ensure that other implementing provisions adopted by the Member States do not compromise the alleviation of the burden on those responsible for providing information; whereas the Commission should be assisted in this task by the Committee on Statistics relating to the Trading of Goods between Member States,

HAS ADOPTED THIS REGULATION

Article 1

1. With a view to compiling transit statistics and storage statistics, Member States may collect data on the trading of goods between Member States, acting in conformity with the rules laid down in this Regulation.

2. Member States which exercise this option shall accordingly inform the Commission.

Article 2

1. For the purposes of this Regulation, the definitions given in Article 2(*a*), (*b*), (*c*), (*d*), (*e*) and (*f*) of Regulation (EEC) No 3330/91 shall apply.

2. For the purpose of this Regulation:

(*a*) transit: means the crossing of a given Member State by goods which are being transported between two places situated outside that Member State;

(*b*) interrupted transit: means transit during which a break in transport occurs; this also includes transhipment;

(*c*) customs warehousing procedure: means the customs warehousing procedure as defined in Articles 1 and 2 of Council Regulation (EEC) No 2503/88 of 25 July 1988 on customs warehouses (OJ L225, 15.8.1988, p 1);

(*d*) competent statistical services: means those services in each Member State which are responsible for compiling statistics on the trading of goods between Member States.

Article 3

Of the goods referred to in Article 3 of Regulation (EEC) No 3330/91, data shall be collected for the purpose of compiling statistics on transit through a given Member State on those goods which are in interrupted transit in that Member State, with the exception of goods which having entered that Member State as non-Community goods, have subsequently been put into free circulation there.

Article 4

Of the goods referred to in Article 3 of Regulation (EEC) No 3330/91, data shall be collected for the purpose of compiling storage statistics in a given Member State on:

(*a*) those which, though the customs warehousing procedure has not terminated, are transferred, within the meaning of Article 20 of Regulation (EEC) No 2503/88, from a customs warehouse situated in that Member State to one situated in another Member State;

(*b*) those which, though the customs warehousing procedure has not terminated, are transferred, within the meaning of Article 20 of Regulation (EEC) No 2503/88, to a customs warehouse situated in that Member State from a customs warehouse situated in another Member State;

(*c*) those which are subject to the customs warehousing procedure in that Member State and are sent to another Member State under the procedure for external Community transit;

(*d*) those which are subject to the customs warehousing procedure in that Member State, having come from another Member State under the procedure for external Community transit.

Article 5

1. Under conditions which they themselves shall determine, Member States shall authorise those responsible for providing statistical information to use administrative or commercial documents already required for other purposes as the statistical data medium.

However, with a view to the standardisation of their basic documentation, Member States may establish exclusively statistical media provided that those required to provide statistical information are free to choose which of these media they use.

2. Member States shall inform the Commission of the media which they authorise or establish.

Article 6

1. In a given Member State, the person responsible for providing statistical information as referred to in Article 8 of Regulation (EEC) No 3330/91 shall be the natural or legal person who, engaged in that Member State in the trading of goods between Member States, draws up the administrative or commercial document designated as the statistical data medium pursuant to the first subparagraph of Article 5(1).

In the absence of such a person and by way of derogation from Article 8 of Regulation (EEC) No 3330/91, each Member State shall designate from among the administrative services to which the document referred to in the first subparagraph is made available, one service which shall provide the information.

2. Member States shall be entitled to proceed in accordance with the second subparagraph of paragraph 1 in order to relieve persons responsible for supplying information of their obligations, in whole or in part.

3. The person or service referred to in paragraph 1 shall conform to the provisions of this Regulation, the provisions adopted pursuant to Article 30 of Regulation (EEC) No 3330/91 and the measures taken by Member States to implement those provisions.

Article 7

1. On the statistical data medium to be sent to the competent services:

— without prejudice to Article 34 of Regulation (EEC) No 3330/91, goods shall be designated according to their usual trade description in sufficiently precise terms to permit their identification and their immediate and unequivocal classification in the most detailed relevant subdivision of the current version of either the classification of the harmonised system for transit statistics or the combined nomenclature for storage statistics, irrespective of the level at which these classifications are applied; however, this provision shall not prevent the Member States applying the standard goods classification for transport statistics—revised (NST/R) instead of the abovementioned classifications, where permissible under the rules governing the medium used,

— the code number corresponding to the abovementioned nomenclature subdivision may also be required by type of goods.

2. On the statistical data medium, countries shall be described by the alphabetical or numerical codes laid down in Council Regulation (EEC) No 1736/75 of 24 June 1975 on the external trade statistics of the Community and statistics of trade between Member States (as last amended by Council Regulation 1629/88/EEC; see respectively OJ L183, 14.7.1975, p 3 and OJ L147, 14.6.1988, p 1).

For the purposes of the first subparagraph, the parties responsible for providing information shall comply with the instructions issued by the national services competent for compiling statistics on trade between Member States.

Article 8

1. Member States which compile transit statistics shall determine which of the following data are to be included on the statistical data medium, by type of goods:

(*a*) the country of consignment, within the meaning of Article 9;

(*b*) the country of destination, within the meaning of Article 9;

(*c*) the quantity of goods in gross mass, within the meaning of Article 9;

(*d*) the mode of transport in accordance with Article 9(*f*)(1);

(*e*) the place where the interruption in transit took place in accordance with Article 9.

2. Member States which compile storage statistics shall determine which of the following data are to be included on the statistical data medium, by type of goods:

(*a*) the Member State of consignment, in the Member State which the goods enter within the meaning of Article 9;

(*b*) the Member State of destination, in the Member State which goods leave within the meaning of Article 9;

(*c*) the country of origin, within the meaning of Article 9; however, this item may be required only as allowed by Community law;

(*d*) the quantity of goods expressed in gross mass or net mass within the meaning of Article 9 and in supplementary units in accordance with the combined nomenclature, where it is used pursuant to Article 7(1);

(*e*) the customs value;

(*f*) the presumed mode of transport, in accordance with Article 9(f)(2);

(*g*) the region of destination, in the Member State which the goods enter.

3. In so far as is not laid down in this Regulation, the data referred to in paragraphs 1 and 2 and the rules governing their inclusion on the statistical data medium shall be defined in accordance with the procedure laid down in Article 30 of Regulation (EEC) No 3330/91.

Article 9

For the purposes of applying Article 8:

(*a*) country/Member State of consignment: means the last country/Member State in which the goods were subject to halts or legal operations not inherent in their transport:

(*b*) country/Member State of destination: means the last country/Member State to which it is known, at the time the statistical data medium is drawn up, that the goods are to be sent;

(*c*) country of origin: means the country in which the goods originated within the meaning of Council Regulation (EEC) No 802/68 of 27 June 1968 on the common definition of the concept of origin of goods (as last amended by Council Regulation 456/91/EEC; see respectively OJ L148, 28.6.1968, p 1 and OJ L54, 28.2.1991, p 4);

(*d*) gross mass: means the cumulated mass of the goods and all their packaging with the exclusion of the transport equipment, and in particular containers;

(*e*) net mass: means the mass of the goods, all packaging removed;

(*f*) mode of transport: means that actually used

1 before or after the interruption of transit;
2 on entry to or exit from the warehouse.

Modes of transport are as follows:

Code	Designation
1	Sea transport
2	Rail transport
3	Road transport
4	Air transport
5	Post
7	Fixed transport installations
8	Inland waterway transport
9	Self-propelled

If the mode of transport is given as one of those listed under codes 1, 2, 3, 4 or 8, Member States may require that it also be stated whether the goods are transported in containers within the meaning of Article 15(3) of Regulation (EEC) No 1736/75;

(*g*) place of interruption of transit: means the port, airport or any other place where transit is interrupted within the meaning of Article 2(2)(*b*).

Article 10

1. Where the data referred to in Articles 7 and 8 need not be shown on the administrative or commercial document referred to in the first subparagraph of Article 5(1) for the purposes for which such documents are required, Member States shall instruct the administrative service referred to in the second subparagraph of Article 6(1) to collect them and transmit them to the competent statistical services in accordance with procedures which they shall lay down, bearing in mind the stated requirements of these statistical services.

2. Without prejudice to the second subparagraph of Article 5(1), Member States shall establish the media to be used by the abovementioned administrative service for transmitting these data.

Article 11

1. For the purposes of this Regulation, statistical thresholds shall be defined as limits, expressed in gross mass for transit statistics and in terms of value or in mass for storage statistics, below which the obligations on those responsible for providing information are suspended.

2. The threshold for transit statistics shall be fixed per type of goods at least:

— 50 kg in the case of air transport,

— 1 000 kg for other modes of transport.

3. The threshold for storage statistics shall be fixed at least ECU 800 per type of goods, irrespective of the mass of the goods, or at least 50 kg per type of goods in the case of air transport or at least 1 000 kg per type of goods for other modes of transport, irrespective of the value of the goods.

Article 12

1. The provisions necessary for implementing this Regulation shall be adopted in accordance with the procedure laid down in Article 30 of Regulation (EEC) No 3330/91.

2. Member States may adopt the provisions required for collecting information in order to compile transit and storage statistics where such provisions are not laid down in this Regulation or adopted in accordance with paragraph 1.

However, if the effect of these national arrangements is to compromise the alleviation of the burden on those responsible for providing information, provisions to restore the conditions for alleviating that burden shall be adopted in accordance with the abovementioned Article.

Article 13

Member States shall communicate to the Commission the measures which they take to implement this Regulation.

Article 14

The Committee on Statistics relating to the Trading of Goods between Member States, set up by Article 29 of Regulation (EEC) No 3330/91, may examine any question, relating to the implementation of this Regulation raised by its chairman, either on his own initiative or at the request of the representative of a Member State.

Article 15

This Regulation shall enter into force on the third day following its publication in the Official Journal of the European Communities.

The Regulation shall remain in force until 31 December 1996. No later than three months before this date, the Commission shall present a report on the application of this Regulation and if necessary put forward a proposal.

This Regulation shall be binding in its entirety and directly applicable in all Member States.

COMMISSION REGULATION

of 2 July 1993

93/2454/EEC

Commission Regulation 2 July 1993 provisions for the implementation of Council Regulation (EEC) No 2913/92 establishing the Community Customs Code

PART I: GENERAL IMPLEMENTING PROVISIONS

TITLE I: GENERAL

TITLE V: CUSTOMS VALUE

TITLE VI: INTRODUCTION OF GOODS INTO THE CUSTOMS TERRITORY

TITLE VII: CUSTOMS DECLARATIONS — NORMAL PROCEDURE

TITLE VIII: EXAMINATION OF THE GOODS, FINDINGS OF THE CUSTOMS OFFICE AND OTHER MEASURES TAKEN BY THE CUSTOMS OFFICE

PART IV: CUSTOMS DEBT

TITLE I: SECURITY

TITLE II: INCURRENCE OF THE DEBT

PART V: FINAL PROVISIONS

THE COMMISSION OF THE EUROPEAN COMMUNITIES,

Having regard to the Treaty establishing the European Economic Community,

Having regard to Council Regulation (EEC) No 2913/92 of 12 October 1992 establishing the Community Customs Code (OJ No L 302, 19.10.1992), hereinafter referred to as the "Code", and in particular Article 249 thereof,

Whereas the Code assembled all existing customs legislation in a single legal instrument; whereas at the same time the Code made certain modifications to this legislation to make it more coherent, to simplify it and to plug certain loopholes; whereas it therefore constitutes complete Community legislation in this area;

Whereas the same reasons which led to the adoption of the Code apply equally to the customs implementing legislation; whereas it is therefore desirable to bring together in a single regulation those customs implementing provisions which are currently scattered over a large number of Community regulations and directives;

Whereas the implementing code for the Community Customs Code hereby established should set out existing customs implementing rules; whereas it is nevertheless necessary, in the light of experience:

— to make some amendments in order to adapt the said rules to the provisions of the Code;

— to extend the scope of certain provisions which currently apply only to specific customs procedures in order to take account of the Code's comprehensive application;

— to formulate certain rules more precisely in order to achieve greater legal security in their application;

Whereas the changes made relate mainly to the provisions concerning customs debt;

Whereas it is appropriate to limit the application of Article 791(2) until 1 January 1995 and to review the subject matter in the light of experience gained before that time;

Whereas the measures provided for by this Regulation are in accordance with the opinion of the Customs Code Committee,

HAS ADOPTED THIS REGULATION:

PART I
GENERAL IMPLEMENTING PROVISIONS

TITLE I
GENERAL

CHAPTER 1
Definitions

Article 1

For the purposes of this Regulation

1. Code means: Council Regulation (EEC) No 2913/92 of 12 October 1992 establishing a Community Customs Code;

[2. *ATA carnet* means: the international customs document for temporary importation established by virtue of the ATA Convention or the Istanbul Convention;][1]

3. *Committee* means: the Customs Code Committee established in Article 247 of the Code;

4. *Customs Cooperation Council* means: the organization set up by the Convention establishing a Customs Cooperation Council, done at Brussels on 15 December 1950;

5. *Particulars required for identification of the goods* means: on the one hand, the particulars used to identify the goods commercially allowing the customs authorities to determine the tariff classification and, on the other hand, the quantity of the goods;

6. *Goods of a non-commercial nature* means: goods whose entry for the customs procedure in question is on an occasional basis and whose nature and quantity indicate that they are intended for the private, personal or family use of the consignees or persons carrying them, or which are clearly intended as gifts;

7. *Commercial policy measures* means: non-tariff measures established, as part of the common commercial policy, in the form of Community provisions governing the import and export of goods, such as surveillance or safeguard measures, quantitative restrictions or limits and import or export prohibitions;

8. *Customs nomenclature* means: one of the nomenclatures referred to in Article 20(6) of the Code;

9. *Harmonised System* means: the Harmonised Commodity Description and Coding System;

10. *Treaty* means: the Treaty establishing the European Economic Community.

[11. Istanbul Convention means: the Convention on Temporary Admission agreed at Istanbul on 26 June 1990.][2]

Amendments

[1]   Substituted by Commission Regulation (EC) No 1762/95 Art 2(1)(*a*). See OJ L171, 21.7.95, p 8.
[2]   Inserted by Commission Regulation (EC) No 1762/95 Art 2(1)(*b*). See OJ L171, 21.7.95, p 8.

[Article 1a

For the purposes of applying Articles 16 to 34 and 291 to 308, the countries of the Benelux Economic Union shall be considered as a single Member State.][1]

Amendments

[1]   Inserted by Commission Regulation 3665/93 EEC. See OJ L335, 31.12.93, p 1.

CHAPTER 2
Decisions

Article 2

Where a person making a request for a decision is not in a position to provide all the documents and information necessary to give a ruling, the customs authorities shall provide the documents and information at their disposal.

Article 3

A decision concerning security favourable to a person who has signed an undertaking to pay the sums due at the first written request of the customs authorities, shall be revoked where the said undertaking is not fulfilled.

Article 4

A revocation shall not affect goods which, at the moment of its entry into effect, have already been placed under a procedure by virtue of the revoked authorization.

However, the customs authorities may require that such goods be assigned to a permitted customs-approved treatment or use within the period which they shall set.

[CHAPTER 3
Data processing techniques

Article 4a

1. Under the conditions and in the manner which they shall determine, and with due regard to the principles laid down by customs rules, the customs authorities may provide that formalities shall be carried out by a data-processing technique. For this purpose:

— **"a data-processing technique"** means:

(*a*)   the exchange of EDI standard messages with the customs authorities;

(*b*)   the introduction of information required for completion of the formalities concerned into customs data-processing systems;

— **"EDI"** (electronic data interchange) means, the transmission of data structured according to agreed message standards, between one computer system and another, by electronic means,

— **"standard message"** means a predefined structure recognized for the electronic transmission of data.

2. The condition laid down for carrying out formalities by a data-processing technique shall include inter alia measures for checking the source of data and for protecting data against the risk of unauthorized access, loss alteration or destruction.

Article 4b

Where formalities are carried out by a data-processing technique, the customs authorities shall determine the rules for replacement of the handwritten signature by another technique which may be based on the use of codes.]¹

Amendments

¹   Inserted by EC Commission Regulation 3665/93. See OJ L335 of 31.12.93 p 1.

Articles 5–140

Notes

Articles 5–140 are outside the scope of this work.

TITLE V
CUSTOMS VALUE

CHAPTER 1
General provisions

Article 141

1. In applying the provisions of Articles 28 to 36 of the Code and those of this title, Member States shall comply with the provisions set out in Annex 23.

The provisions as set out in the first column of Annex 23 shall be applied in the light of the interpretative note appearing in the second column.

2. If it is necessary to make reference to generally accepted accounting principles in determining the customs value, the provisions of Annex 24 shall apply.

Article 142

1. For the purposes of this title:

(*a*)   **"the Agreement"** means the Agreement on implementation of Article VII of the General Agreement on Tariffs and Trade concluded in the framework of the multilateral trade negotiations of 1973 to 1979 and referred to in the first indent of Article 31(1) of the Code.

(*b*)   **"produced goods"** includes goods grown, manufactured and mined;

(*c*)   **"identical goods"** means goods produced in the same country which are the same in all respects, including physical characteristics, quality and reputation. Minor differences in appearance shall not preclude goods otherwise conforming to the definition from being regarded as identical;

(*d*)   **"similar goods"** means goods produced in the same country which, although not alike in all respects, have like characteristics and like component materials which enable them to perform the same functions and to be commercially interchangeable; the quality of the goods, their reputation and the existence of a trademark are among the factors to be considered in determining whether goods are similar;

(*e*)   **"goods of the same class or kind"** means goods which fall within a group or range of goods produced by a particular industry or industry sector, and includes identical or similar goods.

2. "Identical goods" and "similar goods", as the case may be, do not include goods which incorporate or reflect engineering, development, artwork, design work, and plans and sketches for which no adjustment has been made under Article 32 (1)(*b*)(iv) of the Code because such elements were undertaken in the Community.

Article 143

1. For the purposes of Articles 29(1)(*d*) and 30(2)(*c*) of the Code, persons shall be deemed to be related only if:

(*a*)   they are officers or directors of one another's businesses;

(*b*)   they are legally recognized partners in business;

(*c*)   they are employer and employee;

(*d*)   any person directly or indirectly owns, controls or holds 5% or more of the outstanding voting stock or shares of both of them;

(*e*)   one of them directly or indirectly controls the other;

(*f*)   both of them are directly or indirectly controlled by a third person;

(*g*)   together they directly or indirectly control a third person; or

(*h*)   they are members of the same family. Persons shall be deemed to be members of the same family only if they stand in any of the following relationships to one another:

— husband and wife,

— parent and child,

— brother and sister (whether by whole or half blood),

— grandparent and grandchild,

— uncle or aunt and nephew or niece,

— parent-in-law and son-in-law or daughter-in-law,

— brother-in-law and sister- in-law.

2. For the purposes of this title, persons who are associated in business with one another in that one is the sole agent, sole distributor or sole concessionaire, however described, of the other shall be deemed to be related only if they fall within the criteria of paragraph 1.

Article 144

1. For the purposes of determining customs value under Article 29 of the Code of goods in regard to which the price has not actually been paid at the material time for valuation for customs purposes, the price payable for settlement at the said time shall as a general rule be taken as the basis for customs value.

2. The Commission and the Member States shall consult within the Committee concerning the application of paragraph 1.

Article 145

Where goods declared for free circulation are part of a larger quantity of the same goods purchased in one transaction, the price actually paid or payable for the purposes of Article 29(1) of the Code shall be that price represented by the proportion of the total price which the quantity so declared bears to the total quantity purchased.

Apportioning the price actually paid or payable shall also apply in the case of the loss of part of a consignment or when the goods being valued have been damaged before entry into free circulation.

Article 146

Where the price actually paid or payable for the purposes of Article 29(1) of the Code includes an amount in respect of any internal tax applicable within the country of origin or export in respect of the goods in question, the said amount shall not be incorporated in the customs value provided that it can be demonstrated to the satisfaction of the customs authorities concerned that the goods in question have been or will be relieved therefrom for the benefit of the buyer.

Article 147

1. For the purposes of Article 29 of the Code, the fact that the goods which are the subject of a sale are declared for free circulation shall be regarded as adequate indication that they were sold for export to the customs territory of the Community. [In the case of successive sales before valuation, only the last sale, which led to the introduction of the goods into the customs territory of the Community, or a sale taking place in the customs territory of the Community before entry for free circulation of the goods shall constitute such indication.

Where a price is declared which relates to a sale taking place before the last sale on the basis of which the goods were introduced into the customs territory of the Community, it must be demonstrated to the satisfaction of the customs authorities that this sale of goods took place for export to the customs territory in question.

The provisions of Articles 178 to 181a shall apply.][1]

2. ...[2], where goods are used in a third country between the time of sale and the time of entry into free circulation the customs value need not be the transaction value.

3. The buyer need satisfy no condition other than that of being a party to the contract of sale.

Amendments

[1] Substituted by Commission Regulation (EC) No 1762/95 Art 1(2)(*a*). See OJ L 171, 21.7.95, p 8.
[2] Deleted by Commission Regulation (EC) No 1762/95 Art 1(2)(*b*). See OJ L 171, 21.7.95, p 8.

Article 148

Where, in applying Article 29(1)(*b*) of the Code, it is established that the sale or price of imported goods is subject to a condition or consideration the value of which can be determined with respect to the goods being valued, such value shall be regarded as an indirect payment by the buyer to the seller and part of the price actually paid or payable provided that the condition or consideration does not relate to either:

(*a*) an activity to which Article 29(3)(*b*) of the Code applies, or

(*b*) a factor in respect of which an addition is to be made to the price actually paid or payable under the provisions of Article 32 of the Code.

Article 149

1. For the purposes of Article 29(3)(*b*) of the Code, the term "marketing activities" means all activities relating to advertising and promoting the sale of the goods in question and all activities relating to warranties or guarantees in respect of them.

2. Such activities undertaken by the buyer shall be regarded as having been undertaken on his own account even if they are performed in pursuance of an obligation on the buyer following an agreement with the seller.

Article 150

1. In applying Article 30(2)(*a*) of the Code (the transaction value of identical goods), the customs value shall be determined by reference to the transaction value of identical goods in a sale at the same commercial level and in substantially the same quantity as the goods being valued. Where no such sale is found, the transaction value of identical goods sold at a different commercial level and/or in different quantities, adjusted to take account of differences attributable to commercial level and/or to quantity, shall be used, provided that such adjustments can be made on the basis of demonstrated evidence which clearly establishes the reasonableness and accuracy of the adjustment, whether the adjustment leads to an increase or a decrease in the value.

2. Where the costs and charges referred to in Article 32(1)(*e*) of the Code are included in the transaction value, an adjustment shall be made to take account of significant differences in such costs and charges between the imported goods and the identical goods in question arising from differences in distances and modes of transport.

3. If, in applying this Article, more than one transaction value of identical goods is found, the lowest such value shall be used to determine the customs value of the imported goods.

4. In applying this Article, a transaction value for goods produced by a different person shall be taken into account only when no transaction value can be found under paragraph 1 for identical goods produced by the same person as the goods being valued.

5. For the purposes of this Article, the transaction value of identical imported goods means a customs value previously determined under Article 29 of the Code, adjusted as provided for in paragraphs 1 and 2 of this Article.

Article 151

1. In applying Article 30(2)(*b*) of the Code (the transaction value of similar goods), the customs value shall be determined by reference to the transaction value of similar goods in a sale at the same commercial level and in substantially the same quantity as the goods being valued. Where no such sale is found, the transaction value of similar goods sold at a different commercial level and/or in different quantities, adjusted to take account of differences attributable to commercial level and/or to quantity, shall be used, provided that such adjustments can be made on the basis of demonstrated evidence which clearly establishes the reasonableness and accuracy of the adjustment, whether the adjustment leads to an increase or a decrease in the value.

2. Where the costs and charges referred to in Article 32(1)(*e*) of the Code are included in the transaction value, an adjustment shall be made to take account of significant differences in such costs and charges between the imported goods and the similar goods in question arising from differences in distances and modes of transport.

3. If, in applying this Article, more than one transaction value of similar goods is found, the lowest such value shall be used to determine the customs value for the imported goods.

4. In applying this Article, a transaction value for goods produced by a different person shall be taken into account only when no transaction value can be found under paragraph 1 for similar goods produced by the same person as the goods being valued.

5. For the purposes of this Article, the transaction value of similar imported goods means a customs value previously determined under Article 29 of the Code, adjusted as provided for in paragraphs 1 and 2 of this Article.

Article 152

1. (*a*) If the imported goods or identical or similar imported goods are sold in the Community in the condition as imported, the customs value of imported goods, determined in accordance with Article 30(2)(*c*) of the Code, shall be based on the unit price at which the imported goods or identical or similar imported goods are so sold in the greatest aggregate quantity, at or about the time of the importation of the goods being valued, to persons who are not related to the persons from whom they buy such goods, subject to deductions for the following:

    (i) either the commissions usually paid or agreed to be paid or the additions usually made for profit and general expenses (including the direct and indirect costs of marketing the goods in question) in connection with sales in the Community of imported goods of the same class or kind;

    (ii) the usual costs of transport and insurance and associated costs incurred within the Community;

    (iii) the import duties and other charges payable in the Community by reason of the importation or sale of the goods.

  (*b*) If neither the imported goods nor identical nor similar imported goods are sold at or about the time of importation of the goods being valued, the customs value of imported goods determined under this Article shall, subject otherwise to the provisions of paragraph 1(*a*), be based on the unit price at which the imported goods or identical or similar imported goods are sold in the Community in the condition as imported at the earliest date after the importation of the goods being valued but before the expiration of 90 days after such importation.

2. If neither the imported goods nor identical nor similar imported goods are sold in the Community in the condition as imported, then, if the importer so requests, the customs value shall be based on the unit price at which the imported goods, after further processing, are sold in the greatest aggregate quantity to persons in the Community who are not related to the persons from whom they buy such goods, due allowance being made for the value added by such processing and the deductions provided for in paragraph 1(*a*).

3. For the purposes of this Article, the unit price at which imported goods are sold in the greatest aggregate quantity is the price at which the greatest number of units is sold in sales to persons who are not related to the persons from whom they buy such goods at the first commercial level after importation at which such sales take place.

4. Any sale in the Community to a person who supplies directly or indirectly free of charge or at reduced cost for use in connection with the production and sale for export of the imported goods any of the elements specified in Article 32(1)(*b*) of the Code should not be taken into account in establishing the unit price for the purposes of this Article.

5. For the purposes of paragraph 1(*b*), the "earliest date" shall be the date by which sales of the imported goods or of identical or similar imported goods are made in sufficient quantity to establish the unit price.

Article 153

1. In applying Article 30(2)(*d*) of the Code (computed value), the customs authorities may not require or compel any person not resident in the Community to produce for examination, or to allow access to, any account or other record for the purposes of determining this value. However, information supplied by the producer of the goods for the purposes of determining the customs value under this Article may be verified in a non-Community country by the customs authorities of a Member State with the agreement of the producer and provided that such authorities give sufficient advance notice to the authorities of the country in question and the latter do not object to the investigation.

2. The cost or value of materials and fabrication referred to in the first indent of Article 30(2)(*d*) of the Code shall include the cost of elements specified in Article 32(1)(*a*)(ii) and (iii) of the Code.

It shall also include the value, duly apportioned, of any product or service specified in Article 32(1)(*b*) of the Code which has been supplied directly or indirectly by the buyer for use in connection with the production of the imported goods. The value of the elements specified in Article 32(1)(*b*)(iv) of the Code which are undertaken in the Community shall be included only to the extent that such elements are charged to the producer.

3. Where information other than that supplied by or on behalf of the producer is used for the purposes of determining a computed value, the customs authorities shall inform the declarant, if the latter so requests, of the source of such information, the data used and the calculations based on such data, subject to Article 15 of the Code.

4. The "general expenses" referred to in the second indent of Article 30(2)(*d*) of the Code, cover the direct and indirect costs of producing and selling the goods for export which are not included under the first indent of Article 30(2)(*d*) of the Code.

Article 154

Where containers referred to in Article 32(1)(*a*)(ii) of the Code are to be the subject of repeated importations, their cost shall, at the request of the declarant, be apportioned, as appropriate, in accordance with generally accepted accounting principles.

Article 155

For the purposes of Article 32(1)(*b*)(iv) of the Code, the cost of research and preliminary design sketches is not to be included in the customs value.

Article 156

Article 33(*c*) of the Code shall apply *mutatis mutandis* where the customs value is determined by applying a method other than the transaction value.

CHAPTER 2
Provisions concerning royalties and licence fees

Article 157

1. For the purposes of Article 32(1)(*c*) of the Code, royalties and licence fees shall be taken to mean in particular payment for the use of rights relating:

— to the manufacture of imported goods (in particular, patents, designs, models and manufacturing know-how), or

— to the sale for exportation of imported goods (in particular, trade marks, registered designs), or

— to the use or resale of imported goods (in particular, copyright, manufacturing processes inseparably embodied in the imported goods).

2. Without prejudice to Article 32(5) of the Code, when the customs value of imported goods is determined under the provisions of Article 29 of the Code, a royalty or licence fee shall be added to the price actually paid or payable only when this payment:

— is related to the goods being valued, and

— constitutes a condition of sale of those goods.

Article 158

1. When the imported goods are only an ingredient or component of goods manufactured in the Community, an adjustment to the price actually paid or payable for the imported goods shall only be made when the royalty or licence fee relates to those goods.

2. Where goods are imported in an unassembled state or only have to undergo minor processing before resale, such as diluting or packing, this shall not prevent a royalty or licence fee from being considered related to the imported goods.

3. If royalties or licence fees relate partly to the imported goods and partly to other ingredients or component parts added to the goods after their importation, or to post-importation activities or services, an appropriate apportionment shall be made only on the basis of objective and quantifiable data, in accordance with the interpretative note to Article 32(2) of the Code in Annex 23.

Article 159

A royalty or licence fee in respect of the right to use a trade mark is only to be added to the price actually paid or payable for the imported goods where:

— the royalty or licence fee refers to goods which are resold in the same state or which are subject only to minor processing after importation,

— the goods are marketed under the trade mark, affixed before or after importation, for which the royalty or licence fee is paid, and

— the buyer is not free to obtain such goods from other suppliers unrelated to the seller.

Article 160

When the buyer pays royalties or licence fees to a third party, the conditions provided for in Article 157(2) shall not be considered as met unless the seller or a person related to him requires the buyer to make that payment.

Article 161

Where the method of calculation of the amount of a royalty or licence fee derives from the price of the imported goods, it may be assumed in the absence of evidence to the contrary that the payment of that royalty or licence fee is related to the goods to be valued.

However, where the amount of a royalty or licence fee is calculated regardless of the price of the imported goods, the payment of that royalty or licence fee may nevertheless be related to the goods to be valued.

Article 162

In applying Article 32(1)(c) of the Code, the country of residence of the recipient of the payment of the royalty or licence fee shall not be a material consideration.

CHAPTER 3
Provisions concerning place of introduction into the Community

Article 163

1. For the purposes of Article 32(1)(e) and Article 33(a) of the Code, the place of introduction into the customs territory of the Community shall be:

(a) for goods carried by sea, the port of unloading, or the port of transhipment, subject to transhipment being certified by the customs authorities of that port;

(b) for goods carried by sea and then, without transhipment, by inland waterway, the first port where unloading can take place either at the mouth of the river or

— compliance with all the obligations relating to the entry of the goods in question under the procedure concerned.

[2. Where the declarant uses data-processing systems to produce his customs declarations, the customs authorities may provide that the handwritten signature may be replaced by another identification technique which may be based on the use of codes. This facility shall be granted only if the technical and administrative conditions laid down by the customs authorities are complied with.

The customs authorities may also provide that declarations produced using customs data- processing systems may be directly authenticated by those systems, in place of the manual or mechanical application of the customs office stamp and the signature of the competent official.

3. Under the conditions and in the manner which they shall determine, the customs authorities may allow some of the particulars of the written declaration referred to in Annex 37 to be replaced by sending these particulars to the customs office designated for that purpose by electronic means, where appropriate in coded form.]¹

Amendments

¹   Inserted by EC Commission Regulation 3665/93 Art 1(11). See OJ L335 of 31.12.93, p 1.

Article 200

Documents accompanying a declaration shall be kept by the customs authorities unless the said authorities provide otherwise or unless the declarant requires them for other operations. In the latter case the customs authorities shall take the necessary steps to ensure that the documents in question cannot subsequently be used except in respect of the quantity or value of goods for which they remain valid.

Article 201

1. The declaration shall be lodged with the customs office where the goods were presented. It may be lodged as soon as such presentation has taken place.

2. The customs authorities may authorize the declaration to be lodged before the declarant is in a position to present the goods. In this case, the customs authorities may set a time limit, to be determined according to the circumstances, for presentation of the goods. If the goods have not been presented within this time limit, the declaration shall be considered not to have been lodged.

3. Where a declaration has been lodged before the goods to which it relates have arrived at the customs office or at another place designated by the customs authorities, it may be accepted only after the goods in question have been presented to customs.

Article 202

1. The declaration shall be lodged with the competent customs office during the days and hours appointed for opening.

However, the customs authorities may, at the request of the declarant and at his expense, authorize the declaration to be lodged outside the appointed days and hours.

2. Any declaration lodged with the officials of a customs office in any other place duly designated for that purpose by agreement between the customs authorities and the person concerned shall be considered to have been lodged in the said office.

Article 203

The date of acceptance of the declaration shall be noted thereon.

Article 204

The customs authorities may allow or require the corrections referred to in Article 65 of the Code to be made by the lodging of a new declaration intended to replace the original declaration. In that event, the relevant date for determination of any duties payable and for the application of any other provisions governing the customs procedure in question shall be the date of the acceptance of the original declaration.

SECTION 2
FORMS TO BE USED

Article 205

1. The official model for written declarations to customs by the normal procedure, for the purposes of placing goods under a customs procedure or re-exporting them in accordance with Article 182(3) of the Code, shall be the Single Administrative Document.

2. Other forms may be used for this purpose where the provisions of the customs procedure in question permit.

3. The provisions of paragraphs 1 and 2 shall not preclude:

waiver of the written declaration prescribed in Articles 225 to 236 for release for free circulation, export or temporary importation,

— waiver by the Member States of the form referred to in paragraph 1 where the special provisions laid down in Articles 237 and 238 with regard to consignments by letter or parcel-post apply,

— use of special forms to facilitate the declaration in specific cases, where the customs authorities so permit,

— waiver by the Member States of the form referred to in paragraph 1 in the case of existing or future agreements or arrangements concluded between the administrations of two or more Member States with a view to greater simplification of formalities in all or part of the trade between those Member States,

— use by the persons concerned of loading lists for the completion of Community transit formalities in the case of consignments composed of more than one kind of goods,

— printing of export, transit or import declarations and documents certifying the Community status of goods not being moved under internal Community transit

canal or further inland, subject to proof being furnished to the customs office that the freight to the port of unloading is higher than that to the first port;

(c) for goods carried by rail, inland waterway, or road, the place where the first customs office is situated;

(d) for goods carried by other means, the place where the land frontier of the customs territory of the Community is crossed.

[2. The customs value of goods introduced into the customs territory of the Community and then carried to a destination in another part of that territory through the territories of Belarus, Bulgaria, the Czech Republic, Estonia, Hungary, Latvia, Lithuania, Poland, Russia, Romania, the Slovak Republic, Switzerland, or former Yugoslavia in its borders of 1 January 1991 shall be determined by reference to the first place of introduction into the customs territory of the Community, provided that goods are carried direct through the territories of those countries by a usual route across such territory to the place of destination.][1]

3. The customs value of goods introduced into the customs territory of the Community and then carried by sea to a destination in another part of that territory shall be determined by reference to the first place of introduction into the customs territory of the Community, provided the goods are carried direct by a usual route to the place of destination.

[4. Paragraphs 2 and 3 of this Article shall also apply where the goods have been unloaded, transhipped or temporarily immobilized in the territories of Belarus, Bulgaria, the Czech Republic, Estonia, Hungary, Latvia, Lithuania, Poland, Russia, Romania, the Slovak Republic, Switzerland, or former Yugoslavia in its borders of 1 January 1991 for reasons related solely to their transport.][1]

5. For goods introduced into the customs territory of the Community and carried directly from one of the French overseas departments to another part of the customs territory of the Community or vice versa, the place of introduction to be taken into consideration shall be the place referred to in paragraphs 1 and 2 situated in that part of the customs territory of the Community from which the goods came, if they were unloaded or transhipped there and this was certified by the customs authorities.

6. When the conditions specified at paragraphs 2, 3 and 5 are not fulfilled, the place of introduction to be taken into consideration shall be the place specified in paragraph 1 situated in that part of the customs territory of the Community to which the goods are consigned.

Amendments

[1]   Substituted by the Act of Accession of Austria, Finland and Sweden. See OJ C 241 of 29.8.94, p 1.

CHAPTER 4
Provisions concerning transport costs

Article 164

In applying Article 32(1)(e) and 33(a) of the Code:

(a) where goods are carried by the same mode of transport to a point beyond the place of introduction into the customs territory of the Community, transport costs shall be assessed in proportion to the distance covered outside and inside the customs territory of the Community, unless evidence is produced to the customs authorities to show the costs that would have been incurred under a general compulsory schedule of freight rates for the carriage of the goods to the place of introduction into the customs territory of the Community;

(*b*)   where goods are invoiced at a uniform free domicile price which corresponds to the price at the place of introduction, transport costs within the Community shall not be deducted from that price. However, such deduction shall be allowed if evidence is produced to the customs authorities that the free- frontier price would be lower than the uniform free domicile price;

(*c*)   where transport is free or provided by the buyer, transport costs to the place of introduction, calculated in accordance with the schedule of freight rates normally applied for the same modes of transport, shall be included in the customs value.

Article 165

1. All postal charges levied up to the place of destination in respect of goods sent by post shall be included in the customs value of these goods, with the exception of any supplementary postal charge levied in the country of importation.

2. No adjustment to the declared value shall, however, be made in respect of such charges in determining the value of consignments of a non-commercial nature.

3. Paragraphs 1 and 2 are not applicable to goods carried by the express postal services known as EMS — Datapost (in Denmark, EMS — Jetpost, in Germany, EMS Kurierpostsendungen, in Italy, CAI-Post).

Article 166

The air transport costs to be included in the customs value of goods shall be determined by applying the rules and percentages shown in Annex 25.

CHAPTER 5
Valuation of certain carrier media for use in ADP equipment

Article 167

1. Notwithstanding Articles 29 to 33 of the Code, in determining the customs value of imported carrier media bearing data or instructions for use in data processing equipment, only the cost or value of the carrier medium itself shall be taken into account. The customs value of imported carrier media bearing data or instructions shall not, therefore, include the cost or value of the data or instructions, provided that such cost or value is distinguished from the cost or value of the carrier medium in question.

2. For the purposes of this Article:

(*a*)   the expression "carrier medium" shall not be taken to include integrated circuits, semiconductors and similar devices or articles incorporating such circuits or devices;

(*b*) the expression "data or instructions" shall not be taken to include sound, cinematographic or video recordings.

CHAPTER 6
Provisions concerning rates of exchange

Article 168

For the purposes of Articles 169 to 171 of this chapter:

(*a*) **"rate recorded"** shall mean:

— the latest selling rate of exchange recorded for commercial transactions on the most representative exchange market or markets of the Member State concerned, or

— some other description of a rate of exchange so recorded and designated by the Member State as the "rate recorded" provided that it reflects as effectively as possible the current value of the currency in question in commercial transactions;

(*b*) **"published"** shall mean made generally known in a manner designated by the Member State concerned;

(*c*) **"currency"** shall mean any monetary unit used as a means of settlement between monetary authorities or on the international market.

Article 169

1. Where factors used to determine the customs value of goods are expressed at the time when that value is determined in a currency other than that of the Member State where the valuation is made, the rate of exchange to be used to determine that value in terms of the currency of the Member State concerned shall be the rate recorded on the second-last Wednesday of a month and published on that or the following day.

2. The rate recorded on the second-last Wednesday of a month shall be used during the following calendar month unless it is superseded by a rate established under Article 171.

3. Where a rate of exchange is not recorded on the second-last Wednesday indicated in paragraph 1, or, if recorded, is not published on that or the following day, the last rate recorded for the currency in question published within the preceding 14 days shall be deemed to be the rate recorded on that Wednesday.

Article 170

Where a rate of exchange cannot be established under the provisions of Article 169, the rate of exchange to be used for the application of Article 35 of the Code shall be designated by the Member State concerned and shall reflect as effectively as possible the current value of the currency in question in commercial transactions in terms of the currency of that Member State.

Article 171

1. Where a rate of exchange recorded on the last Wednesday of a month and published on that or the following day differs by 5% or more from the rate established in accordance with Article 169 for entry into use the following month, it shall replace the latter rate from the first Wednesday of that month as the rate to be applied for the application of Article 35 of the Code.

2. Where in the course of a period of application as referred to in the preceding provisions, a rate of exchange recorded on a Wednesday and published on that or the following day differs by 5% or more from the rate being used in accordance with this Chapter, it shall replace the latter rate and enter into use on the Wednesday following as the rate to be used for the application of Article 35 of the Code. The replacement rate shall remain in use for the remainder of the current month, provided that this rate is not superseded due to operation of the provisions of the first sentence of this paragraph.

3. Where, in a Member State, a rate of exchange is not recorded on a Wednesday or, if recorded, is not published on that or the following day, the rate recorded shall, for the application in that Member State of paragraphs 1 and 2, be the rate most recently recorded and published prior to that Wednesday.

Article 172

When the customs authorities of a Member State authorize a declarant to furnish or supply at a later date certain details concerning the declaration for free circulation of the goods in the form of a periodic declaration, this authorization may, at the declarant's request, provide that a single rate be used for conversion into that Member State's currency of elements forming part of the customs value as expressed in a particular currency. In this case, the rate to be used shall be the rate, established in accordance with this Chapter, which is applicable on the first day of the period covered by the declaration in question.

CHAPTER 7
Simplified procedures for certain perishable goods

Article 173

1. For the purpose of determining the customs value of products referred to in Annex 26, the Commission shall establish for each classification heading a unit value per 100 kg net expressed in the currencies of the Member States. The unit values shall apply for periods of 14 days, each period beginning on a Friday.

2. Unit values shall be established on the basis of the following elements, which are to be supplied to the Commission by Member States, in relation to each classification heading:

    (*a*) the average free-at-frontier unit price, not cleared through customs, expressed in the currency of the Member State in question per 100 kg net and calculated on the basis of prices for undamaged goods in the marketing centres referred to in Annex 27 during the reference period referred to in Article 174(1);

(*b*) the quantities entered into free circulation over the period of a calendar year with payment of import duties.

3. The average free-at-frontier unit price, not cleared through customs, shall be calculated on the basis of the gross proceeds of sales made between importers and wholesalers. However, in the case of the London, Milan and Rungis marketing centres the gross proceeds shall be those recorded at the commercial level at which those goods are most commonly sold at those centres.

There shall be deducted from the figures so arrived at:

— a marketing margin of 15% for the marketing centres of London, Milan and Rungis and of 8% for the other marketing centres,

— costs of transport and insurance within the customs territory,

— a standard amount of ECU 5 representing all the other costs which are not to be included in the customs value.

   This amount shall be converted into the currencies of the Member States on the basis of the latest rates in force established in accordance with Article 18 of the Code.

— import duties and other charges which are not to be included in the customs value.

4. The Member States may fix standard amounts for deduction in respect of transport and insurance costs in accordance with paragraph 3. Such standard amounts and the methods for calculating them shall be made known to the Commission immediately.

Note

Annex 26 is not reproduced because it is subject to frequent changes.

Article 174

1. The reference period for calculating the average unit prices referred to in Article 173(2)(*a*) shall be the period of 14 days ending on the Thursday preceding the week during which new unit values are to be established.

2. Average unit prices shall be notified by Member States not later than 12 noon on the Monday of the week during which unit values are established pursuant to Article 173. If that day is a non-working day, notification shall be made on the working day immediately preceding that day.

3. The quantities entered into free circulation during a calendar year for each classification heading shall be notified to the Commission by all Member States before 15 June in the following year.

Article 175

1. The unit values referred to in Article 173(1) shall be established by the Commission on alternate Tuesdays on the basis of the weighted average of the average unit prices referred to in Article 173(2)(*a*) in relation to the quantities referred to in Article 173(2)(*b*).

2. For the purpose of determining the weighted average, each average unit price as referred to in Article 173(2)(*a*) shall be converted into ecu on the basis of the last conversion rates determined by the Commission and published in the *Official Journal of the European Communities* prior to the week during which the unit values are to be established. The same conversion rates shall be applied in converting the unit values so obtained back into the currencies of the Member States.

3. The last published unit values shall remain applicable until new values are published. However, in the case of major fluctuations in price in one or more Member States, as a result, for example, of an interruption in the continuity of imports of a particular product, new unit values may be determined on the basis of actual prices at the time of fixing those values.

Article 176

1. Consignments which at the material time for valuation for customs purposes contain not less than 5% of produce unfit in its unaltered state for human consumption or the value of which has depreciated by not less than 20% in relation to average market prices for sound produce, shall be treated as damaged.

2. Consignments which are damaged may be valued:

— either, after sorting, by application of unit values to the sound portion, the damaged portion being destroyed under customs supervision, or

— by application of unit values established for the sound produce after deduction from the weight of the consignment of a percentage equal to the percentage assessed as damaged by a sworn expert and accepted by the customs authorities, or

— by application of unit values established for the sound produce reduced by the percentage assessed as damaged by a sworn expert and accepted by the customs authorities.

Article 177

1. In declaring or causing to be declared the customs value of one or more products which he imports by reference to the unit values established in accordance with this Chapter, the person concerned joins the simplified procedure system for the current calendar year in respect of the product or products in question.

2. If subsequently the person concerned requires the use of a method other than the simplified procedures for the customs valuation of one or more of the products he imports, the customs authorities of the Member State concerned shall be entitled to notify him that he will not be allowed to benefit from the simplified procedures for the remainder of the current calendar year in regard to the product or products concerned; this exclusion can be extended for the following calendar year. Such notified exclusion shall be communicated without delay to the Commission, which shall in turn immediately inform the customs authorities of the other Member States.

CHAPTER 8
Declarations of particulars and documents to be furnished

Article 178

1. Where it is necessary to establish a customs value for the purposes of Articles 28 to 36 of the Code, a declaration of particulars relating to customs value (value declaration) shall accompany the customs entry made in respect of the imported goods. The value declaration shall be drawn up on a form D.V. 1 corresponding to the specimen in Annex 28, supplemented where appropriate by one or more forms D.V. 1 *bis* corresponding to the specimen in Annex 29.

2. It shall be a particular requirement that the value declaration prescribed in paragraph 1 shall be made only by a person who has his residence or place of business in the customs territory of the Community and is in possession of the relevant facts.

3. The customs authorities may waive the requirement of a declaration on the form referred to in paragraph 1 where the customs value of the goods in question cannot be determined under the provisions of Article 29 of the Code. In such cases the person referred to in paragraph 2 shall furnish or cause to be furnished to the customs authorities such other information as may be requested for the purposes of determining the customs value under another Article of the said Code; and such other information shall be supplied in such form and manner as may be prescribed by the customs authorities.

4. The lodging with a customs office of a declaration required by paragraph 1 shall, without prejudice to the possible application of penal provisions, be equivalent to the engagement of responsibility by the person referred to in paragraph 2 in respect of:

— the accuracy and completeness of the particulars given in the declaration,

— the authenticity of the documents produced in support of these particulars, and

— the supply of any additional information or document necessary to establish the customs value of the goods.

5. This Article shall not apply in respect of goods for which the customs value is determined under the simplified procedure system established in accordance with the provisions of Articles 173 to 177.

Article 179

1. Except where it is essential for the correct application of import duties, the customs authorities shall waive the requirement of all or part of the declaration provided for in Article 178(1):

(*a*) where the customs value of the imported goods in a consignment does not exceed ECU 5 000, provided that they do not constitute split or multiple consignments from the same consignor to the same consignee; or

(*b*) where the importations involved are of a non- commercial nature; or

(*c*) where the submission of the particulars in question is not necessary for the application of the Customs Tariff of the European Communities or where the customs duties provided for in the Tariff are not chargeable pursuant to specific customs provisions.

2. The amount in ecu referred to in Paragraph 1(*a*) shall be converted in accordance with Article 18 of the Code. The customs authorities may round-off upwards or downwards the sum arrived at after conversion.

The customs authorities may maintain unamended the exchange value in national currency of the amount determined in ecu if, at the time of the annual adjustment provided for in Article 18 of the Code, the conversion of this amount, before the rounding-off provided for in this paragraph, leads to an alteration of less than 5% in the exchange value expressed in national currency or to a reduction thereof.

3. In the case of continuing traffic in goods supplied by the same seller to the same buyer under the same commercial conditions, the customs authorities may waive the requirement that all particulars under Article 178(1) be furnished in support of each customs declaration, but shall require them whenever the circumstances change and at least once every three years.

4. A waiver granted under this Article may be withdrawn and the submission of a D.V. 1 may be required where it is found that a condition necessary to qualify for that waiver was not or is no longer met.

Article 180

Where computerized systems are used, or where the goods concerned are the subject of a general, periodic or recapitulative declaration, the customs authorities may authorize variations in the form of presentation of data required for the determination of customs value.

Article 181

1. The person referred to in Article 178(2) shall furnish the customs authorities with a copy of the invoice on the basis of which the value of the imported goods is declared. Where the customs value is declared in writing this copy shall be retained by the customs authorities.

2. In the case of written declarations of the customs value, when the invoice for the imported goods is made out to a person established in a Member State other than that in which the customs value is declared, the declarant shall furnish the customs authorities with two copies of the invoice. One of these copies shall be retained by the customs authorities; the other, bearing the stamp of the office in question and the serial number of the declaration at the said customs office shall be returned to the declarant for forwarding to the person to whom the invoice is made out.

3. The customs authorities may extend the provisions of paragraph 2 to cases where the person to whom the invoice is made out is established in the Member State in which the customs value is declared.

[Article 181a

1. The customs authorities need not determine the customs valuation of imported goods on the basis of the transaction value method if, in accordance with the procedure set out in paragraph 2, they are not satisfied, on the basis of reasonable doubts, that the declared value represents the total amount paid or payable as referred to in Article 29 of the Code

2. Where the customs authorities have the doubts described in paragraph 1 they may ask for additional information in accordance with article 178(4). If those doubts continue, the customs authorities must, before reaching a final decision, notify the person concerned, in writing if requested, of the grounds for those doubts and provide him with a reasonable opportunity to respond. A final decision and the grounds therefor shall be communicated in writing to the person concerned.][1]

Amendments

[1]   Inserted by EC Commission Regulation 3254/94. See OJ L 346 of 31.12.94, p 1.

TITLE VI
INTRODUCTION OF GOODS INTO THE CUSTOMS TERRITORY

CHAPTER 1
Examination of the goods and taking of samples by the person concerned

Article 182

TITLE VII
CUSTOMS DECLARATIONS — NORMAL PROCEDURE

CHAPTER 1
Customs declaration in writing

SECTION 1
GENERAL PROVISIONS

Article 198

1. Where a customs declaration covers two or more articles, the particulars relating to each article shall be regarded as constituting a separate declaration.

2. Component parts of industrial plant coming under a single Combined Nomenclature Code shall be regarded as constituting a single item of goods.

Article 199

Without prejudice to the possible application of penal provisions, the lodging with a customs office of a declaration signed by the declarant or his representative shall render him responsible under the provisions in force for:

— the accuracy of the information given in the declaration,

— the authenticity of the documents attached,

and

procedure by means of official or private-sector data-processing systems, if necessary on plain paper, on conditions laid down by the Member States,

— provision by the Member States to the effect that where a computerized declaration-processing system is used, the declaration, within the meaning of paragraph 1, may take the form of the Single Administrative Document printed out by that system.

4. ...[1].

5. Where in Community legislation, reference is made to an export, re-export or import declaration or a declaration placing goods under another customs procedure, Member States may not require any administrative documents other than those which are:

— expressly created by Community acts or provided for by such acts,

— required under the terms of international conventions compatible with the Treaty,

— required from operators to enable them to qualify, at their request, for an advantage or specific facility,

— required, with due regard for the provisions of the Treaty, for the implementation of specific regulations which cannot be implemented solely by the use of the document referred to in paragraph 1.

Amendments

[1]   Deleted by EC Commission Regulation 3665/93 Art 1(12). See OJ L 335 of 31.12.93, p 1.

Article 206

The Single Administrative Document form shall, where necessary, also be used during the transitional period laid down in the Act of Accession of Spain and Portugal in connection with trade between the Community as constituted on 31 December 1985 and Spain or Portugal and between those two last-mentioned Member States in goods still liable to certain customs duties and charges having equivalent effect or which remain subject to other measures laid down by the Act of Accession.

For the purposes of the first paragraph, copy 2 or where applicable copy 7 of the forms used for trade with Spain and Portugal or trade between those Member States shall be destroyed.

It shall also be used in trade in Community goods between parts of the customs territory of the Community to which the provisions of Council Directive 77/388/EEC (OJ No L 145, 13.6.1977, p 1) apply and parts of that territory where those provisions do not apply, or in trade between parts of that territory where those provisions do not apply.

Article 207

Without prejudice to Article 205(3), the customs administrations of the Member States may in general, for the purpose of completing export or import formalities, dispense with the production of one or more copies of the Single Administrative Document intended for use by the authorities of that Member State, provided that the information in question is available on other media.

Article 208

1. The Single Administrative Document shall be presented in subsets containing the number of copies required for the completion of formalities relating to the customs procedure under which the goods are to be placed.

2. Where the Community transit procedure or the common transit procedure is preceded or followed by another customs procedure, a subset containing the number of copies required for the completion of formalities relating to the transit procedure and the preceding or following procedure may be presented.

3. The subsets referred to in paragraphs 1 and 2 shall be taken from:

— either the full set of eight copies, in accordance with the specimen contained in Annex 31,

— or, particularly in the event of production by means of a computerized system for processing declarations, two successive sets of four copies, in accordance with the specimen contained in Annex 32.

4. Without prejudice to Articles 205(3), 222 to 224 or 254 to 289, the declaration forms may be supplemented, where appropriate, by one or more continuation forms presented in subsets containing the declaration copies needed to complete the formalities relating to the customs procedure under which the goods are to be placed. Those copies needed in order to complete the formalities relating to preceding or subsequent customs procedures may be attached where appropriate.

The continuation subsets shall be taken from:

— either a set of eight copies, in accordance with the specimen contained in Annex 33,

— or two sets of four copies, in accordance with the specimen contained in Annex 34.

The continuation forms shall be an integral part of the Single Administrative Document to which they relate.

5. By way of derogation from paragraph 4, the customs authorities may provide that continuation forms shall not be used where a computerized system is used to produce such declarations.

Article 209

1. Where Article 208(2) is applied, each party involved shall be liable only as regards the particulars relating to the procedure for which he applied as declarant, principal or as the representative of one of these.

2. For the purposes of paragraph 1, where the declarant uses a Single Administrative Document issued during the preceding customs procedure, he shall be required, prior to lodging his declaration, to verify the accuracy of the existing particulars for the boxes for which he is responsible and their applicability to the goods in question and the procedure applied for, and to supplement them as necessary.

In the cases referred to in the first subparagraph, the declarant shall immediately inform the customs office where the declaration is lodged of any discrepancy found between the goods in question and the existing particulars. In this case the declarant shall then draw up his declaration on fresh copies of the Single Administrative Document.

Article 210

Where the Single Administrative Document is used to cover several successive customs procedures, the customs authorities shall satisfy themselves that the particulars given in the declarations relating to the various procedures in question all agree.

Article 211

The declaration must be drawn up in one of the official languages of the Community which is acceptable to the customs authorities of the Member State where the formalities are carried out.

If necessary, the customs authorities of the Member State of destination may require from the declarant or his representative in that Member State a translation of the declaration into the official language or one of the official languages of the latter. The translation shall replace the corresponding particulars in the declaration in question.

By way of derogation from the preceding subparagraph, the declaration shall be drawn up in an official language of the Community acceptable to the Member State of destination in all cases where the declaration in the latter Member State is made on copies other than those initially presented to the customs office of the Member State of departure.

Article 212

1. The Single Administrative Document must be completed in accordance with the explanatory note in Annex 37 and any additional rules laid down in other Community legislation.

2. The customs authorities shall ensure that users have ready access to copies of the explanatory note referred to in paragraph 1.

3. The customs administrations of each Member State may, if necessary, supplement the explanatory note.

Article 213

The codes to be used in completing the forms referred to in Article 205(1) are listed in Annex 38.

Article 214

In cases where the rules require supplementary copies of the form referred to in Article 205(1), the declarant may use additional sheets or photocopies of the said form for this purpose.

Such additional sheets or photocopies must be signed by the declarant, presented to the customs authorities and endorsed by the latter under the same conditions as the Single Administrative Document. They shall be accepted by the customs authorities as if they were original documents provided that their quality and legibility are considered satisfactory by the said authorities.

Article 215

1. The forms referred to in Article 205(1) shall be printed on self-copying paper dressed for writing purposes and weighing at least 40 g/m^2 per square metre. The paper must be sufficiently opaque for the information on one side not to affect the legibility of the information on the other side and its strength should be such that in normal use it does not easily tear or crease.

The paper shall be white for all copies. However, on the copies used for Community transit (1,4,5 and 7), box 1 (first and third subdivisions), 2, 3, 4, 5, 6, 8, 15, 17, 18, 19, 21, 25, 27, 31, 32, 33 (first subdivision on the left), 35, 38, 40, 44, 50, 51, 52, 53, 55 and 56 shall have a green background.

The forms shall be printed in green ink.

2. The boxes are based on a unit of measurement of one tenth of an inch horizontally and one sixth of an inch vertically. The subdivisions are based on a unit of measurement of one-tenth of an inch horizontally.

3. A colour marking of the different copies shall be effected in the following manner:

(*a*)   on forms conforming to the specimens shown in Annexes 31 and 33:

— copies 1, 2, 3 and 5 shall have at the right hand edge a continuous margin, coloured respectively red, green, yellow and blue,

— copies 4, 6, 7 and 8 shall have at the right hand edge a broken margin coloured respectively blue, red, green and yellow.

(*b*)   on forms conforming to the specimens shown in Annexes 32 and 34, copies 1/6, 2/7, 3/8 and 4/5 shall have at the right hand edge a continuous margin and to the right of this a broken margin coloured respectively red, green, yellow and blue.

The width of these margins shall be approximately 3 mm. The broken margin shall comprise a series of squares with a side measurement of 3 mm each one separated by 3 mm.

4. The copies on which the particulars contained in the forms shown in Annexes 31 and 33 must appear by a self-copying process are shown in Annex 35.

The copies on which the particulars contained in the forms shown in Annexes 32 and 34 must appear by a self-copying process are shown in Annex 36.

5. The forms shall measure 210 by 297 mm with a maximum tolerance as to length of 5 mm less and 8 mm more.

6. The customs administrations of the Member States may require that the forms show the name and address of the printer or a mark enabling the printer to be identified. They may also make the printing of the forms conditional on prior technical approval.

SECTION 3
PARTICULARS REQUIRED ACCORDING TO THE CUSTOMS PROCEDURE CONCERNED

Article 216

1. The maximum list of boxes to be used for declarations of entry for a particular customs procedure using the Single Administrative Document is contained in Annex 37.

2. Annex 37 also contains the minimum list of boxes to be used of declarations of entry for a particular customs procedure.

Article 217

The particulars required when one of the forms referred to in Article 205(2) is used depend on the form in question. They shall be supplemented where appropriate by the provisions relating to the customs procedure in question.

SECTION 4
DOCUMENTS TO ACCOMPANY THE CUSTOMS DECLARATION

Article 218

1. The following documents shall accompany the customs declaration for release for free circulation:

(*a*) the invoice on the basis of which the customs value of the goods is declared, as required under Article 181;

(*b*) where it is required under Article 178, the declaration of particulars for the assessment of the customs value of the goods declared, drawn up in accordance with the conditions laid down in the said Article;

(*c*) the documents required for the application of preferential tariff arrangements or other measures derogating from the legal rules applicable to the goods declared;

(*d*) all other documents required for the application of the provisions governing the release for free circulation of the goods declared.

2. The customs authorities may require transport documents or documents relating to the previous customs procedure, as appropriate, to be produced when the declaration is lodged.

Where a single item is presented in two or more packages, they may also require the production of a packing list or equivalent document indicating the contents of each package.

3. However, where goods qualify for duties under Article 81 of the Code, the documents referred to in paragraph 1(*b*) and (*c*) need not be required.

In addition, where goods qualify for relief from import duty, the documents referred to in paragraph 1(*a*), (*b*) and (*c*) need not be required unless the customs authorities consider it necessary for the purposes of applying the provisions governing the release of the goods in question for free circulation.

Article 219

1. The transit declaration shall be accompanied by the transport document. The office of departure may dispense with the presentation of this document at the time of completion of the formalities. However, the transport document shall be presented at the request of the customs office or any other competent authority in the course of transport.

2. Without prejudice to any applicable simplification measures, the customs document of export/dispatch or re-exportation of the goods from the customs territory of the Community or any document of equivalent effect shall be presented to the office of departure with the transit declaration to which it relates.

3. The customs authorities may, where appropriate, require production of the document relating to the preceding customs procedure.

Article 220

1. The documents to accompany the declaration of entry for a customs procedure with economic impact, except for the outward processing procedure, shall be as follows:

(*a*)   the documents laid down in Article 218, except in cases of entry for the customs warehousing procedure in a warehouse other than type D;

(*b*)   the authorization for the customs procedure in question or a copy of the application for authorization where the second sub-paragraph of Article 556(1) applies, except in cases of entry for the customs warehousing procedure or where Articles 568(3), 656(3) or 695(3) apply.

2. The documents to accompany the declaration of entry for the outward processing procedure shall be as follows:

(*a*)   the documents laid down in Article 221;

(*b*)   the authorization for the procedure or a copy of the application for authorization where the second subparagraph of Article 751(1) applies, except where Article 760(2) applies.

3. Article 218(2) shall apply to declarations of entry for any customs procedure with economic impact.

4. The customs authorities may allow the documents referred to in paragraphs 1(*b*) and 2(*b*) to be kept at their disposal instead of accompanying the declaration.

Article 221

1. The export or re-export declaration shall be accompanied by all documents necessary for the correct application of export duties and of the provisions governing the export of the goods in question.

2. Article 218(2) shall apply to export or re-export declarations.

CHAPTER 2
[Customs declarations made using a data-processing technique

Article 222

1. Where the customs declaration is made by a data-processing technique, the particulars of the written declaration referred to in Annex 37 shall be replaced by sending to the customs office designated for that purpose, with a view to their processing by computer, data in codified form, or data made out in any other form specified by the customs authorities and corresponding to the particulars required for written declarations.

2. A customs declaration made by EDI shall be considered to have been lodged when the EDI message is received by the customs authorities.

Acceptance of a customs declaration made by EDI shall be communicated to the declarant by means of a response message containing at least the identification details of the message received and/or the registration number of the customs declaration and the date of acceptance.

3. Where the customs declaration is made by EDI, the customs authorities shall lay down the rules for implementing the provisions laid down in Article 247.

4. Where the customs declaration is made by EDI, the release of the goods shall be notified to the declarant, indicating at least the identification details of the declaration and the date of release.

5. Where the particulars of the customs declaration are introduced into customs data-processing systems, paragraphs 2, 3 and 4 shall apply *mutatis mutandis.*

[Article 223

Where a paper copy of the customs declaration is required for the completion of other formalities, this shall, at the request of the declarant, be produced and authenticated, either by the customs office concerned, or in accordance with the second subparagraph of Article 199(2).][1]

Amendments

[1]   Substituted by EC Commission Regulation 3665/93 Art 1(13). See OJ L 335 of 31.12.93, p 1.

[Article 224

Under the conditions and in the manner which they shall determine, the customs authorities may authorize the documents required for the entry of goods for a customs procedure to be made out and transmitted by electronic means.][1]

Amendments

[1]   Substituted by EC Commission Regulation 3665/93 Art 1(13). See OJ L 335 of 31.12.93, p 1.

CHAPTER 3
Customs declarations made orally or by any other act

SECTION 1
ORAL DECLARATIONS

Article 225

Customs declarations may be made orally for the release for free circulation of the following goods:

(*a*) goods of a non-commercial nature:

— contained in travellers' personal luggage, or

— sent to private individuals, or

— in other cases of negligible importance, where this is authorized by the customs authorities;

(*b*) goods of a commercial nature provided:

— the total value per consignment and per declarant does not exceed the statistical threshold laid down in the Community provisions in force, and

— the consignment is not part of a regular series of similar consignments, and

— the goods are not being carried by an independent carrier as part of a larger freight movement;

(*c*) the goods referred to in Article 229, where these qualify for relief as returned goods;

(*d*) the goods referred to in Article 230(*b*) and (*c*).

Article 226

Customs declarations may be made orally for the export of:

(*a*) goods of a non-commercial nature:

— contained in travellers' personal luggage, or
— sent by private individuals;

(*b*) the goods referred to in Article 225(*b*);

(*c*) the goods referred to in Article 231(*b*) and (*c*);

(*d*) other goods in cases of negligible economic importance, where this is authorized by the customs authorities.

Article 227

1. The customs authorities may provide that Articles 225 and 226 shall not apply where the person clearing the goods is acting on behalf of another person in his capacity as customs agent.

2. Where the customs authorities are not satisfied that the particulars declared are accurate or that they are complete, they may require a written declaration.

Article 228

Where goods declared to customs orally in accordance with Articles 225 and 226 are subject to import or export duty the customs authorities shall issue a receipt to the person concerned against payment of the duty owing.

Article 229

1. Customs declarations may be made orally for the temporary importation of the following goods, in accordance with the conditions laid down in Article 696:

[(*a*) animals for the uses referred to in points 12 and 13 of Annex 93a and equipment satisfying the conditions laid down in point (*b*) of Article 685(2),

— packings listed in Article 679, imported filled, bearing the permanent, indelible markings of a person established outside the customs territory of the Community,]¹

— radio and television production and broadcasting equipment and vehicles specially adapted for use for the above purpose and their equipment imported by public or private organizations established outside the customs territory of the Community and approved by the customs authorities issuing the authorization for the procedure to import such equipment and vehicles,

— instruments and apparatus necessary for doctors to provide assistance for patients awaiting an organ transplant pursuant to Article 671(2)(*c*).

(*b*) the goods referred to in Article 232;

(*c*) other goods, where this is authorized by the customs authorities.

2. The goods referred to in paragraph 1 may also be the subject of an oral declaration for re-exportation discharging a temporary importation procedure.

Amendments

¹ Substituted by EC Commission Regulation 3665/93 Art 1(14). See OJ L 335 of 31.12.93, p 1.

SECTION 2

CUSTOMS DECLARATIONS MADE BY ANY OTHER ACT

Article 230

The following, where not expressly declared to customs, shall be considered to have been declared for release for free circulation by the act referred to in Article 233:

(*a*) goods of a non-commercial nature contained in travellers' personal luggage entitled to relief either under Chapter I, Title XI of Council Regulation (EEC) No 918/83 (OJ No L 105, 23.4.1983, p 1), or as returned goods;

(*b*) goods entitled to relief under Chapter I, Titles IX and X of Council Regulation (EEC) No 918/83;

(*c*) means of transport entitled to relief as returned goods;

(*d*) goods imported in the context of traffic of negligible importance and exempted from the requirement to be conveyed to a customs office in accordance with Article 38(4) of the Code, provided they are not subject to import duty.

Article 231

The following, where not expressly declared to customs, shall be considered to have been declared for export by the act referred to in Article 233(*b*):

(*a*) goods of a non-commercial nature not liable for export duty contained in travellers' personal luggage;

(*b*) means of transport registered in the customs territory of the Community and intended to be re-imported;

(*c*) goods referred to in Chapter II of Council Regulation (EEC) No 918/83;

(*d*) other goods in cases of negligible economic importance, where this is authorized by the customs authorities.

Article 232

1. The following, where not declared to customs in writing or orally, shall be considered to have been declared for temporary importation by the act referred to in Article 233, in accordance with Articles 698 and 735:

(*a*) travellers' personal effects and goods imported for sports purposes listed in Article 684;

(*b*) the means of transport listed in Articles 718 to 725.

2. Where they are not declared to customs in writing or orally, the goods referred to in paragraph 1 shall be considered to have been declared for re-exportation discharging the temporary importation procedure by the act referred to in Article 233.

Article 233

[1]. [1] For the purposes of Articles 230 to 232, the act which is considered to be a customs declaration may take the following forms:

(*a*) in the case of goods conveyed to a customs office or to any other place designated or approved in accordance with Article 38(1)(*a*) of the Code:

— going through the green or "nothing to declare" channel in customs offices where the two-channel system is in operation,

— going through a customs office which does not operate the two-channel system without spontaneously making a customs declaration,

— affixing a "nothing to declare" sticker or customs declaration disc to the windscreen of passenger vehicles where this possibility is provided for in national provisions;

(*b*) in the case of exemption from the obligation to convey goods to customs in accordance with the provisions implementing Article 38(4) of the Code, in the case of export in accordance with Article 231 and in the case of re-exportation in accordance with Article 232(2):

— the sole act of crossing the frontier of the customs territory of the Community.

[**2.** Where goods covered by point (*a*) of Article 230, point (*a*) of Article 231, point (*a*) of Article 232(1) or Article 232(2) contained in a passenger's baggage are carried by rail unaccompanied by the passenger and are declared to customs without the passenger being present in person the document referred to in Annex 38a may be used within the terms and limitations set out in it.][2]

Amendments

[1]   Inserted by Commission Regulation (EC) No 1762/95 Art 1(3)(*a*). See OJ L 171, 21.7.95, p 8.

[2]   Inserted by Commission Regulation (EC) No 1762/95 Art 1(3)(*b*). See OJ L 171, 21.7.95, p 8.

Article 234

1. Where the conditions of Articles 230 to 232 are fulfilled, the goods shall be considered to have been presented to customs within the meaning of Article 63 of the Code, the declaration to have been accepted and release to have been granted, at the time when the act referred to in Article 233 is carried out.

2. Where a check reveals that the act referred to in Article 233 has been carried out but the goods imported or taken out do not fulfil the conditions in Articles 230 to 232, the goods concerned shall be considered to have been imported or exported unlawfully.

SECTION 3
PROVISIONS COMMON TO SECTIONS 1 AND 2

Article 235

The provisions of Articles 225 to 232 shall not apply to goods in respect of which the payment of refunds or other amounts or the repayment of duties is sought, or which are subject to a prohibition or restriction or to any other special formality.

Article 236

For the purposes of Sections 1 and 2, **"traveller"** means:

A. on import:

1. any person temporarily entering the customs territory of the Community, not normally resident there, and

2 any person returning to the customs territory of the Community where he is normally resident, after having been temporarily in a third country.

B. on export:

1. any person temporarily leaving the customs territory of the Community where he is normally resident, and

2. any person leaving the customs territory of the Community after a temporary stay, not normally resident there.

SECTION 4
POSTAL TRAFFIC

Article 237

1. The following postal consignments shall be considered to have been declared to customs:

A. for release for free circulation:

(*a*) at the time when they are introduced into the customs territory of the Community:

— postcards and letters containing personal messages only,

— braille letters,

— printed matter not liable for import duties, and

— all other consignments sent by letter or parcel post which are exempt from the obligation to be conveyed to customs in accordance with provisions pursuant to Article 38(4) of the Code;

(*b*) at the time when they are presented to customs:

— consignments sent by letter or parcel post other than those referred to at (*a*), provided they are accompanied by a C1 and/or C2/CP3 declaration.

B. for export:

(*a*) at the time when they are accepted by the postal authorities, in the case of consignments by letter and parcel post which are not liable to export duties.

(*b*) at the time of their presentation to customs, in the case of consignments sent by letter or parcel post which are liable to export duties, provided they are accompanied by a C1 and/or a C2/CP3 declaration.

2. The consignee, in the cases referred to in paragraph 1A, and the consignor, in the cases referred to in paragraph 1B, shall be considered to be the declarant and, where applicable, the debtor. The customs authorities may provide that the postal administration shall be considered as the declarant and, where applicable, as the debtor.

3. For the purposes of paragraph 1, goods not liable to duty shall be considered to have been presented to customs within the meaning of Article 63 of the Code, the customs declaration to have been accepted and release granted:

(*a*) in the case of imports, when the goods are delivered to the consignee;

(*b*) in the case of exports, when the goods are accepted by the postal authorities.

4. Where a consignment sent by letter or parcel post which is not exempt from the obligation to be conveyed to customs in accordance with provisions pursuant to Article 38(4) of the Code is presented without a C1 and/or C2/CP3 declaration or where such declaration is incomplete, the customs authorities shall determine the form in which the customs declaration is to be made or supplemented.

Article 238

Article 237 shall not apply:

— to consignments containing goods for commercial purposes of an aggregate value exceeding the statistical threshold laid down by the Community provisions in force; the customs authorities may lay down higher thresholds;

— to consignments containing goods for commercial purposes which form part of a regular series of like operations;

— where a customs declaration is made in writing, orally or using a data-processing technique;

— to consignments containing the goods referred to in Article 235.

TITLE VIII
EXAMINATION OF THE GOODS, FINDINGS OF THE CUSTOMS OFFICE AND OTHER MEASURES TAKEN BY THE CUSTOMS OFFICE

Articles 239–856

Note

Articles 239–856 are outside the scope of this work.

PART IV
CUSTOMS DEBT

TITLE I
SECURITY

Article 857

1. The types of security other than cash deposits or guarantors, within the meaning of Articles 193, 194 and 195 of the Code, and the cash deposit or the submission of securities for which Member States may opt even if they do not comply with the conditions laid down in Article 194(1) of the Code, shall be as follows:

(*a*) the creation of a mortgage, a charge on land, an antichresis or other right deemed equivalent to a right pertaining to immovable property;

(*b*) the cession of a claim, the pledging, with or without surrendering possession, of goods, securities or claims or, in particular, a savings bank book or entry in the national debt register;

(*c*) the assumption of joint contractual liability for the full amount of the debt by a third party approved for that purpose by the customs authorities and, in particular, the lodging of a bill of exchange the payment of which is guaranteed by such third party;

(*d*) a cash deposit or security deemed equivalent thereto in a currency other than that of the Member State in which the security is given;

(*e*) participation, subject to payment of a contribution, in a general guarantee scheme administered by the customs authorities.

2. The circumstances in which and the conditions under which recourse may be had to the types of security referred to in paragraph 1 shall be determined by the customs authorities.

Article 858

Where security is given by making a cash deposit, no interest thereon shall be payable by the customs authorities.

TITLE II
INCURRENCE OF THE DEBT

CHAPTER 1
Failures which have no significant effect on the operation of temporary storage or of the customs procedure

Article 859

The following failures shall be considered to have no significant effect on the correct operation of the temporary storage or customs procedure in question within the meaning of Article 204(1) of the Code, provided:

— they do not constitute an attempt to remove the goods unlawfully from customs supervision,

— they do not imply obvious negligence on the part of the person concerned, and

— all the formalities necessary to regularize the situation of the goods are subsequently carried out:

1. exceeding the time limit allowed for assignment of the goods to one of the customs-approved treatments or uses provided for under the temporary storage or customs procedure in question, where the time limit would have been extended had an extension been applied for in time;

2. in the case of goods placed under a transit procedure, exceeding the time limit for presentation of the goods to the office of destination, where such presentation takes place later;

3. in the case of goods placed in temporary storage or under the customs warehousing procedure, handling not authorized in advance by the customs authorities, provided such handling would have been authorized if applied for;

4. in the case of goods placed under the temporary importation procedure, use of the goods otherwise than as provided for in the authorization, provided such use would have been authorized under that procedure if applied for;

5. in the case of goods in temporary storage or placed under a customs procedure, unauthorized movement of the goods, provided the goods can be presented to the customs authorities at their request;

6. in the case of goods in temporary storage or placed under a customs procedure, removal of the goods from the customs territory of the

Community or their entry into a free zone or free warehouse without completion of the necessary formalities;

7. in the case of goods having received favourable tariff treatment by reason of their end-use, transfer of the goods without notification to the customs authorities, before they have been put to the intended use, provided that:

(*a*) the transfer is recorded in the transferor's stock records, and

(*b*) the transferee is the holder of an authorization for the goods in question.

Article 860

The customs authorities shall consider a customs debt to have been incurred under Article 204(1) of the Code unless the person who would be the debtor establishes that the conditions set out in Article 859 are fulfilled.

Article 861

The fact that the failures referred to in Article 859 do not give rise to a customs debt shall not preclude the application of provisions of criminal law in force or of provisions allowing cancellation and withdrawal of authorizations issued under the customs procedure in question.

CHAPTER 2
Natural wastage

Article 862

1. For the purposes of Article 206 of the Code, the customs authorities shall, at the request of the person concerned, take account of the quantities missing wherever it can be shown that the losses observed result solely from the nature of the goods and not from any negligence or manipulation on the part of that person.

2. In particular, negligence or manipulation shall mean any failure to observe the rules for transporting, storing, handling, working or processing the goods in question imposed by the customs authorities or by normal practice.

Article 863

The customs authorities may waive the obligation for the person concerned to show that the goods were irretrievably lost for reasons inherent in their nature where they are satisfied that there is no other explanation for the loss.

Article 864

The national provisions in force in the Member States concerning standard rates for irretrievable loss due to the nature of the goods themselves shall be applied where the person concerned fails to show that the real loss exceeds that calculated by application of the standard rate for the goods in question.

CHAPTER 3
[Goods in special situations]¹

Amendments

¹　Substituted by EC Commission Regulation 3665/93 Art 1(68). See OJ L335 of 31.12.93, p 1.

Article 865

The presentation of a customs declaration for the goods in question, or any other act having the same legal effects, and the production of a document for endorsement by the competent authorities, shall be considered as removal of goods from customs supervision within the meaning of Article 203(1) of the Code, where these acts have the effect of wrongly conferring on them the customs status of Community goods.

Article 866

Without prejudice to the provisions laid down concerning prohibitions or restrictions which may be applicable to the goods in question, where a customs debt on importation is incurred pursuant to Articles 202, 203, 204 or 205 of the Code and the import duties have been paid, those goods shall be deemed to be Community goods without the need for a declaration for entry into free circulation.

Article 867

The confiscation of goods pursuant to Article 233(*c*) and (*d*) of the Code shall not affect the customs status of the goods in question.

[Article 867a

1. Non-Community goods which have been abandoned to the Exchequer or seized or confiscated shall be considered to have been entered for the customs warehousing procedure.

2. The goods referred to in paragraph 1 may be sold by the customs authorities only on the condition that the buyer immediately carries out the formalities to assign them a customs-approved treatment or use.

Where the sale is at a price inclusive of import duties, the sale shall be considered as equivalent to release for free circulation, and the customs authorities themselves shall calculate the duties and enter them in the accounts.

In these cases, the sale shall be conducted according to the procedures in force in the Member States.

3. Where the administration decides to deal with the goods referred to in paragraph otherwise than by sale, it shall immediately carry out the formalities to assign them one of the customs-approved treatments or uses laid down in Article 4(15)(*a*),(*b*),(*c*) and (*d*) of the code.]¹

Amendments

¹　Art 867a inserted by Commission Regulation 3665/93/EEC. See OJ L335, 31.12.93, p 1.

PART V
FINAL PROVISIONS

Article 913

1. The following Regulation and Directives shall be repealed:

— Commission Regulation (EEC) No 1494/80 of 11 June 1980 on interpretative notes and generally accepted accounting principles for the purposes of customs value (OJ No L 154, 21.6.1980, p 3),

— Commission Regulation (EEC) No 1495/80 of 11 June 1980 implementing certain provisions of Council Regulation (EEC) No 1224/80 on the valuation of goods for customs purposes (OJ No L 154, 21.6.1980, p 14), as last amended by Regulation (EEC) No 558/91 (OJ No L 62, 8.3.1991, p 24),

— Commission Regulation (EEC) No 1496/80 of 11 June 1980 on the declaration of particulars relating to customs value and on documents to be furnished (OJ No L 154, 21.6.1980, p 16), as last amended by Regulation (EEC) No 979/93 (OJ No L 101, 27.4.1993, p 7),

— Commission Regulation (EEC) No 3177/80 of 5 December 1980 on the place of introduction to be taken into consideration in applying Article 14 (2) of Council Regulation (EEC) No 1224/80 on the valuation of goods for customs purposes (OJ No L 335, 12.12.1980, p 1) as last amended by Regulation (EEC) No 2779/90 (OJ No L 267, 29.9.1990, p 36),

— Commission Regulation (EEC) No 3179/80 of 5 December 1980 on postal charges to be taken into consideration when determining the customs value of goods sent by post (OJ No L 335, 12.12.1980, p 62), as last amended by Regulation (EEC) No 1264/90 (OJ No L 124, 15.5.1990, p 32),

— Commission Regulation (EEC) No 1577/81 of 12 June 1981 establishing a system of simplified procedures for the determination of the customs value of certain perishable goods (OJ No L 154, 13.6.1981, p 26), as last amended by Regulation (EEC) No 3334/90 (OJ No L 321, 21.11.1990, p 6),

— Commission Regulation (EEC) No 3158/83 of 9 November 1983 on the incidence of royalties and licence fees in customs value (OJ No L 309, 10.11.1983, p 19),

— Commission Regulation (EEC) No 1766/85 of 27 June 1985 on the rates of exchange to be used in the determination of customs value (OJ No L 168, 28.6.1985, p 21), as last amended by Regulation (EEC) No 593/91 (OJ No L 66, 13.3.1991, p 14),

— Commission Regulation (EEC) No 3903/92 of 21 December 1992 on air transport costs (OJ No L 393, 31.12.1992, p 1).

Article 914

References to the provisions repealed shall be understood as referring to this Regulation.

Article 915

This Regulation shall enter into force on the third day following its publication in the *Official Journal of the European Communities*.

It shall apply from 1 January 1994.

...

This Regulation shall be binding in its entirety and directly applicable in all Member States.

Note

Words omitted are outside the scope of this work.

ANNEX 23
INTERPRETATIVE NOTES ON CUSTOMS VALUE

First column	*Second column*
Reference to provisions of the Customs Code	*Notes*

Article 29(1)	The price actually paid or payable refers to the price for the imported goods. Thus the flow of dividends or other payments from the buyer to the seller that do not relate to the imported goods are not part of the customs value.
Article 29(1)(*a*) third indent	An example of such restriction would be the case where a seller requires a buyer of automobiles not to sell or exhibit them prior to a fixed date which represents the beginning of a model year.
Article 29(1)(*b*)	Some examples of this include:

(*a*) the seller establishes the price of the imported goods on condition that the buyer will also buy other goods in specified quantities;

(*b*) the price of the imported goods is dependent upon the price or prices at which the buyer of the imported goods sells other goods to the seller of the imported goods;

(*c*) the price is established on the basis of a form of payment extraneous to the imported goods, such as where the imported goods are semi-finished goods which have been provided by the seller on condition that he will receive a specified quantity of the finished goods.

However, conditions or considerations relating to the production or marketing of the imported goods shall not result in rejection of the transaction value. For example, the fact that the buyer furnishes the seller with engineering and plans undertaken in the country of importation shall not result in rejection of the transaction value for the purposes of Article 29(1).

Article 29(2)	1 Paragraphs 2(*a*) and (*b*) provide different means of establishing the acceptability of a transaction value.

2 Paragraph 2(*a*) provides that where the buyer and the seller are related, the circumstances surrounding the sale shall be examined and the transaction value shall be accepted as the customs value provided that the relationship did not influence the price. It is not intended

that there should be an examination of the circumstances in all cases where the buyer and the seller are related. Such examination will only be required where there are doubts about the acceptability of the price. Where the customs authorities have no doubts about the acceptability of the price, it should be accepted without requesting further information from the declarant. For example, the relationship, or it may already have detailed information concerning the buyer and the seller, and may already be satisfied from such examination or information that the relationship did not influence the price.

3 Where the customs authorities are unable to accept the transaction value without further inquiry, it should give the declarant an opportunity to supply such further detailed information as may be necessary to enable it to examine the circumstances surrounding the sale. In this context, the customs authorities should be prepared to examine relevant aspects of the transaction, including the way in which the buyer and seller organise their commercial relations and the way in which the price in question was arrived at, in order to determine whether the relationship influenced the price. Where it can be shown that the buyer and seller, although related under the provisions of Article 143 of this Regulation, buy from and sell to each other as if they were not related, this would demonstrate that the price had not been influenced by the relationship. As an example of this, if the price had been settled in a manner consistent with the normal pricing practices of the industry in question or with the way the seller settles prices for sales to buyers who are not related to him, this would demonstrate that the price had not been influenced by the relationship. As a further example, where it is shown that the price is adequate to ensure recovery of all costs plus a profit which is representative of the firm's overall profit realised over a representative period of time (eg on an annual basis) in sales of goods of the same class or kind, this would demonstrate that the price had not been influenced.

4 Paragraph 2(*b*) provides an opportunity for the declarant to demonstrate that the transaction value closely approximates to a "test" value previously accepted by the customs authorities and is therefore acceptable under the provisions of Article 29. Where a test under paragraph 2(*b*) is met, it is not necessary to

examine the question of influence under paragraph 2(*a*). If the customs authorities already have sufficient information to be satisfied, without further detailed inquiries, that one of the tests provided in paragraph (2)(*b*) has been met, there is no reason for them to require the declarant to demonstrate that the test can be met.

Article 29(2)(*b*)

A number of factors must be taken into consideration in determining whether one value "closely approximates" to another value. These factors include the nature of the imported goods, the nature of the industry itself, the season in which the goods are imported, and, whether the difference in values is commercially significant. Since these factors may vary from case to case, it would be impossible to apply a uniform standard such as a fixed percentage, in each case. For example, a small difference in value in a case involving one type of goods could be unacceptable while a large difference in a case involving another type of goods might be acceptable in determining whether the transaction value closely approximates to the "test" values set forth in Article 29(2)(*b*).

Article 29(3)(*a*)

An example of an indirect payment would be the settlement by the buyer, whether in whole or in part, of a debt owed by the seller.

Article 30(2)(*a*),(*b*)

1 In applying these provisions, the customs authorities shall, wherever possible, use a sale of identical or similar goods, as appropriate, at the same commercial level and in substantially the same quantity as the goods being valued. Where no such sale is found, a sale of identical or similar goods, as appropriate, that takes place under any one of the following three conditions may be used:

(*a*) a sale at the same commercial level but in a different quantity;

(*b*) a sale at a different commercial level but in substantially the same quantity; or

(*c*) a sale at a different commercial level and in a different quantity.

2 Having found a sale under any one of these three conditions adjustments will then be made, as the case may be, for:

(*a*) quantity factors only;

(*b*) commercial level factors only; or

(*c*) both commercial level and quantity factors.

3 The expression "and/or" allows the flexibility to use the sales and make the necessary adjustments in any one of the three conditions described above.

4 A condition for adjustment because of different commercial levels or different quantities is that such adjustment, whether it leads to an increase or a decrease in value, be made only on the basis of demonstrated evidence that clearly establishes the reasonableness and accuracy of the adjustment, eg valid price lists containing prices referring to different levels or different quantities. As an example of this, if the imported goods being valued consist of a shipment of 10 units and the only identical or similar imported goods, as appropriate, for which a transaction value exists involved a sale of 500 units, and it is recognised that the seller grants quantity discounts, the required adjustment may be accomplished by resorting to the seller's price list and using that price applicable to a sale of 10 units. This does not require that a sale had to have been made in quantities of 10 as long as the price list has been established as being bona fide through sales at other quantities. In the absence of such an objective measure, however, the determination of a customs value under the provisions of Article 30(2)(*a*) and (*b*) is not appropriate.

Article 30(2)(*d*)

1 As a general rule, customs value is determined under these provisions on the basis of information readily available in the Community. In order to determine a computed value, however, it may be necessary to examine the costs of producing the goods being valued and other information which has to be obtained from outside the Community. Furthermore, in most cases the producer of the goods will be outside the jurisdiction of the authorities of the Member States. The use of the computed value method will generally be limited to those cases where the buyer and seller are related, and the producer is prepared to supply to the authorities of the country of importation the necessary costings and to provide facilities for any subsequent verification which may be necessary.

2 The "cost or value" referred to in Article 30(2)(*d*), first indent, is to be determined on the basis of information

relating to the production of the goods being valued supplied by or on behalf of the producer. It is to be based upon the commercial accounts of the producer, provided that such accounts are consistent with the generally accepted accounting principles applied in the country where the goods are produced.

3 The "amount for profit and general expenses" referred to in Article 30(2)(*d*), second indent, is to be determined on the basis of information supplied by or on behalf of the producer unless his figures are inconsistent with those usually reflected in sales of goods of the same class or kind as the goods being valued which are made by producers in the country of exportation for export to the country of importation.

4 No cost or value of the elements referred to in this Article shall be counted twice in determining the computed value.

5 It should be noted in this context that the "amount for profit and general expenses" has to be taken as a whole. It follows that if, in any particular case, the producer's profit figure is low and his general expenses are high, his profit and general expenses taken together may nevertheless be consistent with that usually reflected in sales of goods of the same class or kind. Such a situation might occur, for example of a product were being launched in the Community and the producer accepted a nil or low profit to offset high general expenses associated with the launch. Where the producer can demonstrate that he is taking a low profit on his sales of the imported goods because of particular commercial circumstances, his actual profit figures should be taken into account provided that he has valid commercial reasons to justify them and his pricing policy reflects usual pricing policies in the branch of industry concerned. Such a situation might occur, for example, where producers have been forced to lower prices temporarily because of an unforeseeable drop in demand, or where they sell goods to complement a range of goods being produced in the country of importation and accept a low profit to maintain competitivity. Where the producer's own figures for profit and general expenses are not consistent with those usually reflected in sales of goods of the same class or kind as the goods being valued which are made by producers in the country of exportation for export to the country of

importation, the amount for profit and general expenses may be based upon relevant information other than that supplied by or on behalf of the producer of the goods.

6 Whether certain goods are "of the same class or kind" as other goods must be determined on a case-by-case basis with reference to the circumstances involved. In determining the usual profits and general expenses under the provisions of Article 30(2)(*d*), sales for export to the country of importation of the narrowest group or range of goods, which includes the goods being valued, for which the necessary information can be provided, should be examined. For the purposes of Article 30(2)(*d*), "goods of the same class or kind" must be from the same country as the goods being valued.

Article 31(1)

1 Customs values determined under the provisions of Article 31(1) should, to the greatest extent possible, be based on previously determined customs values.

2 The methods of valuation to be employed under Article 31(1) should be those laid down in Articles 29 and 30(2), but a reasonable flexibility in the application of such methods would be in conformity with the aims and provisions of Article 31(1).

3 Some examples of reasonable flexibility are as follows:

(*a*) *Identical goods* — the requirement that the identical goods should be exported at or about the same time as the goods being valued could be flexibly interpreted; identical imported goods produced in a country other than the country of exportation of the goods being valued could be the basis for customs valuation; customs values of identical imported goods already determined under the provisions of Article 30(2)(*c*) and (*d*) could be used.

(*b*) *Similar goods* — the requirement that the similar goods should be exported at or about the same time as the goods being valued could be flexibly interpreted; similar imported goods produced in a country other than the country of exportation of the goods being valued could be the basis for customs valuations; customs values of similar imported goods already determined under the provisions of Article 30(2)(*c*) and (*d*) could be used.

(c) *Deductive method* — the requirement that the goods shall have been sold in the "condition as imported" in Article 152(1)(*a*) could be flexibly interpreted the "90 days" requirement could be administered flexibly.

Article 32(1)(*b*)(ii)

1 There are two factors involved in the apportionment of the elements specified in Article 32(1)(*b*)(ii) to the imported goods — the value of the element itself and the way in which that value is to be apportioned to the imported goods. The apportionment of these elements should be made in a reasonable manner appropriate to the circumstances and in accordance with generally accepted accounting principles.

2 Concerning the value of the element, if the buyer acquires the element from a seller not related to him at a given cost, the value of the element is that cost. If the element was produced by the buyer or by a person related to him, its value would be the cost of producing it. If the element had been previously used by the buyer, regardless of whether it had been acquired or produced by him, the original cost of acquisition or production would have to be adjusted downwards to reflect its use in order to arrive at the value of the element.

3 Once a value has been determined for the element, it is necessary to apportion that value to the imported goods. Various possibilities exist. For example, the value might be apportioned to the first shipment, if the buyer wishes to pay duty on the entire value at one time. As another example, he may request that the value be apportioned over the number of units produced up to the time of the first shipment. As a further example, he may request that the value be apportioned over the entire anticipated production where contracts of firm commitments exist for the production. The method of apportionment used will depend upon the documentation provided by the buyer.

4 As an illustration of the above, a buyer provides the producer with a mould to be used in the production of the imported goods and contracts with him to buy 10,000 units. By the time of arrival of the first shipment of 1,000 units, the producer has already produced 4,000 units. The buyer may request the customs authorities to apportion the value of the mould over 1,000, 4,000 or 10,000 units.

Article 32(1)(*b*)(iv)

1 Additions for the elements specified in Article 32(1)(*b*)(iv) should be based on objective and quantifiable data. In order to minimise the burden for both the declarant and customs authorities in determining the values to be added, data readily available in the buyers commercial record system should be used in so far as possible.

2 For those elements supplied by the buyer which were purchased or leased by the buyer, the addition would be the cost of the purchase or the lease. No addition shall be made for those elements available in the public domain, other than the cost of obtaining copies of them.

3 The ease with which it may be possible to calculate the values to be added will depend on a particular firm's structure and management practice, as well as its accounting methods.

4 For example, it is possible that a firm which imports a variety of products from several countries maintains the records of its design centre outside the country of importation in such as way as to show accurately the costs attributable to a given product. In such cases, a direct adjustment may appropriately be made under the provisions of Article 32.

5 In another case, a firm may carry the cost of the design centre outside the country of importation as a general overhead expense without allocation to specific products. In this instance, an appropriate adjustment could be made under the provisions of Article 32 with respect to the imported goods by apportioning total design centre costs over total production benefiting from the design centre and adding such apportioned cost on a unit basis to imports.

6 Variations in the above circumstances will, of course, require different factors to be considered in determining the proper method of allocation.

7 In cases where the production of the element in question involves a number of countries and over a period of time, the adjustment should be limited to the value actually added to that element outside the country of importation.

Article 32(1)(*c*)

The royalties and licence fees referred to in Article 32(1)(*c*) may include, among other things, payments in respect of patents, trademarks and copyrights.

Article 32(2)

Where objective and quantifiable data do not exist with regard to the additions required to be made under the provisions of Article 32, the transaction value cannot be determined under the provisions of Article 29. As an illustration of this, a royalty is paid on the basis of the price in a sale in the importing country of a litre of a particular product that was imported by the kilogram and made up into a solution after importation. If the royalty is based partially on the imported goods and partially on other factors which have nothing to do with the imported goods (such as when the imported goods are mixed with domestic ingredients and are no longer separately identifiable, or when the royalty cannot be distinguished from special financial arrangements between the buyer and the seller), it would be inappropriate to attempt to make an addition for the royalty. However, if the amount of this royalty is based only on the imported goods and can be readily quantified, an addition to the price actually paid or payable can be made.

Article 143(1)(*e*)

One person shall be deemed to control another when the former is legally or operationally in a position to exercise restraint or direction over the latter.

Article 152(1)(*a*)(i)

1 The words "profit and general expenses" should be taken as a whole. The figure for the purposes of this deduction should be determined on the basis of information supplied by the declarant unless his figures are inconsistent with those obtaining in sales in the country of importation of imported goods of the same class or kind. Where the declarant's figures are inconsistent with such figures, the amount for profit and general expenses may be based upon relevant information other than that supplied by the declarant.

2 In determining either the commissions or the usual profits and general expenses under this provision, the question whether certain goods are of the same class or kind as other goods must be determined on a case-by-case basis by reference to the circumstances involved. Sales in the country of importation of the narrowest group or range of imported goods of the same class or kind, which includes the goods being valued, for which the necessary information can be provided, should be examined. For the purposes of this provision, "goods of the same class or kind" includes goods imported from

the same country as the goods being valued as well as goods imported from other countries.

Article 152(2)

1 Where this method of valuation is used, deductions made for the value added by further processing shall be based on objective and quantifiable data relating to the cost of such work. Accepted industry formulas, recipes, methods of construction, and other industry practices would form the basis of the calculations.

2 This method of valuation would normally not be applicable when, as a result of the further processing, the imported goods lose their identity. However, there can be instances where, although the identity of the imported goods is lost, the value added by the processing can be determined accurately without unreasonable difficulty.

On the other hand, there can also be instances where the imported goods maintain their identity but form such a minor element in the goods sold in the country of importation that the use of this valuation method would be unjustified. In view of the above, each situation of this type must be considered on a case-by-case basis.

Article 152(3)

1 As a example of this, goods are sold from a price list which grants favourable unit prices for purchases made in larger quantities.

Sale quantity	*Unit price*	*Number of sales*	*Total quantity sold at each price*
One to 10 units	100	10 sales of five units	65
		Five sales of three units	
11 to 25 units	95	Five sales of 11 units	55
Over 25 units	90	One sale of 30 units	80
		One sale of 50 units	

The greatest number of units sold at a price is 80; therefore, the unit price in the greatest aggregate quantity is 90.

2 As another example of this, two sales occur. In the first sale 500 units are sold at a price of 95 currency units each. In the second sale 400 units are sold at price of 90 currency units each. In this example, the greatest number

of units sold at a particular price is 500; therefore, the unit price in the greatest aggregate quantity is 95.

3 A third example would be the following situation where various quantities are sold at various prices.

(a) Sales

Sale quantity	unit price
40 units	100
30 units	90
15 units	100
50 units	95
25 units	105
35 units	90
5 units	100

(b) Total

65	90
50	95
60	100
25	105

In this example, the greatest number of units sold at a particular price is 65; therefore, the unit price in the greatest aggregate quantity is 90.

ANNEX 24
APPLICATION OF GENERALLY ACCEPTED ACCOUNTING PRINCIPLES FOR THE DETERMINATION OF CUSTOMS VALUE

1 "Generally accepted accounting principles" refers to the recognised consensus or substantial authoritative support within a country at a particular time as to which economic resources and obligations should be recorded as assets and liabilities, which changes in assets and liabilites should be recorded, how the assets and liabilities and changes in them should be measured, what information should be disclosed and how it should be disclosed, and which financial statements should be prepared. These standards may be broad guidelines of general application as well as detailed practices and procedures.

2 For the purposes of the application of the customs valuation provisions, the customs administration concerned shall utilise information prepared in a manner consistent with generally accepted accounting principles in the country which is appropriate for the Article in question. For example, the determination of usual profit and general expenses under the provisions of Article 152(1)(*a*)(i) of this Regulation would be carried out utilising information prepared in a manner consistent with generally accepted accounting principles of the country of importation. On the other hand, the determination of usual profit and general expenses under the provisions of Article 30(2)(*d*) of the Code would be carried out utilising information prepared in a manner consistent with generally accepted accounting principles of the country of production. As a further example, the determination of an element provided for in Article 32(1)(*b*)(ii) of the Code undertaken in the country of importation would be carried out utilising information in a manner consistent with the generally accepted accounting principles of that country.

ANNEX 25
AIR TRANSPORT COSTS TO BE INCLUDED IN THE CUSTOMS VALUE

INTRODUCTION

1 The following table showed:

(*a*)   third countries listed by continent (column 1);

(*b*)   airports of departure in third countries (column 2);

(*c*)   airports of arrival in the Community with the percentages which represent the part of the air transport costs to be included in the customs value (column 3 and following columns).

2 When the goods are shipped to or from airports not included in the following table, other than the airports referred to in paragraph 3, the percentage given for the airport nearest to that of departure or arrival shall be taken.

3 As regards the French overseas departments of Guadeloupe, Guyana, Martinique and Reunion, of which territories the airports are not included in the table, the following rules shall apply:-

(*a*)   for goods shipped direct to those departments from third countries, the whole of the air transport cost is to be included in the customs value;

(*b*)   for goods shipped to the European part of the Community from third countries and transhipped or unloaded in one of those departments, the air transport costs which would have been incurred for carrying the goods only as far as the place of transhipment or unloading are to be included in the customs value;

(*c*)   for goods shipped to those departments from third countries and transhipped or unloaded in an airport in the European part of the Community, the air transport costs to be included in the customs value are those which result from the application of the percentages given in the following table to the costs which would have been incurred for carrying the goods from the airport of departure to the airport of transhipment or unloading.

The transhipment or unloading shall be certified by an appropriate endorsement by the customs authorities on the air waybill or other air transport document, with the official stamp of the office concerned; failing this certification the provisions of the last subparagraph of Article 14(3) of Regulation (EEC) No 1224/80 shall apply.

Percentages of air transport costs to be included in the customs value

LIST I (Federal Republic of Germany) (not reproduced)

LIST II (*Benelux*) (not reproduced)

LIST III (*France*) (not reproduced)

LIST IV (*Italy*) (not reproduced)

LIST V (*Ireland*) (reproduced)

LIST VI (*Greece*) (not reproduced)

LIST VII (*Spain*) (not reproduced)

LIST VIII (*Portugal*) (not reproduced)

LIST V (Ireland)

Third countries	Airport of departure	Ireland all airports
1	2	3
[I. EUROPE		
Albania	all airports	38
Armenia	all airports	58
Belarus	all airports	38
Bosnia-Herzogovina	all airports	18
Bulgaria	all airports	33
Croatia	all airports	17
Cyprus	see Asia	
Czech Republic	Ostrava	21
	Prague	9
Estonia	all airports	44
Faroe Islands	all airports	36
Georgia	all airports	64
Gibraltar	all airports	0
Hungary	all airports	8
Iceland	all airports	59
Latvia	all airports	24
Lithuania	all airports	34
Former Yugoslav Republic of Macedonia	all airports	37
Malta	all airports	6
Moldova	all airports	35
Montenegro	all airports	34
Norway	Ålesund, Bodø, Trondheim,	
	Alta, Kirkenes	73
	Bergen	51
	Kristiansand	51
	Oslo	59
	Stavanger	47
Poland	Bydgoszcz, Cracow, Gdansk,	
	Rzeszow, Wroclaw	33
	Poznan	13
	Szczecin (Stettin)	0
	Warsaw	25
Romania	all airports	32

Russia	Gorky, Kuibishev, Perm,	
	Rostov, Volgograd	48
	St. Petersburg	29
	Moscow, Orel, Voronej	49
	Irkutsk, Kirensk, Krasnoyarsk, Novosibirsk, Khabarovsk,	
	Vladivostok	74
	Omsk, Sverdlovsk	69
Serbia	all airports	19
Slovakia	Bratislava	0
	Kosice, Presov	31
Slovenia	all airports	10
Switzerland	Basel	0
	Bern	4
	Geneva	0
	Zurich	2
Turkey (European part)	all airports	7
Turkey (Asian part)	Adana, Afyon, Antalya, Elâzig, Gasziantep, Iskenderun, Kastamonu, Konya, Malatya,	
	Samsun, Trabzon	20
	Agri, Diyarbakir, Erzurum,	
	Kars, Van	30
	Akhisar, Ankara, Balikezir, Bandirma, Bursa, Kütahya,	
	Zonguldak	17
	Izmir	16
Ukraine	all airports	44][2]

II. AFRICA

Algeria	Algiers	16

	Annaba, Constantine	23
	El Golea	34
Angola	all airports	79
Benin	all airports	61
Botswana	all airports	68
Burkina Faso	all airports	42
Burundi	all airports	54
Cameroon	all airports	74
Republic of Cape Verde	all airports	27
Central African Republic	all airports	75
Chad	all airports	70
Comoros	all airports	64
Congo	all airports	78
Djibouti	all airports	48
Egypt	all airports	18
Equatorial Guinea	all airports	77
Ethiopia	all airports	44
Gabon	all airports	74
Gambia	all airports	27
Ghana	all airports	61
Guinea	all airports	39
Guinea Bissau	all airports	39
Ivory Coast	all airports	61
Kenya	all airports	55
Lesotho	all airports	68
Liberia	all airports	39
Libya	Benghazi	24
	Sebha	41
	Tripoli	28
Madagascar	all airports	64
Malawi	all airports	59
Mali	all airports	42
Mauritania	all airports	27
Mauritius	all airports	64
Morocco	Casablanca	12
	Fez, Rabat	12
	Ifni	27
	Tangiers, Tetuan	0
Mozambique	all airports	65
Namibia	all airports	68

Niger	all airports	42
Nigeria	all airports	61
Rwanda	all airports	54
Saò Tomé and Principe	all airports	77
Senegal	all airports	27
Seychelles	all airports	64
Sierra Leone	all airports	39
Somalia	all airports	55
Republic of South Africa	all airports	68
St. Helena	all airports	73
Sudan	all airports	40
Swaziland	all airports	68
Tanzania	all airports	59
Togo	all airports	61
Tunisia	Djerba	22
	Tunis	11
Uganda	all airports	54
Zaire	all airports	78
Zambia	all airports	64
Zimbabwe	all airports	64

III. AMERICA

1. *North America*

Canada	Edmonton, Vancouver, Winnipeg	85
	Gander, Moncton	76
	Halifax, Montreal, Ottawa, Quebec,	
	Toronto	76
Greenland	all airports	75
United States of America	Akron, Albany, Atlanta, Baltimore,	
	Boston, Buffalo, Charleston,	
	Chicago, Cincinnati, Columbus,	
	Detroit, Indianapolis, Jacksonville,	
	Kansas City, New Orleans,	

Lexington, Louisville, Memphis, Milwaukee, Minneapolis, Nashville, New York, Philadelphia, Pittsburgh, St. Louis, Washington DC		81
Albuquerque, Austin, Billings, Dallas, Denver, Houston, Las Vegas, Los Angeles, Oklahoma, Phoenix, Portland, Salt Lake City, San Francisco, Seattle		87
Anchorage, Fairbanks, Juneau		82
Honolulu		94
Miami		85
Puerto Rico		86

2. Central America

Bahamas	all airports	83
Belize	all airports	84
Bermuda	all airports	83
Costa Rica	all airports	84
Cuba	all airports	84
Curacao	all airports	71
Dominican Republic	all airports	83
El Salvador	all airports	84
Guatemala	all airports	84
Haiti	all airports	83
Honduras	all airports	84
Jamaica	all airports	84
Mexico	all airports	86
Nicaragua	all airports	84
Panama	all airports	84

Virgin Islands	see West Indies	
West Indies	all airports	71

3. *South America*

Argentina	all airports	71
Aruba	all airports	71
Bolivia	all airports	71
Brazil	all airports	71
Chile	all airports	71
Colombia	all airports	71
Ecuador	all airports	71
Guyana	all airports	71
Paraguay	all airports	71
Peru	all airports	71
Suriname	all airports	71
Trinidad and Tobago	all airports	71
Uruguay	all airports	71
Venezuela	all airports	71

IV. ASIA

Afghanistan	all airports	59
Azerbaijan	all airports	64
Bahrain	all airports	37
Bangladesh	all airports	59
Bhutan	see Nepal	
Brunei	see Malaysia	
Burma	all airports	69
China	all airports	72
Cyprus	all airports	13
Hong Kong	all airports	72
India	all airports	59
Indonesia	all airports	72
Iran	all airports	37
Iraq	all airports	30
Israel	all airports	18
Japan	all airports	78
Jordan	all airports	19
Kampuchea	all airports	69
Kazakhstan	all airports	65
North Korea	all airports	72

South Korea	all airports	72
Kuwait	all airports	38
Kyrgyzstan	all airports	65
Laos	all airports	69
Lebanon	all airports	16
Macao	all airports	72
Malaysia	all airports	72
Maldives	all airports	65
Mongolia	all airports	74
Muscat and Oman	all airports	48
Nepal	all airports	59
Oman	see Muscat and Oman	
Uzbekistan	all airports	65
Pakistan	all airports	59
Philippines	all airports	72
Qatar	all airports	37
Saudi Arabia	all airports	37
Singapore	all airports	72
Sri Lanka	all airports	72
Syria	all airports	19
Tajikistan	all airports	19
Taiwan	all airports	65
Thailand	all airports	69
Turkey	see Europe	
Turkmenistan	all airports	65
United Arab Emirates	all airports	48
Vietnam	all airports	72
Yemen Arab Republic	all airports	45

V. AUSTRALIA
and OCEANIA   all airports   79

COUNCIL REGULATION

of 17 June 1997

97/1103/EC

on certain provisions relating to the introduction of the euro

(OJ L162 , 19/06/1997 p 1–3)

THE COUNCIL OF THE EUROPEAN UNION,

Having regard to the Treaty establishing the European Community, and in particular Article 235 thereof,

Having regard to the proposal of the Commission (OJ No C 369, 7. 12. 1996, p 8),

Having regard to the opinion of the European Parliament (OJ No C 380, 16. 12. 1996, p 49),

Having regard to the opinion of the European Monetary Institute (Opinion delivered on 29 November 1996),

(1) Whereas, at its meeting held in Madrid on 15 and 16 December 1995, the European Council confirmed that the third stage of Economic and Monetary Union will start on 1 January 1999 as laid down in Article 109j (OJ No L 350, 31. 12. 1994, p 27) of the Treaty; whereas the Member States which will adopt the euro as the single currency in accordance with the Treaty will be defined for the purposes of this Regulation as the "participating Member States";

(2) Whereas, at the meeting of the European Council in Madrid, the decision was taken that the term "ECU" used by the Treaty to refer to the European currency unit is a generic term; whereas the Governments of the fifteen Member States have achieved the common agreement that this decision is the agreed and definitive interpretation of the relevant Treaty provisions; whereas the name given to the European currency shall be the "euro"; whereas the euro as the currency of the participating Member States will be divided into one hundred sub-units with the name "cent"; whereas the European Council furthermore considered that the name of the single currency must be the same in all the official languages of the European Union, taking into account the existence of different alphabets;

(3) Whereas a Regulation on the introduction of the euro will be adopted by the Council on the basis of the third sentence of Article 109l (4) of the Treaty as soon as the participating Member States are known in order to define the legal framework of the euro; whereas the Council, when acting at the starting date of the third stage in accordance with the first sentence of Article 109l (4) of the Treaty, shall adopt the irrevocably fixed conversion rates;

(4) Whereas it is necessary, in the course of the operation of the common market and for the changeover to the single currency, to provide legal certainty for citizens and firms in all Member States on certain provisions relating to the introduction of the euro well

before the entry into the third stage; whereas this legal certainty at an early stage will allow preparations by citizens and firms to proceed under good conditions;

(5) Whereas the third sentence of Article 109l (4) of the Treaty, which allows the Council, acting with the unanimity of participating Member States, to take other measures necessary for the rapid introduction of the single currency is available as a legal basis only when it has been confirmed, in accordance with Article 109j(4) of the Treaty, which Member States fulfil the necessary conditions for the adoption of a single currency; whereas it is therefore necessary to have recourse to Article 235 of the Treaty as a legal basis for those provisions where there is an urgent need for legal certainty; whereas therefore this Regulation and the aforesaid Regulation on the introduction of the euro will together provide the legal framework for the euro, the principles of which legal framework were agreed by the European Council in Madrid; whereas the introduction of the euro concerns day-to-day operations of the whole population in participating Member States; whereas measures other than those in this Regulation and in the Regulation which will be adopted under the third sentence of Article 109l(4) of the Treaty should be examined to ensure a balanced changeover, in particular for consumers;

(6) Whereas the ECU as referred to in Article 109g of the Treaty and as defined in Council Regulation (EC) No 3320/94 of 22 December 1994 on the consolidation of the existing Community legislation on the definition of the ECU following the entry into force of the Treaty on European Union (4) will cease to be defined as a basket of component currencies on 1 January 1999 and the euro will become a currency in its own right; whereas the decision of the Council regarding the adoption of the conversion rates shall not in itself modify the external value of the ECU; whereas this means that one ECU in its composition as a basket of component currencies will become one euro; whereas Regulation (EC) No 3320/94 therefore becomes obsolete and should be repealed; whereas for references in legal instruments to the ECU, parties shall be presumed to have agreed to refer to the ECU as referred to in Article 109g of the Treaty and as defined in the aforesaid Regulation; whereas such presumption should be rebuttable taking into account the intentions of the parties;

(7) Whereas it is a generally accepted principle of law that the continuity of contracts and other legal instruments is not affected by the introduction of a new currency; whereas the principle of freedom of contract has to be respected; whereas the principle of continuity should be compatible with anything which parties might have agreed with reference to the introduction of the euro; whereas, in order to reinforce legal certainty and clarity, it is appropriate explicitly to confirm that the principle of continuity of contracts and other legal instruments shall apply between the former national currencies and the euro and between the ECU as referred to in Article 109g of the Treaty and as defined in Regulation (EC) No 3320/94 and the euro; whereas this implies, in particular, that in the case of fixed interest rate instruments the introduction of the euro does not alter the nominal interest rate payable by the debtor; whereas the provisions on continuity can fulfil their objective to provide legal certainty and transparency to economic agents, in particular for consumers, only if they enter into force as soon as possible;

(8) Whereas the introduction of the euro constitutes a change in the monetary law of each participating Member State; whereas the recognition of the monetary law of a State is a universally accepted principle; whereas the explicit confirmation of the principle of continuity should lead to the recognition of continuity of contracts and other legal instruments in the jurisdictions of third countries;

(9) Whereas the term "contract' used for the definition of legal instruments is meant to include all types of contracts, irrespective of the way in which they are concluded;

(10) Whereas the Council, when acting in accordance with the first sentence of Article 109l (4) of the Treaty, shall define the conversion rates of the euro in terms of each of the national currencies of the participating Member States; whereas these conversion rates should be used for any conversion between the euro and the national currency units or between the national currency units; whereas for any conversion between national currency units, a fixed algorithm should define the result; whereas the use of inverse rates for conversion would imply rounding of rates and could result in significant inaccuracies, notably if large amounts are involved;

(11) Whereas the introduction of the euro requires the rounding of monetary amounts; whereas an early indication of rules for rounding is necessary in the course of the operation of the common market and to allow a timely preparation and a smooth transition to Economic and Monetary Union; whereas these rules do not affect any rounding practice, convention or national provisions providing a higher degree of accuracy for intermediate computations;

(12) Whereas, in order to achieve a high degree of accuracy in conversion operations, the conversion rates should be defined with six significant figures; whereas a rate with six significant figures means a rate which, counted from the left and starting by the first non-zero figure, has six figures,

HAS ADOPTED THIS REGULATION:

Article 1

For the purpose of this Regulation:

— **"legal instruments"** shall mean legislative and statutory provisions, acts of administration, judicial decisions, contracts, unilateral legal acts, payment instruments other than banknotes and coins, and other instruments with legal effect,

— **"participating Member States"** shall mean those Member States which adopt the single currency in accordance with the Treaty,

— **"conversion rates"** shall mean the irrevocably fixed conversion rates which the Council adopts in accordance with the first sentence of Article 109l(4) of the Treaty,

— **"national currency units"** shall mean the units of the currencies of participating Member States, as those units are defined on the day before the start of the third stage of Economic and Monetary Union,

— **"euro unit"** shall mean the unit of the single currency as defined in the Regulation on the introduction of the euro which will enter into force at the starting date of the third stage of Economic and Monetary Union.

Article 2

1. Every reference in a legal instrument to the ECU, as referred to in Article 109g of the Treaty and as defined in Regulation (EC) No 3320/94, shall be replaced by a reference to the euro at a rate of one euro to one ECU. References in a legal instrument to the ECU without such a definition shall be presumed, such presumption being rebuttable taking into account the intentions of the parties, to be references to the ECU as referred to in Article 109g of the Treaty and as defined in Regulation (EC) No 3320/94.

2. Regulation (EC) No 3320/94 is hereby repealed.

3. This Article shall apply as from 1 January 1999 in accordance with the decision pursuant to Article 109j(4) of the Treaty.

Article 3

The introduction of the euro shall not have the effect of altering any term of a legal instrument or of discharging or excusing performance under any legal instrument, nor give a party the right unilaterally to alter or terminate such an instrument. This provision is subject to anything which parties may have agreed.

Article 4

1. The conversion rates shall be adopted as one euro expressed in terms of each of the national currencies of the participating Member States. They shall be adopted with six significant figures.

2. The conversion rates shall not be rounded or truncated when making conversions.

3. The conversion rates shall be used for conversions either way between the euro unit and the national currency units. Inverse rates derived from the conversion rates shall not be used.

4. Monetary amounts to be converted from one national currency unit into another shall first be converted into a monetary amount expressed in the euro unit, which amount may be rounded to not less than three decimals and shall then be converted into the other national currency unit. No alternative method of calculation may be used unless it produces the same results.

Article 5

Monetary amounts to be paid or accounted for when a rounding takes place after a conversion into the euro unit pursuant to Article 4 shall be rounded up or down to the nearest cent. Monetary amounts to be paid or accounted for which are converted into a national currency unit shall be rounded up or down to the nearest sub-unit or in the absence of a sub-unit to the nearest unit, or according to national law or practice to a multiple or fraction of the sub-unit or unit of the national currency unit. If the application of the conversion rate gives a result which is exactly half-way, the sum shall be rounded up.

Article 6

This Regulation shall enter into force on the day following that of its publication in the Official Journal of the European Communities.

This Regulation shall be binding in its entirety and directly applicable in all Member States.

COUNCIL REGULATION

of 3 May 1998

98/974/EC

on the introduction of the euro

(OJ L139, 11/05/1998 p 1–5)

THE COUNCIL OF THE EUROPEAN UNION,

Having regard to the Treaty establishing the European Community, and in particular Article 109l(4), third sentence thereof,

Having regard to the proposal from the Commission (OJ C 369, 7. 12. 1996, p 10),

Having regard to the opinion of the European Monetary Institute (OJ C 205, 5. 7. 1997, p 18),

Having regard to the opinion of the European Parliament (OJ C 380, 16. 12. 1996, p 50),

(1) Whereas this Regulation defines monetary law provisions of the Member States which have adopted the euro; whereas provisions on continuity of contracts, the replacement of references to the ecu in legal instruments by references to the euro and rounding have already been laid down in Council Regulation (EC) No 1103/97 of 17 June 1997 on certain provisions relating to the introduction of the euro (OJ L 162, 19. 6. 1997, p 1); whereas the introduction of the euro concerns day-to-day operations of the whole population in participating Member States; whereas measures other than those in this Regulation and in Regulation (EC) No 1103/97 should be examined to ensure a balanced changeover, in particular for consumers;

(2) Whereas, at the meeting of the European Council in Madrid on 15 and 16 December 1995, the decision was taken that the term "ecu" used by the Treaty to refer to the European currency unit is a generic term; whereas the Governments of the 15 Member States have reached the common agreement that this decision is the agreed and definitive interpretation of the relevant Treaty provisions; whereas the name given to the European currency shall be the "euro"; whereas the euro as the currency of the participating Member States shall be divided into one hundred sub-units with the name "cent"; whereas the definition of the name "cent" does not prevent the use of variants of this term in common usage in the Member States; whereas the European Council furthermore considered that the name of the single currency must be the same in all the official languages of the European Union, taking into account the existence of different alphabets;

(3) Whereas the Council when acting in accordance with the third sentence of Article 109l(4) of the Treaty shall take the measures necessary for the rapid introduction of the euro other than the adoption of the conversion rates;

(4) Whereas whenever under Article 109k(2) of the Treaty a Member State becomes a participating Member State, the Council shall according to Article 109l(5) of the Treaty

take the other measures necessary for the rapid introduction of the euro as the single currency of this Member State;

(5) Whereas according to the first sentence of Article 109l(4) of the Treaty the Council shall at the starting date of the third stage adopt the conversion rates at which the currencies of the participating Member States shall be irrevocably fixed and at which irrevocably fixed rate the euro shall be substituted for these currencies;

(6) Whereas given the absence of exchange rate risk either between the euro unit and the national currency units or between these national currency units, legislative provisions should be interpreted accordingly;

(7) Whereas the term "contract" used for the definition of legal instruments is meant to include all types of contracts, irrespective of the way in which they are concluded;

(8) Whereas in order to prepare a smooth changeover to the euro a transitional period is needed between the substitution of the euro for the currencies of the participating Member States and the introduction of euro banknotes and coins; whereas during this period the national currency units will be defined as sub-divisions of the euro; whereas thereby a legal equivalence is established between the euro unit and the national currency units;

(9) Whereas in accordance with Article 109g of the Treaty and with Regulation (EC) No 1103/97, the euro will replace the ECU as from 1 January 1999 as the unit of account of the institutions of the European Communities; whereas the euro should also be the unit of account of the European Central Bank (ECB) and of the central banks of the participating Member States; whereas, in line with the Madrid conclusions, monetary policy operations will be carried out in the euro unit by the European System of Central Banks (ESCB); whereas this does not prevent national central banks from keeping accounts in their national currency unit during the transitional period, in particular for their staff and for public administrations;

(10) Whereas each participating Member State may allow the full use of the euro unit in its territory during the transitional period;

(11) Whereas during the transitional period contracts, national laws and other legal instruments can be drawn up validly in the euro unit or in the national currency unit; whereas during this period, nothing in this Regulation should affect the validity of any reference to a national currency unit in any legal instrument;

(12) Whereas, unless agreed otherwise, economic agents have to respect the denomination of a legal instrument in the performance of all acts to be carried out under that instrument;

(13) Whereas the euro unit and the national currency units are units of the same currency; whereas it should be ensured that payments inside a participating Member State by crediting an account can be made either in the euro unit or the respective national currency unit; whereas the provisions on payments by crediting an account should also apply to those cross-border payments, which are denominated in the euro unit or the national currency unit of the account of the creditor; whereas it is necessary to ensure the smooth functioning of payment systems by laying down provisions dealing

with the crediting of accounts by payment instruments credited through those systems; whereas the provisions on payments by crediting an account should not imply that financial intermediaries are obliged to make available either other payment facilities or products denominated in any particular unit of the euro; whereas the provisions on payments by crediting an account do not prohibit financial intermediaries from coordinating the introduction of payment facilities denominated in the euro unit which rely on a common technical infrastructure during the transitional period;

(14) Whereas in accordance with the conclusions reached by the European Council at its meeting held in Madrid, new tradeable public debt will be issued in the euro unit by the participating Member States as from 1 January 1999; whereas it is desirable to allow issuers of debt to redenominate outstanding debt in the euro unit; whereas the provisions on redenomination should be such that they can also be applied in the jurisdictions of third countries; whereas issuers should be enabled to redenominate outstanding debt if the debt is denominated in a national currency unit of a Member State which has redenominated part or all of the outstanding debt of its general government; whereas these provisions do not address the introduction of additional measures to amend the terms of outstanding debt to alter, among other things, the nominal amount of outstanding debt, these being matters subject to relevant national law; whereas it is desirable to allow Member States to take appropriate measures for changing the unit of account of the operating procedures of organised markets;

(15) Whereas further action at the Community level may also be necessary to clarify the effect of the introduction of the euro on the application of existing provisions of Community law, in particular concerning netting, set-off and techniques of similar effect;

(16) Whereas any obligation to use the euro unit can only be imposed on the basis of Community legislation; whereas in transactions with the public sector participating Member States may allow the use of the euro unit; whereas in accordance with the reference scenario decided by the European Council at its meeting held in Madrid, the Community legislation laying down the time frame for the generalisation of the use of the euro unit might leave some freedom to individual Member States;

(17) Whereas in accordance with Article 105a of the Treaty the Council may adopt measures to harmonise the denominations and technical specifications of all coins;

(18) Whereas banknotes and coins need adequate protection against counterfeiting;

(19) Whereas banknotes and coins denominated in the national currency units lose their status of legal tender at the latest six months after the end of the transitional period; whereas limitations on payments in notes and coins, established by Member States for public reasons, are not incompatible with the status of legal tender of euro banknotes and coins, provided that other lawful means for the settlement of monetary debts are available;

(20) Whereas as from the end of the transitional period references in legal instruments existing at the end of the transitional period will have to be read as references to the euro unit according to the respective conversion rates; whereas a physical redenomination of existing legal instruments is therefore not necessary to achieve this result; whereas the

rounding rules defined in Regulation (EC) No 1103/97 shall also apply to the conversions to be made at the end of the transitional period or after the transitional period; whereas for reasons of clarity it may be desirable that the physical redenomination will take place as soon as appropriate;

(21) Whereas paragraph 2 of Protocol 11 on certain provisions relating to the United Kingdom of Great Britain and Northern Ireland stipulates that, inter alia, paragraph 5 of that Protocol shall have effect if the United Kingdom notifies the Council that it does not intend to move to the third stage; whereas the United Kingdom gave notice to the Council on 30 October 1997 that it does not intend to move to the third stage; whereas paragraph 5 stipulates that, inter alia, Article 109l(4) of the Treaty shall not apply to the United Kingdom;

(22) Whereas Denmark, referring to paragraph 1 of Protocol 12 on certain provisions relating to Denmark has notified, in the context of the Edinburgh decision of 12 December 1992, that it will not participate in the third stage; whereas, therefore, in accordance with paragraph 2 of the said Protocol, all Articles and provisions of the Treaty and the Statute of the ESCB referring to a derogation shall be applicable to Denmark;

(23) Whereas, in accordance with Article 109l(4) of the Treaty, the single currency will be introduced only in the Member States without a derogation;

(24) Whereas this Regulation, therefore, shall be applicable pursuant to Article 189 of the Treaty, subject to Protocols 11 and 12 and Article 109k(1),

HAS ADOPTED THIS REGULATION:

PART I
DEFINITIONS

Article 1

For the purpose of this Regulation:

— **"participating Member States"** shall mean Belgium, Germany, [Greece,][1] Spain, France, Ireland, Italy, Luxembourg, Netherlands, Austria, Portugal and Finland,

— **"legal instruments"** shall mean legislative and statutory provisions, acts of administration, judicial decisions, contracts, unilateral legal acts, payment instruments other than banknotes and coins, and other instruments with legal effect,

— **"conversion rate"** shall mean the irrevocably fixed conversion rate adopted for the currency of each participating Member State by the Council according to the first sentence of Article 109l(4) of the Treaty, [or in accordance with paragraph 5 of that Article][2]

— **"euro unit"** shall mean the currency unit as referred to in the second sentence of Article 2,

— **"national currency units"** shall mean the units of the currencies of participating Member States, as those units are defined on the day before the start of the third stage of economic and monetary union, [or, as the case may be, on the day before the euro is substituted for the currency of a Member State which adopts the euro at a later date][3]

— **"transitional period"** shall mean the period beginning on 1 January 1999 and ending on 31 December 2001,

— **"redenominate"** shall mean changing the unit in which the amount of outstanding debt is stated from a national currency unit to the euro unit, as defined in Article 2, but which does not have through the act of redenomination the effect of altering any other term of the debt, this being a matter subject to relevant national law.

Amendments

[1]   Inserted by Council Regulation 2000/2596/EC of 27 November 2000 (OJ L300, 29/11/2000 p 2–3) Art 1(*a*) with effect from 1 January 2001.

[2]   Inserted by Council Regulation 2000/2596/EC of 27 November 2000 (OJ L300, 29/11/2000 p 2–3) Art 1(*b*) with effect from 1 January 2001.

[3]   Inserted by Council Regulation 2000/2596/EC of 27 November 2000 (OJ L300, 29/11/2000 p 2–3) Art 1(*c*) with effect from 1 January 2001.

PART II
SUBSTITUTION OF THE EURO FOR THE CURRENCIES OF THE PARTICIPATING MEMBER STATES

Article 2

[As from 1 January 1999 the currency of the participating Member States except Greece shall be the euro. As from 1 January 2001 the currency of Greece shall be the euro.][1] The currency unit shall be one euro. One euro shall be divided into one hundred cent.

Amendments

[1]   Substituted by Council Regulation 2000/2596/EC of 27 November 2000 (OJ L300, 29/11/2000 p 2–3) Art 1(2) with effect from 1 January 2001.

Article 3

The euro shall be substituted for the currency of each participating Member State at the conversion rate.

Article 4

The euro shall be the unit of account of the European Central Bank (ECB) and of the central banks of the participating Member States.

PART III
TRANSITIONAL PROVISIONS

Article 5

Articles 6, 7, 8 and 9 shall apply during the transitional period.

Article 6

1. The euro shall also be divided into the national currency units according to the conversion rates. Any subdivision thereof shall be maintained. Subject to the provisions of this Regulation the monetary law of the participating Member States shall continue to apply.

2. Where in a legal instrument reference is made to a national currency unit, this reference shall be as valid as if reference were made to the euro unit according to the conversion rates.

Article 7

The substitution of the euro for the currency of each participating Member State shall not in itself have the effect of altering the denomination of legal instruments in existence on the date of substitution.

Article 8

1. Acts to be performed under legal instruments stipulating the use of or denominated in a national currency unit shall be performed in that national currency unit. Acts to be performed under legal instruments stipulating the use of or denominated in the euro unit shall be performed in that unit.

2. The provisions of paragraph 1 are subject to anything which parties may have agreed.

3. Notwithstanding the provisions of paragraph 1, any amount denominated either in the euro unit or in the national currency unit of a given participating Member State and payable within that Member State by crediting an account of the creditor, can be paid by the debtor either in the euro unit or in that national currency unit. The amount shall be credited to the account of the creditor in the denomination of his account, with any conversion being effected at the conversion rates.

4. Notwithstanding the provisions of paragraph 1, each participating Member State may take measures which may be necessary in order to:

— redenominate in the euro unit outstanding debt issued by that Member State's general government, as defined in the European system of integrated accounts, denominated in its national currency unit and issued under its own law. If a Member State has taken such a measure, issuers may redenominate in the euro unit debt denominated in that Member State's national currency unit unless redenomination is expressly excluded by the terms of the contract; this provision shall apply to debt issued by the general government of a Member State as well as to bonds and other forms of securitised debt negotiable in the capital markets, and to money market instruments, issued by other debtors,

— enable the change of the unit of account of their operating procedures from a national currency unit to the euro unit by:

    (*a*) markets for the regular exchange, clearing and settlement of any instrument listed in section B of the Annex to Council Directive 93/22/EEC of 10 May 1993 on investment services in the securities field (OJ L141, 11. 6. 1993, p 27. Directive as amended by Directive 95/26/EC of the European

Parliament and of the Council (OJ L 168, 18. 7. 1995, p 7)) and of commodities; and

(*b*)   systems for the regular exchange, clearing and settlement of payments.

5. Provisions other than those of paragraph 4 imposing the use of the euro unit may only be adopted by the participating Member States in accordance with any time-frame laid down by Community legislation.

6. National legal provisions of participating Member States which permit or impose netting, set-off or techniques with similar effects shall apply to monetary obligations, irrespective of their currency denomination, if that denomination is in the euro unit or in a national currency unit, with any conversion being effected at the conversion rates.

Article 9

Banknotes and coins denominated in a national currency unit shall retain their status as legal tender within their territorial limits as of the day before the entry into force of this Regulation [or, in the case of Greece, up to and including 31 December 2000].[1]

Amendments

[1]   Inserted by Council Regulation 2000/2596/EC of 27 November 2000 (OJ L300, 29/11/2000 p 2–3) Art 1(3) with effect from 1 January 2001.

PART IV
EURO BANKNOTES AND COINS

Article 10

As from 1 January 2002, the ECB and the central banks of the participating Member States shall put into circulation banknotes denominated in euro. Without prejudice to Article 15, these banknotes denominated in euro shall be the only banknotes which have the status of legal tender in all these Member States.

Article 11

As from 1 January 2002, the participating Member States shall issue coins denominated in euro or in cent and complying with the denominations and technical specifications which the Council may lay down in accordance with the second sentence of Article 105a(2) of the Treaty. Without prejudice to Article 15, these coins shall be the only coins which have the status of legal tender in all these Member States. Except for the issuing authority and for those persons specifically designated by the national legislation of the issuing Member State, no party shall be obliged to accept more than 50 coins in any single payment.

Article 12

Participating Member States shall ensure adequate sanctions against counterfeiting and falsification of euro banknotes and coins.

PART V
FINAL PROVISIONS

Article 13

Articles 14, 15 and 16 shall apply as from the end of the transitional period.

Article 14

Where in legal instruments existing at the end of the transitional period reference is made to the national currency units, these references shall be read as references to the euro unit according to the respective conversion rates. The rounding rules laid down in Regulation (EC) No 1103/97 shall apply.

Article 15

1. Banknotes and coins denominated in a national currency unit as referred to in Article 6(1) shall remain legal tender within their territorial limits until six months after the end of the transitional period at the latest; this period may be shortened by national law.

2. Each participating Member State may, for a period of up to six months after the end of the transitional period, lay down rules for the use of the banknotes and coins denominated in its national currency unit as referred to in Article 6(1) and take any measures necessary to facilitate their withdrawal.

Article 16

In accordance with the laws or practices of participating Member States, the respective issuers of banknotes and coins shall continue to accept, against euro at the conversion rate, the banknotes and coins previously issued by them.

PART VI
ENTRY INTO FORCE

Article 17

This Regulation shall enter into force on 1 January 1999.

This Regulation shall be binding in its entirety and directly applicable in all Member States, in accordance with the Treaty, subject to Protocols 11 and 12 and Article 109k(1).

COUNCIL REGULATION

of 31 December 1998

98/2866/EC

on the conversion rates between the euro and the currencies of the Member States adopting the euro

(OJ L139, 11/05/1998 p 1–5)

THE COUNCIL OF THE EUROPEAN UNION,

Having regard to the Treaty establishing the European Community, and in particular Article 109l(4), first sentence thereof,

Having regard to the proposal from the Commission,

Having regard to the opinion of the European Central Bank (OJ C 412, 31. 12. 1998, p 1),

(1) Whereas according to Article 109j(4) of the Treaty, the third stage of Economic and Monetary Union shall start on 1 January 1999; whereas the Council, meeting in the composition of Heads of State or Government, has confirmed on 3 May 1998 that Belgium, Germany, Spain, France, Ireland, Italy, Luxembourg, the Netherlands, Austria, Portugal and Finland fulfil the necessary conditions for the adoption of a single currency on 1 January 1999 (Council Decision 98/317/EC of 3 May 1998 in accordance with Article 109j(4) of the Treaty (OJ L 139, 11. 5. 1998, p 30));

(2) Whereas according to Council Regulation (EC) No 974/98 of 3 May 1998 on the introduction of the euro (OJ L 139, 11. 5. 1998, p 1), the euro shall be the currency of the Member States which adopt the single currency as from 1 January 1999; whereas the introduction of the euro requires the adoption of the conversion rates at which the euro will be substituted for the national currencies and at which rates the euro will be divided into national currency units; whereas the conversion rates in Article 1 are the conversion rates referred to in the third indent of Article 1 of Regulation (EC) No 974/98;

(3) Whereas according to Council Regulation (EC) No 1103/97 of 17 June 1997 on certain provisions relating to the introduction of the euro (OJ L 162, 19. 6. 1997, p 1), every reference to the ECU in a legal instrument shall be replaced by a reference to the euro at a rate of one euro to one ECU; whereas Article 109l(4), second sentence, of the Treaty, provides that the adoption of the conversion rates shall by itself not modify the external value of the ECU; whereas this is ensured by adopting as the conversion rates, the exchange rates against the ECU of the currencies of the Member States adopting the euro, as calculated by the Commission on 31 December 1998 according to the established procedure for the calculation of the daily official ECU rates;

(4) Whereas the Ministers of the Member States adopting the euro as their single currency, the Governors of the Central Banks of these Member States, the Commission and the European Monetary Institute/the European Central Bank, have issued two Communiqués on the determination and on the adoption of the irrevocable conversion

1691

rates for the euro dated 3 May 1998 (OJ C 160, 27. 5. 1998, p 1) and 26 September 1998, respectively;

(5) Whereas Regulation (EC) No 1103/97 stipulates that the conversion rates shall be adopted as one euro expressed in terms of each of the national currencies of the Member States adopting the euro; whereas in order to ensure a high degree of accuracy, these rates will be adopted with six significant figures and no inverse rates nor bilateral rates between the currencies of the Member States adopting the euro will be defined,

HAS ADOPTED THIS REGULATION:

Article 1

The irrevocably fixed conversion rates between the euro and the currencies of the Member States adopting the euro are:

1 euro //	=	40,3399 Belgian francs
//	=	1,95583 German marks
//	=	166,386 Spanish pesetas
//	=	6,55957 French francs
//	=	0,787564 Irish pounds
//	=	1 936,27 Italian lire
//	=	40,3399 Luxembourg francs
//	=	2,20371 Dutch guilders
//	=	13,7603 Austrian schillings
//	=	200,482 Portuguese escudos
//	=	5,94573 Finnish marks.

Article 2

This Regulation shall enter into force on 1 January 1999.

This Regulation shall be binding in its entirety and directly applicable in all Member States.

COUNCIL REGULATION

of 19 June 2000

00/1478/EC

amending Regulation (EC) No 2866/98 on the conversion rates between the euro and the currencies of the Member States adopting the euro

(OJ L167, 07/07/2000 p 1)

THE COUNCIL OF THE EUROPEAN UNION,

Having regard to the Treaty establishing the European Community, and in particular Article 123(5) thereof,

Having regard to the proposal from the Commission,

Having regard to the opinion of the European Central Bank (Opinion delivered on 16 June 2000 (not yet published in the Official Journal)),

Whereas:

(1) Council Regulation (EC) No 2866/98 of 31 December 1998 on the conversion rates between the euro and the currencies of the Member States adopting the euro (OJ L 359, 31.12.1998, p 1) determines the conversion rates as from 1 January 1999 pursuant to Council Regulation (EC) No 974/98 of 3 May 1998 on the introduction of the euro (OJ L 139, 11.5.1998, p 1).

(2) Council Decision 98/317/EC of 3 May 1998 in accordance with Article 121(4) of the Treaty (OJ L 139, 11.5.1998, p 30) stipulated that Greece did not fulfil the necessary conditions for the adoption of the single currency.

(3) Pursuant to Council Decision 2000/427/EC of 19 June 2000 in accordance with Article 122(2) of the Treaty on the adoption by Greece of the single currency on 1 January 2001 (See page 19 of this Official Journal) Greece now fulfils the necessary conditions, and the derogation of Greece should be abrogated with effect from 1 January 2001.

(4) The introduction of the euro in Greece requires the adoption of the conversion rate between the euro and the drachma,

HAS ADOPTED THIS REGULATION:

Article 1

In the list of conversion rates in Article 1 of Regulation (EC) No 2866/98, the following shall be inserted between the rates of the German mark and the Spanish peseta: "= 340,750 Greek drachma."

Article 2

This Regulation shall enter into force on 1 January 2001.

This Regulation shall be binding in its entirety and directly applicable in all Member States.

COMMISSION REGULATION

of 7 September 2000

00/1901/EC

Official Journal L 228, 08/09/2000 p 28–49

laying down certain provisions for the implementation of Council Regulation (EEC) No 3330/91 on the statistics relating to the trading of goods between Member States

Amendment

Regulation 2000/1901/EC repealed by Commission Regulation of 18 November 2004 (04/1982/EC) art 27 with effect from 1 January 2005.

COUNCIL REGULATION

of 27 November 2000

00/2596/EC

amending Regulation (EC) No 974/98 on the introduction of the euro

(OJ L300, 29/11/2000 p 2–3)

THE COUNCIL OF THE EUROPEAN UNION,

Having regard to the Treaty establishing the European Community, and in particular Article 123(5) thereof,

Having regard to the proposal from the Commission (OJ C 177 E, 27.6.2000, p 98),

Having regard to the opinion of the European Parliament (Opinion delivered on 16 June 2000 (not yet published in the Official Journal)),

Having regard to the opinion of the European Central Bank (OJ C 177, 27.6.2000, p 11),

Whereas:

(1) Council Regulation (EC) No 974/98 of 3 May 1998 on the introduction of the euro (OJ L 139, 11.5.1998, p 1) provides for the substitution of the euro for the currencies of the Member States which fulfilled the necessary conditions for the adoption of the single currency at the time when the Community entered the third stage of economic and monetary union. That Regulation also includes rules which apply to the national currency units of these Member States during the transitional period ending on 31 December 2001, and rules on banknotes and coins.

(2) Council Decision 98/317/EC of 3 May 1998 in accordance with Article 121(4) of the Treaty (OJ L 139, 11 5.1998, p 30) stipulated that Greece did not fulfil the necessary conditions for the adoption of the single currency.

(3) Pursuant to Council Decision 2000/427/EC of 19 June 2000 in accordance with Article 122(2) of the Treaty on the adoption by Greece of the single currency on 1 January 2001 (OJ L 167, 7.7.2000, p 19) Greece now fulfils the necessary conditions and the derogation in favour of Greece is to be abrogated with effect from 1 January 2001.

(4) The introduction of the euro in Greece requires the extension to Greece of the provisions on the introduction of the euro which are applicable in the Member States in which the euro was introduced when the Community entered the third stage of economic and monetary union.

(5) For Member States whose currency is replaced by the euro after the date at which the Community entered the third stage of economic and monetary union, the definition of "national currency units" should refer to the unit of the Member State's currency as it was defined immediately before the introduction of the euro in that Member State.

(6) The provisions on the transitional period apply as from 1 January 2001 in the case of Greece,

HAS ADOPTED THIS REGULATION:

Article 1

Notes

Para 1(*a*) inserted "Greece" between "Germany" and "Spain" in Regulation 98/974/EC, Art 1 (first indent) with effect from 1 January 2001.

Para 1(*b*) inserted "or in accordance with paragraph 5 of that Article" at the end of Regulation 98/974/EC, Art 1 (third indent) with effect from 1 January 2001.

Para 1(c) inserted "or, as the case may be, on the day before the euro is substituted for the currency of a Member State which adopts the euro at a later date" at the end of Regulation 98/974/EC, Art 1 (fifth indent) with effect from 1 January 2001.

Para 2 substituted "As from 1 January 1999 the currency of the participating Member States except Greece shall be the euro. As from 1 January 2001 the currency of Greece shall be the euro." for the first sentence in Regulation 98/974/EC, Art 2 with effect from 1 January 2001.

Para 3 inserted "or, in the case of Greece, up to and including 31 December 2000" to Regulation 98/974/EC, Art 9 with effect from 1 January 2001.

Article 2

This Regulation shall enter into force on 1 January 2001.

This Regulation shall be binding in its entirety and directly applicable in the Member States in accordance with the Treaty establishing the European Community.

COUNCIL REGULATION

of 7 May 2002

02/792/EC

(OJ L128, 15.5.2002, p 1)

amending temporarily Regulation (EEC) No 218/92 on administrative cooperation in the field of indirect taxation (VAT) as regards additional measures regarding electronic commerce

THE COUNCIL OF THE EUROPEAN UNION,

Having regard to the Treaty establishing the European

Community, and in particular Article 93 thereof,

Having regard to the proposal from the Commission (OJ C 337 E, 28.11.2000, p 63),

Having regard to the opinion of the European Parliament (OJ C 232, 17.8.2001, p 202, and the Opinion of 25 April 2002 (not yet published in the Official Journal)),

Having regard to the opinion of the Economic and Social Committee (OJ C 116, 20.4.2001, p 59),

Whereas:

(1) Council Directive 2002/38/EC of 7 May 2002 amending and amending temporarily Directive 77/388/EEC as regards the value added tax arrangements applicable to radio and television broadcasting services and certain electronically supplied services (See page 41 of this Official Journal) provides for the framework for taxing electronic supplies in the Community by taxable persons who are neither established nor required to be identified for tax purposes within the Community.

(2) The Member State of consumption has primary responsibility for assuring the compliance with their obligations by non-established suppliers. To this end, the information necessary to operate the special scheme for electronically supplied services that is provided for in Article 26c of sixth Council Directive 77/388/EEC of 17 May 1977 on the harmonisation of the laws of the Member States relating to turnover taxes — Common system of value added tax: uniform basis of assessment (OJ L 145, 13.6.1977, p 1, as last amended by Directive 2002/38/EC) must be transmitted to those Member States.

(3) It is necessary to provide that the value added tax due in respect of such supplies transferred to accounts designated by the Member States of consumption.

(4) The rules laid down in Directive 77/388/EEC require the non-established taxable person supplying services referred to in the last indent of Article 9(2)e of the Directive to charge VAT to his customer, established or resident in the Community, unless he is satisfied that his customer is a taxable person. The special scheme provided for in Article 26c of the Directive applies only for services provided to non-taxable persons

established or resident in the Community. It is thus clear that the non-established taxable person needs certain information about his customer.

(5) To this end, use could in most cases be made of the facility that is available in Member States in the form of electronic databases which contain a register of persons to whom value added tax identification numbers have been issued in that Member State.

(6) It is accordingly necessary to extend the common system for the exchange of certain information on intra-Community transaction provided for in Article 6 of Regulation (EEC) No 218/92 (OJ L 24, 1.2.1992, p 1).

(7) The provisions of the Regulation should operate for a temporary period of three years which may be extended for practical reasons and Regulation (EEC) No 218/92 should therefore be temporarily amended accordingly,

HAS ADOPTED THIS REGULATION:

Article 1

Notes

Para 1 substituted Regulation 92/218/EEC, Art 1 2nd para.
Para 2 substituted Regulation 92/218/EEC, Art 2(1) 9th indent.
Para 3 substituted Regulation 92/218/EEC, Art 6(4).
Para 4 inserted Regulation 92/218/EEC Title IIIA Arts 9*a*–9*f*.
Para 5 renumbered Regulation 92/218/EEC, Art 13 as para 2 and inserted a new para 1.

Article 2

Article 1 shall apply for a period provided for in Article 4 of Directive 2002/38/EC.

No exchange of information under this Regulation shall take place before 1 July 2003.

Article 3

This Regulation shall enter into force on the seventh day following its publication in the Official Journal of the European Communities.

This Regulation shall be binding in its entirety and directly applicable in all Member States.

Done at Brussels, 7 May 2002.

COUNCIL REGULATION

of 7 October 2003

03/1798/EC

OJ L 264, 15/10/2003 p 1–11

on administrative cooperation in the field of value added tax
and repealing Regulation (EEC) No 218/92

THE COUNCIL OF THE EUROPEAN UNION,

Having regard to the Treaty establishing the European Community, and in particular Article 93 thereof,

Having regard to the proposal from the Commission (OJ C 270 E, 25.9.2001, p 87),

Having regard to the opinion of the European Parliament (OJ C 284 E, 21.11.2002, pp 121 and 191),

Having regard to the opinion of the European Economic and Social Committee (OJ C 80, 3.4.2002, p 76),

Whereas:

(1) Tax evasion and tax avoidance extending across the frontiers of Member States lead to budget losses and violations of the principle of fair taxation and are liable to bring about distortions of capital movements and of the conditions of competition. They therefore affect the operation of the internal market.

(2) Combating value added tax (VAT) evasion calls for close cooperation between the administrative authorities in each Member State responsible for the application of the provisions in that field.

(3) The tax harmonisation measures taken to complete the internal market should therefore include the establishment of a common system for the exchange of information between the Member States whereby the Member States' administrative authorities are to assist each other and cooperate with the Commission in order to ensure the proper application of VAT on supplies of goods and services, intra-Community acquisition of goods and importation of goods.

(4) Electronic storage and transmission of certain data for VAT control purposes is indispensable for the proper functioning of the VAT system.

(5) The conditions for the exchange of, and direct access of Member States to, electronically stored data in each Member State should be clearly defined. Operators should have access to certain of such data where required for the fulfilment of their obligations.

(6) The Member State of consumption has primary responsibility for assuring that non-established suppliers comply with their obligations. To this end, the application of the temporary special scheme for electronically supplied services that is provided for in Article 26c of Sixth Council Directive 77/388/EEC of 17 May 1977 on the

harmonisation of the laws of Member States relating to turnover taxes, Common system of value added tax: uniform basis of assessment (OJ L 145, 13.6.1977, p 1. Directive as last amended by Directive 2002/92/EC (OJ L 331, 7.12.2002, p 27)), requires the definition of rules concerning the provision of information and transfer of money between the Member State of identification and the Member State of consumption.

(7) Council Regulation (EEC) No 218/92 of 27 January 1992 on administrative cooperation in the field of indirect taxation (VAT) (OJ L 24, 1.2.1992, p 1. Regulation as last amended by Regulation (EC) No 792/2002 (OJ L 128, 15.5.2002, p 1)) established in this respect a system of close cooperation amongst the Member States' administrative authorities and between those authorities and the Commission.

(8) Regulation (EEC) No 218/92 supplements Council Directive 77/799/EEC of 19 December 1977 concerning mutual assistance by the competent authorities of the Member States in the field of direct and indirect taxation (OJ L 336, 27.12.1977, p 15. Directive as last amended by the 1994 Act of Accession).

(9) Those two legal instruments have proved to be effective but are no longer able to meet the new requirements of administrative cooperation resulting from the ever closer integration of economies within the internal market.

(10) The existence of two separate instruments for cooperation on VAT has, moreover, hampered effective cooperation between tax administrations.

(11) The rights and obligations of all parties concerned are currently ill-defined. Clearer and binding rules governing cooperation between Member States are therefore necessary.

(12) There is not enough direct contact between local or national anti-fraud offices, with communication between central liaison offices being the rule. This leads to inefficiency, under-use of the arrangements for administrative cooperation and delays in communication. Provision should therefore be made to bring about more direct contacts between services with a view to making cooperation more efficient and faster.

(13) Cooperation is also not intensive enough, in that, apart from the VAT information exchange system (VIES), there are not enough automatic or spontaneous exchanges of information between Member States. Exchanges of information between the respective administrations as well as between administrations and the Commission should be made more intensive and swifter in order to combat fraud more effectively.

(14) The provisions on VAT administrative cooperation of Regulation (EEC) No 218/92 and of Directive 77/799/EEC should therefore be joined and strengthened. For reasons of clarity this should be done in a single new instrument which replaces Regulation (EEC) No 218/92.

(15) This Regulation should not affect other Community measures which contribute to combating VAT fraud.

(16) For the purposes of this Regulation, it is appropriate to consider limitations of certain rights and obligations laid down by Directive 95/46/EC of the European Parliament and of the Council of 24 October 1995 on the protection of individuals with regard to the processing of personal data and on the free movement of such data (OJ L

281, 23.11.1995, p 31) in order to safeguard the interests referred to in Article 13(1)(e) of that Directive.

(17) The measures necessary for the implementation of this Regulation should be adopted in accordance with Council Decision 1999/468/EC of 28 June 1999 laying down the procedures for the exercise of implementing powers conferred on the Commission (OJ L 184, 17.7.1999, p 23).

(18) This Regulation respects the fundamental rights and observes the principles which are recognised in particular by the Charter of Fundamental Rights of the European Union,

HAS ADOPTED THIS REGULATION:

CHAPTER I
GENERAL PROVISIONS

Article 1

1. This Regulation lays down the conditions under which the administrative authorities in the Member States responsible for the application of the laws on VAT on supplies of goods and services, intra-Community acquisition of goods and importation of goods are to cooperate with each other and with the Commission to ensure compliance with those laws.

To that end, it lays down rules and procedures to enable the competent authorities of the Member States to cooperate and to exchange with each other any information that may help them to effect a correct assessment of VAT.

This Regulation also lays down rules and procedures for the exchange of certain information by electronic means, in particular as regards VAT on intra-Community transactions.

For the period provided for in Article 4 of Directive 2002/38/EC (OJ L 128, 15.5.2002, p 41), it also lays down rules and procedures for the exchange by electronic means of value added tax information on services supplied electronically in accordance with the special scheme provided for in Article 26c of Directive 77/388/EEC, and also for any subsequent exchange of information and, as far as services covered by that special scheme are concerned, for the transfer of money between Member States' competent authorities.

2. This Regulation shall not affect the application in the Member States of the rules on mutual assistance in criminal matters.

Article 2

For the purposes of this Regulation:

1. "competent authority of a Member State", means:

— in Belgium:
   Le ministre des finances
   De Minister van financiën,

— in Denmark:
    Skatteministeren,

— in Germany:
    Bundesministerium der Finanzen,

— in Greece:
    Υπουργειο Οικονομίας και Οικονομικων,

— in Spain:
    El Secretario de Estado de Hacienda,

— in France:
    le ministre de l'économie, des finances et de l'industrie,

— in Ireland:
    The Revenue Commissioners,

— in Italy:
    il Capo del Dipartimento delle Politiche Fiscali,

— in Luxembourg:
    L'Administration de l'Enregistrement et des Domaines,

— in the Netherlands:
    De minister van Financiën,

— in Austria:
    Bundesminister für Finanzen,

— in Portugal:
    O Ministro das Finanças,

— in Finland:
    Valtiovarainministeriö
    Finansministeriet,

— in Sweden:
    Chefen för Finansdepartementet,

— in the United Kingdom:
    The Commissioners of Customs and Excise;

2. "central liaison office", means the office which has been designated under Article 3(2) with principal responsibility for contacts with other Member States in the field of administrative cooperation;

3. "liaison department", means any office other than the central liaison office with a specific territorial competence or a specialised operational responsibility which has been designated by the competent authority pursuant to Article 3(3) to exchange directly information on the basis of this Regulation;

4. "competent official", means any official who can directly exchange information on the basis of this Regulation for which he has been authorised pursuant to Article 3(4);

5. "requesting authority", means the central liaison office, a liaison department or any competent official of a Member State who makes a request for assistance on behalf of the competent authority;

6. "requested authority", means the central liaison office, a liaison department or any competent official of a Member State who receives a request for assistance on behalf of the competent authority;

7. "intra-Community transactions", means the intra-Community supply of goods or services;

8. "intra-Community supply of goods", means any supply of goods which must be declared in the recapitulative statement provided for in Article 22(6)(*b*) of Directive 77/388/EEC;

9. "intra-Community supply of services", means any supply of services covered by Article 28b(C), (D), (E) and (F) of Directive 77/388/EEC;

10. "intra-Community acquisition of goods", means acquisition of the right to dispose as owner of movable tangible property under Article 28a(3) of Directive 77/388/EEC;

11. "VAT identification number", means the number provided for in Article 22(1)(*c*), (*d*) and (*e*) of Directive 77/388/EEC;

12. "administrative enquiry", means all the controls, checks and other action taken by Member States in the performance of their duties with a view to ensuring proper application of VAT legislation;

13. "automatic exchange", means the systematic communication of predefined information to another Member State, without prior request, at pre-established regular intervals;

14. "structured automatic exchange", means the systematic communication of predefined information to another Member State, without prior request, as and when that information becomes available;

15. "spontaneous exchange", means the irregular communication without prior request of information to another Member State;

16. "person", means:

    (*a*) a natural person;

    (*b*) a legal person; or

    (*c*) where the legislation in force so provides, an association of persons recognised as having the capacity to perform legal acts but lacking the legal status of a legal person;

17. "to grant access", means to authorise access to the relevant electronic database and to obtain data by electronic means;

18. "by electronic means", means using electronic equipment for the processing (including digital compression) and storage of data, and employing wires, radio transmission, optical technologies or other electromagnetic means;

19. "CCN/CSI network", means the common platform based on the common communication network (CCN) and common system interface (CSI), developed by the

Community to ensure all transmissions by electronic means between competent authorities in the area of customs and taxation.

Article 3

1. The competent authorities referred to in point 1 of Article 2 are the authorities in whose name this Regulation is to be applied, whether directly or by delegation.

2. Each Member State shall designate a single central liaison office to which principal responsibility shall be delegated for contacts with other Member States in the field of administrative cooperation. It shall inform the Commission and the other Member States thereof.

3. The competent authority of each Member State may designate liaison departments. The central liaison office shall be responsible for keeping the list of those departments up to date and making it available to the central liaison offices of the other Member States concerned.

4. The competent authority of each Member State may in addition designate, under the conditions laid down by it, competent officials who can directly exchange information on the basis of this Regulation. When it does so, it may limit the scope of such designation. The central liaison office shall be responsible for keeping the list of those officials up to date and making it available to the central liaison offices of the other Member States concerned.

5. The officials exchanging information under Articles 11 and 13 shall in any case be deemed to be competent officials for this purpose, in accordance with conditions laid down by the competent authorities.

6. Where a liaison department or a competent official sends or receives a request or a reply to a request for assistance, it shall inform the central liaison office of its Member State under the conditions laid down by the latter.

7. Where a liaison department or a competent official receives a request for assistance requiring action outside its territorial or operational area, it shall forward such request without delay to the central liaison office of its Member State and inform the requesting authority thereof. In such a case, the period laid down in Article 8 shall start the day after the request for assistance has been forwarded to the central liaison office.

Article 4

1. The obligation to give assistance as provided for in this Regulation shall not cover the provision of information or documents obtained by the administrative authorities referred to in Article 1 acting with the authorisation or at the request of the judicial authority.

2. However, where a competent authority has the powers in accordance with national law to communicate the information referred to in paragraph 1, it may be communicated as a part of the administrative cooperation provided for in this Regulation. Any such communication must have the prior authorisation of the judicial authority if the necessity of such authorisation derives from national law.

CHAPTER II
EXCHANGE OF INFORMATION ON REQUEST

Article 5

1. At the request of the requesting authority, the requested authority shall communicate the information referred to in Article 1, including any information relating to a specific case or cases.

2. For the purpose of forwarding the information referred to in paragraph 1, the requested authority shall arrange for the conduct of any administrative enquiries necessary to obtain such information.

3. The request referred to in paragraph 1 may contain a reasoned request for a specific administrative enquiry. If the Member State takes the view that no administrative enquiry is necessary, it shall immediately inform the requesting authority of the reasons thereof.

4. In order to obtain the information sought or to conduct the administrative enquiry requested, the requested authority or the administrative authority to which it has recourse shall proceed as though acting on its own account or at the request of another authority in its own Member State.

Article 6

Requests for information and for administrative enquiries pursuant to Article 5 shall, as far as possible, be sent using a standard form adopted in accordance with the procedure referred to in Article 44(2).

Article 7

1. At the request of the requesting authority, the requested authority shall communicate to it any pertinent information it obtains or has in its possession as well as the results of administrative enquiries, in the form of reports, statements and any other documents, or certified true copies or extracts thereof.

2. Original documents shall be provided only where this is not contrary to the provisions in force in the Member State in which the requested authority is established.

SECTION 2

TIME LIMIT FOR PROVIDING INFORMATION

Article 8

The requested authority shall provide the information referred to in Articles 5 and 7 as quickly as possible and no later than three months following the date of receipt of the request.

However, where the requested authority is already in possession of that information, the time limit shall be reduced to a maximum period of one month.

Article 9

In certain special categories of cases, time limits different from the ones provided for in Article 8 may be agreed between the requested and the requesting authorities.

Article 10

Where the requested authority is unable to respond to the request by the deadline, it shall inform the requesting authority in writing forthwith of the reasons for its failure to do so, and when it considers it would be likely to be able to respond.

SECTION 3
PRESENCE IN ADMINISTRATIVE OFFICES AND
PARTICIPATION IN ADMINISTRATIVE ENQUIRIES

Article 11

1. By agreement between the requesting authority and the requested authority and in accordance with the arrangements laid down by the latter, officials authorised by the requesting authority may, with a view to exchanging the information referred to in Article 1, be present in the offices where the administrative authorities of the Member State in which the requested authority is established carry out their duties. Where the requested information is contained in documentation to which the officials of the requested authority have access, the officials of the requesting authority shall be given copies of the documentation containing the requested information.

2. By agreement between the requesting authority and the requested authority, and in accordance with the arrangements laid down by the latter, officials designated by the requesting authority may, with a view to exchanging the information referred to in Article 1, be present during the administrative enquiries. Administrative enquiries shall be carried out exclusively by the officials of the requested authority. The requesting authority's officials shall not exercise the powers of inspection conferred on officials of the requested authority. They may, however, have access to the same premises and documents as the latter, through their intermediary and for the sole purpose of the administrative enquiry being carried out.

3. The officials of the requesting authority present in another Member State in accordance with paragraphs 1 and 2 must at all times be able to produce written authority stating their identity and their official capacity.

SECTION 4
SIMULTANEOUS CONTROLS

Article 12

With a view to exchanging the information referred to in Article 1, two or more Member States may agree to conduct simultaneous controls, in their own territory, of the tax situation of one or more taxable persons who are of common or complementary interest, whenever such controls would appear to be more effective than controls carried out by only one Member State.

Article 13

1. A Member State shall identify independently the taxable persons whom it intends to propose for a simultaneous control. The competent authority of that Member State shall notify the competent authority in the other Member States concerned of the cases proposed for simultaneous controls. It shall give reasons for its choice, as far as possible, by providing the information which led to its decision. It shall specify the period of time during which such controls should be conducted.

2. The Member States concerned shall then decide whether they wish to take part in the simultaneous controls. On receipt of a proposal for a simultaneous control, the competent authority of the Member State shall confirm its agreement or communicate its reasoned refusal to its counterpart authority.

3. Each competent authority of the Member States concerned shall appoint a representative to be responsible for supervising and coordinating the control operation.

CHAPTER III
REQUEST FOR ADMINISTRATIVE NOTIFICATION

Article 14

The requested authority shall, at the request of the requesting authority and in accordance with the rules governing the notification of similar instruments in the Member State in which it is established, notify the addressee of all instruments and decisions which emanate from the administrative authorities and concern the application of VAT legislation in the territory of the Member State in which the requesting authority is established.

Article 15

Requests for notification, mentioning the subject of the instrument or decision to be notified, shall indicate the name, address and any other relevant information for identifying the addressee.

Article 16

The requested authority shall inform the requesting authority immediately of its response to the request for notification and notify it, in particular, of the date of notification of the decision or instrument to the addressee.

CHAPTER IV
EXCHANGE OF INFORMATION WITHOUT PRIOR REQUEST

Article 17

Without prejudice to the provisions of Chapters V and VI, the competent authority of each Member State shall, by automatic or structured automatic exchange, forward the information referred to in Article 1 to the competent authority of any other Member State concerned, in the following cases:

1. where taxation is deemed to take place in the Member State of destination and the effectiveness of the control system necessarily depends on the information provided by the Member State of origin;
2. where a Member State has grounds to believe that a breach of VAT legislation has been committed or is likely to have been committed in the other Member State;
3. where there is a risk of tax loss in the other Member State.

Article 18

The following shall be determined in accordance with the procedure referred to in Article 44(2):

1. the exact categories of information to be exchanged;
2. the frequency of the exchanges;
3. the practical arrangements for the exchange of information.

Each Member State shall determine whether it will take part in the exchange of a particular category of information, as well as whether it will do so in an automatic or structured automatic way.

Article 19

The competent authorities of the Member States may, in any case by spontaneous exchange, forward to each other, any information referred to in Article 1 of which they are aware.

Article 20

Member States shall take the necessary administrative and organisational measures to facilitate the exchanges provided for in this Chapter.

Article 21

A Member State cannot be obliged, for the purposes of implementing the provisions of this Chapter, to impose new obligations on persons liable for VAT with a view to collecting information nor to bear disproportionate administrative burdens.

CHAPTER V
STORAGE AND EXCHANGE OF INFORMATION SPECIFIC TO INTRA-COMMUNITY TRANSACTIONS

Article 22

1. Each Member State shall maintain an electronic database in which it shall store and process the information that it collects in accordance with Article 22(6)(*b*) in the version given in Article 28h of Directive 77/388/EEC.

To enable that information to be used in the procedures provided for in this Regulation, the information shall be stored for at least five years from the end of the calendar year in which access to the information is to be granted.

2. Member States shall ensure that their databases are kept up to date, and are complete and accurate.

Criteria shall be defined, in accordance with the procedure referred to in Article 44(2), to determine which changes are not pertinent, essential or useful and therefore need not be made.

Article 23

On the basis of the data stored in accordance with Article 22, the competent authority of a Member State shall have communicated to it automatically and without delay by any other Member State the following information, to which it may also have direct access:

1 VAT identification numbers issued by the Member State receiving the information;

2 the total value of all intra-Community supplies of goods to persons holding a VAT identification number by all operators identified for the purposes of VAT in the Member State providing the information.

The values referred to in point 2 shall be expressed in the currency of the Member State providing the information and shall relate to calendar quarters.

Article 24

On the basis of the data stored in accordance with Article 22 and solely in order to prevent a breach of VAT legislation, the competent authority of a Member State shall, wherever it considers it necessary for the control of intra-Community acquisitions of goods, obtain directly and without delay, or have direct access to by electronic means, any of the following information:

1 the VAT identification numbers of the persons who effected the supplies referred to in point 2 of Article 23, and

2 the total value of such supplies from each such person to each person holding a VAT identification number referred to in point 1 of Article 23.

The values referred to in point 2 shall be expressed in the currency of the Member State providing the information and shall relate to calendar quarters.

Article 25

1. Where the competent authority of a Member State is obliged to grant access to information under Articles 23 and 24, it shall do so as soon as possible and within three months at the latest of the end of the calendar quarter to which the information relates.

2. By way of derogation from paragraph 1, where information is added to a database in the circumstances provided for in Article 22, access to such additional information shall be granted as quickly as possible and no later than three months from the end of the quarter in which it was collected.

3. The conditions under which access to the corrected information may be granted shall be laid down in accordance with the procedure referred to in Article 44(2).

Article 26

Where, for the purposes of Articles 22 to 25, the competent authorities of the Member States store information in electronic databases and exchange such information by electronic means, they shall take all measures necessary to ensure compliance with Article 41.

Article 27

1. Each Member State shall maintain an electronic database containing a register of persons to whom VAT identification numbers have been issued in that Member State.

2. At any time the competent authority of a Member State may obtain directly or have communicated to it, from the data stored in accordance with Article 22, confirmation of the validity of the VAT identification number under which a person has effected or received an intra-Community supply of goods or services.

On specific request, the requested authority shall also communicate the date of issue and, where appropriate, the expiry date of the VAT identification number.

3. On request, the competent authority shall also provide without delay the name and address of the person to whom the number has been issued, provided that such information is not stored by the requesting authority with a view to possible use at some future time.

4. The competent authorities of each Member State shall ensure that persons involved in the intra-Community supply of goods or of services and, for the period provided for in Article 4 of Directive 2002/38/EC, persons supplying services referred to in the last indent of Article 9(2)e of Directive 77/388/EEC are allowed to obtain confirmation of the validity of the VAT identification number of any specified person.

For the period provided for in Article 4 of Directive 2002/38/EC Member States shall, in particular, provide such confirmation by electronic means in accordance with the procedure referred to in Article 44(2).

5. Where, for the purposes of paragraphs 1 to 4, the competent authorities of the Member States store information in electronic databases and exchange such information by electronic means, they shall take all measures necessary to ensure compliance with Article 41.

CHAPTER VI
PROVISIONS CONCERNING THE SPECIAL SCHEME IN ARTICLE 26C OF DIRECTIVE 77/388/EEC

Article 28

The following provisions shall apply concerning the special scheme provided for in Article 26c in Directive 77/388/EEC. The definitions contained in point A of that Article shall also apply for the purpose of this Chapter.

Article 29

1. The information from the non-established taxable person to the Member State of identification when his activities commence set out in the second subparagraph of

Article 26c(B)(2) of Directive 77/388/EEC is to be submitted in an electronic manner. The technical details, including a common electronic message, shall be determined in accordance with the procedure provided for in Article 44(2).

2. The Member State of identification shall transmit this information by electronic means to the competent authorities of the other Member States within 10 days from the end of the month during which the information was received from the non-established taxable person. In the same manner the competent authorities of the other Member States shall be informed of the allocated identification number. The technical details, including a common electronic message, by which this information is to be transmitted, shall be determined in accordance with the procedure provided for in Article 44(2).

3. The Member State of identification shall without delay inform by electronic means the competent authorities of the other Members States if a non-established taxable person is excluded from the identification register.

Article 30

The return with the details set out in the second subparagraph of Article 26c(B)(5) of Directive 77/388/EEC is to be submitted in an electronic manner. The technical details, including a common electronic message, shall be determined in accordance with the procedure provided for in Article 44(2).

The Member State of identification shall transmit this information by electronic means to the competent authority of the Member State concerned at the latest 10 days after the end of the month that the return was received. Member States which have required the tax return to be made in a national currency other than euro, shall convert the amounts into euro using the exchange rate valid for the last date of the reporting period. The exchange shall be done following the exchange rates published by the European Central Bank for that day, or, if there is no publication on that day, on the next day of publication. The technical details by which this information is to be transmitted shall be determined in accordance with the procedure provided for in Article 44(2).

The Member State of identification shall transmit by electronic means to the Member State of consumption the information needed to link each payment with a relevant quarterly tax return.

Article 31

The provisions in Article 22 shall apply also to information collected by the Member State of identification in accordance with Article 26c(B)(2) and (5) of Directive 77/388/EEC.

Article 32

The Member State of identification shall ensure that the amount the non-established taxable person has paid is transferred to the bank account denominated in euro, which has been designated by the Member State of consumption to which the payment is due. Member States which required the payments in a national currency other than euro, shall convert the amounts into euro using the exchange rate valid for the last date of the reporting period. The exchange shall be done following the exchange rates published by the European Central Bank for that day, or, if there is no publication on that day, on the next day of publication. The transfer shall take place at the latest 10 days after the end of the month that the payment was received.

If the non-established taxable person does not pay the total tax due, the Member State of identification shall ensure that the payment is transferred to the Member States of consumption in proportion to the tax due in each Member State. The Member State of identification shall inform by electronic means the competent authorities of the Member States of consumption thereof.

Article 33

Member States shall notify by electronic means the competent authorities of the other Member States of the relevant bank account numbers for receiving payments according to Article 32.

Member States shall without delay notify by electronic means the competent authorities of the other Member States and the Commission of changes in the standard tax rate.

Article 34

Articles 28 to 33 shall apply for a period provided for in Article 4 of Directive 2002/38/EC.

CHAPTER VII
RELATIONS WITH THE COMMISSION

Article 35

1. The Member States and the Commission shall examine and evaluate how the arrangements for administrative cooperation provided for in this Regulation are working. The Commission shall pool the Member States' experience with the aim of improving the operation of those arrangements.

2. The Member States shall communicate to the Commission any available information relevant to their application of this Regulation.

3. A list of statistical data needed for evaluation of this Regulation shall be determined in accordance with the procedure referred to in Article 44(2). The Member States shall communicate these data to the Commission in so far as they are available and the communication is not likely to involve administrative burdens which would be unjustified.

4. With a view to evaluating the effectiveness of this system of administrative cooperation in combating tax evasion and tax avoidance, Member States may communicate to the Commission any other information referred to in Article 1.

5. The Commission shall forward the information referred to in paragraphs 2, 3 and 4 to the other Member States concerned.

CHAPTER VIII
RELATIONS WITH THIRD COUNTRIES

Article 36

1. When the competent authority of a Member State receives information from a third country, that authority may pass the information on to the competent authorities of Member States which might be interested in it and, in any event, to all those which request it, in so far as permitted by assistance arrangements with that particular third country.

2. Provided the third country concerned has given an undertaking to provide the assistance required to gather evidence of the irregular nature of transactions which appear to contravene VAT legislation, information obtained under this Regulation may be communicated to that third country, with the consent of the competent authorities which supplied the information, in accordance with their domestic provisions applying to the communication of personal data to third countries.

CHAPTER IX
CONDITIONS GOVERNING THE EXCHANGE OF INFORMATION

Article 37

Information communicated pursuant to this Regulation shall, as far as possible, be provided by electronic means under arrangements to be adopted in accordance with the procedure referred to in Article 44(2).

Article 38

Requests for assistance, including requests for notification, and attached documents may be made in any language agreed between the requested and requesting authority. The said requests shall only be accompanied by a translation into the official language or one of the official languages of the Member State in which the requested authority is established, in special cases when the requested authority gives a reason for asking for such a translation.

Article 39

For the period provided for in Article 4 of Directive 2002/38/EC, the Commission and the Member States shall ensure that such existing or new communication and information exchange systems which are necessary to provide for the exchanges of information described in Articles 29 and 30 are operational. The Commission will be responsible for whatever development of the common communication network/common system interface (CCN/CSI) is necessary to permit the exchange of this information between Member States. Member States will be responsible for whatever development of their systems is necessary to permit this information to be exchanged using the CCN/CSI.

Member States shall waive all claims for the reimbursement of expenses incurred in applying this Regulation except, where appropriate, in respect of fees paid to experts.

Article 40

1. The requested authority in one Member State shall provide a requesting authority in another Member State with the information referred to in Article 1 provided that:

(*a*) the number and the nature of the requests for information made by the requesting authority within a specific period do not impose a disproportionate administrative burden on that requested authority;

(*b*) that requesting authority has exhausted the usual sources of information which it could have used in the circumstances to obtain the information requested, without running the risk of jeopardising the achievement of the desired end.

2. This Regulation shall impose no obligation to have enquiries carried out or to provide information if the laws or administrative practices of the Member State which would have to supply the information do not authorise the Member State to carry out those enquiries or collect or use that information for that Member State's own purposes.

3. The competent authority of a Member State may refuse to provide information where the Member State concerned is unable, for legal reasons, to provide similar information. The Commission shall be informed of the grounds of the refusal by the requested Member State.

4. The provision of information may be refused where it would lead to the disclosure of a commercial, industrial or professional secret or of a commercial process, or of information whose disclosure would be contrary to public policy.

5. The requested authority shall inform the requesting authority of the grounds for refusing a request for assistance.

6. A minimum threshold triggering a request for assistance may be adopted in accordance with the procedure referred to in Article 44(2).

Article 41

1. Information communicated in any form pursuant to this Regulation shall be covered by the obligation of official secrecy and enjoy the protection extended to similar information under both the national law of the Member State which received it and the corresponding provisions applicable to Community authorities.

Such information may be used for the purpose of establishing the assessment base or the collection or administrative control of tax for the purpose of establishing the assessment base.

The information may also be used for the assessment of other levies, duties, and taxes covered by Article 2 of Council Directive 76/308/EEC of 15 March 1976 on mutual assistance for the recovery of claims relating to certain levies, duties, taxes and other measures (OJ L 73, 19.3.1976, p 18. Directive as last amended by Directive 2001/44/EC (OJ L 175, 28.6.2001, p 17)).

In addition, it may be used in connection with judicial proceedings that may involve penalties, initiated as a result of infringements of tax law without prejudice to the general rules and legal provisions governing the rights of defendants and witnesses in such proceedings.

2. Persons duly accredited by the Security Accreditation Authority of the European Commission may have access to this information only in so far as it is necessary for care, maintenance and development of the CCN/CSI network.

3. By way of derogation from paragraph 1, the competent authority of the Member State providing the information shall permit its use for other purposes in the Member State of the requesting authority, if, under the legislation of the Member State of the requested authority, the information can be used for similar purposes.

4. Where the requesting authority considers that information it has received from the requested authority is likely to be useful to the competent authority of a third Member State, it may transmit it to the latter authority. It shall inform the requested authority thereof in advance. The requested authority may require that the transmission of the information to a third party be subject to its prior agreement.

5. Member States shall, for the purpose of the correct application of this Regulation, restrict the scope of the obligations and rights provided for in Article 10, Article 11(1), Articles 12 and 21 of Directive 95/46/EC to the extent required in order to safeguard the interests referred to in Article 13(e) of that Directive.

Article 42

Reports, statements and any other documents, or certified true copies or extracts thereof, obtained by the staff of the requested authority and communicated to the requesting authority under the assistance provided for by this Regulation may be invoked as evidence by the competent bodies of the Member State of the requesting authority on the same basis as similar documents provided by another authority of that country.

Article 43

1. For the purpose of applying this Regulation, Member States shall take all necessary measures to:

(*a*) ensure effective internal coordination between the competent authorities referred to in Article 3;

(*b*) establish direct cooperation between the authorities authorised for the purposes of such coordination;

(*c*) ensure the smooth operation of the information exchange arrangements provided for in this Regulation.

2. The Commission shall communicate to each Member State, as quickly as possible, any information which it receives and which it is able to provide.

CHAPTER X
GENERAL AND FINAL PROVISIONS

Article 44

1. The Commission shall be assisted by the Standing Committee on Administrative Cooperation, (hereinafter referred to as the Committee).

2. Where reference is made to this paragraph, Articles 5 and 7 of Decision 1999/468/EC shall apply, having regard to the provisions of Article 8 thereof.

The period laid down in Article 5(6) of Decision 1999/468/EC shall be set at three months.

3. The Committee shall adopt its rules of procedure.

Article 45

1. Every three years from the date of entry into force of this Regulation, the Commission shall report to the European Parliament and the Council on the application of this Regulation.

2. Member States shall communicate to the Commission the text of any provisions of national law, which they adopt in the field covered by this Regulation.

Article 46

1. The provisions of this Regulation shall be without prejudice to the fulfilment of any wider obligations in relation to mutual assistance ensuing from other legal acts, including bilateral or multilateral agreements.

2. Where the Member States conclude bilateral arrangements on matters covered by this Regulation other than to deal with individual cases, they shall inform the Commission without delay. The Commission shall in turn inform the other Member States.

Article 47

Regulation (EEC) No 218/92 is hereby repealed.

References made to the repealed Regulation shall be construed as references to this Regulation.

Article 48

This Regulation shall enter into force on 1 January 2004.

This Regulation shall be binding in its entirety and directly applicable in all Member States.

Done at Luxembourg, 7 October 2003.

REGULATION OF THE EUROPEAN PARLIAMENT AND OF THE COUNCIL

of 31 March 2004

04/638/EC

OJ L 102, 07/04/2004 p 1–8

on Community statistics relating to the trading of goods between Member States and repealing Council Regulation (EEC) No 3330/91

THE EUROPEAN PARLIAMENT AND THE COUNCIL OF THE EUROPEAN UNION,

Having regard to the Treaty establishing the European Community, and in particular Article 285(1) thereof,

Having regard to the proposal from the Commission,

Having regard to the opinion of the European Economic and Social Committee (OJ C 32, 5.2.2004, p 92),

Acting in accordance with the procedure laid down in Article 251 of the Treaty (Opinion of the European Parliament of 16 December 2003 (not yet published in the Official Journal) and Council Decision of 22 March 2004),

Whereas:

(1) Council Regulation (EEC) No 3330/91 of 7 November 1991 on the statistics relating to the trading of goods between Member States (OJ L 316, 16.11.1991, p 1. Regulation as last amended by Regulation (EC) No 1882/2003 of the European Parliament and of the Council (OJ L 284, 31.10.2003, p 1)) introduced a completely new system of data collection, which has been simplified on two occasions. In order to improve the transparency of this system and to make it easier to understand, Regulation (EEC) No 3330/91 should be replaced by this Regulation.

(2) This system should be retained, as a sufficiently detailed level of statistical information is still required for the Community policies involved in the development of the internal market and for Community enterprises to analyse their specific markets. Aggregated data also need to be available quickly in order to analyse the development of the Economic and Monetary Union. Member States should have the possibility of collecting information which meets their specific needs.

(3) There is, however, a need to improve the wording of the rules on compiling statistics relating to the trading of goods between Member States so that they can be more easily understood by the companies responsible for providing the data, the national services collecting the data and users.

(4) A system of thresholds should be retained, but in a simplified form, in order to provide a satisfactory response to users' needs whilst reducing the burden of response on the parties responsible for providing statistical information, particularly small and medium-sized enterprises.

(5) A close link should be maintained between the system for collecting statistical information and the fiscal formalities which exist in the context of trade of goods between Member States. This link makes it possible, in particular, to check the quality of the information collected.

(6) The quality of the statistical information produced, its evaluation by means of common indicators and transparency in this field are important objectives, which call for regulation at Community level.

(7) Since the objective of the planned action, namely the creation of a common legal framework for the systematic production of Community statistics relating to the trading of goods between Member States, cannot be sufficiently achieved at national level and can be better achieved at Community level, the Community may adopt measures, in accordance with the principle of subsidiarity as set out in Article 5 of the Treaty. In accordance with the principle of proportionality, as set out in that Article, this Regulation does not go beyond what is required to achieve this objective.

(8) Council Regulation (EC) No 322/97 of 17 February 1997 on Community statistics (OJ L 52, 22.2.1997, p. 1. Regulation as amended by Regulation (EC) No 1882/2003) provides a reference framework for this Regulation. However, the very detailed level of information in the field of statistics relating to the trading of goods requires specific rules with regard to confidentiality.

(9) It is important to ensure the uniform application of this Regulation and, in order to do so, to make provision for a Community procedure to help determine the implementing arrangements within an appropriate timescale and to make the necessary technical adaptations.

(10) The measures necessary for implementation of this Regulation should be adopted in accordance with Council Decision 1999/468/EC of 28 June 1999 laying down the procedures for the exercise of implementing powers conferred on the Commission (OJ L 184, 17.7.1999, p 23),

HAVE ADOPTED THIS REGULATION:

Article 1

Subject matter

This Regulation establishes a common framework for the systematic production of Community statistics relating to the trading of goods between Member States.

Article 2

Definitions

For the purpose of this Regulation, the following definitions shall apply:

- (*a*) **"goods"**: all movable property, including electric current;
- (*b*) **"specific goods or movements"**: goods or movements which, by their very nature, call for specific provisions, and in particular industrial plants, vessels and aircraft, sea products, goods delivered to vessels and aircraft, staggered

consignments, military goods, goods to or from offshore installations, spacecraft, motor vehicle and aircraft parts and waste products;

(*c*) **"national authorities"**: national statistical institutes and other bodies responsible in each Member State for producing Community statistics relating to the trading of goods between Member States;

(*d*) **"Community goods"**:

    (i) goods entirely obtained in the customs territory of the Community, without addition of goods from third countries or territories which are not part of the customs territory of the Community;

    (ii) goods from third countries or territories which are not part of the customs territory of the Community, which have been released for free circulation in a Member State;

    (iii) goods obtained in the customs territory of the Community either from the goods referred to exclusively in point (ii) or from the goods referred to in points (i) and (ii);

(*e*) **"Member State of dispatch"**: the Member State as defined by its statistical territory from which goods are dispatched to a destination in another Member State;

(*f*) **"Member State of arrival"**: the Member State as defined by its statistical territory in which goods arrive from another Member State;

(*g*) **"goods in simple circulation between Member States"**: Community goods dispatched from one Member State to another, which, on the way to the Member State of destination, travel directly through another Member State or stop for reasons related only to the transport of the goods.

Article 3

Scope

1. Statistics relating to the trading of goods between Member States shall cover dispatches and arrivals of goods.

2. Dispatches shall cover the following goods leaving the Member State of dispatch for a destination in another Member State:

(*a*) Community goods, except goods which are in simple circulation between Member States;

(*b*) goods placed in the Member State of dispatch under the inward processing customs procedure or the processing under customs control procedure.

3. Arrivals shall cover the following goods entering the Member State of arrival, which were initially dispatched from another Member State:

(*a*) Community goods, except goods which are in simple circulation between Member States;

(*b*) goods formerly placed in the Member State of dispatch according to the inward processing customs procedure or the processing according to customs control procedure, which are maintained according to the inward processing customs procedure or the processing according to customs control procedure or released for free circulation in the Member State of arrival.

4. Different or specific rules, to be determined in accordance with the procedure referred to in Article 14(2), may apply to specific goods or movements.

5. Some goods, a list of which shall be drawn up in accordance with the procedure referred to in Article 14(2), shall be excluded from the statistics for methodological reasons.

Article 4

Statistical territory

1. The statistical territory of the Member States shall correspond to their customs territory as defined in Article 3 of Council Regulation (EEC) No 2913/92 (OJ L 302, 19.10.1992, p 1. Regulation as last amended by Regulation (EC) No 2700/2000 of the European Parliament and of the Council (OJ L 311, 12.12.2000, p 17)) of 12 October 1992 establishing the Community Customs Code.

2. By way of derogation from paragraph 1, the statistical territory of Germany shall include Heligoland.

Article 5

Data sources

1. A specific data collection system, hereinafter referred to as the "Intrastat" system, shall apply for the provision of the statistical information on dispatches and arrivals of Community goods which are not the subject of a single administrative document for customs or fiscal purposes.

2. The statistical information on dispatches and arrivals of other goods shall be provided directly by customs to the national authorities, at least once a month.

3. For specific goods or movements, sources of information other than the Intrastat system or customs declarations may be used.

4. Each Member State shall organise the way Intrastat data is supplied by the parties responsible for providing information. To facilitate the task of these parties, the conditions for increased use of automatic data processing and electronic data transmission shall be promoted by the Commission (Eurostat) and the Member States.

Article 6

Reference period

1. The reference period for the information to be provided in accordance with Article 5 shall be the calendar month of dispatch or arrival of the goods.

2. The reference period may be adapted to take into account the linkage with value added tax (VAT) and customs obligations, pursuant to provisions adopted in accordance with the procedure referred to in Article 14(2).

Article 7
Parties responsible for providing information

1. The parties responsible for providing the information for the Intrastat system shall be:

    (*a*)   the natural or legal person registered for VAT in the Member State of dispatch who:

        (i)   has concluded the contract, with the exception of transport contracts, giving rise to the dispatch of goods or, failing that,

        (ii)   dispatches or provides for the dispatch of the goods or, failing that,

        (iii)   is in possession of the goods which are the subject of the dispatch;

    (*b*)   the natural or legal person registered for VAT in the Member State of arrival who:

        (i)   has concluded the contract, with the exception of transport contracts, giving rise to the delivery of goods or, failing that,

        (ii)   takes delivery or provides for delivery of the goods or, failing that,

        (iii)   is in possession of the goods which are the subject of the delivery.

2. The parties responsible for providing information may transfer the task to a third party, but such transfer shall in no way reduce the responsibility of the said party.

3. Failure by any party responsible for providing information to fulfil his/her obligations under this Regulation shall render him/her liable to the penalties which the Member States shall lay down.

Article 8
Registers

1. National authorities shall set up and manage a register of intra-Community operators containing at least the consignors, upon dispatch, and the consignees, upon arrival.

2. In order to identify the parties responsible for providing information referred to in Article 7 and to check the information which is provided, the tax administration responsible in each Member State shall furnish the national authority:

    (*a*)   at least once a month, with the lists of natural or legal persons who have declared that, during the period in question, they have supplied goods to other Member States or acquired goods from other Member States. The lists shall show the total values of the goods declared by each natural or legal person for fiscal purposes;

    (*b*)   on its own initiative or at the request of the national authority, with any information provided for fiscal purposes which could improve the quality of statistics.

The arrangements for the communication of the information shall be determined in accordance with the procedure referred to in Article 14(2).

This information shall be treated by the national authority in accordance with the rules applied to it by the tax administration.

3. The tax administration shall bring to the attention of VAT-registered traders the obligations which they may incur as parties responsible for providing the information required by Intrastat.

Article 9
Intrastat information to be collected

1. The following information shall be collected by the national authorities:

(*a*) the identification number allocated to the party responsible for providing information in accordance with Article 22(1)(c) of the Sixth Council Directive 77/388/EEC of 17 May 1977 on the harmonisation of the laws of the Member States relating to turnover taxes — common system of value added tax: uniform basis of assessment (OJ L 145, 13.6.1977, p 1. Directive as last amended by Directive 2004/15/EC (OJ L 52, 21.2.2004, p 61)), in the version given in Article 28h thereof;

(*b*) the reference period;

(*c*) the flow (arrival, dispatch);

(*d*) the commodity, identified by the eight-digit code of the Combined Nomenclature as defined in Council Regulation (EEC) No 2658/87 of 23 July 1987 on the tariff and statistical nomenclature and on the Common Customs Tariff (OJ L 256, 7.9.1987, p 1. Regulation as last amended by Commission Regulation (EC) No 2344/2003 (OJ L 346, 31.12.2003, p 38));

(*e*) the partner Member State;

(*f*) the value of the goods;

(*g*) the quantity of the goods;

(*h*) the nature of the transaction.

Definitions of the statistical data referred to in points (e) to (h) are given in the Annex. Where necessary, the arrangements for the collection of this information, particularly the codes to be employed, shall be determined in accordance with the procedure referred to in Article 14(2).

2. Member States may also collect additional information, for example:

(*a*) the identification of the goods, at a more detailed level than the Combined Nomenclature;

(*b*) the country of origin, on arrival;

(*c*) the region of origin, on dispatch, and the region of destination, on arrival;

(*d*) the delivery terms;

(*e*) the mode of transport;

(*f*) the statistical procedure.

Definitions of the statistical data referred to in points (b) to (f) are given in the Annex. Where necessary, the arrangements for the collection of this information, particularly the codes to be employed, shall be determined in accordance with the procedure referred to in Article 14(2).

Article 10
Simplification within the Intrastat system

1. In order to satisfy users' needs for statistical information without imposing excessive burdens on economic operators, Member States shall define each year thresholds expressed in annual values of intra-Community trade, below which parties are exempted from providing any Intrastat information or may provide simplified information.

2. The thresholds shall be defined by each Member State, separately for arrivals and dispatches.

3. For defining thresholds below which parties are exempted from providing any Intrastat information, Member States shall ensure that information referred to in Article 9(1), first subparagraph, points (a) to (f), made available by the parties responsible for providing information, is such that at least 97% of the relevant Member State's total trade expressed in value is covered.

4. Member States may define other thresholds below which parties may benefit from the following simplification:

    (*a*) exemption from providing information about the quantity of the goods;

    (*b*) exemption from providing information about the nature of the transaction;

    (*c*) possibility of reporting a maximum of 10 of the detailed relevant subheadings of the Combined Nomenclature, that are the most used in terms of value, and regrouping the other products in accordance with rules determined in accordance with the procedure referred to in Article 14(2).

Every Member State applying these thresholds shall ensure that the trade of these parties shall amount to a maximum of 6 % of its total trade.

5. Member States may, under certain conditions, which meet quality requirements and which shall be defined in accordance with the procedure referred to in Article 14(2), simplify the information to be provided for small individual transactions.

6. The information on the thresholds applied by the Member States shall be sent to the Commission (Eurostat) no later than 31 October of the year preceding the year to which they apply.

Article 11
Statistical confidentiality

Where the parties who have provided information so request, the national authorities shall decide whether statistical results which make it possible indirectly to identify the said provider(s) are to be disseminated or are to be amended in such a way that their dissemination does not prejudice statistical confidentiality.

Article 12
Transmission of data to the Commission

1. Member States shall transmit to the Commission (Eurostat) the monthly results of their statistics relating to the trading of goods between Member States no later than:

    (*a*) 40 calendar days after the end of the reference month for the aggregated data to be defined in accordance with the procedure referred to in Article 14(2);

(*b*)   70 calendar days after the end of the reference month in the case of detailed results including the information referred to in Article 9(1), first subparagraph, points (*b*) to (*h*).

As regards the value of the goods, the results shall include the statistical value only, as defined in the Annex.

Member States shall transmit to the Commission (Eurostat) the data which are confidential.

2. Member States shall provide the Commission (Eurostat) with monthly results which cover their total trade in goods by using estimates, where necessary.

3. Member States shall transmit the data to the Commission (Eurostat) in electronic form, in accordance with an interchange standard. The practical arrangements for the transmission of data shall be determined in accordance with the procedure referred to in Article 14(2).

Article 13

Quality

1. Member States shall take all measures necessary to ensure the quality of the data transmitted according to the quality indicators and standards in force.

2. Member States shall present to the Commission (Eurostat) a yearly report on the quality of the data transmitted.

3. The indicators and standards enabling the quality of the data to be assessed, the structure of the quality reports to be presented by the Member States and any measures necessary for assessing or improving the quality of the data shall be determined in accordance with the procedure referred to in Article 14(2).

Article 14

Committee procedure

1. The Commission shall be assisted by a Committee for the statistics on the trading of goods between Member States.

2. Where reference is made to this paragraph, Articles 5 and 7 of Decision 1999/468/EC shall apply, having regard to the provisions of Article 8 thereof.

The period laid down in Article 5(6) of Decision 1999/468/EC shall be set at three months.

3. The Committee shall adopt its Rules of Procedure.

Article 15

Repeal

1. Regulation (EEC) No 3330/91 is hereby repealed.

2. References to the repealed regulation shall be construed as being made to this Regulation.

Article 16

Entry into force

This Regulation shall enter into force on the 20th day following that of its publication in the Official Journal of the European Union.

It shall apply from 1 January 2005.

This Regulation shall be binding in its entirety and directly applicable in all Member States.

Done at Strasbourg, 31 March 2004.

ANNEX
DEFINITIONS OF STATISTICAL DATA

1. Partner Member State

(*a*) The partner Member State is the Member State of consignment, on arrival. This means the presumed Member State of dispatch in cases where goods enter directly from another Member State. Where, before reaching the Member State of arrival, goods have entered one or more Member States in transit and have been subject in those States to halts or legal operations not inherent in their transport (e.g. change of ownership), the Member State of consignment shall be taken as the last Member State where such halts or operations occurred.

(*b*) The partner Member State is the Member State of destination, on dispatch. This means the last Member State to which it is known, at the time of dispatch, that the goods are to be dispatched.

2. Quantity of the goods

The quantity of the goods can be expressed in two ways:

(*a*)   the net mass, which means the actual mass of the goods excluding all packaging;

(*b*) the supplementary units, which mean the possible units measuring quantity other than net mass, as detailed in the annual Commission regulation updating the Combined Nomenclature.

3. Value of the goods

The value of the goods can be expressed in two ways:

(*a*) the taxable amount, which is the value to be determined for taxation purposes in accordance with Directive 77/388/EEC;

(*b*) the statistical value, which is the value calculated at the national borders of the Member States. It includes only incidental expenses (freight, insurance) incurred, in the case of dispatches, in the part of the journey located on the territory of the Member State of dispatch and, in the case of arrivals, in the part of the journey located outside the territory of the Member State of arrival. It is said to be a fob value (free on board) for dispatches, and a cif value (cost, insurance, freight) for arrivals.

4. Nature of the transaction

The nature of transaction means the different characteristics (purchase/sale, work under contract, etc.) which are deemed to be useful in distinguishing one transaction from another.

5. Country of origin

(*a*) The country of origin, on arrivals only, means the country where the goods originate.

(*b*) Goods which are wholly obtained or produced in a country originate in that country.

(*c*) Goods whose production involved more than one country shall be deemed to originate in the country where they underwent their last, substantial, economically justified processing or working in a company equipped for that purpose, resulting in the manufacture of a new product or representing an important stage of manufacture.

6. Region of origin or destination

(*a*) The region of origin, on dispatch, means the region of the Member State of dispatch where the goods were produced or were erected, assembled, processed, repaired or maintained; failing that, the region of origin is the region where the goods were dispatched, or, failing that, the region where the commercial process took place.

(*b*) The region of destination, on arrival, means the region of the Member State of arrival where the goods are to be consumed or erected, assembled, processed, repaired or maintained; failing that, the region of destination is the region to which the goods are to be dispatched, or, failing that, the region where the commercial process is to take place.

7. Delivery terms

The delivery terms mean those provisions of the sales contract which lay down the obligations of the seller and the buyer respectively, in accordance with the Incoterms of the International Chamber of Commerce (cif, fob, etc.).

8. Mode of transport

The mode of transport is determined by the active means of transport by which the goods are presumed to be going to leave the statistical territory of the Member State of dispatch, on dispatch, and by the active means of transport by which the goods are presumed to have entered the statistical territory of the Member State of arrival, on arrival.

9. Statistical procedure

The statistical procedure means the different characteristics which are deemed to be useful in distinguishing different types of arrivals/dispatches for statistical purposes.

COMMISSION REGULATION

of 18 November 2004

04/1982/EC

OJ L 343, 19/11/2004 p 3

implementing Regulation (EC) No 638/2004 of the European Parliament and of the Council on Community statistics relating to the trading of goods between Member States and repealing Commission Regulations (EC) No 1901/2000 and (EEC) No 3590/92

THE COMMISSION OF THE EUROPEAN COMMUNITIES,

Having regard to the Treaty establishing the European Community,

Having regard to Regulation (EC) No 638/2004 of the European Parliament and of the Council of 31 March 2004 on Community statistics relating to the trading of goods between Member States (OJ L 102, 7.4.2004, p 1) and in particular Articles 3(4) and (5), 6(2), 8(2), 9, 10, 12 and 13(3) thereof,

Whereas:

(1) Statistics relating to the trading of goods between Member States are based on the Regulation (EC) No 638/2004 of the European Parliament and of the Council which reconsiders the statistical provisions with a view to improving transparency and facilitating comprehension and which is adapted to meet current data requirements. Particular implementation arrangements are assigned to the Commission in accordance with Article 14(2) of the said Regulation.

Therefore it is necessary to adopt a new Commission Regulation which should refer in a restrictive manner to the assigned responsibility and specify the implementing provisions. Commission Regulations (EC) No 1901/2000 of 7 September 2000 laying down certain provisions for the implementation of Council Regulation (EEC) No 3330/91 on the statistics relating to the trading of goods between Member States (OJ L 228, 8.9.2000, p 28. Regulation as last amended by Regulation (EC) 2207/2003 (OJ L 330, 18.12.2003, p 15)) and (EEC) No 3590/92 of 11 December 1992 concerning the statistical information media for statistics on trade between Member States (OJ L 364, 12.12.1992, p 32) should therefore be repealed.

(2) For methodological reasons a number of types of goods and movements should be exempted. It is necessary to draw up a comprehensive list of those goods to be excluded from the statistics to be sent to the Commission (Eurostat).

(3) Goods are to be included in trade statistics at the time when they enter or leave the statistical territory of a country. However, special arrangements are needed when data collection takes account of fiscal and customs procedures.

(4) A link between value added tax information and Intrastat declarations should be maintained in order to check the quality of the collected information. It is appropriate to determine the information to be transmitted by the national tax administration to the national authorities responsible for statistics.

(5) Common definitions and concepts should apply to data collected within the Intrastat system in order to facilitate a harmonised application of the system.

(6) With a view to transparency and equal treatment of the companies, harmonised and accurate provisions should be applied for the setting up of thresholds.

(7) Appropriate provisions have to be determined for some specific goods and movements in order to ensure that the necessary information is collected in a harmonised way.

(8) Common and appropriate timetables as well as provisions on adjustments and revisions have to be included in order to satisfy users' needs for timely and comparable figures.

(9) A regular assessment of the system is planned in order to improve the data quality and ensure the transparency of the functioning of the system.

(10) The measures provided for in this Regulation are in accordance with the opinion of the Committee on the statistics relating to the trading of goods between Member States,

HAS ADOPTED THIS REGULATION:

CHAPTER 1
GENERAL PROVISIONS

Article 1
Subject matter

This Regulation sets up the necessary measures for implementing Regulation (EC) No 638/2004 of the European Parliament and of the Council.

Article 2
Excluded goods

The goods listed in Annex I to this Regulation shall be excluded from statistics relating to the trading of goods between Member States to be transmitted to the Commission (Eurostat).

Article 3
Period of reference

1. Member States may adapt the period of reference for Community goods on which VAT becomes chargeable on intra-Community acquisitions according to Article 6(2) of Regulation (EC) No 638/2004.

The reference period may then be defined as the calendar month during which the chargeable event occurs.

2. Member States may adapt the period of reference where the Customs declaration is used in support of the information according to Article 6(2) of Regulation (EC) No 638/ 2004.

The reference period may then be defined as the calendar month during which the declaration is accepted by Customs.

CHAPTER 2
COMMUNICATION OF INFORMATION BY THE TAX ADMINISTRATION

Article 4

1. The parties responsible for providing the information for the Intrastat System have the obligation to prove, at the request of the national authority, the correctness of the provided statistical information.

2. The obligation according to paragraph 1 is limited to data which the provider of statistical information has to deliver to the competent tax administration in connection with his or her intra-Community movements of goods.

Article 5

1. The tax administration responsible in each Member State shall provide to the national authorities the following information in order to identify the persons who have declared goods for fiscal purposes:

    (*a*)　full name of the natural or legal person;

    (*b*)　full address including post code;

    (*c*)　identification number according to Article 9(1)(*a*) of Regulation (EC) No 638/2004.

2. The tax administration responsible in each Member State shall provide to the national authorities for each natural or legal person in accordance with Directive 77/388/EEC (OJ L 145, 13.6.1977, p 1. Directive as last amended by Directive 2004/66/EC (OJ L 168, 1.5.2004, p 35)):

    (*a*)　the taxable amount of intra-Community acquisitions and deliveries of goods;

    (*b*)　the tax period.

Article 6

The additional information referred to in Article 8(2)(*b*) of Regulation (EC) No 638/2004 concerns at least the national VIES data (VAT Information Exchange System data).

CHAPTER 3
COLLECTION OF INTRASTAT INFORMATION

Article 7
Partner Member State and country of origin

The partner Member States and where collected, the country of origin shall be reported according to the version of the nomenclature of countries and territories in force.

Article 8
Value of the goods

1. The value of the goods shall be the taxable amount which is the value to be determined for taxation purposes in accordance with Directive 77/388/EEC.

For products subject to duties, the amount of these duties shall be excluded.

Whenever the taxable amount does not have to be declared for taxation purposes, a positive value has to be reported which shall correspond to the invoice value, excluding VAT, or, failing this, to an amount which would have been invoiced in the event of any sale or purchase.

In the case of processing, the value to be collected, with a view to and following such operations, shall be the total amount which would be invoiced in case of sale or purchase.

2. Additionally, Member States may also collect the statistical value of the goods, as defined in the Annex to Regulation (EC) No 638/2004, from part of the providers of information whose trade shall amount to a maximum of 70 % of the relevant Member State's total trade expressed in value.

3. The value of the goods defined in paragraphs 1 and 2 shall be expressed in the national currency. The exchange rate to be applied shall be:

(*a*)   the rate of exchange applicable for determining the taxable amount for taxation purposes, when this is established; or

(*b*)   the official rate of exchange at the time of completing the declaration or that applicable to calculating the value for customs purposes, in the absence of any special provisions decided by the Member States.

Article 9

Quantity of the goods

1. The net mass shall be given in kilograms. However, the specification of net mass for the subheadings of the Combined Nomenclature hereinafter referred to as 'CN' as established by Council Regulation (EEC) No 2658/87 (OJ L 256, 7.9.1987, p 1. Regulation as last amended by Regulation (EC) No 1558/2004 (OJ L 283, 2.9.2004, p 7)) set out in Annex II to this Regulation shall not be requested from the parties responsible for providing information.

2. The supplementary units shall be mentioned in accordance with the information set out in Council Regulation (EEC) No 2658/87, opposite the subheadings concerned, the list of which is published in Part I 'Preliminary provisions' of the said Regulation.

Article 10

Nature of transaction

The nature of transaction shall be reported according to the codes specified in the list of Annex III to this Regulation. Member States shall apply the codes of column A or a combination of the code numbers in column A and their subdivisions in column B indicated in this list.

Article 11

Delivery terms

Member States which collect the delivery terms according to Article 9(2)(*d*) of Regulation (EC) No 638/2004 may use the codes specified in Annex IV to this Regulation.

Article 12

Mode of transport

Member States which collect the mode of transport according to Article 9(2)(*e*) of Regulation (EC) No 638/2004 may use the codes specified in Annex V to this Regulation.

CHAPTER 4

SIMPLIFICATION WITHIN INTRASTAT

Article 13

1. Member States shall calculate their thresholds for the year following the current calendar year on the basis of the latest available results for their trade with other Member States over a period of at least 12 months. The provisions adopted at the start of a year shall apply for the whole year.

2. The value of the trade of a party responsible for providing information is considered to be above the thresholds:

(*a*) when the value of trade with other Member States during the previous year exceeds the applicable thresholds, or

(*b*) when the cumulative value of trade with other Member States since the beginning of the year of application exceeds the applicable thresholds. In that case, information shall be provided from the month in which thresholds are exceeded.

3. Parties responsible for providing information according to the simplified rules of Article 10(4)(*c*) of Regulation (EC) No 638/2004 shall use the code 9950 00 00 for reporting the residual products.

4. For individual transactions whose value is less than EUR 200, the parties responsible for providing information may report the following simplified information:

— the product code 9950 00 00,

— the partner Member State,

— the value of the goods. National authorities:

(*a*) may refuse or limit application of this simplification if they consider that the aim of maintaining a satisfactory quality of statistical information overrides the desirability of reducing the reporting burden;

(*b*) may require parties responsible for providing information to ask in advance to be allowed to make use of the simplification.

CHAPTER 5
RULES CONCERNING SPECIFIC GOODS AND MOVEMENTS

Article 14

In addition to the provisions of the Regulation (EC) No 638/2004, specific goods and movements shall be subject to the rules set out in this Chapter for data to be transmitted to the Commission (Eurostat).

Article 15
Industrial plant

1. For the purpose of this Article:

(*a*) '**industrial plant**' is a combination of machines, apparatus, appliances, equipment, instruments and materials which together make up large-scale, stationary units producing goods or providing services;

(*b*) '**component part**' means a delivery for an industrial plant which is made up of goods which all belong to the same chapter of the CN.

2. Statistics on trade between Member States may cover only dispatches and arrivals of component parts used for the construction of industrial plants or the re-use of industrial plants.

3. Member States applying paragraph 2 may apply the following particular provisions on condition that the overall statistical value of a given industrial plant exceeds 3 million EUR, unless they are complete industrial plants for re-use:

(*a*) The commodity codes shall be composed as follows:
— the first four digits shall be 9880,
— the fifth and the sixth digits shall correspond to the CN chapter to which the goods of the component part belong,
— the seventh and the eighth digits shall be 0.

(*b*) The quantity shall be optional.

Article 16
Staggered consignments

1. For the purpose of this Article 'staggered consignments' means the delivery of components of a complete item in an unassembled or disassembled state which are shipped during more than one reference period for commercial or transport-related reasons.

2. Member States shall transmit data on arrivals or dispatches of staggered consignments only once, in the month that the last consignment arrives or is dispatched.

Article 17
Vessels and aircraft

1. For the purposes of this Article:

(*a*) '**vessel**' means a vessel used for sea transport, referred to in Additional Notes 1 and 2 of Chapter 89 of the CN, and warships;

(*b*) **'aircraft'** means aeroplanes falling within CN code 8802 for civilian use, provided they are used by an airline, or for military use;

(*c*) **'ownership of a vessel or aircraft'** means the fact of a natural or legal person's registration as owner of a vessel or an aircraft.

2. Statistics relating to the trading of goods between Member States on vessels and aircraft shall cover only the following dispatches and arrivals:

(*a*) the transfer of ownership of a vessel or aircraft, from a natural or legal person established in another Member State to a natural or legal person established in the reporting Member State. This transaction shall be treated as an arrival;

(*b*) the transfer of ownership of a vessel or aircraft from a natural or legal person established in the reporting Member State to a natural or legal person established in another Member State. This transaction shall be treated as a dispatch.

If the vessel or aircraft is new the dispatch is recorded in the Member State of construction;

(*c*) the dispatches and arrivals of vessels or aircraft pending or following processing under contract as defined in Annex III, footnote (e).

3. Member States shall apply the following specific provisions on statistics relating to the trading of goods between Member States:

(*a*) the quantity shall be expressed in number of items and any other supplementary units laid down in the CN, for vessels, and in net mass and supplementary units, for aircraft;

(*b*) the statistical value shall be the total amount which would be invoiced - transport and insurance costs being excluded -in case of sale or purchase of the whole vessel or aircraft;

(*c*) the partner Member State for the reporting Member State shall be:

— the Member State of construction, on arrival in the case of new vessel or aircraft constructed in the European Union,

— in the other cases the partner Member State shall be the Member State where the natural or legal person transferring the ownership of the vessel or aircraft is established, on arrival, or the natural or legal person to whom the ownership of the vessel or aircraft is transferred, on dispatch.

(*d*) the reference period for arrivals and dispatches referred to in paragraphs 2(*a*) and (*b*) shall be the month where the transfer of ownership takes place.

4. Provided that there is no conflict with other national or Community legislation, national authorities responsible for Intrastat shall have access to additional data sources other than those of the Intrastat System or the Single Administrative Document for customs or fiscal purposes which they may need to apply this Article.

Article 18
Motor vehicle and aircraft parts

Member States may apply simplified national provisions for motor vehicle and aircraft parts, provided that they keep the Commission (Eurostat) informed on their particular practice before application.

Article 19
Goods delivered to vessels and aircraft

1. For the purposes of this Article:

(*a*) '**delivery of goods to vessels and aircraft**' means the delivery of products for the crew and passengers, and for the operation of the engines, machines and other equipment of vessels or aircraft;

(*b*) vessels or aircraft shall be deemed to belong to the Member State in which the vessel or aircraft is registered.

2. Statistics relating to the trading of goods between Member States shall cover only dispatches of goods delivered on the territory of the reporting Member State to vessels and aircraft belonging to another Member State. Dispatches shall cover all goods defined in Article 3(2)(*a*) and (*b*) of Regulation (EC) No 638/2004.

3. Member States shall use the following commodity codes for goods delivered to vessels and aircraft:

— 9930 24 00 goods from CN chapters 1 to 24,
— 9930 27 00 goods from CN chapters 1 to 24,
— 9930 99 00: goods classified elsewhere.

The transmission of data on the quantity is optional. However, the data on net mass shall be transmitted on goods belonging to chapter 27.

In addition, the simplified partner country code 'QR' may be used.

Article 20
Offshore installations

1. For the purposes of this Article:

(*a*) '**offshore installation**' means the equipment and devices installed and stationary in the sea outside the statistical territory of any given country;

(*b*) these offshore installations shall be deemed to belong to that Member State in which the natural or legal person responsible for their commercial use is established.

2. Statistics relating to the trading of goods between Member States shall cover dispatches and arrivals of goods delivered to and from these offshore installations.

3. Member States shall use the following commodity codes for goods destined for the operators of the offshore installation or for the operation of the engines, machines and other equipment of the offshore installation:

— 9931 24 00: goods from the CN chapters 1 to 24,
— 9931 27 00: goods from the CN Chapter 27,
— 9931 99 00: goods classified elsewhere.

The transmission of data on the quantity is optional. However, the data on net mass shall be transmitted on goods belonging to chapter 27.

The simplified partner country code 'QV' may be used.

Article 21
Sea products

1. For the purposes of this Article:

(*a*) '**sea products**' means fishery products, minerals, salvage and all other products which have not yet been landed by sea going vessels;

(*b*) sea products shall be deemed to belong to that Member State where the vessel, which is carrying out the capturing, is registered.

2. Statistics relating to the trading of goods between Member States shall cover the following dispatches and arrivals:

(*a*) arrivals when sea products are landed in the reporting Member State's ports or acquired by vessels registered in the reporting Member State from a vessel registered in another Member State;

(*b*) dispatches when sea products are landed in another Member State's ports or acquired by vessels registered in another Member State from a vessel registered in the reporting Member State.

3. The partner Member State shall be, on arrival, the Member State where the vessel, which is carrying out the capturing, is registered and, on dispatch, the Member State where the sea product is landed or the vessel acquiring the sea product is registered.

4. Provided that there is no conflict with other national or Community legislation, national authorities responsible for Intrastat shall have access to additional data sources other than those of the Intrastat System or the Single Administrative Document for customs or fiscal purposes which they may need to apply this Article.

Article 22
Spacecraft

1. For the purposes of this Article, 'spacecraft' means vehicles which are able to travel outside the earth's atmosphere.

2. Statistics relating to the trading of goods between Member States shall cover the following dispatches and arrivals of spacecraft:

(*a*) the dispatch or arrival of a spacecraft pending or following processing under contract as defined in Annex III footnote (*e*) to this Regulation;

(*b*) the launching into space of a spacecraft which was the subject of a transfer of ownership between two natural or legal persons established in different Member States is to be considered:

(i) as a dispatch in the Member State of construction of the finished spacecraft,

(ii) as an arrival in the Member State where the new owner is established.

3. The following specific provisions shall apply to the statistics referred to in paragraph 2(*b*):

(*a*) the data on the statistical value shall be defined as the value of the spacecraft ex-works in accordance with the delivery terms specified in Annex IV to this Regulation.

(*b*) The data on the partner Member State shall be the Member State of construction of the finished spacecraft, on arrival, and the Member State where the new owner is established, on dispatch.

4. Provided that there is no conflict with other national or Community legislation, national authorities responsible for Intrastat shall have access to additional data sources other than those of the Intrastat System or the Single Administrative Document for customs or fiscal purposes which they may need to apply this Article.

Article 23
Electricity

1. Statistics relating to the trading of goods between Member States shall cover dispatches and arrivals of electricity.

2. Provided that there is no conflict with other national or Community legislation, national authorities responsible for Intrastat shall have access to additional data sources other than those of the Intrastat System or the Single Administrative Document for customs or fiscal purposes which they may need to transmit data on the trading of electricity between Member States to the Commission (Eurostat).

3. The statistical value transmitted to the Commission (Eurostat) may be based on estimates. Member States have to inform the Commission (Eurostat) on the methodology used for the estimate before application.

Article 24
Military goods

1. Statistics relating to the trading of goods between Member States shall cover dispatches and arrivals of goods intended for military use.

2. Member States may transmit less detailed information than indicated in Article 9(1) points (*b*) to (*h*) of Regulation (EC) No 638/2004 when the information falls under military secrecy in compliance with the definitions in force in the Member States. However, as a minimum, data on the total monthly statistical value of the dispatches and arrivals shall be transmitted to the Commission (Eurostat).

CHAPTER 6
DATA TRANSMISSION TO EUROSTAT

Article 25

1. Aggregated results referred to in Article 12(1)(*a*) of Regulation (EC) No 638/2004 are defined, for each flow, as the total value of the trade with other Member States. In addition, Member States belonging to the euro area shall provide a breakdown of their trade outside the euro area by products according to Sections of the Standard International Trade Classification, Revision 3.

2. Member States shall take all necessary measures to ensure that the collection of trade data from companies above the threshold of 97 % is exhaustive.

3. Adjustments made in application of Article 12 of Regulation (EC) No 638/2004 shall be transmitted to Eurostat with at least a breakdown by partner country and commodity code at two digit level of the CN.

4. As regards the statistical value of the goods, Member States shall estimate this value, where not collected.

5. Member States having adapted the reference period according to Article 3(1) shall ensure that monthly results are transmitted to the Commission (Eurostat), using estimates if necessary, when the reference period for fiscal purposes does not correspond with a calendar month.

6. Member States shall transmit data declared confidential to the Commission (Eurostat) so that they may be published at least under the original first two-digits of the CN code if the confidentiality is thereby assured.

7. When monthly results already transmitted to the Commission (Eurostat) are subject to revisions, Member States shall transmit revised results no later than in the month following the availability of revised data.

CHAPTER 7
QUALITY REPORT

Article 26

1. Member States shall supply the Commission (Eurostat) no later than 10 months following the calendar year with a quality report containing all information that it requests to assess the quality of the data transmitted.

2. The quality report aims at covering quality of statistics with reference to the following dimensions:
- relevance of statistical concepts,
- accuracy of estimates,
- timeliness in transmission of results to the Commission (Eurostat),
- accessibility and clarity of the information,
- comparability of statistics,
- coherence,
- completeness.

3. The quality indicators are defined in Annex VI to this Regulation.

CHAPTER 8
FINAL PROVISIONS

Article 27

Regulation (EC) No 1901/2000 and Regulation (EEC) No 3590/92 are hereby repealed with effect from 1 January 2005.

Article 28

This Regulation shall enter into force on the twentieth day following its publication in the Official Journal of the European Union.

It shall apply from 1 January 2005.

This Regulation shall be binding in its entirety and directly applicable in all Member States.

Done at Brussels, 18 November 2004.

For the Commission

Joaquín ALMUNIA
Member of the Commission

ANNEX I

LIST OF GOODS EXCLUDED FROM STATISTICS RELATING TO THE TRADING OF GOODS BETWEEN MEMBER STATES TO BE TRANSMITTED TO THE COMMISSION (EUROSTAT)

- (*a*) means of payment which are legal tender and securities
- (*b*) monetary gold
- (*c*) emergency aid for disaster areas
- (*d*) goods benefiting from diplomatic, consular or similar immunity
- (*e*) goods for and following temporary use, provided all the following conditions are met:
  1. no processing is planned or made
  2. the expected duration of the temporary use is not longer than 24 months
  3. the dispatch/arrival has not to be declared as a delivery/acquisition for VAT purposes
- (*f*) goods used as carriers of information such as floppy disks, computer tapes, films, plans, audio and videotapes, CD-ROMs with stored computer software, where developed to order for a particular client or where they are not subject of a commercial transaction, as well as complements for a previous delivery eg updates for which the consignee is not invoiced.
- (*g*) provided that they are not the subject of a commercial transaction: 1. advertising material 2. commercial samples
- (*h*) goods for and after repair and the associated replacement parts. A repair entails the restoration of goods to their original function or condition. The objective of the operation is simply to maintain the goods in working order; this may involve some rebuilding or enhancements but does not change the nature of the goods in any way
- (*i*) goods dispatched to national armed forces stationed outside the statistical territory and goods received from another Member State which had been conveyed outside the statistical territory by the national armed forces, as well as goods acquired or disposed of on the statistical territory of a Member State by the armed forces of another Member State which are stationed there
- (*j*) spacecraft launchers, on dispatch and on arrival pending launching into space, and at the time of launching into space

(k) sales of new means of transport by natural or legal persons liable to VAT to private individuals from other Member States

ANNEX II
LIST OF CN SUBHEADINGS REFERRED TO ARTICLE 9(1)

0105 11 11	2204 21 26	2204 21 91	2204 29 91
0105 11 19	2204 21 27	2204 21 92	2204 29 92
0105 11 91	2204 21 28	2204 21 94	2204 29 94
0105 11 99	2204 21 32	2204 21 95	2204 29 95
0105 12 00	2204 21 34	2204 21 96	2204 29 96
0105 19 20	2204 21 36	2204 21 98	2204 29 98
0105 19 90	2204 21 37	2204 21 99	2204 29 99
*********	2204 21 38	2204 29 10	*********
0407 00 11	2204 21 42	2204 29 11	2205 10 10
*********	2204 21 43	2204 29 12	2205 10 90
2202 10 00	2204 21 44	2204 29 13	2205 90 10
2202 90 10	2204 21 46	2204 29 17	2205 90 90
2202 90 91	2204 21 47	2204 29 18	*********
2202 90 95	2204 21 48	2204 29 42	2206 00 10
2202 90 99	2204 21 62	2204 29 43	2206 00 31
*********	2204 21 66	2204 29 44	2206 00 39
2203 00 01	2204 21 67	2204 29 46	2206 00 51
2203 00 09	2204 21 68	2204 29 47	2206 00 59
2203 00 10	2204 21 69	2204 29 48	2206 00 81
*********	2204 21 71	2204 29 58	*********
2204 10 11	2204 21 74	2204 29 62	2207 10 00
2204 10 19	2204 21 76	2204 29 64	2207 20 00
2204 10 91	2204 21 77	2204 29 65	*********
2204 10 99	2204 21 78	2204 29 71	2209 00 99
2204 21 10	2204 21 79	2204 29 72	*********
2204 21 11	2204 21 80	2204 29 75	2716 00 00
2204 21 12	2204 21 81	2204 29 77	*********
2204 21 13	2204 21 82	2204 29 78	3702 51 00
2204 21 17	2204 21 83	2204 29 82	3702 53 00
2204 21 18	2204 21 84	2204 29 83	3702 54 10
2204 21 19	2204 21 85	2204 29 84	3702 54 90
2204 21 22	2204 21 87	2204 29 87	*********
2204 21 23	2204 21 88	2204 29 88	5701 10 10
2204 21 24	2204 21 89	2204 29 89	5701 10 90
5701 90 10	5705 00 10	6103 49 00	6106 90 10

5701 90 90	5705 00 30	*********	6106 90 30
*********	5705 00 90	6104 11 00	6106 90 50
5702 20 00	*********	6104 12 00	6106 90 90
5702 31 10	6101 10 10	6104 13 00	*********
5702 31 80	6101 10 90	6104 19 00	6107 11 00
5702 32 10	6101 20 10	6104 21 00	6107 12 00
5702 32 90	6101 20 90	6104 22 00	6107 19 00
5702 39 00	6101 30 10	6104 23 00	6107 21 00
5702 41 00	6101 30 90	6104 29 00	6107 22 00
5702 42 00	6101 90 10	6104 31 00	6107 29 00
5702 49 00	6101 90 90	6104 32 00	6107 91 00
5702 51 00	*********	6104 33 00	6107 92 00
5702 52 10	6102 10 10	6104 39 00	6107 99 00
5702 52 90	6102 10 90	6104 41 00	*********
5702 59 00	6102 20 10	6104 42 00	6108 11 00
5702 91 00	6102 20 90	6104 43 00	6108 19 00
5702 92 10	6102 30 10	6104 44 00	6108 21 00
5702 92 90	6102 30 90	6104 49 00	6108 22 00
5702 99 00	6102 90 10	6104 51 00	6108 29 00
*********	6102 90 90	6104 52 00	6108 31 00
5703 10 00	*********	6104 53 00	6108 32 00
5703 20 11	6103 11 00	6104 59 00	6108 39 00
5703 20 19	6103 12 00	6104 61 00	6108 91 00
5703 20 91	6103 19 00	6104 62 00	6108 92 00
5703 20 99	6103 21 00	6104 63 00	6108 99 00
5703 30 11	6103 22 00	6104 69 00	*********
5703 30 19	6103 23 00	*********	6109 10 00
5703 30 81	6103 29 00	6105 10 00	6109 90 10
5703 30 89	6103 31 00	6105 20 10	6109 90 30
5703 90 10	6103 32 00	6105 20 90	6109 90 90
5703 90 90	6103 33 00	6105 90 10	*********
*********	6103 39 00	6105 90 90	6110 11 10
5704 10 00	6103 41 00	*********	6110 11 30
5704 90 00	6103 42 00	6106 10 00	6110 11 90
*********	6103 43 00	6106 20 00	6110 12 10
6110 12 90	6211 32 42	6402 99 98	6403 99 93
6110 19 10	6211 33 31	*********	6403 99 96
6110 19 90	6211 33 41	6403 12 00	6403 99 98
6110 20 10	6211 33 42	6403 19 00	*********
6110 20 91	6211 42 31	6403 20 00	6404 11 00

Comparability over time is another important aspect of quality. Member States shall report any changes to definitions, coverage or methods that will have an impact on continuity.

6. Coherence is defined by how well sets of statistics can be used together. Apart from External Trade Statistics, information on external trade can be found in National Accounts, Business Statistics and Balance of Payments.

In this context, Member States shall report any information concerning the coherence of foreign trade statistics and statistics originating from other sources.

7. Completeness refers to the fact that the themes for which statistics are available reflect the needs and the priorities expressed by users of the European Statistical System.

COUNCIL REGULATION

of 17 October 2005

05/1777/EC

OJ L 343, 29/10/2005 p 1

laying down implementing measures for Directive 77/388/EEC
on the common system of value added tax

THE COUNCIL OF THE EUROPEAN UNION,

Having regard to the Treaty establishing the European Community,

Having regard to the Sixth Council Directive 77/388/EEC of 17 May 1977 on the harmonisation of the laws of the Member States relating to turnover taxes — Common system of value added tax: uniform basis of assessment (OJ L 145, 13.6.1977, p 1. Directive as last amended by Directive 2004/66/EC (OJ L 168, 1.5.2004, p 35)), hereinafter referred to as 'Directive 77/388/EEC', and in particular Article 29a thereof,

Having regard to the proposal from the Commission,

Whereas:

(1) Directive 77/388/EEC contains rules on value added tax which, in some cases, are subject to interpretation by the Member States. The adoption of common provisions implementing Directive 77/388/EEC should ensure that application of the value added tax system complies more fully with the objective of the internal market, in cases where divergences in application have arisen or may arise which are incompatible with the proper functioning of the said market. These implementing measures are legally binding only from the date of the entry into force of this Regulation and are without prejudice to the validity of the legislation and interpretation previously adopted by the Member States.

(2) It is necessary for the achievement of the basic objective of ensuring a more uniform application of the current value added tax system to lay down rules implementing Directive 77/388/EEC, in particular in respect of taxable persons, the supply of goods and services, and the place of their supply. In accordance with the principle of proportionality as set out in the third subparagraph of Article 5 of the Treaty, this Regulation does not go beyond what is necessary in order to achieve the objective pursued. Since it is binding and directly applicable in all Member States, uniformity of application will be best ensured by a Regulation.

(3) These implementing provisions contain specific rules in response to selective questions of application and are designed to bring uniform treatment throughout the Community to those specific circumstances only. They are therefore not conclusive for other cases and, in view of their formulation, are to be applied restrictively.

(4) The further integration of the internal market has led to an increased need for cooperation by economic operators established in different Member States across internal borders and the development of European economic interest groupings (EEIGs), constituted in accordance with Regulation (EEC) No 2137/85 (OJ L 199, 31.7.1985, p 1), it should therefore be provided that such EEIGs are also taxable persons where they supply goods or services for consideration.

(5) The sale of an option as a financial instrument should be treated as a supply of services separate from the underlying transactions to which the option relates.

(6) It is necessary, on the one hand, to establish that a transaction which consists solely of assembling the various parts of a machine provided by a customer must be considered as a supply of services, and, on the other hand, to establish the place of such supply.

(7) Where various services supplied in the framework of organising a funeral form a part of a single service, the rule on the place of supply should also be determined.

(8) Certain specific services such as the assignment of television broadcasting rights in respect of football matches, the translation of texts, services for claiming value added tax refunds, certain services as an agent, the hiring of means of transport and certain electronic services involve cross-border scenarios or even the participation of economic operators established in third countries. The place of supply of these services needs to be clearly determined in order to create greater legal certainty. It should be noted that the services identified as electronic services or otherwise do not constitute a definitive, exhaustive list.

(9) In certain specific circumstances a credit or debit card handling fee which is paid in connection with a transaction should not reduce the taxable amount for the latter.

(10) Vocational training or retraining should include instruction relating directly to a trade or profession as well as any instruction aimed at acquiring or updating knowledge for vocational purposes, regardless of the duration of a course.

(11) 'Platinum nobles' should be treated as being excluded from the exemptions for currency, bank notes and coins.

(12) Goods transported outside the Community by the purchaser thereof and used for the equipping, fuelling or provisioning of means of transport used for non-business purposes by persons other than natural persons, such as bodies governed by public law and associations, should be excluded from the exemption for export transactions.

(13) To guarantee uniform administrative practices for the calculation of the minimum value for exemption on exportation of goods carried in the personal luggage of travellers, the provisions on such calculations should be harmonised.

(14) Electronic import documents should also be admitted to exercise the right to deduct, where they fulfil the same requirements as paper-based documents.

(15) Weights for investment gold which are definitely accepted by the bullion market should be named and a common date for establishing the value of gold coins be determined to ensure equal treatment of economic operators.

(16) The special scheme for taxable persons not established in the Community, supplying electronic services to non-taxable persons established or resident within the Community is subject to certain conditions. Where those conditions are no longer fulfilled, the consequences thereof should, in particular, be made clear.

(17) In the case of intra-Community acquisition of goods, the right of the Member State of acquisition to tax the acquisition should remain unaffected by the value added tax treatment of the transaction in other Member States.

(18) Rules should be established to ensure the uniform treatment of supplies of goods once a supplier has exceeded the distance selling threshold for supplies to another Member State,

HAS ADOPTED THIS REGULATION:

CHAPTER I
SUBJECT MATTER

Article 1

This Regulation lays down measures for the implementation of Articles 4, 6, 9, 11, 13, 15, 18, 26b, 26c, 28a and 28b of Directive 77/388/EEC, and of Annex L thereto.

CHAPTER II
TAXABLE PERSONS AND TAXABLE TRANSACTIONS

SECTION 1
(ARTICLE 4 OF DIRECTIVE 77/388/EEC)

Article 2

A European Economic Interest Grouping (EEIG) constituted in accordance with Regulation (EEC) No 2137/85 which supplies goods or services for consideration to its members or to third parties shall be a taxable person within the meaning of Article 4(1) of Directive 77/388/EEC.

SECTION 2
(ARTICLE 6 OF DIRECTIVE 77/388/EEC)

Article 3

1. The sale of an option, where such a sale is a transaction within the scope of point (5) of Article 13(B)(*d*) of Directive 77/388/EEC, shall be a supply of services within the meaning of Article 6(1) of that Directive. That supply of services shall be distinct from the underlying operations to which the services relate.

2. Where a taxable person only assembles the different parts of a machine all of which were provided to him by his customer, that transaction shall be a supply of services within the meaning of Article 6(1) of Directive 77/388/EEC.

CHAPTER III
PLACE OF TAXABLE TRANSACTIONS

SECTION 1
(Article 9(1) of Directive 77/388/EEC)

Article 4

Insofar as they constitute a single service, services supplied in the framework of organising a funeral shall fall within the scope of Article 9(1) of Directive 77/388/EEC.

SECTION 2
(ARTICLE 9(2) OF DIRECTIVE 77/388/EEC)

Article 5

Except where the goods being assembled become part of immovable property, the place of the supply of services specified in Article 3(2) of this Regulation shall be established in accordance with Article 9(2)(c) or Article 28b(F) of Directive 77/388/EEC.

Article 6

The service of translation of texts shall be covered by Article 9(2)(e) of Directive 77/388/EEC.

Article 7

Where a body established in a third country assigns television broadcasting rights in respect of football matches to taxable persons established in the Community, that transaction shall be covered by the first indent of Article 9(2)(e) of Directive 77/388/EEC.

Article 8

The supply of services which consist in applying for or receiving refunds under Directive 79/1072/EEC (Eighth Council Directive 79/1072/EEC of 6 December 1979 on the harmonisation of the laws of the Member States relating to turnover taxes — Arrangements for the refund of value added tax to taxable persons not established in the territory of the country (OJ L 331, 27.12.1979, p. 11). Directive as last amended by the 2003 Act of Accession) shall be covered by the third indent of Article 9(2)(e) of Directive 77/388/EEC.

Article 9

The supply of services of agents as referred to in the seventh indent of Article 9(2)(e) of Directive 77/388/EEC shall cover the services of agents acting in the name and for the account of the recipient of the service procured and services performed by the agents acting in the name and for the account of the provider of the service procured.

Article 10

Trailers and semi-trailers, as well as railway wagons, shall be forms of transport for the purposes of the eighth indent of Article 9(2)(*e*) of Directive 77/388/EEC.

Article 11

1. 'Electronically supplied services' as referred to in the 12th indent of Article 9(2)(*e*) of Directive 77/388/EEC and in Annex L to Directive 77/388/EEC shall include services which are delivered over the Internet or an electronic network and the nature of which renders their supply essentially automated and involving minimal human intervention, and in the absence of information technology is impossible to ensure.

2. The following services, in particular, shall, where delivered over the Internet or an electronic network, be covered by paragraph 1:

- (*a*) the supply of digitised products generally, including software and changes to or upgrades of software;
- (*b*) services providing or supporting a business or personal presence on an electronic network such as a website or a webpage;
- (*c*) services automatically generated from a computer via the Internet or an electronic network, in response to specific data input by the recipient;
- (*d*) the transfer for consideration of the right to put goods or services up for sale on an Internet site operating as an online market on which potential buyers make their bids by an automated procedure and on which the parties are notified of a sale by electronic mail automatically generated from a computer;
- (*e*) Internet Service Packages (ISP) of information in which the telecommunications component forms an ancillary and subordinate part (i.e. packages going beyond mere Internet access and including other elements such as content pages giving access to news, weather or travel reports; playgrounds; website hosting, access to online debates etc.);
- (*f*) the services listed in Annex I.

Article 12

The following, in particular, shall not be covered by the 12th indent of Article 9(2)(*e*) of Directive 77/388/EEC:

1. radio and television broadcasting services as referred to in the 11th indent of Article 9(2)(*e*) of Directive 77/388/EEC;

2. telecommunications services, within the meaning of the 10th indent of Article 9(2)(*e*) of Directive 77/388/EEC;

3. supplies of the following goods and services:

- (*a*) goods, where the order and processing is done electronically;
- (*b*) CD-ROMs, floppy disks and similar tangible media;
- (*c*) printed matter, such as books, newsletters, newspapers or journals;
- (*d*) CDs, audio cassettes;
- (*e*) video cassettes, DVDs; (f) games on a CD-ROM;

(g) services of professionals such as lawyers and financial consultants, who advise clients by e-mail;

(h) teaching services, where the course content is delivered by a teacher over the Internet or an electronic network, (namely via a remote link);

(i) offline physical repair services of computer equipment;

(j) offline data warehousing services;

(k) advertising services, in particular as in newspapers, on posters and on television;

(l) telephone helpdesk services;

(m) teaching services purely involving correspondence courses, such as postal courses;

(n) conventional auctioneers' services reliant on direct human intervention, irrespective of how bids are made;

(o) telephone services with a video component, otherwise known as videophone services;

(p) access to the Internet and World Wide Web;

(q) telephone services provided through the Internet.

CHAPTER IV
TAXABLE AMOUNT

(ARTICLE 11 OF DIRECTIVE 77/388/EEC)

Article 13

Where a supplier of goods or services, as a condition of accepting payment by credit or debit card, requires the customer to pay an amount to himself or another undertaking, and where the total price payable by that customer is unaffected irrespective of how payment is accepted, that amount shall constitute an integral part of the taxable amount for the supply of the goods or services, under Article 11 of Directive 77/388/EEC.

CHAPTER V
EXEMPTIONS

SECTION 1
(ARTICLE 13 OF DIRECTIVE 77/388/EEC)

Article 14

Vocational training or retraining services provided under the conditions set out in Article 13(A)(1)(i) of Directive 77/388/EEC shall include instruction relating directly to a trade or profession as well as any instruction aimed at acquiring or updating knowledge for vocational purposes. The duration of a vocational training or retraining course shall be irrelevant for this purpose.

Article 15

The exemption referred to in Article 13(B)(d)(4) of Directive 77/388/EEC shall not apply to platinum nobles.

SECTION 2
(ARTICLE 15 OF DIRECTIVE 77/388/EEC)

Article 16

'**Means of transport for private use**' as referred to in the first subparagraph of Article 15(2) of Directive 77/388/EEC shall include means of transport used for non-business purposes by persons other than natural persons, such as bodies governed by public law within the meaning of Article 4(5) of that Directive and associations.

Article 17

In order to determine whether the threshold set by a Member State in accordance with the third indent of the second subparagraph of Article 15(2) of Directive 77/388/EEC has been exceeded, the calculation shall be based on the invoice value. The aggregate value of several goods may be used only if all those goods are included on the same invoice issued by the same taxable person supplying goods to the same customer.

CHAPTER VI
DEDUCTIONS

(ARTICLE 18 OF DIRECTIVE 77/388/EEC)

Article 18

Where the importing Member State has introduced an electronic system for completing customs formalities, the expression 'import document' as referred to in Article 18(1)(*b*) of Directive 77/388/EEC shall cover electronic versions of such documents, provided that they allow for the exercise of the right of deduction to be checked.

CHAPTER VII
SPECIAL SCHEMES

(ARTICLES 26B AND 26C OF DIRECTIVE 77/388/EEC)

Article 19

1. '**Weights accepted by the bullion markets**' as referred to in Article 26b(A)(i), first paragraph, of Directive 77/388/EEC shall at least cover the units and the weights traded as set out in Annex II to this Regulation.

2. For the purposes of establishing the list referred to in the third subparagraph of Article 26b(A) of Directive 77/388/EEC, 'price' and 'open market value' as referred to in the fourth indent of point (ii) of the first subparagraph shall be the price and open market value on 1 April of each year. If 1 April does not fall on a day on which those values are fixed, the values of the next day on which they are fixed shall be used.

Article 20

1. Where, in the course of a calendar quarter, a non-established taxable person using the special scheme provided for in Article 26c(B) of Directive 77/388/EEC meets at least

one of the criteria for exclusion laid down in Article 26c(B)(4), the Member State of identification shall exclude that non-established taxable person from the special scheme. In such cases the non-established taxable person may subsequently be excluded from the special scheme at any time during that quarter.

In respect of electronic services supplied prior to exclusion but during the calendar quarter in which exclusion occurs, the non-established taxable person shall submit a return for the entire quarter in accordance with Article 26c(B)(5) of Directive 77/388/ EEC. The requirement to submit this return shall have no effect on the requirement, if any, to register under the normal rules in a Member State.

2. A Member State of identification which receives a payment in excess of that resulting from the return submitted under Article 26c(B)(5) of Directive 77/388/EEC shall reimburse the overpaid amount directly to the taxable person concerned.

Where the Member State of identification has received an amount pursuant to a return subsequently found to be incorrect, and that Member State has already distributed that amount among the Member States of consumption, those Member States shall directly reimburse the overpayment to the non-established taxable person and inform the Member State of identification of the adjustment to be made.

3. Any return period (quarter) within the meaning of Article 26c(B)(5) of Directive 77/ 388/EEC shall be a separate return period.

Once a return under Article 26c(B)(5) of Directive 77/388/EEC has been rendered, any subsequent changes to the figures contained therein may be made only by means of an amendment to that return and not by an adjustment to a subsequent return.

Amounts of value added tax paid under Article 26c(B)(7) of Directive 77/388/EEC shall be specific to that return. Any subsequent amendments to the amounts paid may be effected only by reference to that return and may not be allocated to another return, or adjusted on a subsequent return.

4. Amounts on value added tax returns made under the special scheme provided for in Article 26c(B) of Directive 77/388/EEC shall not be rounded up or down to the nearest whole monetary unit. The exact amount of value added tax shall be reported and remitted.

CHAPTER VIII
TRANSITIONAL MEASURES

(ARTICLES 28A AND 28B OF DIRECTIVE 77/388/EEC)

Article 21

Where an intra-Community acquisition of goods within the meaning of Article 28a of Directive 77/388/EEC has taken place, the Member State in which the dispatch or transport ends shall exercise its power of taxation irrespective of the VAT treatment applied to the transaction in the Member State in which the dispatch or transport began.

Any request by a supplier of goods for a correction in the tax invoiced by him and reported by him to the Member State where the dispatch or transport of the goods began shall be treated by that State in accordance with its own domestic rules.

Article 22

Where in the course of a calendar year the threshold applied by a Member State in accordance with Article 28b(B)(2) of Directive 77/388/EEC is exceeded, Article 28b(B) of that Directive shall not modify the place of supplies of goods other than products subject to excise duty carried out in the course of the same calendar year which are made before the threshold applied by the Member State for the calendar year then current is exceeded provided that the supplier:

(a) has not exercised the option under Article 28b(B)(3) of that Directive and

(b) did not exceed the threshold in the course of the preceding calendar year.

However, Article 28b(B) of Directive 77/388/EEC shall modify the place of the following supplies to the Member State in which the dispatch or transport ends:

(a) the supply by which the threshold applied by the Member State for the calendar year then current was exceeded in the course of the same calendar year;

(b) any subsequent supplies within that Member State in that calendar year;

(c) supplies within that Member State in the calendar year following the calendar year in which the event referred to in point (a) occurred.

CHAPTER IX
FINAL PROVISIONS

Article 23

This Regulation shall enter into force on 1 July 2006

Article 13 shall be applicable from 1 January 2006.

This Regulation shall be binding in its entirety and directly applicable in all Member States.

Done at Luxembourg, 17 October 2005.

For the Council The President

M. BECKETT

ANNEX I
ARTICLE 11 OF THIS REGULATION

1. Item 1 of Annex L to Directive 77/388/EEC

(a) Website hosting and webpage hosting

(b) Automated, online and distance maintenance of programmes

(c) Remote systems administration

(*d*) Online data warehousing where specific data is stored and retrieved electronically

(*e*) Online supply of on-demand disc space.

2. Item 2 of Annex L to Directive 77/388/EEC

(*a*) Accessing or downloading software (including procurement/accountancy programmes and anti-virus software) plus updates

(*b*) Software to block banner adverts showing, otherwise known as Bannerblockers

(*c*) Download drivers, such as software that interfaces computers with peripheral equipment (such as printers)

(*d*) Online automated installation of filters on websites

(*e*) Online automated installation of firewalls.

3. Item 3 of Annex L to Directive 77/388/EEC

(*a*) Accessing or downloading desktop themes

(*b*) Accessing or downloading photographic or pictorial images or screensavers

(*c*) The digitised content of books and other electronic publications

(*d*) Subscription to online newspapers and journals

(*e*) Weblogs and website statistics

(*f*) Online news, traffic information and weather reports

(*g*) Online information generated automatically by software from specific data input by the customer, such as legal and financial data, (in particular such data as continually updated stock market data, in real time)

(*h*) The provision of advertising space including banner ads on a website/web page

(*i*) Use of search engines and Internet directories.

4. Item 4 of Annex L to Directive 77/388/EEC

(*a*) Accessing or downloading of music on to computers and mobile phones

(*b*) Accessing or downloading of jingles, excerpts, ringtones, or other sounds

(*c*) Accessing or downloading of films

(*d*) Downloading of music on to computers and mobile phones

(*e*) Accessing automated online games which are dependent on the Internet, or other similar electronic networks, where players are geographically remote from one another.

5. Item 5 of Annex L to Directive 77/388/EEC

(*a*) Automated distance teaching dependent on the Internet or similar electronic network to function and the supply of which requires limited or no human intervention, including virtual classrooms, except where the Internet or similar electronic network is used as a tool simply for communication between the teacher and student

(*b*) Workbooks completed by pupils online and marked automatically, without human intervention.

ANNEX II
ARTICLE 19 OF THIS REGULATION

Unit	Weights traded
Kg	12,5/1
Gram	500/250/100/50/20/10/5/2,5/2
Ounce (1 oz = 31,1035 g)	100/10/5/1/$^1/_2$/$^1/_4$
Tael (1 tael = 1,193 oz.) (^{1})	10/5/1
Tola (10 tolas = 3,75 oz.) (^{2})	10

(1) Tael = a traditional Chinese unit of weight. The nominal fineness of a Hong Kong tael bar is 990 but in Taiwan 5 and 10 tael bars can be 999,9 fineness.

(2) Tola = a traditional Indian unit of weight for gold. The most popular sized bar is 10 tola, 999 fineness.

TABLE OF CASES

1763

INDEX